The Broadview Introduction

to Philosophy

The Broadview Introduction to

PHILOSOPHY

CONCISE EDITION

edited by **ANDREW BAILEY**

broadview press

BROADVIEW PRESS – www.broadviewpress.com
Peterborough, Ontario, Canada

Founded in 1985, Broadview Press remains a wholly independent publishing house. Broadview's focus is on academic publishing; our titles are accessible to university and college students as well as scholars and general readers. With over 800 titles in print, Broadview has become a leading international publisher in the humanities, with world-wide distribution. Broadview is committed to environmentally responsible publishing and fair business practices.

Library and Archives Canada Cataloguing in Publication

Title: The Broadview introduction to philosophy / edited by Andrew Bailey.
Other titles: Introduction to philosophy
Names: Bailey, Andrew, 1969- editor.
Description: Concise edition. | Includes bibliographical references.
Identifiers: Canadiana (print) 20230596401 | Canadiana (ebook) 2023059641X | ISBN 9781554816538 (softcover) | ISBN 9781770489561 (PDF) | ISBN 9781460408810 (EPUB)
Subjects: LCSH: Philosophy—Textbooks. | LCSH: Philosophy—Introductions. | LCGFT: Textbooks.
Classification: LCC BD21 .B767 2024 | DDC 100—dc23

Broadview Press handles its own distribution in Canada and the United States:
PO Box 1243, Peterborough, Ontario K9J 7H5, Canada
555 Riverwalk Parkway, Tonawanda, NY 14150, USA
Tel: (705) 482-5915
email: customerservice@broadviewpress.com

For all territories outside of Canada and the United States, distribution is handled by Eurospan Group.

Canada

Broadview Press acknowledges the financial support of the Government of Canada for our publishing activities.

Book design by Michel Vrana
Cover image: borojoint, istockphoto.com

CONTRIBUTING EDITORS AND WRITERS

Editor
Andrew Bailey

Editorial Coordinator
Stephen Latta

Assistant Editors
Tara Bodie
Archie Fields III

Copyeditor
Robert M. Martin

Proofreaders
Stacey Aspinall
Joe Davies
Michel Pharand
Paige Pinto
Michael Roberts
Helena Snopek

Production Editors
Tara Lowes
Tara Trueman

Permissions Coordinator
Jacqueline Kwan

Contributing Writers
Andrew Bailey
Laura Buzzard
Leslie Dema
Stephen Latta
Melissa MacAulay
Robert M. Martin
Andrew Reszitnyk
Nora Ruddock

CONTENTS

ACKNOWLEDGMENTS

A number of academics provided valuable comments and input that helped to shape this book, including (but not limited to):

Ardis Anderson, University of Lethbridge
Shannon Dea, University of Waterloo
William J. Devlin, Bridgewater State University
Leigh Duffy, Buffalo State College
Mark Ereshefsky, University of Calgary
Erin Frykholm, University of Kansas
Hans V. Hansen, University of Windsor
W. Jim Jordan, University of Waterloo
Karl Laderoute, University of Lethbridge
Christinia Landry, Wilfrid Laurier University
Alison K. McConwell, University of Calgary
Joshua Mugg, Park University
Csaba Nyiri, Lourdes University
Brian Orend, University of Waterloo
Tina Strasbourg, Grande Prairie Regional College
Brynn Welch, University of Alabama at Birmingham
Byron Williston, Wilfrid Laurier University

This book is a successor to *First Philosophy: Fundamental Problems and Readings in Philosophy* (2nd ed.; Broadview Press, 2011). Thanks to Alan Belk, Lance Hickey, Peter Loptson, and Mark Migotti for pointing out errors and omissions in the first edition of that book. The editor would warmly welcome further corrections or suggestions for improvement.

Andrew Bailey
Department of Philosophy
The University of Guelph
abailey@uoguelph.ca

HOW TO USE THIS BOOK

This book is an introduction to philosophy. It is intended to be a reasonably representative—though very far from exhaustive—sampling of important philosophical questions, major philosophers and their most important works, periods of philosophical history, and styles of philosophical thought.* Roughly half of the included readings, however, were published since 1950, and another important aim of the book is to provide some background for *current* philosophical debates, to give the interested reader a springboard for the plunge into the exciting world of contemporary philosophy (debates about the nature of consciousness, say, or quantum theories of free will, or feminist ethics, or the status of scientific knowledge, or welfarist vs. libertarian accounts of social justice, or ...).

The aim of this book is to introduce philosophy through philosophy itself: it is not a book *about* philosophy but a book *of* philosophy, in which more than forty great philosophers speak for themselves. Each of the readings is prefaced by a set of notes, but these notes are not intended to explain or summarize the reading. Instead, the goal of the notes is to provide *background information* helpful for understanding the reading—to remove as many of the unnecessary barriers to comprehension as possible, and to encourage a deeper and more sophisticated encounter with great works of philosophy. The notes to selections, therefore, do not stand alone and *certainly* are not a substitute for the reading itself: they are meant to be consulted in combination with the reading.

Readers can of course take or leave these notes as they choose, and read them (or not) in any order. One good way of proceeding, however, would be the following. First, read the selection (so that nothing said in the notes inadvertently taints your first impression of the piece). Then, go back and read some of the notes—the biographical sketch, information on the author's philosophical project, structural and background information—and with these things in mind read the selection again. Spend some time *thinking* about the reading: ask yourself if you really feel you have a good grasp of what the author is trying to say, and then—no less importantly—ask yourself whether the author gives good reasons to believe that what is said is *true*. (The general Introduction tries to give some helpful suggestions for this process of critical reflection.) After this, it should be worthwhile going back to the notes, checking your impressions against any 'common misconceptions,' and then running through at least some of the suggestions for critical reflection. Finally, you might want to go on and read more material by the philosopher in question, or examine what other philosophers have said about those ideas: the suggestions for further reading, available at the companion website, will point you in the right direction.

The philosophical selections are also quite heavily annotated throughout by the editors, again in an effort to get merely contingent difficulties for comprehension out of the way and allow the reader to devote all her or his effort to understanding the philosophy itself. Many of the original texts also include their own notes, all of which have been presented here as endnotes following the reading, so as to keep those notes separate from the editors' annotations. The original endnotes are marked with numbers, while the added annotations are marked with symbols (*, †, ‡, etc.) and placed at the bottom of each page.

A word of explanation about the 'Suggestions for Critical Reflection' section: although the notes to the readings contain no philosophical critique of the selection, the questions in this section are largely intended to help the reader generate his or her own critique. As

---

* There are two major exceptions to this. First, this book focuses exclusively on 'Western' philosophy—that is, roughly, on the philosophical traditions of Europe and of the descendants of European settlers in North America and Australasia. In particular, it does not attempt to encompass the rich philosophical heritage of Asia or Africa. Second, this collection under-represents an important strain of twentieth-century philosophy, 'Continental' philosophy, which includes thinkers such as Husserl, Heidegger, Sartre, Foucault, Derrida, and Habermas, and is characterized by such movements as existentialism, hermeneutics, structuralism, and deconstructionism.

such, they are supposed to be thought-provoking, rather than straightforwardly easy to answer. They try to suggest fruitful avenues for critical thought (though they do not cover every possible angle of questioning, or even all the important ones), and only very rarely is there some particular 'right answer' to the question. Thus, these questions should not be considered a kind of 'self-test' to see if you understand the material: even people with a very good grasp of the material will typically be puzzled by the questions—because they are *supposed* to be puzzling questions.

The readings and their accompanying notes are designed to be 'modular'; that is, in general, one reading can be understood without the benefit of having read any of the other selections. This means that the selections can be read in any order. The current arrangement of the readings groups them by topic, and then orders them so that they follow a reasonably natural progression through a particular philosophical problem. However, quite different courses of study could be plotted through this book, emphasizing, say, philosophers grouped by nationality, by historical period, by philosophical approach, and so on. Furthermore, often readings from one section can quite naturally be brought into another (e.g., Descartes' *Meditations* into the Philosophy of Mind section, or Plato's *Republic* into the section on justice).

Many of the readings in this anthology are complete: The editors feel it is important for students to be able to see an argument in the context in which it was originally presented; also, the fact that the readings are not edited to include only what is relevant to one particular philosophical concern means that they can be used in a variety of different ways following a variety of different lines of thought across the ages. Some instructors will wish to assign for their students shorter excerpts of some of these readings, rather than having them read all of the work included: the fact that complete, or almost complete, works of philosophy are included in this anthology gives instructors the freedom to select the excerpts that best fit their pedagogical aims.

The notes to the readings in this anthology are almost entirely a work of synthesis, and many books and articles were consulted in their preparation; it is impossible—without adding an immense apparatus of notes and references—to acknowledge them in detail. This is, I believe, appropriate for a textbook, but it is not intended to model good referencing practices for student essays. All the material and annotations accompanying the readings was written by the editors, and none of it (unless otherwise noted) was copied from other sources. Typically, the notes for each reading amalgamate information from up to a dozen or so sources; in a few instances, especially for biographical information on still-living philosophers, the notes rely heavily on a smaller number of sources (and I tried to indicate this in the text when it occurred).

INTRODUCTION

What Is Philosophy?

Philosophy, at least according to the origin of the word in classical Greek, is the "love of wisdom"—philosophers are lovers of wisdom. The first philosophers of the Western tradition lived on the shores of the Mediterranean in the sixth century BCE (that is, more than 2,500 years ago);* thinkers such as Thales, Xenophanes, Pythagoras, Heraclitus, and Protagoras tried systematically to answer questions about the ultimate nature of the universe, the standards of knowledge, the objectivity of moral claims, and the existence and nature of God. Questions like these are still at the core of the discipline today.

So what is philosophy? It can be characterized either as a particular sort of *method*, or in terms of its *subject matter*, or as a kind of intellectual *attitude*.

busily mapping out correlations between brain states and mental states—finding which parts of the visual cortex play a role in dreaming, for example—and building computer models of intelligent information processing (such as software for self-driving vehicles). Philosophers are also involved in cognitive science, trying to discover just what would *count* as discovering that dreaming is really nothing more than certain electro-chemical events in the brain, or would count as building a computer which feels pain or genuinely has beliefs. These second kinds of questions are crucial to the whole project of cognitive science, but they are not empirical, scientific questions: there simply is no fact about the brain that a scientist could observe to answer them. And so these questions—which are part of cognitive science—are dealt with by philosophers.

Here are two more examples. Economists study the distribution of wealth in society, and develop theories about how wealth and other goods can come to be distributed one way rather than another (e.g., concentrated in a small proportion of the population, as in Brazil, or spread more evenly across society, as in Sweden). However, questions about which kind of distribution is more *just*, which kind of society is best to live in, are not answered within economic theory—these are philosophical questions. Medical professionals are concerned with facts about sickness and death, and often have to

PHILOSOPHY AS A METHOD

One view is that philosophers study the same things—the same world—as, for example, scientists do, but that they do so in a different, and complementary, way. In particular, it is often claimed that while scientists draw conclusions from empirical *observations* of the world, philosophers use *rational arguments* to justify claims about the world. For instance, both scientists and philosophers are involved in contemporary studies of the human mind. Neuroscientists and psychologists are

---

*   In the East, Lao-Tzu, the founder of Taoism, probably lived at about the same time in China. Buddha and Confucius were born a few decades later. In India, an oral literature called the Veda had been asking philosophical questions since at least 1500 BCE.

make decisions about the severity of an illness or weigh the risk of death from a certain procedure. Philosophers also examine the phenomenon of death, but ask different questions: for example, they ask whether people can survive their own deaths (i.e., if there is a soul), whether death is really a harm for the person who dies, under what conditions—if any—we should assist people in committing suicide, and so on.

One reason why philosophers deal differently with phenomena than scientists do is that philosophers are using different techniques of investigation. The core of the philosophical method is the application of *rational thought* to problems. There are (arguably) two main aspects to this: the use of conceptual or linguistic *analysis* to clarify ideas and questions, and the use of formal or informal *logic* to argue for certain answers to those questions.

For example, questions about the morality of abortion often pivot on the following question: is a fetus a *person* or not? A person is, roughly, someone who has a similar moral status to a normal adult human being. Being a person is not simply *the same thing* as being a member of the human species, however, since it is at least possible that some human beings are not persons (brain-dead individuals in permanent comas, for example?) and some persons might not be human beings (intelligent life from other planets, or gorillas, perhaps?). If it turns out that a fetus *is* a person, abortion will be morally problematic—it may even be a kind of murder. On the other hand, if a fetus is no more a person than, say, one of my kidneys, abortion may be as morally permissible as a transplant. So *is* a fetus a person? How would one even go about discovering the answer to this question? Philosophers proceed by using *conceptual analysis*. What we need to find out, first of all, is what makes something a person—what the essential difference is between persons and non-persons—and then we can apply this general account to human fetuses to see if they satisfy the definition. Put another way, we need to discover precisely what the word "person" means.

Since different conceptual analyses will provide importantly different answers to questions about the morality of abortion, we need to *justify* our definition: we need to give reasons to believe that one particular analysis of personhood is correct. This is where logic comes in: logic is the study of arguments, and its techniques are designed to distinguish between good arguments—by which we should be persuaded—and bad

arguments, which we should not find persuasive. (The next main section of this introduction will tell you a little more about logic.)

PHILOSOPHY AS A SUBJECT MATTER

Another way of understanding philosophy is to say that philosophers study a special set of issues, and that it is this subject matter which defines the subject. Philosophical questions fit three major characteristics:

1. They are of deep and lasting interest to human beings;
2. They have answers, but the answers have not yet been settled on;
3. The answers cannot be decided by science, faith, or common sense.

Philosophers try to give the best possible answers to such questions. That is, they seek the one answer which is more justified than any other possible answer. There are lots of questions which count as philosophical, according to these criteria. All can be classified as versions of one of three basic philosophical questions.

The first foundational philosophical question is *What exists?* For example: Does God exist? Are quarks really real, or are they just fictional postulates of a particular scientific theory? Are numbers real? Do persons exist, and what is the difference between a person and her physical body, or between a person and a 'mere animal'? The various questions of existence are studied by the branch of philosophy called Metaphysics, and by its various sub-fields such as Philosophy of Mind and the study of Personal Identity.

The second fundamental philosophical question is *What do we know?* For example, can we be sure that a scientific theory is actually true, or is it merely the currently dominant simplification of reality? The world appears to us to be full of colors and smells, but can we ever find out whether it really is colored or smelly (i.e., even if no one is perceiving it)? Everyone believes that 5+6=11, but what makes us so sure of this—could we be wrong, and if not, why not? The branch of philosophy which deals with these kinds of questions is called Epistemology. Philosophy of Science examines the special claims to knowledge made by the natural sciences, and Logic is the study of the nature of rational justification.

The third major philosophical question is *What should we do?* If I make a million dollars selling widgets or playing basketball, is it okay for me to keep all of that money and do what I want with it, or do I have some kind of moral obligation to give a portion of my income to the less well off? If I could get out of trouble by telling a lie, and no one else will really be harmed by my lie, is it alright to do so? Is Mozart's *Requiem* more or less artistically valuable than The Beatles' *Sgt. Pepper's Lonely Hearts Club Band*? Questions like these are addressed by Value Theory, which includes such philosophical areas as Ethics, Aesthetics, Political Philosophy, and Philosophy of Law.

PHILOSOPHY AS AN ATTITUDE

A third view is that philosophy is a state of being—a kind of intellectual independence. Philosophy is a reflective activity, an attitude of critical and systematic thoughtfulness. To be philosophical is to continue to question the assumptions behind every claim until we come to our most basic beliefs about reality, and then to critically examine those beliefs. For example, most of us assume that criminals are responsible for their actions, and that this is at least partly why we punish them. But *are* they responsible for what they do? We know that social pressures are very powerful in affecting our behavior. Is it unfair to make individuals entirely responsible for society's effects on them when those effects are negative? How much of our personal identity is bound up with the kind of community we belong to, and how far are we free to choose our own personalities and values? Furthermore, it is common to believe that the brain is the physical cause of all our behavior, that the brain is an entirely physical organ, and that all physical objects are subject to deterministic causal laws. If all of this is right, then presumably all human behavior is just the result of complex causal laws affecting our brain and body, and we could no more choose our actions than a falling rock could choose to take a different route down the mountainside. If this is true, then can we even make sense of the notion of moral responsibility? If it is not true, then where does free will come from and how (if at all) does it allow us to escape the laws of physics? Here, a questioning attitude towards our assumptions about criminals has shown that we might not have properly considered the bases of our assumptions. This ultimately leads us to fundamental questions about the place of human beings in the world.

Here are three quotations from famous philosophers which give the flavor of this view of philosophy as a critical attitude:

Socrates, one of the earliest Western philosophers, who lived in Greece around 400 BCE, is said to have declared that it "is the greatest good for a man, to talk every day about virtue and the other things you hear me converse about when I examine both myself and others, and that the unexamined life is not worth living for a man."[*]

Immanuel Kant—the most important thinker of the late eighteenth century—called this philosophical state of being "Enlightenment."

> Enlightenment is the emergence of man from the immaturity for which he is himself responsible. Immaturity is the inability to use one's understanding without the guidance of another. Man is responsible for his own immaturity, when it is caused, by lack not of understanding, but of the resolution and the courage to use it without the guidance of another. *Sapere aude!* Have the courage to use your own reason! is the slogan of Enlightenment.[†]

Finally, in the twentieth century, Bertrand Russell wrote the following assessment of the value of philosophy:

> Philosophy is to be studied, not for the sake of any definite answers to its questions, since no definite answers can, as a rule, be known to be true, but rather for the sake of the questions themselves; because these questions enlarge our conception of what is possible, enrich our intellectual imagination and diminish the dogmatic assurance which closes the mind against speculation; but above all because, through the greatness of the universe which philosophy contemplates, the mind also is rendered

---

* Plato, *Apology* 38a, in *The Apology and Related Dialogues*, ed. Andrew Bailey, trans. Cathal Woods and Ryan Pack (Broadview, 2016), 75–76.
† Immanuel Kant, "An Answer to the Question: What Is Enlightenment?" in *Practical Philosophy*, ed. Mary J. Gregor (Cambridge University Press, 1996), 17.

great, and becomes capable of that union with the universe which constitutes its highest good.*

SUGGESTIONS FOR CRITICAL REFLECTION

1. Here are some more examples of phenomena which are studied by both scientists and philosophers: color, sense perception, medical practices like abortion and euthanasia, human languages, mathematics, quantum mechanics, the evolution of species, democracy, taxation. What contribution (if any) might philosophers make to the study of these topics?

2. How well does *mathematics* fit into the division between science and philosophy described above? How does *religion* fit into this classification?

3. Here are a few simple candidate definitions of "person": a person is anything which is capable of making rational decisions; a person is any creature who can feel pain; a person is any creature with a soul; a person is any creature which has the appropriate place in a human community. Which of these, if any, do you think are plausible? What are the consequences of these definitions for moral issues like abortion or vegetarianism? Try to come up with a more sophisticated conceptual analysis of personhood.

4. Do you think criminals are responsible for their actions?

5. Should society support philosophy, and to what degree (e.g., should tax dollars be spent paying philosophers to teach at public universities? Why (not)?)?

A Brief Introduction to Arguments

EVALUATING ARGUMENTS

The main tool of philosophy is the *argument*. An argument is any sequence of statements intended to establish—or at least to make plausible—some particular claim. For example, if I say that Vancouver is a better place to live in than Toronto because it has a beautiful setting between the mountains and the ocean, is more relaxed, and has a lower cost of living, then I am making an argument. The claim which is being defended is called the *conclusion*, and the statements which together are supposed to show that the conclusion is (likely to be) true are called the *premises*. Often arguments will be strung together in a sequence, with the conclusions of earlier arguments featuring as premises of the later ones. For example, I might go on to argue that since Vancouver is a better place to live in than Toronto, and since one's living conditions are a big part of what determines one's happiness, then the people who live in Vancouver must, in general, be happier than those living in Toronto. Usually, a work of philosophy is primarily made up of chains of argumentation: good philosophy consists of good arguments; bad philosophy contains bad arguments.

What makes the difference between a good and a bad argument? It's important to notice, first of all, that the difference is *not* that good arguments have true conclusions and bad arguments have false ones. A perfectly good argument might, unluckily, happen to have a conclusion that is false. For example, you might argue that you know this rope will bear my weight because you know that the rope's rating is greater than my weight, you know that the rope's manufacturer is a reliable one, you have a good understanding of the safety standards which are imposed on rope makers and vendors, and you have carefully inspected this rope for flaws. Nevertheless, it still might be the case that this rope is the one in 50 million which has a hidden defect causing it to snap. If so, that makes me unlucky, but it doesn't suddenly make your argument a bad one—we were still being quite reasonable when we trusted the rope. On the other hand, it is very easy to give appallingly bad arguments for true conclusions: Every sentence beginning with the letter "c" is true; "Chickens lay eggs" begins with the letter "c"; therefore, chickens lay eggs.

But there is a deeper reason why the evaluation of arguments doesn't begin by assessing the truth of the conclusion. The whole point of making arguments is to

---

* Bertrand Russell, *The Problems of Philosophy* (Oxford University Press, 1912), 93–94.

establish *whether or not* some particular claim is true or false. An argument works by starting from some claims which, ideally, everyone is willing to accept as true—the premises—and then showing that something interesting—something *new*—follows from them: i.e., an argument tells you that *if* you believe these premises, *then* you should also believe this conclusion. In general, it would be unfair, therefore, to simply reject the conclusion and suppose that the argument must be a bad one—in fact, it would often be intellectually dishonest. If the argument *were* a good one, then it would show you that you might be *wrong* in supposing its conclusion to be false; and to refuse to accept this is not to respond to the argument but simply to ignore it.*

It follows that there are exactly two reasonable ways to criticize an argument. The first is to question the truth of the *premises*. The second is to question the claim that if the premises are true then the conclusion is true as well—that is, one can critique the *strength* of the argument. Querying the truth of the premises (i.e., asking whether it's really true that Vancouver is cheaper than Toronto) is fairly straightforward. The thing to bear in mind is that you will usually be working backwards down a chain of argumentation: that is, each premise of a philosopher's main argument will often be supported by sub-arguments, and the controversial premises in these sub-arguments might be defended by further arguments, and so on. Normally it is not enough to merely demand to know whether some particular premise is true: one must look for *why* the arguer thinks it is true, and then engage with *that* argument.

Understanding and critiquing the strength of an argument (either your own or someone else's) is somewhat more complex. In fact, this is the main subject of most books and courses in introductory logic. When dealing with the strength of an argument, it is usual to divide arguments into two classes: *deductive* arguments and *inductive* arguments. Good deductive arguments are the strongest possible kind of argument: if their premises are true, then their conclusion *must necessarily* be true. For example, if all bandicoots are rat-like marsupials, and if Billy is a bandicoot, then it cannot possibly be false that Billy is a rat-like marsupial. On the other hand, good inductive arguments establish that, if the premises are true, then the conclusion is *highly likely* (but not absolutely certain) to be true as well. For example, I may notice that the first bandicoot I see is rat-like, and the second one is, and the third, and so on; eventually, I might reasonably conclude that all bandicoots are rat-like. This is a good argument for a probable conclusion, but nevertheless the conclusion can never be shown to be *necessarily* true. Perhaps a non-rat-like bandicoot once existed before I was born, or perhaps there is one living now in an obscure corner of New Guinea, or perhaps no bandicoot so far has ever been non-rat-like but at some point, in the future, a bandicoot will be born that in no way resembles a rat, and so on.

DEDUCTIVE ARGUMENTS AND VALIDITY

The strength of deductive arguments is an on/off affair, rather than a matter of degree. Either these arguments are such that if the premises are true then the conclusion necessarily must be, or they are not. Strong deductive arguments are called *valid*; otherwise, they are called *invalid*. The main thing to notice about validity is that its definition is an *if ... then ...* statement: *if* the premises were true, *then* the conclusion would be true as well. An argument can be valid even if its premises and its conclusion are not true: all that matters is that if the premises *had* been true, the conclusion necessarily would have been as well. This is an example of a valid argument:

1. Either bees are rodents or they are birds.
2. Bees are not birds.
3. Therefore bees are rodents.

If the first premise were true, then (since the second premise is already true) the conclusion would *have* to be true—that's what makes this argument valid. This example makes it clear that validity, though a highly desirable property in an argument, is not enough all by itself to make

---

*   Of course, occasionally, you might legitimately know for sure that the conclusion is false, and then you could safely ignore arguments which try to show it is true: for example, after the rope breaks, I could dismiss your argument that it is safe (again, though, this would not show that your argument was bad, just that I need not be persuaded that the conclusion is true). However, this will not do for philosophical arguments: all interesting philosophy deals with issues where, though we may have firm opinions, we cannot just insist that we know all the answers and can therefore afford to ignore relevant arguments.

a good argument: good deductive arguments are both valid *and* have true premises. When arguments are good in this way they are called *sound*: sound arguments have the attractive feature that they necessarily have true conclusions. To show that an argument is unsound, it is enough to show that it is either invalid or has a false premise.

It bears emphasizing that even arguments which have true premises and a true conclusion can be unsound. For example:

1. Only US citizens can become the President of America.
2. George W. Bush is a US citizen.
3. Therefore, George W. Bush was elected President of America.

This argument is not valid, and therefore it should not convince anyone who does not already believe the conclusion to start believing it. It is not valid because the conclusion could have been false even though the premises were true: Bush could have lost to Gore in 2000, for example. The question to ask, in thinking about the validity of arguments, is this: Is there a coherent possible world, which I can even *imagine*, in which the premises are true and the conclusion false? If there is, then the argument is invalid.

When assessing the deductive arguments that you encounter in philosophical work, it is often useful to try to lay out, as clearly as possible, their *structure*. A standard and fairly simple way to do this is simply to pull out the logical connecting phrases and to replace, with letters, the sentences they connect. Five of the most common and important 'logical operators' are *and, or, it is not the case that, if ... then ...*, and *if and only if....* For example, consider the following argument: "If God is perfectly powerful (omnipotent) and perfectly good, then no evil would exist. But evil does exist. Therefore, God cannot be both omnipotent and perfectly good; so either God is not all-powerful or he is not perfectly good." The structure of this argument could be laid bare as follows:

1. If (O and G) then not-E.
2. E.

3. Therefore, not-(O and G).
4. Therefore, either not-O or not-G.

Revealing the structure in this way can make it easier to see whether or not the argument is valid. And in this case, it is valid. In fact, no matter what O, G, and E stand for—no matter how we fill in the blanks—*any* argument of this form must be valid. You could try it yourself—invent random sentences to fill in for O, G, and E, and no matter how hard you try, you will never produce an argument with all true premises and a false conclusion.* What this shows is that validity is often a property of the *form* or structure of an argument. (This is why deductive logic is known as "formal logic." It is not formal in the sense that it is stiff and ceremonious, but because it has to do with argument forms.)

Using this kind of shorthand, therefore, it is possible to describe certain general argument forms which are *invariably* valid and which—since they are often used in philosophical writing—it can be handy to look out for. For example, a very common and valuable form of argument looks like this: if P then Q; P; therefore Q. This form is often called *modus ponens*. Another—which appears in the previous argument about God and evil—is *modus tollens*: if P then Q; not-Q; therefore not-P. A *disjunctive syllogism* works as follows: either P or Q; not-P; therefore Q. A *hypothetical syllogism* has the structure: if P then Q; if Q then R; therefore if P then R. Finally, a slightly more complicated but still common argument structure is sometimes called a *constructive dilemma*: either P or Q; if P then R; if Q then R; therefore R.

INDUCTIVE ARGUMENTS AND INDUCTIVE STRENGTH

I noted above that the validity of deductive arguments is a yes/no affair—that a deductive argument is either extremely strong or it is hopelessly weak. This is not true for inductive arguments. The strength of an inductive argument—the amount of support the premises give to the conclusion—is a matter of degree, and there is no clear dividing line between the 'strong' inductive arguments and the 'weak' ones. Nevertheless, some inductive arguments

---

* Since the argument about God and evil is valid, then we are left with only two possibilities. Either all its premises are true, and then it is sound and its conclusion must inescapably be true. Or one of its premises is false, in which case the conclusion might be false (though we would still not have shown that it is false). The only way to effectively critique this argument, therefore, is to argue against one of the claims 1 and 2.

are obviously much stronger than others, and it is useful to think a little bit about what factors make a difference.

There are lots of different types and structures of inductive arguments; here I will briefly describe four which are fairly representative and commonly encountered in philosophy. The first is *inductive generalization*. This type of argument is the prototypical inductive argument—indeed, it is often what people mean when they use the term "induction"—and it has the following form:

1.   *x* per cent of observed Fs are G.
2.   Therefore *x* per cent of all Fs are G.

That is, inductive generalizations work by inferring a claim about an entire *population* of objects from data about a *sample* of those objects. For example:

(a)   Every swan I have ever seen is white, so all swans (in the past and future, and on every part of the planet) are white.
(b)   Every swan I have ever seen is white, so probably all the swans around here are white.
(c)   800 of the 1,000 rocks we have taken from the Moon contain silicon, so probably around 80% of the Moon's surface contains silicon.
(d)   We have tested two very pure samples of copper in the lab and found that each sample has a boiling point of 2,567°C; we conclude that 2,567°C is the boiling point for copper.
(e)   Every intricate system I have seen created (such as houses and watches) has been the product of intelligent design, so therefore all intricate systems (including, for example, frogs and volcanoes) must be the product of intelligent design.

The two main considerations when assessing the strength of inductive generalizations are the following. First, ask how *representative* is the sample? How likely is it that whatever is true of the sample will also be true of the population as a whole? For instance, although the sample size in argument (c) is much larger than that in argument (d), it is much more likely to be biased: we know that pure copper is very uniform, so a small sample will do; but the surface of the Moon might well be highly variable, and so data about the areas around moon landings may not be representative of the surface as a whole. Second, it is important to gauge how cautious and *accurate* the conclusion is, given the data—how far beyond the evidence

does it go? The conclusion to argument (a) is a much more radical inference from the data than that in argument (b); consequently, though less exciting, the conclusion of argument (b) is much better supported by the premise.

A second type of inductive argument is an *argument from analogy*. It most commonly has the following form:

1.   Object (or objects) *A* and object (or objects) *B* are alike in having features F, G, H, ...
2.   *B* has feature X.
3.   Therefore *A* has feature X as well.

These examples illustrate arguments from analogy:

(a)   Human brains and dolphin brains are large, compared to body size. Humans are capable of planning for the future. So, dolphins must also be capable of planning for the future.
(b)   Humans and dolphins are both mammals and often grow to more than five feet long. Humans are capable of planning for the future. So, dolphins must also be capable of planning for the future.
(c)   Eagles and robins are alike in having wings, feathers, claws, and beaks. Eagles kill and eat sheep. Therefore, robins kill and eat sheep.
(d)   Anselm's ontological argument has the same argumentative form as Gaunilo's "Lost Island" argument. But Gaunilo's argument is a patently bad argument. So there must be something wrong with the ontological argument.
(e)   An eye and a watch are both complex systems in which all of the parts are inter-dependent and where any small misadjustment could lead to a complete failure of the whole. A watch is the product of intelligent design. Therefore, the eye must also be the product of intelligent design (i.e., God exists).

The strength of an argument from analogy depends mostly on two things: first, the degree of *positive relevance* that the noted similarities (F, G, H ...) have to the target property X; and second, the absence of *relevant dissimilarities*—properties which *A* has but *B* does not, which make it *less* likely that *A* is X. For example, the similarity (brain size) between humans and dolphins cited in argument (a) is much more relevant to the target property (planning) than are the similarities cited in argument (b). This, of course, makes (a) a much stronger argument than (b). The primary problem with argument (c), on the other hand, is that we know that robins are much smaller and weaker than eagles and this dissimilarity makes it far less likely that they kill sheep.

A third form of inductive argument is often called *inference to the best explanation* or sometimes *abduction*. This kind of argument works in the following way. Suppose we have a certain quantity of data to explain (such as the behavior of light in various media, or facts about the complexity of biological organisms, or a set of ethical claims). Suppose also that we have a number of theories which account for this data in different ways (e.g., the theory that light is a particle, or the theory that light is a wave, or the theory that it is somehow both). One way of arguing for the truth of one of these theories, over the others, is to show that one theory provides a much *better explanation* of the data than the others. What counts as making a theory a better explanation can be a bit tricky, but some basic criteria would be:

1. The theory predicts all the data we know to be true.
2. The theory explains all this data in the most economical and theoretically satisfying way (scientists and mathematicians often call this the most *beautiful* theory).
3. The theory predicts some *new* phenomena which turn out to exist and which would be a big surprise if one of the competing theories were true. (For example, one of the clinchers for Einstein's theory of relativity was the observation that starlight is bent by the sun's gravity. This would have been a big surprise under the older Newtonian theory, but was predicted by Einstein's theory.)

Here are some examples of inferences to the best explanation:

(a) When I inter-breed my pea plants, I observe certain patterns in the properties of the plants produced (e.g., in the proportion of tall plants, or of plants which produce wrinkled peas). If the properties of pea plants were generated randomly, these patterns would be highly surprising. However, if plants pass on packets of information (genes) to their offspring, the patterns I have observed would be neatly explained. Therefore, genes exist.

(b) The biological world is a highly complex and inter-dependent system. It is highly unlikely that such a system would have come about (and would

continue to hang together) from the purely random motions of particles. It would be much less surprising if it were the result of conscious design from a super-intelligent creator. Therefore, the biological world was deliberately created (and therefore, God exists).

(c) The biological world is a highly complex and inter-dependent system. It is highly unlikely that such a system would have come about (and would continue to hang together) from the purely random motions of particles. It would be much less surprising if it were the result of an evolutionary process of natural selection which mechanically preserves order and eliminates randomness, and which (if it existed) would produce a world much like the one we see around us. Therefore, the theory of evolution is true.

The final type of inductive argument that I want to mention here is usually called *reductio ad absurdum*, which means "reduction to absurdity." It is always a negative argument, and has this structure:

1. Suppose (for the sake of argument) that position p were true.
2. If p were true then something else, q, would also have to be true.
3. However q is absurd—it can't possibly be true.
4. Therefore p can't be true either.

In fact, this argument style can be either inductive or deductive, depending on how rigorous premises 2 and 3 are. If p logically implies q, and if q is a logical contradiction, then it is deductively certain that p can't be true (at least, assuming the classical laws of logic). On the other hand, if q is merely absurd but not literally *impossible*, then the argument is inductive: it makes it highly likely that p is false, but does not prove it beyond all doubt.

Here are a few examples of *reductio* arguments:

(a) Suppose that gun control were a good idea. That would mean it's a good idea for the government to gather information on anything we own which, in the wrong hands, could be a lethal weapon, such as kitchen knives and baseball bats. But that would be ridiculous. This shows gun control cannot be a good idea.

(b) If you think that fetuses have a right to life because they have hearts and fingers and toes, then you must believe that anything with a heart, fingers, and toes has a right to life. But that would be absurd. Therefore, a claim like this about fetuses cannot be a good argument against abortion.

(c) Suppose, for the sake of argument, that this is not the best possible world. But that would mean God had either deliberately chosen to create a sub-standard world or had failed to notice that this was not the best of all possible worlds, and either of these options is absurd. Therefore, it must be true that this is the best of all possible worlds.

(d) "The anti-vitalist says that there is no such thing as vital spirit. But this claim is self-refuting. The speaker can be taken seriously only if his claim cannot. For if the claim is true, then the speaker does not have vital spirit and must be dead. But if he is dead, then his statement is a meaningless string of noises, devoid of reason and truth."*

The critical questions to ask about *reductio* arguments are simply: *Does* the supposedly absurd consequence follow from the position being attacked? and Is it *really* absurd?

A FEW COMMON FALLACIES

Just as it can be useful to look for common patterns of reasoning in philosophical writing, it can also be helpful to be on guard for a few recurring fallacies—and, equally importantly, to take care not to commit them in your own philosophical writing. Here are four common ones:

Begging the question does not mean, as the media would have us believe, stimulating one to ask a further question; instead, it means to assume as true (as one of your premises) the very same thing which you are supposedly attempting to prove. This fallacy is sometimes called *circular reasoning* or even (the old Latin name) *petitio principii*. To argue, for example, that God exists because (a) the Bible says that God exists, (b) God wrote the Bible, and (c) God would not lie, is to commit a blatant case of begging the question. In this case, of course, one would have no reason to accept the premises as true unless one *already* believed the conclusion. Usually, however, arguments that beg the question are a little more

disguised. For example, "Adultery is immoral, since sexual relations outside marriage violate ethical principles," or "Terrorism is bad, because it encourages further acts of terrorism," are both instances of circular reasoning.

Arguing *ad hominem* means attacking or rejecting a position not because the arguments for it are poor, but because the person presenting those arguments is unattractive in some way: i.e., an attack is directed at the person (which is what *ad hominem* means) rather than at their argument. The following are implicit *ad hominem* arguments: "You say churches have too much influence on society? Well, Hitler and Stalin would agree with you!" and "We shouldn't trust the claim, by philosophers such as Anselm, Aquinas, and Leibniz, that God exists, since they were all Christian philosophers and so of course they were biased." Such attacks are fallacious because they have nothing at all to do with how reasonable a claim is: even if the claim is false, *ad hominem* attacks do nothing to show this.

Straw person arguments are particularly devious, and this fallacy can be hard to spot (or to avoid committing) unless great care is taken. The *straw person* fallacy consists in misrepresenting someone else's position so that it can be more easily criticized. It is like attacking a dummy stuffed with straw instead of a real opponent. For example, it's not uncommon to see attacks on "pro-choice" activists for thinking that abortion is a good thing. However, whatever the merits of either position, this objection is clearly unfair—no serious abortion advocates think it is a positively *good thing* to have an abortion; at most they claim that (at least in some circumstances) it is a lesser evil than the alternative. Here's an even more familiar example, containing two straw persons, one after the other: "We should clean out the closets. They're getting a bit messy." "Why, we just went through those closets last year. Do we have to clean them out every day?" "I never said anything about cleaning them out every day. You just want to keep all your junk forever, which is simply ridiculous."

Arguments from ignorance, finally, are based on the assumption that lack of evidence *for* something is evidence that it is false, or that lack of evidence *against* something is evidence for its truth. Generally, neither of these assumptions is reliable. For example, even if we

---

* This example is from Paul Churchland's "Eliminative Materialism and the Propositional Attitudes," *Journal of Philosophy* 78 (1981). (Note, however, that it is not Churchland's argument.)

could find no good proof to show that God exists, this would not, all by itself, suffice to show that God does *not* exist: it would still be possible, for example, that God exists but transcends our limited human reason. Consider the following 'argument' by Senator Joseph McCarthy, about some poor official in the State Department: "I do not have much information on this except the general statement of the agency that there is nothing in the files to disprove his Communist connections."*

SUGGESTIONS FOR CRITICAL REFLECTION

1. Suppose some deductive argument has a premise which is necessarily false. Is it a valid argument?
2. Suppose some deductive argument has a conclusion which is necessarily true. Is it a valid

3. Is the following argument form valid: if P then Q; Q; therefore P? How about: if P then Q; not-P; so not-Q?
4. No inductive argument is strong enough to *prove* that its conclusion is true: the best it can do is to show that the conclusion is highly probable. Does this make inductive arguments bad or less useful? Why don't we restrict ourselves to using only deductive arguments?
5. Formal logic provides mechanical and reliable methods for assessing the validity of deductive arguments. Do you think there might be some similar system for evaluating the strength of inductive arguments?
6. I have listed four important fallacies; can you identify any other common patterns of poor reasoning?

Introductory Tips on Reading and Writing Philosophy

READING PHILOSOPHY

As you will soon find out, if you haven't already, it is not easy to read philosophy. It can be exhilarating, stimulating, life-changing, or even annoying, but it isn't easy. There are no real shortcuts for engaging with philosophy (though the notes accompanying the readings in this book are intended to remove a few of the more unnecessary barriers); however, there are two things to remember which will help you get the most out of reading philosophy—*read it several times*, and *read it actively*.

Philosophical writing is not like a novel, a historical narrative, or even a textbook: it is typically dense, compressed, and written to contribute to an on-going debate with which you may not yet be fully familiar. This means, no matter how smart you are, it is highly unlikely that you will get an adequate understanding of any halfway interesting piece of philosophy the first time through, and it may even take two or three more readings before it really becomes clear. Furthermore, even after that point, repeated readings of good philosophy will usually reveal

new and interesting nuances to the writer's position, and occasionally you will notice some small point that seems to open a mental door and show you what the author is trying to say in a whole new way. As they say, if a piece of philosophy isn't worth reading at least twice, it isn't worth reading once. Every selection in this book, I guarantee, is well worth reading once.

As you go through a piece of philosophy, it is very important to engage with it: instead of just letting the words wash over you, you should make a positive effort, first, to understand, and then, to critically assess the ideas you encounter. On your first read-through it is a good idea to try to formulate a high-level understanding of what the philosopher is attempting: What are the main claims? What is the overall structure of the arguments behind them? At this stage, it can be useful to pay explicit attention to section headings and introductory paragraphs.

Ideally during a second reading, you should try to reconstruct the author's arguments and sub-arguments in more detail. To help yourself understand them, consider jotting down their outlines on a sheet of paper. At

---

* McCarthy on the Senate floor, quoted by Richard H. Rovere in *Senator Joe McCarthy* (University of California Press, 1996), 132.

this point, it can be extremely fruitful to pay attention to special definitions or distinctions used by the author in the arguments. It is also helpful to consider the historical context in which the philosopher wrote, and to look for connections to ideas found in other philosophical works.

Finally, on third and subsequent readings, it is valuable to expressly look for *objections* to the writer's argument (Are the premises true? Is the argument strong?), *unclarities* in position statements, or *assumptions* they depend upon, but do not argue for. I make these suggestions partly because the process of critical assessment is helpful in coming to understand a philosopher's work; but more importantly for the reason that—perhaps contrary to popular opinion—philosophers are typically playing for very high stakes. When philosophers write about whether God exists, whether science is a rational enterprise, or whether unfettered capitalism creates a just society, they are seriously interested in discovering the *answers* to these questions. The arguments they make, if they are good enough, will be strong reasons to believe one thing rather than another. If you are reading philosophy properly, you must sincerely join the debate and be honestly prepared to be persuaded—but it is also important not to let yourself be persuaded too easily.

WRITING PHILOSOPHY

Writing philosophy consists, in roughly equal measures, of *thinking* about philosophy and then of trying to express your ideas *clearly and precisely*. This makes it somewhat unlike other writing: the point of writing philosophy is not, alas, to entertain, nor to explain some chunk of knowledge, nor to trick or cajole the reader into accepting a certain thesis. The point of philosophical writing is, really, to *do* philosophy. This means that, since philosophy is based on arguments, most philosophical essays will have the underlying structure of an argument. They will seek to defend some particular philosophical claim by developing one or more good arguments for that claim.*

There is no particular template to follow for philosophical writing (there are lots of different kinds of good philosophical writing—lots of different ways of arguing well), but here are seven suggestions you might find useful:

1. Take your time. Spend time thinking, and then leave yourself enough time to get the writing right.
2. After you've thought for a while, begin by making an outline of the points you want to make (rather than immediately launching into prose). Then write several drafts, preferably allowing some cooling-off time between drafts so you can come back refreshed and with a more objective eye. Be prepared for the fact that writing a second draft doesn't mean merely tinkering with what you've already got, but starting at the beginning and writing it again.
3. Strive to be clear. Avoid unnecessary jargon, and use plain, simple words whenever possible; concrete examples can be extremely useful in explaining what you mean. It's also worth remembering that the clarity of a piece of writing has a lot to do with its structure. Ideally, the argumentative structure of your essay should be obvious to the reader, and it is a good idea to use your introduction to give the reader a 'road map' of the argument to follow.
4. Aim for precision. Make sure the *thesis* of your essay is spelled out in sufficient detail that the reader is left in no doubt about what you are arguing for (and therefore what the implications will be, if your arguments are strong ones). Also, take care to define important terms so the reader knows exactly what you mean by them. Terms should normally be defined under any of the following three conditions: (a) the word is a technical term whose meaning a layperson probably won't know (e.g., "intrinsic value"); (b) it is an ordinary word whose meaning is not sufficiently clear or precise for philosophical purposes (e.g., "abortion"); or (c) it is an ordinary word that you are going to use to mean something other than what it normally means (e.g., "person").
5. Focus. Everything you write should directly contribute to establishing your thesis. Anything

---

* The conclusion of a philosophical essay, however, need not always be something like: "God exists," or "Physical objects are not colored." It could just as legitimately be something like: "Philosopher A's third argument is flawed," or "When the arguments of philosopher A and those of philosopher B are compared, B wins," or "No one has yet given a good argument to show either P or not-P," or even "Philosopher A's argument is not, as is widely thought, X, but instead it is Y." Though these kinds of claims are, perhaps, less immediately exciting than the first two examples, they are still philosophical claims, they still need to be argued for, and they can be extremely important in an overall debate about, say, the existence of God.

which is unnecessary for your arguments should be eliminated. Make every word count. Also, don't be over-ambitious; properly done, philosophy moves at a fairly slow pace—it is unlikely that anyone could show adequately that, for example, there is no such thing as matter in three pages or less.

6. Argue as well and as carefully as you can. Defend your position using reason and not rhetoric; critically assess the strength of your arguments, and consider the plausibility of your premises. It's important to consider alternatives to your own position and possible counter-arguments; don't be afraid to raise and attempt to reply to objections to your position. (If you make a serious objection, one which you cannot answer, perhaps you should change your position.)

7. When you think you are finished, read the essay out loud and/or give it to someone else to read—at a minimum, this is a good way of checking for ease of reading, and it may reveal problems with your essay or argument that hadn't previously occurred to you.

PART I: PHILOSOPHY OF RELIGION

Does God Exist?

The philosophy of religion is the sub-field of philosophy concerned with the rational evaluation of the truth of religious claims; in particular, the philosophy of religion deals most centrally with claims about the existence, nature, and activities of God. For example, one might ask, is it coherent to say that God is absolutely all-powerful?* Can God be *both* all-knowing and unchanging?† If God is all-knowing—and so knows everything that I am going to do—then in what sense can human beings really be said to have free will? Does God exist eternally, or instead is God somehow 'outside' of time altogether? Does God listen to and answer prayers? Does God ever cause miracles to occur? Does God punish sinners, and if so then what counts as sin and how does the deity punish it? How can a deity consign souls to eternal damnation and yet still be considered benevolent? Could God command us to torture little children for fun, and if he did so would this be a moral duty? If God is inexpressibly mysterious, as some religious creeds assert, then how does one know what one believes in if one believes in God? And so on.

The religious proposition singled out for philosophical evaluation in this chapter is something like the following:

---

*   Consider, for instance, this old quandary: can God make a stone so heavy that even God cannot lift it? Whichever way this question is answered, it seems that there must be at least one thing which God cannot do.

†   After all, as the world changes over time, so must the facts which God knows to be true at that time. What God knew to be true ten seconds ago will differ from what he knows to be true now, which will be different again from what will be true in ten seconds, and so on. So (it appears) God's beliefs must be constantly changing if they are to remain true, so God cannot be eternally unchanging.

that there exists one, and exactly one, deity who is eternal, immaterial, all-powerful, all-knowing, and perfectly morally good, and who created the universe and all its inhabitants. The first four readings in this chapter introduce (and evaluate) the three main arguments in favor of the existence of such an entity and the most important argument against its existence.

One of the earliest philosophical arguments for the existence of God comes from Saint Anselm in the eleventh century and is called the *ontological argument*. The ontological argument tries to show that God *necessarily* exists since God's existence is logically entailed by the concept of God. This argument, a version of which also appears in Descartes's *Meditations* in the Theory of Knowledge chapter of this volume, is criticized in the Anselm reading by a monk called Gaunilo, and also in the selection in this chapter from Aquinas.

The second main type of argument for the existence of God is what is called the *cosmological argument*. Arguments of this type start from observations about the world (the 'cosmos'), such as that every event has a cause, or that all natural things depend for their existence on something else, and infer from this that there must be some entity—a creator and a sustainer—which necessarily exists and upon which everything else depends for its existence. Aquinas presents three cosmological arguments, the first three of his 'Five Ways.'

Finally, the third main variety of argument for the existence of God is the so-called *teleological argument*, often known as the *argument from design*. These arguments begin from the premise that the natural world shows signs of intelligent design or purpose (the Greek for purpose is *telos*) and from this draw the conclusion that the universe must have had an intelligent designer—God. The fifth of Aquinas's arguments for God is a member of this species.

Perhaps the most important argument *against* the existence of God is known as the *problem of evil*. This argument essentially claims that the existence of evil is incompatible with the existence of a powerful and be-nevolent God; since evil clearly does exist, God cannot. The problem of evil is addressed briefly by Aquinas, but a modern philosopher, J.L. Mackie, argues that the problem of evil is logically unbeatable.

The final three readings in this chapter, Blaise Pascal's "The Wager," William Clifford's "The Ethics of Belief," and William James's "The Will to Believe," ask what we should do if it turns out that there *is* no rational reason to believe in God. Pascal argues that, even though as finite beings we cannot comprehend God or be sure of his existence, a rational person should nevertheless believe in God. In contrast, Clifford makes a passionate case that "it is wrong always, everywhere, and for anyone, to believe anything upon insufficient evidence," while in response James argues that, even if we can have no good intellectual reasons for faith, we nevertheless have the right to choose to believe in God for emotional or "passional" reasons instead.

If you want to explore this area of philosophy in more depth, there are many books available which discuss the philosophy of religion. Some of the more philosophically informed ones are: Brian Davies, *An Introduction to the Philosophy of Religion* (Oxford University Press, 2004); Anthony Flew, *God, Freedom and Immortality* (Prometheus Books, 1984); John Hick, *Arguments for the Existence of God* (Macmillan, 1970); John Hick, *Philosophy of Religion* (Prentice-Hall, 1990); Anthony Kenny, *The God of the Philosophers* (Oxford University Press, 1987); Alvin Plantinga, *God and Other Minds* (Cornell University Press, 1990); William Rowe, *Philosophy of Religion* (Wadsworth, 2006); Bertrand Russell, *Why I Am Not a Christian* (Simon and Schuster, 1957); Richard Swinburne, *The Existence of God* (Oxford University Press, 1979); Charles Taliaferro, *Contemporary Philosophy of Religion: An Introduction* (Blackwell, 1998); and Keith Yandell, *Philosophy of Religion: A Contemporary Introduction* (Routledge, 2016). Two useful reference texts are *A Companion to Philosophy of Religion*, edited by Philip Quinn and Charles Taliaferro (Blackwell, 2010), and William Wainwright, ed., *The Oxford Handbook of Philosophy of Religion* (Oxford University Press, 2007).

ST. ANSELM OF CANTERBURY

Proslogion

Who Was St. Anselm of Canterbury?

Anselm was born in 1033 to a noble family in Aosta, Italy, but after his mother's death (when he was 23) he repudiated his inherited wealth and the political career for which his father had prepared him and took up the life of a wandering scholar. In 1060 he became a monk at the Benedictine abbey of Bec in Normandy, rose rapidly through various positions of authority, and was elected Abbot in 1078. He was highly successful as Abbot, attracting monks from all over Europe and confirming Bec in its position as one of the main centers of learning of the time; during this time, he became internationally known as a leading intellectual and established himself as a spiritual counselor to kings from Ireland to Jerusalem. In 1093, much against his will, he succeeded his old teacher Lanfranc as Archbishop of Canterbury, the head of the church in England. His tenure as Archbishop was stormy in the extreme: the king of England at the time, William Rufus, "seems to have combined the virtues of an American gangster with those of a South American dictator,"* and was determined to make the wealthy and powerful church subservient to royal authority. Anselm, by contrast, considered himself effectively co-ruler of England on the Pope's behalf, and he resisted William's encroachments fiercely and bravely. Anselm was exiled from England twice (for a total of more than five years), but eventually reached a compromise with William's brother and successor, Henry I, after the Pope threatened the king's excommunication.† He died in Canterbury in 1109, at the age of 76.

Anselm is often considered the most impressive philosopher and theologian of the early Middle Ages (i.e.,

between about 500 and 1100 CE). His major philosophical works are *Monologion* (which means "soliloquy"), *Proslogion* (Latin for "allocution," a formal speech or address), and a series of dialogues: *On the Grammarian*, *On Truth*, and *On Free Will*. His most important theological writing is *Cur Deus Homo*, or "Why God Became Man." In his final, unfinished work he tried to unravel the mystery of how a soul could come into existence. When he was told that he was soon to die, he is supposed to have replied, characteristically, "If it is His will I shall gladly obey, but if He should prefer me to stay with you just long enough to solve the question of the origin of the soul which I have been turning over in my mind, I would gratefully accept the chance, for I doubt whether anybody else will solve it when I am gone."

What Was Anselm's Overall Philosophical Project?

The original title of Anselm's *Proslogion* was *Faith Seeking Understanding*, and this encapsulates Anselm's consuming theological interest: he wanted to apply the tools of reason in order to better understand some (though not all) of what he already believed on the basis of faith. In fact, Anselm is often credited with being the first major thinker in the medieval Christian tradition to place great importance on the rational justification of theology, not (according to Anselm) because faith by itself is inadequate, but because rational proofs can improve our grasp of the nature of God. Anselm thought of the search for religious truth as not so much accumulating facts about God but as coming to a better personal *acquaintance*

---

* Max Charlesworth, from his introduction to *St. Anselm's Proslogion* (Clarendon Press, 1965), p. 17.
† To excommunicate someone is to ban them from membership in the church and so, in the Catholic tradition, to exclude them from all the sacraments, such as attending mass and receiving absolution for sins. Since it was believed that this would prevent those excommunicated from entering heaven, it was considered an extremely serious punishment.

with God, as one might come to know more about a friend over time. Since we clearly cannot sit down with God over a cup of coffee and chat, this process of finding out more about God depends to a large degree on careful, rational thought about God's nature.

Anselm is best remembered for originating one of the most stimulating and controversial of the arguments for the existence of God, the so-called Ontological Argument. ("Ontological" means "concerning what exists"; in this context, the idea is that we can come to know about God's 'pure' existence, without any sensory contact with God or his effects.) The Ontological Argument, if it works, not only proves as a matter of logic that God exists but also proves that God has a certain nature—that he is wise, good, infinite, powerful, and so on. The selection from Anselm given here is his presentation of this argument from the *Proslogion*, then a critique of the argument from Gaunilo, a monk from the Abbey of Marmoutier near Tours, and finally Anselm's response to that criticism. (Although Anselm's response to Gaunilo can be challenging reading, coming to grips with his compressed arguments is exhilarating, and important for better understanding his argument in the *Proslogion*.)

What Is the Structure of This Reading?

After a preface, in which he explains how the idea for the Ontological Argument came to him, Anselm lays out the Ontological Argument in Chapters 2 and 3 of the *Proslogion*. His argument has three parts:

(a) That a being than which nothing greater can be thought must really exist (Chapter 2).
(b) That furthermore it must necessarily exist: that is, it exists in such a way that it cannot be conceived by the human mind as not existing (first part of Chapter 3).
(c) That the entity described in (a) and (b) must be God (second part of Chapter 3).

In Chapter 4 Anselm responds to a possible objection to part (b) of the argument. In Chapter 5 he briefly draws some conclusions about the nature of God.

In the next section Gaunilo of Marmoutiers responds "on behalf of the Fool." Gaunilo's most important objections are:

(a) That God cannot be meaningfully thought about by human beings (Paragraph 4). Anselm responds to this in parts of Replies 1, 2, 8, and 9.
(b) That even if we could think about God, thinking about things doesn't show all by itself that they exist (Paragraphs 2 and 5). Anselm deals with this in Replies 1, 2, and 6.
(c) That if the Ontological Argument establishes the existence of God, it ought also to establish the existence of the "Lost Island," which is absurd (Paragraph 6). Anselm's response—which, rightly or wrongly, doesn't take the objection very seriously—is at the start of Reply 3.
(d) That a being than which nothing greater can be thought can be thought not to exist (Paragraph 7). Anselm answers in Replies 1, 3, and 9.

Some Useful Background Information

1. The Ontological Argument is an "*a priori*" argument: it purports to prove the existence of God on the basis of reason alone, independently of ordinary observation and empirical science. Anselm wants to show that the *idea* of God (all by itself) proves that God must exist.
2. Anselm makes use of various distinctions that it is useful to be aware of. The first is between two kinds of existence: existence in the mind (in Latin, "in intellectu") and existence in actual reality ("in re"). Something can exist in the mind but not in reality: for example, I can imagine a gold dinosaur and this dinosaur exists only *in intellectu* but not *in re*. Or something can exist in reality but not in anyone's mind: for example, a particular rock no one has ever seen, on the dark side of the Moon. Or something can exist in *both* the mind and reality: the Eiffel Tower, for instance, is both *in re* and *in intellectu* since it is both in Paris and in our thoughts. Finally, some unreal thing no one has ever thought of would be neither *in re* nor *in intellectu*.
3. Then there is a distinction between two ways of thinking about an idea: this is the difference between merely thinking the words that express an idea and actually thinking about the thing itself. As Anselm puts it, "in one sense a thing is thought when the word signifying it is thought; in another

sense when the very object which the thing is is understood." For example, the Fool might think to himself, "God does not exist," but if he does not really know what God is, then for him only "the sound of the letters or syllables" exists *in intellectu* and not actually God himself. This is sometimes explained in terms of the meaning of words or ideas: some of the ideas you think about really are meaningful to you (such as "Paris"), but some only *seem* meaningful when all you are really doing is silently mouthing the words (such as, perhaps, "crapulous"). Notice that, on this way of talking, ideas can be meaningful for us even if we do not know *everything* about their objects. For example, I don't need to have ever visited Paris to think meaningfully about that city; similarly, Anselm held that we can think about God even though God might be unimaginably greater than any picture we can form in our mind.

4. Finally, a third distinction is raised by Gaunilo and discussed by Anselm in his reply. This is the technical distinction between *thinking* (in Latin, "cogitare") and *understanding* ("intelligere"). For Anselm and Gaunilo, to think or conceive is to entertain possibilities—it's to consider things that may not actually be true and treat them (perhaps only temporarily) as if they were. For example, although I know I currently exist I could perhaps conceive of myself as not existing; although it may turn out to be false that extraterrestrials will visit the Earth within fifty years, I can certainly think that they will. By contrast, "understanding" is what philosophers today would call a 'success term': by definition, you cannot *understand* something to be true (or real) if it is in fact false (or unreal). Thus, according to Gaunilo, we could, strictly speaking, only understand the phrase "God exists" if in fact God does exist.

One important question we can now ask is the following: can we think meaningfully about things that are *not* possible? For example, can we think about square circles or married bachelors? According to Anselm, the answer to this question is no: we can, as it were, think the *words* "square circle," but we can't really think about the things themselves. What this means, significantly, is that for Anselm anything we can properly think about must really be possible.

Some Common Misconceptions

1. Anselm is not just claiming that we can prove something exists by simply thinking of it existing: he realizes that not every concept which includes the idea of existence is actually exemplified. For example, we can invent a concept of an existing unicorn—a *glunicorn*, defined as a unicorn that exists. But still there is no such thing. He thinks that the concept of God (that is, a being than which nothing greater can be thought) is a *uniquely special* concept in this respect; God, according to Anselm, has a unique kind of reality.

2. The unwary sometimes suppose that Anselm argues in the following way: God exists in our minds (*in intellectu*); our minds exist in the world (*in re*); therefore, God must also exist in the world. This, however, is not his argument. (If it were, it would merely establish that the *concept* of God exists, while Anselm wants to show that God *himself* exists. Furthermore, when Anselm says things exist *in intellectu* it's not at all clear that he literally wants to say they are *located inside our heads*; the Eiffel Tower which is the object of our thoughts is the very same one as that which is located in Paris.)

3. Anselm (perhaps contrary to what Aquinas says about him in the next reading) does not think that the existence of God is simply self-evident: that is, he doesn't think either (a) that we all already know that God exists, or (b) that merely to say "God does not exist" is to say something obviously self-contradictory (like saying "triangles have four sides"). What he does think is that *after* hearing his argument, it becomes obvious that God must exist. Similarly, he does not claim that everyone already has the concept of God (e.g., that we are born with the knowledge of God); his claim is rather that everyone can grasp that concept if it is explained to them.

How Important and Influential Is This Passage?

Rejected as mere verbal trickery by many subsequent philosophers (including St. Thomas Aquinas, in the next selection; the influential nineteenth-century philosopher Arthur Schopenhauer called it a "charming joke"), the

Ontological Argument was nevertheless popular throughout the Middle Ages, was revived by René Descartes and Gottfried Leibniz in the seventeenth and eighteenth centuries, was influentially used by G.W.F. Hegel in the nineteenth century, and is still attractive to some philosophers today. Many more contemporary philosophers think it fallacious, but it has proved frustratingly difficult to uncontroversially pin down precisely what is wrong with this 'many-faced' argument. Early in the twentieth century developments in the logic of predicates (predicates are 'describing phrases' like "... is green" or "... is taller than ...") bolstered Immanuel Kant's objection that "existence is not a predicate" (see question 5 below). However more recent developments in the logic of possibility and necessity (called modal logic) have apparently given the argument a new lease on life.

Proslogion

PREFACE AND CHAPTERS 2–5[*]

Preface

Earlier, urged to do so by some of my brethren, I published a brief work[†] on the theme of how someone might investigate certain matters of which he is ignorant. Because this book was knit together by many linked arguments, I began to ask myself whether there might be a single argument whose proof required nothing more than this very argument, and which by itself would be enough to prove that God exists; and also prove that there is a supreme good which requires nothing else, but which everything else requires for its existence and well-being; and also prove whatever else we believe regarding the divine Being. Although I tried hard to find this argument, and there were times when I thought it was within my reach, it escaped me altogether. At last, in despair, I was about to stop thinking about it, believing that I was looking for something which could not be found. I wished I could stop thinking about it: it seemed to be occupying my mind uselessly, keeping me from other lines of reasoning which would lead somewhere. But despite my unwillingness and my desire to avoid this

line of thought, it began to persistently force itself on me. So, one day, worn out by this resistance and in the midst of these conflicting thoughts, the very proof I had despaired of finding revealed itself, and I eagerly embraced the thoughts which I had been strenuously repelling.

Since I rejoiced to have found this, I thought I should write these thoughts down, and that some readers would welcome them. So I have written the following treatise, from the point of view of a person who tries to lift his mind to the contemplation of God and seeks to understand what he believes. In my judgment, neither this work nor the one I mentioned above deserved to be called a book, or to bear the name of an author. Yet I thought that they should be given titles to invite potential readers to examine them. Accordingly, I gave each a title: *An Example of Meditation on the Grounds of Faith* for the first, and *Faith Seeking Understanding* for its sequel.

But, after many people had copied them,[‡] I was urged to add my name to them, especially by Hugo, the reverend Archbishop of Lyons, holder of the apostolic office in Gaul, who told me to do this under his

---

[*]   The *Proslogion* was written between 1077 and 1078. Gaunilo's reply was written shortly after it appeared, and Anselm's response quickly after that. The translation reprinted here, of all three works, is by Sidney Norton Deane, modernized by Robert M. Martin for this volume. Deane's original appears in *Proslogium; Monologium; an appendix, In behalf of the fool, by Gaunilon; and Cur Deus homo* (Open Court Publishing, 1903).

[†]   The *Monologion*, probably written one year before the *Proslogion*.

[‡]   Prior to the introduction of the printing press in Europe in the mid-1400s, manuscripts were "published" by being copied by hand.

apostolic authority. And I made their titles more apt, naming the first *Monologion*, that is, A Soliloquy, and the second, *Proslogion*, that is, a discourse.
...

Chapter 2. That God truly exists

So, Lord, You who gives understanding to faith, if you think it is useful, give me the understanding that You exist as we believe You to exist, and that You are what we believe you to be. In fact, we believe that You are a being than which nothing greater can be thought. But is there no being like this, since the fool has said in his heart, there is no God?* But, at any rate, this very fool, when he hears of this being of which I speak—a being than which nothing greater can be thought—understands what he hears; although he does not understand that such a being exists. For, it is one thing for an object to be in the mind, and another to understand that the object exists. When a painter first conceives of what he will afterwards portray, he has it in his mind, but he does not yet understand it to exist, because he has not yet painted it. But after he has made the painting—because he has painted it—he has it in his mind *and* he understands that it exists.

Hence, even the fool is convinced that something than which nothing greater can be thought exists in his mind at least. For when he hears of this, he understands the words. He has the notion of such a being in his mind. But that object—the thing than which nothing greater can be thought—cannot exist in the mind alone. For, suppose it exists in the mind alone; then it can also be thought to exist in reality, which is greater. So if that object is exists in the mind alone, something greater *can* be thought. But as it exists only in his mind, is it a thought of that which *nothing* greater can be thought? Obviously this is impossible. Hence, there is no doubt that there exists a being than which nothing greater can be thought, and it exists both in the mind and in reality.

Chapter 3. God cannot be conceived not to exist

It is certain that this object exists so truly that it cannot be thought not to exist. It is possible to think of a being which cannot be thought not to exist; and this is greater than one which *can* be thought not to exist. Hence, if the object, supposedly the thing than which nothing greater can be thought, can be thought not to exist, it is not really the thing than which nothing greater can be thought. This is an irreconcilable contradiction. There exists in reality, then, a being than which nothing greater can be thought to exist, and it cannot even be thought not to exist.

And You are this being, O Lord, our God. You exist so truly, O Lord, my God, that You can not be thought not to exist; and this is the way it should be. For, if a mind could think of a being better than You, the created thinker would rise above the Creator; and this supposition is completely absurd. Except for You alone, everything else can be thought not to exist. You are thought to exist more truly than all other beings, and so in a higher degree than all others. For, whatever else exists does not exist so truly, and so it exists in a smaller degree. Why, then, has the fool said in his heart, there is no God (Psalms xiv. 1), since it is so evident, to a rational mind, that You exist in the highest degree of all? Why, except that he is dull and a fool?

Chapter 4. How the fool has said in his heart what cannot be conceived

How could it be that the fool said in his heart what he could not think? Or, conversely, how could he not think what he said in his heart? (Assuming that thinking and saying in one's heart are the same thing.) If he really—no, *since* he really—said and did not say in his heart, and thought and did not think, that God exists, there must be more than one way that something is said in the heart or thought. For, in one sense, an object is [merely] thought of, when the word signifying it is understood, and in another, when the very entity—the object—is understood. In the former sense, then, God can be thought not to exist; but that is impossible in the latter. For no one who understands what the

---

* This quotation is from the first lines of the Psalms numbered 14 and 53 in later versions of the Bible.

objects, fire and water, are, can think that fire is water. This thought is impossible when one understands real facts, but it is possible to think that the words "fire" and "water" refer to the same thing. So, then, no one who understands what God is can think that God does not exist; although he says these words in his heart, either without any meaning or with some irregular meaning. For, God is that than which a greater cannot be thought. So anyone who thoroughly understands this, definitely understands that this being so truly exists, that not even in thought can it be non-existent. Therefore, he who understands that God so exists, cannot think that He does not exist.

I thank You, gracious Lord, I thank You; because what I formerly believed because of Your gift of faith, now I understand by Your gift of illumination. I now understand by Your illumination, that if I were unwilling to *believe* that You exist, I should not be able not to *understand* this.

Chapter 5. *God is whatever it is better to be than not to be; and He, as the only self-existent being, creates all things from nothing.*

What are You, then, Lord God, than whom nothing greater can be thought? What are You, except that which, as the highest of all beings, alone exists through itself, and creates all other things from nothing? For, whatever is not the highest of all beings is less than something else which can be thought of. But this cannot be thought of You. What good, therefore, does the supreme good lack, when every good is good *through* it? Therefore, You are just, truthful, blessed, and whatever it is better to be than not to be. For it is better to be just than not just, and better to be blessed than not blessed.

Pro Insipiente

("ON BEHALF OF THE FOOL")
BY GAUNILO OF MARMOUTIERS

Paragraph 1 [Gaunilo's summary of Anselm's arguments]

If someone doubts or denies the existence of a being with the characteristic that nothing greater than it can be thought, that person may be answered this way: The existence of this being is proved, in the first place, by the fact that he himself, in his doubt or denial regarding this being, already has it in his mind; for he understands the words used to speak about it. It is proved, therefore, by the fact that what he understands must exist not only in his mind, but in reality also. And the proof of this is as follows: It is a greater thing to exist both in the mind and in reality than to be in the mind alone. And if this being is in the mind alone, whatever has (even in the past) existed in reality will be greater than this being. And so that which was greater than all beings will be less than some beings, and will not be greater than all, which is a manifest contradiction. And hence, that which is greater than all, already proved to be in the mind, must exist not only in the mind, but also in reality: for otherwise it will not be greater than all other beings.

Paragraph 2

The fool might make this reply: This being is supposed to be in my mind already, and the only reason for this is that I understand the words I hear when this being is spoken of. But couldn't it be said, with equal plausibility, that I have in my mind—can think of—all kinds of unreal objects—things that have absolutely no existence in themselves—because I understand the words used to speak of these things, when they are spoken of, whatever they may be?

On the other hand, perhaps it could it be shown that this special being is of a different sort, in that it cannot be thought of like unreal objects, or objects whose existence is uncertain—that in this case alone, my ability to think of it depends on its existence in reality. In ordinary cases, such as a painted picture, first there is a thought in the painter's mind, and afterwards the object exists. But in this special sort of case, this time sequence does not apply: there is no earlier/later distinction between the mere having of an object in mind and the understanding that the object exists.

Moreover, when you spoke of, or heard of, this sort of being—one impossible to think about unless it exists—it would be impossible to think that it didn't exist. But even God can be thought not to exist. If it were impossible to think this, what would be the point of arguing against someone who doubts or denies the existence of that sort of being?

Anyway, it must be proven by indisputable argument that something exists such that it can't be thought of unless it's already understood as existing. What you have said does not prove this. You say that what I understand, when I hear of it, is already in my mind. But this is true of all sorts of things that I hear about whose external existence is uncertain, or which do not exist at all. That happens when someone speaks about them, using words I understand. Often I am deceived, and believe that what they are speaking about exists. But when I hear your descriptions, I don't believe that a real object you were trying to prove exists.

Paragraph 3

So your example of the painter who thinks of what he is about to paint cannot support this argument. For the picture, before it is made, is contained in the painter's visualizing talent itself—one of his mental characteristics. St. Augustine* says that a carpenter, when he is about to make a box, in fact first has the box in his thought. The box which is to be made is not a living thing; but the box which exists in his thought is part of his mind—part of his living being. For the artist's mind is alive, and before things are produced, they are in there. These things, alive in the mind of the artist, must be the mind's know-how. With the exception of facts about mental things, all other facts, when we hear or think of them, are thought to be external existents. Those real external objects are one thing, and the mind, which thinks about such objects, is something else. So even if a being than which a greater is impossible exists, when we hear or think about this being, this is not analogous to the not-yet-created picture in the mind of the painter.

Paragraph 4

With regard to this being which is greater than all which can be thought, and which, it is said, can be none other than God himself, let us consider a point I mentioned above. I cannot think of any being greater than any possible others, in terms of the specific and generic knowledge of objects. I am just as unable to understand God himself; and so, for this very reason, I can think of this being as not existing. For I do not understand that reality itself which God is, by experience of a really existing entity; nor can I speculate on the nature of that reality on the basis of some other similar reality. For you yourself assert that there can be nothing else like that reality.

Now, suppose that I hear something about a man absolutely unknown to me, a man whose existence I was unaware of. Through the special or general knowledge of what *man* is, or of what *men* are, I could think of this person also, according to the reality of men in general. It would be possible, if the person who told me of him deceived me, that the unknown man himself, of whom I thought, did not exist; this would be possible because the reality in terms of which I thought of him was not *that* man but any man, men in general.

But compare the being of which you speak. I am not able to understand or think of that being in the same way, when I hear the word "God" or the words "a being greater than all other beings." I can think of the man in terms of what is real and familiar to me: but I can't think of God, or a being greater than all others, except merely by understanding the words. And it is unlikely or impossible that an object can be thought of merely by thinking of words alone. For when something is really thought of, it is not just the words which are understood (although they are real, as are the sounds of the letters and syllables). What is thought of is what the words signify. But someone who does

---

* St. Augustine of Hippo, a north-African bishop who lived from 354 until 430, was the most important early Christian theologian and Anselm's major intellectual influence. This quote is from his *Treatises on the Gospel of John*.

not know exactly what some words signify, thinks of it only according to the mental associations produced by hearing the words. In this way, he attempts to imagine what the words might signify, and it would be surprising if, by so doing, he could ever get it right. But this is exactly what is going on when I hear and understand what a person says, who tells me that there is a being greater than all possible beings. So much for the assertion that this supreme nature is already in my mind.

Paragraph 5

I accept this reasoning: If something exists in reality, that thing is greater than the mere thought of that thing in the mind. So if some being exists in my mind only, a corresponding being just like it, except that it really exists, would be greater. But what ideas are in my mind? Is there, in my mind, the idea of a being which cannot be thought of in terms of any fact? If that idea were in my mind, I would not deny it. If it is in my mind, it would establish the existence of a corresponding being in reality. However, I do not concede to the existence of that idea in my mind. So I don't accept that it has real external existence, unless some real proof can be given.

The person who says that this external being exists, because otherwise it would not be the greatest of all things, is not paying close attention to what he is saying. I do not admit—I even deny or doubt—that there is a real being greater than any other real object. I do not concede that it has any other existence than perhaps in people's minds—if you can call that existence. When someone tries to think of such a being, the one designated by the words they hear, they try to form an idea of an object completely unknown to them. So, how is the real existence of this being demonstrated to me on the basis that it is greater than all other beings? I deny this, or doubt you have proven it. In connection with the words, what my mind conjures up is not even like its ideas of things whose existence is uncertain and doubtful. The attempted proof starts with the assumption that such a being must exist at least in people's minds, but as I deny this, we cannot infer that it really externally exists itself.

Paragraph 6

Here is an example of an analogous argument. Suppose someone says: somewhere in the ocean there is an island which (because of the difficulty, or rather the impossibility, of discovering what does not exist) is called Lost Island. And imagine that this island is inestimably wealthy—that it has all sorts of riches and delights, much more even than the Islands of the Blessed;* things are even more richly abundant there because the island is uninhabited, so nothing is unavailable because of being owned by someone. Now if someone should tell me that there is such an island, I would easily understand what he says: there is no difficulty in that. But suppose that he went on to say, as if by a logical inference, "You can no longer doubt that this island, which is more excellent than all lands, exists somewhere, since you have no doubt that it is in your mind. Since it is more excellent not to be in the mind alone, but to exist both in the mind and in reality, for this reason it must exist. For if it does not exist, a corresponding land which really exists will be more excellent than it; and so the island already thought by you to be more excellent will not be more excellent." If a man should try to prove to me by such reasoning that this island truly exists, and that its existence should no longer be doubted, I would believe that he was joking; or else that if he thought he had established the existence of this island, he would be more foolish than I would be if I accepted this proof. What is needed for a real proof would be to show that this island was real, not just imaginary.

Paragraph 7

This, first of all, could be the fool's reply. When he is assured in the first place that this being is so great that its non-existence is not even thinkable, and that this in turn is proved on no other ground than the fact that otherwise it will not be greater than all things, the fool can respond the same way, saying, "When did I grant that any such being exists in reality, that is, a being greater than all others? If I did, then that could be used to prove to me that it also exists in reality

---

* The mythical land—often located where the sun sets in the West—where people in classical times believed the souls of heroes lived in bliss.

to such a degree that it cannot even be thought not to exist." However, it must *first* be somehow proven that an object exists which is higher, that is, greater and better, than all other natures; *then*, from this, we could demonstrate that this being necessarily has all those attributes.

Moreover, it is said that the non-existence of this being is unthinkable. Perhaps it might be better to say that its non-existence, or the possibility of its non-existence, is not *understandable*. For according to the true meaning of the word "understanding," unreal objects cannot be understood. Yet their existence is *thinkable* in the way in which the fool thought of the non-existence of God. I am most certainly aware of my own existence; but I know, nevertheless, that my non-existence is possible. As to that supreme being, moreover, which God is, I can think without any doubt of both his existence and the impossibility of his non-existence. I am not sure whether I can think

of myself as non-existing, when I am most definitely and clearly aware of my existence. But if I can, why can I not think of the non-existence of whatever else I know with the same certainty? If I cannot, however, God will not be the only being of which it can be said that it is impossible to think of its non-existence.

Paragraph 8

There are matters at the beginning of your book* which are the result of correct feeling, but which are argued for weakly. However, the other parts of this book are argued for with such truth, such brilliancy, such grandeur, and are so useful, so fragrant with a certain perfume of devout and holy feeling, that the rest of the work should not be rejected. Instead, these earlier matters ought instead to be reasoned more cogently, so that the whole book can be received with great respect and honor.

Anselm's Reply to Gaunilo

I directed the argument of my *Proslogion* against a fool. Seeing, however, that the author of these objections is by no means a fool, and is a Catholic, speaking in behalf of the fool, I think that it is sufficient that I answer the Catholic.

Reply 1

You say: A being than which a greater cannot be thought is in the mind in the same sense that any being whose real existence is altogether impossible is in the mind. You say that the inference from the fact that it is in the mind to the statement that this being exists in reality, is no more correct than the inference that Lost Island certainly exists, from the fact that when it is described the hearer does not doubt that it is in his mind.

But I say: *If* a being than which a greater is thinkable is not understood, and this idea is not in the mind, then either (1) God is not a being than which a greater

is impossible, or else (2) talk about God is not understood. But I call on your faith and conscience to admit that both are entirely false. So a being than which a greater cannot be thought is truly understood, and is in the mind. Therefore, either the supposition on which you try to base your opposition to my argument (that such a being is not in the mind) is not true, or else the inference which you suppose logically follows from that supposition (that therefore it must exist in reality) is not justified.

But your position is this: Supposing that the words "a being than which a greater cannot be thought" are understood, it does not follow that this being is in the mind; but even if it is in the mind, it does not follow that it exists in reality. In answer to this, I maintain positively that if that being can even be thought of, it must exist in reality. For that sort of thing cannot have a beginning. But any non-existent thing can be thought of; if it begins to exist, it has a beginning [and, not being eternal, it is not perfect]. It follows that anything that can be thought to exist but does not really

---

* The *Proslogion* has 26 chapters, of which only Chapters 2 to 5—those containing the ontological argument about which Gaunilo has complaints—are reprinted here.

exist—that thing is not a being than which a greater cannot be thought. But we're talking about the greatest possible being: if such a being can be thought to exist, it must exist.

Again: If it can be thought at all, it must exist. For no one who denies or doubts the existence of a being than which a greater is unthinkable, denies or doubts that *if* it did exist, its non-existence, either in reality or in the mind, would be impossible. (Otherwise it would not be a being than which a greater cannot be thought.)

Consider something that can be thought, but does not exist; if there were such a being, its non-existence, either in reality or in the mind, would be possible. But what about a being than which a greater is cannot be thought? Let us suppose that it does not exist, even if it can be thought. If it can be thought, but does not exist, then if it existed, it would not be a being than which a greater cannot be thought. If, then, there were a being a greater than which cannot be thought, it would *not* be a being than which a greater than cannot be thought: this is an absurd contradiction. Hence, it is false to deny that a being than which a greater cannot be thought exists, if it can be even thought of, and all the more false if it can be understood or can be in the understanding.

I will go further: if something does not exist anywhere at any time, or if it exists somewhere, at some time, but not at other times, that sort of thing can be imagined or thought to exist nowhere and never. For example, consider something that did not exist yesterday and exists today; because it is thought not to have existed yesterday, so it can be imagined by the intelligence never to have existed. Similarly, something that is not here, but is elsewhere, can be imagined to be nowhere. Similarly, consider an object some of whose individual parts do not exist at the same places or times as other individual parts: *all* its parts, and therefore the whole object, can be imagined to exist nowhere or never. For, although time is said to exist always and the universe to be everywhere, yet time does not *as a whole* exist always, nor the world *as a whole* everywhere. And as individual parts of time do not exist when others exist, so they can be imagined never to exist. And so it can be apprehended by the mind that individual parts of the world exist nowhere, as they do not exist where other parts exist. Moreover,

what is composed of parts can be imagined as dissolved and non-existent. Therefore, anything that does not exist as a whole at some place or time, even if it is existent, can be imagined not to exist. But that than which a greater cannot be thought, if it exists, cannot be imagined not to exist. Otherwise, it is not a being than which a greater cannot be thought, which is inconsistent. By no means, then, does it at any place or at any time fail to exist as a whole, but it exists as a whole everywhere and always.

Do you believe that this being can be thought or understood, in some way? That it can be in the mind, in the understanding? For if it cannot, what I have been saying about it cannot be understood. But if you say that it is not thought and that it is not in the mind, because it is not *thoroughly* understood, this is like saying that a man who cannot face the direct rays of the sun does not see sunlight at all. But clearly a being than which a greater cannot be thought exists; and clearly it *is* in the mind, at least to the extent that these statements regarding it are understood.

Reply 2

Part of my argument, with which you disagree, is the assertion that when the fool hears of a being than which a greater is unthinkable, he understands what he hears. Clearly, someone does not understand what is said in a familiar language has no understanding at all, or a very limited one.

Moreover, I have said that if this being is thought of, it is in the mind. Could anything that has been proven to exist be in nobody's mind? But you will say that although it is in the mind, it does not follow that it is thought of. But observe that the fact of its being thought of does necessitate its being in the mind. For what is thought of is in the mind. What can be clearer than this?

I go on to claim that if it is in the mind *alone*, it can be thought of also to exist in reality, which is greater. If, then, it is in the mind alone, it is a being than which a greater *can* be thought. What is more logical? For if it exists in the mind alone, can it not also be thought to exist in reality? And if it can be thought to exist in reality, does not the person who thinks of this really existing object think of a thing greater than the being existing in the mind alone? But this is an entirely consistent inference: if a being than which a greater cannot be thought is in the mind alone, is that being the one than which a greater cannot be thought? But, assuredly, in no mind is there a being than which a greater both is *thought* and is *unthinkable*. Doesn't it follow, then, that if a being than which a greater cannot be thought is in any mind, it does not exist in the mind alone? For if it is in the mind alone, it is a being than which a greater *can* be thought, which is inconsistent with the hypothesis.

Reply 3

But you imagine this story: Someone tells you about an island in the ocean which is more fertile than any other land. Because of the difficulty, or the impossibility, of discovering what does not exist, it is called Lost Island. But then they go on to reason [in a parody of my argument] that it follows that this island truly exists in reality, because one who hears it described easily understands what he hears. Now I assure you that if this is a correct adaptation of my reasoning, that if anyone thinks of anything other than the Divine being, as the being than which nothing greater can be cognized, I will discover that thing and will give him his Lost Island, which will never be lost again.

The greatest being cannot be thought not to exist, because its existence is a necessary truth; otherwise it would not exist at all. Hence, if anyone says that he thinks that this being doesn't exist, he is not thinking about the greatest being. But if he *does* in fact think of the greatest being, he must be thinking of a being which cannot be even thought not to exist. For if it could be thought not to exist, it could be thought to have a beginning and an end. But this is impossible. He, then, who thinks of this sort of greatest being must think that being cannot be thought not to exist. So, he who thinks of this being does not, cannot, think that it does not exist; to do so would be to think what is impossible, not thinkable. The non-existence of that than which a greater cannot be thought is impossible.

Reply 4

According to you, it is better to say that the non-existence (or even the possibility of non-existence) of this supreme being cannot be *thought*, than to say it cannot be *understood*. It is your position that nothing which exists can be *understood* to be non-existent. So it is not the distinguishing characteristic of God that his non-existence or the possibility of his non-existence can be *understood*: that is true for every existent thing.

But this objection surely does not apply to the term "think," if you consider the meaning of that word. For although no objects which exist can be *thought* not to exist, yet all objects, except the one which exists in the highest degree, can be *thought* not to exist. All other objects have a beginning or end, or are made of a composition of parts, or do not exist as a whole at any time or place. On the other hand, the object thought as having no beginning or end, and no composition or parts, and which is always and everywhere found as a whole, cannot be thought as non-existent.

Be assured, then, that you can think of your own non-existence, although you are most certain that you exist. I am surprised that you admit you are ignorant of this. For we think of the non-existence of many objects which we know to exist, and of the existence of many which we know not to exist. We do this not by forming the opinion that they exist (or don't), but by imagining that they are in the opposite state from what we know.

So [*in one sense,*] we can think of the non-existence of an object, although we know that it exists, because at the same time we can think of its non-existence while knowing it exists. But [*in another sense,*] we cannot think of the nonexistence of an object, so long as we know it to exist, because we cannot think at the same time of existence and non-existence. Having distinguished these two senses of this statement, one will understand that [in the first sense] anything (except God) that is known to exist can be thought not to exist, and anything that is known not to exist can be thought to exist. But [in the second sense] we cannot think of the existence of anything that we know does not exist, or of the non-existence of anything we know to exist. So when I say and adequately explain in my book that we cannot think of non-existence of God *alone*, I am using the first sense of "think."

Reply 5

It is easy, even for someone of low intelligence, to meet the other objections you make on behalf of the fool, so I believed it was unnecessary to show this. However, I hear that some readers of these objections think they have some weight against my arguments, so I will discuss them briefly.

In the first place, you often repeat that this is my argument: what is greater than everything else exists in the mind, and if it is in the mind, it exists also in reality, for otherwise the greatest being would not be the greatest. What exists in reality is greater than the same thing existing only in the mind. But nowhere in all my writings do I make this argument. My assumption about the being in question is that it is the thing such that nothing greater *can be thought*. "The being such that nothing is greater" and "the being such that nothing greater *can be thought*": these two formulas are not equivalent in arguments for the real existence of such a thing.

[First we consider the second argument, the one I really make. Here is why the denial of its conclusion is incoherent.] Suppose someone thinks that a thing such that a greater *cannot be thought* does not exist in reality. Now it's clear that what doesn't really exist is also possibly non-existent, that is, not necessarily existent, and that it can be thought to be non-existent. So, logically speaking, that person can think that this entity is at least possibly non-existent. But if this person is thinking about something whose existence is possible—i.e., not necessary—this person cannot be thinking about the being than which a greater cannot be thought. That person can conceive of a greater being: one whose existence is necessary.

The same is true if that person thinks that the being in question exists but not necessarily—that, in other words, the being might be imagined not to exist.

But now compare this proof [the first argument, which is not mine]. This one concerns a being which is said to be greater than all other beings. It is not evident that existing beings are greater than beings that exist in thought only. Consider a being greater than all other beings, but which can nevertheless be thought not to exist. Is it clear that existing beings are greater than this being? This requires the premise that existence is better than non-existence—a premise that I do not affirm. You have unjustly censured me

for saying what I did not say; what you claim I said is not my argument.

If, on the other hand, my real argument is valid, you should not blame me so for having said what can be proved. My proof is that a being than which a greater cannot be thought really must exist. This being must be thought of as the one greater than all. So, this being is the object of thought, is "in the mind," and for that reason is said to exist in the reality of fact. In sum, what is said to be greater than all other beings is thought about and is in the mind, and therefore it is necessarily inferred that it exists in reality. You see, then, with how much justice you have compared me with your fool, who, on the sole ground that he understands what is described to him, would affirm that a lost island exists.

Reply 6

Another claim, in your objections, is that *any* unreal beings, or beings whose existence is uncertain, can be thought about, and be in the mind, *in the same way* as the being which we discussed. This objection surprised me, because at first I merely wanted to show that this being is thought about *in some way or other*, and so is in the mind. I intended to consider whether this being is in the mind alone, like an unreal object, or whether it also exists in fact, as a real being. Given what I wanted to prove, I first assumed that unreal objects, or objects of doubtful existence, could be in the mind, because the hearer understands what the speaker means when such things are spoken of.

But how, moreover, can these two statements of yours be reconciled?: (1) the assertion that if somebody talks about an unreal object, you could understand what is said, and (2) the assertion that you couldn't understand talk of unreal objects—that the only way you have of understanding talk of an object is by thinking that it really exists, not merely in someone's mind? How, I ask, can these two things be reconciled: that unreal objects are thought about, and that thinking about an object is understanding its real existence? This contradiction is not my problem. But if unreal objects are in some way understood, by a particular sort of understanding, you should allow me to first assume that a being than which a greater cannot be thought is thought about before I reached the conclusion that this being exists in reality.

Reply 7

You go on to say that it is unbelievable that this being cannot be thought not to exist, in the same way in which even God may be thought not to exist. That is an objection that even people with little ability to argue could reply to. Is it reasonable to deny the existence of what you understand, because you denied the existence of that thing on the grounds that you didn't understand it? Or, since partial understanding is the same to him as not understanding at all, he denies the existence of something he only partially understands? Isn't it the case that something is more easily proven of what exists in some understanding than of what exists in no understanding? If someone understands to some degree "that which a greater cannot be thought," then it is incredible that he denies the existence of a being to which this applies. I am saying this denial is incredible because it is based on the denial of the existence of God, which it based in turn on the fact that there is no sense-perception of God, of whom he claims no conception. But is the existence of any other object denied, because it is not at all understood? And isn't the existence of what is understood in some degree more easily proved than the existence of an object which is not understood in any way? So, it wasn't irrational of me, in proving the existence of God, to use the hypothesis of a being greater than which cannot be thought. This was the right tactic for convincing the fool, for he would understand such a being to some extent, while not understanding God in any way.

Reply 8

You demonstrated very carefully that the being than which a greater cannot be thought is not analogous to the picture in the mind of the painter, which he has not yet painted. But this demonstration was quite unnecessary. My aim in mentioning the picture was not to draw an analogy with the being I was discussing. What I wanted to show was that something that is not thought to exist in reality can be in the mind.

Again, you say that when you hear "a being than which a greater is not thinkable," you cannot think of it in terms of any real object known to you either specifically or generically, or have it in your mind. For, you say, you neither know such a being in itself, nor can you form an idea of it from anything like it. But obviously this is not true. For everything that is less good, in so far as it is good, is like the greater good. It is therefore evident to any rational mind, that by ascending from the lesser good to the greater, we can obtain a substantial notion of a being than which a greater is inconceivable. Consider someone who supposes that there is some good which has a beginning and an end; wouldn't that person conceive that that good would be much better if it does not cease to be, even though he does not believe that about the good he thinks exists? And just as the second good is better than the first, in the same way a good which has neither beginning nor end, though it is forever passing from the past through the present to the future, is better than the second? And that far better than any of these is a being—whether any being of such a nature exists or not—which doesn't require change or motion, and cannot be forced to change or move? Is this unthinkable? Can we think of something better than this? This thought process is how we obtain an idea of objects for which we can, or cannot, think of better ones, isn't it? So there *is* a way to form a notion of a being than which a greater is unthinkable. This shows how easy it is to refute the fool who does not accept sacred authority and denies that a notion may be formed, from other objects, of a being than which a greater is unthinkable. But if any Christian would deny this, let him remember that "Ever since the creation of the world God's eternal power and divine nature, invisible though they are, have been seen and understood through the things God has made."*

Reply 9

But even if it were true that *a being* than which a greater is inconceivable cannot be thought or understood, yet that doesn't make it true that the *phrase* "a being than which a greater cannot be thought" cannot be thought or understood. There is nothing to prevent one's saying

---

* A biblical quote, from St. Paul's Epistle to the Romans (1:20).

and understanding the word "ineffable,"* although objects said to be ineffable cannot be described. Being unthinkable is thinkable, although things to which the word "unthinkable" applies are not thinkable. So, when one says, "that than which nothing greater is thinkable," undoubtedly what is heard is thinkable and intelligible, even if that being itself, than which a greater is unthinkable, cannot be thought or understood.

Though there is a man so foolish as to say that there is no being than which a greater is unthinkable, he will not be so shameless as to say that he cannot understand or conceive of what he says. Or, if such a man is found, not only ought his words to be rejected, but he himself should be regarded with contempt. Whoever, then, denies the existence of a being than which a greater cannot be thought, at least understands and conceives of the denial which he makes. But to understand his denial he must understand its components; and a component of this statement is the words "a being than which a greater cannot be thought." Whoever, then, makes this denial, understands and conceives of that than which a greater is inconceivable. Similarly, it is evidently possible to conceive of and think of a being whose nonexistence is impossible. Someone who conceives of this conceives of a greater being than one whose nonexistence is possible. So conceptualizing the greatest being that can be thought of is thinking of a being whose nonexistence is impossible, not one whose non-existence is

possible. Therefore, what he conceives of must exist; for anything whose nonexistence is possible, is not that being he conceives of.

Reply 10

I believe that I have shown by a sufficiently strong argument that in my former book I proved the real existence of a being than which a greater cannot be thought, and I believe that this argument cannot be invalidated by any objection. This reasoning validly shows that the being under discussion, because it is understood or thought, must also exist in reality, and to be whatever we should believe of the Divine, for we attribute to the Divine nature whatever characteristics it is better to have than not to have. For example: it is better to be eternal than not eternal; good than not good; better to be, in fact, goodness itself, than not to be goodness itself. It is impossible that such characteristics be true of anything but an object than which a greater is inconceivable. Hence, the being than which a greater is inconceivable must be that being to which we attribute the Divine nature.

I thank you for your kindness both in criticizing and in praising my book. I can conclude, from your generosity in praising the parts you deem worthy, that your criticisms of the parts you think are weak are given with good will. ▪

Suggestions for Critical Reflection

1. If Anselm's argument is sound, what if anything does it tell us about God (in addition to the fact that he exists)?

2. The concepts 'bachelor' or 'unicorn' do not entail that such things exist. Why does Anselm think that the concept 'God' is importantly different? Is he right? What about the concept of 'an integer between 10 and 12': do you think this concept might commit us to the existence of the number 11? Does this show that not all existence claims are empirical?

3. What do you think about Anselm's distinction between two kinds of existence (*in re* and *in intellectu*)? Do you agree that being thought about is a kind of existence?

4. Does Gaunilo's example of the "Lost Island" show that Anselm has made a mistake? If so, does it show *what* mistake (or mistakes) has been made?

5. The famous eighteenth-century German philosopher Immanuel Kant argued that the flaw in the Ontological Argument is that it mistakenly treats existence as a property. When we say that

---

* "Ineffable" means unutterable or indescribable—incapable of being expressed.

leopards are spotted we are ascribing a property (being covered in spots) to leopards; however, Kant would argue, when we say that leopards exist, we are not pointing to all the leopards and saying that they have the property of existence. (If it were a property, then it would make sense to say that some leopards have it, and some don't. But which leopards don't?) Instead, we are saying something not about actual leopards but about the concept 'leopard': we are saying that something in the actual world fits that concept. If we say that Boy Scouts are honest, we might go on to talk about some Boy Scout who is *perfectly* honest—who possesses the property of honesty to perfection. However, if we say that Boy Scouts exist, it is incoherent to try to point to the perfectly existing Boy Scout. Existence, therefore, is not a property, and so (according to Kant's argument) we have no reason to believe that a being which possesses all the properties of the most perfect thing—i.e., a being than which nothing greater can be thought—must exist. What do you think of this objection to the Ontological Argument? Is it decisive?

6. Suppose we agree with Anselm (against Kant) that existence *is* a perfection. Does this mean that an actual serial killer is more perfect than a merely fictional one?

7. Another objection to the Ontological Argument is the following: we may (as human beings) be able to *think* of an absolutely perfect being, but (contrary to Anselm's assumption) it does not follow from this that an absolutely perfect being is actually *possible*. That is, although we are unable to see what is logically impossible in the idea of a perfect being, it might nevertheless still *be* logically impossible; and since we can't rule this out, we can't show *a priori* that God exists. What do you think of this objection? If it works, what implications does it have for our knowledge of possibility?

8. Finally, a third possible objection to Anselm's Ontological Argument: Even if Anselm succeeds in showing that that a being than which nothing greater can be thought must be *thought of* as existing, it still doesn't follow that it actually *does* exist. To conceive of something as being a certain way, the argument goes, does not mean that it actually *is* that way, or even that one must *believe* that it is that way: for example, one can conceive of the sky as being bright green, even though it isn't. So, for God, we can and perhaps must conceive of God as existing, but it doesn't follow that God does exist (or even that we must believe that God exists). What do you think of this objection? How do you think Anselm might respond to it?

ST. THOMAS AQUINAS

The Existence of God
(FROM *SUMMA THEOLOGIAE*)

Who Was St. Thomas Aquinas?

Saint Thomas was born in 1225 in Roccasecca in southern Italy, the son of the count of Aquino. At the age of five he was sent to be educated at the great Benedictine abbey of Monte Casino, and at 14 he went to university in Naples. His father expected him to join the respectable and wealthy Benedictine order of monks. However, when he was 19 Aquinas instead joined the recently formed Dominican order of celibate, mendicant (begging) friars. These monks had adopted a life of complete poverty and traveled Europe studying and teaching the gospel. Thomas's father was outraged, and—according to legend—he locked Aquinas in the family castle for a year and offered him bribes, including a beautiful prostitute, to join the Benedictines instead. Aquinas is said to have grabbed a burning brand from the fire and chased away the prostitute; his family eventually allowed him to leave and travel to Paris. He went on to study Greek and Islamic philosophy, natural science, and theology in Paris and Cologne under Albertus Magnus ("Albert the Great"), a Dominican who was famed for his vast learning. His colleagues in Cologne nicknamed Aquinas "the dumb ox" because of his reserved personality and large size; Albertus is said to have responded that Thomas's bellowing would be heard throughout the world. In 1256 Aquinas was made a regent master (professor) at the University of Paris. He taught in Paris and Naples until, on December 6, 1273, he had a deeply religious experience after which he stopped writing. "All that I have written seems to me like straw compared to what has now been revealed to me," he said. He died four months later.

Aquinas became known to later ages as the Angelic Doctor, and was canonized in 1323. In fact, starting shortly after his death, miraculous powers (such as healing the blind) were attributed to Aquinas's corpse, and the Cistercian monks who possessed the body became concerned that members of the Dominican order would steal their treasure: as a safeguard, they "exhumed the corpse of Brother Thomas from its resting place, cut off the head and placed it in a hiding place in a corner of the chapel," so that even if the body were stolen they would still have the skull. His sister was given one of his hands.

Aquinas wrote voluminously—over eight million words of closely reasoned prose, especially amazing considering he was not yet 50 when he died. He is said to have committed the entire Bible to memory, and was able to dictate to six or seven secretaries at one time. (His own handwriting was so unintelligible it has been dubbed the *litera inintelligibilis*.) His two major works, both written in Latin, are *Summa contra Gentiles* and *Summa Theologiae*. The first (written between 1259 and 1264) defends Christianity against a large number of objections, without assuming in advance that Christianity is true—it was reputedly written as a handbook for missionaries seeking to convert Muslims and others to Catholicism. The second (written between 1265 and 1273) attempts to summarize Catholic doctrine in such a way that it is consistent with rational philosophy and the natural science of the day.

What Was Aquinas's Overall Philosophical Project?

Aquinas was the most important European philosopher of the Middle Ages. His great achievement was that he brought together Christian theology with the insights of classical Greek philosophy—especially the work of Aristotle—and created a formidably systematic and powerful body of thought. Much of this system, as part of the medieval tradition called "scholasticism," became the standard intellectual world view for Christian Europe for hundreds of years: it formed the basis of European science and philosophy until the intellectual Renaissance of the sixteenth century, and still underpins much Catholic theology.* In 1879 Pope Leo XIII recognized the philosophical system of Aquinas as the official doctrine of the Catholic Church.

The writings of the classical philosophers like Plato and Aristotle were lost to Western Europe for centuries after the fall of the Roman empire, but they were preserved by Jewish, Byzantine, and Islamic scholars on the Eastern and Southern shores of the Mediterranean. Starting in the sixth century CE these writings, translated into Latin, trickled back into non-Arabic Europe and by the thirteenth century, when Aquinas was writing, most of the texts of Plato and Aristotle were again available to Western thinkers. In particular, in the second half of the twelfth century, Aristotle's writings on physics and metaphysics came to light, triggering a deep intellectual conflict in Western Europe. Christian theology is ultimately based on *faith* or scriptural revelation, while the conclusions of Plato and Aristotle are supported by *reason*. When theology and philosophy disagree—and in particular, when philosophers provide us with a rationally compelling argument against a theological claim—which are we to believe? Many conservative Christian theologians at the time viewed classical philosophy as a pagan threat to Christian dogma, but Aquinas was deeply impressed by the work of Aristotle—he considered him the greatest of all philosophers, often referring to him in his writings as simply "The Philosopher"—and set out to reconcile Aristotle's writings with Catholic doctrine. He did this, it is important to note, not because he wanted to remove any threat to Christianity from pagan science, but because he thought that much of what Aristotle had to say was *demonstrably true*.

Aquinas's reconciliation project had two prongs. First, he tried to show whenever possible that Aristotelian thought did not conflict with Christianity but actually supported it: thus faith could be conjoined with reason—religion could be combined with science—by showing how the human powers of reason allowed us to *better understand* the revealed truths of Catholicism.

Second, Aquinas argued that when Aristotle's conclusions did conflict with revealed truth, his arguments were not rationally compelling—but that neither were there any rationally compelling arguments on the other side. For example, Aristotle argued that the universe is eternal and uncreated; Christianity holds that the universe was created a finite amount of time ago by God. Aquinas tried to show that *neither* position is provable. In situations like this, Aquinas argued, we discover that reason falls short and some truths can only be known on the basis of faith.

Together, these two kinds of argument were intended to show that there is no conflict between reason and faith and in fact, rational argument, properly carried out, can only strengthen faith, either by further supporting points of doctrine and making them comprehensible to the rational mind, or by revealing the limits of reason. Importantly, this only works when we reason rigorously and *well*. The foolish, according to Aquinas, might be led into error by arguments which are only apparently persuasive, and one important solution to this problem is not to suppress reason but to *encourage* trained, critical, rational reflection on such arguments. (Of course, this solution, Aquinas realized, was not appropriate for the poor and uneducated; the peasants should instead be urged to rely upon their faith.)

Aquinas distinguished sharply between philosophy and theology. He held that theology begins from faith in God and interprets all things as creatures of God, while philosophy moves in the other direction: it starts with the concrete objects of sense perception—such as animals, rocks, and trees—and reasons towards more general conceptions, eventually making its way to God. In our selection from *Summa Theologiae* Aquinas is doing philosophy, and so all five of the proofs for the existence of God given in the Third Article are based upon Aristotelian science—that is, each proof starts from what intellectuals in the thirteenth century thought was a properly rational understanding of ordinary objects, and shows that this scientific understanding leads us to God. Properly understood, according to Aristotle, the natural phenomena appealed to in all of the "five ways" can only be ultimately explained—even *within* a completed science—by bringing in God.

---

* Although Aquinas's work is usually considered the keystone of scholasticism, he didn't create the tradition single-handedly. Other prominent scholastics—who did not all agree with Aquinas—were Peter Abelard (France, 1079–1142), John Duns Scotus (Scotland, c. 1266–1308), William of Occam (England, c. 1285–1349), and Jean Buridan (France, c. 1295–1358).

What Is the Structure of This Reading?

This reading is a good example of the medieval 'scholastic' method of doing philosophy. Aquinas begins by dividing up his subject matter—which is the knowledge of God—into a sequence of more precise questions. Question 2 of Part I of the *Summa Theologiae* is about God's essence, and in particular about whether God exists. He breaks down this question into three parts, and in each part—called an 'Article'—Aquinas lays out his view, and then answers a series of objections. The First Article considers whether God's existence is *self-evident*: that is, whether it is simply obvious to everyone who considers the matter that God must exist. Aquinas claims that it is not self-evident (except to the learned), and so some kind of argument will be needed to convince the unbeliever. In this section Aquinas argues against the Ontological Argument for the existence of God (see the previous section on Anselm's *Proslogion*). The Second Article discusses whether God's existence can be rationally demonstrated at all, or whether it is something that must be merely accepted on faith: Aquinas argues that God's existence can be proven. Finally, the Third Article lays out this proof; in fact, Aquinas thinks there are no fewer than *five* good arguments for the existence of God (his famous "five ways").

Some Useful Background Information

1. All five of Aquinas's arguments for the existence of God have the same basic form. They all move from some familiar empirical fact about the world to the conclusion that there must be some 'transcendent cause' upon which these facts depend. A 'transcendent cause' is a cause which transcends—lies beyond—the natural world; that is, it is a cause which is not itself *part* of the ever-changing physical universe but which *explains* the existence and nature of that universe.

2. In his first argument for the existence of God Aquinas uses the word "motion" in a somewhat technical sense. Aquinas is not just talking about a change of position but about *all* change in the physical world: the motion of the tides, the growth of a plant, the erosion of a mountain range, or someone baking a cake. Furthermore, in Aristotelian science, all motion or change is a transformation from a state of 'potentiality' to a state of 'actuality.' For example, imagine a row of dominoes standing next to each other. Each domino is *actually* standing up, but it is *potentially* falling down. When one domino is knocked down, it bumps into the next domino in the series and converts that potentiality into actuality—it makes the domino fall down. For Aristotle and Aquinas *all* change is this kind of movement, from being only potentially X into being actually X.

3. One important thing to notice about the domino example is that a domino cannot be toppled by something only *potentially* falling down—the domino next to it must be *actually* falling to have any effect. In other words, mere potentiality cannot make anything happen at all—or, to put it yet another way, a domino cannot knock *itself* over. This last claim is crucial for Aquinas's argument in the First Way to work.

4. The Aristotelian notion of an 'efficient cause' plays a key role in Aquinas's Second Way. The 'efficient cause' of something, according to Aristotle, is simply the agent (the object or substance) which brings it about: for example, the 'efficient cause' of tides is the moon's gravity. It's worth noticing that, sometimes, the continuing presence of an effect requires the continuation of the cause. If the moon's gravity went away, ocean tides would also subside; if the force causing the moon to orbit the Earth disappeared, according to Aristotelian science, the moon would stop moving.* Thus, if God is ultimately the 'efficient cause' of, say, the movements of the tides, God must still be presently acting as that cause.

5. When Aquinas talks about 'merely possible' being in the Third Way he again does not use this phrase in quite the modern sense. For modern philosophers, something is 'merely possible' if it might not have existed—for example, the book you are holding has 'merely possible' (or contingent) being,

---

* Notice that this is importantly different from modern science. Today, we know that motions like planetary orbits, once started, simply continue forever unless some force stops them—this is Newton's first law of motion.

in this modern sense, because under other circumstances it might never have been written at all. By contrast, many modern philosophers would agree that mathematical objects, like the number two, have necessary existence—there are no possible circumstances in which the number two could fail to exist. But this is not quite what Aquinas means by 'possible' and 'necessary': for him, something has 'merely possible' being if it is *generated* and *corruptible*. Something is generated if there was a time at which it didn't exist—a time at which it came into being. Something is corruptible if there will be a time at which it ceases to exist. Since things can't come into existence for no reason at all (according to Aquinas), all non-necessary beings must have been generated by *something else*. For example, this book was generated by me, I was generated by my parents, and so on.

6. Aquinas also distinguishes between two different sorts of necessary (i.e., eternal) being. Some entities have necessary being but were nevertheless created by something else (God). For example, suppose that angels are non-corruptible, eternal beings; nevertheless, they have this nature only because God has created them in that way, so their necessary being is derivative of the necessary being of God. God himself, by contrast, is eternal and uncreated—the necessity of his being is, so to speak, built-in, rather than derived from some other source; God is necessarily necessary.

7. In the Fifth Way, the empirical fact from which Aquinas begins is this: different kinds of things, like water and air and plants, co-operate with each other in such a way that a stable order of nature is produced and maintained. They seem to act 'for the sake of a goal,' which is to say, for a particular *purpose*. For example, heat causes water to evaporate; this water then condenses as clouds and falls as rain; as it falls it nourishes plants and animals, and finally runs back into lakes and oceans where it once again evaporates; and so on. This co-operative cycle is stable and self-perpetuating, but the entities that make it up—the water, plants, and so on—do not *intend* for this to happen: they just, as a matter of fact, act in a way that preserves the system.

Some Common Misconceptions

1. Aquinas does not say that *everything* must have a cause, or that all creation involves a change in the creator. If he did say that, he would have to admit that God must himself have a cause, or that God must himself be moved. When Aquinas asserts that God is the 'first' element of a series, he means that God is importantly different than the other members of that series: God is not a changeable thing, for example, but is instead an Unmoved Mover who brings into existence even the phenomenon of change itself.

2. Although Aquinas thinks that the world in fact began a finite amount of time ago, he does not argue that the notion of an infinite time is rationally incoherent: "By faith alone do we hold, and by no demonstration can it be proved, that the world did not always exist," he says in *Summa Theologiae* (Part I, Question 46, Article 2). But this is not inconsistent with Aquinas's attempt to rationally demonstrate that there must have been a first cause. He thinks he can prove that the world must have been created by God—i.e., that God is the ultimate or underlying cause of the world—but, he argues in a treatise called *On the Eternity of the World*, no one can demonstrate that God's on-going creation of the world might not be spread over an infinitely long period of time. (Analogously, we might loosely say that the curvature of space causes gravitational effects and the curvature of space could conceivably continue forever.) Aquinas, that is, thought of God not just as a temporally first cause of the universe, back at the beginning of time like a supernatural Big Bang, but as the most fundamental cause of everything that happens in the natural world throughout time.

3. When Aquinas says that God is a necessary being, he means (roughly) that God's existence does not depend on the existence of anything else. He does not mean that God's existence is what modern philosophers would call "logically necessary." If God were logically necessary, then it would be impossible for God not to exist—it would be self-contradictory to assert that God does not exist, like saying that some bachelors are married. Aquinas does not think that it is self-contradictory to say that God does not exist, just that it is demonstrably false.

4. Aquinas was well aware that his Five Ways, even if they are sound, only prove the *existence* of God and, by themselves, fail to establish important positive conclusions about the nature of God (e.g., his moral goodness). In the section of the *Summa Theologiae* which comes after our selection, he goes on to give arguments about God's nature. Furthermore, Aquinas was aware he had not yet proved that there can be only one God, and he goes on to try to show—on the basis of philosophical arguments—that any entity whose necessary being is essential rather than derived must be simple, perfect, infinite, immutable, eternal, and one—i.e., if there is a God at all, there can be only one God (*Summa Theologiae* Part I, Questions 3 to 11).

5. Although Aquinas appeals to empirical facts as the premises of his arguments for God, he does not think his *conclusion* that God exists is a merely empirical hypothesis. For example, he does not think any amount of future scientific research could ever cast doubt on his arguments. Contrast that with, for example, the claim that electrons are the unseen cause of the pictures that appear on our television sets. It might be that future scientific advances could call into question our present sub-atomic theory, and so cast doubt on the existence of electrons: maybe all the phenomena we explain by talking about electrons can be better explained by talking about some other kind of invisible particle, or about some other category of thing altogether. By contrast, according to Aquinas, our proofs of the existence of God do not depend on the truth of some particular scientific theory; they follow from the mere existence of change, causation, and contingent beings, *however* these things are ultimately explained by science.

How Important and Influential Is This Passage?

Aquinas thought that, although the existence of God is not self-evident, reason is capable of proving to the careful thinker that God exists. The "five ways" he lists in this passage include versions of many of the most important arguments for God's existence, and—as a convenient, short, and very capable outline of the main arguments—this section from Aquinas's *Summa Theologiae* has been at the center of debate about the existence of God for hundreds of years.

Summa Theologiae*

PART I, QUESTION 2: DOES GOD EXIST?

Article 1: Is the Existence of God Self-Evident?

THOMAS'S ANSWER

A proposition can be self-evident in two different ways. In one way, a proposition is self-evident in itself but not to us; in another way, a proposition is self-evident in itself and also to us. A proposition of either sort is self-evident if the meaning of the predicate term is included in the meaning of the subject term. For example, "a human being is an animal" is self-evident, because the meaning of "animal" [the predicate] is included in the meaning of "human being" [the subject], because being an animal is a part of what it means to be human. Now, if the meaning of the subject and predicate is known to everyone, then the proposition will be self-evident to everyone, as is the case in the first principles of demonstration, the terms

---

* This part of the *Summa Theologiae* was written around 1265. The translation used here, by Steven Baldner, is taken from *Thomas Aquinas: Basic Philosophical Writings* (Broadview Press, 2018). This translation rearranges and abridges the original texts for the sake of clarity and understanding.

of which are basic, common, and known to everyone. These are terms like "being" and "non-being," "whole" and "part," and so forth. On the other hand, if the terms of a self-evident proposition are not known to everyone, the proposition will still be self-evident in itself, but it will not be self-evident to those who do not know the meanings of the terms. It can thus happen, as Boethius says, that "some terms and propositions are self-evident only to those with specialized knowledge."* For example, the proposition, "incorporeal beings do not exist in any place," is self-evident only to those with specialized knowledge.

Accordingly, I say that the proposition, "God exists," is self-evident in itself, because the predicate is identical with the subject, for God is his own being, as will be shown later. However, because we do not know what God is, the proposition "God exists" is not self-evident to us and must be demonstrated to us by means of things that are better known to us, although they are of a lesser nature than God. That is, we must demonstrate the existence of God through the effects that God causes.

OBJECTION I

A truth is self-evident if the knowledge of that truth is naturally in us, as is the case with first principles. John of Damascus, in the beginning of his book, says that "the knowledge of the existence of God is naturally implanted in everyone."† Therefore, the existence of God is self-evident.

REPLY TO OBJECTION I

It is true that a general and confused knowledge of God is naturally implanted in everyone. This can be seen in our desire for ultimate happiness, for God is our ultimate happiness, and the fact that we have a natural desire for happiness indicates that we have some natural knowledge of what we desire. Such a natural desire for happiness, however, does not give us any clear knowledge that God exists. If I know, for example, that some person is approaching, that knowledge does not tell me that it is Peter who is approaching, even if in fact it is Peter. Similarly, everyone desires the ultimate human good, but some people think that this good is riches, others think that it is pleasure, and others have other wrong ideas.

OBJECTION 2

A proposition is called self-evident if it is known to be true as soon as the meaning of its terms are known. Aristotle says that the first principles of demonstrations are known to be true in this way.‡ If, for example, you know what a "whole" is and what a "part" is, you immediately know that "any whole is greater than one of its parts." Likewise, if you understand the meaning of the word "God," you immediately know that God exists. The word "God" means "that than which nothing greater can be thought." It is, however, greater to exist both in reality and in the mind than to exist in the mind alone. Hence, when you understand the word "God" and have this meaning in your mind, you immediately know that God also exists in reality. Therefore, the existence of God is self-evident.

REPLY TO OBJECTION 2

It is quite possible that someone who hears the word "God" will not understand it to mean "that than which a greater cannot be thought," because some people think that God is something physical. Still, even if someone should understand the meaning of "God" as "that than which a greater cannot be thought," it does not follow that he or she would understand this to mean that God would exist in reality as something outside of the mind. The real existence of God cannot be shown unless it is granted that "that than which a greater cannot be thought" exists in some way, but this is precisely what atheists deny.

---

* An aristocratic Christian Roman from the early sixth century, Boethius translated Aristotle's logical writings and wrote several theological treatises. See *How Substances Are Good in Virtue of Their Existence without Being Substantial Goods* (*De hebdomadibus*), Rule 1.

† John of Damascus was an eighth-century monk in Jerusalem. This quote is taken from *An Exposition of the Orthodox Faith* (*De fide orthodoxa*), Bk. 1, Chs. 1 and 3.

‡ Aristotle, *Posterior Analytics* 1.3, 72b18–22.

OBJECTION 3

The existence of truth is self-evident, because anyone who attempts to deny the existence of truth must affirm the existence of truth in the process; for if truth did not exist, it would be true that truth did not exist. If anything is true, it is necessary that truth exists. God, however, is Truth Itself, as is written in John 16:6, "I am the way, the truth, and the life." Therefore, the existence of God is self-evident.

REPLY TO OBJECTION 3

The existence of truth in some general sense is self-evident, but the existence of the First Truth [i.e., God] is not self-evident to us.

Article 2: Is It Possible to Prove the Existence of God?

THOMAS'S ANSWER

There are two kinds of proof. One kind of proof is an argument from cause to effect, and this is a proof from what is absolutely prior to what is posterior. The other kind of proof is an argument from effect to cause, and this is an argument from what is prior in our knowledge [to what is posterior in our knowledge]. When an effect is better known to us than its cause, our knowledge proceeds from the effect to the cause of that effect. From any given effect a proof can be given of its proper cause, provided that the effect is better known to us. Since the effect always depends on its cause, for any given effect there must be a pre-existent cause. Hence, the existence of God, which is not self-evident to us, can be proven through the effects that are known to us.

OBJECTION 1

The existence of God is an article of faith. Whatever belongs to the faith cannot be proven, because proofs or demonstrations produce *knowledge*, but faith is about "the things that cannot be known."* Therefore, the existence of God cannot be proven.

REPLY TO OBJECTION 1

The existence of God and other truths of this sort that can be known by natural reason, truths about which Paul was speaking in Romans 1:20,† are not articles of faith; rather, they are *preambles* to the articles of faith. This is an indication that faith presupposes natural knowledge, just as grace‡ presupposes nature, and as whatever is brought to perfection presupposes a prior state of imperfection. Furthermore, there is no reason why a truth that can be proven and known could be taken on faith by someone who does not grasp the proof.

OBJECTION 2

In order to give a proof, the nature of the thing to be proven must be known. It is not possible, however, for us to know what God is, for we can only understand what God is not, according to John of Damascus.§

REPLY TO OBJECTION 2

When a proof is given from effect to cause, it is necessary to understand about the cause only that it is the cause of the given effect, because the proper definition of the cause cannot be given. This is especially so in the case of God. Whenever we prove the existence of something, we can only know what the name of the cause means; we cannot know the real nature of the

---

*   Hebrews 11:1.
†   "The invisible things of God can be known through those things that have been made by God." This verse from St. Paul was generally taken by medieval theologians to indicate that we can know God's existence philosophically from a consideration of the world God has made. St. Paul was a Jewish Roman citizen who lived in Jerusalem in the first century CE and who became an important missionary and the most significant founder of the church after his conversion to Christianity on the road to Damascus. He is often considered to be something like the second founder of Christianity.
‡   Grace is the unmerited favor or protection of God.
§   John of Damascus, *An Exposition of the Orthodox Faith* (*De fide orthodoxa*), Bk. 1, Ch. 4.

cause. This is so because the nature of something cannot be discovered until after its existence is known. The names of God are given to God from the effects that he causes, as will be discussed later.

OBJECTION 3

The only way to prove the existence of God is through the effects caused by God. The effects, however, are not proportionate to the cause, because he is infinite and the effects are finite. There can be no proportion between the infinite and the finite. Since a cause cannot be proven through an effect that is not proportionate to it, it seems that it is not possible to prove the existence of God.

REPLY TO OBJECTION 3

From effects that are not proportionate to their cause it is not possible to have a perfect knowledge of the cause, but nevertheless from any effect known to us it is possible to demonstrate the existence of the cause, as I have said. Hence, from the effects caused by God it is possible to demonstrate that God exists, although we are not able to attain a perfect knowledge of God's essence through such effects.

Article 3: Does God Exist?

THOMAS'S ANSWER

The existence of God can be proven in five ways.

The first and most manifest way is through motion. It is a fact and obvious to our senses that some things are moved in this world. Whatever is moved is moved by something else. This is so because nothing is moved unless it is first in a potential state toward the goal to which it is moved. The cause of motion, on the other hand, is in an actual state. For example, fire, which is actually hot, makes wood, which is potentially hot, to be actually so. In this way the fire moves and changes the wood. It is not possible that the same thing can be simultaneously in an actual and in a potential state in exactly the same way. What is actually hot cannot at the same time be potentially hot but is, rather, potentially cold. It is, therefore, impossible that something be simultaneously, in exactly the same respect, both the mover and the thing moved. In other words, it is impossible that

anything can move itself. Therefore, whatever is moved must be moved by something other than itself.

Furthermore, it is not possible to suppose an infinite number of movers, for if there is no first mover, then there are no other movers, either. The other, secondary movers are only movers because they are moved by the primary mover. For example, the stick [secondary mover] is moved by the hand [primary mover]. It is, therefore, necessary to come to some primary mover, which is moved by no other mover, and this everyone understands to be God.

The second way is taken from what it means to be an efficient cause. We find in the things of our experience that there is an order among efficient causes, which means that it is never possible for anything to be the efficient cause of itself. If something were the efficient cause of itself, it would have to be prior to itself, which is impossible.

Furthermore, it is not possible that there be an infinite number of efficient causes. This is so because in all series of coordinated efficient causes, the first is the cause of the intermediate cause, and the intermediate cause is the cause of the last cause. It does not matter how many intermediate causes there are; if the cause is removed, the effect is removed. Therefore, if there is no first efficient cause, neither will there be any intermediate efficient cause or a last efficient cause. Clearly, however, there *are* efficient causes. It is necessary, therefore, to recognize some first efficient cause, which everyone calls God.

The third way is taken from a consideration of what is possible and what is necessary. It goes like this. We find some things that are possible to be or not to be, because some things are generated and destroyed, and such things have the possibility either to be or not to be. It is impossible, however, that anything of this nature can exist forever, because whatever can possibly not exist at some time will not exist. If, therefore, all things could possibly not exist, at some time or other, nothing would exist. This is clearly not the case, for it would mean that now nothing would exist, since something can only come to exist from what already does exist. If there were nothing in existence, it would have been impossible for anything to begin to exist, and thus there would be nothing existing now, which is clearly false. It cannot, therefore, be the case that all beings are merely possible beings; it must be the case that some are necessarily existing. Whatever is necessarily existing either has the cause of its necessity from something else or not.

Again, it is not possible to have an infinite number of causes of necessity, just as we saw above that it is not possible to have an infinite number of efficient causes. It is, therefore, necessary to recognize the existence of something that exists necessarily through itself and does not have the cause of its necessity from outside of itself. This being is the cause of necessity in other things, and everyone calls this God.

The fourth way is taken from the grades of being in things. We find that some things have more goodness, more truth, more nobility, and so forth, than other things. We say "more" or "less" about different things because we recognize a "most." For example, things are more or less hot, because we recognize a maximum in heat.* Similarly, there is something that is the maximum in truth, goodness, and nobility, and consequently, the maximum in being, as Aristotle said.† Whatever is the maximum in its category is the cause of all the other things in the category. Fire, for example, is the hottest of things and is the cause of heat in all other cases, as Aristotle said in the same place. There is, therefore, something that is the cause of being and goodness in all things, and this we call God.

The fifth way is taken from the order of things. We see that some things that lack knowledge, such as natural bodies, operate for the sake of a goal. This is apparent from the fact that they always or for the most part operate in the same way, and in this way achieve what is best. It is clear that they achieve their goal, not by chance, but by intention. Those things that lack knowledge do not tend toward a goal unless they are so directed by intelligence, as the arrow is directed to the target by the archer. There is, therefore, some intelligent being, by whom all natural things are ordered to a goal, and this we call God.

OBJECTION 1

If one of two contrary things is infinite, the other contrary‡ cannot possibly exist. God, by his very name, is understood to be an infinitely good being. If, therefore, God does exist, no evil could possibly exist. Evil, however, does exist in the world. Therefore, God does not exist.

REPLY TO OBJECTION 1

As Augustine says, "Since God is supremely good, he would not permit anything of evil to exist in his works, unless he were so omnipotent and good that he would bring good even out of evil."§ It is characteristic of the infinite goodness of God that he allows evils to exist and that he brings good out of them.

OBJECTION 2

We must not suppose more causes than we need in order to explain effects. It seems, however, that everything that happens in the world can be explained by causes other than God, if we suppose that God does not exist. Natural things can be explained entirely by causes in nature, and artificial things can be explained by human reason and will. There is no need, therefore, to suppose that God exists.

REPLY TO OBJECTION 2

Since nature operates for determinate goals by the direction of a superior cause, it is necessary to recognize that even those things that occur by nature are caused by God as the first cause. Furthermore, as has been shown, it is necessary to find a cause beyond human reason and will, because these things are changeable and can fail. It is necessary that all moveable and possibly failing beings be caused by something that is absolutely immobile and necessary in itself, as has been shown. ■

---

* For Thomas, the maximum in heat would be the element of fire, understood to be something like one of our chemical elements. Any fire he experienced would have been a lesser version of that elemental fire.

† Aristotle, *Metaphysics* 2.1, 993b22–30.

‡ Contraries are properties which cannot both apply to a thing at the same time, though they can both fail to apply, e.g., being red all over and green all over, or being ugly and beautiful, or being wise and stupid.

§ St. Augustine of Hippo, a north-African bishop who lived from 354 until 430, was the most important early Christian theologian and philosopher. This quote is from his *Enchiridion on Faith, Hope, and Charity*, Ch. 3, 11.

Suggestions for Critical Reflection

1. Do any of Aquinas's five arguments actually prove that God exists? If none of them work, does this show that God does *not* exist?

2. Do Aquinas's five arguments establish the existence of a *personal* God—of a God who resembles the Christian conception of him? Does Aquinas show that there can be only *one* God, or are his arguments compatible with the existence of numerous gods?

3. Aquinas claims that there cannot be an infinite hierarchy of causes. Is he right about this? Do you think he gives compelling arguments for his claim? We are quite familiar with infinite sequences, such as the succession of integers (... -3, -2, -1, 0, 1, 2, 3 ...). Should Aquinas be worried about such infinite series? Why or why not?

4. Aquinas asserts that if everything were merely possible (and not necessary), then there would have to be some time in the past at which nothing at all existed. Does this follow? What might Aquinas have had in mind when he made this move?

5. For Aquinas, could anything have *both* possible and necessary being? Does this fit with your intuitions about possibility and necessity? What, if anything, is the connection between something being eternal and it having necessary being—for example, in your view, could something necessarily exist, but only for a finite amount of time, or could something that might not have existed at all be eternal?

6. Aquinas asserts that we must have an idea of *the best*, before we can judge anything to be *better than* something else. Do you agree with this claim? Support your answer with examples.

7. To what extent do you think that Aquinas's arguments depend on specifically Aristotelian science? How much does the fact that Aristotelian science has now been discredited in favor of post-Newtonian science cast doubt on his arguments?

WILLIAM PALEY

FROM *Natural Theology*

Who Was William Paley?

William Paley (1743–1805) was an Anglican priest and theologian. He was born in Peterborough, the child of an earnest, intelligent mother and a father who became headmaster of Giggleswick School, Yorkshire, where Paley was educated until going up to Christ's College, Cambridge. Paley's first two years at Cambridge were spent "happily, but unprofitably," as he wrote in his memoirs, in company with friends "where we were not immoral, but idle and rather expensive." He enjoyed, then as throughout his life, angling, visiting the theater, and attending trials at the Old Bailey, the central criminal court of England and Wales. At the start of his third year at university, however, he was scolded by one of his friends for wasting his intellectual talents, and this seems to have changed Paley's relatively idle ways. Two years later he graduated from Christ's College as Senior Wrangler, the title given annually to the top mathematics undergraduate at Cambridge University. (This is considered a major intellectual achievement—arguably, between the mid-eighteenth and the early twentieth century, the most prestigious academic prize in the British Empire.)

After three years as a schoolmaster's assistant and then a Latin tutor, Paley returned to Cambridge to become a fellow of Christ's College, where he taught moral philosophy and religion for the following ten years, earning a reputation as one of the University's most popular lecturers.

In 1767 Paley was ordained a priest and became an Anglican clergyman. In 1776 he married Jane Hewitt, the daughter of a local spirit merchant, with whom he went on to have eight children, and took up his first parish in what is now Cumbria, in the northwest of England. Although Paley was unambitious and indifferent to promotion within the church,* he had the respect of several influential clerical friends who moved him around different parishes until eventually he become Archdeacon of Carlisle (1782) and then Subdean of Lincoln (1795). In the same year, 1795, Paley was offered a doctorate of divinity from Cambridge and was also granted one of the most well-paid church positions in England, the rectory of Bishopwearmouth.

Paley was a popular, humorous, and easy-going man—which no doubt, in addition to his prodigious intellect, contributed to his somewhat charmed clerical career—but he was also a sincere and conscientious vicar. He was in favor (within limits) of toleration and free intellectual inquiry within the church, publicly and vehemently campaigned against the slave trade,† and took seriously his pastoral duties—such as visiting the sick, helping feed the poor, writing inspiring sermons, acting as a magistrate, and establishing Sunday Schools—and wrote instructional pamphlets for his curates to guide and encourage them in those activities as well. He does not seem to have been particularly concerned for his own reputation, and some contemporaries found him lacking in the dignity appropriate to a man of his position: "The familiarity of his manners, his almost perpetual jests, his approximations to coarseness of language, weakened the splendour of his literary reputation."‡

Paley's reputation today is not as an original thinker but as a defender of orthodox Anglican views, boiled down to plain language and laid out as arguments that are intended to be rationally compelling. *The Principles*

---

* Paley was contemptuous of patronage (the practice of seeking favors and jobs from wealthy or politically powerful benefactors), coining the term "rooting" for "that baseness and servility which like swine rooting in a dunghill will perform the basest acts for a rich patron, to gain his protection and good benefice." See the entry on Paley by James E. Crimmins in the *Oxford Dictionary of National Biography* (2004).

† He publicly supported the American colonies against the British Crown during the American Revolutionary War (1775–83), believing that an American victory would lead to the end of slavery.

‡ Henry Digby Best, *Literary and Personal Memorials* (1829), 182, cited in James Crimmins's entry on Paley in the *Oxford Dictionary of National Biography* (2004).

of Moral and Political Philosophy is one of the best statements of eighteenth-century (theologically-based) utilitarianism: an ethical view based on the principle that morally appropriate behavior will not harm others but instead will increase their happiness. This book was one of the most influential philosophical texts of its time, even being cited in debates in British Parliament and in US Congress. It was a set textbook at Cambridge until the early twentieth century—it was required reading for Charles Darwin as a student, for instance—and during his lifetime made Paley quite a lot of money.

Natural Theology, the book from which this reading is excerpted, was written at the end of Paley's life, and intended to be a preface or foundation to the rest of Paley's writings. In it he argues that the general happiness or well-being that can be observed in the physical, natural, and social order of things is evidence for God's creation of the universe. This idea was far from original to Paley—but Paley's use of analogies, and especially the analogy between the world and a clockwork watch (though this also is not original to Paley*) made this an especially influential and well-received presentation of the argument. *Natural Theology* was another Paley best-seller, and Darwin also read this book as an undergraduate and reported in his memoirs that he was charmed and initially persuaded by it.

Paley suffered for several years from an intestinal complaint which he nicknamed 'the scorpion' and he was admired by those who knew him for his fortitude in dealing with this illness while he was completing *Natural Theology*. He died in 1805 and is buried in Carlisle Cathedral.

What Is the Structure of This Reading?

Paley argues that, even if we knew nothing at all about watches, just encountering a watch would immediately show to us that it had been created by an intelligent designer (Chapter I). If we were to discover a special watch that was able to somehow produce copies of itself, this would not make us less likely to think that the watch had a designer but in fact we would naturally assume that the original watch—from which all the rest were produced as copies—had an even more intelligent designer (Chapter II). The natural world—and in Paley's specific

example, the eye—is in many respects very similar to a complex mechanism, such as a watch or a telescope. Since these complex mechanisms are the product of intelligent design, this suggests that the natural world must be, too (Chapter III); and this conclusion follows even if some of the processes and structures we observe in nature apparently fall short of perfection, or it is unclear to us what their purposes are (Chapter V).

Some Useful Background Information

1. The Argument from Design, in Paley's version, has the form of an Argument from Analogy (see A Brief Introduction to Arguments in the introductory material to this book). This is a fairly common argument structure that exhibits the following pattern:
    i.   Some thing A is similar to some other thing B, in several key ways that we already know about.
    ii. We know thing A has some additional feature X that is of interest to us.
    iii. Therefore thing B very likely has feature X as well (since A and B are so similar in other ways).

    Assessing the strength of arguments from analogy is a complex matter, but generally the more known similarities there are between A and B, the more fundamental those similarities are, and the more relevant they are to whether something is X or not, the stronger the argument is.

2. The Argument from Design is also often known as the Teleological Argument, from the idea that the universe has a *telos*, ancient Greek for a goal or a purpose.

Some Common Misconceptions

1. Paley begins by asking the reader to imagine finding a watch lying on the ground in a remote natural setting—a heath, or moorland—and wondering how it came to be there. The question Paley is asking is not why the watch is lying on the ground there, but how the watch came to exist

---

*   In fact, this analogy, used as evidence of divine creation, goes back at least to writings in the 1680s.

in the first place. The point of specifying that the watch is discovered in a natural setting is to leave open the (*prima facie*) possibility that the watch might have grown there, or always been there, or been formed by some sort of process of erosion, or in some other way come into existence without having been constructed by some intelligent watch designer. Of course, Paley immediately then suggests that we should be incredulous at any other suggestion than that a sentient watchmaker had created the watch (and it had somehow then found its way onto the heath).

FROM *Natural Theology**

Chapter I: State of the Argument

In crossing a heath, suppose I pitched my foot against a *stone*, and were asked how the stone came to be there, I might possibly answer, that, for anything I knew to the contrary, it had lain there forever: nor would it perhaps be very easy to show the absurdity of this answer. But suppose I had found a *watch* upon the ground, and it should be inquired how the watch happened to be in that place, I should hardly think of the answer which I had before given, that, for anything I knew, the watch might have always been there. Yet why should not this answer serve for the watch as well as for the stone? Why is it not as admissible in the second case, as in the first? For this reason, and for no other, viz.[†] that, when we come to inspect the watch, we perceive (what we could not discover in the stone) that its several parts are framed and put together for a purpose, *e.g.* that they are so formed and adjusted as to produce motion, and that motion so regulated as to point out the hour of the day; that, if the several parts had been differently shaped from what they are, of a different size from what they are, or placed after any other manner, or in any other order, than that in which they are placed, either no motion at all would have been carried on in the machine, or none which would have answered the use that is now served by it. To reckon up a few of the plainest of these parts, and of their offices, all tending to one result:—We see a cylindrical box containing a coiled elastic spring, which, by its endeavour to relax itself, turns round the box. We next observe a flexible chain (artificially wrought for the sake of flexure) communicating the action of the spring from the box to the fusee.[‡] We then find a series of wheels, the teeth of which, catch in, and apply to, each other, conducting the motion from the fusee to the balance, and from the balance to the pointer; and at the same time, by the size and shape of those wheels, so regulating that motion, as to terminate in causing an index,[§] by an equable and measured progression, to pass over a given space in a given time. We take notice that the wheels are made of brass, in order to keep them from rust; the springs of steel, no other metal being so elastic; that over the face of the watch there is placed glass, a material employed in no other part of the work, but, in the room of which, if there had been any other than a transparent substance, the hour could not be seen without opening the case. This mechanism being observed (it requires indeed an examination of the instrument, and perhaps some previous knowledge of the subject, to perceive and understand it; but being once, as we have said, observed and understood), the inference, we think, is inevitable; that the watch must have had a maker; that there must have existed, at some time and at some place or other, an artificer or artificers, who formed it for the purpose which we

---

*   From *Natural Theology: or, Evidences of the Existence and Attributes of the Deity, Collected from the Appearances of Nature* (Philadelphia, 1802), 1–17, 42–43.

†   "Viz.": that is.

‡   A fusee is a cone-shaped pulley with a chain wound around it in a spiral (used so that as the mainspring unwinds it exerts a constant force).

§   In this context, the index is the hand of the watch (in general, something that indicates a value or quantity).

find it actually to answer; who comprehended its construction,* and designed its use.

I. Nor would it, I apprehend, weaken the conclusion, that we had never seen a watch made; that we had never known an artist capable of making one; that we were altogether incapable of executing such a piece of workmanship ourselves, or of understanding in what manner it was performed; all this being no more than what is true of some exquisite remains of ancient art, of some lost arts, and to the generality of mankind, of the more curious productions of modern manufacture. Does one man in a million know how oval frames are turned?† Ignorance of this kind exalts our opinion of the unseen and unknown artist's skill, if he be unseen and unknown, but raises no doubt in our minds of the existence and agency of such an artist, at some former time, and in some place or other. Nor can I perceive that it varies at all the inference, whether the question arise concerning a human agent, or concerning an agent of a different species, or an agent possessing, in some respects, a different nature.

II. Neither, secondly, would it invalidate our conclusion, that the watch sometimes went wrong, or that it seldom went exactly right. The purpose of the machinery, the design, and the designer, might be evident, and in the case supposed would be evident, in whatever way we accounted for the irregularity of the movement, or whether we could account for it or not. It is not necessary that a machine be perfect, in order to shew with what design it was made: still less necessary, where the only question is, whether it were made with any design at all.

III. Nor, thirdly, would it bring any uncertainty into the argument, if there were a few parts of the watch, concerning which we could not discover, or had not yet discovered, in what manner they conduced to the general effect;‡ or even some parts, concerning which we could not ascertain, whether they conduced to that effect in any manner whatever. For, as to the first branch of the case; if, by the loss, or disorder, or

decay of the parts in question, the movement of the watch were found in fact to be stopped, or disturbed, or retarded, no doubt would remain in our minds as to the utility or intention of these parts, although we should be unable to investigate the manner§ according to which, or the connexion by which, the ultimate effect depended upon their action or assistance: and the more complex is the machine, the more likely is this obscurity to arise. Then, as to the second thing supposed, namely, that there were parts which might be spared, without prejudice to the movement of the watch, and that we had proved this by experiment— these superfluous parts, even if we were completely assured that they were such, would not vacate the reasoning¶ which we had instituted concerning other parts. The indication of contrivance** remained, with respect to them, nearly as it was before.

IV. Nor, fourthly, would any man in his sense think the existence of the watch, with its various machinery, accounted for, by being told that it was one out of possible combinations of material forms; that whatever he had found in the place where he found the watch, must have contained some internal configuration or other; and that this configuration might be the structure now exhibited, viz. of the works of a watch, as well as†† a different structure.

V. Nor, fifthly, would it yield his inquiry more satisfaction to be answered, that there existed in things a principle of order, which had disposed the parts of the watch into their present form and situation. He never knew a watch made by the principle of order; nor can he even form to himself an idea of what is meant by a principle of order, distinct from the intelligence of the watchmaker....

Chapter II: State of the Argument Continued

Suppose, in the next place, that the person, who found the watch, should after some time, discover, that, in addition to all the properties which he had

---

* "Comprehended its construction": designed it, worked out how to make it.
† Shaped into a rounded form using a cutting tool.
‡ "Conduced to the general effect": contributed to the overall function of the watch.
§ "Although we should be unable to investigate the manner": even if we couldn't work out how.
¶ "Would not vacate the reasoning": would not make the argument unsound.
** Evidence of design.
†† Just as probably as.

hitherto observed in it, it possessed the unexpected property of producing, in the course of its movement, another watch like itself; (the thing is conceivable;) that it contained within it a mechanism, a system of parts, a mould for instance, or a complex adjustment of lathes, files, and other tools, evidently and separately calculated for this purpose; let us inquire, what effect ought such a discovery to have upon his former conclusion?

I. The first effect would be to increase his admiration of the contrivance, and his conviction of the consummate skill of the contriver. Whether he regarded the object of the contrivance, the distinct apparatus, the intricate, yet in many parts intelligible, mechanism by which it was carried on, he would perceive, in this new observation, nothing but an additional reason for doing what he had already done; for referring the construction of the watch to design, and to supreme art.* If that construction *without* this property, or, which is the same thing, before this property had been noticed, proved intention and art to have been employed about it; still more strong would the proof appear, when he came to the knowledge of this farther property, the crown and perfection of all the rest.

II. He would reflect, that though the watch before him were, *in some sense*, the maker of the watch which was fabricated in the course of its movements, yet it was in a very different sense from that in which a carpenter, for instance, is the maker of a chair; the author of its contrivance, the cause of the relation of its parts to their use. With respect to these, the first watch was no cause at all to the second: in no such sense as this was it the author of the constitution and order, either of the parts which the new watch contained, or of the parts by the aid and instrumentality of which it was produced.... Therefore,

III. Though it be now no longer probable, that the individual watch which our observer had found was made immediately by the hand of an artificer, yet doth not this alteration in any-wise affect the inference, that an artificer had been originally employed

and concerned in the production. The argument from design remains as it was. Marks of design and contrivance are no more accounted for now than they were before. In the same thing, we may ask for the cause of different properties. We may ask for the cause of the colour of a body, of its hardness, of its heat; and these causes may be all different. We are now asking for the cause of that subserviency to an use, that relation to an end,† which we have remarked in the watch before us. No answer is given to the question by telling us that a preceding watch produced it. There cannot be design without a designer; contrivance without a contriver; order without choice; arrangement, without anything capable of arranging; subserviency and relation to a purpose, without that which could intend a purpose; means suitable to an end, and executing their office in accomplishing that end, without the end ever having been contemplated, or the means accommodated to it. Arrangement, disposition of parts, subserviency of means to an end, relation of instruments to a use, imply the presence of intelligence and mind. No one, therefore, can rationally believe, that the insensible, inanimate‡ watch, from which the watch before us issued, was the proper cause of the mechanism we so much admire in it; could be truly said to have constructed the instrument, disposed its parts, assigned their office, determined their order, action, and mutual dependency, combined their several motions into one result, and that also a result connected with the utilities of other beings.§ All these properties, therefore are as much unaccounted for as they were before.

IV. Nor is anything gained by running the difficulty farther back, *i.e.* by supposing the watch before us to have been produced from another watch, that from a former, and so on indefinitely. Our going back ever so far brings us no nearer to the least degree of satisfaction upon the subject. Contrivance is still unaccounted for. We still want a contriver. A designing mind is neither supplied by this supposition, nor dispensed with. If the difficulty were diminished the further we went back, by going back indefinitely we

---

* Skill or craft of the highest order.
† "That subserviency to an use, that relation to an end": the property of the watch as being something that was designed to serve the function ('end') of telling the time.
‡ Not capable of thought or deliberate action.
§ "The utilities of other beings": the needs of other entities, i.e., of human beings to tell what time it is.

might exhaust it. And this is the only case to which this sort of reasoning applies. Where there is a tendency, or, as we increase the number of terms, a continual approach towards a limit, *there*, by supposing the number of terms to be what is called infinite, we may conceive the limit to be attained: but where there is no such tendency, or approach, nothing is effected by lengthening the series. There is no difference, as to the point in question, (whatever there may be as to many points) between one series and another; between a series which is finite, and a series which is infinite.... The machine, which we are inspecting, demonstrates, by its construction, contrivance and design. Contrivance must have had a contriver; design, a designer; whether the machine immediately proceeded from another machine, or not. That circumstance alters not the case. That other machine may, in like manner, have proceeded from a former machine: nor does that alter the case: contrivance must have had a contriver. That former one from one preceding it: no alteration still: a contriver is still necessary. No tendency is perceived, no approach towards a diminution of this necessity. It is the same with any and every succession of these machines; a succession of ten, of a hundred, of a thousand; with one series as with another; a series which is finite, as with a series which is infinite. In whatever other respects they may differ, in this they do not. In all, equally, contrivance and design are unaccounted for.

The question is not simply, How came the first watch into existence? which question, it may be pretended, is done away by supposing the series of watches thus produced from one another to have been infinite, and consequently to have had no such *first*, for which it was necessary to provide a cause. This, perhaps, would have been nearly the state of the question, if nothing had been before us but an unorganized, unmechanised substance, without mark or indication of contrivance. It might be difficult to shew that such substance could not have existed from eternity, either in succession (if it were possible, which I think it is not, for unorganized bodies to spring from one another), or by individual perpetuity.* But that is not the question now. To suppose it to be so, is to suppose that it made no difference whether we had found a watch or a stone. As it is, the metaphysics of that question have no place; for, in the watch which we are examining, are seen contrivance, design; an end, a purpose; means for the end, adaptation to the purpose. And the question, which irresistibly presses upon our thoughts, is, whence this contrivance and design? The thing required is the intending mind, the adapting hand, the intelligence by which that hand was directed. This question, this demand, is not shaken off, by increasing a number or succession of substances, destitute of these properties;† nor the more, by increasing that number to infinity....

V. ...The conclusion which the *first* examination of the watch, of its works, construction, and movement, suggested, was, that it must have had, for the cause and author of that construction, an artificer, who understood its mechanism, and designed its use. This conclusion is invincible. A *second* examination presents us with a new discovery. The watch is found, in the course of its movement, to produce another watch, similar to itself: and not only so, but we perceive in it a system or organization, separately calculated for that purpose. What effect would this discovery have or ought it to have, upon our former inference? What, as hath already been said, but to increase, beyond measure, our admiration of the skill which had been employed in the formation of such a machine? Or shall it, instead of this, all at once turn us round to an opposite conclusion, viz. that no art or skill whatever has been concerned in the business, although all other evidences of art and skill remain as they were, and this last and supreme piece of art be now added to the rest? Can this be maintained without absurdity? Yet this is atheism.

Chapter III: Application of the Argument

This is atheism: for every indication of contrivance, every manifestation of design, which existed in the watch, exists in the works of nature; with the difference, on the side of nature, of being greater and more, and that in a degree which exceeds all computation. I mean that the contrivances of nature surpass the contrivances of art, in the complexity, subtlety, and

---

* By one thing to exist for eternity.

† Lacking the properties of being designed, for a particular purpose, by a designer.

curiosity of the mechanism; and still more, if possible, do they go beyond them in number and variety: yet, in a multitude of cases, are not less evidently accommodated to their end, or suited to their office, than are the most perfect productions of human ingenuity.

I know no better method of introducing so large a subject, than that of comparing a single thing with a single thing; an eye, for example, with a telescope. As far as the examination of the instrument goes, there is precisely the same proof that the eye was made for vision, as there is that the telescope was made for assisting it. They are made upon the same principles; both being adjusted to the laws by which the transmission and refraction of rays of light are regulated. I speak not of the origin of the laws themselves; but, such laws being fixed, the construction, in both cases, is adapted to them. For instance; these laws require, in order to produce the same effect, that the rays of light, in passing from water into the eye, should be refracted by a more convex surface, than when it passes out of air into the eye. Accordingly we find, that the eye of a fish, in that part of it called the crystalline lens, is much rounder than the eye of terrestrial animals. What plainer manifestation of design can there be than this difference? What could a mathematical instrument-maker have done more, to shew his knowledge of his principle, his application of that knowledge, his suiting of his means to his end; I will not say to display the compass* or excellence of his skill and art, for in these all comparison is indecorous, but to testify counsel, choice, consideration, purpose?

To some it may appear a difference sufficient to destroy all similitude between the eye and the telescope, that the one is a perceiving organ, the other an unperceiving instrument. The fact is, that they are both instruments. And, as to the mechanism, at least as to mechanism being employed, and even as to the kind of it, this circumstance varies not the analogy at all. For, observe, what the constitution of the eye is. It is necessary, in order to produce distinct vision, that an image or picture of the object be formed at the bottom of the eye.† Whence this necessity arises, or how the picture is connected with the sensation, or contributes to it, it may be difficult, nay we will confess, if you please, impossible for us to search out. But the present question is not concerned in the inquiry. It may be true, that, in this, and in other instances, we trace mechanical contrivance a certain way; and that then we come to something which is not mechanical, or which is inscrutable. But this affects not the certainty of our investigation, as far as we have gone. The difference between an animal and an automatic statue,‡ consists in this,—that, in the animal, we trace the mechanism to a certain point, and then we are stopped; either the mechanism becoming too subtile§ for our discernment, or something else beside the known laws of mechanism taking place; whereas, in the automaton,¶ for the comparatively few motions of which it is capable, we trace the mechanism throughout. But, up to the limit, the reasoning is as clear and certain in the one case as in the other. In the example before us, it is a matter of certainty, because it is a matter which experience and observation demonstrate, that the formation of an image at the bottom of the eye is necessary to perfect vision. The image itself can be shewn.** Whatever affects the distinctness of the image, affects the distinctness of the vision. The formation then of such an image being necessary (no matter how), to the sense of sight, and to the exercise of that sense, the apparatus by which it is formed is constructed and put together, not only with infinitely more art, but upon the self-same principles of art, as in the telescope or the camera obscura.†† The perception arising from the image may be laid out of

---

*   Extent, range.

†   "At the bottom of the eye": i.e., on the retina (at the back of the eye).

‡   A statue with a hidden mechanism inside, making it move.

§   Subtle; in this context, hard to see or understand.

¶   Automatic statue.

**   For example, French philosopher and scientist René Descartes recommended placing the eye from a fresh corpse in a hole in the wall of a dark box and scraping away the back of the eye until one could see the inverted image cast upon the retina (in *Optics*, published in 1637).

††   A camera obscura is a dark chamber in which an image of the external scene is projected through a pinhole in one wall and appears as a reversed and inverted image on a surface opposite to the opening. This optical phenomenon has been

the question: for the production of the image, these are instruments of the same kind. The end is the same; the means are the same. The purpose in both is alike. The lenses of the telescope, and the humours of the eye* bear a complete resemblance to one another, in their figure, their position, and in their power over the rays of light, viz. in bringing each pencil[†] to a point at the right distance from the lens; namely, in the eye, at the exact place where the membrane is spread to receive it. How is it possible, under circumstances of such close affinity, and under the operation of equal evidence, to exclude contrivance from the one, yet to acknowledge the proof of contrivance having been employed, as the plainest and clearest of all propositions, in the other?

The resemblance between the two cases is still more accurate, and obtains in more points than we have yet represented, or than we are, on the first view of the subject, aware of. In dioptric telescopes[‡] there is an imperfection of this nature. Pencils of light, in passing through glass lenses, are separated into different colours, thereby tingeing the object, especially the edges of it, as if it were viewed through a prism. To correct this inconvenience had been long a desideratum[§] in the art. At last it came into the mind of a sagacious optician, to inquire how this matter was managed in the eye; in which there was exactly the same difficulty to contend with as in the telescope. His observation taught him, that, in the eye, the evil was cured by combining together lenses composed of different substances, i.e. of substances which possessed different refracting powers. Our artist borrowed from thence his hint; and produced a correction of the defect by imitating, in glasses made from different materials, the effects of the different humours through which the rays of light pass before they reach the bottom of the eye. Could this be in the eye without purpose, which

suggested to the optician the only effectual means of attaining that purpose?[¶] ...

Chapter V: Application of the Argument Continued

Every observation which was made in our first chapter, concerning the watch, may be repeated with strict propriety** concerning the eye; concerning animals; concerning plants; concerning, indeed, all the organized parts of the works of nature. As,

I. When we are inquiring simply after the *existence* of an intelligent Creator, imperfection, inaccuracy, liability to disorder, occasional irregularities, may subsist, in a considerable degree, without inducing any doubt into the question: just as a watch may frequently go wrong, seldom perhaps exactly right, may be faulty in some parts, defective in some, without the smallest ground of suspicion from thence arising that it was not a watch; not made; or not made for the purpose ascribed to it. When faults are pointed out, and when a question is started[††] concerning the skill of the artist, or the dexterity with which the work is executed, then indeed, in order to defend these qualities from accusation, we must be able, either to expose some intractableness and imperfection in the materials, or point out some invincible difficulty in the execution, into which imperfection and difficulty, the matter of complaint may be resolved; or if we cannot do this, we must adduce such specimens of consummate art and contrivance, proceeding from the same hand, as may convince the inquirer of the existence, in the case before him, of impediments like those which we have mentioned, although, what from the nature of the case is very likely to happen, they be unknown and unperceived by him. This we must do in order to vindicate the artist's skill, or, at least, the perfection of

---

known for thousands of years, and was in common use in the seventeenth and eighteenth centuries as an aid to drawing.

*   The fluids inside the eyeball.

†   Ray of light.

‡   Telescopes that create their image using a convex lens.

§   Something desired.

¶   That is, could something in the eye that was random and not part of a design have been the only effective solution to the optician's technical difficulty? (This is a rhetorical question, to which Paley thinks the obvious answer is 'no.')

**   "With strict propriety": very properly.

††   "A question is started": someone raises the question.

it; as we must also judge of his intention, and of the provision employed in fulfilling that intention, not from an instance in which they fail, but from the great plurality of instances in which they succeed. But, after all, these are different questions from the question of the artist's existence; or, which is the same, whether the thing before us be a work of art* or not: and the question ought always to be kept separate in the mind. So likewise it is in the works of nature. Irregularities and imperfections are of little or no weight in the consideration, when that consideration relates simply to the existence of a Creator. When the argument respects his attributes, they are of weight; but are then to be taken in conjunction (the attention is not to rest upon them, but they are to be taken in conjunction) with the unexceptionable evidences† which we possess, of skill, power, and benevolence, displayed in other instances; which evidences may, in strength, number, and variety be such, and may so overpower apparent blemishes, as to induce us, upon the most reasonable ground, to believe, that these last ought to be referred to some cause, though we be ignorant of it, other than defect of knowledge or of benevolence‡ in the author.... ■

Suggestions for Critical Reflection

1. Although Paley's key argument is typically described as resting on an analogy between a clockwork watch and the universe, this reading begins with a *disanalogy* between a watch and a stone. What is going on here? How exactly does Paley's larger argument work? It would be a good idea to lay it out according to the Argument from Analogy pattern described above. What precisely is Paley trying to persuade us to believe?

2. Paley distinguishes between arguments for the existence of a creator, and arguments concerning the nature of that creator. Why does he make this distinction? Are both arguments equally persuasive

---

* In this context, a work of art is something created through skilled craftwork.
† Undeniable examples.
‡ "Referred to some cause ... other than defect of knowledge or of benevolence": assumed to be caused by something different from any failing in the creator.

J.L. MACKIE

Evil and Omnipotence

Who Was J.L. Mackie?

John Leslie Mackie was born in Sydney, Australia, in 1917 and educated at the University of Sydney and Oriel College, Oxford. After serving in the Australian army during the Second World War, he taught at the University of Sydney from 1946 to 1954 and then at Otago University in Dunedin, New Zealand. In 1963 he moved permanently to England, and from 1967 until his death in 1981 he was a Fellow of University College, Oxford. He wrote six books and many philosophical papers, mostly on topics in metaphysics, ethics, the history of philosophy, and the philosophy of religion.

Mackie is probably best known for his 'error theory' of moral values. This holds that:

1.   There are no objective moral values.
2.   All ordinary moral judgments include a claim to objectivity, and so,
3.   All ordinary moral judgments are false.

Mackie therefore argued that morality is not discovered but is *created* by human beings. We should scrap traditional moral theory, he said, and, instead of treating moral theory as descriptive of moral facts, we should understand morality as a device for encouraging empathy with the points of view of others.

Mackie's work, like most Australian analytical philosophy of this century, is notable for its dislike of obfuscation and obscurantism, and for its careful attempts at clarity and precision. Evil and Omnipotence" is well known as probably the best short modern defense of an argument called "the problem of evil."

What Is the Structure of This Reading?

Mackie begins by introducing an argument against the existence of God (or, at least, of God as traditionally conceived) called "the problem of evil." He lays out its logical form (as a paradox), and tries to make clear its theological importance. He briefly discusses a kind of response to this paradox, which he does think is adequate, but claims that such a response would be unacceptable to those who believe in God. Believers must thus attempt to give other solutions to the paradox, but Mackie argues that all of these attempts fail (and, he suggests, typically only seem as plausible as they do because of their vagueness and lack of clarity).

First, there are "half-hearted" responses which, Mackie says, really fail to address the problem. Then there are four more serious responses: (1) good cannot exist without evil; (2) evil is necessary as a means to good; (3) the universe is better with some evil in it; (4) evil is due to human free will. (These responses fall naturally into two groups: 1 and 2, and 3 and 4.) Mackie argues carefully that all four of these responses to the problem of evil are fallacious.

In the course of his attack on the free-will response to the problem of evil, Mackie develops a further argument which he calls "the Paradox of Omnipotence." He argues that this paradox shows it is *logically impossible* that any (temporal) being could exist which had absolutely unlimited power.

The upshot of all this, Mackie concludes, is that God (as he is described by, say, Christianity) cannot possibly exist.

Some Useful Background Information

When Mackie talks about "evil" in this article, he follows normal philosophical usage in this context. In everyday language the word "evil" tends to suggest an especially wicked kind of moral badness; however, "the problem of evil," though it certainly includes extreme ethical badness, is much broader in its scope than that. It's important to realize that, according to the argument from evil, any kind of 'sub-optimality' can be a problem for the existence of God. Therefore examples of 'evil' range along the spectrum from such mild harms as a nasty pimple, a job that does not give 100 per cent satisfaction, or a mountain that would be just a little more beautiful if it were a slightly different shape, right up to major earthquakes, epidemics, and oil spills in the Alaskan wilderness. Moral 'evils' can be as minor as breaking a trivial promise or making a slightly cutting remark, or as serious as rape, torture, and genocide.

A Common Misconception

Mackie is not arguing (directly) that God does not exist: he is arguing that nothing like the *theistic conception* of God can exist. That is, although some sort of God—perhaps an extremely powerful but somehow limited being, like, say, the classical Greek god Zeus—can escape the problem of evil, the sort of God envisaged by the main monotheistic religions such as Christianity, Judaism, and Islam cannot possibly be real. For many if not most of the people who believe in God, this is not a trivial conclusion: if it is a sound argument, the problem of evil shows that God, if he exists at all, must be either limited in his power, or limited in his knowledge, or not entirely morally good.

Evil and Omnipotence*

The traditional arguments for the existence of God have been fairly thoroughly criticised by philosophers. But the theologian can, if he wishes, accept this criticism. He can admit that no rational proof of God's existence is possible. And he can still retain all that is essential to his position, by holding that God's existence is known in some other, non-rational way. I think, however, that a more telling criticism can be made by way of the traditional problem of evil. Here it can be shown, not that religious beliefs lack rational support, but that they are positively irrational, that the several parts of the essential theological doctrine are inconsistent with one another, so that the theologian can maintain his position as a whole only by a much more extreme rejection of reason than in the former case. He must now be prepared to believe, not merely what cannot be proved, but what can be *disproved* from other beliefs that he also holds.

The problem of evil, in the sense in which I shall be using the phrase, is a problem only for someone who believes that there is a God who is both omnipotent† and wholly good. And it is a logical problem, the problem of clarifying and reconciling a number of beliefs: it is not a scientific problem that might be solved by further observations, or a practical problem that might be solved by a decision or an action. These points are obvious; I mention them only because they are sometimes ignored by theologians, who sometimes parry a statement of the problem with such remarks as "Well, can you solve the problem yourself?" or "This is a mystery which may be revealed to us later," or "Evil is something to be faced and overcome, not to be merely discussed."

In its simplest form the problem is this: God is omnipotent; God is wholly good; and yet evil exists. There seems to be some contradiction between these three propositions, so that if any two of them were true the third would be false. But at the same time all three are essential parts of most theological positions: the theologian, it seems, at once *must* adhere and *cannot consistently* adhere to all three. (The problem does not arise only for theists,‡ but I shall discuss it in the form in which it presents itself for ordinary theism.)

---

* This article was originally published in 1955 in the journal *Mind* (64, 254 [April 1955]: 200–12).

† "Omnipotent" means all-powerful; able to do anything at all. (Or at least anything that is not logically incoherent: God could make pigs fly, but even God, perhaps, could not make a male vixen or create a leaf that is—at the same time—both entirely green and not entirely green. This issue is discussed later in the article.)

‡ For those who believe in one, powerful, benevolent God who created and watches over the universe.

However, the contradiction does not arise immediately; to show it we need some additional premises, or perhaps some quasi-logical rules connecting the terms 'good,' 'evil,' and 'omnipotent.' These additional principles are that good is opposed to evil, in such a way that a good thing always eliminates evil as far as it can, and that there are no limits to what an omnipotent thing can do. From these it follows that a good omnipotent thing eliminates evil completely, and then the propositions that a good omnipotent thing exists, and that evil exists, are incompatible.

A. Adequate Solutions

Now once the problem is fully stated it is clear that it can be solved, in the sense that the problem will not arise if one gives up at least one of the propositions that constitute it. If you are prepared to say that God is not wholly good, or not quite omnipotent, or that evil does not exist, or that good is not opposed to the kind of evil that exists, or that there are limits to what an omnipotent thing can do, then the problem of evil will not arise for you.

There are, then, quite a number of adequate solutions of the problem of evil, and some of these have been adopted, or almost adopted, by various thinkers. For example, a few have been prepared to deny God's omnipotence, and rather more have been prepared to keep the term 'omnipotence' but severely to restrict its meaning, recording quite a number of things that an omnipotent being cannot do. Some have said that evil is an illusion, perhaps because they held that the whole world of temporal, changing things is an illusion, and that what we call evil belongs only to this world, or perhaps because they held that although temporal things are much as we see them, those that we call evil are not really evil. Some have said that what we call evil is merely the privation of good,* that evil in a positive sense, evil that would really be opposed to good, does not exist. Many have agreed with Pope† that disorder is harmony not understood, and that partial evil is universal good. Whether any of these views is true is, of course, another question. But each of them gives an adequate solution of the problem of evil in the sense that if you accept it this problem does not arise for you, though you may, of course, have *other* problems to face.

But often enough these adequate solutions are only *almost* adopted. The thinkers who restrict God's power, but keep the term 'omnipotence,' may reasonably be suspected of thinking, in other contexts, that his power is really unlimited. Those who say that evil is an illusion may also be thinking, inconsistently, that this illusion is itself an evil. Those who say that "evil" is merely privation of good may also be thinking, inconsistently, that privation of good is an evil. (The fallacy here is akin to some forms of the "naturalistic fallacy" in ethics,‡ where some think, for example, that "good" is just what contributes to evolutionary progress, and that evolutionary progress is itself good.) If Pope meant what he said in the first line of his couplet, that "disorder" is only harmony not understood, the "partial evil" of the second line must, for consistency, mean "that which, taken in isolation, falsely appears to be evil," but it would more naturally mean "that which, in isolation, really is evil." The second line, in fact, hesitates between two views, that "partial evil" isn't really evil, since only the universal quality is real, and that "partial evil" is really an evil, but only a little one.

In addition, therefore, to adequate solutions, we must recognise unsatisfactory inconsistent solutions, in which there is only a half-hearted or temporary rejection of one of the propositions which together constitute the problem. In these, one of the constituent propositions is explicitly rejected, but it is covertly re-asserted or assumed elsewhere in the system.

---

* The privation of good: the absence of good (some sort of regrettable lack or absence in the world).

† Alexander Pope (1688–1744), an English writer best known for his mock-epic poems such as *The Rape of the Lock*. This quotation comes from his *Essay on Man, Epistle I*: "All nature is but art, unknown to thee; All chance, direction, which thou canst not see; All discord, harmony, not understood; All partial evil, universal good: And, spite of pride, in erring reason's spite, One truth is clear, Whatever is, is right."

‡ This is the alleged fallacy of identifying an ethical concept with a "natural" (i.e., non-moral) notion, such as analyzing moral goodness as evolutionary fitness or the sensation of pleasure.

B. Fallacious Solutions

Besides these half-hearted solutions, which explicitly reject but implicitly assert one of the constituent propositions, there are definitely fallacious solutions which explicitly maintain all the constituent propositions, but implicitly reject at least one of them in the course of the argument that explains away the problem of evil.

There are, in fact, many so-called solutions which purport to remove the contradiction without abandoning any of its constituent propositions. These must be fallacious, as we can see from the very statement of the problem, but it is not so easy to see in each case precisely where the fallacy lies. I suggest that in all cases the fallacy has the general form suggested above: in order to solve the problem one (or perhaps more) of its constituent propositions is given up, but in such a way that it appears to have been retained, and can therefore be asserted without qualification in other contexts. Sometimes there is a further complication: the supposed solution moves to and fro between, say, two of the constituent propositions, at one point asserting the first of these but covertly abandoning the second, at another point asserting the second but covertly abandoning the first. These fallacious solutions often turn upon some equivocation with the words 'good' and 'evil,' or upon some vagueness about the way in which good and evil are opposed to one another, or about how much is meant by 'omnipotence.' I propose to examine some of these so-called solutions, and to exhibit their fallacies in detail. Incidentally, I shall also be considering whether an adequate solution could be reached by a minor modification of one or more of the constituent propositions, which would, however, still satisfy all the essential requirements of ordinary theism.

I. "GOOD CANNOT EXIST WITHOUT EVIL" OR "EVIL IS NECESSARY AS A COUNTERPART TO GOOD."

It is sometimes suggested that evil is necessary as a counterpart to good, that if there were no evil there could be no good either, and that this solves the problem of evil. It is true that it points to an answer to the question "Why should there be evil?" But it does so only by qualifying some of the propositions that constitute the problem.

First, it sets a limit to what God can do, saying that God cannot create good without simultaneously creating evil, and this means either that God is not omnipotent or that there are some limits to what an omnipotent thing can do. It may be replied that these limits are always presupposed, that omnipotence has never meant the power to do what is logically impossible, and on the present view the existence of good without evil would be a logical impossibility. This interpretation of omnipotence may, indeed, be accepted as a modification of our original account which does not reject anything that is essential to theism, and I shall in general assume it in the subsequent discussion. It is, perhaps, the most common theistic view, but I think that some theists at least have maintained that God can do what is logically impossible. Many theists, at any rate, have held that logic itself is created or laid down by God, that logic is the way in which God arbitrarily chooses to think. (This is, of course, parallel to the ethical view that morally right actions are those which God arbitrarily chooses to command, and the two views encounter similar difficulties.*) And *this* account of logic is clearly inconsistent with the view that God is bound by logical necessities—unless it is possible for an omnipotent being to bind himself, an issue which we shall consider later, when we come to the Paradox of Omnipotence. This solution of the problem of evil cannot, therefore, be consistently adopted along with the view that logic is itself created by God.

But, secondly, this solution denies that evil is opposed to good in our original sense. If good and evil are counterparts, a good thing will not "eliminate evil as far as it can." Indeed, this view suggests that good and evil are not strictly qualities of things at all. Perhaps the suggestion is that good and evil are related in much the same way as great and small. Certainly, when the term 'great' is used relatively as a condensation of 'greater than so-and-so', and 'small' is used correspondingly, greatness and smallness are

---

* This ethical view is often called Divine Command Theory, and the usual label for its main problem is "the Euthyphro Dilemma" (from a dialogue by Plato in which the problem is first raised).

counterparts and cannot exist without each other. But in this sense greatness is not a quality, not an intrinsic feature of anything; and it would be absurd to think of a movement in favour of greatness and against smallness in this sense. Such a movement would be self-defeating, since relative greatness can be promoted only by a simultaneous promotion of relative smallness. I feel sure that no theists would be content to regard God's goodness as analogous to this—as if what he supports were not the *good* but the *better*, and as if he had the paradoxical aim that all things should be better than other things.

This point is obscured by the fact that 'great' and 'small' seem to have an absolute as well as a relative sense. I cannot discuss here whether there is absolute magnitude or not, but if there is, there could be an absolute sense for 'great,' it could mean of at least a certain size, and it would make sense to speak of all things getting bigger, of a universe that was expanding all over, and therefore it would make sense to speak of promoting greatness. But in *this* sense great and small are not logically necessary counterparts: either quality could exist without the other. There would be no logical impossibility in everything's being small or in everything's being great.

Neither in the absolute nor in the relative sense, then, of 'great' and 'small' do these terms provide an analogy of the sort that would be needed to support this solution of the problem of evil. In neither case are greatness and smallness both necessary counterparts and mutually opposed forces or possible objects for support and attack.

It may be replied that good and evil are necessary counterparts in the same way as any quality and its logical opposite: redness can occur, it is suggested, only if non-redness also occurs. But unless evil is merely the privation of good, they are not logical opposites, and some further argument would be needed to show that they are counterparts in the same way as genuine logical opposites. Let us assume that this could be given. There is still doubt of the correctness of the metaphysical principle that a quality must have a real opposite: I suggest that it is not really impossible that everything should be, say, red, that the truth is merely that if everything were red we should not notice redness,

and so we should have no word 'red'; we observe and give names to qualities only if they have real opposites. If so, the principle that a term must have an opposite would belong only to our language or to our thought, and would not be an ontological principle,* and, correspondingly, the rule that good cannot exist without evil would not state a logical necessity of a sort that God would just have to put up with. God might have made everything good, though we should not have noticed it if he had.

But, finally, even if we concede that this is an ontological principle, it will provide a solution for the problem of evil only if one is prepared to say, "Evil exists, but only just enough evil to serve as the counterpart of good." I doubt whether any theist will accept this. After all, the *ontological* requirement that non-redness should occur would be satisfied even if all the universe, except for a minute speck, were red, and, if there were a corresponding requirement for evil as a counterpart to good, a minute dose of evil would presumably do. But theists are not usually willing to say, in all contexts, that all the evil that occurs is a minute and necessary dose.

2. "EVIL IS NECESSARY AS A MEANS TO GOOD."

It is sometimes suggested that evil is necessary for good not as a counterpart but as a means. In its simple form this has little plausibility as a solution of the problem of evil, since it obviously implies a severe restriction of God's power. It would be a causal law that you cannot have a certain end without a certain means, so that if God has to introduce evil as a means to good, he must be subject to at least some causal laws. This certainly conflicts with what a theist normally means by omnipotence. This view of God as limited by causal laws also conflicts with the view that causal laws are themselves made by God, which is more widely held than the corresponding view about the laws of logic. This conflict would, indeed; be resolved if it were possible for an omnipotent being to bind himself, and this possibility has still to be considered. Unless a favourable answer can be given to this question, the suggestion that evil is necessary as a means to good solves the problem of

---

* That is, not a principle constraining what exists.

evil only by denying one of its constituent propositions, either that God is omnipotent or that 'omnipotent' means what it says.

3. "THE UNIVERSE IS BETTER WITH SOME EVIL IN IT THAN IT COULD BE IF THERE WERE NO EVIL."

Much more important is a solution which at first seems to be a mere variant of the previous one, that evil may contribute to the goodness of a whole in which it is found, so that the universe as a whole is better as it is, with some evil in it, than it would be if there were no evil. This solution may be developed in either of two ways. It may be supported by an aesthetic analogy, by the fact that contrasts heighten beauty, that in a musical work, for example, there may occur discords which somehow add to the beauty of the work as a whole. Alternatively, it may be worked out in connexion with the notion of progress, that the best possible organisation of the universe will not be static, but progressive, that the gradual overcoming of evil by good is really a finer thing than would be the eternal unchallenged supremacy of good.

In either case, this solution usually starts from the assumption that the evil whose existence gives rise to the problem of evil is primarily what is called physical evil, that is to say, pain. In Hume's rather half-hearted presentation of the problem of evil, the evils that he stresses are pain and disease, and those who reply to him argue that the existence of pain and disease makes possible the existence of sympathy, benevolence, heroism, and the gradually successful struggle of doctors and reformers to overcome these evils. In fact, theists often seize the opportunity to accuse those who stress the problem of evil of taking a low, materialistic view of good and evil, equating these with pleasure and pain, and of ignoring the more spiritual goods which can arise in the struggle against evils.

But let us see exactly what is being done here. Let us call pain and misery 'first order evil' or 'evil (1).' What contrasts with this, namely, pleasure and happiness, will be called 'first order good' or 'good (1).' Distinct from this is 'second order good' or 'good (2)' which somehow emerges in a complex situation in which evil (1) is a necessary component—logically, not merely causally, necessary. (Exactly *how* it emerges does not matter: in the crudest version of this solution good (2) is simply the heightening of happiness by the contrast with misery, in other versions it includes sympathy with suffering, heroism in facing danger, and the gradual decrease of first order evil and increase of first order good.) It is also being assumed that second order good is more important than first order good or evil, in particular that it more than outweighs the first order evil it involves.

Now this is a particularly subtle attempt to solve the problem of evil. It defends God's goodness and omnipotence on the ground that (on a sufficiently long view) this is the best of all logically possible worlds, because it includes the important second order goods, and yet it admits that real evils, namely first order evils, exist. But does it still hold that good and evil are opposed? Not, clearly, in the sense that we set out originally: good does not tend to eliminate evil in general. Instead, we have a modified, a more complex pattern. First order good (e.g., happiness) *contrasts with* first order evil (e.g., misery): these two are opposed in a fairly mechanical way; some second order goods (e.g., benevolence) try to maximise first order good and minimise first order evil; but God's goodness is not this, it is rather the will to maximise *second* order good. We might, therefore, call God's goodness an example of a third order goodness, or good (3). While this account is different from our original one, it might well be held to be an improvement on it, to give a more accurate description of the way in which good is opposed to evil, and to be consistent with the essential theist position.

There might, however, be several objections to this solution. First, some might argue that such qualities as benevolence—and *a fortiori*[*] the third order goodness which promotes benevolence—have a merely derivative value, that they are not higher sorts of good, but merely means to good (1), that is, to happiness, so that it would be absurd for God to keep misery in existence in order to make possible the virtues of benevolence, heroism, etc. The theist who adopts the present solution must, of course, deny this, but he can do so with some plausibility, so I should not press this objection.

---

[*] All the more, for an even stronger reason.

Secondly, it follows from this solution that God is not in our sense benevolent or sympathetic: he is not concerned to minimise evil (1), but only to promote good (2); and this might be a disturbing conclusion for some theists.

But, thirdly, the fatal objection is this. Our analysis shows clearly the possibility of the existence of a *second* order evil, an evil (2) contrasting with good (2) as evil (1) contrasts with good (1). This would include malevolence, cruelty, callousness, cowardice, and states in which good (1) is decreasing and evil (1) increasing. And just as good (2) is held to be the important kind of good, the kind that God is concerned to promote, so evil (2) will, by analogy, be the important kind of evil, the kind which God, if he were wholly good and omnipotent, would eliminate. And yet evil (2) plainly exists, and indeed most theists (in other contexts) stress its existence more than that of evil (1). We should, therefore, state the problem of evil in terms of second order evil, and against this form of the problem the present solution is useless.

An attempt might be made to use this solution again, at a higher level, to explain the occurrence of evil (2): indeed the next main solution that we shall examine does just this, with the help of some new notions. Without any fresh notions, such a solution would have little plausibility: for example, we could hardly say that the really important good was a good (3), such as the increase of benevolence in proportion to cruelty, which logically required for its occurrence the occurrence of some second order evil. But even if evil (2) could be explained in this way, it is fairly clear that there would be third order evils contrasting with this third order good: and we should be well on the way to an infinite regress, where the solution of a problem of evil, stated in terms of evil (n), indicated the existence of an evil (n + 1), and a further problem to be solved.

4. "EVIL IS DUE TO HUMAN FREEWILL."

Perhaps the most important proposed solution of the problem of evil is that evil is not to be ascribed to God at all, but to the independent actions of human beings, supposed to have been endowed by God with freedom of the will. This solution may be combined with the preceding one: first order evil (e.g., pain) may be justified as a logically necessary component in second order good (e.g., sympathy) while second order evil (e.g., cruelty) is not *justified*, but is so ascribed to human beings that God cannot be held responsible for it. This combination evades my third criticism of the preceding solution.

The freewill solution also involves the preceding solution at a higher level. To explain why a wholly good God gave men freewill although it would lead to some important evils, it must be argued that it is better on the whole that men should act freely, and sometimes err, than that they should be innocent automata,* acting rightly in a wholly determined way. Freedom, that is to say, is now treated as a third order good, and as being more valuable than second order goods (such as sympathy and heroism) would be if they were deterministically produced, and it is being assumed that second order evils, such as cruelty, are logically necessary accompaniments of freedom, just as pain is a logically necessary pre-condition of sympathy.

I think that this solution is unsatisfactory primarily because of the incoherence of the notion of freedom of the will: but I cannot discuss this topic adequately here, although some of my criticisms will touch upon it.

First I should query the assumption that second order evils are logically necessary accompaniments of freedom. I should ask this: if God has made men such that in their free choices they sometimes prefer what is good and sometimes what is evil, why could he not have made men such that they always freely choose the good? If there is no logical impossibility in a man's freely choosing the good on one, or on several, occasions, there cannot be a logical impossibility in his freely choosing the good on every occasion. God was not, then, faced with a choice between making innocent automata and making beings who, in acting freely, would sometimes go wrong: there was open to him the obviously better possibility of making beings who would act freely but always go right. Clearly, his failure to avail himself of this possibility is inconsistent with his being both omnipotent and wholly good.

If it is replied that this objection is absurd, that the making of some wrong choices is logically necessary

---

* Robots.

for freedom, it would seem that 'freedom' must here mean complete randomness or indeterminacy, including randomness with regard to the alternatives good and evil, in other words that men's choices and consequent actions can be "free" only if they are not determined by their characters. Only on this assumption can God escape the responsibility for men's actions; for if he made them as they are, but did not determine their wrong choices, this can only be because the wrong choices are not determined by men as they are. But then if freedom is randomness, how can it be a characteristic of *will*? And, still more, how can it be the most important good? What value or merit would there be in free choices if these were random actions which were not determined by the nature of the agent?

I conclude that to make this solution plausible two different senses of 'freedom' must be confused, one sense which will justify the view that freedom is a third order good, more valuable than other goods would be without it, and another sense, sheer randomness, to prevent us from ascribing to God a decision to make men such that they sometimes go wrong when he might have made them such that they would always freely go right.

This criticism is sufficient to dispose of this solution. But besides this there is a fundamental difficulty in the notion of an omnipotent God creating men with free will, for if men's wills are really free this must mean that even God cannot control them, that is, that God is no longer omnipotent. It may be objected that God's gift of freedom to men does not mean that he cannot control their wills, but that he always *refrains* from controlling their wills. But why, we may ask, should God refrain from controlling evil wills? Why should he not leave men free to will rightly, but intervene when he sees them beginning to will wrongly? If God could do this, but does not, and if he is wholly good, the only explanation could be that even a wrong free act of will is not really evil, that its freedom is a value which outweighs its wrongness, so that there would be a loss of value if God took away the wrongness and the freedom together. But this is utterly opposed to what theists say about sin in other contexts. The present solution of the problem of evil, then, can be maintained only in the form that God has made men so free that he *cannot* control their wills.

This leads us to what I call the Paradox of Omnipotence: can an omnipotent being make things

which he cannot subsequently control? Or, what is practically equivalent to this, can an omnipotent being make rules which then bind himself? (These are practically equivalent because any such rules could be regarded as setting certain things beyond his control, and *vice versa*.) The second of these formulations is relevant to the suggestions that we have already met, that an omnipotent God creates the rules of logic or causal laws, and is then bound by them.

It is clear that this is a paradox: the questions cannot be answered satisfactorily either in the affirmative or in the negative. If we answer "Yes," it follows that if God actually makes things which he cannot control, or makes rules which bind himself, he is not omnipotent once he has made them: there are *then* things which he cannot do. But if we answer "No," we are immediately asserting that there are things which he cannot do, that is to say that he is already not omnipotent.

It cannot be replied that the question which sets this paradox is not a proper question. It would make perfectly good sense to say that a human mechanic has made a machine which he cannot control: if there is any difficulty about the question it lies in the notion of omnipotence itself.

This, incidentally, shows that although we have approached this paradox from the free will theory, it is equally a problem for a theological determinist. No one thinks that machines have free will, yet they may well be beyond the control of their makers. The determinist might reply that anyone who makes anything determines its ways of acting, and so determines its subsequent behaviour: even the human mechanic does this by his *choice* of materials and structure for his machine, though he does not know all about either of these: the mechanic thus determines, though he may not foresee, his machine's actions. And since God is omniscient, and since his creation of things is total, he both determines and foresees the ways in which his creatures will act. We may grant this, but it is beside the point. The question is not whether God *originally* determined the future actions of his creatures, but whether he can *subsequently* control their actions, or whether he was able in his original creation to put things beyond his subsequent control. Even on determinist principles the answers "Yes" and "No" are equally irreconcilable with God's omnipotence.

Before suggesting a solution of this paradox, I would point out that there is a parallel Paradox of

Sovereignty. Can a legal sovereign* make a law restricting its own future legislative power? For example, could the British parliament make a law forbidding any future parliament to socialise banking, and also forbidding the future repeal of this law itself? Or could the British parliament, which was legally sovereign in Australia in, say, 1899, pass a valid law, or series of laws, which made it no longer sovereign in 1933? Again, neither the affirmative nor the negative answer is really satisfactory. If we were to answer "Yes," we should be admitting the validity of a law which, if it were actually made, would mean that parliament was, no longer sovereign. If we were to answer "No," we should be admitting that there is a law, not logically absurd, which parliament cannot validly make, that is, that parliament is not now a legal sovereign. This paradox can be solved in the following way. We should distinguish between first order laws, that is laws governing the actions of individuals and bodies other than the legislature, and second order laws, that is laws about laws, laws governing the actions of the legislature itself. Correspondingly, we should distinguish two orders of sovereignty, first order sovereignty (sovereignty (1)) which is unlimited authority to make first order laws, and second order sovereignty (sovereignty (2)) which is unlimited authority to make second order laws. If we say that parliament is sovereign we might mean that any parliament at any time has sovereignty (1), or we might mean that parliament has both sovereignty (1) and sovereignty (2) at present, but we cannot without contradiction mean both that the present parliament has sovereignty (2) and that every parliament at every time has sovereignty (1), for if the present parliament has sovereignty (2) it may use it to take away the sovereignty (1) of later parliaments. What the paradox shows is that we cannot ascribe to any continuing institution legal sovereignty in an inclusive sense.

The analogy between omnipotence and sovereignty shows that the paradox of omnipotence can be solved in a similar way. We must distinguish between first order omnipotence (omnipotence (1)), that is

unlimited power to act, and second order omnipotence (omnipotence (2)), that is unlimited power to determine what powers to act things shall have. Then we could consistently say that God all the time has omnipotence (1), but if so no beings at any time have powers to act independently of God. Or we could say that God at one time had omnipotence (2), and used it to assign independent powers to act to certain things, so that God thereafter did not have omnipotence (1). But what the paradox shows is that we cannot consistently ascribe to any continuing being omnipotence in an inclusive sense.

An alternative solution of this paradox would be simply to deny that God is a continuing being, that any times can be assigned to his actions at all. But on this assumption (which also has difficulties of its own) no meaning can be given to the assertion that God made men with wills so free that he could not control them. The paradox of omnipotence can be avoided by putting God outside time, but the freewill solution of the problem of evil cannot be saved in this way, and equally it remains impossible to hold that an omnipotent God *binds himself* by causal or logical laws.

Conclusion

Of the proposed solutions of the problem of evil which we have examined, none has stood up to criticism. There may be other solutions which require examination, but this study strongly suggests that there is no valid solution of the problem which does not modify at least one of the constituent propositions in a way which would seriously affect the essential core of the theistic position.

Quite apart from the problem of evil, the paradox of omnipotence has shown that God's omnipotence must in any case be restricted in one way or another, that unqualified omnipotence cannot be ascribed to any being that continues through time. And if God and his actions are not in time, can omnipotence, or power of any sort, be meaningfully ascribed to him? ■

---

*   A sovereign in Mackie's sense is a person or group with unlimited authority over others.

Suggestions for Critical Reflection

1. Why do responses like "Evil is something to be faced and overcome, not to be merely discussed" or "God works in mysterious ways, but I have faith" fail to deal rationally with the problem of evil (if they do)?

2. What do you think goodness is? Do you think evil is merely the absence of goodness (or *vice versa*), or can something be neither good nor evil (nor both)?

3. Is the universe better with some evil in it than it would be without any? (For example, do you think a life of successful struggle against adversity is more valuable than one of uninterrupted pleasure? If so, why?) What do you make of Mackie's arguments against this claim?

4. Could *all* evil be due to human free will? If even some of it is, should God have given us free will (if he did)? Is it coherent to think that God could have made us so that we have free will but nevertheless always choose some particular option (the best one) on every occasion?

5. Do you agree that the notion of omnipotence must have *some* limits? For example, could God have made the number four smaller than the number three, or created things that are neither rocks nor non-rocks, or made violent murder a moral duty? If even an "omnipotent" deity must be restricted in these ways, how serious a problem is this for the traditional picture of God? How much does Mackie's "paradox of omnipotence" add to these worries?

BLAISE PASCAL

The Wager, FROM *Pensées*

Who Was Blaise Pascal?

Blaise Pascal (1623–62) was a French scientific prodigy, one of the most important mathematicians of the seventeenth century, and a Catholic theologian. He was born in France's Auvergne region and his mother died when he was three. The family moved to Paris in 1631, where Pascal and his siblings were educated entirely by his father Étienne (who never remarried). Pascal was a brilliant child, especially interested in mathematics, and even before he was sixteen was developing new proofs and corresponding with some of the leading mathematicians of his day—some of whom, such as René Descartes, initially refused to believe they were reading the work of a child.

When Pascal was 16 the French government, enmeshed in the very expensive Thirty Years' War, defaulted on the government's bonds where the Pascals' money was invested, and the family was suddenly plunged from living in relative comfort to hard times. To make matters worse, Pascal's father soon had to flee Paris, leaving his children behind, because of his (understandable) opposition to the government's fiscal policies. For several months Blaise and his two sisters were in the care of a neighbor, Madame Sainctot, a society beauty who ran one of the most glamorous 'salons'—regular intellectual gatherings/parties—in Paris.

Pascal's father was eventually able to find an appointment as the king's tax collector for the city of Rouen, and began to rebuild the family's financial fortunes. But Rouen's tax records were in complete disarray because of recent failed popular uprisings, and the job of rebuilding those records was a tedious and grinding one. In order to help his father with the endless calculations required, the 18-year-old Pascal built the first of a series of mechanical calculators, capable of addition and subtraction, which he developed and refined over the following decade. There was a prior abortive attempt by Wilhelm Schickard in Germany in the 1620s to build a mechanical calculator, but Pascal's machine was probably the first properly functional calculator ever built; it would be another 200 years before the study of mechanical calculation took a further jump forward, including the work of Charles Babbage and his difference engine, and eventually became modern computer engineering.

In mathematics, Pascal's role in the development of probability theory was his most influential contribution. Originally applied to gambling—as we see in this selection—his ideas, partly developed in correspondence with the French lawyer and mathematician Pierre de Fermat, have strongly influenced the development of modern economics, actuarial science, and social science, and were an important basis for Leibniz's formulation of the calculus.

In addition to his achievements in mathematics, Pascal did important work in the experimental sciences, especially on the properties of fluids and air pressure, and he created influential experiments which sought to demonstrate the then-controversial existence of a vacuum.

In 1654, when he was 31, Pascal—already dabbling with religion after the illness and death of his father and the departure of his younger sister, Jacqueline, to a convent—had an intense night-time religious vision that changed his life. He followed his sister in converting to a theological movement within Catholicism that emphasized original sin and human depravity, and hence the necessity of divine grace for salvation, as well as the doctrine of predestination, which holds that the fate of individual human souls has already been decided by God.* It was at this time that Pascal began his reli-

---

*   This movement was known by its detractors as Jansenism, after the Dutch theologian Cornelius Jansen (1585–1638). It was suppressed by the French monarch, King Louis XIV, and by the mainstream of the Catholic church, including Pope Alexander VII and the Jesuits.

gious writings, though he also continued his mathematical work.* During this period he was also increasingly plagued by painful poor health—based on an autopsy performed after his death, it's clear he had a brain lesion, but it is speculated that he may also have had both tuberculosis and stomach cancer—and he lived frugally and abstained from sensual pleasures. What he published in this period—including the *Lettres provinciales* (*The Provincial Letters*, 1656–57)—established Pascal's reputation as one of the greatest writers of French prose.

What Is the Structure of This Reading?

Pensées ('Thoughts') is a collection of fragments of writing that Pascal had been preparing to put together as a major defense of Christianity. He died, aged 39, before the book, his life's work, could be completed. Over the centuries since his death several editors and translators have published different arrangements of the material, but the proper order of the fragments is disputed.

The fragment reprinted here is the most well-known section of the *Pensées*, and is part of a series of thoughts where Pascal argues that we do not require certainty in order to believe in religion—and that such a certainty is unavailable because of our limited and finite understanding. It is rational to believe in God even though we cannot be certain of God's existence and nature, Pascal argues, because this is a question on which we are forced to make a choice (with major consequences for how we should live), and since we must choose an option, the rational choice is to believe in God and the Christian religion.

Some Useful Background Information

1. Although Pascal became a fervent defender of Catholicism, and was an internationally known scientist and mathematician with many aristocratic friends, he was not really a member of the establishment and many of his ideas were radical and unsettling at the time. After his conversion to a brand of Catholicism rather like his sister's 'Jansenism,' Pascal became embroiled in a public and legal battle with the powerful Jesuit order. His *Provincial Letters* contained scathing—and humorous—criticisms of Jesuit casuistry and had to be published anonymously, or Pascal was in real danger of prosecution.

2. Pascal's Wager is often described as an example of what has come to be called decision theory, which is the branch of probability theory that examines how to make decisions in situations of uncertainty. The two key concepts of decision theory are *preferences* and *prospects*: how much do you want different outcomes to occur, and how likely are those outcomes? At its simplest, combining weightings for preferences with judgments of prospects will produce an *expected value* for each possible option, and then the rational agent will choose the option with the highest expected value.

    Suppose that you are considering playing a betting game where you toss a fair coin twice and if heads comes up both times you win $8, but on any other result you must pay $2. We can represent the values of the different outcomes in a table:

Option	You win	You lose
1. You bet	$8	-$2
2. You don't bet	$0	$0

Consider option 1. The probability of getting two heads is 1/4. The probability of *not* getting two heads is therefore 3/4. The expected value of choice one, betting, is therefore ($8 x 1/4) + (-$2 x 3/4) = $2 + -$1.50 = $0.50.

If you choose option 2 and don't place a bet, then you are guaranteed to neither gain nor lose money, and so your expected value is $0. The expected value of option 1 thus exceeds the expected value of option 2, so—in this simple version of decision theory—you should take the bet.

---

* Pascal also found time to inaugurate what is probably the first bus line in history, when his plan for a many-seated carriage to move passengers around Paris was implemented.

The Wager, FROM *Pensées**

$233

...We know that there is an infinite, and are ignorant of its nature. As we know it to be false that numbers are finite, it is therefore true that there is an infinity in number. But we do not know what it is. It is false that it is even, it is false that it is odd; for the addition of a unit can make no change in its nature. Yet it is a number, and every number is odd or even (this is certainly true of every finite number). So we may well know that there is a God without knowing what He is. Is there not one substantial truth, seeing there are so many things which are not the truth itself?

We know then the existence and nature of the finite, because we also are finite and have extension.† We know the existence of the infinite, and are ignorant of its nature, because it has extension like us, but not limits like us. But we know neither the existence nor the nature of God, because He has neither extension nor limits.

But by faith we know His existence; in glory‡ we shall know His nature. Now, I have already shown that we may well know the existence of a thing, without knowing its nature.

Let us now speak according to natural lights.§

If there is a God, He is infinitely incomprehensible, since, having neither parts nor limits, He has no affinity to us.¶ We are then incapable of knowing either what He is or if He is. This being so, who will dare to undertake the decision of the question? Not we, who have no affinity to Him.

Who then will blame Christians for not being able to give a reason for their belief, since they profess a religion for which they cannot give a reason? They declare, in expounding it to the world, that it is a foolishness, *stultitiam*;** and then you complain that they do not prove it! If they proved it, they would not keep their word; it is in lacking proofs, that they are not lacking in sense.†† "Yes, but although this excuses those who offer it as such,‡‡ and takes away from them the blame of putting it forward without reason, it does not excuse those who receive it." Let us then examine this point, and say, "God is, or He is not." But to which side shall we incline? Reason can decide nothing here. There is an infinite chaos which separated us. A game is being played at the extremity of this infinite distance where heads§§ or tails will turn up. What will you wager? According to reason, you can do neither the one thing nor the other; according to reason, you can defend neither of the propositions.

Do not then reprove for error those who have made a choice; for you know nothing about it. "No, but I blame them for having made, not this choice, but a choice; for again both he who chooses heads and he who chooses tails are equally at fault, they are both in the wrong. The true course is not to wager at all."

Yes; but you must wager. It is not optional. You are embarked. Which will you choose then? Let us see. Since you must choose, let us see which interests you least. You have two things to lose, the true and the good; and two things to stake, your reason and your will, your knowledge and your happiness; and your

---

* From *Pensées*, trans. W.F. Trotter (E.P. Dutton & Co., 1958).

† "We also are finite and have extension": we are limited beings with spatial boundaries.

‡ In heaven, after death.

§ "According to natural lights": in accord with the power of reasoning we all have by virtue of being human.

¶ No similarity or commonality with us.

** This is a reference to the Bible, 1 Corinthians 1:18: "For the message of the cross is foolishness to those who are perishing, but to us who are being saved it is the power of God." *Stultitiam* is Latin for being a fool.

†† "It is in lacking proofs, that they are not lacking in sense": it is by being without proof that they show that they are not without sense.

‡‡ Propose it without giving a reason.

§§ The word Pascal uses for heads is *croix*, which subtly relates the gambler's choice to the Christian message of the cross referenced just above.

nature has two things to shun, error and misery. Your reason is no more shocked in choosing one rather than the other, since you must of necessity choose. This is one point settled. But your happiness? Let us weigh the gain and the loss in wagering that God is. Let us estimate these two chances. If you gain, you gain all; if you lose, you lose nothing. Wager, then, without hesitation that He is.—"That is very fine. Yes, I must wager; but I may perhaps wager too much."—Let us see. Since there is an equal risk of gain and of loss, if you had only to gain two lives, instead of one,* you might still wager. But if there were three lives to gain, you would have to play (since you are under the necessity of playing), and you would be imprudent, when you are forced to play, not to chance your life† to gain three at a game where there is an equal risk of loss and gain. But there is an eternity of life and happiness. And this being so, if there were an infinity of chances, of which one only would be for you,‡ you would still be right in wagering one to win two, and you would act stupidly, being obliged to play, by refusing to stake one life against three at a game in which out of an infinity of chances there is one for you, if there were an infinity of an infinitely happy life to gain. But there is here an infinity of an infinitely happy life to gain, a chance of gain against a finite number of chances of loss, and what you stake is finite. It is all divided;§ wherever the infinite is and there is not an infinity of chances of loss against that of gain, there is no time to hesitate, you must give all. And thus, when one is forced to play, he must renounce reason to preserve his life, rather than risk it for infinite gain, as likely to happen as the loss of nothingness.¶

For it is no use to say it is uncertain if we will gain, and it is certain that we risk, and that the infinite distance between the *certainty* of what is staked and the *uncertainty* of what will be gained, equals the finite good which is certainly staked against the uncertain infinite. It is not so, as every player stakes a certainty to gain an uncertainty, and yet he stakes a finite certainty to gain a finite uncertainty, without transgressing against reason. There is not an infinite distance between the certainty staked and the uncertainty of the gain; that is untrue. In truth, there is an infinity between the certainty of gain and the certainty of loss. But the uncertainty of the gain is proportioned to the certainty of the stake according to the proportion of the chances of gain and loss. Hence it comes that, if there are as many risks on one side as on the other, the course is to play even;** and then the certainty of the stake is equal to the uncertainty of the gain, so far is it from fact that there is an infinite distance between them. And so our proposition is of infinite force, when there is the finite to stake in a game where there are equal risks of gain and of loss, and the infinite to gain. This is demonstrable; and if men are capable of any truths, this is one.

"I confess it, I admit it. But, still, is there no means of seeing the faces of the cards?"—Yes, Scripture and the rest, etc. "Yes, but I have my hands tied and my mouth closed; I am forced to wager, and am not free. I am not released, and am so made that I cannot believe.†† What, then, would you have me do?"

True. But at least learn your inability to believe, since reason brings you to this, and yet you cannot believe.‡‡ Endeavour then to convince yourself, not by increase of proofs of God, but by the abatement

---

* "To gain two lives, instead of one": to stand to win two lives instead of one.

† To bet your life.

‡ "If there were an infinity of chances, of which one only would be for you": even if there were an infinite number of outcomes where you lose and only one where you win.

§ It is already mathematically determined.

¶ "Infinite gain, as likely to happen as the loss of nothingness": an infinite gain which is just as likely to happen as a loss which (by comparison) amounts to nothing.

** "The course is to play even": the odds are even.

†† "I am not released, and am so made that I cannot believe": I am not free to choose (what I believe) and I am built in such a way that I cannot believe in God.

‡‡ "But at least learn your inability to believe, since reason brings you to this, and yet you cannot believe": but at least realize that if you can't believe it is not because reason prevents you, since it doesn't (but because your emotions or prejudices do).

of your passions. You would like to attain faith, and do not know the way; you would like to cure yourself of unbelief, and ask the remedy for it. Learn of those who have been bound like you, and who now stake all their possessions.* These are people who know the way which you would follow, and who are cured of an ill of which you would be cured. Follow the way by which they began; by acting as if they believed, taking the holy water, having masses said, etc. Even this will naturally make you believe, and deaden your acuteness.†—"But this is what I am afraid of."—And why? What have you to lose?

But to show you that this leads you there, it is this which will lessen the passions, which are your stumbling-blocks.

The end of this discourse.—Now, what harm will befall you in taking this side? You will be faithful, honest, humble, grateful, generous, a sincere friend, truthful. Certainly you will not have those poisonous pleasures, glory and luxury; but will you not have others? I will tell you that you will thereby gain in this life, and that, at each step you take on this road, you will see so great certainty of gain, so much nothingness in what you risk, that you will at last recognise that you have wagered for something certain and infinite, for which you have given nothing.

"Ah! This discourse transports me, charms me," etc.

If this discourse pleases you and seems impressive, know that it is made by a man who has knelt, both before and after it, in prayer to that Being, infinite and without parts,‡ before whom he lays all he has, for you also to lay before Him all you have for your own good and for His glory, that so strength may be given to lowliness.

...

§277

The heart has its reasons, which reason does not know. We feel it in a thousand things. I say that the heart naturally loves the Universal Being, and also itself naturally, according as it gives itself to them; and it hardens itself against one or the other at its will. You have rejected the one, and kept the other. Is it by reason that you love yourself?

Suggestions for Critical Reflection

1. "[Y]ou must wager. It is not optional." Why do you think Pascal insists on this? Is he right?
2. "And so our proposition is of infinite force, when there is the finite to stake in a game where there are equal risks of gain and of loss, and the infinite to gain. This is demonstrable; and if men are capable of any truths, this is one." This is arguably the heart of Pascal's Wager: what exactly is he saying here? How persuasive is it?
3. Some may object that, while it is all very well to say that we should choose to believe in God, beliefs are not the sort of thing we can simply choose to have or not have. This kind of objection has been made to Pascal's Wager many times. How

adequately do you think he deals with the problem? Imagine that somebody offered you $100 if you would sincerely believe that all the dogs and cats on earth were controlled by aliens on the planet Zarkon. Could you sincerely believe it? Suppose we can bring ourselves to believe in something, by a process other than reasoning (i.e., by a process other than relying on evidence or argument): how authentic would such a belief be?
4. Pascal was a scientist and a mathematician, and one of the key figures in the development of the scientific method; in science, reason is supreme in the pursuit of truth and the emotions or presumptions have no role. Yet in the *Pensées* he argues (using

---

* "Stake all their possessions": wager all they have.
† Pascal uses the word *abêtira*, which implies becoming more like an unthinking, instinctive animal than a human being, who is separated from the beasts by possessing the (in this case unhelpful) capacity to reason.
‡ Indivisible.

reason) that reason has no role in the apprehension of religious truth. This can seem to have an air of paradox. Is it in fact paradoxical? What do you think is going on here?

5. Although Pascal's Wager can seem fairly straightforward as an argument, there is disagreement among commentators as to what it is actually supposed to show. Is it intended to establish that *the only rational option* is to bet that God exists (to choose to be religious)? Or is it really meant to show that logical reasoning *cannot support either* faith or a lack of faith and that therefore, since there is no good reason to choose one over the other, we need some other principle to allow us to decide (since we have no choice except to decide)? Think carefully about the difference between these two interpretations. Which do you think is the right one? Irrespective of what Pascal actually intended, which do you think is the more plausible argument?

6. Suppose Pascal persuades us that we should choose to be religious. Which religion should you choose, and how would you make this decision?

7. What are the limits of reason?

WILLIAM K. CLIFFORD

The Ethics of Belief

Who Was William Clifford?

William Kingdon Clifford (1845–79) was an English mathematician and philosopher. Professor of mathematics at Trinity College, Cambridge, and then at University College London, he is credited with formalizing the field of geometric algebra (a system of transformations for geometric objects) and was also the first to suggest that gravitation might be an expression of spatial geometry—preceding Einstein by more than a quarter of a century. As a philosopher his commitment to clarity of thought, and his sense that it was a public duty to combat error and obscurantism, led him to clash with certain aspects of religious feeling. Darwin's ground-shaking work on evolution was still fresh and newly shocking in the 1870s, and was widely perceived to be inconsistent with Christian theology; Clifford was thus writing in an era in which the modern science seemed to be at odds with religion, and he was perceived to be a notorious and outspoken opponent of spirituality. Clifford was indeed an enemy of dogmatic religion, and he also held ethical and metaphysical views that might be seen to be in tension with some religious views, and (as the essay reprinted here demonstrates) fiercely attacked the role of 'blind faith' in belief.*

In both ethics and metaphysics, Clifford—in the spirit of Darwin—was a sort of naturalist and evolutionist. He defended the view that every elementary piece of matter has a mental aspect—indeed, is essentially "mind-stuff" as he put it—and that these atoms of proto-mentality combine together to make glimmerings of sentience in simpler organisms and, eventually, human consciousness. In this way, minds can be seen as the natural result of increasing complexity in the organization of an underlying (quasi-mental) substance rather than something radically new in nature. Ethically, Clifford postulated the existence of a "tribal self" that developed over historical time, as societies changed and the moral law developed, and is expressed in each individual as a conscience that prescribes behaviors that contribute to the good of the whole 'tribe'. One of his philosophical concerns was to fight against the distortion of this moral voice by the improper demands of dogmatic and priest-ridden religion, which he saw as putting the claims of a particular sect above those of society in general. In his 1877 essay "The Ethics of Religion," Clifford proclaimed that "if men were no better than their religions, the world would be a hell, indeed."

Clifford was born in Exeter and educated at Kings College London and Cambridge. In his mid-twenties he took part in an expedition to Italy to observe a solar eclipse, where he survived a shipwreck on the coast of Sicily. In 1875 he married Lucy Lane, who would become a prominent novelist and journalist. He suffered a breakdown, possibly brought on by overwork, in 1876; eventually recovering, he was able to resume his work, but his health remained poor and he died in 1879 of tuberculosis, at the age of only 33.

By all accounts, Clifford was a somewhat eccentric but brilliant person. He was a highly original thinker, with views that were often contentious or ahead of their time, but he was a very popular teacher, a well-respected scholar, and a sociable person who enjoyed parties and (like his counterpart Charles Dodgson, a.k.a. Lewis Carroll) wrote and published fairy stories for children. The contemporary philosopher Edward Clodd wrote in his book *Memories* (1916) that at Clifford's gatherings "you were sure to meet some one worth the knowing. There was no smart set to fill their empty time and waste yours

---

* At the time Clifford was a student and then a Fellow there, all Cambridge students had to sign the Thirty-nine Articles of Protestant Faith each year affirming their allegiance to the Church of England. Clifford signed in 1863 and 1864, fretted over it but eventually signed in 1865, and then refused to sign in 1866. This should have required his expulsion from the university, but for reasons that are unclear this did not happen and he was elected to a Fellowship at Trinity College in 1868.

in inane gossip; no prigs to irritate you with their affectation; and no pedants to bore you with their academic vagueness, but just a company of sane and healthy men and women, gentle and simple, who wanted to meet one another and have a full, free talk."

What Is the Structure of This Reading?

In Part I, Clifford argues for his famous conclusion that "it is wrong always, everywhere, and for anyone, to believe anything upon insufficient evidence." In the second part he argues that this stance—a philosophical position which has come to be called 'evidentialism'—does not lead to radical skepticism or to moral anarchy. Clifford goes on to make a fairly lengthy examination, not included in this reading, of "under what circumstances it is lawful to believe on the testimony of others." (This discussion deals with cases discussed by William James in the next reading of this book: the conflicting testimony of religious prophets such as Mohammed and Buddha, as well as the examples of a chemist and an Arctic explorer. Clifford argues that the testimony of an

individual has weight only insofar as "there are reasonable grounds for supposing that he knew the truth of what he was saying"—and Clifford argues that supernatural or universal claims can never be justified in this way.) In the final section of the essay, Clifford discusses "when and why we may believe that which goes beyond our own experience, or even beyond the experience of mankind."

A Common Misconception

Clifford's conclusion that it is always wrong to believe anything without sufficient evidence applies not only to cases where the available evidence underdetermines a particular conclusion, but also requires us as individuals to *seek out* the evidence on an issue before we reach a conclusion. We should not allow ourselves to believe something based on inadequate evidence, and the evidence we have might be inadequate either because it is a difficult question that is hard to answer conclusively, or because we have been lazy or biased in uncovering and assessing the evidence that does exist.

The Ethics of Belief*

I. The Duty of Inquiry

A shipowner was about to send to sea an emigrant-ship.† He knew that she was old, and not overwell built at the first; that she had seen many seas and climes, and often had needed repairs. Doubts had been suggested to him that possibly she was not seaworthy. These doubts preyed upon his mind, and made him unhappy; he thought that perhaps he ought to have her thoroughly overhauled and refitted, even though this should put him to great expense. Before the ship sailed, however, he succeeded in overcoming these

melancholy reflections. He said to himself that she had gone safely through so many voyages and weathered so many storms that it was idle to suppose she would not come safely home from this trip also. He would put his trust in Providence, which could hardly fail to protect all these unhappy families that were leaving their fatherland to seek for better times elsewhere. He would dismiss from his mind all ungenerous suspicions about the honesty of builders and contractors. In such ways he acquired a sincere and comfortable conviction that his vessel was thoroughly safe and seaworthy; he watched her departure with a light heart, and benevolent wishes

---

* This essay was published in *Contemporary Review* 29 (1877), 289–309, and reprinted in Clifford's *Lectures and Essays* (1879).
† That is, a sailing ship carrying emigrants to start new lives in another country; a common example at the time Clifford was writing would be emigrants from Europe, particularly Germany or Ireland, to the United States.

for the success of the exiles in their strange new home that was to be; and he got his insurance-money when she went down in mid-ocean and told no tales.

What shall we say of him? Surely this, that he was verily guilty of the death of those men. It is admitted that he did sincerely believe in the soundness of his ship; but the sincerity of his conviction can in no wise help him, because *he had no right to believe on such evidence as was before him.* He had acquired his belief not by honestly earning it in patient investigation, but by stifling his doubts. And although in the end he may have felt so sure about it that he could not think otherwise, yet inasmuch as he had knowingly and willingly worked himself into that frame of mind, he must be held responsible for it.

Let us alter the case a little, and suppose that the ship was not unsound after all; that she made her voyage safely, and many others after it. Will that diminish the guilt of her owner? Not one jot. When an action is once done, it is right or wrong for ever; no accidental failure of its good or evil fruits* can possibly alter that. The man would not have been innocent, he would only have been not found out. The question of right or wrong has to do with the origin of his belief, not the matter of it; not what it was, but how he got it; not whether it turned out to be true or false, but whether he had a right to believe on such evidence as was before him.

There was once an island in which some of the inhabitants professed a religion teaching neither the doctrine of original sin nor that of eternal punishment. A suspicion got abroad that the professors of this religion† had made use of unfair means to get their doctrines taught to children. They were accused of wresting the laws of their country in such a way as to remove children from the care of their natural and legal guardians; and even of stealing them away and keeping them concealed from their friends and relations. A certain number of men formed themselves into a society for the purpose of agitating the public about this matter. They published grave accusations against individual citizens of the highest position and character, and did all in their power to injure these citizens in their exercise of their professions. So great was the noise they made,

that a Commission was appointed to investigate the facts; but after the Commission had carefully inquired into all the evidence that could be got, it appeared that the accused were innocent. Not only had they been accused on insufficient evidence, but the evidence of their innocence was such as the agitators might easily have obtained, if they had attempted a fair inquiry. After these disclosures the inhabitants of that country looked upon the members of the agitating society, not only as persons whose judgment was to be distrusted, but also as no longer to be counted honourable men. For although they had sincerely and conscientiously believed in the charges they had made, *yet they had no right to believe on such evidence as was before them.* Their sincere convictions, instead of being honestly earned by patient inquiring, were stolen by listening to the voice of prejudice and passion.

Let us vary this case also, and suppose, other things remaining as before, that a still more accurate investigation proved the accused to have been really guilty. Would this make any difference in the guilt of the accusers? Clearly not; the question is not whether their belief was true or false, but whether they entertained it on wrong grounds. They would no doubt say, "Now you see that we were right after all; next time perhaps you will believe us." And they might be believed, but they would not thereby become honourable men. They would not be innocent, they would only be not found out. Every one of them, if he chose to examine himself *in foro conscientiae,*‡ would know that he had acquired and nourished a belief, when he had no right to believe on such evidence as was before him; and therein he would know that he had done a wrong thing....

In the two supposed cases which have been considered, it has been judged wrong to believe on insufficient evidence, or to nourish belief by suppressing doubts and avoiding investigation. The reason of this judgment is not far to seek: it is that in both these cases the belief held by one man was of great importance to other men. But forasmuch as no belief held by one man, however seemingly trivial the belief, and however obscure the believer, is ever actually insignificant or without its effect on the fate of mankind,

---

* "Its good or evil fruits": the good or bad things that happen because of it.

† People who profess—affirm their allegiance to—the religion.

‡ *In foro conscientiae* is Latin for "before the tribunal of one's personal conscience."

we have no choice but to extend our judgment to all cases of belief whatever. Belief, that sacred faculty which prompts the decisions of our will, and knits into harmonious working all the compacted energies of our being, is ours not for ourselves but for humanity. It is rightly used on truths which have been established by long experience and waiting toil, and which have stood in the fierce light of free and fearless questioning. Then it helps to bind men together, and to strengthen and direct their common action. It is desecrated when given to unproved and unquestioned statements, for the solace and private pleasure of the believer; to add a tinsel splendour* to the plain straight road of our life and display a bright mirage beyond it; or even to drown the common sorrows of our kind by a self-deception which allows them not only to cast down, but also to degrade us. Whoso would deserve well of his fellows in this matter will guard the purity of his beliefs with a very fanaticism of jealous care, lest at any time it should rest on an unworthy object, and catch a stain which can never be wiped away.

It is not only the leader of men, statesmen, philosopher, or poet, that owes this bounden duty to mankind. Every rustic who delivers in the village alehouse his slow, infrequent sentences, may help to kill or keep alive the fatal superstitions which clog his race. Every hard-worked wife of an artisan may transmit to her children beliefs which shall knit society together, or rend it in pieces. No simplicity of mind, no obscurity of station, can escape the universal duty of questioning all that we believe.

It is true that this duty is a hard one, and the doubt which comes out of it is often a very bitter thing. It leaves us bare and powerless where we thought that we were safe and strong. To know all about anything is to know how to deal with it under all circumstances. We feel much happier and more secure when we think we know precisely what to do, no matter what happens, than when we have lost our way and do not know where to turn. And if we have supposed ourselves to know all about anything, and to be capable of doing what is fit in regard to it, we naturally do not like to find that we are really ignorant and powerless, that we

have to begin again at the beginning, and try to learn what the thing is and how it is to be dealt with—if indeed anything can be learnt about it. It is the sense of power attached to a sense of knowledge that makes men desirous of believing, and afraid of doubting.

This sense of power is the highest and best of pleasures when the belief on which it is founded is a true belief, and has been fairly earned by investigation. For then we may justly feel that it is common property, and holds good for others as well as for ourselves. Then we may be glad, not that *I* have learned secrets by which I am safer and stronger, but that *we men* have got mastery over more of the world; and we shall be strong, not for ourselves but in the name of Man and his strength. But if the belief has been accepted on insufficient evidence, the pleasure is a stolen one. Not only does it deceive ourselves by giving us a sense of power which we do not really possess, but it is sinful, because it is stolen in defiance of our duty to mankind. That duty is to guard ourselves from such beliefs as from pestilence,† which may shortly master our own body and then spread to the rest of the town. What would be thought of one who, for the sake of a sweet fruit, should deliberately run the risk of bringing a plague upon his family and his neighbours?

And, as in other such cases, it is not the risk only which has to be considered; for a bad action is always bad at the time when it is done, no matter what happens afterwards. Every time we let ourselves believe for unworthy reasons, we weaken our powers of self-control, of doubting, of judicially and fairly weighing evidence. We all suffer severely enough from the maintenance and support of false beliefs and the fatally wrong actions which they lead to, and the evil born when one such belief is entertained is great and wide. But a greater and wider evil arises when the credulous‡ character is maintained and supported, when a habit of believing for unworthy reasons is fostered and made permanent. If I steal money from any person, there may be no harm done from the mere transfer of possession; he may not feel the loss, or it may prevent him from using the money badly. But I cannot help doing this great wrong towards Man, that I make myself

---

* A superficial or misleading appearance of value.

† Infectious disease.

‡ Too ready to believe things on inadequate evidence; gullible.

dishonest. What hurts society is not that it should lose its property, but that it should become a den of thieves, for then it must cease to be society. This is why we ought not to do evil, that good may come; for at any rate this great evil has come, that we have done evil and are made wicked thereby. In like manner, if I let myself believe anything on insufficient evidence, there may be no great harm done by the mere belief; it may be true after all, or I may never have occasion to exhibit it in outward acts. But I cannot help doing this great wrong towards Man, that I make myself credulous. The danger to society is not merely that it should believe wrong things, though that is great enough; but that it should become credulous, and lose the habit of testing things and inquiring into them; for then it must sink back into savagery.

The harm which is done by credulity in a man is not confined to the fostering of a credulous character in others, and consequent support of false beliefs. Habitual want of care about what I believe leads to habitual want of care in others about the truth of what is told to me. Men speak the truth to one another when each reveres the truth in his own mind and in the other's mind; but how shall my friend revere the truth in my mind when I myself am careless about it, when I believe things because I want to believe them, and because they are comforting and pleasant? Will he not learn to cry, "Peace," to me, when there is no peace?* By such a course I shall surround myself with a thick atmosphere of falsehood and fraud, and in that I must live. It may matter little to me, in my cloud-castle of sweet illusions and darling lies; but it matters much to Man that I have made my neighbours ready to deceive. The credulous man is father to the liar and the cheat; he lives in the bosom of this his family, and it is no marvel if he should become even as they are. So closely are our duties knit together, that whoso shall keep the whole law, and yet offend in one point, he is guilty of all.

To sum up: it is wrong always, everywhere, and for anyone, to believe anything upon insufficient evidence.

If a man, holding a belief which he was taught in childhood or persuaded of afterwards, keeps down and pushes away any doubts which arise about it in his mind, purposely avoids the reading of books and the company of men that call into question or discuss it, and regards as impious those questions which cannot easily be asked without disturbing it—the life of that man is one long sin against mankind....

Inquiry into the evidence of a doctrine is not to be made once for all, and then taken as finally settled. It is never lawful to stifle a doubt; for either it can be honestly answered by means of the inquiry already made, or else it proves that the inquiry was not complete.

"But," says one, "I am a busy man; I have no time for the long course of study which would be necessary to make me in any degree a competent judge of certain questions, or even able to understand the nature of the arguments."

Then he should have no time to believe.

II. *The Weight of Authority*

Are we then to become universal sceptics, doubting everything, afraid always to put one foot before the other until we have personally tested the firmness of the road? Are we to deprive ourselves of the help and guidance of that vast body of knowledge which is daily growing upon the world, because neither we nor any other one person can possibly test a hundredth part of it by immediate experiment or observation, and because it would not be completely proved if we did? Shall we steal and tell lies because we have had no personal experience wide enough to justify the belief that it is wrong to do so?

There is no practical danger that such consequences will ever follow from scrupulous care and self-control in the matter of belief. Those men who have most nearly done their duty in this respect have found that certain great principles, and these most fitted for the guidance of life, have stood out more and more clearly in proportion to the care and honesty with which they were tested, and have acquired in this way a practical certainty. The beliefs about right and wrong which guide our actions in dealing with men in society, and the beliefs about physical nature which guide our actions in dealing with animate and

---

* An allusion to the Bible, Jeremiah 6:14 and 8:11: "They have healed the wound of my people lightly, saying, 'Peace, peace,' when there is no peace."

inanimate bodies, these never suffer from investigation; they can take care of themselves, without being propped up by "acts of faith," the clamour of paid advocates, or the suppression of contrary evidence. Moreover there are many cases in which it is our duty to act upon probabilities, although the evidence is not such as to justify present belief; because it is precisely by such action, and by observation of its fruits, that evidence is got which may justify future belief. So that we have no reason to fear lest a habit of conscientious inquiry should paralyze the actions of our daily life....

What shall we say of that authority, more venerable and august than any individual witness, the time-honoured tradition of the human race? An atmosphere of beliefs and conceptions has been formed by the labours and struggles of our forefathers, which enables us to breathe amid the various and complex circumstances of our life. It is around and about us and within us; we cannot think except in the forms and processes of thought which it supplies. Is it possible to doubt and to test it? and if possible, is it right?

We shall find reason to answer that it is not only possible and right, but our bounden duty; that the main purpose of the tradition itself is to supply us with the means of asking questions, of testing and inquiring into things; that if we misuse it, and take it as a collection of cut-and-dried statements to be accepted without further inquiry, we are not only injuring ourselves here, but, by refusing to do our part towards the building up of the fabric which shall be inherited by our children, we are tending to cut off ourselves and our race from the human line....

In regard, then, to the sacred tradition of humanity, we learn that it consists, not in propositions or statements which are to be accepted and believed on the authority of the tradition, but in questions rightly asked, in conceptions which enable us to ask further questions, and in methods of answering questions. The value of all these things depends on their being tested day by day. The very sacredness of the precious deposit imposes upon us the duty and the responsibility of testing it, of purifying and enlarging it to the utmost of our power. He who makes use of its results to stifle his own doubts, or to hamper the inquiry of others, is guilty of a sacrilege which centuries shall never be able to blot out. When the labours and questionings of honest and brave men shall have built up the fabric of known truth to a glory which we in this generation can neither hope for nor imagine, in that pure and holy temple he shall have no part nor lot, but his name and his works shall be cast out into the darkness of oblivion for ever.

III. The Limits of Inference

The question, in what cases we may believe that which goes beyond our experience, is a very large and delicate one, extending to the whole range of scientific method, and requiring a considerable increase in the application of it before it can be answered with anything approaching to completeness. But one rule, lying on the threshold of the subject, of extreme simplicity and vast practical importance, may here be touched upon and shortly laid down.

A little reflection will show us that every belief, even the simplest and most fundamental, goes beyond experience when regarded as a guide to our actions. A burnt child dreads the fire, because it believes that the fire will burn it to-day just as it did yesterday; but this belief goes beyond experience, and assumes that the unknown fire of to-day is like the known fire of yesterday. Even the belief that the child was burnt yesterday goes beyond *present* experience, which contains only the memory of a burning, and not the burning itself; it assumes, therefore, that this memory is trustworthy, although we know that a memory may often be mistaken. But if it is to be used as a guide to action, as a hint of what the future is to be, it must assume something about that future, namely, that it will be consistent with the supposition that the burning really took place yesterday; which is going beyond experience. Even the fundamental "I am," which cannot be doubted,[*] is no guide to action until it takes to itself "I shall be," which goes beyond experience. The question is not, therefore, "May we believe what goes beyond experience?" for this is involved in the very nature of belief; but "How far and in what manner may we add to our experience in forming our beliefs?"

And an answer, of utter simplicity and universality, is suggested by the example we have taken: a burnt

---

[*] See Descartes's *Meditations* elsewhere in this book.

child dreads the fire. We may go beyond experience by assuming that what we do not know is like what we do know; or, in other words, we may add to our experience on the assumption of a uniformity in nature. What this uniformity precisely is, how we grow in the knowledge of it from generation to generation, these are questions which for the present we lay aside, being content to examine two instances which may serve to make plainer the nature of the rule.

From certain observations made with the spectroscope, we infer the existence of hydrogen in the sun. By looking into the spectroscope when the sun is shining on its slit, we see certain definite bright lines: and experiments made upon bodies on the earth have taught us that when these bright lines are seen hydrogen is the source of them. We assume, then, that the unknown bright lines in the sun are like the known bright lines of the laboratory, and that hydrogen in the sun behaves as hydrogen under similar circumstances would behave on the earth.

But are we not trusting our spectroscope too much? Surely, having found it to be trustworthy for terrestrial substances, where its statements can be verified by man, we are justified in accepting its testimony in other like cases; but not when it gives us information about things in the sun, where its testimony cannot be directly verified by man?

Certainly, we want to know a little more before this inference can be justified; and fortunately we do know this. The spectroscope testifies to exactly the same thing in the two cases; namely, that light-vibrations of a certain rate are being sent through it. Its construction is such that if it were wrong about this in one case, it would be wrong in the other. When we come to look into the matter, we find that we have really assumed the matter of the sun to be like the matter of the earth, made up of a certain number of distinct substances; and that each of these, when very hot, has a distinct rate of vibration, by which it may be recognized and singled out from the rest. But this is the kind of assumption which we are justified in using when we add to our experience. It is an assumption of uniformity in nature, and can only be checked by comparison with many similar assumptions which we have to make in other such cases.

But is this a true belief, of the existence of hydrogen in the sun? Can it help in the right guidance of human action?

Certainly not, if it is accepted on unworthy grounds, and without some understanding of the process by which it is got at. But when this process is taken in as the ground of the belief, it becomes a very serious and practical matter. For if there is no hydrogen in the sun, the spectroscope—that is to say, the measurement of rates of vibration—must be an uncertain guide in recognizing different substances; and consequently it ought not to be used in chemical analysis—in assaying, for example—to the great saving of time, trouble, and money. Whereas the acceptance of the spectroscopic method as trustworthy has enriched us not only with new metals, which is a great thing, but with new processes of investigation, which is vastly greater.

For another example, let us consider the way in which we infer the truth of an historical event—say the siege of Syracuse in the Peloponnesian war.* Our experience is that manuscripts exist which are said to be and which call themselves manuscripts of the history of Thucydides;† that in other manuscripts, stated to be by later historians, he is described as living during the time of the war; and that books, supposed to date from the revival of learning, tell us how these manuscripts had been preserved and were then acquired. We find also that men do not, as a rule, forge books and histories without a special motive; we assume that in this respect men in the past were like men in the present; and we observe that in this case no special motive was present. That is, we add to our experience on the assumption of a uniformity in the characters of men. Because our knowledge of this uniformity is far less complete and exact than our knowledge of that which obtains in physics, inferences of the historical kind are more precarious and less exact than inferences in many other sciences.

---

*   The final phase of the Peloponnesian War (431–404 BCE) began when Athens launched a failed raid against Syracuse, eventually leading to surrender to Sparta.

†   Thucydides (c. 460–c. 400 BCE) was an Athenian general and chronicler of the war, from whom most of the surviving contemporary accounts have come.

But if there is any special reason to suspect the character of the persons who wrote or transmitted certain books, the case becomes altered. If a group of documents give internal evidence that they were produced among people who forged books in the names of others, and who, in describing events, suppressed those things which did not suit them, while they amplified such as did suit them; who not only committed these crimes, but gloried in them as proofs of humility and zeal; then we must say that upon such documents no true historical inference can be founded, but only unsatisfactory conjecture.

We may, then, add to our experience on the assumption of a uniformity in nature; we may fill in our picture of what is and has been, as experience gives it us, in such a way as to make the whole consistent with this uniformity. And practically demonstrative inference—that which gives us a right to believe in the result of it—is a clear showing that in no other way than by the truth of this result can the uniformity of nature be saved.

No evidence, therefore, can justify us in believing the truth of a statement which is contrary to, or outside of, the uniformity of nature. If our experience is such that it cannot be filled up consistently with uniformity, all we have a right to conclude is that there is something wrong somewhere; but the possibility of inference is taken away; we must rest in our experience, and not go beyond it at all. If an event really happened which was not a part of the uniformity of nature, it would have two properties: no evidence could give the right to believe it to any except those whose actual experience it was; and no inference worthy of belief could be founded upon it at all.

Are we then bound to believe that nature is absolutely and universally uniform? Certainly not; we have no right to believe anything of this kind. The rule only tells us that in forming beliefs which go beyond our experience, we may make the assumption that nature is practically uniform so far as we are concerned. Within the range of human action and verification, we may form, by help of this assumption, actual beliefs; beyond it, only those hypotheses which serve for the more accurate asking of questions.

To sum up:—

We may believe what goes beyond our experience, only when it is inferred from that experience by the assumption that what we do not know is like what we know.

We may believe the statement of another person, when there is reasonable ground for supposing that he knows the matter of which he speaks, and that he is speaking the truth so far as he knows it.

It is wrong in all cases to believe on insufficient evidence; and where it is presumption* to doubt and to investigate, there it is worse than presumption to believe. ■

Suggestions for Critical Reflection

1. "But forasmuch as no belief held by one man, however seemingly trivial the belief, and however obscure the believer, is ever actually insignificant or without its effect on the fate of mankind, we have no choice but to extend our judgment to all cases of belief whatever." How plausible is this claim of Clifford's? If it is not plausible, or if things are more complicated than Clifford allows here, what effect does this have on his overall argument and its conclusion?

2. Clifford argues that our duty to believe only on the basis of sufficient evidence is a duty not only to ourselves but to our community and, indeed, to all of humanity. Why do you think he argues for this stronger conclusion? Would it have been sufficient, or even possible, for him to have argued for a weaker one?

3. "[A] bad action is always bad at the time when it is done, no matter what happens afterwards." Is it? Why is this important to Clifford's argument do you think? If you have studied some ethical theory you

* Arrogance, overstepping the bounds of what is appropriate.

might want to consider what sort of general value theory Clifford is committed to: is he a consequentialist, a deontologist, a virtue theorist, or something else? (For instance, one view might be that he is a consequentialist but restricts his concern to a particular *sort* of consequence.)

4. Clifford raises a high bar for belief. In Part II of this essay, he addresses the question of whether this bar is impractically high and argues that it is not. Is he right?

5. "There are many cases in which it is our duty to act upon probabilities, although the evidence is not such as to justify present belief." When Clifford says this, is he being consistent with the rest of his position? What significance do you think this addition has to his view?

6. In Part III of his essay, Clifford appeals to "a uniformity in nature" as part of his justification for our believing things that go beyond our own experience. How well justified is this assumption itself? If it is not well justified, how much of a problem is this for Clifford?

7. Clifford's position in this essay is typically contrasted with William James's response in "The Will to Believe" (see the next reading). Once you have read James's essay, you should carefully consider what exactly these two thinkers disagree about (and whether there are, perhaps surprising, things about which they agree; e.g., the pragmatic nature of belief?), and make your own assessment of which position is the more plausible.

WILLIAM JAMES

The Will to Believe

Who Was William James?

William James was a popular essayist, one of the philosophical originators of pragmatism (often considered the first uniquely American philosophy), and one of the founders of academic psychology in America. He was born in 1842 in a New York hotel room. His family lived on a substantial inheritance from William's paternal grandfather (after whom he was named), and his father spent his time in the independent study of theology. Shortly after the birth of William's brother Henry—who was to become a famous novelist, author of *The Portrait of a Lady* and *The Bostonians*—the family moved to Europe, living in London, Paris, and Windsor. There, while William was still a young boy, his father had a violent nervous breakdown and found solace in religious mysticism and the "theosophy" of Emanuel Swedenborg.* The family sailed back to New York in 1847, only to return to Europe seven years later in search of a good education for the children: William was educated at a multilingual boarding school near Geneva, the Collège Impérial at Boulogne, and finally the University of Geneva.

As a young man, James was interested in science and painting. Back in Newport, Rhode Island, he embarked on a career as a painter, but quickly switched to the study of chemistry at Harvard in 1861. By then James had already begun his life-long habit of ingesting various, often hallucinogenic, chemicals (such as chloral hydrate, amyl nitrate, or mescaline) out of a scientific interest to see what effect they might have on him. After helping to care for his younger brother Wilky, badly wounded during the Civil War (during and after which the James family made attempts to help the enslaved black people of the South), James entered Harvard Medical School

in 1864. He took part in a scientific expedition to Brazil the following year, but was badly seasick on the trip out and suffered temporary blindness from catching a mild form of smallpox in Rio de Janeiro (he suffered from intermittent trouble with his eyes for the rest of his life). Though he decided at that point that he was "cut out for a speculative rather than an active life," he stayed with the expedition as it sailed up the Amazon. Back in Massachusetts, he continued to suffer from ill health and depression, and contemplated suicide.

He spent the period between 1867 and 1868 studying experimental psychology in Germany, and returned to Harvard to take and pass his examination for an M.D. but then sank into black depression, including bouts of insomnia and nervousness. He resolved never to marry for fear of passing mental illness onto his children. One of the causes of his depression in these years was his inability either to convince himself that modern science had not proved that free will was an illusion, or to resign himself to living in a deterministic, mechanical universe. Famously, in 1870, he apparently decided to shake off this particular worry and simply decided to believe in free will *despite* all the evidence against it: he wrote in his diary, "my first act of free will shall be to believe in free will."† Nevertheless, in 1872 James had a "crisis" which probably resembled that which had changed his father's life 28 years earlier: "Suddenly there fell upon me without any warning, just as if it came out of the darkness, a horrible fear of my own existence.... I became a mass of quivering fear. After this the universe was changed for me altogether...."‡

Probably a psychological lifeline for James at this point was the offer in 1873 to teach comparative anatomy and physiology at Harvard (though he hesitated over

---

*   Swedenborg (1688–1772) was a Swedish scientist and mystic, an important influence on the artist William Blake and poet W.B. Yeats, as well as on the James family.

†   William James, "Diary" for April 30th, 1870, in *The Letters of William James*, ed. Henry James, Jr. (Atlantic Monthly Press, 1920), Volume I, 147–48.

‡   William James, *The Varieties of Religious Experience* (1902), Lectures VI and VII. In William James, *The Essential Writings*, ed. Bruce Wilshire (State University of New York Press, 1984), 232.

accepting it, and delayed taking up the appointment for a year due to ill health). By 1877 James was a permanent professor of physiology at Harvard, though he lectured less on physiology than on the relatively new subject of psychology under the auspices of the philosophy department. In 1878 he married Alice Gibbens; "I have found in marriage a calm and repose I never knew before." His first son, Harry, was born the following year.

In 1889 he became the first Alford Professor of Psychology at Harvard University, and the next year he finally completed his first major work, *The Principles of Psychology* (he had signed the book contract in 1878). This book, a modern-day classic, met with instant acclaim. In 1897 he published *The Will to Believe, and Other Essays in Popular Psychology* and the next year, *Human Immortality: Two Supposed Objections to the Doctrine*, then, in 1899, one of his most popular books during his own lifetime, *Talks to Teachers on Psychology, and to Students on Some of Life's Ideals*. The 1902 publication of *The Varieties of Religious Experience* met with international praise and sales that substantially boosted James's income.

Throughout his life James's work was dogged by persistent health problems and nervous exhaustion, and in 1903 he tried to resign from Harvard but was persuaded to stay with a reduced teaching load. In 1906 James took a temporary appointment at Stanford University in California, but it was cut short by the great San Francisco earthquake of that year (which James witnessed, and apparently found quite exhilarating). In 1907 he finally retired from Harvard and published *Pragmatism: A New Name for Some Old Ways of Thinking*; this is arguably the most famous single work of American philosophy. That book was followed by *A Pluralistic Universe*, *The Meaning of Truth*, and the posthumous *Some Problems in Philosophy*, all of which try to develop and defend James's overall philosophical framework. James died of a chronic heart condition at his farmhouse in New Hampshire in 1910.

What Was James's Overall Philosophical Project?

James's philosophical work, including "The Will to Believe" and his other essays on religious belief, is rooted in a general metaphysical framework that James came to call "radical empiricism." Radical empiricism has three central elements, each of which has far-reaching philosophical implications.

First, there is James's emphasis on careful attention to what is "directly experienced." He thought philosophers and psychologists had generally failed to look carefully enough at what is actually delivered in experience, and to counteract this he defended what is called "the introspective method" in psychology—essentially, learning to pay close attention to the contents of one's own thought. James argued, as early as *The Principles of Psychology*, that philosophers have tended to read too much into what we experience: for example, he argued (like David Hume) that there is no soul or ego or spiritual medium of thought to be seen if we actually look inside ourselves for such a thing. On the other hand, according to James, philosophers have failed to notice that there is *more* to our experience than is traditionally assumed. We do not simply undergo discrete, repeatable lumps of experience, but experience a continuous stream of thought which includes transitions and relations between the more stable 'substantive' ideas; thus "we ought to say a feeling of *and*, a feeling of *if*, a feeling of *but*, and a feeling of *by*, quite as readily as we say a feeling of *blue* or a feeling of *cold*."[*]

Second, James rejected the traditional duality of mind and matter. Instead he postulated "a world of pure experience." Ultimately, according to James, the universe is made up not of some kind of 'stuff' but of a huge set of 'pure experiences.' Some of these experiences make up our streams of individual consciousness and, of those, some are taken by us (on the basis of their relations with other experiences) to be 'mental' and some 'physical.'

Third, James felt that he was able, on the basis of this picture of the nature of the universe, to solve the vexing problem of the *meaning of thought* (which philosophers today call "the problem of intentionality"). The problem is this: what is it about your thoughts, your sensations, or your words that makes them *about* some particular object in the external world? What is it, for example, about the word or the thought "cow" that connects it to a certain species of large, smelly mammal? According to James, the answer is relatively simple: your sensation of the cow just is the cow. The succession of pure experiences that makes up the cow, and the sequence of pure experiences that is your stream

[*]   William James, *The Principles of Psychology* (1890) (Harvard University Press, 1981), 238.

of consciousness (which is *you*) simply intersect, just as two lines can cross at a point; at that intersection is an experience that is simultaneously both thought and object of thought, mental and non-mental, you and the cow.

Our *idea* of a cow, then, is certainly *about* cows, but that 'aboutness' can now be understood in terms of the prospects for future intersections between, if you like, cow sequences and our personal autobiography. Roughly, for James, the meaning of an idea—including religious and moral ideas like *God* and *free will*—is its "cash-value" in terms of future experience. Importantly, this includes not only predictions about sensations that we might expect lie in store for us, but also the effects such an idea will have on our future behavior; how it will change *us*, and thus affect our future experience. This is the core doctrine of what James called "Pragmatism." "To attain perfect clearness in our thoughts of an object, then, we need only consider what conceivable effects of a practical kind the object may involve—what sensations we are to expect from it, and what reactions we must prepare."*

Finally, once we know how ideas get their meaning, we can ask what it is for an idea to be *true*. For James, the answer is its "workability." Given his radical empiricism and his pragmatism, truth can't possibly consist, for James, in a kind of correspondence or matching between an idea and some sort of external reality—James has rejected that whole way of talking. For an idea to be called 'true' is not for it to have some special property or value at the moment it occurs but instead it is for it to have particularly *beneficial* effects on our future conduct and our future experiences. An idea might turn out to be true because it is especially valuable for predicting scientific events (such as eclipses, for example), or its truth might lie in the way it is spiritually ennobling to all those who believe in it.

This, then, is a sketch of James's final world-view. This over-arching philosophical structure did not come to James all at once; it was shaped and reshaped, piece by piece, over his lifetime. Its motivation, one of James's key intellectual driving forces, was the tension that he felt between science and religion: between the cold but intelligent detachment and determinism of his 'scientific conscience,' and his attachment to the ideals of free will, morality, and an interested God. "The Will to Believe" was one of James's earlier—and, at the time and ever since, highly popular—attempts to resolve this contradiction.

What Is the Structure of This Reading?

"The Will to Believe," James announces at the outset, is to be "an essay in justification of faith." He starts out by making three distinctions between types of "options" (living or dead, forced or avoidable, momentous or trivial) and suggests that his essay is to be about options that are living, forced, and momentous—what James calls "genuine options."

James begins his discussion of this kind of option—in the second section of the paper—by immediately considering the objection that it is in some way "preposterous" to say that we could or should simply *choose* what to believe. He responds that not only can we and do we believe things on the basis of "our non-intellectual nature," but furthermore that we must and should do so—that willingness to believe is (morally and intellectually) "lawful." He tries to tie this view to the rejection of what he calls "absolutism" in science and the endorsement of "empiricism," and to the quest to "believe truth" rather than merely "avoid error."

In Section VIII James begins to present his actual arguments for the claim that "there are some options between opinions in which [our passional nature] must be regarded both as an inevitable and as a lawful determinant of our choice." He does so partly by arguing that this must be true for what he earlier called *genuine* options, and he gives as examples moral questions, issues to do with personal relationships, and—at greater length—religious faith. One of his central claims in this section is that "a rule of thinking which would absolutely prevent me from acknowledging certain kinds of truth if those truths were really there, would be an irrational rule."

Some Background Information

1. James refers to a number of people in his essay that may no longer be familiar to modern audiences. Here is a run-down of the names James drops, in the order of their appearance:

---

* William James, *Pragmatism* (Harvard University Press, 1975), 29.

- Leslie Stephen (1832–1904): a British writer, editor, and biographer best known as the editor of the *Dictionary of National Biography* and as novelist Virginia Woolf's father.
- Fridtjof Nansen (1861–1930): a Norwegian explorer, zoologist, and politician who led an Arctic expedition from 1893 to 1896.
- Blaise Pascal (1623–62): a French mathematician, physicist and philosopher. James is referring to the book *Pensées*, published (posthumously) in 1670.
- Arthur Hugh Clough (1819–61): a British poet. The quote is from a poem sometimes known as "Steadfast."
- Thomas Henry Huxley (1825–95): a British biologist and writer, known for championing Darwin's theory of evolution. The quotation is from "The Influence upon Morality of a Decline in Religious Belief" (1878, published as part of a symposium to which Clifford also contributed).
- William Kingdon Clifford (1845–79): a British mathematician, philosopher, and well-known agnostic who died an early death from tuberculosis. James quotes extensively from his "The Ethics of Belief," published in *Contemporary Review* 29 (1877).
- Arthur James Balfour (1848–1930): a philosopher who went on to be British prime minister from 1902 to 1905 and then foreign secretary (1916–19). James is thinking of Balfour's essay "Authority and Reason," published in 1895.
- John Henry Newman (1801–91): an English theologian who converted to Roman Catholicism in 1845 and became a cardinal in 1879.
- Johann Zöllner (1834–82): a German astrophysicist who researched psychic phenomena and defended the existence of a "fourth dimension."
- Charles Howard Hinton (1853–1907): an English mathematician who also, independently, postulated a "fourth dimension."
- Thomas Reid (1710–96): a Scottish philosopher and opponent of the 'skepticism' of David Hume.
- Herbert Spencer (1820–1903): an English philosopher who tried to apply the scientific theory of evolution to philosophy and ethics. He coined the phrase "the survival of the fittest."
- August Weismann (1834–1914): a German biologist and one of the founders of modern genetics, who defended the view that hereditary characteristics are transmitted by a germinal plasm (and so ruled out the transmission of acquired characteristics).
- Charles Secrétan (1815–95): A (rather obscure) late nineteenth-century Swiss philosopher.

2. James's position in "The Will to Believe" is often thought to be a good example of the philosophical position called fideism. This is the thesis that religious belief is based on faith and not on either evidence or reasoning. In other words, the fundamental claims of religion cannot be established by either science or reason but nevertheless (perhaps because we should not place reason ahead of God) they should be believed to be true. Fideism comes in various flavors. Perhaps the mildest is the view, held by St. Augustine and Pascal, that faith must come before reason: that is, only faith can persuade us that religious doctrines are true, but once we believe, we can use our intellect to come to better understand them and to see *why* they are true and rational. The most extreme version is typified in the writings of the nineteenth-century Danish philosopher Søren Kierkegaard. Kierkegaard went so far as to say that some central tenets of Christianity—e.g., that God became incarnate in the person of Jesus Christ—are actually self-contradictory, and thus irrational, so belief in them requires a "leap into faith" which cannot in any way be justified.

Some Common Misconceptions

1. James is not anti-science: he does not want to eliminate the scientific attitude in favor of a religious one, but to show that science leaves open the possibility of religious faith and that it can do so without merely ignoring religion or granting it a special sphere insulated from normal rational inquiry.
2. James does not argue that we *must* be religious but only that, even though we are reasonable and scientifically educated people, we still *can* be religious. Religious belief is, for James, a personal choice.

The Will to Believe*

In the recently published *Life* by Leslie Stephen of his brother, Fitz-James, there is an account of a school to which the latter went when he was a boy. The teacher, a certain Mr. Guest, used to converse with his pupils in this wise: "Gurney, what is the difference between justification and sanctification?—Stephen, prove the omnipotence of God!" etc. In the midst of our Harvard freethinking and indifference we are prone to imagine that here at your good old ortho-dox College conversation continues to be somewhat upon this order; and to show you that we at Harvard have not lost all interest in these vital subjects, I have brought with me to-night something like a sermon on justification by faith to read to you,—I mean an essay in justification *of* faith, a defence of our right to adopt a believing attitude in religious matters, in spite of the fact that our merely logical intellect may not have been coerced. "The Will to Believe," accord-ingly, is the title of my paper.

I have long defended to my own students the lawfulness of voluntarily adopted faith; but as soon as they have got well imbued with the logical spirit, they have as a rule refused to admit my contention to be lawful philosophically, even though in point of fact they were personally all the time chock-full of some faith or other themselves. I am all the while, however, so profoundly convinced that my own posi-tion is correct, that your invitation has seemed to me a good occasion to make my statements more clear. Perhaps your minds will be more open than those with which I have hitherto had to deal. I will be as little technical as I can, though I must begin by set-ting up some technical distinctions that will help us in the end.

I.

Let us give the name of *hypothesis* to anything that may be proposed to our belief; and just as the electri-cians speak of live and dead wires, let us speak of any hypothesis as either *live* or *dead*. A live hypothesis is one which appeals as a real possibility to him to whom it is proposed. If I ask you to believe in the Mahdi,[†] the notion makes no electric connection with your nature,—it refuses to scintillate with any credibility at all. As an hypothesis it is completely dead. To an Arab, however (even if he be not one of the Mahdi's followers), the hypothesis is among the mind's possi-bilities: it is alive. This shows that deadness and live-ness in an hypothesis are not intrinsic properties, but relations to the individual thinker. They are measured by his willingness to act. The maximum of liveness in an hypothesis, means willingness to act irrevoca-bly. Practically, that means belief; but there is some believing tendency wherever there is willingness to act at all.

Next, let us call the decision between two hypotheses an *option*. Options may be of several kinds. They may be—1, *living* or *dead*; 2, *forced* or *avoidable*; 3, *momentous* or *trivial*; and for our purposes we may call an option a *genuine* option when it is of the forced, living, and momentous kind.

1. A living option is one in which both hypotheses are live ones. If I say to you: "Be a theosophist[‡] or be a Mohammedan,"[§] it is probably a dead option, because for you neither hypothesis is likely to be alive. But if I say: "Be an agnostic or be a Christian," it is otherwise: trained as you are, each

---

* This essay was an address to the Philosophical Clubs of Yale and Brown Universities, and was first published in the *New World* in June 1896. This reprint is based on the text in *The Will to Believe, and Other Essays in Popular Philosophy* (Longmans, Green & Co., 1897).

† In Islam, a messianic leader who, it is believed, will appear shortly before the end of the world to establish a reign of righteousness.

‡ A member of a religious sect, the Theosophical Society, founded in New York in 1875, which incorporates aspects of Buddhism and Brahmanism.

§ A Muslim.

hypothesis makes some appeal, however small, to your belief.

2. Next, if I say to you: "Choose between going out with your umbrella or without it," I do not offer you a genuine option, for it is not forced. You can easily avoid it by not going out at all. Similarly, if I say, "Either love me or hate me," "Either call my theory true or call it false," your option is avoidable. You may remain indifferent to me, neither loving nor hating, and you may decline to offer any judgment as to my theory. But if I say, "Either accept this truth or go without it," I put on you a forced option, for there is no standing place outside of the alternative. Every dilemma based on a complete logical disjunction, with no possibility of not choosing, is an option of this forced kind.

3. Finally, if I were Dr. Nansen and proposed to you to join my North Pole expedition, your option would be momentous; for this would probably be your only similar opportunity, and your choice now would either exclude you from the North Pole sort of immortality altogether or put at least the chance of it into your hands. He who refuses to embrace a unique opportunity loses the prize as surely as if he tried and failed. *Per contra*,* the option is trivial when the opportunity is not unique, when the stake is insignificant, or when the decision is reversible if it later prove unwise. Such trivial options abound in the scientific life. A chemist finds an hypothesis live enough to spend a year in its verification: he believes in it to that extent. But if his experiments prove inconclusive either way, he is quit for his loss of time,† no vital harm being done.

It will facilitate our discussion if we keep all these distinctions well in mind.

II.

The next matter to consider is the actual psychology of human opinion. When we look at certain facts, it seems as if our passional and volitional nature lay at the root of all our convictions. When we look at others, it seems as if they could do nothing when the intellect had once said its say. Let us take the latter facts up first.

Does it not seem preposterous on the very face of it to talk of our opinions being modifiable at will? Can our will either help or hinder our intellect in its perceptions of truth? Can we, by just willing it, believe that Abraham Lincoln's existence is a myth, and that the portraits of him in *McClure's Magazine*‡ are all of some one else? Can we, by any effort of our will, or by any strength of wish that it were true, believe ourselves well and about when we are roaring with rheumatism in bed, or feel certain that the sum of the two one-dollar bills in our pocket must be a hundred dollars? We can say any of these things, but we are absolutely impotent to believe them; and of just such things is the whole fabric of the truths that we do believe in made up,—matters of fact, immediate or remote, as Hume said and relations between ideas, which are either there or not there for us if we see them so, and which if not there cannot be put there by any action of our own.

In Pascal's *Thoughts* there is a celebrated passage known in literature as Pascal's wager.§ In it he tries to force us into Christianity by reasoning as if our concern with truth resembled our concern with the stakes in a game of chance. Translated freely his words are these: You must either believe or not believe that God is—which will you do? Your human reason cannot say. A game is going on between you and the nature of things which at the day of judgment will bring out either heads or tails. Weigh what your gains and your losses would be if you should stake all you have on heads, or God's existence: if you win in such case, you gain eternal beatitude;¶ if you lose, you lose nothing

---

* "On the other hand."
† That is, free to stop with no penalty except for the loss of his time.
‡ An influential American muckraking periodical, founded in 1893.
§ See the Pascal selection in this chapter.
¶ Blessedness or happiness.

at all. If there were an infinity of chances, and only one for God in this wager, still you ought to stake your all on God; for though you surely risk a finite loss by this procedure, any finite loss is reasonable, even a certain one is reasonable, if there is but the possibility of infinite gain. Go, then, and take holy water, and have masses said; belief will come and stupefy your scruples,—*Cela vous fera croire et vous abêtira.** Why should you not? At bottom, what have you to lose?

You probably feel that when religious faith expresses itself thus, in the language of the gaming table, it is put to its last trumps.† Surely Pascal's own personal belief in masses and holy water had far other springs; and this celebrated page of his is but an argument for others, a last desperate snatch at a weapon against the hardness of the unbelieving heart. We feel that a faith in masses and holy water adopted wilfully after such a mechanical calculation—would lack the inner soul of faith's reality; and if we were ourselves in the place of the Deity, we should probably take particular pleasure in cutting off believers of this pattern from their infinite reward. It is evident that unless there be some pre-existing tendency to believe in masses and holy water, the option offered to the will by Pascal is not a living option. Certainly no Turk ever took to masses and holy water on its account; and even to us Protestants these means of salvation seem such foregone impossibilities that Pascal's logic, invoked for them specifically, leaves us unmoved. As well might the Mahdi write to us, saying, "I am the Expected One whom God has created in his effulgence.‡ You shall be infinitely happy if you confess me; otherwise you shall be cut off from the light of the sun. Weigh, then, your infinite gain if I am genuine against your finite sacrifice if I am not!" His logic would be that of Pascal; but he would vainly use it on us, for the hypothesis he offers us is dead. No tendency to act on it exists in us to any degree.

The talk of believing by our volition seems, then, from one point of view, simply silly. From another point of view it is worse than silly, it is vile. When one turns to the magnificent edifice of the physical sciences, and sees how it was reared; what thousands of disinterested moral lives of men lie buried in its mere foundations; what patience and postponement, what choking down of preference, what submission to the icy laws of outer fact are wrought into its very stones and mortar; how absolutely impersonal it stands in its vast augustness,—then how besotted and contemptible seems every little sentimentalist who comes blowing his voluntary smoke-wreaths, and pretending to decide things from out of his private dream! Can we wonder if those bred in the rugged and manly school of science should feel like spewing such subjectivism out of their mouths? The whole system of loyalties which grow up in the schools of science go dead against its toleration; so that it is only natural that those who have caught the scientific fever should pass over to the opposite extreme, and write sometimes as if the incorruptibly truthful intellect ought positively to prefer bitterness and unacceptableness to the heart in its cup.

It fortifies my soul to know
That, though I perish, Truth is so—

sings Clough, while Huxley exclaims: "My only consolation lies in the reflection that, however bad our posterity may become, so far as they hold by the plain rule of not pretending to believe what they have no reason to believe, because it may be to their advantage so to pretend [the word 'pretend' is surely here redundant], they will not have reached the lowest depth of immorality." And that delicious *enfant terrible*§ Clifford writes: "Belief is desecrated when given to unproved and unquestioned statements for the solace and private pleasure of the believer.... Whoso would deserve well of his fellows in this matter will guard the purity of his belief with a very fanaticism of jealous care, lest at any time it should rest on an unworthy object, and catch a stain which can never be wiped away.... If [a] belief has been accepted on insufficient evidence [even though the belief be true, as Clifford on the same page explains] the pleasure is a stolen

---

* "That will make you believe and will stupefy you."
† Near to death, in desperate straits.
‡ Radiance.
§ 'Bad boy'—a person whose behavior or ideas shock or embarrass those with more conventional attitudes.

one.... It is sinful because it is stolen in defiance of our duty to mankind. That duty is to guard ourselves from such beliefs as from a pestilence which may shortly master our own body and then spread to the rest of the town.... It is wrong always, everywhere, and for every one, to believe anything upon insufficient evidence."

III.

All this strikes one as healthy, even when expressed, as by Clifford, with somewhat too much of robustious pathos in the voice. Free-will and simple wishing do seem, in the matter of our credences,* to be only fifth wheels to the coach. Yet if any one should thereupon assume that intellectual insight is what remains after wish and will and sentimental preference have taken wing, or that pure reason is what then settles our opinions, he would fly quite as directly in the teeth of the facts.

It is only our already dead hypotheses that our willing nature is unable to bring to life again. But what has made them dead for us is for the most part a previous action of our willing nature of an antagonistic kind. When I say 'willing nature,' I do not mean only such deliberate volitions as may have set up habits of belief that we cannot now escape from,—I mean all such factors of belief as fear and hope, prejudice and passion, imitation and partisanship, the circumpressure of our caste and set. As a matter of fact we find ourselves believing, we hardly know how or why. Mr. Balfour gives the name of 'authority' to all those influences, born of the intellectual climate, that make hypotheses possible or impossible for us, alive or dead. Here in this room, we all of us believe in molecules and the conservation of energy, in democracy and necessary progress, in Protestant Christianity and the duty of fighting for 'the doctrine of the immortal Monroe,'† all for no reasons worthy of the name. We see into these matters with no more inner clearness, and probably with much less, than any disbeliever in them might possess. His unconventionality would probably have some grounds to show for its conclusions; but for us, not insight, but the *prestige* of the opinions, is what makes the spark shoot from them and light up our sleeping magazines‡ of faith. Our reason is quite satisfied, in nine hundred and ninety-nine cases out of every thousand of us, if it can find a few arguments that will do to recite in case our credulity is criticized by someone else. Our faith is faith in someone else's faith, and in the greatest matters this is most the case. Our belief in truth itself, for instance, that there is a truth, and that our minds and it are made for each other,—what is it but a passionate affirmation of desire, in which our social system backs us up? We want to have a truth; we want to believe that our experiments and studies and discussions must put us in a continually better and better position towards it; and on this line we agree to fight out our thinking lives. But if a pyrrhonistic sceptic§ asks us *how we know* all this, can our logic find a reply? No! certainly it cannot. It is just one volition against another,—we willing to go in for life upon a trust or assumption which he, for his part, does not care to make.[1]

As a rule we disbelieve all facts and theories for which we have no use. Clifford's cosmic emotions find no use for Christian feelings. Huxley belabors the bishops because there is no use for sacerdotalism¶ in his scheme of life. Newman, on the contrary, goes over to Romanism,** and finds all sorts of reasons good for staying there, because a priestly system is for him an organic need and delight. Why do so few 'scientists' even look at the evidence for telepathy, so called? Because they think, as a leading biologist, now dead, once said to me, that even if such a thing were true, scientists ought to band together to keep it suppressed and concealed. It would undo the uniformity of Nature and all sorts of other things without which scientists cannot carry on their pursuits. But if this

---

* Beliefs.

† This is the "Monroe Doctrine," set out by American president James Monroe in 1823, which states that the US would regard attempts by European powers to establish new colonies or otherwise interfere in the Americas as acts of aggression.

‡ A storehouse of explosive ammunition.

§ A radical skeptic, one who is determined to withhold assent from almost all beliefs.

¶ The institution of the priesthood.

** Roman Catholicism.

very man had been shown something which as a scientist he might *do* with telepathy, he might not only have examined the evidence, but even have found it good enough. This very law which the logicians would impose upon us—if I may give the name of logicians to those who would rule out our willing nature here—is based on nothing but their own natural wish to exclude all elements for which they, in their professional quality of logicians, can find no use.

Evidently, then, our non-intellectual nature does influence our convictions. There are passional tendencies and volitions which run before and others which come after belief, and it is only the latter that are too late for the fair; and they are not too late when the previous passional work has been already in their own direction. Pascal's argument, instead of being powerless, then seems a regular clincher, and is the last stroke needed to make our faith in masses and holy water complete. The state of things is evidently far from simple; and pure insight and logic, whatever they might do ideally, are not the only things that really do produce our creeds.

IV.

Our next duty, having recognized this mixed-up state of affairs, is to ask whether it be simply reprehensible and pathological, or whether, on the contrary, we must treat it as a normal element in making up our minds. The thesis I defend is, briefly stated, this: *Our passional nature not only lawfully may, but must, decide an option between propositions, whenever it is a genuine option that cannot by its nature be decided on intellectual grounds; for to say, under such circumstances, "Do not decide, but leave the question open," is itself a passional decision,—just like deciding yes or no,—and is attended with the same risk of losing the truth.* The thesis thus abstractly expressed will, I trust, soon become quite clear. But I must first indulge in a bit more of preliminary work.

V.

It will be observed that for the purposes of this discussion we are on 'dogmatic' ground,—ground, I mean, which leaves systematic philosophical scepticism altogether out of account. The postulate that there is truth, and that it is the destiny of our minds to attain it, we are deliberately resolving to make, though the sceptic will not make it. We part company with him, therefore, absolutely, at this point. But the faith that truth exists, and that our minds can find it, may be held in two ways. We may talk of the *empiricist* way and of the *absolutist* way of believing in truth. The absolutists in this matter say that we not only can attain to knowing truth, but we can *know* when we have attained to knowing it; while the empiricists think that although we may attain it, we cannot infallibly know when. To *know* is one thing, and to know for certain *that* we know is another. One may hold to the first being possible without the second; hence the empiricists and the absolutists, although neither of them is a sceptic in the usual philosophic sense of the term, show very different degrees of dogmatism in their lives.

If we look at the history of opinions, we see that the empiricist tendency has largely prevailed in science, while in philosophy the absolutist tendency has had everything its own way. The characteristic sort of happiness, indeed, which philosophies yield has mainly consisted in the conviction felt by each successive school or system that by it bottom-certitude had been attained. "Other philosophies are collections of opinions, mostly false; *my* philosophy gives standing-ground forever,"—who does not recognize in this the key-note of every system worthy of the name? A system, to be a system at all, must come as a *closed* system, reversible in this or that detail, perchance, but in its essential features never!

Scholastic orthodoxy,* to which one must always go when one wishes to find perfectly clear statement, has beautifully elaborated this absolutist conviction in a doctrine which it calls that of 'objective evidence.' If, for example, I am unable to doubt that I now exist before you, that two is less than three, or that if all

---

* The dominant philosophy of the Middle Ages, combining remnants of ancient Greek philosophy (especially Aristotle) with Christian theology.

men are mortal then I am mortal too, it is because these things illumine my intellect irresistibly. The final ground of this objective evidence possessed by certain propositions is the *adæquatio intellectus nostri cum rê*.* The certitude it brings involves an *apititudinem ad extorquendum certum assensum*[†] on the part of the truth envisaged, and on the side of the subject a *quietem in cognitione*,[‡] when once the object is mentally received, that leaves no possibility of doubt behind; and in the whole transaction nothing operates but the *entitas ipsa*[§] of the object and the *entitas ipsa* of the mind. We slouchy modern thinkers dislike to talk in Latin,—indeed, we dislike to talk in set terms at all; but at bottom our own state of mind is very much like this whenever we uncritically abandon ourselves: You believe in objective evidence, and I do. Of some things we feel that we are certain: we know, and we know that we do know. There is something that gives a click inside of us, a bell that strikes twelve, when the hands of our mental clock have swept the dial and meet over the meridian hour.¶ The greatest empiricists among us are only empiricists on reflection: when left to their instincts, they dogmatize like infallible popes. When the Cliffords tell us how sinful it is to be Christians on such 'insufficient evidence,' insufficiency is really the last thing they have in mind. For them the evidence is absolutely sufficient, only it makes the other way. They believe so completely in an anti-Christian order of the universe that there is no living option: Christianity is a dead hypothesis from the start.

VI.

But now, since we are all such absolutists by instinct, what in our quality of students of philosophy ought we to do about the fact? Shall we espouse and endorse it? Or shall we treat it as a weakness of our nature from which we must free ourselves, if we can?

I sincerely believe that the latter course is the only one we can follow as reflective men. Objective evidence and certitude are doubtless very fine ideals to play with, but where on this moonlit and dream-visited planet are they found? I am, therefore, myself a complete empiricist so far as my theory of human knowledge goes. I live, to be sure, by the practical faith that we must go on experiencing and thinking over our experience, for only thus can our opinions grow more true; but to hold any one of them—I absolutely do not care which—as if it never could be reinterpretable or corrigible,** I believe to be a tremendously mistaken attitude, and I think that the whole history of philosophy will bear me out. There is but one indefectibly certain truth, and that is the truth that pyrrhonistic scepticism itself leaves standing,—the truth that the present phenomenon of consciousness exists. That, however, is the bare starting-point of knowledge, the mere admission of a stuff to be philosophized about. The various philosophies are but so many attempts at expressing what this stuff really is. And if we repair to our libraries what disagreement do we discover! Where is a certainly true answer found? Apart from abstract propositions of comparison (such as two and two are the same as four), propositions which tell us nothing by themselves about concrete reality, we find no proposition ever regarded by any one as evidently certain that has not either been called a falsehood, or at least had its truth sincerely questioned by some one else. The transcending of the axioms of geometry, not in play but in earnest, by certain of our contemporaries (as Zöllner and Charles H. Hinton), and the rejection of the whole Aristotelian logic by the Hegelians, are striking instances in point.

No concrete test of what is really true has ever been agreed upon. Some make the criterion external to the moment of perception, putting it either in revelation, the *consensus gentium*,[††] the instincts of the heart, or the systematized experience of the race. Others make the perceptive moment its own test,—Descartes, for instance, with his clear and distinct ideas guaranteed by the veracity of God; Reid with his 'common-sense';

---

* "Perfect correspondence of our understanding with the thing."
† "The aptitude to force a certain agreement."
‡ "Repose in knowledge," i.e., passive acceptance of knowledge.
§ "Being itself," real being.
¶ Noon; i.e., the hour when the sun is at its meridian, its highest point in the sky.
** Correctable.
†† "Public consensus."

and Kant with his forms of synthetic judgment *a priori*.* The inconceivability of the opposite; the capacity to be verified by sense; the possession of complete organic unity or self-relation, realized when a thing is its own other,—are standards which, in turn, have been used. The much lauded objective evidence is never triumphantly there; it is a mere aspiration or *Grenzbegriff*,† marking the infinitely remote ideal of our thinking life. To claim that certain truths now possess it, is simply to say that when you think them true and they *are* true, then their evidence is objective, otherwise it is not. But practically one's conviction that the evidence one goes by is of the real objective brand, is only one more subjective opinion added to the lot. For what a contradictory array of opinions have objective evidence and absolute certitude been claimed! The world is rational through and through,—its existence is an ultimate brute fact; there is a personal God,—a personal God is inconceivable; there is an extra-mental physical world immediately known,—the mind can only know its own ideas; a moral imperative exists,—obligation is only the resultant of desires; a permanent spiritual principle is in every one,—there are only shifting states of mind; there is an endless chain of causes,—there is an absolute first cause; an eternal necessity,—a freedom; a purpose,—no purpose; a primal One,—a primal Many; a universal continuity,—an essential discontinuity in things; an infinity,—no infinity. There is this,—there is that; there is indeed nothing which some one has not thought absolutely true, while his neighbor deemed it absolutely false; and not an absolutist among them seems ever to have considered that the trouble may all the time be essential, and that the intellect, even with truth directly in its grasp, may have no infallible signal for knowing whether it be truth or no. When, indeed, one remembers that the most striking practical application to life of the doctrine of objective certitude has been the conscientious labors of the Holy Office of the Inquisition,‡ one feels less tempted than ever to lend the doctrine a respectful ear.

But please observe, now, that when as empiricists we give up the doctrine of objective certitude, we do not thereby give up the quest or hope of truth itself. We still pin our faith on its existence, and still believe that we gain an ever better position towards it by systematically continuing to roll up experiences and think. Our great difference from the scholastic lies in the way we face. The strength of his system lies in the principles, the origin, the *terminus a quo*§ of his thought; for us the strength is in the outcome, the upshot, the *terminus ad quem*.¶ Not where it comes from but what it leads to is to decide. It matters not to an empiricist from what quarter an hypothesis may come to him: he may have acquired it by fair means or by foul; passion may have whispered or accident suggested it; but if the total drift of thinking continues to confirm it, that is what he means by its being true.

VII.

One more point, small but important, and our preliminaries are done. There are two ways of looking at our duty in the matter of opinion,—ways entirely different, and yet ways about whose difference the theory of knowledge seems hitherto to have shown very little concern. *We must know the truth*; and *we must avoid error*,—these are our first and great commandments as would-be knowers; but they are not two ways of stating an identical commandment, they are two separable laws. Although it may indeed happen that when we believe the truth *A*, we escape as an incidental consequence from believing the falsehood *B*, it hardly ever happens that by merely disbelieving *B* we necessarily believe *A*. We may in escaping *B* fall into believing other falsehoods, *C* or *D*, just as bad as *B*; or we may escape *B* by not believing anything at all, not even *A*.

Believe truth! Shun error—these, we see, are two materially different laws; and by choosing between them we may end by coloring differently our whole intellectual life. We may regard the chase for truth

---

*   See the reading from Descartes elsewhere in this volume.
†   From Kant's *Critique of Pure Reason*, this literally means a concept at the edge or limit of our understanding; it is often translated "limiting concept."
‡   A tribunal formerly held in the Roman Catholic Church and directed at the forceful suppression of heresy; its best known variant is the notorious Spanish Inquisition of the late fifteenth century.
§   "The point from which it comes."
¶   "The point to which it goes."

as paramount, and the avoidance of error as secondary; or we may, on the other hand, treat the avoidance of error as more imperative, and let truth take its chance. Clifford, in the instructive passage which I have quoted, exhorts us to the latter course. Believe nothing, he tells us, keep your mind in suspense forever, rather than by closing it on insufficient evidence incur the awful risk of believing lies. You, on the other hand, may think that the risk of being in error is a very small matter when compared with the blessings of real knowledge, and be ready to be duped many times in your investigation rather than postpone indefinitely the chance of guessing true. I myself find it impossible to go with Clifford. We must remember that these feelings of our duty about either truth or error are in any case only expressions of our passional life. Biologically considered, our minds are as ready to grind out falsehood as veracity, and he who says, "Better go without belief forever than believe a lie!" merely shows his own preponderant private horror of becoming a dupe. He may be critical of many of his desires and fears, but this fear he slavishly obeys. He cannot imagine any one questioning its binding force. For my own part, I have also a horror of being duped; but I can believe that worse things than being duped may happen to a man in this world: so Clifford's exhortation has to my ears a thoroughly fantastic[*] sound. It is like a general informing his soldiers that it is better to keep out of battle forever than to risk a single wound. Not so are victories either over enemies or over nature gained. Our errors are surely not such awfully solemn things. In a world where we are so certain to incur them in spite of all our caution, a certain lightness of heart seems healthier than this excessive nervousness on their behalf. At any rate, it seems the fittest thing for the empiricist philosopher.

VIII.

And now, after all this introduction, let us go straight at our question. I have said, and now repeat it, that not only as a matter of fact do we find our passional nature influencing us in our opinions, but that there are some options between opinions in which this influence must be regarded both as an inevitable and as a lawful determinant of our choice.

I fear here that some of you my hearers will begin to scent danger, and lend an inhospitable ear. Two first steps of passion you have indeed had to admit as necessary,—we must think so as to avoid dupery, and we must think so as to gain truth; but the surest path to those ideal consummations, you will probably consider, is from now onwards to take no further passional step.

Well, of course, I agree as far as the facts will allow. Wherever the option between losing truth and gaining it is not momentous, we can throw the chance of *gaining truth* away, and at any rate save ourselves from any chance of *believing falsehood*, by not making up our minds at all till objective evidence has come. In scientific questions, this is almost always the case; and even in human affairs in general, the need of acting is seldom so urgent that a false belief to act on is better than no belief at all. Law courts, indeed, have to decide on the best evidence attainable for the moment, because a judge's duty is to make law as well as to ascertain it, and (as a learned judge once said to me) few cases are worth spending much time over: the great thing is to have them decided on *any* acceptable principle, and got out of the way. But in our dealings with objective nature we obviously are recorders, not makers, of the truth; and decisions for the mere sake of deciding promptly and getting on to the next business would be wholly out of place. Throughout the breadth of physical nature facts are what they are quite independently of us, and seldom is there any such hurry about them that the risks of being duped by believing a premature theory need be faced. The questions here are always trivial options, the hypotheses are hardly living (at any rate not living for us spectators), the choice between believing truth or falsehood is seldom forced. The attitude of sceptical balance is therefore the absolutely wise one if we would escape mistakes. What difference, indeed, does it make to most of us whether we have or have not a theory of the Röntgen rays,[†] whether we believe or not in mind-stuff, or have a conviction about the causality of conscious states? It makes no difference. Such options are not forced on us. On every account it is better not to make them,

---

[*]   Outrageous, unreal—the result of a fantasy.

[†]   Named for Wilhelm Röntgen, the German physicist who discovered them, these are today called X-rays.

but still keep weighing reasons *pro et contra** with an indifferent hand.

I speak, of course, here of the purely judging mind. For purposes of discovery such indifference is to be less highly recommended, and science would be far less advanced than she is if the passionate desires of individuals to get their own faiths confirmed had been kept out of the game. See for example the sagacity which Spencer and Weismann now display. On the other hand, if you want an absolute duffer in an investigation, you must, after all, take the man who has no interest whatever in its results: he is the warranted incapable, the positive fool. The most useful investigator, because the most sensitive observer, is always he whose eager interest in one side of the question is balanced by an equally keen nervousness lest he become deceived.[2] Science has organized this nervousness into a regular *technique*, her so-called method of verification; and she has fallen so deeply in love with the method that one may even say she has ceased to care for truth by itself at all. It is only truth as technically verified that interests her. The truth of truths might come in merely affirmative form, and she would decline to touch it. Such truth as that, she might repeat with Clifford, would be stolen in defiance of her duty to mankind. Human passions, however, are stronger than technical rules. "Le coeur a ses raisons," as Pascal says, "que la raison ne connaît pas;"[†] and however indifferent to all but the bare rules of the game the umpire, the abstract intellect, may be, the concrete players who furnish him the materials to judge of are usually, each one of them, in love with some pet 'live hypothesis' of his own. Let us agree, however, that wherever there is no forced option, the dispassionately judicial intellect with no pet hypothesis, saving us, as it does, from dupery at any rate, ought to be our ideal.

The question next arises: Are there not somewhere forced options in our speculative questions, and can we (as men who may be interested at least as much in positively gaining truth as in merely escaping dupery) always wait with impunity till the coercive evidence shall have arrived? It seems *a priori* improbable that the truth should be so nicely adjusted to our needs and powers as that. In the great boarding-house of nature, the cakes and the butter and the syrup seldom come out so even and leave the plates so clean. Indeed, we should view them with scientific suspicion if they did.

IX.

Moral questions immediately present themselves as questions whose solution cannot wait for sensible proof. A moral question is a question not of what sensibly exists, but of what is good, or would be good if it did exist. Science can tell us what exists; but to compare the *worths*, both of what exists and of what does not exist, we must consult not science, but what Pascal calls our heart. Science herself consults her heart when she lays it down that the infinite ascertainment of fact and correction of false belief are the supreme goods for man. Challenge the statement, and science can only repeat it oracularly,[‡] or else prove it by showing that such ascertainment and correction bring man all sorts of other goods which man's heart in turn declares. The question of having moral beliefs at all or not having them is decided by our will. Are our moral preferences true or false, or are they only odd biological phenomena, making things good or bad for *us*, but in themselves indifferent? How can your pure intellect decide? If your heart does not *want* a world of moral reality, your head will assuredly never make you believe in one. Mephistophelian[§] scepticism, indeed, will satisfy the head's play-instincts much better than any rigorous idealism can. Some men (even at the student age) are so naturally cool-hearted that the moralistic hypothesis never has for them any pungent life, and in their supercilious presence the hot young moralist always feels strangely ill at ease. The appearance of knowingness is on their side, of *naïveté*, and gullibility on his. Yet, in the inarticulate heart of him, he clings to it that he is not a dupe, and that there is

---

* "For and against."
† "The heart has its reasons which reason knows nothing of."
‡ In the manner of an oracle: solemnly and enigmatically, but without giving reasons.
§ Mephistopheles is the devil to whom, according to a sixteenth-century German legend, Faust sold his soul: something is "Mephistophelian," therefore, if it is fiendish and tricky.

a realm in which (as Emerson says) all their wit and intellectual superiority is no better than the cunning of a fox.* Moral scepticism can no more be refuted or proved by logic than intellectual scepticism can. When we stick to it that there *is* truth (be it of either kind), we do so with our whole nature, and resolve to stand or fall by the results. The sceptic with his whole nature adopts the doubting attitude; but which of us is the wiser, Omniscience only knows.

Turn now from these wide questions of good to a certain class of questions of fact, questions concerning personal relations, states of mind between one man and another. *Do you like me or not?*—for example. Whether you do or not depends, in countless instances, on whether I meet you half-way, am willing to assume that you must like me, and show you trust and expectation. The previous faith on my part in your liking's existence is in such cases what makes your liking come. But if I stand aloof, and refuse to budge an inch until I have objective evidence, until you shall have done something apt, as the absolutists say, *ad extorquendum assensum meum*,† ten to one your liking never comes. How many women's hearts are vanquished by the mere sanguine insistence of some man that they *must* love him! he will not consent to the hypothesis that they cannot. The desire for a certain kind of truth here brings about that special truth's existence; and so it is in innumerable cases of other sorts. Who gains promotions, boons, appointments, but the man in whose life they are seen to play the part of live hypotheses, who discounts them, sacrifices other things for their sake before they have come, and takes risks for them in advance? His faith acts on the powers above him as a claim, and creates its own verification.

A social organism of any sort whatever, large or small, is what it is because each member proceeds to his own duty with a trust that the other members will simultaneously do theirs. Wherever a desired result is achieved by the co-operation of many independent persons, its existence as a fact is a pure consequence of the precursive‡ faith in one another of those immediately concerned. A government, an army, a commercial system, a ship, a college, an athletic team, all exist on this condition, without which not only is nothing achieved, but nothing is even attempted. A whole train of passengers (individually brave enough) will be looted by a few highwaymen, simply because the latter can count on one another, while each passenger fears that if he makes a movement of resistance, he will be shot before any one else backs him up. If we believed that the whole car-full would rise at once with us, we should each severally rise, and train-robbing would never even be attempted. There are, then, cases where a fact cannot come at all unless a preliminary faith exists in its coming. *And where faith in a fact can help create the fact*, that would be an insane logic which should say that faith running ahead of scientific evidence is the 'lowest kind of immorality' into which a thinking being can fall. Yet such is the logic by which our scientific absolutists pretend to regulate our lives!

X.

In truths dependent on our personal action, then, faith based on desire is certainly a lawful and possibly an indispensable thing.

But now, it will be said, these are all childish human cases, and have nothing to do with great cosmical matters, like the question of religious faith. Let us then pass on to that. Religions differ so much in their accidents§ that in discussing the religious question we must make it very generic and broad. What then do we now mean by the religious hypothesis? Science says things are; morality says some things are better than other things; and religion says essentially two things.

First, she says that the best things are the more eternal things, the overlapping things, the things in the universe that throw the last stone, so to speak, and say the final word. "Perfection is eternal,"—this phrase of Charles Secrétan seems a good way of putting this first affirmation of religion, an affirmation which obviously cannot yet be verified scientifically at all.

---

* A reference to the poet Ralph Waldo Emerson's essay "The Sovereignty of Ethics" (1884).
† "To force my unqualified assent."
‡ Preceding.
§ Non-essential properties or attributes.

The second affirmation of religion is that we are better off even now if we believe her first affirmation to be true.

Now, let us consider what the logical elements of this situation are *in case the religious hypothesis in both its branches be really true.* (Of course, we must admit that possibility at the outset. If we are to discuss the question at all, it must involve a living option. If for any of you religion be a hypothesis that cannot, by any living possibility be true, then you need go no farther. I speak to the 'saving remnant' alone.) So proceeding, we see, first, that religion offers itself as a *momentous* option. We are supposed to gain, even now, by our belief, and to lose by our non-belief, a certain vital good. Secondly, religion is a *forced* option, so far as that good goes. We cannot escape the issue by remaining sceptical and waiting for more light, because, although we do avoid error in that way *if religion be untrue*, we lose the good, *if it be true*, just as certainly as if we positively chose to disbelieve. It is as if a man should hesitate indefinitely to ask a certain woman to marry him because he was not perfectly sure that she would prove an angel after he brought her home. Would he not cut himself off from that particular angel-possibility as decisively as if he went and married some one else? Scepticism, then, is not avoidance of option; it is option of a certain particular kind of risk. *Better risk loss of truth than chance of error,*—that is your faith-vetoer's exact position. He is actively playing his stake as much as the believer is; he is backing the field against the religious hypothesis, just as the believer is backing the religious hypothesis against the field. To preach scepticism to us as a duty until 'sufficient evidence' for religion be found, is tantamount therefore to telling us, when in presence of the religious hypothesis, that to yield to our fear of its being error is wiser and better than to yield to our hope that it may be true. It is not intellect against all passions, then; it is only intellect with one passion laying down its law. And by what, forsooth, is the supreme wisdom of this passion warranted? Dupery for dupery, what proof is there that dupery through hope is so much worse than dupery through fear? I, for one, can see no proof; and I simply refuse obedience to the scientist's command to imitate his kind of option, in a case where my own stake is important enough to give me the right to choose my own form of risk. If religion be true and the evidence for it be still insufficient, I do not wish, by putting your extinguisher upon my nature (which feels to me as if it had after all some business in this matter), to forfeit my sole chance in life of getting upon the winning side,—that chance depending, of course, on my willingness to run the risk of acting as if my passional need of taking the world religiously might be prophetic and right.

All this is on the supposition that it really may be prophetic and right, and that, even to us who are discussing the matter, religion is a live hypothesis which may be true. Now, to most of us religion comes in a still further way that makes a veto on our active faith even more illogical. The more perfect and more eternal aspect of the universe is represented in our religions as having personal form. The universe is no longer a mere *It* to us, but a *Thou*, if we are religious; and any relation that may be possible from person to person might be possible here. For instance, although in one sense we are passive portions of the universe, in another we show a curious autonomy, as if we were small active centres on our own account. We feel, too, as if the appeal of religion to us were made to our own active good-will, as if evidence might be forever withheld from us unless we met the hypothesis half-way. To take a trivial illustration: just as a man who in a company of gentlemen made no advances, asked a warrant for every concession, and believed no one's word without proof, would cut himself off by such churlishness from all the social rewards that a more trusting spirit would earn—so here, one who should shut himself up in snarling logicality and try to make the gods extort his recognition willy-nilly, or not get it at all, might cut himself off forever from his only opportunity of making the gods' acquaintance. This feeling, forced on us we know not whence, that by obstinately believing that there are gods (although not to do so would be so easy both for our logic and our life) we are doing the universe the deepest service we can, seems part of the living essence of the religious hypothesis. If the hypothesis *were* true in all its parts, including this one, then pure intellectualism, with its veto on our making willing advances, would be an absurdity; and some participation of our sympathetic nature would be logically required. I, therefore, for one, cannot see my way to accepting the agnostic rules for truth-seeking, or wilfully agree to keep my willing nature out of the game. I cannot do so for this plain reason, that *a rule of thinking which would absolutely prevent me from acknowledging certain kinds of truth if those kinds of truth were really there, would be an irrational rule*. That for me is the long and short of the formal logic of the situation, no matter what the kinds of truth might materially be.

I confess I do not see how this logic can be escaped. But sad experience makes me fear that some of you may still shrink from radically saying with me, *in abstracto*,* that we have the right to believe at our own risk any hypothesis that is live enough to tempt our will. I suspect, however, that if this is so, it is because you have got away from the abstract logical point of view altogether, and are thinking (perhaps without realizing it) of some particular religious hypothesis which for you is dead. The freedom to 'believe what we will' you apply to the case of some patent superstition; and the faith you think of is the faith defined by the schoolboy when he said, "Faith is when you believe something that you know ain't true." I can only repeat that this is misapprehension. *In concreto*,† the freedom to believe can only cover living options which the intellect of the individual cannot by itself resolve; and living options never seem absurdities to him who has them to consider. When I look at the religious question as it really puts itself to concrete men, and when I think of all the possibilities which both practically and theoretically it involves, then this command that we shall put a stopper on our heart, instincts, and courage, and *wait*— acting of course meanwhile more or less as if religion were *not* true[3]—till doomsday, or till such time as our intellect and senses working together may have raked in evidence enough,—this command, I say, seems to me the queerest idol ever manufactured in the philosophic cave. Were we scholastic absolutists, there might be more excuse. If we had an infallible intellect with its objective certitudes, we might feel ourselves disloyal to such a perfect organ of knowledge in not trusting to it exclusively, in not waiting for its releasing word. But if we are empiricists, if we believe that no bell in us tolls to let us know for certain when truth is in our grasp, then it seems a piece of idle fantasticality

to preach so solemnly our duty of waiting for the bell. Indeed we *may* wait if we will,—I hope you do not think that I am denying that,—but if we do so, we do so at our peril as much as if we believed. In either case we *act*, taking our life in our hands. No one of us ought to issue vetoes to the other, nor should we bandy words of abuse. We ought, on the contrary, delicately and profoundly to respect one another's mental freedom: then only shall we bring about the intellectual republic; then only shall we have that spirit of inner tolerance without which all our outer tolerance is soulless, and which is empiricism's glory; then only shall we live and let live, in speculative as well as in practical things.

I began by a reference to Fitz-James Stephen; let me end by a quotation from him. "What do you think of yourself? What do you think of the world? ... These are questions with which all must deal as it seems good to them. They are riddles of the Sphinx,‡ and in some way or other we must deal with them.... In all important transactions of life we have to take a leap in the dark.... If we decide to leave the riddles unanswered, that is a choice; if we waver in our answer, that, too, is a choice: but whatever choice we make, we make it at our peril. If a man chooses to turn his back altogether on God and the future, no one can prevent him; no one can show beyond reasonable doubt that he is mistaken. If a man thinks otherwise and acts as he thinks, I do not see that any one can prove that he is mistaken. Each must act as he thinks best; and if he is wrong, so much the worse for him. We stand on a mountain pass in the midst of whirling snow and blinding mist, through which we get glimpses now and then of paths which may be deceptive. If we stand still we shall be frozen to death. If we take the wrong road we shall be dashed to pieces. We do not certainly know whether there is any right one. What must we do? 'Be strong and of a good courage.' Act for the best, hope for the best, and take what comes.... If death ends all, we cannot meet death better."[4] ■

---

* "In the abstract."
† "In concrete (or actual) cases."
‡ In Greek legend, the Sphinx devoured all who could not solve its riddle. (Oedipus succeeded.)

Suggestions for Critical Reflection

1. The American judge Oliver Wendell Holmes, a close friend, once complained that James was inclined "to turn down the lights so as to give miracle a chance," shielding religious issues from the bright light of truth and careful, scientific inquiry. Do you agree with this criticism? How do you think James responded?

2. Do you think James's position in this essay is best understood as saying religious belief is in fact rational, or that religious belief is not rational but nevertheless 'lawful'?

3. James sometimes seems to talk as if we could and should believe things on the basis of our *will*, our decision to do so, and sometimes as if it's a matter of having some beliefs based on *emotion* ("our passional nature") rather than intellect. Do you think there's a conflict between these two ways of talking? If so, which do you think James really meant?

4. James takes W.K. Clifford's essay "The Ethics of Belief"—which is the reading before this one—as a foil to his own position in "The Will to Believe." If you have read Clifford's piece, how do you think his arguments stand up to James's criticisms? Clifford begins his essay with the story of a ship owner who suppresses his own doubts about the seaworthiness of his vessel and, "putting his trust in Providence," allows the ship to sail, carrying its load of immigrants to their death at sea. James never mentions this example—what do you think he would say about it?

5. Some critics of "The Will to Believe" have complained that James seems to be imagining only cases where we have no evidence at all, either for or against a particular possibility, and simply ignoring the much more common case where we are in possession of some evidence and have to weigh the balance of probabilities. Do you agree that James does this, and if so, is it a mistake on his part?

6. Another common criticism of this essay is that the religious belief James defends is highly attenuated: no more than the belief that "perfection is eternal." Do you share this reaction? Is this all that James is defending, in the end? In what way, if so, is this a "momentous" choice?

7. If you have read the Mackie selection "Evil and Omnipotence" you might want to ask yourself how James could respond to Mackie's claim that belief in a Christian/Islamic/Judaic (etc.) God is internally inconsistent and hence that no reasonable person should hold such a belief. Can James and Mackie *both* be right? If not, which of them is (if either)?

8. In *The Varieties of Religious Experience*, James defines 'truth' basically as what's good for you. He argues that religious belief is good for you. It follows that religious belief is true. Is this consistent with the main point in this essay? Is this basically different from Pascal's main point?

Notes

1 Compare the admirable page 310 in S.H. Hodgson's *Time and Space*, London, 1865.

2 Compare Wilfrid Ward's Essay, "The Wish to Believe," in his *Witnesses to the Unseen*, Macmillan & Co., 1893.

3 Since belief is measured by action, he who forbids us to believe religion to be true, necessarily also forbids us to act as we should if we did believe it to be true. The whole defence of religious faith hinges upon action. If the action required or inspired by the religious hypothesis is in no way different from that dictated by the naturalistic hypothesis, then religious faith is a pure superfluity, better pruned away, and controversy about its legitimacy is a piece of idle trifling, unworthy of serious minds. I myself believe, of course, that the religious hypothesis gives to the world an expression which specifically determines our reactions, and makes them in a large part unlike what they might be on a purely naturalistic scheme of belief.

4 *Liberty, Equality, Fraternity*, p. 353, 2nd edition. London, 1874.

Is the External World the Way It Appears to Be?

'Epistemology' is the theory of knowledge (the word comes from the Greek *epistēmē*, meaning knowledge). Epistemology can be thought of as arranged around three fundamental questions:

i) *What is knowledge?* For example, what is the difference between believing something that happens to be true and actually *knowing* it to be true? How much justification or proof do we need (if any) before we can be said to know something? Or does knowledge have more to do with, say, the *reliability* of our beliefs than our arguments for them? What is the difference between the

conclusions of good science and those of, for example, astrology? Or between astrology and religion?

ii) *What can we know?* What are the scope and limits of our knowledge? Can we ever really *know* about the real, underlying nature of the universe? Can we aspire to religious knowledge (e.g., of the true nature of God), or to ethical knowledge (as opposed to mere ethical belief or opinion), or to reliable knowledge of the historical past or the future? Can I ever know what you are thinking, or even *that* you are thinking? Do I even really know what *I* am thinking: e.g., might I have beliefs and desires that I am unaware of, perhaps because they are repressed or simply non-conscious?

iii) *How do we know that we know?* That is, how can we *justify* our claims to know things? What counts as 'enough' justification for a belief? Where does our knowledge—if we have any at all—come from in the first place? Do we acquire knowledge only through sense-experience, or can we also come to know important things through the power of our own naked reason? Do we have some beliefs which are especially 'basic'—which can be so reliably known that they can form a foundation for all our other beliefs? Or, by contrast, do all our pieces of knowledge fit together like the answers in a giant crossword puzzle, with each belief potentially up for grabs if the rest of the puzzle changes?

The epistemological question that is the focus of this chapter is sometimes called 'the problem of the external world.' In its starkest form, it is simply this: are *any* of our beliefs about the world outside our own heads justified? Can we be sure that any of them at all are *true*? For example, I currently believe that there is a laptop computer in front of me, and a soft-drink can on the table to my left, and a window to my right out of which I can see trees and grass and other houses. Furthermore, I not only believe that these objects exist but I also believe that they have a certain nature: that the pop can is colored red; that the trees outside are further away from me in space than the window I am looking through; that the houses are three-dimensional objects with solid walls, and that they continue to exist even when I close my eyes or turn away; that my computer will continue to behave in a (relatively!) predictable way in accordance with the laws of physics and of computing. But are any of these beliefs of mine justified: do any of them cross the threshold into being *knowledge*, as opposed to mere conjecture? And if some of them are known and not others, *which* are the ones I really know? Which are the beliefs to which a rational person should be committed, and which are the ones a rational person should jettison?

It may seem that these kinds of questions should be fairly straightforward to answer. *Of course* I know that my soda can exists and is really red; it should be pretty easy just to think for a while and give my compelling reasons for having this belief—the reasons which make this belief much more likely to be true than, say, the belief that the can is a figment of my imagination, or is really colorless. However, it turns out, the problem of the external world is a very challenging problem indeed, and

one which has been an important philosophical issue since at least the seventeenth century.

The first three readings in this chapter explore different aspects of the problem of the external world. First, we might ask, does the external world exist *at all*—is there any such thing as a world outside my own head, or might reality be just a dream or some sort of illusion? Plato uses the analogy of a cave to illustrate the view that the world we perceive is merely a superficial shadow cast by a quite different reality, which can only be known through the intellect and not the senses. In the modern era, Descartes seminally raises the question of whether the world we experience could be radically different from the way we perceive it to be and then tries to satisfactorily answer this conundrum. However, in 'solving' this problem, Descartes comes to the conclusion that only some of the things we commonsensically believe about the real nature of the external world are true or justifiable. The Locke reading can be thought of as extending this insight and making it more precise through his discussion of the distinction between 'primary qualities' (which resemble our ideas of them) and 'secondary qualities' (which do not). Locke also raises a somewhat different question: what can we know about the sort of 'stuff' that the external world is made of—if it is 'matter,' then what can we say about the kind of *substance* which is matter?

The final three readings in this section introduce some key epistemological innovations of the twentieth century. Gettier's article "Is Justified True Belief Knowledge?" presents a deep problem for the basic philosophical intuition—which in some form goes all the way back to Plato—that any belief that is both true and properly justified counts as an instance of knowledge. Jennifer Saul explores the consequences of implicit bias, and argues compellingly that it gives rise to something similar to—and more pressingly serious than—philosophical skepticism. Lastly, the article by Helen Longino asks "Can there be a feminist science?" and if so, how different would it look from historical, supposedly "value-free," science?

There are several good introductory epistemology textbooks currently available if you want more background information. For example: Robert Audi, *Epistemology* (Routledge, 2010); Jonathan Dancy, *Introduction to Contemporary Epistemology* (Blackwell, 1991); Richard Feldman, *Epistemology* (Prentice Hall, 2002); Alvin Goldman and Matthew McGrath, *Epistemology: A Con-*

temporary *Introduction* (Oxford University Press, 2014); Keith Lehrer, *Theory of Knowledge* (Westview, 2000); Robert M. Martin, *Epistemology: A Beginner's Guide* (OneWorld, 2014); Adam Morton, *A Guide through the Theory of Knowledge* (Blackwell, 2008); Jennifer Nagel, *Knowledge: A Very Short Introduction* (Oxford University Press, 2014); Pollock and Cruz, *Contemporary Theories of Knowledge* (Rowman & Littlefield, 1999); Matthias Steup, *An Introduction to Contemporary Epistemology* (Prentice Hall, 1996); Steup and Sosa, eds., *Contemporary Debates in Epistemology* (Blackwell, 2013); and Michael Williams, *Problems of Knowledge* (Oxford University Press, 2001). There are also several useful reference works on epistemology: Dancy, Sosa, and Steup, eds., *A Companion to Epistemology* (Blackwell, 2010); Paul K. Moser, *The Oxford Handbook of Epistemology* (Oxford University Press, 2005); Greco and Sosa, eds., *The Blackwell Guide to Epistemology* (Blackwell, 1999); and Bernecker and Pritchard, eds., *The Routledge Companion to Epistemology* (Routledge, 2011).

PLATO

The Allegory of the Cave

Who Was Plato?

The historical details of Plato's life are shrouded in uncertainty. He is traditionally thought to have been born in about 427 BCE and to have died in 347 BCE. His family, who lived in the Greek city-state of Athens, was aristocratic and wealthy. Legend has it that Plato's father, Ariston, was descended from Codrus, the last king of Athens, and his mother, Perictione, was related to the great Solon, who wrote the first Athenian constitution. While Plato was still a boy, his father died and his mother married Pyrilampes, a friend of the revered Athenian statesman Pericles who in the 450s had transformed Athens into one of the greatest cities in the Greek world.

As a young man, Plato probably fought in the Athenian army against Sparta during the Peloponnesian War (431–404 BCE)—which Athens lost—and he may have served again when Athens was involved in the Corinthian War (395–386 BCE).

Given his family connections, Plato looked set for a prominent role in Athenian political life, and, as it happened, when he was about 23, a political revolution occurred in Athens which could have catapulted Plato into public affairs. The coup swept the previous democratic rulers—who had just lost the war against Sparta—out of power and into exile, and replaced them with the so-called Thirty Tyrants, several of whom were Plato's friends and relatives. Plato, an idealistic young man, expected this would usher in a new era of justice and good government, but he was soon disillusioned when the new regime was even more violent and corrupt than the old. He withdrew from public life in disgust. The rule of the Thirty lasted only about 90 days before the exiled democrats were restored to power, and Plato—impressed

by their relative lenience towards the coup leaders—apparently thought again about entering politics. But then, in 399 BCE, the city rulers arrested Plato's old friend and mentor, Socrates, and accused him of the trumped-up charge of impiety towards the city's gods and of corrupting the youth of Athens. Socrates was convicted by a jury of the townspeople, and—since he declared that he would rather die than give up philosophy, even though he was given a chance to escape—he was executed by being forced to drink poison.

> The result was that I, who had at first been full of eagerness for public affairs, when I considered all this and saw how things were shifting about every which way, at last became dizzy. I didn't cease to consider ways of improving this particular situation, however, and, indeed, of reforming the whole constitution. But as far as action was concerned, I kept waiting for favorable moments and finally saw clearly that the constitutions of all actual cities are bad and that their laws are almost beyond redemption without extraordinary resources and luck as well. Hence I was compelled to say in praise of the true philosophy that it enables us to discern what is just for a city or an individual in every case and that the human race will have no respite from evils until those who are really and truly philosophers acquire political power or until, through some divine dispensation, those who rule and have political authority in cities become real philosophers.*

After the death of Socrates, it appears that Plato, along with some other philosophical followers of Socrates, fled Athens and went to the city of Megara in east-

---

* This is a quotation from the so-called *Seventh Letter*, supposed to have been written by Plato when he was 70 years old. It is not certain that Plato actually wrote this document, but if it was not his, it was probably written by one of his disciples shortly after his death. See Plato, *Seventh Letter*, translated by C.D.C. Reeve in his "Introduction" to Plato's *Republic*, trans. G.M.A. Grube, revised by C.D.C. Reeve (Hackett, 1992), ix–x. The later fragmentary quote is from the translation of the *Seventh Letter* by Glen R. Morrow, in *Plato: Complete Works*, ed. John M. Cooper and D.S. Hutchinson (Hackett, 1997), 1648.

central Greece to stay with the philosopher Eucleides (a follower of the great Greek philosopher Parmenides of Elea). He may also have visited Egypt, though his travels at this time are shrouded in myth. It appears that Plato started doing philosophy in earnest at about this time, and his earliest writings date from this point. Almost all of Plato's writings are in the form of dialogues between two or more characters and, in most of them, the character leading the discussion is Socrates. Since Plato never wrote himself into any of his dialogues, it is usually—though not uncontroversially—assumed that the views expressed by the character of Socrates more or less correspond with those that Plato is trying to put forward in his dialogues.

Later, when Plato was about 40, he made another trip away from Athens, visiting Italy to talk with the Pythagorean philosophers. Plato was deeply impressed by Pythagorean philosophy—especially their emphasis on mathematics—but he was horrified by the luxury and sensuality of life in Italy, "with men gorging themselves twice a day and never sleeping alone at night."

After Italy, Plato visited Syracuse on the island of Sicily where, during a long stay, he became close friends with Dion, the brother-in-law of the ruling tyrant Dionysius I.* Dion became Plato's pupil, and (according to legend) came to prefer the philosophical life of moral goodness to the pleasure, luxury, and power of his surroundings. Exactly what happened next is historically unclear, but there is some reason to believe Plato was captured by a displeased Dionysius, sold into slavery, and subsequently rescued from the slave market when his freedom was purchased by an unidentified benevolent stranger.

On Plato's return to Athens, he bought land in a precinct named for an Athenian hero called Academus, and there, in about 385, he founded the first European university (or at least, the first of which there is any real historical knowledge). Because of its location, this school was called the Academy, and it was to remain in existence for over 900 years, until 529 CE. For most of the rest of his life, Plato stayed at the Academy, directing its stud-

ies, and he probably wrote the *Republic* there (in about 380 BCE). Very quickly, the school became a vital center for research in all kinds of subjects, both theoretical and practical. It was probably one of the first cradles for the subjects of metaphysics, epistemology, psychology, ethics, politics, aesthetics, and mathematical science, and members were invited, by various Greek city-states, to help draft new political constitutions.

In 368 Dionysius I of Sicily died and Dion persuaded his successor, Dionysius II, to send for Plato to advise him on how the state should be run. Plato, by now about 60, agreed with some misgivings, possibly hoping to make the younger Dionysius an example of a philosopher-king and to put the doctrines of the *Republic* into practice. However, the experiment was a disastrous failure. Dionysius II—though he gave himself airs as a philosopher—had no inclination to learn philosophy and mathematics in order to become a better ruler. Within four months Dion was banished, and Plato returned to Greece shortly afterwards. However, four years later Dionysius II convinced Plato to return, pressuring him with testimonials from eminent philosophers describing Dionysius's love for philosophy, and bribing him by offering to reinstate Dion at Syracuse within a year. Once again, the king proved false: he not only kept Dion in exile but confiscated and sold his lands and property. Plato was imprisoned on Sicily for nearly two years until, in 360, he finally escaped and returned to Athens for good. He died 13 years later, at the ripe old age of 80.†

What Was Plato's Overall Philosophical Project?

Plato is probably the single person with the best claim to being the inventor of western philosophy. His thought encompassed nearly all the areas central to philosophy today—metaphysics, epistemology, ethics, political theory, aesthetics, and the philosophy of science and mathematics—and, for the first time in European history, dealt with them in a unified way.‡ Plato thought of

---

*   Indeed, Plato later wrote a poem about Dion and spoke of being driven out of his mind with love for him.

†   Dion, meanwhile, attempted to recover his position at Syracuse by force—an endeavor Plato, wisely, refused to support—and was later assassinated by Callippus, a supposed friend and fellow member of the Academy.

‡   In fact the mathematician and philosopher Alfred North Whitehead (1861–1947) famously was moved to say that "The safest general characterization of the European philosophical tradition is that it consists of a series of footnotes

philosophy as a special discipline with its own intellectual method, and he was convinced it had foundational importance in human life. Only philosophy, Plato thought, could provide genuine understanding, since only philosophy scrutinized the assumptions that other disciplines left unquestioned. Furthermore, according to Plato, philosophy reveals a realm of comprehensive and unitary hidden truths—indeed, a whole level of reality that the senses cannot detect—which goes far beyond everyday common sense and which, when properly understood, has the power to revolutionize the way we live our lives and organize our societies. Philosophy, and only philosophy, holds the key to genuine human happiness and well-being.

This realm of objects which Plato claimed to have discovered is generally known as that of the Platonic Forms. The Forms—according to Plato—are changeless, eternal objects, which lie outside of both the physical world and the minds of individuals, and which can only be encountered through pure thought rather than through sensation. One of Plato's favorite examples of a Form is the mathematical property of Equality. In a dialogue called the *Phaedo* he argues that Equality itself cannot be identical with two equal sticks, or with any other group of physical objects of equal length, since we could always be mistaken about whether any two observed objects are really equal with one another, but we could not possibly be mistaken about Equality itself and somehow take *it* to be unequal. When two sticks are equal in length, therefore, they "participate in" Equality—it is their relation to Equality which makes them equal rather than unequal—but Equality itself is an abstract object which exists over and above all the instances of equal things. The form of Equality is what one succeeds in understanding when one has a proper conception of what Equality really is in itself: real knowledge, therefore, comes not from observation but from acquaintance with the Forms. Other central examples of Platonic Forms are Sameness, Number, Motion, Beauty, Justice, Piety, and (the most important Form of all) Goodness.

What Is the Structure of This Reading?

The *Republic* is written in the form of a dramatic dialogue. The narrator, Socrates, speaking directly to the reader, is describing a recent philosophical conversation he had with various other characters. In this excerpt the person he is speaking to is Glaucon (who was actually one of Plato's brothers). In this selection, Socrates—who, in this case, is usually thought to be expressing the views of Plato himself—describes the relation of the ordinary world of perceivable, concrete objects to the realm of the Forms, using the allegory of a cave. Ordinary people, lacking the benefit of a philosophical education, are like prisoners trapped underground in a cave since birth and forced to look only at shadows cast on the wall in front of them by puppets behind their backs, dancing in front of a fire. With the proper philosophical encouragement, they can—if they have the courage to do so—break their bonds and turn around to see that what they believed was reality was really only an illusory puppet show. The philosophers among them can even leave the cave to encounter the true reality—of which even the puppets are only copies—illuminated by the light of the sun which, for Plato, represents the form of the Good. The perceptible world is thus merely an imperfect image of—and sustained by—the quasi-divine, eternal realm of the unchanging and unobservable Forms.

Some Useful Background Information

1. Implicit in the story Socrates tells is a hierarchy of things, each of which corresponds to something in his analogy. From 'worst' to 'best' these are: the shadows of artificial objects (cast by the fire), the artificial objects themselves, the fire, the shadows or reflections of natural objects (cast by the sun), natural objects, and the sun. The corresponding levels in the analogy are (roughly): perceptions or images, material objects, light,* mathematical objects, abstract ideas or forms, and the form of the Good.

---

to Plato." Alfred North Whitehead, *Process and Reality*, corrected edition, ed. D.R. Griffin and D.W. Sherburne (Free Press, 1978), 39.

* So notice that, a bit confusingly, the fire in the cave is an allegory for the sun in real life, while the sun in Socrates's story is an allegory for the Good.

How Important and Influential Is This Passage?

Plato's vivid cave allegory has been influencing Western thought and culture for two thousand years. Sometimes emphasis is placed on its epistemological importance and Plato's theory of Forms as being the fundamental reality. Other readers are most struck by its political resonance, as a plea for the importance of education and philosophical clear-sightedness in our leaders, or as an account of what it means to be really free. In contemporary culture it is frequently referenced either explicitly or implicitly, in movies such as *The Matrix, Dark City, The Truman Show* and *City of Ember*, and books like Ray Bradbury's *Fahrenheit 451* and Emma Donoghue's *Room*.

"The Allegory of the Cave"*

FROM REPUBLIC, BOOK VII (514A–517C)

And now, I said, let me show in a figure† how far our nature is enlightened or unenlightened:—Behold! human beings living in a underground den, which has a mouth open towards the light and reaching all along the den; here they have been from their childhood, and have their legs and necks chained so that they cannot move, and can only see before them, being prevented by the chains from turning round their heads. Above and behind them a fire is blazing at a distance, and between the fire and the prisoners there is a raised way; and you will see, if you look, a low wall built along the way, like the screen which marionette players have in front of them, over which they show the puppets.

I see.

And do you see, I said, men passing along the wall carrying all sorts of vessels, and statues and figures of animals made of wood and stone and various materials, which appear over the wall? Some of them are talking, others silent.

You have shown me a strange image, and they are strange prisoners.

Like ourselves, I replied; and they see only their own shadows, or the shadows of one another, which the fire throws on the opposite wall of the cave?

True, he said; how could they see anything but the shadows if they were never allowed to move their heads?

And of the objects which are being carried in like manner they would only see the shadows?

Yes, he said.

And if they were able to converse with one another, would they not suppose that they were naming what was actually before them?

Very true.

And suppose further that the prison had an echo which came from the other side, would they not be sure to fancy when one of the passers-by spoke that the voice which they heard came from the passing shadow?

No question, he replied.

To them, I said, the truth would be literally nothing but the shadows of the images.

That is certain.

And now look again, and see what will naturally follow if the prisoners are released and disabused of their error. At first, when any of them is liberated and compelled suddenly to stand up and turn his neck round and walk and look towards the light, he will suffer sharp pains; the glare will distress him, and he will be unable to see the realities of which in his former state he had seen the shadows; and then conceive some one saying to him, that what he saw before was an illusion, but that now, when he is approaching nearer to being and his eye is turned towards more real existence, he has a clearer vision,—what will be his reply? And

---

* This translation of the beginning of Book VII of Plato's *Republic* (380 BCE) is by Benjamin Jowett (1888).

† An imaginary form.

you may further imagine that his instructor is pointing to the objects as they pass and requiring him to name them,—will he not be perplexed? Will he not fancy that the shadows which he formerly saw are truer than the objects which are now shown to him?

Far truer.

And if he is compelled to look straight at the light, will he not have a pain in his eyes which will make him turn away to take refuge in the objects of vision which he can see, and which he will conceive to be in reality clearer than the things which are now being shown to him?

True, he said.

And suppose once more, that he is reluctantly dragged up a steep and rugged ascent, and held fast until he is forced into the presence of the sun himself, is he not likely to be pained and irritated? When he approaches the light his eyes will be dazzled, and he will not be able to see anything at all of what are now called realities.

Not all in a moment, he said.

He will require to grow accustomed to the sight of the upper world. And first he will see the shadows best, next the reflections of men and other objects in the water, and then the objects themselves; then he will gaze upon the light of the moon and the stars and the spangled heaven; and he will see the sky and the stars by night better than the sun or the light of the sun by day?

Certainly.

Last of all he will be able to see the sun, and not mere reflections of him* in the water, but he will see him in his own proper place, and not in another; and he will contemplate him as he is.

Certainly.

He will then proceed to argue that this is he who gives the season and the years, and is the guardian of all that is in the visible world, and in a certain way the cause of all things which he and his fellows have been accustomed to behold?

Clearly, he said, he would first see the sun and then reason about him.

And when he remembered his old habitation, and the wisdom of the den and his fellow-prisoners, do you not suppose that he would felicitate† himself on the change, and pity them?

Certainly, he would.

And if they were in the habit of conferring honours among themselves on those who were quickest to observe the passing shadows and to remark which of them went before, and which followed after, and which were together; and who were therefore best able to draw conclusions as to the future, do you think that he would care for such honours and glories, or envy the possessors of them? Would he not say with Homer, "Better to be the poor servant of a poor master,"‡ and to endure anything, rather than think as they do and live after their manner?

Yes, he said, I think that he would rather suffer anything than entertain these false notions and live in this miserable manner.

Imagine once more, I said, such an one coming suddenly out of the sun to be replaced in his old situation; would he not be certain to have his eyes full of darkness?

To be sure, he said.

And if there were a contest, and he had to compete in measuring the shadows with the prisoners who had never moved out of the den, while his sight was still weak, and before his eyes had become steady (and the time which would be needed to acquire this new habit of sight might be very considerable), would he not be ridiculous? Men would say of him that up he went and down he came without his eyes; and that it was better not even to think of ascending; and if any one tried to loose another and lead him up to the light, let them only catch the offender, and they would put him to death.

No question, he said.

---

* Jowett translates Socrates as calling the sun "him," indicating that for Plato the sun represents the form of the Good.

† Congratulate.

‡ Socrates is paraphrasing an exclamation by Achilles's ghost to Odysseus in Homer's epic poem the *Odyssey* (c. 725 BCE): "By god, I'd rather slave on earth for another man—Some dirt-poor tenant farmer who scrapes to keep alive—Than rule down here over all the breathless dead" (trans. Robert Fagles).

This entire allegory, I said, you may now append, dear Glaucon, to the previous argument;* the prison-house is the world of sight, the light of the fire is the sun, and you will not misapprehend me if you interpret the journey upwards to be the ascent of the soul into the intellectual world according to my poor belief, which, at your desire, I have expressed—whether rightly or wrongly God knows. But, whether true or false, my opinion is that in the world of knowledge the idea of good appears last of all, and is seen only with an effort; and, when seen, is also inferred to be the universal author of all things beautiful and right, parent of light and of the lord of light in this visible world, and the immediate source of reason and truth in the intellectual; and that this is the power upon which he who would act rationally either in public or private life must have his eye fixed. ■

Suggestions for Critical Reflection

1. What do you think Socrates has in mind when he talks about certain special people breaking the chains that hold them in the cave and ascending to the light of the sun? What is this an allegory for? How can we achieve this—what sort of process would this be?

2. Given what Socrates says here, what do you think is his view of the knowledge we gain from our senses? Given what Socrates says here, what do you think is his view of material objects—the things that we perceive with our senses?

3. Why do you think Socrates emphasizes how difficult it is to break out of the cave, and how hard it is to get used to the new understanding of reality that this reveals?

---

* These previous arguments are known as the analogy of the sun (*Republic* 508b–509c) and the analogy of the divided line (509d–511e).

RENÉ DESCARTES

Meditations on First Philosophy

Who Was René Descartes?

René Descartes was born in 1596 in a small town nestled below the vineyards of the Loire in western France; at that time the town was called La Haye, but it was later renamed Descartes in his honor. His early life was probably unhappy: he suffered from ill health, his mother had died a year after he was born, and he didn't get on well with his father. (When René sent his father a copy of his first published book, his father's only reported reaction was that he was displeased to have a son "idiotic enough to have himself bound in vellum."*) At the age of about 10 he went to the newly founded college of La Flèche to be educated by the Jesuits. Descartes later called this college "one of the best schools in Europe," and it was there that he learned the medieval 'scholastic' science and philosophy that he was later decisively to reject. Descartes took a law degree at the University of Poitiers and studied mathematics and mechanics; then, at 21, joined first the Dutch army of Prince Maurice of Nassau and then the forces of Maximilian of Bavaria. As a soldier he saw little action, traveling around Europe supported by his family's wealth. During this period, he had resolved "to seek no knowledge other than that which could be found either in myself or in the great book of the world," developing an intense interest in mathematics, which stayed with him for the rest of his life. In fact, Descartes was one of the most important figures in the development of algebra, which is the branch of mathematics that allows abstract relations to be described without using specific numbers, and which is therefore capable of unifying arithmetic and geometry:[†]

I came to see that the exclusive concern of mathematics is with questions of order or method, and that it is irrelevant whether the measure in question involves numbers, shapes, stars, sounds, or any other object whatsoever. This made me realize that there must be a general science which explains all the points that can be raised concerning order and measure irrespective of subject matter. (From *Rules for the Direction of our Native Intelligence* [1628])

This insight led Descartes directly to one of the most significant intellectual innovations of the modern age: the conception of science as the exploration of abstract mathematical descriptions of the world.

It was also during this time—in 1619—that Descartes had the experience said to have inspired him to take up the life of a philosopher, and which, perhaps, eventually resulted in the form of the *Meditations*. Stranded by bad weather near Ulm on the river Danube, Descartes spent the day in a *poêle* (a stoveheated room[‡]) engaged in intense philosophical speculations. That night he had three vivid dreams which he later described as giving him his mission in life. In the first dream Descartes felt himself attacked by phantoms and then a great wind; he was then greeted by a friend who gave him a message about a gift. On awaking after this first dream, Descartes felt a sharp pain which made him fear that the dream was the work of some deceitful evil demon. Descartes eventually fell back asleep and immediately had the second dream: a loud thunderclap, which woke him in terror believing that the room was filled with fiery sparks. The third and last dream was a pleasant one, in which he found an encyclopedia on a table next to a poetry anthol-

---

* Vellum is the parchment made from animal skin that was used to make books.
† He invented the method still used to quantify locations on a graph: Cartesian coordinates (that adjective is derived from the Latin version of his name, 'Cartesius').
‡ Sometimes Descartes's words are taken in what might be their literal meaning, that he spent time in a stove. But although there is other evidence of his eccentricity, this seems an uncharitable translation.

ogy, open to a poem which begins with the line "Which road in life shall I follow?" A man then appeared and said *"Est et non"*—"it is and is not." While still asleep, Descartes apparently began to speculate about the meaning of his dreams, and decided, among other things, that the gift of which his friend spoke in the first dream was the gift of solitude, the dictionary represented systematic knowledge, and *"Est et non"* spoke of the distinction between truth and falsity as revealed by the correct scientific method. Descartes concluded that he had a divine mission to found a new philosophical system to underpin all human knowledge.

In 1628, at the age of 32, Descartes settled in Holland (at the time the most intellectually vibrant nation in Europe), where he lived for most of his remaining life. It was only then that he began sustained work in metaphysics and mathematical physics. His family was wealthy enough that Descartes, who cultivated very modest tastes, was free of the necessity to earn a living and could devote his time to scientific experimentation and writing. By 1633 he had prepared a book on cosmology and physics, called *Le Monde* (*The World*), in which he accepted Galileo's revolutionary claim that the Earth orbits the sun (rather than the other way around), but when he heard that Galileo had been condemned by the Inquisition of the Catholic Church, Descartes withdrew the work from publication.* In 1637 he published (in French) a sample of his scientific work, *Optics, Meteorology, and Geometry*, together with an introduction called *Discourse on the Method of Rightly Conducting One's Reason and Reaching the Truth in the Sciences*. Criticisms of this methodology led Descartes to compose his philosophical masterpiece, *Meditations on First Philosophy*, first published in Latin in 1641. (A French translation, prepared under Descartes's supervision and incorporating his changes, was published in 1647.) In 1644 he published a summary of his scientific and philosophical views, the *Principles of Philosophy*, which he hoped would become a standard university textbook, replacing the medieval texts used at the time. His last work, published in 1649, was *The Passions of the Soul*, which attempted to extend his scientific methodology to ethics and psychology.

Descartes never married, but in 1635 he had a daughter, Francine, with a serving woman called Hélène Jans. He made arrangements for the care and education of the girl, but she died of scarlet fever at the age of five, a devastating shock for Descartes.

In 1649 Descartes accepted an invitation to visit Stockholm and give philosophical instruction to Queen Kristina of Sweden. He was required to give tutorials at the royal palace at five o'clock in the morning; ever since he was a sickly schoolboy he had habitually stayed in bed until 11 am, and it is said that the strain of this sudden break in his habits caused him to catch pneumonia; he died in February 1650. His dying words are said to have been, *"mon âme; il faut partir"*—my soul, it's time to part. His body was returned to France but, apparently, his head was secretly kept in Sweden; in the 1820s a skull bearing the faded inscription "René Descartes" was discovered in Stockholm and is now on display in the Museum of Natural History in Paris.

What Was Descartes's Overall Philosophical Project?

Descartes lived at a time when the accumulated beliefs of centuries—assumptions based on religious doctrine, straightforward observation, and common sense—were being gradually but remorselessly stripped away by exciting new discoveries. (The most striking example of this was the evidence mounting against the centuries-old belief that an unmoving Earth is the center of the universe, orbited by the moon, sun, stars, and all the other planets.) In this intellectual climate, Descartes became obsessed by the thought that no lasting scientific progress was possible without a systematic method for sifting through our preconceived assumptions and distinguishing between those that are reliable and those that are false. Descartes's central intellectual goal was to develop just such a reliable scientific method, and then to construct a coherent and unified theory of the world and of humankind's place within it. This theory, he hoped, would replace scholasticism, the deeply flawed

---

*   Descartes was very aware of the threat from Catholic authorities' opposition to his ideas, and afraid of it. After Descartes's death, all his works were placed on the Index of Prohibited Works by the Church, with the note that they would remain there "until corrected." (The Church announced in 1966 that the prohibition of items on this list was no longer to be considered law, but the Index was still retained as a moral guide.)

medieval system of thought based on the science of Aristotle and Christian theology.

A key feature of Descartes's system is that all knowledge should be based on utterly reliable foundations, discovered through the systematic rejection of any assumptions that can possibly be called into doubt. Then, as in mathematics, complex conclusions could be reliably derived from these foundations by chains of valid reasoning—of simple and certain inferences. The human faculty of *reason* was therefore of the greatest importance. Furthermore, Descartes urged that scientific knowledge of the external world should be rooted, not in the deceptive and variable testimony of the senses, but in the concepts of pure mathematics. That is, Cartesian science tries to reduce all physics to "what the geometers call *quantity*, and take as the object of their demonstrations, i.e., that to which every kind of division shape and motion is applicable" (*Principles of Philosophy*, 1644). (There is, however, for Descartes, a place for empirical investigation in science—not as a tool for producing general understanding, but rather to determine the real external existences of particular things.)

These ideas (though they have never been uncritically and uniformly accepted) have come to permeate the modern conception of science, including Descartes's influential metaphor of a unified "tree of knowledge," with metaphysics as the roots, physics as the trunk, and the special sciences (like biology, anthropology, or ethics) as the branches. His most important and lasting influence on scientific thought is his idea that the physical world is a unified whole, governed by very basic universal mathematical and physical laws, and that finding these is the most basic job of science. One much less familiar, and less lasting, aspect of Descartes's method for the production of knowledge is the central role played by God in his system. For Descartes, all human knowledge of the world around us essentially relies upon our prior knowledge that a non-deceiving God exists. Science, properly understood, not only does not conflict with religion but actually *depends* on religion, he believed.

Finally, one of the best-known results of Descartes's metaphysical reflections is "Cartesian dualism." This doctrine states that mind and body are two completely different substances—that the mind is a nonphysical self in which all the operations of thought take place, and which can be wholly separated from the body after death. Like much of Descartes's work, this theory came to have the status of a more or less standard view for some 300 years after his death, but at the time it was a radical philosophical innovation, breaking with the traditional Aristotelian conception of mental activity as a kind of *attribute* of the physical body (rather than as something entirely separable from the body).

What Is the Structure of This Reading?

The *Meditations* is not intended to be merely an exposition of philosophical arguments and conclusions, but is supposed to be an exercise in philosophical reflection for the reader—as Bernard Williams has put it, "the 'I' that appears throughout them from the first sentence on does not specifically represent [Descartes]: it represents anyone who will step into the position it marks, the position of the thinker who is prepared to reconsider and recast his or her beliefs, as Descartes supposed we might, from the ground up."* Descartes aims to convince us of the truth of his conclusions by making us conduct the arguments ourselves. (It is interesting to note that the structure of the *Meditations* was modeled on the "spiritual exercises" that students at Jesuit schools, such as the one Descartes attended, were required to undertake in order to learn to move away from the world of the senses and to focus on God.)

In the First Meditation the thinker applies a series of progressively more radical doubts to his or her preconceived opinions, which leaves her unsure whether she knows anything at all. But then in the Second Meditation the thinker finds a secure foundational belief in her indubitable awareness of her own existence. The rest of this meditation is a reflection on the thinker's own nature as a "thinking thing." In the Third Meditation the thinker realizes that final certainty can only be achieved through the existence of a non-deceiving God, and argues from the idea of God found in her own mind to the conclusion that God must really exist and be the cause of this idea (this is sometimes nicknamed the "Trademark Argument," from the notion that our possession of the idea of God is God's "trademark" on his creation). The Fourth Meditation urges that the way to avoid error in

---

* This appears in his introductory essay to the Cambridge University Press edition of the *Meditations* (1996).

our judgments is to restrict our beliefs to things of which we are clearly and distinctly certain. The Fifth Meditation introduces Cartesian science by discussing the mathematical nature of our knowledge of matter, and also includes a second proof for God's existence which resembles the eleventh-century "ontological argument" of St. Anselm. Finally, in the Sixth Meditation, the thinker re-establishes our knowledge of the real existence of the external world, argues that mind and body are two distinct substances, and reflects on how mind and body are related.

Some Useful Background Information

1. Descartes makes frequent use of the terms "substance," "essence," and "accident." A substance is, roughly, a bearer of attributes, i.e., a thing that has properties, what the properties are properties *of*. The essence of a substance is its fundamental intrinsic nature, a property without which that thing, of that sort, could not exist. Descartes held that for every substance there is exactly one property which is its essence. A substance's "accidents"* are all the rest of its properties, the ones which are not part of its essence.

    Take, for example, a red ball: its redness, the spherical shape, the rubbery feel, and so on, are all properties—accidents—of the ball, and the ball's substance is the "stuff" that underlies and possesses these properties. According to Descartes, the fundamental nature of this stuff—its essence—is that it is extended in three dimensions, that it fills space.

    For Descartes and his contemporaries there is also another important aspect to the idea of substance. Unlike an instance of a property, which cannot exist all by itself (there can't be an occurrence of redness without there being something which is red—some bit of substance which is the bearer of that property), substances are not dependent for their existence on something else. In fact, for Descartes, this is actually the *definition* of a substance: "By 'substance' we can understand

nothing other than a thing which exists in such a way as to depend on no other things for its existence" (*Principles of Philosophy*). So, for instance, a tree is not really a substance, since trees do depend for their existence on other things (such as soil, light, past trees, and so on). On the other hand, according to Descartes, matter itself—all matter, taken as a whole—is a substance. Matter cannot be destroyed or created (except by God), it can only change its local form, gradually moving from the form of a tree to the form of a rotting tree trunk to the form of soil, for example.

2. Descartes relies quite heavily in the *Meditations* on a three-fold contrast between intellect (or understanding), the will, and sensation and imagination. He explains this distinction in some detail in the Sixth Meditation, but the basic distinction is as follows: Sensation and imagination involve the presentation of ideas, especially mental images. The word 'Imagination' here has a more particular sense than the current one, which includes any sort of speculation or invention; Descartes's notion is an earlier one, involving the having of mental images—pictures in the mind's eye, so to speak. The understanding is our intellectual apprehension of ideas, the faculty by which the mind considers the contents of thoughts (indeed, without understanding, mere sensations have no content at all). The will is our ability to either assent or dissent to these ideas—it is our faculty of judgment. An act of will (assent) is necessary for there to be a belief at all, according to Descartes—a mere idea by itself can be neither accurate nor erroneous.

    Two key details are worth bearing in mind for a fuller appreciation of Descartes's arguments in the *Meditations*. First, although the understanding/ imagination distinction would have been quite familiar at the time, Descartes departs from the intellectual tradition of Aristotle in holding that sensation and imagination, though they certainly intimately involve the body, are modes of the mind. (Aristotle and his followers held that only the intellect is properly mental.) Furthermore, Descartes emphasized that our sensations, by themselves,

---

* Strictly speaking, Descartes thought of accidents as being 'modes' of the one essential property of the substance (rather than being really separate properties): shape, for example, is a mode of being extended in space.

tell us nothing about the world—only our understanding generates judgments. This is arguably the central point of the famous wax example, in the Second Meditation.

Second, Descartes believed that the understanding is a passive, rather than an active, mental faculty: it takes in the deliveries of sensation, for example, and produces thoughts almost automatically, according to the way in which God has created us. By contrast, the will (also given to us by God) is an active mental faculty. We cannot choose how the world appears to us, but we can choose whether or not to certify those judgments as accurate. In this way, for Descartes, error is almost a moral failing—a failure of the will. Our mistakes are not God's fault, but our own.

3. A related phrase frequently used by Descartes in the *Meditations* is the "natural light." Descartes has in mind here what in earlier writings he calls "the light of reason"—the pure inner light of the intellect, a faculty given to us by God, which allows us to see the truth of the world much more clearly than we can with the confused and fluctuating testimony of the senses.

4. Descartes, following the scholastic jargon of the time, calls the representational content of an idea its "objective reality" (he uses this term in his attempted proof of the existence of God in the Third Meditation). Confusingly, for something to have merely objective reality in this sense is for it to belong to the mental world of ideas, and not to the mind-independent external world at all.

For example, if I imagine Santa Claus as being fat and jolly, then Descartes would say that fatness is "objectively" present in my idea—an idea of fatness forms part of my idea of Santa Claus. By contrast, the baby beluga at the Chicago aquarium is fat, but its fatness is not merely the *idea* of fatness but an actual property of the beluga. In general, for any idea *I* that represents a thing *X* which has the property of being F, F-ness will be present formally in *X* but objectively in *I*.

What Descartes and his contemporaries call "formal reality," then, is just the reality something has simply by virtue of existing. Since ideas exist (they are modes of a thinking substance), they have both formal reality—the idea itself—and objective reality—the content of the idea.

5. Although Descartes's talk of a non-physical "soul" was in accord with contemporary Christian theology, his reasons for holding that the mind is immortal and non-material (given largely in the Second and Sixth Meditations) were not primarily religious ones. Descartes does not think of the soul as being especially "spiritual" or as being identical with our "better nature," for example. For Descartes the word "soul" simply means the same as the word "mind," and encompasses the whole range of conscious mental activity, including the sensations of sight, touch, sound, taste, and smell; emotions (such as joy or jealousy); and cognitive activities like believing, planning, desiring, or doubting. For Descartes the mind, or soul, is also to be distinguished from the brain: our brains, since they are extended material things, are part of our body and not our mind.

6. Descartes's metaphysics was a radical departure from the then-prevailing Aristotelian view of nature. In very brief summary, Aristotelians saw natural bodies as being composed of both form and matter. Matter cannot exist without form, and a thing's form determines its nature: that is, a thing's form makes it what it is—a horse, a tree, a cloud—by determining its characteristic development and behavior. There are four basic substances—earth, air, fire, and water—and four basic qualities—hot, cold, wet, and dry. Most natural bodies are made up of mixtures of elements, and they belong to different kinds (such as species, or types of minerals) defined by their forms. In this way, Aristotelian science made no distinction between biological processes, such as growth or nutrition, and other natural phenomena such as burning or gravity: they are all the playing out of essential forms, principles of growth and change, that are 'built in' to the entities involved. For the Aristotelian, then, scientific explanation will be a matter of identifying the multifarious forms—the essential natures—of all the different items in the natural world. Furthermore, the objects that we encounter in nature really have the properties they appear to have to our senses—color, texture, taste, odor, and so on—and what it is for us to perceive the world is a transfer of these qualities from external objects to our sense organs (where they are received in our sensory soul as a "form without

matter"). One final important aspect of Aristotelian science: the changing, natural realm in which we live is located at the center of the universe (due to the tendency of earth and water, because of their natures, to seek the center and thus collect there), but there is a radical discontinuity between this world and the heavenly spheres—literally, crystalline spheres in which the moon, sun, planets, and stars were thought to be embedded—which are unchanging, and not even made of the familiar four elements but of a completely different fifth element (called quintessence).

One of the interpretive tasks in reading the *Meditations* (which Descartes secretly thought of as being designed to present his new and, for his audience highly counter-intuitive, physics) is to discover the differences between the Aristotelian tradition and Descartes's own account. Some of the Cartesian departures to look for are: that different natural kinds differ only in the sizes, shapes, and motions of the particles that make them up; that matter does not contain within it its own principle of motion and change but is 'passive' and subject to external forces; that the qualities we encounter in sense experience do not resemble the causes of those experiences; and that the whole material world, including the heliocentric solar system, is governed by the same small set of laws of motion.

Some Common Misconceptions

1. The *Meditations* describe a process, in which the thinker moves from pre-reflective starting points towards a clearer understanding of knowledge. As a consequence, not everything that Descartes writes—especially in the earlier meditations—is something that he, or the thinker, will agree with by the time they have completed the process. (For example, he begins by saying that "[u]p to this point, what I have accepted as very true I have derived either from the senses or through the senses," which is a principle he later rejects.)

2. Descartes is not a skeptic. Although he is famous for the skeptical arguments put forward in the First Meditation, he uses these only in order to go beyond them.* It is a bit misleading, however, to think of Descartes as setting out in the *Meditations* to defeat skepticism: his main interest is probably not in proving the skeptic wrong, but in discovering the first principles upon which a proper science can be built. He uses skepticism, surprisingly, in order to create knowledge—to show that a properly constituted science would have nothing to fear from even the most radical doubts of the skeptic. Thus, for example, Descartes does not at any point argue that we should actually believe that the external world does not exist—instead, he suspends his belief in external objects until he has a chance to properly build a foundation for this belief (and by the end of the *Meditations* he is quite certain that the external world exists).

3. The "method of doubt" which Descartes uses in the *Meditations* is not an everyday method—it is not supposed to be an appropriate technique for making day-to-day decisions, or even for doing science or mathematics. Most of the time it would be hugely impractical for us to call into question everything that we might possibly doubt, to question all our presuppositions, before we make a judgment. Instead the method of the *Meditations* is supposed to be a once-in-a-lifetime exercise, by which we discover and justify the basic "first principles" that we rely on in everyday knowledge. In short, we always have to rely on certain assumptions when we make decisions or do science, and this is unavoidable but dangerous; the exercise of the *Meditations* can ensure that the assumptions we rely upon are absolutely secure.

4. Although "I think therefore I am" (or "I am, I exist") is the first step in Descartes's reconstruction of human knowledge in the *Meditations*, it is nevertheless not the first piece of *knowledge* that he recognizes—it does not arise out of a complete knowledge vacuum. Before the thinker can come to know that "I think therefore I am" is

---

* In one of his letters, Descartes noted that, when ancient medical authorities such as Galen or Hippocrates wrote about the causes of disease, no one accused them of telling people how to get sick; in the same way, Descartes complained, "I put forward these reasons for doubting not to convince people of them but, on the contrary, in order to refute them."

true, Descartes elsewhere admits that she must know, for example, what is meant by thinking, and that doubting is a kind of thought, and that in order to think one must first exist. Therefore, it is best to think of "I think therefore I am," not as the first item of knowledge, but as the first *non-trivial* piece of secure knowledge about the world that a thinker can have. It's a piece of information not just about concepts or logic but actually about the world— but, according to Descartes, it's information we can only get if we *already* (somehow) possess a certain set of concepts.

5. It is sometimes supposed that Descartes thought that all knowledge could be mathematically deduced from the foundational beliefs that remain after he has applied his method of doubt. But this is not quite right. He thought that the proper *concepts and terms*, which science must use to describe the world, were purely mathematical and were deducible through pure rational reflection. But he also recognized that only through empirical investigation can we discover which scientific descriptions, expressed in the proper mathematical terms, are actually *true* of the world. For example, reason tells us (according to Descartes— and this was a radically new idea at the time) that matter can be defined simply in terms of extension in three dimensions, and that the laws which guide the movements of particles can be understood mathematically. However, only experience can tell us how the bits of matter in, for example, the human body are actually arranged.

6. Descartes does not conclude that error is impossible, even for those who adopt the proper intellectual methods of science. He argues only that *radical and systematic* error is impossible for the conscientious thinker. For example, even after completing Descartes's course of meditations we might still occasionally be tricked by perceptual illusions, or think we are awake when in fact we are dreaming; what Descartes thinks he has blocked, however, is the possibility that such errors show that our entire picture of reality might be wrong.

7. Descartes's project is to show how, by setting our knowledge of the world on firm foundations, we can overcome any skeptical doubts and have confidence in the conception of reality that results. It is less widely appreciated, however, that the common-sense picture of the world, as it is apparently revealed to our senses, with which Descartes begins is very different from the worldview with which we are left at the end of the *Meditations*. Descartes does not merely rescue common sense from skepticism; instead, he replaces a naïve view of the world with a more modern, scientific one.

8. Descartes is sometimes portrayed as making the following (bad) argument to establish that mind is distinct from body: I can doubt that my body exists; I cannot doubt that my mind exists; there is therefore at least one property that my mind has which my body lacks (i.e., being doubtable); and therefore mind and body are not identical. Descartes does seem to make an argument which resembles this (in the Second Meditation), but he later denied that this is really what he meant, and he formulates much stronger—though perhaps still flawed— arguments for dualism in the Sixth Meditation.

How Important and Influential Is This Text?

Descartes is one of the most widely studied Western philosophers, and his *Meditations on First Philosophy* is his philosophical masterpiece and most important work. John Cottingham, an expert on Descartes, has written of the *Meditations* that

> The radical critique of preconceived opinions or prejudices which begins that work seems to symbolize the very essence of philosophical inquiry. And the task of finding secure foundations for human knowledge, a reliable basis for science and ethics, encapsulates, for many, what makes philosophy worth doing.*

"I think therefore I am" ("*cogito ergo sum*" in Latin) is the most famous dictum in the history of philosophy. Note that this is not what it is often popularly taken to be:

---

* This appears in his Introduction to the *Cambridge Companion to Descartes* (1992).

praise of the intellectual life as the real source of human identity. It's rather Descartes's foundational claim beginning his reconstruction of indubitable truth. These exact words, by the way, never appear in the *Meditations*—they are found in other writings by Descartes, including *Discourse on the Method* and the *Principles of Philosophy*; the *Meditations*, however, contains Descartes's most complete account of how this principle, today simply often called "the Cogito," is established.

The importance of Descartes's work to the history of thought is profound. He is commonly considered the first great philosopher of the modern era, since his work was central in sweeping away medieval scholasticism based on Aristotelian science and Christian theology and replacing it with the methods and questions that have dominated philosophy ever since.* This change from scholastic to modern modes of thought was also crucial to the phenomenal growth of natural science and mathematics beginning in the seventeenth century. In recent years, however, it has been fashionable to blame Descartes for what have been seen as philosophical dead ends, and many of the assumptions which he built into philosophy have been questioned (this is one of the reasons why the philosophy of the second half of the twentieth century and beyond has been so exciting).

Meditations on First Philosophy

IN WHICH THE EXISTENCE OF GOD AND THE DIFFERENCE BETWEEN THE HUMAN SOUL AND BODY ARE DEMONSTRATED[†]

Synopsis of the Six Following Meditations

In the First Meditation I set down the reasons which enable us to place everything in doubt, especially material things, at least as long as we do not have foundations for the sciences different from those we have had up to now. Although at first glance the usefulness of such a widespread doubt is not apparent, it is, in fact, very great, because it frees us from all prejudices, sets down the easiest route by which we can detach our minds from our senses, and finally makes it impossible for us to doubt anymore those things which we later discover to be true.

In the Second Meditation, the mind, using its own unique freedom, assumes that all those things about whose existence it can entertain the least doubt do not exist, and recognizes that during this time it is impossible that it itself does not exist. And that is also extremely useful, because in this way the mind can easily differentiate between those things pertaining to it, that is, to its intellectual nature, and those pertaining to the body. However, since at this point

---

* Alan Gewirth went so far as to write, in 1970, "the history of twentieth-century philosophy ... consists in a series of reactions to Descartes's metaphysics. Examples of these reactions are Ryle's castigations of the Cartesian mind-body dualism, Sartre's and Hare's attacks on Cartesian intellectualism and intuitionism, Chomsky's support of Cartesian innatism, and the opposed views taken on Cartesian doubt by Russell and Husserl on the one hand and by Moore, Dewey, Austin, and the later Wittgenstein on the other" ("The Cartesian Circle Reconsidered," *The Journal of Philosophy* 67: 668–85).

† Translated by Ian Johnston, Vancouver Island University, 2012. Translator's Note: This translation is based upon the first Latin edition of Descartes's *Meditations* (1641). I have incorporated most of the relatively few corrections made to that text in the second Latin edition (1642), none of which is particularly important. I have also inserted a number of additions made to the Latin text in the first French edition (1647), which was supervised by Descartes, who approved of the result. These additions from the French edition are inserted here only where they help to clarify the meaning of the original Latin (for example, by clarifying Descartes's Latin pronouns). Other changes in the French text I have ignored. Words in square brackets are insertions and additions from the first French edition.

some people may perhaps expect an argument [proving] the immortality of the soul, I think I should warn them that I have tried to avoid writing anything which I could not accurately demonstrate and that, therefore, I was unable to follow any sequence of reasoning other than the one used by geometers. That means I start by setting down everything on which the proposition we are looking into depends, before I reach any conclusions about it. Now, the first and most important prerequisite for understanding the immortality of the soul is to form a conception of the soul that is as clear as possible, one entirely distinct from every conception [we have] of the body. And that I have done in this section. After that, it is essential also for us to know that all those things we understand clearly and distinctly are true in a way which matches precisely how we think of them. This I was unable to prove before the Fourth Meditation. We also need to have a distinct conception of corporeal* nature. I deal with that point partly in this Second Meditation and partly in the Fifth and Sixth Meditations, as well. And from these we necessarily infer that all those things we conceive clearly and distinctly as different substances, in the same way we think of the mind and the body, are, in fact, truly different substances, distinct from one another, a conclusion I have drawn in the Sixth Meditation. This conclusion is also confirmed in the same meditation from the fact that we cannot think of the body as anything other than something divisible, and, by contrast, [cannot think of] the mind as anything other than something indivisible. For we cannot conceive of half a mind, in the same way we can with a body, no matter how small. Hence, we realize that their natures are not only different but even, in some respects, opposites. However, I have not pursued the matter any further in this treatise for two reasons: (1) because these points are enough to show that the annihilation of the mind does not follow from the corruption of the body, so we mortals thus ought to entertain hopes of another life; and (2) because the premises on the basis of which we can infer the immortality of the mind depend upon an explanation of all the principles of physics. For (2), first of all, we would have to know that all substances without exception—or those things which, in order to exist, must be created by God—are by their very nature incorruptible and can never cease to exist, unless God, by denying them his concurrence,† reduces them to nothing, and then, second, we would have to understand that a body, considered generally, is a substance and thus it, too, never dies. But the human body, to the extent that it differs from other bodies, consists merely of a certain arrangement of parts, with other similar accidental‡ properties; whereas, the human mind is not made up of any accidental properties; in this way, but is a pure substance. For even if all the accidental properties of the mind were changed—if, for example, it were to think of different things or have different desires and perceptions, and so on—that would not mean it had turned into a different mind. But the human body becomes something different from the mere fact that the shape of some of its parts has changed. From this it follows that the [human] body does, in fact, perish very easily, but that the mind, thanks to its nature, is immortal.

In the Third Meditation I have set out what seems to me a sufficiently detailed account of my main argument to demonstrate the existence of God. However, in order to lead the minds of the readers as far as possible from the senses, in this section I was unwilling to use any comparisons drawn from corporeal things, and thus many obscurities may still remain. But these, I hope, have later been entirely removed in the replies [I have made] to the objections.§ For instance, among all the others, there is the issue of how the idea of a supremely perfect being, which is present within us, could have so much objective reality that it is impossible for it not to originate from a supremely perfect cause. This is illustrated [in the replies] by the comparison with a wholly perfect machine, the idea of which exists in the mind of some craftsman. For just as the objective ingenuity of this idea must have some cause, that is, the technical skill of this craftsman or of

---

* Bodily, physical.

† The continuous divine action which many Christians think necessary to maintain things in existence.

‡ See the section in the Introduction, "Some Useful Background Information," for an explanation of "accidental" here, and for a number of other confusing or obscure terms that Descartes uses at various points in *Meditations*.

§ Descartes refers to the set of objections and replies he published at the end of *Meditations*, not reprinted here.

someone else from whom he got the idea, so the idea of God, which is in us, cannot have any cause other than God Himself.

In the Fourth Meditation, I establish that all the things which we perceive clearly and distinctly are true, and at the same time I explain what constitutes the nature of falsity; these are things that we have to know both to confirm what has gone before and to understand what still remains. (However, in the meantime I must observe that in this part I do not deal in any way with sin, that is, with errors committed in pursuit of good and evil, but only with those which are relevant to judgments of what is true and false. Nor do I consider matters relevant to our faith or to the conduct of our lives, but merely those speculative truths we can know only with the assistance of our natural light.)

In the Fifth Meditation, I offer a general explanation of corporeal* nature and, in addition, also demonstrate the existence of God in a new argument, in which, however, several difficulties may, once again, arise. These I have resolved later in my replies to the objections. And finally, I point out in what sense it is true that the certainty of geometrical demonstrations depends upon a knowledge of God.

Finally, in the Sixth Meditation, I differentiate between the understanding and the imagination and describe the principles of this distinction. I establish that the mind is truly distinct from the body, and I point out how, in spite of that, it is so closely joined to the body that they form, as it were, a single thing. I review all the errors which customarily arise through the senses and explain the ways in which such errors can be avoided. And then finally, I set down all the reasons which enable us to infer the existence of material things. I believe these are useful not because they demonstrate the truth of what they prove—for example, that there truly is a world, that human beings have bodies, and things like that, which no one of sound mind ever seriously doubted—but rather because, when we examine these reasons, we see that they are neither as firm or as evident as those by which we arrive at a knowledge of our own minds and of God, so that the latter are the most certain and most evident of all things which can be known by the human intellect. The proof of this one point was the goal I set out to attain in these *Meditations*. For that reason I am not reviewing here, as they arise [in this treatise], various [other] questions I have dealt with elsewhere.

First Meditation: Concerning Those Things Which Can Be Called into Doubt

It is now several years since I noticed how from the time of my early youth I had accepted many false claims as true, how everything I had later constructed on top of those [falsehoods] was doubtful, and thus how at some point in my life I needed to tear everything down completely and begin again from the most basic foundations, if I wished to establish something firm and lasting in the sciences. But this seemed an immense undertaking, and I kept waiting until I would be old enough and sufficiently mature to know that no later period of my life would come [in which I was] better equipped to undertake this disciplined enquiry. This reason made me delay for so long that I would now be at fault if, by [further] deliberation, I used up the time which still remains to carry out that project. And so today, when I have conveniently rid my mind of all worries and have managed to find myself secure leisure in solitary withdrawal, I will at last find the time for an earnest and unfettered general demolition of my [former] opinions.

Now, for this task it will not be necessary to show that every opinion I hold is false, something which I might well be incapable of ever carrying out. But reason now convinces me that I should withhold my assent from opinions which are not entirely certain and indubitable, no less than from those which are plainly false; so if I uncover any reason for doubt in each of them, that will be enough to reject them all. For that I will not need to run through them separately, a task that would take forever, because once the foundations are destroyed, whatever is built above them will collapse on its own. Thus, I shall at once assault the very principles upon which all my earlier beliefs rested.

Up to this point, what I have accepted as true I have derived either from the senses or through the senses. However, sometimes I have discovered that these are mistaken, and it is prudent never to place

---

* Physical (i.e., not mental).

one's entire trust in things which have deceived us even once.

However, although from time to time the senses deceive us about minuscule things or those further away, it could well be that there are still many other matters about which we cannot entertain the slightest doubt, even though we derive [our knowledge] of them from sense experience—for example, the fact that I am now here, seated by the fire, wearing a winter robe, holding this paper in my hands, and so on. And, in fact, how could I deny that these very hands and this whole body are mine, unless perhaps I were to compare myself with certain insane people whose brains are so troubled by the stubborn vapours of black bile* that they constantly claim that they are kings, when, in fact, they are very poor, or that they are dressed in purple, when they are nude, or that they have earthenware heads, or are complete pumpkins, or made of glass? But these people are mad, and I myself would appear no less demented if I took something from them and applied it to myself as an example.

A brilliant piece of reasoning! But nevertheless I am a person who sleeps at night and experiences in my dreams all the things these [mad] people do when wide awake, sometimes even less probable ones. How often have I had an experience like this: while sleeping at night, I am convinced that I am here, dressed in a robe and seated by the fire, when, in fact, I am lying between the covers with my clothes off! At the moment, my eyes are certainly wide open and I am looking at this piece of paper, this head which I am moving is not asleep, and I am aware of this hand as I move it consciously and purposefully. None of what happens while I am asleep is so distinct. Yes, of course—but nevertheless I recall other times when I have been deceived by similar thoughts in my sleep. As I reflect on this matter carefully, it becomes completely clear to me that there are no certain indicators which ever enable us to differentiate between being awake and being asleep, and this is astounding; in my confusion I am almost convinced that I may be sleeping.

So then, let us suppose that I am asleep and that these particular details—that my eyes are open, that I am moving my head, that I am stretching out my hand—are not true, and that perhaps I do not even have hands like these or a whole body like this. We must, of course, still concede that the things we see while asleep are like painted images, which could only have been made as representations of real things. And so these general things—these eyes, this head, this hand, and this entire body—at least are not imaginary things but really do exist. For even when painters themselves take great care to form sirens and satyrs with the most unusual shapes, they cannot, in fact, give them natures which are entirely new. Instead, they simply mix up the limbs of various animals or, if they happen to come up with something so new that nothing at all like it has been seen before and thus [what they have made] is completely fictitious and false, nonetheless, at least the colours which make up the picture certainly have to be real. For similar reasons, although these general things—eyes, head, hand, and so on—could also be imaginary, still we are at least forced to concede the reality of certain even simpler and more universal objects, out of which, just as with real colours, all those images of things that are in our thoughts, whether true or false, are formed.

Corporeal nature appears, in general, to belong to this class [of things], as well as its extension,† the shape of extended things, their quantity or their size and number, the place where they exist, the time which measures how long they last, and things like that.

Thus, from these facts perhaps we are not reaching an erroneous conclusion [by claiming] that physics, astronomy, medicine, and all the other disciplines which rely upon a consideration of composite objects are indeed doubtful, but that arithmetic, geometry, and the other [sciences] like them, which deal with only the simplest and most general matters and have little concern whether or not they exist in the nature of things, contain something certain and indubitable. For whether I am awake or asleep, two and three always add up to five, a square does not have more than four sides, and it does not seem possible to suspect that such manifest truths could be false.

Nevertheless, a certain opinion has for a long time been fixed in my mind—that there is an all-powerful

---

* One of the four basic bodily fluids then thought to be associated with disease when in imbalance.

† Something's extension is its spatial magnitude—the volume of space it occupies.

God who created me and [made me] just as I am. But how do I know He has not arranged things so that there is no earth at all, no sky, no extended thing, no shape, no magnitude, no place, and yet seen to it that all these things appear to me to exist just as they do now? Besides, given that I sometimes judge that other people make mistakes with the things about which they believe they have the most perfect knowledge, might I not in the same way be wrong every time I add two and three together, or count the sides of a square, or do something simpler, if that can be imagined? Perhaps God is unwilling to deceive me in this way, for He is said to be supremely good. But if it is contrary to the goodness of God to have created me in such a way that I am always deceived, it would also seem foreign to His goodness to allow me to be occasionally deceived. The latter claim, however, is not one that I can make.

Perhaps there may really be some people who prefer to deny [the existence of] such a powerful God, rather than to believe that all other things are uncertain. But let us not seek to refute these people, and [let us concede] that everything [I have said] here about God is a fiction. No matter how they assume I reached where I am now, whether by fate, or chance, or a continuous series of events, or in some other way, given that being deceived and making mistakes would seem to be something of an imperfection, the less power they attribute to the author of my being, the greater the probability that I will be so imperfect that I will always be deceived. I really do not have a reply to these arguments. Instead, I am finally compelled to admit that there is nothing in the beliefs which I formerly held to be true about which one cannot raise doubts. And this is not a reckless or frivolous opinion, but the product of strong and well-considered reasoning. And therefore, if I desire to discover something certain, in future I should also withhold my assent from those former opinions of mine, no less than [I do] from opinions which are obviously false.

But it is not sufficient to have called attention to this point. I must [also] be careful to remember it. For these habitual opinions constantly recur, and I have made use of them for so long and they are so familiar that they have, as it were, acquired the right to seize hold of my belief and subjugate it, even against my wishes, and I will never give up the habit of deferring to and relying on them, as long as I continue to assume that they are what they truly are: opinions which are to some extent doubtful, as I have already pointed out, but still very probable, so that it is much more reasonable to believe them than to deny them. For that reason, I will not go wrong, in my view, if I deliberately turn my inclination into its complete opposite and deceive myself, [by assuming] for a certain period that these earlier opinions are entirely false and imaginary, until I have, as it were, finally brought the weight of both my [old and my new] prejudices into an equal balance, so that corrupting habits will no longer twist my judgment away from the correct perception of things. For I know that doing this will not, for the time being, lead to danger or error and that it is impossible for me to indulge in excessive distrust, since I am not concerned with actions at this point, but only with knowledge.

Therefore, I will assume that it is not God, who is supremely good and the fountain of truth, but some malicious demon, at once omnipotent and supremely cunning, who has been using all the energy he possesses to deceive me. I will suppose that sky, air, earth, colours, shapes, sounds, and all other external things are nothing but the illusions of my dreams, set by this spirit as traps for my credulity. I will think of myself as if I had no hands, no eyes, no flesh, no blood, nor any senses, and yet as if I still falsely believed I had all these things. I shall continue to concentrate resolutely on this meditation, and if, in doing so, I am, in fact, unable to learn anything true, I will at least do what is in my power and with a resolute mind take care not to agree to what is false or to enable the deceiver to impose anything on me, no matter how powerful and cunning [he may be]. But this task is onerous, and laziness brings me back to my customary way of life. I am like a prisoner who in his sleep may happen to enjoy an imaginary liberty and who, when he later begins to suspect that he is asleep, fears to wake up and willingly cooperates with the pleasing illusions [in order to prolong them]. In this way, I unconsciously slip back into my old opinions and am afraid to wake up, in case from now on I would have to spend the period of challenging wakefulness that follows this peaceful relaxation not in the light, but in the inextricable darkness of the difficulties I have just raised.

Second Meditation: Concerning the Nature of the Human Mind and the Fact That It Is Easier to Know Than the Body

Yesterday's meditation threw me into so many doubts that I can no longer forget them or even see how they might be resolved. Just as if I had suddenly fallen into a deep eddying current, I am hurled into such confusion that I am unable to set my feet on the bottom or swim to the surface. However, I will struggle along and try once again [to follow] the same path I started on yesterday—that is, I will reject everything which admits of the slightest doubt, just as if I had discovered it was completely false, and I will proceed further in this way, until I find something certain, or at least, if I do nothing else, until I know for certain that there is nothing certain. In order to shift the entire earth from its location, Archimedes asked for nothing but a fixed and immovable point.* So I, too, ought to hope for great things if I can discover something, no matter how small, which is certain and immovable.

Therefore, I assume that everything I see is false. I believe that none of those things my lying memory represents has ever existed, that I have no senses at all, and that body, shape, extension, motion, and location are chimeras.† What, then, will be true? Perhaps this one thing: there is nothing certain.

But how do I know that there exists nothing other than the items I just listed, about which one could not entertain the slightest momentary doubt? Is there not some God, by whatever name I call him, who places these very thoughts inside me? But why would I think this, since I myself could perhaps have produced them? So am I then not at least something? But I have already denied that I have senses and a body. Still, I am puzzled, for what follows from this? Am I so bound up with my body and my senses that I cannot exist without them? But I have convinced myself that there is nothing at all in the universe—no sky, no earth, no minds, no bodies. So then, is it the case that I, too, do not exist? No, not at all: if I persuaded myself of

something, then I certainly existed. But there is some kind of deceiver, supremely powerful and supremely cunning, who is constantly and intentionally deceiving me. But then, if he is deceiving me, there again is no doubt that I exist—for that very reason. Let him trick me as much as he can, he will never succeed in making me nothing, as long as I am aware that I am something. And so, after thinking all these things through in great detail, I must finally settle on this proposition: the statement *I am, I exist* is necessarily true every time I say it or conceive of it in my mind.

But I do yet understand enough about what this *I* is, which now necessarily exists. Thus, I must be careful I do not perhaps unconsciously substitute something else in place of this *I* and in that way make a mistake even here, in the conception which I assert is the most certain and most evident of all. For that reason, I will now reconsider what I once believed myself to be, before I fell into this [present] way of thinking. Then I will remove from that whatever could, in the slightest way, be weakened by the reasoning I have [just] brought to bear, so that, in doing this, by the end I will be left only with what is absolutely certain and immovable.

What then did I believe I was before? Naturally, I thought I was a human being. But what is a human being? Shall I say a *rational animal*? No. For then I would have to ask what an *animal* is and what *rational* means, and thus from a single question I would fall into several greater difficulties. And at the moment I do not have so much leisure time that I wish to squander it with subtleties of this sort. Instead I would prefer here to attend to what used to come into my mind quite naturally and spontaneously in earlier days every time I thought about what I was. The first thought, of course, was that I had a face, hands, arms, and this entire mechanism of limbs, the kind one sees on a corpse, and this I designated by the name *body*. Then it occurred to me that I ate and drank, walked, felt, and thought. These actions I assigned to the *soul*. But I did not reflect on what this *soul* might be, or else I imagined it as some

---

*   Archimedes was an ancient Greek scientist. He also asked for a long-enough lever.

†   In Greek mythology, a female fire-breathing monster with a lion's head, a goat's body, and a serpent's tail; more generally, an absurd or horrible idea or wild fancy.

kind of attenuated substance, like wind, or fire, or aether,* spread all through my denser parts. However, I had no doubts at all about my body—I thought I had a clear knowledge of its nature. Perhaps if I had attempted to describe it using the mental conception I used to hold, I would have explained it as follows: By a *body* I understand everything that is appropriately bound together in a certain form and confined to a place; it fills a certain space in such a way as to exclude from that space every other body; it can be perceived by touch, sight, hearing, taste, or smell, and can also be moved in various ways, not, indeed, by itself, but by something else which makes contact with it. For I judged that possessing the power of self-movement, like the ability to perceive things or to think, did not pertain at all to the nature of body. Quite the opposite in fact, so that when I found out that faculties rather similar to these were present in certain bodies, I was astonished.

But what [am I] now, when I assume that there is some extremely powerful and, if I may be permitted to speak like this, malevolent and deceiving being who is deliberately using all his power to trick me? Can I affirm that I possess even the least of all those things which I have just described as pertaining to the nature of body? I direct my attention [to this], think [about it], and turn [the question] over in my mind. Nothing comes to me. It is tedious and useless to go over the same things once again. What, then, of those things I used to attribute to the soul, like eating, drinking, or walking? But given that now I do not possess a body, these are nothing but imaginary figments. What about sense perception? This, too, surely does not occur without the body. And in sleep I have apparently sensed many objects which I later noticed I had not [truly] perceived. What about thinking? Here I discover something: thinking does exist. This is the only thing which cannot be detached from me. *I am, I exist*—that is certain. But for how long? Surely for as long as I am thinking. For it could perhaps be the case that, if I were to abandon thinking altogether, then in that moment I would completely cease to be. At this point I am not agreeing to anything except what is necessarily true. Therefore, strictly speaking, I am

merely a thinking thing, that is, a mind or spirit, or understanding, or reason—words whose significance I did not realize before. However, I am something real, and I truly exist. But what kind of thing? As I have said, a thing that thinks.

And what else besides? I will let my imagination roam. I am not that interconnection of limbs we call a human body. Nor am I even some attenuated air which filters through those limbs—wind, or fire, or vapour, or breath, or anything I picture to myself. For I have assumed those things were nothing. Let this assumption hold. Nonetheless, I am still something. Perhaps it could be the case that these very things which I assume are nothing, because they are unknown to me, are truly no different from that *I* which I do recognize. I am not sure, and I will not dispute this point right now. I can render judgment only on those things which are known to me: I know that I exist. I am asking what this *I* is—the thing I know. It is very certain that knowledge of this *I*, precisely defined like this, does not depend on things whose existence I as yet know nothing about and therefore on any of those things I conjure up in my imagination. And this phrase *conjure up* warns me of my mistake, for I would truly be conjuring something up if I imagined myself to be something, since imagining is nothing other than contemplating the form or the image of a physical thing. But now I know for certain that I exist and, at the same time, that it is possible for all those images and, in general, whatever relates to the nature of body to be nothing but dreams [or chimeras]. Having noticed this, it seems no less foolish for me to say "I will let my imagination work, so that I may recognize more clearly what I am" than if I were to state, "Now I am indeed awake, and I see some truth, but because I do yet not see it with sufficient clarity, I will quite deliberately go to sleep, so that in my dreams I will get a truer and more distinct picture of it." Therefore, I realize that none of those things which I can understand with the aid of my imagination is pertinent to this idea I possess about myself and that I must be extremely careful to summon my mind back from such things, so that it may perceive its own nature with the utmost clarity, on its own.

---

* Aether is the fifth element of medieval alchemy, and the idea has its origins in the classical Greek notion of the pure atmosphere beyond the sky in which the gods were thought to live, and which they breathed, analogous to (but different from) the air of the terrestrial atmosphere.

But what then am I? A thinking thing. What is this? It is surely something that doubts, understands, affirms, denies, is willing, is unwilling, and also imagines and perceives.

This is certainly not an insubstantial list, if all [these] things belong to me. But why should they not? Surely I am the same I who now doubts almost everything, yet understands some things, who affirms that this one thing is true, denies all the rest, desires to know more, does not wish to be deceived, imagines many things, even against its will, and also notices many things which seem to come from the senses? Even if I am always asleep and even if the one who created me is also doing all he can to deceive me, what is there among all these things which is not just as true as the fact that I exist? Is there something there that I could say is separate from me? For it is so evident that I am the one who doubts, understands, and wills, that I cannot think of anything which might explain the matter more clearly. But obviously it is the same I that imagines, for although it may well be the case, as I have earlier assumed, that nothing I directly imagine is true, nevertheless, the power of imagining really exists and forms part of my thinking. Finally, it is the same I that feels, or notices corporeal things, apparently through the senses: for example, I now see light, hear noise, and feel heat. But these are false, for I am asleep. Still, I certainly seem to see, hear, and grow warm—and this cannot be false. Strictly speaking, this is what in me is called sense perception and, taken in this precise meaning, it is nothing other than thinking.

From these thoughts, I begin to understand somewhat better what I am. However, it still appears that I cannot prevent myself from thinking that corporeal things, whose images are formed by thought and which the senses themselves investigate, are much more distinctly known than that obscure part of me, the *I*, which is not something I can imagine, even though it is really strange that I have a clearer sense of those things whose existence I know is doubtful, unknown, and alien to me than I do of something which is true and known, in a word, of my own self. But I realize what the trouble is. My mind loves to wander and is not yet allowing itself to be confined within the limits of the truth. All right, then, let us at this point for once give it completely free rein, so that a little later on, when the time comes to pull back, it will consent to be controlled more easily.

Let us consider those things we commonly believe we understand most distinctly of all, that is, the bodies we touch and see—not, indeed, bodies in general, for those general perceptions tend to be somewhat more confusing, but rather one body in particular. For example, let us take this [piece of] beeswax. It was collected from the hive very recently and has not yet lost all the sweetness of its honey. It [still] retains some of the scent of the flowers from which it was gathered. Its colour, shape, and size are evident. It is hard, cold, and easy to handle. If you strike it with your finger, it will give off a sound. In short, everything we require to be able to recognize a body as distinctly as possible appears to be present. But watch. While I am speaking, I bring the wax over to the fire. What is left of its taste is removed, its smell disappears, its colour changes, its shape is destroyed, its size increases, it turns to liquid, and it gets hot. I can hardly touch it. And now, if you strike it, it emits no sound. After [these changes], is what remains the same wax? We must concede that it is. No one denies this; no one thinks otherwise. What then was in [this piece of wax] that I understood so distinctly? Certainly nothing I apprehended with my senses, since all [those things] associated with taste, odour, vision, touch, and sound have now changed. [But] the wax remains.

Perhaps what I now think is as follows: the wax itself was not really that sweetness of honey, that fragrance of flowers, that white colour, or that shape and sound, but a body which a little earlier was perceptible to me in those forms, but which is now [perceptible] in different ones. But what exactly is it that I am imagining in this way? Let us consider that point and, by removing those things which do not belong to the wax, see what is left over. It is clear that nothing [remains], other than something extended, flexible, and changeable. But what, in fact, do *flexible* and *changeable* mean? Do these words mean that I imagine that this wax can change from a round shape to a square one or from [something square] to something triangular? No, that is not it at all. For I understand that the wax has the capacity for innumerable changes of this kind, and yet I am not able to run through these innumerable changes by using my imagination. Therefore, this conception [I have of the wax] is not produced by the faculty of imagination. What about extension? Is not the extension of the wax also unknown? For it becomes greater when the wax melts, greater [still] when it boils, and once again [even] greater, if the heat is increased. And I would not be judging correctly what wax is if I did not believe that it could also be extended in various other ways, more than I could ever grasp in my imagination. Therefore, I am forced to admit that my imagination has no idea at all what this wax is and that I perceive it only with my mind. I am talking about this [piece of] wax in particular, for the point is even clearer about wax in general. But what is this wax which can be perceived only by the mind? It must be the same as the wax I see, touch, and imagine—in short, the same wax I thought it was from the beginning. But we should note that the perception of it is not a matter of sight, or touch, or imagination, and never was, even though that seemed to be the case earlier, but simply of mental inspection, which could be either imperfect and confused as it was before, or clear and distinct as it is now, depending on the lesser or greater degree of attention I bring to bear on those things out of which the wax is composed.

However, now I am amazed at how my mind is [weak and] prone to error. For although I am considering these things silently within myself, without speaking aloud, I still get stuck on the words themselves and am almost deceived by the very nature of the way we speak. For if the wax is there [in front of us], we say that we see the wax itself, not that we judge it to be there from the colour or shape. From that I could immediately conclude that I recognized the wax thanks to the vision in my eyes, and not simply by mental inspection. But by analogy, suppose I happen to glance out of the window at people crossing the street; in normal speech I also say I see the people themselves, just as I do with the wax. But what am I really seeing other than hats and coats, which could be concealing automatons* underneath? However, I judge that they are people. And thus what I thought I was seeing with my eyes I understand only with my faculty of judgment, which is in my mind.

But someone who wishes [to elevate] his knowledge above the common level should be ashamed to have based his doubts in the forms of speech which ordinary people use, and so we should move on to consider next whether my perception of what wax is was more perfect and more evident when I first perceived it and believed I knew it by my external senses, or at least by my so-called *common sense*,† in other words, by the power of imagination, or whether it is more perfect now, after I have investigated more carefully both what wax is and how it can be known. To entertain doubts about this matter would certainly be silly. For in my first perception of the wax what was distinct? What did I notice there that any animal might not be capable of capturing? But when I distinguish the wax from its external forms and look at it as something naked, as if I had stripped off its clothing, even though there could still be some error in my judgment, it is certain that I could not perceive it in this way without a human mind.

But what am I to say about this mind itself, in other words, about myself? For up to this point I am not admitting there is anything in me except mind. What, I say, is the *I* that seems to perceive this wax so distinctly? Do I not know myself not only much more truly and certainly, but also much more distinctly and clearly than I know the wax? For if I judge that the wax exists from the fact that I see it, then from the very fact that I see the wax it certainly follows much more clearly that I myself also exist. For it could be that what I see is not really wax. It could be the case that I do not have eyes at all with which to see anything. But when I see or think I see (at the moment I am not differentiating between these two), it is completely impossible that I, the one doing the thinking, am not something. For similar reasons, if I judge that the wax exists from the fact that I am touching it, the same conclusion follows once again, namely, that I exist. The result is clearly the same if [my judgment rests] on the fact that I imagine the wax or on any other reason at all. But these observations I have made about the wax can be applied to all other things located outside of me. Furthermore, if my perception of the wax seemed more distinct after it was drawn to my attention, not merely by sight or touch, but by several [other] causes, I must concede that I now

---

* Mechanical person-imitations; robots.
† This is the supposed mental faculty which unites the data from the five external senses—sight, smell, sound, touch, and taste—into a single sensory experience. The notion goes back to Aristotle, and is different from what we call "common sense" today.

understand myself much more distinctly, since all of those same reasons capable of assisting my perception either of the wax or of any other body whatsoever are even better proofs of the nature of my mind! However, over and above this, there are so many other things in the mind itself which can provide a more distinct conception of its [nature] that it hardly seems worthwhile to review those features of corporeal things which might contribute to it.

And behold—I have all on my own finally returned to the place where I wanted to be. For since I am now aware that bodies themselves are not properly perceived by the senses or by the faculty of imagination, but only by the intellect, and are not perceived because they are touched or seen, but only because they are understood, I realize this obvious point: there is nothing I can perceive more easily or more clearly than my own mind. But because it is impossible to rid oneself so quickly of an opinion one has long been accustomed to hold, I would like to pause here, in order to impress this new knowledge more deeply on my memory with a prolonged meditation.

Third Meditation: Concerning God and the Fact That He Exists

Now I will close my eyes, stop up my ears, and withdraw all my senses. I will even blot out from my thinking all images of corporeal things, or else, since this is hardly possible, I will dismiss them as empty and false images of nothing at all, and by talking only to myself and looking more deeply within, I will attempt, little by little, to acquire a greater knowledge of and more familiarity with myself. I am a thinking thing—in other words, something that doubts, affirms, denies, knows a few things, is ignorant of many things, wills, refuses, and also imagines and feels. For, as I have pointed out earlier, although those things which I sense or imagine outside of myself are perhaps nothing, nevertheless, I am certain that the thought processes I call sense experience and imagination, given that they are only certain modes of thinking, do exist within me.

In these few words, I have reviewed everything I truly know, or at least [everything] that, up to this point, I was aware I knew. Now I will look around more diligently, in case there are perhaps other things in me that I have not yet considered. I am certain that I am a thinking thing. But if that is the case, do I not

then also know what is required for me to be certain about something? There is, to be sure, nothing in this first knowledge other than a certain clear and distinct perception of what I am affirming, and obviously this would not be enough for me to be certain about the truth of the matter, if it could ever happen that something I perceived just as clearly and distinctly was false. And now it seems to me that now I can propose the following general rule: all those things I perceive very clearly and very distinctly are true.

However, before now I have accepted as totally certain and evident many things that I have later discovered to be doubtful. What, then, were these things? [They were], of course, the earth, the sky, the stars, and all the other things I used to grasp with my senses. But what did I clearly perceive in them? Obviously I was observing in my mind ideas or thoughts of such things. And even now I do not deny that those ideas exist within me. However, there was something else which I held to be true and which, because I was in the habit of believing it, I also thought I perceived clearly, although I really was not perceiving it at all, namely, that certain things existed outside of me from which those ideas proceeded and which were like them in every way. And here was where I went wrong, or, if anyway I was judging truthfully, that certainly was not the result of the strength of my perception.

What [then was] true? When I was thinking about something very simple and easy in arithmetic or geometry—for example, that two and three added together make five, and things of that sort—was I not recognizing these with sufficient clarity at least to affirm that they were true? Later on, to be sure, I did judge that such things could be doubted, but the only reason I did so was that it crossed my mind that some God could perhaps have placed within me a certain kind of nature, so that I deceived myself even about those things which appeared most obvious. And every time this preconceived opinion about the supreme power of God occurs to me, I cannot but confess that if He wished, it would be easy for Him to see to it that I go astray, even in those matters which I think I see as clearly as possible with my mind's eye. But whenever I turn my attention to those very things which I think I perceive with great clarity, I am so completely persuaded by them, that I spontaneously burst out with the following words: Let whoever can deceive me, do so; he will still never succeed in making me nothing, not while I think I am something, or in making it true someday that I never existed, since it is true that I exist now, or perhaps even in making two and three, when added together, more or less than five, or anything like that, in which I clearly recognize a manifest contradiction. And since I have no reason to think that some God exists who is a deceiver and since, up to this point, I do not know enough to state whether there is a God at all, it is clear that the reason for any doubt which rests on this supposition alone is very tenuous and, if I may say so, metaphysical. However, to remove even that doubt, as soon as the occasion presents itself, I ought to examine whether God exists and, if He does, whether He can be a deceiver. For as long as this point remains obscure, it seems to me that I can never be completely certain about anything else.

But now an orderly arrangement would seem to require that I first divide all of my thoughts into certain kinds and look into which of these [kinds], strictly speaking, contain truth or error. Some of my thoughts are, so to speak, images of things, and for these alone the name *idea* is appropriate, for example, when I think of a man, or a chimera, or the sky, or an angel, or God. But other thoughts, in addition to these, possess certain other forms. For example, when I will, when I fear, when I affirm, and when I deny, I always apprehend something as the object of my thinking, but in my thought I also grasp something more than the representation of that thing. In this [group of thoughts], some are called volitions* or feelings, and others judgments.

Now, where ideas are concerned, if I consider these only in and of themselves, not considering whether they refer to anything else, they cannot, strictly speaking, be false. For whether I imagine a goat or a chimera, it is no less true that I imagine one than it is that I imagine the other. And we also need have no fear of error in willing or in feeling, for although I can desire something evil or even things which have never existed, that still does not make the fact that I desire them untrue. And thus, all that remains are judgments, in which I must take care not to be deceived. But the most important and most frequent error I can discover in judgments consists of the fact that I judge the ideas within me are similar to or conform to certain things located outside myself. For obviously, if I considered ideas themselves only as certain modes of my thinking, without considering their reference to anything else, they would hardly furnish me any material for making a mistake.

Of these ideas, some, it seems to me, are innate,† others come from outside, and still others I have myself made up. For the fact that I understand what a thing is, what truth is, and what thinking is I seem to possess from no source other than my own nature. But if I now hear a noise, see the sun, or feel heat, I have up to now judged that [these sensations] come from certain things placed outside of me. And, finally, sirens, hippogriffs,‡ and such like are things I myself dream up. But perhaps I could also believe that all [these ideas] come from outside, or else are all innate, or else are all made up, for I have not yet clearly perceived their true origin.

However, the most important point I have to explore here concerns those ideas which I think of as being derived from objects existing outside me: What reason leads me to suppose that these ideas are similar to those objects? It certainly seems that I am taught to think this way by nature. Furthermore, I know by experience that these [ideas] do not depend on my will and therefore not on me myself, for they often present themselves to me even against my will. For example, whether I will it or not, I now feel heat, and thus I believe that the feeling or the idea of heat reaches me from some object apart from me, that is, from [the heat] of the fire I am sitting beside. And nothing is more obvious than my judgment that this object is sending its own likeness into me rather than something else.

I will now see whether these reasons are sufficiently strong. When I say here that I have been taught to think this way by nature, I understand only that I have been carried by a certain spontaneous impulse to believe it, not that some natural light has revealed its truth to me. There is an important difference between

---

*   Acts of decision-making.

†   Inborn—an idea that is already inside me.

‡   In Greek mythology, sirens are half woman, half bird; hippogriffs are combinations of horse and griffin (which is part eagle, part lion).

these two things. For whatever natural light reveals to me—for example, that from the fact that I am doubting it follows that I exist, and things like that—cannot admit of any possible doubt, because there cannot be another faculty [in me] as trustworthy as natural light, one which could teach me that the ideas [derived from natural light] are not true. But where natural impulses are concerned, in the past, when there was an issue of choosing the good thing to do, I often judged that such impulses were pushing me in the direction of something worse, and I do not see why I should place more trust in them in any other matters.

Moreover, although those ideas do not depend on my will, it is not therefore the case that they must come from objects located outside of me. For just as those impulses I have been talking about above are within me and yet seem to be different from my will, so perhaps there is also some other faculty in me, one I do not yet understand sufficiently, which produces those ideas, in the same way they have always appeared to be formed in me up to now while I sleep, without the help of any external objects [which they represent].

Finally, even if these ideas did come from things different from me, it does not therefore follow that they have to be like those things. Quite the contrary, for in numerous cases I seem to have often observed a great difference [between the object and the idea]. So, for example, I find in my mind two different ideas of the sun. One, which is apparently derived from the senses and should certainly be included among what I consider ideas coming from outside, makes the sun appear very small to me. However, the other, which is derived from astronomical reasoning, that is, elicited by certain notions innate in me or else produced by me in some other manner, makes the sun appear many times larger than the earth. Clearly, these two [ideas] cannot both resemble the sun which exists outside of me, and reason convinces [me] that the one which seems to have emanated most immediately from the sun itself is the least like it.

All these points offer me sufficient proof that previously, when I believed that certain things existed apart from me that conveyed ideas or images of themselves, whether by my organs of sense or by some other means, my judgment was not based on anything certain but only on some blind impulse.

However, it crosses my mind that there is still another way of exploring whether certain things of which I have ideas within me exist outside of me. To the extent that those ideas are [considered] merely certain ways of thinking, of course, I do not recognize any inequality among them, and they all appear to proceed from me in the same way. But to the extent that one idea represents one thing, while another idea represents something else, it is clear that they are very different from each other. For undoubtedly those that represent substances to me and contain in themselves more objective reality, so to speak, are something more than those that simply represent modes or accidents.[*] And, once again, that idea thanks to which I am aware of a supreme God—eternal, infinite, omniscient, omnipotent,[†] the Creator of all things that exist outside of Him—certainly has more objective reality in it than those ideas through which finite substances are represented.

Now, it is surely evident by natural light that there must be at least as much [reality] in the efficient and total cause as there is in the effect of this cause. For from where, I would like to know, can the effect receive its reality if not from its cause? And how can the cause provide this reality to the effect, unless the cause also possesses it? But from this it follows that something cannot be made from nothing and also that what is more perfect, that is, contains more reality in itself, cannot be produced from what is less perfect. This is obviously true not only of those effects whose reality is [what the philosophers call] actual or formal, but also of those ideas in which we consider only [what they call] objective reality. For example, some stone which has not previously existed cannot now begin to exist, unless it is produced by something which has in it, either formally or eminently, everything that goes into the stone,[‡] and heat cannot be brought into an object which was not warm previously, except by

---

* See the Introduction for background information on "substance," "accident," "objective reality," and "formal reality."
† To be omniscient is to be all-knowing; to be omnipotent is to be infinitely powerful.
‡ That is, it has either the same properties as the stone (e.g., a certain hardness) or possesses even more perfect or pronounced versions of those properties (e.g., perfect hardness). An effect is "eminently" in a cause when the cause is more perfect than the effect.

something which is of an order at least as perfect as heat, and so on with all the other examples. But beyond this, even the idea of heat or of the stone cannot exist within me, unless it is placed in me by some cause containing at least as much reality as I understand to be in the heat or in the stone. For although that cause does not transfer anything of its own reality, either actual or formal, into my idea, one should not therefore assume that [this cause] must be less real. Instead, [we should consider] that the nature of the idea itself is such that it requires from itself no formal reality other than what it derives from my own thinking, of which it is a mode [that is, a way or style of thinking]. But for the idea to possess this objective reality rather than another, it must surely obtain it from some cause in which there is at least as much formal reality as the objective reality contained in the idea itself. For if we assume that something can be discovered in the idea which was not present in its cause, then it must have obtained this from nothing. But no matter how imperfect the mode of being may be by which a thing is objectively present in the understanding through its idea, that mode is certainly not nothing, and therefore [this idea] cannot come from nothing.

And although the reality which I am considering in my ideas is only objective, I must not imagine that it is unnecessary for the same reality to exist formally in the causes of those ideas, that it is sufficient if [the reality] in them is objective as well. For just as that mode of existing objectively belongs to ideas by their very nature, so the mode of existing formally belongs to the causes of [these] ideas, at least to the first and most important causes, by their nature. And although it may well be possible for one idea to be born from another, still this regress cannot continue on *ad infinitum*,* for we must finally come to some first [idea], whose cause is, as it were, the archetype [or original idea], which formally contains the entire reality that exists only objectively in the idea. And thus natural light makes it clear to me that ideas exist within me as certain images that can, in fact, easily fall short of the perfection of the things from which they were derived but that cannot contain anything greater or more perfect than those things do.

And the more time and care I take examining these things, the more clearly and distinctly I recognize their truth. But what am I finally to conclude from them? It is clear that if the objective reality of any of my ideas is so great that I am certain that the same reality is not in me either formally or eminently and that therefore I myself cannot be the cause of that idea, it necessarily follows that I am not alone in the world but that some other thing also exists which is the cause of that idea. But if I do not find any such idea within me, then I will obviously have no argument that confirms for me the existence of anything beyond myself. For I have been searching very diligently and have not been able to find any other argument up to now.

But of these ideas of mine, apart from the one which reveals my own self to me, about which there can be no difficulty, there is another [that represents] God [to me], and there are others which represent corporeal and inanimate things, as well as others representing angels, animals, and finally other men who resemble me.

As far as concerns those ideas which display other human beings or animals or angels, I understand readily enough that I could have put these together from ideas I have of myself, of corporeal things, and of God, even though there might be no people apart from me or animals or angels in the world.

Where the ideas of corporeal things are concerned, I see nothing in them so great that it seems as if it could not have originated within me. For if I inspect these ideas thoroughly and examine them individually in the same way I did yesterday with the idea of the wax, I notice that there are only a very few things I perceive in them clearly and distinctly—for example, magnitude or extension in length, breadth, and depth; shape, which emerges from the limits of that extension; position, which different forms derive from their relation to each other; and motion or a change of location. To these one can add substance, duration, and number. However, with the other things, like light, colours, sounds, odours, tastes, heat, cold, and other tactile qualities, my thoughts of them involve so much confusion and obscurity, that I still do not know whether they are true or false—in other words, whether the ideas I have of these [qualities] are ideas of things or of non-things. For although I observed a little earlier that falsehood (or, strictly speaking, formal falsehood) could occur only in judgments, nonetheless

---

* Forever (to infinity).

there is, in fact, a certain other material falsehood in ideas, when they represent a non-thing as if it were a thing. Thus, for example, ideas which I have of heat and cold are so unclear and indistinct that I am not able to learn from them whether cold is merely a lack of heat, or heat a lack of cold, or whether both of these are real qualities, or whether neither [of them is]. And because there can be no ideas which are not, as it were, ideas of things, if it is indeed true that cold is nothing other than a lack of heat, the idea which represents cold to me as if it were something positive and real will not improperly be called false, and that will also hold for all other ideas [like this].

To such ideas I obviously do not have to assign any author other than myself, for, if they are, in fact, false, that is, if they represent things which do not exist, my natural light informs me that they proceed from nothing—in other words, that they are in me only because there is something lacking in my nature, which is not wholly perfect. If, on the other hand, they are true, given that the reality they present to me is so slight that I cannot distinguish the object from something which does not exist, then I do not see why I could not have come up with them myself.

As for those details which are clear and distinct in my ideas of corporeal things, some of them, it seems to me, I surely could have borrowed from the idea of myself, namely, substance, duration, number, and other things like that. I conceive of myself as a thinking and non-extended thing, but of the stone as an extended thing which does not think; so there is a great difference between the two; but nevertheless, I think of both as *substance*, something equipped to exist on its own. In the same way, when I perceive that I now exist and also remember that I have existed for some time earlier and when I have various thoughts whose number I recognize, I acquire ideas of *duration* and *number*, which I can then transfer to any other things I choose. As for all the other qualities from which I put together my ideas of corporeal things, that is, extension, shape, location, and motion, they are, it is true, not formally contained in me, since I am nothing other than a thinking thing, but because they are merely certain modes of a substance and I, too, am a substance, it seems that they could be contained in me eminently.

And so the only thing remaining is the idea of God. I must consider whether there is anything in this idea for which I myself could not have been the origin. By the name *God* I understand a certain infinite, [eternal, immutable,] independent, supremely intelligent, and supremely powerful substance by which I myself was created, along with everything else that exists (if, [in fact], anything else does exist). All of these [properties] are clearly [so great] that the more diligently I focus on them, the less it seems that I could have brought them into being by myself alone. And thus, from what I have said earlier, I logically have to conclude that God necessarily exists.

For although the idea of a substance is, indeed, in me—because I am a substance—that still does not mean [that I possess] the idea of an infinite substance, since I am finite, unless it originates in some other substance which is truly infinite.

And I should not think that my perception of the infinite comes, not from a true idea, but merely from a negation of the finite, in [the same] way I perceive rest and darkness by a negation of motion and light. For, on the contrary, I understand clearly that there is more reality in an infinite substance than in a finite one and that therefore my perception of the infinite is somehow in me before my perception of the finite—in other words, my perception of God comes before my perception of myself. For how would I know that I am doubting or desiring, or, in other words, that something is lacking in me and that I am not entirely perfect, unless some idea of a perfect being was in me and I recognized my defects by a comparison?

And one cannot claim that this idea of God might well be materially false and thus could have come from nothing, the way I observed a little earlier with the ideas of heat and cold and things like that. Quite the reverse: for [this idea] is extremely clear and distinct and contains more objective reality than any other, and thus no idea will be found which is more inherently true and in which there is less suspicion of falsehood. This idea, I say, of a supremely perfect and infinite being is utterly true, for although it may well be possible to imagine that such a being does not exist, it is still impossible to imagine that the idea of Him does not reveal anything real to me, in the way I talked above about the idea of cold. This idea of a perfect Being is also entirely clear and distinct, for whatever I see clearly and distinctly which is real and true and which introduces some perfection is totally contained within [this idea]. The fact that I cannot comprehend the infinite or that there are innumerable other things in God that I do not understand or even perhaps have any way of contacting in my thoughts—all this is irrelevant. For something finite, like myself, cannot comprehend the nature of the infinite, and it is sufficient that I understand this very point and judge that all things which I perceive clearly and which I know convey some perfection, as well as innumerable others perhaps which I know nothing about, are in God, either formally or eminently, so that the idea I have of Him is the truest, clearest, and most distinct of all the ideas within me.

But perhaps I am something more than I myself understand, and all those perfections which I attribute to God are potentially in me somehow, even though they are not yet evident and are not manifesting themselves in action. For I already know by experience that my knowledge is gradually increasing, and I do not see anything which could prevent it from increasing more and more to infinity. Nor do I even know of any reasons why, with my knowledge augmented in this way, I could not, with its help, acquire all the other perfections of God or, finally, why, if the power [to acquire] those perfections is already in me, it would not be sufficient to produce the idea of those perfections.

And yet none of these things is possible. For, in the first place, although it is true that my knowledge is gradually increasing and that there are potentially many things within me which have not yet been realized, still none of these is relevant to the idea of God, in which, of course, nothing at all exists potentially. For the very fact that my knowledge is increasing little by little is the most certain argument for its imperfection. Beyond that, even if my knowledge is always growing more and more, nonetheless, that does not convince me that it will ever be truly infinite, since it can never reach a stage where it is not capable of increasing any further. But I judge that God is actually infinite, so that nothing can possibly be added to His perfection. And lastly, I perceive that the objective existence of an idea cannot be produced from a being that is merely potential, which, strictly speaking, is nothing, but only from something which actually or formally exists.

Obviously everything in all these thoughts is evident to the natural light in anyone who reflects carefully [on the matter]. But when I pay less attention and when images of sensible* things obscure the vision in my mind, I do not so readily remember why the idea of a being more perfect than myself must necessarily proceed from some entity that is truly more perfect than me. Therefore, I would like to enquire further whether I, who possess this idea [of God], could exist if such a being did not exist.

If that were the case, then from whom would I derive my existence? Clearly from myself or from my parents or from some other source less perfect than God. For we cannot think of or imagine anything more perfect than God or even anything equally perfect.

However, if I originated from myself, then I would not doubt or hope, and I would lack nothing at all, for I would have given myself all the perfections of which I have any idea within me, and thus I myself would be God. I must not assume that those things which I lack might be more difficult to acquire than those now within me. On the contrary, it clearly would have been much more difficult for me—that is, a thinking thing or substance—to emerge from nothing than to acquire a knowledge of the many things about which I am ignorant, for knowing such things is merely an accident of that thinking substance. And surely if I had obtained from myself that greater perfection [of being the author of my own existence], then I could hardly have denied myself the perfections which are easier to acquire, or, indeed, any of those I perceive contained in the idea of God, since, it seems to me, none of them is more difficult to produce. But if there were some perfections more difficult to acquire, they would certainly appear more difficult to me, too, if, indeed, everything else I possessed was derived from myself, because from them I would learn by experience that my power was limited.

And I will not escape the force of these arguments by assuming that I might perhaps have always been the way I am now, as if it followed from that assumption that I would not have to seek out any author for my own existence. For since the entire period of my life can be divided into innumerable parts each one of which is in no way dependent on the others, therefore, just because I existed a little while ago, it does not follow

---

* I.e., things that can be perceived with the physical senses.

that I must exist now, unless at this very moment some cause is, at it were, creating me once again—in other words, preserving me. For it is clear to anyone who directs attention to the nature of time that, in order for the existence of anything at all to be preserved in each particular moment it lasts, that thing surely needs the same force and action which would be necessary to create it anew if it did not yet exist. Thus, one of the things natural light reveals is that preservation and creation are different only in the ways we think of them.

Consequently, I now ought to ask myself whether I have any power which enables me to bring it about that I, who am now existing, will also exist a little later on, for since I am nothing other than a thinking thing—or at least since my precise concern at the moment is only with that part of me which is a thinking thing—if such a power is in me, I would undoubtedly be conscious of it. But I experience nothing [of that sort], and from this fact alone I recognize with the utmost clarity that I depend upon some being different from myself.

But perhaps that being is not God, and I have been produced by my parents or by some other causes less perfect than God. But [that is impossible]. As I have already said before, it is clear that there must be at least as much [reality] in the cause as in the effect and that thus, since I am a thinking thing and have a certain idea of God within me, I must concede that whatever I finally designate as my own cause is also a thinking substance containing the idea of all the perfections I attribute to God. It is possible once again to ask whether that cause originates from itself or from something else. If it comes from itself, then, given what I have said, it is obvious that the cause itself is God. For clearly, if it derives its power of existing from itself, it also undoubtedly has the power of actually possessing all the perfections whose idea it contains within itself, that is, all those that I think of as existing in God. But if it is produced from some other cause, then I ask once again in the same way whether this cause comes from itself or from some other cause, until I finally reach a final cause, which will be God.

For it is clear enough that this questioning cannot produce an infinite regress, particularly because the issue I am dealing with here is a matter not only of the cause which once produced me but also—and most importantly—of the cause which preserves me at the present time.

And I cannot assume that perhaps a number of partial causes came together to produce me and that from one of them I received the idea of one of the perfections I attribute to God and from another the idea of another perfection, so that all those perfections are indeed found somewhere in the universe, but they are not all joined together in a single being who is God. Quite the contrary, [for] the unity and simplicity—or the inseparability of all those things present in God—is one of the principal perfections which I recognize in Him. And surely the idea of this unity of all His perfections could not have been placed in me by any cause from which I did not acquire ideas of the other perfections as well, for no single cause could have made it possible for me to understand that those perfections were joined together and inseparable, unless at the same time it enabled me to recognize what those perfections were.

And finally, concerning my parents, even if everything I have ever believed about them is true, it is perfectly clear that they are not the ones who preserve me and that, to the extent that I am a thinking thing, there is no way they could have even made me. Instead they merely produced certain arrangements in the material substance which, as I have judged the matter, contains me—that is, contains my mind, for that is all I assume I am at the moment. And thus the fact that my parents contributed to my existence provides no problem for my argument. Given all this, however, from the mere fact that I exist and that I have the idea of a supremely perfect being, or God, I must conclude that I have provided an extremely clear proof that God does, indeed, exist.

All that is left now is to examine how I have received that idea from God. For I have not derived it from the senses, and it has never come to me unexpectedly, as habitually occurs with the ideas of things I perceive with the senses, when those ideas of external substances impinge, or seem to impinge, on my sense organs. Nor is it something I just made up, for I am completely unable to remove anything from it or add anything to it. Thus, all that remains is that the idea is innate in me, just as the idea of myself is also innate in me.

And obviously it is not strange that God, when He created me, placed that idea within me, so that it would be, as it were, the mark of the master craftsman impressed in his own work—not that it is at all necessary for this mark to be different from the work itself. But the fact that God created me makes it highly believable that He made me in some way in His image and likeness, and that I perceive this likeness, which contains the idea of God, by the same faculty with which I perceive myself. In other words, when I turn my mind's eye onto myself, I not only understand that I am an incomplete thing, dependent on something else, and one that aspires [constantly] to greater and better things without limit, but at the same time I also realize that the one I depend on contains within Himself all those greater things [to which I aspire], not merely indefinitely and potentially, but actually and infinitely, and thus that He is God. The entire force of my argument rests on the fact that I recognize I could not possibly exist with the sort of nature I possess, namely, having the idea of God within me, unless God truly existed as well—that God, I say, whose idea is in me—the Being having all those perfections which I do not grasp but which I am somehow capable of touching in my thoughts, and who is entirely free of any defect. These reasons are enough to show that He cannot be a deceiver, for natural light clearly demonstrates that every fraud and deception depends upon some defect.

But before I examine this matter more carefully and at the same time look into other truths I could derive from it, I wish to pause here for a while to contemplate God himself, to ponder His attributes, and to consider, admire, and adore the beauty of His immense light, to the extent that the eyes of my darkened intellect can bear it. For just as we believe through faith that the supreme happiness of our life hereafter consists only in this contemplation of the Divine Majesty, so we know from experience that the same [contemplation] now, though far less perfect, is the greatest joy we are capable of in this life.

Fourth Meditation: Concerning Truth and Falsity

In these last few days, I have grown accustomed to detaching my mind from my senses, and I have clearly noticed that, in fact, I perceive very little with any certainty about corporeal things and that I know a great deal more about the human mind and even more about God. As a result, I now have no difficulty directing my thoughts away from things I [perceive with the senses or] imagine, and onto those purely intellectual matters divorced from all material substance. And clearly the idea I have of the human mind, to the extent that it

is a thinking thing that has no extension in length, breadth, and depth and possesses nothing else which the body has, is much more distinct than my idea of any corporeal substance. Now, when I direct my attention to the fact that I have doubts, in other words, that [I am] something incomplete and dependent, the really clear and distinct idea of an independent and complete being, that is, of God, presents itself to me. From this one fact—that there is an idea like this in me—or else because of the fact that I, who possess this idea, exist, I draw the clear conclusion that God also exists and that my entire existence depends on Him every single moment [of my life]. Thus, I believe that the human intellect can know nothing with greater clarity and greater certainty. And now it seems to me I see a way by which I can go from this contemplation of the true God, in whom all the treasures of science and wisdom are hidden, to an understanding of everything else.

First of all, I recognize that it is impossible that God would ever deceive me, for one discovers some sort of imperfection in everything false or deceptive. And although it may appear that the ability to deceive is evidence of a certain cleverness or power, the wish to deceive undoubtedly demonstrates either malice or mental weakness, and is therefore not found in God.

Then, I know from experience that there is in me a certain faculty of judgment, which I certainly received from God, like all the other things within me. Since He is unwilling to deceive me, He obviously did not give me the kind of faculty that could ever lead me into error, if I used it correctly.

There would remain no doubt about this, if it did not seem to lead to the conclusion that I could never make mistakes. For if whatever is within me I have from God and if He did not give me any power to commit errors, it would appear that I could never make a mistake. Now, it is true that as long as I am thinking only about God and directing myself totally to Him, I detect no reason for errors or falsity. But after a while, when I turn back to myself, I know by experience that I am still subject to innumerable errors. When I seek out their cause, I notice that I can picture not only a certain real and positive [idea] of God, or of a supremely perfect being, but also, so to speak, a certain negative idea of nothingness, or of something removed as far as possible from every perfection, and [I recognize] that I am, as it were, something intermediate between God and nothingness—that is, that

I am situated between a supreme being and non-being in such a way that, insofar as I was created by a supreme being, there is, in fact, nothing in me which would deceive me or lead me into error, but insofar as I also participate, to a certain extent, in nothingness or non-being—in other words, given that I myself am not a supreme being—I lack a great many things. Therefore, it is not strange that I am deceived. From this I understand that error, to the extent that it is error, is not something real which depends on God, but is merely a defect. Thus, for me to fall into error, it is not necessary that I have been given a specific power to do this by God. Instead, I happen to make mistakes because the power I have of judging what is true [and what is false], which I do have from God, is not infinite within me.

However, this is not yet entirely satisfactory, for error is not pure negation, but rather the privation or lack of a certain knowledge that somehow ought to be within me. But to anyone who thinks about the nature of God, it does not seem possible that He would place within me any power that is not a perfect example of its kind or that lacks some perfection it ought to have. For [if it is true] that the greater the skill of the craftsman, the more perfect the works he produces, what could the supreme maker of all things create which was not perfect in all its parts? And there is no doubt that God could have created me in such a way that I was never deceived, and, similarly, there is no doubt that He always wills what is best. So then, is it better for me to make mistakes or not to make them?

As I weigh these matters more attentively, it occurs to me, first, that I should not find it strange if I do not understand the reasons for some of the things God does; thus I should not entertain doubts about His existence just because I happen to learn from experience about certain other things and do not grasp why or how He has created them. For given the fact that I already know my nature is extremely infirm and limited and that, by contrast, the nature of God is immense, incomprehensible, and infinite,

I understand sufficiently well that He is capable of innumerable things about whose causes I am ignorant. For that reason alone, I believe that the entire class of causes we are in the habit of searching out as *final causes** is completely useless in matters of physics, for I do not think I am capable of investigating the final purposes of God without appearing foolhardy.

It also occurs to me that, whenever we look into whether the works of God are perfect, we should not examine one particular creature by itself, but rather the universal totality of things. For something which may well justly appear, by itself, very imperfect, is utterly perfect [if we think of it] as part of the [entire] universe. And although, given my wish to doubt everything, I have up to now recognized nothing as certain, other than the existence of myself and God, nonetheless, since I have observed the immense power of God, I cannot deny that He may have created many other things or at least is capable of creating them and therefore that I may occupy a place in a universe of things.

After that, by examining myself more closely and looking into the nature of my errors (the only things testifying to some imperfection in me), I observe that they proceed from two causes working together simultaneously, namely, from the faculty of knowing, which I possess, and from the faculty of choosing, or from my freedom to choose—in other words from both the intellect and the will together. For through my intellect alone I [do not affirm or deny anything, but] simply grasp the ideas of things about which I can make a judgment, and, if I consider my intellect in precisely this way, I find nothing there which is, strictly speaking, an error. For although countless things may well exist of which I have no idea at all within me, I still should not assert that I am deprived of them, in the proper sense of that word, [as if that knowledge were something my understanding was entitled to thanks to its nature]. I can only make the negative claim that I do not have them, for obviously I can produce no reason which enables me to prove that God ought to have

---

* The final cause of something is (roughly) the purpose or reason for that thing's existence: e.g., the final cause of a statue might be an original idea or artistic goal in the sculptor's head which prompted her to make that particular statue. This terminology goes back to Aristotle, and involves a contrast between final causes and three other sorts of cause—material causes (the marble out of which the statue is hewn), formal causes (the shape—the form—of the statue), and efficient causes (the sculptor's craft in making the statue).

given me a greater power of understanding than He has provided. And although I know that a craftsman is an expert, still I do not assume that he must therefore place in each of his works all the perfections he is capable of placing in some. Moreover, I certainly cannot complain that I have received from God a will or a freedom to choose that is insufficiently ample and perfect. For I clearly know from experience that my will is not circumscribed by any limits. And what seems to me particularly worthy of notice is the fact that, apart from my will, there is nothing in me so perfect or so great that I do not recognize that it could be still more perfect or even greater. For, to consider an example: if I think about the power of understanding, I see at once that in me it is very small and extremely limited. At the same time, I form an idea of another understanding which is much greater, even totally great and infinite, and from the mere fact that I can form this idea, I see that it pertains to the nature of God. By the same reasoning, if I examine my faculty of memory or of imagination or any other faculty, I find none at all which I do not recognize as tenuous and confined in me and immense in God. It is only my will or my freedom to choose which I experience as so great in me that I do not apprehend the idea of anything greater. Thus, through my will, more than through anything else, I understand that I bear a certain image of and resemblance to God. For although the will is incomparably greater in God than in myself—because the knowledge and power linked to it make it much stronger and more efficacious and because, with respect to its object, His will extends to more things—nonetheless, if I think of the will formally and precisely in and of itself, His does not appear greater than mine. For the power of will consists only in the ability to do or not to do [something] (that is, to affirm or to deny, to follow or to avoid)—or rather in this one thing alone, that whether we affirm or deny, follow or avoid [something] which our understanding has set before us, we act in such a way that we do not feel that any external force is determining what we do. For to be free, I do not have to be inclined in two [different] directions. On the contrary, the more I am inclined to one—whether that is because I understand that the principle of the true and the good are manifestly in it or because that is the way God has arranged the inner core of my thinking—the more freely I choose it. Clearly divine grace and natural knowledge never

diminish liberty, but rather increase and strengthen it. However, the indifference I experience when there is no reason urging me to one side more than to the other is the lowest degree of liberty. It does not demonstrate any perfection in [the will], but rather a defect in my understanding or else a certain negation. For if I always clearly perceived what is true and good, I would never need to deliberate about what I ought to be judging or choosing, and thus, although I would be entirely free, I could never be indifferent.

For these reasons, however, I perceive that the power of willing, which I have from God, considered in itself, is not the source of my errors. For it is extremely ample and perfect. And the source is not my power of understanding. For when I understand something, I undoubtedly do so correctly, since my [power of] understanding comes from God, and thus it is impossible for it to deceive me. So from where do my errors arise? Surely from the single fact that my will ranges more widely than my intellect, and I do not keep it within the same limits but extend it even to those things which I do not understand. Since the will does not discriminate among these things, it easily turns away from the true and the good, and, in this way, I make mistakes and transgress.

For example, in the past few days, when I was examining whether anything in the world existed and I observed that, from the very fact that I was exploring this [question], it clearly followed that I existed, I was not able [to prevent myself] from judging that what I understood so clearly was true, not because I was forced to that conclusion by any external force, but because a great light in my understanding was followed by a great inclination in my will, and thus the less I was indifferent to the issue, the more spontaneous and free was my belief. For example: now I know that I exist, to the extent I am a thinking thing; but I am in doubt about whether this thinking nature within me (rather, which I myself *am*) is of that corporeal nature also revealed to me. I assume that up to this point no reason has offered itself to my understanding which might convince me that I am, or am not, of corporeal nature. From this single fact it is clear that I am indifferent as to which of the two I should affirm or deny, or whether I should even make any judgment in the matter.

Furthermore, this indifference extends not merely to those things about which the understanding knows nothing at all, but also, in general, to everything which it does not recognize with sufficient clarity at the time when the will is deliberating about them. For, however probable the conjectures [may be] which draw me in one direction, the mere knowledge that they are only conjectures and not certain and indubitable reasons is enough to urge me to assent to the opposite view. In the past few days I have learned this well enough by experience, once I assumed that all those things I had previously accepted as absolutely true were utterly false, because of the single fact that I discovered they could in some way be doubted.

But when I do not perceive that something is true with sufficient clarity and distinctness, if, in fact, I abstain from rendering judgment, I am obviously acting correctly and am not deceived. But if at that time I affirm or deny, [then] I am not using my freedom to choose properly. If I make up my mind [and affirm] something false, then, of course I will be deceived. On the other hand, if I embrace the alternative, then I may, indeed, hit upon the truth by chance, but that would not free me from blame, since natural light makes it clear that a perception of the understanding must always precede a determination of the will. And it is in this incorrect use of the freedom of the will that one finds the privation which constitutes the nature of error. Privation, I say, inheres in this act of the will, to the extent that it proceeds from me, but not in the faculty I have received from God, nor even in the act, insofar as it depends upon Him.

For I have no cause to complain at all about the fact that God has not given me a greater power of understanding or a more powerful natural light than He has, because it is in the nature of a finite intellect not to understand many things and it is in the nature of a created intellect to be finite. Instead, I should thank Him, who has never owed me anything, for His generosity, rather than thinking that He has deprived me of something He did not provide or else has taken it away.

And I also have no reason to complain on the ground that He gave me a will more extensive than my understanding. For since the will consists of only a single thing and is, so to speak, indivisible, it does not seem that its nature is such that anything could be removed [without destroying it]. And, of course, the more extensive my will, the more I ought to show gratitude to the one who gave it to me.

And finally I also ought not to complain because God concurs with me in bringing out those acts of will or those judgments in which I am deceived. For those actions are true and good in every way, to the extent that they depend on God, and in a certain way there is more perfection in me because I am capable of eliciting these actions than if I were not. But privation, in which one finds the only formal reason for falsity and failure, has no need of God's concurrence, because it is not a thing, and if one links it to Him as its cause, one should not call it privation but merely negation. For obviously it is not an imperfection in God that He has given me freedom to assent or not to assent to certain things, when He has not placed a clear and distinct perception of them in my understanding. However, it is undoubtedly an imperfection in me that I do not use that liberty well and that I bring my judgment to bear on things which I do not properly understand. Nonetheless, I see that God could easily have created me so that I never made mistakes, even though I remained free and had a limited understanding. For example, He could have placed in my intellect a clear and distinct perception of everything about which I would ever deliberate, or He could have impressed on my memory that I should never make judgments about things which I did not understand clearly and distinctly, and done that so firmly that it would be impossible for me ever to forget. And I readily understand that, if God had made me that way, insofar as I have an idea of this totality, I would have been more perfect than I am now. But I cannot therefore deny that there may somehow be more perfection in this whole universe of things because some of its parts are not immune to errors and others are—more perfection than if all things were entirely alike. And I have no right to complain just because the part God wanted me to play in the universe is not the most important and most perfect of all.

Besides, even if I am unable to avoid errors in the first way [mentioned above], which depends upon a clear perception of all those things about which I need to deliberate, I can still use that other [method], which requires me only to remember to abstain from rendering judgment every time the truth of something is not evident. For although experience teaches me that I have a weakness which renders me incapable of keeping [my mind] always focused on one and the same thought, I can still see to it that by attentive and frequently repeated meditation I remember that fact every time the occasion demands. In this way I will acquire the habit of not making mistakes.

Since the greatest and preeminent perfection of human beings consists in this ability to avoid mistakes, I think that with the discovery in today's meditation of the cause of error and falsity I have gained a considerable gift. Clearly the source of mistakes can be nothing other than what I have identified. For as long as I keep my will restrained when I deliver judgments, so that it extends itself only to those things which reveal themselves clearly and distinctly to my understanding, I will surely be incapable of making mistakes, because every clear and distinct perception is undoubtedly something [real]. Therefore, it cannot exist from nothing but necessarily has God as its author—God, I say, that supremely perfect being, who would contradict His nature if He were deceitful. And thus, [such a perception] is unquestionably true. I have learned today not only what I must avoid in order to ensure that I am never deceived, but also at the same time what I must do in order to reach the truth. For I will assuredly reach that if I only pay sufficient attention to all the things I understand perfectly and distinguish these from all the other things which I apprehend confusedly and obscurely. In future, I will pay careful attention to this matter.

Fifth Meditation: Concerning the Essence of Material Things, and, Once Again, Concerning the Fact That God Exists

Many other [issues] concerning the attributes of God are still left for me to examine, [as well as] many things about myself, that is, about the nature of my mind. However, I will perhaps return to those at another time. Now (after I have taken note of what I must avoid and what I must do to arrive at the truth) nothing seems to be more pressing than for me to attempt to emerge from the doubts into which I have fallen in the last few days and to see whether I can know anything certain about material things.

But before I look into whether any such substances exist outside of me, I ought to consider the ideas of them, insofar as they are in my thinking, and see which of them are distinct and which confused.

For example, I distinctly imagine quantity (which philosophers commonly refer to as 'continuous' quantity)—that is, the length, breadth and depth of the quantity, or rather, of the object being quantified. Further, I enumerate the various parts of the object, and assign to those parts all sorts of sizes, shapes, locations, and local movements, and to those movements all sorts of durations.

And in this way I not only clearly observe and acquire knowledge of those things when I examine them in general, but later, by devoting my attention to them, I also perceive innumerable particular details about their shapes, number, motion, and so on, whose truth is so evident and so well suited to my nature, that when I discover them for the first time, it seems that I am remembering what I used to know, rather than learning anything new, or else noticing for the first time things which were truly within me earlier, although I had not previously directed my mental gaze on them.

I believe that the most important issue for me to consider here is that I find within me countless ideas of certain things which, even if they perhaps do not exist outside of me at all, still cannot be called nothing. Although in a certain sense I can think of them whenever I wish, still I do not create them. They have their own true and immutable natures. For example, when I imagine a triangle whose particular shape perhaps does not exist and has never existed outside my thinking, it nevertheless has, in fact, a certain determinate nature or essence or form which is immutable and eternal, which I did not produce, and which does not depend upon my mind; this is clearly shown in the fact that I can demonstrate the various properties of that triangle, namely, that the sum of its three angles is equal to two right angles, that the triangle's longest side has its endpoints on the lines made by the triangle's largest angle, and so on. These properties I now recognize clearly whether I wish to or not, although earlier, when I imagined the triangle [for the first time], I was not thinking of them at all and therefore did not invent them.

In this case it is irrelevant if I tell [myself] that perhaps this idea of a triangle came to me from external things through my sense organs, on the ground that I have certainly now and then seen objects possessing a triangular shape. For I am able to think up countless other shapes about which there can be no suspicion that they ever flowed into me through my senses, and yet [I can] demonstrate various properties about them, no less than I can about the triangle. All these properties are *something* and not pure nothingness, since I conceive of them clearly and distinctly, and, as I have shown above, thus they must be true. Besides, even if I had not proved this, the nature of my mind is certainly such that I cannot refuse to assent to them, at least for as long as I am perceiving them clearly. And I remember that, even in those earlier days, when I was attracted as strongly as possible to objects of sense experience, I always maintained that the most certain things of all were those kinds of truth which I recognized clearly as shapes, numbers, or other things pertinent to arithmetic or geometry or to pure and abstract mathematics generally.

But if it follows from the mere fact that I can draw the idea of some object from my thinking that all things which I perceive clearly and distinctly as pertaining to that object really do belong to it, can I not also derive from this an argument which proves that God exists? For clearly I find the idea of Him, that is, of a supremely perfect being, within me just as much as I do the idea of some shape or number. I know that [actual and] eternal existence belongs to His nature just as clearly and distinctly as [I know] that what I prove about some shape or number also belongs to the nature of that shape or number. And therefore, even if all the things I have meditated on in the preceding days were not true, for me the existence of God ought to have at least the same degree of certainty as [I have recognized] up to this point in the truths of mathematics.

At first glance, however, this argument does not look entirely logical but [appears to] contain some sort of sophistry.* For, since in all other matters I have been accustomed to distinguish existence from essence, I can easily persuade myself that [existence] can also be separated from the essence of God and thus that I [can] think of God as not actually existing. However, when I think about this more carefully, it becomes clear that one cannot separate existence from the essence of God, any more than one can separate the fact that the sum of the three angles in a triangle is equal to two right angles from the essence of a triangle, or separate the idea of a valley from the idea of a mountain. Thus, it is no less contradictory to think of a God (that is, of a supremely perfect being) who lacks existence (that is, who lacks a certain perfection) than it is to think of a mountain without a valley.†

Nonetheless, although I cannot conceive of God other than as something with existence, any more than I can of a mountain without a valley, the truth is that just because I think of a mountain with a valley, it does not therefore follow that there is any mountain in the world. In the same way, just because I think of God as having existence, it does not seem to follow that God therefore exists. For my thinking imposes no necessity on things, and in the same way as I can imagine a horse with wings, even though no horse has wings, so I could perhaps attribute existence to God, even though no God exists.

But this [objection] conceals a fallacy. For from the fact that I cannot think of a mountain without a valley, it does not follow that a mountain and valley exist anywhere, but merely that the mountain and valley, whether they exist or not, cannot be separated from each other. However, from the fact that I cannot think of God without existence, it does follow that existence is inseparable from God, and thus that He truly does exist. Not that my thought brings this about or imposes any necessity on anything, but rather, by contrast, because the necessity of the thing itself, that is, of the existence of God, determines that I must think this way. For I am not free to think of God without existence (that is, of a supremely perfect being lacking a supreme perfection) in the same way that I am free to imagine a horse with wings or without them.

Suppose somebody objects: Agreed that once one has assumed that God has every perfection it is in fact necessary to admit that He exists (because existence is part of perfection), but it is not necessary to make that assumption, just as it is unnecessary to assume that all quadrilaterals [can] be inscribed in a circle. For if one assumed that, one would have to conclude that any rhombus could be inscribed in a circle—but

---

* That is, clever-sounding but deceptive reasoning.
† That is, an upslope without a downslope.

this is clearly false.* But this objection is invalid. For although it may not be necessary for me ever to entertain any thought of God, nevertheless, whenever I do happen to think of a first and supreme being, and, as it were, to derive an idea of Him from the storehouse of my mind, I have to attribute to Him all perfections, even though I do not enumerate them all at that time or attend to each one of them individually. And this necessity is obviously sufficient to make me conclude correctly, once I have recognized that existence is a perfection, that a first and supreme being exists. In the same way, it is not necessary that I ever imagine any triangle, but every time I wish to consider a rectilinear† figure with only three angles, I have to attribute to it those [properties] from which I correctly infer that its three angles are no greater than two right angles, although at that time I may not notice this. But when I think about which figures [are capable of being] inscribed in a circle, it is not at all necessary that I believe every quadrilateral is included in their number. On the contrary, I cannot even imagine anything like that, as long as I do not wish to admit anything unless I understand it clearly and distinctly. Thus, there is a great difference between false assumptions of this kind and the true ideas which are innate in me, of which the first and most important is the idea of God. For, in fact, I understand in many ways that this [idea] is not something made up which depends upon my thought but [is] the image of a true and immutable nature: first, because I cannot think of any other thing whose essence includes existence, other than God alone; second, because I am unable to conceive of two or more Gods of this sort, and because, given that I have already assumed that one God exists, I see clearly that it is necessary that He has previously existed from [all] eternity and will continue [to exist] for all eternity; and finally because I perceive many other things in God, none of which I can remove or change.

But, in fact, no matter what reasoning I finally use by way of proof, I always come back to the point that the only things I find entirely persuasive are those I perceive clearly and distinctly. Among the things I

perceive in this way, some are obvious to everyone, while others reveal themselves only to those who look into them more closely and investigate more diligently, but nevertheless once the latter have been discovered, they are considered no less certain than the former. For example, even though the fact that the hypotenuse of a right triangle is opposite the largest angle of the triangle is more apparent than the fact that the square of the hypotenuse is equal to the sum of the squares of the other two sides, nonetheless, after we have initially recognized the second fact, we are no less certain of its truth [than we are of the other]. But where God is concerned, if I were not overwhelmed with prejudices, and if images of perceptible things were not laying siege to my thinking on all sides, there is certainly nothing I would recognize sooner or more easily than Him. For what is more inherently evident than that there is a supreme being; in other words, that God exists, for existence [necessarily and eternally] belongs to His essence alone?

And although it required careful reflection on my part to perceive this [truth], nonetheless I am now not only as sure about it as I am about all the other things which seem [to me] most certain, but also, I see that the certainty of everything else is so dependent on this very truth that without it nothing could ever be perfectly known.

For although my nature is such that, as long as I perceive something really clearly and distinctly, I am unable to deny that it is true, nevertheless, because I am also by nature incapable of always fixing my mental gaze on the same thing in order to perceive it clearly, [and because] my memory may often return to a judgment I have previously made at a time when I am not paying full attention to the reasons why I made such a judgment, other arguments can present themselves which, if I knew nothing about God, might easily drive me to abandon that opinion. Thus, I would never have any true and certain knowledge, but merely vague and changeable opinions. For example, when I consider the nature of a triangle, it is, in fact, very evident to me (given that I am well versed in the

---

*   Quadrilaterals are four-sided figures. A figure can be inscribed in a circle when a circle can be drawn that passes through each corner. Rhombuses are figures with four sides of equal length. Squares (a type of rhombus) can be inscribed in a circle, but rhombuses not containing four right angles cannot.
†   Formed by straight lines.

principles of geometry) that its three angles are equal to two right angles, and, as long as I focus on the proof of this fact, it is impossible for me not to believe that it is true. But as soon as I turn my mental gaze away from that, although I still remember I perceived it very clearly, it could still easily happen that I doubt whether it is true, if, in fact, I had no knowledge of God. For I can convince myself that nature created me in such a way that I am sometimes deceived by those things I think I perceive as clearly as possible, especially when I remember that I have often considered many things true and certain that I later judged to be false, once other reasons had persuaded me.

However, after I perceived that God exists, because at the same time I also realized that all other things depend on Him and that He is not a deceiver, I therefore concluded that everything I perceive clearly and distinctly is necessarily true. Thus, even if I am not fully attending to the reasons why I have judged that something is true, if I only remember that I have perceived it clearly and distinctly, no opposing argument can present itself that would force me to have doubts. Instead, I possess true and certain knowledge about it—and not just about that, but about all other matters which I remember having demonstrated at any time, for example, [about the truths] of geometry and the like. For what argument could I now bring against them? What about the fact that I am created in such a manner that I often make mistakes? But now I know that I cannot be deceived about those things which I understand clearly. What about the fact that I used to consider many other things true and certain which I later discovered to be false? But I was not perceiving any of these [things] clearly and distinctly, and, in my ignorance of this rule [for confirming] the truth, I happened to believe them for other reasons which I later discovered to be less firm. What then will I say? Perhaps I am dreaming (an objection I recently made to myself), or else everything I am now thinking is no more true than what happens when I am asleep? But even this does not change anything: for surely even though I am asleep, if what is in my intellect is clear, then it is absolutely true.

In this way I fully recognize that all certainty and truth in science depend only on a knowledge of the true God, so much so that, before I knew Him,

I could have no perfect knowledge of anything else. But now I am able to understand innumerable things completely and clearly, about both God Himself and other intellectual matters, as well as about all those things in corporeal nature that are objects of study in pure mathematics.

Sixth Meditation: Concerning the Existence of Material Things and the Real Distinction between Mind and Body

It remains for me to examine whether material things exist. At the moment, I do, in fact, know that they *could* exist, at least insofar as they are objects of pure mathematics, since I perceive them clearly and distinctly. For there is no doubt that God is capable of producing everything which I am capable of perceiving in this way, and I have never judged that there is anything He cannot create, except in those cases where there might be a contradiction in my clear perception of it. Moreover, from my faculty of imagination, which I have learned by experience I use when I turn my attention to material substances, it seems to follow that they exist. For when I consider carefully what the imagination is, it seems nothing other than a certain application of my cognitive faculty to an object which is immediately present to it and which therefore exists.

In order to clarify this matter fully, I will first examine the difference between imagination and pure understanding. For example, when I imagine a triangle, not only do I understand that it is a shape composed of three lines, but at the same time I also see those three lines as if they were, so to speak, present to my mind's eye. This is what I call imagining. However, if I wish to think about a chiliagon, even though I understand that it is a figure consisting of one thousand sides just as well as I understand that a triangle is a figure consisting of three sides, I do not imagine those thousand sides in the same way, nor do I see [them], as it were, in front of me. And although, thanks to my habit of always imagining something whenever I think of a corporeal substance, it may happen that [in thinking of a chiliagon] I create for myself a confused picture of some shape, nevertheless, it is obviously not a chiliagon, because it is no different from the shape I would also picture to myself if I were thinking of a myriagon* or of any other figure with many sides. And that shape is no help at all in recognizing those properties which distinguish the chiliagon from other polygons. However, if it is a question of a pentagon, I can certainly understand its shape just as [well as] I can the shape of a chiliagon, without the assistance of my imagination. But, of course, I can also imagine the pentagon by applying my mind's eye to its five sides and to the area they contain. From this I clearly recognize that, in order to imagine things, I need a certain special mental effort that I do not use to understand them, and this new mental effort reveals clearly the difference between imagination and pure understanding.

Furthermore, I notice that this power of imagining, which exists within me, insofar as it differs from the power of understanding, is not a necessary part of my own essence, that is, of my mind. For even if I did not have it, I would still undoubtedly remain the same person I am now. From this it would seem to follow that my imagination depends upon something different from [my mind]. I understand the following easily enough: If a certain body—my body—exists, and my mind is connected to it in such a way that whenever my mind so wishes it can direct itself (so to speak) to examine that body, then thanks to this particular body it would be possible for me to imagine corporeal things. Thus, the only difference between imagination and pure understanding would be this: the mind, while it is understanding, in some way turns its attention to itself and considers one of the ideas present in itself, but when it is imagining, it turns its attention to the body and sees something in it which conforms to an idea which it has either conceived by itself or perceived with the senses. I readily understand, as I have said, that the imagination *could* be formed in this way, if the body exists, and because I can think of no other equally convenient way of explaining it, I infer from this that the body probably exists—but only probably—and although I am looking into everything carefully, I still do not yet see how from this distinct idea of corporeal nature which I find in my imagination I can derive any argument which necessarily concludes that anything corporeal exists.

However, I am in the habit of imagining many things apart from the corporeal nature which is the object of study in pure mathematics, such as colours, sounds, smells, pain, and things like that, although not so distinctly. And since I perceive these better with my senses, through which, with the help of my memory, they appear to have reached my imagination, then in order to deal with them in a more appropriate manner, I ought to consider the senses at the same time as well and see whether those things which I perceive by this method of thinking, which I call sensation, will enable me to establish some credible argument to prove the existence of corporeal things.

First of all, I will review in my mind the things that I previously believed to be true, because I perceived them with my senses, along with the reasons for those beliefs. Then I will also assess the reasons why I later called them into doubt. And finally I will consider what I ought to believe about them now.

To begin with, then, I sensed that I had a head, hands, feet, and other limbs making up that body which I looked on as if it were a part of me or perhaps even my totality. I sensed that this body moved around among many other bodies which could affect it in different ways, either agreeably or disagreeably. I judged which ones were agreeable by a certain feeling of pleasure and which ones were disagreeable by a feeling of pain. Apart from pain and pleasure, I also felt inside me sensations of hunger, thirst, and other appetites of this kind, as well as certain physical inclinations towards joy, sadness, anger, and other similar emotions. And outside myself, besides the extension, shapes, and motions of bodies, I also had sensations in them of hardness, heat, and other tactile qualities and, in addition, of light, colours, smells, tastes, and sounds. From the variety of these, I distinguished sky, land, sea, and other bodies, one after another. And because of the ideas of all those qualities which presented themselves to my thinking, although I kept sensing these as merely my own personal and immediate ideas, I reasonably believed that I was perceiving certain objects entirely different from my thinking, that is, bodies from which these ideas proceeded. For experience taught me that these ideas reached me without my consent, so that I was unable to sense any object, even if I wanted to, unless it was present to my organs of sense, and I was unable not to sense it when

---

* A myriagon is a 10,000-sided polygon.

it was present. And since the ideas I perceived with my senses were much more vivid, lively, and sharp, and even, in their own way, more distinct than any of those which I myself intentionally and deliberately shaped by meditation or which I noticed impressed on my memory, it did not seem possible that they could have proceeded from myself. Thus, the only conclusion left was that they had come from some other things. Because I had no conception of these objects other than what I derived from those ideas themselves, the only thought my mind could entertain was that [the objects] were similar to [the ideas they produced]. And since I also remembered that earlier I had used my senses rather than my reason and realized that the ideas which I myself formed were not as vivid, lively, and sharp as those which I perceived with my senses and that most of the former were composed of parts of the latter, I easily convinced myself that I had nothing at all in my intellect which I had not previously had in my senses. I also maintained, not without reason, that this body, which, by some special right, I called my own, belonged to me more than any other object, for I could never separate myself from it, as I could from other [bodies], I felt every appetite and emotion in it and because of it, and finally, I noticed pain and the titillation of pleasure in its parts, but not in any objects placed outside it. But why a certain strange sadness of spirit follows a sensation of pain and a certain joy follows from a sensation of [pleasurable] titillation, or why some sort of twitching in the stomach, which I call hunger, is urging me to eat food, while the dryness of my throat [is urging me] to drink, and so on—for that I had no logical explanation, other than that these were things I had learned from nature. For there is clearly no relationship (at least, none I can understand) between that twitching [in the stomach] and the desire to consume food, or between the sensation of something causing pain and the awareness of sorrow arising from that feeling. But it seemed to me that all the other judgments I made about objects of sense experience I had learned from nature. For I had convinced myself that that was how things happened, before I thought about any arguments which might prove it.

However, many later experiences have gradually weakened the entire faith I used to have in the senses. For, now and then, towers which seemed round from a distance appeared square from near at hand, immense statues standing on the tower summits did not seem large when I viewed them from the ground, and in countless other cases like these I discovered that my judgments were deceived in matters dealing with external senses. And not just with external [senses], but also with internal ones as well. For what could be more internal than pain? And yet I heard that people whose legs or arms had been cut off sometimes still seemed to feel pain in the part of their body which they lacked. Thus, even though I were to feel pain in one of my limbs, I did not think I could be completely certain that it was the limb which caused my pain. To these reasons for doubting sense experience, I recently added two extremely general ones. First, there was nothing I ever thought I was sensing while awake that I could not also think I was sensing now and then while asleep, and since I do not believe that those things I appear to sense in my sleep come to me from objects placed outside me, I did not see why I should give more credit to those I appear to sense when I am awake. Second, because I was still ignorant—or at least was assuming I was ignorant—of the author of my being, there seemed to be nothing to prevent nature from constituting me in such a way that I would make mistakes, even in those matters which seemed to me most true. As for the reasons which had previously convinced me of the truth of what I apprehended with my senses, I had no difficulty refuting them. For since nature seemed to push me to accept many things which my reason opposed, I believed I should not place much trust in those things nature taught. And although perceptions of the senses did not depend upon my will, I did not believe that was reason enough for me to conclude that they must come from things different from myself, because there could well be some other faculty in me, even one I did not yet know, which produced them.

But now that I am starting to gain a better understanding of myself and of the author of my being, I do not, in fact, believe that I should rashly accept all those things I appear to possess from my senses, but, at the same time, [I do not think] I should call everything into doubt.

First, since I know that all those things I understand clearly and distinctly could have been created by God in a way that matches my conception of them, the fact that I can clearly and distinctly understand one thing, distinguishing it from something else, is sufficient to convince me that the two of them are different, because they can be separated from each other, at least by God. The power by which this [separation] takes place is irrelevant to my judgment that they are distinct. And therefore, given the mere fact that I know I exist and that, at the moment, I look upon my nature or essence as absolutely nothing other than that I am a thinking thing, I reasonably conclude that my essence consists of this single fact: I am a thinking thing. And although I may well possess (or rather, as I will state later, although I certainly do possess) a body which is very closely joined to me, nonetheless, because, on the one hand, I have a clear and distinct idea of myself, insofar as I am merely a thinking thing, without extension, and, on the other hand, [I have] a distinct idea of body, insofar as it is merely an extended thing which does not think, it is certain that my mind is completely distinct from my body and can exist without it.

Moreover, I discover in myself faculties for certain special forms of thinking, namely, the faculties of imagining and feeling. I can conceive of myself clearly and distinctly as a complete being without these, but I cannot do the reverse and think of these faculties without me, that is, without an intelligent substance to which they belong. For the formal conception of them includes some act of intellection by which I perceive that they are different from me, just as [shapes, movement, and the other] modes [or accidents of bodies are different] from the object [to which they belong]. I also recognize certain other faculties [in me], like changing position, assuming various postures, and so on, which certainly cannot be conceived, any more than those previously mentioned, apart from some substance to which they belong, and therefore they, too, cannot exist without it. However, it is evident that these [faculties], if indeed they [truly] exist, must belong to some corporeal or extended substance, and not to any intelligent substance, since the clear and distinct conception of them obviously contains some [form of] extension, but no intellectual activity whatsoever. Now, it is, in fact, true that I do have a certain passive faculty of perception, that is, of receiving and recognizing ideas of sensible things. But I would be unable to use this power unless some active

faculty existed, as well, either in me or in some other substance capable of producing or forming these ideas. But this [active faculty] clearly cannot exist within me, because it presupposes no intellectual activity at all, and because, without my cooperation and often even against my will, it produces those ideas. Therefore I am left to conclude that it exists in some substance different from me that must contain, either formally or eminently, all the reality objectively present in the ideas produced by that faculty (as I have just observed above).* This substance is either a body, that is, something with a corporeal nature which obviously contains formally everything objectively present in the ideas, or it must be God, or some other creature nobler than the body, one that contains [those same things] eminently. But since God is not a deceiver, it is very evident that He does not transmit these ideas to me from Himself directly or even through the intervention of some other creature in which their objective reality is contained, not formally but only eminently. For since he has given me no faculty whatsoever for recognizing such a source, but by contrast, has endowed me with a powerful tendency to believe that these ideas are sent out from corporeal things, I do not see how it would be possible not to think of Him as a deceiver, if these [ideas] were sent from any source other than corporeal things. And therefore corporeal things exist. However, perhaps they do not all exist precisely in the ways I grasp them with my senses, since what I comprehend with my senses is very obscure and confused in many things. But at least [I should accept as true] all those things in them which I understand clearly and distinctly, that is, generally speaking, everything which is included as an object in pure mathematics.

But regarding other material things which are either merely particular, for example that the sun is of such and such a magnitude and shape, and so on, or less clearly understood, for example light, sound, pain, and things like that, although these may be extremely doubtful and uncertain, nonetheless, because of the very fact that God is not a deceiver and thus it is impossible for there to be any falsity in my opinions which I cannot correct with another faculty God has given me, I have the sure hope that I can reach the

---

* For more on the distinction between formal and objective presence, see the "Some Useful Background Information" section of the introduction to this reading.

truth even in these matters. And clearly there is no doubt that all those things I learn from nature contain some truth. For by the term *nature*, generally speaking, I understand nothing other than either God himself or the coordinated structure of created things established by God, and by the term *my nature*, in particular, nothing other than the combination of all those things I have been endowed with by God.

However, there is nothing that nature teaches me more emphatically than the fact that I have a body, which does badly when I feel pain, which needs food or drink when I suffer from hunger or thirst, and so on. And therefore I should not doubt that there is some truth in this.

For through these feelings of pain, hunger, thirst, and so on, nature teaches me that I am not only present in my body in the same way a sailor is present onboard a ship, but also that I am bound up very closely and, so to speak, mixed in with it, so that my body and I form a certain unity. For if that were not the case, then when my body was injured, I, who am merely a thinking thing, would not feel any pain because of it; instead, I would perceive the wound purely with my intellect, just as a sailor notices with his eyes if something is broken on his ship. And when my body needed food or drink, I would understand that clearly and not have confused feelings of hunger and thirst. For those sensations of thirst, hunger, pain, and so on are really nothing other than certain confused ways of thinking, which arise from the union and, as it were, the mixture of the mind with the body.

Moreover, nature also teaches me that various other bodies exist around my own and that I should pursue some of these and stay away from others. And certainly from the fact that I sense a wide diversity of colours, sounds, odours, tastes, heat, hardness, and similar things, I reasonably conclude that in the bodies from which these different sense perceptions come there are certain variations which correspond to these perceptions, even if they are perhaps not like them. And given the fact that I find some of these sense perceptions pleasant and others unpleasant, it is entirely certain that my body, or rather my totality, since I am composed of body and mind, can be affected by various agreeable and disagreeable bodies surrounding it.

However, many other things which I seemed to have learned from nature I have not really received from her, but rather from a certain habit I have of accepting careless judgments [about things]. And thus it could easily be the case that these judgments are false—for example, [the opinion I have] that all space in which nothing at all happens to stimulate my senses is a vacuum, that in a warm substance there is something completely similar to the idea of heat which is in me, that in a white or green [substance] there is the same whiteness or greenness which I sense, that in [something] bitter or sweet there is the same taste as I sense, and so on, that stars and towers and anything else some distance away have bodies with the same size and shape as the ones they present to my senses, and things of that sort. But in order to ensure that what I perceive in this matter is sufficiently distinct, I should define more accurately what it is precisely that I mean when I say I have learned something from nature. For here I am taking the word *nature* in a more restricted sense than *the combination of all those things which have been bestowed on me by God*. For this combination contains many things which pertain only to the mind, such as the fact that I perceive that what has been done cannot be undone, and all the other things I grasp by my natural light [without the help of the body]. Such things are not under discussion here. This combination also refers to many things which concern only the body, like its tendency to move downward, and so on, which I am also not dealing with [here]. Instead, I am considering only those things which God has given me as a combination of mind and body. And so nature, in this sense, certainly teaches me to avoid those things which bring a sensation of pain and to pursue those which [bring] a sensation of pleasure, and such like, but, beyond that, it is not clear that with those sense perceptions nature teaches us that we can conclude anything about things placed outside of us without a previous examination by the understanding, because to know the truth about them seems to belong only to the mind and not to that combination [of body and mind]. And so, although a star does not make an impression on my eyes any greater than the flame of a small candle, nonetheless, that fact does not incline me, in any real or positive way, to believe that the star is not larger [than the flame], but from the time of my youth I have made this judgment without any reason [to support it]. And although I feel heat when I come near the fire, and even pain if I get too close to it, that is really no reason to believe that there is something in the fire similar to that heat I feel, any more than there is something similar to the pain. The only thing [I can conclude] is that there is something in the fire, whatever it might be, which brings out in us those sensations of heat or pain. So, too, although in some space there is nothing which stimulates my senses, it does not therefore follow that the space contains no substances. But I see that in these and in a great many other matters, I have grown accustomed to undermine the order of nature, because, of course, these sense perceptions are, strictly speaking, given to me by nature merely to indicate to my mind which things are agreeable or disagreeable to that combination of which it is a part, and for that purpose they are sufficiently clear and distinct. But then I use them as if they were dependable rules for immediately recognizing the essence of bodies placed outside me. However, about such bodies they reveal nothing except what is confusing and obscure.

In an earlier section, I have already examined sufficiently why my judgments may happen to be defective, in spite of the goodness of God. However, a new difficulty crops up here concerning those very things which nature reveals to me as objects I should seek out or avoid, and also concerning the internal sensations, in which I appear to have discovered errors: for example, when someone, deceived by the pleasant taste of a certain food, eats a poison hidden within it [and thus makes a mistake]. Of course, in this situation, the person's nature urges him only to eat food which has a pleasant taste and not the poison, of which he has no knowledge at all. And from this, the only conclusion I can draw is that my nature does not know everything. There is nothing astonishing about that, because a human being is a finite substance and thus is capable of only limited perfection.

However, we are frequently wrong even in those things which nature urges [us to seek]. For example, sick people are eager for drink or food which will harm them soon afterwards. One could perhaps claim that such people make mistakes because their nature has been corrupted. But this does not remove the difficulty, for a sick person is no less a true creature of God than a healthy one, and thus it seems no less contradictory that God has given the person a nature which deceives him. And just as a clock made out of wheels and weights observes all the laws of nature with the same accuracy when it is badly made and does not indicate the hours correctly as it does when it completely satisfies the wishes of the person who made it, in the same way, if I look on the human body as some kind of machine composed of bones, nerves, muscles, veins, blood, and skin, as if no mind existed in it, the body would still have all the same motions it now has in those movements that are not under the control of the will and that, therefore, do not proceed from the mind [but merely from the disposition of its organs]. I can readily acknowledge, for example, that in the case of a body sick with dropsy,* it would be quite natural for it to suffer from a parched throat, which usually conveys a sensation of thirst to the mind, and for its nerves and other parts also to move in such a way that it takes a drink and thus aggravates the illness. And when nothing like this is harming the body, it is equally natural for it to be stimulated by a similar dryness in the throat and to take a drink to benefit itself. Now, when I consider the intended purpose of the clock, I could say that, since it does not indicate the time correctly, it is deviating from its own nature, and, in the same way, when I think of the machine of the human body as something formed for the motions which usually take place in it, I might believe that it, too, is deviating from its own nature, if its throat is dry when a drink does not benefit its own preservation. However, I am fully aware that this second meaning of the word *nature* is very different from the first. For it is merely a term that depends on my own thought, a designation with which I compare a sick person and a badly constructed clock with the idea of a healthy person and a properly constructed clock, and thus, the term is extrinsic to these objects. But by that [other use of the term *nature*] I understand something that is really found in things and that therefore contains a certain measure of the truth.

Now, when I consider a body suffering from dropsy, even though I say that its nature has been corrupted, because it has a dry throat and yet does not need to drink, clearly the word *nature* is merely an extraneous term. However, when I consider the composite, that is, the mind united with such a body, I am not dealing with what is simply a term but with a true error of nature, because this composite is thirsty when drinking

---

* An abnormal accumulation of watery fluid in the body (now called edema).

will do it harm. And thus I still have to enquire here why the goodness of God does not prevent its nature, taken in this sense, from being deceitful.

At this point, then, my initial observation is that there is a great difference between the mind and the body, given that the body is, by its very nature, always divisible, whereas the mind is completely indivisible. For, in fact, when I think of [my mind], that is, when I think of myself as purely a thinking thing, I cannot distinguish any parts within me. Instead, I understand that I am something completely individual and unified. And although my entire mind seems to be united with my entire body, nonetheless, I know that if a foot or arm or any other part of the body is sliced off, that loss will not take anything from my mind. And I cannot call the faculties of willing, feeling, understanding, and so on parts of the mind because it is the same single mind that wishes, feels, and understands. By contrast, I cannot think of any corporeal or extended substance that my thought is not capable of dividing easily into parts. From this very fact, I understand that the substance is divisible. (This point alone would be enough to teach me that the mind is completely different from the body, if I did not already know that well enough from other sources.)

Furthermore, I notice that the mind is not immediately affected by all parts of the body, but only by the brain, or perhaps even by just one small part of it, namely, the one in which our *common sense** is said to exist. Whenever this part is arranged in the same particular way, it delivers the same perception to the mind, even though the other parts of the body may be arranged quite differently at the time. This point has been demonstrated in countless experiments, which I need not review here.

In addition, I notice that the nature of my body is such that no part of it can be moved by any other part some distance away which cannot also be moved in the same manner by any other part lying between them, even though the more distant part does nothing. So, for example, in a rope ABCD [which is taut throughout], if I pull on part D at the end, then the movement of the first part, A, will be no different than it would

be if I pulled at one of the intermediate points, B or C, while the last part, D, remained motionless. And for a similar reason, when I feel pain in my foot, physics teaches me that this sensation occurs thanks to nerves spread throughout the foot. These nerves stretch from there to the brain, like cords, and when they are pulled in my foot, they also pull the inner parts of the brain, where they originate, and stimulate in them a certain motion which nature has established to influence the mind with a sense of pain apparently present in the foot. However, since these nerves have to pass through the shin, the thigh, the loins, the back, and the neck in order to reach the brain from the foot, it can happen that, even if that portion of the nerves which is in the foot is not affected, but only one of the intermediate portions, the motion created in the brain is exactly the same as the one created there by an injured foot. As a result, the mind will necessarily feel the identical pain. And we should assume that the same is true with any other sensation whatsoever.

Finally, I notice that, since each of those motions created in that part of the brain which immediately affects the mind introduces into it only one particular sensation, we can, given this fact, come up with no better explanation than that this sensation, out of all the ones which could be introduced, is the one which serves to protect human health as effectively and frequently as possible [when a person is completely healthy]. But experience testifies to the fact that all sensations nature has given us are like this, and thus we can discover nothing at all in them which does not bear witness to the power and benevolence of God. Thus, for example, when the nerves in the foot are moved violently and more than usual, their motion, passing through the spinal cord to the inner core of the brain, gives a signal there to the mind which makes it feel something—that is, it feels as if there is a pain in the foot. And that stimulates [the mind] to do everything it can to remove the cause of the pain as something injurious to the foot. Of course, God could have constituted the nature of human beings in such a way that this same motion in the brain communicated something else to the mind, for example, a sense of

---

* Descartes is probably thinking of the pineal gland here, a tiny structure located between the two hemispheres of the brain; this is because he believed it to be the only anatomical structure of the brain which existed as a single part, rather than one half of a pair.

its own movements, either in the brain, or in the foot, or in any of the places in between—in short, of anything you wish. But nothing else would have served so well for the preservation of the body. In the same way, when we need a drink, a certain dryness arises in the throat which moves its nerves and, with their assistance, the inner parts of the brain. And this motion incites in the mind a sensation of thirst, because in this whole situation nothing is more useful for us to know than that we need a drink to preserve our health. The same is true for the other sensations.

From this it is clearly evident that, notwithstanding the immense goodness of God, human nature, given that it is composed of mind and body, cannot be anything other than something that occasionally deceives us. For if some cause, not in the foot, but in some other part through which the nerves stretch between the foot and the brain, or even in the brain itself, stimulates exactly the same motion as that which is normally aroused when a foot is injured, then pain will be felt as if it were in the foot, and the sensation will naturally be deceiving. Since that same motion in the brain is never capable of transmitting to the mind anything other than the identical sensation and since [the sensation] is habitually aroused much more frequently from an injury in the foot than from anything else in another place, it is quite reasonable that it should always transmit to the mind a pain in the foot rather than a pain in any other part of the body. And if sometimes dryness in the throat does not arise, as it usually does, from the fact that a drink is necessary for the health of the body, but from some different cause, as occurs in a patient suffering from dropsy, it is much better that it should deceive us in a case like that than if it were, by contrast, always deceiving us when the body is quite healthy. The same holds true with the other sensations.

This reflection is the greatest help, for it enables me not only to detect all the errors to which my nature is prone, but also to correct or to avoid them easily. For since I know that, in matters concerning what is

beneficial to the body, all my senses show [me] what is true much more frequently than they deceive me, and since I can almost always use several of them to examine the same matter and, in addition, [can use] my memory, which connects present events with earlier ones, as well as my understanding, which has now ascertained all the causes of my errors, I should no longer fear that those things which present themselves to me every day through my senses are false. And I ought to dismiss all those exaggerated doubts of the past few days as ridiculous, particularly that most important [doubt] about sleep, which I did not distinguish from being awake. For now I notice a significant distinction between the two of them, given that our memory never links our dreams to all the other actions of our lives, as it [usually] does with those things which take place when we are awake. For clearly, if someone suddenly appears to me when I am awake and then immediately afterwards disappears, as happens in my dreams, so that I have no idea where he came from or where he went, I would reasonably judge that I had seen some apparition or phantom created in my brain [similar to the ones created when I am asleep], rather than a real person. But when certain things occur and I notice distinctly the place from which they came, where they are, and when they appeared to me, and when I can link my perception of them to the rest of my life as a totality, without a break, then I am completely certain that this is taking place while I am awake and not in my sleep. And I should not have the slightest doubt about the truth of these perceptions if, after I have called upon all my senses, my memory, and my understanding to examine them, I find nothing in any of them which contradicts any of the others. For since God is not a deceiver, it must follow that in such cases I am not deceived. But because, in dealing with what we need to do, we cannot always take the time for such a scrupulous examination, we must concede that human life is often prone to error concerning particular things and that we need to acknowledge the frailty of our nature. ▪

Suggestions for Critical Reflection

1. Descartes, in the *Meditations*, has traditionally been seen as raising and then trying to deal with the problem of radical skepticism: that is, according to this interpretation, he raises the possibility that (almost) all our beliefs might be radically mistaken and then argues that this is, in fact, impossible. A more recent line of interpretation, though, sees Descartes not as attempting to answer the skeptic, but as trying to replace naïve empirical assumptions about science with a more modern, mathematical view—in particular, that Descartes is trying to show our most fundamental pieces of knowledge about mind, God, and the world come not from sensory experience, but directly from the intellect. Which interpretation do you think is more plausible? Could they both be right? If Descartes does want to refute skepticism, is he successful in doing so? If his goal is to overturn naïve scholastic empiricism, do you think he manages to do that?

2. Descartes's foundational claim is "I think therefore I am." How does Descartes justify this claim? Does he have, or need, an *argument* for it? Is an argument that justifies this claim even possible?

3. Descartes writes, in the Third Meditation, "[t]here cannot be another faculty [in me] as trustworthy as natural light, one which could teach me that the ideas [derived from natural light] are not true." What do you think he means by this? Is he right? How important to his arguments is it that he be right about this?

4. Eighteenth-century Scottish philosopher David Hume dryly said, of the *Meditations*, "To have recourse to the veracity of the supreme Being, in order to prove the veracity of our senses, is surely making a very unexpected circuit" (Section XII of *An Enquiry Concerning Human Understanding*, 1748). What do you think? Does Descartes establish the existence of God?

5. On Descartes's picture, do you think an atheist can have any knowledge? Why or why not?

6. It seems to be crucial to Descartes's arguments (especially those in the Fourth Meditation) that God is not responsible for our errors, that what we believe—and, indeed, whether we believe or simply suspend our belief—is something that is under our direct control: that we can freely will to believe or not. Does this seem plausible to you? (Could you really decide not to believe that, say, your body exists?) How might Descartes argue for this position? If it cannot be defended, how problematic would this be for the project of the *Meditations*?

7. A famous objection to Descartes's conclusions in the *Meditations* (raised for the first time by some of his contemporaries) is today known as the problem of the Cartesian Circle. Descartes says in the Third Meditation, "Whatever I perceive very clearly and distinctly is true." Call this the CDP (Clear and Distinct Perception) Principle. It is this principle that he thinks will allow him to reconstruct a body of reliable scientific knowledge on the foundations of the Cogito. However, he immediately admits, the CDP Principle will only work if we cannot ever make mistakes about what we clearly and distinctly perceive; to show this, Descartes tries to prove that God exists and has created human beings such that what we clearly and distinctly see to be evidently true really is true. But how does Descartes prove God exists? Apparently, by arguing that we have a clear and distinct idea of God, and so it must be true that God exists. That is, the objection runs, Descartes relies upon the CDP Principle to prove that the CDP Principle is reliable—and this argument just goes in a big circle and doesn't prove anything. What do you think of this objection?

8. "How do I know that I am not ten thinkers thinking in unison?" (Elizabeth Anscombe, "The First Person" [1975]). What, if anything, do you think Descartes has proved about the nature of the self?

9. How adequate are Descartes's arguments for mind-body dualism? If mind and body are two different substances, do you think this might cause other philosophical problems to arise? For example, how might mind and body interact if they are radically different and have no properties in common? How could we come to know things about other people's minds? How could we be sure whether animals have minds or not, and if they do what they might be like?

10. Descartes recognized no physical properties but size, shape, and motion. Where do you think Descartes would say colors, tastes, smells, and so on come from?

JOHN LOCKE

FROM *An Essay Concerning Human Understanding*

Who Was John Locke?

John Locke was born in the Somerset countryside, near the town of Bristol, in 1632. His parents were small landowners—minor gentry—who subjected the young Locke to a strict Protestant upbringing. Thanks to the influence of one of his father's friends, Locke was able to gain a place at Westminster School, at the time the best school in England, where he studied Greek, Latin, and Hebrew. He went on to Christ Church College, Oxford, and graduated with a BA in 1656. Shortly afterwards he was made a senior student of his college—a kind of teaching position—which he was to remain at until 1684, when the king of England, Charles II, personally (and illegally) demanded his expulsion.

During the 1650s and early 1660s Locke lectured on Greek and rhetoric at Oxford, but he was idle and unhappy and became increasingly bored by the traditional philosophy of his day. He developed an interest in medicine and physical science (in 1675 he tried and failed to gain the degree of Doctor of Medicine) and in 1665 left the confines of the academic world and began to make his way into the world of politics and science. In the winter of 1665–66 he was ambassador to the German state of Brandenburg, where his first-hand observation of religious toleration between Calvinists, Lutherans, Catholics, and Anabaptists made a big impression on him.

A chance encounter in 1666 was the decisive turning-point in Locke's life: he met a nobleman called Lord Ashley, then the Chancellor of the Exchequer, and soon went to live at Ashley's London house as his confidant and medical advisor. In 1668, Locke was responsible for a life-saving surgical operation on Ashley, implanting a small silver spigot to drain off fluid from a cyst on his liver; the lord never forgot his gratitude (and wore the small tap in his side for the rest of his life). Under Ashley's patronage, Locke had both the leisure to spend several years working on his *Essay Concerning Human Understanding* and a sequence of lucrative and interesting government positions, including one as part of a group drafting the constitution of the new colony of Carolina in the Americas.

Ashley's support was also essential in giving Locke—an introverted and hyper-sensitive soul who suffered for most of his life from bad asthma and general poor health—the confidence to do original philosophy. Locke never married, was a life-long celibate, shied away from drinking parties and a hectic social life, but enjoyed the attentions of lady admirers, and throughout his life he had many loyal friends and got on especially well with some of his friends' children.

Locke spent from 1675 until 1679 traveling in France (where he expected to die of tuberculosis, but survived—Locke spent a large portion of his life confidently expecting an early death), and when he returned to England it was to a very unsettled political situation. The heir to the British throne, Charles II's younger brother James, was a Catholic, and his succession was feared by many politicians, including Ashley—who was, by this time, the Earl of Shaftesbury—and his political party, the Whigs. Their greatest worry was that the return of a Catholic monarchy would mean the return of religious oppression to England, as was happening in parts of Europe. Charles, however, stood by his brother and in 1681 Shaftesbury was sent to prison in the Tower of London, charged with high treason. Shaftesbury was acquitted by a grand jury, but he fled to Holland and died a few months later (spending his last few hours, the story goes, discussing a draft of Locke's *Essay* with his friends). Locke, in danger as a known associate of Shaftesbury's, followed his example in 1683 and secretly moved to the Netherlands, where he had to spend a year underground evading arrest by the Dutch government's agents on King Charles's behalf. While in Holland he rewrote material for the *Essay*, molding it towards its final state, and published an abridgement of the book, which immediately attracted international attention, in a French scholarly periodical.

In 1689 the political tumult in England had subsided enough for Locke to return—James's brief reign (as James II) had been toppled by the Protestant William of Orange and his queen Mary—and he moved as a permanent house-guest to an estate called Oates about 25 miles from London. He returned to political life (though he refused re-appointment as ambassador to Brandenburg, on grounds of ill health), and played a significant role in loosening restrictions on publishers and authors.

It was in this year, when Locke was 57, that the results of his 30 years of thinking and writing were suddenly published in a flood. First, published anonymously, came the *Letter on Toleration*, then *Two Treatises on Government*. In the *Two Treatises*—which proved influential in the liberal movements of the next century that culminated in the French and American revolutions— Locke argued that the authority of monarchs is limited by individuals' rights and the public good. Finally, *An Essay Concerning Human Understanding* was published under his own name, to almost instant acclaim; the publication of this book catapulted Locke overnight to what we would now think of as international superstardom.

These three were his most important works, but Locke—by now one of the most famous men in England—continued to write and publish until his death 15 years later. He wrote, for example, works on the proper control of the currency for the English government; *Some Thoughts Concerning Education* (which, apparently, was historically important in shaping the toilet-training practices of the English educated classes); a work on the proper care and cultivation of fruit trees; and a careful commentary on the *Epistles* of St. Paul. He died quietly, reading in his study, in October 1704.

What Was Locke's Overall Philosophical Project?

Locke is the leading proponent of a school of philosophy now often called "British empiricism." Some of the central platforms of this doctrine are as follows: First, human beings are born like a blank, white sheet of paper—a *tabula rasa*—without any innate knowledge but with certain natural powers, and we use these powers to adapt ourselves to the social and physical environment into which we are born. Two especially important natural powers are the capacity for conscious sense experience and for feeling pleasure and pain, and it is from the interaction of these capacities with the environment that we acquire all of our ideas, knowledge, and habits of mind. All meaningful language must be connected to the ideas that we thus acquire, and the abuse of language to talk about things of which we have no idea is a serious source of intellectual errors—errors that can have harmful consequences for

social and moral life, as well as the growth of the sciences. British empiricism—whose other main exponents were Thomas Hobbes (1588–1679), George Berkeley (1685–1753), and David Hume (1711–76)—was generally opposed to religious fervor and sectarian strife, and cautious about the human capacity for attaining absolute knowledge about things that go beyond immediate experience.

An Essay Concerning Human Understanding is Locke's attempt to present a systematic and detailed empiricist account of the human mind and human knowledge. It also includes an account of the nature of language, and touches on philosophical issues to do with logic, religion, metaphysics, and ethics. Locke was also consciously interested in defending a certain modern way of thinking against the habits of the past: instead of relatively uncritical and conservative acceptance of Greek and Roman history, literature and philosophy, and of Christian theology, Locke defended independent thought, secular values, and the power of modern ideas and social change to produce useful results.

Locke was optimistic about the power and accuracy of his own theory of human understanding—and thus about the powers of human beings to come to know the world— but he nevertheless thought it was a *limited* power. There are some things human beings just cannot ever come to know with certainty, Locke thought, and we should be humble in our attempts to describe reality. Thus, there are some domains in which, according to Locke, our human capacities are sufficient to produce certain knowledge: mathematics, morality, the existence of God, and the existence of things in the world corresponding to our 'simple ideas' (i.e., roughly, the things we perceive). However, there are other areas where the best we can do is to make skillful guesses: these more difficult questions have to do with the underlying nature and workings of nature—that is, with scientific theory—and with the details of religious doctrine. God has given us the capacity to effectively get by in the world by making these careful guesses, according to Locke, but he has not given us the capacity to ever know for sure whether our guesses are correct or not. (This is one reason why Locke believed we should be tolerant of other people's religious beliefs.)

What Is the Structure of This Reading?

An Essay Concerning Human Understanding is divided into four books, each of which is further divided into chapters, which in turn are divided into sections. Book I is primarily an attack on the notion, which Locke found especially in Descartes, that human beings are born with certain "innate ideas"—concepts and knowledge which are not the product of experience but which are, perhaps, implanted in us by God. Book II develops Locke's alternative empiricist theory of ideas: here he describes the different sorts of ideas human beings have (such as our ideas of external objects, space, time, number, cause and effect, and so on), and tries to show how these ideas all derive ultimately from reflection on our own sense-experience. In Book III Locke describes the workings of language, and in particular defends the thesis that all meaningful language derives that meaning from its connections to our ideas. Finally, Book IV is where Locke considers the question of human knowledge and asks how much justification there is for our beliefs about God and nature, concluding that, although limited, the scope of our knowledge is more than enough for practical purposes.

The first two selections collected here come from Book II (and so are about ideas), and the third from Book IV (and so is about knowledge). The first selection asks how much our ideas resemble those things in the world that cause them and, among other things, describes and defends an important distinction between "primary" and "secondary" qualities. The second extract deals with the topic of "substance," the 'stuff' of the material world. The third approaches head-on the issue of the extent and limits of our knowledge of the external world.

Some Useful Background Information

1. Locke writes in a very straightforward and clear style—he deliberately set out to write informally, for a general educated readership—but his language is the English of the seventeenth century and some readers might find this difficult. Here is a short glossary of the words which might be either unfamiliar or used in an unfamiliar way. Other terms are defined in the footnotes of this reading.

   Apprehension: understanding, perception
   Bare/barely: mere/merely
   Denominate: apply a name to something
   Doth: does
   Figure: shape
   Hath: has

   Manna: the sweet dried juice of the Mediterranean ash tree and other plants, which can be used as a mild laxative (also, a substance miraculously supplied as food to the Israelites in the wilderness, according to the Bible)
   Peculiar: particular, specific
   Sensible/insensible: able to be sensed/invisible to the senses
   V.g.: for example
   Viz.: in other words, that is
   Without: outside (of us)

2. Locke's notion of an *idea* is central to his philosophy—which is even sometimes called "the way of ideas"—and he uses the word in his own special and carefully worked out way. For Locke, ideas are not activities of the mind but instead are the *contents* of the mind—they are the things we think about, the objects of our thought. (In fact, for Locke, thought consists entirely in the succession of ideas through consciousness.) Thus, for example, the things we believe, know, remember, or imagine are what Locke would call ideas.

   As the term suggests, Locke probably assumes ideas are mental entities—they are things that exist in our minds rather than in the external world. Certainly, there are no ideas floating around that are not part of someone's consciousness; every idea is necessarily the object of some act of thinking. Furthermore, ideas are the *only* things we directly think about—our thought and our mental experience, for Locke, is internally rather than externally directed: it is an experience of our ideas and the operations of our mind, not directly of the world. When Locke uses the word "perception," for example, he often means the mind's perception (awareness) of its own ideas, not, as we would usually mean, perception of objects outside our own minds.

   However, this is not to say that we don't think about or perceive the external world; Locke commonsensically thought that we saw trees, tasted apples, heard the speech of other human beings, and so on. But it does mean that all our thought and perception is mediated by ideas, which intervene between us and external reality. The ideas we have before our minds are the "immediate objects of perception," and the things those ideas represent are the "indirect objects of perception." Yet it is important to remember that, for Locke, ideas *do* naturally and evidently represent things beyond themselves (although not necessarily the whole, or even the most important aspects, of the nature of those things)—Locke does not believe for a moment that we are locked inside our own heads.

Locke distinguishes between lots of different types of ideas, but one especially important contrast is between simple and complex ideas. A simple idea is "nothing but one uniform appearance, or conception in the mind, and is not distinguishable into different ideas," whereas complex ideas are compounded out of more than one simple idea. For example, redness is a simple idea, while the idea of a London double-decker bus is a complex idea. For Locke, all simple ideas are acquired from experience, either through sense perception or through the perception of our own thoughts (often called "introspection"): we are not free to simply invent or ignore such ideas, as they are physically caused by the things they represent. However, we are free to construct complex ideas out of this raw material as we like, and we can do so in various ways: we can add simple ideas together into a single idea (e.g., the idea of a horse), or we can compare two ideas and perceive the relation that holds between them (e.g., the idea of being taller than), or we can generalize about simple ideas to form abstract ideas (e.g., the idea of time or infinity).

3. Locke held the modern (at the time) "corpuscular" theory of matter, which was developed by Pierre Gassendi (1592–1655) and Robert Boyle (1627–91) and which, though a "mechanical philosophy," contradicted some important elements of Descartes's physical theory. As a corpuscularian, Locke thought that the physical world was made up of tiny indestructible particles, invisible to the human eye, moving around in empty space, and having only the following properties: solidity, extension in three dimensions, shape (or "figure"), motion or rest, number, location ("situation"), volume ("bulk"), and texture. All the phenomena of the material world are built out of or caused by these particles and their properties and powers. Thus, collections of particles big enough to be visible have certain properties (which Locke called "qualities"), e.g., the shape and size of a gold nugget, its color, malleability, luster, chemical inertness, and so on. Our perception of the world—that is to say, our

experience of these qualities—is brought about by invisible streams of tiny particles emanating from the objects in our environment and striking our sense-receptors (our eyes, ears, skin, and so on). Locke and his contemporaries thought this stimulation of our senses causes complex reactions in our "animal spirits," and this is what gives rise to our ideas. Animal spirits were supposed to be a fine fluid (itself made up of tiny particles) flowing through our nervous system and carrying signals from one place to another and ultimately to our brain.

Some Common Misconceptions

1. In reading Locke, it is important not to confuse ideas with qualities. Ideas are mental entities; they constitute our *experience* of the world. Qualities are non-mental attributes of chunks of matter in the world; they are the things ideas are *about*. Thus, in Locke's view, our idea of color should not be confused with the property of color itself. The distinction between primary and secondary qualities, then, is mainly a distinction between types of physical property (though it does have implications for the taxonomy of our ideas).

2. The secondary qualities not only include colors, tastes, smells, sounds, and feels; they also include properties like solubility, brittleness, flammability, being nutritious, being a pain-killer, and so on.

3. It is sometimes thought Locke argued that secondary qualities do not really exist, and that color, smell, taste, and so on are only ideas in our mind. But this is not so. Locke does think that material objects in the world really have secondary qualities, but he argues that we have misunderstood the *nature* of these qualities in a particular way.

4. In thinking about the nature of the secondary qualities it is helpful to consider the nature of their connection with our ideas of them. In this context, two concepts are useful but are sometimes confused with each other. The first notion is that of *perceiver-relativity*: this is the idea that how something *seems* depends on who is perceiving it. To say that "beauty is in the eye of the beholder" is to make a claim about perceiver-relativity; more interestingly, being poisonous is an example of a perceiver-relative property, since substances that are poisonous to one

kind of perceiver might not be poisonous to others (e.g., chemicals called avermectins are lethal to many invertebrates but harmless to mammals). The second, different, notion is of *perceiver-dependence*: this is the idea that the very existence of something depends upon being perceived or thought about. An example of this would be a conscious visual image—there can be no such thing as a conscious image that is not in anybody's consciousness, and so mental images must be mind-dependent.

5. In the third selection below, when Locke is writing about substance, his main topic is the *idea* of substance, not substance itself. That is, he does not ask (directly) whether substance really exists; instead, his question is, do we have an idea of substance? And whatever his conclusions about the idea of substance, Locke denied being skeptical about the actual existence of substance.

How Important and Influential Is This Passage?

"The *Essay* has long been recognized as one of the great works of English literature of the seventeenth century, and one of the epoch-making works in the history of philosophy. It has been one of the most repeatedly reprinted, widely disseminated and read, and profoundly influential books of the past three centuries."* So writes Peter Nidditch, an expert on Locke's philosophy. Locke's *Essay* is often credited with being the most thorough and plausible formulation and defense of empiricism ever written, and it has exercised a huge influence on, especially, English-speaking philosophers right up until the present day (though with a period in the philosophical wilderness during the 1800s). In the eighteenth century Locke was widely considered as important for philosophy, and for what we would today call psychology, as Newton was for physics.

Although the distinction between primary and secondary qualities was certainly not invented by Locke, his account of it was very influential and was taken as the standard line in subsequent discussions of this important idea. Furthermore, the problem Locke raised about the coherence of our idea of material substance has been an important metaphysical problem since he formulated it, and was an important motivator for Berkeley's ideas.

FROM *An Essay Concerning Human Understanding*†

Book II, Chapter VIII: Some Further Considerations Concerning Our Simple Ideas

§1. Concerning the simple ideas of Sensation, it is to be considered, that whatsoever is so constituted in nature as to be able, by affecting our senses, to cause any perception in the mind, doth thereby produce in the understanding a simple idea, which, whatever be the external cause of it, when it comes to be taken notice of by our discerning faculty, it is by the mind looked on and considered there to be a real positive idea in the understanding, as much as any other whatsoever; though, perhaps, the cause of it be but a privation‡ of the subject.

§2. Thus the ideas of heat and cold, light and darkness, white and black, motion and rest, are equally clear and positive ideas in the mind, though, perhaps, some of the causes which produce them are barely

---

* P.H. Nidditch, "Introduction" to *An Essay Concerning Human Understanding* (Oxford University Press, 1975), vii.

† Locke's *An Essay Concerning Human Understanding* was first published in 1690. The excerpts given here are from the sixth edition of 1710, reprinted from Locke's 10-volume *Collected Works* (first published in 1714 and reprinted with corrections in 1823).

‡ A privation is a loss or absence of something.

privations in subjects, from whence our senses derive those ideas. These the understanding, in its view of them, considers all as distinct positive ideas, without taking notice of the causes that produce them; which is an inquiry not belonging to the idea, as it is in the understanding, but to the nature of the things existing without us. These are two very different things, and carefully to be distinguished; it being one thing to perceive and know the idea of white or black, and quite another to examine what kind of particles they must be, and how ranged in the superficies,* to make any object appear white or black.

§3. A painter or dyer, who never inquired into their causes, hath the ideas of white and black, and other colours, as clearly, perfectly, and distinctly in his understanding, and perhaps more distinctly, than the philosopher, who hath busied himself in considering their natures, and thinks he knows how far either of them is in its cause positive or privative; and the idea of black is no less positive in his mind than that of white, however the cause of that colour in the external object may be only a privation.

...

§7. To discover the nature of our ideas the better, and to discourse of them intelligibly, it will be convenient to distinguish them as they are ideas or perceptions in our minds; and as they are modifications of matter in the bodies that cause such perceptions in us: that so we may not think (as perhaps usually is done) that they are exactly the images and resemblances of something inherent in the subject; most of those of sensation being in the mind no more the likeness of something existing without us, than the names that stand for them are the likeness of our ideas, which yet upon hearing they are apt to excite in us.

§8. Whatsoever the mind perceives in itself, or is the immediate object of perception, thought, or understanding, that I call idea; and the power to produce any idea in our mind, I call quality of the subject wherein that power is. Thus a snow-ball having the power to produce in us the ideas of white, cold, and round, the powers to produce those ideas in us, as they are in the snow-ball, I call qualities; and as they are sensations or perceptions in our understandings, I call them ideas; which ideas, if I speak of sometimes

as in the things themselves, I would be understood to mean those qualities in the objects which produce them in us.

§9. Qualities thus considered in bodies are, first, such as are utterly inseparable from the body, in what state soever it be; such as in all the alterations and changes it suffers, all the force can be used upon it, it constantly keeps; and such as sense constantly finds in every particle of matter which has bulk enough to be perceived; and the mind finds inseparable from every particle of matter, though less than to make itself singly be perceived by our senses: *v.g.* take a grain of wheat, divide it into two parts; each part has still solidity, extension, figure, and mobility; divide it again, and it retains still the same qualities, and so divide it on, till the parts become insensible, they must retain still each of them all those qualities. For division (which is all that a mill, or pestle, or any other body, does upon another, in reducing it to insensible parts) can never take away either solidity, extension, figure, or mobility from any body, but only makes two or more distinct separate masses of matter, of that which was but one before; all which distinct masses, reckoned as so many distinct bodies, after division make a certain number. These I call original or primary qualities of body, which I think we may observe to produce simple ideas in us, viz. solidity, extension, figure, motion or rest, and number.

§10. Secondly, such qualities which in truth are nothing in the objects themselves, but powers to produce various sensations in us by their primary qualities, i.e., by the bulk, figure, texture, and motion of their insensible parts, as colours, sounds, tastes, &c. these I call secondary qualities. To these might be added a third sort, which are allowed to be barely powers; though they are as much real qualities in the subject as those which I, to comply with the common way of speaking, call qualities, but for distinction, secondary qualities. For the power in fire to produce a new colour, or consistency, in wax or clay, by its primary qualities, is as much a quality in fire, as the power it has to produce in me a new idea or sensation of warmth or burning, which I felt not before, by the same primary qualities, viz. the bulk, texture, and motion of its insensible parts.

---

* Outside surfaces.

§11. The next thing to be considered is, how bodies produce ideas in us; and that is manifestly by impulse,* the only way which we can conceive bodies to operate in.

§12. If then external objects be not united to our minds, when they produce ideas therein, and yet we perceive these original qualities in such of them as singly fall under our senses, it is evident that some motion must be thence continued by our nerves, or animal spirits, by some parts of our bodies, to the brains or the seat of sensation, there to produce in our minds the particular ideas we have of them. And since the extension, figure, number, and motion of bodies, of an observable bigness, may be perceived at a distance by the sight, it is evident some singly imperceptible bodies must come from them to the eyes, and thereby convey to the brain some motion, which produces these ideas which we have of them in us.

§13. After the same manner, that the ideas of these original qualities are produced in us, we may conceive that the ideas of secondary qualities are also produced, viz. by the operation of insensible particles on our senses. For it being manifest that there are bodies, and good store of bodies, each whereof are so small that we cannot, by any of our senses, discover either their bulk, figure, or motion, as is evident in the particles of the air and water, and others extremely smaller than those; perhaps as much smaller than the particles of air and water as the particles of air and water are smaller than peas or hail-stones: let us suppose at present, that the different motions and figures, bulk and number of such particles, affecting the several organs of our senses, produce in us those different sensations, which we have from the colours and smells of bodies; *v.g.* that a violet, by the impulse of such insensible particles of matter of peculiar figures and bulks, and in different degrees and modifications of their motions, causes the ideas of the blue colour and sweet scent of that flower to be produced in our minds, it being no more impossible to conceive that God should annex such ideas to such motions, with which they have no similitude, than that he should annex the idea of pain to the motion of a piece of steel dividing our flesh, with which that idea hath no resemblance.

§14. What I have said concerning colours and smells may be understood also of tastes and sounds, and other the like sensible qualities; which, whatever reality we by mistake attribute to them, are in truth nothing in the objects themselves, but powers to produce various sensations in us, and depend on those primary qualities, viz. bulk, figure, texture, and motion of parts as I have said.

§15. From whence I think it easy to draw this observation, that the ideas of primary qualities of bodies are resemblances of them, and their patterns do really exist in the bodies themselves, but the ideas produced in us by these secondary qualities have no resemblance of them at all. There is nothing like our ideas, existing in the bodies themselves. They are, in the bodies we denominate from them, only a power to produce those sensations in us; and what is sweet, blue, or warm in idea, is but the certain bulk, figure, and motion of the insensible parts, in the bodies themselves, which we call so.

§16. Flame is denominated hot and light; snow white and cold; and manna white and sweet, from the ideas they produce in us: which qualities are commonly thought to be the same in those bodies that those ideas are in us, the one the perfect resemblance of the other, as they are in a mirror; and it would by most men be judged very extravagant† if one should say otherwise. And yet he that will consider that the same fire, that at one distance produces in us the sensation of warmth, does at a nearer approach produce in us the far different sensation of pain, ought to bethink himself what reason he has to say, that his idea of warmth, which was produced in him by the fire, is actually in the fire; and his idea of pain, which the same fire produced in him the same way, is not in the fire. Why are whiteness and coldness in snow, and pain not, when it produces the one and the other idea in us, and can do neither but by the bulk, figure, number, and motion of its solid parts?

§17. The particular bulk, number, figure, and motion of the parts of fire, or snow, are really in them, whether any one's senses perceive them or no; and therefore they may be called real qualities, because they really exist in those bodies: but light, heat, whiteness,

---

*   Causal impact.

†   Odd or peculiar.

or coldness, are no more really in them than sickness or pain is in manna. Take away the sensation of them; let not the eyes see light or colours, nor the ears hear sounds; let the palate not taste, nor the nose smell; and all colours, tastes, odours, and sounds, as they are such particular ideas, vanish and cease, and are reduced to their causes, i.e., bulk, figure, and motion of parts.

§18. A piece of manna of a sensible bulk is able to produce in us the idea of a round or square figure, and, by being removed from one place to another, the idea of motion. This idea of motion represents it as it really is in manna moving: a circle or square are the same, whether in idea or existence, in the mind or in the manna; and this, both motion and figure, are really in the manna, whether we take notice of them or no: this every body is ready to agree to. Besides, manna, by the bulk, figure, texture, and motion of its parts, has a power to produce the sensations of sickness, and sometimes of acute pains or gripings* in us. That these ideas of sickness and pain are not in the manna, but effects of its operations on us, and are nowhere when we feel them not: this also every one readily agrees to. And yet men are hardly to be brought to think, that sweetness and whiteness are not really in manna; which are but the effects of the operations of manna, by the motion, size, and figure of its particles on the eyes and palate; as the pain and sickness caused by manna are confessedly nothing but the effects of its operations on the stomach and guts, by the size, motion, and figure of its insensible parts, (for by nothing else can a body operate, as has been proved); as if it could not operate on the eyes and palate, and thereby produce in the mind particular distinct ideas, which in itself it has not, as well as we allow it can operate on the guts and stomach, and thereby produce distinct ideas, which in itself it has not. These ideas being all effects of the operations of manna, on several parts of our bodies, by the size, figure, number, and motion of its parts; why those produced by the eyes and palate should rather be thought to be really in the manna than those produced by the stomach and guts; or why the pain and sickness, ideas that are the effect of manna, should be thought to be nowhere when they are not felt: and

yet the sweetness and whiteness, effects of the same manna on other parts of the body, by ways equally as unknown, should be thought to exist in the manna, when they are not seen or tasted, would need some reason to explain.

§19. Let us consider the red and white colours in porphyry:† hinder light from striking on it, and its colours vanish, it no longer produces any such ideas in us; upon the return of light it produces these appearances on us again. Can any one think any real alterations are made in the porphyry by the presence or absence of light; and that those ideas of whiteness and redness are really in porphyry in the light, when it is plain it has no colour in the dark? It has, indeed, such a configuration of particles, both night and day, as are apt, by the rays of light rebounding from some parts of that hard stone, to produce in us the idea of redness, and from others the idea of whiteness; but whiteness or redness are not in it at any time, but such a texture that hath the power to produce such a sensation in us.

§20. Pound an almond, and the clear white colour will be altered into a dirty one, and the sweet taste into an oily one. What real alteration can the beating of the pestle make in any body, but an alteration of the texture of it?

§21. Ideas being thus distinguished and understood, we may be able to give an account how the same water, at the same time, may produce the idea of cold by one hand and of heat by the other; whereas it is impossible that the same water, if those ideas were really in it, should at the same time be both hot and cold: for if we imagine warmth, as it is in our hands, to be nothing but a certain sort and degree of motion in the minute particles of our nerves or animal spirits, we may understand how it is possible that the same water may, at the same time, produce the sensations of heat in one hand, and cold in the other; which yet figure never does, that never producing the idea of a square by one hand, which has produced the idea of a globe by another. But if the sensation of heat and cold be nothing but the increase or diminution of the motion of the minute parts of our bodies, caused by the corpuscles‡ of any other body, it is easy to be understood,

---

* Pains in the bowels.
† A hard red rock filled with large red or white crystals.
‡ Small particles.

that if that motion be greater in one hand than in the other; if a body be applied to the two hands, which has in its minute particles a greater motion, than in those of one of the hands, and a less than in those of the other; it will increase the motion of the one hand and lessen it in the other, and so cause the different sensations of heat and cold that depend thereon.

§22. I have in what just goes before been engaged in physical inquiries a little further than perhaps I intended. But it being necessary to make the nature of sensation a little understood, and to make the difference between the qualities in bodies, and the ideas produced by them in the mind, to be distinctly conceived, without which it were impossible to discourse intelligibly of them, I hope I shall be pardoned this little excursion into natural philosophy, it being necessary in our present inquiry to distinguish the primary and real qualities of bodies, which are always in them (viz. solidity, extension, figure, number, and motion, or rest; and are sometimes perceived by us, viz. when the bodies they are in are big enough singly to be discerned), from those secondary and imputed qualities, which are but the powers of several combinations of those primary ones, when they operate, without being distinctly discerned; whereby we may also come to know what ideas are, and what are not, resemblances of something really existing in the bodies we denominate from them.

§23. The qualities, then, that are in bodies, rightly considered, are of three sorts. First, The bulk, figure, number, situation, and motion, or rest of their solid parts; those are in them, whether we perceive them or no; and when they are of that size that we can discover them, we have by these an idea of the thing, as it is in itself, as is plain in artificial things. These I call primary qualities.

Secondly, The power that is in any body, by reason of its insensible primary qualities, to operate after a peculiar manner on any of our senses, and thereby produce in us the different ideas of several colours, sounds, smells, tastes, &c. These are usually called sensible qualities.

Thirdly, The power that is in any body, by reason of the particular constitution of its primary qualities, to make such a change in the bulk, figure, texture, and motion of another body, as to make it operate on our senses, differently from what it did before. Thus the sun has a power to make wax white, and fire to make lead fluid. These are usually called powers.

The first of these, as has been said, I think may be properly called real, original, or primary qualities; because they are in the things themselves, whether they are perceived or no; and upon their different modifications it is that the secondary qualities depend.

The other two are only powers to act differently upon other things, which powers result from the different modifications of those primary qualities.

§24. But, though the two latter sorts of qualities are powers barely, and nothing but powers, relating to several other bodies, and resulting from the different modifications of the original qualities, yet they are generally otherwise thought of: for the second sort, viz. the powers to produce several ideas in us by our senses, are looked upon as real qualities in the things thus affecting us; but the third sort are called and esteemed barely powers, *v.g.* the idea of heat, or light, which we receive by our eyes or touch from the sun, are commonly thought real qualities, existing in the sun, and something more than mere powers in it. But when we consider the sun in reference to wax, which it melts or blanches, we look on the whiteness and softness produced in the wax, not as qualities in the sun, but effects produced by powers in it: whereas, if rightly considered, these qualities of light and warmth, which are perceptions in me when I am warmed or enlightened by the sun, are no otherwise in the sun, than the changes made in the wax, when it is blanched or melted, are in the sun. They are all of them equally powers in the sun, depending on its primary qualities; whereby it is able, in the one case, so to alter the bulk, figure, texture, or motion of some of the insensible parts of my eyes or hands, as thereby to produce in me the idea of light or heat; and in the other, it is able so to alter the bulk, figure, texture, or motion of the insensible parts of the wax, as to make them fit to produce in me the distinct ideas of white and fluid.

§25. The reason why the one are ordinarily taken for real qualities, and the other only for bare powers, seems to be, because the ideas we have of distinct colours, sounds, &c., containing nothing at all in them of bulk, figure, or motion, we are not apt to think them the effects of these primary qualities, which appear not, to our senses, to operate in their production, and with which they have not any apparent congruity or conceivable connection. Hence it is that we are so forward to imagine, that those ideas are the resemblances of something really existing in the objects themselves: since sensation discovers nothing of bulk, figure, or motion of parts in their production; nor can reason show how bodies, by their bulk, figure, and motion, should produce in the mind the ideas of blue or yellow, &c. But, in the other case, in the operations of bodies changing the qualities one of another, we plainly discover, that the quality produced hath commonly no resemblance with anything in the thing producing it; wherefore we look on it as a bare effect of power. For, through receiving the idea of heat or light from the sun, we are apt to think it is a perception and resemblance of such a quality in the sun; yet when we see wax, or a fair face, receive change of colour from the sun, we cannot imagine that to be the reception or resemblance of anything in the sun, because we find not those different colours in the sun itself. For our senses being able to observe a likeness or unlikeness of sensible qualities in two different external objects, we forwardly enough conclude the production of any sensible quality in any subject to be an effect of bare power, and not the communication of any quality, which was really in the efficient,* when we find no such sensible quality in the thing that produced it. But our senses not being able to discover any unlikeness between the idea produced in us, and the quality of the object producing it, we are apt to imagine, that our ideas are resemblances of something in the objects, and not the effects of certain powers placed in the modification of their primary qualities, with which primary qualities the ideas produced in us have no resemblance.

§26. To conclude, beside those before-mentioned primary qualities in bodies, viz. bulk, figure, extension, number, and motion of their solid parts; all the rest whereby we take notice of bodies, and distinguish them one from another, are nothing else but several powers in them, depending on those primary qualities; whereby they are fitted, either by immediately operating on our bodies to produce several different ideas in us; or else, by operating on other bodies, so to change their primary qualities, as to render them capable of producing ideas in us different from what before they did. The former of these, I think, may be called secondary qualities, immediately perceivable: the latter, secondary qualities, mediately perceivable.

Book II, Chapter XXIII: Of Our Complex Ideas of Substances [§§1–6]

§1. The mind being, as I have declared, furnished with a great number of the simple ideas, conveyed in by the senses, as they are found in exterior things, or by reflection on its own operations, takes notice also, that a certain number of these simple ideas go constantly together; which being presumed to belong to one thing, and words being suited to common apprehensions, and made use of for quick dispatch, are called, so united in one subject, by one name; which, by inadvertency, we are apt afterward to talk of and consider as one simple idea, which indeed is a complication of many ideas together; because, as I have said, not imagining how these simple ideas can subsist by themselves, we accustom ourselves to suppose some substratum wherein they do subsist, and from which they do result; which therefore we call substance.

§2. So that if any one will examine himself concerning his notion of pure substance in general, he will find he has no other idea of it at all, but only a supposition of he knows not what support of such qualities, which are capable of producing simple ideas in us; which qualities are commonly called accidents.† If any one should be asked, what is the subject wherein colour or weight inheres, he would have nothing to say, but the solid extended parts: and if he were demanded, what is it that solidity and extension adhere in, he would not be in a much better case than the Indian‡ before mentioned who, saying that the world was supported by a great elephant, was asked what the elephant rested on; to which his answer was a great tortoise. But being again pressed to know what gave support to the broad-backed tortoise, replied, something, he knew not what. And thus here, as in all other cases where we use words without having clear and distinct ideas, we talk like children; who, being questioned what such a thing is, which they know not, readily give this satisfactory answer, that it is something: which in truth signifies no more, when so used, either by children or men, but that they know not what; and that the thing they pretend to know,

---

* The cause.

† "Accidents" in philosophical usage means non-essential characteristics.

‡ A person from the subcontinent of India (rather than a native of North America).

and talk of, is what they have no distinct idea of at all, and so are perfectly ignorant of it, and in the dark. The idea then we have, to which we give the general name substance, being nothing but the supposed, but unknown support of those qualities we find existing, which we imagine cannot subsist, "*sine re substante*," without something to support them, we call that support *substantia*; which, according to the true import of the word, is, in plain English, standing under or upholding.

§3. An obscure and relative idea of substance in general being thus made, we come to have the ideas of particular sorts of substances, by collecting such combinations of simple ideas as are, by experience and observation of men's senses taken notice of to exist together, and are therefore supposed to flow from the particular internal constitution, or unknown essence of that substance. Thus we come to have the ideas of a man, horse, gold, water, &c. of which substances, whether any one has any other clear idea, farther than of certain simple ideas co-existent together, I appeal to every one's own experience. It is the ordinary qualities observable in iron, or a diamond, put together, that make the true complex idea of those substances, which a smith or a jeweller commonly knows better than a philosopher; who, whatever substantial forms he may talk of, has no other idea of those substances, than what is framed by a collection of those simple ideas which are to be found in them: only we must take notice, that our complex ideas of substances, besides all those simple ideas they are made up of, have always the confused idea of something to which they belong, and in which they subsist. And therefore when we speak of any sort of substance, we say it is a thing having such or such qualities; as body is a thing that is extended, figured, and capable of motion; spirit, a thing capable of thinking; and so hardness, friability,* and power to draw iron, we say, are qualities to be found in a loadstone.† These, and the like fashions of speaking, intimate, that the substance is supposed always something besides the extension, figure, solidity, motion, thinking, or other observable ideas, though we know not what it is.

§4. Hence, when we talk or think of any particular sort of corporeal substances, as horse, stone, &c., though the idea we have of either of them be but the complication or collection of those several simple ideas of sensible qualities, which we used to find united in the thing called horse or stone; yet, because we cannot conceive how they should subsist alone, nor one in another, we suppose them existing in and supported by some common subject; which support we denote by the name substance, though it be certain we have no clear or distinct idea of that thing we suppose a support.

§5. The same thing happens concerning the operations of the mind, viz. thinking, reasoning, fearing, &c., which we concluding not to subsist of themselves, nor apprehending how they can belong to body, or be produced by it, we are apt to think these the actions of some other substance, which we call spirit: whereby yet it is evident, that having no other idea or notion of matter, but something wherein those many sensible qualities which affect our senses do subsist; by supposing a substance wherein thinking, knowing, doubting, and a power of moving, &c. do subsist, we have as clear a notion of the substance of spirit, as we have of body; the one being supposed to be (without knowing what it is) the substratum to those simple ideas we have from without; and the other supposed (with a like ignorance of what it is) to be the substratum to those operations we experiment‡ in ourselves within. It is plain then, that the idea of corporeal substance in matter is as remote from our conceptions and apprehensions, as that of spiritual substance, or spirit: and therefore, from our not having any notion of the substance of spirit, we can no more conclude its non-existence, than we can for the same reason deny the existence of body; it being as rational to affirm there is no body, because we have no clear and distinct idea of the substance of matter, as to say there is no spirit, because we have no clear and distinct idea of the substance of a spirit.

§6. Whatever therefore be the secret, abstract nature of substance in general, all the ideas we have of particular distinct sorts of substances are nothing

---

*   Brittleness, crumbliness.
†   A piece of magnetite (iron oxide) that has magnetic properties.
‡   Here, "experiment" means "experience."

but several combinations of simple ideas co-existing in such, though unknown, cause of their union, as make the whole subsist of itself. It is by such combinations of simple ideas, and nothing else, that we represent particular sorts of substances to ourselves; such are the ideas we have of their several species in our minds; and such only do we, by their specific names, signify to others, *v.g.* man, horse, sun, water, iron: upon hearing which words, every one who understands the language, frames in his mind a combination of those several simple ideas, which he has usually observed, or fancied to exist together under that denomination; all which he supposes to rest in, and be as it were, adherent to that unknown common subject, which inheres not in anything else. Though, in the mean time it be manifest, and every one upon inquiry into his own thoughts will find, that he has no other idea of any substance, *v.g.* let it be gold, horse, iron, man, vitriol,* bread, but what he has barely of those sensible qualities, which he supposes to inhere, with a supposition of such a substratum, as gives, as it were, a support to those qualities or simple ideas, which he has observed to exist united together. Thus the idea of the sun, what is it but an aggregate of those several simple ideas, bright, hot, roundish, having a constant regular motion, at a certain distance from us, and perhaps some other? As he who thinks and discourses of the sun has been more or less accurate in observing those sensible qualities, ideas, or properties, which are in that thing which he calls the sun.

Book IV, Chapter XI: Of Our Knowledge of the Existence of Other Things

§1. The knowledge of our own being we have by intuition. The existence of a God, reason clearly makes known to us, as has been shown.[†]

The knowledge of the existence of any other thing we can have only by sensation: for there being no necessary connection of real existence with any idea a man hath in his memory, nor of any other existence but that of God, with the existence of any particular man; no particular man can know the existence of any other being, but only when, by actual operating upon him, it makes itself perceived by him. For, the having the idea of anything in our mind no more proves the existence of that thing, than the picture of a man evidences[‡] his being in the world, or the visions of a dream make thereby a true history.

§2. It is therefore the actual receiving of ideas from without, that gives us notice of the existence of other things, and makes us know that something doth exist at that time without us, which causes that idea in us, though perhaps we neither know nor consider how it does it: for it takes not from the certainty of our senses, and the ideas we receive by them, that we know not the manner wherein they are produced: *v.g.* whilst I write this, I have, by the paper affecting my eyes, that idea produced in my mind, which, whatever object causes, I call white; by which I know that that quality or accident (i.e., whose appearance before my eyes always causes that idea) doth really exist, and hath a being without me. And of this, the greatest assurance I can possibly have, and to which my faculties can attain, is the testimony of my eyes, which are the proper and sole judges of this thing, whose testimony I have reason to rely on as so certain, that I can no more doubt, whilst I write this, that I see white and black, and that something really exists, that causes that sensation in me, than that I write or move my hand; which is a certainty as great as human nature is capable of, concerning the existence of anything but a man's self alone, and of God.

§3. The notice we have by our senses of the existing of things without us, though it be not altogether so certain as our intuitive knowledge, or the deductions of our reason, employed about the clear abstract ideas of our own minds; yet it is an assurance that deserves the name of knowledge. If we persuade ourselves that our faculties act and inform us right, concerning the existence of those objects that affect them, it cannot pass for an ill-grounded confidence: for I think nobody can,

---

*   Sulfuric acid.

†   These two claims were argued for in his previous two chapters (IX and X). Intuition, for Locke, is roughly direct knowledge—something we can directly see to be true—and is to be contrasted with the indirect knowledge we get from sensation, memory, or reason.

‡   In this context, "evidences" can be read as "shows."

in earnest, be so sceptical as to be uncertain of the existence of those things which he sees and feels. At least, he that can doubt so far (whatever he may have with his own thoughts) will never have any controversy* with me; since he can never be sure I say anything contrary to his own opinion. As to myself, I think God has given me assurance enough of the existence of things without me; since by their different application I can produce in myself both pleasure and pain, which is one great concernment of my present state. This is certain, the confidence that our faculties do not herein deceive us, is the greatest assurance we are capable of concerning the existence of material beings. For we cannot act anything, but by our faculties; nor talk of knowledge itself, but by the helps of those faculties, which are fitted to apprehend even what knowledge is. But besides the assurance we have from our senses themselves, that they do not err in the information they give us, of the existence of things without us, when they are affected by them, we are further confirmed in this assurance by other concurrent reasons.

§4. First, it is plain those perceptions are produced in us by exterior causes affecting our senses; because those that want the organs of any sense never can have the ideas belonging to that sense produced in their minds. This is too evident to be doubted: and therefore we cannot but be assured that they come in by the organs of that sense, and no other way. The organs themselves, it is plain, do not produce them; for then the eyes of a man in the dark would produce colours, and his nose smell roses in the winter: but we see nobody gets the relish of a pine-apple till he goes to the Indies, where it is, and tastes it.

§5. Secondly, because sometimes I find that I cannot avoid the having those ideas produced in my mind. For though when my eyes are shut, or windows fast, I can at pleasure recall to my mind the ideas of light, or the sun, which former sensations had lodged in my memory; so I can at pleasure lay by that idea, and take into my view that of the smell of a rose, or taste of sugar. But, if I turn my eyes at noon towards the sun, I cannot avoid the ideas, which the light, or sun, then produces in me. So that there is a manifest difference between the ideas laid up in my memory (over which,

if they were there only, I should have constantly the same power to dispose of them, and lay them by at pleasure) and those which force themselves upon me, and I cannot avoid having. And therefore it must needs be some exterior cause, and the brisk acting of some objects without me, whose efficacy I cannot resist, that produces those ideas in my mind, whether I will or no. Besides, there is nobody who doth not perceive the difference in himself between contemplating the sun, as he hath the idea of it in his memory, and actually looking upon it; of which two his perception is so distinct, that few of his ideas are more distinguishable one from another. And therefore he hath certain knowledge, that they are not both memory, or the actions of his mind, and fancies only within him; but that actual seeing hath a cause without.

§6. Thirdly, add to this, that many of those ideas are produced in us with pain, which afterwards we remember without the least offence.† Thus, the pain of heat or cold, when the idea of it is revived in our minds, gives us no disturbance; which, when felt, was very troublesome, and is again, when actually repeated; which is occasioned by the disorder the external object causes in our bodies when applied to it. And we remember the pains of hunger, thirst, or the head-ache, without any pain at all; which would either never disturb us, or else constantly do it, as often as we thought of it, were there nothing more but ideas floating in our minds, and appearances entertaining our fancies, without the real existence of things affecting us from abroad. The same may be said of pleasure, accompanying several actual sensations: and though mathematical demonstration depends not upon sense, yet the examining them by diagrams gives great credit to the evidence of our sight, and seems to give it a certainty approaching to that of demonstration itself. For it would be very strange that a man should allow it for an undeniable truth, that two angles of a figure, which he measures by lines and angles of a diagram, should be bigger one than the other; and yet doubt of the existence of those lines and angles, which by looking on he makes use of to measure that by.

§7. Fourthly, our senses in many cases bear witness to the truth of each other's report, concerning the

---

* Disagreement, argument.
† Painful sensation.

existence of sensible things without us. He that sees a fire may, if he doubt whether it be anything more than a bare fancy, feel it too; and be convinced, by putting his hand in it: which certainly could never be put into such exquisite pain by a bare idea or phantom,* unless that the pain be a fancy too; which yet he cannot, when the burn is well, by raising the idea of it, bring upon himself again.

Thus I see, whilst I write this, I can change the appearance of the paper: and by designing the letters, tell beforehand what new idea it shall exhibit the very next moment, by barely drawing my pen over it: which will neither appear (let me fancy as much as I will) if my hands stand still; or though I move my pen, if my eyes be shut: nor, when those characters are once made on the paper, can I choose afterwards but see them as they are; that is, have the ideas of such letters as I have made. Whence it is manifest, that they are not barely the sport and play of my own imagination, when I find that the characters, that were made at the pleasure of my own thought, do not obey them; nor yet cease to be, whenever I shall fancy it; but continue to affect my senses constantly and regularly, according to the figures I made them. To which if we will add, that the sight of those shall, from another man, draw such sounds as I beforehand design they shall stand for; there will be little reason left to doubt that those words I write do really exist without me, when they cause a long series of regular sounds to affect my ears, which could not be the effect of my imagination, nor could my memory retain them in that order.

§8. But yet, if after all this any one will be so sceptical as to distrust his senses, and to affirm that all we see and hear, feel and taste, think and do, during our whole being, is but the series and deluding appearances of a long dream, whereof there is no reality; and therefore will question the existence of all things, or our knowledge of any thing; I must desire him to consider, that, if all be a dream, then he doth but dream that he makes the question; and so it is not much matter that a waking man should answer him. But yet, if he pleases, he may dream that I make him this answer, that the certainty of things existing *in rerum natura*,† when we have the testimony of our senses for it, is not only as great as our frame can attain to, but as our condition needs. For, our faculties being suited not to the full extent of being, nor to a perfect, clear, comprehensive knowledge of things free from all doubt and scruple; but to the preservation of us, in whom they are, and accommodated to the use of life; they serve to our purpose well enough, if they will but give us certain notice of those things which are convenient or inconvenient to us. For he that sees a candle burning, and hath experimented the force of its flame, by putting his finger in it, will little doubt that this is something existing without him, which does him harm, and puts him to great pain: which is assurance enough, when no man requires greater certainty to govern his actions by than what is as certain as his actions themselves. And if our dreamer pleases to try whether the glowing heat of a glass furnace be barely a wandering imagination in a drowsy man's fancy; by putting his hand into it he may perhaps be wakened into a certainty greater than he could wish, that it is something more than bare imagination. So that this evidence is as great as we can desire, being as certain to us as our pleasure or pain, i.e., happiness or misery; beyond which we have no concernment, either of knowing or being. Such an assurance of the existence of things without us is sufficient to direct us in the attaining the good, and avoiding the evil, which is caused by them; which is the important concernment we have of being made acquainted with them.

§9. In fine, then, when our senses do actually convey into our understandings any idea, we cannot but be satisfied that there doth something at that time really exist without us, which doth affect our senses, and by them give notice of itself to our apprehensive faculties, and actually produce that idea which we then perceive: and we cannot so far distrust their testimony, as to doubt that such collections of simple ideas as we have observed by our senses to be united together, do really exist together. But this knowledge extends as far as the present testimony of our senses, employed about particular objects that do then affect them, and no further. For if I saw such a collection of simple ideas, as is wont to be called man, existing together one minute since, and am now alone, I cannot be certain that the same

---

* "Phantom" here and "fancy" earlier both mean illusion, hallucination, imaginary object.

† "In the nature of things," or sometimes, more specifically "in physical reality."

man exists now, since there is no necessary connection of his existence a minute since with his existence now: by a thousand ways he may cease to be, since I had the testimony of my senses for his existence. And if I cannot be certain that the man I saw last to-day is now in being, I can less be certain that he is so who hath been longer removed from my senses, and I have not seen since yesterday, or since the last year: and much less can I be certain of the existence of men that I never saw. And, therefore, though it be highly probable that millions of men do now exist, yet, whilst I am alone writing this, I have not that certainty of it which we strictly call knowledge; though the great likelihood of it puts me past doubt, and it be reasonable for me to do several things upon the confidence that there are men (and men also of my acquaintance, with whom I have to do) now in the world: but this is but probability, not knowledge.

§10. Whereby yet we may observe how foolish and vain a thing it is for a man of a narrow knowledge, who having reason given him to judge of the different evidence and probability of things, and to be swayed accordingly,—how vain, I say, it is to expect demonstration and certainty in things not capable of it, and refuse assent to very rational propositions, and act contrary to very plain and clear truths, because they cannot be made out so evident, as to surmount every the least (I will not say reason but) pretence of doubting. He that, in the ordinary affairs of life would admit of* nothing but direct plain demonstration, would be sure of nothing in this world, but of perishing quickly. The wholesomeness of his meat or drink would not give him reason to venture on it: and I would fain† know, what it is he could do upon such grounds as are capable of no doubt, no objection.

§11. As when our senses are actually employed about any object, we do know that it does exist; so by our memory we may be assured, that heretofore things that affected our senses have existed. And thus we have knowledge of the past existence of several things whereof, our senses having informed us, our memories still retain the ideas; and of this we are past all doubt, so long as we remember well. But this knowledge also reaches no further than our senses have formerly assured us. Thus, seeing water at this instant, it is an unquestionable truth to me that water doth exist: and remembering that I saw it yesterday, it will also be always true, and as long as my memory retains it, always an undoubted proposition to me, that water did exist the 10th of July, 1688, as it will also be equally true that a certain number of very fine colours did exist, which at the same time I saw upon a bubble of that water: but, being now quite out of sight both of the water and bubbles too, it is no more certainly known to me that the water doth now exist, than that the bubbles or colours therein do so; it being no more necessary that water should exist to-day, because it existed yesterday, than that the colours or bubbles exist to-day, because they existed yesterday; though it be exceedingly much more probable, because water hath been observed to continue long in existence but bubbles and the colours on them, quickly cease to be.

§12. What ideas we have of spirits,‡ and how we come by them, I have already shown. But though we have those ideas in our minds, and know we have them there, the having the ideas of spirits does not make us know that any such things do exist without us, or that there are any finite spirits, or any other spiritual beings but the eternal God. We have ground from revelation, and several other reasons, to believe with assurance that there are such creatures: but our senses not being able to discover them, we want the means of knowing their particular existences. For we can no more know, that there are finite spirits really existing, by the idea we have of such beings in our minds, than by the ideas any one has of fairies, or centaurs, he can come to know that things answering those ideas do really exist.

And therefore concerning the existence of finite spirits, as well as several other things, we must content ourselves with the evidence of faith; but universal certain propositions concerning this matter are beyond our reach. For however true it may be, *v.g.* that all the intelligent spirits that God ever created do still exist; yet it can never make a part of our certain knowledge.

---

* "Admit of": accept.

† Gladly, happily.

‡ Spiritual beings such as angels.

These and the like propositions we may assent to as highly probable, but are not, I fear, in this state capable of knowing. We are not then to put others upon demonstrating, nor ourselves upon search of universal certainty, in all those matters, wherein we are not capable of any other knowledge, but what our senses give us in this or that particular.

§13. By which it appears that there are two sorts of propositions: 1. There is one sort of propositions concerning the existence of any thing answerable to such an idea: as having the idea of an elephant, phoenix,* motion, or an angel, in my mind, the first and natural inquiry is, Whether such a thing does anywhere exist? And this knowledge is only of particulars. No existence of anything without us, but only of God, can certainly be known farther than our senses inform us. 2. There is another sort of propositions, wherein is expressed the agreement or disagreement of our abstract ideas, and their dependence on one another. Such propositions may be universal and certain. So having the idea of God and myself, of fear and obedience, I cannot but be sure that God is to be feared and obeyed by me: and this proposition will be certain, concerning man in general, if I have made an abstract idea of such a species, whereof I am one particular. But yet this proposition, how certain soever, that men ought to fear and obey God proves not to me the existence of men in the world, but will be true of all such creatures, whenever they do exist: which certainty of such general propositions depends on the agreement or disagreement to be discovered in those abstract ideas.

§14. In the former case, our knowledge is the consequence of the existence of things producing ideas in our minds by our senses: in the latter, knowledge is the consequence of the ideas (be they what they will) that are in our minds, producing there general certain propositions. Many of these are called *aeternae veritates*,[†] and all of them indeed are so; not from being written all or any of them in the minds of all men; or that they were any of them propositions in any one's mind till he, having got the abstract ideas, joined or separated them by affirmation or negation. But wheresoever we can suppose such a creature as man is, endowed with such faculties, and thereby furnished with such ideas as we have, we must conclude, he must needs, when he applies his thoughts to the consideration of his ideas, know the truth of certain propositions that will arise from the agreement or disagreement which he will perceive in his own ideas. Such propositions are therefore called eternal truths, not because they are eternal propositions actually formed, and antecedent to the understanding, that at any time makes them; nor because they are imprinted on the mind from any patterns, that are anywhere out of the mind, and existed before: but because being once made about abstract ideas, so as to be true, they will, whenever they can be supposed to be made again at any time past or to come, by a mind having those ideas, always actually be true. For names being supposed to stand perpetually for the same ideas, and the same ideas having immutably the same habitudes[‡] one to another; propositions concerning any abstract ideas that are once true, must needs be eternal verities. ■

---

* Mythological bird that dies in flame and is regenerated from its ashes.
† "Eternal verities"—things that are eternally true.
‡ Relations, connections.

Suggestions for Critical Reflection

1. It is relatively easy to see roughly how Locke's distinction between primary and secondary qualities is supposed to go, but harder to see what Locke's *argument* for this distinction is. Do you think Locke backs up his claims with arguments? If so, how strong do you think they are? In the end, how plausible is the primary/secondary quality distinction?

2. Similarly, while it is relatively easy to see roughly how Locke's distinction between primary and secondary qualities is supposed to go, it is harder to see *precisely* how the distinction works. For example, what might Locke mean by saying that our ideas of primary qualities resemble their causes while our ideas of secondary qualities do not? Does this really make any sense? If it doesn't, then what other criterion should we use to help us make the distinction?

3. There has recently been some controversy about Locke's position on substance. The traditional view is that Locke defended substance, but was wrong to do so since his own arguments had effectively shown that we could have no such idea. The notion of substance in question here is that of a "bare particular" or "substratum"—that which underlies properties, as opposed to any of the properties themselves. A more recent interpretation holds that Locke did indeed defend some notion of substance, but one which is more defensible. This is the idea of substance as the "real essence" of something: roughly, for Locke, something's real essence is supposed to be the (unknown) set of properties that forms the causal basis for the observable properties of that thing (just as the atomic structure of gold is responsible for its color, softness, shininess, and so on). Which of these two conceptions of substance do you find the more plausible? (Can you see why philosophers have typically found the notion of a substratum difficult to make sense of?) Which of these notions of substance do you think fits better with what Locke actually says? Do you perhaps prefer a third interpretation?

4. What do you make of Locke's response to skepticism about the existence of the external world? Does it convince you? Do you find plausible the way Locke carefully divides up different types of knowledge about the external world and gives different answers for them?

5. What kind of entity might a Lockean idea be? What, if anything, is it made of? How determinate must it be? For example, if I clearly perceive the idea of a speckled hen, must we say that I perceive (have the idea of) a particular number of speckles, say 12,372? If not, does that mean the idea does not *have* a determinate number of speckles (even though it's a perfectly clear idea and not blurry at all)? What kind of object could *that* be? Some recent commentators, such as John Yolton, have tried to defend Locke from these kinds of puzzles by suggesting that Locke never meant ideas to be mental *things* at all: what, then, could they be instead?

6. How could an idea, in Locke's sense, really be *caused* by material objects in the external world? What could the last few steps of this causal chain be like?

7. If ideas are the objects of our thought—the things we "perceive" in thought—then what is it that does the perceiving, do you think? Can we distinguish it from the succession of ideas?

EDMUND L. GETTIER

Is Justified True Belief Knowledge?

Who Was Edmund Gettier?

Edmund Gettier's career was one of the most unusual in contemporary academic philosophy. His first teaching job was at Wayne State University, in Detroit, Michigan. During the early sixties, the chair of his department suggested that, as tenure consideration approached, some publication might help. The result was "Is Justified True Belief Knowledge?" This article took up all of three pages of a 1963 issue of *Analysis*, but it's the best-known article ever published in epistemology. All Gettier did there was present two examples, but these two showed that the most basic assumption of epistemology since Plato was wrong. Eminent philosopher David Lewis cited Gettier and Gödel as perhaps the only thinkers ever who conclusively refuted a philosophical theory.[*]

As to the extent of Gettier's subsequent publication dossier, beliefs differ. One of his friends thinks there's one other Gettier article in print; another believes there are two.[†] The Philosopher's Index lists only two others, both translations. Despite his limited publication record and his "massive indifference to the usual trappings of an academic career," Gettier's friends agree that he demonstrated an "abiding, deep commitment to philosophy."[‡] Gettier died in 2021 at the age of 93.

What Was Gettier's Overall Philosophical Project?

Gettier attacks a widely-accepted analysis of the concept of *knowledge*. The analysis of knowledge Gettier attacks is the claim that the necessary and sufficient conditions for S (a subject) knowing that P (a proposition) are that (a) P is true; (b) S believes P; and (c) S has justification for this belief.

What Is the Structure of This Reading?

Gettier begins with two assumptions. The first is that one can have justification for believing something that's false.

A tiny bit of background in logic is necessary to understand the second. Logicians say that a statement P is *entailed* by another statement Q when it's logically impossible for P to be false given the truth of Q. So, for example, *The picnic is off* is entailed by *It's raining* and *If it's raining, the picnic is off*.

Gettier's second assumption is that whenever P is entailed by Q, and a person believes Q, and is justified in this belief, and deduces P from Q, and accepts P on this basis, then that person is justified in believing P. Suppose, for example, you believe, with good justification, that it's raining and if it's raining, the picnic is off. And so you deduce from this, and accordingly believe, that the picnic is off. According to Gettier's second assumption, you're justified in believing that the picnic is off.

The second assumption seems quite reasonable. After all, the fact that one's belief that Q is justified means that you'd count Q as likely to be true; and the fact that Q entails P means that P is likely to be true also; so you'd also be justified in believing P.

Applying these reasonable assumptions to Smith's belief in each of Gettier's two examples, we'd conclude that Smith is justified in his belief in both cases. Since both beliefs are true, they should count as knowledge, under the traditional analysis of knowledge as justified

---

[*]   *Philosophical Papers*, Vol. I (Oxford University Press, 1983), x.
[†]   The first opinion is from Robert C. Sleigh, Jr., "Knowing Edmund Gettier," *Philosophical Analysis: A Defense by Example*, ed. David F. Austin (Kluwer, 1987), xiv; the second is from Austin's Preface to that book, xii.
[‡]   Sleigh, xiii.

true belief; but in neither case would we agree that Smith's true beliefs are knowledge.

There has been an enormous amount of discussion in print concerning what to do about Gettier's examples (and other similar sorts of examples, known as Gettier-type cases). Some philosophers have tried to propose a theory of justification that would better account for our judgments about the beliefs of Smith (and the believers in other Gettier-type cases). Others have argued that what's needed is that an additional condition (aside from justified true belief) be added for the correct analysis of knowledge.

Some Useful Background Information

1. In Gettier's time, but less frequently nowadays, philosophers believed their job (or one of them) was to provide analyses of concepts; an analysis, in this sense, provides the conditions for the concept's application, and it was generally thought that the ideal analysis of any concept would provide a list of *necessary* and *sufficient* application conditions.

    The *necessary conditions* for the application of a concept are those such that if something doesn't meet those conditions, the concept doesn't apply to it. Thus, for example, one of the necessary conditions for being someone's brother is being male. You can't be anyone's brother unless you're male. The sufficient conditions are those such that if something does meet these conditions, the concept does apply to it. Thus, being someone's male sibling is sufficient for the application of the concept *brother*. In this case, being someone's male sibling is also necessary. So it's necessary and sufficient; and the successful analysis of the concept *brother* is given by providing this list of conditions which are each necessary and together sufficient: (a) male, (b) somebody's sibling.*

2. It's clear, and hardly needs argument, that believing P is necessary for knowing P. If you don't

believe it, you wouldn't be said to know it. And the truth of P is another obvious necessary condition; your beliefs that are in fact false aren't knowledge, even though you think they are. The third necessary condition—that P be justified—needs a bit more explanation. This is added to distinguish between genuine knowledge and just a lucky guess. If S believes some true P merely because of a hunch, S's belief has no firm grounding, no justification, so it doesn't merit being called knowledge. When Fred wins the lottery, and says he knew he'd win, what he says is false. He may have been firmly convinced he'd win, but he had no justification for this, so he didn't know it. (Note that one may sometimes have justification for a false belief, when a large preponderance of evidence points toward it. But then it's not knowledge either.)

3. The places in Plato's writing Gettier mentions in a footnote, where Plato appears to suggest that knowledge is justified true belief, are these:

From Plato, *Theaetetus*†

SOCRATES: But, my friend, if true opinion and knowledge were the same thing in law courts, the best of judges could never have true opinion without knowledge; in fact, however, it appears that the two are different.

THEAETETUS: Oh yes, I remember now, Socrates, having heard someone make the distinction, but I had forgotten it. He said that knowledge was true opinion accompanied by reason, but that unreasoning true opinion was outside of the sphere of knowledge; and matters of which there is not a rational explanation are unknowable—yes, that is what he called them—and those of which there is are knowable.

From Plato, *Meno*

SOCRATES: Well, and a person who had a right opinion as to which was the way, but had never

---

* This is supposed to be a simple example of a conceptual analysis, but it's worth noticing that even in a case as elementary as this there are hidden complexities: What if the male-female gender binary is problematic? What does it mean to be a sibling—must this be a biological notion? Analysis is rarely as straightforward as it may initially seem.

† Both this and the following translation are from Benjamin Jowett.

been there and did not really know, might give right guidance, might he not?

MENO: Certainly.

SOCRATES: And so long, I presume, as he has right opinion about that which the other man really knows, he will be just as good a guide—if he thinks the truth instead of knowing it—as the man who has the knowledge.

MENO: Just as good.

SOCRATES: Hence true opinion is as good a guide to rightness of action as knowledge; and this is a point we omitted just now in our consideration of the nature of virtue, when we stated that knowledge is the only guide of right action; whereas we find there is also true opinion.

MENO: So it seems.

SOCRATES: Then right opinion is just as useful as knowledge.

MENO: With this difference, Socrates, that he who has knowledge will always hit on the right way, whereas he who has right opinion will sometimes do so, but sometimes not.

SOCRATES: How do you mean? Will not he who always has right opinion be always right, so long as he opines rightly?

MENO: It appears to me that he must; and therefore I wonder, Socrates, this being the case, that knowledge should ever be more prized than right opinion, and why they should be two distinct and separate things.

SOCRATES: Well, do you know why it is that you wonder, or shall I tell you?

MENO: Please tell me.

SOCRATES: It is because you have not observed with attention the images of Daedalus.* But perhaps there are none in your country.

MENO: What is the point of your remark?

SOCRATES: That if they are not fastened up they play truant and run away; but, if fastened, they stay where they are.

MENO: Well, what of that?

SOCRATES: To possess one of his works which is let loose does not count for much in value; it will not stay with you any more than a runaway slave: but when fastened up it is worth a great deal, for his productions are very fine things. And to what am I referring in all this? To true opinion. For these, so long as they stay with us, are a fine possession, and effect all that is good; but they do not care to stay for long, and run away out of the human soul, and thus are of no great value until one makes them fast with causal reasoning. And this process, friend Meno, is recollection,† as in our previous talk we have agreed. But when once they are fastened, in the first place they turn into knowledge, and in the second, are abiding. And this is why knowledge is more prized than right opinion: the one transcends the other by its trammels.

MENO: Upon my word, Socrates, it seems to be very much as you say.

---

* Socrates refers here to the legend that the first sculptor, Daedalus, put mechanisms inside his works that made them move.

† Socrates argues earlier in this dialogue that real knowledge comes from recollection of the general Forms of things encountered before birth.

Is Justified True Belief Knowledge?*

Various attempts have been made in recent years to state necessary and sufficient conditions for someone's knowing a given proposition. The attempts have often been such that they can be stated in a form similar to the following:[1]

(a) S knows that P   *IFF*[†]
   (i) P is true,
   (ii) S believes that P, and
   (iii) S is justified in believing that P.

For example, Chisholm has held that the following gives the necessary and sufficient conditions for knowledge:[2]

(b) S knows that P   *IFF*
   (i)   S accepts P,
   (ii) S has adequate evidence for P, and
   (iii) P is true.

Ayer has stated the necessary and sufficient conditions for knowledge as follows:[3]

(c) S knows that P   *IFF*
   (i)   P is true,
   (ii) S is sure that P is true, and
   (iii) S has the right to be sure that P is true.

I shall argue that (a) is false in that the conditions stated therein do not constitute a *sufficient* condition for the truth of the proposition that S knows that P. The same argument will show that (b) and (c) fail if "has adequate evidence for" or "has the right to be sure that" is substituted for "is justified in believing that" throughout.

I shall begin by noting two points. First, in that sense of 'justified' in which S's being justified in believing P is a necessary condition of S's knowing that P, it is possible for a person to be justified in believing a proposition that is in fact false. Secondly, for any proposition P, if S is justified in believing P, and P entails Q, and S deduces Q from P and accepts Q as a result of this deduction, then S is justified in believing Q. Keeping these two points in mind, I shall now present two cases in which the conditions stated in (a) are true for some proposition, though it is at the same time false that the person in question knows that proposition.

Case I

Suppose that Smith and Jones have applied for a certain job. And suppose that Smith has strong evidence for the following conjunctive proposition:[‡]

(d) Jones is the man who will get the job, and Jones has ten coins in his pocket.

Smith's evidence for (d) might be that the president of the company assured him that Jones would in the end be selected, and that he, Smith, had counted the coins in Jones's pocket ten minutes ago. Proposition (d) entails:

(e) The man who will get the job has ten coins in his pocket.

Let us suppose that Smith sees the entailment from (d) to (e), and accepts (e) on the grounds of (d), for which he has strong evidence. In this case, Smith is clearly justified in believing that (e) is true.

But imagine, further, that unknown to Smith, he himself, not Jones, will get the job. And, also, unknown to Smith, he himself has ten coins in his pocket. Proposition (e) is then true, though proposition (d), from which Smith inferred (e), is false. In our example, then, all of the following are true: (*i*) (e) is true, (*ii*) Smith believes that (e) is true, and (*iii*) Smith is justified in believing that (e) is true. But it is equally

---

*   "Is Justified True Belief Knowledge?" *Analysis* 23 (June 1963): 121–23.
†   'IFF' is an abbreviation for 'If and only if.' 'X if and only if Y' means if X then Y, and if Y then X.
‡   A conjunctive proposition is a statement composed of two propositions connected by 'and.' "It's raining and it's Tuesday" is an example. A conjunctive proposition is true when both of its components are true; otherwise, it's false.

clear that Smith does not *know* that (e) is true; for (e) is true in virtue of the number of coins in Smith's pocket, while Smith does not know how many coins are in Smith's pocket, and bases his belief in (e) on a count of the coins in Jones's pocket, whom he falsely believes to be the man who will get the job.

Case II

Let us suppose that Smith has strong evidence for the following proposition:

(f) Jones owns a Ford.

Smith's evidence might be that Jones has at all times in the past within Smith's memory owned a car, and always a Ford, and that Jones has just offered Smith a ride while driving a Ford. Let us imagine, now, that Smith has another friend, Brown, of whose whereabouts he is totally ignorant. Smith selects three place-names quite at random, and constructs the following three propositions:

(g) Either Jones owns a Ford, or Brown is in Boston;
(h) Either Jones owns a Ford, or Brown is in Barcelona;

(i) Either Jones owns a Ford, or Brown is in Brest-Litovsk.

Each of these propositions is entailed by (f).* Imagine that Smith realizes the entailment of each of these propositions he has constructed by (f), and proceeds to accept (g), (h), and (i) on the basis of (f). Smith has correctly inferred (g), (h), and (i) from a proposition for which he has strong evidence. Smith is therefore completely justified in believing each of these three propositions. Smith, of course, has no idea where Brown is.

But imagine now that two further conditions hold. First, Jones does *not* own a Ford, but is at present driving a rented car. And secondly, by the sheerest coincidence, and entirely unknown to Smith, the place mentioned in proposition (h) happens really to be the place where Brown is. If these two conditions hold then Smith does *not* know that (h) is true, even though (*i*) (h) *is* true, (*ii*) Smith does believe that (h) is true, and (*iii*) Smith is justified in believing that (h) is true.

These two examples show that definition (a) does not state a *sufficient* condition for someone's knowing a given proposition. The same cases, with appropriate changes, will suffice to show that neither definition (b) nor definition (c) do so either. ∎

Suggestions for Critical Reflection

1. Sometimes you say, "I just know that ..." when what you're saying is merely that you feel certain. But most philosophers would say that feeling certain that P is not a sufficient condition for knowing that P. Do you agree? Why or why not? Perhaps a more likely claim is that feeling certain that P is a necessary condition for knowing that P. Do you agree? Why or why not?

2. One suggestion to deal with Gettier-type cases is to add an additional necessary condition to the traditional analysis: that S's belief not be the result of S's inference from a false belief. But consider this example: S believes that there are sheep in the field, and this is true; but what S in fact has seen is really a large furry dog. So S doesn't know there are sheep there. It's sometimes thought that there's no inference from a false belief in this case—why might this be, and do you agree? If so, why might this show the inadequacy of the current proposal?

3. Another suggestion is that S's belief has to have been arrived at by a generally reliable method.

---

* Note that a statement 'P' entails 'P or Q,' where 'Q' is any proposition at all. That's because a disjunctive proposition—one composed by connecting two component propositions with 'or'—is true when (at least) one of its components is true. So assuming that P is true, then it follows that P or anything-at-all must also be true.

But consider this example: S's watch has kept perfect time for years, so looking at her watch is a generally reliable way of finding out what time it is. Today, S looks at her watch at exactly 1 pm, and the watch shows 1:00. S believes correctly that it's 1 pm. But the watch stopped the previous night at 1 am. So S doesn't know that it's 1 pm. This is sometimes taken to show the inadequacy of this proposal—does it?

4. Here's a third troublesome Gettier-type case. S knows a barn when she sees one. But today, unbeknownst to her, she's traveling in an area where they're making a movie, and set designers have built a large number of barn-facades that look just like real barns from the road. By fortunate coincidence, S sees, however, what is the only real barn in the area, and believes (correctly) that there's a real barn there. Does S know that there's a (real) barn there? Is this true belief justified, given that S is an excellent barn-detector?

Notes

1   Plato seems to be considering some such definition at *Theaetetus* 201, and perhaps accepting one at *Meno* 98. [See "Some Useful Background Information" in the introduction to this reading.]

2   Roderick M. Chisholm, *Perceiving: A Philosophical Study* (Ithaca, NY: Cornell University Press, 1957), 16.

3   A.J. Ayer, *The Problem of Knowledge* (London: Macmillan, 1956), 34.

JENNIFER SAUL

Scepticism and Implicit Bias

Who Is Jennifer Saul?

Jennifer Saul is an American-born philosopher who worked for many years at the University of Sheffield in the UK and has recently moved to become Waterloo Chair in Social and Political Philosophy of Language at the University of Waterloo in Ontario, Canada. She is known for her work in both philosophy of language and feminist philosophy. Saul was born in Ohio to a progressive family of academics. She recalls attending her first feminist consciousness-raising meeting at four years old, accompanied by her grandmother, a mathematician who was active in the 1970s feminist movement.* She earned her MA and PhD at Princeton, specializing in analytic philosophy of language. As Saul notes, she hadn't yet entertained the possibility of feminist philosophy during her student years, believing that feminism was "too obviously correct to be something one could do philosophy about."† Ultimately, Saul came to recognize that social justice is connected in important ways to the very aspects of language that were already the focus of her work.

Saul's publications include *Feminism: Issues & Arguments* (2003), *Substitution, Simple Sentences and Intuitions* (2007), and *Lying, Misleading and What Is Said: An Exploration in Philosophy of Language and in Ethics* (2012). Saul co-founded two influential blogs: "Feminist Philosophers" and "What Is It Like to Be a Woman in Philosophy?"‡ She has been a vocal advocate for remedying the race and gender imbalance in academic philosophy, and in 2011 was awarded the Distinguished Woman Philosopher Award by the Society for Women in Philosophy.

What Is the Structure of This Reading?

Saul begins this paper by reviewing the scientific literature surrounding the phenomenon of implicit bias, illustrating a number of ways in which implicit biases appear to disadvantage some people in hiring processes, academic work, and other social interactions. She then argues that the doubt generated by the discovery of implicit bias entails a special sort of skepticism. While traditional philosophical skepticism is often seen as a form of "armchair philosophy," with little practical significance in our lives, the skepticism arising from bias-related doubt is far more troublesome, as it demands both attention and action. According to Saul, we ought to be more "unsettled" by implicit bias than by more traditional skeptical concerns such as the possibility that we are brains in vats. While we may have difficulty proving definitively that we are not brains in vats, in the case of bias-related doubt we actually have strong positive evidence from scientific studies indicating that we are frequently making errors. Moreover, if we are making bias-related errors we really should take action to change this given the harmful social consequences, whereas if we are brains in vats it's not clear that this would actually require us to change our actions.

In the final sections of this paper, Saul asks what we should do about these new concerns. We might attempt to use "counter-intuitive mechanical techniques" to reduce the effects of implicit bias, but Saul notes that the effectiveness of such techniques may be limited, as they typically target very specific associations and behaviors. The only complete solution, according to Saul, is to eradicate all types of prejudice and stereotype, which would result in nothing less than a "sweeping and radical transformation of our social world."

---

* Interview with Jennifer Saul, February 17, 2007, on the "What Is It Like to Be a Philosopher?" blog.

† Ibid.

‡ The title of the latter is an allusion to Thomas Nagel's "What Is It Like to Be a Bat?" (included in the Philosophy of Mind chapter of this volume).

Scepticism and Implicit Bias[*]

The goal of this paper is to explore the idea that what we know about implicit bias gives rise to something *akin to* a new form of scepticism. I am not wedded to the idea that the phenomenon I am pointing to should be called 'scepticism', but I am convinced that it is illuminating to examine the ways in which it does and does not resemble philosophical scepticism. I will call what I am discussing 'bias-related doubt'.

In some ways, bias-related doubt is stronger than traditional forms of scepticism, while in others it is weaker. In brief: I will be arguing that what we know about implicit biases shows us that we have very good reason to believe that we cannot properly trust our knowledge-seeking faculties. This does not mean that we might be mistaken *about everything*, or even everything in the external world (so it is weaker than traditional scepticism). But it does mean that we have *good reason* to believe that we are mistaken about a great deal (so it is stronger than traditional forms of scepticism). A further way in which bias-related doubt is stronger than traditional scepticism: this is doubt that demands action. With traditional scepticism, we feel perfectly fine about setting aside the doubts we have felt when we leave the philosophy seminar room. But with bias-related doubt, we don't feel fine about this at all. We feel a need to *do something* to improve our epistemic situation. Fortunately, though, it turns out that there is much we can do. However, much of what needs to be done cannot be done on a purely individual basis. So although scepticism has sometimes been treated by feminists as a paradigmatic case of the excesses of individualist philosophy,[1] this form of scepticism cannot be fully responded to individualistically.

1 Implicit Biases

There is a vast and still-growing literature on implicit bias, which I'll only be dipping into here. Very broadly speaking, these are largely unconscious tendencies to automatically associate concepts with one another.[2] Put like this, they don't sound very interesting or worrying. But the ones on which attention by philosophers has focused are both very interesting and very worrying. These are unconscious, automatic tendencies to associate certain traits with members of particular social groups, in ways that lead to some very disturbing errors: we tend to judge members of stigmatized groups more negatively, in a whole host of ways. Rather than attempt a general overview, I will give examples of the sorts of errors that will be our concern here.

CURRICULUM VITAE

CV studies take a common, and beautifully simple form. The experimenters ask subjects to rate what is in fact the same CV, varying whatever trait they want to study by (usually) varying the name at the top of it. When they do this, they find that the same CV is considered much better when it has a typically white rather than typically black name, a typically Swedish rather than typically Arab name, a typically male rather than typically female name, and so on. The right name makes the reader rate one as more likely to be interviewed, more likely to be hired, likely to be offered more money, and a better prospect for mentoring. These judgments are very clearly being affected by something that *should* be irrelevant—the social category of the person whose CV is being read. Moreover, the person making these mistaken judgments is surely unaware of the role that social category is playing in the formation of their views of the candidates. Significantly, the most recent of these studies (Moss-Racusin 2012), on the evaluation of women's CVs, showed that women were just as likely to make these problematic judgments as men. It also showed that these problems are not confined to an older generation: the tendencies were equally strong in all age groups.[3]

PRESTIGE BIAS

In a now-classic study, psychologists Peters and Ceci (1982) sent previously published papers to the top

---

[*]   Jennifer Saul, "Scepticism and Implicit Bias," *Disputatio* 5, 37 (2013): 243–63.

psychology journals that had published them, but with false names and non-prestigious affiliations. Only 8% detected that the papers had already been submitted, and 89% were rejected, citing serious methodological errors (and not the one they should have cited—plagiarism). This makes it clear that institutional affiliation has a dramatic effect on the judgments made by reviewers (either positively, negatively, or both). These are experts in their field, making judgments about their area of expertise—psychological methodology—and yet they are making dramatically different judgments depending on the social group to which authors belong (member of prestigious vs non-prestigious psychology department).

PERCEPTION

Studies of so-called 'shooter bias' show us that implicit bias can even influence perception. In these studies, it has been shown that the very same ambiguous object is far more likely to be perceived as a gun when held by a young black man and something innocent (like a phone) when held like by a young white man.[4] (The same effect has been shown with men who appear Muslim versus men who appear non-Muslim (Unkelbach et al. 2008). In some of these experiments, the subjects' task is to shoot in a video game if and only if they see an image of a person carrying a gun. Subjects' 'shooting' is just as you'd expect given their perceptions. These show that implicit bias is getting to us even before we get to the point of reflecting upon the world—it affects our very perceptions of that world, again in worrying ways.[5]

MORAL AND POLITICAL CONSEQUENCES

Now let's explore some consequences of this. First, there are some obvious morally and politically significant consequences. We are very likely to make inaccurate judgments about who is the best candidate for a job, if some of the top candidates are known to be from stigmatised groups. We are very likely to mark inaccurately, if social group membership is known to us and the group we are marking is not socially homogeneous. We are very likely to make inaccurate judgments about which papers deserve to be published, if social group membership is known to us. We may

both over-rate members of some groups and underrate others. Worse yet, we are misperceiving harmless objects as dangerous, and potentially acting on this in truly appalling ways. All of this *should* be tremendously disturbing to us. It means that we are being dramatically *unfair* in our judgments, even though we are doing so unintentionally. We are treating members of stigmatised groups badly, even if we desperately desire to treat them well. Moreover, what we are doing will help to ensure that this unfair treatment is continued: the results of these decisions will help to maintain the stereotypes that currently exist, which cause members of stigmatised groups to be treated unfairly. 'Vicious circle' seems a particularly apt phrase to describe the situation.

EPISTEMOLOGICAL CONSEQUENCES

But I want to focus now on some epistemological aspects of this situation. First, some relatively obvious ones, starting from those within philosophy. The unfairness described above means that there are almost certain to be some excellent students receiving lower marks and less encouragement than they should; some excellent philosophers not getting the jobs they should get; and where anonymous refereeing and editing is not practised, there is some excellent work not being published. Philosophy as a field is the worse for this: it is not as good as it could, or should, be. (For more on this, see Beebee and Saul 2011, Saul forthcoming.) Obviously, much the same will go on in other areas of academia, especially those that are as male-dominated as philosophy. Outside philosophy, there are similar effects, as the testimony of members of stigmatised groups is taken less seriously than it ought to be (Fricker 2007). Their views are less respected, and they are given less of an opportunity to participate fully in discussions and decision-making. As Chris Hookway (2010) has noted, a particular problem may lie in their *questions* not being taken seriously.

Now, some less obvious epistemological aspects of the situation, again focusing on philosophy. When we misjudge a paper's quality, we're making a mistake about the quality of an argument.[6] Moreover, our evaluation of that argument is being influenced by factors totally irrelevant to its quality: it's being influenced by our knowledge of the social group of its author. Worse yet, this influence operates below the level of consciousness—it's unavailable to inspection and rational evaluation. This means we may be accepting arguments we should not accept and rejecting arguments we should not reject. Many of our philosophical beliefs—those beliefs we take to have been arrived at through the most careful exercise of reason—are likely to be wrong.[7]

...

It is important to see that this is not *just* a matter of what Miranda Fricker (2007) has called testimonial injustice. Fricker argues that the social group to which a person belongs will often have a dramatic effect on our willingness to treat them as a credible source of knowledge. We will be less likely to accept the testimony of those from stigmatised groups. One thing implicit bias adds to this picture is just a matter of scale: research shows these problems to be far more widespread than would otherwise be apparent. But another, even more important addition, is that implicit bias doesn't just affect our judgments of people's *credibility* when deciding whether to accept their testimony or not. Mistaken as our credibility judgments are, at least we know that these are judgments about who to take seriously. We recognise that we are making judgments about people, and this is what we mean to be doing. The research on implicit bias shows us that we are actually being affected by biases about social groups *when we think we are evaluating evidence or methodology*. When considering testimony, it makes sense that we need to make judgments about how credible an individual is. But when psychologists assess the methodology of a study—or when philosophers assess the quality of an argument—they shouldn't be looking at the credibility of an individual at all. They should be looking just at the study, or the argument. And yet when implicit bias is at work, we are likely to be affected by the social group of the person presenting evidence or an argument even when we are trying to evaluate that evidence or argument itself. Implicit bias is not just affecting who we trust—it's affecting us when we think we're making judgments that have nothing to do with trust. It's leading us into errors based on social category membership when we

think we're making judgments of scientific or argumentative merit.

But why should that unsettle us? We know already that most of what is currently accepted as science is likely to be proven false within centuries, and possibly decades. But notice: my claim is not that we're likely to be accepting some falsehoods, or even a lot of falsehoods. That's not unsettling. My claim is that we're likely to be *making errors*. Moreover, we're likely to be making errors of a very specific sort. It's *not* that we're likely to get some really difficult technical bits wrong, or that we're likely to get things wrong if we're really exhausted, or drunk. It's that we're likely to let the social identity of the person making an argument affect our evaluation of that argument. It is part of our self-understanding as rational enquirers that we will make certain sorts of mistakes. But not this sort of mistake. These mistakes are ones in which something that we actively think *should not* affect us does.

Worse yet, our errors are not confined to the professional arena, or to what we take to be carefully thought-out judgments about the quality of arguments that we encounter. The studies of shooter bias show us that as humans in the world, we are making errors in *perception* due to implicit bias. The very data from which we begin in thinking about the world—our perceptions—cannot be relied upon to be free of bias. Once more, this is clearly well beyond the worries raised by testimonial injustice.

The best way to see why these mistakes are—and should be—so unsettling to us as enquirers is to compare the situation of one who learns about implicit biases to the situations of people considering various sorts of sceptical scenarios.

2 *Comparison to Sceptical Scenarios*

2.1 COMPARISON TO TRADITIONAL SCEPTICISM

In a traditional sceptical scenario, we are confronted with a possibility that we can't rule out—that we're brains in vats,[*] or that tomorrow gravity might not

---

*   This is an updated version of René Descartes's evil demon thought experiment; see Gilbert Harman, *Thought* (Princeton University Press, 1973), 5.

work any more.* Considering this scenario is meant to make us worry that we don't know (many of) the things that we take ourselves to know, or that we are unjustified in having (many of) the beliefs that we do. And a standard response is that these worries should not grip us, because we have no reason at all to suppose that these possibilities obtain. Doubt induced by implicit bias is unlike this: we have *very good reason* to suppose that we are systematically making errors caused by our unconscious biases related to social categories. In this way, then, the doubt provoked by implicit bias is stronger than that caused by considering sceptical arguments.

But, one might think, it's not really all that troubling. The doubt caused by implicit bias, surely, is a localized one. It seems, at first, to be like the sort of doubt we experience when we discover how poor we are at probabilistic reasoning. We have extremely good reason to think we're making errors when we make judgments of likelihood. But this sort of doubt doesn't trouble us all that much because we know exactly when we should worry and what we should do about it: if we find ourselves estimating likelihood, we should mistrust our instincts and either follow mechanical procedures we've learned or consult an expert (if not in person, then on the internet). This kind of worry is one that everyone can accept without feeling drawn into anything like scepticism. And it may seem at first that bias-related doubt is like this.

The problem starts to become vivid when we ask ourselves *when* we should be worried about implicit bias influencing our judgments. The answer is that we should be worried about it whenever we consider a claim, an argument, a suggestion, a question, etc. from a person whose apparent social group we're in a position to recognize. Whenever that's the case, there will be room for our unconscious biases to perniciously affect us. Most discussed in the literature so far (see Fricker 2007), we might make a mistaken judgment of credibility when assessing testimony. But we also might fail to listen properly to a contribution; fail to carefully consider a question; judge an argument to be less compelling or original than it is; think the evidence presented is worse than it is. And, importantly,

we can be adversely affected in a positive direction as well. When assessing a contribution from someone who our biases favour, we may grant more credibility than their testimony deserves; we may think their arguments are better than they are, perhaps failing to notice flaws that we would have noticed if the arguments were presented by someone else; we may take their evidence to be better than it is, and so on.

And *this* is going to happen a great deal. It happens whenever we are dealing with the social world in a non-anonymised† manner. Since the world is only rarely anonymised for us, this will happen nearly all the time. Much of our knowledge comes from testimony, or from arguments or evidence that we are presented with. Those testifying, or presenting the arguments or evidence, are usually people. And people are generally (though not always) perceived by us as members of social groups. Moreover, much of the knowledge we already have has come to us in this way. Our acceptance or rejection of testimony, arguments, evidence and the like has shaped the worldviews we have now. And this acceptance or rejection was, we can be fairly certain, distorted by the perceived social groups[8] of those presenting the testimony, arguments or evidence. Worse yet, we cannot even go back and attempt to consider or correct errors that we might have made—we are very unlikely to remember the sources of these beliefs of ours.

...

[Chris] Hookway writes that there are three key features to 'an interesting sceptical challenge'. (1990: 164)

1. It must make reference to 'part of our practice of obtaining information about our surroundings which we find natural, which it does not ordinarily occur to us to challenge.'
2. '[I]t must have a certain generality: challenges to the reliability of particular thermometers may lead us to lose confidence in that particular instrument; they do not lead us to lose confidence in ourselves as inquirers.'
3. '[I]t must intimate that the feature of our practice which it draws attention to *could not* be defended.'

---

* This is an allusion to David Hume's problem of induction.
† Anonymized material has all information about who it came from removed.

It seems to me that bias-related doubt easily meets each of these criteria. The practices called into question are ones that we normally don't think to question: our 'instinctive' sense that someone is credible, that a reason is convincing, or that an argument is compelling. There is definitely generality—this isn't like challenges just to probabilistic reasoning, which Hookway rightly flags as not that worrying because those challenges are very contained. Instead, it's challenges to the ordinary ways that we assess reasons, arguments evidence and testimony. Finally, the feature it calls attention to—our judgments are illicitly influenced by irrelevant matters in a way that frequently leads to injustice—is deeply indefensible.

What the literature on implicit bias shows us is that we *really should not* trust ourselves as inquirers. As Hookway argues (2003: 200), 'we can persevere with our inquiries only if we are confident that … our reflection will take appropriate routes'. But we have now discovered that our reflection takes wholly inappropriate routes: we are not only failing to assess claims or arguments by methods that we endorse but we are instead assessing them by methods that we actively oppose. As he notes, only a part of the process of deliberation is conscious, and we need to be able to trust the habits of thought that underpin the unconscious bits (Hookway 1990: 11). We need to trust not just that they will guide us to truth but that they are based in values that we consider our own. Hookway raises the values concern when discussing an obsessive who is unable to stop repeatedly rehearsing doubts that he does not fully endorse, but the concern arises even more strongly in the case of biases against members of stigmatized groups. The literature on implicit bias shows us not just that our habits can't be relied on to lead us to truth, but also that—insofar as they can be described as based in values at all—they are likely to be based in values that we (most of us, anyway) find repugnant. It is difficult to see how we could ever properly trust these again once we have reflected on implicit bias. And, Hookway (2000: Chapter 10)

argues, self-trust is a necessary condition of responsible inquiry.

2.2 COMPARISON TO LIVE SCEPTICAL SCENARIOS

Bryan Frances's work on 'live sceptical scenarios' (Frances 2005), provides another instructive comparison. Frances characterizes traditional sceptical arguments as relying on the fact that certain hypotheses cannot be ruled out. He notes that responses to these often involve pointing out that, while these hypotheses cannot be ruled out, they are nonetheless not really *live*—they are so implausible that we can't really take them seriously. His book is devoted to arguing that there are sceptical hypotheses that are not like this. In his live sceptical scenarios, 'there are compelling scientific and philosophical reasons to think that the hypotheses are actually true'. Therefore, the traditional replies do not apply.

Now this looks quite a lot like what I have called Bias-Related Doubt. The hypotheses are ones for which there is compelling reason for thinking that they are true. But on closer inspection, it turns out that these reasons are far less compelling. The hypotheses in question are things like eliminativism* about belief and error theory about colour.† And the reasons for thinking that they are still live is that some sensible people who know a great deal endorse (or might endorse) these theories on the grounds of compelling scientific or philosophical reasons. But this falls a good deal short of what I have argued about bias-related doubt. Here the hypothesis is that we are frequently making errors that have their root in implicit bias. My claim is not just that the hypothesis is live—that sensible and knowledgeable people might endorse it on the basis of good reasons. Instead, it's that *we all have very good reason to believe that it is true*. And this is much stronger than the claim that a hypothesis is live. We will see that there are also differences with regard to how we should respond.

---

* Eliminativism about beliefs is the view that beliefs (and, usually, other mental states such as desires, thoughts, etc.) do not in fact exist; when we talk about a person "having a belief," we are simply mistaken; beliefs, etc., are not constituted by brain states or independent mental states either. Like witchcraft, they simply do not exist.

† Error theory (about color) is the view that colors do not exist in reality, and that when we make statements about certain objects having certain colors (e.g., "The sky is blue") we are mistaken.

3 What Should We Do?

The scepticism created by learning about implicit bias differs dramatically from most other forms of scepticism in that it leads to the conclusion that we should change our behaviour. A striking feature of the sorts of scepticism that have tended to dominate discussion in recent times is that *even if* we became convinced by them, we would not feel the need to change anything about our behaviour: accepting that I don't know whether I'm a brain in a vat or not simply doesn't affect how I will go about living my life. Becoming a sceptic of the traditional sort doesn't lead me to decide differently about anything in the course of my every day life, or to alter my behaviour in any way.

But not all forms of scepticism are like these in their lack of impact on behaviour: Pyrrhonian scepticism* was meant to have a large and salutary impact on one's life. The convinced Pyrrhonian sceptic would learn to simply accept appearances rather than striving for belief.

> 'If he avoids "belief", the Pyrrhonist "acquiesces in appearances"': he is guided by sensory appearances and by bodily needs and natural desires; he conforms to the prevailing customs and standards of his society.'9

Accepting appearances and conforming to prevailing customs and standards, of course, is very much *not* what a would-be responsible enquirer should feel moved to do after learning about implicit bias. For the literature on implicit bias shows that the way things appear to us is perniciously affected by biases that we are unaware of and would repudiate if we became aware of them. To put it bluntly, accepting appearances would mean acquiescing in one's reaction of fear at the sight of a black man; and acquiescing in one's greater sense of approval when looking at a CV with a man's name at the top of it. That these would not rise to the level of belief may mean that we're not committed to falsehoods. But the behaviours we would be led to would be just as troubling. As Hookway notes (1990:

18), the Pyrrhonist's 'is a very conservative outlook: the appearances he relies on are salient for him because of their conventional role.' Relying on the conventions of one's society is deeply cast into doubt by the literature on implicit bias.

The scepticism produced by implicit bias demands action. There are several reasons for this. The first reason is that the sceptical scenario is one that is troubling in a very different way from more traditional sceptical scenarios. If you actually are a brain in a vat, you're probably doing about as well with your life as you can. It's not clear that you would make different choices if you knew the scenario to hold. (And this is just as true for the live sceptical scenarios Frances considers, like those based in eliminativism or colour error theory.) But if you actually are basing lots of decisions on the social categories that people you encounter belong to, then you're clearly not doing as well as you can. You're making the wrong decisions epistemically speaking: taking an argument to be better than it is, perhaps; or wrongly discounting the view of someone you should listen to. You're also making the wrong decisions practically speaking: assigning the wrong mark to an essay, or rejecting a paper that you should accept. Finally, you're making the wrong decisions morally speaking: you are treating people unfairly; and you are basing your decisions on stereotypes that you find morally repugnant. So when the possibility is raised that you're doing this, it should not be possible to shrug it off in the way that it's perfectly reasonable to shrug off the brain in a vat possibility. Worse yet, it's not just the *possibility* that's raised: the research on implicit bias suggests that it's very likely that you're doing these things, with respect to at least some social categories.

But usually, you can't do anything at all to rule out the sceptical scenarios. And the same is true when it comes to any particular instance of the implicit bias sceptical scenario. Did I judge that woman's work to be less good than it was due to her gender? I will never know, because I won't get the opportunity to assess it without knowledge of her gender. And the same is true for certain more general versions: have I based much of what I think I know on epistemically

---

* Pyrrho (c. 360–c. 270 BCE) was a Greek philosopher who founded the school of Pyrrhonism, or Pyrrhonian skepticism, which was influential in the ancient Greek and Roman world. Its main tenet is that we should suspend belief concerning any proposition that is not completely evident.

irrelevant factors like social categories? I'm not going to be able to find out. So is there *anything* one can do? Not for past cases like these. However, I can act so as to reduce the likelihood of this happening in future instances.

Importantly, though, some of the most obvious things to do just don't work. Getting a woman to judge another woman's work is a poor check against bias, since both men and women are likely to hold biases causing them to negatively judge women's work (recall Moss-Racusin's 2012 CV study). Trying hard to be unprejudiced can backfire, if one doesn't go about it in just the right way (Legault et al. 2011). Reflecting on past instances in which one managed to do the right thing makes one *more* likely, not less likely to be biased (Moskowitz and Li). So what should one do?

Fortunately, there are some things we can do. Obviously anonymising can prevent us from even being aware of the social group that might trigger our implicit biases.[10] But anonymising is not a solution that's always available or appropriate, so it's fortunate that psychologists are discovering a lot of surprising interventions that seem to reduce the influence of implicit biases. We can spend time thinking about counter-stereotypical exemplars (members of stereotyped groups who don't fit the group stereotypes).[11] We can carefully form implementation intentions—not 'I will not be influenced by race' but 'when I see a black face I will think "safe"' (Stewart and Payne 2008). We can spend a few hours engaging in Kawakami's negation training, in which we practice strongly negating stereotypes (Kawakami et al. 2000). But this might not work, unless we use Johnson's (2009) variant in which we think 'NO, THAT'S WRONG!' while pressing a space bar whenever presented with a stereotypical pairing. We can reflect on past instances in which we *failed* in efforts to be unbiased, thereby activating our motivation to control prejudice (Moskowitz and Li). And these are just a few examples.

Interestingly, some very effective interventions—like Kawakami's negation training—are widely viewed as far too demanding for widespread adoption. Alex Madva (manuscript), however, has argued extremely compellingly that these have been dismissed far too quickly. And he has a point—what's a few hours of slightly tedious exercises if it can actually make me less prejudiced? The arguments I have presented here suggest that we may well also have very strong *epistemic* reasons as well for adopting these techniques. If we don't try to overcome the pernicious influences of these biases, we are not being responsible enquirers.[12]

Importantly, though, we are unlikely to completely eliminate the threat of error. Implicit bias could be affecting one's reasoning at almost any point—it is very hard to judge when social group membership is having a pernicious influence. So it is much trickier to correct for than other factors that are known to make one unreliable (e.g. 'don't make important decisions when drunk'). If we knew that we were about to enter a situation in which implicit biases might impair our thinking, and we knew exactly which biases would be relevant, we could formulate appropriate implementation intentions, like 'If I see black person, I will think "safe".' But we don't in general know which stigmatized social groups we will encounter at which points, or what stereotype will be relevant. (Thinking 'safe' when we see a black person will not help us to more accurately assess the quality of their written work.) Moreover, we don't know what sorts of cognitive task might be relevant. So far, I have focused mostly on assessments of quality of argument, or of believability. But implicit biases surely affect other epistemically relevant matters as well: they might lead me to ask the wrong questions, or to neglect the right ones. Implementation intentions are a powerful device for controlling the expression of biases, but by their nature they target very specific behaviours. They cannot provide the general sort of reshaping of the cognitive faculties that would be needed to fully combat the influence of implicit biases. At the end of the paper, I'll discuss what this limitation to our individual corrective measures means for us.

4 Our Rational Capacities

Miranda Fricker is one of the few epistemologists who has thought long and hard about the negative epistemic effects of stereotypes. Her focus, however, is on the way that these affect evaluations of testimony from those that the stereotypes target, and she does not discuss the literature on implicit bias. This literature (as we have seen) shows the pernicious epistemic influence of stereotypes to extend far beyond evaluation of testimony. Still, Fricker's discussion is highly relevant: she argues that those who underrate the testimonies of others due to wrongful stereotyping of their social group are committing an injustice, and that they suffer from an epistemic vice.* This terminology seems wholly appropriate to apply to those in the grip of pernicious implicit biases. It seems worth examining, then, what she says about correcting for prejudices.

Fricker suggests that there are two ways to be a virtuous agent in terms of accepting testimony. The first is to be 'naively' virtuous—to simply have credibility judgments that are not influenced by prejudice. She admits that this will be difficult to manage with respect to the prejudices of the culture/sub-culture one grows up in. The next is to reflectively correct one's judgments—to, for instance, think 'I'm white, and I may fail to give sufficient credibility judgment to black people as a result.' Or, alternatively, to notice that despite consciously believing women to be the equals of men, one tends to always take a man's word over a woman's. Noticing these things, she suggests, allows one to consciously raise the credibility one assigns to members of stigmatized groups. And this possibility, she suggests, is essential to our status as rational enquirers:

> 'The claim that testimonial sensibility is a capacity of reason crucially depends on its capacity to adapt in this way, for otherwise it would be little more than a dead-weight social conditioning that looked more like a threat to the justification of a hearer's responses than a source of that justification.' (84)

Extending this idea in a natural way, we would expect the capacity to consciously, critically, reflectively correct for one's biases quite generally to be crucial to one's epistemic capacities being capacities of reason.

Before we learn about implicit bias and what to do about it, it is genuinely unclear to me whether we have this ability to critically and reflectively correct for our bias. We could perhaps claim that we had the *ability* to do that (once we learned about the evidence, etc.) but this claim would be so weak as not to amount to actually be very reassuring. Now, however, many of us do have the ability to critically and reflectively correct for our biases—at least once we have learned about their existence and studied the literature on what to do about them. Once we do that (and implement these techniques), we can responsibly claim that these capacities are not just dead-weight social conditioning. Importantly, though, this requires more than what Fricker imagined in her discussion: we are unlikely to notice through individualistic reflection the ways that our judgments are affected by social categories; and even when we do notice this we are unlikely to hit upon the right strategies for fighting it. The only way that we can engage in the necessary sort of correction is not individualistically or introspectively, but by informing ourselves about what scientists have discovered about humans like ourselves. The correction is dependent not just on our rational faculties but on the deliverances of science.

In order to inquire responsibly, we must instead recognize that our epistemic capacities are prone to errors that we cannot learn about through first-person reflection; and that we must correct them using counter-intuitive mechanical techniques that draw not upon our rational agency but upon automatic and unconscious responses. We can consciously enlist these unconscious responses, and use them to improve our epistemic responses, but we cannot do this through rational and critical reflection alone.

Moreover, as I noted in the previous section, individual efforts are inevitably limited.

To fully combat the influence of implicit biases, what we really need to do is to re-shape our social world. The stereotypes underlying implicit biases can only fully be broken down by creating more integrated neighborhoods and workplaces; by having women, people of colour and disabled people in positions of power; by having men in nurturing roles; and so on. The only way to be fully freed from the grip of bias-related doubt is to create a social world where the stereotypes that now warp our judgments no longer hold sway over us. And the way to do this is to end the social regularities that feed and support these stereotypes. Can this be done? Who knows. It is a

---

* Saul describes Fricker's position in terms of virtue and vice, terminology that is often used in contemporary epistemology. An epistemic vice is a character trait that leads to bad knowledge practices; gullibility, dogmatism, and closed-mindedness are common examples, whereas conscientiousness and open-mindedness are epistemic virtues.

massive task—one whose importance and magnitude Elizabeth Anderson makes clear (for the case of race) in her *The Imperative of Integration*. But if it is not, we would seem to be stuck with bias-related doubt, and with the consequent lack of trust in our cognitive faculties. And this is in itself quite a fascinating result. Scepticism is generally thought of as a highly individualistic epistemic issue. It's about the would-be knower doubting the guidance of her own mind. But bias-related doubt shows us a social dimension to this. We have seen that the social world gives rise to a powerful form of doubt, and one that can only be fully answered by a sweeping and radical transformation of our social world.[13] ■

Suggestions for Critical Reflection

1. The main conclusion of this paper is that bias-related skepticism is far more worrisome than traditional philosophical skepticism. In what ways is bias-related skepticism said to be worse than traditional skepticism? Do you agree? What are the main components of Saul's argument for this conclusion?

2. Saul stresses that bias-related doubt is "not *just* a matter of what Miranda Fricker has called testimonial injustice." What does she mean by this? In what way does bias-related doubt go above and beyond testimonial injustice?

3. "The only way that we can engage in the necessary sort of correction is not individualistically or introspectively, but by informing ourselves about what scientists have discovered about humans like ourselves." Why does Saul say this, and how important is it? Is she right?

4. To what extent are people morally responsible for their own biases? Is society on the whole responsible? What are the implications of off-loading responsibility for biases from individuals onto society as a whole?

5. Have you observed implicit bias affecting your own judgment? If you have, how might you attempt to eliminate those biases? If you have not, how might you go about determining whether you are affected by implicit biases?

Notes

1 See, for example, Scheman 2002.

2 For a great deal more precision about the many different ways of characterizing implicit bias, and the many sorts of implicit biases there are, see Holroyd and Sweetman (forthcoming).

3 See, for example, Bertrand and Mullainathan 2004; Rooth 2007; Moss-Racusin et al. 2012; Steinpreis et al. 1999.

4 See, for example Correll et al. 2002, 2007; Greenwald, Oakes, & Hoffman 2003; Payne 2001; Plant & Peruche 2005.

5 For much more on how perception is affected, see Siegel 2013.

6 Here I am assuming that philosophers will be prone to the same sorts of errors as others. They have not actually been studied.

7 I am *not* saying that we are affected only by biases. Of course, a part of what we are doing is applying our skill in evaluating philosophy, and sometimes we will get things right. My claim is just that these judgments will often be distorted, to a variable extent, by biases.

8 I phrase it this way because what affects us as audiences is what social group we *take* the speaker to be a member of, not what social group they are actually a member of.

9 Hookway (1990: 6).

10 This worked beautifully with orchestras, which began holding auditions behind screens, dramatically increasing their percentages of female members. And it is now standard practice in the UK to mark students' work anonymously, which is supported by the Union of Students for just this reason: <http://www.nusconnect.org.uk/campaigns/highereducation/archived/learning-and-teaching-hub/anonymous-marking/>.
For research on anonymous marking see Bradley 1984, 1993.

11 Blair 2002; Kang and Banaji 2006.

12 Madva also responds to criticisms that these techniques are not effective enough, and that they are too individualistic, focusing as they do on individual thinkers rather than societal reform.

13 I had very useful discussions of this paper with several different audiences: The ENFA5 Conference in Braga, Portugal; the Eastern APA audience in Washington DC; and the departmental seminars at Nottingham and Southampton. I have also benefitted enormously from discussions with Louise Antony, Ray Drainville, Miranda Fricker, Teresa Marques and especially Chris Hookway—to whom this paper owes an obvious and enormous debt. (Though the errors are all mine.)

References

Anderson, E. 2010. *The Imperative of Integration*. Princeton: Princeton University Press.

Beebee, H. and Saul, J. 2011. *Women in Philosophy in the UK: A Report*, published by the British Philosophical Association and the Society for Women in Philosophy. (<9-08/Women%20in%20Philosophy%20in%20the%20UK%20(BPA-SWIPUK%20Report).pdf>)

Bertrand, M. and Mullainathan, S. 2004. Are Emily and Greg more employable than Lakisha and Jamal? *American Economic Review*, 94, 991–1013.

Blair, I. 2002. The Malleability of Automatic Stereotypes and Prejudice. *Personality and Social Psychology Review*, 3, 242–261.

Bradley, C. 1984. Sex bias in the evaluation of students. *British Journal of Social Psychology*, 23: 2, 147–153.

Bradley, C. 1993. Sex bias in student assessment overlooked? *Assessment and Evaluation in Higher Education* 18:1, 3–8.

Correll, J., Park, B., Judd, C., & Wittenbrink, B. 2002. The police officer's dilemma: Using ethnicity to disambiguate potentially threatening individuals. *Journal of Personality and Social Psychology*, 83, 1314–1329.

Correll, J., Park, B., Judd, C., Wittenbrink, B., Sadler, M.S., & Keesee, T. 2007. Across the thin blue line: Police officers and racial bias in the decision to shoot. *Journal of Personality and Social Psychology*, 92, 1006–1023.

Frances, B. 2005. *Scepticism Comes Alive*. Oxford: Oxford University Press.

Fricker, M. 2007. *Epistemic Injustice: Power and the Ethics of Knowing*. Oxford: Oxford University Press.

Goldin, C. and Rouse, C. 2000. Orchestrating Impartiality: The Impact of 'Blind' Auditions on Female Musicians. *The American Economic Review*, 90:4, 715–741.

Greenwald, A.G., Oakes, M.A. and Hoffman, H. 2003b. Targets of discrimination: Effects of race on responses to weapons holders. *Journal of Experimental Social Psychology*, 39 399–405.

Holroyd, J. and Sweetman, J. Forthcoming.* The Heterogeneity of Implicit Bias. In *Implicit Bias and Philosophy*, ed. by M. Brownstein and J. Saul. Oxford: Oxford University Press.

Hookway, C. 1990. *Scepticism*. London: Routledge.

Hookway, C. 2000. *Truth, Rationality, and Pragmatism: Themes From Peirce*. Oxford: Oxford University Press.

Hookway, C. 2003. How to Be a Virtue Epistemologist. In *Intellectual Virtue: Perspectives from Ethics and Epistemology*, ed. by M. DePaul and L. Zagzebski. Oxford University Press.

Hookway, C. 2010. Some Varieties of Epistemic Injustice: Response to Fricker. *Episteme* 7:2, 151–163.

Johnson, I.R. 2009. *Just say 'No' (and mean it): Meaningful negation as a tool to modify automatic racial prejudice*. Doctoral dissertation, Ohio State University.

Kang, J. and Banaji, M. 2006. Fair Measures: A Behavioral Realist Revision of 'Affirmative Action'. *California Law Review* 94, 1063–1118.

Kawakami, K., Dovidio, J.F., Moll, J., Hermsen, S., and Russin, A. 2000. Just say no (to stereotyping): effects of training in the negation of stereotypic associations on stereotype activation. *Journal of Personality and Social Psychology*, 78, 871–888.

Legault, L., Gutsell, J., and Inzlicht, M. 2011. Ironic Effects of Antiprejudice Messages: How Motivational Interventions Can Reduce (But also Increase) Prejudice. *Psychological Science* 22(12), 1472–1477.

Madva, A. 2013. The Biases Against Debiasing. Paper presented at *Implicit Bias, Philosophy and Psychology Conference*, Sheffield, April 2013.

Moskowitz, G. and Li, P. 2011. Egalitarian Goals Trigger Stereotype Inhibition: A Proactive Form of Stereotype Control. *Journal of Experimental Social Psychology* 47, 103–16.

Moss-Racusin, C., Dovidio, J., Brescoll, V., Graham, M., Handelsman, J. 2012. Science Faculty's Subtle Gender Biases Favor Male Students. *PNAS* 109(41), 16395–16396.

Payne, B.K. 2001. Prejudice and perception: The role of automatic and controlling processes in misperceiving a

* Now published: 2016.

weapon. *Journal of Personality and Social Psychology*, 81, 181–192.

Peters, Douglas P. and Stephen J. Ceci. 1982. Peer-review practices of psychological journals: The fate of published articles, submitted again. *Behavioral and Brain Sciences* 5, 187–255.

Plant, E.A. and Peruche, B.M. 2005. The consequences of race for police officers' responses to criminal suspects. *Psychological Science*, 16, 180–183.

Rooth, D. 2007. Implicit discrimination in hiring: Real world evidence (IZA Discussion Paper No. 2764). Bonn, Germany: Forschungsinstitut zur Zukunft der Arbeit (Institute for the Study of Labor).

Saul, J. Forthcoming. Implicit Bias, Stereotype Threat and Women in Philosophy. In *Women in Philosophy: What Needs to Change?*, ed. by F. Jenkins and K. Hutchison. Oxford: Oxford University Press. (Formerly titled 'Unconscious Influences and Women in Philosophy'.)*

Scheman, N. 2002. Though This Be Method, Yet There Is Madness in It: Paranoia and Liberal Epistemology. In *A Mind of One's Own: Feminist Essays on Reason and Objectivity*, ed. by L. Antony and C. Witt. Cambridge, MA: Westview.

Siegel, S. 2013. Can Selection Effects on Experience Influence Its Rational Role? *Oxford Studies in Epistemology* Vol. 4: 240–270.

Steinpreis, R., Anders, K., and Ritzke, D. 1999. The Impact of Gender on the Review of the Curricula Vitae of Job Applicants and Tenure Candidates: A National Empirical Study. *Sex Roles*, 41:7/8, 509–528.

Stewart, B.D. and Payne, B.K. 2008. Bringing Automatic Stereotyping under Control: Implementation Intentions as Efficient Means of Thought Control. *Personality and Social Psychology Bulletin*, 34, 1332–1345.

Unkelbach, C., Forgas, J., and Denson, T. 2008. The Turban Effect: The Influence of Muslim Headgear and Induced Affect on Aggressive Responses in the Shooter Bias Paradigm. *Journal of Experimental Social Psychology* 44:5, 1409–1413.

---

*   Now published: 2013.

HELEN LONGINO

Can There Be a Feminist Science?

Who Is Helen Longino?

Helen E. Longino (born 1944) has been perhaps the most influential philosopher to apply contemporary feminist approaches to epistemology and philosophy of science. As an undergraduate, she majored in literary studies, moving to logic and philosophy of science for her graduate work at Johns Hopkins University. During the 1960s and 1970s, she was active in anti-war and feminist political action movements. As a faculty member at Mills College, Rice University, and University of Minnesota, she was strongly influential in establishing women's studies courses and programs. Her books include *Studying Human Behavior: How Scientists Investigate Aggression and Sexuality* (2013), *The Fate of Knowledge* (2001), and *Science as Social Knowledge* (1990). Longino is currently the Clarence Irving Lewis Professor of Philosophy at Stanford University. She has served as President of the Philosophy of Science Association and was elected to the American Academy of Arts and Sciences in 2016.

Some Useful Background Information

Longino's target for criticism is the long-held and (for a long time) universal view that the most important feature of good science is its *objectivity*—which was taken to mean that scientific practice, when working right, should be utterly uninfluenced by any values of the scientist, or of her culture or society—any values, that is, other than the internal scientific values of care in observation, honesty, thoroughness, and so on. The idea here was that nature itself—the external facts—should determine what's taken to be true by scientists.

Nobody thinks that real science always works this way: there are numerous high-profile examples brought to light of outright fraud, or unconscious bias, the result of what the scientist himself or the source of his funding, or the dominant culture, hopes to find. But the traditional view counts these as bad science. A very moderate feminist critique of science has, for decades, pointed out how male bias is among the factors that can make for bad science in this sense. Feminists point to deeply flawed scientific studies of the following sort: a study of the causes of heart-attack which studied only males as subjects, blithely considering their conclusions to be applicable to all humans; a study of societal dynamics which looked only at traditional male activities and roles; a study of cognitive abilities that rated subjects on the basis of typically male abilities, leading to the conclusion that women are intellectually less able.

But this is not Longino's critique. She does not merely point out that male-oriented assumptions lead to bad science, nor does she defend a distinctively female way of doing science. Instead, she notes that observations and data inevitably fall short of providing objective justification for scientific knowledge—science is never value free, because we always bring some values or other to bear on the connection between our evidence and our hypotheses. The objectivity of science does not consist in eliminating value judgments. Rather, science is properly objective only when it incorporates *diverse* values—when it avoids privileging one set of social values while ignoring others, and instead allows its claims to be scrutinized by a wide range of participants in an open and democratic way. "Her key idea is that the production of knowledge is a social enterprise, secured through the critical and cooperative interactions of inquirers. The products of this social enterprise are more objective, the more responsive they are to criticism from all points of view."[*]

---

[*]   Elizabeth Anderson, "Feminist Epistemology and Philosophy of Science," *The Stanford Encyclopedia of Philosophy*, ed. Edward N. Zalta (Spring 2017).

What Is the Structure of This Reading?

Longino begins by mentioning various sorts of feminist approaches to science that her article will not take. Her subject will instead be a feminist critique of the idea that science should be impersonal, objective, and value-free; feminists, she argues, offer an alternative that makes for better science.

After a number of preliminaries, she reveals her central argument: that confirmation in science often essentially involves background assumptions, and that these assumptions are sometimes not merely established by simple observation or common sense, but are rather tied in with "contextual values"—not mere internal rules of science, but personal, social, or cultural values.

Some Common Misconceptions

1. Longino does not argue that there are typically feminine characteristics that should be represented more in scientific investigations. She does not reject this view wholesale; she merely argues that this is not what she will talk about.
2. Neither does Longino argue here for a position that some readers, seeing that this is a feminist treatment of scientific practice, might expect: that the current male science gets things all wrong, and that a replacement female science would do better. She mentions that her aim is not to replace one "absolutism" by another.

Can There Be a Feminist Science?*

This paper explores a number of recent proposals regarding "feminist science" and rejects a content-based approach in favor of a process-based approach to characterizing feminist science. Philosophy of science can yield models of scientific reasoning that illuminate the interaction between cultural values and ideology and scientific inquiry. While we can use these models to expose masculine and other forms of bias, we can also use them to defend the introduction of assumptions grounded in feminist political values.

I

The question of this title conceals multiple ambiguities. Not only do the sciences consist of many distinct fields, but the term "science" can be used to refer to a method of inquiry, a historically changing collection of practices, a body of knowledge, a set of claims, a profession, a set of social groups, etc. And as the sciences are many, so are the scholarly disciplines that seek to understand them: philosophy, history, sociology, anthropology, psychology. Any answer from the perspective of some one of these disciplines will, then, of necessity, be partial. In this essay, I shall be asking about the possibility of theoretical natural science that is feminist and I shall ask from the perspective of a philosopher. Before beginning to develop my answer, however, I want to review some of the questions that could be meant, in order to arrive at the formulation I wish to address.

The question could be interpreted as factual, one to be answered by pointing to what feminists in the sciences are doing and saying: "Yes, and this is what it is." Such a response can be perceived as question-begging, however. Even such a friend of feminism as Stephen Gould dismisses the idea of a distinctively feminist or even female contribution to the sciences. In a generally positive review of Ruth Bleier's book, *Science and Gender*, Gould (1984) brushes aside her connection between women's attitudes and values and the interactionist science she calls for. Scientists (male, of course) are already proceeding with wholist[†] and

* *Hypatia* 2, 3 (1987): 51–64.

† Wholism (usually spelled "holism") denotes a variety of positions which resist understanding larger unities as merely the sum of their parts, and asserts that we cannot explain or understand the parts without treating them as belonging to such larger wholes. This contrasts with positivism, which relies upon the assumption that observation is independent from theory and that confirming or disconfirming observations can be specified independently of the theory they are supposed to confirm or disconfirm.

interactionist* research programs. Why, he implied, should women or feminists have any particular, distinctive, contributions to make? There is not masculinist and feminist science, just good and bad science. The question of a feminist science cannot be settled by pointing, but involves a deeper, subtler investigation.

The deeper question can itself have several meanings. One set of meanings is sociological, the other conceptual. The sociological meaning proceeds as follows. We know what sorts of social conditions make misogynist science possible. The work of Margaret Rossiter (1982) on the history of women scientists in the United States and the work of Kathryn Addelson (1983) on the social structure of professional science detail the relations between a particular social structure for science and the kinds of science produced. What sorts of social conditions would make feminist science possible? This is an important question, one I am not equipped directly to investigate, although what I can investigate is, I believe, relevant to it. This is the second, conceptual, interpretation of the question: what sort of sense does it make to talk about a feminist science? Why is the question itself not an oxymoron,† linking, as it does, values and ideological commitment with the idea of impersonal, objective, value-free, inquiry? This is the problem I wish to address in this essay.

The hope for a feminist theoretical natural science has concealed an ambiguity between content and practice. In the content sense the idea of a feminist science involves a number of assumptions and calls a number of visions to mind. Some theorists have written as though a feminist science is one of the theories which encode a particular world view, characterized by complexity, interaction and wholism. Such a science is said to be feminist because it is the expression and valorization‡ of a female sensibility or cognitive temperament. Alternatively, it is claimed that women have certain traits (dispositions to attend to particulars, interactive rather than individualist and controlling social attitudes and behaviors) that enable them to understand the true character of natural processes (which are complex and interactive).[1] While proponents of this interactionist view see it as an improvement over most contemporary science, it has also been branded as soft—misdescribed as non-mathematical. Women in the sciences who feel they are being asked to do not better science, but inferior science, have responded angrily to this characterization of feminist science, thinking that it is simply new clothing for the old idea that women can't do science. I think that the interactionist view can be defended against this response, although that requires rescuing it from some of its proponents as well. However, I also think that the characterization of feminist science as the expression of a distinctive female cognitive temperament has other drawbacks. It first conflates feminine with feminist. While it is important to reject the traditional derogation of the virtues assigned to women, it is also important to remember that women are *constructed* to occupy positions of social subordinates. We should not uncritically embrace the feminine.

This characterization of feminist science is also a version of recently propounded notions of a 'women's standpoint' or a 'feminist standpoint' and suffers from the same suspect universalization that these ideas suffer from. If there is one such standpoint, there are many: as Maria Lugones and Elizabeth Spelman spell out in their tellingly entitled article, "Have We Got a Theory for You: Feminist Theory, Cultural Imperialism, and the Demand for 'The Woman's Voice,'" women are too diverse in our experiences to generate a single cognitive framework (Lugones and Spelman 1983). In addition, the sciences are themselves too diverse for me to think that they might be equally transformed by such a framework. To reject this concept of a feminist science, however, is not to disengage science from feminism. I want to suggest that we focus on science as practice rather than content, as process rather than product; hence, not on feminist science, but on doing science as a feminist.

The doing of science involves many practices: how one structures a laboratory (hierarchically or collectively), how one relates to other scientists (competitively

---

* This is the view, taken from a theoretical position in sociology, that derives social processes—in this case, the practice of science—from human interaction.

† Oxymoron: a contradictory or incongruous combination of terms.

‡ To valorize something is to enhance its value, usually artificially, or to assign a value to it.

or cooperatively), how and whether one engages in political struggles over affirmative action. It extends also to intellectual practices, to the activities of scientific inquiry, such as observation and reasoning. Can there be a feminist scientific inquiry? This possibility is seen to be problematic against the background of certain standard presuppositions about science. The claim that there could be a feminist science in the sense of an intellectual practice is either nonsense because oxymoronic as suggested above or the claim is interpreted to mean that established science (science as done and dominated by men) is wrong about the world. Feminist science in this latter interpretation is presented as correcting the errors of masculine, standard science and as revealing the truth that is hidden by masculine 'bad' science, as taking the sex out of science.

Both of these interpretations involve the rejection of one approach as incorrect and the embracing of the other as the way to a truer understanding of the natural world. Both trade one absolutism for another. Each is a side of the same coin, and that coin, I think, is the idea of a value-free science. This is the idea that scientific methodology guarantees the independence of scientific inquiry from values or value-related considerations. A science or a scientific research program informed by values is *ipso facto** "bad science." "Good science" is inquiry protected by methodology from values and ideology. This same idea underlies Gould's response to Bleier, so it bears closer scrutiny. In the pages that follow, I shall examine the idea of value-free science and then apply the results of that examination to the idea of feminist scientific inquiry.

II

I distinguish two kinds of values relevant to the sciences. Constitutive values, internal to the sciences, are the source of the rules determining what constitutes acceptable scientific practice or scientific method. The personal, social and cultural values, those group or individual preferences about what ought to be, I call contextual values, to indicate that they belong to the social and cultural context in which science is done (Longino 1983c). The traditional interpretation of the value-freedom of modern natural science amounts to a claim that its constitutive and contextual features are clearly distinct from and independent of one another, that contextual values play no role in the inner workings of scientific inquiry, in reasoning and observation. I shall argue that this construal of the distinction cannot be maintained.

There are several ways to develop such an argument. One scholar is fond of inviting her audience to visit any science library and peruse the titles on the shelves. Observe how subservient to social and cultural interests are the inquiries represented by the book titles alone! Her listeners would soon abandon their ideas about the value-neutrality of the sciences, she suggests. This exercise may indeed show the influence of external, contextual considerations on what research gets done/supported (i.e., on problem selection). It does not show that such considerations affect reasoning or hypothesis acceptance. The latter would require detailed investigation of particular cases or a general conceptual argument. The conceptual arguments involve developing some version of what is known in philosophy of science as the underdetermination thesis, i.e., the thesis that a theory is always underdetermined by the evidence adduced in its support, with the consequence that different or incompatible theories are supported by or at least compatible with the same body of evidence. I shall sketch a version of the argument that appeals to features of scientific inference.

One of the rocks on which the logical positivist program foundered was the distinction between theoretical and observational language. Theoretical statements contain, as fundamental descriptive terms, terms that do not occur in the description of data. Thus, hypotheses in particle physics contain terms like "electron," "pion," "muon," "electron spin," etc. The evidence for a hypothesis such as "A pion decays sequentially into a muon, then a positron" is obviously not direct observations of pions, muons and positrons, but consists largely in photographs taken in large and complex experimental apparati: accelerators, cloud chambers, bubble chambers. The photographs show all sorts of squiggly lines and spirals. Evidence for the hypotheses of particle physics is presented as statements that describe these photographs. Eventually, of

---

*   Latin: by that very fact.

course, particle physicists point to a spot on a photograph and say things like "Here a neutrino hits a neutron." Such an assertion, however, is an interpretive achievement which involves collapsing theoretical and observational moments. A skeptic would have to be supplied a complicated argument linking the elements of the photograph to traces left by particles and these to particles themselves. What counts as theory and what as data in a pragmatic sense change over time, as some ideas and experimental procedures come to be securely embedded in a particular framework and others take their place on the horizons. As the history of physics shows, however, secure embeddedness is no guarantee against overthrow.

Logical positivists and their successors hoped to model scientific inference formally. Evidence for hypotheses, data, were to be represented as logical consequences of hypotheses. When we try to map this logical structure onto the sciences, however, we find that hypotheses are, for the most part, not just generalizations of data statements. The links between data and theory, therefore, cannot be adequately represented as formal or syntactic, but are established by means of assumptions that make or imply substantive claims about the field over which one theorizes. Theories are confirmed via the confirmation of their constituent hypotheses, so the confirmation of hypotheses and theories is relative to the assumptions relied upon in asserting the evidential connection. Confirmation of such assumptions, which are often unarticulated, is itself subject to similar relativization. And it is these assumptions that can be the vehicle for the involvement of considerations motivated primarily by contextual values (Longino 1979, 1983a).

The point of this extremely telescoped argument is that one can't give an a priori specification of confirmation that effectively eliminates the role of value-laden assumptions in legitimate scientific inquiry without eliminating auxiliary hypotheses (assumptions) altogether. This is not to say that all scientific reasoning involves value-related assumptions. Sometimes auxiliary assumptions will be supported by mundane inductive reasoning. But sometimes they will not be. In any given case, they may be metaphysical in character; they may be untestable with present investigative techniques; they may be rooted in contextual, value-related considerations. If, however, there is no a priori way to eliminate such assumptions

from evidential reasoning generally, and, hence, no way to rule out value-laden assumptions, then there is no formal basis for arguing that an inference mediated by contextual values is thereby bad science.

A comparable point is made by some historians investigating the origins of modern science. James Jacob (1977) and Margaret Jacob (1976) have, in a series of articles and books, argued that the adoption of conceptions of matter by 17th century scientists like Robert Boyle was inextricably intertwined with political considerations. Conceptions of matter provided the foundation on which physical theories were developed and Boyle's science, regardless of his reasons for it, has been fruitful in ways that far exceed his imaginings. If the presence of contextual influences were grounds for disallowing a line of inquiry, then early modern science would not have gotten off the ground.

The conclusion of this line of argument is that constitutive values conceived as epistemological (i.e., truth-seeking) are not adequate to screen out the influence of contextual values in the very structuring of scientific knowledge. Now the ways in which contextual values do, if they do, influence this structuring and interact, if they do, with constitutive values has to be determined separately for different theories and fields of science. But this argument, if it's sound, tells us that this sort of inquiry is perfectly respectable and involves no shady assumptions or unargued intuitively based rejections of positivism. It also opens the possibility that one can make explicit value commitments and still do "good" science. The conceptual argument doesn't show that all science is value-laden (as opposed to metaphysics-laden)—that must be established on a case-by-case basis, using the tools not just of logic and philosophy but of history and sociology as well. It does show that not all science is value-free and, more importantly, that it is not necessarily in the nature of science to be value-free. If we reject that idea we're in a better position to talk about the possibilities of feminist science.

III

In earlier articles (Longino 1981, 1983b; Longino and Doell 1983), I've used similar considerations to argue that scientific objectivity has to be reconceived as a function of the communal structure of scientific inquiry rather than as a property of individual scientists. I've then used these notions about scientific methodology to show that science displaying masculine bias is not *ipso facto* improper or 'bad' science; that the fabric of science can neither rule out the expression of bias nor legitimate it. So I've argued that both the expression of masculine bias in the sciences and feminist criticism of research exhibiting that bias are—shall we say—business as usual; that scientific inquiry should be expected to display the deep metaphysical and normative* commitments of the culture in which it flourishes; and finally that criticism of the deep assumptions that guide scientific reasoning about data is a proper part of science.

The argument I've just offered about the idea of a value-free science is similar in spirit to those earlier arguments. I think it makes it possible to see these questions from a slightly different angle.

There is a tradition of viewing scientific inquiry as somehow inexorable. This involves supposing that the phenomena of the natural world are fixed in determinate relations with each other, that these relations can be known and formulated in a consistent and unified way. This is not the old "unified science" idea of the logical positivists, with its privileging of physics. In its "unexplicated" or "pre-analytic" state, it is simply the idea that there is one consistent, integrated or coherent, true theoretical treatment of all natural phenomena. (The indeterminacy principle of quantum physics is restricted to our understanding of the behavior of certain particles which themselves underlie the fixities of the natural world. Stochastic† theories reveal fixities, but fixities among ensembles rather than fixed relations among individual objects or events.) The scientific inquirer's job is to discover those fixed relations. Just as the task of Plato's philosophers was to discover the fixed relations among forms and the task of Galileo's scientists was to discover the laws written in the language of the grand book of nature, geometry, so the scientist's task in this tradition remains the discovery of fixed relations however conceived. These ideas are part of the realist tradition in the philosophy of science.

It's no longer possible, in a century that has seen the splintering of the scientific disciplines, to give such a unified description of the objects of inquiry. But the belief that the job is to discover fixed relations of some sort, and that the application of observation, experiment and reason leads ineluctably to unifiable, if not unified, knowledge of an independent reality, is still with us. It is evidenced most clearly in two features of scientific rhetoric: the use of the passive voice as in "it is concluded that ..." or "it has been discovered that ..." and the attribution of agency to the data, as in "the data suggest...." Such language has been criticized for the abdication of responsibility it indicates. Even more, the scientific inquirer, and we with her, become passive observers, victims of the truth. The idea of a value-free science is integral to this view of scientific inquiry. And if we reject that idea we can also reject our roles as passive onlookers, helpless to affect the course of knowledge.

Let me develop this point somewhat more concretely and autobiographically. Biologist Ruth Doell and I have been examining studies in three areas of research on the influence of sex hormones on human behavior and cognitive performance: research on the influence of pre-natal, *in utero*, exposure to higher or lower than normal levels of androgens and estrogens on so-called 'gender-role' behavior in children, influence of androgens (pre- and post-natal) on homosexuality in women, and influence of lower than normal (for men) levels of androgen at puberty on spatial abilities (Doell and Longino, forthcoming).

The studies we looked at are vulnerable to criticism of their data and their observation methodologies. They also show clear evidence of androcentric bias‡—in the assumption that there are just two sexes and two genders (us and them), in the designation of appropriate and inappropriate behaviors for male and female children, in the caricature of lesbianism, in the assumption of male mathematical superiority. We did not find, however, that these assumptions mediated the inferences from data to theory that we found objectionable. These sexist assumptions did affect the way the data were described. What mediated the inferences from the alleged data (i.e., what functioned as auxiliary hypotheses or what provided auxiliary

---

* Normative means having to do with a value—a prescribed norm.

† Probabilistic.

‡ I.e., a bias in favor of the male point of view.

hypotheses) was what we called the linear model—the assumption that there is a direct one-way causal relationship between pre- or post-natal hormone levels and later behavior or cognitive performance. To put it crudely, fetal gonadal hormones organize the brain at critical periods of development. The organism is thereby disposed to respond in a range of ways to a range of environmental stimuli. The assumption of unidirectional programming is supposedly supported by the finding of such a relationship in other mammals; in particular, by experiments demonstrating the dependence of sexual behaviors—mounting and lordosis*—on peri-natal hormone exposure and the finding of effects of sex hormones on the development of rodent brains. To bring it to bear on humans is to ignore, among other things, some important differences between human brains and those of other species. It also implies a willingness to regard humans in a particular way—to see us as produced by factors over which we have no control. Not only are we, as scientists, victims of the truth, but we are the prisoners of our physiology.[2] In the name of extending an explanatory model, human capacities for self-knowledge, self-reflection, self-determination are eliminated from any role in human action (at least in the behaviors studied).

Doell and I have therefore argued for the replacement of that linear model of the role of the brain in behavior by one of much greater complexity that includes physiological, environmental, historical and psychological elements. Such a model allows not only for the interaction of physiological and environmental factors but also for the interaction of these with a continuously self-modifying, self-representational (and self-organizing) central processing system. In contemporary neurobiology, the closest model is that being developed in the group selectionist approach to higher brain function of Gerald Edelman and other researchers (Edelman and Mountcastle 1978). We argue that a model of at least that degree of complexity is necessary to account for the human behaviors studies in the sex hormones and behavior research and that if gonadal hormones function at all at these levels, they will probably be found at most to facilitate or inhibit neural processing in general. The strategy we take in our argument is to show that the degree of intentionality involved in the behaviors in question is greater than is presupposed by the hormonal influence researchers and to argue that this degree of intentionality implicates the higher brain processes.

To this point Ruth Doell and I agree. I want to go further and describe what we've done from the perspective of the above philosophical discussion of scientific methodology.

Abandoning my polemical mood for a more reflective one, I want to say that, in the end, commitment to one or another model is strongly influenced by values or other contextual features. The models themselves determine the relevance and interpretation of data. The linear or complex models are not in turn independently or conclusively supported by data. I doubt for instance that value-free inquiry will reveal the efficacy or inefficacy of intentional states or of physiological factors like hormone exposure in human action. I think instead that a research program in neuro-science that assumes the linear model and sex-gender dualism will show the influence of hormone exposure on gender-role behavior. And I think that a research program in neuroscience and psychology proceeding on the assumption that humans do possess the capacities for self-consciousness, self-reflection, and self-determination, and which then asks how the structure of the human brain and nervous system enables the expression of these capacities, will reveal the efficacy of intentional states (understood as very complex sorts of brain states).

While this latter assumption does not itself contain normative terms, I think that the decision to adopt it is motivated by value-laden considerations—by the desire to understand ourselves and others as self-determining (at least some of the time), that is, as capable of acting on the basis of concepts or representations of ourselves and the world in which we act. (Such representations are not necessarily correct, they are surely mediated by our cultures; all we wish to claim is that they are efficacious.) I think further that this desire on Ruth Doell's and my part is, in several ways, an aspect of our feminism. Our preference for a neurobiological model that allows for agency, for the efficacy of intentionality, is partly a validation of our (and everyone's) subjective experience of thought, deliberation, and choice. One of the tenets of feminist

---

*   Arching the spine backwards or downwards, which is a sexual response in some mammals (such as cats and mice).

research is the valorization of subjective experience, and so our preference in this regard conforms to feminist research patterns. There is, however, a more direct way in which our feminism is expressed in this preference. Feminism is many things to many people, but it is at its core in part about the expansion of human potentiality. When feminists talk of breaking out and do break out of socially prescribed sex-roles, when feminists criticize the institutions of domination, we are thereby insisting on the capacity of humans—male and female—to act on perceptions of self and society and to act to bring about changes in self and society on the basis of those perceptions. (Not overnight and not by a mere act of will. The point is that we act.) And so our criticism of theories of the hormonal influence or determination of so-called gender-role behavior is not just a rejection of the sexist bias in the description of the phenomena—the behavior of the children studied, the sexual lives of lesbians, etc.—but of the limitations on human capacity imposed by the analytic model underlying such research.[3]

While the argument strategy we adopt against the linear model rests on a certain understanding of intention, the values motivating our adoption of that understanding remain hidden in that polemical context. Our political commitments, however, presuppose a certain understanding of human action, so that when faced with a conflict between these commitments and a particular model of brain-behavior relationships we allow the political commitments to guide the choice.

The relevance of my argument about value-free science should be becoming clear. Feminists—in and out of science—often condemn masculine bias in the sciences from the vantage point of commitment to a value-free science. Androcentric bias, once identified, can then be seen as a violation of the rules, as "bad" science. Feminist science, by contrast, can eliminate that bias and produce better, good, more true or gender free science. From that perspective the process I've just described is anathema.* But if scientific methods generated by constitutive values cannot guarantee independence from contextual values, then that approach to sexist science won't work. We cannot restrict ourselves simply to the elimination of bias, but must expand our scope to include the detection of

limiting and interpretive frameworks and the finding or construction of more appropriate frameworks. We need not, indeed should not, wait for such a framework to emerge from the data. In waiting, if my argument is correct, we run the danger of working unconsciously with assumptions still laden with values from the context we seek to change. Instead of remaining passive with respect to the data and what the data suggest, we can acknowledge our ability to affect the course of knowledge and fashion or favor research programs that are consistent with the values and commitments we express in the rest of our lives. From this perspective, the idea of a value-free science is not just empty, but pernicious.

Accepting the relevance to our practice as scientists of our political commitments does not imply simple and crude impositions of those ideas onto the corner of the natural world under study. If we recognize, however, that knowledge is shaped by the assumptions, values and interests of a culture and that, within limits, one can choose one's culture, then it's clear that as scientists/theorists we have a choice. We can continue to do establishment science, comfortably wrapped in the myths of scientific rhetoric, or we can alter our intellectual allegiances. While remaining committed to an abstract goal of understanding, we can choose to whom, socially and politically, we are accountable in our pursuit of that goal. In particular we can choose between being accountable to the traditional establishment or to our political comrades.

Such accountability does not demand a radical break with the science one has learned and practiced. The development of a "new" science involves a more dialectical evolution and more continuity with established science than the familiar language of scientific revolutions implies.

In focusing on accountability and choice, this conception of feminist science differs from those that proceed from the assumption of a congruence between certain models of natural processes and women's inherent modes of understanding.[4] I am arguing instead for the deliberate and active choice of an interpretive model and for the legitimacy of basing that choice on political considerations in this case. Obviously model choice is also constrained by (what we know of) reality, that is,

---

* Something one vehemently dislikes.

by the data. But reality (what we know of it) is, I have already argued, inadequate to uniquely determine model choice. The feminist theorists mentioned above have focused on the relation between the content of a theory and female values or experiences, in particular on the perceived congruence between interactionist, wholist visions of nature and a form of understanding and set of values widely attributed to women. In contrast, I am suggesting that a feminist scientific practice admits political considerations as relevant constraints on reasoning, which, through their influence on reasoning and interpretation, shape content. In this specific case, those considerations in combination with the phenomena support an explanatory model that is highly interactionist, highly complex. This argument is so far, however, neutral on the issue of whether an interactionist and complex account of natural processes will always be the preferred one. If it is preferred, however, this will be because of explicitly political considerations and not because interactionism is the expression of "women's nature."

The integration of a political commitment with scientific work will be expressed differently in different fields. In some, such as the complex of research programs having a bearing on the understanding of human behavior, certain moves, such as the one described above, seem quite obvious. In others it may not be clear how to express an alternate set of values in inquiry, or what values would be appropriate. The first step, however, is to abandon the idea that scrutiny of the data yields a seamless web of knowledge. The second is to think through a particular field and try to understand just what its unstated and fundamental assumptions are and how they influence the course of inquiry. Knowing something of the history of a field is necessary to this process, as is continued conversation with other feminists.

The feminist interventions I imagine will be local (i.e., specific to a particular area of research); they may not be exclusive (i.e., different feminist perspectives may be represented in theorizing); and they will be in some way continuous with existing scientific work. The accretion of such interventions, of science done by feminists as feminists, and by members of other disenfranchised groups, has the potential, nevertheless, ultimately to transform the character of scientific discourse.

Doing science differently requires more than just the will to do so and it would be disingenuous to pretend that our philosophies of science are the only barrier. Scientific inquiry takes place in a social, political and economic context which imposes a variety of institutional obstacles to innovation, let alone to the intellectual working out of oppositional and political commitments. The nature of university career ladders means that one's work must be recognized as meeting certain standards of quality in order that one be able to continue it. If those standards are intimately bound up with values and assumptions one rejects, incomprehension rather than conversion is likely. Success requires that we present our work in a way that satisfies those standards and it is easier to do work that looks just like work known to satisfy them than to strike out in a new direction. Another push to conformity comes from the structure of support for science. Many of the scientific ideas argued to be consistent with a feminist politics have a distinctively non-production orientation.[5] In the example discussed above, thinking of the brain as hormonally programmed makes intervention and control more likely than does thinking of it as a self-organizing complexly interactive system. The doing of science, however, requires financial support and those who provide that support are increasingly industry and the military. As might be expected they support research projects likely to meet their needs, projects which promise even greater possibilities for intervention in and manipulation of natural processes. Our sciences are being harnessed to the making of money and the waging of war. The possibility of alternate understandings of the natural world is irrelevant to a culture driven by those interests. To do feminist science we must change the social and political context in which science is done.

So: can there be a feminist science? If this means: is it in principle possible to do science as a feminist?, the answer must be: yes. If this means: can we in practice do science as feminists?, the answer must be: not until we change present conditions. ■

Suggestions for Critical Reflection

1. Longino writes that she "rejects a content-based approach in favor of a process-based approach to characterizing feminist science." What do you think she means by this? Why is it important?

2. Longino describes a distinction between "contextual" and "constitutive" values in science? What is supposed to be the difference between them? What is Longino's own attitude towards this distinction in the end?

3. "If … there is no a priori way to eliminate such [auxiliary] assumptions from evidential reasoning generally, and, hence, no way to rule out value-laden assumptions, then there is no formal basis for arguing that an inference mediated by contextual values is thereby bad science." What exactly is Longino saying here? Is she right?

4. How does Longino use her example of the study of the influence of sex hormones? What is the "background assumption" she thinks was at work in this study? What would a better version of this study look like?

5. "The idea of a value-free science is not just empty, but pernicious." Is it? Why?

6. A simple definition of feminism sees it as a movement to counter discrimination and injustice toward women. What else might be involved in feminism as an intellectual commitment? Is Longino's view of science properly conceived of as feminist—why or why not?

7. Longino does not advocate replacement of scientifically harmful "androcentric" values by supposedly scientifically superior feminist ones. What, exactly, does she advocate?

Notes

I am grateful to the Wellesley Center for Research on Women for the Mellon Scholarship during which I worked on the ideas in this essay. I am also grateful to audiences at UC Berkeley, Northeastern University, Brandeis University and Rice University for their comments and to the anonymous reviewers for *Hypatia* for their suggestions. An earlier version appeared as Wellesley Center for Research on Women Working Paper #63.

1 This seems to be suggested in Bleier (1984), Rose (1983) and in Sandra Harding's (1980) early work.

2 For a striking expression of this point of view see Witelson (1985).

3 Ideological commitments other than feminist ones may lead to the same assumptions and the variety of feminisms means that feminist commitments can lead to different and incompatible assumptions.

4 Cf. note [1], above.

5 This is not to say that interactionist ideas may not be applied in productive contexts, but that, unlike linear causal models, they are several steps away from the manipulation of natural processes immediately suggested by the latter. See Keller (1985), especially Chapter 10.

References

Addelson, Kathryn Pine. 1983. The man of professional wisdom. In *Discovering reality*, ed. Sandra Harding and Merrill Hintikka. Dordrecht: Reidel.

Bleier, Ruth. 1984. *Science and gender*. Elmsford, NY: Pergamon.

Doell, Ruth, and Helen E. Longino. N.d. *Journal of Homosexuality*. Forthcoming.*

Edelman, Gerald, and Vernon Mountcastle. 1978. *The mindful brain*. Cambridge, MA: MIT Press.

* Now in print: Ruth Doell and Helen Longino, "Sex Hormones and Human Behavior: A Critique of the Linear Model." *Journal of Homosexuality* 15, 3/4 (1988): 55–79.

Gould, Stephen J. 1984. Review of Ruth Bleier, *Science and gender*. *New York Times Book Review*, VVI, 7 (August 12): 1.

Harding, Sandra. 1980. The norms of inquiry and masculine experience. In *PSA 1980*, Vol. 2, ed. Peter Asquith and Ronald Giere. East Lansing, MI: Philosophy of Science Association.

Jacob, James R. 1977. *Robert Boyle and the English Revolution. A study in social and intellectual change*. New York: Franklin.

Jacob, Margaret C. 1976. *The Newtonians and the English Revolution, 1689–1720*. Ithaca, NY: Cornell University Press.

Keller, Evelyn Fox. 1985. *Reflections on gender and science*. New Haven, CT: Yale University Press.

Longino, Helen. 1979. Evidence and hypothesis. *Philosophy of Science* 46 (1): 35–56.

———. 1981. Scientific objectivity and feminist theorizing. *Liberal Education* 67 (3): 33–41.

———. 1983a. The idea of a value free science. Paper presented to the Pacific Division of the American Philosophical Association, March 25, Berkeley, CA.

———. 1983b. Scientific objectivity and logics of science. *Inquiry* 26 (1): 85–106.

———. 1983c. Beyond "bad science." *Science, Technology and Human Values* 8 (1): 7–17.

Longino, Helen, and Ruth Doell. 1983. Body, bias and behavior. *Signs* 9 (2): 206–227.

Lugones, Maria, and Elizabeth Spelman. 1983. Have we got a theory for you! Feminist theory, cultural imperialism and the demand for "the woman's voice." *Hypatia 1*, published as a special issue of *Women's Studies International Forum* 6 (6): 573–581.

Rose, Hilary. 1983. Hand, brain, and heart: A feminist epistemology for the natural sciences. *Signs* 9 (1): 73–90.

Rossiter, Margaret. 1982. *Women scientists in America: Struggles and strategies to 1940*. Baltimore, MD: Johns Hopkins University Press.

Witelson, Sandra. 1985. An exchange on gender. *New York Review of Books* (October 24).

PART III: METAPHYSICS
Philosophy of Mind

WHAT IS THE PLACE OF MIND IN THE PHYSICAL WORLD?

The philosophy of mind has three main parts: the philosophy of psychology, philosophical psychology, and the metaphysics of mental phenomena. The philosophy of psychology (which can also be thought of as a branch of the philosophy of science) consists in the critical evaluation of the claims and methodologies of cognitive science. For example, in the first half of the twentieth century philosophers were involved with assessing the claims made by psychoanalytic theory (such as that of Sigmund Freud) and of psychological behaviorism, which controversially held that the only legitimate subject of psychological study is external human behavior. More recently, philosophers have played a role in creating and critiquing psychological models which are based on analogies between the human mind and computer programs. For example, philosophers of mind examine the question of whether computers can "think"—manifest or model genuine intelligence—and whether the kind of information processing which is performed by the brain more resembles a familiar 'computational' type or a variety of more diffuse 'neural net' processing.

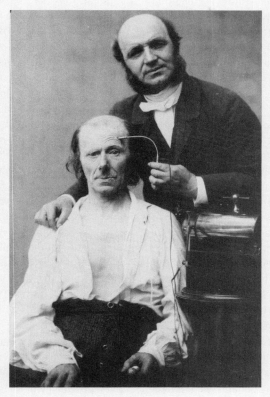

Philosophical psychology, by contrast, does not examine the science of psychology but instead engages in analysis of our ordinary, commonsensical concepts of the mental. It deals with such conceptual questions as the difference between deliberate action and mere behavior, the nature of memory and of perception, the no-

tion of rationality, the concept of personal identity, and so on.

Lastly, the metaphysics of the mind has to do with coming to understand the inherent nature of mental phenomena. The questions asked in this area are really at the heart of the philosophy of mind, and the four most important of them are the following:

1) What is the relationship between mind and brain? Of course, everyone knows that our minds and brains are closely connected: when certain things happen in our brains (perhaps caused by the ingestion of hallucinogenic chemicals), certain corresponding things happen in our minds. But what is the nature of this connection? Is the mind *nothing but* the physical brain (so that the brain processes *just are* the hallucinations), or is it something distinct from the brain, either because it is made of some different metaphysical 'stuff' (such as soul-stuff) or because it belongs to a different level or category of being (as a software program belongs to a different metaphysical category than the hard drive on which it is stored)?

2) What explains the fact that some of our mental states are directed at the world: how do some of our mental states come to be *meaningful*? The words on this page are meaningful because we use them as signs—when we learn to read, what we are learning is how to connect certain squiggles on the page with meaningful ideas. It is a much harder problem, however, to understand how bits

of our mind or brain can become signs, all by themselves, even though there is no one inside the head to 'read' them and give them meaning.

3) What explains the fact that some of our mental states have a certain qualitative *feel*? Put another way, where does *consciousness* come from? For example, the sensation of being tickled, or the smell of cooking onions, both have a distinctive feel to them: there is 'something it is like' for you to be tickled. However, if you think about it, this is a very unusual and quite puzzling fact; after all, for the vast majority of physical objects in the world, if you tickle them they don't feel a thing. So what makes *minds* special and unique in this respect? How do minds come to have a 'light on inside'—to be centers of consciousness and feeling in an unconscious, unfeeling universe? This is manifestly puzzling if you think of the mind as being nothing more than the three-and-a-bit-pound physico-chemical blob inside our skulls, but it turns out to be an extremely difficult problem for any theory of the mind. (In fact, arguably, it is the most difficult and pressing problem in all of philosophy.)

4) How do our mental states interact causally with the physical world? In particular, if our thoughts obey the laws of rationality instead of brute causality, then how can the workings of our mind be part of, or related to, the natural world? When I believe that this pesto sauce contains pine nuts, and I know that I am allergic to pine nuts and that if I eat any I will swell up like a balloon, and I don't want to swell up like a balloon, then it is (apparently) for this *reason* that I refuse to eat the pesto: my behavior is to be explained by the logical, rational connections between my beliefs and desires. The laws of physics, by contrast, are not rational laws. If a bullet ricochets off a lamppost and hits an innocent bystander during a bank robbery, it does not do so because it *ought* to bounce that way (nor does it do a bad thing because it has bounced *irrationally* or illogically)—its path is merely a physical consequence of the way it glanced off the metal of the lamppost. So, the laws of thought are rational and the laws of nature are non-rational: the problem is, then, how can thought be part of nature (be *both* rational and arational)? And if it is *not* part of nature, then how can it make things happen in the physical world (and vice versa)?

It is worth noting that, today, all of these questions are asked against the background of a default position called *physicalism*. Generally, in the sciences, we assume that the real world is nothing more than the physical world:

that all the things which exist are physical (roughly, made of either matter or energy) and obey exclusively physical laws (e.g., those described by fundamental physics). In most domains—such as chemistry, biology, or geology—this methodological assumption has proved fruitful; however, in psychology the question is much more vexed. In fact, the mind seems to be the last holdout of the non-physical in the natural world. How can the feeling of pain or the taste of honey be made of either matter or energy? How can falling in love or choosing to become a politician be subject to the laws of physics? If the study of the human mind is ever to be integrated within the rest of (scientific) human knowledge, these phenomena will need to be accounted for in a physicalist framework: the big question is, can this be done, and how?

The issue in the philosophy of mind which is focused on in this chapter is the mind-body problem—what is the relationship between the mind and the brain?—and in particular the relationship between consciousness and the brain. Historically, there have been five main mind-body theories. The traditional mind-body theory—the dominant story until about the middle of the twentieth century—is called *substance dualism*: on this view, mind and body are two completely different entities made up of two quite different substances: spirit and matter. The classic source for this view is Descartes's *Meditations*, which appears in the Theory of Knowledge chapter of this volume.

In the first reading of this chapter, Thomas Nagel argues that some facts about consciousness are subjective in a particular way that poses problems for physicalism. As he puts it: "Without consciousness the mind-body problem would be much less interesting. With consciousness it seems hopeless." The piece by David Chalmers re-emphasizes the difficulty of explaining consciousness in physical terms and proposes "that conscious experience be considered a fundamental feature [of the universe], irreducible to anything more basic" and describes what sort of theory that might look like. Lastly, the article by Amy Kind addresses head-on the following question: If consciousness is such a problem for physicalism or naturalism, why do we need to believe in (that kind of) consciousness at all?

The philosophy of mind has been a particularly active field for the past 50 years or so, and there are any number of good books available which will take you further into these fascinating questions. Some of the best are these: David Armstrong, *The Mind-Body Problem* (Westview,

1999); Keith Campbell, *Body and Mind* (University of Notre Dame Press, 1984); David Chalmers, *The Conscious Mind* (Oxford University Press, 1996); Paul Churchland, *Matter and Consciousness* (MIT Press, 2013); Tim Crane, *The Mechanical Mind* (Routledge, 2015); Daniel Dennett, *Consciousness Explained* (Little, Brown, 1991); Fred Dretske, *Naturalizing the Mind* (MIT Press, 1995); Edward Feser, *Philosophy of Mind: A Beginner's Guide* (OneWorld, 2006); Owen Flanagan, *The Science of the Mind* (MIT Press, 1991); Jerry Fodor, *Psychosemantics* (MIT Press, 1989); Stewart Goetz and Charles Taliaferro, *A Brief History of the Soul* (Wiley-Blackwell, 2011); John Heil, *Philosophy of Mind: A Contemporary Introduction* (Routledge, 2012); Ted Honderich, *Mind and Brain* (Oxford University Press, 1990); Jaegwon Kim, *Philosophy of Mind* (Routledge, 2010); Pete Mandik, *This Is Philosophy of Mind: An Introduction* (Wiley-Blackwell 2013); Colin McGinn, *The Character of Mind* (Oxford University Press, 1997); John Searle, *Mind: A Brief Introduction* (Oxford University Press, 2005); and Peter Smith and O.R. Jones, *The Philosophy of Mind* (Cambridge University Press, 1986). A good reference work on the philosophy of mind is *The Oxford Handbook of Philosophy of Mind*, edited by Brian P. McLaughlin and Ansgar Beckermann (Oxford University Press, 2011).

THOMAS NAGEL

What Is It Like to Be a Bat?

Who Is Thomas Nagel?

Thomas Nagel, an important American philosopher, was Professor of Law and Philosophy at New York University until his retirement in 2016. He was born in 1937 in Belgrade, Serbia, to German Jewish refugees, and the family moved to the US in 1939. Nagel was educated at Cornell (BA), Corpus Christi College, Oxford (BPhil), and Harvard (PhD, awarded in 1963). After working at Berkeley and Princeton, he moved to New York University in 1980. He is the author of a dozen books, including *The View from Nowhere* (1986) and *Mind and Cosmos: Why the Materialist Neo-Darwinian Conception of Nature Is Almost Certainly False* (2012), and many articles.

What Is Nagel's Overall Philosophical Project?

Throughout his career a main theme of Nagel's philosophical writing has been the difficulty of reconciling two fundamentally different points of view: our first-person, subjective, personal point of view, and the impartial, third-person, objective perspective.* The first-person perspective is typically thought of as being more partial than the third-person—partial both in the sense of being constrained by local horizons, and of being infected with personal concerns and biases. (For example, from *my* point of view it is right and natural to eat with a knife and fork, but this seems natural to me only because of the place and manner of my upbringing: speaking objectively, forks are no more nor less 'natural' than chopsticks or fingers.) As a result, subjective impressions are often thought of as being less reliable or 'true' than objective claims, and the first-person perspective tends to be treated as something to be avoided in serious

knowledge-gathering enterprises such as science or good journalism. Nagel's guiding philosophical question is this: *could* we completely understand the universe from the third-person point of view—that is, is the subjective completely reducible to (or eliminable in favor of) the objective? As he puts it in one of his books, he wants to know "how to combine the perspective of a particular person inside the world with an objective view of that same world, the person and his viewpoint included."†

The short version of Nagel's response to this problem is the following:

1. The subjective perspective is ineliminable in various highly important ways, and a refusal to notice this can lead to philosophical errors. "Appearance and perspective are essential parts of what there is." Our objectivity is limited by the fact that we cannot leave our own viewpoints entirely behind.
2. However, objectivity is also to be valued and fostered as a crucial method of coming to understand aspects of the world as it is in itself. It is important that we struggle to transcend our local horizons and try to get a better view of our place in the universe.

Many of Nagel's books trace these themes, in one way or another. *The View from Nowhere*, published in 1986, is explicitly about the relation between the subjective and the objective. His first book, *The Possibility of Altruism* (1970), dealt with the conflict between personal and impersonal reasons for individual action, and one of his later books, *Equality and Partiality* (1991), examines the issue of reconciling individual claims with those of a group.

"What Is It Like to Be a Bat?" is Nagel's most famous and influential article. In it he applies his theme to the

---

* "First-person" and "third-person" are terms taken from grammatical categories: "I am hungry" is a first-person sentence, as it's about the speaker; "She/he/it is hungry" is a third-person sentence, as it's about a third party. ("You are hungry" would be an example of a second-person sentence.)

† Thomas Nagel, *The View from Nowhere* (Oxford University Press, 1986), 3.

philosophy of mind, and contends that all current third-person theories of the mind (such as identity-theory, behaviorism, or functionalism) are radically incomplete since they fail to capture "what it is like to be" conscious, and this subjective character of experience, Nagel suggests, is a central aspect of mentality. Nagel's most recent book, *Mind and Cosmos* (2012), argues controversially against a reductionist view of the emergence of consciousness.

In the preface to his book *Mortal Questions*, Nagel describes his view of philosophy, and it is worth repeating here:

> I believe one should trust problems over solutions, intuition over arguments, and pluralistic discord over systematic harmony. Simplicity and elegance are never reasons to think that a philosophical theory is true: on the contrary, they are usually grounds for thinking it false. Given a knockdown argument for an intuitively unacceptable conclusion, one should assume there is probably something wrong with the argument that one cannot detect—though it is always possible that the source of the intuition has been misidentified.... Often the problem has to be reformulated because an adequate answer to the original formulation fails to make the *sense* of the problem disappear.... Superficiality is as hard to avoid in philosophy as it is anywhere else. It is too easy to reach solutions that fail to do justice to the difficulty of the problems. All one can do is try to maintain a desire for answers, a tolerance for long periods without any, an unwillingness to brush aside unexplained intuitions, and an adherence to reasonable standards of clear expression and cogent argument.*

What Is the Structure of This Reading?

Nagel begins by saying that the problem of reducing the mental to the physical—of completely describing and explaining our mental life in physical, non-psychological terms—is uniquely difficult because of the nature of conscious experience, and he goes on to explain this by discussing the relation between subjective and objective facts, using bats as an example.

After an aside, where he discusses the relation between facts and conceptual schemes for representing those facts, Nagel proceeds to argue that subjective facts about consciousness make the mind-body problem intractable. One of his central claims is that the reduction of experience to neurophysiology (i.e., the physiology of the brain and nervous system) is importantly different from standard cases of reduction (e.g., the reduction of heat to mean molecular motion). Nagel then discusses what philosophical moral should be drawn from all this—what implications it has, for example, for the claim that mental states are identical with brain states. He closes by suggesting that we pursue a solution to the problem he has raised by trying to develop an "objective phenomenology" of the mental.

Some Useful Background Information

Nagel is reacting against attempts in the 1960s and early 1970s to *reduce* the mental to the physical—that is, to show that, properly understood, mental phenomena are nothing more than physical phenomena. There are two central varieties of reduction, sometimes called "ontological reduction" and "theory reduction." Ontological reduction consists in showing that objects (or properties or events) of the first type are identical with—or "realized by"—objects (properties, events) of the second: for example, it might be that genes are identical with DNA molecules, or that lightning is nothing but a kind of electrical discharge, or that the color purple is just reflected light of a particular wavelength. Theory reduction consists in showing that all the statements of one higher-level theory can be translated into (or otherwise deduced from) statements of another more fundamental theory: for example (roughly speaking), the Mendelian laws of genetics are entailed by molecular biology, and our commonsense 'theory' of temperature can be translated into the kinetic theory of matter.

Nagel's anti-reductive claim is, therefore, that any optimism we might feel, that mental entities such as beliefs and emotions can be shown to be identical with neurological or functional states, or that psychological theories can someday be translated into some non-psychological language, is seriously misguided.

---

* Thomas Nagel, *Mortal Questions* (Cambridge University Press, 1979), x–xi.

Some Common Misconceptions

1. It is sometimes thought Nagel argues that physicalism is false: that is, that the mental involves something *extra* over and above the physical. (This would make Nagel some kind of dualist.) However, Nagel does not claim this: instead, he argues that *existing* physicalist theories of the mental (behaviorism, identity theory, functionalism) must be wrong, and he suggests that, although physicalism may be true—or even demonstrably true—it will be very hard for us to understand *how* it can be true. That is, he worries about the difficulty of giving any kind of objective theory of the mind.

2. There are various kinds of 'subjectivity,' and it has sometimes puzzled people exactly which kind Nagel is worrying about (perhaps because Nagel himself does not distinguish between some of them). One variety of non-objectivity that Nagel is clear he is *not* endorsing, however, is a particular kind of privacy of the mental. Some philosophers (such as Descartes) have held that consciousness is radically private in the sense that we have a special kind of access to our own mental states which, in principle, we cannot have to physical states. If this were true, then I could look as hard as I liked at your brain (which is a physical object) and *never* see any of your mental states; it would mean that the only access to consciousness must necessarily be from the first person, and thus that science would be forever excluded from studying and describing it. It is easy to see how this view might be confused with the one Nagel develops in this article, but nevertheless it is importantly different. For example, Nagel actually *denies* that we could never come to know anything at all about other people's consciousness, and even asserts that we can be corrected by other people when we make mistakes about what we ourselves are feeling (i.e., we are not 'incorrigible'). For Nagel, the problem is not some metaphysical difference of access to the mental and physical, but a problem about reconciling subjective and objective categories. Other versions of 'subjectivity' which may (or may not) be in play in this article include:

   - having a particular point of view or perspective;
   - being phenomenal or experiential (i.e., feeling a certain way);
   - having a sense of oneself as being a subject—as being a creature that, for example, undergoes sensations, forms intentions to do things, and controls its own actions;
   - being infallibly known or present to one's awareness (like the kind of raging toothache which is impossible to ignore and which one couldn't possibly be mistaken about).

What Is It Like to Be a Bat?*

Consciousness is what makes the mind-body problem really intractable. Perhaps that is why current discussions of the problem give it little attention or get it obviously wrong. The recent wave of reductionist euphoria has produced several analyses of mental phenomena and mental concepts designed to explain the possibility of some variety of materialism, psychophysical identification, or reduction.[1] But the problems dealt with are those common to this type of reduction and other types, and what makes the mind-body problem unique, and unlike the water–H_2O problem or the Turing machine–IBM machine problem† or the lightning–electrical discharge problem or

---

* This article was first published in *The Philosophical Review* 83, 4 (1974): 435–50, published by Duke University Press.

† By "IBM machine" Nagel simply means a computer. Turing argued that any effective mathematical method or "algorithm"—and thus any computer program whatever—can in principle be run on a Turing machine; thus the "reduction" of any computation to the very few operations of that machine.

the gene-DNA problem or the oak tree–hydrocarbon problem, is ignored.

Every reductionist has his favorite analogy from modern science. It is most unlikely that any of these unrelated examples of successful reduction will shed light on the relation of mind to brain. But philosophers share the general human weakness for explanations of what is incomprehensible in terms suited for what is familiar and well understood, though entirely different. This has led to the acceptance of implausible accounts of the mental largely because they would permit familiar kinds of reduction. I shall try to explain why the usual examples do not help us to understand the relation between mind and body—why, indeed, we have at present no conception of what an explanation of the physical nature of a mental phenomenon would be. Without consciousness the mind-body problem would be much less interesting. With consciousness it seems hopeless. The most important and characteristic feature of conscious mental phenomena is very poorly understood. Most reductionist theories do not even try to explain it. And careful examination will show that no currently available concept of reduction is applicable to it. Perhaps a new theoretical form can be devised for the purpose, but such a solution, if it exists, lies in the distant intellectual future.

Conscious experience is a widespread phenomenon. It occurs at many levels of animal life, though we cannot be sure of its presence in the simpler organisms, and it is very difficult to say in general what provides evidence of it. (Some extremists have been prepared to deny it even of mammals other than man.) No doubt it occurs in countless forms totally unimaginable to us, on other planets in other solar systems throughout the universe. But no matter how the form may vary, the fact that an organism has conscious experience *at all* means, basically, that there is something it is like to *be* that organism. There may be further implications about the form of the experience; there may even

(though I doubt it) be implications about the behavior of the organism. But fundamentally an organism has conscious mental states if and only if there is something that it is like to *be* that organism—something it is like *for* the organism.

We may call this the subjective character of experience. It is not captured by any of the familiar, recently devised reductive analyses of the mental, for all of them are logically compatible with its absence. It is not analyzable in terms of any explanatory system of functional states, or intentional states,* since these could be ascribed to robots or automata that behaved like people though they experienced nothing.[2] It is not analyzable in terms of the causal role of experiences in relation to typical human behavior—for similar reasons.[3] I do not deny that conscious mental states and events cause behavior, nor that they may be given functional characterizations. I deny only that this kind of thing exhausts their analysis. Any reductionist program has to be based on an analysis of what is to be reduced. If the analysis leaves something out, the problem will be falsely posed. It is useless to base the defense of materialism on any analysis of mental phenomena that fails to deal explicitly with their subjective character. For there is no reason to suppose that a reduction which seems plausible when no attempt is made to account for consciousness can be extended to include consciousness. Without some idea, therefore, of what the subjective character of experience is, we cannot know what is required of a physicalist theory.

While an account of the physical basis of mind must explain many things, this appears to be the most difficult. It is impossible to exclude the phenomenological† features of experience from a reduction in the same way that one excludes the phenomenal features of an ordinary substance from a physical or chemical reduction of it—namely, by explaining them as effects on the minds of human observers.[4] If physicalism is to be defended, the phenomenological features must

---

* An intentional state is one which has what philosophers call "intentionality," a technical term for 'aboutness' or, roughly, meaningfulness. Thus an intentional state is one which is about something else (such as the state of a register in a computer's CPU, as compared with, say, the position of a randomly chosen pebble on a beach).

† "Phenomenological" means having to do with phenomenology, and phenomenology is the description of the features of our lived conscious experience (as opposed to the features of what it is experience *of*). So, for example, the phenomenology of our perception of trees does not concern itself with actual trees and their relations to perceivers, but instead examines what it *feels* like to see a tree—what kind of (moving, temporal, emotionally resonant) picture we have in our head, if you like.

themselves be given a physical account. But when we examine their subjective character it seems that such a result is impossible. The reason is that every subjective phenomenon is essentially connected with a single point of view, and it seems inevitable that an objective, physical theory will abandon that point of view.

Let me first try to state the issue somewhat more fully than by referring to the relation between the subjective and the objective, or between the *pour-soi* and the *en-soi*.* This is far from easy. Facts about what it is like to be an *X* are very peculiar, so peculiar that some may be inclined to doubt their reality, or the significance of claims about them. To illustrate the connection between subjectivity and a point of view, and to make evident the importance of subjective features, it will help to explore the matter in relation to an example that brings out clearly the divergence between the two types of conception, subjective and objective.

I assume we all believe that bats have experience. After all, they are mammals, and there is no more doubt that they have experience than that mice or pigeons or whales have experience. I have chosen bats instead of wasps or flounders because if one travels too far down the phylogenetic tree,† people gradually shed their faith that there is experience there at all. Bats, although more closely related to us than those other species, nevertheless present a range of activity and a sensory apparatus so different from ours that the problem I want to pose is exceptionally vivid (though it certainly could be raised with other species). Even without the benefit of philosophical reflection, anyone who has spent some time in an enclosed space with an excited bat knows what it is to encounter a fundamentally *alien* form of life.

I have said that the essence of the belief that bats have experience is that there is something that it is like to be a bat. Now we know that most bats (the microchiroptera, to be precise) perceive the external world primarily by sonar, or echolocation, detecting the reflections, from objects within range, of their own rapid, subtly modulated, high-frequency shrieks. Their brains are designed to correlate the outgoing impulses with the subsequent echoes, and the information thus acquired enables bats to make precise discriminations of distance, size, shape, motion, and texture comparable to those we make by vision. But bat sonar, though clearly a form of perception, is not similar in its operation to any sense that we possess, and there is no reason to suppose that it is subjectively like anything we can experience or imagine. This appears to create difficulties for the notion of what it is like to be a bat. We must consider whether any method will permit us to extrapolate to the inner life of the bat from our own case,[5] and if not, what alternative methods there may be for understanding the notion.

Our own experience provides the basic material for our imagination, whose range is therefore limited. It will not help to try to imagine that one has webbing on one's arms, which enables one to fly around at dusk and dawn catching insects in one's mouth; that one has very poor vision, and perceives the surrounding world by a system of reflected high-frequency sound signals; and that one spends the day hanging upside down by one's feet in an attic. In so far as I can imagine this (which is not very far), it tells me only what it would be like for *me* to behave as a bat behaves. But that is not the question. I want to know what it is like for a *bat* to be a bat. Yet if I try to imagine this, I am restricted to the resources of my own mind, and those resources are inadequate to the task. I cannot perform it either by imagining additions to my present experience, or by imagining segments gradually subtracted from it, or by imagining some combination of additions, subtractions, and modifications.

To the extent that I could look and behave like a wasp or a bat without changing my fundamental structure, my experiences would not be anything like the experiences of those animals. On the other hand, it is doubtful that any meaning can be attached to the supposition that I should possess the internal neurophysiological constitution of a bat. Even if I could by gradual degrees be transformed into a bat, nothing in my present constitution enables me to imagine what the experiences of such a future stage of myself thus metamorphosed would be like. The best evidence

---

* *Pour-soi* (French) means "for itself" and *en-soi* means "in itself." In this context, the phrase refers to the contrast between consciousness and mere thing-hood.
† (Roughly) the scale of evolutionary development.

would come from the experiences of bats, if we only knew what they were like.

So if extrapolation from our own case is involved in the idea of what it is like to be a bat, the extrapolation must be incompletable. We cannot form more than a schematic conception of what it is like. For example, we may ascribe general *types* of experience on the basis of the animal's structure and behavior. Thus we describe bat sonar as a form of three-dimensional forward perception; we believe that bats feel some versions of pain, fear, hunger, and lust, and that they have other, more familiar types of perception besides sonar. But we believe that these experiences also have in each case a specific subjective character, which it is beyond our ability to conceive. And if there is conscious life elsewhere in the universe, it is likely that some of it will not be describable even in the most general experiential terms available to us.[6] (The problem is not confined to exotic cases, however, for it exists between one person and another. The subjective character of the experience of a person deaf and blind from birth is not accessible to me, for example, nor presumably is mine to him. This does not prevent us each from believing that the other's experience has such a subjective character.)

If anyone is inclined to deny that we can believe in the existence of facts like this whose exact nature we cannot possibly conceive, he should reflect that in contemplating the bats we are in much the same position that intelligent bats or Martians[7] would occupy if they tried to form a conception of what it was like to be us. The structure of their own minds might make it impossible for them to succeed, but we know they would be wrong to conclude that there is not anything precise that it is like to be us: that only certain general types of mental state could be ascribed to us (perhaps perception and appetite would be concepts common to us both; perhaps not). We know they would be wrong to draw such a skeptical conclusion because we know what it is like to be us. And we know that while it includes an enormous amount of variation and complexity, and while we do not possess the vocabulary to describe it adequately, its subjective character is

highly specific, and in some respects describable in terms that can be understood only by creatures like us. The fact that we cannot expect ever to accommodate in our language a detailed description of Martian or bat phenomenology should not lead us to dismiss as meaningless the claim that bats and Martians have experiences fully comparable in richness of detail to our own. It would be fine if someone were to develop concepts and a theory that enabled us to think about those things; but such an understanding may be permanently denied to us by the limits of our nature. And to deny the reality or logical significance of what we can never describe or understand is the crudest form of cognitive dissonance.

This brings us to the edge of a topic that requires much more discussion than I can give it here: namely, the relation between facts on the one hand and conceptual schemes or systems of representation on the other. My realism about the subjective domain in all its forms implies a belief in the existence of facts beyond the reach of human concepts. Certainly it is possible for a human being to believe that there are facts which humans never *will* possess the requisite concepts to represent or comprehend. Indeed, it would be foolish to doubt this, given the finiteness of humanity's expectations. After all, there would have been transfinite numbers even if everyone had been wiped out by the Black Death before Cantor* discovered them. But one might also believe that there are facts which *could* not ever be represented or comprehended by human beings, even if the species lasted forever—simply because our structure does not permit us to operate with concepts of the requisite type. This impossibility might even be observed by other beings, but it is not clear that the existence of such beings, or the possibility of their existence, is a precondition of the significance of the hypothesis that there are humanly inaccessible facts. (After all, the nature of beings with access to humanly inaccessible facts is presumably itself a humanly inaccessible fact.) Reflection on what it is like to be a bat seems to lead us, therefore, to the conclusion that there are facts that do not consist in the truth of propositions expressible in

---

* Georg Cantor (1845–1918) was a German mathematician. His theory of transfinite numbers is a mathematical theory of infinity which introduces a sequence of infinite cardinal numbers (called 'aleph-numbers' and written $\aleph_0$, $\aleph_1$, $\aleph_2$, ...) of increasing size. That is, intuitively, Cantor formalized the fact that some infinities are bigger than others.

a human language. We can be compelled to recognize the existence of such facts without being able to state or comprehend them.

I shall not pursue this subject, however. Its bearing on the topic before us (namely, the mind-body problem) is that it enables us to make a general observation about the subjective character of experience. Whatever may be the status of facts about what it is like to be a human being, or a bat, or a Martian, these appear to be facts that embody a particular point of view.

I am not adverting here to the alleged privacy of experience to its possessor. The point of view in question is not one accessible only to a single individual. Rather it is a *type*. It is often possible to take up a point of view other than one's own, so the comprehension of such facts is not limited to one's own case. There is a sense in which phenomenological facts are perfectly objective: one person can know or say of another what the quality of the other's experience is. They are subjective, however, in the sense that even this objective ascription of experience is possible only for someone sufficiently similar to the object of ascription to be able to adopt his point of view—to understand the ascription in the first person as well as in the third, so to speak. The more different from oneself the other experiencer is, the less success one can expect with this enterprise. In our own case we occupy the relevant point of view, but we will have as much difficulty understanding our own experience properly if we approach it from another point of view as we would if we tried to understand the experience of another species without taking up *its* point of view.[8]

This bears directly on the mind-body problem. For if the facts of experience—facts about what it is like *for* the experiencing organism—are accessible only from one point of view, then it is a mystery how the true character of experiences could be revealed in the physical operation of that organism. The latter is a domain of objective facts *par excellence**—the kind that can be observed and understood from many points of view and by individuals with differing perceptual systems. There are no comparable imaginative obstacles to the acquisition of knowledge about bat neurophysiology by human scientists, and

intelligent bats or Martians might learn more about the human brain than we ever will.

This is not by itself an argument against reduction. A Martian scientist with no understanding of visual perception could understand the rainbow, or lightning, or clouds as physical phenomena, though he would never be able to understand the human concepts of rainbow, lightning, or cloud, or the place these things occupy in our phenomenal world. The objective nature of the things picked out by these concepts could be apprehended by him because, although the concepts themselves are connected with a particular point of view and a particular visual phenomenology, the things apprehended from that point of view are not: they are observable from the point of view but external to it; hence they can be comprehended from other points of view also, either by the same organisms or by others. Lightning has an objective character that is not exhausted by its visual appearance, and this can be investigated by a Martian without vision. To be precise, it has a *more* objective character than is revealed in its visual appearance. In speaking of the move from subjective to objective characterization, I wish to remain noncommittal about the existence of an end point, the completely objective intrinsic nature of the thing, which one might or might not be able to reach. It may be more accurate to think of objectivity as a direction in which the understanding can travel. And in understanding a phenomenon like lightning, it is legitimate to go as far away as one can from a strictly human viewpoint.[9]

In the case of experience, on the other hand, the connection with a particular point of view seems much closer. It is difficult to understand what could be meant by the *objective* character of an experience, apart from the particular point of view from which its subject apprehends it. After all, what would be left of what it was like to be a bat if one removed the viewpoint of the bat? But if experience does not have, in addition to its subjective character, an objective nature that can be apprehended from many different points of view, then how can it be supposed that a Martian investigating my brain might be observing physical processes which were my mental processes (as he might observe physical processes which were bolts of

---

* French: "the best example of its kind."

lightning), only from a different point of view? How, for that matter, could a human physiologist observe them from another point of view?[10]

We appear to be faced with a general difficulty about psychophysical reduction. In other areas the process of reduction is a move in the direction of greater objectivity, toward a more accurate view of the real nature of things. This is accomplished by reducing our dependence on individual or species-specific points of view toward the object of investigation. We describe it not in terms of the impressions it makes on our senses, but in terms of its more general effects and of properties detectable by means other than the human senses. The less it depends on a specifically human viewpoint, the more objective is our description. It is possible to follow this path because although the concepts and ideas we employ in thinking about the external world are initially applied from a point of view that involves our perceptual apparatus, they are used by us to refer to things beyond themselves—toward which we *have* the phenomenal point of view. Therefore we can abandon it in favor of another, and still be thinking about the same things.

Experience itself, however, does not seem to fit the pattern. The idea of moving from appearance to reality seems to make no sense here. What is the analogue in this case to pursuing a more objective understanding of the same phenomena by abandoning the initial subjective viewpoint toward them in favor of another that is more objective but concerns the same thing? Certainly it *appears* unlikely that we will get closer to the real nature of human experience by leaving behind the particularity of our human point of view and striving for a description in terms accessible to beings that could not imagine what it was like to be us. If the subjective character of experience is fully comprehensible only from one point of view, then any shift to greater objectivity—that is, less attachment to a specific viewpoint—does not take us nearer to the real nature of the phenomenon: it takes us farther away from it.

In a sense, the seeds of this objection to the reducibility of experience are already detectable in successful cases of reduction; for in discovering sound to be, in reality, a wave phenomenon in air or other media, we leave behind one viewpoint to take up another, and the auditory, human or animal viewpoint that we leave behind remains unreduced. Members of radically different species may both understand the same physical events in objective terms, and this does not require that they understand the phenomenal forms in which those events appear to the senses of members of the other species. Thus it is a condition of their referring to a common reality that their more particular viewpoints are not part of the common reality that they both apprehend. The reduction can succeed only if the species-specific viewpoint is omitted from what is to be reduced.

But while we are right to leave this point of view aside in seeking a fuller understanding of the external world, we cannot ignore it permanently, since it is the essence of the internal world, and not merely a point of view on it. Most of the neobehaviorism of recent philosophical psychology results from the effort to substitute an objective concept of mind for the real thing, in order to have nothing left over which cannot be reduced. If we acknowledge that a physical theory of mind must account for the subjective character of experience, we must admit that no presently available conception gives us a clue how this could be done. The problem is unique. If mental processes are indeed physical processes, then there is something it is like, intrinsically,[11] to undergo certain physical processes. What it is for such a thing to be the case remains a mystery.

What moral should be drawn from these reflections, and what should be done next? It would be a mistake to conclude that physicalism must be false. Nothing is proved by the inadequacy of physicalist hypotheses that assume a faulty objective analysis of mind. It would be truer to say that physicalism is a position we cannot understand because we do not at present have any conception of how it might be true. Perhaps it will be thought unreasonable to require such a conception as a condition of understanding. After all, it might be said, the meaning of physicalism is clear enough: mental states are states of the body; mental events are physical events. We do not know *which* physical states and events they are, but that should not prevent us from understanding the hypothesis. What could be clearer than the words "is" and "are"?

But I believe it is precisely this apparent clarity of the word "is" that is deceptive. Usually, when we are told that *X* is *Y* we know *how* it is supposed to be true, but that depends on a conceptual or theoretical background and is not conveyed by the "is" alone. We know how both "*X*" and "*Y*" refer, and the kinds of things to which they refer, and we have a rough idea how the two referential paths* might converge on a single thing, be it an object, a person, a process, an event, or whatever. But when the two terms of the identification are very disparate it may not be so clear how it could be true. We may not have even a rough idea of how the two referential paths could converge, or what kind of things they might converge on, and a theoretical framework may have to be supplied to enable us to understand this. Without the framework, an air of mysticism surrounds the identification.

This explains the magical flavor of popular presentations of fundamental scientific discoveries, given out as propositions to which one must subscribe without really understanding them. For example, people are now told at an early age that all matter is really energy. But despite the fact that they know what "is" means, most of them never form a conception of what makes this claim true, because they lack the theoretical background.

At the present time the status of physicalism is similar to that which the hypothesis that matter is energy would have had if uttered by a pre-Socratic philosopher.† We do not have the beginnings of a conception of how it might be true. In order to understand the hypothesis that a mental event is a physical event, we require more than an understanding of the word "is." The idea of how a mental and a physical term might refer to the same thing is lacking, and the usual analogies with theoretical identification in other fields fail to supply it. They fail because if we construe the reference of mental terms to physical events on the usual model, we either get a reappearance of separate subjective events as the effects through which mental reference to physical events is secured, or else we get a false account of how mental terms refer (for example, a causal behaviorist‡ one).

Strangely enough, we may have evidence for the truth of something we cannot really understand. Suppose a caterpillar is locked in a sterile safe by someone unfamiliar with insect metamorphosis, and weeks later the safe is reopened, revealing a butterfly. If the person knows that the safe has been shut the whole time, he has reason to believe that the butterfly is or was once the caterpillar, without having any idea in what sense this might be so. (One possibility is that the caterpillar contained a tiny winged parasite that devoured it and grew into the butterfly.)

It is conceivable that we are in such a position with regard to physicalism. Donald Davidson has argued that if mental events have physical causes and effects, they must have physical descriptions. He holds that we have reason to believe this even though we do not—and in fact *could* not—have a general psychophysical theory.[12] His argument applies to intentional mental events, but I think we also have some reason to believe that sensations are physical processes, without being in a position to understand how. Davidson's position is that certain physical events have irreducibly mental properties, and perhaps some view describable in this way is correct. But nothing of which we can now form a conception corresponds to it; nor have we any idea what a theory would be like that enabled us to conceive of it.[13]

Very little work has been done on the basic question (from which mention of the brain can be entirely omitted) whether any sense can be made of experiences' having an objective character at all. Does it make sense, in other words, to ask what my experiences are *really* like, as opposed to how they appear to me? We cannot genuinely understand the hypothesis that their nature is captured in a physical description unless we understand the more fundamental idea that they *have* an objective nature (or that objective processes can have a subjective nature).[14]

I should like to close with a speculative proposal. It may be possible to approach the gap between subjective and objective from another direction. Setting aside temporarily the relation between the mind and the brain, we can pursue a more objective

---

* By "referential paths" Nagel means something like the various ways in which we fix the reference of our words to a certain thing (e.g., by personal acquaintance or by a description in a textbook). For example, I have at least two "referential paths" to the stuff picked out by the word *water*: it is the liquid which comes out of the tap in my kitchen, and it is the substance which has the molecular composition H_2O.

† A philosopher who lived before or around the time of Socrates (d. 399 BCE).

‡ Nagel presumably means the idea that our mental states are defined as whatever physically causes certain characteristic patterns of behavior (e.g., the word "pain" refers to the cause of pain behavior).

understanding of the mental in its own right. At present we are completely unequipped to think about the subjective character of experience without relying on the imagination—without taking up the point of view of the experiential subject. This should be regarded as a challenge to form new concepts and devise a new method—an objective phenomenology not dependent on empathy or the imagination. Though presumably it would not capture everything, its goal would be to describe, at least in part, the subjective character of experiences in a form comprehensible to beings incapable of having those experiences.

We would have to develop such a phenomenology to describe the sonar experiences of bats; but it would also be possible to begin with humans. One might try, for example, to develop concepts that could be used to explain to a person blind from birth what it was like to see. One would reach a blank wall eventually, but it should be possible to devise a method of expressing in objective terms much more than we can at present, and with much greater precision. The loose intermodal* analogies—for example, "Red is like the sound of a trumpet"—which

crop up in discussions of this subject are of little use. That should be clear to anyone who has both heard a trumpet and seen red. But structural features of perception might be more accessible to objective description, even though something would be left out. And concepts alternative to those we learn in the first person may enable us to arrive at a kind of understanding even of our own experience which is denied us by the very ease of description and lack of distance that subjective concepts afford.

Apart from its own interest, a phenomenology that is in this sense objective may permit questions about the physical[15] basis of experience to assume a more intelligible form. Aspects of subjective experience that admitted this kind of objective description might be better candidates for objective explanations of a more familiar sort. But whether or not this guess is correct, it seems unlikely that any physical theory of mind can be contemplated until more thought has been given to the general problem of subjective and objective. Otherwise we cannot even pose the mind-body problem without sidestepping it.[16] ∎

Suggestions for Critical Reflection

1. Many commentators suggest that Nagel collapses together two or three different kinds of subjectivity that would be better kept separate. Do you agree with this criticism? If so, how much of a problem (if any) does this cause for Nagel's arguments?

2. Do you think Nagel makes a good case for the claim that the reduction of, say, pain to some objectively-describable physical state is a very different ball game than the reduction of, for example, heat or liquidity to microphysical properties? If he's right about this, what philosophical implications are there (if any)?

3. Do you agree that there must be some facts—some things which are true—which could never be known by any human being, no matter how intelligent or well-informed?

4. Given Nagel's arguments, do you think that physicalism could possibly be true? That is, does Nagel leave open the possibility that everything that exists is, at bottom, physical (e.g., composed out of matter and energy)?

5. What do you think of Nagel's proposal for an "objective phenomenology"? What might such a theory look like? Is it even possible? Does Nagel *really* hold open the possibility of an objective description of the subjective character of experience?

---

* Crossing between modes of sensation, such as sight and touch.

Notes

1   Examples are J.J.C. Smart, *Philosophy and Scientific Realism* (London, 1963); David K. Lewis, "An Argument for the Identity Theory," *Journal of Philosophy*, LXIII (1966), reprinted with addenda in David M. Rosenthal, *Materialism & the Mind-Body Problem* (Englewood Cliffs, N.J., 1971); Hilary Putnam, "Psychological Predicates" in Capitan and Merrill, *Art, Mind, & Religion* (Pittsburgh, 1967), reprinted in Rosenthal, *op. cit.*, as "The Nature of Mental States"; D.M. Armstrong, *A Materialist Theory of the Mind* (London, 1968); D.C. Dennett, *Content and Consciousness* (London, 1969). I have expressed earlier doubts in "Armstrong on the Mind," *Philosophical Review*, LXXIX (1970), 394–403; "Brain Bisection and the Unity of Consciousness," *Synthèse*, 22 (1971); and a review of Dennett, *Journal of Philosophy*, LXIX (1972). See also Saul Kripke, "Naming and Necessity" in Davidson and Harman, *Semantics of Natural Language* (Dordrecht, 1972), esp. pp. 334–342; and M.T. Thornton, "Ostensive Terms and Materialism," *The Monist*, 56 (1972).

2   Perhaps there could not actually be such robots. Perhaps anything complex enough to behave like a person would have experiences. But that, if true, is a fact which cannot be discovered merely by analyzing the concept of experience.

3   It is not equivalent to that about which we are incorrigible, both because we are not incorrigible about experience and because experience is present in animals lacking language and thought, who have no beliefs at all about their experiences.

4   Cf. Richard Rorty, "Mind-Body Identity, Privacy, and Categories," *The Review of Metaphysics*, XIX (1965), esp. 37–38.

5   By "our own case" I do not mean just "my own case," but rather the mentalistic ideas that we apply unproblematically to ourselves and other human beings.

6   Therefore the analogical form of the English expression "what it is *like*" is misleading. It does not mean "what (in our experience) it *resembles*," but rather "how it is for the subject himself."

7   Any intelligent extraterrestrial beings totally different from us.

8   It may be easier than I suppose to transcend inter-species barriers with the aid of the imagination. For example, blind people are able to detect objects near them by a form of sonar, using vocal clicks or taps of a cane. Perhaps if one knew what that was like, one could by extension imagine roughly what it was like to possess the much more refined sonar of a bat. The distance between oneself and other persons and other species can fall anywhere on a continuum. Even for other persons the understanding of what it is like to be them is only partial, and when one moves to species very different from oneself, a lesser degree of partial understanding may still be available. The imagination is remarkably flexible. My point, however, is not that we cannot *know* what it is like to be a bat. I am not raising that epistemological problem. My point is rather that even to form a *conception* of what it is like to be a bat (and a fortiori to know what it is like to be a bat) one must take up the bat's point of view. If one can take it up roughly, or partially, then one's conception will also be rough or partial. Or so it seems in our present state of understanding.

9   The problem I am going to raise can therefore be posed even if the distinction between more subjective and more objective descriptions or viewpoints can itself be made only within a larger human point of view. I do not accept this kind of conceptual relativism, but it need not be refuted to make the point that psychophysical reduction cannot be accommodated by the subjective-to-objective model familiar from other cases.

10 The problem is not just that when I look at the "Mona Lisa," my visual experience has a certain quality, no trace of which is to be found by someone looking into my brain. For even if he did observe there a tiny image of the "Mona Lisa," he would have no reason to identify it with the experience.

11 The relation would therefore not be a contingent one, like that of a cause and its distinct effect. It would be necessarily true that a certain physical state felt a certain way. Saul Kripke (*op. cit.*) argues that causal behaviorist and related analyses of the mental fail because they construe, e.g., "pain" as a merely contingent name of pains. The subjective character of an experience ("its immediate phenomenological quality" Kripke calls it [p. 340]) is the essential property left out by such analyses, and the one in virtue of which it is, necessarily, the experience it is. My view is closely related to his. Like Kripke, I find the hypothesis that a certain brain state should *necessarily* have a certain subjective character incomprehensible without further explanation. No such explanation emerges from theories which view the mind-brain relation as contingent, but perhaps there are other alternatives, not yet discovered.

A theory that explained how the mind-brain relation was necessary would still leave us with Kripke's problem of explaining why it nevertheless appears contingent. That difficulty seems to me surmountable, in the following way. We may imagine something by representing it to ourselves either perceptually, sympathetically, or symbolically. I shall not try to say how symbolic imagination works, but part of what happens in the other two cases is this. To imagine something perceptually, we put ourselves in a conscious state resembling the state we would be in if we perceived it. To imagine something sympathetically, we put ourselves in a conscious state resembling the thing itself. (This method can be used only to imagine mental events and states—our own or another's.) When we try to imagine a mental state occurring without its associated brain state, we first sympathetically imagine the occurrence of the mental state: that is, we put ourselves into a state that resembles it mentally. At the same time, we attempt to perceptually imagine the non-occurrence of the associated physical state, by putting ourselves into another state unconnected with the first: one resembling that which we would be in if we perceived the nonoccurrence of the physical state. Where the imagination of physical features is perceptual and the imagination of mental features is sympathetic, it appears to us that we can imagine any experience occurring without its associated brain state, and vice versa. The relation between them will appear contingent even if it is necessary, because of the independence of the disparate types of imagination.

(Solipsism, incidentally, results if one misinterprets sympathetic imagination as if it worked like perceptual imagination: it then seems impossible to imagine any experience that is not one's own.)

12 See "Mental Events" in Foster and Swanson, *Experience and Theory* (Amherst, 1970); though I don't understand the argument against psychophysical laws.

13 Similar remarks apply to my paper "Physicalism," *Philosophical Review* LXXIV (1965), 339–356, reprinted with postscript in John O'Connor, *Modern Materialism* (New York, 1969).

14 This question also lies at the heart of the problem of other minds, whose close connection with the mind-body problem is often overlooked. If one understood how subjective experience could have an objective nature, one would understand the existence of subjects other than oneself.

15 I have not defined the term "physical." Obviously it does not apply just to what can be described by the concepts of contemporary physics, since we expect further developments. Some may think there is nothing to prevent mental phenomena from eventually being recognized as physical in their own right. But whatever else may be said of the physical, it has to be objective. So if our idea of the physical ever expands to include mental phenomena, it will have to assign them an objective character—whether or not this is done by analyzing them in terms of other phenomena already regarded as physical. It seems to me more likely, however, that mental-physical relations will eventually be expressed in a theory whose fundamental terms cannot be placed clearly in either category.

16 I have read versions of this paper to a number of audiences, and am indebted to many people for their comments.

DAVID CHALMERS

The Puzzle of Conscious Experience

Who Is David Chalmers?

David Chalmers was born in Sydney, Australia, in 1966. As a child he excelled in the sciences, especially mathematics, and he earned a bronze medal representing Australia at the notoriously challenging International Mathematical Olympiad in 1982. As a boy he also had synaesthesia, which is a condition where the stimulation of one sensory or cognitive pathway leads to experiences in a second, normally unconnected, sensory or cognitive pathway. In Chalmers, music produced strong color sensations in his mind. "Somewhat disappointingly most songs were murky shades of brown or olive green, but every now and then there was something distinctive. I remember that 'Here, There, and Everywhere' by the Beatles was bright red."*

His undergraduate degree, at the University of Adelaide, concentrated in mathematics and computer science, and he went to the University of Oxford as a Rhodes Scholar to do graduate work in mathematics. However, he had a growing interest in philosophy, and especially the problem of explaining consciousness. Influenced by Douglas Hofstadter's 1979 book *Gödel, Escher, Bach*, about the emergence of cognition from hidden neurological mechanisms, he made the radical decision to switch fields and moved to Indiana University to work in Hofstadter's Center for Research on Concepts and Cognition there. After completing his PhD in 1993 and a two-year post-doctoral fellowship at Washington University in St. Louis, Chalmers taught at UC Santa Cruz and the University of Arizona. In 1994 he gave an influential talk introducing what he called the "hard problem of consciousness" at the inaugural Toward a Science of Consciousness conference, and in 1996 he published the highly influential book *The Conscious Mind*.

Chalmers moved to the Australian National University in Canberra in 2004, and then to New York University, where he is University Professor of Philosophy and Neural Science and—along with Ned Block—co-director of the Center for Mind, Brain and Consciousness. He is also lead singer of the Zombie Blues band, and co-founder of the supremely useful PhilPapers,[†] a comprehensive online index, archive, and bibliography of philosophical writing.

What Is Chalmers's Overall Philosophical Project?

Chalmers is best known for arguing that the problem of integrating phenomenal consciousness—the subjective smells, sights, tastes and so on that make up our flow of conscious experience—into the physical world (and the natural sciences) is a uniquely difficult problem: indeed, what he calls "the hard problem." He does not argue specifically for dualism, but he does think we have compelling reasons to think that no physicalist account of consciousness could ever be successful. This is the subject of the article reprinted here.

In support of this, one of his central arguments is the so-called Zombie Argument (which lies in the background to, but is not explicitly described in, this paper). Zombies—of the philosophical rather than the Haitian or Hollywood variety—are theoretically constructed creatures stipulated to be identical in certain respects with ordinary human beings, but lacking in other respects. In Chalmers's argument, the zombies in question are identical to regular human beings in every physical way—they have brains just like ours, behave just like us, talk in the same way we do, etc.—but are different from human beings in that they lack conscious experience. From the outside your zombie twin is completely indiscernible from you, no matter what behavioral or scientific tests are performed; but 'from the inside' your zombie twin is

---

* From an interview on the website "What Is It Like to Be a Philosopher?" (28 September 2016).
† PhilPapers can be found at https://philpapers.org.

dark within. Its actions and utterances are not accompanied by any conscious sensations, such as pain, the taste of coffee, the sensation of seeing the vivid yellow of a maple tree in the fall....

The Zombie Argument itself can get somewhat complicated, and extensive discussion of the argument over the past twenty years has given rise to a substantial supporting philosophical apparatus. But the basic idea is fairly straightforward:

1. The zombies I have just described are *conceivable*. No one thinks they actually exist, but it is hard to deny that we can imagine them. We could, for example, write a perfectly coherent science fiction story in which a zombie is the protagonist.

2. Conceivability is a guide to logical possibility. We cannot imagine a square triangle or a male vixen, and these things are logically impossible. We can imagine a universe in which the laws of physics allow a pig-like creature to have wings and fly, or that we are subject to a complex deception and cats are actually robotic spies placed on Earth by an alien race, and—although these things are not true, or likely, or (at least in the first case) physically possible—they are nevertheless *logically* possible.

3. So zombies are logically possible.

4. But the logical possibility of zombies is incompatible with the truth of physicalism.

5. So physicalism is false.

A lot of the action here happens in premise 4, of course. Why should we believe it? The central idea is that if consciousness *just is* something physical, then it should not make sense to hold the physical constant while *changing* consciousness. That would be like trying to leave your house exactly as it is in every detail, while simultaneously performing home improvements; this doesn't even make sense, unless your house somehow is not the same thing as your home. Consider the case of 'zombie water': water that is physically exactly like regular water, but that has some difference such as that it is solid at room temperature. If you think hard about this case, you should see that it is actually logically impossible—it

is incoherent—because of the stipulation that zombie water is physically exactly like regular water. Nothing could have all the same microphysical properties and also be subject to all the same laws of physics and yet *not* be liquid at room temperature. Physics explains natural phenomena by showing that, if the physical theory is true, the thing to be explained *had* to be that way. So the apparent conceivability of zombies, while it might seem trivial at first sight, turns out to be hugely significant.*

The center of gravity of Chalmers's work is the problem of consciousness and its consequences, but he has also done influential work on language and meaning (including developing "two-dimensional semantics"), the metaphysics and epistemology of possibility, and artificial minds (including the threat of a "singularity"—a point beyond which artificial intelligence will enter a phase of runaway development beyond human control).

What Is the Structure of This Reading?

Chalmers begins with a distinction he thinks is fundamental to the philosophy of mind: between the functions carried out by the mental faculties, of gathering information from sensation, directing muscular activity, and so on, on the one hand, and the experiences of conscious life—of our impressions of shapes and colors, our feelings of pain and pleasure, our emotions and thoughts: in sum, our mental life—on the other. He's willing to grant that neuroscience could give a physicalist explanation of all of the former phenomena; his argument is that science can never begin to explain our mental life, to answer questions like: Why do we have *that* experience when we eat strawberries? Why are there any experiences at all? The first job of explanation he calls the "easy problem"—not meaning that it's easy to do, but rather just that science knows how to approach it, and it's scientifically doable; the second he calls the "hard problem"—not meaning that it's simply more difficult, but rather that it's really impossible for physical science.

After raising several examples that seem to show that neuroscience is inadequate to explain consciousness, Chalmers briefly considers and rejects the prospect of

---

* Chalmers's landmark 1995 article laying out this argument and more than 20 responses by other philosophers are collected in *Explaining Consciousness: The Hard Problem*, ed. Jonathan Shear (MIT Press, 1999).

solving the problem with "new tools of physical explanation." He proposes that the way forward instead is to postulate a new "fundamental component" for our theories that would allow them to connect together the physical and the phenomenal. He explores this idea—which, he suggests, is the only possible fruitful way of moving forward on the problem of consciousness—tentatively suggesting a version of this theory whereby "[p]erhaps information, or at least some information, has two basic aspects: a physical one and an experiential one." If this were so, he notes, then it might be that in some sense consciousness would be ubiquitous, making this a version of a theory called "panpsychism."

Some Useful Background Information

As science made enormous progress during the nineteenth and early twentieth centuries, a growing number of philosophers came to believe that the physical, scientific categories that had been deployed so successfully in explaining events elsewhere would someday have equal success in dealing with the mental; equally, more and more philosophers came to think that a unified view of reality was the correct one: a view that everything was made of one sort of physical stuff.

These two ideas, however, were separable. While (probably) most philosophers remained physicalist—believing that everything was ultimately constructed out of the same sort of matter, basically obeying the same sorts of laws—doubts grew during the second half of the twentieth century that physical explanation for mental events would be possible; that is, that there was, for example, a kind of brain event that happened every time anyone thought about dinner, that *constituted* thinking about dinner.

The most common theory denying the explicability of the mental by the physical came from the functionalists, who typically held that mental events were classified functionally—that is, by their typical causes and effects—and instances of a single mental type (e.g., wishing you had a hamburger now) might be realized by any of a possibly infinite number of different physical types of event. We can imagine, for example, that a Martian, whose brain was built on entirely different principles from ours, might also yearn for a hamburger, but this yearning might be identical in his case to a totally different physical brain event than in you. If there could not be a physical type corresponding, in an exceptionless way, to any mental type, then there could not be mental-physical bridge laws, and thus no physical explanation of the mental. (Most functionalists are, however, physicalists in the important sense that they believe that each particular mental event is also a physical event.)

Other arguments to the same conclusion relied on the basically normative character of mental ascriptions; the idea here is that whenever we assign beliefs and desires to others, we assume their rationality (otherwise their behavior might be correlated with any beliefs and desires whatever). Rationality is essentially an evaluative notion, thus having no place in physical sciences, like neurophysiology. Thus mental categories must cut up phenomena differently from physical ones; and again exceptionless "bridge" laws linking the two would be impossible. (Again, philosophers who accept this argument are generally physicalists.)

Chalmers, by contrast, accepts the idea that there are relations between the mental and the physical that can be described in terms of scientific laws. He denies, however, that these can be completely physical laws: they would have to describe correlations between the physical and the irreducibly mental.

The Puzzle of Conscious Experience*

Conscious experience is at once the most familiar thing in the world and the most mysterious. There is nothing we know about more directly than consciousness, but it is extraordinarily hard to reconcile it with everything else we know. Why does it exist? What does it do? How could it possibly arise from neural processes in the brain? These questions are among the most intriguing in all of science.

From an objective viewpoint, the brain is relatively comprehensible. When you look at this page, there is a whir of processing: photons strike your retina, electrical signals are passed up your optic nerve and between different areas of your brain, and eventually you might respond with a smile, a perplexed frown or a remark. But there is also a subjective aspect. When you look at the page, you are conscious of it, directly experiencing the images and words as part of your private, mental life. You have vivid impressions of the colors and shapes of the images. At the same time, you may be feeling some emotions and forming some thoughts. Together such experiences make up consciousness: the subjective, inner life of the mind.

For many years, consciousness was shunned by researchers studying the brain and the mind. The prevailing view was that science, which depends on objectivity, could not accommodate something as subjective as consciousness. The behaviorist movement in psychology, dominant earlier in this century, concentrated on external behavior and disallowed any talk of internal mental processes. Later, the rise of cognitive science focused attention on processes inside the head. Still, consciousness remained off-limits, fit only for late-night discussion over drinks.

Over the past several years, however, an increasing number of neuroscientists, psychologists and philosophers have been rejecting the idea that consciousness cannot be studied and are attempting to delve into its secrets. As might be expected of a field so new, there is a tangle of diverse and conflicting theories, often using basic concepts in incompatible ways. To help unsnarl the tangle, philosophical reasoning is vital.

The myriad views within the field range from reductionist theories, according to which consciousness can be explained by the standard methods of neuroscience and psychology, to the position of the so-called mysterians, who say we will never understand consciousness at all. I believe that on close analysis both of these views can be seen to be mistaken and that the truth lies somewhere in the middle.

Against reductionism I will argue that the tools of neuroscience cannot provide a full account of conscious experience, although they have much to offer. Against mysterianism I will hold that consciousness might be explained by a new kind of theory. The full details of such a theory are still out of reach, but careful reasoning and some educated inferences can reveal something of its general nature. For example, it will probably involve new fundamental laws, and the concept of information may play a central role. These faint glimmerings suggest that a theory of consciousness may have startling consequences for our view of the universe and of ourselves.

The Hard Problem

Researchers use the word "consciousness" in many different ways. To clarify the issues, we first have to separate the problems that are often clustered together under the name. For this purpose, I find it useful to distinguish between the "easy problems" and the "hard problem" of consciousness. The easy problems are by no means trivial—they are actually as challenging as most in psychology and biology—but it is with the hard problem that the central mystery lies.

The easy problems of consciousness include the following: How can a human subject discriminate sensory stimuli and react to them appropriately? How does the brain integrate information from many different sources and use this information to control behavior? How is it that subjects can verbalize their internal states? Although all these questions are associated with consciousness, they all concern the objective mechanisms

---

* This article was published in *Scientific American* in December 1995. It was reprinted, slightly updated, in the Scientific American Special Edition *The Hidden Mind* 12, 1 (2002): 90–100.

of the cognitive system. Consequently, we have every reason to expect that continued work in cognitive psychology and neuroscience will answer them.

The hard problem, in contrast, is the question of how physical processes in the brain give rise to subjective experience. This puzzle involves the inner aspect of thought and perception: the way things feel for the subject. When we see, for example, we experience visual sensations, such as that of vivid blue. Or think of the ineffable sound of a distant oboe, the agony of an intense pain, the sparkle of happiness or the meditative quality of a moment lost in thought. All are part of what I call consciousness. It is these phenomena that pose the real mystery of the mind.

To illustrate the distinction, consider a thought experiment devised by the Australian philosopher Frank Jackson. Suppose that Mary, a neuroscientist in the 23rd century, is the world's leading expert on the brain processes responsible for color vision. But Mary has lived her whole life in a black-and-white room and has never seen any other colors. She knows everything there is to know about physical processes in the brain— its biology, structure and function. This understanding enables her to grasp all there is to know about the easy problems: how the brain discriminates stimuli, integrates information and produces verbal reports. From her knowledge of color vision, she knows how color names correspond with wave-lengths on the light spectrum. But there is still something crucial about color vision that Mary does not know: what it is like to experience a color such as red. It follows that there are facts about conscious experience that cannot be deduced from physical facts about the functioning of the brain.

Indeed, nobody knows why these physical processes are accompanied by conscious experience at all. Why is it that when our brains process light of a certain wavelength, we have an experience of deep purple? Why do we have any experience at all? Could not an unconscious automaton have performed the same tasks just as well? These are questions that we would like a theory of consciousness to answer.

Is Neuroscience Enough?

I am not denying that consciousness arises from the brain. We know, for example, that the subjective experience of vision is closely linked to processes in the visual cortex. It is the link itself that perplexes, however. Remarkably, subjective experience seems to emerge from a physical process. But we have no idea how or why this is.

Given the flurry of recent work on consciousness in neuroscience and psychology, one might think this mystery is starting to be cleared up. On closer examination, however, it turns out that almost all the current work addresses only the easy problems of consciousness. The confidence of the reductionist view comes from the progress on the easy problems, but none of this makes any difference where the hard problem is concerned.

Consider the hypothesis put forward by neurobiologists Francis Crick of the Salk Institute for Biological Studies in San Diego and Christof Koch of the California Institute of Technology. They suggest that consciousness may arise from certain oscillations in the cerebral cortex, which become synchronized as neurons fire 40 times per second. Crick and Koch believe the phenomenon might explain how different attributes of a single perceived object (its color and shape, for example), which are processed in different parts of the brain, are merged into a coherent whole. In this theory, two pieces of information become bound together precisely when they are represented by synchronized neural firings.

The hypothesis could conceivably elucidate one of the easy problems about how information is integrated in the brain. But why should synchronized oscillations give rise to a visual experience, no matter how much integration is taking place? This question involves the hard problem, about which the theory has nothing to offer. Indeed, Crick and Koch are agnostic about whether the hard problem can be solved by science at all.

The same kind of critique could be applied to almost all the recent work on consciousness. In his 1991 book *Consciousness Explained*, philosopher Daniel C. Dennett laid out a sophisticated theory of how numerous independent processes in the brain combine to produce a coherent response to a perceived event. The theory might do much to explain how we produce verbal reports on our internal states, but it tells us very little about why there should be a subjective experience behind these reports. Like other reductionist theories, Dennett's is a theory of the easy problems.

The critical common trait among these easy problems is that they all concern how a cognitive or behavioral function is performed. All are ultimately questions about how the brain carries out some task—how it discriminates stimuli, integrates information, produces reports and so on. Once neurobiology specifies appropriate neural mechanisms, showing how the functions are performed, the easy problems are solved.

The hard problem of consciousness, in contrast, goes beyond problems about how functions are performed. Even if every behavioral and cognitive function related to consciousness were explained, there would still remain a further mystery: Why is the performance of these functions accompanied by conscious experience? It is this additional conundrum that makes the hard problem hard.

The Explanatory Gap

Some have suggested that to solve the hard problem, we need to bring in new tools of physical explanation: nonlinear dynamics, say, or new discoveries in neuroscience, or quantum mechanics. But these ideas suffer from exactly the same difficulty. Consider a proposal from Stuart R. Hameroff of the University of Arizona and Roger Penrose of the University of Oxford. They hold that consciousness arises from quantum-physical processes taking place in microtubules, which are protein structures inside neurons. It is possible (if not likely) that such a hypothesis will lead to an explanation of how the brain makes decisions or even how it proves mathematical theorems, as Hameroff and Penrose suggest. But even if it does, the theory is silent about how these processes might give rise to conscious experience. Indeed, the same problem arises with any theory of consciousness based only on physical processing.

The trouble is that physical theories are best suited to explaining why systems have a certain physical structure and how they perform various functions. Most problems in science have this form; to explain life, for example, we need to describe how a physical system can reproduce, adapt and metabolize. But consciousness is a different sort of problem entirely, as it goes beyond the scientific explanation of structure and function.

Of course, neuroscience is not irrelevant to the study of consciousness. For one, it may be able to reveal the nature of the neural correlate of consciousness—the brain processes most directly associated with conscious experience. It may even give a detailed correspondence between specific processes in the brain and related components of experience. But until we know why these processes give rise to conscious experience at

all, we will not have crossed what philosopher Joseph Levine has called the explanatory gap between physical processes and consciousness. Making that leap will demand a new kind of theory.

In searching for an alternative, a key observation is that not all entities in science are explained in terms of more basic entities. In physics, for example, space-time, mass and charge (among other things) are regarded as fundamental features of the world, as they are not reducible to anything simpler. Despite this irreducibility, detailed and useful theories relate these entities to one another in terms of fundamental laws. Together these features and laws explain a great variety of complex and subtle phenomena.

A True Theory of Everything

It is widely believed that physics provides a complete catalogue of the universe's fundamental features and laws. As physicist Steven Weinberg puts it in his 1992 book *Dreams of a Final Theory*, the goal of physics is a "theory of everything" from which all there is to know about the universe can be derived. But Weinberg concedes that there is a problem with consciousness. Despite the power of physical theory, the existence of consciousness does not seem to be derivable from physical laws. He defends physics by arguing that it might eventually explain what he calls the objective correlates of consciousness (that is, the neural correlates), but of course to do this is not to explain consciousness itself. If the existence of consciousness cannot be derived from physical laws, a theory of physics is not a true theory of everything. So a final theory must contain an additional fundamental component.

Toward this end, I propose that conscious experience be considered a fundamental feature, irreducible to anything more basic. The idea may seem strange at first, but consistency seems to demand it. In the 19th century it turned out that electromagnetic phenomena could not be explained in terms of previously known principles. As a consequence, scientists introduced electromagnetic charge as a new fundamental entity and studied the associated fundamental laws. Similar reasoning should be applied to consciousness. If existing fundamental theories cannot encompass it, then something new is required.

Where there is a fundamental property, there are fundamental laws. In this case, the laws must relate experience to elements of physical theory. These laws will almost certainly not interfere with those of the physical world; it seems that the latter form a closed system in their own right. Rather the laws will serve as a bridge, specifying how experience depends on underlying physical processes. It is this bridge that will cross the explanatory gap.

Thus, a complete theory will have two components: physical laws, telling us about the behavior of physical systems from the infinitesimal to the cosmological, and what we might call psychophysical laws, telling us how some of those systems are associated with conscious experience. These two components will constitute a true theory of everything.

Supposing for the moment that they exist, how might we uncover such psychophysical laws? The greatest hindrance in this pursuit will be a lack of data. As I have described it, consciousness is subjective, so there is no direct way to monitor it in others. But this difficulty is an obstacle, not a dead end. For a start, each one of us has access to our own experiences, a rich trove that can be used to formulate theories. We can also plausibly rely on indirect information, such as subjects' descriptions of their experiences. Philosophical arguments and thought experiments also have a role to play. Such methods have limitations, but they give us more than enough to get started.

These theories will not be conclusively testable, so they will inevitably be more speculative than those of more conventional scientific disciplines. Nevertheless, there is no reason they should not be strongly constrained to account accurately for our own first-person experiences, as well as the evidence from subjects' reports. If we find a theory that fits the data better than any other theory of equal simplicity, we will have good reason to accept it. Right now we do not have even a single theory that fits the data, so worries about testability are premature.

We might start by looking for high-level bridging laws, connecting physical processes to experience at an everyday level. The basic contour of such a law might be gleaned from the observation that when we are conscious of something, we are generally able to act on it and speak about it—which are objective, physical functions. Conversely, when some information is directly available for action and speech, it is generally conscious. Thus, consciousness correlates well with what we might call "awareness": the process by which information in the brain is made globally available to motor processes such as speech and bodily action.

Objective Awareness

The notion may seem trivial. But as defined here, awareness is objective and physical, whereas consciousness is not. Some refinements to the definition of awareness are needed, in order to extend the concept to animals and infants, which cannot speak. But at least in familiar cases, it is possible to see the rough outlines of a psychophysical law: where there is awareness, there is consciousness, and vice versa.

To take this line of reasoning a step further, consider the structure present in the conscious experience. The experience of a field of vision, for example, is a constantly changing mosaic of colors, shapes and patterns and as such has a detailed geometric structure. The fact that we can describe this structure, reach out in the direction of many of its components and perform other actions that depend on it suggests that the structure corresponds directly to that of the information made available in the brain through the neural processes of objective awareness.

Similarly, our experiences of color have an intrinsic three-dimensional structure that is mirrored in the structure of information processes in the brain's visual cortex. This structure is illustrated in the color wheels and charts used by artists. Colors are arranged in a systematic pattern—red to green on one axis, blue to yellow on another, and black to white on a third. Colors that are close to one another on a color wheel are experienced as similar. It is extremely likely that they also correspond to similar perceptual representations in the brain, as one part of a system of complex three-dimensional coding among neurons that is not yet fully understood. We can recast the underlying concept as a principle of structural coherence: the structure of conscious experience is mirrored by the structure of information in awareness, and vice versa.

Another candidate for a psychophysical law is a principle of organizational invariance. It holds that physical systems with the same abstract organization will give rise to the same kind of conscious experience, no matter what they are made of. For example, if the precise interactions between our neurons could be duplicated with silicon chips, the same conscious experience would arise. The idea is somewhat controversial, but I believe it is strongly supported by thought experiments describing the gradual replacement of neurons by silicon chips. The remarkable implication is that consciousness might someday be achieved in machines.

Theory of Consciousness

The ultimate goal of a theory of consciousness is a simple and elegant set of fundamental laws, analogous to the fundamental laws of physics. The principles described above are unlikely to be fundamental, however. Rather they seem to be high-level psychophysical laws, analogous to macroscopic principles in physics such as those of thermodynamics or kinematics. What might the underlying fundamental laws be? No one really knows, but I don't mind speculating.

I suggest that the primary psychophysical laws may centrally involve the concept of information. The abstract notion of information, as put forward in the 1940s by Claude E. Shannon of the Massachusetts Institute of Technology, is that of a set of separate states with a basic structure of similarities and differences between them. We can think of a 10-bit binary code as an information state, for example. Such information states can be embodied in the physical world. This happens whenever they correspond to physical states (voltages, say) and when differences between them can be transmitted along some pathway, such as a telephone line.

We can also find information embodied in conscious experience. The pattern of color patches in a visual field, for example, can be seen as analogous to that of the pixels covering a display screen. Intriguingly, it turns out that we find the same information states embedded in conscious experience and in underlying physical processes in the brain. The three-dimensional encoding of color spaces, for example, suggests that the information state in a color experience corresponds directly to an information state in the brain. Thus, we might even regard the two states as distinct aspects of a single information state, which is simultaneously embodied in both physical processing and conscious experience.

Aspects of Information

A natural hypothesis ensues. Perhaps information, or at least some information, has two basic aspects: a physical one and an experiential one. This hypothesis has the status of a fundamental principle that might underlie the relation between physical processes and experience. Wherever we find conscious experience, it exists as one aspect of an information state, the other aspect of which is embedded in a physical process in the brain. This proposal needs to be fleshed out to make a satisfying theory. But it fits nicely with the principles mentioned earlier—systems with the same organization will embody the same information, for example—and it could explain numerous features of our conscious experience.

The idea is at least compatible with several others, such as physicist John A. Wheeler's suggestion that information is fundamental to the physics of the universe. The laws of physics might ultimately be cast in informational terms, in which case we would have a satisfying congruence between the constructs in both physical and psychophysical laws. It may even be that a theory of physics and a theory of consciousness could eventually be consolidated into a single grander theory of information.

A potential problem is posed by the ubiquity of information. Even a thermostat embodies some information, for example, but is it conscious? There are at least two possible responses. First, we could constrain the fundamental laws so that only some information has an experiential aspect, perhaps depending on how it is physically processed. Second, we might bite the bullet and allow that all information has an experiential aspect—where there is complex information processing, there is complex experience, and where there is simple information processing, there is simple experience. If this is so, then even a thermostat might have experiences, although they would be much simpler than even a basic color experience, and there would certainly be no accompanying emotions or thoughts. This seems odd at first, but if experience is truly fundamental, we might expect it to be widespread. In any case, the choice between these alternatives should depend on which can be integrated into the most powerful theory.

Of course, such ideas may be all wrong. On the other hand, they might evolve into a more powerful proposal that predicts the precise structure of our conscious experience from physical processes in our brains. If this project succeeds, we will have good reason to accept the theory. If it fails, other avenues will be pursued, and alternative fundamental theories may be developed. In this way, we may one day resolve the greatest mystery of the mind. ■

Suggestions for Critical Reflection

1. Chalmers says "I am not denying that consciousness arises from the brain." This is accurate, but perhaps a bit surprising. What does he think is the relationship between the brain and consciousness?

2. Valerie Gray Hardcastle suggests we

    Consider the following exchange. A water-mysterian wonders why water has this peculiar property [being wet]. She inquires and you give an explanation of the molecular composition of water and a brief story about the connection between micro-chemical properties and macro-phenomena. Ah, she says ... I am convinced that you have properly correlated water with its underlying molecular composition. I also have no reason to doubt ... your story about the macro-effects of chemical properties to be wrong. But I still am not satisfied, for you have left off in your explanation what I find most puzzling. Why *is* water H$_2$O? Why couldn't it be XYZ? Why couldn't it have some other radically different chemical story behind it? I can imagine a possible world in which water has all the macro-properties that it has now, but is not composed of H$_2$O ... What *can* one say? I think nothing. Water-mysterians are antecedently convinced of the mysteriousness of water and no amount of scientific data is going to change that perspective. Either you already believe that science is going to give you a correct identity statement, or you don't and you think that there is always going to be something left over, the wateriness of water.*

    What analogy is Hardcastle drawing with Chalmers's position? The suggestion here is that consciousness-mysterianism is just as baseless as water-mysterianism, but that there are no arguments that could convince either mysterian that their positions are wrong. Do you agree?

3. Hardcastle points out that both materialists and dualists accept some facts as "brute facts"—unexplainable features of the universe, just the way it is; but she remarks that "it seems highly unlikely that some relatively chauvinistic *biological* fact should ever be brute." If this is to be a criticism of Chalmers, what's the "relatively chauvinistic biological fact" in his view? (What does "chauvinistic" mean in this context?) See if you can explain why Hardcastle thinks that this view is "highly unlikely."

4. What is Chalmers's "principle of organizational invariance"? What are its implications, if it's true? (Is it true?)

5. Chalmers imagines that some day psychophysical laws will be discovered. But if that's the case, would that allow "facts about conscious experience" to be "deduced from physical facts about the functioning of the brain"? If so, does this contradict what Chalmers claims about the "Mary" story?

6. At the end of the reading, Chalmers raises the prospect of panpsychism: the view that everything (or at least everything that "processes information," including certainly thermostats and All Wheel Drive traction systems, and possibly even natural processes such as convection) is conscious. How palatable is this notion? If we must reject it, what problems might this cause for Chalmers?

---

* "The Why of Consciousness: A Non-issue for Materialists," *Journal of Consciousness Studies* 3, 1 (1996): 7–13.

AMY KIND

How to Believe in Qualia

Who Is Amy Kind?

Amy Kind is an American philosopher who writes mainly about imagination, consciousness, and experience. She earned her MA and PhD at the University of California Los Angeles, and is now Russell K. Pitzer Professor of Philosophy at Claremont McKenna College in California. Kind co-edited two major texts on philosophy and the imagination—the *Routledge Handbook of Philosophy of Imagination* (2016) and *Knowledge Through Imagination* (2016)—and authored the textbook *Persons and Personal Identity* (2015) as well as numerous articles on cognition, qualia, and experience. Kind has described her research as an attempt to "put the image back in imagination."[*] She also runs a scholarly blog called "The Junkyard," which publishes posts about the philosophy of imagination by current academic philosophers. "Historically," she writes, "imagination has played a central role in the work of philosophers such as Aristotle, Descartes, Hume, Kant, Sartre, and many others...."[†]

What Is the Structure of This Reading?

In this paper, Kind addresses the issue of "qualia"—that is, the subjective, what-it's-like qualities of conscious experience. When we see a certain shade of color on an object, for example, our experience itself seems to be colorful in that way. When we hear a certain sound from an instrument, our experience may seem to have certain distinctive qualities that can be isolated and that are something other than representations of the instrument. These properties of experience are what philosophers call qualia (or, in the singular, a quale), and—largely because they appear to be in tension with

our best scientific theories of the world—some philosophers deny that they exist.

Kind's goal is to convince us that we should believe in qualia. The main motivation for "qualia realism," according to Kind, is simply the fact that we seem to experience qualia all the time. Some philosophers, however, deny this claim. According to these "opponents of qualia," we don't actually experience qualia; rather, what we experience is simply *things*, out there in the world, like trees, faces, thunder claps, coffee cups, etc. This claim—that we experience things directly, without any mysterious mediating mental objects like qualia—is what Kind refers to as the "transparency thesis." Kind's aim in this paper is to disprove this thesis, and in doing so demonstrate that qualia realism should be our default philosophical position. She does so by considering a number of mundane experiences (such as seeing a tree) and exotic ones (such as the afterimage on the back of your closed eyelids), arguing that these experiences give us good reason to think that qualia exist.

Some Useful Background Information

Kind writes that "[g]enerally speaking, the main proponents of the transparency thesis are representationalists." Representationalism about consciousness is the view that what is sometimes called phenomenal content—what it is like to eat an egg or watch a sunset—is (nothing more than) a variety of representational content. That is, the "pink" experience of watching a sunset is nothing other than the fact that the experience represents—is about—a pink sunset. The advantage of this approach is that representational content is, arguably, fairly well understood and able to be accounted for naturalistically. That is, we have theories of how

---

[*] Kind, "Putting the Image Back in Imagination," *Philosophy and Phenomenological Research* 62, 1 (2001): 85–109.

[†] Kind, "Welcome to the Junkyard" (2017), at *The Junkyard*, https://junkyardofthemind.com/blog/2017/4/3/welcome-to-the-junkyard-1

our mental states come to be about the things they are about, and those theories are compatible with a generally physicalist, naturalistic view of the world. If we can use these sorts of theories to explain phenomenal consciousness, then consciousness also can be naturalised. A key commitment of representationalism about consciousness, then, is that everything that makes consciousness special can be accounted for in terms of the *contents* of conscious states—what conscious states are *about*. Tacitly, this is a denial that conscious states—the vehicles carrying that content—have any properties *themselves* that are special in any mysterious way. That is, representationalism denies that qualia, understood as properties *of* conscious states, exist.*

How to Believe in Qualia†

Why should we believe that qualia‡ exist? It would not be surprising if, when confronted with this question, the qualia realist were puzzled. "Look around you," she might say, "and then pause for just a moment and reflect on your experiences. Isn't there a redness to your experience of that soda can on your desk? And isn't there a sweetness to your experience as you take a sip from it? Surely your experiences have qualitative aspects—surely there is something your experiences are like." And thus, to many a qualia realist, the answer to the question posed above is simple. Why believe in qualia? Because our every experience reveals their existence.

Unfortunately, the matter cannot be resolved this easily. (If it could, then there would be no need to produce a collection of papers making the case for qualia.) The existence of qualia has long been under attack. Opponents of qualia typically fall into two camps. In the first camp, we have philosophers who admit that, at least on the face of it, the phenomenological§ data support the existence of qualia. By their lights, however, there are strong theoretical reasons that count against qualia (typically that they cannot be accommodated within a physicalist¶ framework). These opponents thus have the task of explaining why we should disregard the phenomenology of our experience. They must convince us why we should *not* believe in qualia.

In the second camp, however, are philosophers who deny the phenomenological data. Qualia realists have it wrong, they say. In fact, our experience does not reveal the existence of any qualia, for our experience is *transparent*—when we attend to our experiences, our attention goes right through to their objects. Such philosophers typically take these considerations of transparency to support a representationalist view

---

*   Confusingly, there is also a position in the philosophy of perception called "representationalism" which holds that the world we see in conscious experience is not 'directly' the real world itself, but a virtual-reality replica of that world in an internal representation and hence that our perceptual access to reality is only 'indirect.' This is a distinct position from representationalism about consciousness—and is actually one that these kinds of representationalists typically deny. (Because otherwise the colors, smells, and tastes we experience would have to be properties of the inner representations somewhere between us and the world, and that is just another version of the problem of consciousness. Much more attractive, from a representationalist about consciousness's point of view, is to take the colors etc. we experience to be physical properties of objects out there in the world.)

†   Amy Kind, "How to Believe in Qualia," in *The Case for Qualia*, ed. Edmond Wright (MIT Press, 2008), 285–98.

‡   In philosophy, "qualia" refers to the qualities of our subjective, conscious experiences—or what it is *like* to have a given experience.

§   In this context, "phenomenological" can be read roughly as "experiential," and "phenomenology" as something like "immediate first-hand experience."

¶   Physicalism is the view that the only things that exist are physical things.

of consciousness according to which the qualitative content of experience supervenes on,* or even reduces to, the intentional content† of experience. But for our purposes, what's important is that these philosophers deny that we have any reasons to believe in qualia—or, at the very least, that if we do have any such reasons, they are not provided by our experience. These opponents of qualia thus shift the burden of argument to the qualia realist. It is the qualia realist's responsibility, they say, to convince us why we should believe in qualia.

This essay aims to do just that. As I will suggest, these philosophers in the second camp are mistaken—the phenomenological data do support the existence of qualia. I will not address those philosophers in the first camp, that is, I do not take up the question of how qualia can be accommodated in a physicalist, or even naturalist, account of the mind (though the argument may suggest that it needs to be). But by showing that experience does, after all, support the existence of qualia, I aim to show that qualia realism should be our default position.

1 The Transparency Thesis

The view that our experience is transparent is generally thought to trace back at least to G.E. Moore,‡ who wrote, "When we try to introspect the sensation of blue, all we can see is the blue: the other element is as if it were diaphanous" (Moore 1903: 450). Although Moore subsequently qualifies this characterization of experience,[1] this remark has inspired many contemporary philosophers who present similar phenomenological descriptions. For example, consider the following passages from Michael Tye:

> Focus your attention on a square that has been painted blue. Intuitively, you are directly aware of blueness and squareness as out there in the world

away from you, as features of an external surface. Now shift your gaze inward and try to become aware of your experience itself, inside you, apart from its objects. Try to focus your attention on some intrinsic feature of the experience that distinguishes it from other experiences, something other than what it is an experience *of*. The task seems impossible: one's awareness seems always to slip through the experience to blueness and squareness, as instantiated together in an external object. In turning one's mind inward to attend to the experience, one seems to end up concentrating on what is outside again, on external features or properties. (Tye 1995: 30)[2]

> If you are attending to how things *look* to you, as opposed to how they are independent of how they look, you are bringing to bear your faculty of introspection. But in so doing, you are not aware of any inner object or thing. The only objects of which you are aware are the external ones making up the scene before your eyes. Nor, to repeat, are you directly aware of any qualities of your experience. (Tye 2000: 46–47)

Likewise, consider Gilbert Harman's characterization of experience:

> When Eloise sees a tree before her, the colors she experiences are all experienced as features of the tree and its surroundings. None of them are experienced as intrinsic features of her experience. Nor does she experience any features of anything as intrinsic features of her experiences. And that is true of you too. There is nothing special about Eloise's visual experience. When you see a tree, you do not experience any features as intrinsic features of your experience. Look at a tree and try to turn your attention to intrinsic features of your visual

---

* Some set of facts or properties A supervenes on another set of properties B just in case A cannot vary unless B varies. For example, facts about chairs supervene on facts about the atoms that those chairs are made of: a chair cannot change position, for example, unless its atoms do too.

† By "intentional content," Kind means the things that our experiences are *about*. "Representationalism," then, is the view that our experiences are nothing more than the things our experiences are about, and a theory of consciousness will be complete if it can fully explain the contents of our conscious experiences without needing to also explain any 'left over' properties of those experiences themselves (such as qualia).

‡ G.E. Moore (1873–1958) was a British philosopher known especially for his work in ethics and analytic philosophy.

experience. I predict you will find that the only features there to turn your attention to will be features of the presented tree.... (Harman 1990: 39)

These passages support what I'll call the *transparency thesis*, that is, the claim that experience is transparent. Some philosophers who endorse considerations of transparency intend only a very weak claim, namely, that is *difficult* to attend directly to our experience, or that *typically* we don't attend directly to our experience. But I take it that philosophers like Harman and Tye want to endorse a stronger version of the claim. On their view, it is not simply difficult but *impossible* to attend directly to our experience. The only way to attend to our experience is by attending to the objects represented by that experience.[3] In what follows, I reserve the label "transparency thesis" for this strong claim.

As stated, even in this strong form, the transparency thesis is not itself a denial of the existence of qualia—or at least not straightforwardly so. In claiming that we cannot attend to qualia in attending to our experience, the transparency thesis remains silent on the question of whether qualia exist. But the transparency thesis nonetheless poses quite a threat to the qualia realist. First of all, we might plausibly suppose that any qualia worthy of the name must be introspectible, that is, introspectibility is essential to the nature of qualia.[4] If this is right, then the fact that the transparency thesis denies that qualia are available to introspection ends up being tantamount to a denial of their existence. But even if we were to accept that there could exist non-introspectible qualia, the transparency thesis would still have anti-qualia ramifications. For even if the transparency thesis is strictly speaking compatible with the existence of qualia, if qualia cannot be introspectively attended to then it looks like we no longer have any reason to believe that they exist. Insofar as our belief in qualia is driven by phenomenological considerations, our being deprived of those considerations leaves the belief entirely unjustified.[5]

Generally speaking, the main proponents of the transparency thesis are representationalists. In fact, many representationalists use the transparency thesis as support for their theory, claiming that representationalism offers the best explanation of the phenomenon of transparency. Tye, for example, claims that phenomenal content reduces to a special sort of intentional content.[6] According to Tye, this helps us see "why visual phenomenal character is not a quality of an experience to which we have direct access (representational content is not a quality of the thing that has representational content)" (Tye 2000: 48–49).

In what follows, I will not take up the question of whether the transparency thesis can help motivate representationalism. Rather, I would like to focus instead on the prior question of whether the transparency thesis is true. To some extent, this will require us to look at the relationship between transparency and representationalism, since the defense of the first thesis often goes hand in hand with the defense of the second. But my primary focus here will be on transparency, not representationalism. To my mind, the pro-qualia case against transparency has not yet been satisfactorily made in the literature. Granted, qualia realists have produced numerous cases of apparent counterexamples to the transparency thesis—and I find many of these cases quite compelling. But, as you might expect, such examples are by no means uncontroversial. More important, however, is that most of the cases that have generated discussion are unusual in various respects—involving illusions, blurriness, or other non-ideal circumstances. Thus, the transparency theorist can often blunt the force of such examples. Even if he concedes that transparency fails in these "exotic" cases, he can still maintain that transparency holds for the vast majority of our experiences.[7] And it is not very satisfying for the qualia realist to rest her belief in qualia on a few unusual cases.

This essay thus aims to advance the debate past a discussion of these exotic examples. Once we understand how the exotic cases get their purchase as counterexamples to the transparency thesis, we can use this understanding to think about the more mundane cases for which the transparency thesis is supposed to be obvious. Having seen that we attend to qualia in certain exotic cases, we are reminded how we attend to qualia in the mundane cases as well. In short, by seeing why the transparency thesis is false, we are reminded how, and why, to believe in qualia.

2 The Exotic

The first exotic case to consider comes from blurry vision.[8] Suppose that someone who needs reading glasses peruses the morning newspaper while wearing his glasses. He sees the front page headlines clearly and sharply. When he takes off his glasses, however, his perception changes—he now has a blurry experience of those same headlines. Of course, this phenomenon is not limited to those who need reading glasses. Someone with perfect vision may achieve the same effect by unfocusing her eyes while reading the paper. When someone takes off his reading glasses, or unfocuses her eyes, there is a difference experientially—a phenomenal difference. How should this difference be best described? Does it seem that the words themselves are blurry, that is, that the blurriness is on the newspaper page itself? Or does it seem that the experience itself is blurry? Many people have the strong intuition that attending to the blurriness is different from attending to the words on the page. So insofar as the blurriness feels like an aspect of one's experience rather than an aspect of the headlines themselves, the case of blurry vision presents a problem for the transparency thesis.

A related case comes from phosphene experiences, that is, the color sensations created by pressure on the eyeball when one's eyelids are closed (Wright 1981; Block 1996). In offering this example, Block suggests that the phosphene experiences do not seem to be representing anything; we don't take the experience to suggest that there are colored moving expanses *out there* somewhere. Likewise in attending to the phosphene experiences, we don't seem to be attending to the object of the experience (some colored expanse *out there*) but rather to the experiences themselves.

A third kind of case comes from considering afterimages (see, e.g., Boghossian and Velleman 1989). In general, afterimages occur subsequent to the removal of some original (usually intense) stimulus. When a camera flash goes off, you might experience an afterimage in front of the photographer's face.[9] If you stare intently at a bright light for a little while and then close your eyes, there will be a lingering glow in the darkness. And if you stare at a green dot for half a minute and then shift your attention to a bright white piece of paper, you will visually experience a red dot similar in size and location to the green dot you had been staring at. But in none of these cases does it seem as if the afterimage represents something that is really there. When you close your eyes after looking at the bright light, for example, you don't take the lingering glow to be on the inner surface of your eyelids. When you see the red afterimage against the white page, you don't take the redness to suggest the existence of a red

dot on the page. As Block has suggested, afterimages "don't look as if they are really objects or as if they are really red. They look ... illusory" (Block 1996: 32, ellipsis in original; see also Wright 1983: 57–58).

If the above descriptions of these cases are correct, they seem to pose a significant threat both to representationalism and to the transparency thesis. Each of these cases suggests that there can be phenomenal content that does not reduce to representational content—either because there is no representational content (as in the afterimage and the phosphene cases), or because there is a difference in phenomenal content that does not correspond to representational content (as in the case of blurry vision). The cases thus pose a problem for the representationalists. And each of these cases also suggests that we can attend directly to our experiences without attending to the objects of our experiences—either because there is no object of our experience (again, as in the afterimage and the phosphene cases), or because the experience comes apart from the object that it represents (as in the case of blurry vision). They thus pose a problem for the transparency thesis.

Much of the ink spilled in response to these cases has focused specifically on defusing the threat to representationalism. Tye, for example, claims that in cases of blurry vision there is indeed a representational difference that can account for the phenomenal difference. Less information is presented when one takes off one's glasses: "In seeing blurrily, one undergoes sensory representations that fail to specify just where the boundaries and contours lie" (Tye 2000: 80). In the phosphene and afterimage cases, Tye thinks that by distinguishing what the experience represents *conceptually* from what it represents *nonconceptually*, we can dissipate the threat to representationalism (ibid.: 81–82).

These responses, however, do not do anything to dissipate the threat to the transparency thesis.[10] As a general strategy, the representationalist responses suggest that the proponents of the exotic cases understate the representational richness of the experiences. There is more representational content there than we might have initially believed. But admitting this does nothing to change our original sense of the phenomenology of the experience. It still seems to us, when we are having a blurry experience, that we can focus on the blurriness itself, rather than on just what the blurriness is blurriness *of*. Our attention to an afterimage does not seem to be attention to some worldly content—we do not see "right through" the experience in this case. Even if we can be convinced that the blurry image, the phosphene experience, and the afterimage have representational content, that in itself does not convince us that they are transparent.

3 Between the Exotic and the Mundane

We see something similar by considering a set of cases that fall on the spectrum somewhere between the exotic cases considered in section 2 and the mundane cases for which the transparency thesis has the most force. Recall that the transparency thesis derives its primary support from mundane visual experiences of, say, seeing a tree. But having begun with visual experience, proponents of transparency typically move on to perceptual experience generally, and then even to nonperceptual experiences as well. Tye, for example, explicitly claims that transparency holds across sensory modalities: "[T]he qualities of which we are directly aware via introspection ... are not qualities of the experiences of hearing, smelling, and tasting. Rather, they are qualities of public surfaces, sounds, odors, tastes, and so forth" (Tye 2000: 50). He also claims that transparency applies to bodily sensations, such as pains or itches. For the moment, let's grant the move from mundane visual cases to mundane cases in other perceptual modalities. Insofar as transparency is plausible for the mundane visual cases, it will be plausible for the mundane auditory cases, and similarly for the other perceptual modalities. Nonetheless, as we will see in this section, the plausibility of the transparency thesis becomes considerably more strained once we leave the perceptual realm.

One example frequently invoked in this context is the orgasm. As Block has forcefully argued (in, e.g., Block 1996: 33–34), it is difficult to specify what the representational content of an orgasm could be. All attempts seem to fall far short of capturing this phenomenally "impressive" experience. Similarly, if we think about introspecting an orgasm experience, it is difficult to see what it would mean to say that our experience is transparent. In attending to our experience, our attention goes right through to ... to where? In the mundane visual case, when I introspect my experience of a tree, my attention is supposed to go right through to the tree. But what would be the analogue of the

tree in this case? The only possible suggestion would be some bodily location, but this doesn't seem faithful to the phenomenology of orgasms. And even if in attending to the orgasm we must attend to a particular bodily location, that doesn't seem to be all that we're doing.

A similar point can be made by thinking about pains. Does introspecting an experience of pain amount solely to attending to a particular bodily location? Here the transparency theorist must answer affirmatively. But this is a very hard position to defend. Moreover, it is not adequately defended simply by claiming, as Tye does, that whenever you become introspectively aware of a painful sensation, "your attention goes to *wherever you feel the pain*" (Tye 2000: 50). This claim is much weaker than the claim that your attention to the pain *consists* in your attention to the bodily location. Opponents of transparency can grant that when, for example, I have a pain in my toe, in order to focus on the pain I will have to focus at least in part on my toe. But there is a difference between saying that introspecting an experience of pain *involves* or even *requires* attending to a particular bodily location and saying that *all that there is* to introspecting an experience of pain is attending to a particular bodily location. Even if the former, weaker claim is plausible, it's the latter, stronger claim that the transparency thesis requires.

It's worth noting, however, that the weaker claim too can be called into question. In at least some cases, it seems that we can introspect pain without attending to a particular bodily location where the pain is felt. With some kinds of throbbing headaches, for example, I can introspectively attend to the throbbing pain without my attention going through to a particular part of my head—or so it seems to me. Some headaches are confined to one side or another, other headaches do not even seem to be especially localized. Given that I lack any sense of "where" the headache is, it seems odd to claim that my attention is directed in any but the most general sense at a bodily location.[11]

The same point applies to certain kinds of toothaches. I was once in need of a root canal in a tooth in the lower right side of my mouth, but I didn't know which particular tooth was the problem. I was in pain—in intense pain, in fact—and yet I could not myself pinpoint the precise location of the pain—even when I probed each tooth with my tongue or my finger. Eventually, the dentist pinpointed the problem spot for me by whacking the decaying tooth with a dental instrument. (I don't recommend having your dentist do this.) But his doing so changed my introspective experience. Only after he whacked the relevant tooth could I "find" the pain, and thus, only after he whacked the relevant tooth could I attend to the pain by attending to the tooth.[12]

The plausibility of the transparency thesis erodes further when considering emotions and moods. Emotional transparency is supposed to be relatively unproblematic, especially in comparison with the transparency of moods, since emotions at least tend to be associated with bodily occurrences. As Tye notes, "the qualities of which one is directly aware in introspecting felt emotions are frequently localized in particular parts of the body and experienced as such" (Tye 2000: 51). Anger might involve an increased pulse rate, fear might involve a tingling sensation along one's neck or a queasiness in one's stomach, and so on. This point enables Tye to treat emotional transparency analogously to the transparency of pain and other sensations. When we introspect pain, our attention is supposed to go to wherever we feel the pain. Likewise, when we introspect emotion, our attention is supposed to go wherever we feel the emotion: introspecting anger involves attention to one's increased pulse rate, introspecting fear involves attention to one's queasy stomach, and so on.

Is this all it involves? For the transparency theorist, the answer must be "yes." When we introspect an emotional experience, our attention must go right through to some bodily quality or other.[13] But this seems even less plausible for the case of emotions than it did for the case of pains. The typically tight connection between pains and bodily locations lends plausibility to the claim that we attend to bodily locations when we introspectively attend to pains. As I suggested above, however, the transparency theorist needs to defend a stronger claim—that attention to pain *wholly consists* in attending to bodily locations—to show that experience is transparent. Since there is a much looser connection between emotions and bodily locations, it is harder to establish even the weak claim that we always attend to bodily locations when we introspectively attend to emotions. Matters are even worse for the transparency theorist when it comes to moods, where there is virtually no connection to bodily location. But even if Tye is right that the weak claim is true for emotions or moods, that would not be enough to show that our experience of emotions or moods is transparent.

4 The Mundane

At this point, it will be useful to distinguish explicitly four claims about experience that have been playing a role in our discussion. These claims split into two pairs. We can set out the claims as follows, letting "E" stand for an experience:

1. E has representational content.
2. The qualitative character of E consists wholly in its representational content (i.e., representationalism is true).
3. Attending to E involves attending to its representational content.
4. Attending to E consists wholly in attending to its representational content (i.e., the transparency thesis is true).[14]

Just as we should not confuse (1) with (2), we should not confuse (3) with (4). Moreover, just as (1) does not imply (2), (3) does not imply (4). Claim (1) is a necessary but not sufficient* condition for (2), just as (3) is a necessary but not sufficient condition for (4). Finally, whatever the relationship between (2) and (4)—a question I am here setting aside—it is clear that the truth of (1) implies neither (3) nor a fortiori† (4). On the other hand, however, the falsity of (1) implies the falsity of both (3) and (4). If an experience lacks representational content, then our

---

* P is a necessary condition for Q if P must be true in order for Q to be true; P is a sufficient condition for Q if Q must be true in order for P to be true. So if P is a necessary but not sufficient condition for Q, P could be true while Q is false (but not vice versa).

† Latin: "from the stronger." An *a fortiori* inference is one that draws a weaker conclusion on the basis of a stronger conclusion that has already been reached.

introspective attention to it cannot consist even in part of attention to representational content. So (1) is a necessary but not sufficient condition for all three of the subsequent claims.

Now let's think about how the transparency theorist attempts to accommodate apparent counterexamples to his thesis such as the exotic cases of section 2 and the nonperceptual cases of section 3. The exotic experiences like blurry vision and afterimages that we considered in section 2 threaten (4) primarily because they do not typically seem to have any representational content; for these experiences, that is, (1) seems false. But to defuse the threat of these cases, it is not enough for the transparency theorist to defend (1), that is, to find some representational content that they might have. Since (1) is not a sufficient condition for (4), defending (1) is only the first step. Even if these experiences do have some representational content, we need to be convinced that in attending to these experiences what we are doing— and *all* that we are doing—is attending to that representational content. And here the transparency theorist does not seem to have much to say.

For at least some of the nonperceptual experiences considered in section 3, the transparency theorist is on the same shaky ground that he is on with respect to the exotic cases. When it comes to orgasms and moods, it is hard to identify any representational content of the experience, that is, (1) seems false. But even for the nonperceptual experiences that plausibly do have representational content—experiences like pains and emotions—the transparency theorist is not on solid ground. The considerations he advances to help us see that we are attending to the representational content when we are attending to those experiences do not go far enough. They do not show us that *all* we are attending to when we are attending to the experiences is the representational content of the experience. In other words, even if (3) is true of these experiences, we need to be convinced of something more. And here again the transparency theorist does not seem to have much to say.

With these lessons learned from consideration of the apparent counterexamples to the transparency thesis, we are ready now to turn back to the mundane cases with which the transparency theorist begins— the very cases that are supposed to motivate the transparency thesis. What I want to suggest is that our discussion of the apparent counterexamples to the transparency thesis opens up some new logical space

for the opponents of the thesis to make a case against it. Once we see why transparency fails in the exotic cases, we can raise parallel questions about the mundane cases. Upon reflection, even the supposedly paradigmatic examples of transparency no longer seem as obviously transparent as they initially may have.

Look at a tree, we are instructed, and we are asked to try to turn our attention to intrinsic features of our visual experience. Proponents of transparency predict that we will fail. The only features there for us to turn our attention to are features of the presented tree (Harman 1990: 39). Our attention will always slip through to the greenness, and so on, as instantiated in the tree (see Tye 1995: 30). Keeping in mind our discussion above of the various counterexamples to transparency, however, I think this prediction is now called into question.

First, recall our discussion of the introspection of pain. Pain experience was alleged to be transparent because we cannot introspect it without attention to the bodily location where the pain is felt. However, as I discussed above, this fact alone does not establish the transparency of pain experience. The fact we attend to bodily location in introspectively attending to pain, even essentially so, does not mean that this is all we do. Likewise, the fact that we attend to worldly objects in introspectively attending to our perceptual experiences of worldly objects, even essentially so, does not mean that this is all we do. Compare a visual experience of a tree with a pain in your toe. The fact that you cannot help but attend to the tree when introspecting your visual experience of it no more establishes the transparency of visual experience than the fact that you cannot help but attend to your toe when introspecting the pain in your toe.

This conceptual point helps to create logical space for the failure of transparency, even with respect to perceptual experience. But of course, mere logical space is not enough. When we introspect our visual experiences, if we do not, or cannot, find anything else to attend to, then it looks like the transparency thesis will be correct for these experiences.

Here is where the moral gleaned from the exotic cases comes into play. Those cases showed us that transparency fails for at least some visual experiences. Insofar as those cases showed us how our introspective attention comes apart from the representational content of the experience, we can apply the lessons to the mundane cases. Consider again your visual experience of a tree. How can you attend to that experience without attending to the tree itself? To try to focus your attention away from the tree itself, think about afterimages, and about what you attend to when you are introspectively attending to your experience of afterimages. Now, once again, try to focus on that same aspect of your experience in your experience of the tree. You might try the following. Look at a tree, focus on your experience, and then close your eyes and image the tree. Focus in on the greenness on your imaged experience. Now reopen your eyes, so that you're looking at the tree. I predict that you *will* find features there, other than features of the presented tree, on which to train your attention. In particular, you can continue to attend to the greenness that you were attending to while your eyes were closed.

If I am right about this, the problems for the transparency thesis extend beyond the exotic cases. Even mundane visual experience—the very kind of experience that was supposed to be a paradigm case of transparency—is not transparent. Interestingly, we are helped to understand what's going on in the introspection of mundane cases by better understanding what's going on in the introspection of the exotic cases. Our reflection on why the counterexamples are problematic for the transparency thesis—on what we attend to when we are attending to our exotic experiences—enables us also to see what we are attending to in mundane experience.

5 Conclusion

When we introspect our ordinary perceptual experiences, the world gets in the way. The presence of external objects—the representational content of our experience—threatens to crowd out the qualia. But that doesn't mean the qualia are not there. As I have suggested in this essay, we are reminded that the qualia are there in ordinary experience by thinking carefully about experiences that are more out of the ordinary. In these other cases, there is no external object crowding out the qualia, and we can thus more easily focus our attention directly on them. And having reminded ourselves what we do in these more exotic cases, we can gain a better understanding of what we do in the more mundane cases.

In particular, I contend that when we attend introspectively to our experience—whether exotic or mundane—we are attending at least in part to qualia. Our experience is not, in fact, transparent. And thus, based on the support of the phenomenological data, it seems that we have every reason—or at least, all the reason we initially thought we had—to believe in the existence of qualia. ▪

Suggestions for Critical Reflection

1. Explain Kind's overarching argument against the "transparency thesis." On which points does Kind disagree with advocates of the transparency thesis?

2. Try to think of your own "exotic" instance of perception (akin to blurred vision, afterimages, and phosphene experiences, etc.). What makes this example different from more mundane cases? Does your example provide further evidence against the transparency thesis? Why or why not?

3. According to Kind, the transparency theorist is committed to the view that the experience of pain amounts "solely to attending to a particular bodily location"? Do you think this is a fair representation of the transparency theorist's account of pain? Can you think of a more refined account of pain that is compatible with the transparency thesis?

4. Suppose that representationalists about consciousness are correct and that when we perceive things we see "right through" the experience to the object itself, so that the properties we encounter, such as yellowness, pain, blurriness, or sweetness, are properties of the object not of our experience. The expectation is that the natural sciences will have no difficulty explaining these properties, since they are no longer mysterious mental qualia but just colors on the surfaces of objects and so on. But is this right—do the properties we encounter in experience, such as colors or tastes, really become less mysterious on this account? What about the properties we encounter when we

hallucinate or make mistakes (e.g., if we think we see a ghost)—that is, what if there is no object in our environment to actually have these properties (or to put it the way a representationalist might, what if the object of our experience is "merely intentional")?

5. On the other hand, if colors, smells, and so on are not properties 'in the world' but are properties of our mental experiences, then isn't this *even more* peculiar and problematic? For example, what sort of property is *only* 'visible' introspectively and (apparently) completely invisible when we look at brains 'from the outside'? Given what we know about the rest of science, can we really take the idea of qualia seriously?

6. A painting of a unicorn is called 'representational,' even though there's nothing it represents. What does that mean? Something like: we see it "as if" it could be a picture of something (even though we know it isn't). Does this analogy help the representationalist deal with after-images and other "exotic" perceptions?

7. Consider the following passage and try Kind's suggested experiment (whether with a tree or any other convenient object). Is this an accurate account of your experience?

> You might try the following. Look at a tree, focus on your experience, and then close your eyes and image the tree. Focus in on the greenness on your imaged experience. Now reopen your eyes, so that you're looking at the tree. I predict that you will find features there, other than features of the presented tree, on which to train your attention. In particular, you can continue to attend to the greenness that you were attending to while your eyes were closed.

Notes

1 The very next sentence (which, oddly, is often ignored) reads: "Yet it can be distinguished if we look attentively enough, and if we know that there is something to look for." See Kind 2003 for further discussion.

2 The quotation continues, "And this remains so, even if there really is no blue square in front of one—if, for example, one is subject to an illusion." As we will see in section 2, however, intuitions about transparency are much weaker with respect to illusions.

3 See Kind 2003, 2007, for further discussion of weak versus strong transparency.

4 See Kind 2001.

5 There might, however, be other (nonphenomenological) reasons to believe in qualia. See, e.g., Shoemaker 1994.

6 In particular, Tye thinks that the intentional content must be poised, abstract, and nonconceptual. This is what he calls his PANIC theory. See Tye 1995, 2000.

7 However, in Kind 2007, I deny that this sort of concessionary strategy saves representationalism.

8 See Block 1996; Boghossian and Velleman 1989; Wright 1975: 278.

9 It seems to me that this phenomenon was more dramatic in the "olden days" of actual flashbulbs. The flashes produced by today's digital cameras don't have quite the same effect.

10 For the purposes of this essay, I have set aside the question of the relationship between representationalism and the transparency thesis, but it's worth noting the following. If representationalism entails the transparency thesis, then showing that representationalism can accommodate the exotic cases would at least indirectly show that these cases do not pose a threat to the transparency thesis. But this alone would not help us to see where we went wrong in believing that we could attend directly to our experiences in the exotic cases.

11 Further support for this point might be derived from Ramachandran and Blakeslee's work on pain remapping (Ramachandran and Blakeslee 1999). In some amputees, touching one part of the body (such as the face) produces pain in the phantom limb.

12 For a different kind of example supporting this point, see Wright 1990: 3–14.

13 Strictly speaking, our attention need only go right through to some representational content or other, so if there were a plausible candidate for the representational content of emotions other than bodily states, the transparency theorist would not need to claim that attending to emotions involves attending to some bodily quality or other. Given the absence of a plausible alternative, however, the transparency theorist tends

to interpret emotional experience along similar lines to pain experience, i.e., as representing states of the body.

14 Although (3) is weaker than (4), it does not correspond directly to what I have elsewhere called weak transparency (Kind 2003). Whereas strong transparency claims that it is impossible to attend directly to our experience, weak transparency claims only that it is difficult (but not impossible) to do so. Nonetheless, if strong transparency turns out to be false, the truth of (3) might help to explain why weak transparency is true.

References

Block, N. 1996. Mental paint and mental latex. In *Philosophical Issues*, vol. 7: *Perception*, ed. E. Villanueva, 18–49. Atascadero, Calif.: Ridgeview.

Boghossian, P., and D. Velleman. 1989. Color as a secondary quality. *Mind* 98: 81–103.

Harman, G. 1990. The intrinsic quality of experience. In *Philosophical Perspectives*, vol. 4: *Action Theory and the Philosophy of Mind*, ed. J. Tomberlin, 31–52. Atascadero, Calif.: Ridgeview.

Kind, A. 2001. Qualia realism. *Philosophical Studies* 104: 143–162.

Kind, A. 2003. What's so transparent about transparency? *Philosophical Studies* 115: 225–244.

Kind, A. 2007. Restrictions on representationalism. *Philosophical Studies* 134, 3: 405–427.

Moore, G.E. 1903. The refutation of idealism. *Mind*, new series, 12: 433–453.

Ramachandran, V.S., and S. Blakeslee. 1999. *Phantoms in the Brain: Human Nature and the Architecture of the Mind*. London: Fourth Estate.

Shoemaker, S. 1994. Self-knowledge and "inner sense." *Philosophy and Phenomenological Research* 54: 249–314.

Tye, M. 1995. *Ten Problems of Consciousness*. Cambridge, Mass.: MIT Press/A Bradford Book.

Tye, M. 2000. *Consciousness, Color, and Content*. Cambridge, Mass.: MIT Press/A Bradford Book.

Wright, E.L. 1975. Perception: A new theory. *American Philosophical Quarterly* 14: 273–286.

Wright, E.L. 1981. Yet more on non-epistemic seeing. *Mind* 90: 586–591.

Wright, E.L. 1983. Introspecting images. *Philosophy* 58: 57–72.

Wright, E.L. 1990. Two more proofs of present qualia. *Theoria* 56: 3–22.

Free Will

The metaphysical topic which is addressed in this chapter is the problem of free will. This problem is generated by the following argument:

i. All human behavior is determined: that is, the state of the world at a particular time (e.g., the moment of your birth) entirely fixes what the state of the world will be at every moment into the future (e.g., now), and that includes fixing what actions you will ever perform.

ii. If determinism is true, then human beings are (in at least one important sense) not free to choose their actions—we could not have done otherwise than we did, and so we do not possess genuine free will.

iii. Therefore human beings do not have free will (and, furthermore, may lack moral responsibility for their actions, lead lives that have no meaning, and so on).

This is a straightforwardly valid argument. The problem, of course, is that both premises (i) and (ii) are highly plausible (or at least, can be made to seem so with a certain amount of argumentation), and yet the conclusion is, we hope and believe, *false*: we feel like free agents, able to choose to do one thing rather than another; we

believe that people often have moral (and other kinds of) responsibility for their action; we think that people can guide their own destinies in a meaningful way. The philosophical problem, therefore, is to say what, if anything, is wrong with the argument, and since the argument is valid the only way to criticize it is to call into question the truth of the premises. This means there are exactly three broad philosophical positions on the problem of free will:

The first position, usually called *hard determinism* or just *determinism*, is the view that the argument is sound: that is, both of the premises are true and hence freedom (and moral responsibility and so on) is a mere illusion. This stance is represented here by the reading from Paul Rée.

The second position, usually called *libertarianism* (or *metaphysical libertarianism*), accepts premise (ii) but argues that premise (i) is false—that is, libertarians agree that determinism is incompatible with freedom, but argue that we have free will because *indeterminism* is true. This stance is not fully represented in the readings in this chapter, but a key component of the argument—the defense of premise (ii)—is explored by Ishtiyaque Haji in the second reading. It is important to note that libertarianism is not the (very implausible) position that *none* of our actions are determined—it is the more limited view that *some*, probably the most important, of our actions are free in the sense that they are not fixed by what came before. So even if most of what we do is habitual, for example, as long as we have the capacity to wrestle with the big moral questions and make a (by their lights) genuinely free, genuinely novel, choice, then libertarianism would be true.

The third, and most popular (at least among philosophers), approach to free will is known as *soft determinism* or *compatibilism*. Compatibilists typically accept premise (i), determinism, but deny premise (ii): that is, they deny that the truth of determinism implies that we lack at least one important variety of freedom. Instead, they argue in a variety of ways that determinism is compatible with all the types of freedom worth wanting: that we can be *both* free and determined. Included in this chapter is an extremely influential argument by Harry Frankfurt against the principle of alternate possibilities (PAP), a principle which if true would hold that an agent is morally responsible for an action only if that person could have done otherwise.

Two quick notes about the terminology in this area, which can be confusing: First, "libertarianism" is the label both for a position in political philosophy that prioritizes political freedom, and for a position on the metaphysical question of free will. Although both stress human freedom, they are not deeply related: the first emphasizes political freedom—e.g., the freedom to vote or to practice your religion—while the latter affirms that the actions of human beings are sometimes undetermined and therefore free. We could be politically free even though we are, say, entirely physically or socially determined. It is, of course, the metaphysical and not the political usage of the term that we have in mind in this chapter.

Second, there are labels for *theoretical positions* about free will—"hard determinism," "libertarianism," and "compatibilism"—and labels for *premises* for the arguments for these positions—"determinism" or "indeterminism," "incompatibilism" or "compatibilism," and "moral responsibility." The labels are sometimes similar, and it is important to keep them straight as you think and write about free will. For example, "determinism" (used in this way) is the view that every action is completely fixed by what has happened in the past, and

so we could never have done otherwise than we did. But this in itself is *not* a theory of free will—if it's true then it's the input to a theory, or a constraint on theories ... but both the hard determinist and the compatibilist endorse determinism.

There are many decent collections of articles on the problem of free will, including Robert Kane, ed., *Free Will* (Blackwell, 2009) and *The Oxford Handbook of Free Will* (Oxford University Press, 2011); Derk Pereboom, ed., *Free Will* (Hackett, 2009); Timothy O'Connor, ed., *Agents, Causes, and Events* (Oxford University Press, 1995); and Gary Watson, ed., *Free Will* (Oxford University Press, 2003). Useful and accessible single-author discussions of the problem of free will include Daniel Dennett, *Elbow Room* (MIT Press, 1985); Sam Harris, *Free Will* (Free Press, 2012); Ted Honderich, *How Free Are You?* (Oxford University Press, 1993); Robert Kane, *A Contemporary Introduction to Free Will* (Oxford University Press, 2005); Graham McFee, *Free Will* (McGill-Queen's University Press, 2000); Fischer, Kane, Pereboom, and Vargas, *Four Views on Free Will* (Wiley-Blackwell, 2007); Michael McKenna and Derk Pereboom, *Free Will: A Contemporary Introduction* (Routledge, 2016); Timothy O'Connor, *Persons and Causes* (Oxford University Press, 2000); Matthew Talbert, *Moral Responsibility: An Introduction* (Polity, 2016); and Jennifer Trusted, *Free Will and Responsibility* (Oxford University Press, 1984).

Finally, here are a few influential books on free will: Richard Double, *The Non-Reality of Free Will* (Oxford University Press, 1991); John Martin Fischer, *The Metaphysics of Free Will* (Blackwell, 1996); Ted Honderich, *A Theory of Determinism* (2 vols., Oxford University Press, 1988); Alfred Mele, *Free: Why Science Hasn't Disproved Free Will* (Oxford University Press, 2014); Murphy and Brown, eds., *Did My Neurons Make Me Do It?: Philosophical and Neurobiological Perspectives on Moral Responsibility and Free Will* (Oxford University Press, 2009); Derk Pereboom, *Living without Free Will* (Cambridge University Press, 2001); Galen Strawson, *Freedom and Belief* (Oxford University Press, 1986); Peter van Inwagen, *An Essay on Free Will* (Oxford University Press, 1983); and Daniel Wegner, *The Illusion of Conscious Will* (MIT Press, 2005).

PAUL RÉE

FROM *The Illusion of Free Will*

Who Was Paul Rée?

Paul Rée, a German philosopher and psychologist, is most remembered for his association with the German philosopher Friedrich Nietzsche and for his uncompromising moral relativism and atheism. Born in 1849, Rée was the son of a wealthy Prussian landowner. In his early twenties he fought in the Franco-Prussian war of 1870–71, in which Prussian troops advanced into France and decisively defeated the French army at Sedan (a town near the Belgian border). The outcome was the fall of the French Second Empire and the establishment of a new, united German Empire—the first Reich—under its first chancellor, Prince Otto Leopold von Bismarck. On his return from the war, wounded, Rée went to Switzerland to recuperate and, abandoning the law studies he had begun before the war, devoted himself to the study of philosophy and psychology. In 1875 he received a doctorate in philosophy from the University of Halle (a city in central Germany), and also published a book of psychological aphorisms, *Psychologische Beobachtungen*.

In 1873 Rée had met Nietzsche in Basel, and after the publication of Rée's *Psychological Observations*, Nietzsche wrote him a letter complimenting the work. As a result, the two struck up a close friendship—which Nietzsche's biographer, Walter Kaufmann, has called "among the best things which ever happened to Nietzsche"*—that lasted about seven years. However, Rée was ethnically Jewish (though not a religious practitioner), and several of Nietzsche's anti-Semitic friends and his unpleasant sister resented Rée's influence on Nietzsche.† In 1882, after Nietzsche bitterly broke off his relationship with the tempestuous and bewitching Lou Salomé, to whom Rée had originally introduced him, Rée's friendship with the famous philosopher came to an end, and they never spoke again. Later, Rée was to

dismiss Nietzsche's ethical writings as "a mixture of insanity and nonsense."

In 1877 Rée published *Ursprung der moralischen Empfindungen* (*The Origin of the Moral Sentiments*). In this book, strongly influenced by Charles Darwin and David Hume, Rée argued that there are no universally true moral principles, and that what is regarded as morally right or wrong, in any given society, is a function of its needs and cultural conditions. *The Illusion of Free Will*, in which Rée advocates abandoning notions of moral responsibility in practical as well as philosophical life, was published in 1885, when Rée was 36. In the same year, he published *Die Entstehung des Gewissens* (*The Origin of Conscience*) and in the process of writing this book he became concerned about his own lack of knowledge of the natural sciences. The next year Rée enrolled at the University of Munich to study medicine. After obtaining his MD, Rée returned to his family estate in Stibbe, West Prussia. There he practiced medicine, charging no fees, and when his own medical knowledge fell short in particular cases, paid all the hospital expenses for the peasants and laborers who were his patients.

For the last 10 years of his life, Rée led an isolated, ascetic existence living at Stibbe with his brother, and spent much of his time working on a major book that would encapsulate all his philosophical reflections. Rée told a friend that when it was finished he would give up philosophy, but that since he could not live without doing philosophy, there would be nothing left for him but to die. This is more or less what happened: in 1900, when his book was almost completed, Rée, a passionate mountain climber, returned to live in Switzerland and the following year fell to his death from the icy ridge of a Swiss mountain. His book, *Philosophie*, was published posthumously in 1903 and, to this day, has been almost completely ignored. In this work, Rée roundly

---

*   Walter Kaufmann, *Nietzsche: Philosopher, Psychologist, Antichrist* (Princeton University Press, 1978), 48.
†   There's some controversy about whether Nietzsche himself was anti-Semitic.

condemned metaphysics as a system of "fairy tales" and "lies," and argued that religions "are true neither in the literal nor in an allegorical sense—they are untrue in every sense. Religion issues from a marriage of error and fear."

What Is the Structure of This Reading?

This selection contains most of Chapters 1 and 2 of Paul Rée's 1885 book *Die Illusion der Willensfreiheit* (*The Illusion of Free Will*). The final (third) chapter of the book, which is not reprinted here, contains a detailed critique of Immanuel Kant's views on free will. Rée begins by defining freedom of the will as the ability to act as "an absolute beginning"—i.e., a thought or action is free, according to Rée, only in the case where it is not the necessary result of prior causes. Rée then goes on to argue that *no* event is uncaused, and thus that there can be no such thing as free will. To show this, he first examines the example of an act of decision in a donkey and then extends similar considerations to human beings. He insists that even actions performed solely from a sense of duty are not genuinely free, and he argues that one must be careful to distinguish between correct and incorrect senses of the claim "I can do what I want." Finally, he diagnoses our mistaken belief in free will as being the result of ignorance of the causes of our own actions. Because we do not see how our actions are caused, we fallaciously assume that they are not caused.

In section 5, which marks the start of Chapter 2 of his book, Rée explores the implications for morality of the truth of determinism. He argues that if all our actions are necessary effects of prior causes, then we cannot be held morally responsible for them: we cannot legitimately be praised or blamed for our actions. True philosophers, Rée hints, will try to rid themselves of the bad habit of assigning moral responsibility. On the other hand, we certainly do *prefer* some actions (and some types of people) over others, and this is legitimate; but our preferences themselves are to be explained as causal effects of our genetic inheritance and social upbringing.

Some Useful Background Information

There is a useful and commonly made philosophical distinction which is helpful for understanding Rée's position on free will: the contrast between necessary and sufficient conditions. *A* is a *necessary* condition for *B* if *B* could not have occurred (or been true) without *A*— that is, if there would be no *B* unless *A*. For example, being connected to a power supply is a necessary condition for a bulb to light up (the bulb could not light unless connected to a source of electricity). On the other hand, *A* is a *sufficient* condition for *B* if the occurrence (or truth) of *A* is *sufficient* for the occurrence (or truth) of *B*—that is, if *B* happens every time *A* does. Being connected in the right way to a properly functioning circuit with an adequate source of power, under normal physical circumstances, with the power switch in the "on" position is, altogether, a sufficient circumstance for a bulb to light.

It follows from this that if *A* is a sufficient condition for *B*, then if *A* occurs *B* must *necessarily* occur as well.* (On the other hand, if *A* is merely a necessary condition for *B*, the occurrence of *A* only tells us that *B* may happen, but not that it actually will.)

---

* This claim is a bit more complicated than it seems, however, because of the various flavors which necessity can come in: for example, the fact that *B* always follows *A* in the actual world perhaps means that *B* is a '*physically* necessary' consequence of *A*, but it need not follow that *B* follows from *A* by *logical* necessity.

FROM *The Illusion of Free Will**

CHAPTERS I AND 2

1. Nothing Happens without a Cause

... To say that the will is not free means that it is subject to the law of causality. Every act of will is in fact preceded by a sufficient cause. Without such a cause the act of will cannot occur; and, if the sufficient cause is present, the act of will must occur.

To say that the will is free would mean that it is not subject to the law of causality. In that case every act of will would be an absolute beginning [a first cause] and not a link [in a chain of events]: it would not be the effect of preceding causes.

The reflections that follow may serve to clarify what is meant by saying that the will is not free.... Every object—a stone, an animal, a human being—can pass from its present state to another one. The stone that now lies in front of me may, in the next moment, fly through the air, or it may disintegrate into dust or roll along the ground. If, however, one of these *possible* states is to be *realized*, its sufficient cause must first be present. The stone will fly through the air if it is tossed. It will roll if a force acts upon it. It will disintegrate into dust, given that some object hits and crushes it.

It is helpful to use the terms "potential" and "actual" in this connection. At any moment there are innumerably many potential states. At a given time, however, only *one* can become actual, namely, the one that is triggered by its sufficient cause.

The situation is no different in the case of an animal. The donkey that now stands motionless between two piles of hay[†] may, in the next moment, turn to the left or to the right, or he may jump into the air or put his head between his legs. But here, too, the sufficient cause must first be present if of the *possible* modes of behavior one is to be *realized*.

Let us analyze one of these modes of behavior. We shall assume that the donkey has turned toward the bundle on his right. This turning presupposes that certain muscles were contracted. The cause of this muscular contraction is the excitation of the nerves that lead to them. The cause of this excitation of the nerves is a state of the brain. It was in a state of decision. But how did the brain come to be in that condition? Let us trace the states of the donkey back a little farther.

A few moments before he turned, his brain was not yet so constituted as to yield the sufficient cause for the excitation of the nerves in question and for the contraction of the muscles; for otherwise the movement would have occurred. The donkey had not yet "decided" to turn. If he then moved at some subsequent time, his brain must in the meantime have become so constituted as to bring about the excitation of the nerves and the movement of the muscles. Hence the brain underwent some change. To what causes is this change to be attributed? To the effectiveness of an impression that acts as an external stimulus, or to a sensation that arose internally; for example, the sensation of hunger and the idea of the bundle on the right, by jointly affecting the brain, change the way in which it is constituted so that it now yields the sufficient cause for the excitation of the nerves and the contraction of the muscles. The donkey now "wants" to turn to the right; he now turns to the right.

Hence, just as the position and constitution of the stone, on the one hand and the strength and direction of the force that acts upon it, on the other, necessarily determine the kind and length of its flight, so the

---

* Paul Rée's *Die Illusion der Willensfreiheit* was first published in Berlin in 1885. This selection was translated by Stefan Bauer-Mengelberg and edited by Paul Edwards and Arthur Pap (who also supplied the section headings) in 1973.

† This philosophical example is known as "Buridan's Ass," named for the fourteenth-century French philosopher Jean Buridan. The example is not found in Buridan's writing, but was used by critics to parody his account of free will in similar situations. Aristotle gives this example in *On the Heavens* 295b. In the usual use of the donkey example, it is halfway between two equally attractive bundles, so is unable to move and starves.

movement of the donkey—his turning to the bundle on the right—is no less necessarily the result of the way in which the donkey's brain and the stimulus are constituted at a given moment. That the donkey turned toward this particular bundle was determined by something trivial. If the bundle that the donkey did not choose had been positioned just a bit differently, or if it had smelled different, or if the subjective factor—the donkey's sense of smell or his visual organs—had developed in a somewhat different way, then, so we may assume, the donkey would have turned to the left. But the cause was not complete there, and that is why the effect could not occur, while with respect to the other side, where the cause was complete, the effect could not fail to appear.

For the donkey, consequently, just as for the stone, there are innumerably many *potential* states at any moment; he may walk or run or jump, or move to the left, to the right, or straight ahead. But only the one whose sufficient cause is present can ever become *actual*.

At the same time, there is a difference between the donkey and the stone in that the donkey moves because he wants to move, while the stone moves because it is moved. We do not deny this difference. There are, after all, a good many other differences between the donkey and the stone. We do not by any means intend to prove that this dissimilarity does not exist. We do not assert that the donkey is a stone, but only that the donkey's every movement and act of will has causes just as the motion of the stone does. The donkey moves because he wants to move. But that he wants to move at a given moment, and in this particular direction, is causally determined.

Could it be that there was no sufficient cause for the donkey's wanting to turn around—that he simply wanted to turn around? His act of will would then be an absolute beginning. An assumption of that kind is contradicted by experience and the universal validity of the law of causality. By experience, since observation teaches us that for every act of will some causes were the determining factors. By the universal validity of the law of causality, since, after all, nothing happens anywhere in the world without a sufficient cause. Why, then, of all things should a donkey's act of will come into being without a cause? Besides, the state of willing, the one that immediately precedes the excitation of the motor nerves, is no different in principle from other states—that of indifference, of lassitude, or of

weariness. Would anyone believe that all of these states exist without a cause? And if one does not believe that, why should just the state of willing be thought to occur without a sufficient cause?

It is easy to explain why it seems to us that the motion of the stone is necessary while the donkey's act of will is not. The causes that move the stone are, after all, external and visible. But the causes of the donkey's act of will are internal and invisible; between us and the locus of their effectiveness lies the skull of the donkey. Let us consider this difference somewhat more closely. The stone lies before us as it is constituted. We can also see the force acting upon it, and from these two factors, the constitution of the stone and the force, there results, likewise visible, the rolling of the stone. The case of the donkey is different. The state of his brain is hidden from our view. And, while the bundle of hay is visible, its effectiveness is not. It is an internal process. The bundle does not come into visible contact with the brain but acts at a distance. Hence the subjective and the objective factor—the brain and the impact that the bundle has upon it—are invisible.

Let us suppose that we could depict the donkey's soul in high relief, taking account of and making visible all those states, attitudes, and feelings that characterize it before the donkey turns. Suppose further that we could see how an image detaches itself from the bundle of hay and, describing a visible path through the air, intrudes upon the donkey's brain and how it produces a change there in consequence of which certain nerves and muscles move. Suppose, finally, that we could repeat this experiment arbitrarily often, that, if we returned the donkey's soul into the state preceding his turning and let exactly the same impression act upon it, we should always observe the very same result. Then we would regard the donkey's turning to the right as necessary. We would come to realize that the brain, constituted as it was at that moment, had to react to such an impression in precisely that way.

In the absence of this experiment it seems as though the donkey's act of will were not causally determined. We just do not see its being causally determined and consequently believe that no such determination takes place. The act of will, it is said, is the cause of the turning, but it is not itself determined; it is said to be an absolute beginning.

The opinion that the donkey's act of will is not causally determined is held not only by the outsider;

the donkey himself, had he the gift of reflection, would share it. The causes of his act of will would elude him, too, since in part they do not become conscious at all and in part pass through consciousness fleetingly, with the speed of lightning. If, for example, what tipped the scales was that he was closer by a hair's breadth to the bundle on the right, or that it smelled a shade better, how should the donkey notice something so trivial, something that so totally fails to force itself upon his consciousness?

In *one* sense, of course, the donkey is right in thinking "I could have turned to the left." His state at the moment, his position relative to the bundle, or its constitution need merely have been somewhat different, and he really would have turned to the left. The statement "I could have acted otherwise" is, accordingly, true in this sense: turning to the left is one of the movements possible for me (in contrast, for example, to the movement of flying); it lies within the realm of my possibilities.

We arrive at the same result if we take the law of inertia as our point of departure. It reads: every object strives to remain in its present state. Expressed negatively this becomes: without a sufficient cause no object can pass from its present state to another one. The stone will lie forever just as it is lying now; it will not undergo the slightest change if no causes—such as the weather or a force—act upon it to bring about a change. The donkey's brain will remain in the same state unchanged for all eternity if no causes—the feeling of hunger or fatigue, say, or external impressions—bring about a change.

If we reflect upon the entire life of the donkey *sub specie necessitatis*,* we arrive at the following result. The donkey came into the world with certain properties of mind and body, his genetic inheritance. Since the day of his birth, impressions—of the companions with whom he frolicked or worked, his feed, the climate— have acted upon these properties. These two factors, his inborn constitution and the way in which it was formed through the impressions of later life, are the cause of

all of his sensations, ideas, and moods, and of all of his movements, even the most trivial ones. If, for example, he cocks his left ear and not the right one, that is determined by causes whose historical development could be traced back ad infinitum;† and likewise when he stands, vacillating,‡ between the two bundles. And when action, the act of feeding, takes the place of vacillation, that, too, is determined: the idea of the one bundle now acts upon the donkey's mind, when it has become receptive to the idea of that particular sheaf, in such a way as to produce actions.

2. Human Beings and the Law of Causality

Let us now leave the realm of animals and proceed to consider man. Everything is the same here. Man's every feeling is a necessary result. Suppose, for example, that I am stirred by a feeling of pity at this moment. To what causes is it to be attributed? Let us go back as far as possible. An infinite amount of time has elapsed up to this moment. Time was never empty; objects have filled it from all eternity. These objects ... have continually undergone change. All of these changes were governed by the law of causality; not one of them took place without a sufficient cause.

We need not consider what else may have characterized these changes. Only their *formal* aspect, only this *one* point is of concern to us: no change occurred without a cause.

At some time in the course of this development, by virtue of some causes, organic matter was formed, and finally man. Perhaps the organic world developed as Darwin described it. Be that as it may, it was in any case due to causes that I was born on a particular day, with particular properties of body, of spirit, and of heart. Impressions then acted upon this constitution; I had particular governesses, teachers, and playmates. Teaching and example in part had an effect and in part were lost upon me; the former, when my inborn constitution made me receptive to them, when I had an affinity for them. And that is how it has come to be, through

---

* Latin: "under the aspect of necessity"—that is, seen from the standpoint of necessity. (This expression is modeled on philosopher Baruch Spinoza's coinage *sub specie aeternitatis*, "under the aspect of eternity," which Spinoza uses in his *Ethics* [1677] to characterize the highest form of knowledge as that in which the world is seen from the standpoint of timelessness or eternity.)

† Latin: "without limit, forever."

‡ Swaying indecisively between one course of action and another.

the operation of [a chain of] causes, that I am stirred by a feeling of pity at this moment. The course of the world would have had to be somewhat different if my feelings were to be different now.

It is of no consequence for the present investigation whether the inborn capacity for pity, for taking pleasure in another's pain, or for courage remains constant throughout life or whether teaching, example, and activity serve to change it. In any case the pity or pleasure in another's pain, the courage or cowardice, that a certain person feels or exhibits at a given moment is a necessary result, whether these traits are inborn—an inheritance from his ancestors—or were developed in the course of his own life.

Likewise every intention, indeed, every thought that ever passes through the brain, the silliest as well as the most brilliant, the true as well as the false, exists of necessity. In that sense there is no freedom of thought. It is necessary that I sit in this place at this moment, that I hold my pen in my hand in a particular way, and that I write that every thought is necessary; and if the reader should perchance be of the opinion that this is not the case, i.e., if he should believe that thoughts may not be viewed as effects, then he holds this false opinion of necessity also.

Just as sensations and thoughts are necessary, so, too, is action. It is, after all, nothing other than their externalization, their objective embodiment. Action is born of sensations and thoughts. So long as the sensations are not sufficiently strong, action cannot occur, and when the sensations and thoughts are constituted so as to yield the sufficient cause for it, then it must occur; then the appropriate nerves and muscles are set to work. Let us illustrate this by means of an action that is judged differently at different levels of civilization, namely, murder.* Munzinger,† for example, says that among the Bogos‡ the murderer, the terror of the neighborhood, who never tires of blood and murder, is a man of respect. Whoever has been raised with such views will not be deterred from murder either by external or by internal obstacles. Neither the police nor his conscience forbids him to commit it. On the contrary, it is his habit to praise murder; his parents and his gods stimulate him to commit it, and his companions encourage him by their example. And so it comes to be that, if there is a favorable opportunity, he does the deed. But is this not terribly trivial? After all, everyone knows that an act of murder is due to *motives*! True, but almost no one (except perhaps a philosopher) knows that an act of murder, and indeed every action, has a *cause*. Motives are a part of the cause. But to admit that there are motives for an action is not yet to recognize that it is causally determined, or to see clearly that the action is determined by thoughts and sensations—which in turn are effects—just as the rolling of a ball is determined by a force. But it is this point, and only this one, to which we must pay heed.

Let us now consider the act of murder from the same point of view in the case of civilized peoples. Someone raised at a higher level of civilization has learned from childhood on to disapprove of murder and to regard it as deserving punishment. God, his parents, and his teachers—in short, all who constitute an authority for him—condemn acts of this kind. It is, moreover, inconsistent with his character, which has been formed in an era of peace. Lastly, too, fear of punishment will deter him. Can murder prosper on such soil? Not easily. Fear, pity, the habit of condemning murder—all these are just so many bulwarks that block the path to such an action. Nevertheless need, passion, or various seductive influences will perhaps remove one after another of these bulwarks. Let us consider the cause of an act of murder more closely. First it is necessary to distinguish between two components, the subjective and the objective, in the total cause. The *subjective* part of the cause consists of the state of the murderer at the moment of the deed. To this we must assign all ideas that he had at the time, the conscious as well as the unconscious ones, his sensations, the temperature of his blood, the state of his stomach, of his liver—of each and every one of his bodily organs. The *objective* component consists of the appearance of the victim, the locality in which the deed took place,

---

* The German word Rée used here was *Raubmord*, a compound noun denoting a combination of murder and robbery (with overtones of pillage and rape).

† Werner Munzinger (1832–75) was a Swiss linguist and explorer. He spent many years traveling in Eritrea, Abyssinia, and the Sudan, three countries in northeast Africa south of Egypt (Abyssinia is now called Ethiopia).

‡ The Bogos were a tribe living in the highlands of northern Abyssinia and southern Eritrea. Munzinger described the customs of the Bogos in his 1859 book *Über die Sitten und das Recht der Bogos*.

and the way it was illuminated. The act of murder was necessarily consummated at that moment because these impressions acted upon a human being constituted in that particular way at the time. "Necessarily" means just that the act of murder is an effect; the state of the murderer and the impressions acting upon it are its cause. If the cause had not been complete, the effect could not have occurred. If, for example, the murderer had felt even a trifle more pity at that moment, if his idea of God or of the consequences that his deed would have here on earth had been somewhat more distinct, or if the moon had been a little brighter, so that more light would have fallen upon the victim's face and his pleading eyes—then, perhaps, the cause of the act of murder would not have become complete, and in consequence the act would not have taken place.

Thus for man, as for animal and stone, there are at any moment innumerably many *potential* states. The murderer might, at the moment when he committed the murder, have climbed a tree instead or stood on his head. If, however, instead of the murder one of these actions were to have become *actual*, then its sufficient cause would have had to be present. He would have climbed a tree if he had had the intention of hiding, or of acting as a lookout, that is to say, if at that moment he had had other ideas and sensations. But this could have been the case only if the events that took place in the world had been somewhat different [stretching back in time] ad infinitum.

3. Determinism and Will-Power

But I can, after all, break through the network of thoughts, sensations, and impressions that surrounds me by resolutely saying "I will not commit murder!" No doubt. We must, however, not lose sight of the fact that a resolute "I will" or "I will not" is also, wherever it appears, a necessary result; it does not by any means exist without a cause. Let us return to our examples. Although the Bogo really has reasons only to commit murder, it is nevertheless possible for a resolute "I will not commit murder" to assert itself. But is it conceivable that this "I will not" should occur without a sufficient cause? Fear, pity, or some other feeling, which in turn is an effect, overcomes him and gives rise to this "I will

not" before the cause of the murder has yet become complete. Perhaps Christian missionaries have had an influence upon him; hence the idea of a deity that will visit retribution on him for murder comes before his soul, and that is how the "I will not" comes to be. It is easier to detect the causes of the resolute "I will not commit murder" in someone raised at a higher level of civilization; fear, principles, or the thought of God in most cases produce it in time.

A resolute will can be characteristic of a man. No matter how violently jealousy, greed, or some other passion rages within him, he does not want to succumb to it; he does not succumb to it. The analogue of this constitution is a ball that, no matter how violent a force acts upon it, does not budge from its place. A billiard cue will labor in vain to shake the earth. The earth victoriously resists the cue's thrusts with its mass. Likewise man resists the thrusts of greed and jealousy with the mass of his principles. A man of that kind, accordingly, is free—from being dominated by his drives. Does this contradict determinism? By no means. A man free from passion is still subject to the law of causality. He is necessarily free. It is just that the word "free" has different meanings. It may be correctly predicated of man in every sense except a single one: he is not free from the law of causality. Let us trace the causes of his freedom from the tyranny of the passions.

Let us suppose that his steadfastness of will was not inherited, or, if so, merely as a disposition. Teaching, example, and, above all, the force of circumstances developed it in him. From early childhood on he found himself in situations in which he had to control himself if he did not want to perish. Just as someone standing at the edge of an abyss can banish dizziness by thinking "If I become dizzy, then I will plunge," so thinking "If I yield to my excitation—indeed, if I so much as betray it*—I will perish" has led him to control of his drives.

It is often thought that those who deny that the will is free want to deny that man has the ability to free himself from being dominated by his drives. However, one can imagine man's power to resist passions to be as great as one wants, even infinitely great; that is to say, a man may possibly resist even the most violent passion: his love of God or his principles have still more power over him than the passion. The question whether even

---

*   Reveal it, let it show.

the most resolute act of will is an effect is entirely independent of this.

But is being subject to the law of causality not the weak side of the strong? By no means. Is a lion weak if he can tear a tiger apart? Is a hurricane weak if it can uproot trees? And yet the power by means of which the lion dismembers and the storm uproots is an effect, and not an absolute beginning. By having causes, by being an effect, strength is not diminished.

Just as resolute willing is to be considered an effect, so is irresolute willing. A vacillating man is characterized by the fact that he alternately wants something and then doesn't want it. To say that someone contemplating murder is still vacillating means that at one time the desire for possessions, greed, and jealousy predominate—then he wants to commit murder, at another time fear of the consequences, the thought of God, or pity overcomes him, and then he does not want to commit murder. In the decisive moment, when his victim is before him, everything depends upon which feeling has the upper hand. If at that moment passion predominates, then he wants to commit murder; and then he commits murder.

We see that, from whatever point of view we look at willing, it always appears as a necessary result, as a link [in a chain of events], and never as an absolute beginning.

But can we not prove by means of an experiment that willing is an absolute beginning? I lift my arm because I *want* to lift it.... Here my *wanting* to lift my arm is the cause of the lifting, but this wanting, we are told, is not itself causally determined; rather, it is an absolute beginning. I simply want to lift my arm, and that is that. We are deceiving ourselves. This act of will, too, has causes; my intention to demonstrate by means of an experiment that my will is free gives rise to my wanting to lift my arm. But how did this intention come to be? Through a conversation, or through reflecting on the freedom of the will. Thus the thought "I want to demonstrate my freedom" has the effect that I want to lift my arm. There is a gap in this chain. Granted that my intention to demonstrate that my will is free stands in some relation to my wanting to lift my arm, why do I not demonstrate my freedom by means of some other movement? Why is it *just my arm* that I want to lift? This specific act of will on my part has not yet been causally explained. Does it perhaps not have causes? Is it an uncaused act of will? Let us note first that someone who

wishes to demonstrate that his will is free will usually really extend or lift his arm, and in particular his right arm. He neither tears his hair nor wiggles his belly. This can be explained as follows. Of all of the parts of the body that are subject to our voluntary control, there is none that we move more frequently than the right arm. If, now, we wish to demonstrate our freedom by means of some movement, we will automatically make that one to which we are most accustomed.... Thus we first have a conversation about or reflection on the freedom of the will; this leads to the intention of demonstrating our freedom; this intention arises in an organism with certain [physiological] habits [such as that of readily lifting the right arm], and as a result we want to lift (and then lift) the right arm.

I remember once discussing the freedom of the will with a left-handed man. He asserted "My will is free; I can do what I want." In order to demonstrate this he extended his *left* arm.

It is easy to see, now, what the situation is with regard to the assertion "I can do what I want." In one sense it is indeed correct; in another, however, it is wrong. The *correct* sense is to regard willing as a cause and action as an effect. For example, I can kill my rival if I want to kill him. I can walk to the left if I want to walk to the left. The causes are *wanting* to kill and *wanting* to walk; the effects are killing and walking. In some way every action must be preceded by the act of willing it, whether we are aware of it or not. According to this view, in fact, I can do *only* what I want to do, and only if I want to do it. The *wrong* sense is to regard willing *merely* as a cause, and not at the same time as the effect of something else. But, like everything else, it is cause *as well as effect*. An absolutely initial act of will does not exist. Willing stands in the middle: it brings about killing and walking to the left; it is the effect of thoughts and sensations (which in turn are effects).

4. Ignorance of the Causation of Our Actions

Hence our volition (with respect to some action) is always causally determined. But it seems to be free (of causes); it seems to be an absolute beginning. To what is this appearance due?

We do not perceive the causes by which our volition is determined, and that is why we believe that it is not causally determined at all.

How often do we do something while "lost in thought"! We pay no attention to what we are doing, let alone to the causes from which it springs. While we are thinking, we support our head with our hand. While we are conversing, we twist a piece of paper in our hand. If we then reflect on our behavior—stimulated perhaps by a conversation about the freedom of the will—and if we are quite incapable of finding a sufficient cause for it, then we believe that there was no sufficient cause for it at all, that, consequently, we could have proceeded differently at that moment, e.g., supporting our head with the left hand instead of the right....

To adduce yet another example: suppose that there are two eggs on the table. I take one of them. Why not the other one? Perhaps the one I took was a bit closer to me, or some other trivial matter, which would be very difficult to discover and is of the kind that almost never enters our consciousness, tipped the scales. If I now look back but do not see why I took *that* particular egg, then I come to think that I could just as well have taken the other.

Let us replace "I could have taken the other egg" by other statements containing the expression "I could have." For example, I could, when I took the egg, have chopped off my fingers instead, or I could have jumped at my neighbor's throat. Why do we never adduce such statements ... but always those contemplating an action close to the one that we really carried out? Because at the moment when I took the egg, chopping off my fingers and murder were far from my mind. From this point of view the two aspects of our subject matter—the fact that acts of will are necessary and that they appear not to be necessary—can be perceived especially clearly. *In fact* taking the other egg was at that moment just as impossible as chopping off a finger. For, whether a nuance of a sensation or a whole army of sensations and thoughts is lacking in the complete cause obviously does not matter; the effect cannot occur so long as the cause is incomplete. But it *seems* as though it would have been possible to take the other egg at that moment; if something almost happened, we think that it could have happened.

While in the case of unimportant matters we perhaps do not notice the causes of our act of will and therefore think that it has no causes, the situation is quite different—it will be objected—in the case of important matters. We did not, after all, marry one girl rather than another while "lost in thought." We did not close the sale of our house while "lost in thought." Rather, everyone sees that motives determined such decisions. In spite of this, however, we think "I could have acted differently." What is the source of this error?

In the case of unimportant matters we do not notice the cause of our action at all; in the case of important ones we perceive it, but not adequately. We do, to be sure, see the separate parts of the cause, but the special relation in which they stood to one another at the moment of the action eludes us.

Let us first consider another example from the realm of animals. A vixen* vacillated whether to sneak into the chicken coop, to hunt for mice, or to return to her young in her den. At last she sneaked into the chicken coop. Why? Because she wanted to. But why did she want to? Because this act of will on her part resulted from the relation in which her hunger, her fear of the watchdog, her maternal instinct, and her other thoughts, sensations, and impressions stood to one another at that time. But a vixen with the gift of reflection would, were she to look back upon her action, say "I could have willed differently." For, although she realizes that hunger influenced her act of will, the *degree* of hunger on the one hand, and of fear and maternal instinct on the other, present at the moment of the action elude her. Having become a different animal since the time of the action, perhaps because of it, she thinks—by way of a kind of optical illusion—that she was that other animal already then. It is the same in the case of man. Suppose, for example, that someone has slain his rival out of jealousy. What does he himself, and what do others, perceive with respect to this action? We see that on the one hand jealousy, the desire for possessions, hatred, and rage were present in him, and on the other fear of punishment, pity, and the thought of God. We do not, however, see the particular relation in which hatred and pity, and rage and fear of punishment, stood to one another at the moment of the deed. If we could see this, keep it fixed, and recreate it experimentally, then everyone would regard this action as an effect, as a necessary result.

---

*   Female fox.

Let us now, with the aid of our imagination, suppose that the sensations and thoughts of the murderer at the moment of the deed were spread out before us, clearly visible as if on a map. From this reflection we shall learn that *in fact* we are lacking such an overview, and that this lack is the reason why we do not ascribe a cause (or "necessity") to the action.

The kaleidoscopically changing sensations, thoughts, and impressions would, in order for their relation to one another to become apparent, have to be returned to the state in which they were at the moment of the deed, and then made rigid, as if they were being nailed to their place. But beyond that, the thoughts and sensations would have to be spatially extended and endowed with a colored surface; a stronger sensation would have to be represented by a bigger lump. A clearer thought would have to wear, say, a bright red color, a less clear one a gray coloration. Jealousy and rage, as well as pity and the thought of God, would have to be plastically exhibited* for us in this way. We would, further, have to see how the sight of the victim acts upon these structures of thoughts and sensations, and how there arises from these two factors first the desire to commit murder and then the act of murder itself.

Moreover, we would have to be able to repeat the process, perhaps as follows: we return the murderer to the state of mind that he had some years before the act of murder; we equip his mind with precisely the same thoughts and sensations, and his body with the same constitution. Then we let the very same impressions act upon them; we bring him into contact with the same people, let him read the same books, nourish him with the same food, and, finally, we will place the murdered person, after having called him back to life, before the murderer with the very same facial expression, in the same illumination and at the same distance. Then, as soon as the parts of the cause have been completely assembled, we would always see that the very same effect occurs, namely, wanting to commit, and then committing, murder.

Finally, too, we would have to vary the experiment, in the manner of the chemists; we would have to be able now to weaken a sensation, now to strengthen it, and to observe the result that this produces.

If these conditions were fulfilled, if we could experimentally recreate the process and also vary it, if we were to see its components and, above all, their relation to one another with plastic clarity before us—on the one hand, the *degree* of jealousy and of rage present at the moment; on the other, the *degree* of fear of punishment and of pity—then we would acknowledge that wanting to commit murder and committing murder are necessary results. But as it is we merely see that, on the one hand, jealousy and related feelings, and, on the other, pity and the idea of God, were present in the murderer. But, since we do not see the particular relation in which the sensations and thoughts stood to one another at the moment of the deed, we simply think that the *one* side could have produced acts of will and actions as well as the *other*, that the murderer could, at the moment when he wanted to commit and did commit murder, just as well have willed and acted differently, say compassionately.

It is the same if we ourselves are the person who acts. We, too, think "I could have willed differently." Let us illustrate this by yet another example. Yesterday afternoon at 6:03 o'clock I sold my house. Why? Because I wished to do so. But why did I wish to do so? Because my intention to change my place of residence, and other circumstances, caused my act of will. But was I compelled to will? Could I not have postponed the sale or forgone it altogether? It seems so to me, because I do not see the particular relation in which my thoughts, sensations, and impressions stood to one another yesterday afternoon at 6:03 o'clock.

Thus: we do not see the sufficient cause (either not at all, in the case of unimportant matters; or inadequately, in the case of important ones); consequently it does not exist for us; consequently we think that our volition and our actions were not causally determined at all, that we could just as well have willed and acted differently. No one would say "I could have willed differently" if he could see his act of will and its causes displayed plastically before him, in an experiment permitting repetition.

But who are the mistaken "we" of whom we are speaking here? Patently the author does not consider himself to be one of them. Does he, then, set himself, along with a few fellow philosophers, apart from the

---

* Modeled in three dimensions.

rest of mankind, regarding them as ignorant of the truth? Well, it really is not the case that mankind has always concerned itself with the problem of the freedom of the will and only a small part arrived at the result that the will is not free; rather, in precivilized ages no one, and in civilized ages almost no one, concerned himself with this problem. But of the few who did address themselves to this question, as the history of philosophy teaches us, almost all recognized that there is no freedom of the will. The others became victims of the illusion described above, without ever coming to grips with the problem in its general form (is the will subject to the law of causality or not?)....

5. Determinism Is Inconsistent with Judgments of Moral Responsibility

We hold ourselves and others responsible without taking into account the problem of the freedom of the will.

Experience shows that, if someone has lied or murdered, he is told that he has acted reprehensibly and deserves punishment. Whether his action is uncaused or whether, like the other processes in nature, it is subject to the law of causality—how would people come to raise such questions in the ordinary course of their lives? Or has anyone ever heard of a case in which people talking about an act of murder, a lie, or an act of self-sacrifice discussed these actions in terms of the freedom of the will? It is the same if we ourselves are the person who acted. We say to ourselves "Oh, if only I had not done this! Oh, if only I had acted differently!" or "I have acted laudably, as one should act." At best a philosopher here or there chances upon the question whether our actions are causally determined or not, certainly not the rest of mankind.

Suppose, however, that someone's attention is directed to the fact that the will is not free. At first it will be very difficult to make this plausible to him. His volition is suspended from threads that are too nearly invisible, and that is why he comes to think that it is not causally determined at all. At last, however—so we shall assume—he does come to recognize that actions are effects, that their causes are thoughts and impressions, that these must likewise be viewed as effects, and

so on. How will he then judge these actions? Will he continue to maintain that murder is to be punished by *reprisal* and that benevolent actions are to be considered *meritorious*? By no means. Rather, the first conclusion that he will—validly—draw from his newly acquired insight is that we cannot hold anyone responsible. "*Tout comprendre c'est tout pardonner*";* no one can be made to answer for an *effect*.

In order to illustrate this important truth, that whoever considers intentions to be effects will cease to assign merit or blame for them, let us resume discussion of the examples above. From early childhood on the Bogo ... has learned to praise murder. The praiseworthiness of such an action already penetrated the consciousness of the child as a secondary meaning of the word "murder," and afterward it was confirmed by every impression: his gods and his fellow men praise murder. In consequence he involuntarily judges acts of murder to be praiseworthy, no matter whether it was he himself or someone else who committed them. Let us assume, now, that a philosopher had succeeded in persuading the Bogos that the act of murder and the intention to practice cruelty are causally determined. Then their judgment would undergo an essential modification.

To conceive of actions and intentions as causally determined, after all, means the following. We go back in the history of the individual, say to his birth, and investigate which of his characteristics are inborn and to what causes they are due.[1] Then, ever guided by the law of causality, we trace the development or transformation of these properties; we see how impressions, teachings, and examples come to him and, if his inborn constitution has an affinity for them, are taken up and transformed by it, otherwise passing by without leaving a trace. Finally we recognize that the keystone, the necessary result of this course of development, is the desire to commit murder and the act of murder.

A Bogo who looks upon murder and the intention to practice cruelty in this way—that is, as an effect—will say that it is impossible to regard them as meritorious.

But will he now look upon these actions with apathy, devoid of all feeling? By no means. He will still consider them to be pleasant or unpleasant, agreeable or disagreeable.

---

* French: "To understand all is to forgive all," a European proverb dating back to at least the eighteenth century, expressed most famously using these words by Tolstoy in *War and Peace* (1868).

When the action is directed against himself, he will perceive it as pleasant or as unpleasant; the prospect of being murdered is unpleasant for everyone, whether he considers the action to be causally determined or uncaused.

Similarly our liking or dislike for the character of a human being will persist even if we regard it as the result of causes. To say that I find someone agreeable means that I am drawn to him; I like him. Of a landscape, too, one says that it is agreeable, and, just as this liking cannot be diminished even if we consider the trees, meadows, and hills to be the result of causes, so our liking for the character of a human being is not diminished if we regard it *sub specie necessitatis*. Hence to the Bogo who has come to see that murder is causally determined it is still agreeable or disagreeable. Usually he will consider it to be agreeable. He will say that it warms the cockles of his heart to observe such an action; it accords with his wild temperament, as yet untouched by civilization. Therefore he will, in view of the necessity, suspend only the specifically moral practice of regarding it as meritorious. But his liking may become love, and even esteem and reverence. It will be objected, however, that "I revere a mode of behavior" entails "I consider it meritorious for a person to behave in that way," and similarly for esteem. To be sure, the words "reverence" and "esteem" *frequently* have this meaning, and *to the extent that they do* a determinist would cease using them. But all words that denote human feelings have not only one, but several meanings. They have, if I may express it in that way, a harem of meanings, and they couple now with this one, now with that one. So, if I "revere" someone, it means also that I esteem him, that he impresses me, and that I wish to be like him.... Reverence and esteem in *this* sense can coexist with determinism.

Hence the Bogo who conceives of the intention to practice cruelty and the act of murder as effects can nevertheless consider them to be agreeable or disagreeable, and in a certain sense he can also have esteem and reverence for them, but he will not regard them as meritorious.

Let us now consider the act of murder at high levels of civilization. Civilization, as it progressed, stigmatized murder and threatened penalties for it on earth and in heaven. This censure already penetrates the consciousness of the child as a secondary meaning of the word "murder" and afterward is confirmed through every impression. All the people whom one knows, all the books that one reads, the state with its institutions, pulpit and stage always use "murder" in a censorious sense. That is how it comes to be that we involuntarily declare an act of murder to be blameworthy, be it that others or that we ourselves, driven by passion, committed it. Whether the action was determined by causes or uncaused—that question is raised neither by the person who acted nor by the uninvolved observers. But *if* it is raised, if someone considers the act of murder *sub specie necessitatis*, then he ceases to regard it as blameworthy. He will then no longer want to see punishment in the proper sense—suffering as retribution—meted out for it, but merely punishment as a safety measure.[2] The feelings of liking and dislike, however, will continue to exist even then. On the whole, someone raised at a high level of civilization will have a feeling of dislike for acts of murder; he will not feel drawn to whoever commits it; he will not like him. For such an act does not accord with his temperament, which was formed as he was engaged in non-violent occupations. In spite of the recognition that the action was necessary, this dislike can at times grow to revulsion, and even to contempt—given that the latter notion is stripped of the specifically moral elements that it contains (the attribution of blame). It will then mean something like this: I do not want to be like that person.

The situation is the same in the case of benevolent actions and those performed out of a sense of duty; we cease to regard them as meritorious if we consider them to be effects. Let us look more closely at actions performed out of a sense of duty. To say that someone acts out of a sense of duty means that he performs an action, perhaps contrary to his inclinations, because his conscience commands him to do it. But how does conscience come to issue such commandments? As follows: with some actions (and intentions) there is linked for us from early childhood on a categorical "thou shalt do (or have) them"; for example, "you *should* help everyone as much as possible." If someone then makes this habitual judgment into the guiding principle of his behavior, if he helps a person because his conscience commands "thou *shalt* help thy fellow man," then he is acting "out of a sense of duty".... If we want to consider such an action from the point of view of eternity and necessity, we shall have to proceed as follows: we investigate (1) the constitution of the child who receives the teaching "thou shalt help," (2) the constitution of those who give it to him. The child absorbing this doctrine has some inborn constitution of nerves, of blood, of imagination, and of reason. The commandment "thou shalt help" is impressed upon this substance with some degree of insistence; the deity, heaven, hell, approval of his fellow men and of his own conscience—these ideas are presented to him, depending upon his teachers, as being more or less majestic and inspiring. And the child transforms them with greater or lesser intensity, depending upon his receptivity. The ultimate constitution of a man, the preponderance within him of the sense of duty over his own desires, is in any case a necessary result, a product of his inborn constitution and the impressions received. To someone who contemplates this, such a temperament may, to be sure, still seem agreeable (perhaps because he himself is or would like to be similarly constituted), but no one can regard as *meritorious* behavior that he conceives to be an *effect*.

But what if we ourselves are the person who acted? Then the circumstances are analogous; then, too, liking and dislike remain, while the attribution of merit or blame (the "pangs of conscience") disappears.

Our own action, too, can remain agreeable or become disagreeable for us after it has occurred. It is agreeable if the disposition from which we acted persists after the action; it will become disagreeable if we change our frame of mind. Suppose, for example, that we have acted vengefully and are still in the same mood; then the act of revenge is still agreeable, whether we conceive it to be an effect or not. If, however, a feeling of pity takes the place of our desire for revenge, then we come to dislike our action; we cannot stand our earlier self—the less so, the more pronounced our feeling of pity is. The reflection that the action is an effect in no way affects this feeling of dislike, perhaps of disgust, or even of revulsion for ourselves. We say to ourselves that the desire for revenge was, to be sure, necessarily stronger than the ideas and impressions that stood in its way, hence the action took place necessarily, too; but now it happens that pity is necessarily present, and, along with it, regrets that we acted as we did....

6. Can We Abandon Judgments of Moral Responsibility?

But is it really possible to shake off feelings of guilt so easily? Do they disappear, like a spook, when the magic word *effect* is pronounced? Is the situation with respect to this feeling not quite like that with regard to dislike? It was, to be sure, necessary that I took revenge, but now

I necessarily feel dislike for my own action, along with guilt. I can no more prevent the onset of the one feeling than of the other. But if the feeling of guilt asserts itself in spite of the recognition that actions are effects, should we not suspect that our holding others responsible, too, will persist in spite of this insight? Did we commit an error somewhere? Is it that responsibility and necessity do not exclude each other? The situation is as follows. The reason why we assign moral praise to some actions and moral censure to others has already been mentioned repeatedly. Censure already penetrates the consciousness of the child as a secondary meaning of the words "murder," "theft," "vengefulness," and "pleasure in another's pain," and praise as a secondary meaning of the words "benevolence" and "mercy." That is why censure seems to him to be a constituent part of murder, and praise, of benevolence. At a later point in his life, perhaps in his twentieth year, the insight comes to him from somewhere that all actions are effects and therefore cannot earn merit or blame. What can this poor little insight accomplish against the accumulated habits of a lifetime of judging? The habit of mind of assigning blame for actions like murder makes it very difficult to think of them without this judgment. It is all very well for reason to tell us that we may not assign blame for such actions, since they are effects—our habit of judging, which has become a feeling, will see to it that it is done anyway. But—let habit confront habit! Suppose that, whenever someone involuntarily wants to assign blame or merit for an action, he ascends to the point of view of eternity and necessity. He then regards the action as the necessary result of [a chain of events stretching back into] the infinite past. Through that way of looking at things the *instinctive* association between the action and the judgment will be severed, if not the first time, then perhaps by the thousandth. Such a man will shed the habit of assigning blame or merit for any action whatsoever.

In fact, of course, human beings almost never behave like that; this way of looking at things is completely foreign to them. Furthermore, human beings determine their actions by considering whether they will make them happy or unhappy; but shedding the habit of making judgments [of moral responsibility] would hardly increase their happiness....

The situation with respect to a person's character is no different from that with respect to his individual actions. *Customarily* one assigns blame or merit, whether to himself or to others, for a single action: a single act of cheating or of giving offense. But *sometimes* we go back from the action to its source, to a person's character. In reality, of course, character, in its broadest as well as its smallest traits, is just as necessary as an individual action; it is the product of [a chain of events stretching back into] the infinite past, be it that it was inherited in its entirety or that it was formed in part during the individual's lifetime. But with regard to character, too, hardly anyone adopts this point of view. Just as in the case of particular actions, character is regarded neither as free nor as necessary; that is to say, people do not raise the question at all whether the law of causality is applicable also to actions and character. Hence one assigns blame and merit for character as for actions, though they are effects; for one does not see that they are effects. If one sees this, if one regards character *sub specie necessitatis*, then he ceases to assign blame or merit for it. Liking and dislike, on the other hand, nevertheless persist even then: a character closely related to mine will garner my liking, my love, and perhaps even, in the sense mentioned above, my esteem and reverence—whether I conceive of it as an effect or not.

Hence we assign blame or merit for character and actions out of the habit of judging, without concerning ourselves with the question whether they are causally determined or not. We cease to assign blame or merit for character and actions as soon as we recognize that they are causally determined (if we ignore the remnants of our habits).

Let us recapitulate: the character, the intentions, and the actions of every human being are effects, and it is impossible to assign blame or merit for effects. ■

Suggestions for Critical Reflection

1. "To say that the will is not free means that it is subject to the law of causality." Is this right? Or could the will somehow be *both* free and subject to causal laws?

2. Rée admits that "man has the ability to free himself from being dominated by his drives." Does this undermine his claim that determinism is incompatible with moral responsibility?

3. Rée suggests that anyone who comes to properly grasp the truth of determinism will immediately abandon any belief in moral responsibility (though perhaps will be unable to shake off the habit of making moral judgments). Is this claim plausible? How strong are his reasons for making it?

4. Here are two claims:
   a. Some event *A* will occur *whenever* its sufficient cause is present.
   b. Some event *A* will occur *only* when its sufficient cause is present.

   Do these two claims say different things (i.e., could one be true when the other one is false)? Does Rée clearly differentiate between the two of them? How might the difference between the two claims cause problems for Rée's argument?

5. "Observation teaches us that for every act of will, some causes were the determining factors." Is this true and, if so, is it sufficient to establish determinism?

6. One of the consequences of Rée's determinism, he suggests, is that people can *only* do what they want to do—that is, according to Rée, it is impossible to deliberately do something that you do not want to do. Does this seem right to you? Does it actually follow from the thesis of determinism?

7. Is it *fair* to prefer some people over others, to seek the company of the former, and to shun the latter, if they are not responsible for their character traits? For example, is it okay to dislike depressed people if it's not their fault they are depressed? Is the question of 'fairness' even appropriate, if human beings have no free will?

Notes

1 An investigation as detailed as that is, of course, never possible in practice.

2 Punishments are causes that prevent the repetition of the action punished.

ISHTIYAQUE HAJI

FROM *Incompatibilism's Allure*

Who Is Ishtiyaque Haji?

Ishtiyaque Haji is a Professor of Philosophy at the University of Calgary, Alberta. He is the author of seven books and many papers on free will, moral responsibility, and philosophical psychology. He studied at Simon Fraser University and received his PhD from the University of Massachusetts, Amherst.

What Is the Structure of This Reading?

This reading summarizes some of the main reasons why "a number of thoughtful people might be drawn to libertarianism. The libertarian affirms that determinism is incompatible with moral responsibility and free action but at least some of us, at times, perform free actions for which we are morally responsible. These people might reason that it seems much more plausible that we are, at least on occasion, morally responsible for what we do than that we are not responsible for any of our behavior."*

The chapter begins by describing two case studies that encourage the reader to reflect on our judgments about moral responsibility, and in particular to consider the intuition that blame-worthiness is *incompatible* with certain kinds of determination of our behavior. Haji then organizes this intuition into five possible arguments for incompatibilism, plus a further sixth argument to the effect that we are not responsible for any of our actions regardless of the truth of determinism. Finally, Haji briefly considers a different route to incompatibilism that starts from a principled defense of libertarianism against its alternatives, and then concludes from this that compatibilism must be false.

Haji is agnostic about the truth of determinism, and his concern here is to assess the *compatibility* of determinism, if it turned out to be true, with free will and moral responsibility. His own position, at the end of his book, is that, despite its attractions the main libertarian positions "have significant shortcomings" and we might have to be content with what he calls "semicompatibilism": the view that although determinism is incompatible with our freedom to do otherwise, it does not undermine moral responsibility. He has developed a more restricted form of responsibility that he calls "moral appraisability"—and argues that using this notion allows us to make progress on the "age-old grand puzzle" of free will.

FROM *Incompatibilism's Allure*†

1.1 The Robert Harris Case

Robert Alton Harris' heartrending story is the sort of tragic drama that impels many of us to think deeply about free action, responsibility, and moral luck. The kind of impact, pertinent to our concerns, which Harris' case may well have on our moral thinking can be highlighted perspicuously by following Gary Watson's presentation of its details.[1] The picture of Harris that emerges from the *Los Angeles Times* article, "Icy Killer's Life Steeped in Violence," is one of a ruthless, brutal murderer.[2] This is a portrayal which,

---

* *Incompatibilism's Allure*, 27.

† This is taken from the introductory chapter to Haji's *Incompatibilism's Allure: Principal Arguments for Incompatibilism* (Broadview Press, 2009).

at least initially and customarily, foments attitudes of anger and resentment toward Harris. But as the history of the young man's life on Death Row unravels—as we learn, Watson explains, about how Harris came to be the mean and perverse youth that he was—typically, our negative attitudes are held in check. Some of the details of the case should bear this out.

On July 5, 1978, Robert, 25, and his brother, Daniel, 18, were trying to hotwire a car that they intended to use in a bank robbery. Unable to start the car, Harris decided to take another car in which two youths, John Mayeski and Michael Baker, on their way to a nearby lake for a day of fishing, were eating lunch. Approaching the car and pointing a Luger* at Mayeski's head, Harris crawled into the back seat and ordered the 16-year-olds to drive east. Daniel followed in the Harrises' car. On reaching a secluded canyon area, Harris informed the boys about the planned robbery, and assured them that they would not be hurt. He even offered to leave some of the stolen money in their car to pay for its use. It was agreed that the Harris brothers would leave to rob the bank and that Mayeski and Baker would walk back into town and report the car stolen. As the two boys started to walk away, Harris slowly raised the Luger and shot Mayeski in the back. Harris then chased Baker down a hill and shot him four times. Mayeski was still alive when Harris made his way back. Harris walked over to the boy, put the Luger to his head and fired. Recalling the aftermath of the shooting, Daniel remarked, "[Robert] was swinging the rifle and pistol in the air and laughing. God, that laugh made blood and bone freeze in me."[3]

After the shooting, the Harris brothers drove to a friend's house. Harris began to feast on what was left of the slain youths' lunch. He offered his brother an apple turnover; Daniel became nauseated and ran into the bathroom. "Harris was in an almost lighthearted mood. He smiled and told Daniel that it would be amusing if the two of them were to pose as police officers and inform the parents that their sons were killed."[4] Thinking that somebody might have heard the shots and that the police could be searching for the bodies, Harris told Daniel that they should scout the street near the bodies and perhaps kill some police in the area. Later, as they prepared to rob the bank,

"Harris pulled out the Luger, noticed blood stains and remnants of flesh on the barrel as a result of the point-blank shot, and said, 'I really blew that guy's brains out.' And then, again, he started laughing."[5]

Does it matter to our first reaction—that Harris is an archetypal candidate for blame—how he came to be so? The article is sensitive to this issue as well. During an interview with one of Robert's sisters, Barbara, Barbara "put her palms over her eyes and said softly, 'I saw every grain of sweetness, pity and goodness in him destroyed.... It was a long and ugly journey before he reached that point.'"[6]

Harris was born on January 15, 1953, several hours after his mother, six and one-half months pregnant, was kicked in the stomach by her insanely jealous husband who claimed that the child was not his. Because of the premature birth, Robert was a tiny baby; he was kept alive in an incubator and spent months at the hospital. All of the children had horrendous childhoods, but Robert fell victim to abuse that was unusually brutal even in the Harris family. The pain and permanent injury Robert's mother suffered because of the birth, and the constant abuse to which her husband subjected her, turned her against her son. She began to blame all of her problems on Robert and grew to hate the child. Harris suffered from a learning disability and a speech problem. There was no money, though, for therapy. Barbara reported that when he was at school Harris felt stupid and his classmates teased him, and when he was at home he was abused.

"He wanted love so bad he would beg for any kind of physical contact.... He'd come up to my mother and just try to rub his little hands on her leg or her arm. He just never got touched at all. She'd just push him away or kick him".... All nine children are psychologically crippled ... [Barbara continued], but most have been able to lead useful lives. But Robert was too young, and the abuse lasted too long ... for him ever to have had a chance to recover.... [At age 14] Harris was sentenced to a federal youth detention center [for car theft]. He was one of the youngest inmates there, Barbara Harris said, and he grew up "hard and fast." ... Harris was raped several times ... and he slashed

---

* A World War II-era pistol.

his wrists twice in suicide attempts. He spent more than four years behind bars as a result of an escape, an attempted escape and a parole violation.... The centers were "gladiator schools," Barbara Harris said, and Harris learned to fight and to be mean. By the time he was released from federal prison at 19, all his problems were accentuated.... "The only way he could vent his feelings was to break or kill something," Barbara Harris said. "He took out all the frustrations of his life on animals. He had no feeling for life, no sense of remorse. He reached the point where there wasn't that much left of him."[7]

Reflecting on this section of the *Times'* report, it is natural to wonder to what extent Harris was responsible for becoming the sort of person that he was. Was the pathway of his life fully set in stone by parental and societal neglect, social or genetic conditioning, sheer bad luck, and the like, or did he have any hand in molding it? If the former, and this inclines us to mitigate or remove blame, then we may be well on the way toward *incompatibilism*, loosely, the view that blameworthiness—or, more generally, moral responsibility—is incompatible with being "determined" in certain ways. We might see Harris's actions as "determined" in the sense that their sources—the desires, beliefs, values, and so forth—the springs of action that collectively made up his psychological life—were "foreign" or "alien" to him; "foreign" in a robust sense in which, for example, we are comfortable in proclaiming that the desires that a child acquires as a result of *indoctrination* rather than as an outcome of *education* are not "really" the child's own. Is this ever the case? Real-life cases are engagingly (and sometimes, for purposes of analysis, distressingly) messy. For this reason, to unearth different routes to incompatibilism ... it may be more helpful to turn to thought experiments in which various parameters can be controlled.

1.2 *The Ann/Beth Cases*

Ponder, then, a more clinical imaginary case that Alfred Mele advances. The case resembles Harris' in one vital respect: the central figure's springs of action do not seem to be "truly the agent's own" in that she did not have a hand in their acquisition. Ann and Beth are both philosophy professors but Ann is far more dedicated to the discipline. Wanting more production out of Beth and not scrupulous about how he gets it, the dean of the University enlists the help of new-wave neurologists who "implant" Ann's hierarchy of values into easy-going Beth. Understand 'values' in this way: "*S* at least *thinly values X* at a time if and only if at that time *S* both has a positive motivational attitude toward *X* [for instance, *S* is favorably inclined toward *X* or *S* wants *X*] and believes *X* to be good."[8] The pro-attitudes* "implanted" in Beth are *practically unsheddable*. A pro-attitude is practically unsheddable for a person at a time if, given her psychological constitution at that time, ridding herself of that attitude is not a "psychologically genuine option" under any but extraordinary circumstances.[9] It is important to keep in mind that if, for example, a desire is unsheddable for a person at a time, that desire need not be irresistible at that time. A parent's desire to care for her child may be unsheddable at some time but it need not then be irresistible. This "induction" of values into Beth results in her becoming the psychological twin of Ann in some respects. But the induction leaves unscathed values, beliefs, desires, and so forth which pre-manipulated Beth possessed and which can co-exist more or less harmoniously with the newly engineered-in pro-attitudes. Such psychological tampering is, thus, consistent with failing to undermine personal identity: pre-manipulated Beth is identical to† her post-manipulated later self.

An agent's action expresses a belief, or it expresses a pro-attitude such as a desire, or, more generally, it expresses an actional spring, only if that actional spring plays a (nondeviant) causal role in the production of

---

* A pro-attitude is a favorable attitude towards, or preference for, something.

† Haji does not mean that Beth is exactly the same in every way after her dean's psychological meddling (which of course she is not); he means that she nevertheless is *the same person* as she was before, and she hasn't turned into a different individual—just as you are the same person as the 13-year-old you, although you may have quite different attributes now than you had then.

that action. Again, an actional spring just is a causal antecedent of an action such as a desire, belief, or value. Regarding the first few actions of Beth which express engineered-in actional springs, we would want to say that these implanted elements are not "truly Beth's own." Owing to their not being Beth's own, a number of us would be inclined to agree that these actions of Beth are not free and that Beth is not morally responsible for them. We may refer to this case as **"Ann/Beth-1."**

"**Ann/Beth-2**" is just like **Ann/Beth-1** save that in **Ann/Beth-2** the implanted desires are both unsheddable for Beth *and* irresistible. Again, many of us would be drawn to the view that victimized Beth's actions that express these desires (and other implanted antecedents of action) in this second variation of the case are not ones for which she is responsible. And at least some of us would want to add that Beth is not responsible for these actions because, among other things, they are the inevitable causal upshots of antecedents, such as irresistible engineered-in desires, with respect to the acquisition of which she had no control. But then it is a short step from this sort of reasoning to the much more troubling conclusion that all our actions are already determined—"in the cards" so to speak, because they are the *inevitable* causal consequences, not of manipulators, but of facts in the far distant past and the laws of nature. And if this is so, then none of us is responsible for any of our actions. As some theorists steeped in the free will literature will put it, it appears that causal determinism is incompatible with free action and moral responsibility, or more simply, it appears that incompatibilism may well be true.

...

1.4 Different Pathways to Incompatibilism

... [I]t is not so difficult to see why one might think that determinism rules out free action and, thus, moral responsibility on the credible assumption that if a person is morally responsible for an action, then that action is free. In the second version of the **Ann/Beth** case—**Ann/Beth-2**—Beth's first post-transformation action, *A*, causally issues from an irresistible desire. (Assume that *A* consists in Beth's

expending considerable time on refereeing a paper.) Some may find it tempting to argue in this way:

THE LACK OF FREEDOM ARGUMENT

(1) The causal antecedents of Beth's *A*-ing (her pertinent desires, for example) are irresistible.

(2) If the causal antecedents of Beth's *A*-ing are irresistible, then Beth cannot but do *A*.

(3) If Beth cannot but do *A*, then Beth does not do *A* freely.

(4) If Beth does not do *A* freely, then Beth is not morally responsible for *A*-ing.

(5) Therefore, Beth is not morally responsible for *A*-ing.

What underlies this argument is the intuitive and highly attractive picture that *free* agents have more than one path or option genuinely open to them on various occasions in their lives. On this picture, the paths into the future branch out from the present—"the future is a garden of forking paths," as John Martin Fischer following Borges* says—and it is "up to us" on which pathway we tread; it is "up to us" how we choose and act.[10] So although we may have chosen and acted in one way, we could, given the same past and the laws, have chosen and acted in another way. If determinism is true, though, then at every instant, the future is a branchless extension of the past. So if determinism is true, no one is free to choose among alternative pathways into the future.

It is worth probing deeper into how, precisely, **Ann/Beth-2** motivates *incompatibilism*—it's worth examining how exactly this case helps to energize the view that determinism is incompatible with free action and responsibility. Among others, Peter van Inwagen has argued that if determinism is true, then none of our actions is "up to us"; they are not up to us in the sense that *we could not have done otherwise*. He summarizes his intriguing **Consequence Argument** in this way:

> If determinism is true, then our acts are the consequences of the laws of nature and events in the remote past. But it is not up to us what went

---

* See Jorge Luis Borges's 1941 short story "The Garden of Forking Paths."

on before we were born, and neither is it up to us what the laws of nature are. Therefore, the consequences of these things (including our present acts) are not up to us.[11]

Conjoined with the premise that if our acts are not up to us—if we lack the freedom to do otherwise—we do not perform them freely and are not morally responsible for them, the **Consequence Argument** yields incompatibilism as its conclusion. In **Ann/Beth-2**, Beth's first post-transformation act, A, is inevitable because this action is performed, in part, on the basis of a desire that is irresistible. Suppose we accept van Inwagen's conclusion that if determinism is true, then we never have the freedom to do other than what we in fact do; all our actions are inevitable insofar as they are the causal upshots of the distant past and the laws. We can then avail ourselves of this sort of argument:

THE PROTO-CONSEQUENCE ARGUMENT

(1A) If determinism is true, then Beth cannot but do A.

(2A) If Beth cannot but do A, then Beth does not do A freely.

(3A) If Beth does not do A freely, then Beth is not morally responsible for A-ing.

(4A) Therefore, if determinism is true, then Beth is not morally responsible for A-ing.

The second version of the **Ann/Beth** case suggests another route to incompatibilism. One might reason that manipulated Beth is not responsible for acquiring the engineered-in springs of action, including the irresistible desire, on the basis of which she exerts considerable efforts in refereeing a paper. Nor is she responsible for the fact that if she acquires these springs, then she referees the paper. But then it seems to follow that she is not responsible for refereeing the paper either. In short, this line of reasoning relies on a principle of this sort: if you are not responsible for one thing, and you are not responsible for this thing's leading to a second—that is, you are not responsible for the "conditional fact" that if the first occurs or obtains, so does the second—you are not responsible for the second thing. Exploiting this principle, it may be proposed that,

pretty clearly, no one is even partly morally responsible for the state of the universe at a distant time in the past—a time at which there were no human beings, for instance—and no one is even partly morally responsible for the laws being what they are. Assuming that determinism is true, no one is even partly morally responsible for the fact that the combination of the distant past (the complete state of the universe at a time in the past) and the laws entail all events, including our actions. These two claims appear to sanction the result that no one is even partly responsible for one's actions. Unlike the **Proto-Consequence Argument**, in working toward incompatibilism this **Direct Argument** does not invoke the **Principle of Alternative Possibilities**—that persons are morally responsible for what they have done only if they could have done otherwise. It appears to sidestep this principle altogether. In brief, compare this direct argument for Beth's not being responsible—*direct* because it works around the **Principle of Alternative Possibilities** altogether—with the prior argument for the same conclusion:

THE DIRECT ARGUMENT

(1B) No one is even partly responsible for what the state of the universe at a time close to the Big Bang was and for the laws being what they are.

(2B) Assuming determinism, no one is even partly responsible for the fact that the combination of the distant past (the complete state of the universe at a time close to the Big Bang) and the laws entails that Beth performs A (at the time when she does perform A).

(3B) If (1B) and (2B), then Beth is not morally responsible for performing A.

(4B) Therefore, Beth is not morally responsible for performing A.

Inspection reveals that there is no premise in the **Direct Argument** that neatly corresponds to premise (2A) of the **Proto-Consequence Argument**. So, it seems, there is no premise in the **Direct Argument** that appeals to the **Principle of Alternative Possibilities**.

Reflecting on Harris' case, we might be tempted by the view that it is obvious that Harris did moral wrong in killing the youths; he ought not to have killed them. If we think of the morally deontic* notions of right, wrong, and obligation, it would not be unusual to be drawn to the principle that "ought" implies "can": if you morally ought to do something, then you can do it. If it is true, for example, that you cannot open the safe and defuse the bomb therein because you don't know the combination, then you can't have a moral *obligation* to open the safe. The moral "ought" expresses a kind of necessity or requirement. Morality cannot *require* you to do what you *cannot* do. But if "ought" implies "can," then surely "ought not" implies "can refrain from"; if you ought not to do something—if it is wrong for you to do it—then you can refrain from doing it. So it seems that there is a requirement of alternative possibilities for wrongness: you can't do wrong unless you could have refrained from doing what you do. Suppose, though, that determinism *does* undermine alternative possibilities; suppose, that is, that if determinism is true, then you cannot refrain from doing what you do. We now have another pathway that the **Deontic Argument** exposes to incompatibilism:

THE DEONTIC ARGUMENT

(1C) If determinism is true, then you can't refrain from doing what you do.

(2C) If you can't refrain from doing what you do, then whatever you do is not wrong (because you can't do wrong unless you could have avoided doing what you did).

(3C) If whatever you do is not wrong, then you can't be morally blameworthy for anything that you do.

(4C) Therefore, if determinism is true, you can't be morally blameworthy for anything that you do.

Harris' case and both **Ann/Beth** cases invite yet another argument for incompatibilism. Various varieties of manipulation, or social conditioning, or indoctrination undermine moral responsibility. Arguably, the kind of treatment to which Harris was subject during his early childhood is responsibility-subverting. The manipulation in the **Ann/Beth** cases also seems to be manipulation of a responsibility-subverting sort. Focusing on the **Ann/Beth** cases, one might plausibly propose that the type of manipulation involved in these

cases undercuts responsibility because its victim (Beth), as a result of being manipulated, is not the "ultimate originator" of her engineered-in springs of action; so she is not the ultimate source of the actions that causally derive from these springs. To be responsible, though, for our choices, actions, and so forth, these things must originate "in us." It is a condition of responsibility that we be the ultimate originators or sources of our intentional behavior. As Beth fails to satisfy this condition, Beth is not morally responsible for them. *She* is not the ultimate source of her actions that express her implanted desires, beliefs, etc.; maybe the *manipulator* carries the burden of responsibility. But now assume, again, that determinism is true. Then there is a sense in which all our actions, including all our decisions, originate in the distant past and the laws of nature, sources over which we have no control. Given the thought that if we are not the ultimate sources of our actions we are not responsible for them, it follows that if determinism is true, we are not responsible for any of our actions. So we have this sort of argument for incompatibilism:

THE MANIPULATION ARGUMENT

(1D) Actions that result from manipulation of the sort displayed in the **Ann/Beth** cases are actions for which an agent is not morally responsible. (Or, as we may say, actions that derive from a causal history involving *menacing manipulation*—manipulation that undermines responsibility—aren't ones for which an agent is responsible.)

(2D) Actions that result from a deterministic causal history are relevantly similar to those that derive from a causal history involving menacing manipulation (in either case, the agent is not the ultimate source of her actions).

(3D) If (1D) and (2D), then determinism undermines moral responsibility.

(4D) Therefore, determinism undermines moral responsibility.

This version of the **Manipulation Argument** attempts to convince us that cases of responsibility-undercutting manipulation are relevantly similar to

---

* *Intrinsically* right or wrong, and so *intrinsically* obligatory or forbidden. 'Intrinsically' here is in contrast to: because of consequences, because of (in)compatibility with good character, etc.

actions that are causally determined: just as, in virtue of being manipulated in the manner in which she is, Beth is not the ultimate originator of her actions, and, thus, is not morally responsible for them, so in virtue of her actions being causally determined, Beth is not their ultimate originator and, hence, bears no responsibility for them.

Finally, all the cases with which we commenced might spur an argument—the **Impossibility Argument**—for the stronger conclusion that we are not responsible for any of our actions *regardless* of the truth of determinism. This conclusion is, of course, consistent with the incompatibilist's claim that determinism rules out moral responsibility. In roughly hewn strokes, the line of reasoning for this forceful conclusion unfolds in this way: If Beth is not responsible for the way she is at a particular time—if she is not, for example, responsible for having the desires, values, or beliefs with which she finds herself at a particular time—then she is not responsible for actions that express these causal antecedents. But if she is to be responsible for these causal antecedents—if she is to be responsible for these desires, for instance—she must be responsible for earlier actions or behavior as a result of which she acquired these desires. To be responsible, though, for these earlier actions, she would have had to have been responsible for the springs of these earlier actions. But to have been responsible for these earlier springs, she would have had to have been responsible for still earlier actions that led to the acquisition of these earlier springs, and so forth. Thus, responsibility for an action requires what is impossible: it requires having made an *infinite* number of choices. In premise and conclusion form, the **Impossibility Argument** can be restated in this way:

THE IMPOSSIBILITY ARGUMENT

(1E) The actions we perform depend on certain facts about what we are like in relevant mental respects, or *how we are*.

(2E) If (1E), then if we are responsible for any of our acts, then we are responsible for being in the relevant ways how we are.

(3E) If we are responsible for being in the relevant ways how we are, then we can or could be responsible for an *infinite* series of "character-forming" actions.

(4E) It is not the case that we can or could be responsible for an *infinite* series of "character-forming" actions.

(5E) Therefore, it is false that we are responsible for any of our acts.

The **Impossibility Argument** and the **Manipulation Argument** share a common kernel: both place a great deal of stock in the idea that if we are to be responsible for our actions, these actions must originate "in us"; we must be their "final source." The **Manipulation Argument** seeks to convince us that, just as in cases involving manipulation that is responsibility-undermining, we are not responsible for our actions because our actions ultimately originate in sources external to us (they originate in the manipulator), so with causally determined actions, we are not responsible for them because they have their ultimate sources in the distant past and the laws. The **Impossibility Argument**, in slight contrast, seeks to persuade us that responsibility does require that we be the ultimate originators of our actions, but that it is impossible for us to be such originators. If this skeptical argument is sound, then it indirectly supports incompatibilism in this way: if we are not responsible for our actions regardless of whether determinism is true, then we are not responsible for our actions even if determinism is true.

Some theorists may be drawn to incompatibilism via yet another route. These theorists may first affirm that we *are* morally responsible for at least some of our behavior. This leaves open two possibilities:

1. The incompatibilist account is true, so this moral responsibility is consistent only with a libertarian account of action.*

2. The *compatibilist account of free action and responsibility* is true: this attempts to show that free action and responsibility are compatible with determinism.

---

* A view combining the positions that we have free will and that (therefore) determinism is false.

Then they might reason that, among the leading competing compatibilist and libertarian accounts of free action and responsibility, the best account is a libertarian one. They may, for example, call upon the **Manipulation Argument** to cast doubt on compatibilist rivals. Or, for instance, they might reason that ultimate origination is a requirement of free action and responsibility but no compatibilist competitor is up to the task of providing a suitably rich account of such origination. Their overall strategy would be to examine critically both compatibilist and libertarian contenders and then see which wins the day. In the view of these theorists it is a form of libertarianism that prevails. But if some version of libertarianism is true, then incompatibilism is victorious.

On one libertarian snapshot of free action, if you perform an action at a certain time, that action is free only if, given *exactly* the same past and the laws up until the time (or just prior to the time) at which you perform the action, you could then have performed some alternative instead. If determinism is true, this is impossible; you do not have such "genuine alternatives." For, assuming determinism, if you perform an action at a certain time, the past and the laws entail that you perform that action at that time. So if the past and the laws are "held fixed" right up to or just prior to the time at which you perform an action, it appears that it is not possible that, at that time, you perform some alternative instead. What may underlie this libertarian vision of free action? Either the garden-of-forking-paths picture of free action—the thought that free action and responsibility require that you have genuine alternatives so that it is "up to you" on which pathway into the future you tread; or the idea that responsibility requires that you be an ultimate originator of your choices or actions, something that is not possible if determinism is true; or, perhaps, both of these things. ■

Suggestions for Critical Reflection

1. What is your reaction to the Harris case? Do the details of Harris's life make you less inclined to blame him for his actions, and if so why do you think that is?

2. What is the stipulated difference between the Ann/Beth-1 and Ann/Beth-2 cases? Why does this change matter to the question of free will, do you think?

3. Which of the six arguments for incompatibilism raised by Haji do you think is the strongest? Are there any reasons to believe in incompatibilism that you think Haji might have missed?

4. The arguments for incompatibilism described in this reading tend to move from an intuition that Harris and/or Beth are not free or responsible, to a general claim that (if determinism is true) none of us are ever free. Examine how the arguments make this transition (if they do), and assess how plausibly they do so.

5. Haji says that "if 'ought' implies 'can,' then surely 'ought not' implies 'can refrain from.'" Does this follow? Even if it does not, how plausible do you find the latter claim?

Notes

1 Gary Watson, "Responsibility, and the Limits of Evil: Variations on a Strawsonian Theme," in Fisher and Ravizza, eds., *Perspectives on Moral Responsibility* (Ithaca, NY: Cornell UP, 1993).

2 Miles Corwin, *Los Angeles Times* (16 May 1982). Copyright, 1982, *Los Angeles Times*.

3 Watson 1993, p. 132.

4 Watson 1993, p. 132.

5 Watson 1993, p. 132.

6 Watson 1993, p. 134.

7 Watson 1993, pp. 135–36.

8 Alfred Mele, *Irrationality: An Essay on Akrasia, Self-Deception, and Self-Control* (NY: Oxford UP, 1995), 116.

9   Mele 1995, p. 172; Mele, *Free Will and Luck* (NY: Oxford UP, 2006), 164–65.

10 John M. Fischer, "Compatibilism," in Fischer, Kane, Pereboom and Vargas, *Four Views on Free Will* (Oxford: Blackwell, 2007), 46.

11 Peter van Inwagen, *An Essay on Free Will* (Oxford: Oxford UP, 1983), 16.

HARRY G. FRANKFURT

Alternate Possibilities and Moral Responsibility

Who Was Harry Frankfurt?

Harry Frankfurt (1929–2023) taught at Ohio State University, Yale University, Harpur College, Rockefeller University, and Princeton University. He published eight books and dozens of academic articles on topics in ethics, free will, philosophy of mind, and early modern philosophy. Frankfurt is perhaps best remembered for his work on autonomy and moral responsibility, and his writing has been widely praised for its clarity and concision. In addition to his academic scholarship, Frankfurt also published non-fiction writing suitable to a general audience.

His 2005 book *On Bullshit* was a *New York Times* bestseller, receiving popular media coverage and leading to a television interview on *The Daily Show with Jon Stewart*. *On Bullshit* examines acts of deceptive communication in which the speaker attempts to persuade others by disregarding the truth of what is being said, as opposed to lies, in which the speaker attempts to deliberately hide the truth. In 2006 he published a follow-up book, *On Truth*.

What Is the Structure of This Reading?

Frankfurt frames this paper as an argument against what he calls "the principle of alternate possibilities." This widely-held principle, which has at times been used in arguments against the possibility of free will, holds that "a person is morally responsible for what he has done only if he could have done otherwise." The intuitive appeal of this principle can be seen most easily in cases of coercion: we don't typically say that someone is guilty of a crime or other moral transgression if that person was coerced into action by someone else—say, by being held at gunpoint. Similarly, if we found that someone had caused unwarranted harm to another but we then discovered that some sort of physical obstruction would have made it impossible for them to do otherwise, we might conclude that they are not morally responsible for what they've done. If, for example, a person knowingly drove their vehicle into someone else, we would likely find them innocent of what would otherwise be a horrific moral transgression if in fact the vehicle's steering and braking mechanisms had malfunctioned, preventing any other course of action.

Frankfurt argues that the principle of alternate possibilities is false. In order to do this, he needs only to show that there is at least one case in which a person is responsible for their actions and yet could not have done otherwise. Frankfurt offers a series of related examples involving a fictional person named Jones, distinguishing them from one another by the use of subscript numbers: $Jones_1$, $Jones_2$, $Jones_3$, and $Jones_4$. In each of these cases, Jones is said to have performed some immoral action, and in each case Jones is unable to do other than he has done due to some external condition: a coercive threat in the first three cases; a more direct form of control in the fourth. If the principle of alternate possibilities were true, then Jones would not be responsible for his actions in any of these scenarios. And yet, Frankfurt argues, he is clearly morally responsible in at least some of them (in particular, $Jones_4$), and so the principle of alternate possibilities cannot be true. Toward the end of this reading, Frankfurt proposes that a modified version of the principle may be true, and this revised version would accurately distinguish between the cases in which Jones is responsible and those in which he is not.

A Common Misconception

This paper concerns the moral responsibility of people, not their legal responsibility. In order to establish his arguments, Frankfurt stipulates the intentions and reasoning of the people in his examples. In reality, and in a courtroom, we cannot, of course, know a person's intentions with certainty. So, even if Frankfurt is right about the truth of the principle of alternate possibilities, this may not mean that we should abandon the principle in our legal and everyday practices.

Alternate Possibilities and Moral Responsibility*

A dominant role in nearly all recent inquiries into the free-will problem has been played by a principle which I shall call "the principle of alternate possibilities." This principle states that a person is morally responsible for what he has done only if he could have done otherwise. Its exact meaning is a subject of controversy, particularly concerning whether someone who accepts it is thereby committed to believing that moral responsibility and determinism are incompatible. Practically no one, however, seems inclined to deny or even to question that the principle of alternate possibilities (construed in some way or other) is true. It has generally seemed so overwhelmingly plausible that some philosophers have even characterized it as an *a priori* truth.† People whose accounts of free will or of moral responsibility are radically at odds evidently find in it a firm and convenient common ground upon which they can profitably take their opposing stands.

But the principle of alternate possibilities is false. A person may well be morally responsible for what he has done even though he could not have done otherwise. The principle's plausibility is an illusion, which can be made to vanish by bringing the relevant moral phenomena into sharper focus.

I

In seeking illustrations of the principle of alternate possibilities, it is most natural to think of situations in which the same circumstances both bring it about that a person does something and make it impossible for him to avoid doing it. These include, for example, situations in which a person is coerced into doing something, or in which he is impelled to act by a hypnotic suggestion, or in which some inner compulsion drives him to do what he does. In situations of these kinds there are circumstances that make it impossible for the person to do otherwise, and these very circumstances also serve to bring it about that he does whatever it is that he does.

However, there may be circumstances that constitute sufficient conditions‡ for a certain action to be performed by someone and that therefore make it impossible for the person to do otherwise, but that do not actually impel the person to act or in any way produce his action. A person may do something in circumstances that leave him no alternative to doing it, without these circumstances actually moving him or leading him to do it—without them playing any role, indeed, in bringing it about that he does what he does.

An examination of situations characterized by circumstances of this sort casts doubt, I believe, on the relevance to questions of moral responsibility of the fact that a person who has done something could not have done otherwise. I propose to develop some examples of this kind in the context of a discussion of coercion and to suggest that our moral intuitions concerning these examples tend to disconfirm the principle of alternate possibilities. Then I will discuss the principle in more general terms, explain what I think is wrong with it, and describe briefly and without argument how it might appropriately be revised.

II

It is generally agreed that a person who has been coerced to do something did not do it freely and is not morally responsible for having done it. Now the doctrine that coercion and moral responsibility are mutually exclusive may appear to be no more than a somewhat particularized version of the principle of alternate possibilities. It is natural enough to say of a person who has been coerced to do something that he could not have done otherwise. And it may easily seem that being coerced deprives a person of freedom and of moral responsibility simply because it is a special

---

* Harry Frankfurt, "Alternate Possibilities and Moral Responsibility," *The Journal of Philosophy* 66, 23 (1969): 829–39.

† A truth that can be derived from reason alone, independent of experience. In this context, the expression may be taken to mean that the principle is thought to be necessarily true, without the need of further evidence.

‡ A set of conditions is *sufficient* for X if those conditions will cause X regardless of whether or not any other conditions hold.

case of being unable to do otherwise. The principle of alternate possibilities may in this way derive some credibility from its association with the very plausible proposition that moral responsibility is excluded by coercion.

It is not right, however, that it should do so. The fact that a person was coerced to act as he did may entail both that he could not have done otherwise and that he bears no moral responsibility for his action. But his lack of moral responsibility is not entailed by his having been unable to do otherwise. The doctrine that coercion excludes moral responsibility is not correctly understood, in other words, as a particularized version of the principle of alternate possibilities.

Let us suppose that someone is threatened convincingly with a penalty he finds unacceptable and that he then does what is required of him by the issuer of the threat. We can imagine details that would make it reasonable for us to think that the person was coerced to perform the action in question, that he could not have done otherwise, and that he bears no moral responsibility for having done what he did. But just what is it about situations of this kind that warrants the judgment that the threatened person is not morally responsible for his act?

This question may be approached by considering situations of the following kind. Jones decides for reasons of his own to do something, then someone threatens him with a very harsh penalty (so harsh that any reasonable person would submit to the threat) unless he does precisely that, and Jones does it. Will we hold Jones morally responsible for what he has done? I think this will depend on the roles we think were played, in leading him to act, by his original decision and by the threat.

One possibility is that Jones$_1$ is not a reasonable man: he is, rather, a man who does what he has once decided to do no matter what happens next and no matter what the cost. In that case, the threat actually exerted no effective force upon him. He acted without any regard to it, very much as if he were not aware that it had been made. If this is indeed the way it was, the situation did not involve coercion at all. The threat did not lead Jones$_1$ to do what he did. Nor was it in fact sufficient to have prevented him from doing otherwise: if his earlier decision had been to do something else, the threat would not have deterred him in the slightest. It seems evident that in these circumstances

the fact that Jones$_1$ was threatened in no way reduces the moral responsibility he would otherwise bear for his act. This example, however, is not a counterexample either to the doctrine that coercion excuses or to the principle of alternate possibilities. For we have supposed that Jones$_1$ is a man upon whom the threat had no coercive effect and, hence, that it did not actually deprive him of alternatives to doing what he did.

Another possibility is that Jones$_2$ was stampeded by the threat. Given that threat, he would have performed that action regardless of what decision he had already made. The threat upset him so profoundly, moreover, that he completely forgot his own earlier decision and did what was demanded of him entirely because he was terrified of the penalty with which he was threatened. In this case, it is not relevant to his having performed the action that he had already decided on his own to perform it. When the chips were down he thought of nothing but the threat, and fear alone led him to act. The fact that at an earlier time Jones$_2$ had decided for his own reasons to act in just that way may be relevant to an evaluation of his character; he may bear full moral responsibility for having made *that* decision. But he can hardly be said to be morally responsible for his action. For he performed the action simply as a result of the coercion to which he was subjected. His earlier decision played no role in bringing it about that he did what he did, and it would therefore be gratuitous to assign it a role in the moral evaluation of his action.

Now consider a third possibility. Jones$_3$ was neither stampeded by the threat nor indifferent to it. The threat impressed him, as it would impress any reasonable man, and he would have submitted to it wholeheartedly if he had not already made a decision that coincided with the one demanded of him. In fact, however, he performed the action in question on the basis of the decision he had made before the threat was issued. When he acted, he was not actually motivated by the threat but solely by the considerations that had originally commended the action to him. It was not the threat that led him to act, though it would have done so if he had not already provided himself with a sufficient motive for performing the action in question.

No doubt it will be very difficult for anyone to know, in a case like this one, exactly what happened. Did Jones$_3$ perform the action because of the threat, or were his reasons for acting simply those which had already persuaded him to do so? Or did he act on the basis of two motives, each of which was sufficient for his action? It is not impossible, however, that the situation should be clearer than situations of this kind usually are. And suppose it is apparent to us that Jones₃ acted on the basis of his own decision and not because of the threat. Then I think we would be justified in regarding his moral responsibility for what he did as unaffected by the threat even though, since he would in any case have submitted to the threat, he could not have avoided doing what he did. It would be entirely reasonable for us to make the same judgment concerning his moral responsibility that we would have made if we had not known of the threat. For the threat did not in fact influence his performance of the action. He did what he did just as if the threat had not been made at all.

III

The case of Jones₃ may appear at first glance to combine coercion and moral responsibility, and thus to provide a counterexample to the doctrine that coercion excuses. It is not really so certain that it does so, however, because it is unclear whether the example constitutes a genuine instance of coercion. Can we say of Jones₃ that he was coerced to do something, when he had already decided on his own to do it and when he did it entirely on the basis of that decision? Or would it be more correct to say that Jones₃ was not coerced to do what he did, even though he himself recognized that there was an irresistible force at work in virtue of which he had to do it? My own linguistic intuitions lead me toward the second alternative, but they are somewhat equivocal.* Perhaps we can say either of these things, or perhaps we must add a qualifying explanation to whichever of them we say.

This murkiness, however, does not interfere with our drawing an important moral from an examination of the example. Suppose we decide to say that Jones₃ was *not* coerced. Our basis for saying this will clearly be that it is incorrect to regard a man as being coerced to do something unless he does it *because of* the coercive force exerted against him. The fact that an

irresistible threat is made will not, then, entail that the person who receives it is coerced to do what he does. It will also be necessary that the threat is what actually accounts for his doing it. On the other hand, suppose we decide to say that Jones₃ *was* coerced. Then we will be bound to admit that being coerced does not exclude being morally responsible. And we will also surely be led to the view that coercion affects the judgment of a person's moral responsibility only when the person acts as he does because he is coerced to do so—i.e., when the fact that he is coerced is what accounts for his action.

Whichever we decide to say, then, we will recognize that the doctrine that coercion excludes moral responsibility is not a particularized version of the principle of alternate possibilities. Situations in which a person who does something cannot do otherwise because he is subject to coercive power are either not instances of coercion at all, or they are situations in which the person may still be morally responsible for what he does if it is not because of the coercion that he does it. When we excuse a person who has been coerced, we do not excuse him because he was unable to do otherwise. Even though a person is subject to a coercive force that precludes his performing any action but one, he may nonetheless bear full moral responsibility for performing that action.

IV

To the extent that the principle of alternate possibilities derives its plausibility from association with the doctrine that coercion excludes moral responsibility, a clear understanding of the latter diminishes the appeal of the former. Indeed the case of Jones₃ may appear to do more than illuminate the relationship between the two doctrines. It may well seem to provide a decisive counterexample to the principle of alternate possibilities and thus to show that this principle is false. For the irresistibility of the threat to which Jones₃ is subjected might well be taken to mean that he cannot but perform the action he performs. And yet the threat, since Jones₃ performs the action without regard to it, does not reduce his moral responsibility for what he does.

---

*	In describing this question in terms of "linguistic intuitions," Frankfurt emphasizes that the answer depends on how we define and use the term "coercion," and competent English-speakers may disagree about this.

The following objection will doubtless be raised against the suggestion that the case of Jones$_3$ is a counterexample to the principle of alternate possibilities. There is perhaps a sense in which Jones$_3$ cannot do otherwise than perform the action he performs, since he is a reasonable man and the threat he encounters is sufficient to move any reasonable man. But it is not this sense that is germane to the principle of alternate possibilities. His knowledge that he stands to suffer an intolerably harsh penalty does not mean that Jones$_3$, strictly speaking, *cannot* perform any action but the one he does perform. After all it is still open to him, and this is crucial, to defy the threat if he wishes to do so and to accept the penalty his action would bring down upon him. In the sense in which the principle of alternate possibilities employs the concept of "could have done otherwise," Jones$_3$'s inability to resist the threat does not mean that he cannot do otherwise than perform the action he performs. Hence the case of Jones$_3$ does not constitute an instance contrary to the principle.

I do not propose to consider in what sense the concept of "could have done otherwise" figures in the principle of alternate possibilities, nor will I attempt to measure the force of the objection I have just described.[1] For I believe that whatever force this objection may be thought to have can be deflected by altering the example in the following way.[2] Suppose someone—Black, let us say—wants Jones$_4$ to perform a certain action. Black is prepared to go to considerable lengths to get his way, but he prefers to avoid showing his hand unnecessarily. So he waits until Jones$_4$ is about to make up his mind what to do, and he does nothing unless it is clear to him (Black is an excellent judge of such things) that Jones$_4$ is going to decide to do something *other* than what he wants him to do. If it does become clear that Jones$_4$ is going to decide to do something else, Black takes effective steps to ensure that Jones$_4$ decides to do, and that he does do, what he wants him to do.[3] Whatever Jones$_4$'s initial preferences and inclinations, then, Black will have his way.

What steps will Black take, if he believes he must take steps, in order to ensure that Jones$_4$ decides and acts as he wishes? Anyone with a theory concerning what "could have done otherwise" means may answer this question for himself by describing whatever measures he would regard as sufficient to guarantee that, in the relevant sense, Jones$_4$ cannot do otherwise. Let Black pronounce a terrible threat, and in this way both force Jones$_4$ to perform the desired action and prevent him from performing a forbidden one. Let Black give Jones$_4$ a potion, or put him under hypnosis, and in some such way as these generate in Jones$_4$ an irresistible inner compulsion to perform the act Black wants performed and to avoid others. Or let Black manipulate the minute processes of Jones$_4$'s brain and nervous system in some more direct way, so that causal forces running in and out of his synapses and along the poor man's nerves determine that he chooses to act and that he does act in the one way and not in any other. Given any conditions under which it will be maintained that Jones$_4$ cannot do otherwise, in other words, let Black bring it about that those conditions prevail. The structure of the example is flexible enough, I think, to find a way around any charge of irrelevance by accommodating the doctrine on which the charge is based.[4]

Now suppose that Black never has to show his hand because Jones$_4$, for reasons of his own, decides to perform and does perform the very action Black wants him to perform. In that case, it seems clear, Jones$_4$ will bear precisely the same moral responsibility for what he does as he would have borne if Black had not been ready to take steps to ensure that he do it. It would be quite unreasonable to excuse Jones$_4$ for his action, or to withhold the praise to which it would normally entitle him, on the basis of the fact that he could not have done otherwise. This fact played no role at all in leading him to act as he did. He would have acted the same even if it had not been a fact. Indeed, everything happened just as it would have happened without Black's presence in the situation and without his readiness to intrude into it.

In this example there are sufficient conditions for Jones$_4$'s performing the action in question. What action he performs is not up to him. Of course it is in a way up to him whether he acts on his own or as a result of Black's intervention. That depends upon what action he himself is inclined to perform. But whether he finally acts on his own or as a result of Black's intervention, he performs the same action. He has no alternative but to do what Black wants him to do. If he does it on his own, however, his moral responsibility for doing it is not affected by the fact that Black was lurking in the background with sinister intent, since this intent never comes into play.

V

The fact that a person could not have avoided doing something is a sufficient condition of his having done it. But, as some of my examples show, this fact may play no role whatever in the explanation of why he did it. It may not figure at all among the circumstances that actually brought it about that he did what he did, so that his action is to be accounted for on another basis entirely. Even though the person was unable to do otherwise, that is to say, it may not be the case that he acted as he did *because* he could not have done otherwise. Now if someone had no alternative to performing a certain action but did not perform it because he was unable to do otherwise, then he would have performed exactly the same action even if he *could* have done otherwise. The circumstances that made it impossible for him to do otherwise could have been subtracted from the situation without affecting what happened or why it happened in any way. Whatever it was that actually led the person to do what he did, or that made him do it, would have led him to do it or made him do it even if it had been possible for him to do something else instead.

Thus it would have made no difference, so far as concerns his action or how he came to perform it, if the circumstances that made it impossible for him to avoid performing it had not prevailed. The fact that he could not have done otherwise clearly provides no basis for supposing that he *might* have done otherwise if he had been able to do so. When a fact is in this way irrelevant to the problem of accounting for a person's action it seems quite gratuitous to assign it any weight in the assessment of his moral responsibility. Why should the fact be considered in reaching a moral judgment concerning the person when it does not help in any way to understand either what made him act as he did or what, in other circumstances, he might have done?

This, then, is why the principle of alternate possibilities is mistaken. It asserts that a person bears no moral responsibility—that is, he is to be excused—for having performed an action if there were circumstances that made it impossible for him to avoid performing it. But there may be circumstances that make it impossible for a person to avoid performing some action without those circumstances in any way bringing it about that he performs that action.

It would surely be no good for the person to refer to circumstances of this sort in an effort to absolve himself of moral responsibility for performing the action in question. For those circumstances, by hypothesis, actually had nothing to do with his having done what he did. He would have done precisely the same thing, and he would have been led or made in precisely the same way to do it, even if they had not prevailed.

We often do, to be sure, excuse people for what they have done when they tell us (and we believe them) that they could not have done otherwise. But this is because we assume that what they tell us serves to explain why they did what they did. We take it for granted that they are not being disingenuous, as a person would be who cited as an excuse the fact that he could not have avoided doing what he did but who knew full well that it was not at all because of this that he did it.

What I have said may suggest that the principle of alternate possibilities should be revised so as to assert that a person is not morally responsible for what he has done if he did it because he could not have done otherwise. It may be noted that this revision of the principle does not seriously affect the arguments of those who have relied on the original principle in their efforts to maintain that moral responsibility and determinism are incompatible. For if it was causally determined that a person perform a certain action, then it will be true that the person performed it because of those causal determinants. And if the fact that it was causally determined that a person perform a certain action means that the person could not have done otherwise, as philosophers who argue for the incompatibility thesis characteristically suppose, then the fact that it was causally determined that a person perform a certain action will mean that the person performed it because he could not have done otherwise. The revised principle of alternate possibilities will entail, on this assumption concerning the meaning of 'could have done otherwise', that a person is not morally responsible for what he has done if it was causally determined that he do it. I do not believe, however, that this revision of the principle is acceptable.

Suppose a person tells us that he did what he did because he was unable to do otherwise; or suppose he makes the similar statement that he did what he did because he had to do it. We do often accept statements like these (if we believe them) as valid excuses, and such statements may well seem at first glance to invoke the revised principle of alternate possibilities. But I think that when we accept such statements as valid excuses it is because we assume that we are being told more than the statements strictly and literally convey. We understand the person who offers the excuse to mean that he did what he did *only because* he was unable to do otherwise, or *only because* he had to do it. And we understand him to mean, more particularly, that when he did what he did it was not because that was what he really wanted to do. The principle of alternate possibilities should thus be replaced, in my opinion, by the following principle: a person is not morally responsible for what he has done if he did it only because he could not have done otherwise. This principle does not appear to conflict with the view that moral responsibility is compatible with determinism.

The following may all be true: there were circumstances that made it impossible for a person to avoid doing something; these circumstances actually played a role in bringing it about that he did it, so that it is correct to say that he did it because he could not have done otherwise; the person really wanted to do what he did; he did it because it was what he really wanted to do, so that it is not correct to say that he did what he did only because he could not have done otherwise. Under these conditions, the person may well be morally responsible for what he has done. On the other hand, he will not be morally responsible for what he has done if he did it only because he could not have done otherwise, even if what he did was something he really wanted to do. ■

Suggestions for Critical Reflection

1. The effectiveness of Frankfurt's argument depends on the success of his purported counter-examples. Do you agree with Frankfurt's intuitions about which versions of Jones are responsible? Why or why not?

2. In Frankfurt's counter-examples, Jones is alleged to be morally responsible because he has decided on a course of action independent of the restrictions on his alternate possibilities. But if coercion is not the cause of Jones's decisions, what is? Are these decisions themselves determined by prior conditions, and if so, does this have any bearing on the question of Jones's responsibility?

3. The broader philosophical debate on free will often assumes that either a great many of our actions are performed freely or none of them are, and so we're either very often responsible for our actions (if we have free will) or never responsible (if we do not). In this paper, Frankfurt's claims about moral responsibility seem to pertain to only a much smaller subset of actions involving uncommon scenarios of restriction on possible action. How does Frankfurt's argument bear on the broader debate about free will and responsibility?

4. Suppose you are tasked with assessing the moral guilt of an apparently-coerced person, and yet you are unable to determine the interplay between the apparent coercion and the person's actions. That is, because you can't directly observe the person's reasoning, you don't know whether their case is more similar to that of $Jones_1$, $Jones_2$, etc. How should you proceed? Is it best to adopt something like the principle of alternate possibilities as a practical rule in guiding our judgments about responsibility? Why or why not?

5. Consider this case: A child has fallen into a swimming pool, and $Jones_4$ hears her cries for help. He can swim, and could easily have saved the child, but he's too busy watching TV and doesn't want to get his clothes wet, so he does nothing. But he couldn't have saved the child even had he decided to, because the gate to the swimming pool had (unknown to anybody) been locked, and nobody could have gotten in on time. Is $Jones_4$ morally responsible for the child's death? Does Frankfurt's analysis apply here? Is it helpful?

Notes

1 The two main concepts employed in the principle of alternate possibilities are "morally responsible" and "could have done otherwise." To discuss the principle without analyzing either of these concepts may well seem like an attempt at piracy. The reader should take notice that my Jolly Roger is now unfurled.

2 After thinking up the example that I am about to develop I learned that Robert Nozick, in lectures given several years ago, had formulated an example of the same general type and had proposed it as a counterexample to the principle of alternate possibilities.

3 The assumption that Black can predict what $Jones_4$ will decide to do does not beg the question of determinism. We can imagine that $Jones_4$ has often confronted the alternatives—*A* and *B*—that he now confronts, and that his face has invariably twitched when he was about to decide to do *A* and never when he was about to decide to do *B*. Knowing this, and observing the twitch, Black would have a basis for prediction. This does, to be sure, suppose that there is some sort of causal relation between $Jones_4$'s state at the time of the twitch and his subsequent states. But any plausible view of decision or of action will allow that reaching a decision and performing an action both involve earlier and later phases, with causal relations between them, and such that the earlier phases are not themselves part of the decision or of the action. The example does not require that these earlier phases be deterministically related to still earlier events.

4 The example is also flexible enough to allow for the elimination of Black altogether. Anyone who thinks that the effectiveness of the example is undermined by its reliance on a human manipulator, who imposes his will on $Jones_4$, can substitute for Black a machine programmed to do what Black does. If this is still not good enough, forget both Black and the machine and suppose that their role is played by natural forces involving no will or design at all.

Personal Identity

Who are you? What makes you *you*? One way to think about this is to think about the things about yourself that could be changed while still leaving you the same person. We'll approach this issue by imagining changes over time: you start out being just the way you are now, and have been, and then a radical change happens. The question is: will you still exist in a quite different form? Or would this mean that you cease to exist? How different could your body be? You could lose a limb or change sex and still be you, most people assume, but what if 'you' changed into a different species, or lost your biological body (if you became a robot or a ghost, for example)? How much could your psychology change while still being the psychology of the same person? How much personality change would result in you becoming a different person? What if you had severe amnesia and could no longer remember anything that happened to you before last week, or if all your memories of that time were

replaced by false memories—are you still the same person 'you' were then?

This chapter deals with these issues. The approach we take to them is broadly metaphysical. Informally, one might think of their 'personal identity' as involving the values and beliefs about oneself that one feels especially committed to: perhaps you define yourself as being a musician, being from New Zealand, being a lesbian, being a good hockey player, or having red hair. This kind of self-identity might be something that is largely up to you—you can decide what it is about yourself that you think is particularly important—and it might change over time. It might even involve beliefs about yourself that aren't true (if you falsely believe that you are the lost heir to the Russian throne, for example). In this chapter, however, when we talk about personal identity what we have in mind is some fact of the matter that is not up to you—that is what it is independently of what you believe about it. Just as, we might think, there is something that makes gold gold, or a giraffe a giraffe, or the White House the White House, in the same way there is something that makes you you—our task is to work out what it is.* And, many philosophers think, the question of *personal* identity—what makes individual persons the persons they are—is especially interesting and significant. It turns out (arguably) to be a lot more philosophically puzzling than the question of what makes gold gold. Furthermore, the stakes are higher: we are especially interested in what it takes for a person—ourselves, for example—to continue to exist, rather than to cease to exist; and we are also interested in what makes something a person rather than a non-person, since this might well have important moral and legal implications.

The question of personal identity is one that has a long and complex philosophical history, but to simplify the terrain somewhat we can say that there are four basic positions on the self:

1. Biological views. Roughly, we are our bodies, or parts of our bodies. If your body changes enough you will cease to exist (and possibly another different person will come into existence). On some versions of this view, what makes a human person the particular person that they are is a biological fact about them, not all that different from what makes any animal the animal it is.
2. Psychological views. There is something about our psychological states that makes us the persons we are. For us to persist through time as the same person only requires that there be some appropriate kind of continuity in our psychology—for example, for our past and present mental states to be connected through memories, or by an unbroken stream of consciousness, or for our psychology to be unified by our status as agents who can make plans and carry them out.
3. Substance dualist views. Our selves are a special kind of non-physical object—something like a soul or an ego. These selves typically are intimately attached to a physical body, but that connection is only contingent and we would continue to be the

same person even with a different body or no body at all so long as our soul persists.
4. Non-self views. Personal identity is a comforting myth. There is no such thing as the persistence of a person through time, and none of the biological and psychological facts about us require appeal to the notion of a self. (Consider the Buddhist doctrine of *anattā* or non-self, for example.)

The readings in this chapter focus on the strategy of understanding personal identity in terms of psychological continuity—that is, option 2. above. The modern form of this view originates with John Locke, in the first selection in this chapter. There, Locke argues that what makes us the person we are is our consciousness, rather than our bodies, and furthermore that an individual consciousness is tied together over time by being connected through memories. The following article by Daniel Dennett hammers home, in a very entertaining way, the complexities and perplexities of the issue. The next reading is a very influential article by Derek Parfit in which he argues that psychological continuity fails as an account of personal identity, and suggests that psychological *connectedness*—which can be a matter of degree, and can connect us to more than one possible past or future self—is a more important element in personal survival than continuity.

If you want to explore the philosophy of the self further—and perhaps investigate the other three approaches that are not foregrounded here—there are many resources available. Some good collections of articles include: John Perry, ed., *Personal Identity* (University of California Press, 2008); Martin and Barresi, eds., *Personal Identity* (Blackwell, 2003); Bermúdez, Marcel, and Eilan, eds., *The Body and the Self* (MIT Press, 1995); S. Gallagher, ed., *The Oxford Handbook of the Self* (Oxford University Press, 2011); Gallagher and Shear, eds., *Models of the Self* (Imprint Academic, 1999); and Amelie O. Rorty, ed., *The Identities of Persons* (University of California Press, 1976).

Some relatively recent influential books are: L.R. Baker, *Persons and Bodies: A Constitution View* (Cambridge University Press, 2000); R. Chisholm, *Person and Object* (Open Court, 1976); B. Garrett, *Personal Identity and*

---

* The identity relation in question, then, is what is sometimes known as 'numerical identity': it is a relation every thing bears to itself, and to nothing else.

Self-Consciousness (Routledge, 1998); A. Kind, *Persons and Personal Identity* (Polity Press, 2015); G. Kopf, *Beyond Personal Identity: Dōgen, Nishida, and a Phenomenology of No-Self* (Routledge, 2001); E.J. Lowe, *Subjects of Experience* (Cambridge University Press, 1996); H. Noonan, *Personal Identity* (Routledge, 2003); E. Olson, *The Human Animal: Personal Identity without Psychology* (Oxford University Press, 1997); D. Parfit, *Reasons and Persons* (Oxford University Press, 1984); J. Perry, *Identity, Personal Identity, and the Self* (Hackett, 2002); Shoemaker and Swinburne, *Personal Identity* (Wiley-Blackwell, 1991); P. Snowdon, *Persons, Animals, Ourselves* (Oxford University Press, 2014); P. Unger, *Identity, Consciousness, and Value* (Oxford University Press, 1990); and K.V. Wilkes, *Real People: Personal Identity without Thought Experiments* (Oxford University Press, 1988).

A few representative articles include: W.R. Carter, "How to Change Your Mind," *Canadian Journal of Philosophy* 19 (1989): 1–14; M. Johnston, "Human Beings," *Journal of Philosophy* 84 (1987): 59–83; T. Nagel, "Brain Bisection and the Unity of Consciousness," *Synthèse* 22 (1971): 396–413; and D. Parfit, "We Are Not Human Beings," *Philosophy* 87 (2012): 5–28.

JOHN LOCKE

FROM *An Essay Concerning Human Understanding*

For information on Locke's life and overall philosophical project, please see the introduction to Locke earlier in the Theory of Knowledge chapter of this volume.

What Is the Structure of This Reading?

In this selection from the *Essay Concerning Human Understanding* (1690), Locke evaluates the concept of identity to determine how we decide that one thing is the same at different intervals in time. In the case of living beings, Locke argues, identity is based upon participation in the same life. It is possible for a living thing to change particles and still be the same: a tree may shed its leaves, and still have the same identity.

For people, Locke notes, the situation is more complex. It is difficult to determine what we mean when we say that a young person in the past and an old person in the present share an identity (that is, are the same individual). Locke proposes that we distinguish between one's identity as a "human" (or "man," in Locke's dated phrasing) and as a "person." In his view, a human persists over time much as a tree does, in that one can be called the same human so long as the same living body has persisted from one moment to the next. A person, on the other hand, is "a thinking intelligent being, that has reason and reflection, and can consider itself as itself, the same thinking thing, in different times and places; which it does only by that consciousness which is inseparable from thinking, and, as it seems to me, essential to it." Because it is consciousness that makes one a person, it is the persistence of consciousness that makes one the same person from one moment to the next, according to Locke.

A person's body may change—it may, for example, develop wrinkles—but the person will remain the same as long as they have the same consciousness. And what counts as the same consciousness, from an earlier time to a later, is that the later one can remember the experiences of the earlier one. Memory conjoins the past and present, allowing a person to persist over time. Locke offers the example of a prince's consciousness and memories suddenly transferring into the body of a cobbler. Locke claims that in

such a scenario, we would hold that the prince now *is* the person inhabiting the cobbler's body; his ability to recollect the prince's memories establishes that he is the same person that previously inhabited the princely body. This shows that personal identity is a matter of shared consciousness and memory, and not a matter of bodily continuity.

Some Useful Background Information

1. Locke's contention that consciousness is the seat of personal identity builds upon the ideas of his philosophical predecessor René Descartes (see the Descartes selection from the Theory of Knowledge chapter of this volume). Descartes famously held that the thinking subject or "cogito" is the foundation of the self. Locke's contribution to Descartes's theory of identity is the notion that personhood is found in connected consciousness: a person's identity stretches only as far back as they can recall.

2. On the other hand Locke, unlike Descartes, asserts that selves are not substances—continuity of substance is a quite different issue than continuity of self, writes Locke, and it is quite coherent to suppose one self surviving through a change of substance, or two substances combining to compose one connected consciousness and hence one self, or even one substance composing two different selves at different times. This is in line with Locke's general skepticism about the possibility of having a clear idea what substance actually is. (See the Locke reading in the Theory of Knowledge chapter for more on this.)

3. When Locke brings up the possibility of a cat or parrot exercising reason, he is responding to Aristotle's famous definition of "man" as a "rational animal." Locke rejects Aristotle's account of human existence, because it is possible to imagine an animal gaining intellectual and discursive capabilities on par with those of a human. If a parrot is able to reason as well as a human, this does not mean that a parrot is therefore human, as Aristotle's theory would seem to require.

FROM *An Essay Concerning Human Understanding**
BOOK II, CHAPTER XXVII: OF IDENTITY AND DIVERSITY

§8. An animal is a living organized body; and consequently the same animal, as we have observed, is the same continued life communicated to different particles of matter, as they happen successively to be united to that organized living body. And whatever is talked of other definitions, ingenious observation puts it past doubt, that the idea in our minds, of which the sound man in our mouths is the sign,† is nothing else but of an animal of such a certain form: since I think I may be confident, that, whoever should see a creature of his own shape or make, though it had no more reason all its life than a cat or a parrot, would call him still a man; or whoever should hear a cat or a parrot discourse, reason, and philosophize, would call or think it nothing but a cat or a parrot; and say, the one was a dull irrational man, and the other a very intelligent rational parrot.... For I presume it is not the idea of a thinking or rational being alone that makes the idea of a man in most people's sense: but of a body, so and so shaped, joined to it: and if that be the idea of a man, the same successive body not shifted all at once, must, as well as the same immaterial spirit, go to the making of the same man.

§9. This being premised, to find wherein personal identity consists, we must consider what *person* stands for; which, I think, is a thinking intelligent being, that has reason and reflection, and can consider itself as itself, the same thinking thing, in different times and places; which it does only by that consciousness which is inseparable from thinking, and, as it seems to me, essential to it: it being impossible for anyone to perceive without perceiving that he does perceive. When we see, hear, smell, taste, feel, meditate, or will anything, we know that we do so. Thus it is always as to our present sensations and perceptions: and by this everyone is to himself that which he calls self; it not being considered in this case whether the same self be continued in the same or diverse substances. For, since consciousness always accompanies thinking, and it is that which makes everyone to be what he calls self, and thereby distinguishes himself from all other thinking things, in this alone consists personal identity, i.e. the sameness of a rational being: and as far as this consciousness can be extended backwards to any past action or thought, so far reaches the identity of that person; it is the same self now it was then; and it is by the same self with this present one that now reflects on it, that that action was done.

§10. But it is farther inquired, whether it be the same identical substance. This few would think they had reason to doubt of, if these perceptions, with their consciousness, always remained present in the mind, whereby the same thinking thing would be always consciously present, and, as would be thought, evidently the same to itself. But that which seems to make the difficulty is this, that this consciousness being interrupted always by forgetfulness, there being no moment of our lives wherein we have the whole train of all our past actions before our eyes in one view, but even the best memories losing the sight of one part whilst they are viewing another; and we sometimes, and that the greatest part of our lives, not reflecting on our past selves, being intent on our present thoughts, and in sound sleep having no thoughts at all, or at least none with that consciousness which remarks our waking thoughts: I say, in all these cases, our consciousness being interrupted, and we losing the sight of our past selves, doubts are raised whether we are the same thinking thing, i.e. the same substance or no. Which, however reasonable or unreasonable, concerns not personal identity at all: the question being what makes the same person; and not whether it be the same identical

---

* Locke's *An Essay Concerning Human Understanding* was first published in 1690. The excerpts given here are from the sixth edition of 1710, reprinted from Locke's 10-volume *Collected Works* (first published in 1714 and reprinted with corrections in 1823).

† "Of which the sound man in our mouths is the sign": of which the symbol (for the idea) is the word "man."

substance, which always thinks in the same person; which in this case matters not at all: different substances, by the same consciousness (where they do partake in it) being united into one person, as well as different bodies by the same life are united into one animal, whose identity is preserved, in that change of substances, by the unity of one continued life. For, it being the same consciousness that makes a man be himself to himself, personal identity depends on that only, whether it be annexed solely to one individual substance, or can be continued in a succession of several substances. For as far as any intelligent being can repeat the idea of any past action with the same consciousness it had of it at first, and with the same consciousness it has of any present action; so far it is the same personal self. For it is by the consciousness it has of its present thoughts and actions, that it is self to itself now, and so will be the same self, as far as the same consciousness can extend to actions past or to come; and would be by distance of time, or change of substance, no more two persons, than a man be two men by wearing other clothes today than he did yesterday, with a long or a short sleep between: the same consciousness uniting those distant actions into the same person, whatever substances contributed to their production.

§11. That this is so, we have some kind of evidence in our very bodies, all whose particles, whilst vitally united to this same thinking conscious self, so that we feel when they are touched, and are affected by, and conscious of good or harm that happens to them, are a part of ourselves; i.e. of our thinking conscious self. Thus, the limbs of his body are to everyone a part of himself; he sympathizes and is concerned for them. Cut off a hand, and thereby separate it from that consciousness he had of its heat, cold, and other affections, and it is then no longer a part of that which is himself, any more than the remotest part of matter. Thus, we see the substance whereof personal self consisted at one time may be varied at another, without the change of personal identity; there being no question about the same person, though the limbs which but now were a part of it, be cut off.

§12. But the question is, "whether if the same substance which thinks be changed, it can be the same person; or, remaining the same, it can be different persons?"

And to this I answer, first, This can be no question at all to those who place thought in a purely material animal constitution, void of an immaterial substance. For whether their supposition be true or no, it is plain they conceive personal identity preserved in something else than identity of substance; as animal identity is preserved in identity of life, and not of substance. And therefore those who place thinking in an immaterial substance only, before they can come to deal with these men, must show why personal identity cannot be preserved in the change of immaterial substances, or variety of particular immaterial substances, as well as animal identity is preserved in the change of material substances, or variety of particular bodies: unless they will say, it is one immaterial spirit that makes the same life in brutes,* as it is one immaterial spirit that makes the same person in men; which the Cartesians† at least will not admit, for fear of making brutes thinking things too.

§13. But next, as to the first part of the question, "whether, if the same thinking substance (supposing immaterial substances only to think) be changed, it can be the same person?" I answer, that cannot be resolved, but‡ by those who know what kind of substances they are that do think; and whether the consciousness of past actions can be transferred from one thinking substance to another. I grant, were the same consciousness the same individual action, it could not: but it being a present representation of a past action, why it may not be possible, that that may be represented to the mind to have been, which really never was, will remain to be shown. And therefore how far the consciousness of past actions is annexed to any individual agent, so that another cannot possibly have it, will be hard for us to determine, till we know what kind of action it is that cannot be done without a reflex act of perception accompanying it, and how performed by thinking substances, who cannot think without being conscious of it. But that which we call the same

---

* Animals.
† Followers of French philosopher René Descartes.
‡ In this context, "but" means "except."

consciousness, not being the same individual act, why one intellectual substance may not have represented to it, as done by itself, what it never did, and was perhaps done by some other agent; why, I say, such a representation may not possibly be without reality of matter of fact, as well as several representations in dreams are, which yet whilst dreaming we take for true, will be difficult to conclude from the nature of things. And that it never is so, will by us, till we have clearer views of the nature of thinking substances, be best resolved into the goodness of God, who, as far as the happiness or misery of any of his sensible creatures is concerned in it, will not, by a fatal error of theirs, transfer from one to another that consciousness which draws reward or punishment with it. How far this may be an argument against those who would place thinking in a system of fleeting animal spirits, I leave to be considered. But yet to return to the question before us, it must be allowed, that, if the same consciousness (which, as has been shown, is quite a different thing from the same numerical figure or motion in body) can be transferred from one thinking substance to another, it will be possible that two thinking substances may make but one person. For the same consciousness being preserved, whether in the same or different substances, the personal identity is preserved.

§14. As to the second part of the question, "whether the same immaterial substance remaining, there may be two distinct persons?" which question seems to me to be built on this, whether the same immaterial being, being conscious of the action of its past duration, may be wholly stripped of all the consciousness of its past existence, and lose it beyond the power of ever retrieving it again; and so as it were beginning a new account from a new period, have a consciousness that cannot reach beyond this new state. All those who hold pre-existence* are evidently of this mind; since they allow the soul to have no remaining consciousness of what it did in that pre-existent state, either wholly separate from body, or informing any other body; and if they should not, it is plain, experience would be against them. So that personal identity, reaching no further than consciousness reaches, a pre-existent spirit not having continued so many ages in a state of silence, must needs make different persons. Suppose a Christian, Platonist,† or a Pythagorean‡ should, upon God's having ended all his works of creation the seventh day, think his soul hath existed ever since; and should imagine it has revolved in several human bodies, as I once met with one, who was persuaded his had been the soul of Socrates; (how reasonably I will not dispute; this I know, that in the post he filled, which was no inconsiderable one, he passed for a very rational man, and the press§ has shown that he wanted¶ not parts or learning) would anyone say, that he, being not conscious of any of Socrates's actions or thoughts, could be the same person with Socrates? Let anyone reflect upon himself, and conclude that he has in himself an immaterial spirit, which is that which thinks in him, and, in the constant change of his body keeps him the same; and is that which he calls himself: Let his also suppose it to be the same soul that was in Nestor** or Thersites,†† at the siege of Troy (for souls being, as far as we know anything of them in their nature, indifferent to any parcel of matter, the supposition has no apparent absurdity in it), which it may have been, as well as it is now the soul of any other man: but he now having no consciousness of any of the actions either of Nestor or Thersites, does or can he conceive himself the same person with either of them? can he be concerned in either of their actions? attribute them to himself, or think them his own more than the actions of any other men that ever existed? So that this consciousness not reaching to any of the actions of either of those men, he is no more one self with either of them, than if the soul of immaterial spirit that now informs‡‡ him, had been created, and began to exist, when it began to inform his present body; though it were ever so true,

* The existence of the soul before birth in a body.
† A follower of the philosophy of Plato, who maintained that the soul is the seat of a person's identity.
‡ A follower of the Greek philosopher Pythagoras, who believed in reincarnation and the immortality of the soul.
§ Media publicity.
¶ Lacked.
** In Homer's *Odyssey*, Nestor is an Argonaut and king of Pylos.
†† In Homer's *Iliad*, Thersites was a Greek soldier.
‡‡ Directs, guides.

that the same spirit that informed Nestor's or Thersites's body were numerically the same that now informs his. For this would no more make him the same person with Nestor, than if some of the particles of matter that were once a part of Nestor were now a part of this man; the same immaterial substance, without the same consciousness, no more making the same person, by being united to any body, than the same particle of matter, without consciousness united to any body, makes the same person. But let him once find himself conscious of any of the actions of Nestor, he then finds himself the same person with Nestor.

§15. And thus may we be able, without any difficulty, to conceive the same person at the resurrection, though in a body not exactly in make or parts the same which he had here, the same consciousness going along with the soul that inhabits it. But yet the soul alone, in the change of bodies, would scarce to anyone, but to him that makes the soul the man, be enough to make the same man. For should the soul of a prince, carrying with it the consciousness of the prince's past life, enter and inform the body of a cobbler, as soon as deserted by his own soul, everyone sees he would be the same person with the prince, accountable only for the prince's actions: but who would say it was the same man? The body too goes to the making the man, and would, I guess, to every body determine the man in this case; wherein the soul, with all its princely thoughts about it, would not make another man: but he would be the same cobbler to everyone besides himself. I know that, in the ordinary way of speaking, the same person, and the same man, stand for one and the same thing. And indeed everyone will always have a liberty to speak as he pleases, and to apply what articulate sounds to what ideas he thinks fit, and change them as often as he pleases. But yet when we will inquire what makes the same spirit, man, or person, we must fix the ideas of spirit, man, or person in our minds; and having resolved with ourselves what we mean by them, it will not be hard to determine, in either of them, or the like, when it is the same, and when not.

§16. But though the same immaterial substance or soul does not alone, wherever it be, and in whatsoever state, make the same man; yet it is plain, consciousness, as far as ever it can be extended, should it be to ages past, unites existences and actions, very remote in time, into the same person, as well as it does the existences and actions of the immediately preceding moment: so that whatever has the consciousness of present and past actions, is the same person to whom they both belong. Had I the same consciousness that I saw the ark and Noah's flood, as that I saw an overflowing of the Thames last winter, or as that I write now; I could no more doubt that I who write this now, that saw the Thames overflowed last winter, and that viewed the flood at the general deluge, was the same self, place that self in what substance you please, than that I who write this am the same myself now whilst I write (whether I consist of all the same substance material or immaterial, or no) that I was yesterday. For as to this point of being the same self, it matters not whether this present self be made up of the same or other substances; I being as much concerned, and as justly accountable for any action that was done a thousand years since, appropriated to me now by this self-consciousness, as I am for what I did the last moment.

§17. Self is that conscious thinking thing, whatever substance made up of (whether spiritual or material, simple or compounded, it matters not), which is sensible, or conscious of pleasure and pain, capable of happiness or misery, and so is concerned for itself, as far as that consciousness extends. Thus everyone finds that, whilst comprehended under that consciousness, the little finger is as much a part of himself as what is most so. Upon separation of this little finger, should this consciousness go along with the little finger, and leave the rest of the body, it is evident the little finger would be the person, the same person; and self then would have nothing to do with the rest of the body. As in this case it is the consciousness that goes along with the substance, when one part is separate from another, which makes the same person, and constitutes this inseparable self; so it is in reference to substances remote in time. That with which the consciousness of this present thinking thing can join itself, makes the same person, and is one self with it, and with nothing else; and so attributes to itself, and owns all the actions of that thing, as its own, as far as that consciousness reaches, and no further; as everyone who reflects will perceive.

§18. In this personal identity, is founded all the right and justice of reward and punishment; happiness and misery being that for which everyone is concerned for himself, and not mattering what becomes of any substance not joined to, or affected with that consciousness. For as it is evident in the instance I gave but now, if the consciousness went along with the little finger when it was cut off, that would be the same self which was concerned for the whole body yesterday, as making part of itself, whose actions then it cannot but admit as its own now. Though if the same body should still live, and immediately from the separation of the little finger have its own peculiar consciousness, whereof the little finger knew nothing; it would not at all be concerned for it, as a part of itself, or could own any of its actions, or have any of them imputed to him.

§19. This may show us wherein personal identity consists; not in the identity of substance, but, as I have said, in the identity of consciousness; wherein if Socrates and the present mayor of Queenborough* agree, they are the same person: if the same Socrates waking and sleeping do not partake of the same consciousness, Socrates waking and sleeping is not the same person. And to punish Socrates waking for what sleeping Socrates thought, and waking Socrates was never conscious of, would be no more of right, than to punish one twin for what his brother-twin did, whereof he knew nothing, because their outsides were so like, that they could not be distinguished; for such twins have been seen.

§20. But yet possibly it will still be objected, suppose I wholly lose the memory of some parts of my life, beyond a possibility of retrieving them, so that perhaps I shall never be conscious of them again; yet am I not the same person that did those actions, had those thoughts that I once was conscious of, though I have now forgot them? To which I answer, that we must here take notice what the word I is applied to: which, in this case, is the man only. And the same man being presumed to be the same person, I is easily here supposed to stand also for the same person. But if it be possible for the same man to have distinct incommunicable consciousness at different times, it is past doubt the same man would at different times make different persons; which, we see, is the sense of

mankind in the solemnest declaration of their opinions; human laws not punishing the mad man for the sober man's actions, nor the sober man for what the mad man did, thereby making them two persons: which is somewhat explained by our way of speaking in English when we say such an one is not himself, or is beside himself; in which phrases it is insinuated, as if those who now, or at least first used them, thought that self was changed; the self-same person was no longer in that man.

§21. But yet it is hard to conceive that Socrates, the same individual man, should be two persons. To help us a little in this, we must consider what is meant by Socrates, or the same individual man.

First, it must be either the same individual, immaterial, thinking substance; in short, the same numerical soul, and nothing else.

Secondly, or the same animal, without any regard to an immaterial soul.

Thirdly, or the same immaterial spirit united to the same animal.

Now, take which of these suppositions you please, it is impossible to make personal identity to consist in anything but consciousness, or reach any further than that does.

For, by the first of them, it must be allowed possible that a man born of different women, and in distant times, may be the same man. A way of speaking, which whoever admits, must allow it possible for the same man to be two distinct persons, as any two that have lived in different ages, without the knowledge of one another's thoughts.

By the second and third, Socrates in this life, and after it, cannot be the same man any way, but by the same consciousness; and so making human identity to consist in the same thing wherein we place personal identity, there will be difficulty to allow the same man to be the same person. But then they who place human identity in consciousness only, and not in something else, must consider how they will make the infant Socrates the same man with Socrates after the resurrection. But whatsoever to some men makes a man, and consequently the same individual man, wherein perhaps few are agreed, personal identity can

---

* A small town in Kent, in southeast England.

by us be placed in nothing but consciousness (which is that alone which makes what we call self) without involving us in great absurdities.

§22. But is not a man drunk and sober the same person? Why else is he punished for the fact he commits when drunk, though he be never afterwards conscious of it? Just as much the same person as a man that walks, and does other things in his sleep, is the same person, and is answerable for any mischief he shall do in it. Human laws punish both, with a justice suitable to their way of knowledge; because, in these cases, they cannot distinguish certainly what is real, what counterfeit: and

so the ignorance in drunkenness or sleep is not admitted as a plea. For though punishment be annexed to personality, and personality to consciousness, and the drunkard perhaps be not conscious of what he did; yet human judicatures* justly punish him, because the fact is proved against him, but want of consciousness cannot be proved for him. But in the great day,† wherein the secrets of all hearts shall be laid open, it may be reasonable to think, no one shall be made to answer for what he knows nothing of; but shall receive his doom,‡ his conscience accusing or excusing him. ...

Suggestions for Critical Reflection

1. Locke argues as follows: "since consciousness always accompanies thinking, and it is that which makes everyone to be what he calls self, and thereby distinguishes himself from all other thinking things, in this alone consists personal identity." Is this a good argument?

2. Locke seems to emphasize a first-person, subjective perspective on personal identity—"being the same consciousness that makes a man be himself to himself"—rather than a third-person or objective perspective. Is this the right approach to personal identity? Are we experts on what makes us us?

3. Locke recognizes that it is possible for humans to "lose themselves," and cease to be the person they once were. Do you agree with this idea? Why or why not? Are there circumstances in which someone can become a different person?

4. How would Locke respond to the phenomenon of "false memories," that is, memories that are influenced by external pressures? Would he suggest that a person who misremembers their past experiences is identical with their past self? Why or why not?

5. Locke's theory entails that a person who cannot remember committing a crime while drunk should not be held responsible, because "they" did not really perform the criminal acts. Locke suggests that the law punishes people for acts committed while drunk simply because it is difficult to determine when people are lying about their memories. Do you agree with Locke's position in this issue? Why or why not?

6. You most probably remember nothing from age one. Does that mean that the one-year-old was not you? Suppose you remember nothing that happened to you ten days ago. But nine days ago, you remembered what had happened to you ten days ago; and eight days ago you remembered experiences from nine days ago, and so on up to today. Would that make you the same person you were ten days ago, according to Locke?

7. Thomas Reid argued that Locke mistakes the evidence we have for the existence of a stable personal identity—memory—with personal identity itself.§ Memory, Reid claims, is the testimony of the self, but not the cause of the self. Analyze this claim. To what extent might Reid's revision of

---

* Law courts
† The Last Judgment, or Judgment Day, at the Second Coming of Christ.
‡ Judgment, reward or punishment.
§ Thomas Reid, "Of Mr. Locke's Account of Our Personal Identity," in *Essays on the Intellectual Powers of Man* (1785).

Locke's theory eradicate the "strange" suppositions that Locke's ideas necessitate? How would Locke respond to Reid's objection?

8. David Hume suggests that we never actually experience a "self." Instead, we only ever encounter a flow of changing sensations. The self, he argues, is nothing more than a cluster of perceptions. How might Locke answer Hume? Which view do you find more persuasive? Why?

DANIEL C. DENNETT

Where Am I?

Who Is Daniel Dennett?

Born in Boston in 1942, Daniel Clement Dennett spent his early childhood in Beirut, Lebanon, where his father was stationed as a secret agent in the OSS.* After his father died on a mission in 1947, Dennett returned to the United States. He began his post-secondary studies at Wesleyan University, then transferred to Harvard, where he attended courses taught by the celebrated philosopher W.V.O. Quine. At Quine's recommendation, Dennett pursued his graduate studies at Oxford, where he was supervised by Gilbert Ryle, a towering figure in Anglophone philosophy at the time. At the age of 23, Dennett received an Assistant Professorship at the University of California at Irvine, where he taught until 1971. Dennett then moved to Tufts University in Massachusetts, where he is now University Professor and Austin B. Fletcher Professor of Philosophy, and Director of the Center for Cognitive Studies.

Although his formal education was almost exclusively devoted to philosophy, Dennett has a strong bent for practical issues and problems and for finding out "how things work." He has described himself as "playing catch-up" since graduate school on the scientific areas most closely connected to his research, especially psychology, biology, and computer science.

What Is Dennett's Overall Philosophical Project?

One of the first thinkers to seriously consider the philosophical significance of artificial intelligence and cognitive science, Dennett believes that it is deeply incorrect to identify our self with a *res cogitans*, or "mental substance." It is possible, he claims, to perceive mind-like qualities in objects that cannot possibly contain mental "stuff." Through what he calls "the intentional stance," we can interpret non-thinking objects—such as computers—as though they were rational agents with motivations and beliefs.

The central plank of Dennett's theory of mental content is that, as he puts it, "brains are syntactic engines that can mimic the competence of semantic engines." By this he means that brains are complex, mechanical systems which follow the laws of physics and not the principles of rationality. However, Dennett suggests, evolution has 'designed' the human brain so that its mechanical (or "syntactic") processes closely resemble those of a system intelligently manipulating meaningful symbols (semantics). Meaning is something that brains—and thus human beings—seem to have only *from the outside*. Moreover, since this is, in Dennett's view, all there is to having mental content, any system which is complex enough to act as if it has beliefs or desires—such as a thermostat, a simple robot, or an ant—really does have those mental states in just the same way as a human being, though in a more rudimentary form.

Dennett's theory of consciousness is equally radical and is called the Multiple Drafts Model. He develops it as a foil to a more traditional model of consciousness, which he labels (after René Descartes) the "Cartesian Theater." According to this traditional picture, consciousness consists in a sort of metaphorical theater where all the data of consciousness 'come together' into a single experience at a particular time, which is 'observed' by the self. Dennett rejects nearly all the elements of the Cartesian theater: the idea of a self, a mind's eye, or a central place where all the pieces of a single conscious image come together.

Instead, he thinks of consciousness as the multiple, simultaneous processing of various different bits of data, distributed across the brain and even across time. For example, the processing of the visual information about my room as it was at 11:29 a.m. might be occurring a few moments later than the processing of the aural information about the room at that time, and will certainly take place

---

* The Office of Strategic Services, a wartime intelligence agency of the United States during World War II and predecessor of the CIA.

at a different location in my brain. Furthermore, there is no particular point at which this processing 'stops' and spills its results into consciousness—my perceptions of the state of my office at 11:29 are subject to constant adjustment and revision as they go on, and there is no particular threshold they cross to become conscious. Thus, according to Dennett, there just *is* no "mental image" in our minds when we are conscious and so, roughly, the traditional "problem of consciousness" is dissolved.

What Is the Structure of This Reading?

Dennett begins by providing a lengthy fictional introduction about being tasked by the government to carry out a secret mission, which sets the stage for a thought experiment about a human body operated remotely by a brain in a vat. Dennett describes a situation in which his brain is preserved in Texas, and responsible for electronically controlling his body in Oklahoma. Dennett's opening is noteworthy, not only for its creativity and comedy, but also for its personalization of a philosophical issue. The thought experiment in the text concerns not an abstract individual or token figure, but the author, Daniel C. Dennett himself.

Following his description of the fictional circumstances that led to the disconnection of his body and brain, Dennett raises his essay's central question: in a situation where a person's body is separated from—but still controlled by—their brain, "where" in space is that person? Dennett suggests that there are three possible answers to this question. The first is that "he" is located in his body. The second is that "he" is located in his brain. The third is that "he" is wherever his point of view is located—that is, "wherever he thinks he is." It may be possible, Dennett suggests, for a person to change where they are in space through acts of imagination.

Dennett imagines changes that might occur in his experience of the world as a result of the separation of brain and body. Via a discussion of his body being lost, and his brain being linked to a new body, Dennett then considers a series of possible complications that the ability to separate a person's brain and body would cause. For example, Dennett wonders whether it is possible for a person to be in two places at once, to exist as a disembodied self, to switch bodies while remaining the same person, to make a computer reproduction of a human brain, or for two persons to share the same identity.

Where Am I?*

Now that I've won my suit under the Freedom of Information Act,[†] I am at liberty to reveal for the first time a curious episode in my life that may be of interest not only to those engaged in research in the philosophy of mind, artificial intelligence, and neuroscience but also to the general public.

Several years ago I was approached by Pentagon[‡] officials who asked me to volunteer for a highly dangerous and secret mission. In collaboration with NASA and Howard Hughes,[§] the Department of

Defense was spending billions to develop a Supersonic Tunneling Underground Device, or STUD. It was supposed to tunnel through the earth's core at great speed and deliver a specially designed atomic warhead "right up the Red's[¶] missile silos," as one of the Pentagon brass put it.

The problem was that in an early test they had succeeded in lodging a warhead about a mile deep under Tulsa, Oklahoma, and they wanted me to retrieve it for them. "Why me?" I asked. Well, the mission

---

* Daniel C. Dennett, "Where Am I?" in *Brainstorms: Philosophical Essays on Mind and Psychology* (MIT Press, 1978). This talk was presented first at the Chapel Hill Colloquium, October 1976, and subsequently at MIT, in December 1976, and at the University of Alabama, in April 1978.

† An American law that allows ordinary citizens to access information from the government.

‡ The headquarters of the United States Department of Defense.

§ Hughes was a wealthy American businessperson and pilot well known for his eccentric behavior.

¶ "Red" is a pejorative term for communist. In this context, it refers to the Soviet Union.

involved some pioneering applications of current brain research, and they had heard of my interest in brains and of course my Faustian* curiosity and great courage and so forth.... Well, how could I refuse? The difficulty that brought the Pentagon to my door was that the device I'd been asked to recover was fiercely radioactive, in a new way. According to monitoring instruments, something about the nature of the device and its complex interactions with pockets of material deep in the earth had produced radiation that could cause severe abnormalities in certain tissues of the brain. No way had been found to shield the brain from these deadly rays, which were apparently harmless to other tissues and organs of the body. So it had been decided that the person sent to recover the device should *leave his brain behind*. It would be kept in a safe place where it could execute its normal control functions by elaborate radio links. Would I submit to a surgical procedure that would completely remove my brain, which would then be placed in a life-support system at the Manned Spacecraft Center in Houston? Each input and output pathway, as it was severed, would be restored by a pair of microminiaturized radio transceivers, one attached precisely to the brain, the other to the nerve stumps in the empty cranium. No information would be lost, all the connectivity would be preserved. At first I was a bit reluctant. Would it really work? The Houston brain surgeons encouraged me. "Think of it," they said, "as a mere *stretching* of the nerves. If your brain were just moved over an *inch* in your skull, that would not alter or impair your mind. We're simply going to make the nerves indefinitely elastic by splicing radio links into them."

I was shown around the life-support lab in Houston and saw the sparkling new vat in which my brain would be placed, were I to agree. I met the large and brilliant support team of neurologists, hematologists, biophysicists, and electrical engineers, and after several days of discussions and demonstrations I agreed to give it a try. I was subjected to an enormous array of blood tests, brain scans, experiments, interviews, and the like. They took down my autobiography at great length, recorded tedious lists of my beliefs, hopes, fears, and tastes. They even listed my favorite stereo recordings and gave me a crash session of psychoanalysis.

The day for surgery arrived at last and of course I was anesthetized and remember nothing of the operation itself. When I came out of anesthesia, I opened my eyes, looked around, and asked the inevitable, the traditional, the lamentably hackneyed postoperative question: "Where am I?" The nurse smiled down at me. "You're in Houston," she said, and I reflected that this still had a good chance of being the truth one way or another. She handed me a mirror. Sure enough, there were the tiny antennae poling up through their titanium ports cemented into my skull.

"I gather the operation was a success," I said. "I want to go see my brain." They led me (I was a bit dizzy and unsteady) down a long corridor and into the life-support lab. A cheer went up from the assembled support team, and I responded with what I hoped was a jaunty salute. Still feeling lightheaded, I was helped over to the life-support vat. I peered through the glass. There, floating in what looked like ginger ale, was undeniably a human brain, though it was almost covered with printed circuit chips, plastic tubules, electrodes, and other paraphernalia. "Is that mine?" I asked. "Hit the output transmitter switch there on the side of the vat and see for yourself," the project director replied. I moved the switch to OFF, and immediately slumped, groggy and nauseated, into the arms of the technicians, one of whom kindly restored the switch to its ON position. While I recovered my equilibrium and composure, I thought to myself: "Well, here I am sitting on a folding chair, staring through a piece of plate glass at my own brain ... But wait," I said to myself, "shouldn't I have thought, 'Here I am, suspended in a bubbling fluid, being stared at by my own eyes'?" I tried to think this latter thought. I tried to project it into the tank, offering it hopefully to my brain, but I failed to carry off the exercise with any conviction. I tried again. "Here am *I*, Daniel Dennett, suspended in a bubbling fluid, being stared at by my own eyes." No, it just didn't work. Most puzzling and confusing. Being a philosopher of firm physicalist conviction, I believed unswervingly that the tokening† of my thoughts

---

* Faust is a character from literature and folklore who made a deal with the devil to exchange his soul for knowledge.

† Some type of thing is *tokened* when a particular instance of that type is brought into existence.

was occurring somewhere in my brain: yet, when I thought "Here I am," where the thought occurred to me was *here*, outside the vat, where I, Dennett, was standing staring at my brain.

I tried and tried to think myself into the vat, but to no avail. I tried to build up to the task by doing mental exercises. I thought to myself, "The sun is shining *over there*," five times in rapid succession, each time mentally ostending* a different place: in order, the sunlit corner of the lab, the visible front lawn of the hospital, Houston, Mars, and Jupiter. I found I had little difficulty in getting my "there"s to hop all over the celestial map with their proper references. I could loft a "there" in an instant through the farthest reaches of space, and then aim the next "there" with pinpoint accuracy at the upper left quadrant of a freckle on my arm. Why was I having such trouble with "here"? "Here in Houston" worked well enough, and so did "here in the lab," and even "here in this part of the lab," but "here in the vat" always seemed merely an unmeant mental mouthing. I tried closing my eyes while thinking it. This seemed to help, but still I couldn't manage to pull it off, except perhaps for a fleeting instant. I couldn't be sure. The discovery that I couldn't be sure was also unsettling. How did I know *where* I meant by "here" when I thought "here"? Could I *think* I meant one place when in fact I meant another? I didn't see how that could be admitted without untying the few bonds of intimacy between a person and his own mental life that had survived the onslaught of the brain scientists and philosophers, the physicalists and behaviorists. Perhaps I was incorrigible† about where I *meant* when I said "here." But in my present circumstances it seemed that either I was doomed by sheer force of mental habit to thinking systematically false indexical‡ thoughts, or where a person is (and hence where his thoughts are tokened for purposes of semantic analysis) is not necessarily where his brain, the physical seat of his soul, resides. Nagged by confusion, I attempted to orient myself by

falling back on a favorite philosopher's ploy. I began naming things.

"Yorick,"§ I said aloud to my brain, "you are my brain. The rest of my body, seated in this chair, I dub 'Hamlet.'" So here we all are: Yorick's my brain, Hamlet's my body, and I am Dennett. *Now*, where am I? And when I think "where am I?", where's that thought tokened? Is it tokened in my brain, lounging about in the vat, or right here between my ears where it *seems* to be tokened? Or nowhere? Its *temporal* coordinates give me no trouble; must it not have spatial coordinates as well? I began making a list of the alternatives.

1. *Where Hamlet goes there goes Dennett*. This principle was easily refuted by appeal to the familiar brain-transplant thought experiments so enjoyed by philosophers. If Tom and Dick switch brains, Tom is the fellow with Dick's former body—just ask him; he'll claim to be Tom and tell you the most intimate details of Tom's autobiography. It was clear enough, then, that my current body and I could part company, but not likely that I could be separated from my brain. The rule of thumb that emerged so plainly from the thought experiments was that in a brain-transplant operation, one wanted to be the *donor* not the recipient. Better to call such an operation a *body* transplant, in fact. So perhaps the truth was,

2. *Where Yorick goes there goes Dennett*. This was not at all appealing, however. How could I be in the vat and not about to go anywhere, when I was so obviously outside the vat looking in and beginning to make guilty plans to return to my room for a substantial lunch? This begged the question¶ I realized, but it still seemed to be getting at something important. Casting about for some support for my intuition, I hit upon a legalistic sort of argument that might have appealed to Locke.

Suppose, I argued to myself, I were now to fly to California, rob a bank, and be apprehended. In which state would I be tried: in California, where the

---

* Pointing out, indicating, referring to.

† Incapable of being corrected—in this context because no one else can have better evidence than you can and so no one could be in a position to correct you.

‡ An indexical is an expression whose reference can shift from context to context, such as "here," "now," and "I."

§ A character in Shakespeare's *Hamlet*, whose skull is held by the protagonist during the famous "Alas, poor Yorick! I knew him, Horatio ..." speech.

¶ Presupposed what was supposed to be proved.

robbery took place, or in Texas, where the brains of the outfit were located? Would I be a California felon with an out-of-state brain, or a Texas felon remotely controlling an accomplice of sorts in California? It seemed possible that I might beat such a rap just on the undecidability of that jurisdictional question, though perhaps it would be deemed an interstate, and hence Federal, offense. In any event, suppose I were convicted. Was it likely that California would be satisfied to throw Hamlet into the brig, knowing that Yorick was living the good life and luxuriously taking the waters in Texas? Would Texas incarcerate Yorick, leaving Hamlet free to take the next boat to Rio? This alternative appealed to me. Barring capital punishment or other cruel and unusual punishment, the state would be obliged to maintain the life-support system for Yorick though they might move him from Houston to Leavenworth,* and aside from the unpleasantness of the opprobrium, I, for one, would not mind at all and would consider myself a free man under those circumstances. If the state has an interest in forcibly relocating persons in institutions, it would fail to relocate *me* in any institution by locating Yorick there. If this were true, it suggested a third alternative.

3. *Dennett is wherever he thinks he is.* Generalized, the claim was as follows: At any given time a person has a *point of view* and the location of the point of view (which is determined internally by the content of the point of view) is also the location of the person.

Such a proposition is not without its perplexities, but to me it seemed a step in the right direction. The only trouble was that it seemed to place one in a heads-I-win/tails-you-lose situation of unlikely infallibility as regards location. Hadn't I myself often been wrong about where I was, and at least as often uncertain? Couldn't one get lost? Of course, but getting lost *geographically* is not the only way one might get lost. If one were lost in the woods one could attempt to reassure oneself with the consolation that at least one knew where one was: one was right *here* in the familiar surroundings of one's own body. Perhaps in

this case one would not have drawn one's attention to much to be thankful for. Still, there were worse plights imaginable, and I wasn't sure I wasn't in such a plight right now.

Point of view clearly had something to do with personal location, but it was itself an unclear notion. It was obvious that the content of one's point of view was not the same as or determined by the content of one's beliefs or thoughts. For example, what should we say about the point of view of the Cinerama† viewer who shrieks and twists in his seat as the roller-coaster footage overcomes his psychic distancing? Has he forgotten that he is safely seated in the theater? Here I was inclined to say that the person is experiencing an illusory shift in point of view. In other cases, my inclination to call such shifts illusory was less strong. The workers in laboratories and plants who handle dangerous materials by operating feedback-controlled mechanical arms and hands undergo a shift in point of view that is crisper and more pronounced than anything Cinerama can provoke. They can feel the heft and slipperiness of the containers they manipulate with their metal fingers. They know perfectly well where they are and are not fooled into false beliefs by the experience, yet it is as if they were inside the isolation chamber they are peering into. With mental effort, they can manage to shift their point of view back and forth, rather like making a transparent Necker cube‡ or an Escher§ drawing change orientation before one's eyes. It does seem extravagant to suppose that in performing this bit of mental gymnastics, they are transporting *themselves* back and forth.

Still their example gave me hope. If I was in fact in the vat in spite of my intuitions, I might be able to train myself to adopt that point of view even as a matter of habit. I should dwell on images of myself comfortably floating in my vat, beaming volitions to that familiar body *out there*. I reflected that the ease or difficulty of this task was presumably independent of the truth about the location of one's brain. Had I been practicing before the operation, I might now

---

* A US federal prison located in Kansas.
† A wide-screen movie projection process producing a strong illusion of surrounding reality.
‡ An optical illusion—a cube that seems to shift front surfaces from lower-left to upper-right.
§ An artist whose woodcuts, lithographs, and mezzotints are noted for their inclusion of mathematical themes and impossible objects.

be finding it second nature. You might now yourself try such a *trompe l'oeil*.* Imagine you have written an inflammatory letter which has been published in the *Times*, the result of which is that the government has chosen to impound your brain for a probationary period of three years in its Dangerous Brain Clinic in Bethesda, Maryland. Your body of course is allowed freedom to earn a salary and thus to continue its function of laying up income to be taxed. At this moment, however, your body is seated in an auditorium listening to a peculiar account by Daniel Dennett of his own similar experience. Try it. Think yourself to Bethesda, and then hark back longingly to your body, far away, and yet *seeming* so near. It is only with long-distance restraint (yours? the government's?) that you can control your impulse to get those hands clapping in polite applause before navigating the old body to the rest room and a well-deserved glass of evening sherry in the lounge. The task of imagination is certainly difficult, but if you achieve your goal the results might be consoling.

Anyway, there I was in Houston, lost in thought as one might say, but not for long. My speculations were soon interrupted by the Houston doctors, who wished to test out my new prosthetic nervous system before sending me off on my hazardous mission. As I mentioned before, I was a bit dizzy at first, and not surprisingly, although I soon habituated myself to my new circumstances (which were, after all, well nigh indistinguishable from my old circumstances). My accommodation was not perfect, however, and to this day I continue to be plagued by minor coordination difficulties. The speed of light is fast, but finite, and as my brain and body move farther and farther apart, the delicate interaction of my feedback systems is thrown into disarray by the time lags. Just as one is rendered close to speechless by a delayed or echoic hearing of one's speaking voice so, for instance, I am virtually unable to track a moving object with my eyes whenever my brain and my body are more than a few miles apart. In most matters my impairment is scarcely detectable, though I can no longer hit a slow curve ball with the authority of yore. There are some compensations of course. Though liquor tastes as good as ever, and warms my gullet while corroding my liver, I can drink it in any quantity I please, without becoming the slightest bit inebriated, a curiosity some of my close friends may have noticed (though I occasionally have *feigned* inebriation, so as not to draw attention to my unusual circumstances). For similar reasons, I take aspirin orally for a sprained wrist, but if the pain persists I ask Houston to administer codeine to me *in vitro*.† In times of illness the phone bill can be staggering.

But to return to my adventure. At length, both the doctors and I were satisfied that I was ready to undertake my subterranean mission. And so I left my brain in Houston and headed by helicopter for Tulsa. Well, in any case, that's the way it seemed to me. That's how I would put it, just off the top of my head as it were. On the trip I reflected further about my earlier anxieties and decided that my first postoperative speculations had been tinged with panic. The matter was not nearly as strange or metaphysical as I had been supposing. Where was I? In two places, clearly: both inside the vat and outside it. Just as one can stand with one foot in Connecticut and the other in Rhode Island, I was in two places at once. I had become one of those scattered individuals we used to hear so much about. The more I considered this answer, the more obviously true it appeared. But, strange to say, the more true it appeared, the less important the question to which it could be the true answer seemed. A sad, but not unprecedented, fate for a philosophical question to suffer. This answer did not completely satisfy me, of course. There lingered some question to which I should have liked an answer, which was neither "Where are all my various and sundry parts?" nor "What is my current point of view?" Or at least there seemed to be such a question. For it did seem undeniable that in some sense *I* and not merely *most of me* was descending into the earth under Tulsa in search of an atomic warhead.

When I found the warhead, I was certainly glad I had left my brain behind, for the pointer on the specially built Geiger counter I had brought with me was

---

* French: "deceive the eye"; an artistic technique that allows three-dimensional objects to be rendered in two dimensions so realistically that they seem to be real objects, not paintings.
† Latin: "in the glass"; normally used with reference to experiments and procedures done in test tubes, petri dishes, etc.

off the dial. I called Houston on my ordinary radio and told the operation control center of my position and my progress. In return, they gave me instructions for dismantling the vehicle, based upon my on-site observations. I had set to work with my cutting torch when all of a sudden a terrible thing happened. I went stone deaf. At first I thought it was only my radio earphones that had broken, but when I tapped on my helmet, I heard nothing. Apparently the auditory transceivers had gone on the fritz. I could no longer hear Houston or my own voice, but I could speak, so I started telling them what had happened. In mid-sentence, I knew something else had gone wrong. My vocal apparatus had become paralyzed. Then my right hand went limp—another transceiver had gone. I was truly in deep trouble. But worse was to follow. After a few more minutes, I went blind. I cursed my luck, and then I cursed the scientists who had led me into this grave peril. There I was, deaf, dumb, and blind, in a radioactive hole more than a mile under Tulsa. Then the last of my cerebral radio links broke, and suddenly I was faced with a new and even more shocking problem: whereas an instant before I had been buried alive in Oklahoma, now I was disembodied in Houston. My recognition of my new status was not immediate. It took me several very anxious minutes before it dawned on me that my poor body lay several hundred miles away, with heart pulsing and lungs respiring, but otherwise as dead as the body of any heart-transplant donor, its skull packed with useless, broken electronic gear. The shift in perspective I had earlier found well nigh impossible now seemed quite natural. Though I could think myself back into my body in the tunnel under Tulsa, it took some effort to sustain the illusion. For surely it was an illusion to suppose I was still in Oklahoma: I had lost all contact with that body.

It occurred to me then, with one of those rushes of revelation of which we should be suspicious, that I had stumbled upon an impressive demonstration of the immateriality of the soul based upon physicalist principles and premises. For as the last radio signal between Tulsa and Houston died away, had I not changed location from Tulsa to Houston at the speed of light? And had I not accomplished this without any increase in mass? What moved from A to B at such speed was surely myself, or at any rate my soul or mind—the massless center of my being and home of my consciousness. My *point of view* had lagged somewhat behind, but I had already noted the indirect bearing of point of view on personal location. I could not see how a physicalist philosopher could quarrel with this except by taking the dire and counterintuitive route of banishing all talk of persons. Yet the notion of personhood was so well entrenched in everyone's world view, or so it seemed to me, that any denial would be as curiously unconvincing, as systematically disingenuous, as the Cartesian negation, "non sum."[1]*

The joy of philosophic discovery thus tided me over some very bad minutes or perhaps hours as the helplessness and hopelessness or my situation became more apparent to me. Waves of panic and even nausea swept over me, made all the more horrible by the absence of their normal body-dependent phenomenology.† No adrenaline rush of tingles in the arms, no pounding heart, no premonitory salivation. I did feel a dread sinking feeling in my bowels at one point, and this tricked me momentarily into the false hope that I was undergoing a reversal of the process that landed me in this fix—a gradual undisembodiment. But the isolation and uniqueness of that twinge soon convinced me that it was simply the first of a plague of phantom body hallucinations that I, like any other amputee, would be all too likely to suffer.

My mood then was chaotic. On the one hand, I was fired up with elation of my philosophic discovery and was wracking my brain (one of the few familiar things I could still do), trying to figure out how to communicate my discovery to the journals; while on the other, I was bitter, lonely, and filled with dread and uncertainty. Fortunately, this did not last long, for my technical support team sedated me into a dreamless sleep from which I awoke, hearing with magnificent fidelity the familiar opening strains of my favorite Brahms piano trio. So that was why they had wanted a list of my favorite recordings! It did not take me long to realize that I was hearing the music without ears. The

---

* René Descartes suggested that the thinking subject is the site of the self, famously declaring *cogito ergo sum*, "I think therefore I am." Here, Dennett is negating the Cartesian self, as *non sum* literally means "I am not."

† "Phenomenology" can be read, roughly, as "experiences" in this context.

output from the stereo stylus was being fed through some fancy rectification circuitry directly into my auditory nerve. I was mainlining Brahms, an unforgettable experience for any stereo buff. At the end of the record it did not surprise me to hear the reassuring voice of the project director speaking into a microphone that was now my prosthetic ear. He confirmed my analysis of what had gone wrong and assured me that steps were being taken to re-embody me. He did not elaborate, and after a few more recordings, I found myself drifting off to sleep. My sleep lasted, I later learned, for the better part of a year, and when I awoke, it was to find myself fully restored to my senses. When I looked into the mirror, though, I was a bit startled to see an unfamiliar face. Bearded and a bit heavier, bearing no doubt a family resemblance to my former face, and with the same look of spritely intelligence and resolute character, but definitely a new face. Further self-explorations of an intimate nature left me no doubt that this was a new body, and the project director confirmed my conclusions. He did not volunteer any information on the past history of my new body and I decided (wisely, I think in retrospect) not to pry. As many philosophers unfamiliar with my ordeal have more recently speculated, the acquisition of a new body leaves one's *person* intact. And after a period of adjustment to a new voice, new muscular strengths and weaknesses, and so forth, one's *personality* is by and large also preserved. More dramatic changes in personality have been routinely observed in people who have undergone extensive plastic surgery, to say nothing of sex-change operations, and I think no one contests the survival of the person in such cases. In any event I soon accommodated to my new body, to the point of being unable to recover any of its novelties to my consciousness or even memory. The view in the mirror soon became utterly familiar. That view, by the way, still revealed antennae, and so I was not surprised to learn that my brain had not been moved from its haven in the life-support lab.

I decided that good old Yorick deserved a visit. I and my new body, whom we might as well call Fortinbras,* strode into the familiar lab to another

round of applause from the technicians, who were of course congratulating themselves, not me. Once more I stood before the vat and contemplated poor Yorick, and on a whim I once again cavalierly flicked off the output transmitter switch. Imagine my surprise when nothing unusual happened. No fainting spell, no nausea, no noticeable change. A technician hurried to restore the switch to ON, but still I felt nothing. I demanded an explanation, which the project director hastened to provide. It seems that before they had even operated on the first occasion, they had constructed a computer duplicate of my brain, reproducing both the complete information-processing structure and the computational speed of my brain in a giant computer program. After the operation, but before they had dared to send me off on my mission to Oklahoma, they had run this computer system and Yorick side by side. The incoming signals from Hamlet were sent simultaneously to Yorick's transceivers and to the computer's array of inputs. And the outputs from Yorick were not only beamed back to Hamlet, my body; they were recorded and checked against the simultaneous output of the computer program, which was called "Hubert"† for reasons obscure to me. Over days and even weeks, the outputs were identical and synchronous, which of course did not *prove* that they had succeeded in copying the brain's functional structure, but the empirical support was greatly encouraging.

Hubert's input, and hence activity, had been kept parallel with Yorick's during my disembodied days. And now, to demonstrate this, they had actually thrown the master switch that put Hubert for the first time in on-line control of my body—not Hamlet, of course, but Fortinbras. (Hamlet, I learned, had never been recovered from its underground tomb and could be assumed by this time to have largely returned to the dust. At the head of my grave still lay the magnificent bulk of the abandoned device, with the word STUD emblazoned on its side in large letters—a circumstance which may provide archeologists of the next century with a curious insight into the burial rites of their ancestors.)

---

* A character in *Hamlet* who arrives at the end of the play, after most of the main characters are dead, and is crowned king of Denmark.
† A Germanic name that literally means "bright mind." It is also the first name of Dennett's contemporary, Hubert Dreyfus, a well-known critic of the idea that the mind can be replicated by computer software.

The laboratory technicians now showed me the master switch, which had two positions, labeled *B*, for Brain (they didn't know my brain's name was Yorick), and *H*, for Hubert. The switch did indeed point to *H*, and they explained to me that if I wished, I could switch it back to *B*. With my heart in my mouth (and my brain in its vat), I did this. Nothing happened. A click, that was all. To test their claim, and with the master switch now set at *B*, I hit Yorick's output transmitter switch on the vat and sure enough, I began to faint. Once the output switch was turned back on and I had recovered my wits, so to speak, I continued to play with the master switch, flipping it back and forth. I found that with the exception of the transitional click, I could detect no trace of a difference. I could switch in mid-utterance, and the sentence I had begun speaking under the control of Yorick was finished without a pause or hitch of any kind under the control of Hubert. I had a spare brain, a prosthetic device which might some day stand me in very good stead, were some mishap to befall Yorick. Or alternatively, I could keep Yorick as a spare and use Hubert. It didn't seem to make any difference which I chose, for the wear and tear and fatigue on my body did not have any debilitating effect on either brain, whether or not it was actually causing the motions of my body, or merely spilling its output into thin air.

The one truly unsettling aspect of this new development was the prospect, which was not long in dawning on me, of someone detaching the spare—Hubert or Yorick, as the case might be—from Fortinbras and hitching it to yet another body—some Johnny-come-lately Rosencrantz or Guildenstern.* Then (if not before) there would be *two* people, that much was clear. One would be me, and the other would be a sort of super-twin brother. If there were two bodies, one under the control of Hubert and the other being controlled by Yorick, then which would the world recognize as the true Dennett? And whatever the rest of the world decided, which one would be *me*? Would I be the Yorick-brained one, in virtue of Yorick's causal priority and former intimate relationship with

the original Dennett body, Hamlet? That seemed a bit legalistic, a bit too redolent of the arbitrariness of consanguinity† and legal possession, to be convincing at the metaphysical level. For suppose that before the arrival of the second body on the scene, I had been keeping Yorick as the spare for years, and letting Hubert's output drive my body—that is, Fortinbras—all that time. The Hubert-Fortinbras couple would seem then by squatter's rights (to combat one legal intuition with another) to be the true Dennett and the lawful inheritor of everything that was Dennett's. This was an interesting question, certainly, but not nearly so pressing as another question that bothered me. My strongest intuition was that in such an eventuality *I* would survive so long as *either* brain-body couple remained intact, but I had mixed emotions about whether I should want both to survive.

I discussed my worries with the technicians and the project director. The prospect of two Dennetts was abhorrent to me, I explained, largely for social reasons. I didn't want to be my own rival for the affections of my wife, nor did I like the prospect of the two Dennetts sharing my modest professor's salary. Still more vertiginous and distasteful, though, was the idea of knowing *that much* about another person, while he had the very same goods on me. How could we ever face each other? My colleagues in the lab argued that I was ignoring the bright side of the matter. Weren't there many things I wanted to do but, being only one person, had been unable to do? Now one Dennett could stay at home and be the professor and family man while the other could strike out on a life of travel and adventure—missing the family of course, but happy in the knowledge that the other Dennett was keeping the home fires burning. I could be faithful and adulterous at the same time. I could even cuckold myself—to say nothing of other more lurid possibilities my colleagues were all too ready to force upon my overtaxed imagination. But my ordeal in Oklahoma (or was it Houston?) had made me less adventurous, and I shrank from this opportunity that was being offered (though of course I was never quite sure it was being offered to *me* in the first place).

---

* In *Hamlet*, they are friends of prince Hamlet who are used as pawns by King Claudius to influence young Hamlet's behavior.

† The property of being a blood relation to another person; it is carefully defined in many legal codes to specify when marriages are permitted and how the inheritance of property occurs.

There was another prospect even more disagreeable: that the spare, Hubert or Yorick as the case might be, would be detached from any input from Fortinbras and just left detached. Then, as in the other case, there would be two Dennetts, or at least two claimants to my name and possessions, one embodied in Fortinbras, and the other sadly, miserably disembodied. Both selfishness and altruism bade me take steps to prevent this from happening. So I asked that measures be taken to ensure that no one could ever tamper with the transceiver connections or the master switch without my (our? no, *my*) knowledge and consent. Since I had no desire to spend my life guarding the equipment in Houston, it was mutually decided that all the electronic connections in the lab would be carefully locked. Both those that controlled the life-support system for Yorick and those that controlled the power supply for Hubert would be guarded with fail-safe devices, and I would take the only master switch, outfitted for radio remote control, with me wherever I went. I carry it strapped around my waist and—wait a moment—here it is. Every few months I reconnoiter the situation by switching channels. I do this only in the presence of friends, of course, for if the other channel were, heaven forbid, either dead or otherwise occupied, there would have to be somebody who had my interests at heart to switch it back, to bring me back from the void. For while I could feel, see, hear, and otherwise sense whatever befell my body, subsequent to such a switch, I'd be unable to control it. By the way, the two positions on the switch are intentionally unmarked, so I never have the faintest idea whether I am switching from Hubert to Yorick or vice versa. (Some of you may think that in this case I really don't know *who* I am, let alone where I am. But such reflections no longer make much of a dent on my essential Dennettness, on my own sense of who I am. If it is true that in one sense I don't know who I am then that's another one of your philosophical truths of underwhelming significance.)

In any case, every time I've flipped the switch so far, nothing has happened. *So let's give it a try ...*

"THANK GOD! I THOUGHT YOU'D NEVER FLIP THAT SWITCH! You can't imagine how horrible it's been these last two weeks—but now you know, it's your turn in purgatory. How I've longed for this moment! You see, about two weeks ago—excuse me, ladies and gentlemen, but I've got to explain this to my ... um, brother, I guess you could say, but he's just told you the facts, so you'll understand—about two weeks ago our two brains drifted just a bit out of synch. I don't know whether *my* brain is now Hubert or Yorick, any more than you do, but in any case, the two brains drifted apart, and of course once the process started, it snowballed, for I was in a slightly different receptive state for the input we both received, a difference that was soon magnified. In no time at all the illusion that I was in control of my body—our body—was completely dissipated. There was nothing I could do—no way to call you. YOU DIDN'T EVEN KNOW I EXISTED! It's been like being carried around in a cage, or better, like being possessed—hearing my own voice say things I didn't mean to say, watching in frustration as my own hands performed deeds I hadn't intended. You'd scratch our itches, but not the way I would have, and you kept me awake, with your tossing and turning. I've been totally exhausted, on the verge of a nervous breakdown, carried around helplessly by your frantic round of activities, sustained only by the knowledge that some day you'd throw the switch.

"Now it's your turn, but at least you'll have the comfort of knowing *I* know you're in there. Like an expectant mother, I'm eating—or at any rate tasting, smelling, seeing—for *two* now, and I'll try to make it easy for you. Don't worry. Just as soon as this colloquium is over, you and I will fly to Houston, and we'll see what can be done to get one of us another body. You can have a female body—your body could be any color you like. But let's think it over. I tell you what—to be fair, if we both want this body, I promise I'll let the project director flip a coin to settle which of us gets to keep it and which then gets to choose a new body. That should guarantee justice, shouldn't it? In any case, I'll take care of you, I promise. These people are my witnesses.

"Ladies and gentlemen, this talk we have just heard is not exactly the talk *I* would have given, but I assure you that everything he said was perfectly true. And now if you'll excuse me, I think I'd—we'd—better sit down."[2] ▪

Suggestions for Critical Reflection

1. What is the relationship between brain and body? In Dennett's story, would it be more accurate to say that Dennett "is" the disembodied brain, or that he is the brain-less body? Does either explanation seem correct?

2. At one point in his story, Dennett considers what would occur if he committed a crime while his body and brain were separated. He wonders if the trial would occur in the state where his body was located, or the state where his brain was preserved. What does this rumination indicate about the broader implications of Dennett's inquiry? Are there practical reasons why it is important to figure out where the self really is? Imagine that you are standing on the Connecticut–Rhode Island border, and you shoot somebody also standing on the border. Which state would you be tried in? The one in which the gun was? Or the one with the bullet-hole? Or the one with your brain? Or the one with most of your brain (in case the border bisects your head)?

3. Dennett imagines the existence of an electronically reproduced brain. If the technology to replicate brains electronically existed, what would the implications be for artificial intelligence? Would this entail that robots could be given brains, and therefore selves? Does Dennett leave open the possibility of ascribing personhood to machines?

4. René Descartes argued that, because it is possible to imagine living on without a body, the foundation of the self must be found within the mind, within the mental substance he believed to underwrite thinking (see the reading from Descartes in the Theory of Knowledge chapter, especially meditations 2, 3, and 6). What might Descartes say about the situations described in Dennett's story?

5. Dennett couches his speculations about personal identity within a short piece of narrative fiction, rather than a more conventional philosophical essay. Why do you think he chose to do this? What effect does the form of Dennett's text have upon its content? In other words, what are the consequences, benefits, and drawbacks of these arguments appearing within a short story?

Notes

1 Cf. Jaakko Hintikka, "Cogito ergo sum: Inference or Performance?" *The Philosophical Review*, LXXI, 1962, pp. 3–22.

2 Anyone familiar with the literature on this topic will recognize that my remarks owe a great deal to the explorations of Sydney Shoemaker, John Perry, David Lewis and Derek Parfit, and in particular to their papers in Amelie Rorty, ed., *The Identities of Persons*, 1976.

DEREK PARFIT

Personal Identity

Who Was Derek Parfit?

Derek Antony Parfit was born in 1942 in Chengdu, China, the son of two doctors who provided training to a Chinese Christian mission.* After studying at Eton College, England, he earned a degree in history in 1964 from the University of Oxford, and then pursued a fellowship at Harvard and Columbia. In 1984, Parfit published *Reasons and Persons*, a text that earned him a reputation as one of the world's leading philosophers. He served as a research fellow at All Soul's College, Oxford, and was also a visiting professor at Harvard, Rutgers, and New York University. In two volumes in 2011, and a third in 2017, he published his second and final book *On What Matters*, which synthesized the three leading ethical theories: virtue ethics, deontology, and consequentialism. Parfit thought and wrote about philosophy almost continuously, all day every day, but he was also an extreme perfectionist, constantly revising and distilling his writing down to shorter and clearer passages, and so he published relatively sparsely. Outside of his academic career, Parfit was an amateur photographer, especially of architecture, and a philanthropist known to be generous both intellectually and financially. Parfit died in 2017 at the age of 74. Fortified by his philosophical beliefs, Parfit was reportedly unfrightened by death (though he regretted not being able to do all the philosophy he still wished to do): "My death will break the more direct relations between my present experiences and future experiences, but it will not break various other relations. This is all there is to the fact that there will be no one living who will be me. Now that I have seen this, my death seems to me less bad."†

What Is Parfit's Overall Philosophical Project?

Parfit's central purpose is to take on metaphysical questions that make a difference in how humans lead their lives. To this end, he primarily engages philosophical questions that relate to ethical conduct, such as those involved with free will, time, and personal identity. Parfit attacks the idea that individuals exist in isolation, and that self-interest should be the primary criterion for rational action. In his view, personal identity—the notion that an enduring self connects me to "my" past and future experiences—is misguided. What matters, Parfit claims, are our psychological relations to people, who may be "future selves" separated from us by time, or people across the world separated from us by space. Because personal identity is unimportant, Parfit argues, we have just as much of an obligation to help the world's poor in the present as we do to accumulate wealth for ourselves in the future.

What Is the Structure of This Reading?

Parfit begins by observing that there are situations where the criteria we typically use to determine personal identity fail. He suggests that these situations reveal that some questions about personal identity have no definite answer. But, he wants to show, this isn't a problem because the important philosophical questions that seem to be connected to the issue of personal identity can be separated from it and answered independently.

In section I he closely examines a situation where one self becomes divided into two, and argues that the best

---

* His parents gradually grew disillusioned with evangelizing Christianity in a culture already rich with sophisticated value systems and religious beliefs; meanwhile, the seven-year-old Derek became devout, declaring that he wanted to become a monk. By the age of eight, however, he too had lost his Christian faith, deciding that a good God would not send people to Hell ("How to Be Good," profile of Parfit in *The New Yorker* by Larissa MacFarquhar, 5 September 2011).

† Reported in Derek Parfit's obituary in the London *Times*, 4 January 2017.

response to this kind of case is to accept that one person can survive as two different people. From this it follows that survival cannot be a matter of continuing personal identity, since two different things cannot both be identical to—the same thing as—one thing. In section II, Parfit endorses psychological continuity as a criterion of identity: it works well, he suggests, in cases where there are no splits—non-branching cases—and if there *are* splits or branches, then identity does not apply in any case so the search for a criterion is inapplicable.

In section III Parfit explains how we can make sense of psychological continuity—for example, remembering your past—without presupposing personal identity. Then in section IV he uses the idea of the fusion of two selves to argue that survival can be a matter of degree, rather than something which is all-or-nothing. In doing so, he distinguishes the relations of psychological continuity and psychological *connectedness*, and argues that connectedness is a more important element in survival than continuity. In section V he draws upon his analysis of psychological connectedness to develop a way of talking about important philosophical issues, such as the survival of the self, without depending on the (binary, one-to-one) idea of personal identity.

He concludes by suggesting that there are two significant ethical consequences that arise when we replace the concept of identity with relations of degree. The first is that there is no pressing reason to care more for your future self than for people in the world not identical to you, because many other people may be just as related to you as your own future self. The second is that selfish fears about death can be diminished, because the relationship between one's present and one's future self is not as strong as we ordinarily think.

Personal Identity[*1]

We can, I think, describe cases in which, though we know the answer to every other question, we have no idea how to answer a question about personal identity. These cases are not covered by the criteria of personal identity that we actually use.

Do they present a problem?

It might be thought that they do not, because they could never occur. I suspect that some of them could. (Some, for instance, might become scientifically possible.) But I shall claim that even if they did they would present no problem.

My targets are two beliefs: one about the nature of personal identity, the other about its importance.

The first is that in these cases the question about identity must have an answer.

No one thinks this about, say, nations or machines. Our criteria for the identity of these do not cover certain cases. No one thinks that in these cases the questions "Is it the same nation?" or "Is it the same machine?" must have answers.

Some people believe that in this respect they are different. They agree that our criteria of personal identity do not cover certain cases, but they believe that the nature of their own identity through time is, somehow, such as to guarantee that in these cases questions about their identity must have answers. This belief might be expressed as follows: "Whatever happens between now and any future time, either I shall still exist, or I shall not. Any future experience will either be *my* experience, or it will not."

This first belief—in the special nature of personal identity—has, I think, certain effects. It makes people assume that the principle of self-interest is more rationally compelling than any moral principle. And it makes them more depressed by the thought of aging and of death.

I cannot see how to disprove this first belief. I shall describe a problem case. But this can only make it seem implausible.

Another approach might be this. We might suggest that one cause of the belief is the projection of our emotions. When we imagine ourselves in a problem case, we do feel that the question "Would it be me?" must have an answer. But what we take to be a

* Derek Parfit, "Personal Identity," *The Philosophical Review* 80, 1 (1971): 3–27. This was Parfit's first published philosophy paper.

bafflement about a further fact may be only the bafflement of our concern.

I shall not pursue this suggestion here. But one cause of our concern is the belief which is my second target. This is that unless the question about identity has an answer, we cannot answer certain important questions (questions about such matters as survival, memory, and responsibility).

Against this second belief my claim will be this. Certain important questions do presuppose a question about personal identity. But they can be freed of this presupposition. And when they are, the question about identity has no importance.

I

We can start by considering the much-discussed case of the man who, like an amoeba, divides.[2]

Wiggins has recently dramatized this case.[3] He first referred to the operation imagined by Shoemaker.[4] We suppose that my brain is transplanted into someone else's (brainless) body, and that the resulting person has my character and apparent memories of my life. Most of us would agree, after thought, that the resulting person is me. I shall here assume such agreement.[5]

Wiggins then imagined his own operation. My brain is divided, and each half is housed in a new body. Both resulting people have my character and apparent memories of my life.

What happens to me? There seem only three possibilities: (1) I do not survive; (2) I survive as one of the two people; (3) I survive as both.

The trouble with (1) is this. We agreed that I could survive if my brain were successfully transplanted. And people have in fact survived with half their brains destroyed. It seems to follow that I could survive if half my brain were successfully transplanted and the other half were destroyed. But if this is so, how could I *not* survive if the other half were also successfully transplanted? How could a double success be a failure?

We can move to the second description. Perhaps one success is the maximum score. Perhaps I shall be one of the resulting people.

The trouble here is that in Wiggins' case each half of my brain is exactly similar, and so, to start with, is each resulting person. So how can I survive as only one of the two people? What can make me one of them rather than the other?

It seems clear that both of these descriptions— that I do not survive, and that I survive as one of the people—are highly implausible. Those who have accepted them must have assumed that they were the only possible descriptions.

What about our third description: that I survive as both people?

It might be said, "If 'survive' implies identity, this description makes no sense—you cannot be two people. If it does not, the description is irrelevant to a problem about identity."

I shall later deny the second of these remarks. But there are ways of denying the first. We might say, "What we have called 'the two resulting people' are not two people. They are one person. I do survive Wiggins' operation. Its effect is to give me two bodies and a divided mind."

It would shorten my argument if this were absurd. But I do not think it is. It is worth showing why.

We can, I suggest, imagine a divided mind. We can imagine a man having two simultaneous experiences, in having each of which he is unaware of having the other.

We may not even need to imagine this. Certain actual cases, to which Wiggins referred, seem to be best described in these terms. These involve the cutting of the bridge between the hemispheres of the brain.* The aim was to cure epilepsy. But the result appears to be, in the surgeon's words, the creation of "two separate spheres of consciousness,"[6] each of which controls one half of the patient's body. What is experienced in each is, presumably, experienced by the patient.

There are certain complications in these actual cases. So let us imagine a simpler case.

Suppose that the bridge between my hemispheres is brought under my voluntary control. This would enable me to disconnect my hemispheres as easily as if I were blinking. By doing this I would divide my mind.

---

* The corpus callosum, a thick bundle of nerves connecting the two cerebral hemispheres of the brain (in placental mammals) enabling communication between them.

And we can suppose that when my mind is divided I can, in each half, bring about reunion.

This ability would have obvious uses. To give an example: I am near the end of a maths exam, and see two ways of tackling the last problem. I decide to divide my mind, to work, with each half, at one of two calculations, and then to reunite my mind and write a fair copy of the best result.

What shall I experience?

When I disconnect my hemispheres, my consciousness divides into two streams. But this division is not something that I experience. Each of my two streams of consciousness seems to have been straightforwardly continuous with my one stream of consciousness up to the moment of division. The only changes in each stream are the disappearance of half my visual field and the loss of sensation in, and control over, half my body.

Consider my experiences in what we can call my "right-handed" stream. I remember that I assigned my right hand to the longer calculation. This I now begin. In working at this calculation I can see, from the movements of my left hand, that I am also working at the other. But I am not aware of working at the other. So I might, in my right-handed stream, wonder how, in my left-handed stream, I am getting on.

My work is now over. I am about to reunite my mind. What should I, in each stream, expect? Simply that I shall suddenly seem to remember just having thought out two calculations, in thinking out each of which I was not aware of thinking out the other. This, I submit, we can imagine. And if my mind was divided, these memories are correct.

In describing this episode, I assumed that there were two series of thoughts, and that they were both mine. If my two hands visibly wrote out two calculations, and if I claimed to remember two corresponding series of thoughts, this is surely what we should want to say.

If it is, then a person's mental history need not be like a canal, with only one channel. It could be like a river, with islands, and with separate streams.

To apply this to Wiggins' operation: we mentioned the view that it gives me two bodies and a divided mind. We cannot now call this absurd. But it is, I think, unsatisfactory.

There were two features of the case of the exam that made us want to say that only one person was involved. The mind was soon reunited, and there was only one body. If a mind was permanently divided and its halves developed in different ways, the point of speaking of one person would start to disappear. Wiggins' case, where there are also two bodies, seems to be over the borderline. After I have had his operation, the two "products" each have all the attributes of a person. They could live at opposite ends of the earth. (If they later met, they might even fail to recognize each other.) It would become intolerable to deny that they were different people.

Suppose we admit that they are different people. Could we still claim that I survived as both, using "survive" to imply identity?

We could. For we might suggest that two people could compose a third. We might say, "I do survive Wiggins' operation as two people. They can be different people, and yet be me, in just the way in which the Pope's three crowns are one crown."[*7]

This is a possible way of giving sense to the claim that I survive as two different people, using "survive" to imply identity. But it keeps the language of identity only by changing the concept of a person. And there are obvious objections to this change.[8]

The alternative, for which I shall argue, is to give up the language of identity. We can suggest that I survive as two different people without implying that I am these people.

When I first mentioned this alternative, I mentioned this objection: "If your new way of talking does not imply identity, it cannot solve our problem. For that is about identity. The problem is that all the possible answers to the question about identity are highly implausible."

We can now answer this objection.

We can start by reminding ourselves that this is an objection only if we have one or both of the beliefs which I mentioned at the start of this paper.

The first was the belief that to any question about personal identity, in any describable case, there must

---

* The tiara worn by the Catholic pope includes three tiers or "crowns"; there are various interpretations as to the meaning of these crowns.

Derek Parfit · Personal Identity

be a true answer. For those with this belief, Wiggins' case is doubly perplexing. If all the possible answers are implausible, it is hard to decide which of them is true, and hard even to keep the belief that one of them must be true. If we give up this belief, as I think we should, these problems disappear. We shall then regard the case as like many others in which, for quite unpuzzling reasons, there *is* no answer to a question about identity. (Consider "Was England the same nation after 1066?")*

Wiggins' case makes the first belief implausible. It also makes it trivial. For it undermines the second belief. This was the belief that important questions turn upon the question about identity. (It is worth pointing out that those who have only this second belief do not think that there must *be* an answer to this question, but rather that we must decide upon an answer.)

Against this second belief my claim is this. Certain questions do presuppose a question about personal identity. And because these questions *are* important, Wiggins' case does present a problem. But we cannot solve this problem by answering the question about identity. We can solve this problem only by taking these important questions and prizing them apart from the question about identity. After we have done this, the question about identity (though we might for the sake of neatness decide it) has no further interest.

Because there are several questions which presuppose identity, this claim will take some time to fill out.

We can first return to the question of survival. This is a special case, for survival does not so much presuppose the retaining of identity as seem equivalent to it. It is thus the general relation which we need to prize apart from identity. We can then consider particular relations, such as those involved in memory and intention.

"Will I survive?" seems, I said, equivalent to "Will there be some person alive who is the same person as me?"

If we treat these questions as equivalent, then the least unsatisfactory description of Wiggins' case is, I

think, that I survive with two bodies and a divided mind.

Several writers have chosen to say that I am neither of the resulting people. Given our equivalence, this implies that I do not survive, and hence, presumably, that even if Wiggins' operation is not literally death, I ought, since I will not survive it, to regard it *as* death. But this seemed absurd.

It is worth repeating why. An emotion or attitude can be criticized for resting on a false belief, or for being inconsistent. A man who regarded Wiggins' operation as death must, I suggest, be open to one of these criticisms.

He might believe that his relation to each of the resulting people fails to contain some element which is contained in survival. But how can this be true? We agreed that he *would* survive if he stood in this very same relation to only *one* of the resulting people. So it cannot be the nature of this relation which makes it fail, in Wiggins' case, to be survival. It can only be its duplication.

Suppose that our man accepts this, but still regards division as death. His reaction would now seem wildly inconsistent. He would be like a man who, when told of a drug that could double his years of life, regarded the taking of this drug as death. The only difference in the case of division is that the extra years are to run concurrently. This is an interesting difference. But it cannot mean that there are *no* years to run.

I have argued this for those who think that there must, in Wiggins' case, be a true answer to the question about identity. For them, we might add, "Perhaps the original person does lose his identity. But there may be other ways to do this than to die. One other way might be to multiply. To regard these as the same is to confuse nought† with two."

For those who think that the question of identity is up for decision, it would be clearly absurd to regard Wiggins' operation as death. These people would have to think, "We could have chosen to say that I should be one of the resulting people. If we had, I should not have regarded it as death. But since we have chosen to

---

* The date of the successful invasion of England, and overthrow of its monarchy, by the Norman-French William the Conqueror.

† Zero.

say that I am neither person, I *do*." This is hard even to understand.[9]

My first conclusion, then, is this. The relation of the original person to each of the resulting people contains all that interests us—all that matters—in any ordinary case of survival. This is why we need a sense in which one person can survive as two.[10]

One of my aims in the rest of this paper will be to suggest such a sense. But we can first make some general remarks.

II

Identity is a one–one relation.* Wiggins' case serves to show that what matters in survival need not be one–one.

Wiggins' case is of course unlikely to occur. The relations which matter are, in fact, one–one. It is because they are that we can imply the holding of these relations by using the language of identity.

This use of language is convenient. But it can lead us astray. We may assume that what matters *is* identity and, hence, has the properties of identity.

In the case of the property of being one–one, this mistake is not serious. For what matters is in fact one–one. But in the case of another property, the mistake *is* serious. Identity is all-or-nothing. Most of the relations which matter in survival are, in fact, relations of degree. If we ignore this, we shall be led into quite ill-grounded attitudes and beliefs.

The claim that I have just made—that most of what matters are relations of degree—I have yet to support. Wiggins' case shows only that these relations need not be one–one. The merit of the case is not that it shows this in particular, but that it makes the first break between what matters and identity. The belief that identity *is* what matters is hard to overcome. This is shown in most discussions of the problem cases which actually occur: cases, say, of amnesia or of brain damage. Once Wiggins' case has made one breach in this belief, the rest should be easier to remove.[11]

To turn to a recent debate: most of the relations which matter can be provisionally referred to under the heading "psychological continuity" (which includes causal continuity). My claim is thus that we use the language of personal identity in order to imply such continuity. This is close to the view that psychological continuity provides a criterion of identity.

Williams has attacked this view with the following argument. Identity is a one–one relation. So any criterion of identity must appeal to a relation which is logically one–one. Psychological continuity is not logically one–one. So it cannot provide a criterion.[12]

Some writers have replied that it is enough if the relation appealed to is always in fact one–one.[13]

I suggest a slightly different reply. Psychological continuity is a ground for speaking of identity when it is one–one.

If psychological continuity took a one–many or branching form, we should need, I have argued, to abandon the language of identity. So this possibility would not count against this view.

We can make a stronger claim. This possibility would count in its favor.

The view might be defended as follows. Judgments of personal identity have great importance. What gives them their importance is the fact that they imply psychological continuity. This is why, whenever there is such continuity, we ought, if we can, to imply it by making a judgment of identity.

If psychological continuity took a branching form, no coherent set of judgments of identity could correspond to, and thus be used to imply, the branching form of this relation. But what we ought to do, in such a case, is take the importance which would attach to a judgment of identity and attach this importance directly to each limb of the branching relation. So this case helps to show that judgments of personal identity do derive their importance from the fact that they imply psychological continuity. It helps to show that when we can, usefully, speak of identity, this relation is our ground.

This argument appeals to a principle which Williams put forward.[14] The principle is that an important judgment should be asserted and denied only on importantly different grounds.

---

* A relation of one thing to one thing (as opposed to, say, a two–one relation—such as the typical relation of biological parents to their first child, or a three–one relation—such as the way the three branches of the federal government make up the US government).

Williams applied this principle to a case in which one man is psychologically continuous with the dead Guy Fawkes,* and a case in which two men are. His argument was this. If we treat psychological continuity as a sufficient ground for speaking of identity, we shall say that the one man is Guy Fawkes. But we could not say that the two men are, although we should have the same ground. This disobeys the principle. The remedy is to deny that the one man is Guy Fawkes, to insist that sameness of the body is necessary for identity.

Williams' principle can yield a different answer. Suppose we regard psychological continuity as more important than sameness of the body.[15] And suppose that the one man really is psychologically (and causally) continuous with Guy Fawkes. If he is, it would disobey the principle to deny that he is Guy Fawkes, for we have the same important ground as in a normal case of identity. In the case of the two men, we again have the same important ground. So we ought to take the importance from the judgment of identity and attach it directly to this ground. We ought to say, as in Wiggins' case, that each limb of the branching relation is as good as survival. This obeys the principle.

To sum up these remarks: even if psychological continuity is neither logically, nor always in fact, one–one, it can provide a criterion of identity. For this can appeal to the relation of *non-branching* psychological continuity, which is logically one–one.[16]

The criterion might be sketched as follows. "*X* and *Y* are the same person if they are psychologically continuous and there is no person who is contemporary with either and psychologically continuous with the other." We should need to explain what we mean by "psychologically continuous" and say how much continuity the criterion requires. We should then, I think, have described a sufficient condition for speaking of identity.[17]

We need to say something more. If we admit that psychological continuity might not be one–one, we need to say what we ought to do if it were not one–one. Otherwise our account would be open to the objections that it is incomplete and arbitrary.[18]

I have suggested that if psychological continuity took a branching form, we ought to speak in a new way, regarding what we describe as having the same significance as identity. This answers these objections.[19]

We can now return to our discussion. We have three remaining aims. One is to suggest a sense of "survive" which does not imply identity. Another is to show that most of what matters in survival are relations of degree. A third is to show that none of these relations needs to be described in a way that presupposes identity.

We can take these aims in the reverse order.

III

The most important particular relation is that involved in memory. This is because it is so easy to believe that its description must refer to identity.[20] This belief about memory is an important cause of the view that personal identity has a special nature. But it has been well discussed by Shoemaker[21] and by Wiggins.[22] So we can be brief.

It may be a logical truth that we can only remember our own experiences. But we can frame a new concept for which this is not a logical truth. Let us call this "*q*-memory."

To sketch a definition[23] I am *q*-remembering an experience if (1) I have a belief about a past experience which seems in itself like a memory belief, (2) someone did have such an experience, and (3) my belief is dependent upon this experience in the same way (whatever that is) in which a memory of an experience is dependent upon it.

According to (1) *q*-memories seem like memories. So I *q*-remember *having* experiences.

This may seem to make *q*-memory presuppose identity. One might say, "My apparent memory of *having* an experience is an apparent memory of *my* having an experience. So how could I *q*-remember my having other people's experiences?"

This objection rests on a mistake. When I seem to remember an experience, I do indeed seem to remember *having* it.[24] But it cannot be a part of what I seem to remember about this experience that I, the person who now seems to remember it, am the person who had this experience.[25] That I am is something that I

---

* Guy Fawkes (1570–1606) attempted to assassinate King James I of England and blow up the English Parliament as part of the so-called Gunpowder Plot in 1605.

automatically assume. (My apparent memories sometimes come to me simply as the belief that *I* had a certain experience.) But it is something that I am justified in assuming only because I do not in fact have *q*-memories of other people's experiences.

Suppose that I did start to have such *q*-memories. If I did, I should cease to assume that my apparent memories must be about my own experiences. I should come to assess an apparent memory by asking two questions: (1) Does it tell me about a past experience? (2) If so, whose?

Moreover (and this is a crucial point) my apparent memories would now come to me *as q*-memories. Consider those of my apparent memories which do come to me simply as beliefs about my past: for example, "I did that." If I knew that I could *q*-remember other people's experiences, these beliefs would come to me in a more guarded form: for example, "Someone—probably I—did that." I might have to work out who it was.

I have suggested that the concept of *q*-memory is coherent. Wiggins' case provides an illustration. The resulting people, in his case, both have apparent memories of living the life of the original person. If they agree that they are not this person, they will have to regard these as only *q*-memories. And when they are asked a question like "Have you heard this music before?" they might have to answer "I am sure that I *q*-remember hearing it. But I am not sure whether I remember hearing it. I am not sure whether it was I who heard it, or the original person."

We can next point out that on our definition every memory is also a *q*-memory. Memories are, simply, *q*-memories of one's own experiences. Since this is so, we could afford now to drop the concept of memory and use in its place the wider concept *q*-memory. If we did, we should describe the relation between an experience and what we now call a "memory" of this experience in a way which does not presuppose that they are had by the same person.[26]

This way of describing this relation has certain merits. It vindicates the "memory criterion" of personal identity against the charge of circularity.[27] And it might, I think, help with the problem of other minds.

But we must move on. We can next take the relation between an intention and a later action. It may be a logical truth that we can intend to perform only our own actions. But intentions can be redescribed as *q*-intentions. And one person could *q*-intend to perform another person's actions.

Wiggins' case again provides the illustration. We are supposing that neither of the resulting people is the original person. If so, we shall have to agree that the original person can, before the operation, *q*-intend to perform their actions. He might, for example, *q*-intend, as one of them, to continue his present career, and, as the other, to try something new.[28] (I say "*q*-intend *as* one of them" because the phrase "*q*-intend *that* one of them" would not convey the directness of the relation which is involved. If I intend that someone else should do something, I cannot get him to do it simply by forming this intention. But if I am the original person, and he is one of the resulting people, I can.)

The phrase "*q*-intend *as* one of them" reminds us that we need a sense in which one person can survive as two. But we can first point out that the concepts of *q*-memory and *q*-intention give us our model for the others that we need: thus, a man who can *q*-remember could *q*-recognize, and be a *q*-witness of, what he has never seen; and a man who can *q*-intend could have *q*-ambitions, make *q*-promises, and be *q*-responsible for.

To put this claim in general terms: many different relations are included within, or are a consequence of, psychological continuity. We describe these relations in ways which presuppose the continued existence of one person. But we could describe them in new ways which do not.

This suggests a bolder claim. It might be possible to think of experiences in a wholly "impersonal" way. I shall not develop this claim here. What I shall try to describe is a way of thinking of our own identity through time which is more flexible, and less misleading, than the way in which we now think.

This way of thinking will allow for a sense in which one person can survive as two. A more important feature is that it treats survival as a matter of degree.

IV

We must first show the need for this second feature. I shall use two imaginary examples.

The first is the converse of Wiggins' case: fusion. Just as division serves to show that what matters in survival need not be one—one, so fusion serves to show that it can be a question of degree.

Physically, fusion is easy to describe. Two people come together. While they are unconscious, their two bodies grow into one. One person then wakes up.

The psychology of fusion is more complex. One detail we have already dealt with in the case of the exam. When my mind was reunited, I remembered just having thought out two calculations. The one person who results from a fusion can, similarly, *q*-remember living the lives of the two original people. None of their *q*-memories need be lost.

But some things must be lost. For any two people who fuse together will have different characteristics, different desires, and different intentions. How can these be combined?

We might suggest the following. Some of these will be compatible. These can coexist in the one resulting person. Some will be incompatible. These, if of equal strength, can cancel out, and if of different strengths, the stronger can be made weaker. And all these effects might be predictable.

To give examples—first, of compatibility: I like Palladio* and intend to visit Venice. I am about to fuse with a person who likes Giotto† and intends to visit Padua. I can know that the one person we shall become will have both tastes and both intentions. Second, of incompatibility: I hate red hair, and always vote Labour. The other person loves red hair, and always votes Conservative.‡ I can know that the one person we shall become will be indifferent to red hair, and a floating voter.§

If we were about to undergo a fusion of this kind, would we regard it as death?

Some of us might. This is less absurd than regarding division as death. For after my division the two resulting people will be in every way like me, while after my fusion the one resulting person will not be wholly similar. This makes it easier to say, when faced with fusion, "I shall not survive," thus continuing to regard survival as a matter of all-or-nothing.

This reaction is less absurd. But here are two analogies which tell against it.

First, fusion would involve the changing of some of our characteristics and some of our desires. But only the very self-satisfied would think of this as death. Many people welcome treatments with these effects.

Second, someone who is about to fuse can have, beforehand, just as much "intentional control" over the actions of the resulting individual as someone who is about to marry can have, beforehand, over the actions of the resulting couple. And the choice of a partner for fusion can be just as well considered as the choice of a marriage partner. The two original people can make sure (perhaps by "trial fusion") that they do have compatible characters, desires, and intentions.

I have suggested that fusion, while not clearly survival, is not clearly failure to survive, and hence that what matters in survival can have degrees.

To reinforce this claim we can now turn to a second example. This is provided by certain imaginary beings. These beings are just like ourselves except that they reproduce by a process of natural division.

We can illustrate the histories of these imagined beings with the aid of a diagram. (See below.) The lines on the diagram represent the spatiotemporal paths which would be traced out by the bodies of these beings. We can call each single line (like the double line) a "branch"; and we can call the whole structure a "tree." And let us suppose that each "branch" corresponds to what is thought of as the life of one individual. These individuals are referred to as "A," "B + 1," and so forth.

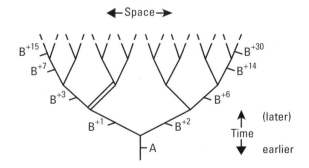

* Andrea Palladio was a sixteenth-century Italian architect best known for the buildings he designed in Venice.
† Giotto di Bondone was an Italian painter and architect whose most famous work is the decoration of the Scrovegni Chapel in Padua, c. 1305.
‡ Labour refers to the most prominent left-wing political party in Britain, and Conservative to the most prominent right-wing party.
§ Someone with no allegiance to any one political party.

Now, each single division is an instance of Wiggins' case. So A's relation to both $B + 1$ and $B + 2$ is just as good as survival. But what of A's relation to $B + 30$?

I said earlier that what matters in survival could be provisionally referred to as "psychological continuity." I must now distinguish this relation from another, which I shall call "psychological connectedness."

Let us say that the relation between a q-memory and the experience q-remembered is a "direct" relation. Another "direct" relation is that which holds between a q-intention and the q-intended action. A third is that which holds between different expressions of some lasting q-characteristic.

"Psychological connectedness," as I define it, requires the holding of these direct psychological relations. "Connectedness" is not transitive, since these relations are not transitive.* Thus, if X q-remembers most of Y's life, and Y q-remembers most of Z's life, it does not follow that X q-remembers most of Z's life. And if X carries out the q-intentions of Y, and Y carries out the q-intentions of Z, it does not follow that X carries out the q-intentions of Z.

"Psychological continuity," in contrast, only requires overlapping chains of direct psychological relations. So "continuity" *is* transitive.

To return to our diagram. A *is* psychologically continuous with $B + 30$. There are between the two continuous chains of overlapping relations. Thus, A has q-intentional control over $B + 2$, $B + 2$ has q-intentional control over $B + 6$, and so on up to $B + 30$. Or $B + 30$ can q-remember the life of $B + 14$, $B + 14$ can q-remember the life of $B + 6$, and so on back to A.[29]

A, however, need *not* be psychologically connected to $B + 30$. Connectedness requires direct relations. And if these beings are like us, A cannot stand in such relations to every individual in his indefinitely long "tree." Q-memories will weaken with the passage of time, and then fade away. Q-ambitions, once fulfilled, will be replaced by others. Q-characteristics will gradually change. In general, A stands in fewer and fewer direct psychological relations to an individual in his "tree" the more remote that individual is. And if the individual is (like $B + 30$) sufficiently remote, there may be between the two *no* direct psychological relations.

Now that we have distinguished the general relations of psychological continuity and psychological connectedness, I suggest that connectedness is a more important element in survival. As a claim about our own survival, this would need more arguments than I have space to give. But it seems clearly true for my imagined beings. A is as close psychologically to $B + 1$ as I today am to myself tomorrow. A is as distant from $B + 30$ as I am from my great-great-grandson.

Even if connectedness is not more important than continuity, the fact that one of these is a relation of degree is enough to show that what matters in survival can have degrees. And in any case the two relations are quite different. So our imagined beings would need a way of thinking in which this difference is recognized.

V

What I propose is this.

First, A can think of any individual, anywhere in his "tree," as "a descendant self." This phrase implies psychological continuity. Similarly, any later individual can think of any earlier individual on the single path[30] which connects him to A as "an ancestral self."

Since psychological continuity is transitive, "being an ancestral self of" and "being a descendant self of" are also transitive.

To imply psychological connectedness I suggest the phrases "one of my future selves" and "one of my past selves."

These are the phrases with which we can describe Wiggins' case. For having past and future selves is, what we needed, a way of continuing to exist which does not imply identity through time. The original person does, in this sense, survive Wiggins' operation: the two resulting people are his later selves. And they can each refer to him as "my past self." (They can share a past self without being the same self as each other.)

Since psychological connectedness is not transitive, and is a matter of degree, the relations "being a past self of" and "being a future self of" should themselves be treated as relations of degree. We allow for

---

* A relation R is transitive when, if a is related by R to b, and b is related by R to c, then a must be related by R to c. "Is larger than" is an example of a transitive relation, while "gave birth to" is not.

this series of descriptions: "my most recent self," "one of my earlier selves," "one of my distant selves," "hardly one of *my* past selves (I can only *q*-remember a few of his experiences)," and, finally, "not in any way one of *my* past selves—just an ancestral self."

This way of thinking would clearly suit our first imagined beings. But let us now turn to a second kind of being. These reproduce by fusion as well as by division.[31] And let us suppose that they fuse every autumn and divide every spring. This yields the following diagram:

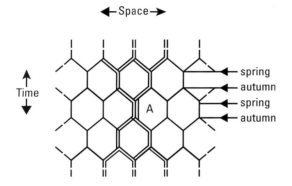

If *A* is the individual whose life is represented by the three-lined "branch," the two-lined "tree" represents those lives which are psychologically continuous with *A's* life. (It can be seen that each individual has his own "tree," which overlaps with many others.)

For the imagined beings in this second world, the phrases "an ancestral self" and "a descendant self" would cover too much to be of much use. (There may well be pairs of dates such that every individual who ever lived before the first date was an ancestral self of every individual who ever will live after the second date.) Conversely, since the lives of each individual last for only half a year, the word "I" would cover too little to do all of the work which it does for us. So part of this work would have to be done, for these second beings, by talk about past and future selves.

We can now point out a theoretical flaw in our proposed way of thinking. The phrase "a past self of" implies psychological connectedness. Being a past self of is treated as a relation of degree, so that this phrase can be used to imply the varying degrees of psychological connectedness. But this phrase can imply only the degrees of connectedness between different lives. It cannot be used within a single life. And our way

of delimiting successive lives does not refer to the degrees of psychological connectedness. Hence there is no guarantee that this phrase, "a past self of," could be used whenever it was needed. There is no guarantee that psychological connectedness will not vary in degree within a single life.

This flaw would not concern our imagined beings. For they divide and unite so frequently, and their lives are in consequence so short, that within a single life psychological connectedness would always stand at a maximum.

But let us look, finally, at a third kind of being.

In this world there is neither division nor union. There are a number of everlasting bodies, which gradually change in appearance. And direct psychological relations, as before, hold only over limited periods of time. This can be illustrated with a third diagram (given below). In this diagram the two shadings represent the degrees of psychological connectedness to their two central points.

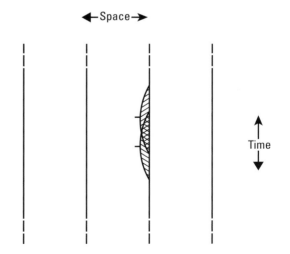

These beings could not use the way of thinking that we have proposed. Since there is no branching of psychological continuity, they would have to regard themselves as immortal. It might be said that this is what they are. But there is, I suggest, a better description.

Our beings would have one reason for thinking of themselves as immortal. The parts of each "line" are all psychologically continuous. But the parts of each "line" are not all psychologically connected. Direct psychological relations hold only between those parts which are close to each other in time. This gives our beings a reason for *not* thinking of each "line" as corresponding to one single life. For if they did, they would have no way of implying these direct relations. When a speaker says, for example, "I spent a period doing such and such," his hearers would not be entitled to assume that the speaker has any memories of this period, that his character then and now are in any way similar, that he is now carrying out any of the plans or intentions which he then had, and so forth. Because the word "I" would carry none of these implications, it would not have for these "immortal" beings the usefulness which it has for us.[32]

To gain a better way of thinking, we must revise the way of thinking that we proposed above. The revision is this. The distinction between successive selves can be made by reference, not to the branching of psychological continuity, but to the degrees of psychological connectedness. Since this connectedness is a matter of degree, the drawing of these distinctions can be left to the choice of the speaker and be allowed to vary from context to context.

On this way of thinking, the word "I" can be used to imply the greatest degree of psychological connectedness. When the connections are reduced, when there has been any marked change of character or style of life, or any marked loss of memory, our imagined beings would say, "It was not I who did that, but an earlier self." They could then describe in what ways, and to what degree, they are related to this earlier self.

This revised way of thinking would suit not only our "immortal" beings. It is also the way in which we ourselves could think about our lives. And it is, I suggest, surprisingly natural.

One of its features, the distinction between successive selves, has already been used by several writers. To give an example, from Proust:* "we are incapable, while we are in love, of acting as fit predecessors of the next persons who, when we are in love no longer, we shall presently have become...."[33]

Although Proust distinguished between successive selves, he still thought of one person as being these different selves. This we would not do on the way of thinking that I propose. If I say, "It will not be me, but one of my future selves," I do not imply that I will be that future self. He is one of my later selves, and I am one of his earlier selves. There is no underlying person who we both are.

To point out another feature of this way of thinking. When I say, "There is no person who we both are," I am only giving my decision. Another person could say, "It will be you," thus deciding differently. There is no question of either of these decisions being a mistake. Whether to say "I," or "one of my future selves," or "a descendant self" is entirely a matter of choice. The matter of fact, which must be agreed, is only whether the disjunction applies. (The question "Are *X* and *Y* the same person?" thus becomes "Is *X* at least an ancestral [or descendant] self of *Y*?")

VI

I have tried to show that what matters in the continued existence of a person are, for the most part, relations of degree. And I have proposed a way of thinking in which this would be recognized.

I shall end by suggesting two consequences and asking one question.

It is sometimes thought to be especially rational to act in our own best interests. But I suggest that the principle of self-interest has no force. There are only two genuine competitors in this particular field. One is the principle of biased rationality: do what will best achieve what you actually want. The other is the principle of impartiality: do what is in the best interests of everyone concerned.

The apparent force of the principle of self-interest derives, I think, from these two other principles.

The principle of self-interest is normally supported by the principle of biased rationality. This is because most people care about their own future interests.

Suppose that this prop is lacking. Suppose that a man does not care what happens to him in, say, the

---

*   Marcel Proust was a French author, best known for his novel, *À la recherche du temps perdu* ("In Search of Lost Time"), published in seven parts between 1913 and 1927. Proust's writing is characterized by detailed reminiscences on the past, which are often sparked by chance encounters with objects in the present.

more distant future. To such a man, the principle of self-interest can only be propped up by an appeal to the principle of impartiality. We must say, "Even if you don't care, you ought to take what happens to you then equally into account." But for this, as a special claim, there seem to me no good arguments. It can only be supported as part of the general claim, "You ought to take what happens to everyone equally into account."[34]

The special claim tells a man to grant an *equal* weight to all the parts of his future. The argument for this can only be that all the parts of his future are *equally* parts of *his* future. This is true. But it is a truth too superficial to bear the weight of the argument. (To give an analogy: The unity of a nation is, in its nature, a matter of degree. It is therefore only a superficial truth that all of a man's compatriots are *equally* his compatriots. This truth cannot support a good argument for nationalism.)[35]

I have suggested that the principle of self-interest has no strength of its own. If this is so, there is no special problem in the fact that what we ought to do

can be against our interests. There is only the general problem that it may not be what we want to do.

The second consequence which I shall mention is implied in the first. Egoism, the fear not of near but of distant death, the regret that so much of one's *only* life should have gone by—these are not, I think, wholly natural or instinctive. They are all strengthened by the beliefs about personal identity which I have been attacking. If we give up these beliefs, they should be weakened.

My final question is this. These emotions are bad, and if we weaken them we gain. But can we achieve this gain without, say, also weakening loyalty to, or love of, other particular selves? As Hume* warned, the "refined reflections which philosophy suggests ... cannot diminish ... our vicious passions ... without diminishing ... such as are virtuous. They are ... applicable to all our affections. In vain do we hope to direct their influence only to one side."[36]

That hope *is* vain. But Hume had another: that more of what is bad depends upon false belief. This is also my hope. ∎

Suggestions for Critical Reflection

1. Parfit's theory of personal identity is often compared to the Buddhist doctrine of no-self—to the point that Tibetan monks have been reported to chant excerpts from his books. To what extent does Parfit advocate the erasure of the self? How does Parfit's theory of degrees of relation relate to the Buddhist idea that all things in the universe are related to one another?

2. Parfit develops a concept he calls *q*-memory. Why does he do this—what part of his overall argument is this? How clear is his explanation of *q*-memory? Are all our memories really *q*-memories?

3. "Now that we have distinguished the general relations of psychological continuity and psychological connectedness, I suggest that connectedness is a more important element in survival." Is Parfit able to show this? How radical is this conclusion, if it is true?

4. Parfit recognizes that a weakened conception of personal identity may inadvertently result in people losing loyalty towards or love for others. Is identity a precondition for love or loyalty? Why or why not?

5. Parfit suggests that his critique of personal identity may soften fears that people have around death. Do you agree with this claim? Why or why not?

6. Parfit claims that his view has practical ethical consequences, in that it may lead us to abandon the principle of self-interest. Does his view also suggest that we should change our understanding of personal responsibility? Does our criminal justice system rely on a certain conception of the self?

7. The Mississippi river has, at several places in it, long islands dividing it into two streams which

---

* David Hume (1711–76) was an important Scottish philosopher.

rejoin down-river. Suppose we drive to the bank of the east stream at one such place. (Call that stream 'Eastie'.) "That's the Mississippi!" I say. But later we drive on the other side to the west stream ('Westie'). "That's the Mississippi again!" I say. If what I said was true, then Eastie = the Mississippi (where the equals sign means *identity*), and Westie = the Mississippi, but Eastie ≠ Westie. Does this approach to identity conflict with Parfit's? If so, who is correct?

8. Suppose that you can expect to live for another 60 years, and that you're pretty sure that 60 years from now you'll have no psychological connectedness whatever with your present self. On those grounds, would Parfit say that you really should have no motivation to think long-term: don't bother brushing your teeth, or putting money into a retirement fund?

Notes

1 I have been helped in writing this by D. Wiggins, D.F. Pears, P.F. Strawson, A.J. Ayer, M. Woods, N. Newman, and (through his publications) S. Shoemaker.

2 Implicit in John Locke, *Essay Concerning Human Understanding*, ed. by John W. Yolton (London, 1961), Vol. II, Ch. XXVII, sec. 18, and discussed by (among others) A.N. Prior in "Opposite Number," *Review of Metaphysics*, II (1957–1958), and "Time, Existence and Identity," *Proceedings of the Aristotelian Society*, LVII (1965–1966); J. Bennett in "The Simplicity of the Soul," *Journal of Philosophy*, LXIV (1967); and R. Chisholm and S. Shoemaker in "The Loose and Popular and the Strict and the Philosophical Senses of Identity," in *Perception and Personal Identity: Proceedings of the 1967 Oberlin Colloquium in Philosophy*, ed. by Norman Care and Robert H. Grimm (Cleveland, 1967).

3 In *Identity and Spatio-Temporal Continuity* (Oxford, 1967), p. 50.

4 In *Self-Knowledge and Self-Identity* (Ithaca, N.Y., 1963), p. 22.

5 Those who would disagree are not making a mistake. For them my argument would need a different case. There must be some multiple transplant, faced with which these people would both find it hard to believe that there must be an answer to the question about personal identity, and be able to be shown that nothing of importance turns upon this question.

6 R.W. Sperry, in *Brain and Conscious Experience*, ed. by J.C. Eccles (New York, 1966), p. 299.

7 Cf. David Wiggins, *op. cit*, p. 40.

8 Suppose the resulting people fight a duel. Are there three people fighting, one on each side, and one on both? And suppose one of the bullets kills. Are there two acts, one murder and one suicide? How many people are left alive? One? Two? (We could hardly say, "One and a half.") We could talk in this way. But instead of saying that the resulting people *are* the original person—so that the pair is a trio—it would be far simpler to treat them as a pair, and describe their relation to the original person in some new way. (I owe this suggested way of talking, and the objections to it, to Michael Woods.)

9 Cf. Sydney Shoemaker, in *Perception and Personal Identity: Proceedings of the 1967 Oberlin Colloquium in Philosophy, loc. cit*.

10 Cf. David Wiggins, *op. cit.*, p. 54.

11 Bernard Williams' "The Self and the Future," *Philosophical Review*, LXXIX (1970), 161–180, is relevant here. He asks the question "Shall I survive?" in a range of problem cases, and he shows how natural it is to believe (1) that this question must have an answer, (2) that the answer must be all-or-nothing, and (3) that there is a "risk" of our reaching the *wrong* answer. Because these beliefs are so natural, we should need in undermining them to discuss their causes. These, I think, can be found in the ways in which we misinterpret what it is to remember (cf. Sec. III below) and to anticipate (cf. Williams' "Imagination and the Self," *Proceedings of the British Academy*, LII [1966], 105–124); and also in the way in which certain features of our egoistic concern—e.g., that it is simple, and applies to all imaginable cases—are "projected" onto its object. (For another relevant discussion, see Terence Penelhum's *Survival and Disembodied Existence* [London, 1970], final chapters.)

12 "Personal Identity and Individuation," *Proceedings of the Aristotelian Society*, LVII (1956–1957), 229–253; also *Analysis*, 21 (1960–1961), 43–48.

13 J.M. Shorter, "More about Bodily Continuity and Personal Identity," *Analysis*, 22 (1961–1962), 79–85; and Mrs. J.M.R. Jack (unpublished), who requires that this truth be embedded in a causal theory.

14 *Analysis*, 21 (1960–1961), 44.

15 For the reasons given by A.M. Quinton in "The Soul," *Journal of Philosophy*, LIX (1962), 393–409.

16 Cf. S. Shoemaker, "Persons and Their Pasts," to appear in the *American Philosophical Quarterly*, and "Wiggins on Identity," *Philosophical Review*, LXXIX (1970), 542.

17 But not a necessary condition, for in the absence of psychological continuity bodily identity might be sufficient.

18 Cf. Bernard Williams, "Personal Identity and Individuation," *Proceedings of the Aristotelian Society*, LVII (1956–1957), 240–241, and *Analysis*, 21 (1960–1961), 44; and also Wiggins, *op. cit.*, p. 38: "if coincidence under [the concept] *f* is to be *genuinely* sufficient we must not withhold identity … simply because transitivity is threatened."

19 Williams produced another objection to the "psychological criterion," that it makes it hard to explain the difference between the concepts of identity and exact similarity (*Analysis*, 21 [1960–1961], 48). But if we include the requirement of causal continuity we avoid this objection (and one of those produced by Wiggins in his note 47).

20 Those philosophers who have held this belief, from Butler onward, are too numerous to cite.

21 *Op. cit.*

22 In a paper on Butler's objection to Locke (not yet published).

23 I here follow Shoemaker's "quasi-memory." Cf. also Penelhum's "retrocognition," in his article on "Personal Identity," in the *Encyclopedia of Philosophy*, ed. by Paul Edwards.

24 As Shoemaker put it, I seem to remember the experience "from the inside" (*op. cit.*).

25 This is what so many writers have overlooked. Cf. Thomas Reid: "My memory testifies not only that this was done, but that it was done by me who now remember it" ("Of Identity," in *Essays on the Intellectual Powers of Man*, ed. by A.D. Woozley [London, 1941], p. 203). This mistake is discussed by A.B. Palma in "Memory and Personal Identity," *Australasian Journal of Philosophy*, 42 (1964), 57.

26 It is not logically necessary that we only *q*-remember our own experiences. But it might be necessary on other grounds. This possibility is intriguingly explored by Shoemaker in his "Persons and Their Pasts" (*op. cit.*). He shows that *q*-memories can provide a knowledge of the world only if the observations which are *q*-remembered trace out fairly continuous spatiotemporal paths. If the observations which are *q*-remembered traced out a network of frequently interlocking paths, they could not, I think, be usefully ascribed to persisting observers, but would have to be referred to in some more complex way. But in fact the observations which are *q*-remembered trace out single and separate paths; so we can ascribe them to ourselves. In other words, it is epistemologically necessary that the observations which are *q*-remembered should satisfy a certain general condition, one particular form of which allows them to be usefully self-ascribed.

27 Cf. Wiggins' paper on Butler's objection to Locke.

28 There are complications here. He could form *divergent* *q*-intentions only if he could distinguish, in advance, between the resulting people (e.g., as "the left-hander" and "the right-hander"). And he could be confident that such divergent *q*-intentions would be carried out only if he had reason to believe that neither of the resulting people would change their (inherited) mind. Suppose he was torn between duty and desire. He could not solve this dilemma by *q*-intending, as one of the resulting people, to do his duty, and, as the other, to do what he desires. For the one he *q*-intended to do his duty would face the same dilemma.

29 The chain of continuity must run in one direction of time. $B + 2$ is not, in the sense I intend, psychologically continuous with $B + 1$.

30 Cf. David Wiggins, *op. cit.*

31 Cf. Sydney Shoemaker in "Persons and Their Pasts," *op. cit.*

32 Cf. Austin Duncan Jones, "Man's Mortality," *Analysis*, 28 (1967–1968), 65–70.

33 *Within a Budding Grove* (London, 1949), I, 226 (my own translation).

34 Cf. Thomas Nagel's *The Possibility of Altruism* (Oxford, 1970), in which the special claim is in effect defended as part of the general claim.

35 The unity of a nation we seldom take for more than what it is. This is partly because we often think of nations, not as units, but in a more complex way. If we thought of ourselves in the way that I proposed, we might be less likely to take our own identity for more than what it is. We are, for example, sometimes told, "It is irrational to act against your own interests. After all, it will be *you* who will regret it." To this we could reply, "No, not me. Not even one of my future selves. Just a descendant self."

36 "The Sceptic," in "Essays Moral, Political and Literary," *Hume's Moral and Political Philosophy* (New York, 1959), p. 349.

How Ought We to Live Our Lives?

Ethics, of course, is the philosophical sub-discipline which examines morality;* along with metaphysics and epistemology, it is one of the largest and most important areas of philosophy. It can usefully be thought of as divided into three main parts: *normative ethics*, *applied ethics,* and *metaethics*.

i) Normative ethics is the philosophical study of the standards of right and wrong, or of good and bad. Normative ethical theories do not attempt to merely *describe* how people actually do behave, or report what people *think* is right: they lay out prescriptions (rooted in rationally supported philosophical theory) for how people *really ought* to think and behave. It is common—though by no means universal—to assume that the proper aim of normative ethics should be to develop a systematic and comprehensive moral theory which has as many of the virtues of a scientific theory as possible: it should capture all the phenomena of moral life, place them within a simple and unified theoretical structure, and provide the resources for answering any ethical question whatsoever—i.e.,

an adequate moral theory should always be able to tell you what to do, and it should always give you the correct answer.

One way of classifying different normative moral theories is in terms of their emphasis on 'the Right' or 'the Good.' Some moral theories—such as that of Kant—are primarily theories of *right action*: they are moral codes (usually derived from, and justified by, some fundamental principle or set of principles, such as Kant's Categorical Imperative) that define the duties human beings have to themselves and others. A (morally) good life is then defined simply as a life of duty—a life spent doing the right thing. By contrast, other moral theories—such as Mill's utilitarianism—*begin* by developing a theory of the good: they are accounts of those things that are *good in themselves* (or at least which are essential components of human flourishing). For example, for Mill, what is good is the happiness of sentient creatures. Right actions are then defined derivatively as those (whichever they are) that best contribute to the good.

---

* There are various important philosophical usages which treat 'ethical' and 'moral' as meaning slightly different things. For example, some philosophers (such as Bernard Williams) use the word 'ethics' to denote systems of *rules* for conduct, while 'morality' has a more open-ended, less institutionalized content ... while others (such as Jürgen Habermas), interestingly, use the terms in almost exactly the opposite way! I am ignoring such niceties here, however, and simply treat the two words as being interchangeable.

ii) Applied ethics is the study of how ethical norms or rules ought to be applied in particular cases of unusual difficulty, such as abortion, mercy-killing, the treatment of animals, genetic research, corporate responsibility to the community, "just" wars, and so on. It encompasses several sub-fields, such as bioethics, business ethics, environmental ethics, legal ethics, and so forth.

iii) Metaethics deals with the philosophical underpinnings of normative ethics: that is, it applies philosophical scrutiny to a part of philosophy itself. The main kinds of metaethical inquiry are the study of the ethical *concepts* used in normative ethics (such as 'duty,' 'right,' 'good,' 'responsibility'), moral *epistemology* (questions about whether and how moral truths can be known), and moral *ontology* (which is concerned with the nature of 'moral reality'—e.g., whether it is objective or subjective, relative or absolute).

The sequence of readings in this section begins in the realm of metaethics, then moves into normative ethics; some applied ethical issues are dealt with in the next section. The question which is being pursued throughout this section is simple, but profound: "How should I live my life?" That is, what kind of *person* should I be? What *values* should guide my plans and choices? Which kinds of *behavior* are morally acceptable, and which unacceptable?

The first selection, from Plato, is a metaethical consideration of the notion of moral value itself: what exactly is the connection between moral virtue and 'the good life'? Are moral goodness and well-being *simply the same thing* (perhaps because only the virtuous are really happy, as Plato goes on to argue, or because what is morally good just is happiness, which is Mill's view)? Or do happiness and virtue come apart (as Kant believes): could one be moral but miserable, vicious yet fulfilled? Along similar lines, another excerpt from Plato asks: what is the connection between moral virtue and religion? Are certain behaviors morally good because the gods (or God) approve of them, or do the gods approve of them because they are good?

The next readings introduce three of the historically most important and influential theories of normative ethics. Aristotle lays the foundations for a theory called 'virtue ethics,' which holds that morality cannot be captured by any set of moral rules or principles—instead, what is

right or wrong will vary from situation to situation and the trick is to educate people to be wise in their ethical judgments. Kant defends the view that moral actions have to be understood independently of their merely contingent motivations, and thus that certain actions are simply right or wrong *in themselves*. Mill lays out a moral theory, called utilitarianism, which is based on the principle that the moral value of actions must be understood in terms of their effect on human happiness or well-being.

In the next reading, Virginia Held presents a feminist critique of traditional moral theory, arguing that the history of ethical thought has been dominated by sexist attitudes towards women and that only a *radical transformation* of moral philosophy will allow us to escape from these distorting preconceptions. One of the things this article does is to introduce a recent approach called "care ethics."

Finally, an influential article by Judith Jarvis Thomson introduces the famous "trolley problem," which illustrates the use of imaginary scenarios to tease out our ethical intuitions and to assess how adequately different moral theories can deal with them.

Several good introductory books on moral philosophy are available, including Piers Benn, *Ethics* (McGill-Queen's University Press, 1998); Simon Blackburn, *Being Good: A Short Introduction to Ethics* (Oxford University Press, 2003); Julia Driver, *Ethics: The Fundamentals* (Blackwell, 2013); Gilbert Harman, *The Nature of Morality* (Oxford University Press, 1977); Colin McGinn, *Moral Literacy, or How to Do The Right Thing* (Hackett, 1992); Pojman and Fieser, *Ethics: Discovering Right and Wrong* (Cengage, 2016); Rachels, *The Elements of Moral Philosophy* (McGraw Hill, 2018); Russ Shafer-Landau, *The Fundamentals of Ethics* (Oxford University Press, 2017); Peter Singer, *Practical Ethics* (Cambridge University Press, 2011); Bernard Williams, *Morality: An Introduction to Ethics* (Cambridge University Press, 1993); and Lewis Vaughn, *Beginning Ethics: An Introduction to Moral Philosophy* (W.W. Norton, 2014). Good reference works are David Copp, ed., *The Oxford Handbook of Ethical Theory* (Oxford University Press, 2007), LaFollette and Persson, eds., *The Blackwell Guide to Ethical Theory* (Blackwell, 2013), and Peter Singer, ed., *A Companion to Ethics* (Blackwell, 1993).

PLATO

FROM *Republic* AND *Euthyphro*

Who Was Plato?

The historical details of Plato's life are shrouded in uncertainty. He is traditionally thought to have been born in about 427 BCE and to have died in 347 BCE. His family, who lived in the Greek city-state of Athens, was aristocratic and wealthy. Legend has it that Plato's father, Ariston, was descended from Codrus, the last king of Athens, and his mother, Perictione, was related to the great Solon, who wrote the first Athenian constitution. While Plato was still a boy, his father died and his mother married Pyrilampes, a friend of the revered Athenian statesman Pericles, who in the 450s had transformed Athens into one of the greatest cities in the Greek world.

As a young man, Plato probably fought with the Athenian army against Sparta during the Peloponnesian war (431–404 BCE)—which Athens lost—and he may have served again when Athens was involved in the Corinthian war (395–386 BCE).

Given his family connections, Plato looked set for a prominent role in Athenian political life and, as it happens, when he was about 23, a political revolution occurred in Athens which could have catapulted Plato into public affairs. The coup swept the previous democratic rulers—who had just lost the war against Sparta—out of power and into exile, and replaced them with the so-called Thirty Tyrants, several of whom were Plato's friends and relatives. Plato, an idealistic young man, expected this would usher in a new era of justice and good government, but he was soon disillusioned when the new regime was even more violent and corrupt than the old. He withdrew from public life in disgust. The rule of the Thirty lasted only about 90 days before the exiled democrats were restored to power, and Plato—impressed

by their relative lenience towards the coup leaders—apparently thought again about entering politics. But then, in 399 BCE, the city rulers arrested Plato's old friend and mentor, Socrates, and accused him of the trumped-up charge of impiety towards the city's gods and of corrupting the youth of Athens. Socrates was convicted by a jury of the townspeople and—since he declared that he would rather die than give up philosophy, even though he was given a chance to escape—he was executed by being forced to drink poison.

> The result was that I, who had at first been full of eagerness for public affairs, when I considered all this and saw how things were shifting about every which way, at last became dizzy. I didn't cease to consider ways of improving this particular situation, however, and, indeed, of reforming the whole constitution. But as far as action was concerned, I kept waiting for favorable moments and finally saw clearly that the constitutions of all actual cities are bad and that their laws are almost beyond redemption without extraordinary resources and luck as well. Hence I was compelled to say in praise of the true philosophy that it enables us to discern what is just for a city or an individual in every case and that the human race will have no respite from evils until those who are really and truly philosophers acquire political power or until, through some divine dispensation, those who rule and have political authority in cities become real philosophers.*

After the death of Socrates, it appears that Plato, along with some other philosophical followers of Socrates, fled Athens and went to the city of Megara in east-

---

* This is a quotation from the so-called *Seventh Letter*, supposed to have been written by Plato when he was 70 years old. It is not certain that Plato actually wrote this document, but if it was not his, it was probably written by one of his disciples shortly after his death. See Plato, *Seventh Letter*, translated by C.D.C. Reeve in his Introduction to Plato's *Republic*, trans. G.M.A. Grube, revised by C.D.C. Reeve (Indianapolis: Hackett, 1992), ix–x. The later fragmentary quote is from the translation of the *Seventh Letter* by Glen R. Morrow, in *Plato: Complete Works*, ed. John M. Cooper and D.S. Hutchinson (Indianapolis: Hackett, 1997), 1648.

central Greece to stay with the philosopher Eucleides (a follower of the great Greek philosopher Parmenides of Elea). He may also have visited Egypt, though his travels at this time are shrouded in myth. It appears that Plato started doing philosophy in earnest at about this time, and his earliest writings date from this point. Almost all of Plato's writings are in the form of dialogues between two or more characters and, in most of them, the character leading the discussion is Socrates. Since Plato never wrote himself into any of his dialogues, it is usually—though not uncontroversially—assumed that the views expressed by the character of Socrates more or less correspond with those that Plato is trying to put forward in his dialogues.

Later, when Plato was about 40, he made another trip away from Athens, visiting Italy to talk with the Pythagorean philosophers. Plato was deeply impressed by Pythagorean philosophy—especially their emphasis on mathematics—but he was horrified by the luxury and sensuality of life in Italy, "with men gorging themselves twice a day and never sleeping alone at night."

After Italy, Plato visited Syracuse on the island of Sicily where, during a long stay, he became close friends with Dion, the brother-in-law of the ruling tyrant Dionysius I.* Dion became Plato's pupil, and (according to legend) came to prefer the philosophical life of moral goodness to the pleasure, luxury, and power of his surroundings. Exactly what happened next is historically unclear, but there is some reason to believe Plato was captured by a displeased Dionysius, sold into slavery, and subsequently rescued from the slave market when his freedom was purchased by an unidentified benevolent stranger.

On Plato's return to Athens, he bought land in a precinct named for an Athenian hero called Academus, and there, in about 385, he founded the first European university (or at least, the first of which there is any real historical knowledge). Because of its location, this school was called the Academy, and it was to remain in existence for over 900 years, until 529 CE. For most of the rest of his life, Plato stayed at the Academy, directing its stud-

ies, and he probably wrote the *Republic* there (in about 380 BCE). Very quickly, the school became a vital center for research in all kinds of subjects, both theoretical and practical. It was probably one of the first cradles for the subjects of metaphysics, epistemology, psychology, ethics, politics, aesthetics, and mathematical science, and members were invited, by various Greek city-states, to help draft new political constitutions.

In 368 Dionysius I of Sicily died and Dion persuaded his successor, Dionysius II, to send for Plato to advise him on how the state should be run. Plato, by now about 60, agreed with some misgivings, possibly hoping to make the younger Dionysius an example of a philosopher-king and to put the doctrines of the *Republic* into practice. However, the experiment was a disastrous failure. Dionysius II—though he gave himself airs as a philosopher—had no inclination to learn philosophy and mathematics in order to become a better ruler. Within four months Dion was banished, and Plato returned to Greece shortly afterwards. However, four years later Dionysius II convinced Plato to return, pressuring him with testimonials from eminent philosophers describing Dionysius's love for philosophy, and bribing him by offering to reinstate Dion at Syracuse within a year. Once again, the king proved false: he not only kept Dion in exile but confiscated and sold his lands and property. Plato was imprisoned on Sicily for nearly two years until, in 360, he finally escaped and returned to Athens for good. He died 13 years later, at the ripe old age of 80.[†]

What Was Plato's Overall Philosophical Project?

Plato is probably the single person with the best claim to being the inventor of western philosophy. His thought encompassed nearly all the areas central to philosophy today—metaphysics, epistemology, ethics, political theory, aesthetics, and the philosophy of science and mathematics—and, for the first time in European history, dealt with them in a unified way.[‡] Plato thought of

---

[*]   Indeed, Plato later wrote a poem about Dion and spoke of being driven out of his mind with love for him.

[†]   Dion, meanwhile, attempted to recover his position at Syracuse by force—an endeavor Plato, wisely, refused to support—and was later assassinated by a supposed friend, and fellow member of the Academy, called Callippus.

[‡]   In fact the mathematician and philosopher Alfred North Whitehead (1861–1947) famously was moved to say that "The safest general characterization of the European philosophical tradition is that it consists of a series of footnotes

philosophy as a special discipline with its own intellectual method, and he was convinced it had foundational importance in human life. Only philosophy, Plato thought, could provide genuine understanding, since only philosophy scrutinized the assumptions that other disciplines left unquestioned. Furthermore, according to Plato, philosophy reveals a realm of comprehensive and unitary hidden truths—indeed, a whole level of reality that the senses cannot detect—which goes far beyond everyday common sense and which, when properly understood, has the power to revolutionize the way we live our lives and organize our societies. Philosophy, and only philosophy, holds the key to genuine human happiness and well-being.

This realm of objects which Plato claimed to have discovered is generally known as that of the Platonic Forms. The Forms—according to Plato—are changeless, eternal objects, which lie outside of both the physical world and the minds of individuals, and which can only be encountered through pure thought rather than through sensation. One of Plato's favorite examples of a Form is the mathematical property of Equality. In a dialogue called the *Phaedo* he argues that Equality itself cannot be identical with two equal sticks, or with any other group of physical objects of equal length, since we could always be mistaken about whether any two observed objects are really equal with one another, but we could not possibly be mistaken about Equality itself and somehow take *it* to be unequal. When two sticks are equal in length, therefore, they "participate in" Equality—it is their relation to Equality which makes them equal rather than unequal—but Equality itself is an abstract object which exists over and above all the instances of equal things. The form of Equality is what one succeeds in understanding when one has a proper conception of what Equality really is in itself: real knowledge, therefore, comes not from observation but from acquaintance with the Forms. Other central examples of Platonic Forms, are Sameness, Number, Motion, Beauty, Justice, Piety, and (the most important Form of all) Goodness.

Plato describes the relation of the ordinary world of perceivable, concrete objects to the realm of the Forms in Book VII of the *Republic*, using the allegory of a cave. Ordinary people, lacking the benefit of a philosophical education, are like prisoners trapped underground in a cave since birth and forced to look only at shadows cast on the wall in front of them by puppets behind their backs, dancing in front of a fire. With the proper philosophical encouragement, they can—if they have the courage to do so—break their bonds and turn around to see that what they believed was reality was really only an illusory puppet show. The philosophers among them can even leave the cave to encounter the true reality— of which even the puppets are only copies—illuminated by the light of the sun which, for Plato, represents the form of the Good. The perceptible world is thus merely an imperfect image of—and sustained by—the quasi-divine, eternal realm of the unchanging and unobservable Forms.

What Is the Structure of This Reading?

The *Republic* is written in the form of a dramatic dialogue. The narrator, Socrates, speaking directly to the reader, describes a conversation in which he took part and which is supposed to have happened the previous day at the Athenian port city of Piraeus. The dialogue is traditionally divided into ten parts or "Books," and the first half of Book II is reprinted here. In the first book, Thrasymachus, a boorish character, has asserted that justice, or morality, is simply the rule of the strong over the weak, and that it is, in fact, not in everybody's self-interest to be just—it is only in the best interests of the ruling powers for everyone else to follow the social rules they lay down. Socrates has, characteristically, attempted to show that Thrasymachus' reasons for this claim are muddled and confused, but although Thrasymachus is unable to defend himself against Socrates' attacks he remains convinced of the truth of his position. As Book II opens, two brothers, Glaucon and Adeimantus, take up Thrasymachus' cause not because they think he is right, but because they want to challenge Socrates to defeat it properly and to conclusively show that being a just and moral person is valuable *in itself*.

Glaucon begins by introducing a classification of "goods" into three types and asks Socrates to which class justice belongs. Socrates replies it belongs to the

---

to Plato." (Alfred North Whitehead, *Process and Reality*, corrected edition, ed. D.R. Griffin and D.W. Sherburne [Free Press, 1978], 39.)

highest type of good, but Glaucon points out that this conflicts with the popularly held assumption that justice belongs in the lowest class of good. Glaucon then presents three arguments in favor of this common view. First, he describes an account of the "origin and essence of justice" which treats it as only a 'second best' solution to a social problem. Second, he uses the myth of the Ring of Gyges to argue that people are unwillingly just and that, given the chance, anyone would behave immorally. Finally, he describes 'ideal cases' of just and unjust people to show that, if one had the option of living a perfectly just or a totally unjust life, the only rational choice would be the latter. When Glaucon has finished, Adeimantus argues at length that even those who defend justice—parents, poets, and politicians—defend it on the basis of its beneficial *effects* only, and never go so far as to claim it is intrinsically worthwhile to be a morally just person. Glaucon and Adeimantus challenge Socrates to refute all of these arguments.

The reading breaks off just as Socrates is about to respond to this challenge (a response not completed until at least the end of Book IX of the *Republic*). Socrates argues, in effect, that the virtue of justice is such a good thing that it is better to be a just person, even if severe misfortune and loss of reputation occur, than it is to be unjust and to enjoy all possible social rewards; that being a just person always makes you *happier* than being an unjust one, no matter what other circumstances may hold.

In crude outline, Plato's response goes like this. There are three fundamentally different kinds of psychological impulses in human beings: *appetitive desires* (e.g., food, sex, money), *spirited desires* (e.g., fame, power, honor), and *rational desires* (knowledge and truth). Because of this three-fold division of desire, the human soul must also be divided into three parts, and people can be classified according to the dominant part of their soul: that

is, people are either money-lovers, honor-lovers, or wisdom-lovers (philosophers). Since these three types of people have very different sorts of desires, they must also have quite different views of what it is to lead a good and morally virtuous life. For one, it is a life of hedonistic pleasure, for the second, a life of political power and influence, and for the philosopher, a life spent in the pursuit of knowledge.

However, according to Plato, only one of these views of the good life is *correct*. Only the philosopher, he argues, has access to the genuinely good life. This is so because the true nature of reality—including moral reality—is the realm of the Forms, and only the philosopher has knowledge of this fundamental reality. Since philosophers are the only ones to understand the true nature of virtue, it seems to Plato to follow that they are the only ones with the specialized knowledge necessary to live a truly good life.* Since capacity for the good life is thus connected with the *kind of person* one is (i.e., a money-lover, an honor-lover, or a philosopher), the Platonic conception of virtue can thus be understood as a particular kind of hierarchy in the soul. According to Plato, to be virtuous is to have a soul ruled by its rational part. Morality, properly understood, fulfils one's highest nature—it is a kind of psychic harmony or mental health—and so leads to the deepest and most genuine form of happiness.†

After the selection from the *Republic* we have included an excerpt from another Socratic dialogue by Plato called the *Euthyphro*. This dialogue was written about fifteen years before the *Republic*, and is set a few weeks before Socrates' trial and conviction for impiety. Socrates is waiting to attend a preliminary hearing before the city's magistrates when he strikes up a conversation with another legal petitioner, Euthyphro, who—to Socrates' amazement—is suing his own father for the crime of murder.

---

* There is also a quasi-religious interpretation of Plato which sees him holding that the Forms—rather than anything in the shifting, illusory spatio-temporal world—are the supreme objects of value. Instead of wealth, power, or pleasure, the most perfect object of devotion is the realm of the Forms, and in particular the Form of the Good (which Plato seems to think of as almost a kind of divinity).

† Plato introduces and explains this account of justice in the human soul by drawing an analogy with the structure of an ideal city-state (which is why the dialogue is called the *Republic*). Briefly, a properly run state would contain three specialized types of citizens: craftspeople, warrior-guardians, and rulers. The rulers would have to have a proper philosophical education, in order to truly know what is best for the state and its citizens, and for this reason they are often called "philosopher kings." The state only functions properly and justly, according to Plato, when these three classes work together in harmony—for example, the craftspeople must be appropriately skilled and must also be properly subservient to the other two classes.

The main subject of the *Euthyphro* is a particular moral virtue: that of piety or holiness, which is to say showing proper respect for religion and the gods (literally, knowledge of how to properly perform ritual prayers and sacrifices). However, the notion is somewhat broader than it might initially seem: insofar as the gods approve on the whole of morally good behavior, to show proper respect for the gods will involve behaving well more generally. Socrates fairly quickly turns the discussion to an attempt to find the essence or definition of piety—the fundamental thing that all pious actions have in common—and this is the point at which this selection begins. Euthyphro's first attempt to answer this question is to say that "what is beloved by the gods is pious, and what is not beloved by them is impious," but Socrates shows him that this is inadequate as a definition. He argues against it in two ways, but it is the second that really counts; this more fundamental objection to the definition emerges when Socrates asks, "Is the pious loved by the gods because it's pious, or it is pious because it is loved?"

Some Useful Background Information

1. All the characters who take part in discussions in the *Republic* were historical figures. Of those mentioned here, Glaucon and Adeimantus were actually Plato's brothers and Thrasymachus was a well-known contemporary teacher of rhetoric, oratory, and "sophist" philosophy (roughly, what we might think of today as a "self-help" guru).* The main character of the *Republic*, however, is its narrator Socrates, Plato's primary intellectual influence. Though he left no writings, Socrates' personality and ideas were so powerful that he appears to have had a tremendous impact upon everyone he encountered, inspiring either fervent devotion or intense irritation. Socrates' main philosophical concern was the ethical question of how one's life should best be lived, and his method was to engage in systematic cross-examination (*elenchus*) of those he encountered, challenging them to state and then justify their beliefs about justice and virtue. The effect of this was to demonstrate to them that their uncritically held beliefs about moral virtue are self-contradictory and hence *have* no justification. The state of bewildered awareness of their own ignorance in which Socrates left his unfortunate victims is called *aporia*, and Socrates' technique of remorseless questioning is sometimes known as the "aporetic method."

2. Though famous for insisting he was wiser than his fellow Athenians only because he alone realized that he knew nothing, Socrates did subscribe to a handful of substantive philosophical positions, at least two of which he passed on to Plato. First, for Socrates, virtue (*aretē*) is a kind of knowledge. To be a virtuous person is, fundamentally, to *understand* what virtue is, in much the same way as being an expert shoemaker consists in knowing everything there is to know about shoes. Socrates (and Plato after him) held that it was vitally important to find correct definitions—to understand the essence (*eidos*)—of ethical concepts, otherwise we will not know how to live.

   The second crucial Socratic doctrine is that the real essence of a person is not their body but their soul, and that this soul is immortal. The health of one's own soul is thus of paramount importance, far more significant than the mere slings and arrows of physical life. Indeed, Socrates was convinced that, even while we are living in the physical world, the quality of our souls is a far more important determinant of our happiness than external circumstances like health, wealth, popularity, or power.

3. The topic of the *Republic* is *dikaiosúnē*, a Greek word usually translated into English as "justice." Strangely enough, it is a matter of some controversy just what Plato means by *dikaiosúnē* (and thus just what, exactly, the *Republic* is about); clearly, though, the notion covers more than we might normally understand by the word "justice," though probably somewhat less than we would, today, understand by "morality." Plato is not merely interested in the virtue of treating other people fairly and impartially (and, in the *Republic*, he is hardly interested at all in the formulation and

---

* Similarly, Euthyphro was a real person and one of Socrates' contemporaries: he was a seer or prophet—that is, someone who was a professional interpreter of the wishes of the gods.

administration of civil and criminal law). Rather, Plato is discussing something like *the right way to live*, where it is understood (as was generally assumed by the ancient Greeks) that human beings are *social* animals, for whom the good life can only exist in a particular sort of political context and all the virtues—such as courage, moderation, generosity, and even piety—have to do, in one way or another, with our relationships with other people. Therefore, by "justice," Plato probably means all the areas of morality that regulate our relationships with other people.

On the other hand, it is important to notice that Plato does *not* think of justice as primarily a way of behaving, as a set of rules for correct action, or as a kind of relationship between people. Justice, for Plato, is an *internal property of individual souls*, and only secondarily of their actions. You have the virtue of justice if your soul has a certain configuration, and then it is this virtue of yours which regulates your treatment of other people; but your treatment of other people is not *itself* justice, it is just the manifestation of your justice. To put it another way, you are not a just person because your actions are just—on the contrary, your actions are just because you are.

4. The description of the "popular view" of justice by Glaucon and Adeimantus is philosophically more complicated than it might at first seem, and the following distinction is a useful one to bear in mind when you are trying to get it straight. This distinction is one between what are often called the "artificial" and the "natural" consequences of justice. The artificial consequences of justice are those "rewards and reputations" which society provides for those who give the appearance of being just. They are artificial rewards because they would not exist if it were not for human social conventions and practices and, more importantly, because they are connected only to the *appearance* of justice rather than justice itself. Thus, someone who appeared just, but was not, would still get all of the artificial rewards of justice. On the other hand, the natural rewards of being just are supposed to follow simply from justice itself, in the same way that health, sight, and knowledge have, in themselves, beneficial consequences for their possessors.

Some Common Misconceptions

1. All the protagonists in this selection from the *Republic*—Glaucon, Adeimantus, and Socrates—*agree* that justice is good in itself. Glaucon and Adeimantus present certain arguments as strongly as they can in order to force Socrates to properly respond to them, but they do not, themselves, endorse the conclusion of those arguments (and they hope Socrates will give them a way to legitimately evade that conclusion).

2. The discussion is about the benefits of justice *for just people themselves*, not for those with whom they interact or for society generally. The topic asks whether *acting justly* is intrinsically worthwhile (rather than whether it is nice to be *treated* justly).

How Important and Influential Is This Passage?

The *Republic* is generally acknowledged to be Plato's greatest work (indeed, one of the very greatest works in all philosophy), and is often thought of as the centerpiece of Plato's philosophy. Though it presents only a partial picture of his developing philosophical views, it is the dialogue where most of Plato's central ideas about ethics, metaphysics, epistemology, politics, psychology, aesthetics, and so on, come together into a single unified theory. This excerpt from the *Republic* is by no means the best-known part of the work, but it is where Plato sets up the philosophical question his book is intended to answer. As with much of Plato's writing, it is the questions he asked which have proved to be of enduring philosophical importance as much as the answers he gave to them. The questions developed here about the relationship between morality and self-interest lie at the very foundation of ethical study, and the myth of the Ring of Gyges, in particular, has been a particularly evocative image through the centuries for exploring these issues.

The *Euthyphro*, also, is a very influential Socratic dialogue and the key argument that Socrates makes there—known as the Euthyphro dilemma—has been an important problem for theists who argue that god is the source of morality (a stance sometimes called Divine Command Theory) for hundreds of years.

FROM *Republic*

BOOK II (357A–367E)*

When I said this, I thought I had done with the discussion, but it turned out to have been only a prelude. Glaucon showed his characteristic courage on this occasion too and refused to accept Thrasymachus' abandonment of the argument. Socrates, he said, do you want to seem to have persuaded us that it is better in every way to be just than unjust, or do you want truly to convince us of this?

I want truly to convince you, I said, if I can.

Well, then, you certainly aren't doing what you want. Tell me, do you think there is a kind of good we welcome, not because we desire what comes from it, but because we welcome it for its own sake—joy, for example, and all the harmless pleasures that have no results beyond the joy of having them?

Certainly, I think there are such things.

And is there a kind of good we like for its own sake and also for the sake of what comes from it—knowing, for example, and seeing and being healthy? We welcome such things, I suppose, on both counts.

Yes.

And do you also see a third kind of good, such as physical training, medical treatment when sick, medicine itself, and the other ways of making money? We'd say that these are onerous† but beneficial to us, and we wouldn't choose them for their own sakes, but for the sake of the rewards and other things that come from them.

There is also this third kind. But what of it?

Where do you put justice?

I myself put it among the finest goods, as something to be valued by anyone who is going to be blessed with happiness, both because of itself and because of what comes from it.

That isn't most people's opinion. They'd say that justice belongs to the onerous kind, and is to be practiced for the sake of the rewards and popularity that come from a reputation for justice, but is to be avoided because of itself as something burdensome.

I know that's the general opinion. Thrasymachus faulted justice on these grounds a moment ago and praised injustice, but it seems that I'm a slow learner.

Come, then, and listen to me as well, and see whether you still have that problem, for I think that Thrasymachus gave up before he had to, charmed by you as if he were a snake.‡ But I'm not yet satisfied by the argument on either side. I want to know what justice and injustice are and what power each itself has when it's by itself in the soul. I want to leave out of account their rewards and what comes from each of them. So, if you agree, I'll renew the argument of Thrasymachus. First, I'll state what kind of thing people consider justice to be and what its origins are. Second, I'll argue that all who practice it do so unwillingly, as something necessary, not as something good. Third, I'll argue that they have good reason to act as they do, for the life of an unjust person is, they say, much better than that of a just one.

It isn't, Socrates, that I believe any of that myself. I'm perplexed, indeed, and my ears are deafened listening to Thrasymachus and countless others. But I've yet to hear anyone defend justice in the way I want, proving that it is better than injustice. I want to hear it praised *by itself*, and I think that I'm most likely to hear this from you. Therefore, I'm going to speak at length in praise of the unjust life, and in doing so I'll show you the way I want to hear you praising justice and denouncing injustice. But see whether you want me to do that or not.

I want that most of all. Indeed, what subject could someone with any understanding enjoy discussing more often?

* The *Republic* was probably written in about 380 BCE. This translation is by G.M.A. Grube, revised by C.D.C. Reeve, and was published in 1992 by the Hackett Publishing Company. Reprinted by permission of Hackett Publishing Company, Inc. All rights reserved.

† Burdensome, troublesome.

‡ As if he were calmed by the music of a snake-charmer.

Excellent. Then let's discuss the first subject I mentioned—what justice is and what its origins are.

They say that to do injustice is naturally good and to suffer injustice bad, but that the badness of suffering it so far exceeds the goodness of doing it that those who have done and suffered injustice and tasted both, but who lack the power to do it and avoid suffering it, decide that it is profitable to come to an agreement with each other neither to do injustice nor to suffer it. As a result, they begin to make laws and covenants, and what the law commands they call lawful and just. This, they say, is the origin and essence of justice. It is intermediate between the best and the worst. The best is to do injustice without paying the penalty; the worst is to suffer it without being able to take revenge. Justice is a mean between these two extremes. People value it not as a good but because they are too weak to do injustice with impunity. Someone who has the power to do this, however, and is a true man wouldn't make an agreement with anyone not to do injustice in order not to suffer it. For him that would be madness. This is the nature of justice, according to the argument, Socrates, and these are its natural origins.

We can see most clearly that those who practice justice do it unwillingly and because they lack the power to do injustice, if in our thoughts we grant to a just and an unjust person the freedom to do whatever they like. We can then follow both of them and see where their desires would lead. And we'll catch the just person red-handed travelling the same road as the unjust. The reason for this is the desire to outdo others and get more and more.* This is what anyone's nature naturally pursues as good, but nature is forced by law into the perversion of treating fairness with respect.

The freedom I mentioned would be most easily realized if both people had the power they say the ancestor of Gyges of Lydia† possessed. The story goes that he was a shepherd in the service of the ruler of Lydia. There was a violent thunderstorm, and an earthquake broke open the ground and created a chasm at the place where he was tending his sheep. Seeing this, he was filled with amazement and went down into it. And there, in addition to many other wonders of which we're told, he saw a hollow bronze horse. There were windowlike openings in it, and, peeping in, he saw a corpse, which seemed to be of more than human size, wearing nothing but a gold ring on its finger. He took the ring and came out of the chasm. He wore the ring at the usual monthly meeting that reported to the king on the state of the flocks. And as he was sitting among the others, he happened to turn the setting‡ of the ring towards himself to the inside of his hand. When he did this, he became invisible to those sitting near him, and they went on talking as if he had gone. He wondered at this, and, fingering the ring, he turned the setting outwards again and became visible. So he experimented with the ring to test whether it indeed had this power—and it did. If he turned the setting inward, he became invisible; if he turned it outward, he became visible again. When he realized this, he at once arranged to become one of the messengers sent to report to the king. And when he arrived there, he seduced the king's wife, attacked the king with her help, killed him, and took over the kingdom.

Let's suppose, then, that there were two such rings, one worn by a just and the other by an unjust person. Now, no one, it seems, would be so incorruptible that he would stay on the path of justice or stay away from other people's property, when he could take whatever he wanted from the marketplace with impunity, go into people's houses and have sex with anyone he wished, kill or release from prison anyone he wished, and do all the other things that would make him like a god among humans. Rather his actions would be in no way different from those of an unjust person and both would follow the same path. This, some would say, is a great proof that one

---

* This is the vice of *pleonexia*, the desire to out-compete everybody else and get more than you are entitled to. According to Plato, *pleonexia* is the root cause of injustice, and proper virtue consists in keeping *pleonexia* in check; Thrasymachus, however, has argued that *pleonexia* is not a vice at all, but a reasonable impulse which is only stifled by artificial social conventions.

† Lydia was an ancient kingdom located in western Asia Minor, where northwestern Turkey lies today. Gyges was king of Lydia from 670 to 652 BCE. Probably the first realm to use coins as money, Lydia was renowned for its immense wealth and reached the height of its power in the seventh century BCE. In 546 BCE its final king, Croesus, was defeated by the Persians, and Lydia was absorbed into the Persian Empire.

‡ The setting for a jewel.

is never just willingly but only when compelled to be. No one believes justice to be a good when it is kept private, since, wherever either person thinks he can do injustice with impunity, he does it. Indeed, every man believes that injustice is far more profitable to himself than justice. And any exponent of this argument will say he's right, for someone who didn't want to do injustice, given this sort of opportunity, and who didn't touch other people's property would be thought wretched and stupid by everyone aware of the situation, though, of course, they'd praise him in public, deceiving each other for fear of suffering injustice. So much for my second topic.

As for the choice between the lives we're discussing, we'll be able to make a correct judgment about that only if we separate the most just and the most unjust. Otherwise we won't be able to do it. Here's the separation I have in mind. We'll subtract nothing from the injustice of an unjust person and nothing from the justice of a just one, but we'll take each to be complete in his own way of life. First, therefore, we must suppose that an unjust person will act as clever craftsmen do: A first-rate captain or doctor, for example, knows the difference between what his craft can and can't do. He attempts the first but lets the second go by, and if he happens to slip, he can put things right. In the same way, an unjust person's successful attempts at injustice must remain undetected, if he is to be fully unjust. Anyone who is caught should be thought inept, for the extreme of injustice is to be believed to be just without being just. And our completely unjust person must be given complete injustice; nothing may be subtracted from it. We must allow that, while doing the greatest injustice, he has nonetheless provided himself with the greatest reputation for justice. If he happens to make a slip, he must be able to put it right. If any of his unjust activities should be discovered, he must be able to speak persuasively or to use force. And if force is needed, he must have the help of courage and strength and of the substantial wealth and friends with which he has provided himself.

Having hypothesized such a person, let's now in our argument put beside him a just man, who is simple and noble and who, as Aeschylus* says, doesn't want to be believed to be good but to be so.† We must take away his reputation, for a reputation for justice would bring him honour and rewards, so that it wouldn't be clear whether he is just for the sake of justice itself or for the sake of those honours and rewards. We must strip him of everything except justice and make his situation the opposite of an unjust person's. Though he does no injustice, he must have the greatest reputation for it, so that his justice may be tested full-strength and not diluted by wrong-doing and what comes from it. Let him stay like that unchanged until he dies—just, but all his life believed to be unjust. In this way, both will reach the extremes, the one of justice and the other of injustice, and we'll be able to judge which of them is happier.

Whew! Glaucon, I said, how vigorously you've scoured each of the men for our competition, just as you would a pair of statues for an art competition.

I do the best I can, he replied. Since the two are as I've described, in any case, it shouldn't be difficult to complete the account of the kind of life that awaits each of them, but it must be done. And if what I say sounds crude, Socrates, remember that it isn't I who speak but those who praise injustice at the expense of justice. They'll say that a just person in such circumstances will be whipped, stretched on a rack, chained, blinded with fire, and, at the end, when he has suffered every kind of evil, he'll be impaled, and will realize then that one shouldn't want to be just but to be believed to be just. Indeed, Aeschylus' words are far more correctly applied to unjust people than to just ones, for the supporters of injustice will say that a really unjust person, having a way of life based on the truth about things and not living in accordance with opinion, doesn't want simply to be believed to be unjust but actually to be so—

Harvesting a deep furrow in his mind,
Where wise counsels propagate.

---

* Aeschylus (525–456 BCE) was a great and influential Greek tragic dramatist. He is sometimes said to have created drama itself, through his innovative introduction of multiple actors speaking different parts. His most famous plays are the *Oresteia* trilogy—*Agamemnon*, *The Libation Bearers*, and *The Eumenides*.

† This refers to Aeschylus' play *Seven Against Thebes*. It is said of a character that "he did not wish to be believed to be the best but to be it." The next two lines of the passage are quoted by Glaucon below.

He rules his city because of his reputation for justice; he marries into any family he wishes; he gives his children in marriage to anyone he wishes; he has contracts and partnerships with anyone he wants; and besides benefiting himself in all these ways, he profits because he has no scruples about doing injustice. In any contest, public or private, he's the winner and outdoes his enemies. And by outdoing them, he becomes wealthy, benefiting his friends and harming his enemies. He makes adequate sacrifices to the gods and sets up magnificent offerings to them. He takes better care of the gods, therefore, (and, indeed, of the human beings he's fond of) than a just person does. Hence it's likely that the gods, in turn, will take better care of him than of a just person. That's what they say, Socrates, that gods and humans provide a better life for unjust people than for just ones.

When Glaucon had said this, I had it in mind to respond, but his brother Adeimantus intervened: You surely don't think that the position has been adequately stated?

Why not? I said.

The most important thing to say hasn't been said yet.

Well, then, I replied, a man's brother must stand by him, as the saying goes.* If Glaucon has omitted something, you must help him. Yet what he has said is enough to throw me to the canvas† and make me unable to come to the aid of justice.

Nonsense, he said. Hear what more I have to say, for we should also fully explore the arguments that are opposed to the ones Glaucon gave, the ones that praise justice and find fault with injustice, so that what I take to be his intention may be clearer.

When fathers speak to their sons, they say that one must be just, as do all the others who have charge of anyone. But they don't praise justice itself, only the high reputations it leads to and the consequences of being thought to be just, such as the public offices, marriages, and other things Glaucon listed. But they elaborate even further on the consequences of reputation. By bringing in the esteem of the gods, they are able to talk about the abundant good things that they themselves and the noble Hesiod and Homer say that the gods give to the pious, for Hesiod says that the gods make the oak trees

Bear acorns at the top and bees in the middle
And make fleecy sheep heavy laden with wool‡

for the just, and tells of many other good things akin to these. And Homer is similar:

When a good king, in his piety,
Upholds justice, the black earth bears
Wheat and barley for him, and his trees are heavy
*   with fruit.*
His sheep bear lambs unfailingly, and the sea yields up
*   its fish.§*

Musaeus¶ and his son make the gods give the just more headstrong goods than these. In their stories, they lead the just to Hades,** seat them on couches, provide them with a symposium†† of pious people, crown them with wreaths, and make them spend all their time drinking—as if they thought drunkenness was the finest wage of virtue. Others stretch even further the wages that virtue receives from the gods, for they

---

* In Homer's *Odyssey* (part 16, lines 97–98).
† To throw me to the floor of a wrestling ring.
‡ Hesiod, *Works and Days*, lines 232–34. Hesiod was an early Greek poet—widely considered the second greatest Greek epic poet after Homer—who lived around 700 BCE. His poem *Works and Days* reflects his experiences as a farmer, giving practical advice on how to live, and also shows Hesiod lamenting the loss of a historic Golden Age which has been replaced, he complains, with a modern era of immorality and suffering.
§ Homer, *Odyssey*, part 19, lines 109 and 111–13.
¶ This Musaeus (as opposed to a Greek poet of the same name, who lived some 1,000 years later) was a mythical poet and singer connected with the cult of Orphism, a Greek mystery religion of the sixth century BCE. His son, Eumolpus, is said to have founded the Eleusinian mysteries, an annual celebration to honor Demeter, goddess of agriculture and fertility.
** The site of the Greek afterlife, where the good were rewarded and the wicked punished.
†† A gathering for drinking, music, and intellectual conversation. (Greek: *sumposion*, literally, 'drinking party.')

say that someone who is pious and keeps his promises leaves his children's children and a whole race behind him. In these and other similar ways, they praise justice. They bury the impious and unjust in mud in Hades; force them to carry water in a sieve; bring them into bad repute while they're still alive, and all those penalties that Glaucon gave to the just person they give to the unjust. But they have nothing else to say. This, then, is the way people praise justice and find fault with injustice.

Besides this, Socrates, consider another form of argument about justice and injustice employed both by private individuals and by poets. All go on repeating with one voice that justice and moderation are fine things, but hard and onerous, while licentiousness and injustice are sweet and easy to acquire and are shameful only in opinion and law. They add that unjust deeds are for the most part more profitable than just ones, and, whether in public or private, they willingly honour vicious people* who have wealth and other types of power and declare them to be happy. But they dishonour and disregard the weak and the poor, even though they agree that they are better than the others.

But the most wonderful of all these arguments concerns what they have to say about the gods and virtue. They say that the gods, too, assign misfortune and a bad life to many good people, and the opposite fate to their opposites. Begging priests and prophets frequent the doors of the rich and persuade them that they possess a god-given power founded on sacrifices and incantations. If the rich person or any of his ancestors has committed an injustice, they can fix it with pleasant rituals. Moreover, if he wishes to injure some enemy, then, at little expense, he'll be able to harm just and unjust alike, for by means of spells and enchantments they can persuade the gods to serve

them. And the poets are brought forward as witnesses to all these accounts. Some harp on the ease of vice, as follows:

> *Vice in abundance is easy to get;*
> *The road is smooth and begins beside you,*
> *But the gods have put sweat between us and virtue,*†

and a road that is long, rough, and steep. Others quote Homer to witness that the gods can be influenced by humans, since he said:

> *The gods themselves can be swayed by prayer,*
> *And with sacrifices and soothing promises,*
> *Incense and libations, human beings turn them from*
> *   their purpose*
> *When someone has transgressed and sinned.*‡

And they present a noisy throng of books by Musaeus and Orpheus,§ offspring as they say of Selene and the Muses,¶ in accordance with which they perform their rituals. And they persuade not only individuals but whole cities that the unjust deeds of the living or the dead can be absolved or purified through sacrifices and pleasant games, whether those who have committed them are still alive, or have died. These initiations, as they call them, free people from punishment hereafter, while a terrible fate awaits those who have not performed rituals.

When all such sayings about the attitudes of gods and humans to virtue and vice are so often repeated, Socrates, what effect do you suppose they have on the souls of young people? I mean those who are clever and are able to flit from one of these sayings to another, so to speak, and gather from them an impression of what sort of person he should be and of how best to

---

* Those having many vices, wicked people.
† Hesiod, *Works and Days*, lines 287–89.
‡ *Iliad*, part 9, lines 497 and 499–501.
§ Orpheus was a legendary poet who lived (if he is a real figure at all) in the sixth or seventh century BCE. According to Greek myth, he was the first living mortal to travel to the underworld, on a quest to retrieve his dead wife Eurydice. Hades, ruler of the underworld, was so moved by the poet's music that he gave back Eurydice, on the condition that Orpheus not look back at her until they reached the world of the living. Orpheus glanced back a moment too soon, and Eurydice vanished. Heart-broken, he wandered alone in the wilds until a band of Thracian women killed him and threw his severed head in the river, where it continued to call for his lost love, Eurydice.
¶ Selene is the Greek goddess of the Moon. The Muses were nine goddesses, daughters of Zeus, who presided over the arts and sciences.

travel the road of life. He would surely ask himself Pindar's* question, "Should I by justice or by crooked deceit scale this high wall and live my life guarded and secure?" And he'll answer: "The various sayings suggest that there is no advantage in my being just if I'm not also thought just, while the troubles and penalties of being just are apparent. But they tell me that an unjust person, who has secured for himself a reputation for justice, lives the life of a god. Since, then, 'opinion forcibly overcomes truth' and 'controls happiness,' as the wise men† say, I must surely turn entirely to it. I should create a façade of illusory virtue around me to deceive those who come near, but keep behind it the greedy and crafty fox of the wise Archilochus."‡

"But surely," someone will object, "it isn't easy for vice to remain always hidden." We'll reply that nothing great is easy. And, in any case, if we're to be happy, we must follow the path indicated in these accounts. To remain undiscovered we'll form secret societies and political clubs. And there are teachers of persuasion to make us clever in dealing with assemblies and law courts. Therefore, using persuasion in one place and force in another, we'll outdo others without paying a penalty.

"What about the gods? Surely, we can't hide from them or use violent force against them!" Well, if the gods don't exist or don't concern themselves with human affairs, why should we worry at all about hiding from them? If they do exist and do concern themselves with us, we've learned all we know about them from the laws and the poets who give their genealogies—nowhere else. But these are the very people who tell us that the gods can be persuaded and influenced by sacrifices, gentle prayers, and offerings. Hence, we should believe them on both matters or neither. If we believe them, we should be unjust and offer sacrifices from the fruits of our injustice. If we are just, our only gain is not to be punished by the gods, since we lose the profits of injustice. But if we are unjust, we get the profits of our crimes and transgressions and

afterwards persuade the gods by prayer and escape without punishment.

"But in Hades won't we pay the penalty for crimes committed here, either ourselves or our children's children?" "My friend," the young man will say as he does his calculation, "mystery rites have great power and the gods have great power of absolution. The greatest cities tell us this, as do those children of the gods who have become poets and prophets."

Why, then, should we still choose justice over the greatest injustice? Many eminent authorities agree that, if we practice such injustice with a false façade, we'll do well at the hands of gods and humans, living and dying as we've a mind to. So, given all that has been said, Socrates, how is it possible for anyone of any power—whether of mind, wealth, body, or birth—to be willing to honor justice and not laugh aloud when he hears it praised? Indeed, if anyone can show that what we've said is false and has adequate knowledge that justice is best, he'll surely be full not of anger but of forgiveness for the unjust. He knows that, apart from someone of godlike character who is disgusted by injustice or one who has gained knowledge and avoids injustice for that reason, no one is just willingly. Through cowardice or old age or some other weakness, people do indeed object to injustice. But it's obvious that they do so only because they lack the power to do injustice, for the first of them to acquire it is the first to do as much injustice as he can.

And all of this has no other cause than the one that led Glaucon and me to say to you: "Socrates, of all of you who claim to praise justice, from the original heroes of old whose words survive, to the men of the present day, not one has ever blamed injustice or praised justice except by mentioning the reputations, honours, and rewards that are their consequences. No one has ever adequately described what each itself does of its own power by its presence in the soul of the person who possesses it, even if it remains hidden from gods and humans. No one, whether in poetry or in private

---

*   Pindar (520–440 BCE) was a Greek lyric poet.
†   Simonides of Ceos (c. 556–468 BCE), a Greek poet.
‡   Archilochus of Paros (who lived around 650 BCE), yet another Greek poet, and author of the famous fable about a fox and a hedgehog. All that remains of his writing now is this quotation: "a fox knows many things, but a hedgehog one important thing." In the fable, apparently, the clever fox tries many strategies to eat the hedgehog, who simply repels each attempt by rolling up into a spiny ball. It's not clear how the moral of this story—the success of the hedgehog—applies here, other than by its reference to a greedy and crafty animal.

conversations, has adequately argued that injustice is the worst thing a soul can have in it and that justice is the greatest good. If you had treated the subject in this way and persuaded us from youth, we wouldn't now be guarding against one another's injustices, but each would be his own best guardian, afraid that by doing injustice he'd be living with the worst thing possible."

Thrasymachus or anyone else might say what we've said, Socrates, or maybe even more, in discussing justice and injustice—crudely inverting their powers, in my opinion. And, frankly, it's because I want to hear the opposite from you that I speak with all the force I can muster. So don't merely give us a theoretical argument that justice is stronger than injustice, but tell us what each itself does, because of its own powers, to someone who possesses it, that makes injustice bad and justice good. Follow Glaucon's advice, and don't take reputations into account, for if you don't deprive justice and injustice of their true reputations and attach false ones to them, we'll say that you are not praising them but their reputations and that you're encouraging us to be unjust in secret. In that case, we'll say that you agree with Thrasymachus that justice is the good

of another, the advantage of the stronger, while injustice is one's own advantage and profit, though not the advantage of the weaker.

You agree that justice is one of the greatest goods, the ones that are worth getting for the sake of what comes from them, but much more so for their own sake, such as seeing, hearing, knowing, being healthy, and all other goods that are fruitful by their own nature and not simply because of reputation. Therefore, praise justice as a good of that kind, explaining how—because of its very self—it benefits its possessors and how injustice harms them. Leave wages and reputations for others to praise.

Others would satisfy me if they praised justice and blamed injustice in that way, extolling the wages of one and denigrating those of the other. But you, unless you order me to be satisfied, wouldn't, for you've spent your whole life investigating this and nothing else. Don't, then, give us only a theoretical argument that justice is stronger than injustice, but show what effect each has because of itself on the person who has it—the one for good and the other for bad—whether it remains hidden from gods and human beings or not....

FROM *Euthyphro**

SOCRATES: ... So now, by Zeus, explain to me what you were just now claiming to know clearly: what sort of thing do you say holiness is, and unholiness, with respect to murder and everything else as well? Or isn't the pious the same as itself in every action,[†] and the impious in turn is the complete opposite of the pious but the same as itself, and everything that in fact turns out to be impious has a single form with respect to its impiousness?

EUTHYPHRO: It certainly is, Socrates.

SOCRATES: So tell me, what do you say the pious is, and what is the impious?

EUTHYPHRO: Well then, I claim that the pious is what I am doing now, prosecuting someone who is guilty of wrongdoing—either of murder or temple robbery or anything else of the sort, whether it happens to be one's father or mother or whoever else—and the impious is failing to prosecute. For observe, Socrates, how great a proof I will give you that this is how the law stands, one I have already given to others as well, which shows such actions to be correct—not yielding to impious people, that is, no matter who they happen to be. Because these very people also happen to worship Zeus as the best and most just of the gods, and agree that he put his own father in bonds because he unjustly swallowed his sons, and the father too castrated his own father for other similar reasons.[‡] Yet

---

* The *Euthyphro* was probably written in about 395 BCE. This translation is by Cathal Woods and Ryan Pack and was published in 2016 by Broadview Press.

† That is, there is just one kind of piety—all pious actions have something in common.

‡ For the stories of Zeus, Cronos, and Ouranos, see Hesiod, *Theogony*, 154–82 and 453–506.

they are sore at me because I am prosecuting my father for his injustice. And so they say contradictory things about the gods and about me.

SOCRATES: Maybe this, Euthyphro, is why I am being prosecuted for this crime, that whenever someone says such things about the gods, for some reason I find them hard to accept? For this reason, I suppose, someone will claim I misbehave. But now if you, with your expertise in such matters, also hold these beliefs, it's surely necessary, I suppose, that we too must accept them—for indeed what *can* we say, we who admit openly that we know nothing about these matters? But before the god of friendship* tell me, do you truly believe these things happened like this?

EUTHYPHRO: These and still more amazing things, Socrates, that most people are unaware of.

SOCRATES: And do you believe there is really a war amongst the gods, with terrible feuds, even, and battles and many other such things, such as are recounted by the poets and the holy artists, and that have been elaborately adorned for us on sacred objects, too, and especially the robe covered with such designs which is brought up to the acropolis at the great Panathenaea?† Are we to say that these things are true, Euthyphro?

EUTHYPHRO: Not only these, Socrates, but as I said just now, I could also describe many other things about the gods to you, if you want, which I am sure you will be astounded to hear.

SOCRATES: I wouldn't be surprised. But you can describe these to me at leisure some other time. For the time being, however, try to state more clearly what I asked you just now, since previously, my friend, you did not teach me well enough when I asked what the pious was but you told me that what you're doing is something pious, prosecuting your father for murder.

EUTHYPHRO: And I spoke the truth, too, Socrates.

SOCRATES: Perhaps. But in fact, Euthyphro, you say there are many other pious things.

EUTHYPHRO: Indeed there are.

SOCRATES: So do you remember that I did not request this from you, to teach me one or two of the many pious things, but to teach me the form itself by which everything pious is pious? For you said that it's by one form that impious things are somehow impious and pious things pious. Or don't you remember?

EUTHYPHRO: I certainly do.

SOCRATES: So then tell me whatever this form itself is, so that, by looking at it and using it as a paradigm, if you or anyone else do anything of that kind I can say that it is pious, and if it is not of that kind, that it is not.

EUTHYPHRO: Well if that's what you want, Socrates, that's what I'll tell you.

SOCRATES: That's exactly what I want.

EUTHYPHRO: Well, what is beloved by the gods is pious, and what is not beloved by them is impious.

SOCRATES: Excellent, Euthyphro! And you have answered in the way I was looking for you to answer. Whether you have done so truly or not, that I don't quite know—but you will obviously spell out how what you say is true.

EUTHYPHRO: Absolutely.

SOCRATES: Come then, let's look at what we said. An action or a person that is beloved by the gods is pious, while an action or person that is despised by the gods is impious. It is not the same, but the complete opposite, the pious to the impious. Isn't that so?

EUTHYPHRO: Indeed it is.

---

*   Zeus Philios, or Zeus in his aspect of the champion of friendship.
†   The Panathenaea was an annual celebration of Athena's birthday, with a larger ("great") celebration every four years. A new robe would be presented to the statue of the goddess Athena.

SOCRATES: And this seems right?

EUTHYPHRO: I think so, Socrates.

SOCRATES: But wasn't it also said that the gods are at odds with each other and disagree with one another and that there are feuds among them?

EUTHYPHRO: Yes, it was.

SOCRATES: What is the disagreement about, my good man, that causes hatred and anger? Let's look at it this way. If we disagree, you and I, about quantity, over which of two groups is greater, would our disagreement over this make us enemies and angry with each other, or wouldn't we quickly resolve the issue by resorting to counting?

EUTHYPHRO: Of course.

SOCRATES: And again, if we disagreed about bigger and smaller, we would quickly put an end to the disagreement by resorting to measurement?

EUTHYPHRO: That's right.

SOCRATES: And we would weigh with scales, I presume, to reach a decision about heavier and lighter?

EUTHYPHRO: How else?

SOCRATES: Then what topic, exactly, would divide us and what difference would we be unable to settle such that we would be enemies and angry with one another? Perhaps you don't have an answer at hand, so as I'm talking, see if it's the just and the unjust, the noble and the shameful, and the good and the bad. Isn't it these things that make us enemies of one another, any time that happens, whether to me and you or to any other men, when we quarrel about them and are unable to come to a satisfactory judgment about them?

EUTHYPHRO: It is indeed this disagreement, Socrates, and over these things.

SOCRATES: And what about the gods, Euthyphro? If they indeed disagree over something, don't they disagree over these very things?

EUTHYPHRO: It's undoubtedly necessary.

SOCRATES: Then some of the gods think different things are just—according to you, worthy Euthyphro—and noble and shameful, and good and bad, since they surely wouldn't be at odds with one another unless they were disagreeing about these things. Right?

EUTHYPHRO: You're right.

SOCRATES: And so whatever each group thinks is noble and good and just, they also love these things, and they hate the things that are the opposites of these?

EUTHYPHRO: Certainly.

SOCRATES: Then according to you the things some of them think are just, others think are unjust, and by disagreeing about these things they are at odds and at war with each other. Isn't this so?

EUTHYPHRO: It is.

SOCRATES: The same things, it seems, are both hated by the gods and loved, and so would be both despised and beloved by them?

EUTHYPHRO: It seems so.

SOCRATES: And the same things would be both pious and impious, Euthyphro, according to this argument?

EUTHYPHRO: I'm afraid so.

SOCRATES: So you haven't answered what I was asking, you remarkable man! I didn't ask you for what is both pious and impious at once: what is beloved by the gods is also hated by the gods, as it appears. As a result, Euthyphro, it wouldn't be surprising if in doing what you're doing now—punishing your father—you were doing something beloved by Zeus but despised by Cronos and Uranus, and while it is dear to Hephaestus, it is despised by Hera, and if any other god disagrees with another on the subject, your action will also appear to them similarly.

EUTHYPHRO: But I believe, Socrates, that none of the gods will disagree with any other on this matter at least: that any man who has killed another person unjustly need not pay the penalty.

SOCRATES: What's that? Have you never heard any *man* arguing that someone who killed unjustly or did something else unjustly should not pay the penalty?

EUTHYPHRO: There's no end to these arguments, both outside and inside the courts, since people commit so many injustices and do and say anything to escape the punishment.

SOCRATES: Do they actually agree that they are guilty, Euthyphro, and despite agreeing they nonetheless say that they shouldn't pay the penalty?

EUTHYPHRO: They don't agree on that at all.

SOCRATES: So they don't do or say *everything*, since, I think, they don't dare to claim or argue for this: that if they are in fact guilty they should *not* pay the penalty. Rather, I think they claim that they're not guilty. Right?

EUTHYPHRO: That's true.

SOCRATES: So they don't argue, at least, that the guilty person shouldn't pay the penalty, but perhaps they argue about who the guilty party is and what he did and when.

EUTHYPHRO: That's true.

SOCRATES: Doesn't the very same thing happen to the gods, too, if indeed, as you said, they are at odds about just and unjust things, some saying that a god commits an injustice against another one, while others deny it? But absolutely no one at all, you remarkable man, either god or human, dares to say that the guilty person need not pay the penalty.

EUTHYPHRO: Yes. What you say is true, Socrates, for the most part.

SOCRATES: But I think that those who quarrel, Euthyphro, both men and gods, if the gods actually quarrel, argue over the particulars of what was done. Differing over a certain action, some say that it was done justly, others that it was done unjustly. Isn't that so?

EUTHYPHRO: Certainly.

SOCRATES: Come now, my dear Euthyphro. So that I can become wiser, teach me too what evidence you have that all gods think the man was killed unjustly—the one who committed murder while he was working for you, and was bound by the master of the man he killed, and died from his bonds before the servant could learn from the interpreters what ought to be done in his case, and is the sort of person on whose behalf it is proper for a son to prosecute his father and make an allegation of murder. Come, try to give me a clear indication of how in this case all the gods believe beyond doubt that this action is proper. If you could show me this satisfactorily I would never stop praising you for your wisdom.

EUTHYPHRO: But this is probably quite a task, Socrates, though I could explain it to you very clearly, even so.

SOCRATES: I understand. It's because you think I'm a slower learner than the judges, since you could make it clear to *them* in what way these actions are unjust and how the gods all hate such things.

EUTHYPHRO: Very clear indeed, Socrates, if only they would listen to me when I talk.

SOCRATES: Of course they'll listen, so long as they think you speak well. But while you were speaking the following occurred to me: I'm thinking to myself, "Even if Euthyphro convincingly shows me that every god thinks this kind of death is unjust, what more will I have learned from Euthyphro about what the pious and the impious are? Because while this particular deed might be despised by the gods, as is likely, it was already apparent, just a moment ago, that the pious and impious aren't defined this way, since we saw that what is despised by the gods is also beloved by them." So I acquit you of this, Euthyphro. If you want, let us allow that all gods think this is unjust and that all of them despise it. But this current correction to the definition—that what all the gods despise is impious while what they love is pious, and what some love and some hate is neither or both—do you want us to now define the pious and the impious in this way?

EUTHYPHRO: Well, what is stopping us, Socrates?

SOCRATES: For my part nothing, Euthyphro, but think about whether adopting this definition will make it easiest for you to teach me what you promised.

EUTHYPHRO: I do indeed say that the pious is what all the gods love, and the opposite, what all gods hate, is impious.

SOCRATES: Then let's look again, Euthyphro, to see whether it's well stated. Or will we be content to simply accept our own definition or someone else's, agreeing that it is right just because somebody says it is? Or must we examine what the speaker is saying?

EUTHYPHRO: We must examine it. But I'm quite confident that what we have now is well put.

SOCRATES: We'll soon know better, my good man. Think about this: Is the pious loved by the gods because it's pious, or it is pious because it is loved?

EUTHYPHRO: I don't know what you mean, Socrates.

SOCRATES: I'll try to express myself more clearly. We speak of something being carried and of carrying, and being led and leading, and being seen and seeing, and so you understand that all of these are different from one another and how they are different?

EUTHYPHRO: I think I understand.

SOCRATES: So there's a thing loved and different from this there's the thing that loves?

EUTHYPHRO: How could there not be?

SOCRATES: Then tell me whether what is carried is a carried thing because it is carried, or because of something else?

EUTHYPHRO: No, it's because of this.

SOCRATES: And also what is led because it is led, and what is seen because it is seen?

EUTHYPHRO: Absolutely.

SOCRATES: So it is not that because it is something seen, it is seen, but the opposite, that because it is seen it is something seen. And it is not because it is something led that it is led, but because it is led it is something led. And it is not because it is something carried that it is carried, but because it is carried, it is something carried. Is it becoming clear what I'm trying to say, Euthyphro? I mean this: that if something becomes or is affected by something, it's not because it is a thing coming to be that it comes to be; but because it comes to be it is a thing coming into being. Nor is it affected by something because it is a thing that is affected; but because it is affected, it is a thing that is being affected. Or don't you agree?

EUTHYPHRO: I do.

SOCRATES: And is a loved thing either a thing coming to be or a thing affected by something?

EUTHYPHRO: Certainly.

SOCRATES: And does the same apply to this as to the previous cases: it is not because it is a loved thing that it is loved by those who love it, but it is a loved thing because it is loved?

EUTHYPHRO: Necessarily.

SOCRATES: So what do we say about the pious, Euthyphro? Precisely that is it loved by all the gods, according to your statement?

EUTHYPHRO: Yes.

SOCRATES: Is it because of this: that it is pious? Or because of something else?

EUTHYPHRO: No, it's because of that.

SOCRATES: Because it is pious, then, it is loved, rather than being pious because it is loved?

EUTHYPHRO: It seems so.

SOCRATES: Then because it loved by the gods it is a loved thing and beloved by the gods?

EUTHYPHRO: How could it not?

SOCRATES: So the beloved is not pious, Euthyphro, nor is the pious beloved by the gods, as you claim, but the one is different from the other.

EUTHYPHRO: How so, Socrates?

SOCRATES: Because we agree that the pious is loved because of this—that is, because it's pious—and not that it is pious because it is loved. Right?

EUTHYPHRO: Yes.

SOCRATES: The beloved, on the other hand, because it is loved by gods, is beloved due to this very act of being loved, rather than being loved because it is beloved?

EUTHYPHRO: That's true.

SOCRATES: But if the beloved and the pious were in fact the same, my dear Euthyphro, then, if the pious were loved because of being the pious, the beloved would be loved because of being the beloved; and again, if the beloved was beloved because of being loved by gods, the pious would also be pious by being loved. But as it is, you see that the two are opposites and are completely different from one another, since the one, because it is loved, is the kind of thing that is loved, while the other is loved because it is the kind of thing that is loved.

So I'm afraid, Euthyphro, that when you were asked what in the world the pious is, you did not want to reveal its nature to me, but wanted to tell me some one of its qualities—that the pious has the quality of being loved by all the gods—but as for what it *is*, you did not say at all. So if I am dear to you, don't keep me in the dark but tell me again from the beginning what in the world the pious is. And we won't differ over whether it is loved by the gods or whatever else happens to it, but tell me without delay, what is the pious, and the impious?

... ■

Suggestions for Critical Reflection

1. How does Glaucon distinguish between the three different kinds of good? Do his examples make sense, and can you think of any examples of goods that do not fit easily into his classification? Into which of the three classes would *you* place justice?

2. Many modern debates about justice or morality tend to assume that there are only two fundamental, mutually exclusive positions one might take. Either something is morally right in itself, *regardless* of its consequences—often called a "deontological" view—or things are morally right or wrong *because* of their consequences (a view called "consequentialism"). For example, one might hold that taking human life is intrinsically morally wrong, no matter what the justification (e.g., because human life is 'sacred'); alternately, one might believe killing is wrong because of its harmful consequences (suffering, death, etc.), or perhaps even that sometimes it can be morally justified to kill human beings if the net consequences of doing so are sufficiently desirable (e.g., if a killing prevents more deaths than it brings about). How does the view of justice Socrates is being asked to defend fit here? Is his position *either* deontological or consequentialist? If not, what is it? How tenable a view is it?

3. How plausible is Glaucon's story of the origin of justice? If he were historically right about it, what would this show us (if anything) about the *moral* value of behaving justly?

4. If you had the Ring of Gyges, how would you behave? Do you agree with the claim that nearly everybody who possessed such a ring would behave immorally? What, if anything, would the answer to this question show about how people *ought* to behave?

5. Do unjust people generally lead more pleasant lives than just people? If so, what, if anything, would this show about the nature of morality?

6. Some commentators have claimed that the speeches of Glaucon and Adeimantus are not, as they purport to be, making the same point, but, in fact, are arguing for two quite *different* conclusions. Glaucon, it is said, emphasizes the need to defend justice *in itself*, without concern for the consequences, while Adeimantus urges that the virtue of justice must be shown to have beneficial *consequences* for those who have it. What do you think about this? Is this characterization of the speeches correct and, if so, does it mean they must be arguing for different conclusions?

7. Socrates agrees with Glaucon and Adeimantus that if justice is to be properly defended, it must be defended in isolation from its artificial or conventional consequences (such as reputation, wealth, and political influence). He also agrees that a good theory of justice must be capable of accommodating such extreme and unrealistic examples as the Ring of Gyges. But is this the right methodology to adopt? Couldn't we say that an essential part of what makes justice valuable is its pragmatic role in regulating social interactions in the kind of political societies in which we find ourselves? For example, perhaps part of the *point* of being just *is* that it entitles us to certain social rewards, or allows us to escape social penalties, and so justice does lose at least some of its value if this connection to social reality breaks down. What do you think?

8. If being just would make a person unhappy, would it then be irrational to be moral? Does Plato think so? Why does Socrates accept the challenge of showing that being just is in one's self-interest? Why not agree that justice is onerous, but is, nevertheless, our moral duty?

9. In the *Euthyphro*, Socrates famously asks whether right action (piety) is loved by the gods because it is right, or if an action is right simply because it is approved of by the gods. What is the difference between the two options? Socrates does not seem to take the second option seriously, instead focusing on the first; why do you think this might be?

10. Socrates claims that "the beloved is not pious, Euthyphro, nor is the pious beloved by the gods, as you claim, but the one is different from the other." How does he reach this conclusion?

ARISTOTLE

FROM *Nicomachean Ethics*

Who Was Aristotle?

Aristotle was born in 384 BCE in Stageira, a small town in the northeast corner of the Chalcidicé peninsula in the kingdom of Macedon, many days journey north of the intellectual centers of Greece. His father—Nicomachus, a physician at the Macedonian court—died when Aristotle was young, and he was brought up by his mother's wealthy family. At 17 Aristotle traveled to Athens to study at Europe's most important center of learning, the Academy, set up and presided over by Plato. As a young philosopher, Aristotle showed exceptional promise and made a name for himself as being industrious and clever, a good speaker, argumentative (if rather sarcastic), original, and an independent thinker. He was apparently a bit of a dandy—cutting his hair in a fashionably short style, and wearing jeweled rings—and is said to have suffered from poor digestion, to have lisped, and to have had spindly legs.

After Plato's death in about 347 BCE, Aristotle left Athens (possibly pushed out by a surge of anti-Macedonian feeling in the city—though one story suggests he left in a fit of pique after failing to be granted leadership of the Academy, and yet another account has it that Aristotle was unhappy with the Academy's turn towards pure mathematics under Plato's successor Speusippus). He traveled to Atarneus on the coast of Asia Minor (present-day Turkey) where his mother's family had connections and where the pro-Macedonian tyrant, Hermias, was a patron of philosophical studies. There, with three colleagues from the Academy, Aristotle started his own school at the town of Assos. Aristotle married Hermias's niece and adopted daughter, Pythias, and they had a daughter, also called Pythias.

This happy familial situation did not last long, however. In about 345 BCE Hermias was betrayed and executed (in a particularly grisly fashion) by the Persians.

Aristotle and his family fled to the nearby island of Lesbos, in the eastern Aegean Sea, where Aristotle founded another school at a town called Mytilene. There, with his student Theophrastus, he engaged in a hugely impressive series of studies in botany, zoology, and marine biology, collecting observations which were still of unrivaled scientific interest 2,000 years later. (Indeed, as late as the nineteenth century, Charles Darwin was able to praise Aristotle's biological researches as a work of genius which every professional biologist should read.)

Aristotle's stay on Lesbos was of short duration. In 343 BCE, invited by Philip II, the ruler of Macedonia, he returned home to tutor the 13-year-old prince Alexander. Little is reliably known about Aristotle's life during this period, though many fanciful stories have been written, clouding it in myth. Three years later, on Philip's death, Alexander became king and launched the military career which, in fairly short order, made him ruler of a massive empire and earned him the epithet Alexander the Great. (One history claims that when Alexander embarked on his conquest of the East—his armies advanced as far as the Indian sub-continent—he took along scientists whose sole job it was to report their discoveries back to Aristotle.)

In 335 BCE, after Alexander's troops had completed their conquest of the Greek city-states, Aristotle moved back to Athens where, once again, he started his own research institute. This university became known as the Lyceum (after the grove, dedicated to the god Apollo Lyceus, where it was located), and it continued to flourish for 500 years after Aristotle's death.* There he spent the next twelve years teaching, writing, and building up the first great library of the ancient world. Most of his known philosophical writings probably date from this time. After his wife Pythias died, Aristotle became the lover of a woman called Herpyllis. Their son Nicomachus was named, following the Greek custom, after his grandfather.

---

* Because philosophical discussions at the Lyceum were often conducted while strolling around a colonnaded walk called a *peripatos*, Aristotle's group became known as "the Peripatetics" (the walkers).

This peaceful existence was shattered in 323 BCE by news of Alexander's death in Babylon at the age of 33. Almost instantly, open revolt against the Macedonian conquerors broke out, and Aristotle—because of his connection with Alexander—was suddenly no longer welcome in Athens. One of the citizens brought an indictment of impiety towards him—the same "crime" for which the Athenians had executed Socrates three-quarters of a century earlier. It is said that in order to prevent the Athenians from sinning against philosophy a second time, Aristotle and his family beat a hasty retreat to Chalcis, on the island of Euboea, where his mother's family had estates. There Aristotle soon died, in November 322 BCE, at age 62. In his humane and sensible will, which has been preserved for posterity, Aristotle directed that Pythias's bones should be placed in his grave, in accordance with her wishes. He also freed several of his slaves and made generous and flexible financial provisions for Herpyllis and Nicomachus.

What Was Aristotle's Overall Philosophical Project?

Aristotle's life-work was nothing less than the attempt to collect together and systematically arrange all human knowledge. His consuming ambition was to get as close as possible to *knowing everything*—about the natural world, the human social world, and even the unchanging and eternal world of the heavens and the gods. However, unlike many other philosophers with similar ambitions before and since, Aristotle probably did not believe that there is some single, unified set of truths—some single *theory*—which provides the key to unlocking all of reality. He was not looking for a deeper, more authentic realm lying behind and explaining the world we live in, but instead was simply trying to find out as much as he could about *our* world, as we experience it. Thus, it is sometimes said, Aristotle's basic theoretical commitment was to *common sense*: he wanted to develop a system that provided a place for both scientific and moral-political truths, but did not depend on mysteriously invisible and inaccessible objects such as Plato's Forms (see the notes to the previous reading).* For Aristotle, the ultimate reality is the concrete world with which we are already acquainted—people, animals, plants, minerals—which Aristotle thought of as *substances* and their properties.

Often, Aristotle worked in the following way: after choosing a domain of study (such as rhetoric or metaphysics), he would begin by summarizing and laying out all the serious claims made about it—"what seems to be the case," including all the "reputable opinions." He would also pay attention to the way in which the matters in question were ordinarily spoken of—the assumptions about them built into everyday language. Then, Aristotle would survey the puzzles or problems generated by this material, and would set out to solve those puzzles, preferably without disturbing too many of the received opinions. Typically he would not stop there: new puzzles or objections would be raised by the solutions, and he would try to clear up those matters, and then new puzzles would be generated, and so on, each time, he hoped, getting closer to the final truth.

Since Aristotle did not believe in a single "theory of everything," he divided the branches of knowledge, or "sciences," into three main groups: theoretical sciences (whose aim is to discover truths), practical sciences (governing the performance of actions), and productive sciences (whose goal is the making of objects). The major theoretical sciences, according to Aristotle, are theology (which he thought of as the study of "changeless items"), mathematics, and the natural sciences. The chief practical sciences are ethics and politics. Examples of productive sciences are poetics, rhetoric, medicine, and agriculture. According to Aristotle, these various sciences are quite different: although they add up to a composite picture of reality, they share no single set of theoretical concepts or assumptions, no single methodology, and no single set of standards for scientific rigor. The proper methods of mathematics differ from those of zoology, which differ again from those of ethics.

---

* Another, then contemporary, theory which Aristotle opposed, also on the grounds of mystery-mongering, was a theory called "atomism," put forward by philosophers like Leucippus (who flourished between 450 and 420 BCE) and Democritus (c. 460–371 BCE). This theory postulated the existence of huge numbers of invisibly tiny, eternal, unchangeable particles—*atoma*, Greek for "uncuttables"—whose hidden behaviors and interactions were supposed to explain all the observable properties of the visible spatio-temporal world.

On the other hand, Aristotle hoped each science, or at least all theoretical sciences, would share the same *structure*: Aristotle was the first philosopher to conceive of science as a body of knowledge arranged according to a particular logical structure, which he modeled on that of geometry. As in geometry, there are two kinds of scientific truth, according to Aristotle: truths which are simply "evident" and need no explanation, and a much larger body of further truths which are justified or explained by being logically derived from the self-evident truths. (Aristotle, more or less single-handedly, invented the study of logic—which he called the science of "syllogisms"—partly to be able to describe the proper structure of scientific knowledge.) Unlike the case with geometry, however, Aristotle insisted that the "axioms" of any theoretical science—the self-evident truths upon which it is based—should ideally capture the *essences* of the things being described by that science. In this way, according to Aristotle, the logical structure of science would exactly reflect the structure of the world itself. Just as the properties of things (say, plants) are caused by their essential natures, so will the claims of the relevant science (e.g., botany) be logically derived from its basic assumptions about the essences of the things in its domain.

So where, according to Aristotle, do we get these first principles of the different sciences? The answer, Aristotle believed, was not from the exercise of pure reason but from careful *observation* of the world around us. By looking very hard and carefully at a particular domain (such as botany or ethics) we discern some fundamental truths about the things in that domain, from which everything else about it will follow. Because of this practical emphasis on observation rather than mere thought, Aristotle is described as "the father of modern empiricism." On the other hand, Aristotle never developed anything like an experimental method: his method for testing theories—verifying and falsifying them—consisted more in reasoned analysis than in empirical testing.

What Is the Structure of This Reading?

Judging by Alexandrian-age library catalogues, Aristotle wrote some 150 works in his lifetime—ranging in length from essays to books—covering a huge variety of topics: logic, physics, biology, meteorology, philosophy of science, history of science, metaphysics, psychology (including works on love, friendship, and the emotions), ethics and political theory, political science, rhetoric, poetics (and some original poetry), and political and legal history. Only a fraction of these writings—perhaps less than a fifth—survive: many of Aristotle's works, including all the dialogues he wrote for popular consumption, are now lost.* Most of what remains are summaries of lectures delivered at various times during his career, which were deposited in Aristotle's own library at the Lyceum to be consulted by teachers and students. Most of these notes were probably edited and re-edited, both by Aristotle and his successors; the *Nicomachean Ethics*, for example, is so-called because it is thought to have been edited by Aristotle's son Nicomachus after his father's death.†

The *Nicomachean Ethics* is traditionally divided into 10 books (though the divisions were probably not Aristotle's own). Book I examines the nature of the good for human beings—happiness—and divides it into two categories: intellectual excellence and moral excellence. Books II to IV deal with moral excellence, beginning with a general account of it and going on to discuss several of the moral virtues in detail. Book V looks at the virtue of justice, while Book VI describes some of the forms of intellectual excellence. Book VII deals with moral self-control and the nature of pleasure, and Books VIII and IX are about friendship. Finally, Book X concludes with a discussion of *eudaimonia* or well-being, and of the role that education and society play in bringing about individual happiness.

Excerpted here are the first few pages of Book I, which introduce Aristotle's view of the study of ethics, and then section 7 of Book I, where Aristotle lays out his so-called function argument for the view that human

---

* This lost *oeuvre* is a particular tragedy because Aristotle's prose style was greatly admired by the ancients—more so than Plato's, for example—and yet (not unnaturally, considering their purpose) the lecture notes, which are the only things of Aristotle's we have left to us, are generally agreed to be rather dryly written: terse and elliptical, full of abrupt transitions, inadequate explanations, and technical jargon.

† Aristotle's other main ethical work—an earlier set of lecture notes, generally thought to be superseded by the more mature *Nicomachean Ethics*—is similarly called the *Eudemian Ethics*, possibly after its ancient editor Eudemus of Rhodes.

happiness consists in a life of excellent activity in accordance with reason. There follows the second half of Book II, where Aristotle defines moral virtue as a disposition to choose the mean—illustrating this with examples of particular moral virtues—and then discusses the practical corollaries of this account of virtue. Finally, part of Book X is included: here, Aristotle discusses further the nature of happiness and argues that the highest form of happiness is to be found in a life of philosophical "contemplation."

Some Useful Background Information

1. Aristotle categorized ethics as a practical, rather than a theoretical, science. The *Nicomachean Ethics* is written "not in order to know what virtue is, but in order to become good." In other words, for Aristotle, the point of ethics is not merely to know what good people are like, but to learn to act as good people do: the *Nicomachean Ethics* is intended to foster what he calls "practical wisdom" (*phronesis*) in those who study it. The science of ethics is continuous, for Aristotle, with two others—biology and politics. It is continuous with biology because ethics is the study of the good life for humankind *as a biological species*. A good life for the member of *any* species (whether a horse or a daffodil) is a life of continuous flourishing, but what *counts* as flourishing will depend upon the biological nature of that species. Ethics is continuous with politics—the study of human society—because the arena in which human beings live their lives, in which they develop as moral agents and exercise their moral capacities, is necessarily a social one.
2. According to Aristotle, the goal of human life is to achieve *eudaimonia*. *Eudaimonia* is usually—as it is in our selection—translated as "happiness," but this can be misleading. The Greek word does not refer to a psychological state or feeling, such as pleasure, but instead means a certain kind of desirable *activity* or *way of life*—it is the activity of living well. The happy person is, for Aristotle, someone who has lived a genuinely *successful* or fulfilling life.
3. Aristotle's understanding of nature, and in particular of biology, is what is called *teleological*: a

thing's *telos* is its goal or purpose and, for Aristotle, all of nature is goal-directed. For example, the nature of some processes (such as digestion) or biological organs (such as the eye) is plausibly determined by their *function*—their goal or *telos*—and not by their physical composition at some particular time. Eyes are things, any things, that have the function of seeing. Aristotle extended this model to the entire natural world, so that, in his view, the essence of fire consists in its goal (of, roughly, rising upwards), the essence of an acorn is its purpose to grow into an oak tree, and the essence of the species *horse* is to flourish and procreate as horses are supposed to do. Since human beings are as much a part of the biological world as anything else, it follows that a proper understanding of human nature—and thus of the good life for human beings—must involve an investigation into the function of the human species.

Some Common Misconceptions

1. When Aristotle refers to the *telos*—the function or goal—of living creatures like plants, animals, and human beings, he is not thinking of these creatures as having a purpose for *something else*. He is not, for example, assuming that there is some great universal plan (perhaps God's plan) and that living creatures have a role to play in fulfilling this plan. Instead, the *telos* of living creatures is *internal* to them: it is, so to speak, built into their biological natures. So, for another example, the fact that apples serve our purposes as food does not mean that this is their *telos*.
2. It is sometimes easy to forget that Aristotle's Doctrine of the Mean urges us to avoid *both* excess and deficiency. Aristotle's account not only instructs us to moderate our anger or curb our drinking, it also warns us against feeling too *little* anger or not drinking *enough* wine.
3. When Aristotle refers to "the mean" of a spectrum of behavior, he does not intend to speak of something like an arithmetical average, and thus does not suggest we should, literally, choose the *mid-point* of that range of behavior. The mean or mid-point of two numbers (as 6 is the mean of 2 and 10) is an example of what Aristotle calls a mean "in the object."

Aristotle contrasts this mathematical use with his own usage of "mean," which is a mean "relative to us." For example, we should eat neither too many, nor too few, cookies; but exactly how many cookies we should eat depends on our personal circumstances (our weight, our lifestyle, how many other people also want cookies, whether we are allergic to ingredients in the cookies, and so on). Certainly, Aristotle does not want to say that we should eat *exactly half* of all the available cookies.

4. Aristotle does not think of his ethical theory as a sort of moral rulebook. Unlike most modern moral philosophers, such as Immanuel Kant and J.S. Mill, Aristotle is not trying to find a theory that will, by itself, generate moral principles to tell us how to act. Instead, he is trying to develop an account of moral *character*—a theory of the good person. It is salutary to recall that, although the topic of Aristotle's book is indeed *ēthika*, which is usually translated as "ethics," the Greek word means "matters to do with character." Similarly, when Aristotle writes of *ēthikē aretē*—which is almost invariably translated as "moral virtue"—the literal meaning is "excellence of character," and by "excellence" is meant simply what we would mean if we spoke of an excellent horse or an excellent phone. The modern sense of ethics, as involving *obedience to some sort of moral law*, is substantially more recent than Aristotle, and arose (more or less) with the monotheistic religions of Judaism, Christianity, and Islam.

5. The Doctrine of the Mean does not apply to particular *actions*, but to *virtues*—to states of character. Thus, the idea is not that one always *acts* in a way which is intermediate between two extremes, but that one's actions are guided by a *character trait* which is neither excessive nor insufficient. For example, in certain situations, someone possessing the virtue of generosity might nevertheless refuse to give anything at all to a particular person in a particular circumstance (or, conversely, might give away everything they own); or a person with the virtue of being even-tempered might nevertheless find it appropriate, sometimes, to become very angry (or, in another situation, to meekly suppress any angry feelings whatsoever).

How Important and Influential Is This Passage?

Many professional philosophers consider Aristotle to be the greatest philosopher who ever lived (for example, Oxford philosopher J.L. Ackrill called him "a philosophical super-genius"*); throughout the Middle Ages he was simply "the Philosopher." The system of ethics developed in the *Nicomachean Ethics* has had a profound effect on all subsequent moral philosophy. In every age of philosophy it has been either fervently embraced or fiercely rejected, but never ignored. Several of its central tenets—that morality consists in finding a "golden mean," or that the rational aim of human life is happiness (though not necessarily pleasure)—have become part of our everyday moral consciousness. On the other hand, for much of the post-medieval period, Aristotle's emphasis on the *virtues*, rather than on *types of action*, as the basis of morality was paid relatively little attention. More recently, there has been a surge of interest in so-called virtue ethics, and Aristotle is generally considered the original source for this 'new' theory. (Modern virtue theories, however, diverge from Aristotle's ethical philosophy in important ways. In particular, they tend to reject or ignore his emphasis on *eudaimonia* as the ultimate moral good.)

---

*   J.L. Ackrill, *Aristotle the Philosopher* (Oxford University Press, 1981), 8.

FROM *Nicomachean Ethics**

BOOK I

1 [Ends and Goods]

Every craft and every line of inquiry, and likewise every action and decision, seems to seek some good; that is why some people were right to describe the good as what everything seeks.† But the ends‡ [that are sought] appear to differ; some are activities, and others are products apart from the activities. Wherever there are ends apart from the actions, the products are by nature better than the activities.

Since there are many actions, crafts, and sciences, the ends turn out to be many as well; for health is the end of medicine, a boat of boat building, victory of generalship, and wealth of household management. But some of these pursuits are subordinate to some one capacity; for instance, bridle making and every other science producing equipment for horses are subordinate to horsemanship, while this and every action in warfare are, in turn, subordinate to generalship, and in the same way other pursuits are subordinate to further ones. In all such cases, then, the ends of the ruling sciences are more choiceworthy§ than all the ends subordinate to them, since the lower ends are also pursued for the sake of the higher. Here it does not matter whether the ends of the actions are the activities themselves, or something apart from them, as in the sciences we have mentioned.

2 [The Highest Good and Political Science]

Suppose, then, that the things achievable by action have some end that we wish for because of itself, and because of which we wish for the other things, and that we do not choose everything because of something else—for if we do, it will go on without limit, so that desire will prove to be empty and futile. Clearly, this end will be the good, that is to say, the best good.

Then does knowledge of this good carry great weight for [our] way of life, and would it make us better able, like archers who have a target to aim at, to hit the right mark? If so, we should try to grasp, in outline at any rate, what the good is, and which is its proper science or capacity.

It seems proper to the most controlling science—the highest ruling science. And this appears characteristic of political science.¶ For it is the one that prescribes which of the sciences ought to be studied in cities, and which ones each class in the city should learn, and how far; indeed we see that even the most honored capacities—generalship, household management, and rhetoric, for instance—are subordinate to it. And since it uses the other sciences concerned with action, and moreover legislates what must be done and what avoided, its end will include the ends of the other sciences, and so this will be the human good. For even

---

* The *Nicomachean Ethics* was probably written, as a series of lecture notes which would have undergone frequent revision, sometime between 334 and 322 BCE. This selection is reprinted from *Aristotle, Nicomachean Ethics*, 2nd edition, translated, with introduction, notes, and glossary by Terence Irwin (Hackett, 1999). The section headings are not Aristotle's own, but are supplied by the translator.

† This definition is consistent with the views of Plato, but Aristotle is probably thinking mostly of the work of a philosopher, mathematician, and astronomer called Eudoxus of Cnidus. Eudoxus taught at Plato's Academy in Athens from 368 until his death in 355 BCE, and was in charge of the school (during one of Plato's absences in Sicily) when Aristotle arrived there to study at the age of 17.

‡ Here, and throughout this reading, "end" means "goal" or "purpose," rather than merely "stopping place."

§ More worthy of pursuit, to be preferred.

¶ For Aristotle the study of politics (*politikē*) would be broader than our modern political science, and would include all aspects of the study of society. The goal of political science, according to Aristotle, ought to be to achieve happiness (*eudaimonia*) for all the citizens of the state, and this is why he thinks that the investigation into human happiness (ethics) is continuous with politics.

if the good is the same for a city as for an individual, still the good of the city is apparently a greater and more complete good to acquire and preserve. For while it is satisfactory to acquire and preserve the good even for an individual, it is finer and more divine to acquire and preserve it for a people and for cities. And so, since our line of inquiry seeks these [goods, for an individual and for a community], it is a sort of political science.

3 [The Method of Political Science]

Our discussion will be adequate if we make things perspicuous enough to accord with the subject matter; for we would not seek the same degree of exactness in all sorts of arguments alike, any more than in the products of different crafts. Now, fine and just things, which political science examines, differ and vary so much as to seem to rest on convention only, not on nature. But [this is not a good reason, since] goods also vary in the same way, because they result in harm to many people—for some have been destroyed because of their wealth, others because of their bravery. And so, since this is our subject and these are our premises, we shall be satisfied to indicate the truth roughly and in outline; since our subject and our premises are things that hold good usually [but not universally], we shall be satisfied to draw conclusions of the same sort.

Each of our claims, then, ought to be accepted in the same way [as claiming to hold good usually]. For the educated person seeks exactness in each area to the extent that the nature of the subject allows; for apparently it is just as mistaken to demand demonstrations from a rhetorician as to accept [merely] persuasive arguments from a mathematician....

7 [An Account of the Human Good]

But let us return once again to the good we are looking for, and consider just what it could be. For it is apparently one thing in one action or craft, and another thing in another; for it is one thing in medicine, another in generalship, and so on for the rest. What, then, is the good of each action or craft? Surely it is that for the sake of which the other things are done; in medicine this is health, in generalship victory, in house-building a house, in another case something else, but in every action and decision it is the end, since it is for the sake of the end that everyone does the other actions. And so, if there is some end of everything achievable in action, the good achievable in action will be this end; if there are more ends than one, [the good achievable in action] will be these ends.

Our argument, then, has followed a different route to reach the same conclusion. But we must try to make this still more perspicuous. Since there are apparently many ends, and we choose some of them (for instance, wealth, flutes,* and, in general, instruments) because of something else, it is clear that not all ends are complete. But the best good is apparently something complete. And so, if only one end is complete, the good we are looking for will be this end; if more ends than one are complete, it will be the most complete end of these.

We say that an end pursued in its own right is more complete than an end pursued because of something else, and that an end that is never choiceworthy because of something else is more complete than ends that are choiceworthy both in their own right and because of this end. Hence an end that is always choiceworthy in its own right, never because of something else, is complete without qualification.

Now happiness,† more than anything else, seems complete without qualification. For we always choose it because of itself, never because of something else. Honor, pleasure, understanding, and every virtue we certainly choose because of themselves, since we would choose each of them even if it had no further result; but we also choose them for the sake of happiness, supposing that through them we shall be happy. Happiness, by contrast, no one ever chooses for their sake, or for the sake of anything else at all.

The same conclusion [that happiness is complete] also appears to follow from self-sufficiency. For the complete good seems to be self-sufficient. What we count as self-sufficient is not what suffices for a solitary person by himself, living an isolated life, but what suffices also for parents, children, wife, and, in general,

---

* Strictly speaking, Aristotle means an *aulos*, an ancient Greek double-reed instrument.

† *Eudaimonia* (see the "Some Useful Background Information" section of the introduction to this reading).

for friends and fellow citizens, since a human being is a naturally political [animal]. Here, however, we must impose some limit; for if we extend the good to parents' parents and children's children and to friends of friends, we shall go on without limit; but we must examine this another time.

Anyhow, we regard something as self-sufficient when all by itself it makes a life choiceworthy and lacking nothing; and that is what we think happiness does. Moreover, we think happiness is most choiceworthy of all goods, [since] it is not counted as one good among many. [If it were] counted as one among many, then, clearly, we think it would be more choiceworthy if the smallest of goods were added; for the good that is added becomes an extra quantity of goods, and the larger of two goods is always more choiceworthy.

Happiness, then, is apparently something complete and self-sufficient, since it is the end of the things achievable in action.

But presumably the remark that the best good is happiness is apparently something [generally] agreed, and we still need a clearer statement of what the best good is. Perhaps, then, we shall find this if we first grasp the function of a human being. For just as the good, i.e., [doing] well, for a flautist, a sculptor, and every craftsman, and, in general, for whatever has a function and [characteristic] action, seems to depend on its function, the same seems to be true for a human being, if a human being has some function.

Then do the carpenter and the leather worker have their functions and actions, but has a human being no function? Is he by nature idle, without any function?* Or, just as eye, hand, foot, and, in general, every [bodily] part apparently has its function, may we likewise ascribe to a human being some function apart from all of these?

What, then, could this be? For living is apparently shared with plants, but what we are looking for is the special function of a human being; hence we should set aside the life of nutrition and growth. The life next in order is some sort of life of sense perception; but this too is apparently shared with horse, ox, and every animal.

The remaining possibility, then, is some sort of life of action of the [part of the soul] that has reason. One [part] of it has reason as obeying reason; the other has it as itself having reason and thinking. Moreover, life is also spoken of in two ways [as capacity and as activity], and we must take [a human being's special function to be] life as activity, since this seems to be called life more fully. We have found, then, that the human function is activity of the soul[†] in accord with reason or requiring reason.

Now we say that the function of a [kind of thing]—of a harpist, for instance—is the same in kind as the function of an excellent individual of the kind—of an excellent harpist, for instance. And the same is true without qualification in every case, if we add to the function the superior achievement in accord with the virtue; for the function of a harpist is to play the harp, and the function of a good harpist is to play it well. Moreover, we take the human function to be a certain kind of life, and take this life to be activity and actions of the soul that involve reason; hence the function of the excellent man is to do this well and finely.

Now each function is completed well by being completed in accord with the virtue proper [to that kind of thing]. And so the human good proves to be activity of the soul in accord with virtue, and indeed with the best and most complete virtue, if there are more virtues than one. Moreover, in a complete life. For one swallow does not make a spring,[‡] nor does one

---

* In the original Greek, this would have been a pun: the word for being "without function" (*argon*) was also used colloquially to mean a "good for nothing" or a "dropout."

† By "soul"—*psuchē*—Aristotle means, very roughly, that which makes us alive or animates us. The religious or Cartesian connotations of the word—the notion of the soul as a sort of substantial spiritual self, housed in a temporary material vessel (the body)—only came about much later in history.

‡ An allusion to the return of migrating swallows at the start of the summer, this remark has become a well-known cliché—the idea is that seeing the first swallow of the year does not mean that spring has fully arrived yet. (Aristotle himself, as it happens, believed that swallows hibernated over winter in holes in the ground—and claimed that this was something he had personally observed—and his authority was so great that this 'scientific fact' was believed for centuries.)

day; nor, similarly, does one day or a short time make us blessed and happy.

This, then, is a sketch of the good; for, presumably, we must draw the outline first, and fill it in later. If the sketch is good, anyone, it seems, can advance and articulate it, and in such cases time discovers more, or is a good partner in discovery. That is also how the crafts have improved, since anyone can add what is lacking [in the outline].

We must also remember our previous remarks, so that we do not look for the same degree of exactness in all areas, but the degree that accords with a given subject matter and is proper to a given line of inquiry. For the carpenter's and the geometer's inquiries about the right angle are different also; the carpenter restricts himself to what helps his work, but the geometer inquires into what, or what sort of thing, the right angle is, since he studies the truth. We must do the same, then, in other areas too, [seeking the proper degree of exactness], so that digressions do not overwhelm our main task.

Nor should we make the same demand for an explanation in all cases. On the contrary, in some cases it is enough to prove rightly that [something is true, without also explaining why it is true]. This is so, for instance, with principles, where the fact that [something is true] is the first thing, that is to say, the principle.

Some principles are studied by means of induction,* some by means of perception,† some by means of some sort of habituation,‡ and others by other means. In each case we should try to find them out by means suited to their nature, and work hard to define them rightly. For they carry great weight for what follows; for the principle seems to be more than half the whole,§ and makes evident the answer to many of our questions.

...

BOOK II

5 [Virtue of Character: Its Genus¶]

Next we must examine what virtue is. Since there are three conditions arising in the soul—feelings, capacities, and states—virtue must be one of these.

By feelings I mean appetite, anger, fear, confidence, envy, joy, love, hate, longing, jealousy, pity, and in general whatever implies pleasure or pain. By capacities I mean what we have when we are said to be capable of these feelings—capable of being angry, for instance, or of being afraid or of feeling pity. By states I mean what we have when we are well or badly off in relation to feelings. If, for instance, our feeling is too intense or slack, we are badly off in relation to anger, but if it is intermediate, we are well off; the same is true in the other cases.

First, then, neither virtues nor vices are feelings. For we are called excellent or base insofar as we have virtues or vices, not insofar as we have feelings. Further, we are neither praised nor blamed insofar as we have feelings; for we do not praise the angry or the frightened person, and do not blame the person who is simply angry, but only the person who is angry in a particular way. We are praised or blamed, however,

* This, for Aristotle, is the process of moving from particular facts, observations, or examples to a general or universal claim (for example, from particular examples of courage and cowardice to a general understanding of the relation between them). The Greek word is *epagōgē*, which literally means "leading on."
† The word Aristotle uses, *aisthēsis*, can be used to mean sense-perception, but Aristotle probably means something more like "direct intuition" of (moral) facts—just *seeing* that something is right or wrong.
‡ This, in Aristotle's view, is how the moral virtues are inculcated: by repeatedly and self-consciously acting in a particular way (e.g., bravely) until that manner of behaving (e.g., bravery) becomes a habit or a character trait.
§ This was apparently a Greek proverb.
¶ Aristotle defined a category by stating the family—what genus—it belonged to, then by explaining what differentiated it from other categories in the same family—the differentia: that is, what species it was among others in the genus. For example, humans are defined as belonging to the genus animals, and were, in particular, the species of animals that are rational.

insofar as we have virtues or vices. Further, we are angry and afraid without decision; but the virtues are decisions of some kind, or [rather] require decision. Besides, insofar as we have feelings, we are said to be moved; but insofar as we have virtues or vices, we are said to be in some condition rather than moved.

For these reasons the virtues are not capacities either; for we are neither called good nor called bad, nor are we praised or blamed, insofar as we are simply capable of feelings. Further, while we have capacities by nature, we do not become good or bad by nature; we have discussed this before.

If, then, the virtues are neither feelings nor capacities, the remaining possibility is that they are states. And so we have said what the genus of virtue is.

6 [Virtue of Character: Its Differentia]

But we must say not only, as we already have, that it is a state, but also what sort of state it is.

It should be said, then, that every virtue causes its possessors to be in a good state and to perform their functions well. The virtue of eyes, for instance, makes the eyes and their functioning excellent, because it makes us see well; and similarly, the virtue of a horse makes the horse excellent, and thereby good at galloping, at carrying its rider, and at standing steady in the face of the enemy. If this is true in every case, the virtue of a human being will likewise be the state that makes a human being good and makes him perform his function well.

We have already said how this will be true, and it will also be evident from our next remarks, if we consider the sort of nature that virtue has.

In everything continuous and divisible we can take more, less, and equal, and each of them either in the object itself or relative to us; and the equal is some intermediate between excess and deficiency. By the intermediate in the object I mean what is equidistant from each extremity; this is one and the same for all. But relative to us the intermediate is what is neither superfluous nor deficient; this is not one, and is not the same for all.

If, for instance, ten are many and two are few, we take six as intermediate in the object, since it exceeds [two] and is exceeded [by ten] by an equal amount, [four]. This is what is intermediate by numerical proportion. But that is not how we must take the intermediate that is relative to us. For if ten pounds [of food], for instance, are a lot for someone to eat, and two pounds a little, it does not follow that the trainer will prescribe six, since this might also be either a little or a lot for the person who is to take it—for Milo* [the athlete] a little, but for the beginner in gymnastics a lot; and the same is true for running and wrestling. In this way every scientific expert avoids excess and deficiency and seeks and chooses what is intermediate—but intermediate relative to us, not in the object.

This, then, is how each science produces its product well, by focusing on what is intermediate and making the product conform to that. This, indeed, is why people regularly comment on well-made products that nothing could be added or subtracted; they assume that excess or deficiency ruins a good [result], whereas the mean preserves it. Good craftsmen also, we say, focus on what is intermediate when they produce their product. And since virtue, like nature, is better and more exact than any craft, it will also aim at what is intermediate.

By virtue I mean virtue of character; for this is about feelings and actions, and these admit of excess, deficiency, and an intermediate condition. We can be afraid, for instance, or be confident, or have appetites, or get angry, or feel pity, and in general have pleasure or pain, both too much and too little, and in both ways not well. But having these feelings at the right times, about the right things, toward the right people, for the right end, and in the right way, is the intermediate and best condition, and this is proper to virtue. Similarly, actions also admit of excess, deficiency, and an intermediate condition.

Now virtue is about feelings and actions, in which excess and deficiency are in error and incur blame, whereas the intermediate condition is correct and wins praise, which are both proper to virtue. Virtue, then, is a mean, insofar as it aims at what is intermediate.

---

*   Milo of Croton, supposed to have lived in the second half of the sixth century BCE in southern Italy, was a legendary wrestler and athlete, famous for his immense strength.

Moreover, there are many ways to be in error—for badness is proper to the indeterminate, as the Pythagoreans* pictured it, and good to the determinate. But there is only one way to be correct. That is why error is easy and correctness is difficult, since it is easy to miss the target and difficult to hit it. And so for this reason also excess and deficiency are proper to vice, the mean to virtue; "for we are noble in only one way, but bad in all sorts of ways."†

Virtue, then, is a state that decides, consisting in a mean, the mean relative to us, which is defined by reference to reason, that is to say, to the reason by reference to which the prudent person would define it. It is a mean between two vices, one of excess and one of deficiency.

It is a mean for this reason also: Some vices miss what is right because they are deficient, others because they are excessive, in feelings or in actions, whereas virtue finds and chooses what is intermediate.

That is why virtue, as far as its essence and the account stating what it is are concerned, is a mean, but, as far as the best [condition] and the good [result] are concerned, it is an extremity.

Now not every action or feeling admits of the mean. For the names of some automatically include baseness—for instance, spite, shamelessness, envy [among feelings], and adultery, theft, murder, among actions. For all of these and similar things are called by these names because they themselves, not their excesses or deficiencies, are base. Hence in doing these things we can never be correct, but must invariably be in error. We cannot do them well or not well—by committing adultery, for instance, with the right woman at the right time in the right way. On the contrary, it is true without qualification that to do any of them is to be in error.

[To think these admit of a mean], therefore, is like thinking that unjust or cowardly or intemperate action also admits of a mean, an excess and a deficiency. If it did, there would be a mean of excess, a mean of deficiency, an excess of excess and a deficiency of deficiency. On the contrary, just as there is no excess or deficiency of temperance or of bravery (since the intermediate is a sort of extreme), so also there is no mean of these vicious actions either, but whatever way anyone does them, he is in error. For in general there is no mean of excess or of deficiency, and no excess or deficiency of a mean.

7 [The Particular Virtues of Character]

However, we must not only state this general account but also apply it to the particular cases. For among accounts concerning actions, though the general ones are common to more cases, the specific ones are truer, since actions are about particular cases, and our account must accord with these. Let us, then, find these from the chart.‡

First, then, in feelings of fear and confidence the mean is bravery. The excessively fearless person is nameless (indeed many cases are nameless), and the one who is excessively confident is rash. The one who is excessive in fear and deficient in confidence is cowardly.

In pleasures and pains—though not in all types, and in pains less than in pleasures—the mean is temperance and the excess intemperance. People deficient in pleasure are not often found, which is why they also lack even a name; let us call them insensible.

In giving and taking money the mean is generosity, the excess wastefulness and the deficiency ungenerosity. Here the vicious people have contrary excesses and defects; for the wasteful person is excessive in spending and deficient in taking, whereas the ungenerous person is excessive in taking and deficient in spending. At the moment we are speaking in outline and summary, and that is enough; later we shall define these things more exactly.

In questions of money there are also other conditions. Another mean is magnificence; for the magnificent person differs from the generous by being concerned with large matters, while the generous person is concerned with small. The excess is ostentation and vulgarity, and the deficiency is stinginess. These differ

---

* The followers of philosopher and mystic Pythagoras of Samos (c. 570–495 BCE). One of their most influential beliefs was that everything in the universe can be understood in terms of *harmonia* or number, and the notion of a "limit" which Aristotle refers to here is a quasi-mathematical notion.

† The source of this quotation is unknown.

‡ Aristotle must have used a diagram at this point during his lectures, to illustrate graphically the various virtues and their extremes.

from the vices related to generosity in ways we shall describe later.

In honor and dishonor the mean is magnanimity, the excess something called a sort of vanity, and the deficiency pusillanimity. And just as we said that generosity differs from magnificence in its concern with small matters, similarly there is a virtue concerned with small honors, differing in the same way from magnanimity, which is concerned with great honors. For honor can be desired either in the right way or more or less than is right. If someone desires it to excess, he is called an honor-lover, and if his desire is deficient he is called indifferent to honor, but if he is intermediate he has no name. The corresponding conditions have no name either, except the condition of the honor-lover, which is called honor-loving.

This is why people at the extremes lay claim to the intermediate area. Moreover, we also sometimes call the intermediate person an honor-lover, and sometimes call him indifferent to honor; and sometimes we praise the honor-lover, sometimes the person indifferent to honor. We will mention later the reason we do this; for the moment, let us speak of the other cases in the way we have laid down.

Anger also admits of an excess, deficiency, and mean. These are all practically nameless; but since we call the intermediate person mild, let us call the mean mildness. Among the extreme people, let the excessive person be irascible, and his vice irascibility, and let the deficient person be a sort of inirascible person, and his deficiency inirascibility.

There are also three other means, somewhat similar to one another, but different. For they are all concerned with common dealings in conversations and actions, but differ insofar as one is concerned with truth telling in these areas, the other two with sources of pleasure, some of which are found in amusement, and the others in daily life in general. Hence we should also discuss these states, so that we can better observe that in every case the mean is praiseworthy, whereas the extremes are neither praiseworthy nor correct, but blameworthy. Most of these cases are also nameless, and we must try, as in the other cases also, to supply names ourselves, to make things clear and easy to follow.

In truth-telling, then, let us call the intermediate person truthful, and the mean truthfulness; pretense that overstates will be boastfulness, and the person who has it boastful; pretense that understates will be self-deprecation, and the person who has it self-deprecating.

In sources of pleasure in amusements let us call the intermediate person witty, and the condition wit; the excess buffoonery and the person who has it a buffoon; and the deficient person a sort of boor and the state boorishness.

In the other sources of pleasure, those in daily life, let us call the person who is pleasant in the right way friendly, and the mean state friendliness. If someone goes to excess with no [ulterior] aim, he will be ingratiating; if he does it for his own advantage, a flatterer. The deficient person, unpleasant in everything, will be a sort of quarrelsome and ill-tempered person.

There are also means in feelings and about feelings. Shame, for instance, is not a virtue, but the person prone to shame as well as [the virtuous people we have described] receives praise. For here also one person is called intermediate, and another—the person excessively prone to shame, who is ashamed about everything—is called excessive; the person who is deficient in shame or never feels shame at all is said to have no sense of disgrace; and the intermediate one is called prone to shame.

Proper indignation is the mean between envy and spite; these conditions are concerned with pleasure and pain at what happens to our neighbors. For the properly indignant person feels pain when someone does well undeservedly; the envious person exceeds him by feeling pain when anyone does well, while the spiteful person is so deficient in feeling pain that he actually enjoys [other people's misfortunes].

There will also be an opportunity elsewhere to speak of these. We must consider justice after these. Since it is spoken of in more than one way, we shall distinguish its two types and say how each of them is a mean. Similarly, we must also consider the virtues that belong to reason.

8 [Relations between Mean and Extreme States]

Among these three conditions, then, two are vices—one of excess, one of deficiency—and one, the mean, is virtue. In a way, each of them is opposed to each of the others, since each extreme is contrary both to the intermediate condition and to the other extreme, while the intermediate is contrary to the extremes.

For, just as the equal is greater in comparison to the smaller, and smaller in comparison to the greater, so also the intermediate states are excessive in comparison to the deficiencies and deficient in comparison to the excesses—both in feelings and in actions. For the brave person, for instance, appears rash in comparison to the coward, and cowardly in comparison to the rash person; the temperate person appears intemperate in comparison to the insensible person, and insensible in comparison with the intemperate person; and the generous person appears wasteful in comparison to the ungenerous, and ungenerous in comparison to the wasteful person. That is why each of the extreme people tries to push the intermediate person to the other extreme, so that the coward, for instance, calls the brave person rash, and the rash person calls him a coward, and similarly in the other cases.

Since these conditions of soul are opposed to each other in these ways, the extremes are more contrary to each other than to the intermediate. For they are further from each other than from the intermediate, just as the large is further from the small, and the small from the large, than either is from the equal.

Further, sometimes one extreme—rashness or wastefulness, for instance—appears somewhat like the intermediate state, bravery or generosity. But the extremes are most unlike one another; and the things that are furthest apart from each other are defined as contraries. And so the things that are further apart are more contrary.

In some cases the deficiency, in others the excess, is more opposed to the intermediate condition. For instance, cowardice, the deficiency, not rashness, the excess, is more opposed to bravery, whereas intemperance, the excess, not insensibility, the deficiency, is more opposed to temperance.

This happens for two reasons: One reason is derived from the object itself. Since sometimes one extreme is closer and more similar to the intermediate condition, we oppose the contrary extreme, more than this closer one, to the intermediate condition.

Since rashness, for instance, seems to be closer and more similar to bravery, and cowardice less similar, we oppose cowardice, more than rashness, to bravery; for what is further from the intermediate condition seems to be more contrary to it. This, then, is one reason, derived from the object itself.

The other reason is derived from ourselves. For when we ourselves have some natural tendency to one extreme more than to the other, this extreme appears more opposed to the intermediate condition. Since, for instance, we have more of a natural tendency to pleasure, we drift more easily toward intemperance than toward orderliness. Hence we say that an extreme is more contrary if we naturally develop more in that direction; and this is why intemperance is more contrary to temperance, since it is the excess [of pleasure].

9 [How Can We Reach the Mean?]

We have said enough, then, to show that virtue of character is a mean and what sort of mean it is; that it is a mean between two vices, one of excess and one of deficiency; and that it is a mean because it aims at the intermediate condition in feelings and actions.

That is why it is also hard work to be excellent. For in each case it is hard work to find the intermediate; for instance, not everyone, but only one who knows, finds the midpoint in a circle. So also getting angry, or giving and spending money, is easy and everyone can do it; but doing it to the right person, in the right amount, at the right time, for the right end, and in the right way is no longer easy, nor can everyone do it. Hence doing these things well is rare, praiseworthy, and fine.

That is why anyone who aims at the intermediate condition must first of all steer clear of the more contrary extreme, following the advice that Calypso* also gives: "Hold the ship outside the spray and surge."† For one extreme is more in error, the other less. Since, therefore, it is hard to hit the intermediate extremely accurately, the second-best tack, as they say, is to take

---

* In Homer's *Odyssey*, Calypso is a sea nymph who is in love with Odysseus and keeps him on her island for seven years.
† A line from Homer's *Odyssey* (part 12, lines 219–20). However, it is actually Circe (an enchantress), not Calypso (the nymph who detained Odysseus and his crew on her island), who gave the advice. The actual quotation is from Odysseus's orders to his steersman when he acts on Circe's suggestion that he take the ship closer to Scylla (a sea monster) than to Charybdis (a great whirlpool). Aristotle's quotations from Homer were apparently made from memory, and are rarely exact.

the lesser of the evils. We shall succeed best in this by the method we describe.

We must also examine what we ourselves drift into easily. For different people have different natural tendencies toward different goals, and we shall come to know our own tendencies from the pleasure or pain that arises in us. We must drag ourselves off in the contrary direction; for if we pull far away from error, as they do in straightening bent wood, we shall reach the intermediate condition.

And in everything we must beware above all of pleasure and its sources; for we are already biased in its favor when we come to judge it. Hence we must react to it as the elders reacted to Helen, and on each occasion repeat what they said;* for if we do this, and send it off, we shall be less in error.

In summary, then, if we do these things we shall best be able to reach the intermediate condition. But presumably this is difficult, especially in particular cases, since it is not easy to define the way we should be angry, with whom, about what, for how long. For sometimes, indeed, we ourselves praise deficient people and call them mild, and sometimes praise quarrelsome people and call them manly.

Still, we are not blamed if we deviate a little in excess or deficiency from doing well, but only if we deviate a long way, since then we are easily noticed. But how great and how serious a deviation receives blame is not easy to define in an account; for nothing else perceptible is easily defined either. Such things are among particulars, and the judgment depends on perception.

This is enough, then, to make it clear that in every case the intermediate state is praised, but we must sometimes incline toward the excess, sometimes toward the deficiency; for that is the easiest way to hit the intermediate and good condition. ...

BOOK X

6 [Conditions for Happiness]

We have now finished our discussion of the types of virtue; of friendship; and of pleasure. It remains for us to discuss happiness in outline, since we take this to be the end of human [aims]. Our discussion will be shorter if we first take up again what we said before.

We said, then, that happiness is not a state. For if it were, someone might have it and yet be asleep for his whole life, living the life of a plant, or suffer the greatest misfortunes. If we do not approve of this, we count happiness as an activity rather than a state, as we said before.

Some activities are necessary, i.e., choiceworthy for some other end, while others are choiceworthy in their own right. Clearly, then, we should count happiness as one of those activities that are choiceworthy in their own right, not as one of those choiceworthy for some other end. For happiness lacks nothing, but is self-sufficient.

An activity is choiceworthy in its own right if nothing further apart from it is sought from it. This seems to be the character of actions in accord with virtue; for doing fine and excellent actions is choiceworthy for itself. But pleasant amusements also [seem to be choiceworthy in their own right]; for they are not chosen for other ends, since they actually cause more harm than benefit, by causing neglect of our bodies and possessions. Moreover, most of those people congratulated for their happiness resort to these sorts of pastimes. That is why people who are witty participants in them have a good reputation with tyrants, since they offer themselves as pleasant [partners] in the tyrant's aims, and these are the sort of people the tyrant requires. And so these amusements seem

---

* See Homer's *Iliad*, part 3, lines 156–60 (here translated by Richmond Lattimore):
    Surely there is no blame on Trojans and strong-greaved Achaians
    if for long time they suffer hardship for a woman like this one.
    Terrible is the likeness of her face to immortal goddesses.
    Still, though she be such, let her go away in the ships, lest
    she be left behind, a grief for us and our children.

to have the character of happiness because people in supreme power spend their leisure in them.

These sorts of people, however, are presumably no evidence. For virtue and understanding, the sources of excellent activities, do not depend on holding supreme power. Further, these powerful people have had no taste of pure and civilized pleasure, and so they resort to bodily pleasures. But that is no reason to think these pleasures are most choiceworthy, since boys also think that the things they honor are best. Hence, just as different things appear honorable to boys and to men, it is reasonable that in the same way different things appear honorable to base and to decent people.

As we have often said, then, what is honorable and pleasant is what is so to the excellent person. To each type of person the activity that accords with his own proper state is most choiceworthy; hence the activity in accord with virtue is most choiceworthy to the excellent person [and hence is most honorable and pleasant].

Happiness, then, is not found in amusement; for it would be absurd if the end were amusement, and our lifelong efforts and sufferings aimed at amusing ourselves. For we choose practically everything for some other end—except for happiness, since it is [the] end; but serious work and toil aimed [only] at amusement appears stupid and excessively childish. Rather, it seems correct to amuse ourselves so that we can do something serious, as Anacharsis* says; for amusement would seem to be relaxation, and it is because we cannot toil continuously that we require relaxation. Relaxation, then, is not [the] end; for we pursue it [to prepare] for activity. But the happy life seems to be a life in accord with virtue, which is a life involving serious actions, and not consisting in amusement.

Besides, we say that things to be taken seriously are better than funny things that provide amusement, and that in each case the activity of the better part and the better person is more serious and excellent; and

the activity of what is better is superior, and thereby has more the character of happiness.

Besides, anyone at all, even a slave, no less than the best person, might enjoy bodily pleasures; but no one would allow that a slave shares in happiness, if one does not [also allow that the slave shares in the sort of] life [needed for happiness]. Happiness, then, is found not in these pastimes, but in the activities in accord with virtue, as we also said previously.

7 [Happiness and Theoretical Study]

If happiness is activity in accord with virtue, it is reasonable for it to accord with the supreme virtue, which will be the virtue of the best thing. The best is understanding, or whatever else seems to be the natural ruler and leader, and to understand what is fine and divine, by being itself either divine or the most divine element in us. Hence complete happiness will be its activity in accord with its proper virtue; and we have said that this activity is the activity of study.†

This seems to agree with what has been said before, and also with the truth. For this activity is supreme, since understanding is the supreme element in us, and the objects of understanding are the supreme objects of knowledge.

Further, it is the most continuous activity, since we are more capable of continuous study than any continuous action.

Besides, we think pleasure must be mixed into happiness; and it is agreed that the activity in accord with wisdom is the most pleasant of the activities in accord with virtue. Certainly, philosophy seems to have remarkably pure and firm pleasures, and it is reasonable for those who have knowledge to spend their lives more pleasantly than those who seek it.

Moreover, the self-sufficiency we spoke of will be found in study more than in anything else. For admittedly the wise person, the just person, and the other

---

* Anacharsis was a prince of Scythia (today the southern Ukraine), said to have lived early in the sixth century BCE, whose travels throughout the Greek world gave him a reputation for wisdom. He was known for his aphorisms, which were believed to be particularly profound.

† The Greek word *theōria*, translated here as "study," denotes something like the theoretical study of reality for the sake of knowledge alone, and would include, for example, astronomy, biology, mathematics, and anthropology as well as what we call philosophy. Furthermore, it is not so much the *search* for this knowledge that Aristotle is thinking of, but the quasi-aesthetic *appreciation* of it—a tranquil surveying of it in one's mind—once it has been acquired. (*Theōrein* is a Greek verb which originally meant to look at something, to gaze at it steadily.)

virtuous people all need the good things necessary for life. Still, when these are adequately supplied, the just person needs other people as partners and recipients of his just actions; and the same is true of the temperate person, the brave person, and each of the others. But the wise person is able, and more able the wiser he is, to study even by himself; and though he presumably does it better with colleagues, even so he is more self-sufficient than any other [virtuous person].

Besides, study seems to be liked because of itself alone, since it has no result beyond having studied. But from the virtues concerned with action we try to a greater or lesser extent to gain something beyond the action itself.

Besides, happiness seems to be found in leisure; for we deny ourselves leisure so that we can be at leisure, and fight wars so that we can be at peace. Now the virtues concerned with action have their activities in politics or war, and actions here seem to require trouble. This seems completely true for actions in war, since no one chooses to fight a war, and no one continues it, for the sake of fighting a war; for someone would have to be a complete murderer if he made his friends his enemies so that there could be battles and killings. But the actions of the politician also deny us leisure; apart from political activities themselves, those actions seek positions of power and honors, or at least they seek happiness for the politician himself and for his fellow citizens, which is something different from political science itself, and clearly is sought on the assumption that it is different.

Hence among actions in accord with the virtues those in politics and war are preeminently fine and great; but they require trouble, aim at some [further] end, and are choiceworthy for something other than themselves. But the activity of understanding, it seems, is superior in excellence because it is the activity of study, aims at no end apart from itself, and has its own proper pleasure, which increases the activity. Further, self-sufficiency, leisure, unwearied activity (as far as is possible for a human being), and any other features ascribed to the blessed person, are evidently features of this activity. Hence a human being's complete happiness will be this activity, if it receives a complete span of life, since nothing incomplete is proper to happiness.

Such a life would be superior to the human level. For someone will live it not insofar as he is a human being, but insofar as he has some divine element in him. And the activity of this divine element is as much superior to the activity in accord with the rest of virtue as this element is superior to the compound.* Hence if understanding is something divine in comparison with a human being, so also will the life in accord with understanding be divine in comparison with human life. We ought not to follow the makers of proverbs and 'Think human, since you are human', or 'Think mortal, since you are mortal'. Rather, as far as we can, we ought to be pro-immortal, and go to all lengths to live a life in accord with our supreme element; for however much this element may lack in bulk, by much more it surpasses everything in power and value.

Moreover, each person seems to be his understanding, if he is his controlling and better element. It would be absurd, then, if he were to choose not his own life, but something else's. And what we have said previously will also apply now. For what is proper to each thing's nature is supremely best and most pleasant for it; and hence for a human being the life in accord with understanding will be supremely best and most pleasant, if understanding, more than anything else, is the human being. This life, then, will also be happiest.

8 [Theoretical Study and the Other Virtues]

The life in accord with the other kind of virtue [i.e., the kind concerned with action] is [happiest] in a secondary way, because the activities in accord with this virtue are human. For we do just and brave actions, and the other actions in accord with the virtues, in relation to other people, by abiding by what fits each person in contracts, services, all types of actions, and also in feelings; and all these appear to be human conditions. Indeed, some feelings actually seem to arise from the body; and in many ways virtue of character seems to be proper to feelings.

Besides, prudence is inseparable from virtue of character, and virtue of character from prudence. For the principles of prudence accord with the virtues

---

* The view that human beings are made up of both soul and body, while the divine is pure intellect.

of character; and correctness in virtues of character accords with prudence. And since these virtues are also connected to feelings, they are concerned with the compound. Since the virtues of the compound are human virtues, the life and the happiness in accord with these virtues is also human. The virtue of understanding, however, is separated [from the compound]. Let us say no more about it, since an exact account would be too large a task for our present project.

Moreover, it seems to need external supplies very little, or [at any rate] less than virtue of character needs them. For let us grant that they both need necessary goods, and to the same extent; for there will be only a very small difference, even though the politician labors more about the body and suchlike. Still, there will be a large difference in [what is needed] for the [proper] activities [of each type of virtue]. For the generous person will need money for generous actions; and the just person will need it for paying debts, since wishes are not clear, and people who are not just pretend to wish to do justice. Similarly, the brave person will need enough power, and the temperate person will need freedom [to do intemperate actions], if they are to achieve anything that the virtue requires. For how else will they, or any other virtuous people, make their virtue clear?

Moreover, it is disputed whether decision or action is more in control of virtue, on the assumption that virtue depends on both. Well, certainly it is clear that the complete [good] depends on both; but for actions many external goods are needed, and the greater and finer the actions the more numerous are the external goods needed.

But someone who is studying needs none of these goods, for that activity at least; indeed, for study at least, we might say they are even hindrances. Insofar as he is a human being, however, and [hence] lives together with a number of other human beings, he chooses to do the actions that accord with virtue. Hence he will need the sorts of external goods [that are needed for the virtues], for living a human life.

In another way also it appears that complete happiness is some activity of study. For we traditionally suppose that the gods more than anyone are blessed and happy; but what sorts of actions ought we to ascribe to them? Just actions? Surely they will appear ridiculous making contracts, returning deposits, and so on. Brave actions? Do they endure what [they find] frightening and endure dangers because it is fine? Generous actions? Whom will they give to? And surely it would be absurd for them to have currency or anything like that. What would their temperate actions be? Surely it is vulgar praise to say that they do not have base appetites. When we go through them all, anything that concerns actions appears trivial and unworthy of the gods. Nonetheless, we all traditionally suppose that they are alive and active, since surely they are not asleep like Endymion.* Then if someone is alive, and action is excluded, and production even more, what is left but study? Hence the gods' activity that is superior in blessedness will be an activity of study. And so the human activity that is most akin to the gods' activity will, more than any others, have the character of happiness.

A sign of this is the fact that other animals have no share in happiness, being completely deprived of this activity of study. For the whole life of the gods is blessed, and human life is blessed to the extent that it has something resembling this sort of activity; but none of the other animals is happy, because none of them shares in study at all. Hence happiness extends just as far as study extends, and the more someone studies, the happier he is, not coincidentally but insofar as he studies, since study is valuable in itself. And so [on this argument] happiness will be some kind of study.

But happiness will need external prosperity also, since we are human beings; for our nature is not self-sufficient for study, but we need a healthy body, and need to have food and the other services provided. Still, even though no one can be blessedly happy without external goods, we must not think that to be happy we will need many large goods. For self-sufficiency and action do not depend on excess.

Moreover, we can do fine actions even if we do not rule earth and sea; for even from moderate resources we can do the actions that accord with virtue. This is evident to see, since many private citizens seem to do decent actions no less than people in power do—even

---

* According to Greek myth, Endymion was such a beautiful man that the Moon fell in love with him. She made him immortal, but cast him into an eternal sleep so that she could descend and embrace him every night.

more, in fact. It is enough if moderate resources are provided; for the life of someone whose activity accords with virtue will be happy.

Solon* surely described happy people well, when he said† they had been moderately supplied with external goods, had done what he regarded as the finest actions, and had lived their lives temperately. For it is possible to have moderate possessions and still to do the right actions. And Anaxagoras‡ would seem to have supposed that the happy person was neither rich nor powerful, since he said he would not be surprised if the happy person appeared an absurd sort of person to the many. For the many judge by externals, since these are all they perceive. Hence the beliefs of the wise would seem to accord with our arguments.

These considerations, then, produce: some confidence. But the truth in questions about action is judged from what we do and how we live, since these are what control [the answers to such questions]. Hence we ought to examine what has been said by applying it to what we do and how we live; and if it harmonizes with what we do, we should accept it, but if it conflicts we should count it [mere] words.

The person whose activity accords with understanding and who takes care of understanding would seem to be in the best condition, and most loved by the gods. For if the gods pay some attention to human beings, as they seem to, it would be reasonable for them to take pleasure in what is best and most akin to them, namely understanding; and reasonable for them to benefit in return those who most of all like and honor understanding, on the assumption that these people attend to what is beloved by the gods, and act correctly and finely. Clearly, all this is true of the wise person more than anyone else; hence he is most loved by the gods. And it is likely that this same person will be happiest; hence, by this argument also, the wise person, more than anyone else, will be happy. ■

Suggestions for Critical Reflection

1. When Aristotle talks of the "precision" of a subject matter, what exactly does he mean? What kind of precision can mathematics have which ethics must always lack? Does this mean there can be no universally true moral principles (but, perhaps, just 'rules of thumb')?

2. Does Aristotle assume there is just one thing which is the goal of every human life? Is he right?

3. Aristotle seems to define the (biological) function of human beings as the thing "which is peculiar to man"—i.e., as something only human beings can do. Is this a plausible way of identifying the human function? Is reason the *only* capacity which human beings have uniquely? Does Aristotle believe that only human beings are rational, or does he say things elsewhere which are inconsistent with this?

4. What if human beings do not *have* a function? How much damage would this do to Aristotle's moral theory?

5. Aristotle concedes that not every *vice* is a matter of degree, but he does seem to hold that every *virtue is* in the middle between two vices. Does this claim seem plausible? What about, for example, the virtue of kindness?

6. Does Aristotle's Doctrine of the Mean actually help us at all in making moral decisions? If not, how much of a problem is this for Aristotle's ethics? Do you think Aristotle *expects* his Doctrine of the Mean to guide our moral behavior? If the Doctrine of the Mean *cannot* tell us what to do, then what (if anything) is its point?

7. Many commentators on Aristotle's ethics have worried about what is sometimes called the

---

* Solon (c. 640–558 BCE) was an Athenian lawmaker and poet, considered the founder of Athenian democracy, whose name was a byword for wisdom.
† As quoted in Book I of Herodotus' *History*.
‡ Anaxagoras of Clazomenae (c. 500–428 BCE) was the first philosopher to teach in Athens—though he, like Socrates and Plato, was prosecuted for impiety by the Athenians (in part for believing that the sun is a fiery body larger than Greece and that the light of the moon is reflected light from the sun).

"Aristotelian circle." Aristotle can be seen as making the following claims: virtuous action is what the practically wise person would choose; the practically wise are those who can successfully act in such a way as to achieve *eudaimonia*; but *eudaimonia*, for Aristotle, simply consists in wise action (it is "activity of soul exhibiting excellence"). If this is an accurate description of Aristotle's claims, how are we to *recognize* wise or virtuous action without an independent standard by which to judge it, and when Aristotle's inter-connected definitions go around in an endless circle? Do you agree that Aristotle's theory is circular? If so, do you think that makes it simply vacuous?

8. How plausible do you find Aristotle's arguments that the life of a philosopher is the best and happiest possible kind of life for human beings? How consistent is the emphasis in Book X on the activity of *theoria*—on *theoretical* reason—with Aristotle's earlier focus on *practical* wisdom?

9. Is Aristotle too egoistic? Does he pay too much attention to the question of how we as *individuals* can lead a good life, and not enough on moral issues to do with helping other people? For example, is generosity a virtue just because of its good effects on others, or simply because being generous makes one happy?

IMMANUEL KANT

FROM *Foundations of the Metaphysics of Morals*

Who Was Immanuel Kant?

Immanuel Kant—by common consent the most important philosopher of the past 300 years, and arguably the most important of the past 2,300—was born in 1724 on the coast of the Baltic Sea, in Königsberg, a regionally important harbor city in East Prussia.* Kant spent his whole life living in this town, and never ventured outside its region. His family were devout members of an evangelical Protestant sect (rather like the Quakers or early Methodists) called the Pietists, and Pietism's strong emphasis on moral responsibility, hard work, and distrust of religious dogma had a deep effect on Kant's character. Kant's father was a craftsman (making harnesses and saddles for horses) and his family was fairly poor; Kant's mother, whom he loved deeply, died when he was 13.

Kant's life is notorious for its outward uneventfulness. He was educated at a strict Lutheran school in Königsberg, and after graduating from the University of Königsberg in 1746 (where he supported himself by some tutoring but also by his skill at billiards and card games) he served as a private tutor to various local families until he became a lecturer at the university in 1755. However his position—that of *Privatdozent*—carried no salary, and Kant was expected to support himself by the income from his lecturing; financial need caused Kant to lecture for 30 or more hours a week on a huge range of subjects (including mathematics, physics, geography, anthropology, ethics, and law). During this period Kant published several scientific works and his reputation as a scholar grew; he turned down opportunities for professorships in other towns (Erlangen and Jena), having his heart set on a professorship in Königsberg. Finally, at the

age of 46, Kant became professor of logic and metaphysics at the University of Königsberg, a position he held until his retirement 26 years later in 1796. After a tragic period of senility he died in 1804, and was buried with pomp and circumstance in the "professors' vault" at the Königsberg cathedral.†

Kant's days were structured by a rigorous and unvarying routine—indeed, it is often said that the housewives of Königsberg were able to set their clocks by the regularity of his afternoon walk. He never married (though twice he nearly did), had very few close friends, and lived by all accounts an austere and outwardly unemotional life. He was something of a hypochondriac, hated noise, and disliked all music except for military marches. Nevertheless, anecdotes by those who knew him give the impression of a warm, impressive, rather noble human being, capable of great kindness and dignity and sparkling conversation. He did not shun society, and in fact his regular daily routine included an extended lunchtime gathering at which he and his guests—drawn from the cosmopolitan stratum of Königsberg society—would discuss politics, science, philosophy, and poetry.

Kant's philosophical life is often divided into three phases: his "pre-Critical" period, his "silent" period, and his "Critical" period. His pre-Critical period began in 1747 when he published his first work (*Thoughts on the True Estimation of Living Forces*) and ended in 1770 when he wrote his Inaugural Dissertation—*Concerning the Form and Principles of the Sensible and Intelligible World*—and became a professor. Between 1770 and 1780, Kant published almost nothing. In 1781, however, at the age of 57, Kant made his first major contribution to philosophy with his monumental *Critique of Pure Rea-*

---

* Prussia is a historical region which included what is today northern Germany, Poland, and the western fringes of Russia. It became a kingdom in 1701, and then a dominant part of the newly unified Germany in 1871. Greatly reduced after World War I, the state of Prussia was formally abolished after World War II, and Königsberg—renamed Kaliningrad during the Soviet era, after one of Stalin's henchmen—now sits on the western rump of Russia (between Poland and Lithuania).

† His body no longer remains there: in 1950 his sarcophagus was broken open by unknown vandals and his corpse was stolen and never recovered.

son (written, Kant said, over the course of a few months "as if in flight"). He spent the next 20 years in unrelenting intellectual labor, trying to develop and answer the new problems laid out in this masterwork. First, in order to clarify and simplify the system of the *Critique* for the educated public, Kant published the much shorter *Prolegomena to Any Future Metaphysics* in 1783. In 1785 came Kant's *Foundations of the Metaphysics of Morals*, and in 1788 he published what is now known as his "second Critique": the *Critique of Practical Reason*. His third and final Critique, the *Critique of Judgement*, was published in 1790—an amazing body of work produced in less than 10 years.

By the time he died, Kant had already become known as a great philosopher, with a permanent place in history. Over his grave was inscribed a quote from the *Critique of Practical Reason*, which sums up the impulse for his philosophy: "Two things fill the mind with ever new and increasing admiration and reverence, the more often and more steadily one reflects on them: the starry heavens above me and the moral law within me."*

What Was Kant's Overall Philosophical Project?

Kant's core ethical idea is that the guiding principle for morality is delivered by pure reason—it is an objectively rational way to behave, and any other way of behaving is irrational—and that all particular moral injunctions are either justified or shown to be unjustified by this principle of reason. This supreme principle of morality is called the Categorical Imperative, and it is introduced and explained in this reading.

Kant argues that the Categorical Imperative is rational in a particular, and somewhat unfamiliar, way. Often, when we speak of something being rational, we really mean that it is *instrumentally* rational: that is, *if* you wish to achieve a certain outcome, *then* the rational thing to do is such-and-such. For example, if you want to make a sandwich then it is rational to collect bread and sandwich fillings, and to put them together with the bread on the outside and the fillings inside; if you want to win a battle under certain circumstances then it might be rational to send your cavalry around to the left to outflank

the enemy's artillery; and so on. But is it rational to *want* to make a sandwich or win a battle? That depends: it might be instrumentally rational to seek these outcomes, depending on what else you want (to give yourself energy for a busy afternoon of study, or to win the war), but if you had different overall goals (to avoid procrastination, to preserve your forces to fight in a later more important battle) it might not. Instrumental rationality can tell you how to achieve your goals effectively, but it cannot by itself tell you what those goals should be.

Another way in which we often think about being rational has to do with consistency. For example, in logic, *if* you begin from particular premises, *then* you are required to conclude that some other claim is true as well. To believe in the truth of the premises while asserting the falsity of the conclusion would be logically inconsistent and hence irrational. For example, suppose you believe that ice is cold, and that if you put something cold in contact with something warm then the warm thing will lose its heat to the cold thing; then it would be irrational, because inconsistent, to believe that you can heat up your coffee by adding ice cubes to it. But, just as with instrumental rationality what it is rational to do depends on some ultimately non-rational fact about what you want to achieve, this kind of appeal to consistency is relative to what else you already happen to believe. If you thought that ice was hot then it would be quite rational to try and use it to heat up a drink.

The way in which the Categorical Imperative is rational is neither of these. It is, according to Kant, *unconditionally* rational (otherwise, he thinks, it wouldn't really be moral). The Categorical Imperative specifies a principle of action that is rational all by itself, under any circumstances, no matter what else we want or believe, or what else is true. Any rational agent whatever can recognize that the Categorical Imperative is true and, because they are rational agents, they will *want* to act in accordance with it. People don't need to be (in fact can't be) externally compelled to behave morally, according to Kant; once they think reflectively about the principles that are guiding their behavior, they will freely bind their will to the moral law because choosing anything else is irrational. It is impossible to want to violate the Categorical Imperative (though of course we might unreflectively do so by mistake), similar to the way it is impossible to

---

* Immanuel Kant, *Critique of Practical Reason*, ed. Mary Gregor (Cambridge University Press, 1997), 133.

consciously believe that P is true and that it is false at the same time.

Where does the Categorical Imperative come from? How do we discover it and come to know that it is true? This is a complex issue for Kant, and he considers it a branch of metaphysics—the metaphysics of practical reason. Prior to Kant, seventeenth- and eighteenth-century philosophers divided knowledge into exactly two camps: "truths of reason" (or "relations of ideas") on the one hand, and "truths of fact" (or "matters of fact") on the other. A major school of thought called rationalism was characterized by the doctrine that all final, complete knowledge was a truth of reason: that is, it was made up entirely of claims that could be proven *a priori* (without the need for sensory observations) as being necessarily true, as a matter of logic, since it would be self-contradictory for them to be false. The opposing school, empiricists, on the other hand, believed that all genuinely *informative* claims were truths of fact: if we wanted to find out about the world itself, rather than merely the logical relations between our own concepts, we had to rely upon the (*a posteriori*) data of sensory experience. At the center of Kant's contribution to the history of thought was the way he reshaped this distinction in a new framework. Instead of merely drawing a distinction between truths of reason and truths of fact, Kant replaced this with *two* separate distinctions: that between "*a priori*" and "*a posteriori*" propositions, and that between "analytic" and "synthetic" judgments.* On this more complex scheme, the rationalists' truths of reason turn out to be "analytic *a priori*" knowledge, while empirical truths of fact are "synthetic *a posteriori*" propositions. But, Kant pointed out, this leaves open the possibility that there is at least a *third* type of knowledge: *synthetic a priori* judgments. These are judgments which we know *a priori* and thus do not need to learn from experience, but which nevertheless go beyond merely "analytic" claims about our own concepts.

Kant's question therefore becomes: *How* is synthetic *a priori* knowledge possible? After all, the source of this knowledge can be neither experience (since it is *a priori*) nor the logical relations of ideas (since it is synthetic), so where could this kind of knowledge possibly come from? In bald (and massively simplified) summary, Kant's answer to these questions in the *Critique of Pure Reason* is the following. Synthetic *a priori* knowledge is possible insofar as it is knowledge of the *conditions of our experience of the world* (or indeed, of any *possible* experience). For example, for Kant, our judgments about the fundamental nature of space and time are not claims about our experiences themselves, nor are they the results of logic: instead, the forms of space and time are the conditions under which we are capable of having experience *at all*—we *can* only undergo sensations (either perceived or imaginary) that are arranged in space, and spread out in time; anything else is just impossible for us. So we can know *a priori*, but not analytically, that space and time must have a certain nature, since they are the forms of (the very possibility of) our experience.

Kant sets out to address the question of the Categorical Imperative in a similar way. The Categorical Imperative, he argues is *a priori* and necessary, but it is not analytic—it is not to be discovered merely by analysis of certain concepts (such as our concept of "good" or "right"; it isn't merely true by definition). As such it is a synthetic *a priori* claim. If we are to establish it, it must be required by some sort of built-in condition or limit of an appropriate domain of human experience. In the case of morality, the domain is not perception but what Kant called *practical reason*, because we are dealing here with a law that should govern our behavior, rather than laws that describe how the world is. The Categorical Imperative, according to Kant, is made necessary by the structure or limits of our freedom to act—the common features of our practical life. For Kant, genuine freedom does not consist in lawlessness but in being bound by laws that are of one's own making: freedom is autonomy. A rational will is one that operates on the basis of reasons, and this means that a free will is one that is not influenced by non-rational factors—such as psychological impulses or the laws of neuroscience—but only by its grasp of rational principles. For this to be true—for us to be genuinely free, as we believe we are—there therefore must *be* a rational law to which we can conform our behavior: there must be a Categorical Imperative.

---

* "Analytic" judgments are true due to the meanings of their words alone (e.g., "All bachelors are unmarried"), while synthetic truths are true at least in part due to the way the world is (e.g., "The sky is blue").

What Is the Structure of This Reading?

Kant's *Foundations of the Metaphysics of Morals* was written not just for professional philosophers, but for the general educated reader. Nevertheless, it can be pretty hard going, especially for those coming to Kant for the first time; the effort, however, is richly rewarded.

The *Foundations* forms a single, continuous argument running the whole length of the book, and each step of that overall argument is supported by sub-arguments. Kant's goals for the work are first, to establish that there is such a thing as morality—that there really are laws that should govern our conduct—and, second, to discover and justify the "supreme principle of morality." This "supreme principle," which Kant announces he has uncovered, is now famous as the Categorical Imperative.

Each section of the *Foundations* plays a role in Kant's overall argument. He begins, in the First Section, by simply trying to discover *what we already think morality is*. He is not, at this stage, trying to *justify* these beliefs: he merely wants to analyze our moral "common sense" to bring to light the principle behind it. He argues that the only thing which is "unconditionally" morally good is a good will, and that this insight is embedded in our ordinary moral judgments. (He then backs this argument with another, longer but less plausible—not included here—which appeals to "the purpose of nature.") The key to understanding morality, therefore, must be a proper understanding of the good will; if we can understand the principles that people of good will try to act on, Kant thinks, then we can see what the moral law tells us to do. In order to carry out this investigation, Kant announces he will focus on examples that make the moral will especially clear: i.e., on cases where the person performing an action has other motives that would normally lead to *not* doing that thing, but where she does it anyway because she recognizes it as her moral duty. He illustrates this contrast between people doing things "from duty" and doing them for some other reason by giving examples (each of which can be done for the sake of duty or not): a merchant who does not overcharge customers, a person who refrains from committing suicide, a man who performs kind actions to help others, and someone taking care to preserve their own happiness.

Consideration of examples like these shows us, Kant argues, that what gives a particular action moral worth is not the kind of action it is, nor the consequences of that action, nor even the purpose for which the action is performed, but the psychological rule, or *maxim*, motivating that action. This in turn, Kant claims, shows moral worth is a kind of *respect for moral law* and that, in order to have the form of a law, moral principles must be *universalizable*.* This important result is then illustrated and further explained using the example of truth-telling.

Kant concludes the First Section by explaining the need for philosophy to bolster these insights of common sense. The Second Section, therefore, is devoted to developing the fundamental elements of a proper "metaphysics of morals," which, in turn, Kant argues, must ultimately be embedded within a general theory of *practical reason*. Since the theory of practical reason is a theory of what reason tells us we ought to do (whether or not we actually do it), it must be a theory of what Kant calls *imperatives*. Kant therefore embarks on a discussion of the different types of imperative, distinguishing between *hypothetical* imperatives and *categorical* imperatives. Moral imperatives, he argues, must be categorical and not hypothetical.

He then asks: What makes these imperatives "possible," that is, what makes them legitimate requirements of rationality? Why are they *laws* that are binding on rational beings? The answer for hypothetical imperatives, Kant argues, is easy: that hypothetical imperatives are laws of reason is an *analytic* truth. However, in the case of categorical imperatives, the issue is more difficult. That these imperatives are rationally binding can only be, in Kant's terms, a *synthetic a priori* practical principle—something which we can know, independently of experience, to be true, but which is not merely true 'logically' or by virtue of the meanings of the words involved. Thus, showing there really *are* moral laws that are binding on all rational creatures is a difficult problem for Kant—and he postpones it until the Third Section of his book.

---

* That is, a rule that can rationally be applied to everyone. Kant does not mean that we should act only in ways we'd want others to act. He means that in some sense it's impossible to conceive of the universalization of some maxims (such as 'tell lies when it's beneficial to you'); as these maxims are not universalizable, they cannot be moral principles. See the "Misconceptions" section below for further explanation.

First, he turns to a more detailed analysis of the concept of a categorical imperative and, by emphasizing the *unconditional* character of categorical imperatives, arrives at his first major formulation of the moral law: the so-called Formula of Universal Law. Kant then illustrates how this law constrains our duties by ruling out certain maxims as being immoral. He gives four (carefully chosen) examples: someone contemplating suicide, someone considering borrowing money by making a false promise to repay it, someone wasting their talents in a life of self-indulgence and idleness, and someone refusing to help others.

If this helps us see *what* the categorical imperative requires us, morally, to do, the next issue is to discover *why* our wills should be consistent with the categorical imperative: what could motivate us to adopt universalizable maxims? The imperative is categorical and not hypothetical, so we cannot appeal to any contingent or variable motivations: the goal of morality—the *value* of being moral—must be something shared by every possible rational creature, no matter how they are situated. This, Kant argues, means all rational creatures must be ends-in-themselves and the ultimate source of all objective value. The categorical imperative can thus be expressed according to the Formula of Humanity as End in Itself. The reason non-universalizable maxims are immoral is, according to Kant, because they fail to properly respect rational creatures as ends in themselves; Kant illustrates this by reconsidering his four examples in light of this latest formulation.

This notion of rational beings as having (and indeed being the source of) objective, intrinsic worth leads Kant to the idea of the *kingdom of ends*: an ideal human community in which people treat each other as ends in themselves. Acting morally, Kant claims, can be thought of as *legislating* moral laws for this ideal community: we guide our own behavior by principles which we realize should be followed by all the free and equal members of the kingdom of ends. This formulation of the categorical imperative is often called the Formula of Autonomy (autonomy comes from the Greek words for self—*autos*—and law—*nomos*—and hence means something like

"following one's own laws"). Again, this shows us something new about the categorical imperative: the reason we ought to follow the moral law is not because we are forced to conform to it by something outside ourselves (such as society or God), but because these are laws that rational people lay down *for themselves*.* Morality, thus, does not infringe on freedom—on the contrary, it is the fullest expression of freedom, and also of respect for the freedom of others. Furthermore, it is the capacity of rational creatures to be legislators in the kingdom of ends which is the source of what Kant calls their *dignity*.

This brings us to the final stage of Kant's argument: the last problem he faces is that of showing moral law really does exist—that we really are rationally bound by it. He has shown that we *would* be bound by it if we were autonomous, rational beings capable of being legislative citizens in the kingdom of ends; now Kant has to show that human beings really do have an autonomous will, and this is the project of the Third Section (which is not reprinted here). To do this, Kant needs to show that the human will is not subject to the laws of nature, for otherwise we would not be free to legislate the moral law for ourselves. On the other hand, if we are free, then—since our wills must be governed by *some* law or other or they would not be causal—we must be governed by the moral law. Morality and freedom are thus intimately connected, for Kant, and we cannot have one without the other. He then argues that if we are to think of ourselves as *rational*, we must necessarily think of ourselves as free. Thus, to be rational just is to be governed by the moral law.

But how is this freedom possible—how *can* human beings be rational, given that we are surely part of the natural world and hence entangled in the web of the laws of nature? Here Kant appeals to and summarizes parts of his *Critique of Pure Reason*, where he argued that the empirical world of appearance—the world of nature—is not the way things are in themselves, but merely how they appear to us: 'behind' this world of appearance is the deeper reality of things as they are in themselves. Human beings, too, are subject to this duality: as members of the natural world, we are subject to

---

* Moreover, we do not need to be told, by some external authority, what the moral law is. We can each reliably discover *for ourselves* what we ought to do. In fact, for Kant, acting in accordance with a moral law merely because some moral authority has told you to does not make you a good person. That would be to obey a merely hypothetical, and not a categorical, imperative.

the laws of causality, but our real selves—our *egos*—are "above nature" and so, at least potentially, are autonomous. Kant's overall conclusion in the *Foundations of the Metaphysics of Morals*, then, is not that we can actually know there *is* a moral law, but that a) if there were a moral law it would have to be the way he has described, b) it is at least possible the moral law really does exist, and c) in any case we are forced to *believe* the moral law exists, simply in virtue of thinking of ourselves as rational beings.

Some Useful Background Information

1. The goal of Kant's *Foundations* is not to tell people how to act or to introduce a new theory of morality. Kant thought that, on the whole, people know perfectly well what they are and are not supposed to do and, indeed, that any moral theory having prescriptions that substantially diverged from "common sense" beliefs about morality was likely to be erroneous. When criticized by his contemporaries for merely providing a new formula for old beliefs, Kant replied, "... who would even want to introduce a new principle of all morality and, as it were, first invent it? Just as if, before him, the world had been ignorant of what duty is, or in thoroughgoing error about it."* Instead, Kant aimed to provide a new philosophical *underpinning* for morality: he thought people had misunderstood *why* the prescriptions of morality are the way they are, and that they lacked a reliable *method* for making sure they always did the right thing.

2. In the Preface to the *Foundations of the Metaphysics of Morals* Kant divides philosophy into three parts: logic (the study of thought), physics (the study of the way the world is), and ethics (the study of what we ought to do). Kant thinks of each of these as a domain of *laws*: logic deals with the laws of thought, physics deals with the laws of nature, and ethics deals with what Kant calls the *laws of freedom*—that is, with laws governing the conduct of those beings not subject to the laws of nature. In this way, Kant sets up the study of morality as the study of a particular kind of law

(as opposed to, say, of character traits, states of affairs, or types of actions), and he thinks of these laws as being analogous to, but different from, laws of nature.

3. According to Kant, there are in general two routes to knowledge: experience and reason. The study of logic is within the domain of pure reason, but for Kant physics and ethics each have both a "pure" and an empirical part. Particular physical laws—for example that infection is transmitted by micro-organisms—are empirical, but the general *framework* for these laws—the idea that all events must have a lawlike cause—is not itself empirical (after all, we have not *seen* every event and its cause). That ethics must be built upon a non-empirical foundation is even more obvious, according to Kant. Ethics is the study, not of how things actually are, but of how things *ought* to be. Scrutinizing the way human beings actually behave, and describing the things they actually believe, will never be sufficient to tell you what we *ought* to do and think. Moral laws and concepts, therefore, must be established by pure reason alone (though experience will certainly play a role in determining the *concrete content* of moral principles in actual circumstances). This body of non-empirical knowledge, which sets out what Kant calls the "synthetic *a priori*" framework for physics and ethics, is called *metaphysics*; that is why Kant labels the subject of this work the "metaphysics of morals."

4. While all things in nature are bound by laws, rational beings instead govern their behavior by their *conception* of laws. For example, while objects fall because of the law of gravity, rational entities refrain from stepping off high places, not because of this law itself, but because of their *understanding* or conception of the law. A *maxim*, for Kant, is the subjective psychological principle that lies behind volition. It is, roughly, a stable motive that makes people do things in one way rather than another, a tacit 'rule' that guides their behavior. Examples of maxims might be "never kill innocent people," "don't tell lies unless it is clearly to your advantage to do so," "don't eat meat (except on special occasions)," "always give people the

---

* Immanuel Kant, *Critique of Practical Reason*, Preface, footnote to p. 7. This translation is by Mary Gregor.

correct change," "never sleep with someone before the third date," and "never shop-lift, but it's okay to take office supplies from your workplace."

Some Common Misconceptions

1. Kant is not an ethical grinch or an unfeeling puritan. He does not claim that we cannot be glad to perform a moral action, that we only act morally when we do something we don't want to do, or that happiness is incompatible with goodness. Kant's examples in the *Foundations* are only supposed to be thought experiments which pull apart, as clearly as possible, actions we *want* to do from actions we *ought* to do, in order to show what makes actions distinctively moral. He does not claim that the mere presence of an inclination to do something detracts from its moral worth: the key idea is just that one's *motive* must be duty and not inclination. (In fact, Kant argues that we have a kind of indirect moral duty to seek our own happiness, and that since generous inclinations are helpful in doing good actions, we should cultivate these feelings in ourselves.)

2. Similarly, Kant does not—as is sometimes claimed—assert that the good will is the *only thing* which is good, that everything else which is good is merely a *means* to the achievement of a good will, or even that a good will is *all* we require for a completely good life. It is perfectly consistent with Kant's views to point out that, say, health or pleasure are valuable for their own sake. Kant's claim is that the good will is the *highest* good, and that it is the *precondition* of all the other goods (i.e., nothing else is good unless it is combined with a good will). When Kant says health is not "unconditionally" good, what he means is that it is not good at all unless it is combined with a good will—though when it *is* so combined, it really does have value in itself. By contrast, a good will is unconditionally good: it has its goodness in all possible circumstances, independently of its relation to anything else, and this is what makes it the "highest" good.

3. The categorical imperative is (arguably) not intended by Kant to be *itself* a recipe for moral action. It does not, and is not supposed to, tell you what you ought to do. Instead, the categorical imperative acts as a *test* for particular maxims—permitting some and prohibiting others. To put it another way, Kant does not expect us to *deduce* particular moral maxims from the categorical imperative alone; rather, we take the maxims upon which we are *already* disposed to act and scrutinize them to see if they are formally consistent with the moral law.

4. The categorical imperative—say, the Formula of Universal Law—applies to maxims, not to actions or even intentions. Thus, for example, there is no requirement that our *actions* be universalizable: it need not be immoral for me to use my toothbrush or live in my house, even though not *everyone* could do those things. Instead, the *maxims* which guide my actions must be universalizable, and one and the same maxim (e.g., the principle of taking care of one's teeth) can give rise to different actions by different people in different circumstances. Conversely, two actions of exactly the same type (e.g., refusing to give someone a loan) could be of vastly different moral significance since the maxims that lie behind them might be of vastly different moral worth. It is also important to notice that maxims are not the same thing as *intentions*: one can intend to do something (such as make someone happy) for any of several quite different maxims (e.g., because you realize that being nice to people is part of moral duty, or because you want to be remembered in their will), and thus sometimes this intention is moral and sometimes it is not.*

5. When Kant claims certain maxims cannot be universalized, he cannot mean by this merely that it would be *immoral* or *bad* if these maxims were universal laws. (This would make his reasoning

---

* One significant consequence of this is that Kant is not coldly saying that all of our actions should be done *because* it is our duty, in the sense that the purpose of our acting is to be dutiful. On the contrary, good people will typically do the things they do because they want to help others, or to cultivate their own talents, or to be good parents, and so on: it is just that the maxims they are following in acting on these intentions are maxims which are consistent with the moral law.

circular; if he is trying to define immorality in terms of non-universalizable maxims, he can't turn around and define universalizability in terms of immorality. Also, Kant has disavowed the relevance of the *consequences* of an action as part of what makes it moral or immoral, so he cannot now appeal to the consequences of making a maxim universal.) Instead, Kant means it is *literally impossible* to will that certain maxims be universal laws—that it would go against rationality itself to do so, rather like willing that 2+2=5 or wanting my desires to be always and everywhere frustrated.

6. Kant did not hold that *all* universalizable maxims are moral; it would be a problem for his account if he had done so, since some obviously trivial and non-moral maxims appear to be consistent with the categorical imperative (e.g., a policy of always wearing socks on Tuesdays). Kant is able to exclude such examples from the sphere of the moral by distinguishing between actions that merely *conform* to a law, and actions performed *because* of a law. It is these latter kind of actions that are genuinely moral, since in these cases I decide what to do *by* working out what I would will that every rational being should do (rather than doing something for *other* reasons—e.g., to keep my feet warm—that also happens to be something that every rational being could do).

7. Kant's philosophy is not, as is often assumed, authoritarian or dictatorial. Although he places great emphasis on a rigid adherence to duty, it is important to realize that, for Kant, this duty is not imposed from the outside: it is not a matter of the laying down of moral laws by the state, society, or even by God. Quite the opposite: for Kant, constraining one's own behavior by the moral law actually *constitutes* genuine freedom or autonomy, which is being guided by rationality and not by mere inclination. Moral duty, for Kant, is *self*-legislated.

How Important and Influential Is This Passage?

Kant's *Foundations of the Metaphysics of Morals* is one of the most important ethical works ever written. Philosopher H.J. Paton called it "one of the small books which are truly great: it has exercised on human thought an influence almost ludicrously disproportionate to its size.... Its main topic—the supreme principle of morality—is of the utmost importance to all who are not indifferent to the struggle of good against evil."* Since their introduction in this work, some of Kant's themes—the idea that human beings are ends-in-themselves and so not to be treated as mere means by others; that our own humanity finds its greatest expression through the respect we have for others; that morality is freedom and vice a form of enslavement—have become central parts of contemporary moral culture. Many modern moral philosophers have been heavily influenced by his work, and descendants of his moral theory form one of the main strands in contemporary ethical theory. Kant's ethical theory is very much a 'live' philosophical position today.

---

* H.J. Paton, "Preface" to his translation of *The Moral Law, or Kant's Groundwork of the Metaphysics of Morals* (Hutchinson University Library, 1949), 7.

FROM *Foundations of the Metaphysics of Morals**

FIRST SECTION

Transition from the Common Rational Moral Cognition to the Philosophical Moral Cognition

Nothing can possibly be conceived in the world, or even out of it, which can be called good without qualification, except a *good will*. Intelligence, wit, judgment, and the other *talents* of the mind, however they may be named, or courage, resolution, perseverance, as qualities of *temperament*, are undoubtedly good and desirable in many respects; but these gifts of nature may also become extremely bad and mischievous if the will which is to make use of them, and which, therefore, constitutes what is called *character*, is not good. It is the same with the *gifts of fortune*. Power, riches, honor, even health, and the general well-being and contentment with one's condition which is called *happiness*, inspire pride, and often presumption, if there is not a good will to correct the influence of these on the mind, and with this also to rectify the whole principle of acting, and adapt it to its end. The sight of a being who is not adorned with a single feature of a pure and good will, enjoying unbroken prosperity, can never give pleasure to an impartial spectator. Thus a good will appears to constitute the indispensable condition even of being worthy of happiness.

There are even some qualities which are of service to this good will itself, and may facilitate its action, yet which have no inner unconditional value, but always presuppose a good will, and this qualifies the esteem that we justly have for them, and does not permit us to regard them as absolutely good. Moderation in the affections and passions, self-control, and calm deliberation are not only good in many respects, but even seem to constitute part of the *inner* worth of the person; but they are far from deserving to be called good without qualification, although they have been so unconditionally praised by the ancients. For without the principles of a good will, they may become extremely evil; and the coldness of a villain not only makes him far more dangerous, but also directly makes him more abominable in our eyes than he would have been without it.

A good will is good not because of what it accomplishes or effects, not by its aptness for the attainment of some proposed end, but simply by virtue of the volition—that is, it is good in itself, and considered by itself is to be esteemed much higher than all that can be brought about by it in favor of any inclination, or even the sum total of all inclinations.[†] Even if it should happen that, owing to a step-motherly nature,[‡] this will should wholly lack power to accomplish its purpose, if with its greatest efforts it should yet achieve nothing, and there should remain only the good will (not, to be sure, a mere wish, but the summoning of all means in our power), then, like a jewel, it would still shine by its own light, as a thing which has its whole value in itself. Its usefulness or fruitlessness can neither add to nor take away anything from this value. It would be, as it were, only the setting to enable us to handle it more conveniently in common commerce, or to attract to it the attention of those who are not yet connoisseurs, but not to recommend it to true connoisseurs, or to determine its value....

We have then to develop the concept of a will which deserves to be highly esteemed for itself, and is good without a view to anything further, a concept which exists already in the sound natural understanding, requiring rather to be clarified than to be taught, and which in estimating the value of our actions always takes the first place and constitutes the condition of all the rest. In order to do this, we will take concept of duty, which includes that of a

---

* Kant's *Grundlegung zur Metaphysik der Sitten* was first published in Riga in 1785. This translation is by Thomas K. Abbott with revisions by Lara Denis, from *Groundwork for the Metaphysics of Morals* (Broadview Press, 2005).

† One's inclinations are things one wants or likes to do.

‡ Owing to a step-motherly nature: because the world is ungenerous or uncooperative.

good will, although implying certain subjective limitations and hindrances. These, however, far from concealing it or rendering it unrecognizable, rather bring it out by contrast and make it shine forth so much the brighter.

I omit here all actions which are already recognized as contrary to duty, although they may be useful for this or that purpose, for with these the question whether they are done *from duty* cannot arise at all, since they even conflict with it. I also set aside those actions which really conform to duty, but to which men have *no* immediate *inclination*, performing them because they are impelled thereto by some other inclination. For in this case we can readily distinguish whether the action which agrees with duty is done *from duty* or from a selfish purpose. It is much harder to make this distinction when the action accords with duty, and the subject has besides an *immediate* inclination to it. For example, it is always a matter of duty that a dealer should not overcharge an inexperienced purchaser; and wherever there is much commerce the prudent tradesman does not overcharge, but keeps a fixed price for everyone, so that a child buys from him as well as any other. People are thus *honestly* served; but this is not enough to make us believe that the tradesman has so acted from duty and from principles of honesty; his own advantage required it; it is unwarranted in this case to suppose that he might besides have an immediate inclination in favor of the buyers, so that, as it were, from love he should give no advantage to one over another. Accordingly the action was done neither from duty nor from immediate inclination, but merely with a selfish purpose.

On the other hand, it is a duty to preserve one's life; and, in addition, everyone has also an immediate inclination to do so. But on this account the often anxious care which most people take for it has no intrinsic worth, and their maxim* has no moral content. They preserve their life *in conformity with duty*, no doubt, but not *from duty*. On the other hand, if adversity and hopeless sorrow have completely taken away the relish for life, if the unfortunate one, strong in mind, indignant to his fate rather than desponding or dejected, wishes for death, and yet preserves his life without loving it—not from inclination or fear, but from duty—then his maxim has moral content.

To be beneficent† when one can is a duty; and besides this, there are many minds so sympathetically constituted that, without any other motive of vanity or self-interest, they find a pleasure in spreading joy around them, and can take delight in the satisfaction of others so far as it is their own work. But I maintain that in such a case an action of this kind, however proper, however amiable it may be, has nevertheless no true moral worth, but is on a level with other inclinations, for example, the inclination to honor, which if it is happily directed to that which is in fact of public utility and accordant with duty, and consequently honorable, deserves praise and encouragement, but not esteem. For the maxim lacks the moral content, namely, that such actions be done *from duty*, not from inclination. Put the case that the mind of that philanthropist was clouded by sorrow of his own, extinguishing all sympathy with the lot of others, and that while he still has the power to benefit others in distress, he is not touched by their trouble because he is absorbed with his own; and now suppose that he tears himself out of this dead insensibility and performs the action without any inclination to it, but simply from duty, then for the first time his action has its genuine moral worth. Further still, if nature has put little sympathy in the heart of this or that man, if he, supposed to be an upright man, is by temperament cold and indifferent to the sufferings of others, perhaps because in respect of his own he is provided with the special gifts of patience and fortitude, and supposes, or even requires, that others should have the same—and such a man would certainly not be the meanest product of nature—but if nature had not specially framed him for a philanthropist, would he not still find in himself a source from which to give himself a far higher worth than that of a good-natured temperament could be? Unquestionably. It is just in this that the moral worth of the character is brought out which is incomparably the highest of all, namely, that he is beneficent, not from inclination, but from duty....

---

* A general rule of conduct.

† Generous, kind.

The second proposition* is: That an action done from duty derives its moral worth, *not from the purpose* which is to be attained by it, but from the maxim by which it is determined, and therefore does not depend on the realization of the object of the action, but merely on the *principle of volition* by which the action has taken place, without regard to any object of desire. It is clear from what precedes that the purposes which we may have in view in our action, or their effects regarded as ends and incentives of the will, cannot give to actions any unconditional or moral worth. In what, then, can their worth lie if it is not to consist in the will in reference to its expected effect? It cannot lie anywhere but in the *principle of the will* without regard to the ends which can be attained by the action. For the will stands between its *a priori* principle, which is formal, and its *a posteriori* incentive, which is material, as between two roads, and as it must be determined by something, it follows that it must be determined by the formal principle of volition when an action is done from duty, in which case every material principle has been withdrawn from it.

The third proposition, which is a consequence of the two preceding, I would express thus: *Duty is the necessity of acting from respect for the law.* I may have *inclination* for an object as the effect of my proposed action, but *never respect* for it, just because it is an effect and not an activity of will. Similarly, I cannot have respect for inclination, whether my own or another's; I can at most, if my own, approve it; if another's, sometimes even love it, that is, look on it as favorable to my own interest. It is only what is connected with my will as a principle, by no means as an effect—what does not serve my inclination, but outweighs it, or at least in case of choice excludes it from its calculation—in other words, simply the law of itself, which can be an object of respect, and hence a command. Now an action done from duty must wholly exclude the influence of inclination, and with it every object of the will, so that nothing remains which can determine the will except objectively the *law*, and subjectively *pure respect* for this practical law, and consequently the maxim[1] that I should follow this law even to the thwarting of all my inclinations.

Thus the moral worth of an action does not lie in the effect expected from it, nor in any principle of action which needs to borrow its motive from this expected effect. For all these effects—agreeableness of one's condition, and even the promotion of the happiness of others—could have been also brought about by other causes, so that for this there would have been no need of the will of a rational being; whereas it is in this alone that the supreme and unconditional good can be found. The pre-eminent good which we call moral can therefore consist in nothing else than *the representation of the law* in itself, *which certainly is only possible in a rational being*, insofar as this representation, and not the expected effect, determines the will. This is a good which is already present in the person who acts accordingly, and we need not wait for it to appear first in the result....

But what sort of law can that be, the conception of which must determine the will, even without paying any regard to the effect experienced from it, in order that this will may be called good absolutely and without qualification? As I have deprived the will of every impulse which could arise for it from obedience to any particular law, there remains nothing but the universal conformity of its actions to law in general, which alone is to serve the will as a principle, that is, I am never to act otherwise than so *that I could also will that my maxim should become a universal law*. Here, now, it is the simple lawfulness in general, without assuming any particular law applicable to certain actions, that serves the will as its principle, and must so serve it if duty is not to be a vain† delusion and a chimerical‡ notion. The common reason of human beings in its practical judgments perfectly coincides with this, and always has in view the principle here suggested.

Let the question be, for example: May I when in distress make a promise with the intention not to keep it? I readily distinguish here between the two significations which the question may have: whether it is prudent or whether it is right to make such a false promise. The former may undoubtedly often be the case. I see clearly indeed that it is not enough to extricate myself from a present difficulty by means

---

*   Kant does not say explicitly what the first proposition was—it is that only an action done from duty has moral worth.
†   Pointless, useless.
‡   A product of fantasy.

of this subterfuge, but it must be well considered whether there may not hereafter spring from this lie much greater inconvenience than that from which I now seek to free myself, and as, with all my supposed *cunning*, the consequences cannot be so easily foreseen but that credit once lost may be much more injurious to me than any mischief which I seek to avoid at present, it should be considered whether it would not be *more prudent* to act herein according to a universal maxim, and to make it a habit to promise nothing except with the intention of keeping it. But it is soon clear to me that such a maxim will still only be based on the fear of consequences. Now it is a wholly different thing to be truthful from duty than to be so from apprehension of injurious consequences. In the first case, the very notion of the action already implies a law for me; in the second case, I must first look about elsewhere to see what results may be combined with it which would affect myself. For to deviate from the principle of duty is beyond all doubt evil; but to be unfaithful to my maxim of prudence may often be very advantageous to me, although to abide by it is certainly safer. The shortest way, however, and an unerring one, to discover the answer to this question whether a lying promise is consistent with duty, is to ask myself: Would I be content that my maxim (to extricate myself from difficulty by a false promise) should hold as a universal law, for myself as well as for others? And would I be able to say to myself, "Everyone may make a deceitful promise when he finds himself in a difficulty from which he cannot otherwise extricate himself"? Then I presently become aware that, while I can will the lie, I can by no means will that lying become a universal law. For with such a law there would be no promises at all, since it would be in vain to profess my intention in regard to my future actions to those who would not believe this profession, or if they over-hastily did

so, would pay me back in my own coin. Hence my maxim, as soon as it should be made a universal law, would necessarily destroy itself.

I do not, therefore, need any far-reaching penetration* to discern what I have to do in order that my volition may be morally good. Inexperienced in the course of the world, incapable of being prepared for all its contingencies, I only ask myself: Can you also will that your maxim should be a universal law? If not, then it must be rejected, and that not because of a disadvantage accruing from it to myself or even to others, but because it cannot enter as a principle into a possible universal legislation, and reason extorts from me immediate respect for such legislation. I do not indeed as yet *discern* on what this respect is based (this the philosopher may inquire), but at least I understand this—that it is an estimation of the worth which far outweighs all worth of what is recommended by inclination, and that the necessity of acting from *pure* respect for the practical law is what constitutes duty, to which every other motive must give place because it is the condition of a will that is good *in itself*, and the worth of such a will is above everything.

Thus, then, without quitting the moral cognition of common human reason, we have arrived at its principle. And although, no doubt, common human reason does not conceive it in such an abstract and universal form, yet it really always has it before its eyes and uses it as the standard of judgment. Here it would be easy to show how, with this compass in hand, common human reason is well able to distinguish, in every case that occurs, what is good, what evil, conformably to duty or inconsistent with it, if, without in the least teaching it anything new, we only, like Socrates,† direct its attention to the principle it itself employs; and that, therefore, we do not need science and philosophy to know what we should do to be honest and good, yes, even to be wise and virtuous....

---

*   Extreme cleverness or deep insight.

†   This ancient Athenian is famous for (among other things) a technique of teaching—today called the "Socratic method"—in which the master, instead of imparting knowledge, asks a sequence of questions to prompt the pupil to reflect on their own ideas and to uncover knowledge they already have within themselves. Because of this technique, Socrates compared himself to a midwife helping people give birth to philosophical ideas. See the Plato readings from earlier in this section for examples of this method.

Transition from Popular Moral Philosophy to the Metaphysics of Morals

If we have so far drawn our notion of duty from the common use of our practical reason, it is by no means to be inferred that we have treated it as an empirical concept. On the contrary, if we attend to the experience of human conduct, we meet frequent and, as we ourselves allow, just complaints that one cannot find a single, certain example of the disposition to act from pure duty. Although many things are done *in conformity with* what *duty* prescribes, it is nevertheless always doubtful whether they are done strictly *from duty*, and so have moral worth. Hence there have at all times been philosophers who have altogether denied that this disposition actually exists at all in human actions, and have ascribed everything to a more or less refined self-love. Not that they have on that account questioned the soundness of the conception of morality; on the contrary, they spoke with sincere regret of the frailty and impurity of human nature, which, though noble enough to take as its rule an idea so worthy of respect, is yet too weak to follow it; and employs reason, which ought to give it the law, only for the purpose of providing for the interest of the inclinations, whether singly or at the best in the greatest possible harmony with one another.

In fact, it is absolutely impossible to make out by experience with complete certainty a single case in which the maxim of an action, however right in itself, rested simply on moral grounds and on the representation of duty. Sometimes it happens that with the sharpest self-examination we can find nothing beside the moral principle of duty which could have been powerful enough to move us to this or that action and to so great a sacrifice; yet we cannot from this infer with certainty that it was not really some secret impulse of self-love, under the false appearance of duty, that was the actual determining cause of the will. We like then to flatter ourselves by falsely taking credit for a more noble motive; whereas in fact we can never, even by the strictest examination, get completely behind the secret incentives, since, when the question is of moral worth, it is not with the actions which we see that we are concerned, but with those inward principles of them which we do not see.

Moreover, we cannot better serve the wishes of those who ridicule all morality as mere chimera of human imagination overstepping itself from vanity, than by conceding to them that concepts of duty must be drawn only from experience (as, from indolence, people are ready to think is the case with all other concepts also); for this is to prepare for them a certain triumph. I am willing to admit out of love for humanity that even most of our actions are in conformity with duty; but if we look closer at them we everywhere come upon the dear self which is always prominent; and it is this they have in view, and not the strict command of duty, which would often require self-denial. Without being an enemy of virtue, a cool observer, one that does not mistake the wish for good, however lively, for its reality, may sometimes doubt whether true virtue is actually found anywhere in the world, and this especially as years increase and the judgment is partly made wiser by experience, and partly also more acute in observation. This being so, nothing can secure us from falling away altogether from our ideas of duty, or maintain in the soul a well-grounded respect for its law, but* the clear conviction that although there should never have been actions which really sprang from such pure sources, yet whether this or that takes place is not at all the question; but that reason itself, independent of all experience, ordains what ought to take place, that accordingly actions of which perhaps the world has so far never given an example, the feasibility even of which might be very much doubted by one who founds everything on experience, are nevertheless inflexibly commanded by reason; that, for example, even though there might never have been a sincere friend, yet not a whit less is pure sincerity in friendship required of everyone, because, prior to all experience, this duty is involved (as duty in general) in the idea of a reason determining the will by *a priori* principles.

---

* Except.

When we add further that, unless we deny that the notion of morality has any truth or reference to any possible object, we must admit that its law must be valid, not merely for human beings, but for all *rational beings as such*, not merely under certain contingent conditions or with exceptions, but with *absolute necessity*, then it is clear that no experience could enable us to infer even the possibility of such apodictic* laws. For with what right could we bring into unbounded respect as a universal precept for all rational nature that which perhaps holds only under the contingent conditions of humanity? Or how could laws of the determination of *our* will be regarded as laws of the determination of the will of rational beings as such, and for us only as such, if they were merely empirical and did not take their origin wholly *a priori* from pure but practical reason?

Nor could anything be more fatal to morality than that we should wish to derive it from examples. For every example of it that is set before me must first itself be judged by principles of morality, as to whether it is worthy to serve as an original example, that is, as a model; but by no means can it authoritatively furnish the conception of morality. Even the Holy One of the Gospels† must first be compared with our ideal of moral perfection before we can recognize Him as such; and so He says of Himself, "Why do you call Me (whom you see) good; none is good (the model of good) but God only (whom you do not see)?"‡ But whence have we the conception of God as the supreme good? Simply from the *idea* of moral perfection, which reason frames *a priori* and connects inseparably with the notion of a free will. Imitation finds no place at all in morality, and examples serve only for encouragement, that is, they put beyond all doubt the feasibility of what the law commands, they make visible that which the practical rule expresses more generally, but they can never authorize us to set aside the true original which lies in reason, and to guide ourselves by examples....

Such a metaphysics of morals, completely isolated, not mixed with any anthropology, theology, physics, or hyperphysics, and still less with occult qualities (which we might call hypophysical),§ is not only an indispensable substratum of all sound theoretical knowledge of duties, but is at the same time a desideratum¶ of the highest importance to the actual fulfilment of their precepts. For the pure thought of duty, unmixed with any foreign addition of empirical attractions, and, in a word, the thought of the moral law, exercises on the human heart, by way of reason alone (which first becomes aware with this that it can of itself be practical), an influence so much more powerful than all other incentives ... which may be derived from the field of experience that in the consciousness of its dignity** it despises the latter, and can by degrees become their master; whereas a mixed doctrine of morals, compounded partly of incentives drawn from feelings and inclinations, and partly also of conceptions of reason, must make the mind waver between motives which cannot be brought under any principle, which lead to good only by mere accident, and very often also to evil.

From what has been said, it is clear that all moral concepts have their seat and origin completely *a priori* in reason, and that, moreover, in the commonest reason just as truly as in that which is in the highest degree speculative; that they cannot be obtained by abstraction from any empirical, and therefore merely contingent, cognitions; that it is just this purity of their origin that makes them worthy to serve as our supreme practical principle, and that just in proportion as we add anything empirical, we detract from their genuine influence and from the absolute value of actions; that it is not only of the greatest necessity, in a purely speculative point of view, but is also of the greatest practical importance, to derive these concepts and laws from pure reason, to present them pure and unmixed, and even to determine the compass of this practical or pure rational cognition, that is,

---

*   Necessarily true, clearly demonstrated or established.
†   Jesus Christ.
‡   Matthew 19:17.
§   Hyperphysics is that which goes beyond physics. The term is usually used in a similar way as "paranormal" or "supernatural." "Hypophysics" is a coinage meaning that which lies *below* physics.
¶   Something very much needed or desired.
**   For Kant, "dignity" is a technical term meaning something like *intrinsic worth*.

to determine the whole faculty of pure practical reason; and, in doing so, we must not make its principles dependent on the particular nature of human reason, though in speculative philosophy this may be permitted, or may even at times be necessary; but since moral laws ought to hold good for every rational being, we must derive them from the universal concept of a rational being. In this way, although for its *application* to human beings morality has need of anthropology, yet, in the first instance, we must treat it in itself (a thing which in such distinct branches of science is easily done); knowing well that, unless we are in possession of this, it would not only be vain to determine the moral element of duty in right actions for purposes of speculative criticism, but it would be impossible to base morals on their genuine principles, even for common practical purposes, especially for moral instruction, so as to produce pure moral dispositions, and to engraft them on people's minds to the promotion of the greatest possible good in the world.

But in order that in this study we may not merely advance by the natural steps from the common moral judgment (in this case very worthy of respect) to the philosophical, as has been already done, but also from a popular philosophy, which goes no further than it can reach by groping with the help of examples, to metaphysics (which does not allow itself to be checked by anything empirical and, as it must measure the whole extent of this kind of rational knowledge, goes as far as ideal conceptions, where even examples fail us), we must follow and clearly describe the practical faculty of reason, from the general rules of its determination to the point where the concept of duty springs from it.

Everything in nature works according to laws. Rational beings alone have the capacity to act *in accordance with the representation* of laws—that is, according to principles, that is, have a *will*. Since the deduction of actions from principles requires *reason*, the will is nothing but practical reason. If reason infallibly determines the will, then the actions of such a being which are recognized as objectively necessary* are subjectively necessary also, that is, the will is a capacity to choose *that only* which reason independent of inclination recognizes as practically necessary, that is, as good. But if reason of itself does not sufficiently determine the will, if the latter is subject also to subjective conditions (particular incentives) which do not always coincide with the objective conditions, in a word, if the will does not *in itself* completely accord with reason (which is actually the case with human beings), then the actions which objectively are recognized as necessary are subjectively contingent, and the determination of such a will according to objective laws is *necessitation*, that is to say, the relation of the objective laws to a will that is not thoroughly good is conceived as the determination of the will of a rational being by principles of reason, but which the will from its nature does not necessarily follow.

The conception of an objective principle, in so far as it is obligatory for a will, is called a command (of reason), and the formula of the command is called an *imperative*.

All imperatives are expressed through an *ought*, and thereby indicate the relation of an objective law of reason to a will which from its subjective constitution is not necessarily determined by it (a necessitation). They say that something would be good to do or to forbear, but they say it to a will which does not always do a thing because it is represented to be good to do it. That is *practically good*, however, which determines the will by means of the representations of reason, and consequently not from subjective causes, but objectively, that is, on principles which are valid for every rational being as such. It is distinguished from the agreeable as that which influences the will only by means of feeling from merely subjective causes, valid only for the senses of this or that one, and not as a principle of reason which holds for everyone....

A perfectly good will would therefore be equally subject to objective laws (viz. laws of good), but could not be conceived as *necessitated* thereby to act lawfully, because of itself from its subjective constitution it can only be determined by the conception of good. Therefore no imperatives hold for the Divine will, or in general for a *holy* will; *ought* is here out of place because the volition is already of itself necessarily in unison with the law. Therefore imperatives are only formulae to express the relation of objective laws of all volition to the subjective imperfection of the will of this or that rational being, for example, a human will.

---

* As determined by the objective principles of rationality.

Now all imperatives command either *hypothetically* or *categorically*. The former represent the practical necessity of a possible action as means to something else that is willed (or at least which one might possibly will). The categorical imperative would be that which represented an action as necessary of itself without reference to another end, that is, as objectively necessary.

Since every practical law represents a possible action as good, and on this account, for a subject who is practically determinable by reason, as necessary, all imperatives are formulae determining an action which is necessary according to the principle of a will good in some respects. If now the action is good only as a means *to something else*, then the imperative is *hypothetical*; if it is conceived as good *in itself* and consequently as being necessarily the principle of a will which of itself conforms to reason, then it is *categorical*.

Thus the imperative declares what action possible by me would be good, and presents the practical rule in relation to a will which does not forthwith perform an action simply because it is good, whether because the subject does not always know that it is good, or because, even if it know this, yet its maxims might be opposed to the objective principles of practical reason.

Accordingly the hypothetical imperative only says that the action is good for some purpose, *possible* or *actual*. In the first case, it is a *problematic*, in the second an *assertoric*, practical principle. The categorical imperative which declares an action to be objectively necessary in itself without reference to any purpose, without any other end, is valid as an *apodictic* (practical) principle.

Whatever is possible only by the power of some rational being may also be conceived as a possible purpose of some will; and therefore the principles of action as regards the means necessary to attain some possible purpose are in fact infinitely numerous. All sciences have a practical part consisting of problems expressing that some end is possible for us, and of imperatives directing how it may be attained. These may, therefore, be called in general imperatives of *skill*. Here there is no question whether the end is rational and good, but only what one must do in order to attain it. The precepts for the physician to make his patient thoroughly healthy, and for a poisoner to ensure certain death, are of equal value in this respect, that each serves to effect its purpose perfectly. Since in early youth it cannot be known what ends are likely to occur to us in the course of life, parents seek to have their children taught a *great many things*, and provide for their *skill* in the use of means for all sorts of *discretionary* ends, of none of which can they determine whether it may not perhaps hereafter be an object to their pupil, but which it is at all events *possible* that he might aim at; and this anxiety is so great that they commonly neglect to form and correct their children's judgment of the value of the things which may be chosen as ends.

There is *one* end, however, which may be assumed to be actually such to all rational beings (so far as imperatives apply to them, viz. as dependent beings), and therefore, one purpose which they not merely *may* have, but which we may with certainty assume that they all actually *do have* by a natural necessity, and this is *happiness*. The hypothetical imperative which expresses the practical necessity of an action as means to the advancement of happiness is *assertoric*. We are not to present it as necessary for an uncertain and merely possible purpose, but for a purpose which we may presuppose with certainty and *a priori* in every human being, because it belongs to his being. Now skill in the choice of means to his own greatest well-being may be called *prudence*, ... in the narrowest sense. And thus the imperative which refers to the choice of means to one's own happiness, that is, the precept of prudence, is still always *hypothetical*; the action is not commanded absolutely, but only as means to another purpose.

Finally, there is an imperative which commands a certain conduct immediately, without having as its condition any other purpose to be attained by it. This imperative is *categorical*. It concerns not the matter of the action, or its intended result, but its form and the principle of which it is itself a result; and what is essentially good in it consists in the mental disposition, let the consequence be what it may. This imperative may be called that of *morality*.

There is a marked distinction also between the volitions on these three sorts of principles in the *dissimilarity* of the necessitation of the will. In order to mark this difference more clearly, I think they would be most suitably named in their order if we said they are either *rules* of skill, or *counsels* of prudence, or *commands* (*laws*) of morality. For it is law only that involves the concept of an *unconditional* and objective necessity, which is consequently universally valid; and commands are laws which must be obeyed, that is, must be followed, even in opposition to inclination. *Counsels*, indeed, involve necessity, but one which can only hold under a contingent subjective condition, viz., they depend on whether this or that human being counts this or that as part of his happiness; the categorical imperative, on the contrary, is not limited by any condition, and as being absolutely, although practically, necessary may be quite properly called a command. We might also call the first kind of imperatives *technical* (belonging to art), the second *pragmatic* ... (belonging to welfare), and the third *moral* (belonging to free conduct as such, that is, to morals).

Now arises the question, how are all these imperatives possible? This question does not seek to know how we can conceive the performance of the action which the imperative ordains, but merely how we can conceive the necessitation of the will which the imperative expresses. No special explanation is needed to show how an imperative of skill is possible. Whoever wills the end wills also (so far as reason has decisive influence on his action) the means in his power which are indispensably necessary to it. This proposition is, as regards the volition, analytic;* for in willing an object as my effect there is already thought the causality of myself as an acting cause, that is to say, the use of the means; and the imperative educes† from the concept of a volition of an end the concept of actions necessary to this end. Synthetic propositions must no doubt be employed in defining the means to a proposed end; but they do not concern the principle, the act of the will, but the object and its realization. For example, that in order to bisect a line on an unerring principle I must draw from its extremities two intersecting arcs; this no doubt is taught by mathematics only in synthetic propositions; but if I know that it is only by this process that the intended operation can be performed, then to say that if I fully will the operation, I also will the action required for it, is an analytic proposition; for it is one and the same thing to represent something as an effect which I can produce in a certain way, and to represent myself as acting in this way.

If it were only equally easy to give a definite conception of happiness, the imperatives of prudence would correspond exactly with those of skill, and would likewise be analytic. For in this case as in that, it could be said whoever wills the end wills also (necessarily in accordance with reason) the indispensable means thereto which are in his power. But, unfortunately, the notion of happiness is so indeterminate that although every human being wishes to attain it, yet he never can say definitely and consistently what it is that he really wishes and wills. The reason for this is that all the elements which belong to the concept of happiness are altogether empirical, that is, they must be borrowed from experience, and nevertheless the idea of happiness requires an absolute whole, a maximum of welfare in my present and all future circumstances. Now it is impossible that the most clear-sighted and at the same time most powerful being (supposed finite) should frame for himself a definite conception of what he really wills in this. If he wills riches, how much anxiety, envy, and snares might he not thereby draw upon his shoulders? If he wills knowledge and discernment, perhaps it might prove to be only an eye so much sharper to show him so much the more fearfully the evils that are now concealed from him and that cannot be avoided, or to impose more wants on his desires, which already give him concern enough. Would he have long life? Who guarantees to him that it would not be a long misery? Would he at least have health? How often has uneasiness of the body restrained from excesses into which perfect health would have allowed one to fall, and so on? In short, he is unable, on any principle, to determine with certainty what would make him truly happy; because to do so he would need to be omniscient. We cannot therefore act on any definite principles to secure happiness, but only on empirical counsels, for example, of regimen, frugality, courtesy, reserve, etc., which experience teaches do, on the average, most promote well-being. Hence it follows that the imperatives of prudence do not, strictly speaking,

---

* Something is analytically true if it is true in virtue of the meanings involved, particularly in cases where, as Kant put it, the concept of the predicate is "contained in" the concept of the subject (e.g., "All aunts are female" or "This poodle is a dog"). Synthetic propositions, according to Kant, are simply propositions that are not analytic: thus, in synthetic propositions, the predicate provides *new* information about the subject (e.g., "My aunt is called Dora" or "Poodles come in many colors").

† Brings out, makes explicit.

command at all, that is, they cannot present actions objectively as practically *necessary*; that they are rather to be regarded as counsels (*consilia*) than precepts (*praecepta*) of reason, that the problem to determine certainly and universally what action would promote the happiness of a rational being is completely insoluble, and consequently no imperative respecting it is possible which would, in the strict sense, command him to do what makes him happy; because happiness is not an ideal of reason but of imagination, resting solely on empirical grounds, and it is vain to expect that these should determine an action by which one could attain the totality of a series of consequences which is really endless. This imperative of prudence would, however, be an analytic proposition if we assume that the means to happiness could be certainly assigned; for it is distinguished from the imperative of skill only by this, that in the latter the end is merely *possible*, in the former it is *given*; as, however, both only ordain the means to that which we suppose to be willed as an end, it follows that the imperative which ordains the willing of the means to him who wills the end is in both cases analytic. Thus there is no difficulty in regard to the possibility of an imperative of this kind either.

On the other hand, the question, how the imperative of *morality* is possible, is undoubtedly one, the only one, demanding a solution, as this is not at all hypothetical, and the objective necessity which it presents cannot rest on any hypothesis, as is the case with the hypothetical imperatives. Only here we must never leave out of consideration that we *cannot* make out *by means of any example*, in other words, empirically, whether there is such an imperative at all; but it is rather to be feared that all those which seem to be categorical may yet be at bottom hypothetical. For instance, when the precept is: "You ought not to promise deceitfully," and it is assumed that the necessity of this is not a mere counsel to avoid some other ill, so that it should mean: "You shall not make a lying promise, lest if it become known you should destroy your credit," but that an action of this kind must be regarded as evil in itself, so that the imperative of the prohibition is categorical; then we cannot show with certainty in any example that the will was determined merely by the law, without any other incentives, although it may appear to be so. For it is always possible that fear of disgrace, perhaps also obscure dread

of other dangers, may have a secret influence on the will. Who can prove by experience the non-existence of a cause when all that experience tells us is that we do not perceive it? But in such a case the so-called moral imperative, which as such appears to be categorical and unconditional, would in reality be only a pragmatic precept, drawing our attention to our own interests, and merely teaching us to take these into consideration.

We will therefore have to investigate *a priori* the possibility of a *categorical* imperative, as we have not in this case the advantage of its reality being given in experience, so that [the elucidation of] its possibility should be requisite only for its explanation, not for its establishment. In the meantime it may be discerned beforehand that the categorical imperative alone has the purport of a practical law; and the rest may indeed be called *principles* of the will but not laws, since whatever is only necessary for the attainment of some discretionary purpose may be considered as in itself contingent, and we can at any time be free from the precept if we give up the purpose; on the contrary, the unconditional command leaves the will no liberty to choose the opposite, consequently it alone carries with it that necessity which we require of a law.

Secondly, in the case of this categorical imperative or law of morality, the difficulty (of describing its possibility) is a very profound one. It is an *a priori* synthetic practical proposition; ... and as there is so much difficulty in discerning the possibility of speculative propositions of this kind, it may readily be supposed that the difficulty will be no less with the practical.

In this problem we will first inquire whether the mere concept of a categorical imperative may not perhaps supply us also with the formula of it, containing the proposition which alone can be a categorical imperative; for even if we know the tenor of such an absolute command, yet how it is possible will require further special and laborious study, which we postpone to the last section.

When I conceive a hypothetical imperative, in general I do not know beforehand what it will contain until I am given the condition. But when I conceive a categorical imperative, I know at once what it contains. For as the imperative contains besides the law only the necessity that the maxims[2] shall conform to this law, while the law contains no conditions restricting it, there remains nothing but the general statement that the maxim of the action should conform to universal law, and it is this conformity alone that the imperative properly represents as necessary.

There is therefore but one categorical imperative, namely, this: *Act only on that maxim whereby you can at the same time will that it become a universal law.**

Now if all imperatives of duty can be deduced from this one imperative as their principle, then, although it should remain undecided whether what is called duty is not merely a vain notion, yet at least we shall be able to show what we understand by it and what this notion means.

Since the universality of the law according to which effects are produced constitutes what is properly called *nature* in the most general sense (as to form)—that is, the existence of things so far as it is determined by general laws—the imperative of duty may be expressed thus: *Act as if the maxim of your action were to become by your will a universal law of nature.*†

We will now enumerate a few duties, adopting the usual division of them into duties to ourselves and duties to others, and into perfect and imperfect duties.[3]

1. Someone reduced to despair by a series of misfortunes feels wearied of life, but is still so far in possession of his reason that he can ask himself whether it would not be contrary to his duty to himself take his own life. Now he inquires whether the maxim of his action could become a universal law of nature. His maxim is: From self love I adopt it as my principle to shorten my life when its longer duration is likely to bring more ill than satisfaction. It is asked then simply whether this principle founded on self-love can become a universal law of nature. Now we can see at once that a system of nature of which it should be a law to destroy life by means of the very feeling whose vocation it is to impel to the improvement of life would contradict itself, and therefore could not exist as a system of nature; hence that maxim cannot possibly exist as a universal law of nature, and consequently would be wholly inconsistent with the supreme principle of all duty.

2. Another finds himself forced by necessity to borrow money. He knows that he will not be able to repay it, but sees also that nothing will be lent to him unless he promises firmly to repay it within in a determinate time. He wants to make this promise, but he has still so much conscience as to ask himself: Is it not unlawful and inconsistent with duty to get out of a difficulty this way? Suppose, however, that he resolves to do so, then the maxim of his action would be expressed thus: When I think myself in want of money, I will borrow money and promise to repay it, although I know that I never can do so. Now this principle of self-love or of one's own advantage may perhaps be consistent with my whole future welfare; but the question now is, Is it right? I change then the suggestion of self-love into a universal law, and state the question thus: How would it be if my maxim were a universal law? Then I see at once that it could never hold as a universal law of nature, but would necessarily contradict itself. For supposing it to be a universal law that everyone when he thinks himself in a difficulty should be able to promise whatever he pleases, with the purpose of not keeping his promise, the promise itself would become impossible, as well as the end that he might have in view in it, since no one would consider that anything was promised to him, but would ridicule all such statements as vain pretenses.

3. A third finds in himself a talent which with the help of some culture might make him a useful human being in many respects. But he finds himself in comfortable circumstances and prefers to indulge in pleasure rather than to take pain in enlarging and improving his fortunate natural predispositions. He asks, however, whether his maxim of neglect of his natural gifts, besides agreeing with his inclination to indulgence, agrees also with what is called duty. He sees then that a system of nature could indeed subsist with such a universal law, although human beings (like the South Sea islanders‡) should let their talents rust and resolve to devote their lives merely to idleness, amusement, and propagation of their species—in a word, to enjoyment; but he cannot possibly *will* that this should be a universal law of nature, or be implanted in us as such by a natural instinct. For as a rational being, he necessarily wills that his faculties be

---

* This formulation of the categorical imperative is often called the Formula of Universal Law.
† This is often called the Formula of the Law of Nature.
‡ The inhabitants of the islands of the southern Pacific, such as Polynesia and Micronesia.

developed, since they serve him, and have been given him, for all sorts of purposes.

4. Yet a fourth, who is in prosperity, while he sees that others have to contend with great wretchedness and that he could help them, thinks: What concern is it of mine? Let everyone be as happy as heaven pleases, or as he can make himself; I will take nothing from him nor even envy him, only I do not wish to contribute anything to his welfare or to his assistance in need! Now no doubt, if such a mode of thinking were a universal law, the human race might very well subsist, and doubtless even better than in a state in which everyone talks of sympathy and good-will, or even takes care occasionally to put it into practice, but, on the other side, also cheats when he can, betrays the rights of human beings, or otherwise violates them. But although it is possible that a universal law of nature might exist in accordance with that maxim, it is impossible to *will* that such a principle should have the universal validity of a law of nature. For a will which resolved this would contradict itself, inasmuch as many cases might occur in which one would have need of the love and sympathy of others, and in which, by such a law of nature, sprung from his own will, he would deprive himself of all hope of the aid he desires.

These are a few of the many actual duties, or at least what we regard as such, which obviously fall into two classes on the one principle that we have laid down. We must *be able to will* that a maxim of our action should be a universal law. This is the canon of the moral judgment of the action generally. Some actions are of such a character that their maxim cannot without contradiction be even *conceived* as a universal law of nature, far from it being possible that we should *will* that it *should* be so. In others, this intrinsic impossibility is not found, but still it is impossible to *will* that their maxim should be raised to the universality of a law of nature, since such a will would contradict itself. It is easily seen that the former violate strict or rigorous (inflexible) duty; the latter only wide (meritorious) duty. Thus it has been completely shown by these examples how all duties depend as regards the nature of the obligation (not the object of the action) on the same principle.

If now we attend to ourselves on occasion of any transgression of duty, we will find that we in fact do not will that our maxim should be a universal law, for that is impossible for us; on the contrary, we will that the opposite should remain a universal law, only we assume the liberty of making an *exception* in our own favor or (just for this time only) in favor of our inclination. Consequently, if we considered all cases from one and the same point of view, namely, that of reason, we should find a contradiction in our own will, namely, that a certain principle should be objectively necessary as a universal law, and yet subjectively should not be universal, but admit of exceptions. As, however, we at one moment regard our action from the point of view of a will wholly conformed to reason, and then again look at the same action from the point of view of a will affected by inclination, there is not really any contradiction, but an opposition (*antagonismus*) of inclination to the precept of reason, whereby the universality (*universalitas*) of the principle is changed into a mere generality (*generalitas*), so that the practical principle of reason shall meet the maxim half way. Now, although this cannot be justified in our own impartial judgment, yet it proves that we do really recognize the validity of the categorical imperative and (with all respect for it) only allow ourselves a few exceptions which we think unimportant and forced upon us.

We have thus established at least this much—that if duty is a conception which is to have any import and real legislative authority for our actions, it can only be expressed in categorical, and not at all in hypothetical, imperatives. We have also, which is of great importance, exhibited clearly and definitely for every practical application the content of the categorical imperative, which must contain the principle of all duty if there is such a thing at all. We have not yet, however, advanced so far as to prove *a priori* that there actually is such an imperative, that there is a practical law which commands absolutely of itself and without any other incentive, and that the following of this law is duty.

With the view of attaining to this it is of extreme importance to remember that we must not allow ourselves to think of deducing the reality of this principle from the *particular attributes of human nature*. For duty is to be a practical, unconditional necessity of action; it must therefore hold for all rational beings (to whom an imperative can apply at all), and *for this reason only* be also a law for all human wills. On the contrary, whatever is deduced from the particular natural characteristics of humanity, from certain feelings and propensities, or even, if possible, from any particular tendency proper to human reason, and which need not necessarily hold for the will of every rational being—this may indeed supply us with a maxim but not with a law; with a subjective principle on which we may have a propensity and inclination to act, but not with an objective principle on which we should be *enjoined* to act, even though all our propensities, inclinations, and natural dispositions were opposed to it. In fact, the sublimity and intrinsic dignity of the command in duty are so much the more evident, the less the subjective impulses favor it and the more they oppose it, without being able in the slightest degree to weaken the obligation of the law or to diminish its validity....

The question then is this: Is it a necessary law *for all rational beings* that they should always judge their actions by maxims of which they can themselves will that they should serve as universal laws? If there is such a law, then it must be connected (altogether *a priori*) with the very concept of the will of a rational being as such. But in order to discover this connection we must, however reluctantly, take a step into metaphysics, although into a domain of it which is distinct from speculative philosophy—namely, the metaphysics of morals....

The will is conceived as a capacity of determining itself to action in accordance with the *representation of certain laws*. And such a capacity can be found only in rational beings. Now that which serves the will as the objective ground of its self-determination is the *end*, and if this is assigned by reason alone, it must hold for all rational beings. On the other hand, that which merely contains the ground of possibility of the action of which the effect is the end, this is called the *means*. The subjective ground of the desire is the *incentive*, the objective ground of the volition is the *motive*; hence the distinction between subjective ends which rest on incentives, and objective ends which depend on motives valid for every rational being. Practical principles are *formal* when they abstract from all subjective ends; they are *material* when they assume these, and therefore particular incentives. The ends which a rational being proposes to himself at pleasure as *effects* of his actions (material ends) are all only relative, for it is only their relation to the particular desires of the subject that gives them their worth, which therefore

cannot furnish principles universal and necessary for all rational beings and for every volition, that is to say, practical laws. Hence all these relative ends can give rise only to hypothetical imperatives.

Supposing, however, that there were something *whose existence* has *in itself* an absolute worth, something which, being *an end in itself*, could be a source of definite laws, then in this and this alone would lie the source of a possible categorical imperative, that is, a practical law.

Now I say: the human being and in general every rational being exists as an end* in itself, *not merely as a means* to be arbitrarily used by this or that will, but in all his actions, whether they concern himself or other rational beings, must be always regarded at the same time as an end. All objects of the inclinations have only a conditional worth; for if the inclinations and the needs founded on them did not exist, then their object would be without any value. But the inclinations themselves, being sources of needs, are so far from having an absolute worth for which they should be desired that, on the contrary, it must be the universal wish of every rational being to be wholly free from them. Thus the worth of any object which is *to be acquired* by our action is always conditional. Beings whose existence depends not on our will but on nature's, have nevertheless, if they are nonrational beings, only a relative value as means, and are therefore called *things*; rational beings, on the contrary, are called *persons*, because their very nature restricts all choice (and is an object of respect). These, therefore, are not merely subjective ends whose existence has a worth *for us* as an effect of our action, but *objective ends*, that is, things whose existence is an end in itself—an end, moreover, for which no other can be substituted, to which they should serve *merely* as means, for otherwise nothing whatever would possess *absolute worth*; but if all worth were conditioned and therefore contingent, then there would be no supreme practical principle of reason whatever.

If then there is a supreme practical principle or, with respect to the human will, a categorical imperative, it must be one which, being drawn from the conception of that which is necessarily an end for everyone because it is *an end in itself*, constitutes an *objective*

---

* A source of value and meaning, a goal or purpose.

principle of will, and can therefore serve as a universal practical law. The foundation of this principle is: *rational nature exists as an end in itself*. The human being necessarily conceives of his own existence as being so; so far then this is a *subjective* principle of human actions. But every other rational being regards its existence similarly, just on the same rational principle that holds for me; ... so that it is at the same time an objective principle from which as a supreme practical law all laws of the will must be capable of being deduced. Accordingly the practical imperative will be as follows: *So act as to treat humanity, whether in your own person or in that of any other, in every case at the same time as an end, never as a means only.** We will now inquire whether this can be practically carried out.

To abide by the previous examples:

First, under the head of necessary duty to oneself: Someone who contemplates suicide should ask himself whether his action can be consistent with the idea of humanity *as an end in itself*. If he destroys himself in order to escape from painful circumstances, he uses a person merely as a *means* to maintain a tolerable condition up to the end of life. But a human being is not a thing, that is to say, something which can be used merely as a means, but must in all his actions be always considered as an end in itself. I cannot, therefore, dispose in any way of a human being in my own person by mutilating, damaging, or killing him. (It belongs to morals proper to define this principle more precisely, so as to avoid all misunderstanding, for example, as to the amputation of the limbs in order to preserve myself; as to exposing my life to danger with a view to preserve it, etc. This question is therefore omitted here.)

Second, as regards necessary duties, or those of strict obligation, towards others: He who is thinking of making a lying promise to others will see at once that he would be using another human being *merely as a means*, without the latter at the same time containing in himself the end. For he whom I propose by such a promise to use for my own purposes cannot possibly assent to my mode of acting toward him, and therefore cannot himself contain the end of this action. This violation of the principle of humanity in other human beings is more obvious if we take in examples of attacks on the freedom and property of others. For then it is clear that he who transgresses the rights of human beings intends to use the person of others merely as means, without considering that as rational beings they ought always to be esteemed also as ends, that is, as beings who must be capable of containing in themselves the end of the very same action.[4]

Third, as regards contingent (meritorious) duties to oneself: It is not enough that the action does not violate humanity in our own person as an end in itself, it must also *harmonize with* it. Now there are in humanity capacities of greater perfection which belong to the end that nature has in view with regard to humanity in ourselves as the subject; to neglect these might perhaps be consistent with the *maintenance* of humanity as an end in itself, but not with the *advancement* of this end.

Fourth, as regards meritorious duties toward others: The natural end which all human beings have is their own happiness. Now humanity might indeed subsist although no one should contribute anything to the happiness of others, provided he did not intentionally withdraw anything from it; but after all, this would only harmonize negatively, not positively, with *humanity as an end in itself*, if everyone does not also endeavor, as far as he can, to forward the ends of others. For the ends of any subject which is an end in itself ought as far as possible to be *my* ends also, if that conception is to have its *full* effect in me.

This principle that humanity and generally every rational nature is *an end in itself* (which is the supreme limiting condition of every human being's freedom of action), is not borrowed from experience, *first*, because it is universal, applying as it does to all rational beings whatever, and experience is not capable of determining anything about them; *second*, because it does not present humanity as an end to human beings (subjectively), that is, as an object which human beings do of themselves actually adopt as an end; but as an objective end which must as a law constitute the supreme limiting condition of all our subjective ends, let them be what they will; it must therefore spring from pure reason. In fact the ground of all practical legislation lies (according to the first principle) *objectively in the rule* and its form of universality which makes it capable of being a law (say, for example, a law of nature);

---

* This is often called the Formula of Humanity as End in Itself.

but *subjectively* in the *end*; now by the second principle, the subject of all ends is each rational being inasmuch as it is an end in itself. From this follows the third practical principle of the will, which is the ultimate condition of its harmony with the universal practical reason, viz., the idea of *the will of every rational being as a will giving universal law.**

On this principle all maxims are rejected which are inconsistent with the will being itself universal legislator. Thus the will is not merely subject to the law, but subject to it so that it must be regarded *as itself giving the law*, and on this ground only subject to the law (of which it can regard itself as the author).

In the previous imperatives, namely, that based on the conception of the conformity of actions to general laws, as in a *system of nature*, and that based on the universal *prerogative* of rational beings as *ends* in themselves—these imperatives just because they were conceived as categorical excluded from any share in their authority all admixture of any interest as an incentive; they were, however, only *assumed* to be categorical, because such an assumption was necessary to explain the conception of duty. But we could not prove independently that there are practical propositions which command categorically, nor can it be proved in this section; one thing, however, could be done, namely, to indicate in the imperative itself, by some determinate expression, that in the case of volition from duty all interest is renounced, which is the specific criterion of categorical as distinguished from hypothetical imperatives. This is done in the present third formula of the principle, namely, in the idea of the will of every rational being as a *will giving universal law*.

For although a will *which is subject to laws* may be attached to this law by means of an interest, yet a will which is itself a supreme lawgiver, so far as it is such, cannot possibly depend on any interest, since a will so dependent would itself still need another law restricting the interest of its self-love by the condition that it should be valid as universal law.

Thus the *principle* of every human will as *a will which in all its maxims ... gives universal laws*, provided it be otherwise correct, would be very *well suited* to be the categorical imperative in this respect,

namely, that just because of the idea of universal legislation it is *not based on any interest*, and therefore it alone among all possible imperatives can be *unconditional*. Or still better, converting the proposition, if there is a categorical imperative (that is, a law for the will of every rational being), it can only command that everything be done from maxims of one's will regarded as a will which could at the same time will that it should itself give universal laws, for in that case only the practical principle and the imperative which it obeys are unconditional, since they cannot be based on any interest.

Looking back now on all previous attempts to discover the principle of morality, we need not wonder why they all failed. It was seen that the human being is bound to laws by duty, but it was not observed that the laws to which he is subject are *only those of his own giving*, though at the same time they are *universal*, and that he is only bound to act in conformity with his own will—a will, however, which is designed by nature to give universal laws. For when one has conceived the human being only as subject to a law (no matter what), then this law required some interest, either by way of attraction or constraint, since it did not originate as a law from *his own* will, but this will was according to a law obliged by *something else* to act in a certain manner. Now by this necessary consequence all the labor spent in finding a supreme principle of *duty* was irrevocably lost. For one never elicited duty, but only a necessity of acting from a certain interest. Whether this interest was private or otherwise, in any case the imperative had to be conditional, and could not by any means be capable of being a moral command. I will therefore call this the principle of *autonomy* of the will, in contrast with every other which I accordingly count under *heteronomy*.†

The concept of every rational being as one which must consider itself as giving in all the maxims of its will universal laws, so as to judge itself and its actions from this point of view—this concept leads to another which depends on it and is very fruitful, namely, that of a *kingdom of ends*.

By a *kingdom* I understand the systematic union of different rational beings through common laws.

---

* This is sometimes called the Formula of Autonomy.
† Autonomy = self-rule. Heteronomy = rule by another.

Now since it is by laws that the universal validity of ends are determined, hence, if we abstract from the personal differences of rational beings, and likewise from all the content of their private ends, we shall be able to conceive all ends combined in a systematic whole (including both rational beings as ends in themselves, and also the special ends which each may propose to himself), that is to say, we can conceive a kingdom of ends, which on the preceding principles is possible.

For all rational beings come under the *law* that each of them must treat itself and all others *never merely as means*, but in every case *at the same time as ends in themselves*. From this results a systematic union of rational beings through common objective laws, that is, a kingdom which may be called a kingdom of ends, since what these laws have in view is just the relation of these beings to one another as ends and means. It is certainly only an ideal.

A rational being belongs as a *member* to the kingdom of ends when, although giving universal laws in it, he is also himself subject to these laws. He belongs to it *as sovereign* when, while giving laws, he is not subject to the will of any other.

A rational being must always regard himself as giving laws either as member or as sovereign in a kingdom of ends which is rendered possible by the freedom of will. He cannot, however, maintain the latter position merely by maxims of his will, but only in case he is a completely independent being without needs and with unrestricted power adequate to his will.

Morality consists then in the reference of all action to the legislation which alone can render a kingdom of ends possible.* This legislation must be capable of existing in every rational being, and of emanating from his will, so that the principle of this will is never to act on any maxim which could not without contradiction be also a universal law, and accordingly always so to act that *the will could at the same time regard itself as giving through its maxims universal laws*. If now the maxims of rational beings are not by their own nature coincident with this objective principle, then the necessity of acting on it is called practical necessitation, that is, *duty*. Duty does not apply to the sovereign in the kingdom of ends, but it does apply to every member of it and to all in the same degree.

The practical necessity of acting on this principle, that is, duty, does not rest at all on feelings, impulses, or inclinations, but solely on the relation of rational beings to one another, a relation in which the will of a rational being must always be regarded as *legislative*, since otherwise it could not be regarded as *an end in itself*. Reason then refers every maxim of the will, regarding it as legislative universally, to every other will and also to every action towards oneself; and this not on account of any other practical motive or any future advantage, but from the idea of the *dignity* of a rational being, obeying no law but that which he himself also gives.

In the kingdom of ends everything has either *price* or *dignity*. Whatever has price can be replaced by something else which is *equivalent*; whatever, on the other hand, is above all price, and therefore admits of no equivalent, has a dignity.

Whatever has reference to the general inclinations and wants of humankind has a *market price*; whatever, without presupposing a need, corresponds to a certain taste, that is, to a delight in the mere purposeless play of our faculties, has a *fancy price*;† but that which constitutes the condition under which alone anything can be an end in itself, this has not merely relative worth, that is, price, but an inner worth, that is, *dignity*.

Now morality is the condition under which alone a rational being can be an end in himself, since by this alone it is possible that he should be a legislating member in the kingdom of ends. Thus morality, and humanity, insofar as it is capable of morality, is that which alone has dignity. Skill and diligence in labor have a market price; wit, lively imagination, and humor have a fancy price; on the other hand, fidelity to promises, benevolence from principle (not from instinct), have an inner worth. Neither nature nor art contains anything which in default of these it could put in their place, for their worth consists not in the effects which spring from them, not in the use and advantage which they secure, but in the disposition, that is, the maxims of the will which are ready to manifest themselves in such actions, even if they do

---

* This is sometimes called the Formula of the Kingdom of Ends.
† A capricious or arbitrary preference; individual taste; an inclination, a liking.

not have the desired effect. These actions also need no recommendation from any subjective taste or sentiment, that they may be looked upon with immediate favor and delight; they need no immediate propensity or feeling for them; they exhibit the will that performs them as an object of an immediate respect, and nothing but reason is required to *impose* them on the will; not to *flatter* it into them, which, in the case of duties, would be a contradiction. This estimation therefore shows that the worth of such a disposition is dignity, and places it infinitely above all price, with which it cannot for a moment be brought into comparison or competition without as it were violating its sanctity.

What then is it which justifies virtue or the morally good disposition, in making such lofty claims? It is nothing less than the *privilege* it secures to the rational being of participating *in the giving of universal laws*, by which it qualifies him to be a member of a possible kingdom of ends, a privilege to which he was already destined by his own nature as being an end in itself, and on that account legislating in the kingdom of ends; free as regards all laws of nature, and obeying only those laws which he himself gives, and by which his maxims can belong to a system of universal law to which at the same time he submits himself. For nothing has any worth except what the law assigns it. Now the legislation itself which assigns the worth of

everything must for that very reason possess dignity, that is, an unconditional incomparable worth; and the word *respect** alone supplies a becoming expression for the esteem which a rational being must have for it. *Autonomy* then is the basis of the dignity of human nature and of every rational nature.

The three modes of presenting the principle of morality that have been adduced are at bottom only so many formulae of the very same law, and each unites in itself the other two. There is, however, a difference among them, but it is subjectively rather than objectively practical, intended, namely, to bring an idea of reason nearer to intuition (by means of a certain analogy), and thereby nearer to feeling. All maxims, in fact, have—

1. A *form*, consisting in universality; and in this view the formula of the moral imperative is expressed thus, that the maxims must be so chosen as if they were to serve as universal laws of nature.

2. A *matter*, namely, an end, and here the formula says that the rational being, as it is an end by its own nature and therefore an end in itself, must in every maxim serve as the condition limiting all merely relative and arbitrary ends.

3. A *complete determination* of all maxims by means of that formula, namely, that all maxims ought, by their own legislation, to harmonize with a possible kingdom of ends as with a kingdom of nature.[5] ... ■

Suggestions for Critical Reflection

1. Kant gives four examples in which it is supposed to be impossible to will that your maxim become universal law. Just exactly *how* does Kant think this is impossible? Is there more than one kind of 'impossibility' here? Is Kant *correct* that it is, in some way, impossible to universalize these four maxims? (If you don't think he is, what does this show about his moral theory?)

2. Could Kant's moral theory lead to a potential conflict of duties? For example, the duty to tell the truth seems to conflict, potentially, with the

duty to save the lives of innocent people: what, for example, if you are faced with a mad axman demanding to know where his victim—whom you happen to know is cowering under your kitchen table—is hiding? (Here the key idea is that, in some situations, two universalizable *maxims* must tend toward different and incompatible actions. Mere conflicts of rules for action—e.g., "always return what you have borrowed"—will tend to miss the mark as criticisms of Kant, as the maxims which lie behind them may well allow for exceptions

---

* Other translators have preferred the English word "reverence." The German word is *Achtung*, which in this context has religious overtones of awe before the sublimity of the moral law.

in particular cases.) If duties mandated by the categorical imperative *can* conflict with each other, how much destruction does this wreak on Kant's moral theory?

3. On the other hand, does Kant's moral theory produce any concrete ethical prescriptions at all? The German philosopher G.W.F. Hegel called Kant's Formula of Universal Law an "empty formalism" and said it reduced "the science of morals to the preaching of duty for duty's sake.... No transition is possible to the specification of particular duties nor, if some such particular content for acting comes under consideration, is there any criterion in that principle for deciding whether it is or is not a duty. On the contrary, by this means any wrong or immoral line of conduct may be justified."* What do you make of this objection?

4. Kant provides several—up to five—different formulations of the categorical imperative. What is the relationship between them? For example, do some of the formulations yield different sets of duties than the others?

5. Kant denies that "the principles of morality are ... to be sought anywhere in knowledge of human nature." Does this seem like a reasonable position to take? What reasons does he have for this striking claim, and how persuasive are they?

6. At one point Kant argues that the function of reason cannot, primarily, be to produce happiness, since then it would not have been well adapted by nature to its purpose, and it must therefore have some other purpose (to produce a will which is good in itself). What do you think of this argument? How much does it rely upon the assumption that nature has purposes?

7. Kant suggests our ordinary, everyday moral beliefs and practices contain within them the "ultimate principle" of morality (the categorical imperative). Is he successful in showing we *already* tacitly believe the categorical imperative? If not, how much of a problem is this for his later arguments?

8. Do all of our actions rest on maxims? Do you think that Kant thinks they do (and if so, how does that affect your understanding of what he means by "maxim")? If they do not, does this cause serious problems for Kant's moral theory?

9. "There are ... many persons so sympathetically constituted that without any motive of vanity or selfishness they find an inner satisfaction in spreading joy and rejoice in the contentment of others which they have made possible. But I say that, however dutiful and however amiable it may be, that kind of action has no true moral worth." What do you think of this claim of Kant's? When properly understood, do you think it is plausible?

10. Does Kant's moral theory require us to be perfectly rational in order to be perfectly moral? If so, is this a reasonable expectation? What place can the irrational elements of human psychology—such as emotions—have in Kant's moral philosophy?

11. How well can Kant's moral theory handle the following question: Now you've shown me what morality is, *why* should I be moral? Why is morality binding on me? For example, when Kant rules out all hypothetical imperatives as grounds for moral behavior, does he thereby rule out all possible *reasons* to be moral?

12. How accurately can we make moral judgments about *other people*, if Kant's theory is correct? How easily could we tell what maxim is guiding their behavior? For that matter, how accurately can we make moral judgments about our *own* behavior? Do we always know our own motives for action? How much, if at all, is any of this a problem for Kant's theory?

13. Even if you disagree with the details in Kant's moral theory, do you think his fundamental claim is sound? Is there a sharp distinction between moral actions and those performed for the sake of self-interest or emotional inclination? Must genuinely moral actions be motivated by a categorical or universally rational duty?

---

* G.W.F. Hegel, *Philosophy of Right*, trans. T.M. Knox (Oxford University Press, 1967), 90.

Notes

1   A maxim is the subjective principle of volition. The objective principle (i.e., that which would serve all rational beings also subjectively as a practical principle if reason had full power over the faculty of desire) is the practical law.

2   A maxim is the subjective principle of acting and must be distinguished from the objective principle (i.e., the practical law). The former contains the practical rule which reason determines according to the conditions of the subject (often his ignorance or inclinations) and is thus the principle according to which the subject acts. The law, on the other hand, is the objective principle valid for every rational being, and the principle by which it ought to act, i.e., an imperative.

3   ... [B]y a perfect duty I here understand a duty which permits no exception in the interest of inclination; thus I have not merely outer but also inner perfect duties....

4   Let it not be thought that the banal "what you do not wish to be done to you ..." could here serve as guide or principle, for it is only derived from the principle and is restricted by various limitations. It cannot be a universal law, because it contains the ground neither of duties to one's self nor of the benevolent duties to others (for many a man would gladly consent that others should not benefit him, provided only that he might be excused from showing benevolence to them). Nor does it contain the ground of obligatory duties to another, for the criminal would argue on this ground against the judge who sentences him. And so on.

5   Teleology considers nature as a realm of ends; morals regards a possible realm of ends as a realm of nature. In the former the realm of ends is a theoretical Idea for the explanation of what actually is. In the latter it is a practical Idea for bringing about that which does not exist but which can become actual through our conduct and for making it conform with this Idea.

JOHN STUART MILL

FROM *Utilitarianism*

Who Was John Stuart Mill?

John Stuart Mill, the most important British philosopher of the nineteenth century, was born in London in 1806, the eldest son of Scottish utilitarian philosopher and political radical James Mill (1773–1836). His childhood was shaped—some might say, misshaped—by his father's fervent belief in the importance of education. James Mill held that every variation in the talents and capacities of individual human beings could be explained by their education and experiences, and therefore he believed that a proper educational regime, beginning more or less from birth, could train any child to be an almost superhuman intellect. To prove these theories, Mill raised his first son, John Stuart, to be the British radical movement's secret weapon: a prodigious intellect who would be a living demonstration of what could be achieved through properly scientific educational methods, and who would go out into the world to spread the secular gospel of utilitarianism and liberalism.

His father took sole charge of little John Stuart's education from the time he was a toddler, keeping him isolated from other children (who might be harmful influences) and even from other adults who were not Mill's own philosophical compatriots. John was therefore kept out of schools—which his father believed reinforced ignorant and immoral social attitudes—and educated at home, learning Greek and Latin in the same large study where his father was hard at work on a monumental history of India (and, since no English-Greek dictionary had yet been written, frequently interrupting his father to ask questions about vocabulary). In his autobiography, the younger Mill wrote, "I have no remembrance of the time when I began to learn Greek. I have been told that it was when I was three years old."[*]

By the time he was eight—the age at which he began to learn Latin and arithmetic—he had studied much of Greek literature in the original, including all of Herodotus' *Histories* and six dialogues by Plato. At 12 he started on logic and the serious study of philosophy; political economy began at 13; and at 20 he was sent to France for a year to become fluent in that language and to study chemistry and mathematics.[†]

Despite these prodigious achievements, Mill's early life seems not to have been a happy one. He had no toys or children's books—not so much, apparently, because his father forbade them as simply because it never occurred to him to provide them—and John Stuart later remarked that he had never learned to play. Until he was 14 he never really mixed with children his own age at all. An early draft of his autobiography contained the following passage, deleted before publication:

> I believe there is less personal affection in England than in any other country of which I know anything, and I give my father's family not as peculiar in this respect but only as a faithful exemplification of the ordinary fact. That rarity in England, a really warm hearted mother, would in the first place have made the children grow up loving and being loved. But my mother with the very best intentions, only knew how to pass her life in drudging for them ... but to make herself loved, looked up to, or even obeyed, required qualities which she unfortunately did not possess. I thus grew up in the absence of love and in the presence of fear: and many and indelible are the effects of this bringing-up, in the stunting of my moral growth.[‡]

---

[*] This and other passages below are from J.S. Mill, *Autobiography* (Penguin Books, 1989), 27, 112, 117, 68.

[†] At around this time Mill was offered a place at Cambridge University. His father refused it for him, saying he already knew more than Cambridge could ever teach him.

[‡] *The Early Draft of John Stuart Mill's "Autobiography,"* ed. Jack Stillinger (University of Illinois Press, 1961), 184.

At the age of 22, Mill suffered a nervous breakdown and was plunged into suicidal despair. The trigger—according to his autobiography—was a sudden realization that living the life for which his father had trained him could not make him happy:

> ... [I]t occurred to me to put the question directly to myself, "Suppose that all your objects in life were realized; that all the changes in institutions and opinions which you are looking forward to, could be completely effected this very instant: would this be a great joy and happiness to you?" And an irrepressible self-consciousness distinctly answered, "No!" At this my heart sank within me: the whole foundation on which my life was constructed fell down. All my happiness was to have been found in the continual pursuit of this end. The end had ceased to charm, and how could there ever again be any interest in the means? I seemed to have nothing left to live for.

Mill's response to this crisis was not to *abandon* utilitarianism and the radical philosophy of his father, but instead to *modify* the theories by which he had been brought up. He came to adopt the view that "those only are happy ... who have their minds fixed on some object other than their own happiness": that is, true happiness—which, as his father had taught him, is the measure of all action—comes not from the pursuit of one's own happiness in itself, but from living a life filled with concern for the happiness of others and with a love of other things, such as poetry and music, for their own sake. Mill, in fact, claimed his sanity was saved by his discovery of Romantic poetry—especially that of William Wordsworth (1770–1850), Samuel Taylor Coleridge (1772–1834), and Johann Wolfgang von Goethe (1749–1832)—and he later placed great emphasis on the proper development of the emotional and sentimental side of one's character, as well as one's intellect.

In 1830, at 24, Mill began a deeply passionate love affair with a beautiful, vivacious, but married woman, Harriet Hardy Taylor (b. 1807), the wife of John Taylor, a merchant. Mill's relationship with Harriet was central to his life, and she had a great influence on his writings.

For 15 years, between 1834 and John Taylor's death in 1849, Harriet and the two Johns lived out a curiously Victorian compromise: Harriet and Mill agreed never to be seen in "society" as a couple—which would cause a scandal—but were allowed by Harriet's husband to go on frequent holidays together. In 1851, two years after her husband's death, Harriet and Mill were finally able to marry, but in 1858, Harriet died of tuberculosis—a disease she probably caught from her new husband, who in turn had probably caught it from his father, who had died of TB in 1836.

Mill never held an academic position, but he spent 35 years working as an administrator for the British East India Company in London. The East India Company, which had also employed Mill's father, was a private trading company formed in 1600 which, by the end of the eighteenth century, had its own army and political service and was effectively administering the sub-continent of India on behalf of the British government. Mill started his career in 1823, at 17, as a clerk in the office of the Examiner of India Correspondence; by 1856 he had become Chief Examiner of India Correspondence, as his father had been before him. In 1858 the East India Company was taken over by the British Crown following the Indian Rebellion of 1857, and Mill retired with a substantial pension.

Mill's work for the company left him plenty of time for his writing, and he was also very active in public life. In 1823 he was arrested for distributing birth-control pamphlets, and in 1825 he helped to found the London Debating Society. In 1824 his father had established the *Westminster Review*, a quarterly magazine advocating a radically liberal political and social agenda, and John Stuart—only 18 years old at the time of its founding—was a frequent and enthusiastic contributor of articles during its early years. In 1835 he started his own radical periodical, the *London Review*, which soon became the influential *London and Westminster Review* and ran, under his editorship, until 1840. Between 1865 and 1868 Mill was the Liberal Member of Parliament for Westminster, and in 1866 he secured a law guaranteeing freedom of speech in London's Hyde Park.* In 1867 he tried, but failed, to amend the second Reform Bill to introduce proportional representation and the vote for women. In

---

* This is the location, since that date, of London's famous Speakers' Corner—a place where "soapbox orators" can say whatever they like with legal impunity.

1866—by now something of a 'grand old man' of English society—he was made Rector of the University of St. Andrews in Scotland. In 1872 he became godfather to the newborn Bertrand Russell.

Mill died suddenly, from a fever, in 1873, at Aix-en-Provence, France. From about 1860 until 1870 he had been at the peak of his powers and influence. The moral philosopher Henry Sidgwick wrote in 1873, "from about 1860–1865 or thereabouts he ruled England in the region of thought as very few men ever did. I do not expect to see anything like it again."[*] A few decades later the former prime minister James Arthur Balfour noted that the authority of Mill's thought in English universities had been "comparable to that wielded ... by Hegel in Germany and in the middle ages by Aristotle."[†] By the First World War, however, Mill's reputation as a philosopher had suffered a precipitous decline, and he remained in ill-favor in the English-speaking philosophical world until the early 1970s, when new scholarship and changing philosophical fashions made possible a gradual increase in the appreciation of Mill as a major philosophical figure—the finest flowering of nineteenth-century British philosophy, and a precursor for the "naturalist" philosophers of the second half of the twentieth century.

What Was Mill's Overall Philosophical Project?

Mill is important less for the *originality* of his philosophic thought than for his brilliant *synthesis* of several major strands in nineteenth-century (and especially British) thought into a single, compelling, well-developed picture. The main ingredients for his worldview were empiricism, associationism, utilitarianism, and elements of German Romanticism. Together, these elements became what John Skorupski has called Mill's "liberal naturalism."[‡]

The bedrock of Mill's philosophy is empiricism: he believed all human knowledge comes ultimately from sense-experience, and his most substantial intellectual project was the attempt to construct a system of empirical knowledge that could underpin not just science but

also moral and social affairs. One of his main interests was in showing that empiricism need not lead to skepticism, such as that espoused by Scottish philosopher David Hume (1711–76). Mill's main discussion of the foundation of knowledge and the principles of inference is the massive *System of Logic*, published in six volumes in 1843. In this work he discusses both deductive inference (including mathematics, which Mill argues is—like all human knowledge—reducible to a set of generalizations of relations among sense-experiences) and inductive inference in the natural sciences. He also tries to show how these methods can be applied in politics and the social sciences. Social phenomena, he argues, are just as much the result of causal laws as are natural events, and thus the social sciences—though they will never make us perfectly able to predict human behavior—are capable of putting social policy on an objective footing that goes beyond the mere "intuitions" of conservative common sense.

His prescriptions for scientific practice—today called "Mill's methods"—were highly influential in the development of the philosophy of science in the twentieth century, and his work is still the foundation of modern methodologies for discovering causal laws. The key engine of science, for Mill, is simply *enumerative induction* or generalization from experience. Crudely put, once we have observed a sequence of events that all obey some regularity—ravens that are black, say, or moving magnetic fields being accompanied by an electrical current—we are justified in inferring that all future events of that type will follow the same law.

Mill's work was also a precursor of what is now called "naturalized epistemology." He proposed that all the phenomena of the human mind, including rationality, be treated as the result of the operation of psychological laws acting upon the data of experience. This psychological theory is called *associationism*—since it holds that ideas arise from the psychological associations between sensations—and is particularly defended by Mill in his *Examination of Sir William Hamilton's Philosophy* (1865).

[*]   Henry Sidgwick, in a May 1873 letter to C.H. Pearson; he is quoted in Stefan Collini, *Public Moralists, Political Thought and Intellectual Life in Great Britain 1850–1930* (Oxford University Press, 1991), 178.

[†]   Arthur James Balfour, *Theism and Humanism* (Hodder and Stoughton, 1915), 138.

[‡]   John Skorupski, "Introduction: The Fortunes of Liberal Naturalism," in *The Cambridge Companion to Mill*, ed. John Skorupski (Cambridge University Press, 1998), 1–34.

In his own time, Mill was for many years most wide-ly known for his *Principles of Political Economy* (1848), which tried to show that the science of economics—criticized by some for its tendency to predict disaster and starvation—could be reformulated as a progres-sive force for social progress. Mill pointed out the mis-match between what economics measures and what human beings really value, and this led him to argue for limiting economic growth for the sake of the environ-ment, for controlling populations in order to allow an ad-equate standard of living for everyone, and for what he considered the economically ideal form of society—a system of worker-owned cooperatives.

Mill's main ethical position is utilitarianism, which is set out in this selection. As he wrote in his autobiog-raphy, of reading Jeremy Bentham's work on utilitari-anism (at the age of 15), "it gave unity to my concep-tions of things. I now had opinions; a creed, a doctrine, a philosophy; in one among all the best senses of the word, a religion; the inculcation and diffusion of which could be made the principal outward purpose of a life." Mill was also concerned to apply this moral theory to wider questions of social policy. Of all social institu-tions—including both formal institutions such as laws and churches, and informal ones like social norms—Mill wants to ask: Does this institution contribute to human welfare, and does it do so better than any of the alternatives? If the answer is "No," Mill argues, then that institution should (gradually and non-violently) be changed for the better.

Mill's *On Liberty* (1859; see elsewhere in this vol-ume)—which, during his lifetime, was probably his most famous writing—is a classic defense of the freedom of thought and discussion, arguing that "the only purpose for which power can be rightfully exercised over any member of a civilized community, against his will, is to prevent harm to others. His own good, either physical or moral, is not a sufficient warrant." This essay was sparked partly by Mill's growing fear of the middle-class conformism (which he saw in America and detected in-creasing signs of in Britain) that he thought dangerously stifled originality and the critical consideration of ideas. Central to these concerns is Mill's view of human nature as "progressive," as well as the importance of individual-ity and autonomy. These themes, with their emphasis on the power and importance of the human spirit, were part of what he took from the European Romantic movement.

One of Mill's last works, *The Subjection of Women* (1869), is a classic statement of liberal feminism. Mill argues that women should have just as much freedom as men, and he attacks the conservative view that women and men have different "natures" that suit them for different spheres of life by arguing that no one could possibly know this—since all knowledge comes only from experience—unless women were first allowed to throw off their oppression and, over several gener-ations, try to do all the things that men were allowed to do.

What Is the Structure of This Reading?

Utilitarianism was not written as a scholarly treatise but as a sequence of articles, published in a monthly magazine and intended for the general educated reader: consequently, although *Utilitarianism* is philosophically weighty and—just below the surface—often difficult, its overall structure is quite straightforward. Mill be-gins by making some general remarks in the first chap-ter, attacking moral intuitionism and suggesting, among other things, that the principle of utilitarianism has always had a major tacit influence on moral beliefs. In Chapter 2, where our selection begins, he defines utili-tarianism, attempts to head off several common misun-derstandings of the doctrine, and raises and responds to about ten possible objections to the theory (such as that utilitarianism is a godless morality worthy only of pigs, or alternatively that it sets an impractically high standard that can never be attained by mere mortal human beings). In the third chapter, Mill considers the question of moral motivation and discusses how peo-ple might come to feel themselves morally bound by the principles of utilitarianism, arguing that utilitarianism is grounded in the natural social feelings of humanity. In Chapter 4 Mill sets out to give a positive "proof" (insofar as that is possible) for the claim that utilitarianism is the correct moral theory: he argues, first, that one's own happiness is desirable to oneself; second that it follows that happiness is simply desirable in itself, no matter whose it is; and third that *only* happiness is intrinsically desirable. It is this third stage in the argument that takes up most of the chapter. The final chapter of *Utilitarian-ism*, not included here, is a long discussion dealing with the relationship between utilitarianism and justice.

Some Useful Background Information

1. Mill frames much of *Utilitarianism* in terms of a debate between two basic positions on the nature of morality: the "intuitive" school and the "inductive" school. The intuitionists, whom Mill attacks, believed that ethical facts—though as real and as objectively true as any others—are *non-empirical*: that is, moral truths cannot be detected or confirmed using the five senses, but instead are known through the special faculty of "moral intuition." This philosophical position was represented in Mill's time by, among others, Sir William Hamilton (1788–1856) and William Whewell (1794–1866), and Mill's frequent criticism of the notion of "transcendental" moral facts is directed at intuitionists such as them. Mill considered intuitionism to be not only false but also a serious obstacle to social and moral progress. He thought the claim that (educated) human beings can "just tell" which moral principles are true, without needing or being able to cite evidence for these beliefs, tended to act as a disguise for prejudice and social conservatism. Mill's own moral methodology, by contrast, was what he called "inductive": he believed that *all* human knowledge, including ethical knowledge, comes ultimately from sense experience and therefore that moral judgments must be explained and defended by showing their connections to actual human experience.

2. The notion of *happiness* is a very important part of Mill's moral philosophy, so it is useful to be clear about exactly what his theory of happiness is. Because of Mill's empiricist and associationist philosophical upbringing, it was most natural for him to adopt a kind of hedonistic view of happiness. In keeping with his emphasis on sense experience as the key to understanding knowledge and the mind, Mill thinks of happiness as a kind of *pleasurable mental state* (*hēdonē* is the classical Greek word for "pleasure"). For Mill, a happy life is, roughly, one filled with as many pleasurable sensations, and as few painful ones, as possible.

Mill followed his philosophical predecessors in thinking that pleasurable experiences can be classified according to their duration and their intensity: thus rational people seeking their own happiness will aim to arrange their lives so that, over time, they will have more longer-lasting pleasures than short-lived ones, and more intense pleasures than dilute ones. For example, the initial painfulness of learning the violin might be more than offset by the intense and long-lasting pleasure of playing it well.* In addition, however, Mill distinguishes between different *qualities* of pleasure. For Mill (unlike, say, Bentham), pleasure is not just one type of mental sensation but comes in "higher" and "lower" varieties. For example, according to Mill, the pleasant feeling that accompanies advanced intellectual or creative activity is a more valuable kind of pleasure—even if it is no more intense or long-lasting—than that which comes from physical satisfactions like eating and sex.

3. One of Mill's philosophical presuppositions that is significant for his moral and social philosophy is *individualism*. Mill assumed that individual persons are the basic unit of political analysis—that social structures are nothing more than constructions out of these individuals and are nothing over and above particular people and the relations between them. It follows that the analysis of social phenomena must be approached through a study of the actions and intentions of individuals (as opposed to the study of larger social groups), and similarly that social change is possible only through a large number of changes to individual people. What matters to Mill is not "the general happiness" in some abstract sense, but the happiness of large numbers of individual human beings. He views social institutions as merely *instruments* for benefiting all these people. Furthermore, for Mill (influenced, as he was, by European Romanticism), there is a special kind of *value* in individuality: the particular uniqueness of each person is a thing to be treasured in itself.

---

* Mill's mentor Jeremy Bentham (1748–1832) even proposed what he called a "felicific calculus": a mathematical system for measuring the total net quantity of pleasure to be expected from a given course of action. Roughly, calculate the balance of pleasure and pain that would accompany a particular outcome of your actions—taking into account their intensity and duration—and then multiply this number by the probability of that outcome actually occurring. This yields what Bentham called the "expected utility" of an action. The rational agent—according to Bentham—acts in a way that has the greatest expected utility.

Some Common Misconceptions

1. For Mill, mere *exemption* from pain is not itself a good. He holds that pleasure is the only good, and pain the only bad, and the overall goodness of states of affairs consists in the *balance* of pleasure over pain. The absence of pain is thus morally neutral, unless it is accompanied by the positive presence of pleasure.

2. Mill is not arguing that people already *do* act in order to produce the greatest happiness of the greatest number: he is arguing that we *should*. He is not merely describing an already prevalent moral psychology, but arguing for a certain set of moral attitudes that he thinks we ought to cultivate in ourselves and in society in general.

3. Utilitarianism is a theory of actions and not motives. It does not require that people *intend* to maximize utility but rather that their behavior, in fact, does so. Mill insists that the criterion for what makes an action right is that it maximize utility; it does not follow from this that all our actions must have the conscious goal of maximizing utility. In fact, there is a good case to be made that a community where everyone is *trying* to maximize utility all the time would actually be self-defeating and a much less happy society than it would be if people acted from other motivations. If this is right, it would follow that, according to utilitarianism itself, it would be immoral to be always consciously trying to maximize utility. This is not a paradox or a problem for the theory, however; it simply shows there is a difference between the criterion of right action and the best advice one can give moral agents for actually meeting that criterion.

    Actions, according to Mill, include within themselves two parts: an *intention* (which is different from a motive—it is not *why* the action is done but *what* the action is intended to achieve), and the action's *effects*. Mill sometimes appeals to differences of intention to distinguish between kinds of actions (as in his Chapter 3 footnote about a tyrant rescuing a drowning man), but, strictly speaking, only the *effects* or consequences of an action can be morally relevant in Mill's view.

4. One common complaint against utilitarianism is that it makes *every* action, no matter how trivial, a moral issue: pretty much everything we do (e.g., getting a haircut) will have *some* effect on someone's pleasure and pain, and so it appears we have a moral duty to ensure we *always* act in such a way as to maximize the general happiness—and this, to say the least, would seem to put a bit of a strain on everyday life. However, even if this is, in fact, an implication of Mill's utilitarian theory, he did not intend to commit us to such an onerous regime. Something that Mill writes elsewhere is illuminating in this regard: "It is not good that persons should be bound, by other people's opinion, to do everything that they would deserve praise for doing. There is a standard of altruism to which all should be required to come up, and a degree beyond which it is not obligatory, but meritorious."[*]

5. Despite how *Utilitarianism* can strike us today, in the aftermath of the grand and often massively destructive social-engineering projects of the twentieth century, Mill was actually a bitter foe of what might be called "social constructivism." He emphatically did *not* see society as merely a machine built to help human beings to live together, a machine that can be broken into bits and reconstructed if it is not working optimally, and one where the rational, technical vision of collective planners should override individual initiative in the public good. On the contrary, Mill was very much an individualist and a humanist. He saw society as built from the actions of separate individual human beings and held that it is a kind of historical "consensus" that has created traditions and cultural practices that are continually but gradually evolving over time. Mill's vision for the reform of society, then, was not the imposition of central planning, but instead the gradual construction of a set of cultural norms—including, especially, a progressive educational system—to create human beings with the best possible moral character.

---

[*] From *Auguste Comte and Positivism*, in *Collected Works of J.S. Mill*, vol. 10 (University of Toronto Press, 1979), 337.

How Important and Influential Is This Work?

John Stuart Mill did not *invent* utilitarianism (and never pretended to have done so). Indeed, he was brought up by people who already considered themselves utilitarians. Mill's importance to utilitarianism is that he gave it what is arguably its single greatest and most influential formulation, in the essay *Utilitarianism*. It is this work that, ever since it was written, has been the starting point for both defenders and foes of utilitarianism. Furthermore, utilitarianism is itself a very important and influential moral theory.

Along with Marxism, it was arguably the most prevalent moral theory among philosophers, economists, political scientists, and other social theorists for much of the twentieth century (completely eclipsing—or in some cases, as with G.E. Moore's moral philosophy, absorbing—the moral "intuitionism" that Mill saw as his theory's main competitor in 1861). Utilitarianism's influence has waned since the 1970s and it has been subjected to several damaging philosophical attacks, but it is still, uncontroversially, one of the four or five most discussed and appealed-to moral theories in contemporary philosophical discourse.

FROM *Utilitarianism**

Chapter 2: What Utilitarianism Is

... The creed which accepts as the foundation of morals, Utility, or the Greatest Happiness Principle, holds that actions are right in proportion as they tend to promote happiness, wrong as they tend to produce the reverse of happiness. By happiness is intended pleasure, and the absence of pain; by unhappiness, pain, and the privation of pleasure. To give a clear view of the moral standard set up by the theory, much more requires to be said; in particular, what things it includes in the ideas of pain and pleasure; and to what extent this is left an open question. But these supplementary explanations do not affect the theory of life on which this theory of morality is grounded—namely, that pleasure, and freedom from pain, are the only things desirable as ends; and that all desirable things (which are as numerous in the utilitarian as in any other scheme) are desirable either for the pleasure inherent in themselves, or as means to the promotion of pleasure and the prevention of pain.

Now, such a theory of life excites in many minds, and among them in some of the most estimable in feeling and purpose, inveterate dislike. To suppose that life has (as they express it) no higher end than pleasure—no better and nobler object of desire and pursuit—they designate as utterly mean and grovelling; as a doctrine worthy only of swine, to whom the followers of Epicurus[†] were, at a very early period, contemptuously likened;[‡] and modern holders of the doctrine are occasionally made the subject of equally polite comparisons by its German, French, and English assailants.

When thus attacked, the Epicureans have always answered, that it is not they, but their accusers, who represent human nature in a degrading light; since the accusation supposes human beings to be capable of no pleasures except those of which swine are capable. If

---

*   *Utilitarianism* was first published in 1861 as a series of three essays in volume 64 of *Fraser's Magazine*. It was first published as a book in 1863; this text is from the fourth edition, published in 1871 (by Longmans, Green, Reader, and Dyer), the last to be printed in Mill's lifetime.
†   Epicurus (341–270 BCE) was a Greek philosopher and founder of the loosely knit school of thought called Epicureanism. A central plank of this doctrine is—as the modern connotations of the word "epicurean" suggest—that the good life is one filled with pleasure. Indeed, for Epicurus, the only rational goal in life is one's own pleasure. However, contrary to the popular association of "Epicureanism" with mere sensual self-indulgence, Epicurus placed much greater emphasis on stable, non-sensory pleasures (say, the pleasures of friendship and psychological contentment) and also stressed the importance of dispensing with unnecessary desires, harmful fears (such as the fear of death), and hollow gratifications. For more on Epicurus, see the reading from Kathy Behrendt later in this volume.
‡   For example, in Diogenes Laertius's *Lives of Eminent Philosophers*, written c. 230 CE.

this supposition were true, the charge could not be gainsaid,* but would then be no longer an imputation; for if the sources of pleasure were precisely the same to human beings and to swine, the rule of life which is good enough for the one would be good enough for the other. The comparison of the Epicurean life to that of beasts is felt as degrading, precisely because a beast's pleasures do not satisfy a human being's conceptions of happiness. Human beings have faculties more elevated than the animal appetites, and when once made conscious of them, do not regard anything as happiness which does not include their gratification. I do not, indeed, consider the Epicureans to have been by any means faultless in drawing out their scheme of consequences from the utilitarian principle. To do this in any sufficient manner, many Stoic,† as well as Christian elements require to be included. But there is no known Epicurean theory of life which does not assign to the pleasures of the intellect, of the feelings and imagination, and of the moral sentiments, a much higher value as pleasures than to those of mere sensation. It must be admitted, however, that utilitarian writers in general have placed the superiority of mental over bodily pleasures chiefly in the greater permanency, safety, uncostliness, etc., of the former—that is, in their circumstantial advantages rather than in their intrinsic nature. And on all these points utilitarians have fully proved their case; but they might have taken the other, and, as it may be called, higher ground, with entire consistency. It is quite compatible with the principle of utility to recognise the fact, that some *kinds* of pleasure are more desirable and more valuable than others. It would be absurd that while, in estimating all other things, quality is considered as well as quantity, the estimation of pleasures should be supposed to depend on quantity alone.

If I am asked, what I mean by difference of quality in pleasures, or what makes one pleasure more valuable than another, merely as a pleasure, except its being greater in amount, there is but one possible answer. Of two pleasures, if there be one to which all or almost all who have experience of both give a decided preference, irrespective of any feeling of moral obligation to prefer it, that is the more desirable pleasure. If one of the two is, by those who are competently acquainted with both, placed so far above the other that they prefer it, even though knowing it to be attended with a greater amount of discontent, and would not resign it for any quantity of the other pleasure which their nature is capable of, we are justified in ascribing to the preferred enjoyment a superiority in quality, so far outweighing quantity as to render it, in comparison, of small account.

Now it is an unquestionable fact that those who are equally acquainted with, and equally capable of appreciating and enjoying, both, do give a most marked preference to the manner of existence which employs their higher faculties. Few human creatures would consent to be changed into any of the lower animals, for a promise of the fullest allowance of a beast's pleasures; no intelligent human being would consent to be a fool, no instructed person would be an ignoramus, no person of feeling and conscience would be selfish and base, even though they should be persuaded that the fool, the dunce, or the rascal is better satisfied with his lot than they are with theirs. They would not resign what they possess more than he for the most complete satisfaction of all the desires which they have in common with him. If they ever fancy they would, it is only in cases of unhappiness so extreme, that to escape from it they would exchange their lot for almost any other, however undesirable in their own eyes. A being of higher faculties requires more to make him happy, is capable probably of more acute suffering, and certainly accessible to it at more points, than one of an inferior type; but in spite of these liabilities, he can never really wish to sink into what he feels to be a lower grade of existence. We may give what explanation we please of this unwillingness; we may attribute it to pride, a name which is given indiscriminately to some of the most and to some of the least estimable feelings of which mankind are capable:

* Denied.
† Stoicism was, with Epicureanism, one of the two main strands of "Hellenistic" philosophy (roughly, that associated with Greek culture during the 300 years after the death of Alexander the Great in 323 BCE). Its main ethical doctrine was that wise and virtuous persons accept, with calm indifference, their place in the impartial, rational, inevitable order of the universe—even if it is their fate to suffer hardship or painful death—but also work dutifully to foster a social order that mirrors the rational order of the cosmos. For more on stoicism, see the reading from Epictetus later in this volume.

we may refer it to the love of liberty and personal independence, an appeal to which was with the Stoics one of the most effective means for the inculcation of it; to the love of power, or to the love of excitement, both of which do really enter into and contribute to it: but its most appropriate appellation* is a sense of dignity, which all human beings possess in one form or other, and in some, though by no means in exact, proportion to their higher faculties, and which is so essential a part of the happiness of those in whom it is strong, that nothing which conflicts with it could be, otherwise than momentarily, an object of desire to them. Whoever supposes that this preference takes place at a sacrifice of happiness—that the superior being, in anything like equal circumstances, is not happier than the inferior—confounds the two very different ideas, of happiness, and content. It is indisputable that the being whose capacities of enjoyment are low, has the greatest chance of having them fully satisfied; and a highly endowed being will always feel that any happiness which he can look for, as the world is constituted, is imperfect. But he can learn to bear its imperfections, if they are at all bearable; and they will not make him envy the being who is indeed unconscious of the imperfections, but only because he feels not at all the good which those imperfections qualify. It is better to be a human being dissatisfied than a pig satisfied; better to be Socrates dissatisfied than a fool satisfied. And if the fool, or the pig, are of a different opinion, it is because they only know their own side of the question. The other party to the comparison knows both sides.

... From this verdict of the only competent judges, I apprehend there can be no appeal. On a question which is the best worth having of two pleasures, or which of two modes of existence is the most grateful† to the feelings, apart from its moral attributes and from its consequences, the judgment of those who are qualified by knowledge of both, or, if they differ, that of the majority among them, must be admitted as final. And there needs be the less hesitation to accept this judgment respecting the quality of pleasures, since

there is no other tribunal to be referred to even on the question of quantity. What means are there of determining which is the acutest of two pains, or the intensest of two pleasurable sensations, except the general suffrage‡ of those who are familiar with both? Neither pains nor pleasures are homogeneous, and pain is always heterogeneous with pleasure. What is there to decide whether a particular pleasure is worth purchasing at the cost of a particular pain, except the feelings and judgment of the experienced? When, therefore, those feelings and judgment declare the pleasures derived from the higher faculties to be preferable *in kind*, apart from the question of intensity, to those of which the animal nature, disjoined from the higher faculties, is susceptible, they are entitled on this subject to the same regard.

I have dwelt on this point, as being a necessary part of a perfectly just conception of Utility or Happiness, considered as the directive rule of human conduct. But it is by no means an indispensable condition to the acceptance of the utilitarian standard; for that standard is not the agent's own greatest happiness, but the greatest amount of happiness altogether; and if it may possibly be doubted whether a noble character is always the happier for its nobleness, there can be no doubt that it makes other people happier, and that the world in general is immensely a gainer by it. Utilitarianism, therefore, could only attain its end§ by the general cultivation of nobleness of character, even if each individual were only benefited by the nobleness of others, and his own, so far as happiness is concerned, were a sheer deduction¶ from the benefit. But the bare enunciation of such an absurdity as this last, renders refutation superfluous.

According to the Greatest Happiness Principle, as above explained, the ultimate end, with reference to and for the sake of which all other things are desirable (whether we are considering our own good or that of other people), is an existence exempt as far as possible from pain, and as rich as possible in enjoyments, both in point of quantity and quality; the test

---

* Name, label.
† Pleasing.
‡ A view expressed by voting (or the right to make such a vote).
§ Here, as elsewhere, 'end' means goal or object aimed at.
¶ Subtraction (as opposed to an inference).

of quality, and the rule for measuring it against quantity, being the preference felt by those who in their opportunities of experience, to which must be added their habits of self-consciousness and self-observation, are best furnished with the means of comparison. This, being, according to the utilitarian opinion, the end of human action, is necessarily also the standard of morality; which may accordingly be defined, the rules and precepts for human conduct, by the observance of which an existence such as has been described might be, to the greatest extent possible, secured to all mankind; and not to them only, but, so far as the nature of things admits, to the whole sentient creation.*

Against this doctrine, however, arises another class of objectors, who say that happiness, in any form, cannot be the rational purpose of human life and action; because, in the first place, it is unattainable: and they contemptuously ask, what right hast thou to be happy? a question which Mr. Carlyle† clenches by the addition, What right, a short time ago, hadst thou even *to be*? Next, they say, that men can do without happiness; that all noble human beings have felt this, and could not have become noble but by learning the lesson of Entsagen,‡ or renunciation; which lesson, thoroughly learnt and submitted to, they affirm to be the beginning and necessary condition of all virtue.

The first of these objections would go to the root of the matter were it well founded; for if no happiness is to be had at all by human beings, the attainment of it cannot be the end of morality, or of any rational conduct. Though, even in that case, something might still be said for the utilitarian theory; since utility includes not solely the pursuit of happiness, but the prevention or mitigation of unhappiness; and if the former aim be chimerical,§ there will be all the greater scope and more imperative need for the latter, so long at least as mankind think fit to live, and do not take refuge in the simultaneous act of suicide recommended under certain conditions by Novalis.¶ When, however, it is thus positively asserted to be impossible that human life should be happy, the assertion, if not something like a verbal quibble, is at least an exaggeration. If by happiness be meant a continuity of highly pleasurable excitement, it is evident enough that this is impossible. A state of exalted pleasure lasts only moments, or in some cases, and with some intermissions, hours or days, and is the occasional brilliant flash of enjoyment, not its permanent and steady flame. Of this the philosophers who have taught that happiness is the end of life were as fully aware as those who taunt them. The happiness which they meant was not a life of rapture; but moments of such, in an existence made up of few and transitory pains, many and various pleasures, with a decided predominance of the active over the passive, and having as the foundation of the whole, not to expect more from life than it is capable of bestowing. A life thus composed, to those who have been fortunate enough to obtain it, has always appeared worthy of the name of happiness. And such an existence is even now the lot of many, during some considerable portion of their lives. The present wretched education, and wretched social arrangements, are the only real hindrance to its being attainable by almost all.

The objectors perhaps may doubt whether human beings, if taught to consider happiness as the end of life, would be satisfied with such a moderate share

---

*   All creatures capable of sensation (and thus of feeling pleasure and pain).

†   Thomas Carlyle (1795–1881) was a popular Scottish writer and (somewhat reactionary) social critic. This quotation is from his 1836 book *Sartor Resartus*. As a young man Mill was heavily influenced by Carlyle's allegiance to German Romanticism, but once Carlyle began to realize that Mill did not see himself as one of his disciples, their relationship took a sharp turn for the worse. (The fact that Mill's maid accidentally used the only manuscript copy of Carlyle's *History of the French Revolution* to light a fire when Carlyle was visiting him—forcing Carlyle to rewrite all of Volume I—cannot have helped.) *Utilitarianism* is largely intended as a response to criticisms of Mill's moral theories leveled by Carlyle and others.

‡   German for "to renounce or abjure." The idea it is supposed to capture is that moral behavior must be painful or difficult to be genuinely virtuous.

§   Unrealistic, fanciful.

¶   Novalis was the pseudonym of an early German poet and philosopher in the Romantic movement, Friedrich von Hardenberg (1772–1801). His most famous poem, "Hymns to the Night," was written after the death of his young fiancée from tuberculosis in 1799. Just months after its publication, von Hardenberg also succumbed to the disease.

of it. But great numbers of mankind have been satisfied with much less. The main constituents of a satisfied life appear to be two, either of which by itself is often found sufficient for the purpose: tranquillity, and excitement. With much tranquillity, many find that they can be content with very little pleasure: with much excitement, many can reconcile themselves to a considerable quantity of pain. There is assuredly no inherent impossibility in enabling even the mass of mankind to unite both; since the two are so far from being incompatible that they are in natural alliance, the prolongation of either being a preparation for, and exciting a wish for, the other. It is only those in whom indolence amounts to a vice, that do not desire excitement after an interval of repose: it is only those in whom the need of excitement is a disease, that feel the tranquillity which follows excitement dull and insipid, instead of pleasurable in direct proportion to the excitement which preceded it. When people who are tolerably fortunate in their outward lot do not find in life sufficient enjoyment to make it valuable to them, the cause generally is, caring for nobody but themselves. To those who have neither public nor private affections, the excitements of life are much curtailed, and in any case dwindle in value as the time approaches when all selfish interests must be terminated by death: while those who leave after them objects of personal affection, and especially those who have also cultivated a fellow-feeling with the collective interests of mankind, retain as lively an interest in life on the eve of death as in the vigour of youth and health. Next to selfishness, the principal cause which makes life unsatisfactory is want* of mental cultivation. A cultivated mind—I do not mean that of a philosopher, but any mind to which the fountains of knowledge have been opened, and which has been taught, in any tolerable degree, to exercise its faculties—finds sources of inexhaustible interest in all that surrounds it; in the objects of nature, the achievements of art, the imaginations of poetry, the incidents of history, the ways of mankind, past and present, and their prospects in the future. It is possible, indeed, to become indifferent to all this, and that too without having exhausted a thousandth part of it; but only when one has had from the beginning no moral or human interest in these

things, and has sought in them only the gratification of curiosity.

Now there is absolutely no reason in the nature of things why an amount of mental culture sufficient to give an intelligent interest in these objects of contemplation, should not be the inheritance of every one born in a civilised country. As little is there an inherent necessity that any human being should be a selfish egotist, devoid of every feeling or care but those which centre in his own miserable individuality. Something far superior to this is sufficiently common even now, to give ample earnest of what the human species may be made. Genuine private affections and a sincere interest in the public good, are possible, though in unequal degrees, to every rightly brought up human being. In a world in which there is so much to interest, so much to enjoy, and so much also to correct and improve, every one who has this moderate amount of moral and intellectual requisites is capable of an existence which may be called enviable; and unless such a person, through bad laws, or subjection to the will of others, is denied the liberty to use the sources of happiness within his reach, he will not fail to find this enviable existence, if he escape the positive evils of life, the great sources of physical and mental suffering—such as indigence, disease, and the unkindness, worthlessness, or premature loss of objects of affection. The main stress of the problem lies, therefore, in the contest with these calamities, from which it is a rare good fortune entirely to escape; which, as things now are, cannot be obviated, and often cannot be in any material degree mitigated. Yet no one whose opinion deserves a moment's consideration can doubt that most of the great positive evils of the world are in themselves removable, and will, if human affairs continue to improve, be in the end reduced within narrow limits. Poverty, in any sense implying suffering, may be completely extinguished by the wisdom of society, combined with the good sense and providence of individuals. Even that most intractable of enemies, disease, may be indefinitely reduced in dimensions by good physical and moral education, and proper control of noxious influences; while the progress of science holds out a promise for the future of still more direct conquests over this detestable foe.

---

* Lack, absence.

And every advance in that direction relieves us from some, not only of the chances which cut short our own lives, but, what concerns us still more, which deprive us of those in whom our happiness is wrapt up.* As for vicissitudes of fortune, and other disappointments connected with worldly circumstances, these are principally the effect either of gross imprudence, of ill-regulated desires, or of bad or imperfect social institutions. All the grand sources, in short, of human suffering are in a great degree, many of them almost entirely, conquerable by human care and effort; and though their removal is grievously slow—though a long succession of generations will perish in the breach before the conquest is completed, and this world becomes all that, if will and knowledge were not wanting, it might easily be made—yet every mind sufficiently intelligent and generous to bear a part, however small and unconspicuous, in the endeavour, will draw a noble enjoyment from the contest itself, which he would not for any bribe in the form of selfish indulgence consent to be without.

And this leads to the true estimation of what is said by the objectors concerning the possibility, and the obligation, of learning to do without happiness. Unquestionably it is possible to do without happiness; it is done involuntarily by nineteen-twentieths of mankind, even in those parts of our present world which are least deep in barbarism; and it often has to be done voluntarily by the hero or the martyr, for the sake of something which he prizes more than his individual happiness. But this something, what is it, unless the happiness of others or some of the requisites of happiness? It is noble to be capable of resigning entirely one's own portion of happiness, or chances of it: but, after all, this self-sacrifice must be for some end; it is not its own end; and if we are told that its end is not happiness, but virtue, which is better than happiness, I ask, would the sacrifice be made if the hero or martyr did not believe that it would earn for others immunity from similar sacrifices? Would it be made if he thought that his renunciation of happiness for himself would produce no fruit for any of his fellow creatures, but to make their lot like his, and place them also in the condition of persons who have renounced happiness? All honour to those who can abnegate for themselves the personal enjoyment of life, when by such renunciation they contribute worthily to increase the amount of happiness in the world; but he who does it, or professes to do it, for any other purpose, is no more deserving of admiration than the ascetic mounted on his pillar.† He may be an inspiriting proof of what men *can* do, but assuredly not an example of what they *should*.

... I must again repeat, what the assailants of utilitarianism seldom have the justice to acknowledge, that the happiness which forms the utilitarian standard of what is right in conduct, is not the agent's own happiness, but that of all concerned. As between his own happiness and that of others, utilitarianism requires him to be as strictly impartial as a disinterested‡ and benevolent spectator. In the golden rule of Jesus of Nazareth, we read the complete spirit of the ethics of utility. To do as you would be done by, and to love your neighbour as yourself, constitute the ideal perfection of utilitarian morality. As the means of making the nearest approach to this ideal, utility would enjoin, first, that laws and social arrangements should place the happiness, or (as speaking practically it may be called) the interest, of every individual, as nearly as possible in harmony with the interest of the whole; and secondly, that education and opinion, which have so vast a power over human character, should so use that power as to establish in the mind of every individual an indissoluble association between his own happiness and the good of the whole; especially between his own happiness and the practice of such modes of conduct, negative and positive, as regard for the universal happiness prescribes; so that not only he may be unable to conceive the possibility of happiness to himself, consistently with conduct opposed to the general good, but also that a direct impulse to promote the general good may be in every individual one of the habitual motives of action, and the sentiments connected therewith may fill a large and prominent

---

* For example, Mill's wife Harriet Taylor, who died of "pulmonary congestion" in 1858.

† Mill is probably thinking of St. Simeon Stylites (c. 390–459), a Syrian ascetic who spent more than 30 years living at the top of various pillars, the highest of which was 20 meters tall.

‡ Free from bias or self-interest (not *un*interested or bored!).

place in every human being's sentient existence. If the impugners of the utilitarian morality represented it to their own minds in this, its true character, I know not what recommendation possessed by any other morality they could possibly affirm to be wanting to it; what more beautiful or more exalted developments of human nature any other ethical system can be supposed to foster, or what springs of action, not accessible to the utilitarian, such systems rely on for giving effect to their mandates.

The objectors to utilitarianism cannot always be charged with representing it in a discreditable light. On the contrary, those among them who entertain anything like a just idea of its disinterested character, sometimes find fault with its standard as being too high for humanity. They say it is exacting too much to require that people shall always act from the inducement of promoting the general interests of society. But this is to mistake the very meaning of a standard of morals, and confound the rule of action with the motive of it. It is the business of ethics to tell us what are our duties, or by what test we may know them; but no system of ethics requires that the sole motive of all we do shall be a feeling of duty; on the contrary, ninety-nine hundredths of all our actions are done from other motives, and rightly so done, if the rule of duty does not condemn them. It is the more unjust to utilitarianism that this particular misapprehension should be made a ground of objection to it, inasmuch as utilitarian moralists have gone beyond almost all others in affirming that the motive has nothing to do with the morality of the action, though much with the worth of the agent. He who saves a fellow creature from drowning does what is morally right, whether his motive be duty, or the hope of being paid for his trouble; he who betrays the friend that trusts him, is guilty of a crime, even if his object be to serve another friend to whom he is under greater obligations.[1]

But to speak only of actions done from the motive of duty, and in direct obedience to principle: it is a misapprehension of the utilitarian mode of thought, to conceive it as implying that people should fix their minds upon so wide a generality as the world, or society at large. The great majority of good actions are intended not for the benefit of the world, but for that of individuals, of which the good of the world is made up; and the thoughts of the most virtuous man need not on these occasions travel beyond the particular persons concerned, except so far as is necessary to assure himself that in benefiting them he is not violating the rights—that is, the legitimate and authorised expectations—of any one else. The multiplication of happiness is, according to the utilitarian ethics, the object of virtue: the occasions on which any person (except one in a thousand) has it in his power to do this on an extended scale, in other words to be a public benefactor, are but exceptional; and on these occasions alone is he called on to consider public utility; in every other case, private utility, the interest or happiness of some few persons, is all he has to attend to. Those alone the influence of whose actions extends to society in general, need concern themselves habitually about so large an object. In the case of abstinences indeed—of things which people forbear to do from moral considerations, though the consequences in the particular case might be beneficial—it would be unworthy of an intelligent agent not to be consciously aware that the action is of a class which, if practised generally, would be generally injurious, and that this is the ground of the obligation to abstain from it. The amount of regard for the public interest implied in this recognition, is no greater than is demanded by every system of morals, for they all enjoin to abstain from whatever is manifestly pernicious to society.

The same considerations dispose of another reproach against the doctrine of utility, founded on a still grosser misconception of the purpose of a standard of morality, and of the very meaning of the words right and wrong. It is often affirmed* that utilitarianism renders men cold and unsympathising; that it chills their moral feelings towards individuals; that it makes them regard only the dry and hard consideration of the consequences of actions, not taking into their moral estimate the qualities from which those actions emanate. If the assertion means that they do not allow their judgment respecting the rightness or wrongness of an action to be influenced by their opinion of the qualities of the person who does it, this is a complaint not against utilitarianism, but against having any standard of morality at all; for certainly no

---

* For example, in Charles Dickens's novel *Hard Times* (1854), especially through the character of Gradgrind.

known ethical standard decides an action to be good or bad because it is done by a good or a bad man, still less because done by an amiable, a brave, or a benevolent man, or the contrary. These considerations are relevant, not to the estimation of actions, but of persons; and there is nothing in the utilitarian theory inconsistent with the fact that there are other things which interest us in persons besides the rightness and wrongness of their actions. The Stoics, indeed, with the paradoxical misuse of language which was part of their system, and by which they strove to raise themselves above all concern about anything but virtue, were fond of saying that he who has that has everything; that he, and only he, is rich, is beautiful, is a king. But no claim of this description is made for the virtuous man by the utilitarian doctrine. Utilitarians are quite aware that there are other desirable possessions and qualities besides virtue, and are perfectly willing to allow to all of them their full worth. They are also aware that a right action does not necessarily indicate a virtuous character, and that actions which are blameable, often proceed from qualities entitled to praise. When this is apparent in any particular case, it modifies their estimation, not certainly of the act, but of the agent. I grant that they are, notwithstanding, of opinion, that in the long run the best proof of a good character is good actions; and resolutely refuse to consider any mental disposition as good, of which the predominant tendency is to produce bad conduct. This makes them unpopular with many people; but it is an unpopularity which they must share with every one who regards the distinction between right and wrong in a serious light; and the reproach is not one which a conscientious utilitarian need be anxious to repel....

It may not be superfluous to notice a few more of the common misapprehensions of utilitarian ethics, even those which are so obvious and gross that it might appear impossible for any person of candour and intelligence to fall into them....

... Utility is often summarily stigmatised as an immoral doctrine by giving it the name of Expediency, and taking advantage of the popular use of that term to contrast it with Principle. But the Expedient, in the sense in which it is opposed to the Right, generally means that which is expedient for the particular interest of the agent himself; as when a minister sacrifices the interests of his country to keep himself in place. When it means anything better than this, it means that which is expedient for some immediate object, some temporary purpose, but which violates a rule whose observance is expedient in a much higher degree. The Expedient, in this sense, instead of being the same thing with the useful, is a branch of the hurtful. Thus, it would often be expedient, for the purpose of getting over some momentary embarrassment, or attaining some object immediately useful to ourselves or others, to tell a lie. But inasmuch as the cultivation in ourselves of a sensitive feeling on the subject of veracity, is one of the most useful, and the enfeeblement of that feeling one of the most hurtful, things to which our conduct can be instrumental; and inasmuch as any, even unintentional, deviation from truth, does that much towards weakening the trustworthiness of human assertion, which is not only the principal support of all present social well-being, but the insufficiency of which does more than any one thing that can be named to keep back civilisation, virtue, everything on which human happiness on the largest scale depends; we feel that the violation, for a present advantage, of a rule of such transcendent expediency, is not expedient, and that he who, for the sake of a convenience to himself or to some other individual, does what depends on him to deprive mankind of the good, and inflict upon them the evil, involved in the greater or less reliance which they can place in each other's word, acts the part of one of their worst enemies. Yet that even this rule, sacred as it is, admits of possible exceptions, is acknowledged by all moralists; the chief of which is when the withholding of some fact (as of information from a malefactor, or of bad news from a person dangerously ill) would save an individual (especially an individual other than oneself) from great and unmerited evil, and when the withholding can only be effected by denial. But in order that the exception may not extend itself beyond the need, and may have the least possible effect in weakening reliance on veracity, it ought to be recognised, and, if possible, its limits defined; and if the principle of utility is good for anything, it must be good for weighing these conflicting utilities against one another, and marking out the region within which one or the other preponderates.

Again, defenders of utility often find themselves called upon to reply to such objections as this—that there is not time, previous to action, for calculating and weighing the effects of any line of conduct on the general happiness. This is exactly as if any one were to say that it is impossible to guide our conduct by Christianity, because there is not time, on every occasion on which anything has to be done, to read through the Old and New Testaments. The answer to the objection is, that there has been ample time, namely, the whole past duration of the human species. During all that time, mankind have been learning by experience the tendencies of actions; on which experience all the prudence, as well as all the morality of life, are dependent. People talk as if the commencement of this course of experience had hitherto been put off, and as if, at the moment when some man feels tempted to meddle with the property or life of another, he had to begin considering for the first time whether murder and theft are injurious to human happiness. Even then I do not think that he would find the question very puzzling; but, at all events, the matter is now done to his hand. It is truly a whimsical supposition that, if mankind were agreed in considering utility to be the test of morality, they would remain without any agreement as to what *is* useful, and would take no measures for having their notions on the subject taught to the young, and enforced by law and opinion. There is no difficulty in proving any ethical standard whatever to work ill, if we suppose universal idiocy to be conjoined with it; but on any hypothesis short of that, mankind must by this time have acquired positive beliefs as to the effects of some actions on their happiness; and the beliefs which have thus come down are the rules of morality for the multitude, and for the philosopher until he has succeeded in finding better. That philosophers might easily do this, even now, on many subjects; that the received code of ethics is by no means of divine right; and that mankind have still much to learn as to the effects of actions on the general happiness, I admit, or rather, earnestly maintain. The corollaries from the principle of utility, like the precepts of every practical art, admit of indefinite improvement, and, in a progressive state of the human mind, their improvement is perpetually going on. But to consider the rules of morality as improvable, is one thing; to pass over the intermediate generalisations entirely, and endeavour to test each individual action directly by the first principle, is another. It is a strange notion that the acknowledgment of a first principle is inconsistent with the admission of secondary ones. To inform a traveller respecting the place of his ultimate destination, is not to forbid the use of landmarks and direction-posts on the way. The proposition that happiness is the end and aim of morality, does not mean that no road ought to be laid down to that goal, or that persons going thither should not be advised to take one direction rather than another. Men really ought to leave off talking a kind of nonsense on this subject, which they would neither talk nor listen to on other matters of practical concernment. Nobody argues that the art of navigation is not founded on astronomy, because sailors cannot wait to calculate the Nautical Almanack.* Being rational creatures, they go to sea with it ready calculated; and all rational creatures go out upon the sea of life with their minds made up on the common questions of right and wrong, as well as on many of the far more difficult questions of wise and foolish. And this, as long as foresight is a human quality, it is to be presumed they will continue to do. Whatever we adopt as the fundamental principle of morality, we require subordinate principles to apply it by; the impossibility of doing without them, being common to all systems, can afford no argument against any one in particular; but gravely to argue as if no such secondary principles could be had, and as if mankind had remained till now, and always must remain, without drawing any general conclusions from the experience of human life, is as high a pitch, I think, as absurdity has ever reached in philosophical controversy.

The remainder of the stock arguments against utilitarianism mostly consist in laying to its charge the common infirmities of human nature, and the general difficulties which embarrass conscientious persons in shaping their course through life. We are told that a utilitarian will be apt to make his own particular case an exception to moral rules, and, when under temptation, will see a utility in the breach of a rule, greater than he will see in its observance. But is utility the only creed which is able to furnish us with excuses for

---

*   An annual government publication that tabulates the astronomical data required for maritime navigation. (For example, the almanac might give the coordinates of a particular star as it would be seen at a particular time and date from various places on the earth's surface: observation will therefore tell you where you are.)

evil doing, and means of cheating our own conscience? They are afforded in abundance by all doctrines which recognise as a fact in morals the existence of conflicting considerations; which all doctrines do, that have been believed by sane persons. It is not the fault of any creed, but of the complicated nature of human affairs, that rules of conduct cannot be so framed as to require no exceptions, and that hardly any kind of action can safely be laid down as either always obligatory or always condemnable. There is no ethical creed which does not temper the rigidity of its laws, by giving a certain latitude, under the moral responsibility of the agent, for accommodation to peculiarities of circumstances; and under every creed, at the opening thus made, self-deception and dishonest casuistry* get in. There exists no moral system under which there do not arise unequivocal cases of conflicting obligation. These are the real difficulties, the knotty points both in the theory of ethics, and in the conscientious guidance of personal conduct. They are overcome practically, with greater or with less success, according to the intellect and virtue of the individual; but it can hardly be pretended that any one will be the less qualified for dealing with them, from possessing an ultimate standard to which conflicting rights and duties can be referred. If utility is the ultimate source of moral obligations, utility may be invoked to decide between them when their demands are incompatible. Though the application of the standard may be difficult, it is better than none at all: while in other systems, the moral laws all claiming independent authority, there is no common umpire entitled to interfere between them; their claims to precedence one over another rest on little better than sophistry,† and unless determined, as they generally are, by the unacknowledged influence of considerations of utility, afford a free scope for the action of personal desires and partialities. We must remember that only in these cases of conflict between secondary principles is it requisite that first principles should be appealed to. There is no case of moral obligation in which some secondary principle is not involved; and if only one, there can seldom be any real doubt which one it is, in the mind of any person by whom the principle itself is recognised.

Chapter 3: Of the Ultimate Sanction‡ of the Principle of Utility

The question is often asked, and properly so, in regard to any supposed moral standard—What is its sanction? what are the motives to obey it? or more specifically, what is the source of its obligation? whence does it derive its binding force? It is a necessary part of moral philosophy to provide the answer to this question; which, though frequently assuming the shape of an objection to the utilitarian morality, as if it had some special applicability to that above others, really arises in regard to all standards....

The principle of utility either has, or there is no reason why it might not have, all the sanctions which belong to any other system of morals. Those sanctions are either external or internal. Of the external sanctions it is not necessary to speak at any length. They are, the hope of favour and the fear of displeasure, from our fellow creatures or from the Ruler of the Universe, along with whatever we may have of sympathy or affection for them, or of love and awe of Him, inclining us to do his will independently of selfish consequences. There is evidently no reason why all these motives for observance should not attach themselves to the utilitarian morality, as completely and as powerfully as to any other. Indeed, those of them which refer to our fellow creatures are sure to do so, in proportion to the amount of general intelligence; for whether there be any other ground of moral obligation than the general happiness or not, men do desire happiness; and however imperfect may be their own practice, they desire and commend all conduct in others towards themselves, by which they think their happiness is promoted. With regard to the religious motive, if men believe, as most profess to do, in the goodness of God, those who think that conduciveness

---

* Unsound and deceptive reasoning; or, reasoning from particular cases rather than general rules.
† Plausible but misleading argument.
‡ "Sanction" was a technical term in eighteenth- and nineteenth-century philosophy. Sanctions are the considerations that motivate adherence to rules of conduct. For example, Bentham—in his *Introduction to the Principles of Morals and Legislation*—distinguished between four different types of sanction: "physical" (e.g., hunger or sexual desire), "political" (e.g., prison), "religious" (e.g., heaven and hell), and "moral" (e.g., social disapproval).

to the general happiness is the essence, or even only the criterion of good, must necessarily believe that it is also that which God approves. The whole force therefore of external reward and punishment, whether physical or moral, and whether proceeding from God or from our fellow men, together with all that the capacities of human nature admit of disinterested devotion to either, become available to enforce the utilitarian morality, in proportion as that morality is recognised; and the more powerfully, the more the appliances of education and general cultivation are bent to the purpose.

So far as to external sanctions. The internal sanction of duty, whatever our standard of duty may be, is one and the same—a feeling in our own mind; a pain, more or less intense, attendant on violation of duty, which in properly cultivated moral natures rises, in the more serious cases, into shrinking from it as an impossibility. This feeling, when disinterested, and connecting itself with the pure idea of duty, and not with some particular form of it, or with any of the merely accessory circumstances, is the essence of Conscience; though in that complex phenomenon as it actually exists, the simple fact is in general all encrusted over with collateral associations, derived from sympathy, from love, and still more from fear; from all the forms of religious feeling; from the recollections of childhood and of all our past life; from self-esteem, desire of the esteem of others, and occasionally even self-abasement. This extreme complication is, I apprehend, the origin of the sort of mystical character which, by a tendency of the human mind of which there are many other examples, is apt to be attributed to the idea of moral obligation, and which leads people to believe that the idea cannot possibly attach itself to any other objects than those which, by a supposed mysterious law, are found in our present experience to excite it. Its binding force, however, consists in the existence of a mass of feeling which must be broken through in order to do what violates our standard of right, and which, if we do nevertheless violate that standard, will probably have to be encountered afterwards in the form of remorse. Whatever theory we have of the nature or origin of conscience, this is what essentially constitutes it.

The ultimate sanction, therefore, of all morality (external motives apart) being a subjective feeling in our own minds, I see nothing embarrassing to those whose standard is utility, in the question, what is the sanction of that particular standard? We may answer, the same as of all other moral standards—the conscientious feelings of mankind. Undoubtedly this sanction has no binding efficacy on those who do not possess the feelings it appeals to; but neither will these persons be more obedient to any other moral principle than to the utilitarian one. On them morality of any kind has no hold but through the external sanctions. Meanwhile the feelings exist, a fact in human nature, the reality of which, and the great power with which they are capable of acting on those in whom they have been duly cultivated, are proved by experience. No reason has ever been shown why they may not be cultivated to as great intensity in connection with the utilitarian, as with any other rule of morals....

It is not necessary, for the present purpose, to decide whether the feeling of duty is innate* or implanted. Assuming it to be innate, it is an open question to what objects it naturally attaches itself, for the philosophic supporters of that theory are now agreed that the intuitive perception is of principles of morality and not of the details. If there be anything innate in the matter, I see no reason why the feeling which is innate should not be that of regard to the pleasures and pains of others. If there is any principle of morals which is intuitively obligatory, I should say it must be that. If so, the intuitive ethics would coincide with the utilitarian, and there would be no further quarrel between them. Even as it is, the intuitive moralists, though they believe that there are other intuitive moral obligations, do already believe this to be one; for they unanimously hold that a large *portion* of morality turns upon the consideration due to the interests of our fellow-creatures. Therefore, if the belief in the transcendental origin of moral obligation gives any additional efficacy to the internal sanction, it appears to me that the utilitarian principle has already the benefit of it.

On the other hand, if, as is my own belief, the moral feelings are not innate, but acquired, they are not for that reason the less natural. It is natural to

---

*   Inborn, possessed at birth.

man to speak, to reason, to build cities, to cultivate the ground, though these are acquired faculties. The moral feelings are not indeed a part of our nature, in the sense of being in any perceptible degree present in all of us; but this, unhappily, is a fact admitted by those who believe the most strenuously in their transcendental origin. Like the other acquired capacities above referred to, the moral faculty, if not a part of our nature, is a natural outgrowth from it; capable, like them, in a certain small degree, of springing up spontaneously; and susceptible of being brought by cultivation to a high degree of development. Unhappily it is also susceptible, by a sufficient use of the external sanctions and of the force of early impressions, of being cultivated in almost any direction: so that there is hardly anything so absurd or so mischievous that it may not, by means of these influences, be made to act on the human mind with all the authority of conscience. To doubt that the same potency might be given by the same means to the principle of utility, even if it had no foundation in human nature, would be flying in the face of all experience.

But moral associations which are wholly of artificial creation, when intellectual culture goes on, yield by degrees to the dissolving force of analysis: and if the feeling of duty, when associated with utility, would appear equally arbitrary; if there were no leading department of our nature, no powerful class of sentiments, with which that association would harmonise, which would make us feel it congenial, and incline us not only to foster it in others (for which we have abundant interested motives), but also to cherish it in ourselves; if there were not, in short, a natural basis of sentiment for utilitarian morality, it might well happen that this association also, even after it had been implanted by education, might be analysed away.

But there is this basis of powerful natural sentiment; and this it is which, when once the general happiness is recognised as the ethical standard, will constitute the strength of the utilitarian morality. This firm foundation is that of the social feelings of mankind; the desire to be in unity with our fellow creatures, which is already a powerful principle in human nature, and happily one of those which tend to become stronger, even without express inculcation,* from the influences of advancing civilisation. The social state is at once so natural, so necessary, and so habitual to man, that, except in some unusual circumstances or by an effort of voluntary abstraction, he never conceives himself otherwise than as a member of a body; and this association is riveted more and more, as mankind are further removed from the state of savage independence. Any condition, therefore, which is essential to a state of society, becomes more and more an inseparable part of every person's conception of the state of things which he is born into, and which is the destiny of a human being. Now, society between human beings, except in the relation of master and slave, is manifestly impossible on any other footing than that the interests of all are to be consulted. Society between equals can only exist on the understanding that the interests of all are to be regarded equally. And since in all states of civilisation, every person, except an absolute monarch, has equals, every one is obliged to live on these terms with somebody; and in every age some advance is made towards a state in which it will be impossible to live permanently on other terms with anybody. In this way people grow up unable to conceive as possible to them a state of total disregard of other people's interests. They are under a necessity of conceiving themselves as at least abstaining from all the grosser injuries, and (if only for their own protection) living in a state of constant protest against them. They are also familiar with the fact of co-operating with others and proposing to themselves a collective, not an individual interest as the aim (at least for the time being) of their actions. So long as they are co-operating, their ends are identified with those of others; there is at least a temporary feeling that the interests of others are their own interests. Not only does all strengthening of social ties, and all healthy growth of society, give to each individual a stronger personal interest in practically consulting the welfare of others; it also leads him to identify his *feelings* more and more with their good, or at least with an even greater degree of practical consideration for it. He comes, as though instinctively, to be conscious of himself as a being who *of course* pays regard to others. The good of others becomes to him a thing naturally and necessarily to be attended to, like any of the physical

---

* Frequent repetition or instruction, intended to firmly impress something in someone's mind.

conditions of our existence. Now, whatever amount of this feeling a person has, he is urged by the strongest motives both of interest and of sympathy to demonstrate it, and to the utmost of his power encourage it in others; and even if he has none of it himself, he is as greatly interested as any one else that others should have it. Consequently the smallest germs of the feeling are laid hold of and nourished by the contagion of sympathy and the influences of education; and a complete web of corroborative association is woven round it, by the powerful agency of the external sanctions. This mode of conceiving ourselves and human life, as civilisation goes on, is felt to be more and more natural. Every step in political improvement renders it more so, by removing the sources of opposition of interest, and levelling those inequalities of legal privilege between individuals or classes, owing to which there are large portions of mankind whose happiness it is still practicable to disregard. In an improving state of the human mind, the influences are constantly on the increase, which tend to generate in each individual a feeling of unity with all the rest; which, if perfect, would make him never think of, or desire, any beneficial condition for himself, in the benefits of which they are not included. If we now suppose this feeling of unity to be taught as a religion, and the whole force of education, of institutions, and of opinion, directed, as it once was in the case of religion, to make every person grow up from infancy surrounded on all sides both by the profession and the practice of it, I think that no one, who can realise this conception, will feel any misgiving about the sufficiency of the ultimate sanction for the Happiness morality....

Chapter 4: Of What Sort of Proof the Principle of Utility Is Susceptible

It has already been remarked, that questions of ultimate ends do not admit of proof, in the ordinary acceptation of the term. To be incapable of proof by reasoning is common to all first principles; to the first premises of our knowledge,* as well as to those of our conduct. But the former, being matters of fact, may be the subject of a direct appeal to the faculties which

judge of fact—namely, our senses, and our internal consciousness.† Can an appeal be made to the same faculties on questions of practical ends? Or by what other faculty is cognisance taken of them?

Questions about ends are, in other words, questions about what things are desirable. The utilitarian doctrine is, that happiness is desirable, and the only thing desirable, as an end; all other things being only desirable as means to that end. What ought to be required of this doctrine—what conditions is it requisite that the doctrine should fulfil—to make good its claim to be believed?

The only proof capable of being given that an object is visible, is that people actually see it. The only proof that a sound is audible, is that people hear it: and so of the other sources of our experience. In like manner, I apprehend, the sole evidence it is possible to produce that anything is desirable, is that people do actually desire it. If the end which the utilitarian doctrine proposes to itself were not, in theory and in practice, acknowledged to be an end, nothing could ever convince any person that it was so. No reason can be given why the general happiness is desirable, except that each person, so far as he believes it to be attainable, desires his own happiness. This, however, being a fact, we have not only all the proof which the case admits of, but all which it is possible to require, that happiness is a good: that each person's happiness is a good to that person, and the general happiness, therefore, a good to the aggregate of all persons. Happiness has made out its title as *one* of the ends of conduct, and consequently one of the criteria of morality.

But it has not, by this alone, proved itself to be the sole criterion. To do that, it would seem, by the same rule, necessary to show, not only that people desire happiness, but that they never desire anything else. Now it is palpable that they do desire things which, in common language, are decidedly distinguished from happiness. They desire, for example, virtue, and the absence of vice, no less really than pleasure and the absence of pain. The desire of virtue is not as universal, but it is as authentic a fact, as the desire of happiness. And hence the opponents of the utilitarian standard deem that they have a right to infer that there are

---

* The foundations of our beliefs.

† Mill means the memory of something previously experienced.

other ends of human action besides happiness, and that happiness is not the standard of approbation and disapprobation.

But does the utilitarian doctrine deny that people desire virtue, or maintain that virtue is not a thing to be desired? The very reverse. It maintains not only that virtue is to be desired, but that it is to be desired disinterestedly, for itself. Whatever may be the opinion of utilitarian moralists as to the original conditions by which virtue is made virtue; however they may believe (as they do) that actions and dispositions are only virtuous because they promote another end than virtue; yet this being granted, and it having been decided, from considerations of this description, what is virtuous, they not only place virtue at the very head of the things which are good as means to the ultimate end, but they also recognise as a psychological fact the possibility of its being, to the individual, a good in itself, without looking to any end beyond it; and hold, that the mind is not in a right state, not in a state conformable to Utility, not in the state most conducive to the general happiness, unless it does love virtue in this manner— as a thing desirable in itself, even although, in the individual instance, it should not produce those other desirable consequences which it tends to produce, and on account of which it is held to be virtue. This opinion is not, in the smallest degree, a departure from the Happiness principle. The ingredients of happiness are very various, and each of them is desirable in itself, and not merely when considered as swelling an aggregate. The principle of utility does not mean that any given pleasure, as music, for instance, or any given exemption from pain, as for example health, is to be looked upon as means to a collective something termed happiness, and to be desired on that account. They are desired and desirable in and for themselves; besides being means, they are a part of the end. Virtue, according to the utilitarian doctrine, is not naturally and originally part of the end, but it is capable of becoming so; and in those who love it disinterestedly it has become so, and is desired and cherished, not as a means to happiness, but as a part of their happiness.

To illustrate this farther, we may remember that virtue is not the only thing, originally a means, and which if it were not a means to anything else, would be and remain indifferent, but which by association with what it is a means to, comes to be desired for itself, and that too with the utmost intensity. What,

for example, shall we say of the love of money? There is nothing originally more desirable about money than about any heap of glittering pebbles. Its worth is solely that of the things which it will buy; the desires for other things than itself, which it is a means of gratifying. Yet the love of money is not only one of the strongest moving forces of human life, but money is, in many cases, desired in and for itself, the desire to possess it is often stronger than the desire to use it, and goes on increasing when all the desires which point to ends beyond it, to be compassed by it, are falling off. It may, then, be said truly, that money is desired not for the sake of an end, but as part of the end. From being a means to happiness, it has come to be itself a principal ingredient of the individual's conception of happiness. The same may be said of the majority of the great objects of human life—power, for example, or fame; except that to each of these there is a certain amount of immediate pleasure annexed, which has at least the semblance of being naturally inherent in them; a thing which cannot be said of money. Still, however, the strongest natural attraction, both of power and of fame, is the immense aid they give to the attainment of our other wishes; and it is the strong association thus generated between them and all our objects of desire, which gives to the direct desire of them the intensity it often assumes, so as in some characters to surpass in strength all other desires. In these cases the means have become a part of the end, and a more important part of it than any of the things which they are means to. What was once desired as an instrument for the attainment of happiness, has come to be desired for its own sake. In being desired for its own sake it is, however, desired as *part* of happiness. The person is made, or thinks he would be made, happy by its mere possession; and is made unhappy by failure to obtain it. The desire of it is not a different thing from the desire of happiness, any more than the love of music, or the desire of health. They are included in happiness. They are some of the elements of which the desire of happiness is made up. Happiness is not an abstract idea, but a concrete whole; and these are some of its parts. And the utilitarian standard sanctions and approves their being so. Life would be a poor thing, very ill provided with sources of happiness, if there were not this provision of nature, by which things originally indifferent, but conducive to, or otherwise associated with, the satisfaction of our primitive desires, become in themselves sources of pleasure more valuable than the primitive pleasures, both in permanency, in the space of human existence that they are capable of covering, and even in intensity.

Virtue, according to the utilitarian conception, is a good of this description. There was no original desire of it, or motive to it, save its conduciveness to pleasure, and especially to protection from pain. But through the association thus formed, it may be felt a good in itself, and desired as such with as great intensity as any other good; and with this difference between it and the love of money, of power, or of fame, that all of these may, and often do, render the individual noxious to the other members of the society to which he belongs, whereas there is nothing which makes him so much a blessing to them as the cultivation of the disinterested love of virtue. And consequently, the utilitarian standard, while it tolerates and approves those other acquired desires, up to the point beyond which they would be more injurious to the general happiness than promotive of it, enjoins and requires the cultivation of the love of virtue up to the greatest strength possible, as being above all things important to the general happiness.

It results from the preceding considerations, that there is in reality nothing desired except happiness. Whatever is desired otherwise than as a means to some end beyond itself, and ultimately to happiness, is desired as itself a part of happiness, and is not desired for itself until it has become so. Those who desire virtue for its own sake, desire it either because the consciousness of it is a pleasure, or because the consciousness of being without it is a pain, or for both reasons united; as in truth the pleasure and pain seldom exist separately, but almost always together, the same person feeling pleasure in the degree of virtue attained, and pain in not having attained more. If one of these gave him no pleasure, and the other no pain, he would not love or desire virtue, or would desire it only for the other benefits which it might produce to himself or to persons whom he cared for.

We have now, then, an answer to the question, of what sort of proof the principle of utility is susceptible. If the opinion which I have now stated is psychologically true—if human nature is so constituted as to desire nothing which is not either a part of happiness or a means of happiness, we can have no other proof, and we require no other, that these are the only things desirable. If so, happiness is the sole end of human action, and the promotion of it the test by which to judge of all human conduct; from whence it necessarily follows that it must be the criterion of morality, since a part is included in the whole.

And now to decide whether this is really so; whether mankind do desire nothing for itself but that which is a pleasure to them, or of which the absence is a pain; we have evidently arrived at a question of fact and experience, dependent, like all similar questions, upon evidence. It can only be determined by practised self-consciousness and self-observation, assisted by observation of others. I believe that these sources of evidence, impartially consulted, will declare that desiring a thing and finding it pleasant, aversion to it and thinking of it as painful, are phenomena entirely inseparable, or rather two parts of the same phenomenon; in strictness of language, two different modes of naming the same psychological fact: that to think of an object as desirable (unless for the sake of its consequences), and to think of it as pleasant, are one and the same thing; and that to desire anything, except in proportion as the idea of it is pleasant, is a physical and metaphysical* impossibility....

But if this doctrine be true, the principle of utility is proved. Whether it is so or not, must now be left to the consideration of the thoughtful reader. ■

---

* Mill probably means "psychological." In his view, not only do human beings actually desire things "in proportion as the idea of it is pleasant," but there is no possible human psychology that would be otherwise.

Suggestions for Critical Reflection

1. One of the attractions of utilitarianism, it is often supposed, is that it is 'scientific' or objective in a way that intuitionism (or other ethical theories such as Kantianism, or virtue theory) is not. The Greatest Happiness Principle apparently provides a quasi-mathematical, bias-free, and theoretically motivated way of working out what we ought to do in literally any moral situation. But is this really so? For example, can the pleasures and pains of sentient creatures really be 'objectively' measured and compared, in order to calculate the net effect of actions on utility? Even if pleasures and pains are measurable, do you think all the consequences of an action can be properly predicted and measured? How serious are these problems for utilitarianism?

2. Does Mill's notion of "higher" or more "noble" pleasure make sense? How could the "nobility" of an experience add to the pleasure of it? Why couldn't an experience be noble but not pleasant? In that case, would Mill be able to say that it is still valuable? In other words, is Mill *really* a hedonist (i.e., someone who thinks that only pleasure has intrinsic value—and only pain intrinsic disvalue)?

3. An influential criticism of the hedonistic component of utilitarianism was invented by philosopher Robert Nozick (1938–2002) and is called the "experience machine." The experience machine is a fictional device that keeps your body alive in a tank of fluids, for a normal human life-span, all the while stimulating your brain so that you continuously feel as if you are having the most pleasant and satisfying experiences imaginable. Since—properly designed—this would be an utterly reliable way of maximizing the quality and number of pleasant sensations during your lifetime, it seems that the utilitarian is forced to conclude that it would be our *moral duty* to plug ourselves into one of these machines (especially if they are such reliable and long-lasting devices that nearly everyone can be plugged in at the same time). But Nozick argues that this result is clearly unsatisfactory: surely there is more to a valuable life than a mere succession of pleasant experiences, and so utilitarianism must be a faulty moral theory. What do you think about Nozick's argument? What exactly does it suggest is wrong with utilitarianism (or at least Mill's version of the theory)? Could this problem—if it is a problem—be fixed?

4. Roger Crisp has called the third paragraph of the fourth chapter of *Utilitarianism* "the most notorious [passage] in Mill's writings."[*] In it Mill compares desirability with visibility in an effort to argue that desire is a faculty that reveals what we morally ought to do. The most famous and apparently devastating criticism of this argument came from G.E. Moore in 1903: "The fact is that 'desirable' does not mean 'able to be desired' as 'visible' means 'able to be seen.' The desirable means simply what *ought* to be desired or deserves to be desired."[†] How does Moore's complaint cause problems for Mill's argument? Does Mill really make the mistake Moore is suggesting? If Mill's own arguments fail to show that we *ought* to desire happiness, is there any other way a utilitarian could consistently argue for this claim? Does utilitarianism need to provide arguments for it?

5. How well does Mill refute moral egoism? That is, does his argument show that I ought to care about *everyone*'s happiness, and not just my own? Does he have an *argument* for the "impartiality" component of utilitarianism? Does he need one?

6. Is Mill right that we desire *only* happiness? In other words, is his claim that, "to desire anything, except in proportion as the idea of it is pleasant, is a physical and metaphysical impossibility," a plausible one? If he is wrong, how seriously does this undercut his argument for the truth of utilitarianism? For example, what about Mill's own example of virtue: is he right in arguing that we value our own virtue only as a "part" of our happiness?

7. Mill appears to argue that happiness is the only thing desired, because the satisfaction of any desire is part of happiness. This seems to *define* happiness as desire satisfaction; if so, what do you

---

[*] Roger Crisp, *The Routledge Philosophy Guidebook to Mill on Utilitarianism* (Routledge, 1997), 73.

[†] G.E. Moore, *Principia Ethica* (Cambridge University Press, 1903), 67.

think of his further claim that this conclusion is an empirical matter, to be settled by observation?

8. Utilitarianism is a kind of moral theory that is sometimes called "welfarist": for such theories, the only thing of intrinsic value is the welfare of moral agents (according to Mill, sentient beings). One consequence of welfarism is that *nothing else* is of intrinsic value. Thus, for example, the beauty of art and nature, ecological sustainability, scientific knowledge, justice, equality, loyalty, kindness, or self-sacrifice—none of these things have any value in themselves but are valuable *only* insofar as they increase the welfare of sentient creatures (and are actually *immoral* if they reduce this welfare). Is this something Mill would agree with? Does this seem to be an acceptable consequence of a moral theory?

9. Utilitarianism is often accused of being an extremely demanding moral theory. According to utilitarianism, a certain unit of pleasure or pain should matter *equally* to me whether it belongs to me, to a member of my family, to a stranger halfway across the world, or even to an animal. Utilitarianism requires us to maximize overall happiness, and does not allow us to think of the happiness of ourselves and our friends as being especially important. If you or I were to spend all of our free time, and use almost all of our money, working to help victims of famine and other natural disasters around the world, this might well produce more overall utility than the lives we currently lead. If so, then utilitarianism apparently commits us to a moral *duty* to behave in this way, and we are being flat-out *immoral* in spending time with our families or watching movies. Does a careful reading support the claim that this is a consequence of Mill's position? Is this acceptable? If not, what is wrong with it?

10. According to utilitarianism, should we be morally responsible for all the consequences of our actions, including the unforeseen ones? What would Mill say (bear in mind his distinction between the morality of actions and of agents)? Are we just as responsible for *not* doing things that could have prevented great pain? For example, according to utilitarianism, am I equally morally deficient if I fail to give money to charity as I am if I send poisoned food to famine-stricken areas (supposing the outcomes in terms of human death and suffering would be the same)?

11. Act (or "direct") utilitarianism is the view that one should act in any circumstance so as to produce the greatest overall balance of pleasure over pain. (You would have a moral duty to break an important promise to your best friend if doing so would increase overall utility by even a tiny amount, for example.) Rule (or "indirect") utilitarianism, on the other hand, is the view that one should act in accordance with certain moral rules, rules fixed as those which, over time, can be expected to maximize utility if they are generally followed. (For example, you should never break an important promise, even if you can foresee that keeping it, in a particular case, will cause far more pain than pleasure.) Is Mill an act or rule utilitarian? Which is the better theory? Is *either* version attractive and, if not, can you think of a third option for utilitarianism?

12. According to utilitarianism, *how* should we maximize utility? Should we aim to maximize the *total* utility of the world, the *average* utility, or what? (For example, if we chose to maximize total utility, we might be morally obliged to aim for an extremely large population, even if each member has only a low level of happiness; on the other hand, if we opt for the highest possible average utility we might be committed to keeping the population small and select, perhaps killing, before birth, people who look as though they might drag the average down.) What would Mill say?

13. Mill thought utilitarianism to be the one true fundamental moral theory and to be consistent with (what is right in) the moral theories of Aristotle and Kant. If you are familiar with Aristotle's and Kant's ethical views, consider whether utilitarianism is in fact consistent with them. For example, could Kant accept that consequences are what is morally important about our actions?

Note

1   An opponent, whose intellectual and moral fairness it is a pleasure to acknowledge (the Rev. J. Llewellyn Davies), has objected to this passage, saying, "Surely the rightness or wrongness of saving a man from drowning does depend very much upon the motive with which it is done. Suppose that a tyrant, when his enemy jumped into the sea to escape from him, saved him from drowning simply in order that he might inflict upon him more exquisite tortures, would it tend to clearness to speak of that action as 'a morally right action'? Or suppose again, according to one of the stock illustrations of ethical inquiries, that a man betrayed a trust received from a friend, because the discharge of it would fatally injure that friend himself or some one belonging to him, would utilitarianism compel one to call the betrayal 'a crime' as much as if it had been done from the meanest motive?"

I submit, that he who saves another from drowning in order to kill him by torture afterwards, does not differ only in motive from him who does the same thing from duty or benevolence; the act itself is different.

The rescue of the man is, in the case supposed, only the necessary first step of an act far more atrocious than leaving him to drown would have been. Had Mr. Davies said, "the rightness or wrongness of saving a man from drowning does depend very much"—not upon the motive but—"upon the *intention*," no utilitarian would have differed from him. Mr. Davies, by an oversight too common not to be quite venial, has in this case confounded the very different ideas of Motive and Intention. There is no point at which utilitarian thinkers (and Bentham pre-eminently) have taken more pains to illustrate than this. The morality of the action depends entirely upon the intention—that is, upon what the agent *wills to do*. But the motive, that is, the feeling which makes him will to do so, when it makes no difference to the act, makes none in the morality: though it makes a great difference in our moral estimation of the agent, especially if it indicates a good or a bad habitual *disposition*—a bent of character from which useful, or from which hurtful actions are likely to arise.

VIRGINIA HELD

Feminist Transformations of Moral Theory

Who Is Virginia Held?

Virginia P. Held (b. 1929) is an influential ethicist and social-political philosopher, known especially as one of the central figures in the development of the "ethics of care," along with Carol Gilligan, Sara Ruddick, Nel Noddings, and others. Before becoming a professional philosopher she was a reporter, working for *The Reporter* magazine and other publications. She obtained her PhD from Columbia University in 1968, going on to spend much of her career teaching at Hunter College in New York. A past President of the Eastern Division of the American Philosophical Society, she is now a Distinguished Professor Emerita in the philosophy program of the Graduate Center at the City University of New York. She is the author of several books, including *Feminist Morality: Transforming Culture, Society and Politics* (1993), *Rights and Goods: Justifying Social Action* (1984), and *The Ethics of Care: Personal, Political, and Global* (2006)—and many articles on social and political philosophy, ethics, and feminist philosophy.

What Is the Structure of This Reading?

Held begins her article by arguing that, historically, all ethical theories have been built upon assumptions biased in favor of men and against women. She then goes on, in the next three sections, to discuss feminist approaches to the transformation of each of these three conceptual areas. In particular, she emphasizes a feminist re-valuing of *emotional responses* in ethics, the importance of *mothering* (which breaks through the public-private distinction), and the notion of the self as being importantly constituted by its *relations* to others.

Some Useful Background Information

The ethics of care, or care ethics, is a modern approach to moral theory that competes with traditional deontological/Kantian and consequentialist/utilitarian ethics. Ethicists working in this mode emphasize the basic moral significance of caring personal relationships, such as those between parents and children, between patients and their care-givers, and between humans and animals. A key moral issue, according to care ethics, is the maintenance of these networks of relationships in such a way that the well-being of each party, including the dependent and the vulnerable, is preserved and fostered; and an important critique of other types of ethical theory is that they are blind to these relationships, and, even worse, by placing an exclusive emphasis on justice and impartiality, that they are positively harmful to them. Care ethicists tend to focus on "actual experience, with an emphasis on reason and emotion, literal rather than hypothetical persons, embodiment, actual dialogue, and contextual, lived methodologies."* Similarly, rather than seeking universalizable moral rules, care ethics somewhat resembles virtue theory (and several non-western ethical traditions) in defining care as more of a lived practice. Two foundational texts for the ethics of care are Carol Gilligan's *In A Different Voice* (Harvard University Press, 1982) and Nel Noddings's *Caring* (University of California Press, 1982).

---

* "Care Ethics" by Maureen Sander-Staudt, in the *Internet Encyclopedia of Philosophy*, 24 October 2018.

Feminist Transformations of Moral Theory*

The history of philosophy, including the history of ethics, has been constructed from male points of view, and has been built on assumptions and concepts that are by no means gender-neutral.[1] Feminists characteristically begin with different concerns and give different emphases to the issues we consider than do nonfeminist approaches. And, as Lorraine Code expresses it, "starting points and focal points shape the impact of theoretical discussion."[2] Within philosophy, feminists often start with, and focus on, quite different issues than those found in standard philosophy and ethics, however "standard" is understood. Far from providing mere additional insights which can be incorporated into traditional theory, feminist explorations often require radical transformations of existing fields of inquiry and theory.[3] From a feminist point of view, moral theory along with almost all theory will have to be transformed to take adequate account of the experience of women.

I shall in this paper begin with a brief examination of how various fundamental aspects of the history of ethics have not been gender-neutral. And I shall discuss three issues where feminist rethinking is transforming moral concepts and theories....

I. Reason and Emotion

In the area of moral theory in the modern era, the priority accorded to reason has taken two major forms. A) On the one hand has been the Kantian, or Kantian-inspired search for very general, abstract, deontological,[†] universal moral principles by which rational beings should be guided. Kant's Categorical Imperative is a foremost example: it suggests that all moral problems can be handled by applying an impartial, pure, rational principle to particular cases. It requires that we try to see what the general features of the problem before us are, and that we apply an abstract principle, or rules derivable from it, to this problem. On this view, this procedure should be adequate for all moral decisions. We should thus be able to act as reason recommends, and resist yielding to emotional inclinations and desires in conflict with our rational wills.

B) On the other hand, the priority accorded to reason in the modern era has taken a Utilitarian form. The Utilitarian approach, reflected in rational choice theory, recognizes that persons have desires and interests, and suggests rules of rational choice for maximizing the satisfaction of these. While some philosophers in this tradition espouse egoism,[‡] especially of an intelligent and long-term kind, many do not. They begin, however, with assumptions that what are morally relevant are gains and losses of utility to theoretically isolatable individuals, and that the outcome at which morality should aim is the maximization of the utility of individuals. Rational calculation about such an outcome will, in this view, provide moral recommendations to guide all our choices. As with the Kantian approach, the Utilitarian approach relies on abstract general principles or rules to be applied to particular cases. And it holds that although emotion is, in fact, the source of our desires for certain objectives, the task of morality should be to instruct us on how to pursue those objectives most rationally. Emotional attitudes toward moral issues themselves interfere with rationality and should be disregarded. Among the questions Utilitarians can ask can be questions about which emotions to cultivate, and which desires to try to change, but these questions are to be handled in the terms of rational calculation, not of what our feelings suggest.

Although the conceptions of what the judgments of morality should be based on, and of how reason should guide moral decision, are different in Kantian and in Utilitarian approaches, both share a reliance on a highly abstract, universal principle as the appropriate source of moral guidance, and both share the view

* This article was originally published in *Philosophy and Phenomenological Research* 50 (Supplement Autumn 1990): 321–44.

† Based on the notion of a duty or a right (rather than on the value of some kind of state of affairs or type of character).

‡ That one either is, or ought to be, exclusively motivated by self-interest.

that moral problems are to be solved by the application of such an abstract principle to particular cases. Both share an admiration for the rules of reason to be appealed to in moral contexts, and both denigrate emotional responses to moral issues.

Many feminist philosophers have questioned whether the reliance on abstract rules, rather than the adoption of more context-respectful approaches, can possibly be adequate for dealing with moral problems, especially as women experience them.[26] Though Kantians may hold that complex rules can be elaborated for specific contexts, there is nevertheless an assumption in this approach that the more abstract the reasoning applied to a moral problem, the more satisfactory. And Utilitarians suppose that one highly abstract principle, The Principle of Utility, can be applied to every moral problem no matter what the context.

A genuinely universal or gender-neutral moral theory would be one which would take account of the experience and concerns of women as fully as it would take account of the experience and concerns of men. When we focus on the experience of women, however, we seem to be able to see a set of moral concerns becoming salient that differs from those of traditional or standard moral theory. Women's experience of moral problems seems to lead us to be especially concerned with actual relationships between embodied persons, and with what these relationships seem to require. Women are often inclined to attend to rather than to dismiss the particularities of the context in which a moral problem arises. And we often pay attention to feelings of empathy and caring to suggest what we ought to do rather than relying as fully as possible on abstract rules of reason.

Margaret Walker, for instance, contrasts feminist moral "understanding" with traditional moral "knowledge." She sees the components of the former as involving "attention, contextual and narrative appreciation, and communication in the event of moral deliberation."[27] This alternative moral epistemology holds that "the adequacy of moral understanding decreases as its form approaches generality through abstraction."[28]

The work of psychologists such as Carol Gilligan and others has led to a clarification of what may be thought of as tendencies among women to approach moral issues differently. Rather than interpreting moral problems in terms of what could be handled by applying abstract rules of justice to particular cases, many of the women studied by Gilligan tended to be more concerned with preserving actual human relationships, and with expressing care for those for whom they felt responsible. Their moral reasoning was typically more embedded in a context of particular others than was the reasoning of a comparable group of men.[29] One should not equate tendencies women in fact display with feminist views, since the former may well be the result of the sexist, oppressive conditions in which women's lives have been lived. But many feminists see our own consciously considered experience as lending confirmation to the view that what has come to be called "an ethic of care" needs to be developed. Some think it should supercede "the ethic of justice" of traditional or standard moral theory. Others think it should be integrated with the ethic of justice and rules.

In any case, feminist philosophers are in the process of reevaluating the place of emotion in morality in at least two respects. First, many think morality requires the development of the moral emotions, in contrast to moral theories emphasizing the primacy of reason. As Annette Baier notes, the rationalism typical of traditional moral theory will be challenged when we pay attention to the role of parent. "It might be important," she writes, "for father figures to have rational control over their violent urges to beat to death the children whose screams enrage them, but more than control of such nasty passions seems needed in the mother or primary parent, or parent-substitute, by most psychological theories. They need to love their children, not just to control their irritation."[30] So the emphasis in many traditional theories on rational control over the emotions, "rather than on cultivating desirable forms of emotion,"[31] is challenged by feminist approaches to ethics.

Secondly, emotion will be respected rather than dismissed by many feminist moral philosophers in the process of gaining moral understanding. The experience and practice out of which feminist moral theory can be expected to be developed will include embodied feeling as well as thought. In a recent overview of a vast amount of writing, Kathryn Morgan states that "feminist theorists begin ethical theorizing with embodied, gendered subjects who have particular histories, particular communities, particular allegiances, and particular visions of human flourishing. The starting point involves valorizing what has frequently been most mistrusted and despised in the western philosophical tradition...."[32] Among the elements being reevaluated are feminine emotions. The "care" of the alternative feminist approach to morality appreciates rather than rejects emotion. The caring relationships important to feminist morality cannot be understood in terms of abstract rules or moral reasoning. And the "weighing" so often needed between the conflicting claims of some relationships and others cannot be settled by deduction or rational calculation. A feminist ethic will not just acknowledge emotion, as do Utilitarians, as giving us the objectives toward which moral rationality can direct us. It will embrace emotion as providing at least a partial basis for morality itself, and for moral understanding.

Annette Baier stresses the centrality of trust for an adequate morality.[33] Achieving and maintaining trusting, caring relationships is quite different from acting in accord with rational principles, or satisfying the individual desires of either self or other. Caring, empathy, feeling with others, being sensitive to each other's feelings, all may be better guides to what morality requires in actual contexts than may abstract rules of reason, or rational calculation, or at least they may be necessary components of an adequate morality.

The fear that a feminist ethic will be a relativistic "situation ethic" is misplaced. Some feelings can be as widely shared as are rational beliefs, and feminists do not see their views as reducible to "just another attitude."[34] In her discussion of the differences between feminist medical ethics and nonfeminist medical ethics, Susan Sherwin gives an example of how feminists reject the mere case by case approach that has come to predominate in nonfeminist medical ethics. The latter also rejects the excessive reliance on abstract rules characteristic of standard ethics, and in this way resembles feminist ethics. But the very focus on cases in isolation from one another deprives this approach from attending to general features in the institutions and practices of medicine that, among other faults,

systematically contribute to the oppression of women.[35] The difference of approach can be seen in the treatment of issues in the new reproductive technologies, where feminists consider how the new technologies may further decrease the control of women over reproduction.

This difference might be thought to be one of substance rather than of method, but Sherwin shows the implications for method also. With respect to reproductive technologies one can see especially clearly the deficiencies of the case by case approach: what needs to be considered is not only choice in the purely individualistic interpretation of the case by case approach, but control at a more general level and how it affects the structure of gender in society. Thus, a feminist perspective does not always counsel attention to specific case vs. appeal to general considerations, as some sort of methodological rule. But the general considerations are often not the purely abstract ones of traditional and standard moral theory, they are the general features and judgments to be made about cases in actual (which means, so far, patriarchal) societies. A feminist evaluation of a moral problem should never omit the political elements involved; and it is likely to recognize that political issues cannot be dealt with adequately in purely abstract terms any more than can moral issues.

The liberal tradition in social and moral philosophy argues that in pluralistic society* and even more clearly in a pluralistic world, we cannot agree on our visions of the good life, on what is the best kind of life for humans, but we can hope to agree on the minimal conditions for justice, for coexistence within a framework allowing us to pursue our visions of the good life.[36] Many feminists contend that the commitment to justice needed for agreement *in actual conditions* on even minimal requirements of justice is as likely to demand relational feelings as a rational recognition of abstract principles. Human beings can and do care, and are capable of caring far more than at present, about the sufferings of children quite distant from them, about the prospects for future generations, and about the well-being of the globe. The liberal tradition's mutually disinterested rational individualists

---

* A society that values (or at least tolerates) a range of different, and even mutually incompatible, views among its members of what constitutes a "good life." For example, toleration of different religions and sexual orientations is a form of pluralism.

would seem unlikely to care enough to take the actions needed to achieve moral decency at a global level, or environmental sanity for decades hence, as they would seem unable to represent caring relationships within the family and among friends. As Annette Baier puts it, "A moral theory, it can plausibly be claimed, cannot regard concern for new and future persons as an optional charity left for those with a taste for it. If the morality the theory endorses is to sustain itself, it must provide for its own continuers, not just take out a loan on a carefully encouraged maternal instinct or on the enthusiasm of a self-selected group of environmentalists, who make it their business or hobby to be concerned with what we are doing to mother earth."[37]

The possibilities as well as the problems (and we are well aware of some of them) in a feminist reenvisioning of emotion and reason need to be further developed, but we can already see that the views of nonfeminist moral theory are unsatisfactory.

II. The Public and the Private

The second questionable aspect of the history of ethics on which I focused was its conception of the distinction between the public and the private. As with the split between reason and emotion, feminists are showing how gender-bias has distorted previous conceptions of these spheres, and we are trying to offer more appropriate understandings of "private" morality and "public" life.

Part of what feminists have criticized has been the way the distinction has been accompanied by a supposition that what occurs in the household occurs as if on an island beyond politics, whereas the personal is highly affected by the political power beyond, from legislation about abortion to the greater earning power of men, to the interconnected division of labor by gender both within and beyond the household, to the lack of adequate social protection for women against domestic violence.[38] Of course we recognize that the family is not identical to the state, and we need concepts for thinking about the private or personal, and the public or political. But they will have to be very different from the traditional concepts.

Feminists have also criticized deeper assumptions about what is distinctively human and what is "natural" in the public and private aspects of human life, and what is meant by "natural" in connection with women.[39] Consider the associations that have traditionally been built up: the public realm is seen as the distinctively human realm in which man transcends his animal nature, while the private realm of the household is seen as the natural region in which women merely reproduce the species.[40] These associations are extraordinarily pervasive in standard concepts and theories, in art and thought and cultural ideals, and especially in politics.

Dominant patterns of thought have seen women as primarily mothers, and mothering as the performance of a primarily biological function. Then it has been supposed that while engaging in political life is a specifically human activity, women are engaged in an activity which is not specifically human. Women accordingly have been thought to be closer to nature than men,[41] to be enmeshed in a biological function involving processes more like those in which other animals are involved than like the rational discussion of the citizen in the polis, or the glorious battles of noble soldiers, or the trading and rational contracting of "economic man." The total or relative exclusion of women from the domain of public life has then been seen as either inevitable or appropriate.

The view that women are more determined by biology than are men is still extraordinarily prevalent. It is as questionable from a feminist perspective as many other traditional misinterpretations of women's experience. Human mothering is an extremely different activity from the mothering engaged in by other animals. The work and speech of men is recognized as very different from what might be thought of as the "work" and "speech" of other animals. Human mothering is fully as different from animal mothering. Of course all human beings are animal as well as human. But to whatever extent it is appropriate to recognize a difference between "man" and other animals, so would it be appropriate to recognize a comparable difference between "woman" and other animals, and between the activities—including mothering—engaged in by women and the behavior of other animals.

Human mothering shapes language and culture, it forms human social personhood, it develops morality. Animal behavior can be highly impressive and complex, but it does not have built into it any of the consciously chosen aims of morality. In creating human social persons, human mothering is different in kind from merely propagating a species. And human mothering can be fully as creative an activity as those activities traditionally thought of as distinctively human, because to create *new* persons, and new types of *persons*, can surely be as creative as to make new objects, products, or institutions. *Human* mothering is no more "natural" or "primarily biological" than is any other human activity.

Consider nursing an infant, often thought of as the epitome of a biological process with which mothering is associated and women are identified. There is no reason to think of human nursing as any more simply biological than there is to think of, say, a businessmen's lunch this way. Eating is a biological process, but what and how and with whom we eat are thoroughly cultural. Whether and how long and with whom a woman nurses an infant, are also human, cultural matters. If men transcend the natural by conquering new territory and trading with their neighbors and making deals over lunch to do so, women can transcend the natural by choosing not to nurse their children when they could, or choosing to nurse them when their culture tells them not to, or singing songs to their infants as they nurse, or nursing in restaurants to overcome the prejudices against doing so, or thinking human thoughts as they nurse, and so forth. Human culture surrounds and characterizes the activity of nursing as it does the activities of eating, or governing, or writing, or thinking.

We are continually being presented with images of the humanly new and creative as occurring in the public realm of the polis, or the realms of marketplace or of art and science outside the household. The very term 'reproduction' suggests mere repetition, the "natural" bringing into existence of repeated instances of the same human animal. But human reproduction is not repetition.[42] This is not to suggest that bringing up children in the interstices* of patriarchal society, in society structured by institutions supporting male dominance, can achieve the potential of transformation latent in the activity of human mothering. But the activity of creating new social persons and new kinds of persons is potentially the most transformative human activity of all. And it suggests that morality should concern itself first of all with this activity, with what its norms and practices ought to be, and with

how the institutions and arrangements throughout society and the world ought to be structured to facilitate the right kinds of development of the best kinds of new persons. The flourishing of children ought to be at the very center of moral and social and political and economic and legal thought, rather than, as at present, at the periphery, if attended to at all.

Revised conceptions of public and private have significant implications for our conceptions of human beings and relationships between them. Some feminists suggest that instead of seeing human relationships in terms of the impersonal ones of the "public" sphere, as standard political and moral theory has so often done, we might consider seeing human relationships in terms of those experienced in the sphere of the "private," or of what these relationships could be imagined to be like in post-patriarchal society.[43] The traditional approach is illustrated by those who generalize, to other regions of human life than the economic, assumptions about "economic man" in contractual relations with other men. It sees such impersonal, contractual relations as paradigmatic, even, on some views, for moral theory. Many feminists, in contrast, consider the realm of what has been misconstrued as the "private" as offering guidance to what human beings and their relationships should be like even in regions beyond those of family and friendship. Sara Ruddick looks at the implications of the practice of mothering for the conduct of peace politics.[44] Marilyn Friedman and Lorraine Code consider friendship, especially as women understand it, as a possible model for human relationships.[45] Others see society as non-contractual rather than as contractual.

Clearly, a reconceptualization is needed of the ways in which every human life is entwined with personal and with social components. Feminist theorists are contributing imaginative work to this project.

III. The Concept of Self

Let me turn now to the third aspect of the history of ethics which I discussed and which feminists are re-envisioning: the concept of self. One of the most important emphases in a feminist approach to morality is the recognition that more attention must be paid

---

* Intervening spaces, cracks.

to the domain between, on the one hand, the self as ego, as self-interested individual, and, on the other hand, the universal, everyone, others in general.[46] Traditionally, ethics has dealt with these poles of individual self and universal all. Usually, it has called for impartiality against the partiality of the egoistic self; sometimes it has defended egoism against claims for a universal perspective. But most standard moral theory has hardly noticed as morally significant the intermediate realm of family relations and relations of friendship, of group ties and neighborhood concerns, especially from the point of view of women. When it has noticed this intermediate realm it has often seen its attachments as threatening to the aspirations of the Man of Reason, or as subversive of "true" morality. In seeing the problems of ethics as problems of reconciling the interests of the self with what would be right or best for "everyone," standard ethics has neglected the moral aspects of the concern and sympathy which people actually feel for particular others, and what moral experience in this intermediate realm suggests for an adequate morality.

The region of "particular others" is a distinct domain, where what can be seen to be artificial and problematic are the very egoistic "self" and the universal "all others" of standard moral theory. In the domain of particular others, the self is already constituted to an important degree by relations with others, and these relations may be much more salient and significant than the interests of any individual self in isolation.[47] The "others" in the picture, however, are not the "all others," or "everyone," of traditional moral theory; they are not what a universal point of view or a view from nowhere could provide.[48] They are, characteristically, actual flesh and blood other human beings for whom we have actual feelings and with whom we have real ties.

From the point of view of much feminist theory, the individualistic assumptions of liberal theory and of most standard moral theory are suspect. Even if we would be freed from the debilitating aspects of dominating male power to "be ourselves" and to pursue our own interests, we would, as persons, still have ties to other persons, and we would at least in part be constituted by such ties. Such ties would be part of what we inherently are. We are, for instance, the daughter or son of given parents, or the mother or father of given children, and we carry with us at least some ties to the racial or ethnic or national group within which we developed into the persons we are.

If we look, for instance, at the realities of the relation between mothering person (who can be female or male) and child, we can see that what we value in the relation cannot be broken down into individual gains and losses for the individual members in the relation. Nor can it be understood in universalistic terms. Self-development apart from the relation may be much less important than the satisfactory development of the relation. What matters may often be the health and growth of and the development of the relation-and-its-members in ways that cannot be understood in the individualistic terms of standard moral theories designed to maximize the satisfaction of self-interest. The universalistic terms of moral theories grounded in what would be right for "all rational beings" or "everyone" cannot handle, either, what has moral value in the relation between mothering person and child.

Feminism is of course not the only locus of criticism of the individualistic and abstractly universalistic features of liberalism and of standard moral theory. Marxists* and communitarians† also see the self as constituted by its social relations. But in their usual form, Marxist and communitarian criticisms pay no more attention than liberalism and standard moral theory to the experience of women, to the context of mothering, or to friendship as women experience it.[49] Some recent nonfeminist criticisms, such as offered by Bernard Williams, of the impartiality required by standard moral theory, stress how a person's identity may be formed by personal projects in ways that do not satisfy universal norms, yet ought to be admired. Such views still interpret morality from the point of

---

* See the section on Justice from this volume for more on Marx.

† Communitarian political theories tend to stress the social role of a shared sense of common purpose and tradition and mutual ties of kinship and affection, as opposed to the typically "liberal" conception of society as constructed out of a set of contractual relations between otherwise unattached individuals. In North America, communitarianism is especially associated with a wave of criticism of liberalism in the 1980s, spearheaded by such philosophers as Alasdair MacIntyre, Michael Sandel, Charles Taylor, and Michael Walzer.

view of an individual and his project, not a social relationship such as that between mothering person and child. And recent nonfeminist criticisms in terms of traditional communities and their moral practices, as seen for instance in the work of Stuart Hampshire and Alasdair MacIntyre, often take traditional gender roles as given, or provide no basis for a radical critique of them.[50] There is no substitute, then, for feminist exploration of the area between ego and universal, as women experience this area, or for the development of a refocused concept of relational self that could be acceptable from a feminist point of view.

Relationships can be evaluated as trusting or mistrustful, mutually considerate or selfish, harmonious or stressful, and so forth. Where trust and consideration are appropriate, which is not always, we can find ways to foster them. But understanding and evaluating relationships, and encouraging them to be what they can be at their best, require us to look at relationships between actual persons, and to see what both standard moral theories and their nonfeminist critics often miss. To be adequate, moral theories must pay attention to the neglected realm of particular others in the actual relationships and actual contexts of women's experience. In doing so, problems of individual self-interest vs. universal rules may recede to a region more like background, out-of-focus insolubility or relative unimportance. The salient problems may then be seen to be how we ought best to guide or to maintain or to reshape the relationships, both close and more distant, that we have, or might have, with actual other human beings. Particular others can be actual children in need in distant continents, or the anticipated children of generations not yet even close to being born. But they are not "all rational beings" or "the greatest number," and the self that is in relationships with particular others and is composed to a significant degree by such relations is not a self whose ego must be pitted against abstract, universal claims. Developing the needed guidance for maintaining and reshaping relationships presents enormous problems, but a first step is to recognize how traditional and nonfeminist moral theory of both an individualistic and communitarian kind falls short in providing it.

The concept of the relational self which is evolving within feminist thought is leading to interesting inquiry in many fields. An example is the work being done at the Stone Center at Wellesley College.[51]

Psychologists there have posited a self-in-relation theory and are conducting empirical inquiries to try to establish how the female self develops. They are working with a theory that a female relational self develops through a mutually empathetic mother-daughter bond.

The work has been influenced by Jean Baker Miller's re-evaluation of women's psychological qualities as strengths rather than weaknesses. In her book *Toward a New Psychology of Women*, published in 1976, Miller identified women's "great desire for affiliation" as one such strength.[52] Nancy Chodorow's *The Reproduction of Mothering*, published in 1978, has also had a significant influence on the work done at the Stone Center, as it has on much feminist inquiry.[53] Chodorow argued that a female affiliative self is reproduced by a structure of parenting in which mothers are the primary caretakers, and sons and daughters develop differently in relation to a parent of the same sex, or a parent of different sex, as primary caretaker. Daughters develop a sense of self by identifying themselves with the mother; they come to define themselves as connected to or in relation with others. Sons, in contrast, develop a sense of self by differentiating themselves from the mother; they come to define themselves as separate from or unconnected to others. An implication often drawn from Chodorow's work is that parenting should be shared equally by fathers and mothers so that children of either sex can develop with caretakers of both same and different sex.

In 1982, Carol Gilligan, building on both Miller and Chodorow, offered her view of the "different voice" with which girls and women express their understanding of moral problems.[54] Like Miller and Chodorow, Gilligan valued tendencies found especially in women to affiliate with others and to interpret their moral responsibilities in terms of their relationships with others. In all, the valuing of autonomy and individual independence over care and concern for relationships, was seen as an expression of male bias. The Stone Center has tried to elaborate and to study a feminist conception of the relational self. In a series of Working Papers, researchers and clinicians have explored the implications of this conception for various issues in women's psychology (e.g., power, anger, work inhibitions, violence, eating patterns) and for therapy.

The self as conceptualized in these studies is seen as having both a need for recognition and a need to understand the other, and these needs are seen as compatible. They are created in the context of mother-child interaction, and are satisfied in a mutually empathetic relationship. This does not require a loss of self, but a relationship of mutuality in which self and other both express intersubjectivity. Both give and take in a way that not only contributes to the satisfaction of their needs as individuals, but also affirms the "larger relational unit" they compose.[55] Maintaining this larger relational unit then becomes a goal, and maturity is seen not in terms of individual autonomy but in terms of competence in creating and sustaining relations of empathy and mutual inter-subjectivity.

The Stone Center psychologists contend that the goal of mutuality is rarely achieved in adult male-female relationships because of the traditional gender system. The gender system leads men to seek autonomy and power over others, and to undervalue the caring and relational connectedness that is expected of women. Women rarely receive the nurturing and empathetic support they provide. Accordingly, these psychologists look to the interaction that occurs in mother-daughter relationships as the best source of insight into the promotion of the healthy, relational self. This research provides an example of exploration into a refocused, feminist conception of the self, and into empirical questions about its development and implications....

To argue for a view of the self as relational does not mean that women need to remain enmeshed in the ties by which they are constituted. In recent decades, especially, women have been breaking free of relationships with parents, with the communities in which they grew up, and with men, relationships in which they defined themselves through the traditional and often stifling expectations of others.[63] These quests for self have often involved wrenching instability and painful insecurity. But the quest has been for a new and more satisfactory relational self, not for the self-sufficient individual of liberal theory. Many might share the concerns expressed by Alison Jaggar that disconnecting ourselves from particular others, as ideals of individual autonomy seem to presuppose we should, might make us incapable of morality, rather than capable of it, if, as so many feminists think, "an ineliminable part of morality consists in responding emotionally to particular others."[64]

I have examined three topics on which feminist philosophers and feminists in other fields are thinking anew about where we should start and how we should focus our attention in ethics. Feminist reconceptualizations and recommendations concerning the relation between reason and emotion, the distinction between public and private, and the concept of the self, are providing insights deeply challenging to standard moral theory. The implications of this work are that we need an almost total reconstruction of social and political and economic and legal theory in all their traditional forms as well as a reconstruction of moral theory and practice at more comprehensive, or fundamental, levels.[65] ■

Suggestions for Critical Reflection

1. Many have argued that the stereotyping of certain characteristics as "female" (e.g., emotional, less concerned with principles, more concerned with relationships than with issues) is harmful for women (not to mention inaccurate). Does an ethics of care risk encouraging these stereotypes?

2. Held draws a contrast between an "ethic of care" and an "ethic of justice," and suggests the former is more appropriate to women's experience than the latter. Does this claim seem right to you? If so, in what ways—if any—does that make an ethic of care a *better moral theory* than an ethic of justice? What potential benefits and pitfalls can you see in the notion of an ethic of care?

3. Held argues that women are no more biologically determined than men, and, in particular, that the activity of mothering is no less "human" than, say, politics or trade. What implications does this have for our view of human relationships, and for morality?

4. Feminist ethicists often pay particular attention to a domain of people intermediate between the self and "everyone": i.e., they focus on our moral relationships to "particular others," our friends, family, and other individuals with whom we have personal relationships. How important, and how defensible, is this shift in focus? *Do* we have special moral responsibilities to particular people—which we do not have to others—just because, for example, they are our friends? If so, is feminist ethics the only theory able to accommodate this insight?

5. Held describes a model of the self which treats it as at least partly constituted by its *relationships* with other people. Does Held mean to suggest that only *women* have a "relational self" or that men do as well? If this model is correct, what are its implications for ethics? For example, how does it affect the problem of moral motivation? What would it do to our conception of justice, rights, and duties? How does it change the nature and value of human autonomy?

Notes

1 See e.g., Cheshire Calhoun, "Justice, Care, Gender Bias," *The Journal of Philosophy* 85 (September, 1988): 451–63.

2 Lorraine Code, "Second Persons," in *Science, Morality and Feminist Theory*, ed. Marsha Hanen and Kai Nielsen (Calgary: University of Calgary Press, 1987), p. 360.

3 See e.g., *Revolutions in Knowledge: Feminism in the Social Sciences*, ed. Sue Rosenberg Zalk and Janice Gordon-Kelter (Boulder: Westview Press, forthcoming).

[...]

26 For an approach to social and political as well as moral issues that attempts to be context-respectful, see Virginia Held, *Rights and Goods. Justifying Social Action* (Chicago: University of Chicago Press, 1989).

27 Margaret Urban Walker, "Moral Understandings: Alternative 'Epistemology' for a Feminist Ethics," *Hypatia* 4 (Summer, 1989): 15–28, p. 19.

28 Ibid., p. 20. See also Iris Marion Young, "Impartiality and the Civic Public. Some Implications of Feminist Critiques of Moral and Political Theory," in Seyla Benhabib and Drucilla Cornell, *Feminism as Critique* (Minneapolis: University of Minnesota Press, 1987).

29 See especially Carol Gilligan, *In a Different Voice. Psychological Theory and Women's Development* (Cambridge, Massachusetts: Harvard University Press, 1988); and Eva Feder Kittay and Diana T. Meyers eds., *Women and Moral Theory* (Totowa, New Jersey: Rowman and Allanheld, 1987).

30 Annette Baier, "The Need for More Than Justice," in *Science, Morality and Feminist Theory*, ed. Hanen and Nielsen, p. 55.

31 Ibid.

32 Kathryn Pauly Morgan, ["Strangers in a Strange Land: Feminists Visit Relativists" in *Perspectives on Relativism*, ed. D. Odegaard and Carole Stewart (Toronto: Agathon Press, 1990),] p. 2.

33 Annette Baier, ["Trust and Anti-Trust," *Ethics* 96 (1986)].

34 See especially Kathryn Pauly Morgan, "Strangers in a Strange Land...."

35 Susan Sherwin, "Feminist and Medical Ethics: Two Different Approaches to Contextual Ethics," *Hypatia* 4 (Summer, 1989): 57–72.

36 See especially the work of John Rawls and Ronald Dworkin; see also Charles Larmore, *Patterns of Moral Complexity* (Cambridge: Cambridge University Press, 1987).

37 Annette Baier, "The Need for More Than Justice," pp. 53–54.

38 See e.g., Linda Nicholson, *Gender and History. The Limits of Social Theory in the Age of the Family* (New York: Columbia University Press, 1986); and Jean Bethke Elshtain, *Public Man, Private Woman* (Princeton, New Jersey: Princeton University Press, 1981). See also Carole Pateman, *The Sexual Contract* (Stanford, California: Stanford University Press, 1988).

39 See e.g., Susan Moller Okin, *Women in Western Political Thought*. See also Alison M. Jaggar, *Feminist Politics and Human Nature* (Totowa, New Jersey: Rowman and Allanheld, 1983).

40 So entrenched is this way of thinking that it was even reflected in Simone de Beauvoir's pathbreaking feminist text *The Second Sex*, published in 1949. Here, as elsewhere, feminists have had to transcend our own early searches for our own perspectives.

41 See e.g., Sherry B. Ortner, "Is Female to Male as Nature Is to Culture?" in *Woman, Culture, and Society*, ed. Michelle Z. Rosaldo and Louise Lamphere (Stanford: Stanford University Press, 1974).

42 For further discussion and an examination of surrounding associations, see Virginia Held, "Birth and Death," in *Ethics* 99 (January 1989): 362–88.

43 See e.g., Virginia Held, "Non-contractual Society: A Feminist View," in *Science, Morality and Feminist Theory*, ed. Hanen and Nielsen.

44 Sarah Ruddick, [*Maternal Thinking: Toward a Politics of Peace* (Boston: Beacon Press, 1989)].

45 See Marilyn Friedman, "Feminism and Modern Friendship: Dislocating the Community," *Ethics* 99 (January 1989): 275–90; and Lorraine Code, "Second Persons."

46 See Virginia Held, "Feminism and Moral Theory," in *Women and Moral Theory*, ed. Kittay and Meyers.

47 See Seyla Benhabib, "The Generalized and the Concrete Other. The Kohlberg-Gilligan Controversy and Moral Theory," in *Women and Moral Theory*, ed. Kittay and Meyers. See also Caroline Whitbeck, "Feminist Ontology: A Different Reality," in *Beyond Domination*, ed. Carol Gould (Totowa, New Jersey: Rowman and Allanheld, 1983).

48 See Thomas Nagel, *The View from Nowhere* (New York: Oxford University Press, 1986). For a feminist critique, see Susan Bordo, "Feminism, Postmodernism, and Gender-Skepticism," in *Feminism/Postmodernism*, ed. Linda Nicholson (New York: Routledge, 1989).

49 On Marxist theory, see e.g., *Women and Revolution*, ed. Lydia Sargent (Boston: South End Press, 1981); Alison Jaggar, *Feminist Politics and Human Nature*; and Ann Ferguson, *Blood at the Root. Motherhood, Sexuality and Male Dominance* (London: Pandora, 1989). On communitarian theory, see Marilyn Friedman, "Feminism and Modern Friendship...," and also her paper "The Social Self and the Partiality Debates," presented at the Society for Women in Philosophy meeting in New Orleans, April 1990.

50 Bernard Williams, *Moral Luck* (Cambridge: Cambridge University Press, 1981); *Public and Private Morality*, ed. Stuart Hampshire (Cambridge: Cambridge University Press, 1978); Alasdair MacIntyre, *After Virtue. A Study in Moral Theory* (Notre Dame, Indiana: University of Notre Dame Press, 1981). For discussion see Susan Moller Okin, *Justice, Gender, and the Family* (New York: Basic Books, 1989).

51 On the Stone Center concept of the self see especially Jean Baker Miller, "The Development of Women's Sense of Self," Wellesley, Massachusetts: Stone Center Working Paper No. 12; Janet Surrey, "The 'Self-in-Relation': A Theory of Women's Development" (Wellesley, Massachusetts: Stone Center Working Paper No. 13); and Judith Jordan, "The Meaning of Mutuality" (Wellesley, Massachusetts: Stone Center Working Paper No. 23). For a feminist but critical view of this work, see Marcia Westkott, "Female Relationality and the Idealized Self," *American Journal of Psychoanalysis* 49 (September, 1989): 239–50.

52 Jean Baker Miller, *Toward a New Psychology of Women* (Boston: Beacon Press, 1976).

53 Nancy Chodorow, *The Reproduction of Mothering: Psychoanalysis and the Sociology of Gender* (Berkeley: University of California Press, 1978).

54 Carol Gilligan, *In a Different Voice*.

55 J.V. Jordan, "The Meaning of Mutuality," p. 2.

[...]

63 See e.g., *Women's Ways of Knowing. The Development of Self, Voice, and Mind*, by Mary Field Belenky, Blyth McVicker Clinchy, Nancy Rule Goldberger, and Jill Mattuck Tarule (New York: Basic Books, 1986).

64 [Alison M. Jaggar, "Feminist Ethics: Some Issues for the Nineties," *Journal of Social Philosophy* 20 (Spring/Fall 1989),] p. 11.

65 This paper is based in part on my Truax Lectures on "The Prospect of Feminist Morality" at Hamilton College on November 2 and 9, 1989. Early versions were also presented at Colgate University; at Queen's University in Kingston, Ontario; at the University of Kentucky; and at the New School for Social Research. I am grateful to all who made possible these occasions and commented on the paper at these times, and to Alison Jaggar, Laura Purdy, and Sara Ruddick for additional discussion.

JUDITH JARVIS THOMSON

The Trolley Problem

Who Was Judith Jarvis Thomson?

A distinguished philosopher of ethics and metaphysics, Judith Jarvis Thomson was born in New York City in 1929. The descendent of a long line of Eastern European rabbis, Thomson officially converted to Judaism when she was 14 years old. After obtaining two BA degrees, one from Barnard College and one from Cambridge University, Thomson completed her PhD in philosophy at Columbia in 1959. She taught at Barnard College from 1956 to 1962 and briefly served as a professor at Boston University before securing a permanent professorship at MIT in 1964. Thomson published numerous influential papers and several books, including *Acts and Other Events* (1977), *The Realm of Rights* (1990), and *Normativity* (2008). She received a prestigious Guggenheim Fellowship in 1986, and was awarded an honorary Doctor of Letters degree from Cambridge in 2015 and from Harvard in 2016. Thomson died in 2020, at the age of 91.

What Is the Structure of This Reading?

Thomson's argument employs a large number of thought experiments—imaginary scenarios with simplified conditions that are meant to draw out the reader's intuitions. Among the thought experiments Thomson discusses are:

1. *Trolley Driver*: An unstoppable trolley is headed toward a group of five workers repairing a section of track and will run down and kill the workers unless the driver diverts the trolley to a different track. The other track contains only one worker, who will inevitably be killed should the driver choose to divert the trolley. Should the driver divert the trolley?
2. *Bystander at the Switch*: A bystander next to the trolley track is observing the above scenario, and sees that the driver of the trolley has fainted without changing the path of the trolley. The bystander is next to a switch which could be used to divert the trolley to the segment of track containing only one worker. Should the bystander flip the switch?
3. *Fat Man*: While standing on a footbridge overlooking a track, a person sees an out-of-control trolley headed toward a group of five workers. The person is standing next to a rather large man, and knows that they could shove the large man off the bridge and onto the trolley tracks below, and that the man's body would then stop the trolley before it kills the five workers. Should this person shove the man onto the tracks?
4. *Transplant*: A surgeon requires five different organs in order to save the lives of five patients, who will otherwise die within a day. A healthy young person shows up at the transplant clinic, requesting only a routine check-up. The young person happens to be a compatible donor for all five of the other patients; however, the potential donor would have to be killed in order to have all five of their organs transplanted, and is unwilling to consent to such an operation. Should the surgeon operate anyway, killing the potential donor in order to save five other people?
5. *Hospital*: Five hospital patients will die unless a certain gas is manufactured to save their lives. However, in order to manufacture this gas, we would have to flood a nearby room with lethal fumes, killing the patient who inhabits that room. Should we manufacture the gas?

Thomson also discusses a number of variations of these scenarios, teasing out the ways in which slight differences can cause us to have very different intuitions about which actions are permissible and which are not.

Each scenario presents a choice that will lead to more-or-less the same two possible outcomes: one in which five people die, and another in which only one person dies. And yet, for many of us (including Thomson), it seems intuitively as though the act leading to only one person's death is permissible in some of these scenarios but not in others. If our intuitions are a reliable guide to right and wrong, then this would seem to show that the morality of an action depends on more than just its outcome. The bulk of Thomson's article is spent considering possible explanations as to why we're permitted to act in some of these situations but not in others. She examines and rejects a number of potential responses before providing her own solution.

Some Useful Background Information

Many of the thought experiments described in this article are of Thomson's own creation. The first variation of the Trolley Driver scenario, however, is borrowed from another important philosopher, Philippa Foot. Foot presented the example as a way of illustrating the "Doctrine of Double Effect," a principle especially influential in Christian philosophy. According to this Doctrine, it is sometimes morally permissible to cause harm when that harm is a side effect of an action intended to bring about something good.

Some Common Misconceptions

1. It's not uncommon for readers of this paper to reject the set of options on offer—to claim, for example, that the trolley driver should instead look for an emergency brake, or derail the trolley, or find some other mechanical solution that would prevent any loss of life. Though it may be commendable to seek out such alternative solutions in real life, to respond to Thomson's thought experiments in this way is to misunderstand their purpose. Thomson deliberately simplifies the mechanics of each scenario and limits the available options so as to focus attention on the comparative merits of only two possible actions. By limiting the options in this way, we may come to better understand the grounds of our moral reasoning.

2. Thomson's claims about which actions are morally permissible are not meant as predictions of how she would behave or of how the majority of people would behave. Rather, they are meant as assessments of the morality of each possible action, regardless of whether we would act accordingly in a situation of high tension and limited time.

How Important and Influential Is This Passage?

Though Thomson's conclusion is itself important, this paper's greater influence is perhaps not so much found in the conclusion itself but rather in the collection of thought experiments it provides. These scenarios, and their use in drawing out intuitions about morality, are well-known not only within academic philosophy but also in other areas of inquiry such as computing science. And over the years they've entered into some areas of popular culture, with variations presented in television, film, and video games.

The Trolley Problem*

I.

Some years ago, Philippa Foot[†] drew attention to an extraordinarily interesting problem.[1] Suppose you are the driver of a trolley.[‡] The trolley rounds a bend, and there come into view ahead five track workmen, who have been repairing the track. The track goes through a bit of a valley at that point, and the sides are steep, so you must stop the trolley if you are to avoid running the five men down. You step on the brakes, but alas

---

* Judith Jarvis Thomson, "The Trolley Problem," *The Yale Law Journal* 94, 6 (May 1985): 1395–1415.

† Philippa Ruth Foot (1920–2010) was an influential British philosopher who wrote primarily on the rationality of morality and helped to re-popularize and modernize virtue ethics.

‡ That is, a tram or streetcar.

they don't work. Now you suddenly see a spur of track leading off to the right. You can turn the trolley onto it, and thus save the five men on the straight track ahead. Unfortunately, Mrs. Foot has arranged that there is one track workman on that spur of track. He can no more get off the track in time than the five can, so you will kill him if you turn the trolley onto him. Is it morally permissible for you to turn the trolley?

Everybody to whom I have put this hypothetical case says, Yes, it is.[2] Some people say something stronger than that it is morally *permissible* for you to turn the trolley: They say that morally speaking, you *must* turn it—that morality requires you to do so. Others do not agree that morality requires you to turn the trolley, and even feel a certain discomfort at the idea of turning it. But everybody says that it is true, at a minimum, that you *may* turn it—that it would not be morally wrong in you to do so.

Now consider a second hypothetical case. This time you are to imagine yourself to be a surgeon, a truly great surgeon. Among other things you do, you transplant organs, and you are such a great surgeon that the organs you transplant always take. At the moment you have five patients who need organs. Two need one lung each, two need a kidney each, and the fifth needs a heart. If they do not get those organs today, they will all die; if you find organs for them today, you can transplant the organs and they will all live. But where to find the lungs, the kidneys, and the heart? The time is almost up when a report is brought to you that a young man who has just come into your clinic for his yearly check-up has exactly the right blood-type, and is in excellent health. Lo, you have a possible donor. All you need do is cut him up and distribute *his* parts among the five who need them. You ask, but he says, "Sorry. I deeply sympathize, but no." Would it be morally permissible for you to operate anyway? Everybody to whom I have put this second hypothetical case says, No, it would not be morally permissible for you to proceed.

Here then is Mrs. Foot's problem: *Why* is it that the trolley driver may turn his trolley, though the surgeon may not remove the young man's lungs, kidneys, and heart?[3] In both cases, one will die if the agent acts, but five will live who would otherwise die—a net saving of

four lives. What difference in the other facts of these cases explains the moral difference between them? I fancy that the theorists of tort and criminal law* will find this problem as interesting as the moral theorist does.

II.

Mrs. Foot's own solution to the problem she drew attention to is simple, straightforward, and very attractive. She would say: Look, the surgeon's choice is between operating, in which case he kills one, and not operating, in which case he lets five die; and killing is surely worse than letting die[4]—indeed, so much worse that we can even say

(I) Killing one is worse than letting five die.

So the surgeon must refrain from operating. By contrast, the trolley driver's choice is between turning the trolley, in which case he kills one, and not turning the trolley, in which case he does not *let five die*, he positively *kills* them. Now surely we can say

(II) Killing five is worse than killing one.

But then that is why the trolley driver may turn his trolley: He would be doing what is worse if he fails to turn it, since if he fails to turn it he kills five.

I do think that that is an attractive account of the matter. It seems to me that if the surgeon fails to operate, he does not kill his five patients who need parts; he merely lets them die. By contrast, if the driver fails to turn his trolley, he does not merely let the five track workmen die; he drives his trolley into them, and thereby kills them.

But there is good reason to think that this problem is not so easily solved as that.

Let us begin by looking at a case that is in some ways like Mrs. Foot's story of the trolley driver. I will call her case *Trolley Driver*; let us now consider a case I will call *Bystander at the Switch*. In that case you have been strolling by the trolley track, and you can see the situation at a glance: The driver saw the five on the track ahead, he stamped on the brakes, the brakes failed, so

---

*   Tort law deals with legal actions seeking a private civil remedy, such as damages, while criminal law addresses criminal wrongs that are punishable by the state.

he fainted. What to do? Well, here is the switch, which you can throw, thereby turning the trolley yourself. Of course you will kill one if you do. But I should think you may turn it all the same.[5]

Some people may feel a difference between these two cases. In the first place, the trolley driver is, after all, captain of the trolley. He is charged by the trolley company with responsibility for the safety of his passengers and anyone else who might be harmed by the trolley he drives. The bystander at the switch, on the other hand, is a private person who just happens to be there.

Second, the driver would be driving a trolley into the five if he does not turn it, and the bystander would not—the bystander will do the five no harm at all if he does not throw the switch.

I think it right to feel these differences between the cases.

Nevertheless, my own feeling is that an ordinary person, a mere bystander, may intervene in such a case. If you see something, a trolley, a boulder, an avalanche, heading towards five, and you can deflect it onto one, it really does seem that—other things being equal—it would be permissible for you to *take* charge, *take* responsibility, and deflect the thing, whoever you may be. Of course you run a moral risk if you do, for it might be that, unbeknownst to you, other things are not equal. It might be, that is, that there is some relevant difference between the five on the one hand, and the one on the other, which would make it morally preferable that the five be hit by the trolley than that the one be hit by it. That would be so if, for example, the five are not track workmen at all, but Mafia members in workmen's clothing, and they have tied the one workman to the right-hand track in the hope that you would turn the trolley onto him. I won't canvass all the many kinds of possibilities, for in fact the moral risk is the same whether you are the trolley driver, or a bystander at the switch.

Moreover, second, we might well wish to ask ourselves what exactly is the difference between what the driver would be doing if he failed to turn the trolley and what the bystander would be doing if he failed to throw the switch. As I said, the driver would be driving a trolley into the five; but what exactly would his driving the trolley into the five consist in? Why, just sitting there, doing nothing! If the driver does just sit there, doing nothing, then that will have been how come he drove his trolley into the five.

I do not mean to make much of that fact about what the driver's driving his trolley into the five would consist in, for it seems to me to be right to say that if he does not turn the trolley, he does drive his trolley into them, and does thereby kill them. (Though this does seem to me to be right, it is not easy to say exactly what makes it so.) By contrast, if the bystander does not throw the switch, he drives no trolley into anybody, and he kills nobody.

But as I said, my own feeling is that the bystander *may* intervene. Perhaps it will seem to some even less clear that morality requires him to turn the trolley than that morality requires the driver to turn the trolley; perhaps some will feel even more discomfort at the idea of the bystander's turning the trolley than at the idea of the driver's turning the trolley. All the same, I shall take it that he *may*.

If he may, there is serious trouble for Mrs. Foot's thesis (I). It is plain that if the bystander throws the switch, he causes the trolley to hit the one, and thus he kills the one. It is equally plain that if the bystander does not throw the switch, he does not cause the trolley to hit the five, he does not kill the five, he merely fails to save them—he lets them die. His choice therefore is between throwing the switch, in which case he kills one, and not throwing the switch, in which case he lets five die. If thesis (I) were true, it would follow that the bystander may not throw the switch, and that I am taking to be false.

III.

I have been arguing that

(I) Killing one is worse than letting five die

is false, and a fortiori* that it cannot be appealed to to explain why the surgeon may not operate in the case I shall call *Transplant*.

I think it pays to take note of something interesting which comes out when we pay close attention to

---

* Latin: "from the stronger." An *a fortiori* inference is one that draws a weaker conclusion on the basis of a stronger conclusion that has already been reached.

(II) Killing five is worse than killing one.

For let us ask ourselves how we would feel about *Transplant* if we made a certain addition to it. In telling you that story, I did not tell you why the surgeon's patients are in need of parts. Let us imagine that the history of their ailments is as follows. The surgeon was badly overworked last fall—some of his assistants in the clinic were out sick, and the surgeon had to take over their duties dispensing drugs. While feeling particularly tired one day, he became careless, and made the terrible mistake of dispensing chemical X to five of the day's patients. Now chemical X works differently in different people. In some it causes lung failure, in others kidney failure, in others heart failure. So these five patients who now need parts need them because of the surgeon's carelessness. Indeed, if he does not get them the parts they need, so that they die, he will have killed them. Does that make a moral difference? That is, does the fact that he will have killed the five if he does nothing make it permissible for him to cut the young man up and distribute his parts to the five who need them?

We could imagine it to have been worse. Suppose what had happened was this: The surgeon was badly overextended last fall, he had known he was named a beneficiary in his five patients' wills, and it swept over him one day to give them chemical X to kill them. Now he repents, and would save them if he could. If he does not save them, he will positively have murdered them. Does *that* fact make it permissible for him to cut the young man up and distribute his parts to the five who need them?

I should think plainly not. The surgeon must not operate on the young man. If he can find no other way of saving his five patients, he will *now* have to let them die—despite the fact that if he now lets them die, he will have killed them.

We tend to forget that some killings themselves include lettings die, and do include them where the act by which the agent kills takes time to cause death—time in which the agent can intervene but does not.

In face of these possibilities, the question arises what we should think of thesis (II), since it *looks* as if it tells us that the surgeon ought to operate, and thus that he may permissibly do so, since if he operates he kills only one instead of five.

There are two ways in which we can go here. First, we can say: (II) does tell us that the surgeon ought to operate, and that shows it is false. Second, we can say: (II) does not tell us that the surgeon ought to operate, and it is true.

For my own part, I prefer the second. If Alfred kills five and Bert kills only one, then questions of motive apart, and other things being equal, what Alfred did *is* worse than what Bert did. If the surgeon does not operate, so that he kills five, then it will later be true that he did something worse than he would have done if he had operated, killing only one—especially if his killing of the five was murder, committed out of a desire for money, and his killing of the one would have been, though misguided and wrongful, nevertheless a well-intentioned effort to save five lives. Taking this line would, of course, require saying that assessments of which acts are worse than which other acts do not by themselves settle the question what it is permissible for an agent to do.

But it might be said that we ought to by-pass (II), for perhaps what Mrs. Foot would have offered us as an explanation of why the driver may turn the trolley in *Trolley Driver* is not (II) itself, but something more complex, such as

(II') If a person is faced with a choice between doing something *here and now* to five, by the doing of which he will kill them, and doing something else *here and now* to one, by the doing of which he will kill only the one, then (other things being equal) he ought to choose the second alternative rather than the first.

We may presumably take (II') to tell us that the driver ought to, and hence permissibly may, turn the trolley in *Trolley Driver*, for we may presumably view the driver as confronted with a choice between here and now driving his trolley into five, and here and now driving his trolley into one. And at the same time, (II') tells us nothing at all about what the surgeon ought to do in *Transplant*, for he is not confronted with such a choice. If the surgeon operates, he does do something by the doing of which he will kill only one; but if the surgeon does not operate, he does not do something by the doing of which he kills five; he merely fails to do something by the doing of which he would make it be the case that he has not killed five.

I have no objection to this shift in attention from (II) to (II'). But we should not overlook an interesting question that lurks here. As it might be put: *Why* should the present tense matter so much? Why should a person prefer killing one to killing five if the alternatives are wholly in front of him, but not (or anyway, not in every case) where one of them is partly behind him? I shall come back to this question briefly later.

Meanwhile, however, even if (II′) can be appealed to in order to explain why the trolley driver may turn his trolley, that would leave it entirely open why the bystander at the switch may turn *his* trolley. For he does not drive a trolley into each of five if he refrains from turning the trolley; he merely lets the trolley drive into each of them.

So I suggest we set *Trolley Driver* aside for the time being. What I shall be concerned with is a first cousin of Mrs. Foot's problem, viz.: Why is it that the bystander may turn his trolley, though the surgeon may not remove the young man's lungs, kidneys, and heart? Since *I* find it particularly puzzling that the bystander may turn his trolley, I am inclined to call this The Trolley Problem. Those who find it particularly puzzling that the surgeon may not operate are cordially invited to call it The Transplant Problem instead.

IV.

It should be clear, I think, that "kill" and "let die" are too blunt to be useful tools for the solving of this problem. We ought to be looking within killings and savings for the ways in which the agents would be carrying them out.

It would be no surprise, I think, if a Kantian* idea occurred to us at this point. Kant said: "Act so that you treat humanity, whether in your own person or in that of another, always as an end and never as a means only." It is striking, after all, that the surgeon who proceeds in *Transplant* treats the young man he cuts up "as a means only": He literally uses the young man's body to save his five, and does so without the young man's consent. And perhaps we may say that the agent in *Bystander at the Switch* does not use his victim to save his five, or (more generally) treat his victim as a means only, and that that is why he (unlike the surgeon) may proceed.

But what exactly is it to treat a person as a means only, or to use a person? And why exactly is it wrong to do this? These questions do not have obvious answers.[6]

Suppose an agent is confronted with a choice between doing nothing, in which case five die, or engaging in a certain course of action, in which case the five live, but one dies. Then perhaps we can say: If the agent chooses to engage in the course of action, then he uses the one to save the five only if, had the one gone out of existence just before the agent started, the agent would have been unable to save the five. That is true of the surgeon in *Transplant*. He needs the young man if he is to save his five; if the young man goes wholly out of existence just before the surgeon starts to operate, then the surgeon cannot save his five. By contrast, the agent in *Bystander at the Switch* does not need the one track workman on the right-hand track if he is to save his five; if the one track workman goes wholly out of existence before the bystander starts to turn the trolley, then the bystander *can* all the same save his five. So here anyway is a striking difference between the cases.

It does seem to me right to think that solving this problem requires attending to the means by which the agent would be saving his five if he proceeded. But I am inclined to think that this is an overly simple way of taking account of the agent's means.

One reason for thinking so[7] comes out as follows. You have been thinking of the tracks in *Bystander at the Switch* as not merely diverging, but continuing to diverge, as in the following picture:

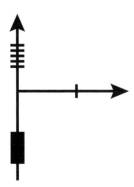

---

* Immanuel Kant (1724–1804) was an influential German philosopher. The adjective "Kantian" refers here to Kant's moral philosophy, which emphasized duties, in particular the "Categorical Imperative," a variation of which is quoted by Thomson. See the reading from Kant earlier in this chapter.

Consider now what I shall call "the loop variant" on this case, in which the tracks do not continue to diverge—they circle back, as in the following picture:

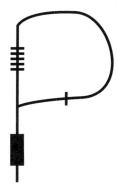

Let us now imagine that the five on the straight track are thin, but thick enough so that although all five will be killed if the trolley goes straight, the bodies of the five will stop it, and it will therefore not reach the one. On the other hand, the one on the right-hand track is fat, so fat that his body will by itself stop the trolley, and the trolley will therefore not reach the five. May the agent turn the trolley? Some people feel more discomfort at the idea of turning the trolley in the loop variant than in the original *Bystander at the Switch*. But we cannot really suppose that the presence or absence of that extra bit of track makes a major moral difference as to what an agent may do in these cases, and it really does seem right to think (despite the discomfort) that the agent may proceed.

On the other hand, we should notice that the agent here needs the one (fat) track workman on the right-hand track if he is to save his five. If the one goes wholly out of existence just before the agent starts to turn the trolley, then the agent cannot save his five[8]— just as the surgeon in *Transplant* cannot save his five if the young man goes wholly out of existence just before the surgeon starts to operate.

Indeed, I should think that there is no plausible account of what is involved in, or what is necessary for, the application of the notions "treating a person as a means only," or "using one to save five," under which the surgeon would be doing this whereas the agent in this variant of *Bystander at the Switch* would

not be. If that is right, then appeals to these notions cannot do the work being required of them here.

V.

Suppose the bystander at the switch proceeds: He throws the switch, thereby turning the trolley onto the right-hand track, thereby causing the one to be hit by the trolley, thereby killing him—but saving the five on the straight track. There are two facts about what he does which seem to me to explain the moral difference between what he does and what the agent in *Transplant* would be doing if *he* proceeded. In the first place, the bystander saves his five by making something that threatens them instead threaten one. Second, the bystander does not do that by means which themselves constitute an infringement of any right of the one's.

As is plain, then, my hypothesis as to the source of the moral difference between the cases makes appeal to the concept of a right. My own feeling is that solving this problem requires making appeal to that concept—or to some other concept that does the same kind of work.[9] Indeed, I think it is one of the many reasons why this problem is of such interest to moral theory that it does force us to appeal to that concept; and by the same token, that we learn something from it about that concept.

Let us begin with an idea, held by many friends of rights, which Ronald Dworkin* expressed crisply in a metaphor from bridge: Rights "trump" utilities.[10] That is, if one would infringe a right in or by acting, then it is not sufficient justification for acting that one would thereby maximize utility. It seems to me that something like this must be correct.

Consideration of this idea suggests the possibility of a very simple solution to the problem. That is, it might be said (i) The reason why the surgeon may not proceed in *Transplant* is that if he proceeds, he maximizes utility, for he brings about a net saving of four lives, but in so doing he would infringe a right of the young man's.

Which right? Well, we might say: The right the young man has against the surgeon that the surgeon

---

* Ronald Dworkin (1931–2013) was an American philosopher and jurist.

not kill him—thus a right in the cluster of rights that the young man has in having a right to life.

Solving this problem requires being able to explain also why the bystander may proceed in *Bystander at the Switch*. So it might be said (ii) The reason why the bystander may proceed is that if he proceeds, he maximizes utility, for he brings about a net saving of four lives, and in so doing he does *not* infringe any right of the one track workman's.

But I see no way—certainly there is no easy way—of establishing that these ideas are true.

Is it clear that the bystander would infringe no right of the one track workman's if he turned the trolley? Suppose there weren't anybody on the straight track, and the bystander turned the trolley onto the right-hand track, thereby killing the one, but not saving anybody, since nobody was at risk, and thus nobody needed saving. Wouldn't that infringe a right of the one workman's, a right in the cluster of rights that he has in having a right to life?

So should we suppose that the fact that there are five track workmen on the straight track who are in need of saving makes the one lack that right—which he would have had if that had not been a fact?

But then why doesn't the fact that the surgeon has five patients who are in need of saving make the young man also lack that right?

I think some people would say there is good (excellent, conclusive) reason for thinking that the one track workman lacks the right (given there are five on the straight track) lying in the fact that (given there are five on the straight track) it is morally permissible to turn the trolley onto him. But if your reason for thinking the one lacks the right is that it is permissible to turn the trolley onto him, then you can hardly go on to explain its being permissible to turn the trolley onto him by appeal to the fact that he lacks the right. It pays to stress this point: If you want to say, as (ii) does, that the bystander may proceed because he maximizes utility and infringes no right, then you need an independent account of what makes it be the case that he infringes no right—independent, that is, of its being the case that he may proceed.

There is *some* room for maneuver here. Any plausible theory of rights must make room for the possibility of waiving a right, and within that category, for the possibility of failing to have a right by virtue of assumption of risk; and it might be argued that that is what is involved here, i.e., that track workmen know of the risks of the job, and consent to run them when signing on for it.

But that is not really an attractive way of dealing with this difficulty. Track workmen certainly do not explicitly consent to being run down with trolleys when doing so will save five who are on some other track—certainly they are not asked to consent to this at the time of signing on for the job. And I doubt that they consciously assume the risk of it at that or any other time. And in any case, what if the six people involved had not been track workmen? What if they had been young children? What if they had been people who had been shoved out of helicopters? Wouldn't it all the same be permissible to turn the trolley?

So it is not clear what (independent) reason could be given for thinking that the bystander will infringe no right of the one's if he throws the switch.

I think, moreover, that there is *some* reason to think that the bystander will infringe a right of the one if he throws the switch, even though it is permissible for him to do so. What I have in mind issues simply from the fact that if the bystander throws the switch, then he does what will kill the one. Suppose the bystander proceeds, and that the one is now dead. The bystander's motives were, of course, excellent—he acted with a view to saving five. But the one did not volunteer his life so that the five might live; the bystander volunteered it for him. The bystander made him pay with his life for the bystander's saving of the five. This consideration seems to me to lend some weight to the idea that the bystander did do him a wrong—a wrong it was morally permissible to do him, since five were saved, but a wrong *to him* all the same.

Consider again that lingering feeling of discomfort (which, as I said, some people do feel) about what the bystander does if he turns the trolley. No doubt it is permissible to turn the trolley, but still ... but still .... People who feel this discomfort also think that, although it is permissible to turn the trolley, it is not morally required to do so. My own view is that they are right to feel and think these things. We would be able to explain why this is so if we supposed that if the bystander turns the trolley, then he does do the one track workman a wrong—if we supposed, in particular, that he infringes a right of the one track workman's which is in that cluster of rights which the workman has in having a right to life.[11]

I do not for a moment take myself to have established that (ii) is false. I have wished only to draw attention to the difficulty that lies ahead of a person who thinks (ii) true, and also to suggest that there is some reason to think that the bystander would infringe a right of the one's if he proceeded, and thus some reason to think that (ii) is false. It can easily be seen that if there is some reason to think the bystander would infringe a right of the one's, then there is also some reason to think that (i) is false—since if the bystander does infringe a right of the one's if he proceeds, and may nevertheless proceed, then it cannot be the fact that the surgeon infringes a right of the young man's if *he* proceeds which makes it impermissible for *him* to do so.

Perhaps a friend of (i) and (ii) can establish that they are true. I propose that, just in case he can't, we do well to see if there isn't some other way of solving this problem than by appeal to them. In particular, I propose we grant that both the bystander and the surgeon would infringe a right of their ones, a right in the cluster of rights that the ones' have in having a right to life, and that we look for some *other* difference between the cases which could be appealed to to explain the moral difference between them.

Notice that accepting this proposal does not commit us to rejecting the idea expressed in that crisp metaphor of Dworkin's. We can still say that rights trump utilities—if we can find a further feature of what the bystander does if he turns the trolley (beyond the fact that he maximizes utility) which itself trumps the right, and thus makes it permissible to proceed.

VI.

As I said, my own feeling is that the trolley problem can be solved only by appeal to the concept of a right—but not by appeal to it in as simple a way as that discussed in the preceding section. What we were attending to in the preceding section was only the fact that the agents would be killing and saving if they proceeded; what we should be attending to is the means by which they would kill and save.[12] (It is very tempting, because so much simpler, to regard a human act as a solid nugget, without internal structure, and to try to trace its moral value to the shape of its surface, as it were. The trolley problem seems to me to bring home that that will not do.)

I said earlier that there seem to me to be two crucial facts about what the bystander does if he proceeds in *Bystander at the Switch*. In the first place, he saves his five by making something that threatens them instead threaten the one. And second, he does not do that by means which themselves constitute infringements of any right of the one's.

Let us begin with the first.

If the surgeon proceeds in *Transplant*, he plainly does not save his five by making something that threatens them instead threaten one. It is organ-failure that threatens his five, and it is not *that* which he makes threaten the young man if he proceeds.

Consider another of Mrs. Foot's cases, which I shall call *Hospital*.

> Suppose [Mrs. Foot says] that there are five patients in a hospital whose lives could be saved by the manufacture of a certain gas, but that this will inevitably release lethal fumes into the room of another patient whom for some reason we are unable to move.[13]

Surely it would not be permissible for us to manufacture the gas.

In *Transplant* and *Hospital*, the five at risk are at risk from their ailments, and this might be thought to make a difference. Let us by-pass it. In a variant on *Hospital*—which I shall call *Hospital'*—all six patients are convalescing. The five at risk are at risk, not from their ailments, but from the ceiling of their room, which is about to fall on them. We can prevent this by pumping on a ceiling-support-mechanism; but doing so will inevitably release lethal fumes into the room of the sixth. Here too it is plain we may not proceed.

Contrast a case in which lethal fumes are being released by the heating system in the basement of a building next door to the hospital. They are headed towards the room of five. We can deflect them towards the room of one. Would that be permissible? I should think it would be—the case seems to be in all relevant respects like *Bystander at the Switch*.

In *Bystander at the Switch*, something threatens five, and if the agent proceeds, he saves the five by making that very thing threaten the one instead of the five. That is not true of the agents in *Hospital'* or *Hospital* or *Transplant*. In *Hospital'*, for example, what threatens the five is the ceiling, and the agent does not save them by making *it* threaten the one, he saves them by doing what will make something wholly different (some lethal fumes) threaten the one.

Why is this difference morally important? Other things being equal, to kill a man is to infringe his right to life, and we are therefore morally barred from killing. It is not enough to justify killing a person that if we do so, five others will be saved: To say that if we do so, five others will be saved is merely to say that utility will be maximized if we proceed, and that is not by itself sufficient to justify proceeding. Rights trump utilities. So if that is all that can be said in defense of killing a person, then killing that person is not permissible.

But that five others will be saved is not all that can be said in defense of killing in *Bystander at the Switch*. The bystander who proceeds does not merely minimize the number of deaths which get caused: He minimizes the number of deaths which get caused by something that already threatens people, and that will cause deaths whatever the bystander does.

The bystander who proceeds does not make something be a threat to people which would otherwise not be a threat to anyone; he makes be a threat to fewer what is already a threat to more. We might speak here of a "distributive exemption," which permits arranging that something that will do harm anyway shall be better distributed than it otherwise would be—shall (in *Bystander at the Switch*) do harm to fewer rather than more. Not just any distributive intervention is permissible: It is not in general morally open to us to make one die to save five. But other things being equal, it is not morally required of us that we let a burden descend out of the blue onto five when we can make it instead descend onto one.

I do not find it clear why there should be an exemption for, and only for, making a burden which is descending onto five descend, instead, onto one. That there is seems to me very plausible, however. On the one hand, the agent who acts under this exemption makes be a threat to one something that is *already* a threat to more, and thus something that will do harm *whatever* he does; on the other hand, the exemption seems to allow those acts which intuition tells us are clearly permissible, and to rule out those acts which intuition tells us are clearly impermissible.

VII.

More precisely, it is not morally required of us that we let a burden descend out of the blue onto five when we can make it instead descend onto one *if* we can make it descend onto the one by means which do not themselves constitute infringements of rights of the one.

Consider a case—which I shall call *Fat Man*—in which you are standing on a footbridge over the trolley track. You can see a trolley hurtling down the track, out of control. You turn around to see where the trolley is headed, and there are five workmen on the track where it exits from under the footbridge. What to do? Being an expert on trolleys, you know of one certain way to stop an out-of-control trolley: Drop a really heavy weight in its path. But where to find one? It just so happens that standing next to you on the footbridge is a fat man, a really fat man. He is leaning over the railing, watching the trolley; all you have to do is to give him a little shove, and over the railing he will go, onto the track in the path of the trolley. Would it be permissible for you to do this? Everybody to whom I have put this case says it would not be. But why?

Suppose the agent proceeds. He shoves the fat man, thereby toppling him off the footbridge into the path of the trolley, thereby causing him to be hit by the trolley, thereby killing him—but saving the five on the straight track. Then it is true of this agent, as it is true of the agent in *Bystander at the Switch*, that he saves his five by making something which threatens them instead threaten one.

But *this* agent does so by means which themselves constitute an infringement of a right of the one's. For shoving a person is infringing a right of his. So also is toppling a person off a footbridge.

I should stress that doing these things is infringing a person's rights even if doing them does not cause his death—even if doing them causes him no harm at all. As I shall put it, shoving a person, toppling a person off a footbridge, are *themselves* infringements of rights of his. A theory of rights ought to give an account of what makes it be the case that doing either of these things is itself an infringement of a right of his. But I think we may take it to be a datum* that it

---

* Singular of "data"—in this case, meaning something we are entitled to assume as true.

is, the job which confronts the theorist of rights being, not to establish that it is, but rather to explain why it is.

Consider by contrast the agent in *Bystander at the Switch*. He too, if he proceeds, saves five by making something that threatens them instead threaten one. But the means he takes to make that be the case are these: Turn the trolley onto the right-hand track. And turning the trolley onto the right-hand track is not *itself* an infringement of a right of anybody's. The agent would do the one no wrong at all if he turned the trolley onto the right-hand track, and by some miracle the trolley did not hit him.

We might of course have imagined it not necessary to shove the fat man. We might have imagined that all you need do to get the trolley to threaten him instead of the five is to wobble the handrail, for the handrail is low, and he is leaning on it, and wobbling it will cause him to fall over and off. Wobbling the handrail would be impermissible, I should think—no less so than shoving. But then there is room for an objection to the idea that the contrast I point to will help explain the moral differences among these cases. For it might be said that if you wobble the handrail, thereby getting the trolley to threaten the one instead of the five, then the means you take to get this to be the case are just these: Wobble the handrail. But doing that is not *itself* an infringement of a right of anybody's. You would do the fat man no wrong at all if you wobbled the handrail and no harm came to him in consequence of your doing so. In this respect, then, your situation seems to be exactly like that of the agent in *Bystander at the Switch*. Just as the means he would be taking to make the trolley threaten one instead of five would not constitute an infringement of a right, so also would the means you would be taking to make the trolley threaten one instead of five not constitute an infringement of a right.

What I had in mind, however, is a rather tighter notion of "means" than shows itself in this objection. By hypothesis, wobbling the handrail will cause the fat man to topple onto the track in the path of the trolley, and thus will cause the trolley to threaten him instead of the five. But the trolley will not threaten him instead of the five unless wobbling the handrail does cause him to topple. Getting the trolley to threaten the fat man instead of the five *requires* getting him into its path. You get the trolley to threaten him instead of them by wobbling the handrail only if, and only because, by wobbling the handrail you topple him into the path of the trolley.

What I had in mind, then, is a notion of "means" which comes out as follows. Suppose you get a trolley to threaten one instead of five by wobbling a handrail. The means you take to get the trolley to threaten the one instead of the five include wobbling the handrail, *and* all those further things that you have to succeed in doing by wobbling the handrail if the trolley is to threaten the one instead of the five.

So the means by which the agent in *Fat Man* gets the trolley to threaten one instead of five include toppling the fat man off the footbridge; and doing that is itself an infringement of a right of the fat man's. By contrast, the means by which the agent in *Bystander at the Switch* gets the trolley to threaten one instead of five include no more than getting the trolley off the straight track onto the right-hand track; and doing that is not itself an infringement of a right of anybody's.

VIII.

It is arguable, however, that what is relevant is not that toppling the fat man off the footbridge is itself an infringement of *a* right of the fat man's but rather that toppling him off the footbridge is itself an infringement of a particularly stringent right of his.

What I have in mind comes out in yet another variant on *Bystander at the Switch*. Here the bystander must cross (without permission) a patch of land that belongs to the one in order to get to the switch; thus in order to get the trolley to threaten the one instead of five, the bystander must infringe a right of the one's. May he proceed?

Or again, in order to get the switch thrown, the bystander must use a sharply pointed tool, and the only available sharply pointed tool is a nailfile that belongs to the one; here too the bystander must infringe a right of the one's in order to get the trolley to threaten the one instead of five. May he proceed?

For my own part, I do not find it obvious that he may. (Remember what the bystander will be doing to the one by throwing that switch.) But others tell me they think it clear the bystander may proceed in such a case. If they are right—and I guess we should agree that they are—then that must surely be because the rights which the bystander would have to infringe here are minor, trivial, non-stringent—property rights of no great importance. By contrast, the right to not be toppled off a footbridge onto a trolley track is on any view a stringent right. We shall therefore have to recognize that what is at work in these cases is a matter of degree: If the agent must infringe a stringent right of the one's in order to get something that threatens five to threaten the one (as in *Fat Man*), then he may not proceed, whereas if the agent need infringe no right of the one's (as in *Bystander at the Switch*), or only a more or less trivial right of the one's (as in these variants on *Bystander at the Switch*), in order to get something that threatens five to threaten the one, then he may proceed.

Where what is at work is a matter of degree, it should be no surprise that there are borderline cases, on which people disagree. I confess to having been greatly surprised, however, at the fact of disagreement on the following variant on *Bystander at the Switch*:

> The five on the straight track are regular track workmen. The right-hand track is a dead end, unused in ten years. The Mayor, representing the City, has set out picnic tables on it, and invited the convalescents at the nearby City Hospital to have their meals there, guaranteeing them that no trolleys will ever, for any reason, be turned onto that track. The one on the right-hand track is a convalescent having his lunch there; it would never have occurred to him to do so if the Mayor had not issued his invitation and guarantee. The Mayor was out for a walk; he now stands by the switch.[14]

For the Mayor to get the trolley to threaten the one instead of the five, he must turn the trolley onto the right-hand track; but the one has a right against the Mayor that he not turn the trolley onto the right-hand track—a right generated by an official promise, which was then relied on by the one. (Contrast the original *Bystander at the Switch*, in which the one had no such right.) My own feeling is that it is plain the Mayor may not proceed. To my great surprise, I find that some people think he may. I conclude they think the right less stringent than I do.

In any case, that distributive exemption that I spoke of earlier is very conservative. It permits intervention into the world to get an object that already threatens death to those many to instead threaten death to these few, but only by acts that are not themselves gross impingements on the few. That is, the intervenor must not use means that infringe stringent rights of the few in order to get his distributive intention carried out.

It could of course be argued that the fact that the bystander of the original *Bystander at the Switch* makes threaten the one what already threatens the five, and does so by means that do not themselves constitute infringements of any right of the one's (not even a trivial right of the one's), shows that the bystander in that case infringes no right of the one's at all. That is, it could be argued that we have here that independent ground for saying that the bystander does not infringe the one's right to life which I said would be needed by a friend of (ii).[15] But I see nothing to be gained by taking this line, for I see nothing to be gained by supposing it never permissible to infringe a right; and something is lost by taking this line, namely the possibility of viewing the bystander as doing the one a wrong if he proceeds—albeit a wrong it is permissible to do him.

IX.

What counts as "*an* object which threatens death"? What marks one threat off from another? I have no doubt that ingenious people can construct cases in which we shall be unclear whether to say that if the agent proceeds, he makes threaten the one the very same thing as already threatens the five.

Moreover, which are the interventions in which the agent gets a thing that threatens five to instead threaten one by means that themselves constitute infringements of stringent rights of the one's? I have no doubt that ingenious people can construct cases in which we shall all be unclear whether to say that the agent's means do constitute infringements of stringent rights—and cases also in which we shall be unclear whether to say the agent's means constitute infringements of any rights at all.

But it is surely a mistake to look for precision in the concepts brought to bear to solve this problem: There isn't any to be had. It would be enough if cases in which it seems to us unclear whether to say "same threat," or unclear whether to say "non-right-infringing-means," also seemed to us to be cases in which it is unclear whether the agent may or may not proceed; and if also coming to see a case as one to which these expressions do (or do not) apply involves coming to see the case as one in which the agent may (or may not) proceed.

X.

If these ideas are correct, then we have a handle on anyway some of the troublesome cases in which people make threats. Suppose a villain says to us "I will cause a ceiling to fall on five unless you send lethal fumes into the room of one." Most of us think it would not be permissible for us to accede to this threat. Why? We may think of the villain as part of the world around the people involved, a part which is going to drop a burden on the five if we do not act. On this way of thinking of him, nothing *yet* threatens the five (certainly no ceiling as yet threatens them) and a fortiori we cannot save the five by making what (already) threatens them instead threaten the one. Alternatively, we may think of the villain as himself a threat to the five. But sending the fumes in is not making *him* be a threat to the one instead of to the five. The hypothesis I proposed, then, yields what it should: We may not accede.

That is because the hypothesis I proposed says nothing at all about the source of the threat to the five. Whether the threat to the five is, or is caused by, a human being or anything else, it is not permissible to do what will kill one to save the five except by making what threatens the five itself threaten the one.

By contrast, it seems to me very plausible to think that if a villain has started a trolley towards five, we may deflect the trolley towards one—other things being equal, of course. If a trolley is headed towards five, and we can deflect it towards one, we *may*, no matter who or what caused it to head towards the five.

I think that these considerations help us in dealing with a question I drew attention to earlier. Suppose a villain says to us "I will cause a ceiling to fall on five unless you send lethal fumes into the room of one." If we refuse, so that he does what he threatens to do, then he surely does something very much worse than we would be doing if we acceded to his threat and sent the fumes in. If we accede, we do something misguided and wrongful, but not nearly as bad as what he does if we refuse.

It should be stressed: The fact that he will do something worse if we do not send the fumes in does not entail that we ought to send them in, or even that it is permissible for us to do so.

How after all could that entail that we may send the fumes in? The fact that we would be saving five lives by sending the fumes in does not itself make it permissible for us to do so. (Rights trump utilities.) How could adding that the taker of those five lives would be doing what is worse than we would tip the balance? If we may not infringe a right of the one in order to save the five lives, it cannot possibly be thought that we may infringe the right of that one in order, not merely to save the five lives, but to make the villain's moral record better than it otherwise would be.

For my own part, I think that considerations of motives apart, and other things being equal, it does no harm to say that

(II) Killing five is worse than killing one

is, after all, true. *Of course* we shall then have to say that assessments of which acts are worse than which do not by themselves settle the question of what is permissible for a person to do. For we shall have to say that, despite the truth of (II), it is not the case that we are required to kill one in order that another person shall not kill five, or even that it is everywhere permissible for us to do this.

What is of interest is that what holds interpersonally also holds intra-personally. I said earlier that we might imagine the surgeon of *Transplant* to have caused the ailments of his five patients. Let us imagine the worst: He gave them chemical X precisely in order to cause their deaths, in order to inherit from them. Now he repents. But the fact that he would be saving five lives by operating on the one does not itself make it permissible for him to operate on the one. (Rights trump utilities.) And if he may not infringe a right of the one in order to save the five lives, it cannot possibly be thought that he may infringe the right of that one in order, not merely to save the five lives, but to make his own moral record better than it otherwise would be.

Another way to put the point is this: Assessments of which acts are worse than which have to be directly relevant to the agent's circumstances if they are to have a bearing on what he may do. If A threatens to kill five unless B kills one, then although killing five is worse than killing one, these are not the alternatives open to B. The alternatives open to B are: Kill one, thereby forestalling the deaths of five (and making A's moral record better than it otherwise would be), or let it be the case that A kills five. And the supposition that it would be worse for B to choose to kill the one is entirely compatible with the supposition that killing five is worse than killing one. Again, the alternatives open to the surgeon are: Operate on the one, thereby saving five (and making the surgeon's own moral record better than it otherwise would be), or let it be the case that he himself will have killed the five. And the supposition that it would be worse for the surgeon to choose to operate is entirely compatible with the supposition that killing five is worse than killing one.

On the other hand, suppose a second surgeon is faced with a choice between here and now giving chemical X to five, thereby killing them, and operating on, and thereby killing, only one. (It taxes the imagination to invent such a second surgeon, but let that pass. And compare *Trolley Driver*.) Then, other things being equal, it does seem he may choose to operate on the one. Some people would say something stronger, namely that he is required to make this choice. Perhaps they would say that

(II′) If a person is faced with a choice between doing something *here and now* to five, by the doing

of which he will kill them, and doing something else *here and now* to one, by the doing of which he will kill only the one, then (other things being equal) he ought to choose the second alternative rather than the first

is a quite general moral truth. Whether or not the second surgeon is morally required to make this choice (and thus whether or not (II′) is a general moral truth), it does seem to be the case that he may. But this did seem puzzling. As I put it: Why should the present tense matter so much?

It is plausible to think that the present tense matters because the question for the agent at the time of acting is about the present, viz., "What may I here and now do?," and because that question is the same as the question "Which of the alternatives here and now open to me may I choose?" The alternatives now open to the second surgeon are: kill five or kill one. If killing five is worse than killing one, then perhaps he ought to, but at any rate he may, kill the one. ■

Suggestions for Critical Reflection

1. Thomson frequently appeals to her own intuitions about which actions are morally permissible. In responding to the various scenarios, she uses phrases such as "my own feeling is," "it really does seem right to think," and "surely it would not." For the most part, these claims are presented without further argument. Do your own intuitions about these scenarios align with Thomson's, or do they differ? Is there a general moral principle you can think of that would justify your intuitive beliefs about which of the actions are permissible and which are not?

2. If you are familiar with some standard moral theories—represented in this chapter by Aristotle (virtue theory), Kant (deontology), Mill (consequentialism), and Held (care ethics)—consider how these theories would approach the various scenarios Thomson describes. When Thomson endorses Dworkin's dictum "rights trump utilities," is she

opting for one type of moral theory over others? Is she right to do so?

3. Most of us will not, in the course of our lives, encounter life-or-death moral choices closely resembling Thomson's thought experiments. Are there other contexts of ethical and political decision-making in which our intuitions regarding these thought experiments may provide insight? Think especially of contexts in which we are forced to weigh good consequences against other principles or rights.

4. Some have suggested the trolley problem may have practical relevance in connection with self-driving vehicles. Suppose, for example, that a driver realizes the inevitability of a high-speed collision and is able to either swerve left to kill or injure one person or continue in a straight path to kill or injure five. In most contexts, a human driver simply wouldn't have time to compare and decide between these options. However, this decision

might be possible for a vehicle navigated by artificial intelligence, equipped with sensors and programming capable of assessing the physical variables at play and predicting probable outcomes. In programming such an AI, should we design it to maximize the number of lives saved, always sacrificing one life if doing so is likely to spare multiple lives, even if this means veering off course? Should the AI take into account other factors, such as whether the five people at risk are adhering to the rules of the road, or whether they are young or old? Should the AI favor the life of any human passengers it is transporting, over the lives of people outside of the vehicle?

5. In recent decades, some philosophers have used surveys and experimentation to determine our common intuitions regarding thought experiments of the kind Thomson discusses. One such survey found that 81 per cent of American respondents

agreed that one should change the path of the trolley in the "Bystander at the Switch" scenario, while only 63 per cent of Russian respondents and 52 per cent of Chinese respondents agreed.* Does this apparent cultural variation undermine Thomson's argument in any way? Does this kind of experimental data have bearing on the philosophical issues at hand?

6. Also in recent years, some psychologists and philosophers have raised criticisms of trolley-problem type thought experiments, arguing that they are too extreme and unrealistic to elicit genuine moral intuitions (or teach genuine moral lessons), or that forcing people to think about ethics in this kind of calculating way is a distortion of how we really reason, or should reason, in ethical situations.† What do you make of these kinds of worries?

Notes

1 *See* P. FOOT, *The Problem of Abortion and the Doctrine of the Double Effect*, in VIRTUES AND VICES AND OTHER ESSAYS IN MORAL PHILOSOPHY 19 (1978).

2 I think it possible (though by no means certain) that John Taurek would say No, it is not permissible to (all simply) turn the trolley; what you ought to do is flip a coin. *See* Taurek, *Should the Numbers Count?*, 6 PHIL. & PUB. AFF. 293 (1977). (But he is there concerned with a different kind of case, namely that in which what is in question is not whether we may do what harms one to avoid harming five, but whether we may or ought to choose to save five in preference to saving one.) For criticism of Taurek's article, see Parfit, *Innumerate Ethics*, 7 PHIL. & PUB. AFF. 285 (1978).

3 I doubt that anyone would say, with any hope of getting agreement from others, that the surgeon ought to flip a coin. So even if you think that the trolley driver ought to flip a coin, there would remain, for you, an analogue of Mrs. Foot's problem, namely: Why ought the trolley driver flip a coin, whereas the surgeon may not?

4 Mrs. Foot speaks more generally of causing injury and failing to provide aid; and her reason for thinking that the former is worse than the latter is that the negative duty to refrain from causing injury is stricter than the positive duty to provide aid. *See* P. FOOT, *supra* note 1, at 27–29.

5 A similar case (intended to make a point similar to the one that I shall be making) is discussed in Davis, *The Priority of Avoiding Harm*, in KILLING AND LETTING DIE 172, 194–95 (B. Steinbock ed. 1980).

6 For a sensitive discussion of some of the difficulties, see Davis, *Using Persons and Common Sense*, 94 *Ethics* 387 (1984). Among other things, she argues (I think rightly) that the Kantian idea is not to be identified with the common sense concept of "using a person." *Id.* at 402.

7 For a second reason to think so, see *infra* note 13.

8 It is also true that if the five go wholly out of existence just before the agent starts to turn the trolley, then the one will die whatever the agent does. Should we say, then, that the agent uses one to save five if he acts, *and* uses five to save one if he does not act? No: What

---

* Henrik Ahlenius and Torbjörn Tännsjö, "Chinese and Westerners Respond Differently to the Trolley Dilemmas," *Journal of Cognition and Culture* 12, 3–4 (2012): 195–201.

† See, for example, Christopher Bauman et al., "Revisiting External Validity: Concerns about Trolley Problems and Other Sacrificial Dilemmas in Moral Psychology," *Social and Personality Psychology Compass* 8/9 (2014): 536–54.

follows *and* is false. If the agent does not act, he uses nobody. (I doubt that it can even be said that if he does not act, he lets them *be used*. For what is the active for which this is passive? Who or what would be using them if he does not act?)

9 I strongly suspect that giving an account of what makes it wrong to *use* a person, *see supra* text accompanying notes 6–8, would also require appeal to the concept of a right.

10 R. Dworkin, *Taking Rights Seriously* ix (1977).

11 Many of the examples discussed by Bernard Williams and Ruth Marcus plainly call out for this kind of treatment. *See* B. Williams, *Ethical Consistency*, in Problems of the Self 166 (1973); Marcus, *Moral Dilemmas and Consistency*, 77 J. PHIL. 121 (1980).

12 It may be worth stressing that what I suggest calls for attention is not (as some construals of "double effect" would have it) whether the agent's killing of the one is his means to something, and not (as other construals of "double effect" would have it) whether the death of the one is the agent's means to something, but rather what are the means by which the agent both kills and saves.

For a discussion of "the doctrine of double effect," see P. FOOT, *supra* note 1.

13 *Id*. at 29. As Mrs. Foot says, we do not *use* the one if we proceed in *Hospital*. Yet the impermissibility of proceeding in *Hospital* seems to have a common source with the impermissibility of operating in *Transplant*, in which the surgeon *would* be using the one whose parts he takes for the five who need them. This is my second reason for thinking that an appeal to the fact that the surgeon would be using his victim is an over-simple way of taking account of the means he would be employing for the saving of his five. *See supra* note 7.

14 Notice that in this case too the agent does not *use* the one if he proceeds. (This case, along with a number of other cases I have been discussing, comes from Thomson, *Killing, Letting Die, and the Trolley Problem*, 59 THE MONIST 204 (1976). Mrs. Thomson seems to me to have been blundering around in the dark in that paper, but the student of this problem may possibly find some of the cases she discusses useful.)

15 *See supra* text accompanying notes 9–11.

Justice

WHAT IS JUSTICE?

Social and political philosophy is made up of our attempts to understand and map the basic categories of social life, and to ethically evaluate different forms of social organization. It has three closely interwoven strands: *conceptual analysis* of various important social dimensions, *normative assessment* of the ways society ought to be structured along these dimensions, and *empirical investigation* of issues relevant to the implementation of these social ideals. It includes social philosophy, political philosophy, philosophy of law, and philosophy of the social sciences (such as economics and sociology).

Among the central concepts studied within social and political philosophy are society, culture, human nature, political obligation, power, democracy, toleration, rights, equality, autonomy or freedom, justice, merit, welfare, property, social class, public interest, and social stability. Different analyses of these notions, and different emphases on some ideas (e.g., equality) over others (e.g., autonomy), give rise to differing political philosophies—differing ideological stances as to what the ideal society should look like, and thus different views on how current societies should be modified in order to move them closer to this ideal. Some of the main social-political ideologies (not all of which are mutually exclusive) are:

- *Anarchism*, which denies that any coercive government institutions are ever justified;
- *Libertarianism* (or "classical liberalism"), which holds that government infringements on individual liberty are always inappropriate, but accepts that a "minimal" state is consistent with this; libertarians also hold that failing to help people in need is not an infringement on their liberty, and that the state therefore has no duty to provide this form of support for its citizens;
- *Liberalism* (or "welfare liberalism"), which is also concerned with promoting individual liberty but holds that a guaranteed social minimum standard of living and enforced equal opportunity are necessary to provide citizens with genuinely substantive autonomy;
- *Communitarianism*, which denies that the rights of individuals are basic and asserts that collectives (states, cultures, communities) have moral claims that are prior to, and sometimes even opposed to, the rights which liberals ascribe to individuals; usually, this is because communitarians hold some version of the thesis that individual identity is constituted by one's social setting, and thus that the liberal notion of an "isolated individual" who exists independently of society is a mere myth;
- *Fascism*, which is an extreme communitarian view stressing the overriding importance of national culture and giving the state authority to control almost all aspects of social life;
- *Socialism*, which takes neither individual liberty nor community to be a fundamental ideal, but instead emphasizes the value of equality, and justifies coercive social institutions insofar as they promote social equality;
- *Communism*, which advocates a society in which private property is abolished in favor of communal ownership of all goods, in the belief that it is only in such conditions that human beings can truly flourish;
- *Conservatism*, which distrusts naked political power and is skeptical of social planning, and which therefore seeks to channel and constrain government within historically evolved, time-tested social institutions and relationships; and
- *Feminism*, which advocates, among other things, social reform (e.g., to the institution of the family) in order to take better account of the fact that women should have the same basic social rights as men.

In addition to conceptual and ethical analysis, there are also many substantive empirical questions which have an important bearing on the choice and implementation of social philosophies. For example, ethical analysis might lead us to decide on a particular set of principles of distributive justice (indicating the ideal distribution of benefits and burdens in society); then, however, it is still a substantial empirical problem to decide which social and economic arrangements will best instantiate those principles. A sampling of other important questions: What checks and balances on government power will be most effective without being inefficient? How can the self-interest of individuals best be harnessed for the public good? What is the most effective body of legislation for fostering social stability? Can equality of opportunity be preserved without infringing on personal autonomy (e.g., on people's choices about who to hire or rent to)? Which forms of punishment are the most effective deterrent of crime? How much is human nature shaped and changed by social circumstances? What is the relationship between free economic markets and democratic political structures? And so on.

The particular social-political issue which is the focus of this section is the problem of justice. The readings approach the topic in all three of the inter-connected ways identified above: they deal with the philosophical analysis of the concept of justice, make claims about how society should be organized in order to take proper account of justice, and touch on some of the empirical data relevant to the construction of a just society. They also deal with some of the different *aspects* of justice: justice as a property of a political system, a set of social relationships, of actions, or of individuals; and justice considered as a problem of specifying how social benefits and burdens should be distributed among the members of that society (*distributive justice*), and the problem of determining the appropriate way to correct injustices or compensate for illegitimate inequalities (*rectificatory justice*).

The reading from Thomas Hobbes addresses the pressing problem of justifying (and defining the limits of) coercive state power over individuals. Hobbes, famously, answers this question with the device of a "social contract," by which rationally self-interested individuals would agree to leave the "state of nature" and submit themselves to the authority of the state. Mill is also, in the reading reprinted here, concerned with the question of the justice of government intervention in the lives of citizens, and he formulates and defends the classical liberal position which limits government action to the prevention of harm. The following readings then present three of the most important modern political ideologies on justice, and particularly distributive justice. Marx and Engels argue for the inevitable ascendance of communism; Rawls carefully lays out the most influential contemporary version of welfare liberalism; and Nozick attempts to rebut Rawls with a lively and fast-moving defense of libertarianism. The final reading, by Susan Moller Okin, presents a feminist critique of contemporary liberal theory and raises deeper questions about gender and its relationship to justice.

There are a number of good books which will take you deeper into social and political philosophy. Perhaps the best place to start is with Will Kymlicka's excellent *Contemporary Political Philosophy* (Oxford University Press, 2001). Also good are John Christman, *Social and Political Philosophy: A Contemporary Introduction* (Routledge, 2017); Carl Cohen, *Communism, Fascism, and Democracy: The Theoretical Foundations* (McGraw-Hill, 1997); Iain Hampsher-Monk, *A History of Modern Political Thought, Major Political Thinkers from Hobbes to Marx* (Blackwell, 1993); J.R. Lucas, *The Principles of Politics* (Oxford University Press, 1986); Gerald MacCallum, *Political Philosophy* (Prentice Hall, 1987); Michael J. Sandel, *Justice: What's the Right Thing to Do?* (Farrar, Strauss and Giroux, 2009); Adam Swift, *Political Philosophy* (Polity Press, 2013); and Jonathan Wolff, *An Introduction to Political Philosophy* (Oxford University Press, 2006). Goodin and Pettit, eds., *A Companion to Contemporary Political Philosophy* (Blackwell, 1996) and Gaus and D'Agostino, eds., *The Routledge Companion to Social and Political Philosophy* (Routledge, 2017) are both well worth consulting.

The modern literature on justice is rich and extensive. Here are some relevant books: Brian Barry, *Theories of Justice*, Volume 1 (University of California Press, 1991); G.A. Cohen, *Self-Ownership, Freedom, and Equality* (Cambridge University Press, 1995); Ronald Dworkin, *Taking Rights Seriously* (Harvard University Press, 1978); Friedrich A. Hayek, *The Constitution of Liberty* (Routledge and Kegan Paul, 1960); David Miller, *Principles of Social Justice* (Harvard University Press, 2001); Stephen Nathanson, *Economic Justice* (Prentice Hall, 1998); D.D. Raphael, *Concepts of Justice* (Oxford University Press, 2001); John Roemer, *Theories of Distributive Justice* (Harvard University Press, 1996); Michael Sandel, *Liberalism and the Limits of Justice* (Cambridge University Press, 1998); Amartya Sen, *The Idea of Justice* (Harvard University Press, 2009); Arthur and Shaw, eds., *Justice and Economic Distribution* (Prentice Hall, 1991); and Michael Walzer, *Spheres of Justice* (Basic Books, 1984).

THOMAS HOBBES

FROM *Leviathan*

Who Was Thomas Hobbes?

Thomas Hobbes was born, prematurely, in 1588* in the village of Westport near the small town of Malmesbury, in the southern English county of Wiltshire. Though several relatives had grown wealthy in the family's cloth-making business, Hobbes's father was a poor, ill-educated country clergyman, who frequently ran into trouble with the church authorities for disobedience and volatility. Young Thomas was apparently a studious, unhealthy, rather melancholy boy, who loved music. Because of his black hair, he was nicknamed "Crow" by his schoolfellows. When Hobbes was 16, his father's long-running feud with a nearby vicar, whom he had publicly slandered as "a knave† and an arrant knave and a drunken knave," came to a head when (probably drunk) he encountered his enemy in the churchyard at Malmesbury and set about him with his fists. Any act of violence in a church or churchyard was an excommunicable offense at that time, and laying hands on a clergyman was an even more serious crime, subject to corporal punishment and imprisonment. Hobbes's father was forced to flee. It is not known whether Thomas ever again saw his father, who died "in obscurity beyond London."

By the time of his father's disappearance, however, young Hobbes had already been plucked out of his family situation and sent off to Oxford (an education paid for by his uncle Francis, a prosperous glover). There, Hobbes attended Magdalen Hall, one of the poorer foundations at Oxford and one which was renowned for its religious Puritanism.‡ He does not seem to have been impressed by the quality of the education he received. Later in life he was dismissive of the Aristotelian logic and metaphysics he was taught and claimed that, at the time, he was more interested in reading about explorations of newly discovered lands and poring over maps of the world and the stars, than in studying traditional philosophy.

As soon as Hobbes completed his BA, in 1608, he was lucky enough to be offered a job as tutor to the eldest son of William Cavendish, a rich and powerful Derbyshire landowner who owned the great stately home at Chatsworth (and who became the first Earl of Devonshire in 1618). Cavendish's son, also called William, was only a few years younger than Hobbes himself, and Hobbes's position quickly became that of a servant, secretary, and friend, rather than tutor. In 1614, Hobbes and Cavendish toured France and Italy, where they both learned Italian and encountered some of the currents of Italian intellectual thought, including the fiercely anti-Papal writings of several Venetian authors.

William Cavendish succeeded his father as the Earl of Devonshire in 1626, but died of disease just two years later. Hobbes, now 40 years old, signed on as tutor to the son of another rich landowner, Sir Gervase Clifton. During this period, he accompanied his charge on another trip to the continent (France and Switzerland), and it was in Geneva that he picked up a copy of Euclid's *Elements* and fell in love with its method of deductive

---

* This was the year that the Catholic monarch of Spain, Philip II, dispatched a massive fleet of ships—the Armada—to invade Protestant England. Hobbes later wrote, in an autobiographical poem, that "hereupon it was my mother dear/ Did bring forth twins at once, both me and fear," and used to joke that this explained his timid nature. (In the event, however, the Armada was decisively defeated in the English Channel before it could rendezvous with the Spanish invasion force waiting in the Spanish Netherlands, an area comprising modern Belgium, Luxembourg, and part of northern France.) See Thomas Hobbes, *Verse Autobiography* (1670), lines 27–28. This poem is reprinted in the Curley edition of *Leviathan* (Hackett, 1994), liv–lxiv.

† A well-known out-and-out dishonest person.

‡ The Puritans were a group of English Protestants who regarded the Protestant Reformation under Elizabeth I (1558–1603) as incomplete. Influenced by Protestant teachings from continental Europe, such as Calvinism, they advocated strict religious discipline and simplification of the ceremonies and creeds of the Church of England.

reasoning. A contemporary biographer wrote of the incident:

> Being in a gentleman's library, Euclid's *Elements* lay open, and 'twas the 47th Prop. of Book I. He read the proposition. "By G——," said he (he would now and then swear, by way of emphasis), "this is impossible!" So he reads the demonstration of it, which referred him back to such a proposition; which proposition he read. That referred him back to another, which he also read. And so on, until at last he was demonstratively convinced of that truth. This made him in love with geometry.[*]

After his return to England, Hobbes agreed to re-enter the service of the widowed countess of Devonshire as tutor to her 13-year-old son, the third earl. The 1630s were important years for Hobbes's intellectual development. His secure, and relatively undemanding, position allowed him time both to develop the main outlines of his political philosophy and also to pursue his interest in science (especially optics). His connection to a great noble house also gave him contacts with other intellectuals clustered around noble patrons, such as the mathematicians and scientists supported by the Earl of Newcastle, and the theologians, lawyers, and poets associated with the Viscount Falkland.

In 1634, Hobbes embarked on another European tour with his pupil, and spent over a year living in Paris where he met French scientists and mathematicians—and especially the influential and well-connected Marin Mersenne—and became finally and fully gripped by the intellectual excitement of the age. "The extreme pleasure I take in study overcomes in me all other appetites," he wrote at this time in a letter.[†] By 1636, when Hobbes had returned to England, he was devoting as much of his energies as possible to philosophical and scientific work:

the third earl turned 18 in 1637, so—although Hobbes remained in his service—he was no longer needed as a tutor and his time was largely his own.

His earliest surviving work is a treatise on the science of optics, in part of which Hobbes attacks Descartes's *Discourse on the Method* (published in 1637). Hobbes accused Descartes of inconsistency and of not taking seriously enough his own mechanistic physics. Since perception is caused entirely by physical motions or pressures, then the mind—that which does the perceiving—must also be a physical object, capable of being affected by motion, Hobbes argued.[‡] Hobbes, therefore, in his very earliest philosophical writing rejected the dualism of matter and spirit in favor of a purely mechanical view of the world.

Hobbes's philosophical work was pushed in a different direction at the end of the 1630s, as political events unfolded in England. As the country moved towards civil war, during the final years of the so-called personal rule of King Charles I,[§] there was an intense public debate about the degree of absoluteness of the power of the sovereign. The main issue was whether there were any limits to the power of the king at all. It was recognized that the monarch could exceed his normal powers during exceptional circumstances—but the king, himself, claimed to be the judge of which circumstances were exceptional, and this essentially allowed him to exceed his "normal" powers whenever he chose. In 1640, after the Scots invaded and occupied northern England, the King recalled Parliament to grant him extra taxes to raise an army. They refused, and what became known as the "Short Parliament" was abruptly dissolved. In the same year, Hobbes wrote and circulated an unabashedly pro-royalist work called *The Elements of Law*, which attempted to justify the nature and extent of sovereign power from philosophical first principles. By the end of that year, facing a backlash from anti-royalist parliamen-

---

[*] John Aubrey, *Brief Lives, Chiefly of Contemporaries, Set Down by John Aubrey, Between the Years 1669 & 1696*, Vol. 1, ed. A. Clark (Oxford University Press, 1898), 387.

[†] Thomas Hobbes, Letter 21 in Vol. 4 of *The Clarendon Edition of the Works of Thomas Hobbes*, ed. H. Warender et al. (Oxford University Press, 1983).

[‡] "Since vision is formally and really nothing but motion, it follows that that which sees is also formally and strictly speaking nothing other than that which is moved; for nothing other than a body ... can be moved." (Thomas Hobbes, "Tractatus opticus: prima edizione integrale," ed. F. Alessio, *Revista Critica di Storia dela Filosofia* 18 (1963): 147–88. This translation is by Noel Malcolm, p. 207.)

[§] In 1629, after a series of clashes with Parliament, Charles dissolved the legislative body permanently and began an 11-year period of ruling alone, as an absolute monarch.

tarians as tensions grew, Hobbes called in all his investments and left England for Paris.

In Paris, Hobbes was quickly reabsorbed into the intellectual life of the great city, and his reputation was established by the 1642 publication of *De Cive*, a remodeled version of *The Elements of Law*. After this, Hobbes returned to the study of scientific philosophy and theology, and spent several years working on a substantial book on logic, metaphysics, and physics, which was eventually published in 1655 as *De Corpore*. However, his work was frequently interrupted, once by a serious illness from which he nearly died (in 1647), and repeatedly by visitors from England, including royalist exiles from the English Civil War (which had erupted in 1642 and dragged on until 1648). In 1646, Hobbes was made mathematical tutor to the young Prince Charles, now in exile in Paris. This turned Hobbes's thoughts back to politics, and—secretively and rapidly—he completed the major work *Leviathan* between the autumn of 1649 and the spring of 1651.

By this time, Hobbes was keen to return to England. The war had been won by the Parliamentarians (Charles I was beheaded in 1649, the monarchy and House of Lords abolished, and a Commonwealth, led by Oliver Cromwell, set up) and *Leviathan*—which Hobbes took care to ensure was published in London—was partly intended to ease his passage back home. Hobbes did not abandon, or even substantially modify, the central arguments of his earlier, royalist writings, but in *Leviathan* he does emphasize that his project is to justify *political authority* generally (and not necessarily just that of a monarch). He also discusses extensively the question—which at that time was of vital interest to the former aristocratic supporters of the old king—of when it is legitimate to shift allegiance from one ruler to another. Hobbes later said he had written *Leviathan* on behalf of "those many and faithful servants and subjects of His Majesty," who had fought on the royalist side and lost, and who were now in the position of negotiating with the new Parliamentary rulers for their old lands and titles. "They that had done their utmost endeavor to perform their obligation to the King, had done all that they could be obliged unto; and were consequently at liberty to seek the safety of their lives and livelihood wheresover, and without treachery."

Hobbes probably did not expect his work to cause offense among the court-in-exile of the young Charles II in Paris,* and he presented a hand-written copy to the king in 1651. However, because he denied that kings ruled by a divine right handed down directly from God, Hobbes was perceived as turning against the monarchy. Furthermore, the attack on organized religion, and especially Catholicism, that *Leviathan* contained provoked fury among Charles's courtiers. Hobbes was banned from the court, and shortly afterwards the French clergy attempted to have him arrested; Hobbes quickly fled back to England.

There he settled back into the employ of the Earl of Devonshire, and resumed a quiet bachelor life of light secretarial work and intellectual discussion. However, the notoriety of *Leviathan* slowly grew, and—because of its bitter attacks on religion and the universities—Hobbes made enemies of many influential groups. For example, when the Royal Society was formed in 1660, Hobbes was pointedly *not* invited to become a member, partly because his fellow exponents of the new "mechanical philosophy" were highly wary of being associated with atheism and reacted by violently attacking Hobbes's supposedly "atheistic" new world-view. Throughout the 1660s and 1670s, Hobbes and his works were denounced from pulpits all over England for what was said to be his godlessness and denial of objective moral values. There were even rumors that Hobbes—also sometimes known as the "Beast of Malmesbury"—was to be charged for heresy (which could, even then, have resulted in his being burned at the stake, though the last people to be executed for heresy in England died in 1612). In contrast with the general public vilification Hobbes faced in his own country, in France and Holland his reputation was soaring and (after the death of acclaimed scientist Pierre Gassendi in 1655) he was widely regarded by French scientists and men of letters as the greatest living philosopher.

Hobbes, though now well into old age (and suffering severely from Parkinson's disease), continued to write prolifically, including several public defenses of *Leviathan*, several treatises on mathematics, a debate with Robert Boyle about the experimental evidence for vacuums, a short book on six problems in physics, a controversial critical church history in Latin verse, translations

---

* Charles II was eventually restored to the throne, by a vote of Parliament, in 1660.

of Homer's *Iliad* and *Odyssey* into English verse, and a history of the English civil war entitled *Behemoth*. When Hobbes died, shortly after suffering a severe stroke in December 1679, he was 91 years old.

What Was Hobbes's Overall Philosophical Project?

Hobbes thought of himself as primarily a scientist. Not only was he interested in what we would, today, think of as science (optics, physics, geometry), he was also concerned to place the study of human beings—especially psychology, ethics, and politics—on what he considered a *scientific* footing. Hobbes was deeply conscious that he was living during a period of intellectual revolution—a time when the old Aristotelian assumptions were being stripped away by the new mechanical and mathematical science which Hobbes enthusiastically endorsed—as well as during an era of political and religious revolution. He wanted to play a significant role in both these movements.

Since Hobbes considered himself a scientist, his view of what *constitutes* science is particularly significant. Hobbes's scheme of the sciences changes somewhat throughout his writings, but its most stable core looks something like this. The most fundamental science is what Hobbes (like Aristotle) called "first philosophy," and it consists in "universal definitions"—of *body*, *motion*, *time*, *place*, *cause*, and so on—and their logical consequences. Thus the most basic kind of science, for Hobbes, is more purely rational than it is experimental. After first philosophy, comes geometry, which (for Hobbes) was the science of the simple motions of bodies. For example, Hobbes rejected the view that geometry is the study of abstract objects and their relations, but instead insisted that it concerns itself with the movements of concrete objects in real space. The next step in the ladder of the sciences is mechanics, which investigates the more complex motions due to whole bodies working together, and this is followed by physics, the study of the invisible motions of the parts of bodies (including the effects on the human senses of the motions of external bodies). Then comes moral philosophy, which Hobbes thought of as primarily the investigation of passion and volition, which he considered the internal effects of sensation on the human mind. Finally, civil philosophy—the science of politics—formulates the laws of conduct that will ensure peace and self-preservation for communities of creatures with our particular internal psychological constitution.

A central—and at the time infamous—plank of Hobbes's scientific world-view was his unrelenting *materialism*. According to the new "mechanical" philosophy which had caught Hobbes up in its sweep across the thinkers of Europe, all physical phenomena are ultimately to be explained in terms of the motions and interactions of large numbers of tiny, material bodies. Hobbes enthusiastically accepted this view, and was one of the earliest thinkers to extend it to phenomena his peers generally did not think of as "physical." In particular, Hobbes declared that *mental* phenomena ought to be just as susceptible to mechanical explanation as anything else in nature. For Hobbes, then, the natural world did not contain both matter and spirit (minds): it was entirely made up of material bodies, and human beings were to be viewed as nothing more than very complex material objects, like sophisticated robots or automata.

Along similar lines, Hobbes was very skeptical of claims to religious knowledge, and this was one among several reasons why he devoted so much energy to attacks on the authority of the church. According to Hobbes's theory of language, words have meaning only if they express thoughts, and thoughts are nothing more than the residue in our minds of sensations produced by the action of external objects upon our bodies. Since God is supposed to be an infinite, transcendent being, beyond our powers to perceive, Hobbes—although it is not at all clear that he was actually an atheist—was led to assert we can have no meaningful thoughts about God, and thus can say nothing positive about him. Furthermore, according to Hobbes's materialism, the notion of an "incorporeal substance" is simply incoherent, and so, if God exists at all, he must exist as a *material* body (which Hobbes claimed, in fact, to believe).

Like Descartes, Hobbes saw himself as developing the foundations for a completely new and radical philosophy which was to decisively change the way his contemporaries saw the world. Furthermore, Hobbes did not see moral and political philosophy as a purely intellectual exercise. He firmly believed the great and tragic upheaval of the English Civil War was directly caused by the promulgation of false and dangerous moral ideas, and could have been avoided by proper appreciation of the moral truth. In *Leviathan*, then, Hobbes's project was to place social and political philosophy on a *scientific* foundation for the first time (and he thought doing so would be of immense service to humanity). His model for this was geometry: he begins with a sequence of axiomatic definitions—such as "justice," "obligation," "right of nature," and "law of nature"—and then tries to show that his philosophical results are rationally derivable from these basic assumptions. His goal was to derive and prove universal political laws—rather like the laws of physics—from which infallible judgments about particular cases can be made.*

What Is the Structure of This Reading?

Leviathan is divided into four parts: "Of Man," which deals primarily with human psychology and the state of nature; "Of Commonwealth," which discusses the formation of political states and the powers of their sovereigns; "Of a Christian Commonwealth," which examines the relationship between secular and religious law; and "Of the Kingdom of Darkness," which is a vitriolic attack on certain kinds of organized religion, and especially Catholicism. The excerpts given here come from Parts I and II.

First, there is a sequence of three chapters which come nearly at the end of Part I. In these Hobbes describes the unhappy "state of nature" for human beings and argues that several (nineteen, of which the first five are included in this excerpt) moral "laws of nature" or "theorems" arise as "convenient articles of peace upon which men may be drawn to agreement." Then we jump to the first two chapters of "Of Commonwealth," in which Hobbes discusses how political states arise and argues that state sovereigns are entitled to almost absolute power over their subjects.

Some Useful Background Information

1. *Leviathan* was published just 40 years after the first "King James" English translation of the Bible; hence Hobbes's writing style, dating from the same period, is what we might think of today as "biblical."

This makes Hobbes all the more interesting to read, but can impose something of a barrier for modern audiences. Some words in the reading might be unfamiliar or used in an unfamiliar or archaic way (footnotes are provided throughout to assist the modern reader).

2. The fundamental political problem for Hobbes, and the issue *Leviathan* primarily sets out to address, was the following: How can any political system unambiguously and indisputably determine the answer to the question What is the law? How can universally, uncontroversially acceptable rules of conduct by which the citizens of a state must lead their public lives be determined? A precondition, Hobbes thought, was for there to be only a single source of law, and for that source to be absolute in the sense that whatever the legislator declared as law was law. Any other kind of political system, Hobbes believed, would descend inevitably into factionalism, insecurity, and civil war.

3. Hobbes was quite explicit in rejecting the Aristotelian view of human nature which had been passed down to his day. For Aristotle, human beings are naturally social animals, our natural situation is as active members of a political community, and our highest good is the sort of happiness, or flourishing, for which our biological species is best suited. Furthermore, according to Aristotle, there is a natural hierarchy among human beings, with some people being inherently more noble than others. These inequalities are not created by society, on the Aristotelian picture, but ideally should be mirrored in the social order.

    For Hobbes, by contrast, human beings are *not* naturally social animals, and furthermore there is no single conception of happiness tied to the human 'essence.' Instead, according to Hobbes, human happiness is a matter of the continual satisfaction of desires or appetites, and since individual human beings differ in their particular desires, so too will what makes people happy. Because people's desires often come into conflict—especially when several people compete for the same scarce

---

*   On the other hand, it is important to note that, unlike physics, politics is a *normative* science. It does not simply describe what people do do, but in some sense prescribes what they *ought* to do. In this respect, Hobbes's political science resembles modern economics more than mathematics or experimental science.

resource, such as land, money, or honor—human beings are naturally *anti*-social. Furthermore, even when civil society has been established, according to Hobbes, most of its citizens will not, and should not, be active participants in political life, but will simply lead private lives, out of the public sphere, within the constraints of their obedience to the commands of the sovereign. Finally, it was Hobbes's view that human beings, in the state of nature, are in a state of radical equality, where no one is substantially any better (or worse) than anyone else; similarly, in civil society, although there will be gradations of honor among men, everyone is fundamentally equal under the sovereign.

4. Like Aristotle, however, Hobbes sees justice, and morality generally, as applying to character traits—what Hobbes calls "manners"—rather than primarily to states of affairs or types of action. For Hobbes, moral virtues are those habits which it is rational for all people to praise; that is, they are those dispositions which contribute to the preservation, not merely of the individual, but of everyone in the community by contributing to peace and stable society.

Some Common Misconceptions

1. When Hobbes talks about "the state of nature" he is referring *neither* to a particular historical period in human history (such as the age of hunter-gatherers) *nor* to a mere theoretical possibility (a time that never actually occurred). What Hobbes has in mind is any situation, at any time or place, where there is no effective government capable of imposing order on the local population. Thus primitive or prehistoric societies may (or may not) be in the state of nature; but so may modern societies locked in a civil war, destroyed by conflict with other countries, or simply experiencing a constitutional crisis. Likewise, the international community of nations (then, as now) is in a state of nature, lacking any overarching world government capable of determining and enforcing international law. (Hence, as he points out in the text, when Hobbes describes the state of nature as being "a condition of war" he does not mean it will necessarily involve constant fighting and bloodshed, but rather that no one can feel *secure* against the threat of force.)

2. Hobbes is not the "immoralist" he is sometimes taken to be. Far from arguing *against* the existence of universal moral principles, Hobbes is concerned to *combat* the kind of moral relativism which holds that all laws, including moral laws, are mere matters of arbitrary human convention. Hobbes adopts the assumption of the moral skeptic that the only fundamental, universal moral principle is self-interest, but he then argues that, from the skeptic's *own assumption*, certain "natural" laws of justice follow deductively. In this way, he tries to show there can be laws without a lawgiver: moral principles based, not in divine or human command, but in human nature itself. (On the other hand, Hobbes does stress, we are bound by these laws only if we can be sure others will obey them too—that is, on the whole, only once we have agreed to form a civil society. To that extent, at least, the principles of justice remain, for Hobbes, a matter of convention, that is, a societal arrangement for the purpose of mutual advantage.)

3. A mainspring of Hobbes's political philosophy is the claim that human beings seek their own self-preservation. There is textual evidence that Hobbes saw this desire for self-preservation not as merely a non-rational desire, even one which all human beings naturally share, but as actually being a *primary goal of reason*. That is, one of the dictates *of rationality*, for Hobbes, is that we should take all measures necessary for our self-preservation, and so the ethical laws Hobbes generates out of this principle are not merely *hypothetical* commands ("Do this if you care more about your self-preservation than anything else") but are dictates that all rational creatures should recognize as binding.

4. Though Hobbes is, legitimately, often said to be rather pessimistic about human nature, this can be overstated. His view, essentially, is not that *everyone* is selfish, but that *enough* people are fundamentally selfish that it would be unwise to construct a civil society on the assumption that people are generally benevolent. According to Hobbes, children are born concerned only with themselves and, though they can learn to care for others, this can be brought about only with proper moral education. Unfortunately, he believed, not very many children are actually brought up in this

way, and so most of the citizens of a commonwealth will, in fact, care primarily for themselves and their families and not be much moved by the interests of strangers.

5. Hobbes did not think that people *in fact* always act to preserve themselves: his claim is not that people always behave in a way which is optimal in avoiding hardship or death for themselves—on the contrary, Hobbes was convinced that people are often rash and vainglorious and prone to irrational quarrels—but that it is always *reasonable* or *rational* for people to seek self-preservation, and furthermore that this fact is so universally recognized by human beings that it is capable of serving as a solid basis for civil society. (Contrary to popular belief, then, Hobbes is not quite what is technically called a "psychological egoist": someone who believes that all people, as a matter of psychological necessity, always act only in their own self-interest.)

6. Although Hobbes is frequently thought of as a *social contract theorist*, he actually does not see the foundation of the state as involving a contract or covenant between *all* members of that society, but instead as a kind of *free gift* by the citizens to their sovereign. That is, people in the state of nature (covenant together to) freely turn over their right of nature to a sovereign power, in the hope that this sovereign will protect them and allow them to live in greater security. (Importantly, this means the sovereign cannot *break a covenant* if they fail to protect their subjects, though they do come to be bound by the law of nature prohibiting

ingratitude, and so must "endeavour that he which giveth [a gift] have no reasonable cause to repent him of his good will.")

7. Hobbes thought that his new political science could conclusively demonstrate that all states need a sovereign (an absolute dispenser of law). He did not, however, insist that this sovereign must be a *monarch*; he was quite ready to recognize that a republic, led by an assembly of senators for example, could be an equally effective form of government.

How Important and Influential Is This Passage?

Hobbes's *Leviathan* is arguably the most important work of political philosophy in English before the twentieth century, even though the work's *conclusions* have been widely rejected from Hobbes's day to this. The project of justifying and delimiting the extent of the state's power over its subjects, without appeal to such supernatural mechanisms as the divine right of kings, is an immensely important one, and it can be said that Hobbes gave this question its first great answer in modern times. The selections reprinted here include several themes for which Hobbes is most notorious: the doctrine that life in a state of nature is "solitary, poor, nasty, brutish, and short"; the attempt to ground universal principles of justice in the essential selfishness of human nature; the notion that the institution of a political state consists in a kind of "contract" between its members; and the claim that the power of a sovereign is absolute.

FROM *Leviathan**

PART I: OF MAN

Chapter XIII: Of the Natural Condition of Mankind as Concerning Their Felicity and Misery

Nature hath made men so equal in the faculties of body and mind as that, though there be found one man sometimes manifestly stronger in body or of quicker mind than another, yet when all is reckoned together the difference between man and man is not so considerable as that one man can thereupon claim to himself any benefit to which another may not pretend† as well as he. For as to the strength of body, the weakest has strength enough to kill the strongest, either by secret machination‡ or by confederacy§ with others that are in the same danger with himself.

And as to the faculties of the mind—setting aside the arts grounded upon words, and especially that skill of proceeding upon general and infallible rules, called science, which very few have and but in few things, as being not a native faculty born with us, nor attained, as prudence, while we look after somewhat else—I find yet a greater equality amongst men than that of strength. For prudence is but experience, which equal time equally bestows on all men in those things they equally apply themselves unto. That which may perhaps make such equality incredible is but a vain conceit of one's own wisdom, which almost all men think they have in a greater degree than the vulgar;¶ that is, than all men but themselves, and a few others, whom by fame, or for concurring with themselves, they approve. For such is the nature of men that howsoever they may acknowledge many others to be more witty, or more eloquent, or more learned, yet they will hardly believe there be many so wise as themselves; for they see their own wit** at hand, and other men's at a distance. But this proveth rather that men are in that point equal, than unequal. For there is not ordinarily a greater sign of the equal distribution of anything than that every man is contented with his share.

From this equality of ability ariseth equality of hope in the attaining of our ends. And therefore if any two men desire the same thing, which nevertheless they cannot both enjoy, they become enemies; and in the way to their end†† (which is principally their own conservation, and sometimes their delectation‡‡ only) endeavour to destroy or subdue one another. And from hence it comes to pass that where an invader hath no more to fear than another man's single power, if one plant, sow, build, or possess a convenient seat,§§ others may probably be expected to come prepared with forces united to dispossess and deprive him, not only of the fruit of his labour, but also of his life or liberty. And the invader again is in the like danger of another.

And from this diffidence¶¶ of one another, there is no way for any man to secure himself so*** reasonable

---

*   *Leviathan* was first published, in London, in 1651; the excerpts reprinted here are from that edition (with modernized spelling, and partly modernized punctuation). As well as his English version, Hobbes also prepared an edition in Latin (much of which was probably written before the English version), first published in Amsterdam in 1681.

†   Lay claim to or profess (not necessarily deceitfully).

‡   Plotting or scheming.

§   An alliance or league for joint action or mutual support.

¶   Ordinary people.

**   Intelligence.

††   Goal, desire.

‡‡   Delight, pleasure.

§§   An attractive dwelling place.

¶¶   Distrust (as opposed to the more modern sense, timidity).

***   As.

as anticipation;* that is, by force, or wiles, to master the persons of all men he can so long till he see no other power great enough to endanger him: and this is no more than his own conservation requireth, and is generally allowed. Also, because there be some that, taking pleasure in contemplating their own power in the acts of conquest, which they pursue farther than their security requires, if others (that otherwise would be glad to be at ease within modest bounds) should not by invasion increase their power, they would not be able, long time, by standing only on their defence, to subsist. And by consequence, such augmentation of dominion over men being necessary to a man's conservation, it ought to be allowed him.

Again, men have no pleasure (but on the contrary a great deal of grief) in keeping company† where there is no power able to overawe‡ them all. For every man looketh that his companion should value him at the same rate he sets upon himself, and upon all signs of contempt or undervaluing naturally endeavours, as far as he dares (which amongst them that have no common power to keep them in quiet is far enough to make them destroy each other), to extort a greater value from his contemners,§ by damage; and from others, by the example.

So that in the nature of man, we find three principal causes of quarrel. First, competition; secondly, diffidence; thirdly, glory.

The first maketh men invade for gain; the second, for safety; and the third, for reputation. The first use violence, to make themselves masters of other men's persons, wives, children, and cattle; the second, to defend them; the third, for trifles, as a word, a smile, a different opinion, and any other sign of undervalue, either direct in their persons or by reflection in their kindred, their friends, their nation, their profession, or their name.

Hereby it is manifest that during the time men live without a common power to keep them all in awe,¶ they are in that condition which is called war; and such a war as is of every man against every man. For war consisteth not in battle only, or the act of fighting, but in a tract of time, wherein the will to contend by battle is sufficiently known: and therefore the notion of *time* is to be considered in the nature of war, as it is in the nature of weather. For as the nature of foul weather lieth not in a shower or two of rain, but in an inclination thereto of many days together: so the nature of war consisteth not in actual fighting, but in the known disposition thereto during all the time there is no assurance to the contrary. All other time is peace.

Whatsoever therefore is consequent to** a time of war, where every man is enemy to every man, the same consequent to the time wherein men live without other security than what their own strength and their own invention shall furnish them withal. In such condition there is no place for industry,†† because the fruit thereof is uncertain: and consequently no culture of the earth;‡‡ no navigation, nor use of the commodities that may be imported by sea; no commodious§§ building; no instruments of moving and removing such things as require much force; no knowledge of the face of the earth; no account of time; no arts; no letters; no society; and which is worst of all, continual fear, and danger of violent death; and the life of man, solitary, poor, nasty, brutish, and short.

... To this war of every man against every man, this also is consequent; that nothing can be unjust. The notions of right and wrong, justice and injustice, have there no place. Where there is no common power, there is no law; where no law, no injustice. Force and fraud are in war the two cardinal virtues. Justice and injustice are none of the faculties neither of the body nor mind. If they were, they might be in a man that were alone in

---

* To prevent someone's action by acting first.
† Spending time with other people.
‡ To restrain by fear.
§ People who treat others with contempt or scorn.
¶ Fear
** The result of, caused by.
†† Diligent, energetic work.
‡‡ Farming.
§§ Comfortable, pleasant.

the world, as well as* his senses and passions. They are qualities that relate to men in society, not in solitude. It is consequent also to the same condition that there be no propriety,† no dominion, no *mine* and *thine* distinct; but only that to be every man's that he can get, and for so long as he can keep it. And thus much for the ill condition which man by mere nature is actually placed in; though with a possibility to come out of it, consisting partly in the passions, partly in his reason.

The passions that incline men to peace are: fear of death; desire of such things as are necessary to commodious living; and a hope by their industry to obtain them. And reason suggesteth convenient articles of peace‡ upon which men may be drawn to agreement. These articles are they which otherwise are called the laws of nature, whereof I shall speak more particularly in the two following chapters.

Chapter XIV: Of the First and Second Natural Laws, and of Contracts

The *right of nature*, which writers commonly call *jus naturale*, is the liberty each man hath to use his own power as he will himself for the preservation of his own nature; that is to say, of his own life; and consequently, of doing anything which, in his own judgement and reason, he shall conceive to be the aptest means thereunto.

By *liberty* is understood, according to the proper signification of the word, the absence of external impediments; which impediments may oft take away part of a man's power to do what he would, but cannot hinder him from using the power left him according as his judgement and reason shall dictate to him.

A *law of nature*, *lex naturalis*, is a precept, or general rule, found out by reason, by which a man is forbidden to do that which is destructive of his life, or taketh away the means of preserving the same, and to omit that by which he thinketh it may be best preserved. For though they that speak of this subject use to confound§ *jus* and *lex*, *right* and *law*, yet they ought

to be distinguished, because *right* consisteth in liberty to do, or to forbear; whereas *law* determineth and bindeth to one of them: so that law and right differ as much as obligation and liberty, which in one and the same matter are inconsistent.

And because the condition of man (as hath been declared in the precedent chapter) is a condition of war of every one against every one, in which case every one is governed by his own reason, and there is nothing he can make use of that may not be a help unto him in preserving his life against his enemies; it followeth that in such a condition every man has a right to every thing, even to one another's body. And therefore, as long as this natural right of every man to every thing endureth, there can be no security to any man, how strong or wise soever he be, of living out the time which nature ordinarily alloweth men to live.¶ And consequently it is a precept, or general rule of reason: *that every man ought to endeavour peace, as far as he has hope of obtaining it; and when he cannot obtain it, that he may seek and use all helps and advantages of war.* The first branch of which rule containeth the first and fundamental law of nature, which is: *to seek peace and follow it.* The second, the sum of the right of nature, which is: *by all means we can to defend ourselves.*

From this fundamental law of nature, by which men are commanded to endeavour peace, is derived this second law: *that a man be willing, when others are so too, as far forth as for peace and defence of himself he shall think it necessary, to lay down** this right to all things; and be contented with so much liberty against other men as he would allow other men against himself.* For as long as every man holdeth this right, of doing anything he liketh; so long are all men in the condition of war. But if other men will not lay down their right, as well as he, then there is no reason for anyone to divest himself of his: for that were to expose himself to prey, which no man is bound to, rather than to dispose himself to peace. This is that law of the Gospel: Whatsoever you require that others should do to you, that do ye to them. And that law of all men, *quod tibi fieri non vis, alteri ne feceris.*††

---

*   Just as much as.
†   Property, ownership (as opposed to the more modern sense, suitableness).
‡   A peace treaty.
§   Have in the past mixed up or confused (one thing for the other).
¶   That is, people will die young—nobody will be able to live a full natural lifespan.
** To give up.
†† "Do not do to others what you would not want done to yourself."

To *lay down* a man's *right* to anything is to divest himself of the *liberty* of hindering another of the benefit of his own right to the same.* For he that renounceth or passeth away his right giveth not to any other man a right which he had not before, because there is nothing to which every man had not right by nature, but only standeth out of his way that he may enjoy his own original right without hindrance from him, not without hindrance from another. So that the effect which redoundeth to one man by another man's defect of right is but so much diminution of impediments to the use of his own right original.†

Right is laid aside, either by simply renouncing it, or by transferring it to another....

Whensoever a man transferreth his right, or renounceth it, it is either in consideration of some right reciprocally transferred to himself, or for some other good he hopeth for thereby. For it is a voluntary act: and of the voluntary acts of every man, the object is some *good to himself*. And therefore there be some rights which no man can be understood by any words, or other signs, to have abandoned or transferred. As, first, a man cannot lay down the right of resisting them that assault him by force to take away his life, because he cannot be understood to aim thereby at any good to himself. The same may be said of wounds, and chains, and imprisonment, both because there is no benefit consequent to such patience, as there is to the patience of suffering another to be wounded or imprisoned, as also because a man cannot tell when he seeth men proceed against him by violence whether they intend his death or not. And lastly the motive and end for which this renouncing and transferring of right is introduced is nothing else but the security of a man's person, in his life, and in the means of so preserving life as not to be weary of it. And therefore if a man by words, or other signs, seem to despoil‡ himself of the end for which those signs were intended, he is not to be understood as if he meant it, or that it was his will, but that he was ignorant of how such words and actions were to be interpreted.

The mutual transferring of right is that which men call *contract*....

Chapter XV: Of Other Laws of Nature

From that law of nature by which we are obliged to transfer to another such rights as, being retained, hinder the peace of mankind, there followeth a third; which is this: *that men perform their covenants§ made*; without which covenants are in vain, and but empty words; and the right of all men to all things remaining, we are still in the condition of war.

And in this law of nature consisteth the fountain and original of¶ *justice*. For where no covenant hath preceded, there hath no right been transferred, and every man has right to everything and consequently, no action can be unjust. But when a covenant is made, then to break it is *unjust* and the definition of *injustice* is no other than *the not performance of covenant*. And whatsoever is not unjust is *just*.

But because covenants of mutual trust, where there is a fear of not performance on either part (as hath been said in the former chapter), are invalid, though the original of justice be the making of covenants, yet injustice actually there can be none till the cause of such fear be taken away; which, while men are in the natural condition of war, cannot be done. Therefore before the names of just and unjust can have place, there must be some coercive power to compel men equally** to the performance of their covenants, by the terror of some punishment greater than the benefit they expect by the breach of their covenant, and to make good that propriety which by mutual contract men acquire in recompense of the universal right they abandon: and such power there is none before the

---

* To deprive himself of the liberty of blocking someone else from getting the benefit of his right to the same thing.

† "So that the effect on person A from person B's giving up their right to something is only a reduction in a barrier to the use of person A's already-existing (original) right to that thing."

‡ Rob.

§ Promises, solemn agreements.

¶ The origin of.

** To force all people.

erection of a commonwealth.* And this is also to be gathered out of the ordinary definition of justice in the Schools,† for they say that *justice is the constant will of giving to every man his own*. And therefore where there is no *own*, that is, no propriety, there is no injustice; and where there is no coercive power erected, that is, where there is no commonwealth, there is no propriety, all men having right to all things: therefore where there is no commonwealth, there nothing is unjust. So that the nature of justice consisteth in keeping of valid covenants, but the validity of covenants begins not but with‡ the constitution of a civil power sufficient to compel men to keep them: and then it is also that propriety begins.

The fool hath said in his heart, there is no such thing as justice,§ and sometimes also with his tongue, seriously alleging that: every man's conservation and contentment being committed to his own care, there could be no reason why every man might not do what he thought conduced thereunto: and therefore also to make, or not make, keep, or not keep, covenants was not against reason when it conduced to one's benefit.... This specious reasoning is ... false.

For the question is not of promises mutual, where there is no security of performance on either side, as when there is no civil power erected over the parties promising; for such promises are no covenants: but either where one of the parties has performed already, or where there is a power to make him perform, there is the question whether it be against reason; that is, against the benefit of the other to perform, or not. And I say it is not against reason. For the manifestation whereof we are to consider: first, that when a man doth a thing which, notwithstanding anything can be foreseen and reckoned on, tendeth to his own destruction (howsoever some accident, which he could not expect, arriving may turn it to his benefit); yet such events do not make it reasonably or wisely done. Secondly, that in a condition of war, wherein every man to every man, for want of a common power to keep them all in awe, is an enemy, there is no man can hope by his own strength, or wit, to defend himself from destruction without the help of confederates (where every one expects the same defence by the confederation that any one else does); and therefore he which declares he thinks it reason to deceive those that help him can in reason expect no other means of safety than what can be had from his own single power. He, therefore, that breaketh his covenant, and consequently declareth that he thinks he may with reason do so, cannot be received into any society that unite themselves for peace and defence but by the error of them that receive him; nor when he is received be retained in it without seeing the danger of their error; which errors a man cannot reasonably reckon upon as the means of his security: and therefore if he be left or cast out of society, he perisheth; and if he live in society, it is by the errors of other men, which he could not foresee nor reckon upon, and consequently against the reason of his preservation; and so, as all men that contribute not to his destruction forbear him only out of ignorance of what is good for themselves.

...

Whatsoever is done to a man, conformable to¶ his own will signified to the doer, is not injury to him. For if he that doeth it hath not passed away his original right to do what he please by some antecedent covenant, there is no breach of covenant, and therefore no injury done him. And if he have, then his will to have it done, being signified, is a release of that covenant, and so again there is no injury done him.

Justice of actions is by writers** divided into *commutative* and *distributive*: and the former they say consisteth in proportion arithmetical; the latter in proportion geometrical. Commutative, therefore, they place in the equality of value of the things contracted for; and distributive, in the distribution of equal benefit to men of equal merit. As if it were injustice to sell

---

* A political unit (such as a state) founded on law and united by explicit or tacit agreement of the people for the common good.
† The universities or their teachings, the traditional "scholastic" syllabus handed down from the Middle Ages.
‡ Doesn't begin without.
§ A paraphrase from Psalm 14 (and Psalm 53) of the Bible: "The Fool has said in his heart, there is no God."
¶ Consistent with.
** A similar distinction would also have been known to Hobbes from Thomas Aquinas's *Summa Theologiae* (the second part of Part II, question 61).

dearer than we buy, or to give more to a man than he merits. The value of all things contracted for is measured by the appetite of the contractors, and therefore the just value is that which they be contented to give. And merit (besides that which is by covenant, where the performance on one part meriteth the performance of the other part, and falls under justice commutative, not distributive) is not due by justice, but is rewarded of grace* only. And therefore this distinction, in the sense wherein it useth to be expounded, is not right. To speak properly, commutative justice is the justice of a contractor; that is, a performance of covenant in buying and selling, hiring and letting to hire, lending and borrowing, exchanging, bartering, and other acts of contract.

And distributive justice, the justice of an arbitrator; that is to say, the act of defining what is just. Wherein, being trusted by them that make him arbitrator, if he perform his trust, he is said to distribute to every man his own: and this is indeed just distribution, and may be called, though improperly, distributive justice, but more properly equity, which also is a law of nature, as shall be shown in due place.

As justice dependeth on antecedent covenant;[†] so does *gratitude* depend on antecedent grace; that is to say, antecedent free-gift; and is the fourth law of nature, which may be conceived in this form: *that a man which receiveth benefit from another of mere grace endeavour that he which giveth it have no reasonable cause to repent him of his good will.* For no man giveth but with intention of good to himself, because gift is voluntary; and of all voluntary acts, the object is to every man his own good; of which if men see they shall be frustrated, there will be no beginning of benevolence or trust, nor consequently of mutual help, nor of reconciliation of one man to another; and therefore they are to remain still in the condition of war, which is contrary to the first and fundamental law of nature which commandeth men to *seek peace.* The breach of this law is called *ingratitude*, and hath the same relation to grace that injustice hath to obligation by covenant.

A fifth law of nature is *complaisance*;[‡] that is to say, *that every man strive to accommodate himself to the rest.* For the understanding whereof we may consider that there is in men's aptness to society a diversity of nature, rising from their diversity of affections, not unlike to that we see in stones brought together for building of an edifice. For as that stone which by the asperity[§] and irregularity of figure takes more room from others than itself fills, and for hardness cannot be easily made plain,[¶] and thereby hindereth the building, is by the builders cast away as unprofitable and troublesome: so also, a man that by asperity of nature will strive to retain those things which to himself are superfluous, and to others necessary, and for the stubbornness of his passions cannot be corrected, is to be left or cast out of society as cumbersome thereunto. For seeing every man, not only by right, but also by necessity of nature, is supposed to endeavour all he can to obtain that which is necessary for his conservation, he that shall oppose himself against it for things superfluous is guilty of the war that thereupon is to follow, and therefore doth that which is contrary to the fundamental law of nature, which commandeth to *seek peace.* The observers of this law may be called *sociable* (the Latins call them *commodi*); the contrary, *stubborn, insociable, froward,*[**] *intractable.*
...

These are the laws of nature, dictating peace, for a means of the conservation of men in multitudes; and which only concern the doctrine of civil society. There be other things tending to the destruction of particular men; as drunkenness, and all other parts of intemperance, which may therefore also be reckoned amongst those things which the law of nature hath forbidden, but are not necessary to be mentioned, nor are pertinent enough to this place.

And though this may seem too subtle a deduction of the laws of nature to be taken notice of by all men, whereof the most part are too busy in getting food, and the rest too negligent to understand; yet to

---

* Something freely given (even though it may not be deserved—that is, something the giver is entitled to either give or withhold, as they choose).
† A prior (already existing) contract.
‡ A desire to please others, affability.
§ Roughness.
¶ Smooth.
** Difficult to deal with, hard to please.

leave all men inexcusable, they have been contracted into one easy sum, intelligible even to the meanest capacity; and that is: *Do not that to another which thou wouldest not have done to thyself*, which showeth him that he has no more to do in learning the laws of nature but, when weighing the actions of other men with his own they seem too heavy, to put them into the other part of the balance, and his own into their place, that his own passions and self-love may add nothing to the weight; and then there is none of these laws of nature that will not appear unto him very reasonable.

The laws of nature oblige *in foro interno*;* that is to say, they bind to a desire they should take place: but *in foro externo*;† that is, to the putting them in act, not always. For he that should be modest and tractable, and perform all he promises in such time and place where no man else should do so, should but make himself a prey to others, and procure his own certain ruin, contrary to the ground of all laws of nature which tend to nature's preservation. And again, he that having sufficient security that others shall observe the same laws towards him, observes them not himself, seeketh not peace, but war, and consequently the destruction of his nature by violence.

And whatsoever laws bind *in foro interno* may be broken, not only by a fact contrary to the law, but also by a fact according to it, in case a man think it contrary. For though his action in this case be according to the law, yet his purpose was against the law; which, where the obligation is *in foro interno*, is a breach.

The laws of nature are immutable and eternal; for injustice, ingratitude, arrogance, pride, iniquity, acception‡ of persons, and the rest can never be made lawful. For it can never be that war shall preserve life, and peace destroy it.

The same laws, because they oblige§ only to a desire and endeavour (I mean an unfeigned and constant endeavour) are easy to be observed. For in that they require nothing but endeavour, he that endeavoureth their performance fulfilleth them; and he that fulfilleth the law is just.

And the science of them is the true and only moral philosophy. For moral philosophy is nothing else but the science of what is *good* and *evil* in the conversation and society of mankind. *Good* and *evil* are names that signify our appetites and aversions, which in different tempers, customs, and doctrines of men are different: and diverse men differ not only in their judgement on the senses of what is pleasant and unpleasant to the taste, smell, hearing, touch, and sight; but also of what is conformable or disagreeable to reason in the actions of common life. Nay, the same man, in diverse times, differs from himself; and one time praiseth, that is, calleth good, what another time he dispraiseth, and calleth evil: from whence arise disputes, controversies, and at last war. And therefore so long as a man is in the condition of mere nature, which is a condition of war, private appetite is the measure of good and evil: and consequently all men agree on this, that peace is good, and therefore also the way or means of peace, which (as I have shown before) are *justice, gratitude, modesty, equity, mercy*, and the rest of the laws of nature, are good; that is to say, *moral virtues*; and their contrary vices, evil. Now the science of virtue and vice is moral philosophy; and therefore the true doctrine of the laws of nature is the true moral philosophy. But the writers of moral philosophy, though they acknowledge the same virtues and vices; yet, not seeing wherein consisted their goodness, nor that they come to be praised as the means of peaceable, sociable, and comfortable living, place them in a mediocrity¶ of passions: as if not the cause, but the degree of daring, made fortitude; or not the cause, but the quantity of a gift, made liberality.

...

---

*   In the internal domain (literally, the "inner marketplace")—that is, psychologically or with respect to an individual's conscience or judgment.

†   In the external domain—that is, with respect to the social context.

‡   Favoritism, corrupt preference for one person over another.

§   Require (of one).

¶   A moderate amount, a mean (as in Aristotle's moral philosophy).

Chapter XVII: Of the Causes, Generation, and Definition of a Commonwealth

The final cause, end, or design of men (who naturally love liberty, and dominion over others) in the introduction of that restraint upon themselves, in which we see them live in commonwealths, is the foresight of their own preservation, and of a more contented life thereby; that is to say, of getting themselves out from that miserable condition of war which is necessarily consequent, as hath been shown, to the natural passions of men when there is no visible power to keep them in awe, and tie them by fear of punishment to the performance of their covenants, and observation of those laws of nature set down in the fourteenth and fifteenth chapters.

For the laws of nature—as *justice, equity, modesty, mercy*, and, in sum, *doing to others as we would be done to*—of themselves, without the terror of some power to cause them to be observed, are contrary to our natural passions, that carry us to partiality,* pride, revenge, and the like. And covenants, without the sword, are but words and of no strength to secure a man at all. Therefore, notwithstanding the laws of nature (which every one hath then kept, when he has the will to keep them, when he can do it safely), if there be no power erected, or not great enough for our security, every man will and may lawfully rely on his own strength and art for caution† against all other men. And in all places, where men have lived by small families,‡ to rob and spoil one another has been a trade, and so far from being reputed against the law of nature that the greater spoils they gained, the greater was their honour; and men observed no other laws therein but the laws of honour; that is, to abstain from cruelty, leaving to men their lives and instruments of husbandry. And as small families did then; so now do cities and kingdoms, which are but greater families (for their own security), enlarge their dominions upon all pretences of danger, and fear of invasion, or assistance that may be given to invaders; endeavour as much as they can to subdue or weaken their neighbours by open force, and secret arts, for want of other caution, justly; and are remembered for it in after ages with honour.

Nor is it the joining together of a small number of men that gives them this security; because in small numbers, small additions on the one side or the other make the advantage of strength so great as is sufficient to carry the victory, and therefore gives encouragement to an invasion. The multitude sufficient to confide in for our security is not determined by any certain number, but by comparison with the enemy we fear; and is then sufficient when the odds of the enemy§ is not of so visible and conspicuous moment to determine the event of war, as to move him to attempt.

And be there never so great a multitude; yet if their actions be directed according to their particular judgements, and particular appetites, they can expect thereby no defence, nor protection, neither against a common enemy, nor against the injuries of one another. For being distracted in opinions concerning the best use and application of their strength, they do not help, but hinder one another, and reduce their strength by mutual opposition to nothing: whereby they are easily, not only subdued by a very few that agree together, but also, when there is no common enemy, they make war upon each other for their particular interests. For if we could suppose a great multitude of men to consent in the observation of justice, and other laws of nature, without a common power to keep them all in awe, we might as well suppose all mankind to do the same; and then there neither would be, nor need to be, any civil government or commonwealth at all, because there would be peace without subjection.

Nor is it enough for the security, which men desire should last all the time of their life, that they be governed and directed by one judgement for a limited time; as in one battle, or one war. For though they obtain a victory by their unanimous endeavour against a foreign

---

*   Prejudice, bias (probably in favor of oneself).
†   Security, confident lack of anxiety.
‡   That is, in no larger organized groups.
§   The ratio of the enemy's strength to that of the defenders'.

enemy, yet afterwards, when either they have no common enemy, or he that by one part is held for an enemy is by another part held for a friend, they must needs by the difference of their interests dissolve, and fall again into a war amongst themselves....

The only way to erect such a common power, as may be able to defend them from the invasion of foreigners, and the injuries of one another, and thereby to secure them in such sort as that by their own industry and by the fruits of the earth they may nourish themselves and live contentedly, is to confer all their power and strength upon one man, or upon one assembly of men, that may reduce all their wills, by plurality of voices, unto one will: which is as much as to say, to appoint one man, or assembly of men, to bear their person;* and every one to own† and acknowledge himself to be author of whatsoever he that so beareth their person shall act, or cause to be acted, in those things which concern the common peace and safety; and therein to submit their wills, every one to his will, and their judgements to his judgement. This is more than consent, or concord; it is a real unity of them all in one and the same person, made by covenant of every man with every man, in such manner as if every man should say to every man: *I authorise and give up my right of governing myself to this man, or to this assembly of men, on this condition; that thou give up, thy right to him, and authorise all his actions in like manner.* This done, the multitude so united in one person is called a *commonwealth*; in Latin, *civitas*. This is the generation of that great *Leviathan*,‡ or rather, to speak more reverently, of that *Mortal God* to which we owe, under the *Immortal God*, our peace and defence. For by this authority, given him by every particular man in the commonwealth, he hath the use of so much power and strength conferred

on him that, by terror thereof, he is enabled to form the wills of them all, to peace at home, and mutual aid against their enemies abroad. And in him consisteth the essence of the commonwealth; which, to define it, is: *one person, of whose acts a great multitude, by mutual covenants one with another, have made themselves every one the author, to the end he may use the strength and means of them all as he shall think expedient for their peace and common defence.*

And he that carryeth this person is called sovereign, and said to have *sovereign power*; and every one besides,§ his subject.

The attaining to this sovereign power is by two ways. One, by natural force: as when a man maketh his children to submit themselves, and their children, to his government, as being able to destroy them if they refuse; or by war subdueth his enemies to his will, giving them their lives on that condition. The other, is when men agree amongst themselves to submit to some man, or assembly of men, voluntarily, on confidence to be protected by him against all others. This latter may be called a political commonwealth, or commonwealth by *institution*; and the former, a commonwealth by *acquisition*. And first, I shall speak of a commonwealth by institution.

Chapter XVIII: Of the Rights of Sovereigns by Institution

A *commonwealth* is said to be *instituted* when a *multitude* of men do agree, and *covenant*, *every one with every one*, that to whatsoever *man*, or *assembly of men*, shall be given by the major part the *right* to *present* the person of them all, that is to say, to be their *representative*; every

---

*   Act as their representative.

†   Admit, agree.

‡   This is an allusion to the Old Testament book of Job, where Leviathan is described as a fearsome, fire-breathing, many-headed sea monster. Leviathan's symbolic meaning in the Bible is obscure, but it was sometimes associated with the devil by biblical commentators (such as Aquinas). In the book of Revelation, it is written that God's final victory over Leviathan will herald the end of the world. Why Hobbes chose this controversy-inducing label for the state, and even made it the title of his work, is obscure. However, in a later passage (at the end of Chapter XXVIII) Hobbes quotes from Job: "There is nothing on earth to be compared with him. He is made so as not to be afraid. He seeth every high thing below him, and is king of all the children of pride" (Job 41:33–34). Yet, Hobbes points out, Leviathan "is mortal and subject to decay, as all other earthly creatures are, and ... there is that in heaven (though not on earth) that he should stand in fear of, and whose laws he ought to obey."

§   Everyone else.

one, as well* he that *voted for it* as he that *voted against it*, shall *authorize* all the actions and judgements of that man, or assembly of men, in the same manner as if they were his own, to the end to live peaceably amongst themselves, and be protected against other men.

From this institution of a commonwealth are derived all the *rights* and *faculties* of him, or them, on whom the sovereign power is conferred by the consent of the people assembled.

First, because they covenant, it is to be understood they are not obliged by former covenant to anything repugnant hereunto.† And consequently they that have already instituted a commonwealth, being thereby bound by covenant to own the actions and judgements of one, cannot lawfully make a new covenant amongst themselves to be obedient to any other, in anything whatsoever, without his permission. And therefore, they that are subjects to a monarch cannot without his leave cast off monarchy and return to the confusion of a disunited multitude; nor transfer their person from him that beareth it to another man, or other assembly of men: for they are bound, every man to every man, to own and be reputed author of all that he that already is their sovereign shall do and judge fit to be done; so that any one man dissenting, all the rest should break their covenant made to that man, which is injustice: and they have also every man given the sovereignty to him that beareth their person; and therefore if they depose him, they take from him that which is his own, and so again it is injustice....

Secondly, because the right of bearing the person of them all is given to him they make sovereign, by covenant only of one to another, and not of him to any of them, there can happen no breach of covenant on the part of the sovereign; and consequently none of his subjects, by any pretence of forfeiture,‡ can be freed from his subjection. That he which is made sovereign maketh no covenant with his subjects beforehand is manifest; because either he must make it with the whole multitude, as one party to the covenant, or he must make a several§ covenant with every man. With the whole, as one party, it is impossible, because as yet they are not

one person: and if he make so many several covenants as there be men, those covenants after he hath the sovereignty are void; because what act soever can be pretended by any one of them for breach thereof is the act both of himself, and of all the rest, because done in the person and by the right of every one of them in particular. Besides, if any one or more of them pretend a breach of the covenant made by the sovereign at his institution, and others or one other of his subjects, or himself alone, pretend there was no such breach, there is in this case no judge to decide the controversy: it returns therefore to the sword again; and every man recovereth the right of protecting himself by his own strength, contrary to the design they had in the institution. It is therefore in vain to grant sovereignty by way of precedent covenant. The opinion that any monarch receiveth his power by covenant, that is to say, on condition, proceedeth from want of understanding this easy truth: that covenants being but words, and breath, have no force to oblige, contain, constrain, or protect any man, but what it has from the public sword; that is, from the untied hands of that man, or assembly of men, that hath the sovereignty, and whose actions are avouched by them all, and performed by the strength of them all, in him united....

Thirdly, because the major part¶ hath by consenting voices declared a sovereign, he that dissented must now consent with the rest; that is, be contented to avow all the actions he shall do, or else justly be destroyed by the rest. For if he voluntarily entered into the congregation of them that were assembled, he sufficiently declared thereby his will, and therefore tacitly covenanted, to stand to what the major part should ordain: and therefore if he refuse to stand thereto, or make protestation against any of their decrees, he does contrary to his covenant, and therefore unjustly. And whether he be of the congregation or not, and whether his consent be asked or not, he must either submit to their decrees or be left in the condition of war he was in before; wherein he might without injustice be destroyed by any man whatsoever.

Fourthly, because every subject is by this institution author of all the actions and judgements of the

---

* Just as much.
† In conflict with (the present covenant).
‡ Breaking of an agreement.
§ Separate, individual.
¶ The majority.

sovereign instituted, it follows that whatsoever he doth, can be no injury to any of his subjects; nor ought he to be by any of them accused of injustice....

Fifthly, and consequently to that which was said last, no man that hath sovereign power can justly be put to death, or otherwise in any manner by his subjects punished. For seeing every subject is author of the actions of his sovereign, he punisheth another for the actions committed by himself.

And because the end of this institution is the peace and defence of them all, and whosoever has right to the end has right to the means, it belongeth of right to whatsoever man or assembly that hath the sovereignty to be judge both of the means of peace and defence, and also of the hindrances and disturbances of the same; and to do whatsoever he shall think necessary to be done, both beforehand (for the preserving of peace and security, by prevention of discord at home, and hostility from abroad) and when peace and security are lost, for the recovery of the same. And therefore,

Sixthly, it is annexed to the sovereignty to be judge of what opinions and doctrines are averse, and what conducing, to peace; and consequently, on what occasions, how far, and what men are to be trusted withal in speaking to multitudes of people; and who shall examine the doctrines of all books before they be published. For the actions of men proceed from their opinions, and in the well-governing of opinions consisteth the well-governing of men's actions in order to their peace and concord....

Seventhly, is annexed to the sovereignty the whole power of prescribing the rules whereby every man may know what goods he may enjoy, and what actions he may do, without being molested by any of his fellow subjects: and this is it men call *propriety*. For before constitution of sovereign power, as hath already been shown, all men had right to all things, which necessarily causeth war: and therefore this propriety, being necessary to peace, and depending on sovereign power, is the act of that power, in order to the public peace....

Eighthly, is annexed to the sovereignty the right of *judicature*; that is to say, of hearing and deciding all controversies which may arise concerning law, either civil or natural, or concerning fact....

Ninthly, is annexed to the sovereignty the right of making war and peace with other nations and commonwealths; that is to say, of judging when it is for the public good, and how great forces are to be assembled, armed, and paid for that end, and to levy money upon the subjects to defray the expenses thereof....

Tenthly, is annexed to the sovereignty the choosing of all counsellors, ministers, magistrates, and officers, both in peace and war. For seeing the sovereign is charged with the end, which is the common peace and defence, he is understood to have power to use such means as he shall think most fit for his discharge.

Eleventhly, to the sovereign is committed the power of rewarding with riches or honour; and of punishing with corporal or pecuniary punishment,[*] or with ignominy,[†] every subject according to the law he hath formerly made; or if there be no law made, according as he shall judge most to conduce to the encouraging of men to serve the commonwealth, or deterring of them from doing disservice to the same.

Lastly, considering what values men are naturally apt to set upon themselves, what respect they look for from others, and how little they value other men; from whence continually arise amongst them, emulation,[‡] quarrels, factions, and at last war, to the destroying of one another, and diminution of their strength against a common enemy; it is necessary that there be laws of honour, and a public rate of the worth of such men as have deserved or are able to deserve well of the commonwealth, and that there be force in the hands of some or other to put those laws in execution. But it hath already been shown that not only the whole *militia*, or forces of the commonwealth, but also the judicature of all controversies, is annexed to the sovereignty. To the sovereign therefore it belongeth also to give titles of honour, and to appoint what order of place and dignity each man shall hold, and what signs of respect in public or private meetings they shall give to one another.

These are the rights which make the essence of sovereignty, and which are the marks whereby a man may discern in what man, or assembly of men, the sovereign power is placed and resideth.... ■

---

* Monetary punishment, that is, a fine.
† Shame, public disgrace.
‡ Ambitious or envious rivalry for power or honor.

Suggestions for Critical Reflection

1. Hobbes appears to argue that, in the state of nature, everybody is fundamentally equal in ability and in rights. Is that what he means? If so, is he right about this? If he is, does this mean all *social* inequalities are based on nothing more than convention?

2. Hobbes argues that human beings, in the state of nature, are in a continual state of "war of every one against every one." How good are his arguments for this claim? Are there any real-world examples of groups of people who are in the state of nature (as Hobbes defines it) but *not* at war with each other? If Hobbes incorrectly equates the state of nature with a condition of warfare, how seriously does this affect his subsequent arguments?

3. "By *liberty* is understood, according to the proper signification of the word, the absence of external impediments." Is this a fully adequate definition? Is Hobbes's view of liberty significant for the political theory that he develops? (For example, would someone who took a different view of freedom be happy with Hobbes's view of sovereign power?)

4. At one point, Hobbes suggests injustice is a kind of absurdity or inconsistency, and thus to be unjust is simply to be irrational. Is Hobbes right (in the terms of his own theory)? If so, does this show something about Hobbes's *definition* of injustice? Is injustice really nothing more or less than "*the not performance of covenant*"?

5. "Of the voluntary acts of every man, the object is some *good to himself*." Is this true? Is it a realistic assumption, or is Hobbes being excessively pessimistic about human nature? (Taken in the wider context of this reading, does it seem that Hobbes means to describe how human beings invariably *do* behave, or to state how people *should* behave if they are being rational? Does the way his claim is understood make a difference to Hobbes's argument?)

6. Hobbes argues that, in the state of nature, there is no justice. If Hobbes is right about this, does it follow that all human beings are *immoral* by nature?

7. Does Hobbes reconcile morality and self-interest? That is, does he successfully show that they are *the same thing*? (Is this, in fact, what he is trying to do?.

8. "Whatsoever is done to a man, conformable to his own will signified to the doer, is not injury to him." Does this follow logically from Hobbes's assumptions? If it does, is this a problem for those assumptions?

9. Does Hobbes count the exit from the state of nature into a commonwealth as a contract? Is this (or would this be) contrary to his own views? Since there is no mechanism for enforcing agreements in the state of nature, how can people in that state first contract together to form a commonwealth? How could this first crucial covenant be made *before* there exists a power to enforce covenants?

10. Hobbes argues that, once a commonwealth has been set up, every member of the commonwealth must treat the sovereign's actions as being *their own* actions—must "*authorize* all the actions and judgments of that man, or assembly of men, in the same manner as if they were his own"—even if those actions cause them personal hardship. (So, for example, if the state puts you in prison it is no different than if you had voluntarily locked yourself up.) Does this seem reasonable? Is it a crucial part of Hobbes's political theory, or could he have adopted a weaker position on this point?

11. What view do you think Hobbes would take of the notion of *democratically elected* government? What would be his view of civil disobedience or protest movements?

JOHN STUART MILL

FROM *On Liberty*

For some information on Mill's life and his overall philosophical project, please see the introduction to Mill earlier in this volume.

What Is the Structure of This Reading?

On Liberty is a short five-chapter book, parts of the first, second, and fourth chapters of which are reprinted here. Mill's topic is the extent to which the state, and society in general, ought to have authority over the lives of individuals: the problem of setting limits to society's claims upon the individual, Mill asserts, is "the principal question in human affairs" but, he laments, its solution has not yet been put on a properly rational footing. Mill seeks to address this by formulating "one very simple principle"—sometimes today known as the "harm principle"—that should "govern absolutely the dealings of society with the individual in the way of compulsion and control." After some clarificatory remarks about this principle, Mill argues in defense of it beginning, in Chapter II, with the particular case of liberty of thought and discussion.

Mill's argument for the freedom of thought has three parts. He considers, first, the possibility that the received opinions might be false and the heretical ones true; second, the possibility that the received views are completely true and the heresy false; and lastly, a situation where dogma and heresy both contain only a part of the truth. In each case, Mill argues, allowing complete freedom of thought and discussion provides much greater value than harm to society.

In Chapter III (not included here) Mill discusses the importance of individuality to human well-being, describing it as a valuable component of personal happiness and an essential motor of social progress. In Chapter IV, therefore, he goes on to consider the question of the proper borderline between personal individuality and social authority, and uses his "harm principle" to show how this border should be drawn. The final chapter (not included) describes some illustrative applications of the principle to detailed sample cases, such as trade regulation, liquor taxation, and marriage laws.

Some Common Misconceptions

1. In arguing for the freedom of thought and discussion, Mill asserts we can never be *completely sure* that views which oppose our own, and which we might want to suppress, are not true (and thus we can never be completely sure that our own views are not false). However, he stresses that he does not mean that we should never feel certain of our own views, or that we should never act on them, or even that we should not attempt to persuade others of their truth. Mill is by no means a skeptic about the possibility of human knowledge and certainty. Rather, Mill argues that we should not *force* others to adopt our views—even if we are completely satisfied with their truth—by preventing them from hearing or thinking about alternative positions.

2. In arguing for firm limits on the authority of society over the individual, Mill is not arguing for the kind of a *laissez-faire* system in which everyone is assumed to be fundamentally self-interested, and where individuals are thought to have no moral duties towards their fellow-citizens except those arising from their own self-interest. On the contrary, he claims "[h]uman beings owe to each other help to distinguish the better from the worse, and encouragement to choose the former and avoid the latter," and he thought it was very much society's role to provide opportunities and incentives for self-improvement to its citizens.

    Similarly, Mill is not simply claiming that society should interfere with individuals as little as possible—that, for example, the coercion of individuals by the state is always a bad thing and should be resorted to only when necessary. By contrast, he thinks there is a sphere in which society should not interfere with its members but also a sphere in which it *ought* to do so: individuals do have duties to the other members of the societies of which they are a part, and society has the right to force people to perform those duties.

3. Mill's style of argument in this essay includes (appropriately enough) raising objections to his own position and making them as forcefully as he can, and then responding to them. As you read, take care that you distinguish between Mill's own views and those he presents and then argues against.

How Important and Influential Is This Passage?

Mill's *On Liberty* has been a 'classic' since it was first published. To his great satisfaction, it immediately inspired intense debate between fervent supporters of the views expressed in the book and sharp critics of them, and—though many of the ideas it contains have now become quite familiar—the work is still the focus of substantial controversy today. *On Liberty* is generally considered to be one of the central statements of classical liberalism, and one of the finest defenses of individualism and freedom of thought ever written.

FROM *On Liberty**

Chapter I: Introductory

... A time ... came in the progress of human affairs, when men ceased to think it a necessity of nature that their governors should be an independent power, opposed in interest to themselves. It appeared to them much better that the various magistrates of the State should be their tenants or delegates, revocable at their pleasure. In that way alone, it seemed, could they have complete security that the powers of government would never be abused to their disadvantage. By degrees, this new demand for elective and temporary rulers became the prominent object of the exertions of the popular party, wherever any such party existed; and superseded, to a considerable extent, the previous efforts to limit the power of rulers. As the struggle proceeded for making the ruling power emanate from the periodical choice of the ruled, some persons began to think that too much importance had been attached to the limitation of the power itself. That (it might seem) was a resource against rulers whose interests were habitually opposed to those of the people. What

was now wanted was, that the rulers should be identified with the people; that their interest and will should be the interest and will of the nation. The nation did not need to be protected against its own will. There was no fear of its tyrannizing over itself. Let the rulers be effectually responsible to it, promptly removable by it, and it could afford to trust them with power of which it could itself dictate the use to be made. Their power was but the nation's own power, concentrated, and in a form convenient for exercise....

But, in political and philosophical theories, as well as in persons, success discloses faults and infirmities which failure might have concealed from observation. The notion, that the people have no need to limit their power over themselves, might seem axiomatic, when popular government was a thing only dreamed about, or read of as having existed at some distant period of the past. Neither was that notion necessarily disturbed by such temporary aberrations as those of the French Revolution,† the worst of which were the work of an usurping few, and which, in any case, belonged, not to the permanent working of popular institutions, but to

---

* *On Liberty* was first published in London in 1859.

† The French Revolution, which began with the storming of the Bastille prison in 1789, toppled the Bourbon monarchy—King Louis XVI was executed in 1793—but failed to produce a stable form of republican government and, after a period of ruthless extremism known as the Reign of Terror (1793–94), was eventually replaced by Napoleon Bonaparte's imperial reign in 1799.

a sudden and convulsive outbreak against monarchical and aristocratic despotism. In time, however, a democratic republic* came to occupy a large portion of the earth's surface, and made itself felt as one of the most powerful members of the community of nations; and elective and responsible government became subject to the observations and criticisms which wait upon a great existing fact. It was now perceived that such phrases as "self-government," and "the power of the people over themselves," do not express the true state of the case. The "people" who exercise the power, are not always the same people with those over whom it is exercised, and the "self-government" spoken of, is not the government of each by himself, but of each by all the rest. The will of the people, moreover, practically means, the will of the most numerous or the most active *part* of the people; the majority, or those who succeed in making themselves accepted as the majority; the people, consequently, *may* desire to oppress a part of their number; and precautions are as much needed against this, as against any other abuse of power. The limitation, therefore, of the power of government over individuals, loses none of its importance when the holders of power are regularly accountable to the community, that is, to the strongest party therein. This view of things, recommending itself equally to the intelligence of thinkers and to the inclination of those important classes in European society to whose real or supposed interests democracy is adverse, has had no difficulty in establishing itself; and in political speculations "the tyranny of the majority" is now generally included among the evils against which society requires to be on its guard.

Like other tyrannies, the tyranny of the majority was at first, and is still vulgarly,† held in dread, chiefly as operating through the acts of the public authorities. But reflecting persons perceived that when society is itself the tyrant—society collectively, over the separate individuals who compose it—its means of tyrannizing are not restricted to the acts which it may do by the hands of its political functionaries. Society can and does execute its own mandates: and if it issues wrong mandates instead of right, or any mandates at all in things with which it ought not to meddle, it practises

a social tyranny more formidable than many kinds of political oppression, since, though not usually upheld by such extreme penalties, it leaves fewer means of escape, penetrating much more deeply into the details of life, and enslaving the soul itself. Protection, therefore, against the tyranny of the magistrate is not enough; there needs protection also against the tyranny of the prevailing opinion and feeling; against the tendency of society to impose, by other means than civil penalties, its own ideas and practices as rules of conduct on those who dissent from them; to fetter the development, and, if possible, prevent the formation, of any individuality not in harmony with its ways, and compel all characters to fashion themselves upon the model of its own. There is a limit to the legitimate interference of collective opinion with individual independence; and to find that limit, and maintain it against encroachment, is as indispensable to a good condition of human affairs, as protection against political despotism.

But though this proposition is not likely to be contested in general terms, the practical question, where to place the limit—how to make the fitting adjustment between individual independence and social control—is a subject on which nearly everything remains to be done. All that makes existence valuable to any one, depends on the enforcement of restraints upon the actions of other people. Some rules of conduct, therefore, must be imposed, by law in the first place, and by opinion on many things which are not fit subjects for the operation of law. What these rules should be, is the principal question in human affairs; but if we except a few of the most obvious cases, it is one of those which least progress has been made in resolving. No two ages, and scarcely any two countries, have decided it alike; and the decision of one age or country is a wonder to another. Yet the people of any given age and country no more suspect any difficulty in it, than if it were a subject on which mankind had always been agreed. The rules which obtain among themselves appear to them self-evident and self-justifying. This all but universal illusion is one of the examples of the magical influence of custom, which is not only, as the proverb says a second nature, but is continually mistaken for the first. The

---

*   The United States of America.
†   Commonly, popularly.

effect of custom, in preventing any misgiving respecting the rules of conduct which mankind impose on one another, is all the more complete because the subject is one on which it is not generally considered necessary that reasons should be given, either by one person to others, or by each to himself. People are accustomed to believe and have been encouraged in the belief by some who aspire to the character of philosophers, that their feelings, on subjects of this nature, are better than reasons, and render reasons unnecessary. The practical principle which guides them to their opinions on the regulation of human conduct, is the feeling in each person's mind that everybody should be required to act as he, and those with whom he sympathizes, would like them to act....

The likings and dislikings of society, or of some powerful portion of it, are thus the main thing which has practically determined the rules laid down for general observance, under the penalties of law or opinion. And in general, those who have been in advance of society in thought and feeling, have left this condition of things unassailed in principle, however they may have come into conflict with it in some of its details. They have occupied themselves rather in inquiring what things society ought to like or dislike, than in questioning whether its likings or dislikings should be a law to individuals. They preferred endeavouring to alter the feelings of mankind on the particular points on which they were themselves heretical, rather than make common cause in defence of freedom, with heretics generally....

The object of this Essay is to assert one very simple principle, as entitled to govern absolutely the dealings of society with the individual in the way of compulsion and control, whether the means used be physical force in the form of legal penalties, or the moral coercion of public opinion. That principle is, that the sole end for which mankind are warranted, individually or collectively in interfering with the liberty of action of any of their number, is self-protection. That the only purpose for which power can be rightfully exercised over any member of a civilized community, against his will, is to prevent harm to others. His own good, either physical or moral, is not a sufficient warrant. He cannot rightfully be compelled to do or forbear because it will be better for him to do so, because it will make him happier, because, in the opinions of others, to do so would be wise, or even right. These are good reasons for remonstrating* with him, or reasoning with him, or persuading him, or entreating him, but not for compelling him, or visiting him with any evil, in case† he do otherwise. To justify that, the conduct from which it is desired to deter him must be calculated to produce evil to some one else. The only part of the conduct of any one, for which he is amenable to society, is that which concerns others. In the part which merely concerns himself, his independence is, of right, absolute. Over himself, over his own body and mind, the individual is sovereign.

It is, perhaps, hardly necessary to say that this doctrine is meant to apply only to human beings in the maturity of their faculties. We are not speaking of children, or of young persons below the age which the law may fix as that of manhood or womanhood. Those who are still in a state to require being taken care of by others, must be protected against their own actions as well as against external injury. For the same reason, we may leave out of consideration those backward states of society in which the race itself may be considered as in its nonage.‡ The early difficulties in the way of spontaneous progress are so great, that there is seldom any choice of means for overcoming them; and a ruler full of the spirit of improvement is warranted in the use of any expedients that will attain an end, perhaps otherwise unattainable. Despotism is a legitimate mode of government in dealing with barbarians, provided the end be their improvement, and the means justified by actually effecting that end. Liberty, as a principle, has no application to any state of things anterior to the time when mankind have become capable of being improved by free and equal discussion. Until then, there is nothing for them but implicit obedience to an Akbar or a

---

* Forcefully arguing.
† If.
‡ A period of immaturity, being underage.

Charlemagne,* if they are so fortunate as to find one. But as soon as mankind have attained the capacity of being guided to their own improvement by conviction or persuasion (a period long since reached in all nations with whom we need here concern ourselves), compulsion, either in the direct form or in that of pains and penalties for non-compliance, is no longer admissible as a means to their own good, and justifiable only for the security of others.

It is proper to state that I forego any advantage which could be derived to my argument from the idea of abstract right as a thing independent of utility. I regard utility as the ultimate appeal on all ethical questions; but it must be utility in the largest sense, grounded on the permanent interests of man as a progressive being. Those interests, I contend, authorize the subjection of individual spontaneity to external control, only in respect to those actions of each, which concern the interest of other people. If any one does an act hurtful to others, there is a *prima facie*† case for punishing him, by law, or, where legal penalties are not safely applicable, by general disapprobation.‡ There are also many positive acts for the benefit of others, which he may rightfully be compelled to perform; such as, to give evidence in a court of justice; to bear his fair share in the common defence, or in any other joint work necessary to the interest of the society of which he enjoys the protection; and to perform certain acts of individual beneficence, such as saving a fellow-creature's life, or interposing to protect the defenceless against ill-usage, things which whenever it is obviously a man's duty to do, he may rightfully be made responsible to society for not doing. A person may cause evil to others not only by his actions but by his inaction, and in either case he is justly accountable to them for the injury....

But there is a sphere of action in which society, as distinguished from the individual, has, if any, only an indirect interest; comprehending§ all that portion of a person's life and conduct which affects only himself, or, if it also affects others, only with their free, voluntary, and undeceived consent and participation. When I say only himself, I mean directly, and in the first instance: for whatever affects himself, may affect others through himself; and the objection which may be grounded on this contingency, will receive consideration in the sequel. This, then, is the appropriate region of human liberty. It comprises, first, the inward domain of consciousness; demanding liberty of conscience, in the most comprehensive sense; liberty of thought and feeling; absolute freedom of opinion and sentiment on all subjects, practical or speculative, scientific, moral, or theological. The liberty of expressing and publishing opinions may seem to fall under a different principle, since it belongs to that part of the conduct of an individual which concerns other people; but, being almost of as much importance as the liberty of thought itself, and resting in great part on the same reasons, is practically inseparable from it. Secondly, the principle requires liberty of tastes and pursuits; of framing the plan of our life to suit our own character; of doing as we like, subject to such consequences as may follow; without impediment from our fellow-creatures, so long as what we do does not harm them even though they should think our conduct foolish, perverse, or wrong. Thirdly, from this liberty of each individual, follows the liberty, within the same limits, of combination among individuals; freedom to unite, for any purpose not involving harm to others: the persons combining being supposed to be of full age, and not forced or deceived.

No society in which these liberties are not, on the whole, respected, is free, whatever may be its form of government; and none is completely free in which they do not exist absolute and unqualified. The only

---

* Akbar the Great was Mogul emperor of northern India from 1556 to 1605. He is generally considered the founder of the Mogul empire, and was famous for implementing an effective administrative system, imposing religious tolerance, and making his court a center for art and literature. Charlemagne ("Charles the Great") was king of the Franks from 768 to 814. His armies conquered much of central and western Europe—including parts of Spain, Italy, Saxony, Bavaria, Austria, and Hungary—and, in 800, he was anointed the first Holy Roman Emperor by Pope Leo III. Like Akbar, Charlemagne is known for making his court a great center of culture and scholarship, and for imposing an effective legal and administrative structure on his dominions.

† At first sight, on first impression.

‡ Strong (moral) disapproval.

§ Including, covering.

freedom which deserves the name, is that of pursuing our own good in our own way, so long as we do not attempt to deprive others of theirs, or impede their efforts to obtain it. Each is the proper guardian of his own health, whether bodily, or mental or spiritual. Mankind are greater gainers by suffering each other to live as seems good to themselves, than by compelling each to live as seems good to the rest....

Chapter II: Of the Liberty of Thought and Discussion

The time, it is to be hoped, is gone by when any defence would be necessary of the "liberty of the press" as one of the securities against corrupt or tyrannical government. No argument, we may suppose, can now be needed, against permitting a legislature or an executive, not identified in interest with the people, to prescribe opinions to them, and determine what doctrines or what arguments they shall be allowed to hear. This aspect of the question, besides, has been so often and so triumphantly enforced by preceding writers, that it needs not be specially insisted on in this place. Though the law of England, on the subject of the press, is as servile to this day as it was in the time of the Tudors,* there is little danger of its being actually put in force against political discussion, except during some temporary panic, when fear of insurrection drives ministers and judges from their propriety; ... and, speaking generally, it is not, in constitutional countries, to be apprehended that the government, whether completely responsible to the people or not, will often attempt to control the expression of opinion, except when in doing so it makes itself the organ of the general intolerance of the public. Let us suppose, therefore, that the government is entirely at one with the people, and never thinks of exerting any power of coercion unless in agreement with what it conceives to be their voice. But I deny the right of the people to exercise such coercion, either by themselves or by their government. The power itself is illegitimate. The best government has no more title to it than the worst. It is as noxious, or more noxious, when exerted in accordance with public opinion, than when in opposition to it. If all mankind minus one, were of one opinion, and only one person were of the contrary opinion, mankind would be no more justified in silencing that one person, than he, if he had the power, would be justified in silencing mankind. Were an opinion a personal possession of no value except to the owner; if to be obstructed in the enjoyment of it were simply a private injury, it would make some difference whether the injury was inflicted only on a few persons or on many. But the peculiar evil of silencing the expression of an opinion is, that it is robbing the human race; posterity† as well as the existing generation; those who dissent from the opinion, still more than those who hold it. If the opinion is right, they are deprived of the opportunity of exchanging error for truth: if wrong, they lose, what is almost as great a benefit, the clearer perception and livelier impression of truth, produced by its collision with error.

It is necessary to consider separately these two hypotheses, each of which has a distinct branch of the argument corresponding to it. We can never be sure that the opinion we are endeavouring to stifle is a false opinion; and if we were sure, stifling it would be an evil still.

First: the opinion which it is attempted to suppress by authority may possibly be true. Those who desire to suppress it, of course deny its truth; but they are not infallible. They have no authority to decide the question for all mankind, and exclude every other person from the means of judging. To refuse a hearing to an opinion, because they are sure that it is false, is to assume that *their* certainty is the same thing as *absolute* certainty. All silencing of discussion is an assumption of infallibility. Its condemnation may be allowed to rest on this common argument, not the worse for being common.

Unfortunately for the good sense of mankind, the fact of their fallibility is far from carrying the weight in their practical judgment, which is always allowed to it in theory; for while every one well knows himself to be fallible, few think it necessary to take any precautions against their own fallibility, or admit the supposition that any opinion of which they feel very certain, may be one of the examples of the error to which they

---

* The royal dynasty ruling England from 1485 to 1603 (Henry VII–Elizabeth I).

† Future generations of people.

acknowledge themselves to be liable. Absolute princes, or others who are accustomed to unlimited deference, usually feel this complete confidence in their own opinions on nearly all subjects. People more happily situated, who sometimes hear their opinions disputed, and are not wholly unused to be set right when they are wrong, place the same unbounded reliance only on such of their opinions as are shared by all who surround them, or to whom they habitually defer: for in proportion to a man's want of confidence in his own solitary judgment, does he usually repose, with implicit trust, on the infallibility of "the world" in general. And the world, to each individual, means the part of it with which he comes in contact; his party, his sect, his church, his class of society: the man may be called, by comparison, almost liberal and large-minded to whom it means anything so comprehensive as his own country or his own age. Nor is his faith in this collective authority at all shaken by his being aware that other ages, countries, sects, churches, classes, and parties have thought, and even now think, the exact reverse. He devolves upon* his own world the responsibility of being in the right against the dissentient worlds of other people; and it never troubles him that mere accident has decided which of these numerous worlds is the object of his reliance, and that the same causes which make him a Churchman in London, would have made him a Buddhist or a Confucian in Pekin.† Yet it is as evident in itself as any amount of argument can make it, that ages are no more infallible than individuals; every age having held many opinions which subsequent ages have deemed not only false but absurd; and it is as certain that many opinions, now general, will be rejected by future ages, as it is that many, once general, are rejected by the present.

The objection likely to be made to this argument, would probably take some such form as the following. There is no greater assumption of infallibility in forbidding the propagation of error, than in any other thing which is done by public authority on its own judgment and responsibility. Judgment is given to men that they may use it. Because it may be used erroneously, are men to be told that they ought not to use it at all? To prohibit what they think pernicious, is not

claiming exemption from error, but fulfilling the duty incumbent on them, although fallible, of acting on their conscientious conviction. If we were never to act on our opinions, because those opinions may be wrong, we should leave all our interests uncared for, and all our duties unperformed. An objection which applies to all conduct can be no valid objection to any conduct in particular. It is the duty of governments, and of individuals, to form the truest opinions they can; to form them carefully, and never impose them upon others unless they are quite sure of being right. But when they are sure (such reasoners may say), it is not conscientiousness but cowardice to shrink from acting on their opinions, and allow doctrines which they honestly think dangerous to the welfare of mankind, either in this life or in another, to be scattered abroad without restraint, because other people, in less enlightened times, have persecuted opinions now believed to be true. Let us take care, it may be said, not to make the same mistake: but governments and nations have made mistakes in other things, which are not denied to be fit subjects for the exercise of authority: they have laid on bad taxes, made unjust wars. Ought we therefore to lay on no taxes, and, under whatever provocation, make no wars? Men, and governments, must act to the best of their ability. There is no such thing as absolute certainty, but there is assurance sufficient for the purposes of human life. We may, and must, assume our opinion to be true for the guidance of our own conduct: and it is assuming no more when we forbid bad men to pervert society by the propagation of opinions which we regard as false and pernicious.

I answer, that it is assuming very much more. There is the greatest difference between presuming an opinion to be true, because, with every opportunity for contesting it, it has not been refuted, and assuming its truth for the purpose of not permitting its refutation. Complete liberty of contradicting and disproving our opinion, is the very condition which justifies us in assuming its truth for purposes of action; and on no other terms can a being with human faculties have any rational assurance of being right.

When we consider either the history of opinion, or the ordinary conduct of human life, to what is it to

---

* Delegates, transfers to.
† Today called Beijing, the capital of China.

be ascribed that the one and the other are no worse than they are? Not certainly to the inherent force of the human understanding; for, on any matter not self-evident, there are ninety-nine persons totally incapable of judging of it, for one who is capable; and the capacity of the hundredth person is only comparative; for the majority of the eminent men of every past generation held many opinions now known to be erroneous, and did or approved numerous things which no one will now justify. Why is it, then, that there is on the whole a preponderance* among mankind of rational opinions and rational conduct? If there really is this preponderance—which there must be, unless human affairs are, and have always been, in an almost desperate state—it is owing to a quality of the human mind, the source of everything respectable in man, either as an intellectual or as a moral being, namely, that his errors are corrigible.† He is capable of rectifying his mistakes by discussion and experience. Not by experience alone. There must be discussion, to show how experience is to be interpreted. Wrong opinions and practices gradually yield to fact and argument: but facts and arguments, to produce any effect on the mind, must be brought before it. Very few facts are able to tell their own story, without comments to bring out their meaning. The whole strength and value, then, of human judgment, depending on the one property, that it can be set right when it is wrong, reliance can be placed on it only when the means of setting it right are kept constantly at hand. In the case of any person whose judgment is really deserving of confidence, how has it become so? Because he has kept his mind open to criticism of his opinions and conduct. Because it has been his practice to listen to all that could be said against him; to profit by as much of it as was just, and expound to himself, and upon occasion to others, the fallacy of what was fallacious. Because he has felt, that the only way in which a human being can make some approach to knowing the whole of a subject, is by hearing what can be said about it by persons of every variety of opinion, and studying all modes in which it can be looked at by every character of mind. No wise man ever acquired his wisdom in any mode but this; nor is it in the nature of human intellect to become wise in any other manner. The steady habit of correcting and completing his own opinion by collating it with those of others, so far from causing doubt and hesitation in carrying it into practice, is the only stable foundation for a just reliance on it: for, being cognizant of all that can, at least obviously, be said against him, and having taken up his position against all gainsayers knowing that he has sought for objections and difficulties, instead of avoiding them, and has shut out no light which can be thrown upon the subject from any quarter—he has a right to think his judgment better than that of any person, or any multitude, who have not gone through a similar process.

... In order more fully to illustrate the mischief of denying a hearing to opinions because we, in our own judgment, have condemned them, it will be desirable to fix down the discussion to a concrete case; and I choose, by preference, the cases which are least favourable to me—in which the argument against freedom of opinion, both on the score of truth and on that of utility, is considered the strongest. Let the opinions impugned be the belief in a God and in a future state,‡ or any of the commonly received doctrines of morality. To fight the battle on such ground, gives a great advantage to an unfair antagonist; since he will be sure to say (and many who have no desire to be unfair will say it internally), Are these the doctrines which you do not deem sufficiently certain to be taken under the protection of law? Is the belief in a God one of the opinions, to feel sure of which, you hold to be assuming infallibility? But I must be permitted to observe, that it is not the feeling sure of a doctrine (be it what it may) which I call an assumption of infallibility. It is the undertaking to decide that question *for others*, without allowing them to hear what can be said on the contrary side. And I denounce and reprobate this pretension§ not the less, if put forth on the side of my most solemn convictions. However positive any one's

---

* Superiority in weight or number.
† Correctable.
‡ An afterlife.
§ Reject this claim (that is, to infallibility).

persuasion may be, not only of the falsity, but of the pernicious* consequences—not only of the pernicious consequences, but (to adopt expressions which I altogether condemn) the immorality and impiety of an opinion; yet if, in pursuance of that private judgment, though backed by the public judgment of his country or his contemporaries, he prevents the opinion from being heard in its defence, he assumes infallibility. And so far from the assumption being less objectionable or less dangerous because the opinion is called immoral or impious, this is the case of all others in which it is most fatal. These are exactly the occasions on which the men of one generation commit those dreadful mistakes which excite the astonishment and horror of posterity. It is among such that we find the instances memorable in history, when the arm of the law has been employed to root out the best men and the noblest doctrines; with deplorable success as to the men, though some of the doctrines have survived to be (as if in mockery) invoked, in defence of similar conduct towards those who dissent from *them*, or from their received interpretation.

... A theory which maintains that truth may justifiably be persecuted because persecution cannot possibly do it any harm, cannot be charged with being intentionally hostile to the reception of new truths; but we cannot commend the generosity of its dealing with the persons to whom mankind are indebted for them. To discover to† the world something which deeply concerns it, and of which it was previously ignorant; to prove to it that it had been mistaken on some vital point of temporal or spiritual interest, is as important a service as a human being can render to his fellow-creatures, and in certain cases, as in those of the early Christians and of the Reformers,‡ those who think with Dr. Johnson§ believe it to have been the most precious gift which could be bestowed on mankind. That the authors of such splendid benefits should be requited by martyrdom; that their reward should be to be dealt with as the vilest of criminals, is not, upon this theory, a deplorable error and misfortune, for which humanity should mourn in sackcloth and ashes, but the normal and justifiable state of things. The propounder of a new truth, according to this doctrine, should stand, as stood, in the legislation of the Locrians,¶ the proposer of a new law, with a halter round his neck, to be instantly tightened if the public assembly did not, on hearing his reasons, then and there adopt his proposition.

People who defend this mode of treating benefactors, can not be supposed to set much value on the benefit; and I believe this view of the subject is mostly confined to the sort of persons who think that new truths may have been desirable once, but that we have had enough of them now.

But, indeed, the dictum that truth always triumphs over persecution, is one of those pleasant falsehoods which men repeat after one another till they pass into commonplaces, but which all experience refutes. History teems with instances of truth put down by persecution. If not suppressed forever, it may be thrown back for centuries. To speak only of religious opinions: the Reformation broke out at least twenty times before Luther,** and was put down. Arnold of Brescia was put down. Fra Dolcino was put down. Savonarola was put down. The Albigeois were put down. The Vaudois were put down. The Lollards were put down. The Hussites were put down.†† Even after the era of

---

* Harmful.

† Expose, reveal to.

‡ Protestant Reformers, such as Martin Luther and John Calvin, who challenged the doctrines and authority of the Catholic Church in the sixteenth century.

§ Mill has earlier mentioned that Johnson—a well-known eighteenth-century writer and lexicographer—said "that the persecutors of Christianity were in the right; that persecution is an ordeal through which truth ought to pass, and always passes successfully" (recorded in James Boswell's *Life of Johnson* [1791], Volume II, entry for May 7, 1773).

¶ Locris was a minor state in ancient Greece, and among the first to adopt a written code of law (in about 660 BCE). Its regulations were severe: in addition to the principle mentioned in the text, it also enshrined the *lex talionis*, the law of retaliation (of taking an eye for an eye, a tooth for a tooth).

** Martin Luther (1483–1546) was a German theologian who initiated the Protestant Reformation in 1517.

†† Arnold of Brescia was executed as a heretic in 1155; Fra Dolcino of Novara was tortured to death in 1307; Savonarola Girolamo was burned to death in 1498. The Albigeois, or Albigenses, tried to establish a church independent of

Luther, wherever persecution was persisted in, it was successful. In Spain, Italy, Flanders, the Austrian empire, Protestantism was rooted out; and, most likely, would have been so in England, had Queen Mary lived, or Queen Elizabeth died. Persecution has always succeeded, save where the heretics were too strong a party to be effectually persecuted. No reasonable person can doubt that Christianity might have been extirpated* in the Roman empire. It spread, and became predominant, because the persecutions were only occasional, lasting but a short time, and separated by long intervals of almost undisturbed propagandism. It is a piece of idle sentimentality that truth, merely as truth, has any inherent power denied to error, of prevailing against the dungeon and the stake. Men are not more zealous for truth than they often are for error, and a sufficient application of legal or even of social penalties will generally succeed in stopping the propagation of either. The real advantage which truth has, consists in this, that when an opinion is true, it may be extinguished once, twice, or many times, but in the course of ages there will generally be found persons to rediscover it, until some one of its reappearances falls on a time when from favourable circumstances it escapes persecution until it has made such head as to withstand all subsequent attempts to suppress it.

It will be said, that we do not now put to death the introducers of new opinions: we are not like our fathers who slew the prophets, we even build sepulchres† to them. It is true we no longer put heretics to death; and the amount of penal infliction which modern feeling would probably tolerate, even against the most obnoxious opinions, is not sufficient to extirpate them. But let us not flatter ourselves that we are yet free from the stain even of legal persecution. Penalties for opinion, or at least for its expression, still exist by law; and their enforcement is not, even in these times,

so unexampled as to make it at all incredible that they may some day be revived in full force....

But though we do not now inflict so much evil on those who think differently from us, as it was formerly our custom to do, it may be that we do ourselves as much evil as ever by our treatment of them. Socrates‡ was put to death, but the Socratic philosophy rose like the sun in heaven, and spread its illumination over the whole intellectual firmament. Christians were cast to the lions, but the Christian Church grew up a stately and spreading tree, overtopping the older and less vigorous growths, and stifling them by its shade. Our merely social intolerance, kills no one, roots out no opinions, but induces men to disguise them, or to abstain from any active effort for their diffusion. With us, heretical opinions do not perceptibly gain or even lose, ground in each decade or generation; they never blaze out far and wide, but continue to smoulder in the narrow circles of thinking and studious persons among whom they originate, without ever lighting up the general affairs of mankind with either a true or a deceptive light. And thus is kept up a state of things very satisfactory to some minds, because, without the unpleasant process of fining or imprisoning anybody, it maintains all prevailing opinions outwardly undisturbed, while it does not absolutely interdict§ the exercise of reason by dissentients afflicted with the malady of thought. A convenient plan for having peace in the intellectual world, and keeping all things going on therein very much as they do already. But the price paid for this sort of intellectual pacification, is the sacrifice of the entire moral courage of the human mind. A state of things in which a large portion of the most active and inquiring intellects find it advisable to keep the genuine principles and grounds of their convictions within their own breasts, and attempt, in what they address to the public, to fit as much as

---

Roman Catholicism and were exterminated by the Inquisition in the thirteenth century. The Vaudois, or Waldenses, also attempted to break free of Catholicism in the late twelfth century and, though greatly weakened by the oppression of the Inquisition, survived to join the Calvinist movement in the sixteenth century. The Lollards were followers of John Wycliffe (1320–84) and the Hussites of John Huss (1369–1415). Both movements revolted against the authority of the Church, and both were vigorously suppressed.

* Pulled out by the roots—i.e., thoroughly eliminated.

† Tombs; so churches or structures inside them erected in memory of Jesus' tomb; so, figuratively, to build a sepulcher to someone to demonstrate reverential respect to them.

‡ Fifth-century BCE Athenian philosopher and teacher of Plato.

§ Forbid.

they can of their own conclusions to premises which they have internally renounced, cannot send forth the open, fearless characters, and logical, consistent intellects who once adorned the thinking world. The sort of men who can be looked for under it, are either mere conformers to commonplace, or time-servers* for truth whose arguments on all great subjects are meant for their hearers, and are not those which have convinced themselves. Those who avoid this alternative, do so by narrowing their thoughts and interests to things which can be spoken of without venturing within the region of principles, that is, to small practical matters, which would come right of themselves, if but the minds of mankind were strengthened and enlarged, and which will never be made effectually right until then; while that which would strengthen and enlarge men's minds, free and daring speculation on the highest subjects, is abandoned.

Those in whose eyes this reticence on the part of heretics is no evil, should consider in the first place, that in consequence of it there is never any fair and thorough discussion of heretical opinions; and that such of them as could not stand such a discussion, though they may be prevented from spreading, do not disappear. But it is not the minds of heretics that are deteriorated most, by the ban placed on all inquiry which does not end in the orthodox conclusions. The greatest harm done is to those who are not heretics, and whose whole mental development is cramped, and their reason cowed, by the fear of heresy. Who can compute what the world loses in the multitude of promising intellects combined with timid characters, who dare not follow out any bold, vigorous, independent train of thought, lest it should land them in something which would admit of being considered irreligious or immoral?...

Let us now pass to the second division of the argument, and dismissing the supposition that any of the received opinions may be false, let us assume them to be true, and examine into the worth of the manner in which they are likely to be held, when their truth is not freely and openly canvassed. However unwillingly a person who has a strong opinion may admit the possibility that his opinion may be false, he ought to be moved by the consideration that however true it may be, if it is not fully, frequently, and fearlessly discussed, it will be held as a dead dogma, not a living truth.

There is a class of persons (happily not quite so numerous as formerly) who think it enough if a person assents undoubtingly to what they think true, though he has no knowledge whatever of the grounds of the opinion, and could not make a tenable defence of it against the most superficial objections. Such persons, if they can once get their creed taught from authority, naturally think that no good, and some harm, comes of its being allowed to be questioned. Where their influence prevails, they make it nearly impossible for the received opinion to be rejected wisely and considerately, though it may still be rejected rashly and ignorantly; for to shut out discussion entirely is seldom possible, and when it once gets in, beliefs not grounded on conviction are apt to give way before the slightest semblance of an argument. Waiving, however, this possibility—assuming that the true opinion abides in the mind, but abides as a prejudice, a belief independent of, and proof against, argument—this is not the way in which truth ought to be held by a rational being. This is not knowing the truth. Truth, thus held, is but one superstition the more, accidentally clinging to the words which enunciate a truth.

If the intellect and judgment of mankind ought to be cultivated, a thing which Protestants at least do not deny, on what can these faculties be more appropriately exercised by any one, than on the things which concern him so much that it is considered necessary for him to hold opinions on them? If the cultivation of the understanding consists in one thing more than in another, it is surely in learning the grounds of one's own opinions. Whatever people believe, on subjects on which it is of the first importance to believe rightly, they ought to be able to defend against at least the common objections. But, some one may say, "Let them be *taught* the grounds of their opinions. It does not follow that opinions must be merely parroted because they are never heard controverted.† Persons who learn geometry do not simply commit the theorems to memory, but understand and learn likewise the demonstrations; and it would be absurd to say that

---

* People who, for convenience or self-interest, adopt their views to suit circumstances.
† Opposed, disputed.

they remain ignorant of the grounds of geometrical truths, because they never hear any one deny, and attempt to disprove them." Undoubtedly: and such teaching suffices on a subject like mathematics, where there is nothing at all to be said on the wrong side of the question. The peculiarity of the evidence of mathematical truths is, that all the argument is on one side. There are no objections, and no answers to objections. But on every subject on which difference of opinion is possible, the truth depends on a balance to be struck between two sets of conflicting reasons. Even in natural philosophy,* there is always some other explanation possible of the same facts; some geocentric theory instead of heliocentric,† some phlogiston‡ instead of oxygen; and it has to be shown why that other theory cannot be the true one: and until this is shown and until we know how it is shown, we do not understand the grounds of our opinion. But when we turn to subjects infinitely more complicated, to morals, religion, politics, social relations, and the business of life, three-fourths of the arguments for every disputed opinion consist in dispelling the appearances which favour some opinion different from it. The greatest orator, save one, of antiquity,§ has left it on record that he always studied his adversary's case with as great, if not with still greater, intensity than even his own. What Cicero practised as the means of forensic¶ success, requires to be imitated by all who study any subject in order to arrive at the truth. He who knows only his own side of the case, knows little of that. His reasons may be good, and no one may have been able to refute them. But if he is equally unable to refute the reasons on the opposite side; if he does not so much as know what they are, he has no ground for preferring either opinion. The rational position for him would be suspension of judgment, and unless he contents himself with that, he is either led by authority, or adopts, like the generality of the world, the side to which he feels most inclination. Nor is it enough that he should hear the arguments of adversaries from his own teachers, presented as they state them, and accompanied by what they offer as refutations. This is not the way to do justice to the arguments, or bring them into real contact with his own mind. He must be able to hear them from persons who actually believe them; who defend them in earnest, and do their very utmost for them. He must know them in their most plausible and persuasive form; he must feel the whole force of the difficulty which the true view of the subject has to encounter and dispose of, else he will never really possess himself of the portion of truth which meets and removes that difficulty. Ninety-nine in a hundred of what are called educated men are in this condition, even of those who can argue fluently for their opinions. Their conclusion may be true, but it might be false for anything they know: they have never thrown themselves into the mental position of those who think differently from them, and considered what such persons may have to say; and consequently they do not, in any proper sense of the word, know the doctrine which they themselves profess. They do not know those parts of it which explain and justify the remainder; the considerations which show that a fact which seemingly conflicts with another is reconcilable with it, or that, of two apparently strong reasons, one and not the other ought to be preferred. All that part of the truth which turns the scale, and decides the judgment of a completely informed mind, they are strangers to; nor is it ever really known, but to those who have attended equally and impartially to both sides, and endeavoured to see the reasons of both in the strongest light. So essential is this discipline to a real understanding of moral and human subjects, that if opponents of all important truths do not exist, it is indispensable to imagine them

---

*   Science.

†   On the geocentric theory, the sun, planets, and other heavenly bodies circle the Earth. According to heliocentric accounts, the planets orbit the Sun.

‡   Phlogiston is a theoretical substance, which turned out not to exist, once thought to be a volatile constituent of all combustible substances, released as flame in combustion. It is now known that combustion is, in general, a chemical interaction with oxygen.

§   The greatest orator of antiquity was said to be Demosthenes, and the second greatest was Cicero.

¶   Relating to debate or argument, especially in a court of law or public discussion.

and supply them with the strongest arguments which the most skilful devil's advocate* can conjure up.

To abate the force of these considerations, an enemy of free discussion may be supposed to say, that there is no necessity for mankind in general to know and understand all that can be said against or for their opinions by philosophers and theologians. That it is not needful for common men to be able to expose all the misstatements or fallacies of an ingenious opponent. That it is enough if there is always somebody capable of answering them, so that nothing likely to mislead uninstructed persons remains unrefuted. That simple minds, having been taught the obvious grounds of the truths inculcated on them, may trust to authority for the rest, and being aware that they have neither knowledge nor talent to resolve every difficulty which can be raised, may repose in the assurance that all those which have been raised have been or can be answered, by those who are specially trained to the task.

Conceding to this view of the subject the utmost that can be claimed for it by those most easily satisfied with the amount of understanding of truth which ought to accompany the belief of it; even so, the argument for free discussion is no way weakened. For even this doctrine acknowledges that mankind ought to have a rational assurance that all objections have been satisfactorily answered; and how are they to be answered if that which requires to be answered is not spoken? or how can the answer be known to be satisfactory, if the objectors have no opportunity of showing that it is unsatisfactory? If not the public, at least the philosophers and theologians who are to resolve the difficulties, must make themselves familiar with those difficulties in their most puzzling form; and this cannot be accomplished unless they are freely stated, and placed in the most advantageous light which they admit of....

If, however, the mischievous† operation of the absence of free discussion, when the received opinions are true, were confined to leaving men ignorant of the grounds of those opinions, it might be thought that this, if an intellectual, is no moral evil, and does not affect the worth of the opinions, regarded in their influence on the character. The fact, however, is, that not only the grounds of the opinion are forgotten in the absence of discussion, but too often the meaning of the opinion itself. The words which convey it, cease to suggest ideas, or suggest only a small portion of those they were originally employed to communicate. Instead of a vivid conception and a living belief, there remain only a few phrases retained by rote; or, if any part, the shell and husk only of the meaning is retained, the finer essence being lost. The great chapter in human history which this fact occupies and fills, cannot be too earnestly studied and meditated on.

It is illustrated in the experience of almost all ethical doctrines and religious creeds. They are all full of meaning and vitality to those who originate them, and to the direct disciples of the originators. Their meaning continues to be felt in undiminished strength, and is perhaps brought out into even fuller consciousness, so long as the struggle lasts to give the doctrine or creed an ascendancy over other creeds. At last it either prevails, and becomes the general opinion, or its progress stops; it keeps possession of the ground it has gained, but ceases to spread further. When either of these results has become apparent, controversy on the subject flags, and gradually dies away. The doctrine has taken its place, if not as a received opinion, as one of the admitted sects or divisions of opinion: those who hold it have generally inherited, not adopted it; and conversion from one of these doctrines to another, being now an exceptional fact, occupies little place in the thoughts of their professors.‡ Instead of being, as at first, constantly on the alert either to defend themselves against the world, or to bring the world over to them, they have subsided into acquiescence, and neither listen, when they can help it, to arguments against their creed, nor trouble dissentients (if there be such) with arguments in its favour. From this time may usually be dated the decline in the living power of the doctrine....

But what! (it may be asked) Is the absence of unanimity an indispensable condition of true knowledge?

---

* Formerly, one who argued in favor of an evil conclusion; later (and here) one who takes a position in order to test the strength of reasons for and against it.

† Causing harm or injury.

‡ I.e., of those who profess—assert—them.

Is it necessary that some part of mankind should persist in error, to enable any to realize the truth? Does a belief cease to be real and vital as soon as it is generally received—and is a proposition never thoroughly understood and felt unless some doubt of it remains? As soon as mankind have unanimously accepted a truth, does the truth perish within them? The highest aim and best result of improved intelligence, it has hitherto been thought, is to unite mankind more and more in the acknowledgment of all important truths: and does the intelligence only last as long as it has not achieved its object? Do the fruits of conquest perish by the very completeness of the victory?

I affirm no such thing. As mankind improve, the number of doctrines which are no longer disputed or doubted will be constantly on the increase: and the well-being of mankind may almost be measured by the number and gravity of the truths which have reached the point of being uncontested. The cessation, on one question after another, of serious controversy, is one of the necessary incidents of the consolidation of opinion; a consolidation as salutary in the case of true opinions, as it is dangerous and noxious when the opinions are erroneous. But though this gradual narrowing of the bounds of diversity of opinion is necessary in both senses of the term, being at once inevitable and indispensable, we are not therefore obliged to conclude that all its consequences must be beneficial. The loss of so important an aid to the intelligent and living apprehension of a truth, as is afforded by the necessity of explaining it to, or defending it against, opponents, though not sufficient to outweigh, is no trifling drawback from, the benefit of its universal recognition. Where this advantage can no longer be had, I confess I should like to see the teachers of mankind endeavouring to provide a substitute for it; some contrivance for making the difficulties of the question as present to the learner's consciousness, as if they were pressed upon him by a dissentient champion, eager for his conversion.

But instead of seeking contrivances for this purpose, they have lost those they formerly had. The Socratic dialectics, so magnificently exemplified in the dialogues of Plato, were a contrivance of this description. They were essentially a negative discussion of the great questions of philosophy and life, directed with consummate skill to the purpose of convincing any one who had merely adopted the commonplaces of received opinion, that he did not understand the subject—that he as yet attached no definite meaning to the doctrines he professed; in order that, becoming aware of his ignorance, he might be put in the way to attain a stable belief, resting on a clear apprehension both of the meaning of doctrines and of their evidence. The school disputations of the Middle Ages had a somewhat similar object. They were intended to make sure that the pupil understood his own opinion, and (by necessary correlation) the opinion opposed to it, and could enforce the grounds of the one and confute those of the other....

It still remains to speak of one of the principal causes which make diversity of opinion advantageous, and will continue to do so until mankind shall have entered a stage of intellectual advancement which at present seems at an incalculable distance. We have hitherto considered only two possibilities: that the received opinion may be false, and some other opinion, consequently, true; or that, the received opinion being true, a conflict with the opposite error is essential to a clear apprehension and deep feeling of its truth. But there is a commoner case than either of these; when the conflicting doctrines, instead of being one true and the other false, share the truth between them; and the nonconforming opinion is needed to supply the remainder of the truth, of which the received doctrine embodies only a part. Popular opinions, on subjects not palpable to sense,* are often true, but seldom or never the whole truth. They are a part of the truth; sometimes a greater, sometimes a smaller part, but exaggerated, distorted, and disjoined from the truths by which they ought to be accompanied and limited. Heretical opinions, on the other hand, are generally some of these suppressed and neglected truths, bursting the bonds which kept them down, and either seeking reconciliation with the truth contained in the common opinion, or fronting† it as enemies, and setting themselves up, with similar exclusiveness, as the whole truth. The latter case is hitherto the most

---

* Not obvious or easily grasped.
† Confronting.

frequent, as, in the human mind, one-sidedness has always been the rule, and many-sidedness the exception. Hence, even in revolutions of opinion, one part of the truth usually sets while another rises. Even progress, which ought to superadd, for the most part only substitutes one partial and incomplete truth for another; improvement consisting chiefly in this, that the new fragment of truth is more wanted, more adapted to the needs of the time, than that which it displaces. Such being the partial character of prevailing opinions, even when resting on a true foundation; every opinion which embodies somewhat of the portion of truth which the common opinion omits, ought to be considered precious, with whatever amount of error and confusion that truth may be blended. No sober judge of human affairs will feel bound to be indignant because those who force on our notice truths which we should otherwise have overlooked, overlook some of those which we see. Rather, he will think that so long as popular truth is one-sided, it is more desirable than otherwise that unpopular truth should have one-sided asserters too; such being usually the most energetic, and the most likely to compel reluctant attention to the fragment of wisdom which they proclaim as if it were the whole....

We have now recognized the necessity to the mental well-being of mankind (on which all their other well-being depends) of freedom of opinion, and freedom of the expression of opinion, on four distinct grounds; which we will now briefly recapitulate.

First, if any opinion is compelled to silence, that opinion may, for aught we can certainly know, be true. To deny this is to assume our own infallibility.

Secondly, though the silenced opinion be an error, it may, and very commonly does, contain a portion of truth; and since the general or prevailing opinion on any object is rarely or never the whole truth, it is only by the collision of adverse opinions that the remainder of the truth has any chance of being supplied.

Thirdly, even if the received opinion be not only true, but the whole truth; unless it is suffered to be, and actually is, vigorously and earnestly contested, it will, by most of those who receive it, be held in the manner of a prejudice, with little comprehension or feeling of its rational grounds. And not only this, but,

fourthly, the meaning of the doctrine itself will be in danger of being lost, or enfeebled, and deprived of its vital effect on the character and conduct: the dogma becoming a mere formal profession, inefficacious for good, but cumbering* the ground, and preventing the growth of any real and heartfelt conviction, from reason or personal experience....

Chapter IV: Of the Limits to the Authority of Society over the Individual

What, then, is the rightful limit to the sovereignty of the individual over himself? Where does the authority of society begin? How much of human life should be assigned to individuality, and how much to society?

Each will receive its proper share, if each has that which more particularly concerns it. To individuality should belong the part of life in which it is chiefly the individual that is interested; to society, the part which chiefly interests society.

Though society is not founded on a contract, and though no good purpose is answered by inventing a contract in order to deduce social obligations from it, every one who receives the protection of society owes a return for the benefit, and the fact of living in society renders it indispensable that each should be bound to observe a certain line of conduct towards the rest. This conduct consists, first, in not injuring the interests of one another; or rather certain interests, which, either by express legal provision or by tacit understanding, ought to be considered as rights; and secondly, in each person's bearing his share (to be fixed on some equitable principle) of the labours and sacrifices incurred for defending the society or its members from injury and molestation. These conditions society is justified in enforcing, at all costs to those who endeavour to withhold fulfilment. Nor is this all that society may do. The acts of an individual may be hurtful to others, or wanting in due consideration for their welfare, without going the length of violating any of their constituted rights. The offender may then be justly punished by opinion, though not by law. As soon as any part of a person's conduct affects prejudicially the interests of others, society has jurisdiction over it, and the question whether the general welfare will or will

---

* Encumbering.

not be promoted by interfering with it, becomes open to discussion. But there is no room for entertaining any such question when a person's conduct affects the interests of no persons besides himself, or needs not affect them unless they like (all the persons concerned being of full age, and the ordinary amount of understanding). In all such cases there should be perfect freedom, legal and social, to do the action and stand the consequences.

It would be a great misunderstanding of this doctrine, to suppose that it is one of selfish indifference, which pretends that human beings have no business with each other's conduct in life, and that they should not concern themselves about the well-doing or well-being of one another, unless their own interest is involved. Instead of any diminution, there is need of a great increase of disinterested exertion to promote the good of others. But disinterested benevolence can find other instruments to persuade people to their good, than whips and scourges, either of the literal or the metaphorical sort. I am the last person to undervalue the self-regarding virtues; they are only second in importance, if even second, to the social. It is equally the business of education to cultivate both. But even education works by conviction and persuasion as well as by compulsion, and it is by the former only that, when the period of education is past, the self-regarding virtues should be inculcated. Human beings owe to each other help to distinguish the better from the worse, and encouragement to choose the former and avoid the latter. They should be forever stimulating each other to increased exercise of their higher faculties, and increased direction of their feelings and aims towards wise instead of foolish, elevating instead of degrading, objects and contemplations. But neither one person, nor any number of persons, is warranted in saying to another human creature of ripe years, that he shall not do with his life for his own benefit what he chooses to do with it. He is the person most interested in his own well-being, the interest which any other person, except in cases of strong personal attachment, can have in it, is trifling, compared with that which he himself has; the interest which society has in him individually (except as to his conduct to others) is fractional, and altogether indirect: while, with respect to

his own feelings and circumstances, the most ordinary man or woman has means of knowledge immeasurably surpassing those that can be possessed by any one else. The interference of society to overrule his judgment and purposes in what only regards himself, must be grounded on general presumptions; which may be altogether wrong, and even if right, are as likely as not to be misapplied to individual cases, by persons no better acquainted with the circumstances of such cases than those are who look at them merely from without. In this department, therefore, of human affairs, Individuality has its proper field of action. In the conduct of human beings towards one another, it is necessary that general rules should for the most part be observed, in order that people may know what they have to expect; but in each person's own concerns, his individual spontaneity is entitled to free exercise. Considerations to aid his judgment, exhortations to strengthen his will, may be offered to him, even obtruded on* him, by others; but he, himself, is the final judge. All errors which he is likely to commit against advice and warning, are far outweighed by the evil of allowing others to constrain him to what they deem his good.

I do not mean that the feelings with which a person is regarded by others, ought not to be in any way affected by his self-regarding qualities or deficiencies. This is neither possible nor desirable. If he is eminent in any of the qualities which conduce to his own good, he is, so far, a proper object of admiration. He is so much the nearer to the ideal perfection of human nature. If he is grossly deficient in those qualities, a sentiment the opposite of admiration will follow. There is a degree of folly, and a degree of what may be called (though the phrase is not unobjectionable) lowness or depravation of taste, which, though it cannot justify doing harm to the person who manifests it, renders him necessarily and properly a subject of distaste, or, in extreme cases, even of contempt: a person could not have the opposite qualities in due strength without entertaining these feelings. Though doing no wrong to any one, a person may so act as to compel us to judge him, and feel to him, as a fool, or as a being of an inferior order: and since this judgment and feeling are a fact which he would prefer to avoid, it is doing him

---

*   Forced upon, even without that person's permission.

a service to warn him of it beforehand, as of any other disagreeable consequence to which he exposes himself. It would be well, indeed, if this good office* were much more freely rendered than the common notions of politeness at present permit, and if one person could honestly point out to another that he thinks him in fault, without being considered unmannerly or presuming. We have a right, also, in various ways, to act upon our unfavourable opinion of any one, not to the oppression of his individuality, but in the exercise of ours. We are not bound, for example, to seek his society; we have a right to avoid it (though not to parade the avoidance), for we have a right to choose the society most acceptable to us. We have a right, and it may be our duty, to caution others against him, if we think his example or conversation likely to have a pernicious effect on those with whom he associates. We may give others a preference over him in optional good offices, except those which tend to his improvement. In these various modes a person may suffer very severe penalties at the hands of others, for faults which directly concern only himself; but he suffers these penalties only in so far as they are the natural, and, as it were, the spontaneous consequences of the faults themselves, not because they are purposely inflicted on him for the sake of punishment. A person who shows rashness, obstinacy, self-conceit—who cannot live within moderate means—who cannot restrain himself from hurtful indulgences—who pursues animal pleasures at the expense of those of feeling and intellect—must expect to be lowered in the opinion of others, and to have a less share of their favourable sentiments, but of this he has no right to complain, unless he has merited their favour by special excellence in his social relations, and has thus established a title to their good offices, which is not affected by his demerits towards himself.

What I contend for is, that the inconveniences which are strictly inseparable from the unfavourable judgment of others, are the only ones to which a person should ever be subjected for that portion of his conduct and character which concerns his own good, but which does not affect the interests of others in their relations with him. Acts injurious to others require a totally different treatment. Encroachment on their rights; infliction on them of any loss or damage not justified by his own rights; falsehood or duplicity in dealing with them; unfair or ungenerous use of advantages over them; even selfish abstinence from defending them against injury—these are fit objects of moral reprobation, and, in grave cases, of moral retribution and punishment. And not only these acts, but the dispositions which lead to them, are properly immoral, and fit subjects of disapprobation which may rise to abhorrence. Cruelty of disposition; malice and ill-nature; that most anti-social and odious of all passions, envy; dissimulation and insincerity, irascibility on insufficient cause, and resentment disproportioned to the provocation; the love of domineering over others; the desire to engross more than one's share of advantages (the πλεονεξία† of the Greeks); the pride which derives gratification from the abasement of others; the egotism which thinks self and its concerns more important than everything else, and decides all doubtful questions in his own favour;—these are moral vices, and constitute a bad and odious moral character: unlike the self-regarding faults previously mentioned, which are not properly immoralities, and to whatever pitch they may be carried, do not constitute wickedness. They may be proofs of any amount of folly, or want of personal dignity and self-respect; but they are only a subject of moral reprobation when they involve a breach of duty to others, for whose sake the individual is bound to have care for himself. What are called duties to ourselves are not socially obligatory, unless circumstances render them at the same time duties to others. The term duty to oneself, when it means anything more than prudence, means self-respect or self-development; and for none of these is any one accountable to his fellow-creatures, because for none of them is it for the good of mankind that he be held accountable to them.

The distinction between the loss of consideration which a person may rightly incur by defect of prudence or of personal dignity, and the reprobation which is due to him for an offence against the rights of others, is not a merely nominal distinction. It makes a vast difference both in our feelings and in our conduct towards him, whether he displeases us in things

---

* Helpful service, favor.

† πλεονεξία or "pleonexia" is an ancient Greek word meaning greediness or graspingness.

in which we think we have a right to control him, or in things in which we know that we have not. If he displeases us, we may express our distaste, and we may stand aloof from a person as well as from a thing that displeases us; but we shall not therefore feel called on to make his life uncomfortable. We shall reflect that he already bears, or will bear, the whole penalty of his error; if he spoils his life by mismanagement, we shall not, for that reason, desire to spoil it still further: instead of wishing to punish him, we shall rather endeavour to alleviate his punishment, by showing him how he may avoid or cure the evils his conduct tends to bring upon him. He may be to us an object of pity, perhaps of dislike, but not of anger or resentment; we shall not treat him like an enemy of society: the worst we shall think ourselves justified in doing is leaving him to himself, if we do not interfere benevolently by showing interest or concern for him. It is far otherwise if he has infringed the rules necessary for the protection of his fellow-creatures, individually or collectively. The evil consequences of his acts do not then fall on himself, but on others; and society, as the protector of all its members, must retaliate on him; must inflict pain on him for the express purpose of punishment, and must take care that it be sufficiently severe. In the one case, he is an offender at our bar,* and we are called on not only to sit in judgment on him, but, in one shape or another, to execute our own sentence: in the other case, it is not our part to inflict any suffering on him, except what may incidentally follow from our using the same liberty in the regulation of our own affairs, which we allow to him in his.

The distinction here pointed out between the part of a person's life which concerns only himself, and that which concerns others, many persons will refuse to admit. How (it may be asked) can any part of the conduct of a member of society be a matter of indifference to the other members? No person is an entirely isolated being; it is impossible for a person to do anything seriously or permanently hurtful to himself, without mischief reaching at least to his near connections, and often far beyond them. If he injures his property, he does harm to those who directly or indirectly derived

support from it, and usually diminishes, by a greater or less amount, the general resources of the community. If he deteriorates his bodily or mental faculties, he not only brings evil upon all who depended on him for any portion of their happiness, but disqualifies himself for rendering the services which he owes to his fellow-creatures generally; perhaps becomes a burthen† on their affection or benevolence; and if such conduct were very frequent, hardly any offence that is committed would detract more from the general sum of good. Finally, if by his vices or follies a person does no direct harm to others, he is nevertheless (it may be said) injurious by his example; and ought to be compelled to control himself, for the sake of those whom the sight or knowledge of his conduct might corrupt or mislead.

And even (it will be added) if the consequences of misconduct could be confined to the vicious or thoughtless individual, ought society to abandon to their own guidance those who are manifestly unfit for it? If protection against themselves is confessedly due to children and persons under age, is not society equally bound to afford it to persons of mature years who are equally incapable of self-government? If gambling, or drunkenness, or incontinence,‡ or idleness, or uncleanliness, are as injurious to happiness, and as great a hindrance to improvement, as many or most of the acts prohibited by law, why (it may be asked) should not law, so far as is consistent with practicability and social convenience, endeavour to repress these also? And as a supplement to the unavoidable imperfections of law, ought not opinion at least to organize a powerful police against these vices, and visit rigidly with social penalties those who are known to practise them? There is no question here (it may be said) about restricting individuality, or impeding the trial of new and original experiments in living. The only things it is sought to prevent are things which have been tried and condemned from the beginning of the world until now; things which experience has shown not to be useful or suitable to any person's individuality. There must be some length of time and amount of experience, after which a moral or prudential truth may

* Tribunal, place of judgment.
† Burden.
‡ Lack of self-control.

be regarded as established, and it is merely desired to prevent generation after generation from falling over the same precipice which has been fatal to their predecessors.

I fully admit that the mischief which a person does to himself, may seriously affect, both through their sympathies and their interests, those nearly connected with him, and in a minor degree, society at large. When, by conduct of this sort, a person is led to violate a distinct and assignable obligation to any other person or persons, the case is taken out of the self-regarding class, and becomes amenable to moral disapprobation in the proper sense of the term. If, for example, a man, through intemperance or extravagance, becomes unable to pay his debts, or, having undertaken the moral responsibility of a family, becomes from the same cause incapable of supporting or educating them, he is deservedly reprobated, and might be justly punished; but it is for the breach of duty to his family or creditors, not for the extravagance. If the resources which ought to have been devoted to them, had been diverted from them for the most prudent investment, the moral culpability would have been the same. George Barnwell murdered his uncle to get money for his mistress, but if he had done it to set himself up in business, he would equally have been hanged.* Again, in the frequent case of a man who causes grief to his family by addiction to bad habits, he deserves reproach for his unkindness or ingratitude; but so he may for cultivating habits not in themselves vicious, if they are painful to those with whom he passes his life, or who from personal ties are dependent on him for their comfort. Whoever fails in the consideration generally due to the interests and feelings of others, not being compelled by some more imperative duty, or justified by allowable self-preference, is a subject of moral disapprobation for that failure, but not for the cause of it, nor for the errors, merely personal to himself, which may have remotely led to it. In like manner, when a person disables himself, by conduct purely self-regarding, from the performance of some definite duty incumbent on

him to the public, he is guilty of a social offence. No person ought to be punished simply for being drunk; but a soldier or a policeman should be punished for being drunk on duty. Whenever, in short, there is a definite damage, or a definite risk of damage, either to an individual or to the public, the case is taken out of the province of liberty, and placed in that of morality or law.

But with regard to the merely contingent or, as it may be called, constructive injury which a person causes to society, by conduct which neither violates any specific duty to the public, nor occasions perceptible hurt to any assignable individual except himself; the inconvenience is one which society can afford to bear, for the sake of the greater good of human freedom. If grown persons are to be punished for not taking proper care of themselves, I would rather it were for their own sake, than under pretence of preventing them from impairing their capacity of rendering to society benefits which society does not pretend it has a right to exact. But I cannot consent to argue the point as if society had no means of bringing its weaker members up to its ordinary standard of rational conduct, except waiting till they do something irrational, and then punishing them, legally or morally, for it. Society has had absolute power over them during all the early portion of their existence: it has had the whole period of childhood and nonage in which to try whether it could make them capable of rational conduct in life. The existing generation is master both of the training and the entire circumstances of the generation to come; it cannot indeed make them perfectly wise and good, because it is itself so lamentably deficient in goodness and wisdom; and its best efforts are not always, in individual cases, its most successful ones; but it is perfectly well able to make the rising generation, as a whole, as good as, and a little better than, itself. If society lets any considerable number of its members grow up mere children, incapable of being acted on by rational consideration of distant motives, society has itself to blame for the consequences. Armed not only with all the powers of education, but with the ascendancy

---

* This tale was featured in the popular seventeenth-century ballad "George Barnwell," and later formed the subject matter of a play by George Lillo, *The London Merchant, or, the History of George Barnwell* (1731), which was one of the first prose works of domestic tragedy in English. It is the story of a young apprentice's downfall caused by his love for a beautiful, but unfeeling, prostitute.

which the authority of a received opinion always exercises over the minds who are least fitted to judge for themselves; and aided by the *natural* penalties which cannot be prevented from falling on those who incur the distaste or the contempt of those who know them; let not society pretend that it needs, besides all this, the power to issue commands and enforce obedience in the personal concerns of individuals, in which, on all principles of justice and policy, the decision ought to rest with those who are to abide the consequences....

But the strongest of all the arguments against the interference of the public with purely personal conduct, is that when it does interfere, the odds are that it interferes wrongly, and in the wrong place. On questions of social morality, of duty to others, the opinion of the public, that is, of an overruling majority, though often wrong, is likely to be still oftener right; because on such questions they are only required to judge of their own interests; of the manner in which some mode of conduct, if allowed to be practised, would affect themselves. But the opinion of a similar majority, imposed as a law on the minority, on questions of self-regarding conduct, is quite as likely to be wrong as right; for in these cases public opinion means, at the best, some people's opinion of what is good or bad for other people; while very often it does not even mean that; the public, with the most perfect indifference, passing over the pleasure or convenience of those whose conduct they censure, and considering only their own preference. There are many who consider as an injury to themselves any conduct which they have a distaste for, and resent it as an outrage to their feelings; as a religious bigot, when charged with disregarding the religious feelings of others, has been known to retort that they disregard his feelings, by persisting in their abominable worship or creed. But there is no parity between the feeling of a person for his own opinion, and the feeling of another who is offended at his holding it; no more than between the desire of a thief to take a purse, and the desire of the right owner to keep it. And a person's taste is as much his own peculiar concern as his opinion or his purse. It is easy for any one to imagine an ideal public, which leaves the freedom and choice of individuals in all uncertain matters undisturbed, and only requires them to abstain from modes of conduct which universal experience has condemned. But where has there been seen a public which set any such limit to its censorship? or when does the public trouble itself about universal experience? In its interferences with personal conduct it is seldom thinking of anything but the enormity* of acting or feeling differently from itself; and this standard of judgment, thinly disguised, is held up to mankind as the dictate of religion and philosophy, by nine tenths of all moralists and speculative writers. These teach that things are right because they are right; because we feel them to be so. They tell us to search in our own minds and hearts for laws of conduct binding on ourselves and on all others. What can the poor public do but apply these instructions, and make their own personal feelings of good and evil, if they are tolerably unanimous in them, obligatory on all the world? ... ■

Suggestions for Critical Reflection

1. Mill suggests that, in modern democratic societies, the question of individual liberty requires "a different and more fundamental treatment" than it has historically been given, since in the past people were governed by an independent ruler while in a democracy it is "the people" themselves who exercise power. What exactly is the difference that democracy makes to the question of individual liberty, according to Mill? Do you think Mill might say—or should have said—that the rise of democracy, ironically, makes it *harder* for individuals to be free of illegitimate social interference?

2. Mill asserts (famously) that "the only purpose for which power can be rightfully exercised over any member of a civilized community, against his will, is to prevent harm to others." Given this principle, it is obviously crucial to specify what constitutes "harm." Does Mill ever do so adequately? What is

* Outrageousness.

the best way of cashing out this crucial concept? Will it require drawing a distinction between *real* harms and what people merely *perceive* to be a harm to them (such as, say, witnessing a homo-sexual couple kissing)? If so, how can these 'real' harms be distinguished from the merely apparent ones? *Is* there a way of doing so that supports all the conclusions Mill wants to draw?

3. Before he begins his defense of his "harm princi-ple," Mill notes that "I regard utility as the ultimate appeal on all ethical questions." If you have read the selection from Mill's *Utilitarianism* in the Ethics section of this book, you might want to consider how much of his subsequent reasoning is rooted in utilitarianism ... or indeed, whether the principle he defends in *On Liberty* is even *consistent* with Mill's utilitarian theory. What do you think Mill means by "utility in the largest sense, grounded on the perma-nent interests of man as a progressive being"?

4. "The only freedom which deserves the name, is that of pursuing our own good in our own way...." Is this true, or might there be a deeper, more valuable kind of freedom? What if someone's conception of their own good is importantly limited in some way, or is fallacious (even though it causes no harm to other people)? For example, what if I choose to spend my entire life in a basement watching TV, eating pizza, and growing and smoking (but not buying or selling) marijuana—could this really be an example of "the only freedom which deserves the name"? Further, what if I live this way, not through deliberate choice, but simply because it is how I grew up and is all I have ever experienced, and suppose I would, in fact, be much happier if some social authority were empowered to force me to get out more and make some friends. Must Mill still say I am free *only* if society leaves me alone? If so, is he right about that?

5. Part of Mill's argument in Chapter II involves the claim that "[c]omplete liberty of contradicting and disproving our opinion, is the very condition which justifies us in assuming its truth for purposes of action; and on no other terms can a being with human faculties have any rational assurance of being right." Does Mill really mean that we can have *no* "rational assurance" of being right about anything unless there is *complete* freedom of thought on the issue? If so, does he show that this

is a plausible claim? Is there a less black-and-white version of this claim which seems more plausible (and which Mill might really have meant)? If so, does this less extreme version adequately support Mill's conclusions about the value of com-plete freedom of thought?

6. Mill argues that believing something merely on the basis of authority, even if it is true, "is not the way in which truth ought to be held by a rational being." That is, he seems to suggest, believing some claim to be true without first having considered all the available arguments for and against that claim is mere vacant "superstition" and not genuine knowl-edge. Do Mill's arguments make this claim seem plausible, or does it strike you as too extreme? If he is right, how much of what most people believe could count as genuine knowledge? Is there a less contentious intermediate position? If so, would this weaker claim still support Mill's conclusions about the value of complete freedom of thought?

7. Should people be free to express *any* opinion, whatsoever? Imagine the most morally offensive view you can (involving, for example, the horrible torture of innocent toddlers or the most bizarre and uncomfortable kind of sexual act): should society allow people to, for example, make and distribute movies advocating this view? What if, to your horror, these movies prove highly popular and lots of people start watching them: should they still be allowed? Where, if anywhere, should the line be drawn, and does Mill get this line right?

8. Mill begins Chapter IV by stating "every one who receives the protection of society owes a return for the benefit, and the fact of living in society renders it indispensable that each should be bound to observe a certain line of conduct towards the rest." This, according to Mill, is what justifies society in placing at least *some* limits on the freedom of the individual. Does Mill have an argument for this principle, or is it just an assumption he makes? How philosophically significant is this assumption? For example, do you agree (and does Mill mean) that you have duties to your fellow citizens—such as (according to Mill) the duty to serve in the army in times of war, or to perform jury duty when called upon, or to rescue someone who has fallen into an icy river—*merely* by virtue of your living in a society?

9. Mill tries to distinguish between the "natural" social penalties of having a poor and foolish character, and penalties that might be deliberately inflicted on stupid people to punish them for their stupidity. According to Mill, the former kind of harm is an inevitable and acceptable consequence of one's own choices, while the latter constitutes morally unacceptable social interference. Is the crucial distinction between "natural" and punitive social harms an entirely clear one? (For example, what about repeatedly passing someone over for promotion or preventing them from attending a social organization such as a club or educational institution? Would these be "natural" consequences of someone's unpopularity, or a way of punishing them for being unpopular?) If this distinction is unclear, how serious a problem is this for Mill's position?

10. Mill also distinguishes between "self-regarding" and "social" virtues and vices, and claims only the latter are, properly speaking, *moral* virtues and vices, and that only these are properly within the ambit of social control. Again, is this an entirely clear distinction? For example, is it clear which of your character traits affect only you, personally, and which affect other people as well? If this kind of distinction is unclear or unworkable, how serious a blow is this for Mill's account of individual liberty?

KARL MARX AND FRIEDRICH ENGELS

FROM *The Communist Manifesto*

The philosophers have only *interpreted* the world in different ways; the point is to *change* it—Karl Marx (*Theses on Feuerbach*, Thesis 11)

Who Were Karl Marx and Friedrich Engels?

Karl Heinrich Marx was born in 1818 in the town of Trier in the Rhineland, formerly a region of Prussia lying next to the French border that is today part of Germany. Both his parents were Jewish, descended from a long line of rabbis and Jewish intellectuals. They were part of the first generation of German Jews to enjoy equal legal status with Christians and to be granted free choice of residence and profession. The Rhineland had been ruled by the French during the Napoleonic period, from 1792 until 1815, and Marx's father Heinrich had benefited from the relatively enlightened French regime, using the opportunity to forge a successful career as a respected lawyer. However, after Prussian power was restored in Trier in 1815, Marx's father felt obliged to convert himself and his family to Lutheranism in order to protect his career, and so Karl was not brought up as a Jew.

Karl's father wanted him to become a lawyer, but Karl was a rowdy, rebellious child and, as a young man, chose to spend his time studying philosophy and history, dueling, and writing romantic verses to his childhood sweetheart, the daughter of his neighbor, Jenny von Westphalen (whom he married in 1843). From 1835 to 1841 Marx studied at the universities of Bonn (where he spent a year studying law) and Berlin, where he was exposed to, and heavily influenced by, the idealist philosophy of G.W.F. Hegel.* Marx's early writings show his preoccupation with the notion of human self-realization through the struggle for freedom and a view of the nature of reality as turbulently changing, themes which find resonance in Hegel. However, like many contemporary "Young Hegelians," Marx found the Hegelian system, as it was then taught in the Prussian universities, to be politically and religiously much too conservative.

In 1841 Marx successfully submitted a doctoral dissertation (on Greek philosophy) to the university of Jena, but—because his political radicalism made him effectively unhireable in the contemporary political climate— he quickly gave up any prospect of an academic career. Instead, he wrote for a liberal newspaper in Cologne, the *Rheinische Zeitung*, and in short order became its editor. Under Marx, the paper went from cautious criticism of the government to a more radical critique of prevailing conditions, especially issues of economic justice. Inevitably, the paper was first heavily censored and then, in 1843, shut down by the Prussian authorities. At this point Marx and his new wife left for the more bohemian city of Paris, where Marx worked as a journalist for another radical publication, the *Deutsch-Französische Jahrbücher* [*German-French Annals*]. Realizing that he knew little about the economic issues which he saw as so politically significant, Marx threw himself into the study of political economy. Even before these studies began, however, Marx was already—like many of his compatriots—politically left-wing in a way that could loosely be called "communist." He was convinced of the need for "cooperative" rather than individual control of economic resources, and was ferociously concerned about the need to alleviate the living conditions of the swelling numbers of urban poor.

In 1845, pressure from the Prussian government caused Marx to be expelled from France and he and his family moved to Brussels. There he developed a close friendship, begun in France, with Friedrich Engels, the man who was to be Marx's most important intellectual collaborator, supporter, and friend (indeed, the only lasting friend Marx ever had).

---

* Hegel argued that the whole universe ('being')—including thinking subjects such as human beings—is ultimately comprehensible as an all-inclusive rational whole ('the Absolute') governed by dynamic logical principles.

Engels was born in 1820 in Barmen, near Düsseldorf. His family were wealthy mill owners in the rapidly industrializing northwest German Ruhr valley, and although Engels had hoped for a career in literature, his father insisted that he leave school at 17 to work for the family firm. He worked first in a local factory, then in an export office in the port city of Bremen, and finally as an accountant for the English branch of the firm Ermen and Engels. Thus, from the time he was a young man, Engels saw first-hand the profound social changes brought about by the introduction of new methods of production in the textile industry. Although he never formally attended university, he did sit in on lectures at Berlin University during his spell of compulsory military service and, through his exposure to the radical democratic movement, acquired a working knowledge of Hegelian philosophy. He worked for the *Rheinische Zeitung* while Marx was its editor, writing articles from Manchester, England, where, employed by the family firm, he was appalled to witness the living conditions of the English working class. In 1844 he wrote the impassioned *Condition of the Working Classes in England*. He also wrote a critical study of the standard positions in political economy—a work that greatly impressed Marx, and directly intersected with his interests at the time. After Engels's return to Germany in 1844, the two began collaborating on writings, speeches, and debates intended to spread their radical ideas among workers and intellectuals. Their most important publication of this period was the *Communist Manifesto*.

1848, the year *The Communist Manifesto* was published, was a year of revolution in Europe. Most of the countries of Europe, except Britain, Belgium, and Russia, underwent a spasm of social upheaval in which old, aristocratic regimes fell and were replaced (briefly) by bold, new republican governments. Marx and Engels, in their different ways, attempted to play a role in this revolutionary process. Marx, now expelled from Belgium for his activism, returned to Cologne and started up a new radical newspaper, the *Neue Rheinische Zeitung*, his goal being to inspire and educate the revolutionary leaders (along the lines of *The Communist Manifesto*). Meanwhile, Engels was an officer in a short-lived military uprising in the German region of Baden. Within a

matter of months, however, the European upheaval was over and, everywhere except France, the new democratic, republican regimes began to collapse and the old order reasserted itself. Marx and his associates were tried in a Cologne court for charges of inciting revolt and, although Marx successfully defended himself in court, he was nevertheless exiled from Prussian territory in 1849. As a result, Marx and Engels emigrated permanently to England: Marx, to live and write in London, and Engels to work for his family firm in Manchester.

Conditions were extremely hard for the Marx family, especially for the first decade of their lives in London. Marx was unwilling to take work that would interfere with his writing, and when he did seek stable employment he was unable to get it. (At one point he applied for a job as a railway clerk, but was unsuccessful because of the—now notorious—illegibility of his handwriting.) He and his family—his wife, her servant, and six children—subsisted on financial gifts from family and friends and on the income from Marx's occasional freelance journalism (mostly as a European correspondent for the *New York Tribune*, which paid £1 per article). Their main financial benefactor was Engels, who sent them grants and allowances taken from his own income and the money from his investments. Nevertheless, the Marx household lived in relative poverty for many years, enduring poor housing and bad food. Three of Marx's children died young, in part because of these hard conditions, and his own health suffered a collapse from which it never fully recovered.*

Meanwhile, Marx single-mindedly devoted his life to the cause of ending what he saw as the serious, and increasing, inequalities and exploitation inherent in capitalist society. His role, he thought, was to formulate the theoretical framework that would reveal the true state of things to the masses of workers and, by doing so, would both incite and guide the impending revolutionary replacement of capitalism by communism. He saw himself mainly as an 'ideas man' and a publicist for the communist movement, rather than an organizer or leader (and indeed, during his lifetime, his personal political influence was quite small). He spent 10 hours a day, most days, in the Reading Room of the British Museum, conducting research and writing; after returning home, he

---

* Despite these hardships, however, Marx's marriage was apparently a very happy one, and he was a devoted husband and father.

would often continue to write late into the night. His main work during these years, a massive, wide-ranging, detailed analysis of capitalist society and what Marx saw as the tensions intrinsic to it, was eventually published in three substantial volumes as *Das Kapital* (in English, *Capital*).[*]

Engels, meanwhile, ran his family's cotton mills in Lancashire and became a respected figure in Manchester society. He rode horses two days a week with the aristocratic Cheshire Hunt (valuable training, he claimed, for a future leader of the armies of the revolution), but at heart, Engels was unquestionably a devoted revolutionary, sincerely committed to the cause of communism, and he did his best to support Marx's work. He lived with an Irish factory girl called Mary Burns, and when she died he took in, and eventually married, her sister Lizzie.

In 1864 the International Working Men's Association (otherwise known as the First International) was formed. This was a watershed in the history of the working class movement, and for the next eight years the organization was highly influential in European left-wing politics. Marx was one of its main leaders, and was heavily engaged with its internal politics. By the 1870s he had become the leading theoretician for the radical movement in Europe, especially in Germany, and had become notorious across the continent as the "Red Doctor Marx."

Marx died, of chronic respiratory disease, in London in 1883. (Despite Engels's best efforts: he took him on a tour of France, Switzerland, and Algiers in the hope that a change of climate might help his condition.) He is buried next to his wife in Highgate Cemetery.

After 1870, Engels—who retired at 50, an independently wealthy man—had devoted all of his time to helping Marx with his research, and after Marx's death he continued the writing of *Capital* from Marx's notes, completing it in 1894, a year before his own death.

In a speech given at Marx's graveside, Engels said

... Marx was above all else a revolutionist. His real mission in life was to contribute, in one way or another, to the overthrow of capitalist society and of the state institutions which it had brought into being, to contribute to the liberation of the modern proletariat, which *he* was the first to make conscious of its own position and needs, conscious of the conditions of its emancipation. Fighting was his element. And he fought with a passion, a tenacity and a success such as few could rival.[†]

What Was Marx's Overall Philosophical Project?

In 1852, Marx summarized his three most important political ideas in the following way:

1. That social classes are not permanent features of society, but instead are phases in the historical development of the relations of economic production.
2. That the struggle between these classes will necessarily lead to the "dictatorship of the proletariat," in which the working people will forcibly take over political power from the property-owners.
3. That the dictatorship of the proletariat is not an end in itself, but a transition period before the advent of a classless communist society devoted to the free development and flourishing of individuals.

What does Marx mean by these three claims? The first is best approached through Marx's analysis of capitalism. A large proportion of his writing was devoted to this analysis, and it provides the clearest example of how he thought social class divisions were produced and perpetuated by a particular type of economic system.

A society is capitalist, according to Marx, if the production of goods is dominated by the use of wage-labor: that is, by the use of labor power sold, as their only way to make a living, by people who have no significant control over means of production (the proletariat), and bought by other people who do have control over means of production such as raw materials, capital, and machinery (the bourgeoisie). The bourgeoisie make their money mostly by combining the purchased labor power with the means of production they own, and selling the commodities thus produced. Marx held that the relationship between these

---

[*] Marx's mother is said to have commented that it was a shame that her boy merely wrote about capital and never acquired any.

[†] Friedrich Engels, from Marx and Engels, *Collected Works*, Vol. 24 (International Publishers, 1989), 468–69.

two classes, bourgeoisie and proletariat, was intrinsically and inescapably *antagonistic*, and he attempted to explain all the main institutional features of capitalist society in terms of this relation. Since, in Marx's view, the main institutions of a capitalist society have the function of preserving the interests of the bourgeoisie, and since these interests are opposed to those of the proletarians, capitalist society is therefore a kind of class rule, or oppression, of the majority by the minority.

Furthermore, for Marx, social structures, such as capitalism, that are based on the oppression of one class by another, give rise to what he called *ideologies*. An ideology is a (socially influential) system of beliefs or assumptions that reflects a false perception of reality—a perception of reality distorted by the social forces involved in class oppression. Central examples, for Marx, were systems of religious belief and the capitalist doctrine of the "free market." The dominance of a ruling class, whose members usually make up only a tiny minority of society, cannot be preserved through physical coercion alone: it can only survive as long as most people believe (falsely) that the social status quo is in their own interests, or that there is no realistic alternative to the current system, or in a situation where the oppressed classes are divided against each other (e.g., by nationalism, racism, or sexism) and fail to see their own common interest.

Considerations like these give rise to one of the best-known components of Marx's philosophical system, *historical materialism*: "[t]he mode of production of material life conditions the social, political, and intellectual life-process in general."* This is the view that the foundation or "base" of society is its economic structure, which is defined by historical facts about the means of production (for example, facts about the level of agricultural sophistication, industrial technology, trade and transportation networks, and so on). As productive forces change, economic adjustments—changes to the relations of production—give rise to revolutions in society's "superstructure": the political, legal, moral, religious, and philosophical components of culture. In other words, political and social changes do not cause economic change,

but the other way around: political and social systems are determined by their economic basis.

Marx's second main political-philosophical idea, in his 1852 summary, was the view that capitalism contains internal tensions which, in time, will inevitably produce the revolutionary overthrow of the bourgeoisie by the workers and usher in a "dictatorship of the proletariat." This view is, in part, the heritage of Marx's early influence by, and reaction to, the philosophical system of Hegel. For Hegel, history is a "dialectical" movement in which a thesis—a principle or idea—is challenged by its antithesis, and from this conflict there emerges a synthesis of the two, a new principle. In time this new principle meets *its* antithesis, and so on (until the ideal, final synthesis is achieved). Thus Hegel was an *idealist*, in the sense that for him the engine of world change was the clash of *Ideas*.† In Engels's words, Marx "turned the Hegelian system on its head": instead of conflicts between ideas (in the shape of political structures) driving change, Marx held that the world contains its own internal conflicts and that political ideas actually spring up *from* this conflict rather than causing it. These built-in conflicts, the mainspring of historical change, are *economic* in nature, generated by people's attempts to satisfy their material needs—for food, clothing, shelter, and so on—and their subsequent pursuit of personal wealth, within the context of their society's particular level of economic development. (Thus, Marx's system is often called *dialectical materialism*, though Marx himself never used this label.)

Marx's diagnosis of the economic conflicts driving capitalism towards revolution is complex and many-faceted. One of its central notions is that of *alienation*, which in turn arises from two other fundamental ideas in Marx's system: his theory of human nature and his "labor theory of value." According to Marx, human beings are essentially *active* and *creative* beings. Human flourishing consists in the continual transformation of one's inherent creative power into objective products, the constant *realization* of one's "subjectivity." Thus, productive activity—that is, work—is an essential component of human well-being. Marx's concern for the poor was never merely concern for their basic "material

---

* From the preface to *A Contribution to the Critique of Political Economy* in Karl Marx, *Early Writings*, trans. Livingstone and Benton (Penguin Books and New Left Review, 1975), 425.

† This is, of necessity, rather a caricature of Hegel's philosophical system. A good first introduction to Hegel's work is Charles Taylor's *Hegel* (Cambridge University Press, 1977).

needs," such as food and housing, but was part of his view of human flourishing as being a matter of "free self-activity," of true self-expression in a social context.

The institution of private property, in Marx's view, stifles the flourishing of the human spirit. Since private property represents the products of labor as if they were mere *things*, it alienates labor—and thus, human nature—from itself. Workers in a modern economy typically do not experience the economic goods they spend their lives producing as expressions of *themselves*, but merely as things to be sold. Furthermore, capitalism intensifies this process of alienation by treating *labor itself* as a commodity, to be bought and sold. Not only is the product of your creative activity alienated from you, but that very activity, work itself, is alienated—it is no longer *yours*, once you have sold it to an employer.

Furthermore, on Marx's analysis, the capitalist sale of goods for profit is inherently exploitative. According to the labor theory of value, which Marx took over from British economists Adam Smith (1723–90) and David Ricardo (1772–1823) and developed into his own economic theory, the fair value of anything in a free market is determined by the amount of labor required to produce it. This has two major implications. First it means, according to Marx, that *capital* adds no value to goods over and above the labor taken to produce them, and thus the capitalist, after recompensing his workers for the value of the labor they have expended in his factories, simply appropriates the "surplus value" which is generated as profits. Although not economically "unfair," in Marx's view, this is nevertheless a form of exploitation. Second, when the labor theory of value is applied to a free market for *labor itself*, it has the implication that the working classes will necessarily (and not "unjustly," by the lights of capitalism) be forced into permanent poverty. This is because the labor-value of labor itself is simply the amount necessary to keep the worker healthy and ready to work each day—that is, the minimum amount of food and shelter necessary to sustain the worker. This therefore, no more and no less, is the labor wage in a free capitalist market, and this produces a huge class of workers with no security, no prospects, no savings, no interest in preserving the current social conditions—in short, "nothing to lose but their chains."

Finally, there is the third part of Marx's 1852 summary: communism. Marx actually had relatively little to say about the nature of a future communist society, but it is clear that he saw it as a society in which the tensions inherent in capitalism have annihilated themselves and produced an economic system that—because there is no private property or capital—does not generate alienation and exploitation but instead allows for genuine human flourishing as active, creative individuals, self-determined and self-sufficient within a community of other self-determined human beings.

What Is the Structure of This Reading?

The Communist Manifesto was written to be a statement of the ideals and aims of the Communist League. The Communist League, an umbrella organization linking the main centers of communist activity in London, Paris, Brussels, and Cologne, was formed in June 1847, largely at the instigation of Marx and Engels, and was descended from a shadowy Parisian 'secret society' called the League of the Just. Most of its (few) members were German émigrés, and included several tailors, a few students, a typesetter, a cobbler, a watchmaker, a painter of miniatures, a disgraced Prussian officer, and Marx's aristocratic brother-in-law. A Congress of the League was held in London in November of 1847. To quote the eminent British historian A.J.P. Taylor:

> Marx attended in person. He listened impatiently while the worthy tailors lamented the wickedness of capitalism and preached universal brotherhood. He rose and denounced brotherhood in the name of class war. The tailors were entranced. Where they relied on sentiment, a learned man explained to them how society worked and placed the key to the future in their hands. They invited Marx to write a declaration of principles for them. He agreed.*

Engels wrote a first draft—a question-and-answer brief on the main principles of communism—which was then completely rewritten by Marx (who was less than 30 years old at the time) in the space of less than six weeks.

---

* A.J.P. Taylor, "Introduction" to Marx and Engels, *The Communist Manifesto* (Penguin Books, 1967), 22.

The *Manifesto* has four sections. The first part is a history of society from the Middle Ages to the present day, presented as a succession of class struggles, and predicting the imminent victory of the proletariat over the present ruling class, the bourgeoisie. Part II describes the position of communists with respect to the proletarian class and then goes on to reject a sequence of bourgeois objections to communism. This is followed by a brief characterization of the nature of the forthcoming communist revolution. The third part, not included here, contains an extended criticism of other forms of socialism: reactionary, bourgeois, and utopian. The final section provides a short description of communist tactics toward opposition parties and culminates with a call for proletarian unity.

Some Useful Background Information

For Marx, no external force or random accident is required to topple capitalism. He believed the overthrow of capitalism by socialism was inescapable, that it would come about because of the very nature of capitalism itself. An accurate grasp of the forces that sustain almost all social systems throughout history, Marx thought, would show that they must inevitably, as a result of internal processes, decline and be replaced by a radically different social system. However, *inevitably* does not mean *spontaneously*: the actual overthrow of existing society must be performed by a band of determined revolutionaries, joining the already existing, day-to-day class struggles and introducing revolutionary ideas to combat the ruling ideology, emphasizing the need for unity among the oppressed, and, when the time is ripe, boldly leading the revolution. The key is to follow the course of history *knowingly* by controlling the circumstances that generate it.

Some Common Misconceptions

1. Although Marx believed all the main institutions of society function to preserve the interests of the ruling class, he was not a conspiracy theorist. He did not believe, for example, that leading political figures receive covert orders from the business community. Instead, he held that institutional mechanisms press the actions of successful political figures into reflecting the long-term interests of

the bourgeoisie (including the need for social and economic stability and the suppression of revolution). One especially important mechanism for this, according to Marx, is national debt: governments depend on capitalists to renew huge but routine loans, and these financiers could throw national finances into chaos if their interests are too directly threatened. Another major influence is the pace of investment: if capitalists are displeased, the rate of investment slows and this has serious repercussions for employment rates and income levels. A third major factor is bourgeois ownership of the media (in Marx's time, mass-circulation newspapers—today, television or social media networks), and their consequent ability to manipulate and mould public opinion.

2. Marx's philosophy, as it is found in his writings, is not exactly the same thing as the ideological system often called "Marxism" today. His thought has been built on and interpreted by many other writers, starting with Engels and including several prominent Russian thinkers such as Georgy Plekhanov (1856–1918) and Vladimir Ilich Lenin (1870–1924) who formulated an 'orthodox,' systematic Soviet version of Marxism, and the so-called Western Marxists such as Georg Lukács (1885–1971), Theodor Adorno (1903–69), and Louis Althusser (1918–90). Nor is it quite the same thing as communism. The notion of the abolition of private property dates back at least to the early Christians, and was proposed during the French Revolution by a few fringe groups whom even the revolutionaries considered beyond the pale. And of course, the modern association of Communism with the political and economic structures of China and the Soviet Union is a development which occurred after Marx's death (and it is highly unlikely that Marx would have unconditionally approved of those regimes).

How Important and Influential Is This Passage?

The Communist Manifesto is the most successful political pamphlet of all time: for a substantial period of the twentieth century, roughly a third of the human race was ruled by governments that claimed allegiance to the ideas expressed in it. Practically, Marx's thought is the chief inspiration for all modern forms of social radicalism. Intellectually, according to the *Blackwell Encyclopedia of Political Thought*, "[o]ver the whole range of the social sciences, Marx has proved probably the most influential figure of the twentieth century."* Marx's central ideas—"historical materialism," the labor theory of value, the notion of class struggle—have had an inestimable influence on the development of contemporary economics, history, and sociology, even though they are not widely accepted by most Western intellectuals today.

FROM *The Communist Manifesto*[†]

A spectre is haunting Europe—the spectre of Communism. All the Powers of old Europe have entered into a holy alliance to exorcise this spectre: Pope and Tsar, Metternich and Guizot,[‡] French Radicals and German police-spies.

Where is the party in opposition that has not been decried as Communistic by its opponents in power? Where the Opposition that has not hurled back the branding reproach of Communism, against the more advanced opposition parties, as well as against its reactionary adversaries?

Two things result from this fact:

1. Communism is already acknowledged by all European Powers to be itself a Power.
2. It is high time that Communists should openly, in the face of the whole world, publish their views, their aims, their tendencies, and meet this nursery tale of the Spectre of Communism with a Manifesto of the party itself.

To this end, Communists of various nationalities have assembled in London and sketched the following Manifesto, to be published in the English, French, German, Italian, Flemish and Danish languages.[§]

I. Bourgeois and Proletarians[1]

The history of all hitherto existing society[2] is the history of class struggles.

Freeman and slave, patrician and plebeian, lord and serf, guild-master[¶][3] and journeyman,[**] in a word, oppressor and oppressed, stood in constant opposition to one another, carried on an uninterrupted, now

---

* David McLellan in *The Blackwell Encyclopedia of Political Thought*, ed. Miller et al. (Blackwell, 1987), 322.

† *Manifest der Kommunistischen Partei* was first published, in German, in London in 1848. The text reprinted here is the English translation made in 1888 by Samuel Moore, which was edited and authorized by Friedrich Engels. The author's notes in the text are those made by Engels in 1888.

‡ Prince Klemens Metternich (1773–1859) was the conservative chancellor of the Austrian empire; he was the dominant figure in European politics at this time, but was soon to be driven from power by the Revolutions of 1848. François Guizot (1787–1874) was the liberal moderate premier of France until he also was overthrown in the political turbulence of 1848.

§ Only one translation—into Swedish—was published in 1848–49, and widespread translation and reprinting of the *Manifesto* did not begin until after 1870.

¶ 'Master' here means master-craftsman, a medieval independent skilled craftsman, who (as Marx's footnote mentions) was a full member of a guild, a mutual-aid association of similar workers.

** A patrician was a member of one of the noble families of the ancient Roman republic, while plebeians were the common people of Rome. The terminology was also used in later ages (e.g., in the medieval free cities of Italy and Germany) to mark a similar distinction. A serf was a member of a particular feudal class of people in Europe, those bound by law to a particular piece of land and, like the land, owned by a lord. A journeyman was a craftsman who had completed his apprenticeship and was employed at a fixed wage by a master artisan, but who was not yet allowed (by his guild) to work for himself.

hidden, now open fight, a fight that each time ended, either in a revolutionary re-constitution of society at large, or in the common ruin of the contending classes.

In the earlier epochs of history, we find almost everywhere a complicated arrangement of society into various orders, a manifold gradation of social rank. In ancient Rome we have patricians, knights, plebeians, slaves; in the Middle Ages, feudal lords, vassals,* guild-masters, journeymen, apprentices, serfs; in almost all of these classes, again, subordinate gradations.

The modern bourgeois society that has sprouted from the ruins of feudal society has not done away with class antagonisms. It has but established new classes, new conditions of oppression, new forms of struggle in place of the old ones.

Our epoch, the epoch of the bourgeoisie, possesses, however, this distinctive feature: it has simplified class antagonisms. Society as a whole is more and more splitting up into two great hostile camps, into two great classes directly facing each other: Bourgeoisie and Proletariat.

From the serfs of the Middle Ages sprang the chartered burghers† of the earliest towns. From these burgesses the first elements of the bourgeoisie were developed.

The discovery of America, the rounding of the Cape,‡ opened up fresh ground for the rising bourgeoisie. The East-Indian and Chinese markets, the colonisation of America, trade with the colonies, the increase in the means of exchange and in commodities generally, gave to commerce, to navigation, to industry, an impulse never before known, and thereby, to the revolutionary element in the tottering feudal society, a rapid development.

The feudal system of industry, under which industrial production was monopolized by closed guilds, now no longer sufficed for the growing wants of the new markets. The manufacturing system took its place. The guild-masters were pushed on one side by the manufacturing middle class; division of labour between the different corporate guilds vanished in the face of division of labour in each single workshop.

Meantime the markets kept ever growing, the demand ever rising. Even manufacture no longer sufficed. Thereupon, steam and machinery revolutionized industrial production. The place of manufacture was taken by the giant, Modern Industry, the place of the industrial middle class, by industrial millionaires, the leaders of whole industrial armies, the modern bourgeois.

Modern Industry has established the world market, for which the discovery of America paved the way. This market has given an immense development to commerce, to navigation, to communication by land. This development has, in its turn, reacted on the extension of industry; and in proportion as industry, commerce, navigation, railways extended, in the same proportion the bourgeoisie developed, increased its capital, and pushed into the background every class handed down from the Middle Ages.

We see, therefore, how the modern bourgeoisie is itself the product of a long course of development, of a series of revolutions in the modes of production and of exchange.

Each step in the development of the bourgeoisie was accompanied by a corresponding political advance in that class. An oppressed class under the sway of the feudal nobility, an armed and self-governing association in the medieval commune;§ here independent urban republic (as in Italy and Germany), there taxable "third estate"¶ of the monarchy (as in France), afterwards, in the period of manufacture proper, serving either the semi-feudal or the absolute monarchy as a counterpoise against the nobility, and, in fact, cornerstone of the great monarchies in general, the bourgeoisie has at last, since the establishment of Modern Industry and of the world market, conquered for itself, in the modern representative State,** exclusive

---

* A vassal received land and protection from a feudal lord, in return for homage and allegiance.

† Someone who is a citizen of a town in virtue of being a full member of a legally chartered trade association or guild.

‡ The Cape of Good Hope, at the southern tip of Africa.

§ An association of medieval townspeople for mutual defense, often a self-governing "community."

¶ The three divisions of society in pre-Revolutionary France were the first estate (clergy), the second estate (nobility), and the third estate (commoners).

** A modern, rather than a feudal, state: one whose institutions are based on the political representation of *individuals*, rather than of social corporations (such as towns or guilds) or estates (such as the nobility or the clergy).

political sway. The executive of the modern State is but a committee for managing the common affairs of the whole bourgeoisie.

The bourgeoisie, historically, has played a most revolutionary part.

The bourgeoisie, wherever it has got the upper hand, has put an end to all feudal, patriarchal, idyllic relations. It has pitilessly torn asunder the motley feudal ties that bound man to his "natural superiors," and has left no other nexus between man and man than naked self-interest, than callous "cash payment." It has drowned out the most heavenly ecstasies of religious fervour, of chivalrous enthusiasm, of philistine sentimentalism, in the icy water of egotistical calculation. It has resolved personal worth into exchange value, and in place of the numberless indefeasible chartered freedoms,* has set up that single, unconscionable freedom—Free Trade. In one word, for exploitation, veiled by religious and political illusions, it has substituted naked, shameless, direct, brutal exploitation.

The bourgeoisie has stripped of its halo every occupation hitherto honoured and looked up to with reverent awe. It has converted the physician, the lawyer, the priest, the poet, the man of science, into its paid wage-labourers.

The bourgeoisie has torn away from the family its sentimental veil, and has reduced the family relation to a mere money relation.

The bourgeoisie has disclosed how it came to pass that the brutal display of vigour in the Middle Ages, which Reactionists† so much admire, found its fitting complement in the most slothful indolence. It has been the first to show what man's activity can bring about. It has accomplished wonders far surpassing Egyptian pyramids, Roman aqueducts, and Gothic cathedrals; it has conducted expeditions that put in the shade all former Exoduses of nations and crusades.

The bourgeoisie cannot exist without constantly revolutionizing the instruments of production, and thereby the relations of production, and with them the whole relations of society. Conservation of the old modes of production in unaltered form, was, on the contrary, the first condition of existence for all earlier industrial classes. Constant revolutionizing of production, uninterrupted disturbance of all social conditions, everlasting uncertainty and agitation distinguish the bourgeois epoch from all earlier ones. All fixed, fast-frozen relations, with their train of ancient and venerable prejudices and opinions, are swept away, all new-formed ones become antiquated before they can ossify.‡ All that is solid melts into air, all that is holy is profaned, and man is at last compelled to face with sober senses, his real condition of life and his relations with his kind.

The need of a constantly expanding market for its products chases the bourgeoisie over the entire surface of the globe. It must nestle everywhere, settle everywhere, establish connections everywhere.

The bourgeoisie has, through its exploitation of the world market, given a cosmopolitan character to production and consumption in every country. To the great chagrin of Reactionists, it has drawn from under the feet of industry the national ground on which it stood. All old-established national industries have been destroyed or are daily being destroyed. They are dislodged by new industries, whose introduction becomes a life and death question for all civilized nations, by industries that no longer work up indigenous raw material, but raw material drawn from the remotest zones; industries whose products are consumed, not only at home, but in every quarter of the globe. In place of the old wants, satisfied by the production of the country, we find new wants, requiring for their satisfaction the products of distant lands and climes. In place of the old local and national seclusion and self-sufficiency, we have intercourse§ in every direction, universal interdependence of nations. And as in material, so also in intellectual production. The intellectual creations of individual nations become common property. National one-sidedness and narrow-mindedness become more and more impossible, and from the numerous national and local literatures, there arises a world literature.

---

* The charters were granted (or sold) by royalty to associations of townspeople, guaranteeing them protection and certain freedoms.
† Those who resist change and seek to return to an older social and political order.
‡ Turn into stone.
§ Communication and trade between different localities.

The bourgeoisie, by the rapid improvement of all instruments of production, by the immensely facilitated means of communication, draws all, even the most barbarian, nations into civilization. The cheap prices of its commodities are the heavy artillery with which it batters down all Chinese walls, with which it forces the barbarians' intensely obstinate hatred of foreigners to capitulate.* It compels all nations, on pain of extinction, to adopt the bourgeois mode of production; it compels them to introduce what it calls civilization into their midst, *i.e.*, to become bourgeois themselves. In one word, it creates a world after its own image.

The bourgeoisie has subjected the country to the rule of the towns. It has created enormous cities, has greatly increased the urban population as compared with the rural, and has thus rescued a considerable part of the population from the idiocy of rural life. Just as it has made the country dependent on the towns, so it has made barbarian and semi-barbarian countries dependent on the civilized ones, nations of peasants on nations of bourgeois, the East on the West.

The bourgeoisie keeps more and more doing away with the scattered state of the population, of the means of production, and of property. It has agglomerated† population, centralized means of production, and has concentrated property in a few hands. The necessary consequence of this was political centralization. Independent, or but loosely connected provinces with separate interests, laws, governments and systems of taxation, became lumped together into one nation, with one government, one code of laws, one national class-interest, one frontier,‡ and one customs-tariff.

The bourgeoisie, during its rule of scarce one hundred years, has created more massive and more colossal productive forces than have all preceding generations together. Subjection of Nature's forces to man, machinery, application of chemistry to industry and agriculture, steam-navigation, railways, electric telegraphs, clearing of whole continents for cultivation,

canalization of rivers, whole populations conjured out of the ground—what earlier century had even a presentiment that such productive forces slumbered in the lap of social labour?

We see then: the means of production and of exchange, on whose foundation the bourgeoisie built itself up, were generated in feudal society. At a certain stage in the development of these means of production and of exchange, the conditions under which feudal society produced and exchanged, the feudal organization of agriculture and manufacturing industry, in one word, the feudal relations of property became no longer compatible with the already developed productive forces; they became so many fetters.§ They had to be burst asunder; they were burst asunder.

Into their place stepped free competition, accompanied by a social and political constitution adapted in it, and the economical and political sway of the bourgeois class.

A similar movement is going on before our own eyes. Modern bourgeois society, with its relations of production, of exchange and of property, a society that has conjured up such gigantic means of production and of exchange, is like the sorcerer who is no longer able to control the powers of the nether world whom he has called up by his spells. For many a decade past the history of industry and commerce is but the history of the revolt of modern productive forces against modern conditions of production, against the property relations that are the conditions for the existence of the bourgeois and of its rule. It is enough to mention the commercial crises that by their periodical return put on its trial, each time more threateningly, the existence of the entire bourgeois society. In these crises a great part not only of the existing products, but also of the previously created productive forces, are periodically destroyed. In these crises there breaks out an epidemic that, in all earlier epochs, would have seemed an absurdity—the epidemic of over-production.¶ Society suddenly finds itself put back

---

* A reference to the first Opium War in China (1839–43), which forced the Chinese to cede Hong Kong to the British and to open five of their ports to foreign trade.
† Combined together.
‡ External border.
§ Leg chains or shackles.
¶ Such crises occurred regularly in advanced capitalist economies from 1825 until 1939. Periodically, as more and more companies joined a particular industry, firms found themselves facing a glut of their products on the market. This

into a state of momentary barbarism; it appears as if a famine, a universal war of devastation had cut off the supply of every means of subsistence; industry and commerce seem to be destroyed; and why? Because there is too much civilization, too much means of subsistence, too much industry, too much commerce. The productive forces at the disposal of society no longer tend to further the development of the conditions of bourgeois property; on the contrary, they have become too powerful for these conditions, by which they are fettered, and so soon as they overcome these fetters, they bring disorder into the whole of bourgeois society, endanger the existence of bourgeois property. The conditions of bourgeois society are too narrow to comprise the wealth created by them. And how does the bourgeoisie get over these crises? On the one hand by enforced destruction of a mass of productive forces; on the other, by the conquest of new markets, and by the more thorough exploitation of the old ones. That is to say, by paving the way for more extensive and more destructive crises, and by diminishing the means whereby crises are prevented.

The weapons with which the bourgeoisie felled feudalism to the ground are now turned against the bourgeoisie itself.

But not only has the bourgeoisie forged the weapons that bring death to itself; it has also called into existence the men who are to wield those weapons—the modern working class—the proletarians.

In proportion as the bourgeoisie, *i.e.*, capital, is developed, in the same proportion is the proletariat, the modern working class, developed—a class of labourers, who live only so long as they find work, and who find work only so long as their labour increases capital. These labourers, who must sell themselves piecemeal, are a commodity, like every other article of commerce, and are consequently exposed to all the vicissitudes of competition, to all the fluctuations of the market.

Owing to the extensive use of machinery and to division of labour, the work of the proletarians has lost all individual character, and, consequently, all charm for the workman. He becomes an appendage of the machine, and it is only the most simple, most monotonous, and most easily acquired knack, that is required of him. Hence, the cost of production of a workman is restricted, almost entirely, to the means of subsistence that he requires for maintenance, and for the propagation of his race. But the price of a commodity, and therefore also of labour, is equal to its cost of production. In proportion, therefore, as the repulsiveness of the work increases, the wage decreases. Nay more, in proportion as the use of machinery and division of labour increases, in the same proportion the burden of toil also increases, whether by prolongation of the working hours, by the increase of the work exacted in a given time, or by increased speed of the machinery, etc.

Modern industry has converted the little workshop of the patriarchal master into the great factory of the industrial capitalist. Masses of labourers, crowded into the factory, are organized like soldiers. As privates of the industrial army they are placed under the command of a perfect hierarchy of officers and sergeants. Not only are they slaves of the bourgeois class, and of the bourgeois State; they are daily and hourly enslaved by the machine, by the overlooker, and, above all, by the individual bourgeois manufacturer himself. The more openly this despotism proclaims gain to be its end and aim, the more petty, the more hateful and the more embittering it is.

The less the skill and exertion of strength implied in manual labour, in other words, the more modern industry becomes developed, the more is the labour of men superseded by that of women. Differences of age and sex have no longer any distinctive social validity for the working class. All are instruments of labour, more or less expensive to use, according to their age and sex.

No sooner is the exploitation of the labourer by the manufacturer, so far, at an end, and he receives his wages in cash, than he is set upon by the other

---

over-supply depressed prices below expected profit levels, and so companies suddenly began to cut back production. Each time, these cutbacks started a vicious chain reaction, as suppliers were also forced to make cutbacks, which increased the unemployment rate, which reduced consumer spending and so increased over-supply, which depressed prices still further, and so on. At the height of the Great Depression of the 1930s, the worst such crisis, unemployment reached 25 per cent in the United States. Marx provided a sophisticated analysis of this sort of crisis in *Capital*.

portions of the bourgeoisie, the landlord, the shop-keeper, the pawnbroker, etc.

The lower strata of the middle class—the small tradespeople, shopkeepers, and retired tradesmen generally, the handicraftsmen and peasants—all these sink gradually into the proletariat, partly because their diminutive capital does not suffice for the scale on which Modern Industry is carried on, and is swamped in the competition with the large capitalists, partly because their specialized skill is rendered worthless by new methods of production. Thus, the proletariat is recruited from all classes of the population.

The proletariat goes through various stages of development. With its birth begins its struggle with the bourgeoisie. At first, the contest is carried on by individual labourers, then by the workpeople of a factory, then by the operatives of one trade, in one locality, against the individual bourgeois who directly exploits them. They direct their attacks not against the bourgeois condition of production, but against the instruments of production themselves; they destroy imported wares that compete with their labour, they smash to pieces machinery, they set factories ablaze, they seek to restore by force the vanished status of the workman of the Middle Ages.

At this stage the labourers still form an incoherent mass scattered over the whole country, and broken up by their mutual competition. If anywhere they unite to form more compact bodies, this is not yet the consequence of their own active union, but of the union of the bourgeoisie, which class, in order to attain its own political ends, is compelled to set the whole proletariat in motion, and is moreover yet, for a time, able to do so. At this stage, therefore, the proletarians do not fight their enemies, but the enemies of their enemies, the remnants of absolute monarchy, the landowners, the non-industrial bourgeois, the petty bourgeoisie.* Thus, the whole historical movement is concentrated in the hands of the bourgeoisie; every victory so obtained is a victory for the bourgeoisie.

But with the development of industry, the proletariat not only increases in number; it becomes concentrated in greater masses, its strength grows, and it feels that strength more. The various interests and conditions of life within the ranks of the proletariat are more and more equalized, in proportion as machinery obliterates all distinctions of labour, and nearly everywhere reduces wages to the same low level. The growing competition among the bourgeois, and the resulting commercial crises, make the wages of the workers ever more fluctuating. The increasing improvement of machinery, ever more rapidly developing, makes their livelihood more and more precarious; the collisions between individual workmen and individual bourgeois take more and more the character of collisions between two classes. Thereupon, the workers begin to form combinations (Trades' Unions) against the bourgeois; they club together in order to keep up the rate of wages; they found permanent associations in order to make provision beforehand for these occasional revolts. Here and there the contest breaks out into riots.

Now and then the workers are victorious, but only for a time. The real fruit of their battles lies, not in the immediate result, but in the ever expanding union of the workers. This union is helped on by the improved means of communication that are created by modern industry and that place the workers of different localities in contact with one another. It was just this contact that was needed to centralize the numerous local struggles, all of the same character, into one national struggle between classes. But every class struggle is a political struggle. And that union, to attain which the burghers of the Middle Ages, with their miserable highways, required centuries, the modern proletarian, thanks to railways, achieve in a few years.

This organization of the proletarians into a class, and consequently into a political party, is continually being upset again by the competition between the workers themselves. But it ever rises up again, stronger, firmer, mightier. It compels legislative recognition of particular interests of the workers, by taking advantage of the divisions among the bourgeoisie itself. Thus, the ten-hours' bill in England was carried.†

---

*   The petty (i.e., lesser) bourgeoisie, for Marx, are those who control means of production (like the bourgeoisie) but work them with their own labor (like the proletariat): for example, independent shopkeepers or small farmers.

†   This law—part of the 1847 Factory Act—limited the daily working hours of women and children to 58 hours a week. It was highly controversial, and was passed by Parliament only because conservative "Old England" landowners opposed

Altogether collisions between the classes of the old society further, in many ways, the course of development of the proletariat. The bourgeoisie finds itself involved in a constant battle. At first with the aristocracy; later on, with those portions of the bourgeoisie itself, whose interests have become antagonistic to the progress of industry; at all times, with the bourgeoisie of foreign countries. In all these battles it sees itself compelled to appeal to the proletariat, to ask for its help, and thus, to drag it into the political arena. The bourgeoisie itself, therefore, supplies the proletariat with its own elements of political and general education, in other words, it furnishes the proletariat with weapons for fighting the bourgeoisie.

Further, as we have already seen, entire sections of the ruling class are, by the advance of industry, precipitated into the proletariat, or are at least threatened in their conditions of existence. These also supply the proletariat with fresh elements of enlightenment and progress.

Finally, in times when the class struggle nears the decisive hour, the progress of dissolution going on within the ruling class, in fact within the whole range of old society, assumes such a violent, glaring character, that a small section of the ruling class cuts itself adrift, and joins the revolutionary class, the class that holds the future in its hands. Just as, therefore, at an earlier period, a section of the nobility went over to the bourgeoisie, so now a portion of the bourgeoisie goes over to the proletariat, and in particular, a portion of the bourgeois ideologists, who have raised themselves to the level of comprehending theoretically the historical movement as a whole.

Of all the classes that stand face to face with the bourgeoisie today, the proletariat alone is a genuinely revolutionary class. The other classes decay and finally disappear in the face of Modern Industry; the proletariat is its special and essential product.

The lower middle class, the small manufacturer, the shopkeeper, the artisan, the peasant, all these fight against the bourgeoisie, to save from extinction their existence as fractions of the middle class. They are therefore not revolutionary, but conservative. Nay more, they are reactionary, for they try to roll back the wheel of history. If by chance they are revolutionary, they are only so in view of their impending transfer into the proletariat, they thus defend not their present, but their future interests, they desert their own standpoint to place themselves at that of the proletariat.

The "dangerous class," the social scum,* that passively rotting mass thrown off by the lowest layers of the old society may, here and there, be swept into the movement by a proletarian revolution; its conditions of life, however, prepare it far more for the part of a bribed tool of reactionary intrigue.

In the condition of the proletariat, those of old society at large are already virtually swamped. The proletarian is without property; his relation to his wife and children has no longer anything in common with the bourgeois family relations; modern industrial labour, modern subjection to capital, the same in England as in France, in America as in Germany, has stripped him of every trace of national character. Law, morality, religion, are to him so many bourgeois prejudices, behind which lurk in ambush just as many bourgeois interests.

All the preceding classes that got the upper hand sought to fortify their already acquired status by subjecting society at large to their conditions of appropriation. The proletarians cannot become masters of the productive forces of society, except by abolishing their own previous mode of appropriation, and thereby also every other previous mode of appropriation. They have nothing of their own to secure and to fortify; their mission is to destroy all previous securities for, and insurances of, individual property.

All previous historical movements were movements of minorities, or in the interest of minorities. The proletarian movement is the self-conscious, independent movement of the immense majority, in the interest of the immense majority. The proletariat, the lowest stratum of our present society, cannot stir, cannot raise itself up, without the whole super-incumbent strata of official society being sprung into the air.

Though not in substance, yet in form, the struggle of the proletariat with the bourgeoisie is at first

the interests of the ever-more-powerful industrialists and mill owners.

* The original German word here—one that has found its way into English—is *Lumpenproletariat*, literally, "proletariat in rags."

a national struggle. The proletariat of each country must, of course, first of all settle matters with its own bourgeoisie.

In depicting the most general phases of the development of the proletariat, we traced the more or less veiled civil war, raging within existing society, up to the point where that war breaks out into open revolution, and where the violent overthrow of the bourgeoisie lays the foundation for the sway of the proletariat.

Hitherto, every form of society has been based, as we have already seen, on the antagonism of oppressing and oppressed classes. But in order to oppress a class, certain conditions must be assured to it under which it can, at least, continue its slavish existence. The serf, in the period of serfdom, raised himself to membership in the commune, just as the petty bourgeois, under the yoke of the feudal absolutism, managed to develop into a bourgeois. The modern labourer, on the contrary, instead of rising with the progress of industry, sinks deeper and deeper below the conditions of existence of his own class. He becomes a pauper, and pauperism develops more rapidly than population and wealth. And here it becomes evident that the bourgeoisie is unfit any longer to be the ruling class in society, and to impose its conditions of existence upon society as an over-riding law. It is unfit to rule because it is incompetent to assure an existence to its slave within his slavery, because it cannot help letting him sink into such a state, that it has to feed him, instead of being fed by him. Society can no longer live under this bourgeoisie, in other words, its existence is no longer compatible with society.

The essential condition for the existence, and for the sway of the bourgeois class, is the formation and augmentation of capital; the condition for capital is wage-labour. Wage-labour rests exclusively on competition between the labourers. The advance of industry, whose involuntary promoter is the bourgeoisie, replaces the isolation of the labourers, due to competition, by their revolutionary combination, due to association. The development of Modern Industry, therefore, cuts from under its feet the very foundation on which the bourgeoisie produces and appropriates products. What the bourgeoisie, therefore, produces, above all, is its own grave-diggers. Its fall and the victory of the proletariat are equally inevitable.

II. Proletarians and Communists

In what relation do the Communists stand to the proletarians as a whole?

The Communists do not form a separate party opposed to the other working-class parties.

They have no interests separate and apart from those of the proletariat as a whole.

They do not set up any sectarian principles of their own, by which to shape and mold the proletarian movement.

The Communists are distinguished from the other working-class parties by this only: (1) In the national struggles of the proletarians of the different countries, they point out and bring to the front the common interests of the entire proletariat, independently of all nationality. (2) In the various stages of development which the struggle of the working class against the bourgeoisie has to pass through, they always and everywhere represent the interests of the movement as a whole.

The Communists, therefore, are on the one hand, practically, the most advanced and resolute section of the working-class parties of every country, that section which pushes forward all others; on the other hand, theoretically, they have over the great mass of the proletariat the advantage of clearly understanding the line of march, the conditions, and the ultimate general results of the proletarian movement.

The immediate aim of the Communists is the same as that of all other proletarian parties: formation of the proletariat into a class, overthrow of the bourgeois supremacy, conquest of political power by the proletariat.

The theoretical conclusions of the Communists are in no way based on ideas or principles that have been invented, or discovered, by this or that would-be universal reformer.

They merely express, in general terms, actual relations springing from an existing class struggle, from a historical movement going on under our very eyes. The abolition of existing property relations is not at all a distinctive feature of Communism.

All property relations in the past have continually been subject to historical change consequent upon the change in historical conditions.

The French Revolution, for example, abolished feudal property in favour of bourgeois property.

The distinguishing feature of Communism is not the abolition of property generally, but the abolition of bourgeois property. But modern bourgeois private property is the final and most complete expression of the system of producing and appropriating products, that is based on class antagonisms, on the exploitation of the many by the few.

In this sense, the theory of the Communists may be summed up in the single sentence: Abolition of private property.

We Communists have been reproached with the desire of abolishing the right of personally acquiring property as the fruit of a man's own labour, which property is alleged to be the groundwork of all personal freedom, activity and independence.

Hard-won, self-acquired, self-earned property! Do you mean the property of the petty artisan and of the small peasant, a form of property that preceded the bourgeois form? There is no need to abolish that; the development of industry has to a great extent already destroyed it, and is still destroying it daily.

Or do you mean the modern bourgeois private property?

But does wage-labour create any property for the labourer? Not a bit. It creates capital, *i.e.*, that kind of property which exploits wage-labour, and which cannot increase except upon conditions of begetting a new supply of wage-labour for fresh exploitation. Property, in its present form, is based on the antagonism of capital and wage-labour. Let us examine both sides of this antagonism.

To be a capitalist, is to have not only a purely personal, but a social *status* in production. Capital is a collective product, and only by the united action of many members, nay, in the last resort, only by the united action of all members of society, can it be set in motion.

Capital is, therefore, not a personal, it is a social power.

When, therefore, capital is converted into common property, into the property of all members of society, personal property is not thereby transformed into social property. It is only the social character of the property that is changed. It loses its class character.

Let us now take wage-labour.

The average price of wage-labour is the minimum wage, *i.e.*, that quantum of the means of subsistence, which is absolutely requisite to keep the labourer in bare existence as a labourer. What, therefore, the wage-labourer appropriates by means of his labour, merely suffices to prolong and reproduce a bare existence. We by no means intend to abolish this personal appropriation of the products of labour, an appropriation that is made for the maintenance and reproduction of human life, and that leaves no surplus wherewith to command the labour of others. All that we want to do away with is the miserable character of this appropriation, under which the labourer lives merely to increase capital, and is allowed to live only in so far as the interest of the ruling class requires it.

In bourgeois society, living labour is but a means to increase accumulated labour. In Communist society, accumulated labour is but a means to widen, to enrich, to promote the existence of the labourer.

In bourgeois society, therefore, the past dominates the present; in Communist society, the present dominates the past. In bourgeois society capital is independent and has individuality, while the living person is dependent and has no individuality.

And the abolition of this state of things is called by the bourgeois abolition of individuality and freedom! And rightly so. The abolition of bourgeois individuality, bourgeois independence, and bourgeois freedom is undoubtedly aimed at.

By freedom is meant, under the present bourgeois conditions of production, free trade, free selling and buying.

But if selling and buying disappears, free selling and buying disappears also. This talk about free selling and buying, and all the other "brave words" of our bourgeoisie about freedom in general, have a meaning, if any, only in contrast with restricted selling and buying, with the fettered traders of the Middle Ages, but have no meaning when opposed to the Communistic abolition of buying and selling, or the bourgeois conditions of production, and of the bourgeoisie itself.

You are horrified at our intending to do away with private property. But in your existing society, private property is already done away with for nine-tenths of the population; its existence for the few is solely due to its non-existence in the hands of those nine-tenths. You reproach us, therefore, with intending to do away with a form of property, the necessary condition for whose existence is the non-existence of any property for the immense majority of society.

In one word, you reproach us with intending to do away with your property. Precisely so; that is just what we intend.

From the moment when labour can no longer be converted into capital, money, or rent, into a social power capable of being monopolized, *i.e.*, from the moment when individual property can no longer be transformed into bourgeois property, into capital, from that moment, you say, individuality vanishes.

You must, therefore, confess that by "individual" you mean no other person than the bourgeois, than the middle-class owner of property. This person must, indeed, be swept out of the way, and made impossible.

Communism deprives no man of the power to appropriate the products of society; all that it does is to deprive him of the power to subjugate the labour of others by means of such appropriation.

It has been objected that upon the abolition of private property all work will cease, and universal laziness will overtake us.

According to this, bourgeois society ought long ago to have gone to the dogs through sheer idleness; for those who work, acquire nothing, and those who acquire anything, do not work. The whole of this objection is but another expression of the tautology: that there can no longer be any wage-labour when there is no longer any capital.

All objections urged against the Communistic mode of producing and appropriating material products, have, in the same way, been urged against the Communistic mode of producing and appropriating intellectual products. Just as, to the bourgeois, the disappearance of class property is the disappearance of production itself, so the disappearance of class culture is to him identical with the disappearance of all culture.

That culture, the loss of which he laments, is, for the enormous majority, a mere training to act as a machine.

But don't wrangle with us so long as you apply, to our intended abolition of bourgeois property, the standard of your bourgeois notions of freedom, culture, law, etc. Your very ideas are but the outgrowth of the conditions of your bourgeois production and bourgeois property, just as your jurisprudence is but the will of your class made into a law for all, a will, whose essential character and direction are determined by the economical conditions of existence of your class.

The selfish misconception that induces you to transform into eternal laws of nature and of reason, the social forms springing from your present mode of production and form of property—historical relations that rise and disappear in the progress of production—this misconception you share with every ruling class that has preceded you. What you see clearly in the case of ancient property, what you admit in the case of feudal property, you are of course forbidden to admit in the case of your own bourgeois form of property.

Abolition of the family! Even the most radical flare up at this infamous proposal of the Communists.

On what foundation is the present family, the bourgeois family, based? On capital, on private gain. In its completely developed form this family exists only among the bourgeoisie. But this state of things finds its complement in the practical absence of the family among proletarians, and in public prostitution.

The bourgeois family will vanish as a matter of course when its complement vanishes, and both will vanish with the vanishing of capital.

Do you charge us with wanting to stop the exploitation of children by their parents? To this crime we plead guilty.

But, you will say, we destroy the most hallowed of relations, when we replace home education by social.

And your education! Is not that also social, and determined by the social conditions under which you educate, by the intervention, direct or indirect, of society, by means of schools, etc.? The Communists have not invented the intervention of society in education; they do but seek to alter the character of that intervention, and to rescue education from the influence of the ruling class.

The bourgeois clap-trap about the family and education, about the hallowed co-relation of parent and child, becomes all the more disgusting, the more, by the action of Modern Industry, all family ties among the proletarians are torn asunder, and their children transformed into simple articles of commerce and instruments of labour.

But you Communists would introduce community of women, screams the bourgeoisie in chorus.

The bourgeois sees his wife a mere instrument of production. He hears that the instruments of production are to be exploited in common, and, naturally, can come to no other conclusion that the lot of being common to all will likewise fall to the women.

He has not even a suspicion that the real point aimed at is to do away with the status of women as mere instruments of production.

For the rest, nothing is more ridiculous than the virtuous indignation of our bourgeois at the community of women* which, they pretend, is to be openly and officially established by the Communists. The Communists have no need to introduce community of women; it has existed almost from time immemorial.

Our bourgeois, not content with having the wives and daughters of their proletarians at their disposal, not to speak of common prostitutes, take the greatest pleasure in seducing each other's wives.

Bourgeois marriage is in reality a system of wives in common and thus, at the most, what the Communists might possibly be reproached with is that they desire to introduce, in substitution for a hypocritically concealed, an openly legalized community of women. For the rest, it is self-evident that the abolition of the present system of production must bring with it the abolition of the community of women springing from that system, *i.e.*, of prostitution both public and private.

The Communists are further reproached with desiring to abolish countries and nationality.

The workers have no country. We cannot take from them what they have not got. Since the proletariat must first of all acquire political supremacy, must rise to be the leading class of the nation, must constitute itself *the* nation, it is so far, itself national, though not in the bourgeois sense of the word.

National differences and antagonism between peoples are daily more and more vanishing, owing to the development of the bourgeoisie, to freedom of commerce, to the world market, to uniformity in the mode of production and in the conditions of life corresponding thereto.

The supremacy of the proletariat will cause them to vanish still faster. United action, of the leading civilized countries at least, is one of the first conditions for the emancipation of the proletariat.

In proportion as the exploitation of one individual by another is put an end to, the exploitation of one nation by another will also be put an end to. In proportion as the antagonism between classes within the nation vanishes, the hostility of one nation to another will come to an end.

The charges against Communism made from a religious, a philosophical, and, generally, from an ideological standpoint, are not deserving of serious examination.

Does it require deep intuition to comprehend that man's ideas, views, and conception, in one word, man's consciousness, changes with every change in the conditions of his material existence, in his social relations and in his social life?

What else does the history of ideas prove, than that intellectual production changes its character in proportion as material production is changed? The ruling ideas of each age have ever been the ideas of its ruling class.

When people speak of ideas that revolutionize society, they do but express that fact, that within the old society, the elements of a new one have been created, and that the dissolution of the old ideas keeps even pace with the dissolution of the old conditions of existence.

When the ancient world was in its last throes, the ancient religions were overcome by Christianity. When Christian ideas succumbed in the eighteenth century to rationalist ideas, feudal society fought its death battle with the then revolutionary bourgeoisie. The ideas of religious liberty and freedom of conscience merely gave expression to the sway of free competition within the domain of knowledge.

"Undoubtedly," it will be said, "religious, moral, philosophical, and juridical ideas have been modified in the course of historical development. But religion, morality, philosophy, political science, and law, constantly survived this change.

"There are, besides, eternal truths, such as Freedom, Justice, etc., that are common to all states of society. But Communism abolishes eternal truths, it abolishes all religion and all morality, instead of

---

* Women no longer legally bound in couples by marriage.

constituting them on a new basis; it therefore acts in contradiction to all past historical experience."

What does this accusation reduce itself to? The history of all past society has consisted in the development of class antagonisms, antagonisms that assumed different forms at different epochs.

But whatever form they may have taken, one fact is common to all past ages, *viz.*, the exploitation of one part of society by the other. No wonder, then, that the social consciousness of past ages, despite all the multiplicity and variety it displays, moves within certain common forms, or general ideas, which cannot completely vanish except with the total disappearance of class antagonisms.

The Communist revolution is the most radical rupture with traditional relations; no wonder that its development involved the most radical rupture with traditional ideas.

But let us have done with the bourgeois objections to Communism.

We have seen above, that the first step in the revolution by the working class is to raise the proletariat to the position of ruling class, to win the battle of democracy.

The proletariat will use its political supremacy to wrest, by degrees, all capital from the bourgeoisie, to centralize all instruments of production in the hands of the State, *i.e.*, of the proletariat organized as the ruling class; and to increase the total productive forces as rapidly as possible.

Of course, in the beginning, this cannot be effected except by means of despotic inroads on the rights of property, and on the conditions of bourgeois production; by means of measures, therefore, which appear economically insufficient and untenable, but which, in the course of the movement, outstrip themselves, necessitate further inroads upon the old social order, and are unavoidable as a means of entirely revolutionizing the mode of production.

These measures will, of course, be different in different countries.

Nevertheless in most advanced countries, the following will be pretty generally applicable:

1. Abolition of property in land and application of all rents of land to public purposes.
2. A heavy progressive or graduated income tax.
3. Abolition of all right of inheritance.
4. Confiscation of the property of all emigrants and rebels.
5. Centralization of credit in the banks of the State, by means of a national bank with State capital and an exclusive monopoly.
6. Centralization of the means of communication and transport in the hands of the State.
7. Extension of factories and instruments of production owned by the State; the bringing into cultivation of waste-lands, and the improvement of the soil generally in accordance with a common plan.
8. Equal liability of all to labour. Establishment of industrial armies, especially for agriculture.
9. Combination of agriculture with manufacturing industries; gradual abolition of all the distinction between town and country by a more equable distribution of the population over the country.
10. Free education for all children in public schools. Abolition of children's factory labour in its present form. Combination of education with industrial production, etc., etc.

When, in the course of development, class distinctions have disappeared, and all production has been concentrated in the hands of a vast association of the whole nation, the public power will lose its political character. Political power, properly so called, is merely the organized power of one class for oppressing another. If the proletariat during its contest with the bourgeoisie is compelled, by the force of circumstances, to organize itself as a class, if, by means of a revolution, it makes itself the ruling class, and, as such, sweeps away by force the old conditions of production, then it will, along with these conditions, have swept away the conditions for the existence of class antagonisms and of classes generally, and will thereby have abolished its own supremacy as a class.

In place of the old bourgeois society, with its classes and class antagonisms, we shall have an association, in which the free development of each is the condition for the free development of all.

...

IV. Position of the Communists in Relation to the Various Existing Opposition Parties

Section II has made clear the relations of the Communists to the existing working-class parties, such as the Chartists in England and the Agrarian Reformers in America.*

The Communists fight for the attainment of the immediate aims, for the enforcement of the momentary interests of the working class; but in the movement of the present, they also represent and take care of the future of that movement. In France the Communists ally with the Social Democrats, against the conservative and radical bourgeoisie, reserving, however, the right to take up a critical position in regard to phases and illusions traditionally handed down from the great Revolution.

In Switzerland, they support the Radicals, without losing sight of the fact that this party consists of antagonistic elements, partly of Democratic Socialists, in the French sense, partly of radical bourgeois.

In Poland, they support the party that insists on an agrarian revolution as the prime condition for national emancipation, that party which fomented the insurrection of Kraków in 1846.†

In Germany, they fight with the bourgeoisie whenever it acts in a revolutionary way, against the absolute monarchy, the feudal squirearchy,‡ and the petty bourgeoisie.

But they never cease, for a single instant, to instil into the working class the clearest possible recognition of the hostile antagonism between bourgeoisie and proletariat, in order that the German workers may straightway use, as so many weapons against the bourgeoisie, the social and political conditions that the bourgeoisie must necessarily introduce along with its supremacy, and in order that, after the fall of the reactionary classes in Germany, the fight against the bourgeoisie itself may immediately begin.

The Communists turn their attention chiefly to Germany, because that country is on the eve of a bourgeois revolution that is bound to be carried out under more advanced conditions of European civilization, and with a much more developed proletariat, than that of England was in the seventeenth, and France in the eighteenth century, and because the bourgeois revolution in Germany will be but the prelude to an immediately following proletarian revolution.

In short, the Communists everywhere support every revolutionary movement against the existing social and political order of things.

In all these movements they bring to the front, as the leading question in each, the property question, no matter what its degree of development at the time.

Finally, they labour everywhere for the union and agreement of the democratic parties of all countries.

The Communists disdain to conceal their views and aims. They openly declare that their ends can be attained only by the forcible overthrow of all existing social conditions. Let the ruling classes tremble at a Communist revolution. The proletarians have nothing to lose but their chains. They have a world to win.

WORKING MEN OF ALL COUNTRIES, UNITE! ▪

---

* Chartism was a popular reformist movement that lasted from 1837 to 1848. Among its demands (outlined in an 1837 "People's Charter") were universal male voting rights, equal electoral districts, abolition of the property qualification for running for Parliament, and annual parliaments. The National Reform Association was founded in 1844 to campaign for free settlement of the landless on public lands, a moratorium on seizure of family farms for non-payment of debt, and establishment of a 160-acre ceiling on land ownership to ensure there would be enough small-holdings to go around.

† A nationalist, republican uprising in southern Poland against the Russians, Prussians, and Austrians who had jointly occupied it since the collapse of Napoleon's empire in 1815. The rebellion was crushed, and Kraków incorporated into the Austrian empire.

‡ Landed gentry.

Suggestions for Critical Reflection

1. "The history of all hitherto existing society is the history of class struggles." What role does this resounding phrase have in Marx's argument? Is it a *true* claim? (How easy would it be for professional historians to show it to be either true or false?) If its historical truth is open to question, how serious a problem is this for Marx's views?

2. Marx's critique of the bourgeoisie has both positive and negative elements. For example, he notes that they have "accomplished wonders far surpassing ... Gothic cathedrals," but also claims the bourgeois have reduced the family to "a mere money relation." What is Marx's overall judgment of the bourgeoisie? How far do you agree with it?

3. "The executive of the modern State is but a committee for managing the common affairs of the whole bourgeoisie." How does Marx support this claim? What, exactly, do you think he means by it? What implications does it have, if true?

4. Marx suggests modern bourgeois society contains within it the seeds of its own self-destruction (as did feudal society before it). How compelling are his arguments for this claim?

5. Marx says that, for the proletariat, "[l]aw, morality, religion, are to him so many bourgeois prejudices, behind which lurk in ambush just as many bourgeois interests." What are the implications of this statement? Why do you think Marx says it, and do you think he is justified in doing so?

6. Marx addresses the criticism of communism which says that, if private property and personal wealth are abolished, people will have no incentive to be productive at all "and universal laziness will overtake us." How adequately do you think Marx handles this objection?

7. What do you make of Marx's list of 10 components for the dictatorship of the proletariat? How radical or unreasonable do they seem today? How likely would they be to result in the elimination of private property and the emancipation of the proletariat?

8. What, if anything, do historical developments since Marx's death—in particular, the rise and fall of the Soviet Union, and the failure of capitalism to end in revolution in the democratic West—show about the validity of his philosophical thought?

Notes

1 By bourgeoisie is meant the class of modern Capitalists, owners of the means of social production and employers of wage-labour. By proletariat, the class of modern wage-labourers who, having no means of production of their own, are reduced to selling their labour-power in order to live.

2 That is, all *written* history. In 1847, the pre-history of society, the social organization existing previous to recorded history, was all but unknown. Since then, [August von] Haxthausen discovered common ownership of land in Russia, [Georg Ludwig von] Maurer proved it to be the social foundation from which all Teutonic races started in history, and by and by village communities were found to be, or to have been the primitive form of society everywhere from India to Ireland. The inner organization of this primitive Communistic society was laid bare, in its typical form, by [Lewis Henry] Morgan's crowning discovery of the true nature of the *gens* and its relation to the *tribe*. With the dissolution of these primaeval communities society begins to be differentiated into separate and finally antagonistic classes. I have attempted to retrace this dissolution in *Der Ursprung der Familie, des Privateigenthums und des Staats* [*The Origins of the Family, Private Property and the State*], second edition, Stuttgart, 1886.

3 Guild-master, that is, a full member of a guild, a master within, not a head of a guild.

4 "Commune" was the name taken, in France, by the nascent towns even before they had conquered from their feudal lords and masters local self-government and political rights as the "Third Estate." Generally speaking, for the economical development of the bourgeoisie, England is here taken as the typical country; for its political development, France.

JOHN RAWLS

FROM *Justice as Fairness: A Restatement*

Who Was John Rawls?

John Borden Rawls was, until his death in 2002, perhaps the world's most important contemporary political philosopher, and his 1971 book *A Theory of Justice* is generally regarded as the most significant work of political theory published in the twentieth century. Born in 1921 in Baltimore to an upper-class southern family, Rawls's father was a successful tax lawyer and constitutional expert while his mother was the feminist president of the local League of Women Voters. As a boy, the intensely religious Rawls was sent to Kent, a renowned Episcopalian preparatory school in Connecticut, and then went on to Princeton for his undergraduate degree. In 1943, he joined the US infantry and served in New Guinea, the Philippines, and Japan (where he witnessed first-hand the aftermath of the atomic bombing of Hiroshima). The horrors he experienced during the war caused Rawls to lose his Christian faith. Rawls was awarded a Bronze Star for valor in New Guinea, and later promoted to sergeant. However he was demoted back to private for refusing to discipline a soldier because he believed the punishment was unjust, and he left the army as a private in 1946, returning to Princeton to pursue his PhD in philosophy.

After completing the doctorate, he taught at Princeton for two years, visited Oxford University for a year on a Fulbright Fellowship, and was then employed as a professor at Cornell. In 1964 Rawls moved to Harvard University, where he was appointed James Bryant Conant Professor of Philosophy in 1979. During the 1960s, despite his "bat-like horror of the limelight,"* Rawls spoke out publicly against American involvement in the Vietnam War, and he was influenced by this to develop a theoretical underpinning for citizen resistance against a government's unjust policies.

Throughout the 1980s and early 1990s Rawls was an omnipresent figure in political philosophy, and exerted a great influence on the discipline through his teaching and mentoring of younger academics as well as his writings. Former US President Bill Clinton said of him that Rawls "almost singlehandedly ... revived the disciplines of political and ethical philosophy with his argument that a society in which the most fortunate helped the least fortunate is not only a moral society, but a logical one."† Unfortunately, in 1995, Rawls suffered the first of several strokes that seriously impeded his ability to continue working, though he was able to complete his final book, *The Law of Peoples* (1999), which laid out his views on international justice.

What Was Rawls's Overall Philosophical Project?

Though Rawls was always much more the reclusive academic than a campaigning public figure, his work was nevertheless guided by a deep personal commitment to combating injustice. Because of his family's origins in the American south, one of Rawls's earliest moral concerns was the injustice of black slavery. He was interested in formulating a moral theory that not only showed slavery to be unjust, but described its injustice *in the right way*. For Rawls, the immorality of slavery does not lie merely in the fact that benefits for slaveowners were outweighed by harms done to the enslaved—rather, slavery is the kind of thing that should *never* be imposed on any human being, no matter what overall benefits or efficiencies it might bring about. Thus, Rawls found himself opposed to the then-dominant political morality of utilitarianism, and seeking a new foundation for social justice in the work

---

* Ben Rogers, obituary for John Rawls, *The Guardian*, 27 November 2002.
† Speech at the occasion of awarding Rawls the National Humanities Medal in 1999.

of Immanuel Kant and social contract theorists such as John Locke and Jean-Jacques Rousseau.*

Two guiding assumptions behind Rawls's neo-Kantian project (which he called "Kantian constructivism") were, first, that there is such a thing as moral truth—that at least some fundamental moral questions have objectively correct answers, even if it is difficult to discover them—and second, that "the right" is separate from and prior to "the good." This latter claim is the idea (which is found in Kant) that the morally right thing to do cannot be defined as, and will not always be the same thing as, the maximization of some moral good, such as happiness or equality. There are certain constraints on how people can be treated which always take precedence over the general welfare.

The central doctrine which has informed the resulting political morality is what Rawls calls "justice as fairness." This is the view that social institutions should not confer morally arbitrary long-term advantages on some persons at the expense of others. According to Rawls, one's prospects and opportunities in life are strongly influenced by the circumstances of one's birth—one's place in the social, political, and economic structure defined by the basic institutions of one's society. For example, one might have been born to slaveowners or to enslaved people, to a wealthy political dynasty in New England or to a poor family in a Philadelphia ghetto, to an Anglophone or to a Francophone family in 1950s Montréal. These important differences are morally arbitrary—a mere matter of luck—not something for which people deserve to be either rewarded or punished. According to Rawls, therefore, the fundamental problem of social justice is to ensure that the basic institutions of our society are set up in such a way that they do not generate and perpetuate morally arbitrary inequalities.

The upshot of this, in Rawls's view, includes the radical result that inequalities in wealth, income, and other "primary social goods" are justified *only* if they are to the advantage of the least well off in society. Rawls's work has thus been widely seen (and criticized) as the philosophical foundation for a particularly egalitarian and left-wing version of the modern welfare state, and also—because of his emphasis on a set of universal,

indefeasible basic rights and liberties—as an important successor to the rich tradition of liberal political thought.

What Is the Structure of This Reading?

The selection reprinted here comes from Rawls's 2001 book *Justice as Fairness*. In it he sets out to represent, in their final form, the ideas first laid out in his seminal 1971 work *A Theory of Justice*. The heart of his substantive theory is the so-called two principles of justice, and his description of these (though not his extended argument for their adequacy) is included here.

In Part I of *Justice as Fairness* Rawls lays out the fundamental ideas underlying his political theory, including the important notion of society as a fair system of cooperation, and the main concepts involved in arguing for his theory of justice as being justified by a "contract" made in the "original position." Some of these basic notions are briefly described in "Some Useful Background Information," below. Part II of the book presents his two principles of justice, and the first two sections of it are reprinted here. In the first section, Rawls summarizes three basic points which inform and constrain his reasoning, and in the second he describes the two principles themselves. In the rest of Part II (not included) he provides more details about the two principles, and in Part III he lays out the argument from the original position. In Part IV he describes some of the institutions of a just basic structure, and finally in Part V he addresses questions about the political stability of such a society.

Some Useful Background Information

1. Rawls believes democratic societies are always characterized by what he calls "the fact of reasonable pluralism." By this he means "the fact of profound and irreconcilable differences in citizens' reasonable comprehensive religious and philosophical conceptions of the world, and in their views of the moral and aesthetic values to be sought in human life."† A consequence of

---

*   See the Ethics section for readings on utilitarianism and Kant's moral theory. Social contract theory is represented by the Hobbes reading earlier in this section.
†   John Rawls, *Justice as Fairness: A Restatement* (Harvard University Press, 2001), 3.

this reasonable pluralism, Rawls believes, is that a democratic society can never genuinely be a *community*—a collection of persons united in affirming and pursuing the same conception of the good life. Rawls therefore proposes that we adopt—in fact, tacitly already have adopted—a different view of contemporary society: one that sees it as *a fair system of co-operation between free and equal citizens*. The task of a theory of justice then becomes one of specifying the fair terms of co-operation (and doing so in a way that is acceptable—that seems fair—even to citizens who have widely divergent conceptions of the good).

2. Rawls assumes the primary subject of this kind of theory of justice will be what he calls the *basic structure* of society. "[T]he basic structure of society is the way in which the main political and social institutions of society fit together into one system of social co-operation, and the way they assign basic rights and duties and regulate the division of advantages that arises from social co-operation over time.... The basic structure is the background social framework within which the activities of associations and individuals take place."* Examples of components of the basic structure include the political constitution, the relationship between the judiciary and the government, the structure of the economic system, and the social institution of the family. The kinds of things *not* included in the basic structure—and thus affected only indirectly by Rawls's theory of justice— are the internal arrangements of associations such as churches and universities, particular pieces of non-constitutional legislation or legal decisions, and social relationships between individual citizens.

3. If justice consists in the fair terms of co-operation for society viewed as a system of cooperation, then the question becomes: how are these fair terms of cooperation arrived at? Since the fact of reasonable pluralism precludes appeal to any kind of shared moral authority or outlook, Rawls concludes that the free terms of cooperation must be "settled by an agreement reached by free and equal citizens engaged in cooperation, and made in view of what they regard as their reciprocal advantage."†

Furthermore, this contract, like any agreement, must be made under conditions which are fair to all the parties involved. Rawls's attempt to specify the circumstances in which agreement on the basic structure of society would be fair is a thought-experiment called the *original position*.

In the original position, the parties to the contract are imagined placed behind what Rawls calls a *veil of ignorance*: they are not allowed to know their social positions; their particular comprehensive doctrines of the good; their race, sex, or ethnic group; or their genetic endowments of such things as strength and intelligence. In other words, knowledge of all the contingent or arbitrary aspects of one's place in actual society are removed. On the other hand, the parties in the original position are assumed to be well-informed about such things as economic and political theory and human psychology, and to be rational. In this way, all information which would—in Rawls's view—introduce unfair distortions into the social contract is excluded from the original position and only the data needed to make a fair decision are allowed in: thus, for example, there could be no question of rich people trying to establish a basic social structure which protects their wealth by disadvantaging the poor, since nobody in the original position knows whether they are rich or poor.

Rawls's idea is that whatever contract would be agreed to by representatives in the original position must be a fair one, one that any reasonable citizen could accept no matter what their place in society or their conception of the good. This contract is, of course, merely hypothetical (there was never actually any original position). Rawls's point is not that citizens are actually bound by a historical social contract, but that the thought-experiment of making a contract in the original position is a device for showing what principles of justice *we should accept if we are reasonable*. And, Rawls argues, the principles that would be rationally arrived at in the original position will not be, say, utilitarian, or non-egalitarian, but will be something very much like his two principles of justice.

---

* Ibid., 10.
† Ibid., 15.

FROM *Justice as Fairness: A Restatement**

PART II: PRINCIPLES OF JUSTICE, §§ 12–13

§12. *Three Basic Points*

12.1. In Part II we discuss the content of the two principles of justice that apply to the basic structure, as well as various grounds in favor of them and replies to a number of objections. A more formal and organized argument for these principles is presented in Part III, where we discuss the reasoning that moves the parties in the original position. In that argument the original position serves to keep track of all our assumptions and to bring out their combined force by uniting them into one framework so that we can more easily see their implications.

I begin with three basic points which review some matters discussed in Part I and introduce others we are about to examine. Recall first that justice as fairness is framed for a democratic society. Its principles are meant to answer the question: once we view a democratic society as a fair system of social cooperation between citizens regarded as free and equal, what principles are most appropriate to it? Alternatively: which principles are most appropriate for a democratic society that not only professes but wants to take seriously the idea that citizens are free and equal, and tries to realize that idea in its main institutions? The question of whether a constitutional regime is to be preferred to majoritarian democracy, we postpone until later (Part IV, §44).†

12.2. The second point is that justice as fairness takes the primary subject of political justice to be the basic structure of society, that is, its main political and social institutions and how they fit together into one unified system of cooperation (§4). We suppose that citizens are born into society and will normally spend their whole lives within its basic institutions. The nature and role of the basic structure importantly influence social and economic inequalities and enter into determining the appropriate principles of justice.

In particular, let us suppose that the fundamental social and economic inequalities are the differences in citizens' life-prospects (their prospects over a complete life) as these are affected by such things as their social class of origin, their native endowments, their opportunities for education, and their good or ill fortune over the course of life (§16). We ask: by what principles are differences of that kind—differences in life-prospects—made legitimate and consistent with the idea of free and equal citizenship in society seen as a fair system of cooperation?

12.3. The third point is that justice as fairness is a form of political liberalism: it tries to articulate a family of highly significant (moral) values that characteristically apply to the political and social institutions of the basic structure. It gives an account of these values in the light of certain special features of the political relationship as distinct from other relationships, associational, familial, and personal.

1. It is a relationship of persons within the basic structure of society, a structure we enter only by birth and exit only by death (or so we may assume for the moment). Political society is closed, as it were; and we do not, and indeed cannot, enter or leave it voluntarily.

2. Political power is always coercive power applied by the state and its apparatus of enforcement; but

---

* Reprinted with permission of the publisher from "Three Basic Points" and "Two Principles of Justice" in *Justice as Fairness: A Restatement* by John Rawls, edited by Erin Kelly (Cambridge: MA: The Belknap Press of Harvard University Press), 39–50. Copyright © 2001 by the President and Fellows of Harvard College.

† In that section, Rawls explains that "[a] constitutional regime is one in which laws and statutes must be consistent with certain fundamental rights and liberties.... There is in effect a constitution (not necessarily written) with a bill of rights specifying those freedoms and interpreted by the courts as constitutional limits on legislation." By contrast, there are no constitutional limits on legislation in a majoritarian democracy, and whatever the majority decides (according to the proper procedures) is law.

in a constitutional regime political power is at the same time the power of free and equal citizens as a collective body. Thus political power is citizens' power, which they impose on themselves and one another as free and equal.

The idea of political liberalism arises as follows. We start from two facts: first, from the fact of reasonable pluralism, the fact that a diversity of reasonable comprehensive doctrines is a permanent feature of a democratic society; and second, from the fact that in a democratic regime political power is regarded as the power of free and equal citizens as a collective body. These two points give rise to a problem of political legitimacy. For if the fact of reasonable pluralism always characterizes democratic societies and if political power is indeed the power of free and equal citizens, in the light of what reasons and values—of what kind of a conception of justice—can citizens legitimately exercise that coercive power over one another?

Political liberalism answers that the conception of justice must be a political conception, as defined in §9.1.* Such a conception when satisfied allows us to say: political power is legitimate only when it is exercised in accordance with a constitution (written or unwritten) the essentials of which all citizens, as reasonable and rational, can endorse in the light of their common human reason. This is the liberal principle of legitimacy. It is a further desideratum† that all legislative questions that concern or border on these essentials, or are highly divisive, should also be settled, so far as possible, by guidelines and values that can be similarly endorsed.

In matters of constitutional essentials, as well as on questions of basic justice, we try to appeal only to principles and values each citizen can endorse. A political conception of justice hopes to formulate these values: its shared principles and values make reason public, while freedom of speech and thought in a constitutional regime make it free. In providing a public basis of justification, a political conception of justice

provides the framework for the liberal idea of political legitimacy. As noted in §9.4, however, and discussed further in §26, we do not say that a political conception formulates political values that can settle all legislative questions. This is neither possible nor desirable. There are many questions legislatures must consider that can only be settled by voting that is properly influenced by nonpolitical values. Yet at least on constitutional essentials and matters of basic justice we do try for an agreed basis; so long as there is at least rough agreement here, fair social cooperation among citizens can, we hope, be maintained.[1]

12.4. Given these three points, our question is: viewing society as a fair system of cooperation between citizens regarded as free and equal, what principles of justice are most appropriate to specify basic rights and liberties, and to regulate social and economic inequalities in citizens' prospects over a complete life? These inequalities are our primary concern.

To find a principle to regulate these inequalities, we look to our firmest considered convictions about equal basic rights and liberties, the fair value of the political liberties as well as fair equality of opportunity. We look outside the sphere of distributive justice more narrowly construed to see whether an appropriate distributive principle is singled out by those firmest convictions once their essential elements are represented in the original position as a device of representation (§6). This device is to assist us in working out which principle, or principles, the representatives of free and equal citizens would select to regulate social and economic inequalities in these prospects over a complete life when they assume that the equal basic liberties and fair opportunities are already secured.

The idea here is to use our firmest considered convictions about the nature of a democratic society as a fair system of cooperation between free and equal citizens—as modeled in the original position—to see whether the combined assertion of those convictions so expressed will help us to identify an appropriate distributive principle for the basic structure with

---

*   According to Rawls, a conception of justice is *political* if, (a) it applies only to the basic structure of society (and not directly to particular groups of people within those societies); (b) it does not presuppose any particular comprehensive conception of the good life; and (c) it is formulated, as far as possible, from ideas already implicit in the public political culture of a democratic society.

†   Something which is needed or considered highly desirable.

its economic and social inequalities in citizens' life-prospects. Our convictions about principles regulating those inequalities are much less firm and assured; so we look to our firmest convictions for guidance where assurance is lacking and guidance is needed (*Theory*, §§4, 20*).

§13. Two Principles of Justice

13.1. To try to answer our question, let us turn to a revised statement of the two principles of justice discussed in *Theory*, §§11–14. They should now read:[2]

1. Each person has the same indefeasible† claim to a fully adequate scheme of equal basic liberties, which scheme is compatible with the same scheme of liberties for all; and
2. Social and economic inequalities are to satisfy two conditions: first, they are to be attached to offices and positions open to all under conditions of fair equality of opportunity; and second, they are to be to the greatest benefit of the least-advantaged members of society (the difference principle).[3]

As I explain below, the first principle is prior to the second; also, in the second principle fair equality of opportunity is prior to the difference principle. This priority means that in applying a principle (or checking it against test cases) we assume that the prior principles are fully satisfied. We seek a principle of distribution (in the narrower sense) that holds within the setting of background institutions that secure the basic equal liberties (including the fair value of the political liberties)[4] as well as fair equality of opportunity. How far that principle holds outside that setting is a separate question we shall not consider.[5]

13.2. The revisions in the second principle are merely stylistic. But before noting the revisions in the first principle, which are significant,‡ we should attend to

the meaning of fair equality of opportunity. This is a difficult and not altogether clear idea; its role is perhaps best gathered from why it is introduced: namely, to correct the defects of formal equality of opportunity—careers open to talents—in the system of natural liberty, so-called (*Theory*, §12: 62ff.; §14).§ To this end, fair equality of opportunity is said to require not merely that public offices and social positions be open in the formal sense, but that all should have a fair chance to attain them. To specify the idea of a fair chance we say: supposing that there is a distribution of native endowments, those who have the same level of talent and ability and the same willingness to use these gifts should have the same prospects of success regardless of their social class of origin, the class into which they are born and develop until the age of reason. In all parts of society there are to be roughly the same prospects of culture and achievement for those similarly motivated and endowed.

Fair equality of opportunity here means liberal equality. To accomplish its aims, certain requirements must be imposed on the basic structure beyond those of the system of natural liberty. A free market system must be set within a framework of political and legal institutions that adjust the long-run trend of economic forces so as to prevent excessive concentrations of property and wealth, especially those likely to lead to political domination. Society must also establish, among other things, equal opportunities of education for all regardless of family income (§15).[6]

13.3. Consider now the reasons for revising the first principle.[7] One is that the equal basic liberties in this principle are specified by a list as follows: freedom of thought and liberty of conscience; political liberties (for example, the right to vote and to participate in politics) and freedom of association, as well as the rights and liberties specified by the liberty and integrity (physical and psychological) of the person; and finally, the rights and liberties covered by the rule of

---

* *Theory: A Theory of Justice* (Harvard University Press, 1971).
† Cannot, under any circumstances, be annulled.
‡ Rawls's original, 1971 formulation was: "Each person is to have an equal right to the most extensive total system of equal basic liberties compatible with a similar system of liberty for all."
§ The "system of natural liberty," in Rawls's terminology, is one which assumes that, in an economically efficient free market economy, a basic structure "in which positions are open to those able and willing to strive for them will lead to a just distribution" (*A Theory of Justice*, §12), but which makes no effort to correct for arbitrary inequalities in the initial social conditions of the competitors.

law. That the basic liberties are specified by a list is quite clear from *Theory*, §11: 61 (1st ed.); but the use of the singular term "basic liberty" in the statement of the principle in *Theory*, §11: 60 (1st ed.), obscures this important feature of these liberties.

This revision brings out that no priority is assigned to liberty as such, as if the exercise of something called "liberty" had a preeminent value and were the main, if not the sole, end of political and social justice. While there is a general presumption against imposing legal and other restrictions on conduct without a sufficient reason, this presumption creates no special priority for any particular liberty. Throughout the history of democratic thought the focus has been on achieving certain specific rights and liberties as well as specific constitutional guarantees, as found, for example, in various bills of rights and declarations of the rights of man. Justice as fairness follows this traditional view.

13.4. A list of basic liberties can be drawn up in two ways. One is historical: we survey various democratic regimes and assemble a list of rights and liberties that seem basic and are securely protected in what seem to be historically the more successful regimes. Of course, the veil of ignorance means that this kind of particular information is not available to the parties in the original position, but it is available to you and me in setting up justice as fairness.[8] We are perfectly free to use it to specify the principles of justice we make available to the parties.

A second way of drawing up a list of basic rights and liberties is analytical: we consider what liberties provide the political and social conditions essential for the adequate development and full exercise of the two moral powers of free and equal persons (§7.1).* Following this we say: first, that the equal political liberties and freedom of thought enable citizens to develop and to exercise these powers in judging the justice of the basic structure of society and its social policies; and second, that liberty of conscience and freedom of association enable citizens to develop and exercise their moral powers in forming and revising and in rationally pursuing (individually or, more often, in association with others) their conceptions of the good.

Those basic rights and liberties protect and secure the scope required for the exercise of the two moral powers in the two fundamental cases just mentioned: that is to say, the first fundamental case is the exercise of those powers in judging the justice of basic institutions and social policies; while the second fundamental case is the exercise of those powers in pursuing our conception of the good. To exercise our powers in these ways is essential to us as free and equal citizens.

13.5. Observe that the first principle of justice applies not only to the basic structure (both principles do this) but more specifically to what we think of as the constitution, whether written or unwritten. Observe also that some of these liberties, especially the equal political liberties and freedom of thought and association, are to be guaranteed by a constitution (*Theory*, chap. IV). What we may call "constituent power," as opposed to "ordinary power,"[9] is to be suitably institutionalized in the form of a regime: in the right to vote and to hold office, and in so-called bills of rights, as well as in the procedures for amending the constitution, for example.

These matters belong to the so-called constitutional essentials, these essentials being those crucial matters about which, given the fact of pluralism, working political agreement is most urgent (§9.4). In view of the fundamental nature of the basic rights and liberties, explained in part by the fundamental interests they protect, and given that the power of the people to constitute the form of government is a superior power (distinct from the ordinary power exercised routinely by officers of a regime), the first principle is assigned priority.

This priority means (as we have said) that the second principle (which includes the difference principle as one part) is always to be applied within a setting of background institutions that satisfy the requirements of the first principle (including the requirement of securing the fair value of the political liberties), as by definition they will in a well-ordered society.†[10] The

---

* These moral powers are a) the capacity to understand, apply, and act from the principles of political justice, and b) the capacity to have, revise, and rationally pursue a conception of the good (i.e., what is of value in human life).

† By "well-ordered society," Rawls means a society in which the following are true: (a) all citizens accept the same political conception of justice, (b) its basic structure is publicly known to satisfy those shared principles of justice, and

fair value of the political liberties ensures that citizens similarly gifted and motivated have roughly an equal chance of influencing the government's policy and of attaining positions of authority irrespective of their economic and social class.[11] To explain the priority of the first principle over the second: this priority rules out exchanges ("trade-offs," as economists say) between the basic rights and liberties covered by the first principle and the social and economic advantages regulated by the difference principle. For example, the equal political liberties cannot be denied to certain groups on the grounds that their having these liberties may enable them to block policies needed for economic growth and efficiency.

Nor can we justify a selective service act that grants educational deferments or exemptions to some on the grounds that doing this is a socially efficient way both to maintain the armed forces and to provide incentives to those otherwise subject to conscription to acquire valuable skills by continuing their education. Since conscription is a drastic interference with the basic liberties of equal citizenship, it cannot be justified by any needs less compelling than those of the defense of these equal liberties themselves (*Theory*, §58: 333f.).

A further point about priority: in asserting the priority of the basic rights and liberties, we suppose reasonably favorable conditions to obtain. That is, we suppose historical, economic and social conditions to be such that, provided the political will exists, effective political institutions can be established to give adequate scope for the exercise of those freedoms. These conditions mean that the barriers to constitutional government (if such there are) spring largely from the political culture and existing effective interests, and not from, for instance, a lack of economic means, or education, or the many skills needed to run a democratic regime.[12]

13.6. It is important to note a distinction between the first and second principles of justice. The first principle, as explained by its interpretation, covers the constitutional essentials. The second principle requires fair equality of opportunity and that social and economic inequalities be governed by the difference principle, which we discuss in §§17–19. While some principle of opportunity is a constitutional essential—for example, a principle requiring an open society, one with careers open to talents (to use the eighteenth-century phrase)—fair equality of opportunity requires more than that, and is not counted a constitutional essential. Similarly, although a social minimum providing for the basic needs of all citizens is also a constitutional essential (§38.3–4; §49.5), the difference principle is more demanding and is not so regarded.

The basis for the distinction between the two principles is not that the first expresses political values while the second does not. Both principles express political values. Rather, we see the basic structure of society as having two coordinate roles, the first principle applying to one, the second principle to the other (*Theory*, §11: 53). In one role the basic structure specifies and secures citizens' equal basic liberties (including the fair value of the political liberties (§45)) and establishes a just constitutional regime. In the other role it provides the background institutions of social and economic justice in the form most appropriate to citizens seen as free and equal. The questions involved in the first role concern the acquisition and the exercise of political power. To fulfill the liberal principle of legitimacy (§12.3), we hope to settle at least these questions by appeal to the political values that constitute the basis of free public reason (§26).*

The principles of justice are adopted and applied in a four-stage sequence.[13] In the first stage, the parties adopt the principles of justice behind a veil of ignorance. Limitations on knowledge available to the parties are progressively relaxed in the next three stages: the stage of the constitutional convention, the legislative stage in which laws are enacted as the constitution allows and as the principles of justice require and permit, and the final stage in which the rules are applied by administrators and followed by citizens generally and the constitution and laws are

---

(c) citizens have an "effective sense of justice," i.e., they understand and act in accordance with those principles of justice.

* By "free public reason," Rawls means the principles of reasoning and the rules of evidence which are accepted by all the citizens of a well-ordered society (irrespective of their differing conceptions of the good).

interpreted by members of the judiciary. At this last stage, everyone has complete access to all the facts. The first principle applies at the stage of the constitutional convention, and whether the constitutional essentials are assured is more or less visible on the face of the constitution and in its political arrangements and the way these work in practice. By contrast the second principle applies at the legislative stage and it bears on all kinds of social and economic legislation, and on the many kinds of issues arising at this point (*Theory*, §31: 172–176). Whether the aims of the second principle are realized is far more difficult to ascertain. To some degree these matters are always open to reasonable differences of opinion; they depend on inference and judgment in assessing complex social and economic information. Also, we can expect more agreement on constitutional essentials than on issues of distributive justice in the narrower sense.

Thus the grounds for distinguishing the constitutional essentials covered by the first principle and the institutions of distributive justice covered by the second are not that the first principle expresses political values and the second does not. Rather, the grounds of the distinction are four:

1. The two principles apply to different stages in the application of principles and identify two distinct roles of the basic structure;
2. It is more urgent to settle the constitutional essentials;

3. It is far easier to tell whether those essentials are realized; and
4. It seems possible to gain agreement on what those essentials should be, not in every detail, of course, but in the main outlines.

13.7. One way to see the point of the idea of constitutional essentials is to connect it with the idea of loyal opposition, itself an essential idea of a constitutional regime. The government and its loyal opposition agree on these constitutional essentials. Their so agreeing makes the government legitimate in intention and the opposition loyal in its opposition. Where the loyalty of both is firm and their agreement mutually recognized, a constitutional regime is secure. Differences about the most appropriate principles of distributive justice in the narrower sense, and the ideals that underlie them, can be adjudicated, though not always properly, within the existing political framework.

While the difference principle does not fall under the constitutional essentials, it is nevertheless important to try to identify the idea of equality most appropriate to citizens viewed as free and equal, and as normally and fully cooperating members of society over a complete life. I believe this idea involves reciprocity[14] at the deepest level and thus democratic equality properly understood requires something like the difference principle. (I say "something like," for there may be various nearby possibilities.) The remaining sections of this part (§§14–22) try to clarify the content of this principle and to clear up a number of difficulties. ∎

Suggestions for Critical Reflection

1. Rawls restricts the application of his theory of justice to democratic societies. Why do you think he makes this restriction? Is it appropriate to stipulate such preconditions for a philosophical theory of social justice? Could his theory of justice as fairness be recast to apply to *all* kinds of societies, and not just democracies?

2. Rawls argues "the fact of reasonable pluralism" in democratic societies gives rise to a problem of political legitimacy, and offers what he calls a "liberal" solution to that problem via a "political" conception of justice. How plausible is it that democracies really do face the deep problem of political legitimacy which Rawls describes? How adequate and attractive do you find his proposed solution? Is the kind of political conception of justice Rawls describes even *available* in contemporary liberal democratic societies?

3. Rawls appeals several times to "our firmest considered convictions" to help us decide what the basic structure of a just society should look like. Is this kind of appeal to intuition legitimate—or avoidable—in political philosophy?

4. Rawls's theory of justice as fairness is encapsulated in his two principles. How plausible and attractive are they? How radical are they? Might they have any controversial implications? What changes would we have to make to bring our society into accord with these principles (in particular with the second principle, which deals with distributive justice)?

5. The "difference principle" makes a crucial reference to the "least-advantaged members of society." Who exactly is Rawls thinking of here? What difference does it make?

6. The first part of the second principle stipulates "fair equality of opportunity." What does Rawls seem to have in mind? How different is Rawls's idea of fair equality of opportunity from what one might think of as the "free market" view of equal opportunity?

7. Rawls emphasizes that the question of the justice of social inequalities arises, for his theory, only *after* basic equal liberties and fair equality of opportunity have been secured. Why does he prioritize his principles in this way? Is he right to do so? Does this "lexical ordering" of the principles mean substantial social inequalities could, in fact, be justified in a Rawlsian society?

8. Why does Rawls not consider the second principle of justice a "constitutional essential"? What is the significance of this?

9. Rawls suggests the notion of democratic equality "involves reciprocity at the deepest level," and that this in turn requires "something like the difference principle." Is he right? What kind of argument might he have in mind?

Notes

1   It is not always clear whether a question involves a constitutional essential, as will be mentioned in due course. If there is doubt about this and the question is highly divisive, then citizens have a duty of civility to try to articulate their claims on one another by reference to political values, if that is possible.

2   This section summarizes some points from "The Basic Liberties and Their Priority," *Tanner Lectures on Human Values*, vol. 3, ed. Sterling McMurrin (Salt Lake City: University of Utah Press, 1982), §I, reprinted in *Political Liberalism* [New York City: Columbia University Press, 1993]. In that essay I try to reply to what I believe are two of the more serious objections to my account of liberty in *Theory* raised by H.L.A. Hart in his splendid critical review essay, "Rawls on Liberty and Its Priority," *University of Chicago Law Review* 40 (Spring 1975): 551–555, reprinted in his *Essays in Jurisprudence and Philosophy* (Oxford: Oxford University Press, 1983). No changes made in justice as fairness in this restatement are more significant than those forced by Hart's review.

3   Instead of "the difference principle," many writers prefer the term "the maximin principle," or simply "maximin justice," or some such locution. See, for example, Joshua Cohen's very full and accurate account of the difference principle in "Democratic Equality," *Ethics* 99 (July 1989): 727–751. But I still use the term "difference principle" to emphasize first, that this principle and the maximin rule for decision under uncertainty (§28.1) are two very distinct things; and second, that in arguing for the difference principle over other distributive principles (say a restricted principle of (average) utility, which includes a social minimum), there is no appeal at all to the maximin rule for decision under uncertainty. The widespread idea that the argument for the difference principle depends on extreme aversion to uncertainty is a mistake, although a mistake unhappily encouraged by the faults of exposition in *Theory*, faults to be corrected in Part III of this restatement.

4   See *Theory*, §36: 197–199.

5   Some have found this kind of restriction objectionable; they think a political conception should be framed to cover all logically possible cases, or all conceivable cases, and not restricted to cases that can arise only within a specified institutional context. See for example Brian Barry, *The Liberal Theory of Justice* (Oxford: Oxford University Press, 1973), p. 112. In contrast, we seek a principle to govern social and economic inequalities in democratic regimes as we know them, and so we are concerned with inequalities in citizens' life-prospects that may actually arise, given our understanding of how certain institutions work.

6   These remarks are the merest sketch of a difficult idea. We come back to it from time to time.

7   This principle may be preceded by a lexically prior principle requiring that basic needs be met, as least insofar as their being met is a necessary condition

for citizens to understand and to be able fruitfully to exercise the basic rights and liberties. For a statement of such a principle with further discussion, see R.G. Peffer, *Marxism, Morality, and Social Justice* (Princeton: Princeton University Press, 1990), p.14.

8 Here I should mention that there are three points of view in justice as fairness that it is essential to distinguish: the point of view of the parties in the original position, the point of view of citizens in a well-ordered society, and the point of view of you and me who are setting up justice as fairness as a political conception and trying to use it to organize into one coherent view our considered judgments at all levels of generality. Keep in mind that the parties are, as it were, artificial persons who are part of a procedure of construction that we frame for our philosophical purposes. We may know many things that we keep from them. For these three points of view, see *Political Liberalism*, p. 28.

9 This distinction is derived from Locke, who speaks of the people's power to constitute the legislative as the first and fundamental law of all commonwealths. John Locke, *Second Treatise of Government*, §§134, 141, 149.

10 It is sometimes objected to the difference principle as a principle of distributive justice that it contains no restrictions on the overall nature of permissible distributions. It is concerned, the objection runs, solely with the least advantaged. But this objection is incorrect: it overlooks the fact that the parts of the two principles of justice are designed to work in tandem and apply as a unit. The requirements of the prior principles have important distributive effects. Consider the effects of fair equality of opportunity as applied to education, say, or the distributive effects

of the fair value of the political liberties. We cannot possibly take the difference principle seriously so long as we think of it by itself, apart from its setting within prior principles.

11 See *Political Liberalism*, p. 358.

12 The priority (or the primacy) of the basic equal liberties does not, contrary to much opinion, presuppose a high level of wealth and income. See Amartya Sen and Jean Dreze, *Hunger and Public Action* (Oxford: Oxford University Press, 1989), chap. 13; and Partha Dasgupta, *An Inquiry into Well-Being and Destitution* (Oxford: Oxford University Press, 1999), chaps. 1–2, 5 and passim.

13 See *Theory*, §31: 172–176, and *Political Liberalism*, pp. 397–398.

14 As understood in justice as fairness, reciprocity is a relation between citizens expressed by principles of justice that regulate a social world in which all who are engaged in cooperation and do their part as the rules and procedures require are to benefit in an appropriate way as assessed by a suitable benchmark of comparison. The two principles of justice, including the difference principle with its implicit reference to equal division as a benchmark, formulate an idea of reciprocity between citizens. For a fuller discussion of the idea of reciprocity, see *Political Liberalism*, pp. 16–17, and the introduction to the paperback edition, pp. xliv, xlvi, li. The idea of reciprocity also plays an important part in "The Idea of Public Reason Revisited," *University of Chicago Law Review*, 64 (Summer 1997): 765–807, reprinted in *The Law of Peoples* (Cambridge, Mass.: Harvard University Press, 1999) and *Collected Papers* [Cambridge, Mass.: Harvard University Press, 1999].

ROBERT NOZICK

FROM *Anarchy, State, and Utopia*

Who Was Robert Nozick?

Robert Nozick was born in 1938, to Russian Jewish immigrants, and grew up in Brooklyn, New York. He took his undergraduate degree at Columbia College and his PhD, on theories of rational decision-making, at Princeton. He taught at Princeton from 1962 to 1965, Harvard from 1965 to 1967, Rockefeller University from 1967 to 1969, and then returned to Harvard, a full professor of philosophy, at the tender age of 30. Nozick was already well-known in philosophical circles, but his first book, *Anarchy, State, and Utopia* (1974) propelled him into the public eye with its controversial but intellectually dazzling defense of political libertarianism. This book—which was widely perceived as an energetic response to his Harvard colleague John Rawls's liberal *Theory of Justice*—won the National Book Award and was named by *The Times Literary Supplement* as one of "The Hundred Most Influential Books Since the War." In 1998, Nozick was made Joseph Pellegrino University Professor at Harvard. Sadly he died of stomach cancer in 2002, at the relatively young age of 63.

What Was Nozick's Overall Philosophical Project?

As a young man, Nozick was a radical left-winger; he was converted to libertarianism—the view that individual rights should be maximized and the role of the state minimized—as a graduate student, largely through reading *laissez-faire* economists like F.A. Hayek and Milton Friedman. However, he was never fully comfortable with his public reputation as a right-wing ideologue. In

a 1978 article in *The New York Times Magazine*,* he said, "right-wing people like the pro-free-market argument, but don't like the arguments for individual liberty in cases like gay rights—although I view them as an interconnecting whole."†

In the same article, Nozick also described his fresh and lively approach to philosophical writing, noting, "[i]t is as though what philosophers want is a way of saying something that will leave the person they're talking to no escape. Well, why should they be bludgeoning people like that? It's not a nice way to behave."

Nozick's philosophical interests were notably broad. Best known for his work in political philosophy, he also made important contributions to epistemology (especially his notion of knowledge as a kind of "truth tracking"), metaphysics (with his "closest continuer" theory of personal identity), and decision theory (particularly through his introduction of "Newcomb's problem" to the philosophical literature).

What Is the Structure of This Reading?

In Part I of *Anarchy, State, and Utopia*, Nozick argues that a minimal state is justified; then, in Part II, that no state more powerful or extensive than a minimal state is morally justified. In Part III he argues this is not an unfortunate result; rather, the minimal state is "a framework for utopia" and "inspiring as well as right." The material reprinted here is from the first section of the first chapter of Part II, where Nozick argues that considerations of distributive justice do not require going beyond the minimal state, and, in fact, on the contrary, a proper account of distributive justice shows that state

---

* "Harvard's Nozick: Philosopher of the New Right," by Jonathan Lieberson, 17 December 1978.

† As Alan Ryan wrote in his obituary for Nozick in *The Independent* (30 January 2002), "*Anarchy, State and Utopia* is a book that is more misunderstood by its admirers than its critics. It is often thought to have provided philosophical support for the policies of Ronald Reagan and Margaret Thatcher, but its criticism of social conservatism is at least as devastating as its criticism of the redistributive welfare state."

interference in distributive patterns must violate the rights of individuals.

Nozick first outlines what he considers the correct theory of distributive justice. He calls this the *entitlement theory of justice in holdings*, and presents it as made up of exactly three principles of justice. He then distinguishes between two possible varieties of historical principles of justice—*patterned* or *non-patterned*—and claims that his entitlement theory belongs to the latter class. In the next section, Nozick argues that all end-state or patterned theories of distributive justice are inconsistent with liberty—i.e., they are committed to the repeated violation of the rights of individuals.

Some Useful Background Information

Nozick argues in *Anarchy, State, and Utopia* that only a minimal "night-watchman" state is consistent with individual liberty. A minimal state has a monopoly on the use of force within its boundaries (except for force used in immediate self-defense), and it uses this monopoly to guard its citizens against violence, theft, and fraud, and to enforce compliance with legally-made contracts. Beyond this, however, the minimal state has no legitimate function. For example, in the minimal state there can be no central bank or other form of economic regulation, no department of public works, no public education system, no welfare provisions or state pensions, no social healthcare system, no environmental protection regulations or agencies, and so on.

A Common Misconception

Nozick does not believe it is actually *immoral* to help the poor (or preserve the environment, or provide universal healthcare, or foster the arts ...). He argues that it is immoral to *force* people to do these things—in other words, that we have no legally enforceable *duty* to do them—but it is perfectly consistent to believe that it would be *morally good* if we were (voluntarily) to contribute to these ends.

FROM *Anarchy, State, and Utopia**

The minimal state is the most extensive state that can be justified. Any state more extensive violates people's rights. Yet many persons have put forth reasons purporting to justify a more extensive state. It is impossible within the compass of this book to examine all the reasons that have been put forth. Therefore, I shall focus upon those generally acknowledged to be most weighty and influential, to see precisely wherein they fail. In this chapter we consider the claim that a more extensive state is justified, because necessary (or the best instrument) to achieve distributive justice....

The term "distributive justice" is not a neutral one. Hearing the term "distribution," most people presume that some thing or mechanism uses some principle or criterion to give out a supply of things. Into this process of distributing shares some error may have crept. So it is an open question, at least, whether *re*distribution should take place; whether we should do again what has already been done once, though poorly. However, we are not in the position of children who have been given portions of pie by someone who now makes last minute adjustments to rectify careless cutting. There is no *central* distribution, no person or group entitled to control all the resources, jointly deciding how they are to be doled out. What each person gets, he gets from others who give to him in exchange for something, or as a gift. In a free society, diverse persons control different resources, and new holdings arise out of the voluntary exchanges and actions of persons. There is no more a distributing or distribution of shares than there is a distributing of mates in a society in which persons choose whom they shall marry. The total result is the product of many individual decisions which the different individuals involved are entitled to make.

* From Robert Nozick, "Distributive Justice," in *Anarchy, State, and Utopia* by (Basic Books, 1974), 149–53, 155–58, 160–64.

Some uses of the term "distribution," it is true, do not imply a previous distributing appropriately judged by some criterion (for example, "probability distribution"); nevertheless, despite the title of this chapter, it would be best to use a terminology that clearly is neutral. We shall speak of people's holdings; a principle of justice in holdings describes (part of) what justice tells us (requires) about holdings....

The Entitlement Theory

The subject of justice in holdings consists of three major topics. The first is the *original acquisition of holdings*, the appropriation of unheld things. This includes the issues of how unheld things may come to be held, the process, or processes, by which unheld things may come to be held, the things that may come to be held by these processes, the extent of what comes to be held by a particular process, and so on. We shall refer to the complicated truth about this topic, which we shall not formulate here, as the principle of justice in acquisition. The second topic concerns the *transfer of holdings* from one person to another. By what processes may a person transfer holdings to another? How may a person acquire a holding from another who holds it? Under this topic come general descriptions of voluntary exchange, and gift and (on the other hand) fraud, as well as reference to particular conventional details fixed upon in a given society. The complicated truth about this subject (with placeholders for conventional details) we shall call the principle of justice in transfer. (And we shall suppose it also includes principles governing how a person may divest himself of a holding, passing it into an unheld state.)

If the world were wholly just, the following inductive definition* would exhaustively cover the subject of justice in holdings.

1. A person who acquires a holding in accordance with the principle of justice in acquisition is entitled to that holding.
2. A person who acquires a holding in accordance with the principle of justice in transfer, from

someone else entitled to the holding, is entitled to the holding.
3. No one is entitled to a holding except by (repeated) applications of 1 and 2.

The complete principle of distributive justice would say simply that a distribution is just if everyone is entitled to the holdings they possess under the distribution.

A distribution is just if it arises from another just distribution by legitimate means. The legitimate means of moving from one distribution to another are specified by the principle of justice in transfer. The legitimate first "moves" are specified by the principle of justice in acquisition.[1] Whatever arises from a just situation by just steps is itself just. The means of change specified by the principle of justice in transfer preserve justice. As correct rules of inference are truth-preserving, and any conclusion deduced via repeated application of such rules from only true premises is itself true, so the means of transition from one situation to another specified by the principle of justice in transfer are justice-preserving, and any situation actually arising from repeated transitions in accordance with the principle from a just situation is itself just. The parallel between justice-preserving transformations and truth-preserving transformations illuminates where it fails as well as where it holds. That a conclusion could have been deduced by truth-preserving means from premises that are true suffices to show its truth. That from a just situation a situation *could* have arisen via justice-preserving means does *not* suffice to show its justice. The fact that a thief's victims voluntarily *could* have presented him with gifts does not entitle the thief to his ill-gotten gains. Justice in holdings is historical; it depends upon what actually has happened....

Not all actual situations are generated in accordance with the two principles of justice in holdings: the principle of justice in acquisition and the principle of justice in transfer. Some people steal from others, or defraud them, or enslave them, seizing their product and preventing them from living as they choose, or forcibly exclude others from competing in exchanges. None of these are permissible modes of

---

* An inductive definition works by defining a base case and then giving a rule for generalizing from that case which covers everything else in the domain to be defined.

transition from one situation to another. And some persons acquire holdings by means not sanctioned by the principle of justice in acquisition. The existence of past injustice (previous violations of the first two principles of justice in holdings) raises the third major topic under justice in holdings: the rectification of injustice in holdings. If past injustice has shaped present holdings in various ways, some identifiable and some not, what now, if anything, ought to be done to rectify these injustices? What obligations do the performers of injustice have toward those whose position is worse than it would have been had the injustice not been done? Or, than it would have been had compensation been paid promptly? How, if at all, do things change if the beneficiaries and those made worse off are not the direct parties in the act of injustice, but, for example, their descendants? Is an injustice done to someone whose holding was itself based upon an unrectified injustice? How far back must one go in wiping clean the historical slate of injustices? What may victims of injustice permissibly do in order to rectify the injustices being done to them, including the many injustices done by persons acting through their government? I do not know of a thorough or theoretically sophisticated treatment of such issues.[2] Idealizing greatly, let us suppose theoretical investigation will produce a principle of rectification. This principle uses historical information about previous situations and injustices done in them (as defined by the first two principles of justice and rights against interference), and information about the actual course of events that flowed from these injustices, until the present, and it yields a description (or descriptions) of holdings in the society. The principle of rectification presumably will make use of its best estimate of subjunctive information* about what would have occurred (or a probability distribution† over what might have occurred, using the expected value) if the injustice had not taken place. If the actual description of holdings turns out not to be one of the descriptions yielded by the principle, then one of the descriptions yielded must be realized.[3]

The general outlines of the theory of justice in holdings are that the holdings of a person are just if he is entitled to them by the principles of justice in acquisition and transfer, or by the principle of rectification of injustice (as specified by the first two principles). If each person's holdings are just, then the total set (distribution) of holdings is just. To turn these general outlines into a specific theory we would have to specify the details of each of the three principles of justice in holdings: the principle of acquisition of holdings, the principle of transfer of holdings, and the principle of rectification of violations of the first two principles. I shall not attempt that task here....

Patterning

The entitlement principles of justice in holdings that we have sketched are historical principles of justice. To better understand their precise character, we shall distinguish them from another subclass of the historical principles. Consider, as an example, the principle of distribution according to moral merit. This principle requires that total distributive shares vary directly with moral merit; no person should have a greater share than anyone whose moral merit is greater. (If moral merit could be not merely ordered but measured on an interval or ratio scale, stronger principles could be formulated.) Or consider the principle that results by substituting "usefulness to society" for "moral merit" in the previous principle. Or instead of "distribute according to moral merit," or "distribute according to usefulness to society," we might consider "distribute according to the weighted sum‡ of moral merit, usefulness to society, and need," with the weights of the different dimensions equal. Let us call a principle of distribution *patterned* if it specifies that a distribution is to vary along with some natural dimension, weighted sum of natural dimensions, or

---

*   Information about a hypothetical, non-actual situation.

†   A specification of all possible values of a variable along with the probability that each will occur.

‡   A weighted sum is obtained by adding terms, each of which is given a certain value (weight) by using a multiplier which reflects their relative importance.

lexicographic ordering* of natural dimensions. And let us say a distribution is patterned if it accords with some patterned principle. (I speak of natural dimensions, admittedly without a general criterion for them, because for any set of holdings some artificial dimensions can be gimmicked up to vary along with the distribution of the set.) The principle of distribution in accordance with moral merit is a patterned historical principle, which specifies a patterned distribution. "Distribute according to I.Q." is a patterned principle that looks to information not contained in distributional matrices. It is not historical, however, in that it does not look to any past actions creating differential entitlements to evaluate a distribution; it requires only distributional matrices whose columns are labeled by I.Q. scores. The distribution in a society, however, may be composed of such simple patterned distributions, without itself being simply patterned. Different sectors may operate different patterns, or some combination of patterns may operate in different proportions across a society. A distribution composed in this manner, from a small number of patterned distributions, we also shall term "patterned." And we extend the use of "pattern" to include the overall designs put forth by combinations of end-state principles.

Almost every suggested principle of distributive justice is patterned: to each according to his moral merit, or needs, or marginal product,[†] or how hard he tries, or the weighted sum of the foregoing, and so on. The principle of entitlement we have sketched is not patterned.[4] There is no one natural dimension or weighted sum or combination of a small number of natural dimensions that yields the distributions generated in accordance with the principle of entitlement. The set of holdings that results when some persons receive their marginal products, others win at gambling, others receive a share of their mate's income, others receive gifts from foundations, others receive interest on loans, others receive gifts from admirers, others receive returns on investment, others make for themselves much of what they have, others find things, and so on, will not be patterned. Heavy strands of patterns will run through it; significant portions of the variance in holdings will be accounted for by pattern-variables. If most people most of the time choose to transfer some of their entitlements to others only in exchange for something from them, then a large part of what many people hold will vary with what they held that others wanted. More details are provided by the theory of marginal productivity. But gifts to relatives, charitable donations, bequests to children, and the like, are not best conceived, in the first instance, in this manner. Ignoring the strands of pattern, let us suppose for the moment that a distribution actually arrived at by the operation of the principle of entitlement is random with respect to any pattern. Though the resulting set of holdings will be unpatterned, it will not be incomprehensible, for it can be seen as arising from the operation of a small number of principles. These principles specify how an initial distribution may arise (the principle of acquisition of holdings) and how distributions may be transformed into others (the principle of transfer of holdings). The process whereby the set of holdings is generated will be intelligible, though the set of holdings itself that results from this process will be unpatterned....

How Liberty Upsets Patterns

It is not clear how those holding alternative conceptions of distributive justice can reject the entitlement conception of justice in holdings. For suppose a distribution favored by one of these non-entitlement conceptions is realized. Let us suppose it is your favorite one and let us call this distribution D_1; perhaps everyone has an equal share, perhaps shares vary in

---

* Strictly speaking, this means sorting a group of items in the order they would appear if they were listed in a dictionary (i.e., roughly, alphabetically), but listing first all the words made up of only one letter, then all the words made up of two letters, then all those with three letters, and so on. (The main idea here is to impose a useful order on an infinite sequence of formulae.) In the philosophical literature on justice, however, the phrase is generally used to mean a strict *prioritizing* of principles: first principle A must be satisfied, and only then should we worry about principle B; only when both A and B are satisfied can we apply principle C; and so on.

† The contribution that each additional worker makes to total output. Thus, to be rewarded according to one's marginal product is to be paid in proportion to the amount that your contribution has increased output over what it would have been if you hadn't been employed.

accordance with some dimension you treasure. Now suppose that Wilt Chamberlain* is greatly in demand by basketball teams, being a great gate attraction. (Also suppose contracts run only for a year, with players being free agents.) He signs the following sort of contract with a team: In each home game, twenty-five cents from the price of each ticket of admission goes to him. (We ignore the question of whether he is "gouging" the owners, letting them look out for themselves.) The season starts, and people cheerfully attend his team's games; they buy their tickets, each time dropping a separate twenty-five cents of their admission price into a special box with Chamberlain's name on it. They are excited about seeing him play; it is worth the total admission price to them. Let us suppose that in one season one million persons attend his home games, and Wilt Chamberlain winds up with $250,000, a much larger sum than the average income and larger even than anyone else has.† Is he entitled to this income? Is this new distribution D_2, unjust? If so, why? There is *no* question about whether each of the people was entitled to the control over the resources they held in D_1; because that was the distribution (your favorite) that (for the purposes of argument) we assumed was acceptable. Each of these persons *chose* to give twenty-five cents of their money to Chamberlain. They could have spent it on going to the movies, or on candy bars, or on copies of *Dissent* magazine, or of *Monthly Review*.‡ But they all, at least one million of them, converged on giving it to Wilt Chamberlain in exchange for watching him play basketball. If D_1 was a just distribution, and people voluntarily moved from it to D_2, transferring parts of their shares they were given under D_1 (what was it for if not to do something with?), isn't D_2 also just? If the people were entitled to dispose of the resources to which they were entitled (under D_1), didn't this include their being entitled to give it to, or exchange it with, Wilt Chamberlain? Can anyone else complain on grounds of justice? Each other person already has his legitimate share under D_1. Under D_1, there is nothing that anyone has that

anyone else has a claim of justice against. After someone transfers something to Wilt Chamberlain, third parties *still* have their legitimate shares; *their* shares are not changed. By what process could such a transfer among two persons give rise to a legitimate claim of distributive justice on a portion of what was transferred, by a third party who had no claim of justice on any holding of the others *before* the transfer?[7] To cut off objections irrelevant here, we might imagine the exchanges occurring in a socialist society, after hours. After playing whatever basketball he does in his daily work, or doing whatever other daily work he does, Wilt Chamberlain decides to put in *overtime* to earn additional money. (First his work quota is set; he works time over that.) Or imagine it is a skilled juggler people like to see, who puts on shows after hours.

Why might someone work overtime in a society in which it is assumed their needs are satisfied? Perhaps because they care about things other than needs. I like to write in books that I read, and to have easy access to books for browsing at odd hours. It would be very pleasant and convenient to have the resources of Widener Library§ in my back yard. No society, I assume, will provide such resources close to each person who would like them as part of his regular allotment (under D_1). Thus, persons either must do without some extra things that they want, or be allowed to do something extra to get some of these things. On what basis could the inequalities that would eventuate be forbidden? Notice also that small factories would spring up in a socialist society, unless forbidden. I melt down some of my personal possessions (under D_1) and build a machine out of the material. I offer you, and others, a philosophy lecture once a week in exchange for your cranking the handle on my machine, whose products I exchange for yet other things, and so on. (The raw materials used by the machine are given to me by others who possess them under D_1, in exchange for hearing lectures.) Each person might participate to gain things over and above their allotment under D_1. Some persons even might want to leave their job

---

* Wilt Chamberlain was a well-known American basketball player during the 1960s. He was seven-time consecutive winner of the National Basketball Association scoring title from 1960 to 1966, and in 1962 he scored a record 100 points in a single game.
† In 1974, the US average (mean) household income was around $13,000.
‡ *Dissent* and *Monthly Review* are left-wing/socialist periodicals.
§ Harvard University's library.

in socialist industry and work full time in this private sector. I shall say something more about these issues in the next chapter. Here I wish merely to note how private property even in means of production would occur in a socialist society that did not forbid people to use as they wished some of the resources they are given under the socialist distribution D_1.[8] The socialist society would have to forbid capitalist acts between consenting adults.

The general point illustrated by the Wilt Chamberlain example and the example of the entrepreneur in a socialist society is that no end-state principle or distributional patterned principle of justice can be continuously realized without continuous interference with people's lives. Any favored pattern would be transformed into one unfavored by the principle, by people choosing to act in various ways; for example, by people exchanging goods and services with other people, or giving things to other people, things the transferrers are entitled to under the favored distributional pattern. To maintain a pattern one must either continually interfere to stop people from transferring resources as they wish to, or continually (or periodically) interfere to take from some persons resources that others for some reason chose to transfer to them. (But if some time limit is to be set on how long people may keep resources others voluntarily transfer to them, why let them keep these resources for *any* period of time? Why not have immediate confiscation?) It might be objected that all persons voluntarily will choose to refrain from actions which would upset the pattern. This presupposes unrealistically (1) that all will most want to maintain the pattern (are those who don't, to be "reeducated" or forced to undergo "self-criticism"?), (2) that each can gather enough information about his own actions and the ongoing activities of others to discover which of his actions will upset the pattern, and (3) that diverse and far-flung persons can coordinate their actions to dovetail into the pattern. Compare the manner in which the market is neutral among persons' desires, as it reflects and transmits widely scattered information via prices, and coordinates persons' activities.... ■

Suggestions for Critical Reflection

1. What does Nozick mean when he claims that "[t]he term 'distributive justice' is not a neutral one"? Is the terminology he introduces instead any more "neutral"? What is the significance of this issue (if any) for the arguments that follow?

2. "Whatever arises from a just situation by just steps is itself just." Is this apparently straightforward claim *really* true? Can you think of any reasons to doubt it—for example, can you come up with any plausible counter-examples to this general claim? How significant a part of Nozick's general argument is this assertion? If we accept it, might we then be forced to accept a version of libertarianism, or is there a way of making it consistent with a more extensive state?

3. How plausible do you find Nozick's sketch of a principle of rectification of injustice? Is the goal of such rectifications to return injured parties (such as formerly enslaved people or their present-day children) to the position they would have been in

had the injustice not occurred, or do we normally think there is more (or less) to it than that?

4. Is the distinction between historical and end-state principles of justice as clear-cut as Nozick presents it? Are most—or even many—theories of justice pure forms of one or the other? How comfortably, if at all, can historical and end-state views of justice be combined in a single theory (for example, an egalitarian theory)?

5. What do you think of Nozick's Wilt Chamberlain argument? If it is sound, what are its implications? If you think it is not sound, what, exactly, is wrong with it (bearing in mind that it's not enough to simply disagree with its conclusion)?

6. Nozick argues that distributional patterns cannot be "continuously realized without continuous interference with people's lives." Does this, in itself, show that no adequate principles of justice can be patterned? What ethical assumptions might Nozick be making here? Are these assumptions justified?

Notes

1   Applications of the principle of justice in acquisition may also occur as part of the move from one distribution to another. You may find an unheld thing now and appropriate it. Acquisitions also are to be understood as included when, to simplify, I speak only of transitions by transfers.

2   See, however, the useful book by Boris Bittker, *The Case for Black Reparations* (New York: Random House, 1973).

3   If the principle of rectification of violations of the first two principles yields more than one description of holdings, then some choice must be made as to which of these is to be realized. Perhaps the sort of considerations about distributive justice and equality that I argue against play a legitimate role in *this* subsidiary choice. Similarly, there may be room for such considerations in deciding which otherwise arbitrary features a statute will embody, when such features are unavoidable because other considerations do not specify a precise line; yet a line must be drawn.

4   One might try to squeeze a patterned conception of distributive justice into the framework of the entitlement conception, by formulating a gimmicky obligatory "principle of transfer" that would lead to the pattern. For example, the principle that if one has more than the mean income one must transfer everything one holds above the mean to persons below the mean so as to bring them up to (but not over) the mean. We can formulate a criterion for a "principle of transfer" to rule out such obligatory transfers, or we can say that no correct principle of transfer, no principle of transfer in a free society will be like this. The former is probably the better course, though the latter also is true.

Alternatively, one might think to make the entitlement conception instantiate a pattern, by using matrix entries that express the relative strength of a person's entitlements as measured by some real-valued function. But even if the limitation to natural dimensions failed to exclude this function, the resulting edifice would *not* capture our system of entitlements to *particular* things.

[...]

7   Might not a transfer have instrumental effects on a third party, changing his feasible options? (But what if the two parties to the transfer independently had used their holdings in this fashion?) I discuss this question below, but note here that this question concedes the point for distributions of ultimate intrinsic noninstrumental goods (pure utility experiences, so to speak) that are transferrable. It also might be objected that the transfer might make a third party more envious because it worsens his position relative to someone else. I find it incomprehensible how this can be thought to involve a claim of justice. On envy, see Chapter 8 [of *Anarchy, State and Utopia*].

Here and elsewhere in this chapter, a theory which incorporates elements of pure procedural justice might find what I say acceptable, *if* kept in its proper place; that is, if background institutions exist to ensure the satisfaction of certain conditions on distributive shares. But if these institutions are not themselves the sum or invisible-hand result of people's voluntary (nonaggressive) actions, the constraints they impose require justification. At no point does *our* argument assume any background institutions more extensive than those of the minimal night-watchman state, a state limited to protecting persons against murder, assault, theft, fraud, and so forth.

8   See the selection from John Henry MacKay's novel, *The Anarchists*, reprinted in Leonard Krimmerman and Lewis Perry, eds., *Patterns of Anarchy* (New York: Doubleday Anchor Books, 1966), in which an individualist anarchist presses upon a communist anarchist the following question: "Would you, in the system of society which you call 'free Communism' prevent individuals from exchanging their labour among themselves by means of their own medium of exchange? And further: Would you prevent them from occupying land for the purpose of personal use?" The novel continues: "[the] question was not to be escaped. If he answered 'Yes!' he admitted that society had the right of control over the individual and threw overboard the autonomy of the individual which he had always zealously defended; if on the other hand, he answered 'No!' he admitted the right of private property which he had just denied so emphatically.... Then he answered 'In Anarchy any number of men must have the right of forming a voluntary association, and so realizing their ideas in practice. Nor can I understand how any one could justly be driven from the land and house which he uses and occupies ... every serious man must declare himself: for Socialism, and thereby for force and against liberty, or for Anarchism, and thereby for liberty and against force.'" In contrast, we find Noam Chomsky writing, "Any consistent anarchist must oppose private ownership of the means of production," "the consistent anarchist then ... will be a socialist ... of a particular sort." Introduction to Daniel Guerin, *Anarchism: From Theory to Practice* (New York: Monthly Review Press, 1970), pages xiii, xv.

SUSAN MOLLER OKIN

Justice and Gender

Who Was Susan Moller Okin?

Susan Moller Okin, who was once described as "perhaps the best feminist political philosopher in the world,"* was born in 1946 in Auckland, New Zealand, and died suddenly in 2004 at the age of only 57. At the time of her death she was a professor of political science at Stanford University, and she had previously taught at Auckland, Vassar, Brandeis, and Harvard. Her doctorate, which she received in 1975, was from Harvard.

Okin's main importance as a political philosopher lay in her insistence that gender—the status and position of women—is an issue that lies at the heart of political theory, and is not merely a fringe topic that can be addressed after the main principles of justice have been laid down. As the article reprinted here makes clear, at the time that Okin began writing—in the 1970s—this was a radical view: one which, it seems fair to say, had not even occurred to the (male) writers who were mainly responsible for carrying on the liberal political tradition. Okin formulated careful and forceful arguments that, in particular, the role and structure of the family—the so-called domestic sphere, that shaped, and still shapes, the opportunities available to women in society—were crucial to any adequate account of social justice. These arguments brought about a sea change in political philosophy, carrying issues surrounding gender roles and the family to the center of the discipline.

Near the end of her career, Okin's interests shifted towards the situation of women in less developed countries, and she worked on the complex tangle of issues raised by the interaction between gender issues, poverty, and multiculturalism. Once again, she was among the first to identify an issue that at the time was barely on the radar and has since become a main theme in political thought: the potential for conflict between the aim of gender equality, and sensitivity to the customs of other cultures and religions. Okin's own view was a provoca-

tive defense of the liberal egalitarian position that all citizens in a state should have equal rights and privileges and that this trumps certain oppressive cultural practices, such as forced marriage, polygamy, or female genital mutilation. She became a highly visible supporter of the Global Fund for Women, an international foundation devoted to the support of women's human rights.

Probably Okin's best-known work is the book *Justice, Gender and the Family*, published in 1989, and her article "Reason and Feeling in Thinking about Justice." She also wrote two other very influential books—*Women in Western Political Thought* (1979), and *Is Multiculturalism Bad for Women?* (1999)—and many more widely read articles, including the one excerpted here.

What Is the Structure of This Reading?

After introducing the topic "how just is gender?," Okin begins by outlining the role of gender in justifying inequality in the western tradition of political thought, including that of Aristotle, Rousseau, Kant, Hegel, and Bentham. She then asks whether modern political theory fares any better on this front—whether modern theorists are more sensitive to the problem of gender-based inequalities in society—and examines two representative leading writers: John Rawls, the most prominent liberal ideologist, and Michael Walzer, a leading communitarian. In this selection, the discussion of Walzer has been omitted, leaving the focus on Rawls. Okin concludes that insufficient attention is still being devoted to gender. She argues that, although Walzer appears on the surface to be more sympathetic to feminist concerns, in fact it is the Rawlsian tradition that is best able to accommodate feminism. However, she concludes by suggesting that full consideration of the problem of gender in a theory of social justice will require not only modifying contemporary liberal theory but also, potentially, a radical alteration of gender itself.

---

* Debra Satz, a Stanford philosopher, quoted in Okin's obituary in the *Stanford Report*, March 9, 2004.

A Common Misconception

Although Okin, in this article and elsewhere in her work, attacks liberalism for its historical bias against women, she nevertheless does not reject liberal political theory. On the contrary, her view is that liberalism is an emancipatory doctrine that simply has not been taken far enough. The basic idea of freedom and equality for all citizens is the right one—but in order to apply fully to women (and, indeed, to men), these liberal principles must be applied to the family as well as to the public spheres of government and economics.

Justice and Gender [1][*]

Theories of justice are centrally concerned with whether, how, and why persons should be treated differently from each other. Which initial or acquired characteristics or positions in society, they ask, legitimize differential treatment of persons by social institutions, laws, and customs? In particular, how should beginnings affect outcomes? The division of humanity into two sexes would seem to provide an obvious subject for such inquiries. We live in a society in whose past the innate characteristic of sex has been regarded as one of the clearest legitimizers of different rights and restrictions, both formal and informal. While the legal sanctions that uphold male dominance have been to some extent eroded within the past century, and more rapidly in the last twenty years, the heavy weight of tradition, combined with the effects of socialization broadly defined, still work powerfully to reinforce roles for the two sexes that are commonly regarded as of unequal prestige and worth.[2] The sexual division of labor within the family, in particular, is not only a fundamental part of the marriage contract, but so deeply influences us in our most formative years that feminists of both sexes who try to reject it find themselves struggling against it with varying degrees of ambivalence. Based on this linchpin, the deeply entrenched social institutionalization of sex difference, which I will refer to as "the gender system" or simply "gender," still permeates our society.

This gender system has rarely been subjected to the tests of justice. When we turn to the great tradition of Western political thought with questions about the justice of gender in mind, it is to little avail. Bold feminists like Mary Astell, Mary Wollstonecraft, Harriet Taylor, and George Bernard Shaw have occasionally challenged the tradition,[†] often using its own premises and arguments to overturn its justification of the unequal treatment of women. But John Stuart Mill is a rare exception to the rule that those who hold central positions in the tradition almost never questioned the justice of the subordination and oppression of women. This phenomenon is undoubtedly due in part to the fact that Aristotle, whose theory of justice has been so influential, relegated women and slaves to a realm of "household justice," whose participants are not fundamentally equal to the free men who participate in political justice, but inferiors whose natural function is to serve those who are more fully human. The liberal tradition, despite its supposed foundation of individual rights and human equality, is more Aristotelian in this respect than is generally acknowledged.[3] In one way or another, liberals have assumed that the "individual" who is the basic subject of their theories is the male head of a patriarchal household.[4] Thus the application of principles of justice to relations between the sexes, or within the household, has frequently been ruled out from the start.

---

[*]   From *Philosophy and Public Affairs*, 16, 1 (Winter 1987): 42–72.

[†]   Mary Astell (1666–1731) wrote *A Serious Proposal to the Ladies, for the Advancement of Their True and Greatest Interest* (1694) and fought for more equal educational opportunities for women; Mary Wollstonecraft (1759–97) was the author of *A Vindication of the Rights of Woman* (1792); Harriet Taylor (1807–58) worked with John Stuart Mill (her second husband) as a key contributor to *On Liberty* (1859); George Bernard Shaw (1856–1950), the playwright, was a prominent socialist and author of *The Intelligent Woman's Guide to Socialism and Capitalism* (1928).

Other assumptions, too, contribute to the widespread belief that neither women nor the family are appropriate subjects for discussions of justice. One is that women, whether because of their essential disorderliness, their enslavement to nature, their private and particularist inclinations, or their oedipal development,* are incapable of developing a sense of justice. This notion can be found—sometimes briefly suggested, sometimes developed at greater length—in the works of theorists from Plato to Freud, including Bodin, John Knox,† Rousseau, Kant, Hegel and Bentham.[5] The frequent implication is that those who do not possess the qualifications for fully ethical reasoning or action need not have principles of justice applied to them. Finally, in Rousseau (as so often, original) we find the unique claim that woman, being "made to submit to man and even to put up with his injustice," is imbued innately with a capacity to tolerate the unjust treatment with which she is likely to meet.[6]

For those who are not satisfied with these reasons for excluding women and gender from the subject matter of justice, the great tradition has little to offer, directly at least, to our inquiry. When we turn to contemporary theories of justice, however, we can expect to find more illuminating and positive contributions to the subject of gender and justice. I turn to ... John Rawls's *A Theory of Justice* ... in response to the question "How just is gender?"[7]

Justice as Fairness

An ambiguity runs throughout John Rawls's *A Theory of Justice*, continually noticeable to anyone reading it from a feminist perspective. On the one hand, as I shall argue below, a consistent and wholehearted application of Rawls's liberal principles can lead us to challenge fundamentally the gender system of our society. On the other hand, in his own account of his theory, this challenge is barely hinted at, much less developed. The major reason is that throughout most of the argument, it is assumed (as throughout almost the entire liberal tradition) that the appropriate subjects of political theories are heads of families. As a result, although Rawls indicates on several occasions that a person's sex is a morally arbitrary and contingent characteristic, and although he states explicitly that the family itself is one of those basic social institutions to which the principles of justice must apply, his theory of justice fails to develop either of these convictions.

Rawls, like almost all political theorists until very recent years, employs supposedly generic male terms of reference. "Men," "mankind," "he" and "his" are interspersed with nonsexist terms of reference such as "individual" and "moral person." Examples of intergenerational concern are worded in terms of "fathers" and "sons," and the difference principle‡ is said to correspond to "the principle of fraternity."[8] This linguistic usage would perhaps be less significant if it were not for the fact that Rawls is self-consciously a member of a long tradition of moral and political philosophy that has used in its arguments either such supposedly generic masculine terms, or even more inclusive terms of reference ("human beings," "persons," "all rational beings as such"), only to exclude women from the scope of the conclusions reached. Kant is a clear example.[9] But when Rawls refers to the generality and universality of Kant's ethics, and when he compares the principles chosen in his own original position to those regulative of Kant's kingdom of ends,§ "acting from [which] expresses our nature as free and equal rational persons,"[10] he does not mention the fact that women were not included in that category of "free and equal rational persons," to which Kant meant his moral theory to apply. Again, in a brief discussion of

---

* That is, according to Freudian psychoanalytic theory, the psychosexual development of children, passing through a period during which they develop the unconscious desire to possess the parent of the opposite sex and eliminate the parent of the same sex. This has become known as the Oedipus complex.

† Jean Bodin (1530–96) was a French legal theorist who argued for the absolute authority of the sovereign; John Knox (c. 1510–72) was the leading Protestant reformer in Scotland, and author of *The First Blast of the Trumpet against the Monstrous Regiment of Women* (1558).

‡ The principle, developed by Rawls, that inequalities in the distribution of goods are justified only if those inequalities benefit the worst-off members of society. See the selection by Rawls earlier in this section.

§ See the selection by Kant in the Ethics section of this volume.

Freud's account of moral development, Rawls presents Freud's theory of the formation of the male super-ego in largely gender-neutral terms, without mentioning that Freud considered women's moral development to be sadly deficient, on account of their incomplete resolution of the Oedipus complex.[11] Thus there is a certain blindness to the sexism of the tradition in which Rawls is a participant, which tends to render his terms of reference even more ambiguous than they might otherwise be. A feminist reader finds it difficult not to keep asking: "Does this theory of justice apply to women, or not?"

This question is not answered in the important passages that list the characteristics that persons in the original position* are not to know about themselves, in order to formulate impartial principles of justice. In a subsequent article, Rawls has made it clear that sex is one of those morally irrelevant contingencies that is to be hidden by the veil of ignorance.[12] But throughout *A Theory of Justice*, while the list of things unknown by a person in the original position includes

> his place in society, his class position or social status, ... his fortune in the distribution of natural assets and abilities, his intelligence and strength, and the like, ... his conception of the good, the particulars of his rational plan of life, [and] even the special features of his psychology ...[13]

"his" sex is not mentioned. Since the parties also "know the general facts about human society,"[14] presumably including the fact that it is structured along the lines of gender both by custom and by law, one might think that whether or not they knew their sex might matter enough to be mentioned. Perhaps Rawls means to cover it by his phrase "and the like," but it is also possible that he did not consider it significant.

The ambiguity is exacerbated by Rawls's statement that those free and equal moral persons in the original position who formulate the principles of justice are to be thought of not as "single individuals" but as "heads of families" or "representatives of families."[15] He says that it is not necessary to think of the parties as heads of families, but that he will generally do so. The reason he does this, he explains, is to ensure that each person in the original position cares about the well-being of some persons in the next generation. These "ties of sentiment" between generations, which Rawls regards as important in the establishment of his just savings principle,† would otherwise constitute a problem, because of the general assumption that the parties in the original position are mutually disinterested. In spite of the ties of sentiment *within* families, then, "as representatives of families their interests are opposed as the circumstances of justice imply."[16]

The head of a family need not necessarily, of course, be a man. The very fact, however, that in common usage the term "female-headed households" is used *only* in reference to households without resident adult males, tends to suggest that it is assumed that any present male adult takes precedence over a female as the household or family head. Rawls does nothing to dispel this impression when he says of those in the original position that "imagining themselves to be fathers, say, they are to ascertain how much they should set aside for their sons by noting what they would believe themselves entitled to claim of their fathers."[17] He makes the "heads of families" assumption only in order to address the problem of savings between generations, and presumably does not intend it to be a sexist assumption. Nevertheless, Rawls is effectively trapped by this assumption into the traditional mode of thinking that life within the family and relations between the sexes are not properly to be regarded as part of the subject matter of a theory of social justice.

Before I go on to argue this, I must first point out that Rawls states at the outset of his theory that the family *is* part of the subject matter of social justice. "For us" he says,

---

* A hypothetical situation in which people are deprived of all knowledge of their personal and historical circumstances that are irrelevant to justice—they are behind "the veil of ignorance"—in order to ensure that any judgments they make about the proper structure of society will be appropriately impartial.

† Rawls—who is often credited with providing the first thorough discussion of what the current generation owes to future people—argues that the main duty owed to our successors is the saving of sufficient material capital to maintain just institutions over time.

the primary subject of justice is the basic structure of society, or more exactly, the way in which the major social institutions distribute fundamental rights and duties and determine the division of advantages from social cooperation.[18]

He goes on to specify "the monogamous family" as an example of such major social institutions, together with the political constitution, the legal protection of essential freedoms, competitive markets, and private property. The reason that Rawls makes such institutions the primary subject of his theory of social justice is that they have such profound effects on people's lives from the start, depending on where they find themselves placed in relation to them. He explicitly distinguishes between these major institutions and other "private associations," "less comprehensive social groups," and "various informal conventions and customs of everyday life,"[19] for which the principles of justice satisfactory for the basic structure might be less appropriate or relevant. There is no doubt, then, that in his initial definition of the sphere of social justice, the family is included.[20] The two principles of justice that Rawls defends in Part I, the principle of equal basic liberty, and the difference principle combined with the requirement of fair equality of opportunity, are intended to apply to the basic structure of society. They are "to govern the assignment of rights and duties and to regulate the distribution of social and economic advantages."[21] Whenever in these basic institutions there are differences in authority, in responsibility, in the distribution of resources such as wealth or leisure, these differences must be both to the greatest benefit of the least advantaged, and attached to positions accessible to all under conditions of fair equality of opportunity.

In Part II, Rawls discusses at some length the application of his principles of justice to almost all of the major social institutions listed at the beginning of the book. The legal protection of freedom of thought and liberty of conscience is defended, as are just democratic constitutional institutions and procedures; competitive markets feature prominently in the discussion of the just distribution of income; the issue of the private or public ownership of the means of production is explicitly left open, since Rawls argues that justice as fairness might be compatible with certain versions of either. But throughout these discussions,

the question of whether the monogamous family, in either its traditional or any other form, is a just social institution, is never raised. When Rawls announces that "the sketch of the system of institutions that satisfy the two principles of justice is now complete,"[22] he has still paid no attention at all to the internal justice of the family. The family, in fact, apart from passing references, appears in *A Theory of Justice* in only three contexts: as the link between generations necessary for the savings principle, as a possible obstacle to fair equality of opportunity—on account of inequalities amongst families—and as the first school of moral development. It is in the third of these contexts that Rawls first specifically mentions the family as a just institution. He mentions it, however, not to *consider* whether or not the family "in some form" is a just institution, but to *assume* it. Clearly regarding it as important, Rawls states as part of his first psychological law of moral development: "given that family institutions are just...."[23]

Clearly, however, by Rawls's own reasoning about the social justice of major institutions, this assumption is unwarranted. For the central tenet of the theory is that justice characterizes institutions whose members could hypothetically have agreed to their structure and rules from a position in which they did not know which place in the structure they were to occupy. The argument of the book is designed to show that the two principles of justice as fairness are those that individuals in such a hypothetical situation would indeed agree upon. But since those in the original position are the heads or representatives of families, they are *not in a position to determine questions of justice within families*.[24] As far as children are concerned, Rawls makes a convincing argument from paternalism for their temporary inequality. But wives (or whichever adult member[s] of a family are *not* its "head") go completely unrepresented in the original position. If families are just, as Rawls assumes, then they must *get* to be just in some different way (unspecified by Rawls) than other institutions, for it is impossible to see how the viewpoint of their less advantaged members ever gets to be heard....

[N]ot only does Rawls, as noted above, "assume that the basic structure of a well-ordered society includes the family *in some form.*" He adds to this the comment that "in a broader inquiry the institution of the family might be questioned, and other arrangements might indeed prove to be preferable."[32] But why should it require a broader inquiry than that engaged in *A Theory of Justice*, to ask questions about the institution of the family? Surely Rawls is right at the outset when he names it as one of those basic social institutions that most affects the life chances of individuals. The family is not a private association like a church or a university, which vary considerably in type, and which one can join and leave voluntarily. For although one has some choice (albeit highly constrained) about marrying into a gender-structured family, one has no choice at all about being born into one. Given this, Rawls's failure to subject the structure of the family to his principles of justice is particularly serious in the light of his belief that a theory of justice must take account of "how [individuals] get to be what they are" and "cannot take their final aims and interests, their attitudes to themselves and their life, as given."[33] For the family with its gender structure, female parenting in particular, is clearly a crucial determinant in the different socialization of the two sexes—in how men and women "get to be what they are."

If Rawls were to assume throughout the construction of his theory that all human adults are to be participants in what goes on behind the veil of ignorance, he would have no option but to require that the family, as a major social institution affecting the life chances of individuals, be constructed in accordance with the two principles of justice....

Women and Justice in Theory and Practice

... As I have shown above, while Rawls briefly rules out formal, legal discrimination on the grounds of sex (as on other grounds that he regards as "morally irrelevant"), he fails entirely to address the justice of the gender system, which—with its roots in the sex roles of the family and with its branches extending into virtually every corner of our lives—is one of the fundamental structures of our society. If, however, we read Rawls taking seriously both the notion that those behind the veil of ignorance are sexless persons, and the requirement that the family and the gender system—as basic social institutions—are to be subject to scrutiny, constructive feminist criticism of these contemporary institutions follows. So, also, do hidden difficulties for a Rawlsian theory of justice in a gendered society.

I will explain each of these points in turn. But first, both the critical perspective and the incipient problems of a feminist reading of Rawls can perhaps be illuminated by a description of a cartoon I saw a few years ago. Three elderly, robed male justices are depicted, looking down with astonishment at their very pregnant bellies. One says to the others, without further elaboration: "Perhaps we'd better reconsider that decision." This illustration points to several things. First, it graphically demonstrates the importance, in thinking about justice, of a concept like Rawls's original position, which makes us put ourselves into the positions of others—especially positions that we ourselves can never be in. Second, it suggests that those thinking in such a way might well conclude that more than formal legal equality of the sexes is required if justice is to be done. As we have seen in recent years, it is quite possible to institutionalize the formal legal equality of the sexes and at the same time to enact laws concerning pregnancy, abortion, maternity leave, and so on, that in effect discriminate against women, not as women *per se*, but as "pregnant persons." The U.S. Supreme Court decided in 1976, for example, that "an exclusion of pregnancy from a disability benefits plan ... providing general coverage is not a gender-based discrimination at all."[34] One of the virtues of the cartoon is its suggestion that one's thinking on such matters is likely to be affected by the knowledge that one might become a "pregnant person." Finally, however, the illustration suggests the limits of what is possible, in terms of thinking ourselves into the original position, as long as we live in a gender-structured society. While the elderly male justices can, in a sense, imagine *themselves* pregnant, what is much more doubtful is whether, in constructing principles of justice, they can imagine themselves *women*. This raises the question whether, in fact, sex *is* a morally irrelevant and contingent human characteristic, in a society structured by gender.

Let us first assume that sex is contingent in this way, though I will later question this assumption. Let us suppose that it is possible, as Rawls clearly considers that it is, to hypothesize the moral thinking of representative human beings, ignorant of their sex and of all the other things that are hidden by the veil of ignorance. It seems clear that, while Rawls does not do this, we must consistently take the relevant positions of both sexes into account in formulating principles of justice. In particular, those in the original position must take special account of the perspective of women, since their knowledge of "the general facts about human society"[35] must include the knowledge that women have been and continue to be the less advantaged sex in a number of respects. In considering the basic institutions of society, they are more likely to pay special attention to the family than virtually to ignore it, since its unequal assigning of responsibilities and privileges to the two sexes and its socialization of children into sex roles make it, in its current form, a crucial institution for the preservation of sex inequality.

It is impossible to discuss here all the ways in which the principles of justice that Rawls arrives at are inconsistent with a gender-structured society. A general explanation of this point and three examples to illustrate it will have to suffice. The critical impact of a feminist reading of Rawls comes chiefly from his second principle, which requires that inequalities be "to the greatest benefit of the least advantaged" and "attached to offices and positions open to all."[36] This means that if any roles or positions analogous to our current sex roles, including those of husband and wife, mother and father, were to survive the demands of the first requirement, the second requirement would disallow any linkage between these roles and sex. Gender, as I have defined it in this article, with its ascriptive designation of positions and expectations of behavior in accordance with the inborn characteristic of sex, could no longer form a legitimate part of the social structure, whether inside or outside the family. Three illustrations will help to link this conclusion with specific major requirements that Rawls makes of a just or well-ordered society.

First, after the basic political liberties, one of the most essential liberties is "the important liberty of free choice of occupation."[37] It is not difficult to see that this liberty is compromised by the assumption and customary expectation, central to our gender system, that women take far greater responsibility than men for housework and child care, whether or not they also work for wages outside the home. In fact, both the assigning of these responsibilities to women—resulting in their asymmetrical economic dependency on men—and also the related responsibility of husbands to support their wives, compromise the liberty of choice of occupation of both sexes. While Rawls has

no objection to some aspects of the division of labor, he asserts that, in a well-ordered society, "no one need be servilely dependent on others and made to choose between monotonous and routine occupations which are deadening to human thought and sensibility" but that work can be "meaningful for all."[38] These conditions are far more likely to be met in a society which does not assign family responsibilities in a way that makes women into a marginal sector of the paid work force and renders likely their economic dependence upon men.

Second, the abolition of gender seems essential for the fulfillment of Rawls's criteria for political justice. For he argues that not only would equal formal political liberties be espoused by those in the original position, but that any inequalities in the *worth* of these liberties (for example, the effects on them of factors like poverty and ignorance) must be justified by the difference principle. Indeed, "the constitutional process should preserve the equal representation of the original position to the degree that this is practicable."[39] While Rawls discusses this requirement in the context of *class* differences, stating that those who devote themselves to politics should be "drawn more or less equally from all sectors of society,"[40] it is just as clearly applicable to sex differences. And the equal political representation of women and men, especially if they are parents, is clearly inconsistent with our gender system.

Finally, Rawls argues that the rational moral persons in the original position would place a great deal of emphasis on the securing of self-respect or self-esteem. They "would wish to avoid at almost any cost the social conditions that undermine self-respect," which is "perhaps the most important" of all the primary goods.[41] In the interests of this primary value, if those in the original position did not know whether they were to be men or women, they would surely be concerned to establish a thoroughgoing social and economic equality between the sexes that would preserve either from the need to pander to or servilely provide for the pleasures of the other. They would be highly motivated, for example, to find a means of regulating pornography that did not seriously compromise freedom of speech. In general, they would be unlikely to tolerate basic social institutions that asymmetrically either forced or gave strong incentives to members of one sex to become sex objects for the other.

There is, then, implicit in Rawls's theory of justice a potential critique of gender-structured social institutions, which can be made explicit by taking seriously the fact that those formulating the principles of justice do not know their sex....

In the earlier stages of working on this article, I thought mainly in terms of what justice has to say about gender, rather than about the effects of gender on justice.... But, given the reliance of [Rawls's] ... theory on the agreement of representative human beings about the basic moral principles that are to govern their lives, I conclude that, while we can use it along the way to critique existing inequalities, we cannot complete such a theory of justice until the life experiences of the two sexes become as similar as their biological differences permit. Such a theory, and the society that puts it into practice, will be fundamentally influenced by the participation of both women and men in all spheres of human life. Not only is gender incompatible with a just society but the disappearance of gender is likely to lead in turn to important changes in the theory and practices of justice. ■

Suggestions for Critical Reflection

1. Okin writes that, "[i]n one way or another, liberals have assumed that the 'individual' who is the basic subject of their theories is the male head of a patriarchal household." Consider the works from this tradition that you might have read: is Okin right in her judgment? What implications should we draw from this?

2. Is there a difference between the way we should understand justice and equity within families as opposed to in society at large? Does Okin think there should be? Do you?

3. "For the family with its gender structure, female parenting in particular, is clearly a crucial determinant in the different socialization of the two sexes—in how men and women 'get to be what they are.'" Is Okin right about this? What implications does it have?

4. Okin quotes Rawls as assuming "that family institutions are just," and then proceeds to argue that, by Rawls's own lights, the institution of the family cannot be considered just. Does Okin mean by this that it must be considered *unjust*? How effective are Okin's arguments on this point? Do they apply only to Rawls, or do they have wider application?

5. Okin points out Rawls's use of male pronouns and other non-inclusive language. What role does this play in her argument? If Rawls had made the same claims using gender-inclusive language, would this have bearing on the strength of Okin's criticisms?

6. Okin concludes that "gender [is] incompatible with a just society." What does she mean by this? How radical a claim is this? Do you think it is warranted?

7. Okin's points largely concern issues that Rawls neglected to discuss. Do you think that what's left out could be added consistently to what Rawls said, or is Okin's position incompatible with Rawls's?

8. This article was published in 1987. In your view, have there been any significant changes to the attitudes that Okin describes concerning the relevance of gender to justice, or the place of principles of justice within the family?

Notes

1 An earlier version of this article was presented at the 80th Annual Meeting of the American Political Science Association, August 30–September 2, 1984 in Washington, D.C. I gratefully acknowledge the helpful comments of the following people: Robert Amdur, Peter Euben, Robert Goodin, Anne Harper, Robert Keohane, Carole Pateman, John Rawls, Nancy Rosenblum, Robert Simon, Quentin Skinner, Michael Walzer, Iris Young and the Editors of *Philosophy & Public Affairs*. Thanks also to Lisa Carisella and Elaine Herrmann for typing the manuscript.

2 On the history of the legal enforcement of traditional sex roles and recent changes therein, see Leo Kanowitz, *Sex Roles in Law and Society* (Albuquerque:

University of New Mexico Press, 1973, and 1974 Supplement), esp. pts. 2, 4, 5; also Kenneth M. Davidson, Ruth Bader Ginsburg and Henna Hill Kay, *Sex-Based Discrimination* (St. Paul: West Publishing Co., 1974, and 1978 Supplement by Wendy Williams), esp. chap. 2.

3   See Judith Hicks Stiehm, "The Unit of Political Analysis: Our Aristotelian Hangover," in Sandra Harding and Merrill B. Hintikka, eds., *Discovering Reality: Feminist Perspectives on Epistemology, Metaphysics, Methodology, and Philosophy of Science* (Dordrecht: Reidel, 1983), pp. 31–43.

4   See Carole Pateman and Theresa Brennan, "'Mere Auxiliaries to the Commonwealth'; Women and the Origins of Liberalism," *Political Studies* 27, no. 2 (June 1979): 183–200; also Susan Moller Okin, "Women and the Making of the Sentimental Family," *Philosophy & Public Affairs* 11, no. 1 (Winter 1982): 65–88.

5   See Nannerl O. Keohane, "Female Citizenship: The Monstrous Regiment of Women," presented at the Annual Meeting of the Conference for the Study of Political Thought, April 6–8, 1979, on Bodin, John Knox and Rousseau; Carole Pateman, "'The Disorder of Women'; Women, Love, and The Sense of Justice," *Ethics* 81, no. 1 (October 1980): 20–34, on Rousseau and Freud; Susan Moller Okin, "Thinking like a Woman," unpublished ms., 1984, on Plato and Hegel; Terence Ball, "Utilitarianism, Feminism and the Franchise: James Mill and His Critics," *History of Political Thought* 1, no. 1 (Spring 1980): 91–115, on Bentham.

6   Jean-Jacques Rousseau, *Émile*, in *Oeuvres Complètes* 4 (Paris: Pléiade, 1969), pp. 734–35, 750.

7   John Rawls, *A Theory of Justice* (Cambridge, MA: Harvard University Press, 1971), hereafter referred to as *Theory*....

8   *Theory*, pp. 105–106, 208–209, 288–289.

9   See Okin, "Women and the Making of the Sentimental Family," pp. 78–82.

10   *Theory*, pp. 251, 256.

11   Ibid., p. 459.

12   "Fairness to Goodness," *Philosophical Review* 84 (1975): 537. He says: "That we have one conception of the good rather than another is not relevant from a moral standpoint. In acquiring it we are influenced by the same sort of contingencies that lead us to rule out a knowledge of our sex and class."

13   *Theory*, p. 137; see also p. 12.

14   Ibid., p. 137.

15   Ibid., pp. 128, 146.

16   Ibid., p. 128; see also p. 292.

17   Ibid., p. 289.

18   Ibid., p. 8.

19   Ibid., p. 7.

20   It is interesting to note that in a subsequent paper on the question why the basic structure of society is the primary subject of justice, Rawls does not mention the family as part of the basic structure. "The Basic Structure as Subject," *American Philosophical Quarterly* 14, no. 2 (April 1977): 159.

21   *Theory*, p. 61.

22   Ibid., p. 303.

23   *Theory*, p. 490. See Deborah Kearns, "A Theory of Justice—and Love; Rawls on the Family," *Politics* (Australasian Political Studies Association Journal) 18, no. 2 (November 1983): 30–40 for an interesting discussion of the significance of Rawls's failure to address the justice of the family for his theory of moral development.

24   As Jane English says, in a paper that is more centrally concerned with the problems of establishing Rawls's savings principle than with justice within the family *per se*: "By making the parties in the original position heads of families rather than individuals, Rawls makes the family opaque to claims of justice." "Justice between Generations," *Philosophical Studies* 31 (1977): 95.

[...]

32   [*Theory*,] pp. 462–63 (emphasis added).

33   "The Basic Structure as Subject," p. 160.

34   *General Electric vs. Gilbert*, 429, U.S. 125 (1976).

35   *Theory*, p. 137.

36   Ibid., p. 302.

37   Ibid., p. 274.

38   Ibid., p. 529.

39   Ibid., p. 222; see also pp. 202–205, 221–228.

40   Ibid., p. 228.

41   Ibid., pp. 440, 396; see also pp. 178–179.

[...]

Equality and Fairness

The previous chapter introduced some main theories of justice: Hobbes's justification for the almost absolute power of the sovereign; Mill's classic statement of liberalism; Marx's communism; Rawls's modern formulation of welfarist liberalism; and Nozick's libertarian and Okin's feminist responses to Rawls. In this chapter we turn to some pressing real-world examples of injustice.

The first two readings address sexism and the oppression of women. In the first reading Mary Wollstonecraft argues, against prevailing assumptions in the late eighteenth century, that women are just as capable of rational thought and moral virtue as men, and not only deserve equal rights to freedom and independence but would benefit society if they had those rights. In the next reading Simone de Beauvoir, a mid-twentieth-century precursor of what is sometimes called "second-wave feminism,"

goes beyond the demand for equal rights for women within existing legal structures, and argues that, since there is no pre-existing, inborn "female nature," women's whole consciousness is shaped by the patriarchal society into which they are born, and so social change needs to go much deeper than mere equality of opportunity.

The following reading, by Talia Mae Bettcher, is a philosophical examination of the concept of gender and its application to people in the trans community. She argues that, because trans people cannot be adequately understood in terms of the gender definitions already established by dominant culture, these definitions are morally inadequate and should be revised. "Five Faces of Oppression," by Iris Marion Young, lays out an "enabling conception of justice" that, Young argues, provides a more accurate model than the theories we encountered in the last chapter for understanding the varieties of injustice affecting a variety of marginalized groups in liberal democracies: exploitation, marginalization, powerlessness, cultural imperialism, and violence.

The final two selections in this chapter deal with issues of race. Kwame Anthony Appiah critically examines racial categories and argues that, at best, they are socially constructed identities and have no basis in biology. Finally, a moving selection from Ta-Nehisi Coates's semi-autobiographical book *Between the World and Me* describes how his personal and educational experience led him to his current ideological position regarding black oppression.

There is a rich and growing philosophical literature on sexism, racism, homophobia, the treatment of LGBTQ+ groups, economic exploitation, and other forms of injustice. To give just a few illustrative examples: Zack, Shrage, and Sartwell, eds., *Race, Class, Gender, and Sexuality: The Big Questions* (Blackwell, 1998); Susan Ferguson, ed., *Race, Gender, Sexuality and Social Class: Dimensions of Inequality and Identity* (Sage, 2015); Alison Stone, *An Introduction to Feminist Philosophy* (Polity Press, 2007); Cudd and Andreasen, eds., *Feminist Theory: A Philosophical Anthology* (Blackwell, 2005); Georgia Warnke, *Debating Sex and Gender* (Oxford University Press, 2010); Linda Martín Alcoff, *Visible Identities: Race, Gender, and the Self* (Oxford University Press, 2006); Stryker and Whittle, eds., *The Transgender Studies Reader* (Routledge, 2006); Naomi Zack, *Philosophy of Race: An Introduction* (Palgrave, 2018); Taylor, Alcoff, and Anderson, eds., *The Routledge Companion to the Philosophy of Race* (Routledge, 2017); and Andrew Valls, ed., *Race and Racism in Modern Philosophy* (Cornell University Press, 2005).

MARY WOLLSTONECRAFT

FROM *A Vindication of the Rights of Woman*

Who Was Mary Wollstonecraft?

Mary Wollstonecraft, an eighteenth-century British writer, has come to be considered one of the most influential feminist philosophers of the Western tradition. She is also well-known for her turbulent and difficult personal life.

Wollstonecraft was born in 1759 into a comfortably well-off London family. Her father, however, was a drunken, violent spendthrift who squandered the family's modest fortune during Mary's childhood years (including money that Mary was to have inherited from another relative at 21). The family moved frequently as her father tried, and repeatedly failed, to make a go of farming in Epping, Whalebone (East London), Essex, Yorkshire, and Wales before they finally moved back to London when Mary was eighteen.

During these years Mary came to adopt a protective role toward her mother and two younger sisters. She sometimes slept outside the door of her mother's bedroom as a teenager in order to protect her from her father's alcohol-fueled rages. Later she nursed her sister, Eliza, after the difficult birth of her daughter. Eliza was probably suffering from post-partum depression, and Mary also suspected that her husband abused her; Mary convinced her sister to leave her husband, and helped her to do so. Unfortunately she was forced to leave behind her baby, who died within the year; this left Eliza disgraced in society, unable to remarry, and she spent the rest of her life struggling against poverty.

Wollstonecraft was also a passionate friend. A key friendship in her early life was with Fanny Blood, with whom she dreamed of setting up a female utopia. Together with Wollstonecraft's sisters they set up a school in Newington Green, London (a center for non-conformist religious communities*). However it was not long before Blood became engaged and left the school. Blood's hus-band, Hugh Skeys, took her to Europe to try and improve her delicate health, but when she became pregnant she fell seriously ill. Wollstonecraft visited her in Lisbon to try and nurse her to health, but Blood died of complications from premature childbirth in 1785. This was a severe emotional blow for Wollstonecraft, and part of the inspiration for her first novel *Mary, a Fiction* (1788).

On Wollstonecraft's return to England† she closed the school—which had declined in her absence—and took a position as governess to the daughters of Lord Viscount Kingsborough in Ireland. She stayed with the Kingsboroughs for a year, and then made a decision which, for that time, was almost unprecedented: she decided to attempt to support herself as an author. Some of the reasons for this can be seen in her first work, *Thoughts on the Education of Daughters* (1877), subtitled "Unfortunate Situation of Females, Fashionably Educated, and Left without a Fortune," in which she expressed her frustration at the very limited opportunities available for 'respectable' women who nevertheless needed to work.

Wollstonecraft moved to London where, encouraged and assisted by the radical liberal publisher and bookseller Joseph Johnson, she settled down to make her living by writing. She learned French and German so that she could work as a translator of continental texts, and wrote reviews, some of which were published in Johnson's liberal *Analytical Review*. She also published two books. *A Vindication of the Rights of Men* (1790) was a response to Edmund Burke's conservative critique of the French Revolution in *Reflections on the Revolution in France*. Its even more famous and influential partner was *A Vindication of the Rights of Woman* (1792). Wollstonecraft began to move in radical intellectual circles that included Thomas Paine, Joseph Priestley, Samuel Taylor Coleridge, William Blake, William Wordsworth, and William Godwin.

---

* Religious groups that dissented from the Anglican Church.
† One anecdote that shows Wollstonecraft's character is that, on the voyage home from Portugal, she browbeat the captain of the ship into rescuing a wrecked French vessel that he wanted to pass by.

During this period she became enraptured with the painter Henry Fuseli and pursued a relationship with him even though he was married. In a typically forthright fashion, Wollstonecraft proposed that she come to live with Fuseli and his wife in order to carry on a platonic (i.e., non-sexual) relationship with the artist; Fuseli's wife was appalled and he broke off his relationship with Mary.

Humiliated, Wollstonecraft left for Paris late in 1792 in order to escape London and to witness first-hand the revolutionary events in France. She arrived alone in a country in turmoil, only a few weeks before the execution of the deposed King Louis XVI. Wollstonecraft plunged into the excitement, and quickly fell passionately in love with an American adventurer named Gilbert Imlay (formerly an officer in the American Revolutionary War, he was acting as a diplomatic representative of the US while simultaneously lining his pockets by running the British blockade of French ports). Although Imlay had no interest in marrying her—and Wollstonecraft herself had strong reservations about marriage—Mary became pregnant with her first daughter, Fanny. After Britain declared war on France in 1793, Imlay registered Wollstonecraft as his wife in order to protect her from being arrested as a British citizen; however he did not marry her, and after leaving her at Le Havre, where she was to give birth, he never returned. Despite all this Wollstonecraft continued her writing, publishing *An Historical and Moral View of the French Revolution* in 1794. The violent excesses she had witnessed caused her to temper her radical zeal somewhat, but she felt that appropriate changes to education, concurrent with gradual political change, would prevent too much upheaval accompanying social change.

Wollstonecraft finally returned to London in 1795, seeking Imlay who had since left France for England. Imlay, who had begun an affair with a young actress, rejected her,* but when she attempted to kill herself with an overdose of tincture of opium he saved her life. In a last desperate attempt to win back his affections Wollstonecraft undertook to travel to Scandinavia—taking only her maid and young daughter—to attempt to track down a ship's captain who had absconded with a small fortune in Imlay's money intended to buy Swedish goods to import into France. But when she got back to England and found him living with another woman, it became clear to her that Imlay would never return her love. Once again, she attempted suicide—by jumping in the Thames—and once again she was saved, this time by a passing stranger.

Gradually Wollstonecraft's depression began to lift and—throwing off any financial support from Imlay—she returned to the literary life she had previously developed in London. Cautiously, she entered once more into a love affair, this time with the journalist, novelist, and utilitarian philosopher William Godwin. The relationship was a happy and reciprocated one, and when Wollstonecraft became pregnant they decided to marry. This forced Wollstonecraft to reveal publicly that her 'marriage' to Imlay had been a fake one, and once again she was the subject of social scandal. Godwin, too, was attacked, this time for hypocrisy by some of his radical friends, because he had argued in his *Enquiry Concerning Political Justice* (1793) that marriage should be abolished as a social institution.

Nevertheless Wollstonecraft and Godwin were wed in March 1797, and, so that they could retain their independence, moved into adjoining houses in London. Wollstonecraft was full of plans for the future, and had embarked on a new novel, to be called *Maria, or The Wrongs of Woman*. In August, Wollstonecraft gave birth to her second daughter, Mary; but although at first the delivery seemed to go well, Wollstonecraft developed septicemia and died several days later. She was 38.

Godwin was grief-stricken. In 1798 he published his *Memoirs of the Author of a Vindication of the Rights of Woman* which, though deeply felt and sincere, caused yet more scandal for revealing in print the history of his dead wife's love affairs, illegitimate child, and suicide attempts. Their daughter, Mary Godwin, went on to elope outrageously with the Romantic poet Percy Bysshe Shelley, and wrote *Frankenstein* (1818).

---

* Virginia Woolf's diagnosis of Imlay's feelings about Wollstonecraft is delightful (though no doubt too charitable to him): "Tickling minnows he had hooked a dolphin, and the creature rushed him through the waters till he was dizzy and only wanted to escape" (from "Four Figures").

What Was Wollstonecraft's Overall Philosophical Project?

Wollstonecraft is best known for her argument, presented in *A Vindication of the Rights of Woman*, that women and men are inherently equal—equally rational, equally intelligent, equally moral—and that any appearances of intellectual or moral inequality are an artifact of differing education and social upbringing. She argued that men had enslaved women by educating them to care only for romantic love, and by fetishizing weak and passive ideals of femininity. Instead of rational, active, strong, and independent women, society rewarded women who remained childlike, passive, weak, and dependent. Wollstonecraft argued that real social change had to occur at the level of the family, with women educated to rationally fulfill their duties as mothers, wives, and daughters. She proposed a new social order, which would better serve the natural capacities of human beings, in which men and women are both treated as rational, autonomous beings. She argued that social changes of this sort would produce citizens—especially female citizens—that were better able to serve social justice, which would in turn produce a better, more robust and healthy society, that would then raise even more virtuous citizens, and so on in an upward spiral of social progress. Thus, equality for women would benefit all members of society, and not just the female sex.

A key concern for Wollstonecraft was the importance of personal independence. For her, self-government was a key aspect of individual human development. In particular, moral virtue essentially involves acting autonomously on the basis of moral principles. These principles, according to Wollstonecraft, do not arise merely out of sympathy for others or other moral passions, or in accordance with merely social strictures, but are grasped by rational reflection on the attributes of God and God's design manifested through human nature. It was on this basis that she felt the rights of women could be asserted and found indisputable, if people would consider the subject impartially. Arbitrary power structures and entrenched ideologies were under attack in revolutionary France, and Wollstonecraft pointed out that such structures also kept women from being accorded the rights that were demanded for men. "Who," she asked, "made man the exclusive judge, if woman partake with him the gift of reason?"

The principles that shaped Wollstonecraft's political philosophy also shaped her moral philosophy. Reason, because it cultivates virtue, should guide an individual's moral life. Education for girls and young women should focus on nurturing their reason, so they can achieve both economic and psychological independence. (Wollstonecraft even wrote a children's book, *Original Stories from Real Life* [1788], which encourages a balance between reason and emotion.) Not only the mind, but also the body, should be made strong and resilient, in order to meet the changes and difficulties of life with fortitude. Such an education would prevent women from being "blown about by every momentary gust of feeling." Rather, reason and feeling should balance each other, with reason taking the upper hand. A woman so guided, according to Wollstonecraft, would not be entirely subject to the whims of fathers, husbands, and brothers for her well-being and happiness.

What Is the Structure of This Reading?

A Vindication of the Rights of Woman focuses on the condition of women in society, as well as on the social construction of gender. It is a more abstract work of political theory than the preceding *Vindication of the Rights of Men*, expanding to address metaphysical and psychological aspects of the question of universal rights. Wollstonecraft originally planned on writing a second volume, but she completed only the first, which comprises a dedication, an introduction, and 13 chapters.

The dedication to Talleyrand-Périgord, French statesman and former bishop of Autun,* is the first excerpt included here. Talleyrand was one of the writers of the new French Constitution of 1791, as well as the author of a new program for French public education, one that excluded women at the higher levels and sought only to prepare them for domestic life. Wollstonecraft's dedi-

---

* Charles-Maurice de Talleyrand-Périgord (1754–1838) became Bishop of Autun in 1788. A year later he supported anti-clerical revolutionaries and helped in the seizure of Church properties across France. Serving under Louis XVI, the Revolution, Napoleon, and beyond, Talleyrand was considered a crafty and adaptable diplomat and politician. Wollstonecraft met him on one of his diplomatic journeys to England.

cation asks Talleyrand to reconsider the reasoning that prompted the leaders of the Revolution to leave women out of their new Constitution and exclude them from their program for national education. In this Dedication, she outlines her chief argument, that if women are not given social rights and equal educational opportunities, they will resort to power tactics of dubious morality, thereby undermining the family, and by extension, society. She argues that women possess reason, and as such have the right to unfold their talents in society. She calls for the legislators of France to revise their Constitution and to grant equality to women under the law.

The second excerpt is from the Introduction, in which Wollstonecraft considers the situation of women in society and outlines her arguments for changing it. Here she addresses the "false system of education" that trains upper and middle-class women to be ornamental and weak. Conceding that women are physically weaker than men, she asserts that their capacity for reason is equal. An education that undermines reason, she argues, nurtures immorality, and if society is to improve, women must be given opportunity to escape from their "slavish dependence" and to develop themselves as strong and independent human beings.

The last section is from Chapter Two, entitled "The Prevailing Opinion of a Sexual Character Discussed." Here, Wollstonecraft considers the dominant opinions of her society regarding the character of women and the kind of education best suited to them. She outlines the consensus among educational theorists of her day, who thought that women and men had essentially different virtues and should be educated accordingly. Women, it was thought, should be educated for obedience and passivity, to be ruled over by men. Wollstonecraft argues against these ideas, insisting instead that virtue is not relative, and that women should be educated in the same way as men: to strengthen the body, develop reason, and nurture the heart. Give women freedom and independence, she states, and virtue will result, not only in the individual but also in society.

Some Useful Background Information

1. Wollstonecraft argues against women cultivating an excess of what in the eighteenth and nineteenth centuries was called "sensibility." This term referred to a particular kind of refined aesthetic and moral responsiveness and sympathy, particularly to beauty and the sorrows of others. This kind of sentiment became a central motif in literature from the 1740s to the 1770s, particularly in the novels of Laurence Sterne, Jean-Jacques Rousseau, and Johann Wolfgang von Goethe. Wollstonecraft was concerned that women who over-cultivated sensibility were at risk of valuing feeling over common sense and reason. She was, however, herself influenced by this movement, and her political action was in many ways spurred by her sympathetic engagement with the sorrows of others.

2. Two of Wollstonecraft's first publications, *Thoughts on the Education of Daughters* (1787) and *Original Stories from Real Life* (1788), were focused on pedagogy, particularly the education of girls. Education continued to be an abiding interest, and in the *Vindication* Wollstonecraft argues that only by changing educational practices can social and political changes be fostered in society. Wollstonecraft believed that children should be taught at co-educational day schools, while living at home. While this does not seem controversial to us, it was quite radical at a time when children were taught separately, boys at boarding schools to be educated for public life, and girls at home to attend to domestic duties. Many eighteenth-century moralists and philosophers, including Rousseau in his well-known novel *Émile, or On Education* (1762), argued that women and men had different moral natures, and that a woman's education should be limited to what is necessary to form a pleasing companion for man. These opinions of female character were prevalent in society, and Wollstonecraft takes pains to show that they were the opinions of custom and prejudice, not of reason.

A Common Misconception

Wollstonecraft is considered by many to be the "founding mother" of feminism, but 'feminism' was not a term that became current until the late nineteenth century, and Wollstonecraft would not have used it. Her work certainly contains ideas that became foundational to feminism; she was far ahead of her time, for example, in her insistence that women and men were equal in terms of possessing reason, and that a just society must recognize a woman's right to a life that fulfills her utmost potential. Unlike modern feminists, however, Wollstonecraft thought that superior physical strength in men reflected a higher capacity for virtue. She also believed that women's duties were bound first and foremost to the domestic sphere.

How Important and Influential Is This Reading?

Mary Wollstonecraft's reputation—never very secure during her own lifetime—was heavily affected by her husband's memoir of her 'scandalous' and emotionally turbulent life. She was, more than anything else, a figure of derision and pity (see, e.g., Richard Polwhele's 1798 poem "The Unsex'd Females") until the late nineteenth century, when figures within the nascent feminist movement rediscovered the power of her ideas—and, for some, the inspirational example of her own unconventional life story. (For example, Virginia Woolf praised Wollstonecraft for her "experiments in living.") By the 1970s Wollstonecraft was recognized as a key originator of modern feminism, though even then perhaps as much attention was focused on her unconventional life as on her philosophical writings. A further re-evaluation of Wollstonecraft occurred in the 1990s, with more focus on her ideas and the source of those ideas in the intellectual currents of the eighteenth century. Today, *A Vindication of the Rights of Woman* is considered a classic of feminist thought, and an important bridge between Enlightenment and Romantic thought.

FROM *A Vindication of the Rights of Woman**

To M. Talleyrand-Périgord, Late Bishop of Autun

Sir,

Having read with great pleasure a pamphlet which you have lately published,[†] I dedicate this volume to you; to induce you to reconsider the subject, and maturely weigh what I have advanced respecting the rights of woman and national education: and I call with the firm tone of humanity; for my arguments, Sir, are dictated by a disinterested spirit—I plead for my sex—not for myself. Independence I have long considered as the grand blessing of life, the basis of every virtue—and independence I will ever secure by contracting my wants, though I were to live on a barren heath....

Contending for the rights of woman, my main argument is built on this simple principle, that if she be not prepared by education to become the companion of man, she will stop the progress of knowledge and virtue; for truth must be common to all, or it will be inefficacious with respect to its influence on general practice. And how can woman be expected to co-operate unless she know why she ought to be virtuous? unless freedom strengthen her reason till she comprehend her duty, and see in what manner it is connected with her real good? If children are to be educated to understand the true principle of patriotism, their mother must be a patriot; and the love of mankind, from which an orderly train of virtues spring, can only be produced by considering the moral and civil interest of mankind; but the education and situation of woman, at present, shuts her out from such investigations.

In this work I have produced many arguments, which to me were conclusive, to prove that the prevailing notion respecting a sexual[‡] character was subversive of morality, and I have contended, that to render the human body and mind more perfect, chastity[§] must more universally prevail, and that chastity will

---

*   The full title of this work is *A Vindication of The Rights of Woman: with Strictures on Political and Moral Subjects*, and it was first published in 1792.

†   Talleyrand published his *Report on Public Instruction* in 1791. This long treatise was inspired by Enlightenment ideals and argued for national public education from primary to higher levels of education—for men. Talleyrand argued that women should receive no higher education but only instruction that would aid in their domestic duties.

‡   Gender-specific.

§   Modesty, restraint (not necessarily sexual abstinence).

never be respected in the male world till the person of a woman is not, as it were, idolized, when little virtue or sense embellish it with the grand traces of mental beauty, or the interesting simplicity of affection.

Consider, Sir, dispassionately, these observations—for a glimpse of the truth seemed to open before you when you observed, "that to see one half of the human race excluded by the other from all participation of government, was a political phenomenon that, according to abstract principles, it was impossible to explain."[*] If so, on what does your constitution rest? If the abstract rights of man will bear discussion and explanation, those of woman, by a parity of reasoning, will not shrink from the same test: though a different opinion prevails in this country, built on the very arguments which you use to justify the oppression of woman—prescription.[†]

Consider, I address you as a legislator, whether, when men contend for their freedom, and to be allowed to judge for themselves respecting their own happiness, it be not inconsistent and unjust to subjugate women, even though you firmly believe that you are acting in the manner best calculated to promote their happiness? Who made man the exclusive judge, if woman partake with him the gift of reason?

In this style, argue tyrants of every denomination, from the weak king to the weak father of a family; they are all eager to crush reason; yet always assert that they usurp its throne only to be useful. Do you not act a similar part, when you *force* all women, by denying them civil and political rights, to remain immured in their families groping in the dark? For surely, Sir, you will not assert, that a duty can be binding which is not founded on reason? If indeed this be their destination, arguments may be drawn from reason: and thus augustly supported, the more understanding women acquire, the more they will be attached to their duty—comprehending it—for unless they comprehend it,

unless their morals be fixed on the same immutable principle as those of man, no authority can make them discharge it in a virtuous manner. They may be convenient slaves, but slavery will have its constant effect, degrading the master and the abject dependent.

But, if women are to be excluded, without having a voice, from a participation of the natural rights of mankind, prove first, to ward off the charge of injustice and inconsistency, that they want reason[‡]—else this flaw in your NEW CONSTITUTION will ever show that man must, in some shape, act like a tyrant, and tyranny, in whatever part of society it rears its brazen front, will ever undermine morality.

I have repeatedly asserted, and produced what appeared to me irrefragable[§] arguments drawn from matters of fact, to prove my assertion, that women cannot, by force, be confined to domestic concerns; for they will, however ignorant, intermeddle with more weighty affairs, neglecting private duties only to disturb, by cunning tricks, the orderly plans of reason which rise above their comprehension.

Besides, whilst they are only made to acquire personal accomplishments, men will seek for pleasure in variety, and faithless husbands will make faithless wives; such ignorant beings, indeed, will be very excusable when, not taught to respect public good, nor allowed any civil rights, they attempt to do themselves justice by retaliation.

The box of mischief thus opened[¶] in society, what is to preserve private virtue, the only security of public freedom and universal happiness?

Let there be then no coercion *established* in society, and the common law of gravity prevailing, the sexes will fall into their proper places. And, now that more equitable laws are forming your citizens, marriage may become more sacred: your young men may choose wives from motives of affection, and your maidens allow love to root out vanity.

---

[*]   From *Report on Public Instruction*, Appendix B.I.ii. Only men over 25 were recognized as citizens in the French constitution of 1791. French women did not receive the vote until 1944.
[†]   Authority of long-held custom and tradition.
[‡]   Lack reason.
[§]   Irrefutable.
[¶]   This is a reference to the Greek story of Pandora's box. In Hesiod's *Works and Days* (c. 700 BCE), Pandora—the first human woman—is given a receptacle containing all the evils of the world, including death; not knowing what was inside, her curiosity led her to open the box, unleashing its contents on the world. 'Mischief' here means harmful action.

The father of a family will not then weaken his constitution and debase his sentiments, by visiting the harlot, nor forget, in obeying the call of appetite, the purpose for which it was implanted. And, the mother will not neglect her children to practice the arts of coquetry,* when sense and modesty secure her the friendship of her husband.

But, till men become attentive to the duty of a father, it is vain to expect women to spend that time in their nursery which they, "wise in their generation,"† choose to spend at their glass;‡ for this exertion of cunning is only an instinct of nature to enable them to obtain indirectly a little of that power of which they are unjustly denied a share: for, if women are not permitted to enjoy legitimate rights, they will render both men and themselves vicious, to obtain illicit privileges.

I wish, Sir, to set some investigations of this kind afloat in France; and should they lead to a confirmation of my principles, when your constitution is revised the Rights of Woman may be respected, if it be fully proved that reason calls for this respect, and loudly demands JUSTICE for one half of the human race.

I am, SIR,
Yours respectfully,
M.W.

Introduction

After considering the historic page,§ and viewing the living world with anxious solicitude, the most melancholy emotions of sorrowful indignation have depressed my spirits, and I have sighed when obliged to confess, that either nature has made a great difference between man and man, or that the civilization which has hitherto taken place in the world has been very partial. I have turned over various books written on the subject of education, and patiently observed the conduct of parents and the management of schools; but what has been the result?—a profound conviction that the neglected education of my fellow-creatures is the grand source of the misery I deplore; and that women, in particular, are rendered weak and wretched by a variety of concurring causes, originating from one hasty conclusion. The conduct and manners of women, in fact, evidently prove that their minds are not in a healthy state; for, like the flowers which are planted in too rich a soil, strength and usefulness are sacrificed to beauty; and the flaunting leaves, after having pleased a fastidious eye, fade, disregarded on the stalk, long before the season when they ought to have arrived at maturity.—One cause of this barren blooming I attribute to a false system of education, gathered from the books written on this subject by men who, considering females rather as women than human creatures, have been more anxious to make them alluring mistresses than affectionate wives and rational mothers; and the understanding of the sex has been so bubbled by this specious homage, that the civilized women of the present century, with a few exceptions, are only anxious to inspire love, when they ought to cherish a nobler ambition, and by their abilities and virtues exact respect.

In a treatise, therefore, on female rights and manners, the works which have been particularly written for their improvement must not be overlooked; especially when it is asserted, in direct terms, that the minds of women are enfeebled by false refinement; that the books of instruction, written by men of genius, have had the same tendency as more frivolous productions; and that, in the true style of Mahometanism,¶ they are treated as a kind of subordinate beings, and not as a part of the human species, when improveable reason is allowed to be the dignified distinction which raises men above the brute creation, and puts a natural scepter in a feeble hand.

Yet, because I am a woman, I would not lead my readers to suppose that I mean violently to agitate the contested question respecting the equality or inferiority of the sex; but as the subject lies in my way, and I cannot pass it over without subjecting the main tendency of my reasoning to misconstruction, I shall stop

---

*   Flirting and other arts used to gain the affection of men, usually for the sense of power it confers and with no intent of reciprocation.

†   See Luke 16:8.

‡   Mirror.

§   Written histories.

¶   Islam.

a moment to deliver, in a few words, my opinion.—In the government of the physical world it is observable that the female in point of strength is, in general, inferior to the male. This is the law of nature; and it does not appear to be suspended or abrogated in favor of woman. A degree of physical superiority cannot, therefore, be denied—and it is a noble prerogative! But not content with this natural pre-eminence, men endeavor to sink us still lower, merely to render us alluring objects for a moment; and women, intoxicated by the adoration which men, under the influence of their senses, pay them, do not seek to obtain a durable interest in their hearts, or to become the friends of the fellow creatures who find amusement in their society.

I am aware of an obvious inference:—from every quarter have I heard exclamations against masculine women; but where are they to be found? If by this appellation men mean to inveigh against their ardor in hunting, shooting, and gaming, I shall most cordially join in the cry; but if it be against the imitation of manly virtues, or, more properly speaking, the attainment of those talents and virtues, the exercise of which ennobles the human character, and which raise females in the scale of animal being, when they are comprehensively termed mankind;—all those who view them with a philosophic eye must, I should think, wish with me, that they may every day grow more and more masculine.

This discussion naturally divides the subject. I shall first consider women in the grand light of human creatures, who, in common with men, are placed on this earth to unfold their faculties; and afterwards I shall more particularly point out their peculiar designation.

I wish also to steer clear of an error which many respectable writers have fallen into; for the instruction which has hitherto been addressed to women, has rather been applicable to *ladies*, if the little indirect advice, that is scattered through Sandford and Merton,* be excepted; but, addressing my sex in a firmer tone, I pay particular attention to those in the middle class, because they appear to be in the most natural state. Perhaps the seeds of false-refinement, immorality, and

vanity, have ever been shed by the great. Weak, artificial beings, raised above the common wants and affections of their race, in a premature unnatural manner, undermine the very foundation of virtue, and spread corruption through the whole mass of society! As a class of mankind they have the strongest claim to pity; the education of the rich tends to render them vain and helpless, and the unfolding mind is not strengthened by the practice of those duties which dignify the human character.—They only live to amuse themselves, and by the same law which in nature invariably produces certain effects, they soon only afford barren amusement.

But as I purpose taking a separate view of the different ranks of society, and of the moral character of women, in each, this hint is, for the present, sufficient; and I have only alluded to the subject, because it appears to me to be the very essence of an introduction to give a cursory account of the contents of the work it introduces.

My own sex, I hope, will excuse me, if I treat them like rational creatures, instead of flattering their fascinating graces, and viewing them as if they were in a state of perpetual childhood, unable to stand alone. I earnestly wish to point out in what true dignity and human happiness consists—I wish to persuade women to endeavor to acquire strength, both of mind and body, and to convince them that the soft phrases, susceptibility of heart, delicacy of sentiment, and refinement of taste, are almost synonymous with epithets of weakness, and that those beings who are only the objects of pity and that kind of love, which has been termed its sister, will soon become objects of contempt.

Dismissing then those pretty feminine phrases, which the men condescendingly use to soften our slavish dependence, and despising that weak elegancy of mind, exquisite sensibility, and sweet docility of manners, supposed to be the sexual characteristics of the weaker vessel, I wish to show that elegance is inferior to virtue, that the first object of laudable ambition is to obtain a character as a human being, regardless of the distinction of sex; and that secondary views should be brought to this simple touchstone.† ...

---

* Children's novel by Thomas Day (1748–89) featuring two male child protagonists, a farm boy and a rich boy. The novel includes lessons in manners, masculinity, and class politics; Wollstonecraft reviewed the third volume for the *Analytical Review*.

† Test.

Chapter 2: The Prevailing Opinion of a Sexual Character Discussed

To account for, and excuse the tyranny of man, many ingenious arguments have been brought forward to prove, that the two sexes, in the acquirement of virtue, ought to aim at attaining a very different character: or, to speak explicitly, women are not allowed to have sufficient strength of mind to acquire what really deserves the name of virtue. Yet it should seem, allowing them to have souls, that there is but one way appointed by Providence to lead *mankind* to either virtue or happiness....

It is, however, sufficient for my present purpose to assert, that, whatever effect circumstances have on the abilities, every being may become virtuous by the exercise of its own reason; for if but one being was created with vicious inclinations, that is positively bad, what can save us from atheism? or if we worship a God, is not that God a devil?

Consequently, the most perfect education, in my opinion, is such an exercise of the understanding as is best calculated to strengthen the body and form the heart. Or, in other words, to enable the individual to attain such habits of virtue as will render it independent. In fact, it is a farce to call any being virtuous whose virtues do not result from the exercise of its own reason. This was Rousseau's opinion respecting men:* I extend it to women, and confidently assert that they have been drawn out of their sphere by false refinement and not by an endeavor to acquire masculine qualities. Still the regal homage which they receive is so intoxicating that until the manners of the times are changed and formed on more reasonable principles, it may be impossible to convince them that the illegitimate power, which they obtain by degrading themselves, is a curse, and that they must return to nature and equality if they wish to secure the placid satisfaction that unsophisticated affections impart. But for this epoch we must wait—wait, perhaps, till kings and nobles, enlightened by reason, and preferring the real

dignity of man to childish state, throw off their gaudy hereditary trappings: and if then women do not resign the arbitrary power of beauty, they will prove that they have *less* mind than man.

I may be accused of arrogance; still I must declare what I firmly believe, that all the writers who have written on the subject of female education and manners from Rousseau to Dr. Gregory,† have contributed to render women more artificial, weak characters than they would otherwise have been; and, consequently, more useless members of society. I might have expressed this conviction in a lower key; but I am afraid it would have been the whine of affectation, and not the faithful expression of my feelings, of the clear result, which experience and reflection have led me to draw....

Strengthen the female mind by enlarging it, and there will be an end to blind obedience; but, as blind obedience is ever sought for by power, tyrants and sensualists are in the right when they endeavor to keep women in the dark, because the former only want slaves, and the latter a play-thing. The sensualist, indeed, has been the most dangerous of tyrants, and women have been duped by their lovers, as princes by their ministers, whilst dreaming that they reigned over them....

Rousseau declares that a woman should never, for a moment, feel herself independent, that she should be governed by fear to exercise her *natural* cunning, and made a coquettish slave in order to render her a more alluring object of desire, a *sweeter* companion to man, whenever he chooses to relax himself. He carries the arguments, which he pretends to draw from the indications of nature, still further, and insinuates that truth and fortitude, the corner stones of all human virtue, should be cultivated with certain restrictions, because, with respect to the female character, obedience is the grand lesson which ought to be impressed with unrelenting rigor.

What nonsense! When will a great man arise with sufficient strength of mind to puff away the fumes which pride and sensuality have thus spread over the subject! If women are by nature inferior to men, their

---

* In his novel *Émile, or On Education* (1762), French philosopher Jean-Jacques Rousseau (1712–78) asserts that a man's virtues must follow from reason, but he does not assert the same for women. Wollstonecraft frequently argues against the narrow ideas of femininity and female education outlined in *Émile*.
† Scottish moralist John Gregory (1724–73) wrote the best-selling tract *A Father's Legacy to His Daughters* (1774). In it, women and parents are given advice on morality and conduct, and he advises women to hide any learning they might have, in case it scares off suitors.

virtues must be the same in quality, if not in degree, or virtue is a relative idea; consequently, their conduct should be founded on the same principles, and have the same aim.*

Connected with man as daughters, wives, and mothers, their moral character may be estimated by their manner of fulfilling those simple duties; but the end, the grand end of their exertions should be to unfold their own faculties and acquire the dignity of conscious virtue. They may try to render their road pleasant; but ought never to forget, in common with man, that life yields not the felicity which can satisfy an immortal soul. I do not mean to insinuate, that either sex should be so lost in abstract reflections or distant views, as to forget the affections and duties that lie before them, and are, in truth, the means appointed to produce the fruit of life; on the contrary, I would warmly recommend them, even while I assert, that they afford most satisfaction when they are considered in their true, sober light.

Probably the prevailing opinion, that woman was created for man, may have taken its rise from Moses's poetical story;† yet, as very few, it is presumed, who have bestowed any serious thought on the subject, ever supposed that Eve was, literally speaking, one of Adam's ribs, the deduction must be allowed to fall to the ground; or, only be so far admitted as it proves that man, from the remotest antiquity, found it convenient to exert his strength to subjugate his companion, and his invention to show that she ought to have her neck bent under the yoke, because the whole creation was only created for his convenience or pleasure.

Let it not be concluded that I wish to invert the order of things; I have already granted, that, from the constitution of their bodies, men seem to be designed by Providence to attain a greater degree of virtue. I speak collectively of the whole sex; but I see not the shadow of a reason to conclude that their virtues should differ in respect to their nature. In fact, how can they, if virtue has only one eternal standard? I must therefore, if I reason consequentially, as strenuously

maintain that they have the same simple direction, as that there is a God....

Women ought to endeavour to purify their heart;‡ but can they do so when their uncultivated understandings make them entirely dependent on their senses for employment and amusement, when no noble pursuit sets them above the little vanities of the day, or enables them to curb the wild emotions that agitate a reed over which every passing breeze§ has power? To gain the affections of a virtuous man is affectation necessary? Nature has given woman a weaker frame than man; but, to ensure her husband's affections, must a wife, who by the exercise of her mind and body whilst she was discharging the duties of a daughter, wife, and mother, has allowed her constitution to retain its natural strength, and her nerves a healthy tone, is she, I say, to condescend to use art and feign a sickly delicacy in order to secure her husband's affection? Weakness may excite tenderness, and gratify the arrogant pride of man; but the lordly caresses of a protector will not gratify a noble mind that pants for, and deserves to be respected. Fondness is a poor substitute for friendship!

In a seraglio,¶ I grant, that all these arts are necessary; the epicure must have his palate tickled, or he will sink into apathy; but have women so little ambition as to be satisfied with such a condition? Can they supinely dream life away in the lap of pleasure, or the languor of weariness, rather than assert their claim to pursue reasonable pleasures and render themselves conspicuous by practicing the virtues which dignify mankind? Surely she has not an immortal soul who can loiter life away merely employed to adorn her person, that she may amuse the languid hours, and soften the cares of a fellow-creature who is willing to be enlivened by her smiles and tricks, when the serious business of life is over.

Besides, the woman who strengthens her body and exercises her mind will, by managing her family and practicing various virtues, become the friend, and not the humble dependent of her husband; and

---

* In *Émile*, Rousseau argues that men's and women's virtues are essentially different.
† Genesis 2:18–25. Moses was at this time thought to be the author of Genesis.
‡ See Matthew 5:8.
§ See Matthew 11:7.
¶ Harem.

if she, by possessing such substantial qualities, merit his regard, she will not find it necessary to conceal her affection, nor to pretend to an unnatural coldness of constitution to excite her husband's passions. In fact, if we revert to history, we shall find that the women who have distinguished themselves have neither been the most beautiful nor the most gentle of their sex....

It appears to me necessary to dwell on these obvious truths, because females have been insulated, as it were; and, while they have been stripped of the virtues that should clothe humanity, they have been decked with artificial graces that enable them to exercise a short-lived tyranny. Love, in their bosoms, taking place of every nobler passion, their sole ambition is to be fair, to raise emotion instead of inspiring respect; and this ignoble desire, like the servility in absolute monarchies, destroys all strength of character. Liberty is the mother of virtue, and if women be, by their very constitution, slaves, and not allowed to breathe the sharp invigorating air of freedom, they must ever languish like exotics, and be reckoned beautiful flaws in nature.

As to the argument respecting the subjection in which the sex has ever been held, it retorts on man. The many have always been enthralled by the few; and monsters, who scarcely have shown any discernment of human excellence, have tyrannized over thousands of their fellow-creatures. Why have men of superior endowments submitted to such degradation? For, is it not universally acknowledged that kings, viewed collectively, have ever been inferior, in abilities and virtue, to the same number of men taken from the common mass of mankind—yet, have they not, and are they not still treated with a degree of reverence that is an insult to reason? China is not the only country where a living man has been made a God.* Men have submitted to superior strength to enjoy with impunity the pleasure of the moment—women have only done the same, and therefore till it is proved that the courtier, who servilely resigns the birthright of a man, is not a moral agent, it cannot be demonstrated that woman is essentially inferior to man because she has always been subjugated.

Brutal force has hitherto governed the world, and that the science of politics is in its infancy, is evident from philosophers scrupling to give the knowledge most useful to man that determinate distinction.

I shall not pursue this argument any further than to establish an obvious inference, that as sound politics diffuse liberty, mankind, including woman, will become more wise and virtuous. ◼

Suggestions for Critical Reflection

1. How, according to Wollstonecraft, did men justify excluding women from the "abstract rights of man"?
2. Does Wollstonecraft think women, once liberated and educated, could take on roles traditionally filled by men in society? Why or why not?
3. On what class of society does Wollstonecraft focus? Why? How does this choice affect her argument?
4. What are the characteristics that most people thought defined women in Wollstonecraft's day? Does this perception of women still exist in our society? If so, by whom is it held?
5. For Wollstonecraft, what is the relationship between reason and virtue?
6. "Let it not be concluded that I wish to invert the order of things," writes Wollstonecraft—why does she say this? What does she mean?

---

* Wollstonecraft is alluding here to the doctrine of the divine right of kings, which states that a monarch receives his or her authority from God and is not subject to earthly election or oversight. In some cases, notably in Egypt and Rome, some rulers went a step further and claimed divinity for themselves. Chinese Emperors ruled according to what was called the "Mandate of Heaven," and they were considered the "Heavenly Sons" of the universe. Similar beliefs about the divinity of kings existed in most monarchical societies, including England. Wollstonecraft believed that the people should appoint their legislators, and that the so-called divine right of kings was an illegitimate means of usurping that elective power.

7. In the "Dedication" to Talleyrand, Wollstonecraft describes the *Vindication* as a treatise about "the rights of woman and national education." Why, for Wollstonecraft, is educational reform crucial to enacting the social changes she envisions? What, for her, was wrong with the theories of female education that were current in her day?

8. The French Revolution and associated civil rights struggles in the late eighteenth century were concerned with overthrowing "arbitrary" hierarchies based on birth, custom, and the institutions that upheld them. What was that power based in? What, according to Wollstonecraft, is the moral consequence of such power?

SIMONE DE BEAUVOIR

FROM *The Second Sex*

Who Was Simone de Beauvoir?

Born in Paris in 1908, Simone de Beauvoir had become such an important figure in France by the time of her death in 1986 that her funeral was attended by 5,000 people, including four former ministers of the Mitterrand government. A headline announcing her death read "Women, you owe her everything!"

Beauvoir was the eldest of two daughters in a respectable, conservative bourgeois family, and she spent her formative years heatedly reacting against her parents and their values. She became an atheist while still a teenager, and decided early on to devote her life to writing and studying 'rather than' becoming a wife and mother. She studied philosophy at the ancient Sorbonne University in Paris and was the youngest person ever to obtain the *agrégation* (a high-level competitive examination for recruiting teachers in France) in philosophy, in 1929. She was 21. In that same year she met the famous existentialist philosopher Jean-Paul Sartre and began an intense relationship with him—the most important of her life—that lasted until his death in 1980.[*]

Beauvoir and Sartre became notorious throughout France as a couple who were lovers and soul-mates but who maintained an open relationship; both considered themselves highly sexually "liberated," and Beauvoir was openly bisexual. Sartre made what he called a "pact" with her—they could have affairs with other people, but they were required to tell each other everything—and he proceeded to match his actions to this rule. As he put it to Beauvoir: "What *we* have is an *essential* love; but it is a good idea for us also to experience *contingent* love affairs."

Despite the rotating cast of lovers, Beauvoir remained devoted to Sartre all her life and always maintained that he was the most brilliant man she had ever known. Indeed, she once declared that, her many books, literary prizes, and social influence notwithstanding, her greatest achievement in life was her relationship with Sartre.

Between 1932 and 1943, Beauvoir was a high school teacher of philosophy in Rouen, in north-western France. There, she was subject to official reprimands for her protests about male chauvinism and for her pacifism; finally, a parental complaint made against her for 'corrupting' one of her female students caused her dismissal. For the rest of her life, Beauvoir lived in Paris and made her living from her writing. At the end of World War II, she became an editor at *Les Temps Modernes*, a new political journal founded by Sartre and other French intellectuals. She used this journal to disseminate her own work, and several excerpts from *The Second Sex* were first published in it.

Interestingly, part of the impetus to write *The Second Sex* came to her as she gradually realized that, unlike some of her female friends, she did *not* at first feel any sense that she was disadvantaged as a woman, but that this feeling of personal satisfaction and of independence resulted primarily from her relationship with a well-known, influential man—Sartre. When she reflected on this relationship, she realized with astonishment that she was fundamentally different from Sartre "because he was a man and I was only a woman."[†] As she put it, "In writing *The Second Sex* I became aware, for the first time, that I myself was leading a false life, or rather, that I was profiting from this male-oriented society without even knowing it."[‡]

---

[*] When the university *agrégation* results came out, Sartre and Beauvoir tied for first place, although Sartre was subsequently awarded first place with Beauvoir second. Also, incidentally, 1929 was the year Beauvoir acquired her lifelong nickname, le Castor (French for 'beaver,' because of the resemblance of her surname to "beaver").

[†] As cited by Deirdre Bair in her introduction to the 1989 Vintage edition of *The Second Sex*, from interviews Bair conducted with Beauvoir in the 1980s.

[‡] From an interview with Beauvoir published in *Society*, February 1976.

She was also influenced by what she saw in America, during a visit in 1947, of the experience of black people in a segregated society. For example, she was friends with the African American short story writer and novelist Richard Wright, who, with his white wife Ellen, was a tireless advocate for black equality. For Beauvoir, feminism was part of a larger project of social justice and human rights. From the late 1940s until the 1960s she was a very public left-wing political activist and a vocal supporter of communism (and critic of American-style capitalism).

The Second Sex is an extended examination of the problems women have encountered throughout history and of the possibilities left open to them. After the Introduction (reprinted here), the book is divided into two halves: Book One is a historical overview of "Facts and Myths" about women, and Book Two deals with "Women's Life Today." Book One is divided into sections describing the "Destiny" of women according to theories of biology, psychoanalysis, and Marxist historical materialism; the "History" of women from prehistoric times to the granting of the vote to women in France in 1944; and "Myths" about women in literature. Book Two is more personal, and discusses women in childhood, adolescence, sexual initiation, various forms of mature loving and sexual relationships, and old age. The conclusion of the book is positive and optimistic, as Beauvoir tries to set out a model of life and action for future generations of women.

Some Useful Background Information

1. The first words of Book Two of *The Second Sex* are "One is not born, but rather becomes, a woman. No biological, psychological or economic fate determines the figure that the human female presents in society; it is civilization as a whole that determines this creature." This is how Beauvoir most famously expresses an influential central thesis of the book: that "woman," as a biological category, is separable from "feminine," as a social construction—or more generally, that sex is not the same thing as gender. Thus, woman's status under the patriarchy as the Other is a contingent, socially constructed fact rather than an essential truth about the female gender.

   It is important to appreciate that Beauvoir is not denying that there are biological differences between men and women, nor does she insist that these biological differences must be simply ignored in a properly constituted society. Rather, she is arguing that our *biological* constitutions do not determine our *gender* characteristics: such things as "femininity" or "masculinity," being "nurturing" or "modest" or "emotional" or "delicate"—these things are constructed and constrained purely by *social* influences. Under different social conditions women and men might naturally and freely behave in ways radically different from contemporary social norms.

   Thus, according to Beauvoir, gender is more something we *do*—a way we live—than something we *are*. Gender is constrained by social pressures in large part because social pressures constrain how we can legitimately behave. A woman in, say, Canada in the 1950s could not just decide as an individual to behave like a man—or like someone who is neither masculine nor feminine—and in this way change her gender unilaterally. Even if she were brave enough to attempt the experiment, according to Beauvoir—and the other existentialists—one cannot possess a certain trait, such as being masculine, unless others recognize one as doing so.

2. This emphasis on the social construction of gender, race, and other aspects of the reality we experience in our day-to-day lives is related to Beauvoir's commitment to existentialism. Central to existentialism is the doctrine that *existence precedes essence*: humans have no pre-given purpose or essence determined for them by God or by biology. According to existentialism, each consciousness faces the world as an isolated individual, and inevitably creates itself—gives itself determinate form—by making choices. We are forced to make these choices by the need to respond to the things around us, including both passive natural objects and other consciousnesses; but what we choose is not forced.

   Beauvoir and Sartre see the meeting of one consciousness with another as profoundly disturbing: faced with the gaze of an Other, we recognize a point of view which is necessarily different from our own and so we are required to concede our own incompleteness; furthermore, the opposing consciousness must treat *us* as an Other, which we feel as a threat to destroy us by turning us into an object.

Beauvoir's feminism can be seen as a development of this idea: in response to the threat posed by other consciousnesses, according to existentialism, one might retaliate by objectifying and dominating the Other, to be able to control it without destroying it and thus be able to withstand its gaze. Thus, according to Beauvoir, men have objectified and dominated women as the Other, and by succumbing to all-pervasive social pressures women have allowed themselves to be dominated.

3. Towards the end of this essay, Beauvoir mentions the contrast between being *en-soi* (in-itself) and being *pour-soi* (for-itself). Being for-itself is a mode of existence that is purposive and, as it were, constituted by its own activity; being in-itself, by contrast, is a less fully human kind of existence that is more like being a 'thing'—self-sufficient, non-purposive, and driven by merely contingent current conditions.

How Important and Influential Is This Passage?

The Second Sex is often considered the founding work of twentieth-century feminism. It has been called "one of the most important and far-reaching books on women ever published"[*] and "the best book about women ever written."[†] From the day it was published it was both popular and controversial: 22,000 copies of the first volume were sold in France in the first week, and Beauvoir received large quantities of hate mail, including some from "very active members of the First Sex," and from other women: "How courageous you are.... You're going to lose a lot of friends!" one of her friends wrote to her.[‡] She was accused of writing a pornographic book (because of *The Second Sex*'s discussion of female sexuality), and the Vatican put it on the index of prohibited

books. "Once," Beauvoir reported in her autobiography, "during an entire dinner at Nos Provinces on the Boulevard Montparnasse, a table of people nearby stared at me and giggled; I didn't like dragging [her lover, Nelson] Algren into a scene, but as I left I gave them a piece of my mind."[§] On the other hand, some of the contemporary reviews were glowing: *The New Yorker* called it "more than a work of scholarship; it is a work of art, with the salt of recklessness that makes art sting."[¶]

After the initial furor died down, the book was criticized by scholars and critics as having too much of a middle-class, distorted viewpoint—as having been written by someone who had no cause to actually feel the pressures that give life to feminism. The poet Stevie Smith wrote, in 1953: "She has written an enormous book about women and it is soon clear that she does not like them, nor does she like being a woman."[**] This debate continues today, and arguably it is only recently that *The Second Sex* has come to be appreciated seriously as a work of philosophy that stands on its own merits, rather than read solely in terms of Beauvoir's "biography, relationship with ... Sartre, psyche, or feminist credentials."[††]

Simone de Beauvoir is a pivotal figure in the history of feminist thought from the Renaissance to the twenty-first century. In the Renaissance and early modern period, writers that we would today think of as feminist (such as Christine de Pizan [1365–c. 1430] and Mary Astell [1666–1731]) tended to focus on the social asymmetries between women and men. They argued that women have similar innate abilities to men and should be granted opportunities equivalent to those their male counterparts enjoyed in certain key areas, especially education, the family, and sometimes work and politics. The eighteenth and nineteenth centuries (in work by writers such as Olympe de Gouges [1745–93], Mary Wollstonecraft [1759–97], Sojourner Truth [1797–1883], John Stuart Mill [1806–73], and Harriet Taylor [1807–58]) saw a greater accumulation of forceful writings against the oppression of women, combined with more explicit (but only grad-

---

[*] Terry Keefe, *Simone de Beauvoir: A Study of Her Writings* (Barnes & Noble Books, 1983), 111.

[†] Maureen Freely, *The Guardian*, June 6, 1999.

[‡] From a letter by Claudine Chonez and mentioned by Beauvoir in her autobiography *Force of Circumstances* (1963, translated by Richard Howard and published by Penguin in 1968).

[§] Also from Beauvoir's *Force of Circumstances*.

[¶] From a review by Brendan Gill, February 28, 1953.

[**] From Smith's review of the book published in *The Spectator*, November 20, 1953.

[††] Allison Fell, *Times Literary Supplement*, December 9, 2005.

ually successful) political campaigns to have women's equal status with men enshrined in law. It was at the end of the nineteenth century—in France, during the 1890s—that the term "feminism" first appeared.

Up to this point, feminism can be usefully—albeit simplistically—understood as characterized by a demand for equal rights with men. Once women are educated as extensively as men, are given the opportunity to vote, are not forbidden from joining certain professions, and so on, then it was assumed that their innate capacities—in many (though perhaps not all) respects equal to, or even superior to, those of the male sex—would flourish free from oppression. That is, pre-twentieth-century feminism tended to focus on the suppression and distortion of woman's nature by contingent social structures such as laws and institutions. Beauvoir's writings marked a significant shift and deepening in the nature of feminist thought. She denied that there is an inborn "female nature" that just awaits the opportunity to break free from male oppression, and insisted that women are dominated by men in *all* aspects of their lives—that their very consciousness, the very shape of their minds, is formed by the patriarchal society of which they are a part. Feminism cannot aspire simply to change the laws and institutions of a country; this will leave the subordinate position of women essentially untouched. Feminists must fight for much more thoroughgoing change to the basic practices and assumptions of the whole society.

Later twentieth-century feminism, often known as *second-wave feminism*—representatives of which include Susan Moller Okin (1946–2004), Catharine MacKinnon (b. 1946), Martha Nussbaum (b. 1947), and Iris Young (1949–2006)—took up this emphasis on the deep and subtle nature of patriarchal dominance (though often without a very self-conscious sense of the debt to Beauvoir). The distinction between sex and gender—the notion of gender as a social construct—proved especially significant in making this case. For many feminists, this has evolved into a critique of standards that are taken to have an objective and universal status—such as "rational," "true," and "right"—but which, feminists argue, in fact reflect particular gender interests. Thus, for example, to argue—as Wollstonecraft did—that women are "equally rational" as men is to succumb to, rather than combat, one of the hidden patriarchal structures that oppress women.

The so-called *third-wave* (or sometimes, *postmodern*) feminism that began in the 1980s can also be seen as having roots in the work of Beauvoir. Third-wave feminism emphasizes the claim that gender is a social, contingent, rather than a natural category, and adopts an "anti-essentialist" stance about women: that is, there is nothing that can be usefully said about woman 'as such,' and instead we must focus in an explicitly un-unified way on different conceptions of femininity in particular ethnic, religious, and social groups.

FROM *The Second Sex**

INTRODUCTION

I hesitated a long time before writing a book on woman. The subject is irritating, especially for women; and it is not new. Enough ink has flowed over the quarrel about feminism; it is now almost over: let's not talk about it anymore. Yet it is still being talked about. And the volumes of idiocies churned out over this past century do not seem to have clarified the problem. Besides, is there a problem? And what is it? Are there even women? True, the theory of the eternal feminine still has its followers; they whisper, "Even in Russia,† *women* are still very much women"; but other well-informed people—and also at times those same ones—lament, "Woman is losing herself, woman is lost." It is hard to know any longer if women still exist, if they will always exist, if

---

* *The Second Sex* was first published in French in 1949. This translation, by Constance Borde and Sheila Malovany-Chevallier, is from 2009.

† That is, even after the reorganization of society in Russia after the Communist Revolution of 1917 (and the upheaval of World War II).

there should be women at all, what place they hold in this world, what place they should hold. "Where are the women?" asked a short-lived magazine recently.[1] But first, what is a woman? "*Tota mulier in utero*: she is a womb,"* some say. Yet speaking of certain women, the experts proclaim, "They are not women," even though they have a uterus like the others. Everyone agrees there are females in the human species; today, as in the past, they make up about half of humanity; and yet we are told that "femininity is in jeopardy"; we are urged, "Be women, stay women, become women." So not every female human being is necessarily a woman; she must take part in this mysterious and endangered reality known as femininity. Is femininity secreted by the ovaries? Is it enshrined in a Platonic heaven? Is a frilly petticoat enough to bring it down to earth? Although some women zealously strive to embody it, the model has never been patented. It is typically described in vague and shimmering terms borrowed from a clairvoyant's vocabulary. In Saint Thomas's† time it was an essence defined with as much certainty as the sedative quality of a poppy. But conceptualism has lost ground: biological and social sciences no longer believe there are immutably determined entities that define given characteristics like those of the woman, the Jew, or the black; science considers characteristics as secondary reactions to a *situation*. If there is no such thing today as femininity, it is because there never was. Does the word "woman," then, have no content? It is what advocates of Enlightenment philosophy, rationalism, or nominalism‡ vigorously assert: women are, among human beings, merely those who are arbitrarily designated by the word "woman"; American women in particular are inclined to think that woman as such no longer exists. If some backward individual still takes herself for a woman, her friends advise her to undergo

psychoanalysis to get rid of this obsession. Referring to a book—a very irritating one at that—*Modern Woman: The Lost Sex*,§ Dorothy Parker¶ wrote: "I cannot be fair about books that treat women as women. My idea is that all of us, men as well as women, whoever we are, should be considered as human beings." But nominalism is a doctrine that falls a bit short; and it is easy for antifeminists to show that women *are* not men. Certainly woman like man is a human being; but such an assertion is abstract; the fact is that every concrete human being is always uniquely situated. To reject the notions of the eternal feminine, the black soul, or the Jewish character is not to deny that there are today Jews, blacks, or women: this denial is not a liberation for those concerned but an inauthentic flight. Clearly, no woman can claim without bad faith to be situated beyond her sex. A few years ago, a well-known woman writer refused to have her portrait appear in a series of photographs devoted specifically to women writers. She wanted to be included in the men's category; but to get this privilege, she used her husband's influence. Women who assert they are men still claim masculine consideration and respect. I also remember a young Trotskyite** standing on a platform during a stormy meeting, about to come to blows in spite of her obvious fragility. She was denying her feminine frailty; but it was for the love of a militant man she wanted to be equal to. The defiant position that American women occupy proves they are haunted by the feeling of their own femininity. And the truth is that anyone can clearly see that humanity is split into two categories of individuals with manifestly different clothes, faces, bodies, smiles, movements, interests, and occupations; these differences are perhaps superficial; perhaps they are destined to disappear. What is certain is that for the moment they exist in a strikingly obvious way.

---

* Latin for "The whole woman is in her uterus," or, more snappily, "Woman is a womb." This aphorism dates back to medieval scholastic theology.
† St. Thomas Aquinas (1225–74).
‡ Nominalism is the view that only particular things exist, and 'abstract' things—universals—such as beauty, redness, or species-membership, are not real. Conceptualism (mentioned above) is the view that abstractions do exist as mental concepts.
§ By Ferdinand Lundberg and Marynia F. Farnham, published in 1947. Among other things, this book proposed that laws be adopted prohibiting single women from working, thus forcing them into marriage.
¶ Parker (1893–1967) was an American critic, satirical poet, and short-story writer, famous for her acerbic wit.
** A follower of the brand of Marxism advocated by Leon Trotsky (1879–1940), who advocated permanent global revolution on behalf of the world's workers, and was critical of Joseph Stalin's theory of socialism in one country (Russia).

If the female function is not enough to define woman, and if we also reject the explanation of the "eternal feminine," but if we accept, even temporarily, that there are women on the earth, we then have to ask: What is a woman?

Merely stating the problem suggests an immediate answer to me. It is significant that I pose it. It would never occur to a man to write a book on the singular situation of males in humanity.[2] If I want to define myself, I first have to say, "I am a woman"; all other assertions will arise from this basic truth. A man never begins by positing himself as an individual of a certain sex: that he is a man is obvious. The categories masculine and feminine appear as symmetrical in a formal way on town hall records or identification papers. The relation of the two sexes is not that of two electrical poles: the man represents both the positive and the neuter to such an extent that in French *hommes* designates human beings, the particular meaning of the word *vir* being assimilated into the general meaning of the word "homo." Woman is the negative, to such a point that any determination is imputed to her as a limitation, without reciprocity. I used to get annoyed in abstract discussions to hear men tell me: "You think such and such a thing because you're a woman." But I know my only defense is to answer, "I think it because it is true," thereby eliminating my subjectivity; it was out of the question to answer, "And you think the contrary because you are a man," because it is understood that being a man is not a particularity; a man is in his right by virtue of being man; it is the woman who is in the wrong. In fact, just as for the ancients there was an absolute vertical that defined the oblique, there is an absolute human type that is masculine. Woman has ovaries and a uterus; such are the particular conditions that lock her in her subjectivity; some even say she thinks with her hormones. Man vainly forgets that his anatomy also includes hormones and testicles. He grasps his body as a direct and normal link with the world that he believes he apprehends in all objectivity, whereas he considers woman's body an obstacle, a prison, burdened by everything that particularizes it. "The female is female by virtue of a certain *lack* of qualities," Aristotle said. "We should regard women's nature as suffering from natural defectiveness."[*] And Saint Thomas in his turn decreed that woman was an "incomplete man," an "incidental" being. This is what the Genesis story symbolizes, where Eve appears as if drawn from Adam's "supernumerary" bone, in Bossuet's words.[†] Humanity is male, and man defines woman, not in herself, but in relation to himself; she is not considered an autonomous being. "Woman, the relative being," writes Michelet. Thus Monsieur Benda declares in *Le rapport d'Uriel* (Uriel's Report): "A man's body has meaning by itself, disregarding the body of the woman, whereas the woman's body seems devoid of meaning without reference to the male. Man thinks himself without woman. Woman does not think herself without man."[‡] And she is nothing other than what man decides; she is thus called "the sex," meaning that the male sees her essentially as a sexed being; for him she is sex, so she is it in the absolute. She is determined and differentiated in relation to man, while he is not in relation to her; she is the inessential in front of the essential. He is the Subject; he is the Absolute. She is the Other.[3]

The category of *Other* is as original[§] as consciousness itself. The duality between Self and Other can be found in the most primitive societies, in the most ancient mythologies; this division did not always fall into the category of the division of the sexes, it was not based on any empirical given: this comes out in works like Granet's on Chinese thought, and Dumézil's on India and Rome.[¶] In couples such as Varuna–Mitra,

---

*   *On the Generation of Animals*, Book IV.

†   Jacques-Bénigne Bossuet (1627–1704) was a French bishop famous for his brilliant sermons. Supernumerary means "superfluous," "exceeding the required number."

‡   Jules Michelet (1798–1874) was a French historian. Julien Benda (1867–1956) was a French novelist and critic; *Le rapport d'Uriel* was published in 1946.

§   Dating back to origins.

¶   Marcel Granet (1884–1940) was a French sociologist, and Georges Dumézil (1898–1986) was a philologist and historian of religions.

Uranus–Zeus,* Sun–Moon, Day–Night, no feminine element is involved at the outset; neither in Good–Evil, auspicious and inauspicious, left and right, God and Lucifer; alterity† is the fundamental category of human thought. No group ever defines itself as One without immediately setting up the Other opposite itself. It only takes three travelers brought together by chance in the same train compartment for the rest of the travelers to become vaguely hostile "others." Village people view anyone not belonging to the village as suspicious "others." For the native of a country inhabitants of other countries are viewed as "foreigners"; Jews are the "others" for anti-Semites, blacks for racist Americans, indigenous people for colonists, proletarians for the propertied classes. After studying the diverse forms of primitive society in depth, Lévi-Strauss‡ could conclude: "The passage from the state of Nature to the state of Culture is defined by man's ability to think biological relations as systems of oppositions; duality, alternation, opposition, and symmetry, whether occurring in defined or less clear form, are not so much phenomena to explain as fundamental and immediate givens of social reality."[4] These phenomena could not be understood if human reality were solely a *Mitsein*§ based on solidarity and friendship. On the contrary, they become clear if, following Hegel, a fundamental hostility to any other consciousness is found in consciousness itself; the subject posits itself only in opposition; it asserts itself as the essential and sets up the other as inessential, as the object.

But the other consciousness has an opposing reciprocal claim: traveling, a local is shocked to realize that in neighboring countries locals view him as a foreigner; between villages, clans, nations, and classes there are wars, potlatches, agreements, treaties, and struggles that remove the absolute meaning from the idea of the *Other* and bring out its relativity; whether one likes it or not, individuals and groups have no choice but to recognize the reciprocity of their relation. How is it, then, that between the sexes this reciprocity has not been put forward, that one of the terms has been asserted as the only essential one, denying any relativity in regard to its correlative, defining the latter as pure alterity? Why do women not contest male sovereignty? No subject posits itself spontaneously and at once as the inessential from the outset; it is not the Other who, defining itself as Other, defines the One; the Other is posited as Other by the One positing itself as One. But in order for the Other not to turn into the One, the Other has to submit to this foreign point of view. Where does this submission in woman come from?

There are other cases where, for a shorter or longer time, one category has managed to dominate another absolutely. It is often numerical inequality that confers this privilege: the majority imposes its law on or persecutes the minority. But women are not a minority like American blacks, or like Jews: there are as many women as men on the earth. Often, the two opposing groups concerned were once independent of each other; either they were not aware of each other in the past, or they accepted each other's autonomy; and some historical event subordinated the weaker to the stronger: the Jewish Diaspora, slavery in America, and the colonial conquests are facts with dates. In these cases, for the oppressed there was a *before*: they share a past, a tradition, sometimes a religion, or a culture. In this sense, the parallel Bebel¶ draws between

---

*   Varuna and Mitra are Hindu gods (both concerned with upholding law and order), and Uranus and Zeus were Greek gods. One of Dumézil's classic books is *Mitra-Varuna: An Essay on Two Indo-European Representations of Sovereignty* (1948).

†   Alterity is the state of being different, especially lack of identification with some part of one's personality or community. It has come to be a technical, philosophical term for the principle of exchanging one's own perspective for that of the Other.

‡   Claude Lévi-Strauss (1908–2009) was a French anthropologist, famous for developing structuralism as a method of understanding human society and culture (e.g., the structures of kinship systems).

§   A Hegelian term, literally meaning "being with."

¶   August Bebel (1840–1913) was a German Marxist revolutionary. In *Woman and Socialism*, first published in 1879, he argued that the social emancipation of women was a crucial precursor to the overthrow of capitalism. In Marxist theory the proletariat is the lower class of society that does not have ownership of the means of production and must instead work for wages.

women and the proletariat would be the best founded: proletarians are not a numerical minority either, and yet they have never formed a separate group. However, not *one* event but a whole historical development explains their existence as a class and accounts for the distribution of *these* individuals in this class. There have not always been proletarians: there have always been women; they are women by their physiological structure; as far back as history can be traced, they have always been subordinate to men; their dependence is not the consequence of an event or a becoming, it did not *happen*. Alterity here appears to be an absolute, partly because it falls outside the accidental nature of historical fact. A situation created over time can come undone at another time—blacks in Haiti for one are a good example; on the contrary, a natural condition seems to defy change. In truth, nature is no more an immutable given than is historical reality. If woman discovers herself as the inessential and never turns into the essential, it is because she does not bring about this transformation herself. Proletarians say "we." So do blacks. Positing themselves as subjects, they thus transform the bourgeois or whites into "others." Women—except in certain abstract gatherings such as conferences—do not use "we"; men say "women," and women adopt this word to refer to themselves; but they do not posit themselves authentically as Subjects. The proletarians made the revolution in Russia, the blacks in Haiti, the Indo-Chinese are fighting in Indochina.* Women's actions have never been more than symbolic agitation; they have won only what men have been willing to concede to them; they have taken nothing; they have received.[5] It is that

they lack the concrete means to organize themselves into a unit that could posit itself in opposition. They have no past, no history, no religion of their own; and unlike the proletariat, they have no solidarity of labor or interests; they even lack their own space that makes communities of American blacks, the Jews in ghettos, or the workers in Saint-Denis† or Renault‡ factories. They live dispersed among men, tied by homes, work, economic interests, and social conditions to certain men—fathers or husbands—more closely than to other women. As bourgeois women, they are in solidarity with bourgeois men and not with women proletarians; as white women, they are in solidarity with white men and not with black women. The proletariat could plan to massacre the whole ruling class; a fanatic Jew or black could dream of seizing the secret of the atomic bomb and turning all of humanity entirely Jewish or entirely black: but a woman could not even dream of exterminating males. The tie that binds her to her oppressors is unlike any other. The division of the sexes is a biological given, not a moment in human history. Their opposition took shape within an original *Mitsein*, and she has not broken it. The couple is a fundamental unit with the two halves riveted to each other: cleavage of society by sex is not possible. This is the fundamental characteristic of woman: she is the Other at the heart of a whole whose two components are necessary to each other.

One might think that this reciprocity would have facilitated her liberation; when Hercules spins wool at Omphale's§ feet, his desire enchains him. Why was Omphale unable to acquire long-lasting power? Medea, in revenge against Jason, kills her children:¶

---

* The Communist Revolution took place in Russia in 1917. The Haitian Revolution was a slave revolt which broke out in 1791 and ended in 1804 with the former French colony's independence. The First Indochina War lasted from 1945 until 1954 and pushed the French out of their colonies in what are now Vietnam, Laos, and Cambodia. (The Second Indochina War began in 1955 and lasted until 1975, and was known in the West as the Vietnam War.)

† Saint-Denis is a region including the northern suburbs of Paris and has been the scene of several significant worker uprisings and strikes, including the revolt of 1848 (and others as recently as 2003). Saint-Ouen, in Saint-Denis, was one of the first cities where a factory worker was elected mayor.

‡ A French automobile manufacturer.

§ A queen of Lydia, an ancient kingdom in the region that is today Turkey, who is said to have owned Hercules as her slave for three years. (Hercules was being punished for the murder of his friend Iphitus. The story goes that while he was enslaved he became so weak that he wore women's clothes and did 'women's work,' while the queen wore his lion skin and carried his club.)

¶ Medea was a powerful sorceress, the daughter of King Aeëtes of Colchis (at the eastern end of the Black Sea), and the granddaughter of Helios, the sun god. When Jason and the crew of the Argo arrived at Colchis seeking the Golden

this brutal legend suggests that the bond attaching the woman to her child could have given her a formidable upper hand. In *Lysistrata*,* Aristophanes lightheartedly imagined a group of women who, uniting together for the social good, tried to take advantage of men's need for them: but it is only a comedy. The legend that claims that the ravished Sabine women resisted their ravishers with obstinate sterility also recounts that by whipping them with leather straps, the men magically won them over into submission.† Biological need—sexual desire and desire for posterity—which makes the male dependent on the female, has not liberated women socially. Master and slave are also linked by a reciprocal economic need that does not free the slave. That is, in the master-slave relation, the master does not *posit* the need he has for the other; he holds the power to satisfy this need and does not mediate it; the slave, on the other hand, out of dependence, hope, or fear, internalizes his need for the master; however equally compelling the need may be to them both, it always plays in favor of the oppressor over the oppressed: this explains the slow pace of working-class liberation, for example. Now, woman has always been, if not man's slave, at least his vassal; the two sexes have never divided the world up equally; and still today, even though her condition is changing, woman is heavily handicapped. In no country is her legal status identical to man's, and often it puts her at a considerable disadvantage. Even when her rights are recognized abstractly, long-standing habit keeps them from being concretely manifested in customs. Economically, men and women almost form two castes; all things being equal, the former

have better jobs, higher wages, and greater chances to succeed than their new female competitors; they occupy many more places in industry, in politics, and so forth, and they hold the most important positions. In addition to their concrete power, they are invested with a prestige whose tradition is reinforced by the child's whole education: the present incorporates the past, and in the past all history was made by males. At the moment that women are beginning to share in the making of the world, this world still belongs to men: men have no doubt about this, and women barely doubt it. Refusing to be the Other, refusing complicity with man, would mean renouncing all the advantages an alliance with the superior caste confers on them. Lord-man will materially protect liegewoman and will be in charge of justifying her existence: along with the economic risk, she eludes the metaphysical risk of a freedom that must invent its goals without help. Indeed, beside every individual's claim to assert himself as subject—an ethical claim—lies the temptation to flee freedom and to make himself into a thing: it is a pernicious path because the individual, passive, alienated, and lost, is prey to a foreign will, cut off from his transcendence, robbed of all worth. But it is an easy path: the anguish and stress of authentically assumed existence are thus avoided. The man who sets the woman up as an *Other* will thus find in her a deep complicity. Hence woman makes no claim for herself as subject because she lacks the concrete means, because she senses the necessary link connecting her to man without positing its reciprocity, and because she often derives satisfaction from her role as *Other*.

Fleece, Medea fell in love with Jason and used her magic to help him, in return for Jason's promise to marry her. When Jason later deserted her and married the daughter of Creon, the king of Corinth, Medea took her revenge by killing the new bride with a poisoned robe and crown which burned the flesh from her body (and killed King Creon as well when he tried to embrace his dying daughter), and also by murdering the two children she had with Jason.

* A play, written in about 411 BCE, in which the women of Hellas (ancient Greece) agree to withhold sex from their men folk until they agree to end the long-running war between Athens and Sparta.

† At the beginning of Roman history, according to myth, the newly founded city of Rome needed to increase its population quickly in order to defend itself against its neighbors, but it did not have enough women to sustain its numbers. The Romans therefore invited the neighboring community of the Sabines to a religious celebration in honor of Neptune, and during the party the younger Roman men kidnapped the Sabine women and raped them. The Sabines—some months later!—returned with an army to bring back their women by force, but discovered (according to legend) that their erstwhile wives and daughters had reconciled with their new Roman husbands, and borne their children. The women stopped the battle before it started by placing themselves between the two armies; the Romans and the Sabines made peace, and Rome continued to grow.

But a question immediately arises: How did this whole story begin? It is understandable that the duality of the sexes, like all duality, be expressed in conflict. It is understandable that if one of the two succeeded in imposing its superiority, it had to establish itself as absolute. It remains to be explained how it was that man won at the outset. It seems possible that women might have carried off the victory, or that the battle might never be resolved. Why is it that this world has always belonged to men and that only today things are beginning to change? Is this change a good thing? Will it bring about an equal sharing of the world between men and women or not?

These questions are far from new; they have already had many answers; but the very fact that woman is *Other* challenges all the justifications that men have ever given: these were only too clearly dictated by their own interest. "Everything that men have written about women should be viewed with suspicion, because they are both judge and party," wrote Poulain de la Barre,* a little-known seventeenth-century feminist. Males have always and everywhere paraded their satisfaction of feeling they are kings of creation. "Blessed be the Lord our God, and the Lord of all worlds that has not made me a woman," Jews say in their morning prayers; meanwhile, their wives resignedly murmur: "Blessed be the Lord for creating me according to his will." Among the blessings Plato thanked the gods for was, first, being born free and not a slave and, second, a man and not a woman. But males could not have enjoyed this privilege so fully had they not considered it as founded in the absolute and in eternity: they sought to make the fact of their supremacy a right. "Those who made and compiled the laws, being men, favored their own sex, and the jurisconsults† have turned the laws into principles," Poulain de la Barre continues. Lawmakers, priests, philosophers, writers, and scholars have gone to great lengths to prove that women's subordinate condition was willed in heaven and profitable on earth. Religions forged by men reflect this will for domination: they found ammunition in the legends of Eve and Pandora. They have put philosophy and theology in their service, as seen in the previously cited words of Aristotle and Saint Thomas. Since ancient times, satirists and moralists have delighted in depicting women's weaknesses. The violent indictments brought against them all through French literature are well-known: Montherlant, with less verve, picks up the tradition from Jean de Meung.‡ This hostility seems sometimes founded but is often gratuitous; in truth, it covers up a more or less skillfully camouflaged will to self-justification. "It is much easier to accuse one sex than to excuse the other," says Montaigne.§ In certain cases, the process is transparent. It is striking, for example, that the Roman code limiting a wife's rights invokes "the imbecility and fragility of the sex" just when a weakening family structure makes her a threat to male heirs. It is striking that in the sixteenth century, to keep a married woman under wardship, the authority of Saint Augustine¶ affirming "the wife is an animal neither reliable nor stable" is called on, whereas the unmarried woman is recognized as capable of managing her own affairs. Montaigne well understood the arbitrariness and injustice of the lot assigned to women: "Women are not wrong at all when they reject

---

* François Poulain de la Barre, a French Catholic village priest, published three pamphlets urging the equality of the sexes, including "De l'égalité des deux sexes" (1671) from which this quote is taken.

† One learned in law.

‡ Henri de Montherlant (1896–1972) was a French writer, soldier, athlete, and bullfighter whose novels glorify force and masculinity. Jean de Meung (c. 1240–c. 1305) was a French poet and alchemist known for his continuation of the *Roman de la rose* (*Romance of the Rose*), an allegorical poem in the courtly love tradition begun by Guillaume de Lorris in about 1230. His section of the poem is particularly noted for its controversial digressions on a variety of topics, including a quatrain vilifying womankind. (For this offense, it is said, he was cornered by the ladies of the court of Charles VI who tried to have him stripped naked and whipped; only his impish eloquence allowed him to escape.)

§ Michel de Montaigne (1533–92) was a French courtier and the author of *Essais*, which established, as a new literary form, the essay (a short piece dealing with the author's personal thoughts about a particular subject).

¶ St. Augustine of Hippo (354–430), a "church father" whose writings (and political victories) were extremely influential on the future doctrine of the Church. (Not St. Augustine of Canterbury (d. 604), considered the originator of the Christian Church in Britain.)

the rules of life that have been introduced into the world, inasmuch as it is the men who have made these without them. There is a natural plotting and scheming between them and us." But he does not go so far as to champion their cause. It is only in the eighteenth century that deeply democratic men begin to consider the issue objectively. Diderot,* for one, tries to prove that, like man, woman is a human being. A bit later, John Stuart Mill ardently defends women. But these philosophers are exceptional in their impartiality. In the nineteenth century the feminist quarrel once again becomes a partisan quarrel; one of the consequences of the Industrial Revolution is that women enter the labor force: at that point, women's demands leave the realm of the theoretical and find economic grounds; their adversaries become all the more aggressive; even though landed property is partially discredited, the bourgeoisie clings to the old values where family solidity guarantees private property: it insists all the more fiercely that woman's place be in the home as her emancipation becomes a real threat; even within the working class, men tried to thwart women's liberation because women were becoming dangerous competitors—especially as women were used to working for low salaries.[6] To prove women's inferiority, antifeminists began to draw not only, as before, on religion, philosophy, and theology but also on science: biology, experimental psychology, and so forth. At most they were willing to grant "separate but equal status" to the *other* sex.[7] That winning formula is most significant: it is exactly that formula the Jim Crow laws[†] put into practice with regard to black Americans; this so-called egalitarian segregation served only to introduce the most extreme forms of discrimination. This convergence is in no way pure chance: whether it is race, caste, class, or sex reduced to an inferior condition, the justification process is the same. "The

eternal feminine" corresponds to "the black soul" or "the Jewish character." However, the Jewish problem on the whole is very different from the two others: for the anti-Semite, the Jew is more an enemy than an inferior, and no place on this earth is recognized as his own; it would be preferable to see him annihilated. But there are deep analogies between the situations of women and blacks: both are liberated today from the same paternalism, and the former master caste wants to keep them "in their place," that is, the place chosen for them; in both cases, they praise, more or less sincerely, the virtues of the "good black," the carefree, childlike, merry soul of the resigned black, and the woman who is a "true woman"—frivolous, infantile, irresponsible, the woman subjugated to man. In both cases, the ruling caste bases its argument on the state of affairs it created itself. The familiar line from George Bernard Shaw[‡] sums it up: The white American relegates the black to the rank of shoe-shine boy, and then concludes that blacks are only good for shining shoes. The same vicious circle can be found in all analogous circumstances: when an individual or a group of individuals is kept in a situation of inferiority, the fact is that he or they *are* inferior. But the scope of the verb *to be* must be understood; bad faith means giving it a substantive value, when in fact it has the sense of the Hegelian dynamic: *to be* is to have become, to have been made as one manifests oneself. Yes, women in general *are* today inferior to men; that is, their situation provides them with fewer possibilities: the question is whether this state of affairs must be perpetuated.

Many men wish it would be: not all men have yet laid down their arms. The conservative bourgeoisie continues to view women's liberation as a danger threatening their morality and their interests. Some men feel threatened by women's competition. In

---

* Denis Diderot (1713–84) was a French philosopher best known as the chief editor of *Encyclopédie*. Arguably the supreme literary creation of the Age of Enlightenment, *Encyclopédie* attempted to present all the achievements of human learning in a single (28-volume) work.

† From the 1880s until, in many cases, the 1960s, more than half of the US states passed "Jim Crow" laws (so-called after a black character in minstrel shows) to enforce segregation, imposing legal punishments on people for consorting with members of another race. For example, business owners and public institutions were often ordered to keep their black and white clientele separated.

‡ Shaw (1856–1950) was an Irish playwright and critic, awarded the Nobel Prize in Literature in 1925. In addition to his plays, he is also the author of *The Intelligent Woman's Guide to Socialism and Capitalism* (1928).

*Hebdo-Latin** the other day, a student declared: "Every woman student who takes a position as a doctor or lawyer is *stealing* a place from us." That student never questioned his rights over this world. Economic interests are not the only ones in play. One of the benefits that oppression secures for the oppressor is that the humblest among them *feels superior*: in the United States a "poor white" from the South can console himself for not being a "dirty nigger"; and more prosperous whites cleverly exploit this pride. Likewise, the most mediocre of males believes himself a demigod next to women. It was easier for M. de Montherlant to think himself a hero in front of women (handpicked, by the way) than to act the man among men, a role that many women assumed better than he did. Thus, in one of his articles in *Le Figaro Littéraire* in September 1948, M. Claude Mauriac†—whom everyone admires for his powerful originality—could[8] write about women: "*We* listen in a tone [*sic*] of polite indifference ... to the most brilliant one among them, knowing that her intelligence, in a more or less dazzling way, reflects ideas that come from *us*." Clearly his female interlocutor does not reflect M. Mauriac's own ideas, since he is known not to have any; that she reflects ideas originating with men is possible: among males themselves, more than one of them takes as his own opinions he did not invent; one might wonder if it would not be in M. Claude Mauriac's interest to converse with a good reflection of Descartes, Marx, or Gide‡ rather than with himself; what is remarkable is that with the ambiguous "we," he identifies with Saint Paul, Hegel, Lenin, and Nietzsche, and from their heights he looks down on the herd of women who dare to speak to him on an equal footing; frankly, I know of more than one woman who would not put up with M. Mauriac's "tone of polite indifference."

I have stressed this example because of its disarming masculine naïveté. Men profit in many other more subtle ways from woman's alterity. For all those suffering from an inferiority complex, this is a miraculous liniment; no one is more arrogant toward women, more aggressive or more disdainful, than a man anxious about his own virility. Those who are not threatened by their fellow men are far more likely to recognize woman as a counterpart; but even for them the myth of the Woman, of the Other, remains precious for many reasons;[9] they can hardly be blamed for not wanting to lightheartedly sacrifice all the benefits they derive from the myth: they know what they lose by relinquishing the woman of their dreams, but they do not know what the woman of tomorrow will bring them. It takes great abnegation to refuse to posit oneself as unique and absolute Subject. Besides, the vast majority of men do not explicitly make this position their own. They do not *posit* woman as inferior: they are too imbued today with the democratic ideal not to recognize all human beings as equals. Within the family, the male child and then the young man sees the woman as having the same social dignity as the adult male; afterward, he experiences in desire and love the resistance and independence of the desired and loved woman; married, he respects in his wife the spouse and the mother, and in the concrete experience of married life she affirms herself opposite him as a freedom. He can thus convince himself that there is no longer a social hierarchy between the sexes and that on the whole, in spite of their differences, woman is an equal. As he nevertheless recognizes some points of inferiority—professional incapacity being the predominant one—he attributes them to nature. When he has an attitude of benevolence and partnership toward a woman, he applies the principle of abstract equality; and he does not *posit* the concrete inequality he recognizes. But as soon as he clashes with her, the situation is reversed. He will apply the concrete inequality theme and will even allow himself to disavow abstract equality.[10] This is how many men affirm, with quasi good faith, that women *are* equal to men and have no demands to make, and *at the same time* that women will never be equal to men and that their demands are in vain. It is difficult for men to measure the enormous extent of social discrimination that seems insignificant from the outside and whose moral and intellectual

* Like *Franchise*, another ephemeral magazine of the era.

† Claude Mauriac (1914–96) was a French journalist, critic, and avant-garde novelist. Several of his experimental novels (published in the late 1950s and early 1960s) focus on the exploits of a cold-hearted, womanizing egoist named Bertrand Carnéjoux. *Figaro littéraire* is the literary supplement of the French daily newspaper *Le Figaro* (founded 1826).

‡ André Gide (1869–1951), a French novelist, intellectual, literary critic, and social crusader (for, especially, homosexual rights). He received the Nobel Prize for Literature in 1947.

repercussions are so deep in woman that they appear to spring from an original nature.[11] The man most sympathetic to women never knows her concrete situation fully. So there is no good reason to believe men when they try to defend privileges whose scope they cannot even fathom. We will not let ourselves be intimidated by the number and violence of attacks against women; nor be fooled by the self-serving praise showered on the "real woman"; nor be won over by men's enthusiasm for her destiny, a destiny they would not for the world want to share.

We must not, however, be any less mistrustful of feminists' arguments: very often their attempt to polemicize robs them of all value. If the "question of women" is so trivial, it is because masculine arrogance turned it into a "quarrel"; when people quarrel, they no longer reason well. What people have endlessly sought to prove is that woman is superior, inferior, or equal to man: created after Adam, she is obviously a secondary being, some say; on the contrary, say others, Adam was only a rough draft, and God perfected the human being when he created Eve; her brain is smaller, but relatively bigger; Christ was made man, but perhaps out of humility. Every argument has its opposite, and both are often misleading. To see clearly, one needs to get out of these ruts; these vague notions of superiority, inferiority, and equality that have distorted all discussions must be discarded in order to start anew.

But how, then, will we ask the question? And in the first place, who are we to ask it? Men are judge and party: so are women. Can an angel be found? In fact, an angel would be ill qualified to speak, would not understand all the givens of the problem; as for the hermaphrodite, it is a case of its own: it is not both a man and a woman, but neither man nor woman. I think certain women are still best suited to elucidate the situation of women. It is a sophism to claim that Epimenides should be enclosed within the concept of Cretan and all Cretans within the concept of liar:* it is not a mysterious essence that dictates good or bad faith to men and women; it is their situation that disposes them to seek the truth to a greater or lesser extent. Many women today, fortunate to have had all the privileges of the human being restored to them, can afford the luxury of impartiality: we even feel the necessity of it. We are no longer like our militant predecessors; we have more or less won the game; in the latest discussions on women's status, the UN has not ceased to imperiously demand equality of the sexes, and indeed many of us have never felt our femaleness to be a difficulty or an obstacle; many other problems seem more essential than those that concern us uniquely: this very detachment makes it possible to hope our attitude will be objective. Yet we know the feminine world more intimately than men do because our roots are in it; we grasp more immediately what the fact of being female means for a human being, and we care more about knowing it. I said that there are more essential problems; but this one still has a certain importance from our point of view: How will the fact of being women have affected our lives? What precise opportunities have been given us, and which ones have been denied? What destiny awaits our younger sisters, and in which direction should we point them? It is striking that most feminine literature is driven today by an attempt at lucidity more than by a will to make demands; coming out of an era of muddled controversy, this book is one attempt among others to take stock of the current state.

But it is no doubt impossible to approach any human problem without partiality: even the way of asking the questions, of adopting perspectives, presupposes hierarchies of interests; all characteristics comprise values; every so-called objective description is set against an ethical background. Instead of trying to conceal those principles that are more or less explicitly implied, we would be better off stating them from the start; then it would not be necessary to specify on each page the meaning given to the words "superior," "inferior," "better," "worse," "progress," "regression," and so on. If we examine some of the books on women, we see that one of the most frequently held points of view is that of public good or general interest: in reality, this is taken to mean the interest of society as each one wishes to maintain or establish it. In our opinion, there is no public good other than one that assures the citizens' private good; we judge institutions from the point of view

---

*   The Cretan philosopher Epimenides of Knossos (who lived around 600 BCE) invented a famous logical paradox by asserting, "Cretans, always liars." That is, since Epimenides himself was a Cretan, if this sentence is true then it must be false; a bit less obviously, if it is false then (arguably) it is true since it says of itself that it is false, which is true.

of the concrete opportunities they give to individuals. But neither do we confuse the idea of private interest with happiness: that is another frequently encountered point of view; are women in a harem* not happier than a woman voter? Is a housewife not happier than a woman worker? We cannot really know what the word "happiness" means, and still less what authentic values it covers; there is no way to measure the happiness of others, and it is always easy to call a situation that one would like to impose on others happy: in particular, we declare happy those condemned to stagnation, under the pretext that happiness is immobility. This is a notion, then, we will not refer to. The perspective we have adopted is one of existentialist morality. Every subject posits itself as a transcendence concretely, through projects; it accomplishes its freedom only by perpetual surpassing toward other freedoms; there is no other justification for present existence than its expansion toward an indefinitely open future. Every time transcendence lapses into immanence, there is degradation of existence into "in-itself," of freedom into facticity; this fall is a moral fault if the subject consents to it; if this fall is inflicted on the subject, it takes the form of frustration and oppression; in both cases it is an absolute evil. Every individual concerned with justifying his existence experiences his existence as an indefinite need to transcend himself. But what singularly defines the situation of woman is that being, like all humans, an autonomous freedom, she discovers and chooses herself in a world where men force her to assume herself as Other: an attempt is made to freeze her as an object and doom her to immanence, since her transcendence will be forever transcended by another essential and sovereign consciousness. Woman's drama lies in this conflict between the fundamental claim of every subject, which always posits itself as essential, and the demands of a situation that constitutes her as inessential. How, in the feminine condition, can a human being accomplish herself? What paths are open to her? Which ones lead to dead ends? How can she find independence within dependence? What circumstances limit women's freedom and can she overcome them? These are the fundamental questions we would like to elucidate. This means that in focusing on the individual's possibilities, we will define these possibilities not in terms of happiness but in terms of freedom.

Clearly this problem would have no meaning if we thought that a physiological, psychological, or economic destiny weighed on woman. So we will begin by discussing woman from a biological, psychoanalytical, and historical materialist point of view. We will then attempt to positively demonstrate how "feminine reality" has been constituted, why woman has been defined as Other, and what the consequences have been from men's point of view. Then we will describe the world from the woman's point of view such as it is offered to her,[12] and we will see the difficulties women are up against just when, trying to escape the sphere they have been assigned until now, they seek to be part of the human *Mitsein*. ■

Suggestions for Critical Reflection

1. Beauvoir begins her book by asking "what is a woman?" How do you think she answers this question?

2. Beauvoir claims that the terms *masculine* and *feminine* are not symmetrical opposites. What do you make of this claim? How does Beauvoir develop it? What is its importance?

3. "[A]s far back as history can be traced, [women] have always been subordinate to men; their dependence is not a consequence of an event or a becoming, it did not *happen*." Does this claim seem plausible? How important is it to Beauvoir's argument?

4. Beauvoir suggests that for women to renounce their status as an Other would be to abandon "all the advantages an alliance with the superior caste confers on them." What does she mean by this? Is she right? How serious a difficulty is this for feminism?

---

* The private part of an Arab household, traditionally forbidden to male strangers.

5. Beauvoir writes that "there are deep analogies between the situations of women and blacks," and goes on to explain this claim. What do you think of this analogy?

6. "[T]he ruling caste bases its argument on the state of affairs it created itself." Does this ring true? How important is it for the social activist, including the feminist, to notice this? How much does this explain the behavior towards women by even well-intentioned men?

7. "We are no longer like our militant predecessors; we have more or less won the game." Is Beauvoir right about this? Is this claim consistent with her general theory of the oppression of women in society?

8. "One is not born, but rather becomes, a woman." Some commentators have argued that, in making this central claim, Beauvoir herself falls victim to the patriarchal mindset she is criticizing—that she is tacitly assuming that "femaleness is indeed optional and subhuman, and maleness the slipped-from standard."* Does this criticism strike you as plausible? Does it suggest a fundamental problem with Beauvoir's project, or with the way she carries it out?

Notes

1 Out of print today, titled *Franchise*.

2 The Kinsey Report [Alfred C. Kinsey and others: *Sexual Behavior in the Human Male*. (W.B. Saunders Co., 1948)], for example, confines itself to defining the sexual characteristics of the American man, which is completely different.

3 This idea has been expressed in its most explicit form by E. Levinas in his essay *Le temps et l'autre* (*Time and the Other*). He expresses it like this: "Is there not a situation where alterity would be borne by a being in a positive sense, as essence? What is the alterity that does not purely and simply enter into the opposition of two species of the same genus? I think that the absolutely contrary contrary, whose contrariety is in no way affected by the relationship that can be established between it and its correlative, the contrariety that permits its terms to remain absolutely other, is the feminine. Sex is not some specific difference ... Neither is the difference between the sexes a contradiction ... Neither is the difference between the sexes the duality of two complementary terms, for two complementary terms presuppose a preexisting whole ... [A]lterity is accomplished in the feminine. The term is on the same level as, but in meaning opposed to, consciousness." I suppose Mr. Levinas is not forgetting that woman also is consciousness for herself. But it is striking that he deliberately adopts a man's point of view, disregarding the reciprocity of the subject and the object. When he writes that woman is mystery, he assumes that she is mystery for man. So this apparently objective description is in fact an affirmation of masculine privilege.

4 See Claude Lévi-Strauss, *Les structures élémentaires de la parenté* (*The Elementary Structures of Kinship*). I thank Claude Lévi-Strauss for sharing the proofs of his thesis, which I drew on heavily, particularly in the second part, pp. 76–89.

5 See second part, page 126.

6 See Part Two, pp. 135–136.

7 "*L'égalité dans la différence*" in the French text. Literal translation: "different but equal."—TRANS.

8 At least he thought he could.

9 The article by Michel Carrouges on this theme in *Cahiers du Sud*, no. 292, is significant. He writes with indignation: "If only there were no feminine myth but only bands of cooks, matrons, prostitutes, and bluestockings with functions of pleasure or utility!" So, according to him, woman has no existence for herself; he only takes into account her *function* in the male world. Her finality is in man; in fact, it is possible to prefer her poetic "function" to all others. The exact question is why she should be defined in relation to the man.

10 For example, man declares that he does not find his wife in any way diminished just because she does not have a profession: work in the home is just as noble and so on. Yet at the first argument he remonstrates, "You wouldn't be able to earn a living without me."

11 Describing this very process will be the object of Volume II of this study.

12 This will be the subject of a second volume.

---

* From Jane O'Grady, writing in the *Oxford Companion to Philosophy* (1995), 179; O'Grady is not making this claim herself, but only describing it.

TALIA MAE BETTCHER

Trans Women and the Meaning of "Woman"

Who Is Talia Mae Bettcher?

Born in Canada in 1966, Talia Mae Bettcher holds a PhD from UCLA and is Professor and Chair of Philosophy at California State University, Los Angeles, where for several years she served as Director of the Center for the Study of Genders and Sexualities. In recent decades, Bettcher's philosophical work has focused primarily on transgender and gender issues; much of this work, she says, is informed by her own experience as a trans woman and her involvement in trans subculture in Los Angeles. In addition to publishing numerous articles that combine philosophy and trans studies, she explores similar questions in works of performance art. Bettcher was a founding editor of the ground-breaking interdisciplinary journal *Transgender Studies Quarterly* and she co-edited a special issue of the feminist philosophy journal *Hypatia* titled *Transgender Studies and Feminism: Theory, Politics, and Gender Realities* (2009). She has also written two books on the eighteenth-century philosopher George Berkeley: *Berkeley's Philosophy of Spirit: Consciousness, Ontology and the Elusive Subject* (2007) and *Berkeley: A Guide for the Perplexed* (2009).

What Is the Structure of This Reading?

Bettcher opens this article by summarizing the two dominant views that are often used to make sense of trans people's lives: the "Wrong Body Model" and the "Transgender Model." In the course of the article, she argues that both of these models are flawed in multiple ways, and she proposes a new model intended to avoid the pitfalls she has identified.

The first major flaw Bettcher describes is that proponents of both the Wrong Body Model and the Transgender Model adopt what she refers to as a "single-meaning position": they presume, for example, that "woman" has a single definition and argue that this definition should include trans women. Bettcher outlines several variations on the single-meaning position, including definitions that

describe womanhood according to specific biological markers—an approach that falls apart in practice, given the biological variety of human beings. She also discusses definitions that use a "family resemblance" approach in which a person fits into the category of "woman" by possessing a critical number of features of that category. Bettcher argues that even the family resemblance approach is inadequate, since at best it allows that a trans woman is merely "a marginal instance" of womanhood—and at worst it leaves the gender status of trans women more open to questioning if they possess fewer physical features of paradigmatic womanhood.

Bettcher goes on to introduce "semantic contextualism," an alternative to the single-meaning position. According to this approach, the meaning of "woman" changes according to context—which can mean that, in some contexts at least, self-identification is enough to determine that an individual is a woman. But semantic contextualism also has a serious flaw: if it allows for the possibility that trans women are women in some contexts, it also allows for the possibility that trans women are men in other contexts. Which definitions apply in which situations becomes a question of political debate, so that once again trans women must defend their womanhood while the womanhood of non-trans women is taken for granted.

The alternative Bettcher offers is what she calls a "multiple-meaning position." According to this view, the term "trans woman" has a different meaning in dominant culture from the meaning it has in trans subculture—and in trans subculture, if one is a trans woman, one is necessarily a woman. Acknowledging that the terms "woman" and "trans woman" have multiple meanings allows us to assert that trans subculture's understanding of womanhood should be accepted while also leaving room to observe that a dominant definition of womanhood exists, and to critique it.

This leads Bettcher to identify a major problem with both the "Wrong Body Model" and the "Transgender Model": both attempt to describe trans lives in terms of the gender definitions that have already been established by dominant culture. We must start from the ways trans people define gender, she argues, if we are to reach a model that will better help us to understand and resist the oppression of trans people.

Some Useful Background Information

1. Because the question Bettcher discusses underlies the relationship between transfeminism and other forms of feminism, it is worth noting that, while many feminists seek intersections between feminist and trans theory, strongly anti-trans views have also been articulated within feminist thought. Some feminists have argued that trans men are misogynist in their rejection of femininity[*] or that trans women should not be recognized as women in contexts where doing so would interfere with the achievement of feminist objectives.[†] Others have made such overtly transphobic claims as the assertion that trans women appropriate and objectify the female body in a way that is tantamount to rape.[‡] Controversy regarding the relationship between trans and feminist politics was particularly intense in the 1970s, and it continues in the twenty-first century. Is it also worth noting that trans studies as an independent discipline is relatively new; it emerged in the 1990s.

2. A major line of philosophical exploration in trans studies concerns the nature of gender (generally understood as role or identity) and its relationship to sex (generally understood as physical or biological—though the definition of the terms is also part of the inquiry). Bettcher's argument alludes to the idea that gender is socially constructed—an idea that is very important in some feminist theory and is also held by some trans theorists. The nuances of this position are different for different thinkers, but, broadly speaking, advocates of this position hold that gender is produced by culture (rather than gendered characteristics being something we innately possess by virtue of our biology), and that rather than inherently *being* or *possessing* a gender, we *enact* a gender by performing its role over time according to social norms. Some go so far as to say that even physical sex is culturally constructed in the sense that we can only represent or talk about the body in the gendered language offered by our culture; sex is thus really a part of gender. On the other hand, some thinkers—both in feminist and in trans theory—reject the constructionist view entirely.

Trans Women and the Meaning of "Woman"[§]

There is a familiar view of transsexuality that speaks of women trapped inside male bodies and men trapped inside female bodies. On this view—let's call it the "Wrong Body Model"—transsexuality is a misalignment between gender identity and sexed body. At its most extreme, the idea is that one's real sex, given by internal identity, is innate. It is on the basis of this identity that one affirms that one has always really belonged to a particular sex and has a claim to the surgical procedures that bring one's body into alignment with one's identity.[1] However, one of the problems with this account is that it naturalizes sex and gender differences in a troubling way. Christine Overall remarks, for example, "On this theory, gender is

---

[*] Jack (publishing as Judith) Halberstam discusses examples of this in "Transgender Butch: Butch/FTM Border Wars and the Masculine Continuum," *GLQ: A Journal of Lesbian and Gay Studies* 4, 2 (1998): 287–310.

[†] See, for example, Kathleen Stock, "Academic Philosophy and the UK Gender Recognition Act," *Medium* (7 May 2018).

[‡] See, for example, Janice Raymond's influential work *The Transsexual Empire: The Making of the She-Male* (Boston: Beacon Press, 1979).

[§] Talia Mae Bettcher, "Trans Women and the Meaning of 'Woman,'" in *Philosophy of Sex: Contemporary Readings*, 6th ed., ed. A. Soble, N. Power, and R. Halwani (Rowan & Littlefield, 2013), 233–50.

reified,* at least for some individuals. As a member of the social group 'women,' I find this idea frightening."[2] As a (trans) woman and as a feminist, I find this idea frightening, too.

There is another view, explicitly political, that has developed over the past twenty years, which says that trans people challenge the traditional binary† between man and woman. Because, on this view, trans people do not fit neatly into the two categories "man" and "woman," mainstream society attempts to force trans people into this system in order to make it appear that there is a sharp dichotomy between men and women (when trans people show that there is not). The medical establishment is but one way in which society makes trans people disappear. The forces of oppression aim at invisibility, and the strategy of resistance is to come out and make oneself visible.[3] On this view—let's call it the "Transgender Model"—it is not trans people who are the problem but society itself. One of the difficulties with this account is that many trans people don't view themselves as "beyond the binary" at all but as either men or women. Thus, the Transgender Model seems to invalidate the self-identities of some transsexual people.[4]

Due to problems with both models, I am interested in providing an alternative account that relies on a multiple-meaning view (it is not quite yet a model rivaling the above two, but the beginnings of one). Specifically, my aim is to develop an account that accommodates trans people who see themselves as situated in a binary category while avoiding the pathologization and naturalization of gender identity.[5] I aim to probe deeper into the Wrong Body Model and the Transgender Model and to use the results of this investigation to eventually develop a model both more plausible and more accommodating to the experiences of trans people. In this essay, I make a few preliminary moves in that direction.

My claim is that we can understand the gender identities of (at least some) trans people who situate themselves in a binary category to stand in a "meaning conflict" with more mainstream conceptions of what

and who they are. Both the Wrong Body Model and the Transgender Model err in adopting what I call a "single-meaning position"; that is, they assume that a gender term has one meaning only. This leads them to presuppose the dominant meaning of gender terms while erasing resistant ones. Moreover, by presupposing the dominant meanings, both accounts end up accepting the marginal status of trans people. This leads them to try to justify the view that trans people are who they say they are. This is a bad place to start trans theory and politics, I argue, since non-trans people do not need to justify who they say they are in the same way: to accept this asymmetry is to effectively yield political ground from the very beginning. On the contrary, once we accept resistant, subcultural meanings, there is no need to defend the self-identifying claims of trans people. Instead, the power relations by which trans identities are institutionally enforced from without become fully visible.

My work is informed by my own experience as a (white) trans woman living in the trans activist subcultures of Los Angeles. There we've developed different gender practices (including the use of gender terms such as "woman" and "man") that do not always accord with more mainstream ones. It is my methodological starting point to take such practices seriously. As philosophers, we often rely on our intuitions about language use. This case is no different. It is just that my knowledge concerns a subculture that may seem foreign to some. My starting point is that in analyzing the meaning of terms such as "woman," it is inappropriate to dismiss alternative ways in which those terms are actually used in trans subcultures; such usage needs to be taken into consideration as part of the analysis. This is certainly the case when the question precisely concerns whether a trans person *counts* as a woman or a man.

The Single-Meaning Position

Consider a form of transphobia I call "the basic denial of authenticity." A central feature of it is "identity

---

* To reify something is to make that thing (or at least treat it as being) real and definite—for example, to turn something abstract into something concrete.

† A binary is a set of two terms that are deemed to be comprehensive and mutually exclusive; according to a binary conception of gender, one must be either a man or a woman, and one cannot be both or neither.

enforcement," whereby trans women are identified as "really men" and trans men are identified as "really women" (regardless of how we ourselves self-identify). Often this kind of identity enforcement (particularly through pronoun use) occurs repeatedly and runs against the trans person's own frequent requests to be treated otherwise. It can appear in mundane interactions between a trans person and a store clerk (e.g., repeated references to a trans woman as "sir") to cases in which a trans person is "exposed" as "really a man/ woman, disguised as a woman/man" and subjected to extreme forms of violence and murder.[6]

Now consider the self-identifying claim "I am a trans woman." Frequently, in dominant cultural contexts, the expression "trans woman" is understood to mean "a man who lives as a woman." Is this a case in which an individual merely misunderstands the meaning of the expression? No, because that meaning is accepted by many people and, indeed, often by the media, law enforcement agencies, domestic violence and homeless shelters, and so forth. Yet when I use that expression ("I am a trans woman") in trans subcultures, it simply does not mean that. So it is fair to say that identity enforcement does not merely concern whether a gender category expression applies to a person but also what an expression even means. The enforcer thinks (in the case of the trans woman) that the category "man" applies while the category "woman" doesn't. So the enforcer thinks that if "trans woman" is truthfully said, it can't possibly mean that the person is a woman (and isn't actually a man). Instead, it must mean that the person is merely pretending to be a woman. "Trans" would flag something involving pretense and would perhaps have the force of "fake" (as in "fake woman").

There are two ways one might respond to the enforcer. The first involves accepting the single-meaning position; the second involves accepting the multiple-meaning position. In the single-meaning position, "woman" is taken to have a fixed meaning; it is taken for granted that there is one concept. The dispute between the enforcer and the trans woman hinges on whether the concept "woman" applies or doesn't apply to her. On this view, "trans" would qualify the term "woman" (taken in the standard meaning) as a particular kind (one who had been assigned male sex at birth, perhaps, who became a woman later). The disagreement concerning the meaning of "transgender" ("fake" versus "transitional") would then hinge on the correct applicability of the term "woman" (or "female"). So to the enforcer, "trans woman" means "man living as a woman" while to the trans woman, "trans woman" means "woman assigned to the male sex at birth." This obviously raises difficult questions about how we ought to analyze terms such as "woman" and "man."

Most people would define "woman" as "adult female human being" and "man" as "adult male human being," thereby considering the differences as biological. Yet many feminists have argued that "woman" picks out a *social* kind, role, or status.[7] If so, that would require an alternative analysis of "woman." Of course, even if we accept a biological definition, we would still have the difficulty of defining "female" and "male" because there are multiple features involved in sex determination (including chromosomal karyotype,* gonadal structure, genital structure, reproductive capacity, and hormone levels), not to mention cases in which these features come apart. For example, a person with complete androgen insensitivity syndrome will have XY chromosomes and internal male gonads but a female phenotype.† In such cases it may be very difficult to tell whether the person is male, female, or neither. Indeed, it seems plausible that there is no fact of the matter in such cases.

One way to accommodate this multiplicity of features in the single-meaning position is to take gender terms as expressing family resemblance concepts. An analysis of such concepts would not involve specifying their necessary and sufficient conditions but listing their various overlapping features (or family resemblances). This list would include the multiple features above. And one could easily add more cultural features to the list as well, thereby addressing the feminist insight that there is a significant social component to gender categories like "woman."

With this type of account in hand, one could show that at least *some* trans women meet enough of

---

* The observable characteristics (number and appearance) of an individual's chromosomes.

† The observable characteristics of an individual organism, as shaped by genetic and environmental factors.

the conditions required for the application of the category "woman." One might point to hormone levels, surgically altered genitalia, and so forth to defend a claim to womanhood. The enforcer, by contrast, might point to karyotype and birth genitalia in order to defend a verdict of manhood. In such a conflict, the stakes concern which criteria are to weigh more in applying "woman." Notably, however, this strategy does not yield the kind of certainty one wants to validate a trans person's identity claims; at bottom we probably have a factually undecidable question. A trans woman in this case is, far from being a paradigm of womanhood, merely a marginal instance.[8] Whether she counts as a woman would depend on pragmatic and political considerations (concerns about *how best* to draw the line or about which criteria to use and how much weight they have). One might argue that in such hard cases it is best to consider self-identification (rather than karyotype) as decisive.[9] But that decision is not determined by a simple analysis of the concept "woman" but by the view that, in difficult cases, it is better to let people self-identify rather than pick a gender term for them. Despite the fact that the Transgender Model seems to ignore the self-identities of some transsexual people, it actually seems *to get it right* in positioning a postoperative trans woman problematically with respect to the binary. If a postoperative trans woman counts as a woman at all, it is not because she is a paradigmatic woman but because, while problematically positioned with regard to the binary categories, she is, owing to political considerations, *best viewed* as a woman.

The case is grimmer when we consider trans women who have not undergone genital reconstruction surgery and, particularly, those who have not undergone any bodily changes at all (hormone therapy, "top surgery,"* and the like). In terms of governmentally issued IDs, a trans woman who has not undergone any medical intervention is likely to not be allowed any changes (so her documentation will consistently say "male"). In cases of public sex segregation, including public changerooms, domestic violence shelters, homeless shelters, shared hospital rooms, jail and prison housing, and same-sex searches by police officers and other security officials, she is likely viewed

as "really male." To be sure, gender presentation may help secure that claim to womanhood. But that might not be enough. Certainly, it seems very hard to see how a trans woman could claim to be a veritable woman on the basis of gender identity alone (without such presentation). It even seems unclear how she can be recognized as "in-between" or "problematically positioned" with regard to the categories as the transgender model says. On the contrary, she would probably count as a "man" (just as the enforcer claims). The problem with the single-meaning position, then, is that it does not appear to do justice to trans people's self-identifying claims about their gender.

Semantic Contextualism

We can understand this disagreement differently if we understand it in terms of a more robust conflict over the very meaning of the term "woman." Already we have had to allow that the term "trans" means something different to the enforcer and to the trans woman: to the former it means "fake" and to the trans woman it might mean "transitional."[10] In the multiple-meaning account I propose, the same is true in the case of the term "woman." In order to bring out the details of my account, I contrast it with a view that is superficially similar to it, namely semantic contextualism. According to semantic contextualism, the extension of "woman" changes depending on the context. Jennifer Mather Saul considers a definition according to which "*X is a woman* is true in a context C [if and only if] X is human and relevantly similar (according to the standards at work in C) to most of those possessing all of the biological markers of female sex."[11]

On this definition, the term "woman" operates as an indexical: its content is determined by the specific context in which it is used since the standards for correct application of the concept contextually vary. However, despite this variability of content, the meaning of "woman" is still fixed in the sense that there is a single rule-governed way in which the content is determined. By analogy, while the indexical "I" changes its referent when different people utter it, the indexical still has a fixed "meaning" insofar as the referent is determined by the rule: "'I' refers to the person

---

* Surgical procedures on the breasts of transgender patients.

who utters it."[12] Because of this, I consider contextualism to endorse a single-meaning position.

In the account Saul considers, there can be a context C1 in which the relevant similarity (for correct application of the term "woman") involves "sincerely self-identifying as a woman" and another context C2 in which the relevant similarity involves "having XX chromosomes."[13] Thus, whether a trans woman counts as a woman depends on which standards are relevant in a given context. One of the benefits of this view is that it makes it possible for any trans woman (regardless of whether she has undergone medical procedures) to count as woman. It does this by allowing for contexts in which the standard of self-identification is salient in determining correct applicability. It also has the advantage that when trans women count as women in context C1, they do so for metaphysical reasons, that is, for reasons owing to the semantics of the term "woman" and the facts that obtain in the world of that context rather than for political reasons or decisions.

Despite these advantages, however, the account has problems. One major worry Saul raises with this account is that while it allows a trans woman to assert something true when she says, "I am a woman," it trivializes her assertion. For the enforcer is also correct. Explaining the worry, Saul says:

> The reason the trans woman's claims are true, on the contextualist view, is simply that there are a huge range of acceptable ways to use the term "woman" and the trans woman's way of using "woman" isn't ruled out.... What the trans woman needs to do justice to her claim is surely not just the acknowledgement that her claim is true but also the acknowledgement that her opponent's claim is false.[14]

A second, related worry is that in questions concerning whether a trans woman is a woman, there does not seem to be room for metaphysical disagreement. First, note that this question is going to have to be context sensitive. That is, the question whether a trans woman is a woman must be relative to a given context. So the question comes down to which standards are applicable in a given context (say, for example, the context of restroom use). But the only way to make sense of the dispute is to see it as a political

one. That is, the only way to arbitrate the dispute is by appealing to political and moral facts. Meditating on the word "woman" is probably not going to yield an answer. As Saul explains, "On my view of woman, I cannot argue that the lawmakers are making a mistake about how the word 'woman' works. But what I can do is argue that they are morally and politically wrong to apply the standards that they do."[15] While trans women can claim womanhood as a metaphysical fact (relative to a context), in cases of controversy over which standards apply in a particular context, their status as women is once again decided by the political rather than the metaphysical.

Consider two additional concerns. First, there are no similar consequences for most non-trans women because most non-trans women are going to count as women *on almost any reasonable standard* (e.g., self-identification, karyotype, and reproductive capacity). Because of this, there is far less room for somebody to truthfully deny her womanhood (relative to some context). And in cases of dispute over which standards are relevant, most non-trans women count as women regardless of which standards are selected. That is, the question whether non-trans women count as women need not be decided by political decision (largely because the need for a decision would not arise). Most non-trans women would count as women across all or most contexts ("transcontextually"). In this sense, most non-trans women would count as paradigms of "woman." By contrast, trans women would not count as women transcontextually since there are obvious contexts when they do not count (e.g., when karyotype is salient), and so there are cases in which it is controversial whether trans women are women (it is controversial, that is, which standards to apply).

The second, related worry is that there will be certain contexts in which some trans women do count as men due to the fact that they have an XY karyotype, or a penis, or testes. A variation of an example Saul considers is the use of "woman" and "man" by the American Cancer Society when testing for prostate cancer. If it is decided that men of a certain age should be tested, then all trans women who are of that age would count as men in that specific context. The difficulty is that the trans women might not count themselves as men at all in *any* context, or they might not consider their prostates to undermine their claims to (trans) womanhood. Indeed, I know many trans women, for example, who are content with their "male genitalia." However, many do not consider them *male* genitalia in the first place, but the sort of genitalia congruent with transgender femaleness. Similarly, I know many trans men who have no interest in phalloplasty* and who consider their genitalia (transgender) *male* genitalia. Often, what happens is that the social meaning commonly associated with a body part is, in a subcultural context, completely changed. In light of this, a trans woman might reasonably complain that testing for prostate cancer cannot be viewed in terms of testing only men (or males). Such a claim, she might argue, is transphobic in that it erases the existence of trans women by treating them as nothing but (non-trans) men. Instead, once trans women are taken seriously, the testing ought to be framed in terms of testing both non-trans men and trans women of a certain age. More simply, the testing could be done on *people* with prostates. That testicles, penises, XY karyotype, and prostates count as *male* in the first place is precisely what trans subcultures are *contesting*.

The Multiple-Meaning Position

As there are different gendered practices in different cultural contexts, the conflict over meaning exhibits itself in the contrast between dominant or mainstream culture and trans subcultures. This includes the practice of gender attribution. So a trans person can count as "really a man" according to dominant cultural practices while counting as a woman in friendlier trans subcultures.[16]

It is a fact that in some trans community contexts, the meanings of gender terms (such as "woman") are altered and their extensions broadened. This is a two-step process. First, "trans woman" is taken as a basic expression, not as a qualification of the dominant meaning of "woman." This means that whether someone is a trans woman does not depend primarily on questions about the applicability of the terms "man" and "woman." Recall that on the enforcer's view,

"trans woman" means "fake woman" because "woman" does not apply to the individual (despite her "trying to pass herself off" as one). By contrast, on the family resemblance view, being a "trans woman" depends on one's counting as a woman *simpliciter*.† On that view, it seems that only some trans women would count (and marginally so); as we saw above, trans women would have at best a mixture of family resemblance features and so would at best count as difficult cases. As to contextualism, there are at least two possibilities. The first is that when a trans woman does not count as a woman she also does not count as a "trans woman" (i.e., transitional woman). The second is that "trans woman" means "fake woman" in some contexts and "transitional woman" in others.

When I say that "trans woman" is basic I mean that it does not route through the question whether "woman" applies or not; that is, the criteria for the correct application of "trans woman" do not depend on the criteria governing the application of "woman." The criteria are roughly equivalent to the criteria governing "male-to-female trans person." Crudely, a person counts as a trans woman if she was assigned to the male sex at birth, currently lives as a woman, and self-identifies as a trans woman (or as a woman).[17] This means that "trans woman" applies *unproblematically* and *without qualification* to all self-identified trans women. For example, even if a trans woman has no surgical or hormonal changes in her body (while "living as a woman"), she can still count as a paradigm instance of "trans woman."

The second step is that being a trans woman is a sufficient condition for being a woman. "Woman" is then taken to apply to *both* trans and non-trans women (where "non-trans woman" is a person who counts as a woman but who does not count as a trans woman). We thereby end up with entirely new criteria for who is a woman (specified in the criteria for counting a person as a trans woman). And we end up with an extension‡ of "woman" different from the one that refers to only non-trans women (and to trans women who have just enough features to be argued into the category).

---

* Surgical construction of a penis.
† Latin: "in the most complete sense, without qualification."
‡ The extension of a term is the set of things to which that term correctly applies (e.g., the extension of "green" is the set of all and only green things).

Indeed, we end up with a notion of "woman" on which a trans woman is a paradigmatic (rather than a borderline) case. Thus, the expression "non-trans woman" operates in the way that "woman" used to operate. "Woman," by contrast, now operates in such a way that it applies to trans women unproblematically. The same shift can occur with terms such as "female" and "male." Subculturally, what counts as male and female is broadened. So we can have trans women/females with penises and trans men/males with vaginas (although it is not clear even that terms such as "penis" and "vagina" would always be used in such cases). In such a context, a vagina would not necessarily be female and a penis would not necessarily be male.

The worry with this account is that it also (like the semantic contextualist approach but in a different way) trivializes the claims of trans women (and men). One might say, "*Of course* you're a teapot, if by 'teapot' we mean 'human being.' And *of course* you're a woman if by 'woman' we mean 'man who lives as a woman.'" The account, however, is no verbal trick but tracks a difference between cultural practices of gender and the relation of these practices to the interpretation of the body and self-presentation. Whether one is viewed as a "gender rebel" depends on interpretation. If one were viewed as a man, then one's gender presentation would be read as a form of "gender bending" if one wears a skirt. But if the same person were viewed as a woman, then her gender presentation would not be construed as misaligned with her status. The key is whether genitalia are viewed as necessary to one's normative* gender status. Since in trans subcultural practices they are not, then in trans subculture a normative social status is reassigned in a very real way: what would count as gender non-normative (in the mainstream) is entirely normative (in the subculture).

This affects the way sex is segregated. To be sure, in trans subcultural formations there is no control over institutions (such as jail housing and strip-search requirements). But there can certainly be control over the way bodies may be subject to different privacy and decency boundaries. For example, "normally" a man's chest is not subject to taboos against nudity, but in trans subcultures, it might be read as a woman's chest or at least a chest that is subject to such taboos.

So this conflict of meaning is undergirded by a conflict in gender practice. And this gendered practice informs (and is informed by) a basic conception (or narrative) of how the world is composed of various different types of gendered people. There is a genuine dispute concerning two competing visions of gender. And the taken-for-granted assumption that the dominant cultural view is the only valid one can be seen as a kind of cultural arrogance bolstered by institutional power.

Consider someone who lives as a woman, sees herself as a woman, and has been sustained in a subculture that respects her intimacy boundaries, only to find that she is subject to violence because she is "really male." She goes through mainstream institutions (hospitals, jails) where she is housed as male, searched as male, and turned away from a shelter as male. This invalidation is not only of an individual's self-identity but also of an entire life that has been lived with dignity in a competing cultural world.[18] My point is that this conflict over meaning is deeply bound up with the distribution of power and the capacity to enforce a way of life, regardless of the emotional and physical damage done to the individual.

The multiple-meaning view allows us to avoid the difficulties that plague the family resemblance account, for according to my view, all trans women count as women and do so paradigmatically, not marginally. And trans women count as women not owing to a political decision that arises as a consequence of their status as "difficult cases" but owing to the metaphysical facts that accord with the very meaning of the word "man" and "woman" *as deployed in trans subcultures.* That is, from the perspective of trans subculture, the enforcer who denies that a trans woman is a woman would be *making an error* every bit as much as if he were to call a non-trans woman a man.

My view also avoids some of the difficulties that plague semantic contextualism. This might not be obvious since the multiple-meaning account might seem to be merely a version of it, given that it seems I have only added a new context-relative standard. In particular, one might worry that this account is open to the following objections that suggest its similarity to semantic contextualism. First, while it is true that from the perspective of trans subculture the enforcer

---

* Having to do with prevailing social values or norms.

is incorrect in denying that a trans woman is a woman, it is also true that from the perspective of dominant culture he is correct. Since the trans woman cannot claim that the enforcer's view is false, her self-identity claim is trivialized. In this way, the account is similar to semantic contextualism. Second, the decision regarding which perspective to take (the dominant or the resistant one) is a political one. So whether a trans woman counts as a woman is again a political decision. By contrast, a non-trans woman will count as a woman regardless of such political decisions; there is an asymmetry. Again, this is a problem that also plagued semantic contextualism. Replying to these objections helps show how my account differs from contextualism. I start with the first objection.

First, a trans woman can reject the entire dominant gender system as based on false beliefs about gender and gender practices that are harmful and even oppressive.[19] That is, while she might agree that she is not a woman in dominant culture, she can reject, on philosophical grounds, the entire system of gender that dominant cultures circulate. To see this, consider the following analogy. According to an evangelical account of "sinner," I would count as one. But it does not follow that I am one even though I might meet all the criteria of the evangelical account. In rejecting the claim that I'm a sinner, I'm rejecting the entire picture of the world in which that term has its definition fixed. Similarly, a trans woman can reject as false the claim that she is "really a man" by rejecting the entire system of gender in which that claim is true (on the grounds discussed above). This move does not work in the case of semantic contextualism, of course, since a trans woman who fails to accept that there are some contexts (e.g., karyotype-salient contexts) in which she is not a woman is simply wrong. On the multiple-meaning view, a trans woman can say that she is a woman in all legitimate contexts because those contexts in which she is not a woman occur in a dominant culture that has been rejected for the reasons mentioned above. She can argue that the very belief in contexts in which she counts as a man (for example, a context in which genital structure is relevant) rests on the assumption that penises are male and is therefore grounded in a vision that marginalizes trans women from the start.

Once we accept this response, we obviously also need to recognize that the shift in usage is *far more* *radical* than the mere introduction of a new contextually relative standard. It makes more sense to speak of a transformation in meaning or concept than to speak of a new contextually relative standard. Put another way, there are actually two concepts and two meanings of "womanhood." The two concepts (and the two meanings) are related in that the latter is the result of changes performed on the former. One starts with a particular concept and then expands it, for example, to include something that wasn't included in it before. This makes sense if we think of gender concepts as determined, in part, by underlying gender practices and conceptions of what a gendered world is. Once practice and conception seriously change, one can plausibly argue that the concepts change as well.

This allows us to reply to the second objection: we need not think that trans women only count as women on the basis of a political decision while non-trans women do not. Given that we can now speak of two concepts of "womanhood" (a dominant one and a resistant one), the question, "Are trans women really women?" does not get off the ground. Instead, we need to disambiguate the two concepts. A preoperative trans woman might be a woman-R ("woman" in the resistant sense) but not as a woman-D ("woman" in the dominant sense). She would be a woman-R and fail to be a woman-D not as a matter of political decision but metaphysically speaking. The political question, instead, concerns which concept we should take seriously, and this is connected to the larger question regarding which gendered vision of the world (if any) we commit to. Notably, these questions do not arise because of trans women counting as "difficult cases." And these questions also confront non-trans women. A non-trans woman who self-identifies as a woman-D can be seen as taking up a political stance that marginalizes trans women by endorsing a transphobic gendered view of the world. Or a feminist project that proceeds with the concept women-D could be viewed as anti-trans. In my account, the worry is not that non-trans women alone count as paradigmatic women. The worry, rather, is that a non-trans woman can avail herself of a concept (that is part of a larger gendered vision of the world) that marginalizes trans women. When a non-trans woman accepts this concept about what counts as a woman-D, this is the effect of privilege, not of it being the case that she is a paradigmatic woman while trans women are not.

So the multiple-meaning account I have out-lined is not a variant of semantic contextualism, for it can solve the problems that confronted that account. Insofar as it squares with the reality of trans subcultural usage while addressing these problems, it seems to be the best account for our purposes. And by taking the multiple-meaning account seriously, we can now see some basic problems with both the Wrong Body Model and the Transgender Model.

Starting Points for Trans Stories

This distinction between the single-meaning and multiple-meaning positions reveals something important about starting points in trans politics. Consider the question (among some non-trans feminists) whether trans women do or do not count as women. In raising such a question, trans women are viewed as difficult cases with respect to the category "woman." In this way, the inclusion of trans women in the category of "woman" is something in need of defense (unlike the taken-for-granted inclusion of non-trans women). Notably, this asymmetry, which places the womanhood of trans women in jeopardy, arises only if we assume the dominant understanding of "woman." If we assume a resistant understanding of "woman," no question arises since trans women are exemplars of womanhood. While it might sometimes be a useful strategy to assume a dominant understanding of "woman" in order to defend the inclusion of trans women (as difficult cases), an unquestioned assumption of the dominant understanding is a bad starting point in trans politics and theory. It ignores resistant meanings produced in trans subcultures, thereby leaving us scrambling to find a home in the dominant meanings, those meanings that marginalize us from the get-go.

Consider an analogy. When I teach an undergraduate course in the philosophy of gender, I examine arguments that purport to show the immorality of "homosexuality."[20] I try to show students why these arguments are unsound because it is important to debunk the (bad) arguments that harm lesbian, gay, bisexual, and transsexual (LGBT) people. However, in a graduate seminar in LGBT studies, I would not engage this issue because this would play into the hands of a heterosexist cultural asymmetry that places homosexuality in moral jeopardy while leaving the moral status of heterosexuality unquestioned—a questionable political starting point.

Similarly, it is a questionable political starting point to accept as valid the dominant understanding of gender categories that situate trans people as, at best, problematic cases. To be sure, it might be a useful strategy to adopt the dominant understanding in particular situations. But I worry about any theory designed to illuminate trans oppression or resistance that unreflectively accepts a dominant understanding of categories.

In the Wrong Body Model, one counts as a woman-D (at best) to some degree and with qualification, so long as an appropriate authority recognizes one as possessing the right gender identity and one undergoes, as much as possible, a transformative process to conform to the dominant concept of woman. A dominant understanding of the category is presupposed and an asymmetry is tacitly accepted whereby trans membership in the category requires justification. As a consequence, trans people who do not value genital reconstruction surgery are taken not to have the right gender identity, and they are delegitimated as "mere" crossdressers. A result of the Wrong Body Model's affiliation with dominant meanings is that trans people who live their lives with dignity in different subcultural worlds of meaning are simply kicked to the curb.

The Transgender Model also marginalizes trans people. It presupposes a dominant understanding of the categories "man" and "woman" under which trans people fit only marginally or as difficult cases not easily categorized. Here, a trans person would be—at most—legitimized as a (marginal) woman through somehow arguing that she meets enough of the dominant criteria of membership. Similarly, a trans person could be legitimized as "in-between" by showing under which dominant categories the person falls and does not fall. In both cases, the dominant understanding is presupposed and the position of trans people vis-à-vis the categories is justified by pointing to the criteria of membership in *these categories* (unlike non-trans people who are accepted as paradigmatic of the dominant categories and therefore in no need of justification). Once we take resistant meanings seriously, however, it is no longer clear why a trans person who sees herself as a woman is only marginally so at best. And it is far from clear why certain bodies count as in-between. Once trans men and trans women are taken as paradigms of concepts like "man" and "woman," it becomes doubtful that their bodies are problematic or in-between. Perversely, then, the Transgender Model, like the Wrong Body Model, ends up dismissing the lived lives of trans people.

Final Remarks

As I have framed it, there is a different and expanded notion of womanhood in trans subcultures. Although I have spoken as if there is only one understanding, this is misleading because trans subculture is generally replete with multiple and sometimes conflicting accounts of gender. After all, it is hard to be trans and avoid thinking a little bit about what a woman is, what a man is, what gender is, and the like. Gender terms ("trans," "transgender," "transsexual," "woman," etc.) simply won't stay put. Instead of understanding "trans woman" as a subcategory of an expanded category of womanhood, trans women may also be conceptualized as in-between with respect to the traditional categories where they do not count as women *simpliciter* (i.e., as non-trans women) who *are* seen as part of the binary. It is just not obvious how trans people are going to understand the term "woman" when they self-identify (or do not self-identify) with that term.

Such variability is not an "anything goes" approach. In trans subcultures, the use of these gender terms is subject to some constraint. Moreover, there is a fairly common linguistic practice. Claims about self-identity in (some) trans subcultures have the form of first-person, present-tense avowals of mental attitudes (e.g. "I am angry at you").[21] This means that the shift in meaning involves not only an expansion of the category but also a change in use, reflected in the grammar of first- and third-person assertions. It is no longer merely a question whether the category is truthfully predicated of the object in question. Instead, there is a firstperson, present-tense avowal of gender. For example, the claim "I am a trans woman" may be an avowal of a deep sense of "who one is" (that is, of one's deepest values and commitments). And as such, this is the prerogative of the first person alone where

defensible avowals of gender are presumptively taken as authoritative. Fundamental to this practice is the idea that gender categories do not merely apply (or fail to apply) on the basis of objective criteria but are adopted for personal and political reasons. For example, the category "trans woman" might be avowed or disavowed because the category does not speak to "who they are," because it does not fit or feel right. Alternatively, it might be avowed or disavowed on solely political grounds. Insofar as such considerations are fundamental to the very practice of gender attribution in these contexts it is easy to see why this is such a shift from the dominant practice of gender attribution, which operates independently of such considerations. The shift makes room for the multiplicity of meaning by allowing first-person authority over both gender avowal and the very meaning of the avowal.

The point I have defended in this essay is that accounts that take for granted singular, fixed meanings of gender terms cannot plausibly provide a liberatory theory. Not only do such accounts go wrong by failing to square with the actual reality of the situation, namely the fact that central terms are used in trans contexts in multiple and contested ways; they actually undermine trans self-identifications by foreclosing the possibility of multiplicity. These accounts do so, in part, because they aim to justify the categorization of trans people by appealing to the dominant meanings. This, I have argued, implies an acceptance of a marginalizing asymmetry between trans and non-trans people from the beginning. To provide a satisfying account of trans phenomena, gender marginalization cannot be accepted as a starting point. The demand for justification and the demand for illumination are not the same. We need new accounts, I believe, that don't begin with a *justification* for trans self-identity claims but that follow subcultural practice in taking the presumptive legitimacy of such claims for granted. This requires recognizing the multiplicity of resistant meanings rather than acquiescing to the dominant culture's erasure of them. In my view, it is the only way to yield illuminating accounts of trans phenomena that do not proceed from transphobic starting points.[22] ■

Suggestions for Critical Reflection

1. Why does Bettcher object to the "family resemblance" approach to defining "woman"? Evaluate her objections.

2. Why does Bettcher object to the "semantic contextualist" approach to defining "woman"? Evaluate her objections.

3. Bettcher acknowledges that "one might worry" that the multiple-meaning approach "is open to ... objections that suggest its similarity to semantic contextualism." In your view, is the multiple-meaning approach sufficiently different from semantic contextualism to avoid its pitfalls? How clear is the distinction between a "context" and a "world"?

4. Bettcher criticizes definitions of "woman" that proceed from the assumption that non-trans women are women but that the womanhood of trans women requires demonstration. In your view, are there valid reasons to require demonstration of the womanhood of one group but not the other? Why or why not? If there are reasons, are they purely metaphysical or are they also to do with values?

5. Bettcher engages in this article with both metaphysical and political ideas. How are the metaphysical and the political related here? Is one given primacy over the other? Should it be?

6. Regarding the discussion of trans people in philosophy, Bettcher has said the following:

> I'm afraid there's a tendency among some philosophers to suppose that philosophical investigations into race, gender, disability, trans issues, and so forth are no different methodologically from investigations into the question whether tables really exist. One difference, however, is that while tables aren't part of the philosophical conversation, trans people, disabled people, people of color, are part of the conversation.*

How (if at all) is this view reflected in the methodology Bettcher uses in "Trans Women and the Meaning of 'Woman'"? To the extent that it is reflected, does it strengthen—or weaken—the persuasiveness of the article?

Notes

1   For some examples, see Henry Rubin, *Self-Made Men: Identity and Embodiment among Transsexual Men* (Nashville, Tenn.: Vanderbilt University Press, 2003), 150–51. Not all transsexuals have endorsed this view.

2   Christine Overall, "Sex/Gender Transitions and Life-Changing Aspirations," in *"You've Changed": Sex Reassignment and Personal Identity*, edited by Laurie Shrage (Oxford, U.K.: Oxford University Press, 2009), 11–27, at 14. The worry is that culturally determined gender behavior, beliefs, and attitudes are often very harmful to women. So it is troublesome to treat them as natural or as essential because it makes them seem unchangeable and even suggests that this "is how it is meant to be."

3   This account glosses over significant differences among thinkers such as Kate Bornstein, Leslie Feinberg, and Sandy Stone. See Kate Bornstein, *Gender Outlaw: On Men, Women, and the Rest of Us* (New York: Routledge, 1994); Leslie Feinberg, *Stone Butch Blues: A Novel* (Los

Angeles: Alyson Books, 1993); Sandy Stone, "The Empire Strikes Back: A Posttranssexual Manifesto," in *Body Guards: The Cultural Politics of Gender Ambiguity*, edited by Julia Epstein and Kristina Straub (New York: Routledge, 1991), 280–304. However, this account captures the general idea frequently assumed in discussions of trans issues. For a more in-depth discussion of the transgender paradigm, see Talia Mae Bettcher, "Feminist Perspectives on Trans Issues," http://plato.stanford.edu/entries/feminism-trans, *Stanford Encyclopedia of Philosophy*, edited by Edward N. Zalta (accessed March 10, 2012).

4   It is possible for variants of the Transgender Model to appeal to the notion of an innate gender identity. However, social constructionism about gender has definitely figured very prominently in this model.

5   By "naturalization" I mean that something cultural is treated as "natural" (that is, as independent of culture). In this case, I mean that gender identity is treated as

---

*   Talia Mae Bettcher, "'When Tables Speak': On the Existence of Trans Philosophy," *Daily Nous*, May 30, 2018.

innate. By "pathologization" I mean that something nonpathological is treated as though it is pathological.

6 For a more detailed account of the basic denial of authenticity, see Talia Mae Bettcher, "Appearance, Reality, and Gender Deception: Reflections on Transphobic Violence and the Politics of Pretence," in *Violence, Victims, and Justifications*, edited by Felix Ó Murchadha (Bern: Peter Lang, 2006), 175–200.

7 For a detailed discussion of the sex/gender distinction in feminist theory, see Mari Mikkola, "Feminist Perspectives on Sex and Gender," plato.stanford.edu/entries/feminism-gender, *Stanford Encyclopedia of Philosophy*, edited by Edward N. Zalta (accessed March 10, 2012).

8 For this style of approach, see C. Jacob Hale, "Are Lesbians Women?" *Hypatia* 11:2 (Spring 1996): 94–121; John Corvino, "Analyzing Gender," *Southwest Philosophy Review* 17:1 (2000): 173–80; Cressida Heyes, *Line Drawings: Defining Women through Feminist Practice* (Ithaca, N.Y.: Cornell University Press, 2000); and Jennifer McKitrick "Gender Identity Disorder," in *Establishing Medical Reality: Essays in the Metaphysics and Epistemology of Biomedical Science*, edited by Harold Kincaid and Jennifer McKitrick (Dordrecht: Springer, 2007), 137–48.

9 See Corvino, "Analyzing Gender," 179, for this type of view.

10 I say "might" because I argue below that different trans women can mean different things by the expression "trans woman."

11 Jennifer Mather Saul, "Politically Significant Terms and the Philosophy of Language: Methodological Issues," in *Out from the Shadows: Analytical Feminist Contributions to Traditional Philosophy*, edited by Sharon L. Crasnow and Anita M. Superson (Oxford, U.K.: Oxford University Press, 2012), 195–216, at 201. Saul does not accept this account but uses it to develop the methodological point that very different considerations can inform analysis when the term is politically significant. For example, in analyzing "woman," Saul thinks that it is important to do justice to a trans woman's self-identity claims. Such intuitions are not easily explained away as they might be when we are not thinking of politically fraught cases precisely because so much more seems to hinge on them. She then suggests that this is relevant to philosophers of language more generally. My point is less methodological, although I'm obviously concerned to take the claims of trans women seriously. My proposed account does justice to trans women's self-identity claims in a way that a semantic contextualist account does not. Besides, I do draw on trans subcultures' use of gendered language as crucial data in my analysis of gender terms.

Taking seriously how trans people use the terms is often overlooked in analyses of these types.

12 My formulation of the rule is obviously too simple. But that doesn't matter for my purposes.

13 Saul, "Politically Significant Terms," 201, 203.

14 Saul, "Politically Significant Terms," 209–10.

15 Saul, "Politically Significant Terms," 204.

16 I am largely indebted to C. Jacob Hale for this type of view. See his "Leather Dyke Boys and Their Daddies: How to Have Sex without Men and Women," *Social Text* 52/53, 16:3–4 (1997): 223–36.

17 It is also possible to recognize somebody as a trans woman despite the fact that she has not yet "transitioned" and does not yet self-identify as a woman (or a trans woman) in case this person eventually transitions. Explaining this is actually quite tricky, however, so I won't worry about it in this paper. I am grateful to Jennifer Saul for pressing me to think about this more.

18 The notion of "world" originates in the work of Maria Lugones. My understanding of cultural conflicts over meaning is informed by her view. See her "Playfulness, 'World'-Travelling, and Loving Perception," *Hypatia: A Journal of Feminist Philosophy* 2:2 (Summer 1987): 3–19.

19 Here are some examples. One false belief is that gender terms only have single (dominant) meanings. Another is that all people are either "naturally" male or female. And, of course, there are many others that involve treating cultural phenomena as "natural" manifestations of gender. By "harmful gender practices" I mean to include those practices that involve treating trans people with violence and those that are sexist and sexually violent. For a discussion of these practices see Talia Mae Bettcher, "Evil Deceivers and Make-Believers: Transphobic Violence and the Politics of Illusion," *Hypatia: A Journal of Feminist Philosophy* 22:3 (Summer 2007): 43–65.

20 I have worries about the term "homosexuality" as it derives from a sexological framework in which same-sex sexuality is viewed as pathological.

21 For development of this view, see my "Trans Identities and First Person Authority," in *"You've Changed": Sex Reassignment and Personal Identity*, edited by Laurie Shrage (Oxford, U.K.: Oxford University Press, 2009): 98–120.

22 Parts of this essay were published as "Without a Net: Starting Points for Trans Stories," *American Philosophical Association LGBT Newsletter* 10:2 (Spring 2011): 2–5. I am grateful to the editor, William Wilkerson, for his comments. I am also grateful for the extremely helpful feedback by Raja Halwani and Nicholas Power in finalizing this version of the essay. I would also like to thank Jennifer Saul for her (always) insightful and constructive comments.

IRIS MARION YOUNG

Five Faces of Oppression

Who Was Iris Marion Young?

Iris Marion Young (1949–2006) was an American political theorist, philosopher, and activist, who is widely considered to be one of the most important political philosophers of the last quarter of the twentieth century. Her work focused on gender and race theory, global justice, continental political theory, and ethics. She was Professor of Political Science at the University of Chicago and was affiliated with the Center for Gender Studies there. One of her colleagues, Patchen Markell, said of her that "she was one of those scholars who practiced ... what she preached; in her case, a systematic egalitarianism and opposition to hierarchy."*

Young published a great deal of influential work but is best known for *Justice and the Politics of Difference* (1990), a landmark text in moral and political philosophy. In it, she critiques prevalent theories of justice and argues that liberal democracies have not only failed to address the structural oppressions that afflict social groups in capitalist states, but that they may in fact be involved in maintaining those oppressions. The book had an important influence in shaping identity politics and in offering an alternative set of criteria for analyzing the engrained power structures that continue to oppress groups in liberal democracies.

What Is the Structure of This Reading?

The following reading is excerpted from Chapter Two of *Justice and the Politics of Difference* (1990). In it, Young proposes a new conception of justice, which she terms an "enabling conception of justice," that includes but moves beyond distributive patterns to include other social phenomena: decision-making procedures, division of labor, and culture. Injustice, under this model, takes the forms of oppression and domination.

For Young, oppression describes structural phenomena that "immobilize or diminish a group in society." Oppression is a central category for contemporary political discourse, particularly for social movements that seek to free groups from injustice: socialists, feminists, Native American activists, Black activists, and LGBTQ activists (among others). Young focuses her analysis on structural oppression, which, in modern democracies, is embedded in social norms, habits, and symbols, and in the unconscious assumptions that shape institutions, the media, and all the other processes of daily life.

Young argues that social justice can best be achieved not by doing away with group distinctions, but by shaping institutions that respect differences among groups. She argues that groups should be understood in terms of a shared sense of identity. From this perspective, the self does not stand outside and prior to its group membership, but is instead shaped by social processes. Social groups, she states, should be fluid, and one must recognize that they are intersectional: they overlap, cut across one another, and are differentiated by many factors (such as age, nationality, sexuality, region, and class).

According to Young, we cannot use the concepts and language of liberalism effectively to analyze the oppression that is manifested in our social structures, because these concepts focus on the rights and freedoms of individuals rather than the welfare of social groups. With the "five faces of oppression," she offers instead a language and conceptual framework for identifying and analyzing group oppression.

She begins by explaining what she means by treating oppression as a *structural* concept, and then goes on to justify and defend her focus on social groups—rather than individuals—as the subject of oppression. In the

---

* Danielle Allen, Robert Gooding-Williams, Patchen Markell, John P. McCormick, Martha Nussbaum, Cass R. Sunstein, and Nathan Tarcov, "Iris Marion Young: Tributes from Her Colleagues in Political Theory at the University of Chicago," *PS: Political Science and Politics* 40, 1 (January 2007): 168–70.

next, main section of this chapter she introduces each of the "five faces" of oppression in turn: exploitation, marginalization, powerlessness, cultural imperialism, and violence. Her claim is that none of these forms of oppression can be reduced to—analyzed away in terms of—the others, and that together these five forms are adequate for understanding the important ways in which groups are oppressed in contemporary democratic societies, as well as the complex similarities and differences that exist among different groups' experience of oppression.

Some Useful Background Information

Young makes reference to models of distributive justice, such as those developed by John Rawls and Robert Nozick (see the chapter on Justice in this volume), which analyze justice primarily in terms of how society distributes goods—money, jobs, benefits, resources—among individuals in society. Young finds this approach problematic, because it focuses the discussion on possession: how much do individuals have, what don't they have, and how does what one individual has compare with what another has? Young prefers to focus on human behaviors and social processes that take place within institutions, to discover whether or not society is enabling people to flourish. She is also interested in seeking justice not only for the individual, but for groups. For example, even in societies where every individual is given the right to vote, that does not ensure that some oppressed minorities are not prevented by various means from exercising that right. Young is interested in developing a conception of justice that pays attention to oppressive processes and seeks for means to redress them.

Five Faces of Oppression*

Someone who does not see a pane of glass does not know that he does not see it. Someone who, being placed differently, does see it, does not know the other does not see it.

When our will finds expression outside ourselves in actions performed by others, we do not waste our time and our power of attention in examining whether they have consented to this. This is true for all of us. Our attention, given entirely to the success of the undertaking, is not claimed by them as long as they are docile....

Rape is a terrible caricature of love from which consent is absent. After rape, oppression is the second horror of human existence. It is a terrible caricature of obedience.

—Simone Weil[†]

I have proposed an enabling conception of justice. Justice should refer not only to distribution, but also to the institutional conditions necessary for the development and exercise of individual capacities and collective communication and cooperation. Under this conception of justice, injustice refers primarily to two forms of disabling constraints, oppression and domination. While these constraints include distributive patterns,[‡] they also involve matters which cannot easily be assimilated to the logic of distribution: decision-making procedures, division of labor, and culture....

In this chapter I offer some explication of the concept of oppression as I understand its use by new social movements in the United States since the 1960s. My starting point is reflection on the conditions of the groups said by these movements to be oppressed: among others women, Blacks, Chicanos,[§] Puerto Ricans and other Spanish-speaking Americans,

---

* "Five Faces of Oppression" is Chapter 2 of Young's *Justice and the Politics of Difference* (Princeton University Press, 1990).

† French philosopher and mystic (1909–43). This quotation is taken from her 1943 essay, "Are We Struggling for Justice?"

‡ Patterns in how goods are distributed—the subject of distributive justice.

§ Chicano or Chicana is a chosen identity of some Mexican Americans in the United States.

American Indians, Jews, lesbians, gay men, Arabs, Asians, old people, working-class people, and the physically and mentally disabled. I aim to systematize the meaning of the concept of oppression as used by these diverse political movements, and to provide normative argument to clarify the wrongs the term names.

Obviously the above-named groups are not oppressed to the same extent or in the same ways. In the most general sense, all oppressed people suffer some inhibition of their ability to develop and exercise their capacities and express their needs, thoughts, and feelings. In that abstract sense all oppressed people face a common condition. Beyond that, in any more specific sense, it is not possible to define a single set of criteria that describe the condition of oppression of the above groups. Consequently, attempts by theorists and activists to discover a common description or the essential causes of the oppression of all these groups have frequently led to fruitless disputes about whose oppression is more fundamental or more grave. The contexts in which members of these groups use the term oppression to describe the injustices of their situation suggest that oppression names in fact a family of concepts and conditions, which I divide into five categories: exploitation, marginalization, powerlessness, cultural imperialism, and violence.

In this chapter I explicate each of these forms of oppression. Each may entail or cause distributive injustices, but all involve issues of justice beyond distribution. In accordance with ordinary political usage, I suggest that oppression is a condition of groups....

Oppression as a Structural Concept

New left social movements of the 1960s and 1970s ... shifted the meaning of the concept of oppression. In its new usage, oppression designates the disadvantage and injustice some people suffer not because a tyrannical power coerces them, but because of the everyday practices of a well-intentioned liberal* society. In this new left usage, the tyranny of a ruling group over another, as in South Africa, must certainly be called oppressive. But oppression also refers to systemic constraints on groups that are not necessarily the result of the intentions of a tyrant. Oppression in this sense is structural, rather than the result of a few people's choices or policies. Its causes are embedded in unquestioned norms, habits, and symbols, in the assumptions underlying institutional rules and the collective consequences of following those rules. It names, as Marilyn Frye puts it, "an enclosing structure of forces and barriers which tends to the immobilization and reduction of a group or category of people" (Frye, 1983, p. 11). In this extended structural sense oppression refers to the vast and deep injustices some groups suffer as a consequence of often unconscious assumptions and reactions of well-meaning people in ordinary interactions, media and cultural stereotypes, and structural features of bureaucratic hierarchies and market mechanisms—in short, the normal processes of everyday life. We cannot eliminate this structural oppression by getting rid of the rulers or making some new laws, because oppressions are systematically reproduced in major economic, political, and cultural institutions.

The systemic character of oppression implies that an oppressed group need not have a correlate oppressing group. While structural oppression involves relations among groups, these relations do not always fit the paradigm of conscious and intentional oppression of one group by another. Foucault† (1977) suggests that to understand the meaning and operation of power in modern society we must look beyond the model of power as "sovereignty," a dyadic relation‡ of ruler and subject, and instead analyze the exercise of power as the effect of often liberal and "humane" practices of education, bureaucratic administration, production and distribution of consumer goods, medicine, and so on. The conscious actions of many individuals daily contribute to maintaining and reproducing oppression, but those people are usually simply doing their jobs or living their lives, and do not understand themselves as agents of oppression.

---

* The term "liberal" or "liberalism" has been applied to a family of historical and contemporary political views. In this context, liberalism can be broadly characterized as the view that individual freedoms and rights are central to the functioning of society.

† Michel Foucault (1926–84), French philosopher and historian.

‡ A relationship between two individuals.

I do not mean to suggest that within a system of oppression individual persons do not intentionally harm others in oppressed groups. The raped woman, the beaten Black youth, the locked-out worker, the gay man harassed on the street, are victims of intentional actions by identifiable agents. I also do not mean to deny that specific groups are beneficiaries of the oppression of other groups, and thus have an interest in their continued oppression. Indeed, for every oppressed group there is a group that is *privileged* in relation to that group....

I offer below an explication of five faces of oppression as a useful set of categories and distinctions which I believe is comprehensive, in the sense that it covers all the groups said by new left social movements to be oppressed and all the ways they are oppressed. I derive the five faces of oppression from reflection on the condition of these groups. Because different factors, or combinations of factors, constitute the oppression of different groups, making their oppression irreducible, I believe it is not possible to give one essential definition of oppression. The five categories articulated in this chapter, however, are adequate to describe the oppression of any group, as well as its similarities with and differences from the oppression of other groups. But first we must ask what a group is.

The Concept of a Social Group

Oppression refers to structural phenomena that immobilize or diminish a group. But what is a group? Our ordinary discourse differentiates people according to social groups such as women and men, age groups, racial and ethnic groups, religious groups, and so on. Social groups of this sort are not simply collections of people, for they are more fundamentally intertwined with the identities of the people described as belonging to them. They are a specific kind of collectivity, with specific consequences for how people understand one another and themselves. Yet neither social theory nor philosophy has a clear and developed concept of the social group (see Turner et al., 1987).

A social group is a collective of persons differentiated from at least one other group by cultural forms, practices, or way of life. Members of a group have a specific affinity with one another because of their similar experience or way of life, which prompts them to associate with one another more than with those not identified with the group, or in a different way. Groups are an expression of social relations; a group exists only in relation to at least one other group. Group identification arises, that is, in the encounter and interaction between social collectivities that experience some differences in their way of life and forms of association, even if they regard themselves as belonging to the same society....

[Groups] constitute individuals. A person's particular sense of history, affinity, and separateness, even the person's mode of reasoning, evaluating, and expressing feeling, are constituted partly by her or his group affinities. This does not mean that persons have no individual styles, or are unable to transcend or reject a group identity. Nor does it preclude persons from having many aspects that are independent of these group identities.

The social ontology underlying many contemporary theories of justice is methodologically individualist or atomist.* It presumes that the individual is ontologically prior to the social. This individualist social ontology usually goes together with a normative conception of the self as independent. The authentic self is autonomous, unified, free, and self-made, standing apart from history and affiliations, choosing its life plan entirely for itself.

One of the main contributions of poststructuralist† philosophy has been to expose as illusory this

---

* In social and political philosophy, atomist theories are those that view individual action as the basis for understanding the whole—that is, group behaviors can be understood wholly through describing the behaviors of separate individuals, and furthermore that those individual actions can each be fully understood without making reference to the whole. An 'ontology' is a view about what sorts of individual things and groups of things are the basic constituents of some domain.

† Poststructuralism is a mid-twentieth-century European philosophical movement defined by its opposition to the prior theory of structuralism. *Structuralism* is a view of human culture which sees it as a meaningful structure, rather like a conceptual scheme, that is distinct from 'raw' concrete reality and is our way of interpreting that reality—all the phenomena of human life can be made intelligible by revealing their place in this overall, interconnecting structure.

metaphysic of a unified self-making subjectivity, which posits the subject as an autonomous origin or an underlying substance to which attributes of gender, nationality, family role, intellectual disposition, and so on might attach. Conceiving the subject in this fashion implies conceiving consciousness as outside of and prior to language and the context of social interaction, which the subject enters. Several currents of recent philosophy challenge this deeply held Cartesian assumption.* Lacanian psychoanalysis,† for example, and the social and philosophical theory influenced by it, conceive the self as an achievement of linguistic positioning that is always contextualized in concrete relations with other persons, with their mixed identities (Coward and Ellis, 1977). The self is a product of social processes, not their origin.

From a rather different perspective, Habermas‡ indicates that theory of communicative action also must challenge the "philosophy of consciousness" which locates intentional egos as the ontological origins of social relations. A theory of communicative action conceives individual identity not as an origin but as a product of linguistic and practical interaction (Habermas, 1987; pp. 3–40). As Stephen Epstein describes it, identity is a "socialized sense of individuality, an internal organization of self-perception concerning one's relationship to social categories, that also incorporates views of the self perceived to be held by others. Identity is constituted relationally, through involvement with—and incorporation of—significant others and integration into communities" (Epstein, 1987, p. 29). Group categorization and norms are major constituents of individual identity (see Turner et al., 1987).

A person joins an association, and even if membership in it fundamentally affects one's life, one does not take that membership to define one's very identity, in the way, for example, being Navaho might. Group affinity, on the other hand, has the character of what Martin Heidegger§ (1962) calls "thrownness": one *finds oneself* as a member of a group, which one experiences as always already having been. For our identities are defined in relation to how others identify us, and they do so in terms of groups which are always already associated with specific attributes, stereotypes, and norms.

From the thrownness of group affinity it does not follow that one cannot leave groups and enter new ones. Many women become lesbian after first identifying as heterosexual. Anyone who lives long enough becomes old. These cases exemplify thrownness precisely because such changes in group affinity are experienced as transformations in one's identity. Nor does it follow from the thrownness of group affinity that one cannot define the meaning of group identity for oneself; those who identify with a group can redefine the meaning and norms of group identity. The present point is only that one first finds a group identity as given, and then takes it up in a certain way. While groups may come into being, they are never founded....

[S]ome people think that social groups are invidious fictions, essentializing arbitrary attributes. From this point of view problems of prejudice, stereotyping, discrimination, and exclusion exist because some people mistakenly believe that group identification makes a difference to the capacities, temperament, or virtues of group members. This individualist conception of persons and their relation to one another tends to identify oppression with group identification. Oppression, on this view, is something that happens to people when they are classified in groups. Because others identify them as a group, they are excluded and despised. Eliminating oppression thus requires eliminating groups. People should be treated as individuals, not as members of groups, and allowed to form their lives freely without stereotypes or group norms.

There are several varieties of *poststructuralism*, but what they have in common is their rejection of the notion of a unified, universal, ahistorical conceptual structure. Leading poststructuralist figures include Jacques Derrida, Michel Foucault, Gilles Deleuze, Judith Butler, Jean Baudrillard, and Julia Kristeva.

* In this context, the view that a person can be understood as—and begins as—an isolated individual, separate from and prior to any particular social context (e.g., any particular language or set of cultural assumptions). This view is associated with René Descartes (1596–1650), who understood persons as metaphysically self-sufficient non-physical souls that can exist even without a physical body, never mind a social setting.

† Theories of psychoanalysis put forward by French theorist and psychiatrist Jacques Lacan (1901–81).

‡ German philosopher and social theorist Jürgen Habermas (b. 1929).

§ Martin Heidegger (1889–1976) was an influential German philosopher.

[I take] issue with that position. While I agree that individuals should be free to pursue life plans in their own way, it is foolish to deny the reality of groups. Despite the modern myth of a decline of parochial attachments and ascribed identities, in modern society group differentiation remains endemic. As both markets and social administration increase the web of social interdependency on a world scale, and as more people encounter one another as strangers in cities and states, people retain and renew ethnic, locale, age, sex, and occupational group identifications, and form new ones in the processes of encounter (cf. Ross, 1980, p. 19; Rothschild, 1981, p. 130). Even when they belong to oppressed groups, people's group identifications are often important to them, and they often feel a special affinity for others in their group. I believe that group differentiation is both an inevitable and a desirable aspect of modern social processes. Social justice ... requires not the melting away of differences, but institutions that promote reproduction of and respect for group differences without oppression.

Though some groups have come to be formed out of oppression, and relations of privilege and oppression structure the interactions between many groups, group differentiation is not in itself oppressive. Not all groups are oppressed. In the United States Roman Catholics are a specific social group, with distinct practices and affinities with one another, but they are no longer an oppressed group. Whether a group is oppressed depends on whether it is subject to one or more of the five conditions I shall discuss below.

The view that groups are fictions does carry an important antideterminist or antiessentialist intuition. Oppression has often been perpetrated by a conceptualization of group difference in terms of unalterable essential natures that determine what group members deserve or are capable of, and that exclude groups so entirely from one another that they have no similarities or overlapping attributes. To assert that it is possible to have social group difference without oppression, it is necessary to conceptualize groups in a much more relational and fluid fashion....

Arising from social relations and processes, finally, group differences usually cut across one another.

Especially in a large, complex, and highly differentiated society, social groups are not themselves homogeneous, but mirror in their own differentiations many of the other groups in the wider society. In American society today, for example, Blacks are not a simple, unified group with a common life. Like other racial and ethnic groups, they are differentiated by age, gender, class, sexuality, region, and nationality, any of which in a given context may become a salient group identity.

This view of group differentiation as multiple, cross-cutting, fluid, and shifting implies another critique of the model of the autonomous, unified self. In complex, highly differentiated societies like our own, all persons have multiple group identifications. The culture, perspective, and relations of privilege and oppression of these various groups, moreover, may not cohere. Thus individual persons, as constituted partly by their group affinities and relations, cannot be unified, themselves are heterogeneous and not necessarily coherent.

The Faces of Oppression

EXPLOITATION

The central function of Marx's* theory of exploitation is to explain how class structure can exist in the absence of legally and normatively sanctioned class distinctions. In precapitalist societies domination is overt and accomplished through directly political means. In both slave society and feudal society the right to appropriate the product of the labor of others partly defines class privilege, and these societies legitimate class distinctions with ideologies of natural superiority and inferiority.

Capitalist society, on the other hand, removes traditional juridically enforced class distinctions and promotes a belief in the legal freedom of persons. Workers freely contract with employers and receive a wage; no formal mechanisms of law or custom force them to work for that employer or any employer. Thus the mystery of capitalism arises: when everyone is formally free, how can there be class domination? Why do class distinctions persist between the wealthy, who

---

* German political theorist and philosopher Karl Marx (1818–83): see the reading by Marx and Engels in the Justice chapter of this volume.

own the means of production, and the mass of people, who work for them? The theory of exploitation answers this question....

The injustice of capitalist society consists in the fact that some people exercise their capacities under the control, according to the purposes, and for the benefit of other people. Through private ownership of the means of production, and through markets that allocate labor and the ability to buy goods, capitalism systematically transfers the powers of some persons to others, thereby augmenting the power of the latter. In this process of the transfer of powers, according to Macpherson (1973), the capitalist class acquires and maintains an ability to extract benefits from workers. Not only are powers transferred from workers to capitalists, but also the powers of workers diminish by more than the amount of transfer, because workers suffer material deprivation and a loss of control, and hence are deprived of important elements of self-respect. Justice, then, requires eliminating the institutional forms that enable and enforce this process of transference and replacing them with institutional forms that enable all to develop and use their capacities in a way that does not inhibit, but rather can enhance, similar development and use in others.

The central insight expressed in the concept of exploitation, then, is that this oppression occurs through a steady process of the transfer of the results of this labor of one social group to benefit another. The injustice of class division does not consist only in the distributive fact that some people have great wealth while most people have little (cf. Buchanan, 1982, pp. 44–49; Holmstrom 1977). Exploitation enacts a structural relation between social groups. Social rules about what work is, who does what for whom, how work is compensated, and the social process by which the results of work are appropriated operate to enact relations of power and inequality. These relations are produced and reproduced through a systematic process in which the energies of the have-nots are continuously expended to maintain and augment the power, status, and wealth of the haves.

Many writers have cogently argued that the Marxist concept of exploitation is too narrow to encompass all forms of domination and oppression (Giddens, 1981, p. 242; Brittan and Maynard, 1984, p. 93; Murphy, 1985; Bowles and Giotis, 1986, pp. 20–24). In particular, the Marxist concept of class leaves important phenomena of sexual and racial oppression unexplained. Does this mean that sexual and racial oppression are nonexploitative, and that we should reserve wholly distinct categories for these oppressions? Or can the concept of exploitation be broadened to include other ways in which the labor and energy expenditure of one group benefits another, and reproduces a relation of domination between them?

Feminists have had little difficulty showing that women's oppression consists partly in a systematic and unreciprocated transfer of powers from women to men. Women's oppression consists not merely in an inequality of status, power, and wealth resulting from men's excluding them from privileged activities. The freedom, power, status, and self-realization of men is possible precisely because women work for them. Gender exploitation has two aspects, transfer of the fruits of material labor to men and transfer of nurturing and sexual energies to men....

Race is a structure of oppression at least as basic as class or gender. Are there, then, racially specific forms of exploitation? There is no doubt that racialized groups in the United States, especially Blacks and Latinos, are oppressed through capitalist superexploitation* resulting from a segmented labor market that tends to reserve skilled, high-paying, unionized jobs for whites. There is wide disagreement about whether such superexploitation benefits whites as a group or only benefits the capitalist class (see Reich, 1981), and I do not intend to enter into that dispute here.

However one answers the question about capitalist superexploitation of racialized groups, is it possible to conceptualize a form of exploitation that is racially specific on analogy with the gender-specific forms just discussed? I suggest that the category of *menial* labor might supply a means for such conceptualization. In

---

*   A Marxist term to describe the exploitation inflicted on laborers who work in systems creating "superprofits," or above-average profit margins; for example, colonial superexploitation resulted in superprofits for imperial nations. Young is stating here that modern capitalist societies, in this case the United States, have been built and maintained by superprofits harnessed by a white ruling class through the superexploitation of other racial groups.

its derivation "menial" designates the labor of servants. Wherever there is racism, there is the assumption, more or less enforced, that members of the oppressed racial groups are or ought to be servants of those, or some of those, in the privileged group. In most white racist societies this means that many white people have dark- or yellow-skinned domestic servants, and in the United States today there remains significant racial structuring of private household service....

Menial labor usually refers not only to service, however, but also to any servile, unskilled, low-paying work lacking in autonomy, in which a person is subject to taking orders from many people. Menial work tends to be auxiliary work, instrumental to the work of others, where those others receive primary recognition for doing the job. Laborers on a construction site for example are at the beck and call of welders, electricians, carpenters, and other skilled workers, who receive recognition for the job done. In the United States explicit racial discrimination once reserved menial work for Blacks, Chicanos, American Indians, and Chinese, and menial work still tends to be linked to Black and Latino workers (Symanski, 1985). I offer this category of menial labor as a form of racially specific exploitation, as a provisional category in need of exploration....

The injustice of exploitation consists in social processes that bring about a transfer of energies from one group to another to produce unequal distributions, and in the way in which social institutions enable a few to accumulate while they constrain many more. The injustices of exploitation cannot be eliminated by redistribution of goods, for as long as institutionalized practices and structural relations remain unaltered, the process of transfer will re-create an unequal distribution of benefits. Bringing about justice where there is exploitation requires reorganization of institutions and practices of decision-making; alteration of the division of labor, and similar measure of institutional, structural, and cultural change.

MARGINALIZATION

Increasingly in the United States racial oppression occurs in the form of marginalization rather than exploitation. Marginals are people the system of labor cannot or will not use. Not only in Third World capitalist countries, but also in most Western capitalist societies, there is a growing underclass of people permanently confined to lives of social marginality, most of whom are racially marked—Blacks or Indians in Latin America, and Blacks, East Indians, Eastern Europeans, or North Africans in Europe.

Marginalization is by no means the fate only of racially marked groups, however. In the United States a shamefully large proportion of the population is marginal: old people, and increasingly people who are not very old but get laid off from their jobs and cannot find new work: young people, especially Black or Latino, who cannot find first or second jobs; many single mothers and their children; other people involuntarily unemployed; many mentally and physically disabled people; American Indians, especially those on reservations.

Marginalization is perhaps the most dangerous form of oppression. A whole category of people is expelled from useful participation in social life and thus potentially subjected to severe material deprivation and even extermination. The material deprivation marginalization often causes is certainly unjust, especially in a society where others have plenty. Contemporary advanced capitalist societies have in principle acknowledged the injustice of material deprivation caused by marginalization, and have taken some steps to address it by providing welfare payments and services. The continuance of this welfare state is by no means assured, and in most welfare state societies, especially the United States, welfare redistributions do not eliminate large-scale suffering and deprivation.

Material deprivation, which can be addressed by redistributive social policies, is not, however, the extent of the harm caused by marginalization. Two categories of injustice beyond distribution are associated with marginality in advanced capitalist societies. First, the provision of welfare itself produces new injustice by depriving those dependent on it of rights and freedoms that others have. Second, even when material deprivation is somewhat mitigated by the welfare state, marginalization is unjust because it blocks the opportunity to exercise capacities in socially defined and recognized ways. I shall explicate each of these in turn.

Liberalism has traditionally asserted the right of all rational autonomous agents to equal citizenship. Early bourgeois liberalism explicitly excluded from citizenship all those whose reason was questionable or not fully developed, and all those not independent (Pateman, 1988, chap. 3; cf. Bowles and Gintis, 1986, chap. 2). Thus poor people, women, the mad and the feeble-minded, and children were explicitly excluded from citizenship, and many of these were housed in institutions modeled on the modern prison: poorhouses, insane asylums, schools.

Today the exclusion of dependent persons from equal citizenship rights is only barely hidden beneath the surface. Because they depend on bureaucratic institutions for support or services, the old, the poor, and the mentally or physically disabled are subject to patronizing, punitive, demeaning, and arbitrary treatment by the policies and people associated with welfare bureaucracies. Being a dependent in our society implies being legitimately subject to the often arbitrary and invasive authority of social service providers and other public and private administrators, who enforce rules with which the marginal must comply, and otherwise exercise power over the conditions of their lives. In meeting needs of the marginalized, often with aid of social scientific disciplines, welfare agencies also construct the needs themselves. Medical and social service professionals know what is good for those they serve, and the marginals and dependents themselves do not have the right to claim to know what is good for them (Fraser, 1987a; K. Ferguson, 1984, chap. 4). Dependency in our society thus implies, as it has in all liberal societies, a sufficient warrant to suspend basic rights to privacy, respect, and individual choice.

Although dependency produces conditions of injustice in our society, dependency in itself need not be oppressive. One cannot imagine a society in which some people would not need to be dependent on others at least some of the time: children, sick people, women recovering from childbirth, old people who have become frail, depressed or otherwise emotionally needy persons, have the moral right to depend on others for subsistence and support.

An important contribution of feminist moral theory has been to question the deeply held assumption that moral agency and full citizenship require that a person be autonomous and independent. Feminists have exposed this assumption as inappropriately individualistic and derived from a specifically male experience of social relations, which values competition and solitary achievement (see Gilligan, 1982; Friedman, 1985). Female experience of social relations, arising both from women's typical domestic care responsibilities and from the kinds of paid work that many women do, tends to recognize dependence as a basic human condition (cf. Hartsock, 1983, chap. 10). Whereas on the autonomy model a just society would as much as possible give people the opportunity to be independent, the feminist model envisions justice as according respect and participation in decisionmaking to those who are dependent as well as to those who are independent (Held, 1987). Dependency should not be a reason to be deprived of choice and respect, and much of the oppression many marginals experience would be lessened if a less individualistic model of rights prevailed.

Marginalization does not cease to be oppressive when one has shelter and food. Many old people, for example, have sufficient means to live comfortably but remain oppressed in their marginal status. Even if marginals were provided a comfortable material life within institutions that respected their freedom and dignity, injustices of marginality would remain in the form of uselessness, boredom, and lack of self-respect. Most of our society's productive and recognized activities take place in contexts of organized social cooperation, and social structures and processes that close persons out of participation in such social cooperation are unjust. Thus while marginalization definitely entails serious issues of distributive justice, it also involves the deprivation of cultural, practical, and institutionalized conditions for exercising capacities in a context of recognition and interaction....

POWERLESSNESS

While it is false to claim that a division between capitalist and working classes no longer describes our society, it is also false to say that class relations have remained unaltered since the nineteenth century. An adequate conception of oppression cannot ignore the experience of social division reflected in the colloquial distinction between the "middle class" and the "working class," a division structured by the social division of labor between professionals and nonprofessionals. Professionals are privileged in relation to nonprofessionals, by virtue of their position in the division of labor and the status it carries. Nonprofessionals suffer a form of oppression in addition to exploitation, which I call powerlessness.

In the United States, as in other advanced capitalist countries, most workplaces are not organized democratically, direct participation in public policy decisions is rare, and policy implementation is for the most part hierarchical, imposing rules on bureaucrats and citizens. Thus most people in these societies do not regularly participate in making decisions that affect the conditions of their lives and actions, and in this sense most people lack significant power. At the same time, domination in modern society is enacted through the widely dispersed powers of many agents mediating the decisions of others. To that extent many people have some power in relation to others, even though they lack the power to decide policies or results. The powerless are those who lack authority or power even in this mediated sense, those over whom power is exercised without their exercising it; the powerless are situated so that they must take orders and rarely have the right to give them. Powerlessness also designates a position in the division of labor and the concomitant social position that allow persons little opportunity to develop and exercise skills. The powerless have little or no work autonomy, exercise little creativity or judgment in their work, have no technical expertise or authority, express themselves awkwardly, especially in public or bureaucratic settings, and do not command respect....

This powerless status is perhaps best described negatively: the powerless lack the authority, status, and sense of self that professionals tend to have. The status privilege of professionals has three aspects, the lack of which produces oppression for nonprofessionals.

First, acquiring and practicing a profession has an expansive, progressive character. Being professional usually requires a college education and the acquisition of a specialized knowledge that entails working with symbols and concepts. Professionals experience progress first in acquiring the expertise, and then in the course of professional advancement and the rise in status. The life of the nonprofessional by comparison is powerless in the sense that it lacks this orientation toward the progressive development of capacities and avenues for recognition.

Second, while many professionals have supervisors and cannot directly influence many decisions or the actions of many people, most nevertheless have considerable day-to-day work autonomy. Professionals usually have some authority over others, moreover—either over workers they supervise, or over auxiliaries, or over clients. Nonprofessionals, on the other hand, lack autonomy, and in both their working and their consumer-client lives often stand under the authority of professionals.

Though based on a division of labor between "mental" and "manual" work, the distinction between "middle class" and "working class" designates a division not only in working life, but also in nearly all aspects of social life. Professionals and nonprofessionals belong to different cultures in the United States. The two groups tend to live in segregated neighborhoods or even different towns, a process itself mediated by planners, zoning officials, and real estate people. The groups tend to have different tastes in food, decor, clothes, music, and vacations, and often different health and educational needs. Members of each group socialize for the most part with others in the same status group. While there is some intergroup mobility between generations, for the most part the children of professionals become professionals and the children of nonprofessionals do not.

Thus, third, the privileges of the professional extend beyond the workplace to a whole way of life. I call this way of life "respectability." To treat people with respect is to be prepared to listen to what they have to say or to do what they request because they have some authority, expertise, or influence. The norms of respectability in our society are associated specifically with professional culture. Professional dress, speech, tastes, demeanor, all connote respectability. Generally professionals expect and receive respect from others. In restaurants, banks, hotels, real estate offices, and many other such public places, as well as in the media, professionals typically receive more respectful treatment than nonprofessionals. For this reason nonprofessionals seeking a loan or a job, or to buy a house or a car, will often try to look "professional" and "respectable" in those settings.

The privilege of this professional respectability appears starkly in the dynamics of racism and sexism. In daily interchange women and men of color must prove their respectability. At first they are often not treated by strangers with respectful distance or deference. Once people discover that this woman or that Puerto Rican man is a college teacher or a business executive, however, they often behave more respectfully toward her or him. Working-class white men, on the other hand, are often treated with respect until their working-class status is revealed....

CULTURAL IMPERIALISM

To experience cultural imperialism means to experience how the dominant meanings of a society render the particular perspective of one's own group invisible at the same time as they stereotype one's group and mark it out as the Other.

Cultural imperialism involves the universalization of a dominant group's experience and culture, and its establishment as the norm. Some groups have exclusive or primary access to what Nancy Fraser (1987b) calls the means of interpretation and communication in a society. As a consequence, the dominant cultural products of the society, that is, those most widely disseminated, express the experience, values, goals, and achievements of these groups. Often without noticing they do so, the dominant groups project their own experience as a representative of humanity as such. Cultural products also express the dominant group's perspective on and interpretation of events and elements in the society, including other groups in the society, insofar as they attain cultural status at all.

An encounter with other groups, however, can challenge the dominant group's claim to universality. The dominant group reinforces its position by bringing the other groups under the measure of its dominant norms. Consequently, the difference of women from men, American Indians or Africans from Europeans, Jews from Christians, homosexuals from heterosexuals, workers from professionals, becomes reconstructed largely as deviance and inferiority. Since only the dominant group's cultural expressions receive wide dissemination, their cultural expressions become the normal, or the universal, and thereby the unremarkable. Given the normality of its own cultural expressions and identity, the dominant group constructs the differences which some groups exhibit as lack and negation. These groups become marked as Other.

The culturally dominated undergo a paradoxical oppression, in that they are both marked by stereotypes and at the same time rendered invisible. As remarkable, deviant beings, the culturally imperialized are stamped with an essence. The stereotypes confine them to a nature which is often attached in some way to their bodies, and which thus cannot easily be denied. These stereotypes so permeate the society that they are not noticed as contestable. Just as everyone knows that the earth goes around the sun, so everyone knows that gay people are promiscuous, that Indians are alcoholics, and that women are good with children. White males, on the other hand, insofar as they escape group marking, can be individuals....

The group defined by the dominant culture as deviant, as a stereotyped Other, *is* culturally different from the dominant group, because the status of Otherness creates specific experiences not shared by the dominant group, and because culturally oppressed groups also are often socially segregated and occupy specific positions in the social division of labor. Members of such groups express their specific group experiences and interpretations of the world to one another, developing and perpetuating their own culture. Double consciousness, then, occurs because one finds one's being defined by two cultures: a dominant and a subordinate culture. Because they can affirm and recognize one another as sharing similar experiences and perspectives on social life, people in culturally imperialized groups can often maintain a sense of positive subjectivity.

Cultural imperialism involves the paradox of experiencing oneself as invisible at the same time that one is marked out as different. The invisibility comes about when dominant groups fail to recognize the perspective embodied in their cultural expressions as a perspective. These dominant cultural expressions often simply have little place for the experience of other groups, at most only mentioning or referring to them in stereotyped or marginalized ways. This, then is the injustice of cultural imperialism: that the oppressed group's own experience and interpretation of social life finds little expression that touches the dominant culture, while that same culture imposes on the oppressed group its experience and interpretation of social life.

VIOLENCE

Finally, many groups suffer the oppression of systematic violence. Members of some groups live with the knowledge that they must fear random, unprovoked attacks on their persons or property, which have no motive but to damage, humiliate, or destroy the person. In American society women, Blacks, Asians, Arabs, gay men, and lesbians live under such threats of violence, and in at least some regions Jews, Puerto Ricans, Chicanos, and other Spanish-speaking Americans must fear such violence as well. Physical violence against these groups is shockingly frequent.... While the frequency of physical attack on members of these and other racially or sexually marked groups is very disturbing, I also include in this category less severe incidents of harassment, intimidation, or ridicule simply for the purpose of degrading, humiliating, or stigmatizing group members.

Given the frequency of such violence in our society, why are theories of justice usually silent about it? I think the reason is that theorists do not typically take such incidents of violence and harassment as matters of social injustice. No moral theorist would deny that such acts are very wrong. But unless all immoralities are injustices, they might wonder, why should such acts be interpreted as symptoms of social injustice? Acts of violence or petty harassment are committed by particular individuals, often extremists, deviants, or the mentally unsound. How then can they be said to involve the sorts of institutional issues I have said are properly the subject of justice?

What makes violence a face of oppression is less the particular acts themselves, though these are often utterly horrible, than the social context surrounding them, which makes them possible and even acceptable. What makes violence a phenomenon of social injustice, and not merely an individual moral wrong, is its systemic character, its existence as a social practice.

Violence is systemic because it is directed at members of a group simply because they are members of that group. Any woman, for example, has a reason to fear rape. Regardless of what a Black man has done to escape the oppressions of marginality of powerlessness, he lives knowing he is subject to attack or harassment. The oppression of violence consists not only in direct victimization, but in the daily knowledge shared by all members of oppressed groups that they are *liable* to violation, solely on account of their group identity. Just living under such a threat of attack on oneself or family or friends deprives the oppressed of freedom and dignity, and needlessly expends their energy.

Violence is a social practice. It is a social given that everyone knows happens and will happen again. It is always at the horizon of social imagination, even for those who do not perpetrate it. According to the prevailing social logic, some circumstances make such violence more "called for" than others. The idea of rape will occur to many men who pick up a hitch-hiking woman; the idea of hounding or teasing a gay man on their dorm floor will occur to many straight male college students. Often several persons inflict the violence together, especially in all-male groupings. Sometimes violators set out looking for people to beat up, rape, or taunt. This rule-bound, social, and often premeditated character makes violence against groups a social practice.

Group violence approaches legitimacy, moreover, in the sense that it is tolerated. Often third parties find it unsurprising because it happens frequently and lies as a constant possibility at the horizon of the social imagination. Even when they are caught, those who perpetrate acts of group-directed violence or harassment often receive light or no punishment. To that extent society renders their acts acceptable.

An important aspect of random, systematic violence is its irrationality. Xenophobic* violence differs from the violence of states or ruling-class repression. Repressive violence has a rational, albeit evil, motive: rulers use it as a coercive tool to maintain their power. Many accounts of racist, sexist, or homophobic violence attempt to explain its motivation as a desire to maintain group privilege or domination. I do not doubt that fear of violence often functions to keep oppressed groups subordinate, but do not think xenophobic violence is rationally motivated in the way that, for example, violence against strikers is.

On the contrary, the violation of rape, beating, killing, and harassment of women, people of color, gays, and other marked groups is motivated by fear or hatred of those groups. Sometimes the motive may be a simple will to power, to victimize those marked as vulnerable by the very social fact that they are subject to violence. If so, this motive is secondary in the sense that it depends on a social practice of group violence. Violence-causing fear or hatred of the other at least partly involves insecurities on the part of the violators: its irrationality suggests that unconscious processes are at work.

Cultural imperialism, moreover, itself intersects with violence. The culturally imperialized may reject the dominant meanings and attempt to assert their own subjectivity, or the fact of their cultural difference may

---

* Irrationally fearful or mistrustful of what is foreign or strange.

put the lie to the dominant culture's implicit claim to universality. The dissonance generated by such a challenge to the hegemonic* cultural meanings can also be a source of irrational violence.

Violence is a form of injustice that a distributive understanding of justice seems ill equipped to capture. This may be why contemporary discussions of justice rarely mention it. I have argued that group-directed violence is institutionalized and systemic. To the degree that institutions and social practices encourage, tolerate, or enable the perpetration of violence against members of specific groups, those institutions and practices are unjust and should be reformed. Such reform may require the redistribution of resources or positions, but in large part can come only through a change in cultural images, stereotypes, and the mundane reproduction of relations of dominance and aversion in the gestures of everyday life.

Applying the Criteria

Social theories that construct oppression as a unified phenomenon usually either leave out groups that even the theorists think are oppressed, or leave out important ways in which groups are oppressed. Black liberation theorists and feminist theorists have argued persuasively, for example, that Marxism's reduction of all oppressions to class oppression leaves out much about the specific oppression of Blacks and women. By pluralizing the category of oppression in the way explained in this chapter, social theory can avoid the exclusive and oversimplifying effects of such reductionism.

I have avoided pluralizing the category in the way some others have done, by constructing an account of separate systems of oppression for each oppressed group: racism, sexism, classism, heterosexism, ageism, and so on. There is a double problem with considering each group's oppression a unified and distinct structure or system. On the one hand, this way of conceiving oppression fails to accommodate the similarities and overlaps in the oppressions of different groups. On the other hand, it falsely represents the situation of all group members as the same.

I have arrived at the five faces of oppression—exploitation, marginalization, powerlessness, cultural imperialism, and violence—as the best way to avoid such exclusions and reductions. They function as criteria for determining whether individuals and groups are oppressed, rather than as a full theory of oppression. I believe that these criteria are objective. They provide a means of refuting some people's belief that their group is oppressed when it is not, as well as a means of persuading others that a group is oppressed when they doubt it. Each criterion can be operationalized; each can be applied through the assessment of observable behavior, status relationships, distributions, texts and other cultural artifacts. I have no illusions that such assessments can be value-neutral. But these criteria can nevertheless serve as means of evaluating claims that a group is oppressed, or adjudicating disputes about whether or how a group is oppressed.

The presence of any of these five conditions is sufficient for calling a group oppressed. But different group oppressions exhibit different combinations of these forms, as do different individuals in the groups. Nearly all, if not all, groups said by contemporary social movements to be oppressed suffer cultural imperialism. The other oppressions they experience vary. Working-class people are exploited and powerless, for example, but if employed and white do not experience marginalization and violence. Gay men, on the other hand, are not qua gay exploited or powerless, but they experience severe cultural imperialism and violence. Similarly, Jews and Arabs as groups are victims of cultural imperialism and violence, though many members of these groups also suffer exploitation or powerlessness. Old people are oppressed by marginalization and cultural imperialism, and this is also true of physically and mentally disabled people. As a group women are subject to gender-based exploitation, powerlessness, cultural imperialism, and violence. Racism in the United States condemns many Blacks and Latinos to marginalization, and puts many more at risk, even though many members of these groups escape that condition; members of these groups often suffer all five forms of oppression.

---

*   Ruling, dominant.

Applying these five criteria to the situation of groups makes it possible to compare oppressions without reducing them to a common essence or claiming that one is more fundamental than another. One can compare the ways in which a particular form of oppression appears in different groups. For example, while the operations of cultural imperialism are often experienced in similar fashion by different groups, there are also important differences. One can compare the combinations of oppressions groups experience, or the intensity of those oppressions. Thus with these criteria one can plausibly claim that one group is more oppressed than another without reducing all oppressions to a single scale.

Why are particular groups oppressed in the way they are? Are there any causal connections among the five forms of oppression? Causal or explanatory questions such as these are beyond the scope of this discussion. While I think general social theory has a place, causal explanation must always be particular and historical. Thus an explanatory account of why a particular group is oppressed in the ways that it is must trace the history and current structure of particular social relations. Such concrete historical and structural explanations will often show causal connections among the different forms of oppression experienced by a group. The cultural imperialism in which white men make stereotypical assumptions about and refuse to recognize the values of Blacks or women, for example, contributes to the marginalization and powerlessness many Blacks and women suffer. But cultural imperialism does not always have these effects. ■

Suggestions for Critical Reflection

1. Consider the quotation by Simone Weil used as an epigraph to this reading. Why do you think Young chose it to open her argument?

2. Young states that she has "proposed an enabling conception of justice." How, if at all, could the framework of the five faces of oppression be enabling for oppressed groups working to improve their lives? If you have read the selections in this volume by Rawls and Nozick, how do you think it differs from a distributive account of justice?

3. "The systemic character of oppression implies that an oppressed group need not have a correlate oppressing group." What does Young mean by this—what do you think are its implications if she is right?

4. Young claims that the five faces of oppression can serve as criteria for determining whether a group is oppressed. Consider a particular category of people who may be oppressed, such as a specific ethnic or gender group. Do Young's criteria help in assessing the oppression of this group? Does applying the criteria help you to better understand the group's concerns?

5. Philosophers disagree about the role of social groups in society, with some viewing them as positive, a means to create a society in which many interconnecting but distinct groups live together supportively, whereas others believe the best way forward would be to move beyond group membership and into a post-racial, post-gender society. What do you think? Is group membership positive, or is it a source of prejudice and determinism that stands in the way of a just society?

6. Consider Young's discussion of marginalization. What are the two categories of injustice caused by marginalization that she says are beyond the scope of distributive remedy? How do societies try to address these types of structural oppressions?

7. Young writes that "acquiring and practicing a profession has an expansive, progressive character." Why does she say this? Is she right? Could non-professional careers be "expansive" in a similar way, and if so does this have implications for her argument?

8. Are Young's five categories of oppression comprehensive? Are there any forms of oppression which they do not cover? (Does Young mean them to be totally comprehensive?)

9. If you have read the Beauvoir selection in this chapter, consider whether she is one of the people whom Young criticizes as thinking that "social groups are invidious fictions, essentializing arbitrary attributes." If so, how might Beauvoir reply?

References

Bowles, Samuel and Herbert Gintis. 1986. *Democracy and Capitalism*. New York: Basic.

Brittan, Arthur and Mary Maynard. 1984. *Sexism, Racism and Oppression*. Oxford: Blackwell.

Buchanan, Allen. 1982. *Marx and Justice*. Totowa, N.J.: Roman and Allanheld.

Coward, Rosalind and John Ellis. 1977. *Language and Materialism*. London: Routledge and Kegan Paul.

Epstein, Steven. 1987. "Gay Politics, Ethnic Identity: The Limits of Social Constructionism." *Socialist Review* 17 (May–August): 9–54.

Ferguson, Kathy. 1984. *The Feminist Case against Bureaucracy*. Philadelphia: Temple University Press.

Foucault, Michel. 1977. *Discipline and Punish*. New York: Pantheon.

Fraser, Nancy. 1987a. "Women, Welfare, and the Politics of Need Interpretation." *Hypatia: A Journal of Feminist Philosophy* 2 (Winter): 103–22.

———. 1987b. "Social Movements vs. Disciplinary Bureaucracies: The Discourse of Social Needs." CHS Occasional Paper No. 8. Center for Humanistic Studies, University of Minnesota.

Friedman, Marilyn. 1985. "Care and Context in Moral Reasoning." In Carol Harding, ed., *Moral Dilemmas: Philosophical and Psychological Issues in the Development of Moral Reasoning*. Chicago: Precedent.

Friedman, Marilyn and Larry May. 1985. "Harming Women as a Group." *Social Theory and Practice* 11 (Summer): 297–34.

Frye, Marilyn. 1983. "Oppression." In *The Politics of Reality*. Trumansburg, N.Y.: Crossing Press.

Giddens, Anthony. 1981. *A Contemporary Critique of Historical Materialism*. Berkeley and Los Angeles: University of California Press.

Gilligan, Carol. 1982. *In a Different Voice*. Cambridge: Harvard University Press.

Habermas, Jürgen. 1987. *The Theory of Communicative Competence*. Vol. 2: *Lifeworld and System*. Boston: Beacon.

Hartsock, Nancy. 1983. *Money, Sex and Power*. New York: Longman.

Heidegger, Martin. 1962. *Being and Time*. New York: Harper and Row.

Held, Virginia. 1987. "A Non-Contractual Society." In Marsha Hanen and Kai Nielsen, eds., *Science, Morality and Feminist Theory*. Calgary: University of Calgary Press.

Holmstrom, Nancy. 1977. "Exploitation." *Canadian Journal of Philosophy* 7 (June): 353–69.

Macpherson, C.B. 1973. *Democratic Theory: Essays in Retrieval*. Oxford: Oxford University Press.

Murphy, Raymond. 1985. "Exploitation or Exclusion?" *Sociology* 19 (May): 225–43.

Pateman, Carole. 1988. *The Sexual Contract*. Stanford: Stanford University Press.

Reich, Michael. 1981. *Racial Inequality*. Princeton: Princeton University Press.

Ross, Jeffrey. 1980. Introduction to Jeffrey Ross and Ann Baker Cottrell, eds., *The Mobilization of Collective Identity*. Lanham, Md.: University Press of America.

Rothschild, Joseph. 1981. *Ethnopolitics*. New York: Columbia University Press.

Symanski, Al. 1985. "The Structure of Race." *Review of Radical Political Economy* 17 (Winter): 106–20.

Turner, John C., Michael A. Hogg, Penelope V. Oakes, Stephen D. Rucher, and Margaret S. Wethrell. 1987. *Rediscovering the Social Group: A Self-Categorization Theory*. Oxford: Blackwell.

KWAME ANTHONY APPIAH

How to Decide If Races Exist

Who Is Kwame Anthony Appiah?

British-Ghanaian philosopher Kwame Anthony Appiah was born in London in 1954. His father, Joseph Appiah, was a well-known Ghanaian politician and lawyer, and his mother, born Peggy Cripps, was a British writer and art historian. Appiah grew up in Kumasi, Ghana, and attended high school in Britain. He received his BA from Clare College, Cambridge in 1975, and his PhD in philosophy from Cambridge in 1982. His research interests include the philosophy of language, African and African American history and literature, race theory, and moral and political philosophy.

Appiah's work is focused on questions of race, culture, and identity: "The challenge," he writes in *Cosmopolitanism: Ethics in a World of Strangers* (2006), "is to take minds and hearts formed over the long millennia of living in local troops and equip them with ideas and institutions that will allow us to live together as the global tribe we have become." As a proponent of cosmopolitanism, Appiah has argued for moving beyond ethno-racial identities into a "post-racial" world, though he recognizes that this dream is unlikely to be fulfilled any time soon.

Appiah's doctoral thesis and early work focused on the philosophy of language, but he soon began working in African and African-American cultural studies. His first major publication, *In My Father's House: Africa in the Philosophy of Culture* (1992), considers African identity in relation to the West and an increasingly globalized world. Though criticized by some scholars as Eurocentric, the book was generally well received, and it garnered several awards. In *Color Conscious: The Political Morality of Race* (1996) (co-authored with Amy Gutmann), Appiah discusses the falsity of biological concepts of race, and, on the basis of this, criticizes the role that group identities can sometimes play in determining individual identity. This skepticism towards group identities is further explored in *The Ethics of Identity* (2005), in which Appiah considers how group membership can both foster and limit individual freedom. He questions how the ways we categorize ourselves and others determine who we are.

Appiah has taught at Yale, Cornell, Duke, and Harvard Universities, and he is currently Professor of Philosophy and Law at New York University.

What Is the Structure of This Reading?

"How to Decide If Races Exist" analyzes how we think about race, the role racial categories play in identity formation, and whether our categorizations have any basis in biological science.

Appiah opens his argument by considering what he calls "folk races," the racial categories that are commonly used and accepted in society (applications and forms that ask you to identify your race, for example, would list these categories). These "folk races" are the categories we absorb as children that shape our social world. Appiah emphasizes that these categories are essentialized, meaning that they aren't based simply on appearance: people assigned to these categories are also thought to share inherited intrinsic qualities that explain their aptitudes and behaviors.

Appiah notes that racial categories exert a shaping influence on individuals and societies, particularly in the formation of social identities, despite the fact that these categories are not well-grounded in biology. He analyzes our social identities by parsing the labels we give them: What does it mean when we say someone is "Asian," for example, and what does it mean to call oneself "Asian"? Appiah suggests that three things are necessary for a label to function as a social identity: it needs to be applied to a group of people ("ascription"), people need to identify themselves by the label ("identification"), and the group needs to be treated differently from others on account of its label, whether positively, negatively, or both ("treatment"). Most social identities will also have norms attached to them, which are traits that a group is widely held to share. Appiah argues that these elements are present for all social identities—not only ethno-racial, but also sexual, national, professional, and political (among others).

Appiah next considers the possibility that genetic science might reveal a biological grounding for racial identities. As an example, he discusses a trend among African Americans to use genetic testing in order to trace their roots to a particular region and people in Africa, and thereby establish their ethno-racial identity. This testing then connects people across the globe who share African ancestry. While not hostile to this emerging aspect of the Pan-African movement, Appiah is skeptical of the existence of a genetic basis for racial identity, given that almost all people have multiple ancestors from a variety of regions across the globe. Genetics, while it can reveal important information about diseases that are more common in certain places in the world, does not, according to Appiah, lend support for our commonly held essentialized racial categories.

While Appiah does not argue here, as he does elsewhere, that racial categories should be abandoned entirely, he does lay the foundation for this argument. If we want to continue to say there are races, he argues, we should understand them as constructed social identities rather than as biologically based subspecies.

Some Useful Background Information

1. Appiah refers to racial essentialism several times in this piece, which he defines as "the idea that human groups have core properties in common that explain not just their shared superficial appearances but also the deep tendencies of their moral and cultural lives."* Nineteenth-century theorists combined essentialism with a belief in the biological reality of race, and eventually this theory merged with nationalism to produce some of the most hateful and destructive racism the world has yet known. Though we now recognize the horrors caused by racial genocide in past centuries, Appiah notes that belief in essential differences among people persists widely across the world, and that this is unlikely to change drastically very soon.

2. In contemporary philosophical debates about race, Appiah is considered a "racial skeptic." He argues that since essentialist race categories aren't supported by biological evidence, we should stop classifying people according to these categories. Appiah believes that the concept of race hinders us from creating healthier societies. In his 2015 article "Race in the Modern World," he suggests that "the price of trying to move beyond ethno-racial identities is worth paying, not only for moral reasons but also for the sake of intellectual hygiene. It would allow us to live and work together more harmoniously and productively, in offices, neighborhoods, towns, states, and nations. Why, after all, should we tie our fates to groups whose existence seems always to involve misunderstandings about the facts of human difference? Why rely on imaginary natural commonalities rather than build cohesion through intentional communities?" The article printed here, "How to Decide If Races Exist," provides a foundation for this position of racial skepticism.

It is important to note that Appiah's skepticism regarding racial categories does not extend to "race-like social identities," which he says can be positive forces in the struggle against racism. He does, however, approach identity politics with some ambivalence, too, lest our racial (and sexual, gender, national, etc.) identities subject us to "new tyrannies."

---

* See Appiah, "Race in the Modern World: The Problem with the Color Line," *Foreign Affairs*, March/April 2015.

How to Decide If Races Exist*

I

From a very early age, people across cultures classify others on the basis of appearance without any particular encouragement. As Susan Gelman has argued in her fascinating book *The Essential Child*, evidence from developmental psychology shows that by the age of six children treat races as "possessing inborn features, inherent in the ... person, and passed down from parent to child."[1] Young children, she argues, also *essentialize* these groups: they believe that the "outer" characteristics by which they assign people to groups reflect shared "inner" properties that explain both appearance and behavior.[2] So there is a large set of ways of classifying people all around the world and throughout history that reflect this cognitive predisposition.

By talk of "folk races"—and this is just a stipulation—I mean to pick out those folk categories that are based on the idea that membership in the relevant group is determined by intrinsic properties inherited from one's parents, properties that are shared by all normal members of the group. Using this terminology, the hypothesis that there are human folk races is the hypothesis that there are human groups of common ancestry that are (roughly) definable by shared inherited intrinsic properties.

It's a consequence of this stipulation that biological subspecies, at least as many evolutionary biologists have conceived of them, are not likely to be folk races.[3] That's because membership in a subspecies is not an intrinsic property, but a relational one. A subspecies is a kind of biological population. In a sexually reproducing species like ours, a population is a collection of organisms whose members have a significantly higher propensity to reproduce with opposite-sex members of the group than they have to reproduce with organisms outside it. As a result, two organisms that are

quite alike in intrinsic biological properties can belong to different populations, and two organisms that are quite dissimilar in properties can belong to the same population. Indeed, you can have two organisms, *A* and *B*, in the same population where *A* is far more different in intrinsic properties from *B* than from *C*, which is not in the population at all. (Imagine a population split in two by the sudden appearance of a new river formed after an earthquake. Consider *A*, *B* and *C*, who were members of the original population before the split. Suppose *A* and *C* are close kin, but *A* and *B* have no recent common ancestor; suppose that *A* and *B* are now on one side of the river and *C* is on the other. Organisms that can't meet can't mate. So *A* and *C* belong to different populations now.)

I advertise this fact—that what I call folk races aren't likely to behave like modern biological classifications—since it *is* the pretty direct result of a stipulation and some well-known biology. For clarity's sake, I'll use the word "subspecies" for this biological kind. I want to insist that my stipulation isn't arbitrary, though: it is motivated by the fact that folk practices of ethno-racial classification are generally essentialist (in Gelman's sense) because we have the cognitive tendency that Gelman has described so well.

Folk classifications in the modern West are quite typical. We assign people to races in a way that is governed by this rule: if your parents are of the same race, you're of the same race as your parents. Since you get your genetic endowment from your parents, racial identities governed by this rule will sometimes be statistically correlated with genetic characteristics, provided there are genes in the local members of a folk race that are commoner than in the general population. Since people are also often assigned to racial groups in part on the basis of phenotypic characteristics[†] that have a genetic basis, there will often, in fact, be such correlations. But Westerners are inclined to suppose

---

*   Kwame Anthony Appiah, "How to Decide If Races Exist," *Proceedings of the Aristotelian Society* 106 (2006): 365–82. Paper delivered at a meeting of the Aristotelian Society, held in Senate House, University of London, on Monday 19 June 2006.

†   Observable features of the bodies and behaviors of organisms.

not just that there are biologically-based features of people that are statistically characteristic of their race, but also that those features extend far beyond the superficial characteristics on the basis of which racial categorization is usually based. So we *essentialize* race, in Gelman's sense of that term. And a great deal of what people believe about the biological basis of these deeper differences is false.

Because the central beliefs of many people about folk races are mistaken in these ways, we cannot explain how people are assigned to races by discovering some folk theory and supposing it to be roughly true. So—since folk races are, like it or not, an important feature of our social landscape—we need an account of the racial categories actually in place that is consistent with the pervasiveness of erroneous beliefs.

II

Here is such an account.[4] It begins by supposing that folk race is an important kind of social identity. That's because I think that folk races are of interest to us largely because they *are* forms of social identity. They continue to be interesting in that way whether or not they are interesting for biological purposes.

My explication of social identities is nominalist:* it explains how the identities work by talking about the labels for them. The main motivation for the nominalism is that it allows us to leave open the question of whether the empirical presuppositions of a labelling practice are correct. Since many social identities are like folk races in being shot through with false belief, this is a decided advantage. So, take a representative label, X, for some identity.

> IDENTITY: There will be criteria of ascription†
> for the term "X"; some people will identify as Xs;
> some people will treat others as Xs; and there will
> be norms of identification.

Each of these notions—ascription, identification, treatment and norms of identification—requires brief commentary.

III

A person's criteria of ascription for "X" are properties on the basis of which she sorts people into those to whom she does and those to whom she doesn't apply the label "X." The criteria of ascription need not be the same for every user of the term; indeed, there will rarely be a socially agreed set of properties individually necessary and jointly sufficient for being an X.[5]

Here is what characterizes competence with the term "X." There will be certain kinds of people—we can call them "prototypical Xs"—such that your criteria of ascription must pick them out as Xs. There will be other kinds—"antitypes," let us call them—that your criteria of ascription must exclude. A prototype is not an actual person: it is a specification of conditions sufficient for being an X; just so, an antitype specifies conditions sufficient for not-being one. But something may be neither a prototype nor an antitype of an X. A Cuban-American, most of whose ancestors came to Cuba before the eighteenth century, and who arrived in Florida in 1950 is a prototype of a Latino. A normal European or African who does not speak Spanish or Portuguese and does not come from the Iberian peninsula is an antitype. List all the prototypes and antitypes and you may find that they do not divide logical space into two classes.

Because prototypes and antitypes don't always divide logical space in two, criteria of ascription need not divide actual people into Xs and not-Xs, either. Rather, they must divide all actual people roughly into three classes, which we can call (modeling our classification on Max Black's account of metaphor‡) the positive, negative and neutral classes. That is, they must make some people, in the positive class, Xs;

---

* In this context, nominalism is the view that the names or labels for things may not correspond to any actually existing abstract object or property.

† To ascribe a characteristic to someone or something is to say that the characteristic is true of them.

‡ Philosopher Max Black (1909–88) put forward in 1954 what is known as a "semantic twist" account of metaphor. His theory divides a metaphoric utterance into two halves: the focal words (the ones used metaphorically) and the framing words (which are not being used metaphorically). By having the two yoked together by metaphoric utterance, new meaning is imposed on the focal word by the frame—for instance (one of Black's own central examples) "the chairman ploughed through the discussion."

some people, in the negative class, not-Xs; and they may leave some people, in the neutral class, as neither determinately Xs nor determinately not-Xs.[6] Let me underline that, whereas prototypes are abstract, these classes are classes of actual people. I am not trying to get at the way the predicate works across possibilia.*

This is what competence consists in; but people do not need to know that their criteria of ascription have these features to be competent. And, in general, they won't know what the relationship is between their criteria of ascription and the total human population. So they may well think, for example, that they can divide the world precisely into Xs and not-Xs, even though there do in fact exist people (people they have not met) who would be in the neutral class for them, if they did know about them. I shall say that someone who has criteria of ascription for an identity-term "X" that meet the conditions for competence has a *conception* of an X.

This is, no doubt, too abstract; so let me just exemplify. Take the term "Asian" as used by Johnny from Cornwall, who has met very few people from anywhere in Asia and very few British Asians either. Johnny says "Asians are a race" and ascribes the term "Asian" to everyone who looks a certain way, in fact the sort of way most movie stars in Bollywood movies would look to him. (I'll call this "looking Asian to" Johnny.) He also thinks that the label is properly applied to anyone whose ancestors for many generations have come from India, because he supposes that everybody in those countries would look Asian to him. Now Johnny will get all the prototypes and antitypes right. Give him a Bangladeshi? "Asian." Give him most Finns or Congolese? "Not Asian." So he's competent. But presented with a Kirghiz or a Kazakh† (people, let us suppose, of whose existence he is currently unaware) he might not know what to say. So his conception has a neutral class, even though he doesn't know this. He may also have false beliefs—such as that almost everyone in Asia looks roughly the way Indian people look—even though most people in Asia

do not: a couple of billion people in China and South-East Asia, for example.

IV

By itself a way of classifying people that works in this way by ascription would not produce a social identity. What makes it a social identity of the relevant kind is not just that people suppose themselves or others to be Xs but that being-an-X figures in a certain typical way in their thoughts, feelings and acts. When a person thinks of herself as an X in the relevant way, she *identifies as an X*. What this means is that she sometimes *feels like an X* or *acts as an X*.

An agent *acts as an X* when the thought "because I am an *X*" figures in her reasons for acting or abstaining. Perhaps you never act as a British person (hereafter "Brit"). But feelings can constitute identification too. You discover that hundreds of thousands of Brits responded to the Asian tsunami‡ by sending money. You feel proud to be British. To *feel like an X* is for your being an X to figure in the intentional content§ of your feeling. The intentional content doesn't have to be *that you're an X*, though: you may feel proud of Mary, a fellow Brit, say. Here your being British figures in the intentional content of the feeling, because part of the intentional structure of the feeling is that Mary is *British like me*, even though you're not proud *that you're British*.

Similarly, our treatment of and feelings about other people reflect identity. You treat *A* as an *X* when "because *A* is an *X*" figures in your reason for doing something to *A*. Supererogatory¶ kindness is a common form of treatment—as directed towards fellow in-group members. Morally opprobrious unkindness is, alas, a horribly frequent form of treatment—as directed towards out-group members. It takes ascription, identification and treatment for a label to be functioning as the label for a social identity of the sort that I am explicating.

---

* Merely possible (non-actual) things.

† People from the former (central Asian) Soviet republics of Kyrgyzstan and Kazakhstan, respectively, whose citizens belong primarily to the Turkic ethnic group.

‡ The 2004 Indian Ocean earthquake and tsunami that killed more than 250,000 people, mainly in Indonesia, Sri Lanka, India, and Thailand.

§ Intentional content is what a mental state (or other meaningful thing, such as a sentence) is about.

¶ A supererogatory action is one that is morally good but goes beyond what is morally required.

One reason identities are useful is that they allow us to predict how people will behave. This is not just because the existence of criteria of ascription entails that members of the group have or tend to have certain properties. It is also because social identities are associated with *norms* for *X*s. That is the final element of my explication of the notion.

There are things that, *qua X*s,* people ought and ought not to do. The "ought" here is the general practical ought, not some special moral one. Here are some examples. Negatively: men ought not to wear dresses; gay men ought not to fall in love with women; blacks ought not to embarrass the race. Positively: men ought to open doors for women; gay people ought to come out; blacks ought to support affirmative action.† To say that these norms exist is evidently not to endorse them. I don't myself endorse any of the norms I just listed. The existence of a norm that *X*s ought to *A* amounts only to its being widely thought—and widely known to be thought—that many people believe that *X*s ought to *A*.[7]

V

I should underline how many and various are the predicates‡ of persons that fit this general rubric. I started with racial and ethnic terms; and I mentioned a nationality, British. But I could also have mentioned professional identities, vocations, affiliations, formal and informal (like Man U§ fan or Conservative), and other more airy labels ... dandy, say, or cosmopolitan.

I am pointing to this range not just because, like a well-bred philosopher, I am interested in generality, but also because this range invites an obvious question. *Why* do we have such a diverse range of social identities and relations? One answer, an aetiological¶ one, will talk about our evolution as a social species and the fact that we are designed evolutionarily for the social game of coalition-building in search of food, mates and protection. This is, I think, a good explanation for our having the sort of psychology of in-group and out-group solidarities and antagonisms that social and developmental psychologists, like Susan Gelman, have been exploring for the last half-century.

But the psychologies that evolution has given us mean that there is a way the world looks from the inside, from the point of view of a creature with that psychology. And from that point of view I think there is another, equally persuasive answer. Each of us has to make a life and to try to make it go well, and we need identities to make our human lives.

We make our lives, that is, *as* men and *as* women; *as* Americans and *as* Brits; *as* philosophers and novelists. Morality—by which I mean what we owe to one another—is part of the scaffolding on which we make that construction. So are various projects that we voluntarily undertake: Voltaire's garden—the one, perhaps, to whose cultivation he consigned his *picaro* Candide—shaped the last part of his life.** But identities are another central resource for making our lives. Identities are diverse and extensive, I think, because people need an enormous diversity of tools for making their lives. Each person needs many options. And, because people are various, the range of options that would be sufficient for each of us won't be sufficient for us all.

VI

There are positive, negative and neutral classes for each competent speaker: that is, there is a way she would

---

* In the capacity of being an *X*.
† Policies specifically promoting the employment and education of disadvantaged groups who have suffered and continue to suffer discrimination.
‡ Describing terms.
§ The English football club Manchester United.
¶ An explanation in terms of causes.
** French philosopher Voltaire (1694–1778) grew extensive gardens in the estates he rented while exiled to Switzerland in the later years of his life. In his novel *Candide* (1759), the protagonist reflects on the life of a Turkish landowner, who cultivated his land with his own labor and the labor of his children. Working in the garden keeps off "three great evils—idleness, vice, and want." Candide reflects that such a quietly productive life is far preferable to the violent and stressful life of kings. The last words of the novel, spoken by Candide, are: "let us cultivate our garden." The word *picaro* is a Spanish term meaning "rascal." It is also used to refer to the protagonist of picaresque novels.

assign everybody on the planet roughly to one of these three classes, if that person showed up in her environment and answered truthfully questions about herself. The prototypes and antitypes define the socially permissible limits of individual positive and negative classes. So we might ask whether there is an interesting property—intrinsic or relational, simple or logically compound—shared by (most) prototypes that is not shared by (most) antitypes. Can we tell a story about racial identity, for example, that shows it to correspond roughly, in this way, to a biological property of genuine interest? If so, folk races are, in a sense, biologically real.

It's in answering this question that new work on the human genome* strikes some people as helpful. Genomics teaches us not only what genes are, but also how they tend to be associated with each other. This offers the prospect of associating certain social groups statistically with genomic features. And where those statistical correlations are distinctive enough of the group and the genomic feature is of importance—for example, for medical reasons—there can be an obvious sense in which biological claims about the group can turn out to be statistical truths. This has been part of folk wisdom for quite a while for a few cases: sickle-cell disease, glucose-6-phosphate dehydrogenase deficiency, and Tay-Sachs disease,[†] for example, are both rare in human beings generally and much more frequent in some groups of common ancestry than in others.

Sometimes the groups in question are quite small: there are alleles[‡] that have been found in certain families and nowhere else. Sometimes the groups are large: Yoruba people, of whom there are more than thirty million in south-west Nigeria, have a 6% frequency of the gene for haemoglobin C (which produces a relatively mild blood disease even in heterozygotes,[§]

who carry two copies of it); and 25% of the population of Nigeria as a whole carries the gene for haemoglobin S, which produces the classic and serious form of sickle-cell disease in heterozygotes.[8] A normal haemoglobin[¶] molecule is made up of four subunits, two α and two β chains; each chain is produced by a distinct gene, and there are many variants of both the α and the β chains. Since the α and β chains are required in equal numbers to form normal haemoglobin, there is also a range of genetic diseases associated with non-standard haemoglobins—the thalassaemias—in which one or other chain is produced in too small a quantity. 39% of Nigerians have some form of α-thalassaemia, the diseases produced when you have an under-production of α chains. These disorders—sickle-cell and thalassaemia—can be inherited both separately and together, producing a dazzling array of blood diseases, and so there is a very wide range of clinical contexts in which it is relevant to know if someone has Nigerian ancestry.

Of course, it's the differences in frequency between populations that make these correlations significant. As a standard discussion of blood diseases points out:

> α-Thalassemia is perhaps the most common single-gene disorder in the world. The frequency of α-thalassemia alleles is 5–10% in persons from the Mediterranean basin, 20–30% in portions of West Africa, and as high as 68% in the southwest Pacific. The frequency of heterozygote carrier status among the Chinese population has been reported to vary from 5–15%. The frequency of α-thalassemia is less than 0.01% in Great Britain, Iceland, and Japan.[9]

---

* An organism's complete set of genes.

† This is an inherited group of diseases, the most common being sickle-cell anemia, which causes anemia, infections, long-term pain, and possible stroke. About 80 per cent of sickle cell disease cases are believed to occur in Sub-Saharan Africa. G6PDD is a genetic disease that affects the metabolism and predisposes the patient to red blood cell breakdown—patients are often unsymptomatic, and the condition confers an evolutionary advantage, as it gives some protection against malaria. It is particularly common among males from certain parts of Africa, Asia, the Mediterranean, and the Middle East. Tay-Sachs disease is a serious genetic disorder that destroys nerve cells in the brain and spinal cord, and is particularly associated with Ashkenazi Jews.

‡ Variant forms of a gene that have been altered by mutation and are located on the same site on a homologous chromosome (i.e., a chromosome which contains the same genes in the same order).

§ An organism having different alleles at a given genetic locus.

¶ The protein found in red blood cells that carries oxygen.

What is most obviously distinctive of reproductively isolated biological populations is the frequency with which variant alleles occur in that population. As we saw earlier, an *individual* in one biological population could, in principle, have almost the same genotype as an individual in another. That is, in essence, why attempts to define biological populations by biological properties shared by their members won't work. A population is a collection of organisms defined, as I said earlier, by the fact that they have a significantly higher probability of reproducing with opposite-sex members of the group than they have of reproducing with organisms outside it. This is a relational property—though it is one that is sometimes explained by an intrinsic property: some sub-populations of *Drosophila** have male genitalia that don't work with the genitalia of females in others. Sometimes the explanation is not an intrinsic property of the organism: populations may just be separated by a mountain range. And sometimes, in humans at least, the explanation could be cultural. If two human populations had ever lived side by side for a long time with no exchange of genes, indeed that would be the most likely explanation. History does not, so far as I know, afford examples of total reproductive isolation of this kind.

So, for example, a majority of members of the folk race of African-Americans have relatively dark skin for genetic reasons. Biological remains that contain some of the genes that characteristically account for this darker skin colour can therefore reasonably be identified for forensic purposes as (socially) African-American. Here there is a genuine biological trait that can be used to identify a genuine social trait, even though the social trait is not identical with any intrinsic biological property. So the utility of genomic properties in identifying a social group doesn't entail that the social group is a subspecies.

This is all consistent with recognizing that many African-Americans do not bear the genes that produce darker skin; that there are other genomic characteristics statistically distinctive of African populations that a person of African ancestry may share without having the skin-colour genes; and that you can be an African-American while having many fewer of the genomic characteristics statistically distinctive of an African population than many people who are identified as white.

Perhaps all this is obvious. But I find in discussion that people seem not to grasp these points intuitively, so perhaps they are worth making. And if they are worth making, perhaps it is also worth filling in some of the conceptual background.

VII

As we all now know, genes consist of sequences of bases,† and each sequence of three such bases (a *triplet* or DNA *codon*) has a functional significance in determining what protein is produced. Mutations in genes occur when one base is replaced with another. Because the relationship between codons and amino acids is many–one, some such substitutions make little functional difference, since the same polypeptide‡ sequences result and the same proteins are formed. Other substitutions change the polypeptide sequence, by substituting one amino acid for another, but make little difference to the biological functioning of the resulting protein: enzymes, for example, characteristically have certain active regions that are important to their functioning, while other sequences are structural supports for the active regions.

Where a mutation has a functional significance, it is most likely to have a negative effect on the organisms that carry it: we are complex wholes with interdependent parts adapted to one another over a relatively long period in a relatively stable environment, and in general a change in the functioning of one element of this complex stable whole will reduce, not increase, our overall fitness. But where a mutation has little or no functional significance it can survive. There will be no selection pressure against it. And so there will be single nucleotide polymorphisms—DNA sequences that differ in just one base from each other—that produce different forms of a gene that are nevertheless

---

*   Commonly known as fruit flies, drosophila are often used in genetics research.
†   Nitrogen-containing biological compounds including adenine, cytosine, guanine, and thymine, which are the basic building blocks of DNA.
‡   A chain of amino acids, which can be the building block for a protein.

functionally equivalent. ("Single nucleotide polymorphism" is a long expression for a short change. Usually it's abbreviated to SNP, pronounced "snip.") A SNP refers both to a site on a chromosome which is occupied in different people by different bases and to the various bases that can be there.[10] Most loci on most genes are the same in everybody: many of the base sequences it takes to be a functioning organism are identical, because changes in most base sequences don't produce a functioning individual. But it's usually estimated that 0.1% of the DNA consists of sites where SNPs can occur in living people. By October 2005, about 3.6 million SNPs had been "validated."[11]

The *genotype* of a person is a specification of every pair of alleles that she carries for every locus* on the genome. Consider two people, each of whom carries the same two alleles at the same two sites: say, *Aa* and *Bb*. But suppose in John *A* and *B* are on one chromosome and *a* and *b* are on another, while in James *A* and *b* are on the same chromosome and *a* and *B* are on another. Suppose that these sites are close together on the same chromosome: as a result the alleles that they carry are extremely unlikely to be separated in cell division.

Now consider the results of sex with a partner whose genotype is *AABB*. With John, she will have offspring *AABB* or *AaBb*. With James, the options are *AABb* or *AaBB*. While John's and James's genotypes are the same, the genotypes of their offspring with the same partner will be different. We will be able to tell, in particular, if we come across one of these offspring, which of the two males was their father simply by looking at two loci, *even though, for those loci, the two potential fathers have the same genotype*. What determines your propensity to produce offspring of a certain genotype, simply put, isn't just your genotype, it's the way in which that genotype is placed on your chromosomes.

That's why the notion of a haplotype—or haploid genotype—is useful in tracing ancestry. It's the specification not of your genotype, but of the sequence of genes on just one of each pair of your chromosomes.

Each individual can be thought of genetically, then, as having two haplotypes. Of course, because there are twenty-three chromosome pairs, you could specify the haplotype in 2^{23} ways: but once you had picked one such way—by selecting one from each pair of chromosomes—you would also have fixed which other haplotype you needed to specify.

One non-arbitrary way to pick a way of specifying the haplotype would be to specify the sequence of alleles on the chromosomes derived from the mother's egg and then specify the sequence on the chromosomes derived from the father's sperm. In the process of meiosis—the type of cell division that produces sex cells—material can be swapped between the two versions of a chromosome carried in a normal somatic cell,† in the process called "crossing over." But if crossing over did not occur, you could think of a person as the combination of a maternal and a paternal haplotype, since without crossing over each person would get exactly one chromosome of each homologous pair of chromosomes from each parent. (Bear in mind, though, that there are 2^{23}—or 8,388,608—possible haplotypes derivable from each parent without crossing over; that's one reason why children of the same parents would be different from one another even if there were no recombination of genes in meiosis.)[12]

The word "haplotype" is also used to refer to classes of haplotypes in the sense I have just defined: namely, a class of haplotypes that are identical in some sequence of alleles close to each other on a single chromosome, often, more particularly, a set of genes for proteins that carry out related activities. More precisely, a haplotype in this second sense is fixed by the sequence of alleles on a relatively short continuous stretch of a chromosome (modulo‡ a few SNPs that have little functional significance). From now on I'll use "haplotypes" in this second sense. So to say two people have the same haplotype is to say, roughly, that they share an interesting collection of genes on a single chromosome.

Since the genes in short regions of a chromosome seldom get separated in cell division, your haplotype

---

* Fixed position (plural loci).
† A cell making up the body of an organism, and thus (roughly) any cell except a gamete—a sperm or an egg—or stem cell.
‡ Except for differences with respect to x (usually, that make no relevant difference to the case under discussion).

in this sense is almost always derived from a single parent. As a result, when a SNP arises by mutation in an ancestral chromosome, it provides a marker for descendants of that ancestor, so long as that SNP does not undergo further mutation and the sequence of genes that includes it does not get broken by crossing over. And this is the basis on which African-Americans are now seeking to identify ancestral ties to particular places in Africa.

VIII

Many contemporary African-Americans have come to take an interest in Yoruba religion, especially in the forms mediated by Haitian *vodou* and the Afro-Brazilian traditions of Bahia.* To discover that you have SNPs associated with a haplotype distinctive of contemporary Yorubaland† would be, for many African-Americans, therefore, an exciting discovery. But Yoruba identity provides a good paradigm of the difficulties faced by those seeking an African identity through the human genome project.

The HapMap Project‡ has a site in Ibadan in Nigeria, a city that is predominantly Yoruba, and the ninety or so individuals in thirty families whose genes were sampled there identified themselves as having four Yoruba grandparents. The theory is simple enough. Find SNPs (or sets of them) in haplotypes that are common in Ibadan today, and that have not been found elsewhere. While there will be contemporary Yoruba people who don't have this polymorphism, it is extremely unlikely that anyone that does carry it does not share ancestry with those that do.

For someone not descended from the ancestor to have both the haplotype and the SNP, they would both have to have both the same sequence of alleles and have an ancestor who had the same SNP produced by a mutation at exactly the same locus. With 3.6 million SNPs already validated, that is extremely unlikely.

The empirical conditions under which this sort of thing can be reliably done are quite constraining, however. You must first be sure that you have identified SNPs that are in fact distinctive of a certain population. To do that, you have, of course, not only to have detailed knowledge of the genome in Yorubaland, but also knowledge of the genome in other (especially nearby) places. That is the knowledge that the HapMap aims to provide.

Notice that if a SNP originated with a mutation, say a thousand or even five hundred years ago, it may in fact be quite widely dispersed. So, for example, some significant number of the contemporary descendants of that common ancestor might have been living hundreds of miles west of their distant cousins for several centuries. Suppose that the reason you share the Yoruba haplotype is that you are descended from someone who was born in what is now the country of Benin in the early eighteenth century. Then, while your ancestor had cousins in what is now Yorubaland, he never identified as Yoruba. For despite the antiquity of many Yoruba traditions, Yoruba identity itself was developed largely in the last hundred years.

Of course, the city of Ife,§ now regarded as the origin and heartland of the Yoruba people, was founded at least a millennium ago. But the city-state that was there in the eleventh century was superseded in the

---

* Faith practiced by the Yoruba, a West African people. Central to the faith are interactions between people and spirits called "Orishas," each of them associated with various ideas and phenomena. Ancestral reincarnation is also a central belief. Many of the enslaved people taken from Africa were Yoruba, and they brought their faith with them to the various places they were taken, where they would continue to practice it within the Christian context forced upon them by slave owners. Haitian *vodou* is a syncretic faith first practiced by enslaved West Africans in the French Empire during the seventeenth and eighteenth centuries, which blends Roman Catholic practices with those of West African Vodun, as practiced by the Fon and Ewe peoples, as well as by the Yoruba. Bahia is a northeastern state of Brazil: the area was the slaving center of Brazil, and its culture was defined in many ways by the enslaved West Africans who were brought there, and their Yoruba-based religious system, Candomblé.

† The cultural region of the Yoruba people in West Africa, spanning southwest and western Nigeria, south and central Benin, and central Togo, and comprising about 55 million people.

‡ An international project that sought to create a haplotype map of the human genome, in an attempt to find the causes of common genetic diseases. The project concluded in 2009.

§ A city in south-western Nigeria.

fourteenth century by the kingdoms of Oyo and Benin (each of which traced the ancestry of its royal lineage to Ife). As Benin declined, Oyo became the dominant state in the region; by the eighteenth century the kings of Oyo were being paid tribute by the kings of Dahomey, a practice that continued well into the nineteenth century. As a result of warfare and trade in the region—including the trade in slaves—some men travelled widely and took wives from, or had children in, political communities other than their own. Dahomey, a major slave-trading state, sold people from Oyo or Benin into the slave trade. But it was only in the twentieth century that people in south-western Nigeria who spoke related dialects of the Yoruba language, began to think of themselves as a single Yoruba nation. Suppose that your haplotype with some of its distinctive SNPs is very likely derived from someone who has many descendants in Ibadan today. Even if your ancestor had been taken from near Ibadan in the eighteenth century, he would not have thought of himself as Yoruba.

Simply put, the interpretation of haplotype data requires that you know some non-biological history. A couple of thousand years ago, iron-smelting people moved south from somewhere north of the Bight of Biafra,* started migrating south and east into equatorial Africa. We call this the Bantu migration because in many of the languages spoken by their descendants from Congo south to the Cape, the word for people is "Bantu." Haplotypes distinctive of that ancestral population could be spread across half the continent. The Ndebele of southern Zimbabwe are largely descendants of migrants from Zululand who escaped from Shaka† in the early nineteenth century. Haplotypes distinctive of Zululand might be found in a person whose ancestor was taken into slavery from Zimbabwe and exported through Angola to Brazil.

Because pre-existing ethnic solidarities were strongly discouraged among slaves in the New World, they were deliberately introduced into groups of multiple origins and discouraged from holding on to their mother tongues. As a result, by the nineteenth century many slaves in the western Atlantic would have had ancestors from a variety of African societies. Finding that one has ancestry in one place is interesting, I suppose. But, given those facts, it seems odd to insist that this is where one is really from. More than this, the population that we call African-American is likely to have eighteenth-century ancestors from many parts of Europe and from Native American Indian populations as well. The converse is also true. It has been estimated that there are as many US citizens who identify as white descended from American slaves as there are who identify as African-American. This is a consequence of two things: the fact that you may claim African-American ancestry if just one of your parents is African-American, and the fact that many people who could have claimed that ancestry chose, beginning in the nineteenth century, to identify as white, because their skins were light enough for them to be able to "pass." As a result, while not many white Americans are going to go hunting for Yoruba haplotypes in their genomes, perhaps thirty or forty million of them in fact have haplotypes derived from ancestors born in Africa in the last four hundred years.

If you grasp these points you are likely to notice that racial identities in social life tend to be configured in a way that takes account of these sorts of complexities, even while people announce commitments to folk biological theories that are inconsistent with them. In practice, for example, race-like social identities in local contexts are important to patterns of solidarity: in these contexts, people whose (partially genetically determined) physical appearance doesn't fit the physical stereotype of the group are counted in or out in part on the basis of whether they identify with the interests of the group, in part by their utility to the group. As claims to be able to settle issues of ancestry by genomic analysis become more common, it will be interesting to see whether the appeal of the determinateness and objectivity of scientific claims will come to override more flexible and interest-relative folk understandings; or whether, on the other hand, people will become increasingly clear about the gap between folk races and the interests of biology.[13]

---

* A large bay on the West African coast.

† A warrior ruler of the Zulu who, during his short lifetime (c. 1787–1828), combined more than a hundred chiefdoms into a powerful Zulu kingdom in southern Africa. Zulu expansion was a significant factor of the *Mfecane* ("Crushing") that depopulated large areas of southern Africa between 1815 and about 1840.

IX

We live in a scientistic civilization.* That is one reason, I suspect, that people want the categories they care about to be "scientific." There are, as I have suggested, ways in which folk race might be connected with biological facts. But current biology, even after the genome project, is very unlikely to endorse race-like categories that are essentialized (in the psychologist's sense); or to find much interest in human subspecies, given the rather low barriers to gene flow between human groups over the evolutionary timescale. If you want to say there are races, understand race as a social identity, I suggest. But know that as biological and historical knowledge about them is diffused, the criteria of ascription associated with them are likely to change. Know also that as long as they are essentialized they won't correspond to classifications that are likely to be central to theoretical biology, though the statistical distribution of their haplotypes may, from time to time, be of medical interest. ∎

Suggestions for Critical Reflection

1. In a 2016 interview with *The Guardian* magazine, Appiah said, "I do think that in the long run if everybody grasped the facts about the relevant biology and the social facts, they'd have to treat race in a different way and stop using it to define each [other]."† Would widespread belief that race is a social construct make a difference in how we treat each other? Why or why not?

2. What, according to Appiah, is a social identity?

3. Evaluate Appiah's claims about the insight offered by the human genome project into the biological basis of races. What does biology have to teach us about the nature of race? What are the implications?

4. How does Appiah's argument challenge ideas of racial essentialism? To what extent does his argument apply to issues of essentialism in other contexts (in feminist and gender studies, for example)?

5. Why, according to Appiah, might it be useful to know if one had Nigerian ancestry?

6. Think of three group categories with which you self-identify or to which you think others would ascribe you. Examine them using Appiah's various criteria (ascription, identification, treatment, norms). What are the effects of these categories on your life? Would you do better without them, or do they contribute to your life?

7. To what degree would it be difficult to eliminate folk racial categories and move toward a "post-racial" society? To what degree do you think it would be desirable?

Notes

1 Susan Gelman, *The Essential Child*, New York: Oxford University Press, 2003, p. 105.

2 See Gelman 2003, Chapter 11, "Why Do We Essentialize?"

3 See Philip Kitcher, "Race, Ethnicity, Biology, Culture," in Leonard Harris (ed.), *Racism*, Amherst, NY: Humanity, 1999, pp. 87–120.

4 See K.A. Appiah and Amy Gutmann, *Color Conscious: The Political Morality of Race*, Princeton, NJ: Princeton University Press, 1998, and K.A. Appiah, *The Ethics of Identity*, Princeton, NJ: Princeton University Press, 2005.

5 For those who want to go this way, I suggest the best chance you have is to suppose that someone is competent if their conception picks out most of the Xs in their social environment; where what it is to be an X is explicated in terms of the best scientific account of what it is most users are talking about. One reason I don't favour this approach is that I think that for some social identities the best scientific account is that

---

* Culture that places an exaggerated amount of trust in scientific knowledge over other kinds of knowledge.

† Hannah Ellis-Peterson, "Racial Identity Is a Biological Nonsense, Says Reith Lecturer," October 18, 2016.

they're not referring to anything; but then that would make no users competent, if they thought there were any *X*s at all.

6 I say "roughly" to acknowledge a complication that I will ignore from now on: these classes will usually each be fuzzy.

7 I put it this way because I think it sometimes turns out that hardly anybody really believes in the norm; still, it exists if people mostly think most people endorse it.

8 See O.O. Akinyanju, "A Profile of Sickle Cell Disease in Nigeria," *Annals of the New York Academy of Sciences*, 565.1, 1989, pp. 126–36; and Kenneth R. Bridges, *Information Center for Sickle Cell and Thalassemic Disorders*, http://sickle.bwh.harvard.edu/index.html.

9 Alexandra C. Cherva, Afshin Ameri and Ashok Raj, "Hemoglobin H Disease," *eMedicine*, http://www.emedicine.com/ped/topic955.htm. Last updated: April 2, 2002.

10 This is like the word "gene," which is used to refer both to a locus on the chromosome and to the various alleles that can occur at that locus.

11 The International HapMap Consortium, "A Haplotype Map of the Human Genome," *Nature*, 437, 27 October 2005, p. 1316.

12 This is the reason haplotypes are called haplotypes: the spermatozoa and the oocytes are haploid—they have only one member of each type of chromosome—unlike most somatic cells, which are diploid, having two of each.

13 In thinking about their ancestral roots, the descendants of my English grandparents will have to bear in mind that most of Granny and Grandpa's haplotypes had descendant tokens in at least England, Ghana, Kenya, Namibia, Nigeria, Thailand and the United States, in the bodies of people with haplotypes recently derived from England, Ghana, India, Kenya, Nigeria and Norway, less than fifty years after they died.

References

Akinyanju, O.O. 1989: "A Profile of Sickle Cell Disease in Nigeria." *Annals of the New York Academy of Sciences*, 565.1, pp. 126–36.

Appiah, K.A. 2005: *The Ethics of Identity*. Princeton, NJ: Princeton University Press.

Appiah, K.A. and Amy Gutmann 1998: *Color Conscious: The Political Morality of Race*. Princeton, NJ: Princeton University Press.

Bridges, Kenneth R.: *Information Center for Sickle Cell and Thalassemic Disorders*. http://sickle.bwh.harvard.edu/index.html.

Cherva, Alexandra C., Afshin Ameri and Ashok Raj 2002: "Hemoglobin H Disease." *eMedicine*. http://www.emedicine.com/ped/topic955.htm.

Gelman, Susan 2003: *The Essential Child*. New York: Oxford University Press.

International HapMap Consortium 2005: "A Haplotype Map of the Human Genome." *Nature*, 437, 27 October 2005.

Kitcher, Philip 1999: "Race, Ethnicity, Biology, Culture." In Leonard Harris (ed.), *Racism*, Amherst, NY: Humanity, 1999.

TA-NEHISI COATES

FROM *Between the World and Me*

Who Is Ta-Nehisi Coates?

One of North America's most prominent public intellectuals, Ta-Nehisi Coates is best known for his writing on black oppression in the United States. Born in 1975, Coates grew up in inner-city Baltimore, where, as he recounts in his autobiographical writings, he attended a substandard school but received an informal education from his parents; his mother was a teacher and his father was an activist who operated an independent press focused on classic works by black writers. Coates attended Howard University for five years before becoming a journalist. He rose to prominence as a regular blogger for the political magazine *The Atlantic*; his career accelerated around the same time as Barack Obama achieved the presidency, and Coates became known especially as a commentator on race and the Obama administration. His position as a journalist was cemented with "The Case for Reparations" (2014), an extensive feature article in *The Atlantic* that provoked a national conversation with its meticulous account of black oppression as fundamental to American economic, social, and political life. "The Case for Reparations" would later be reprinted in *We Were Eight Years in Power: An American Tragedy* (2017), a collection featuring one of Coates's essays for each year of Obama's presidency.

In 2015, Coates published *Between the World and Me*, a book-length essay in the form of a letter combining memoir, political commentary, and philosophical reflection. With this work, Coates came to be seen as the latest star in an intellectual genealogy of celebrated black American writers and thinkers; Toni Morrison, for example, famously praised him for "fill[ing] the intellectual void" left by the iconic mid-twentieth-century essayist and novelist James Baldwin. Coates received a National Book Award for *Between the World and Me*, and in the same year he was awarded a prestigious MacArthur "Genius Grant." He also broadened his audience considerably by becoming a writer for Marvel comics, first as the author of a *Black Panther* series beginning in 2016, and then as a writer of *Captain America*.

What Is the Structure of This Reading?

Between the World and Me takes the form of an extended letter to Coates's teenage son Samori—an approach many have seen as referencing the opening of Baldwin's important work *The Fire Next Time* (1963), which the author addressed to his nephew. The structure of Coates's book is thus more discursive and less systematic than is typical of academic philosophy; Coates's presentation of his ideas is intermingled with analysis of American politics and history, as well as his own autobiography.

The book as a whole is divided into three sections, and the portion excerpted below is drawn from the first. In this section, Coates traces his own development from childhood to university, outlining how his personal and educational experience led him to his current ideological position regarding black oppression. The rest of the book, not excerpted here, addresses aspects of his life after graduation, including the killing of his friend Prince Jones by police, as well as Coates's travels to France, where he experiences life beyond the shadow of American racism.

Some Useful Background Information

1. Coates's book addresses the full sweep of the history of black oppression in America; thus, it may be helpful to keep the following dates and events in mind:
    - The first enslaved black people taken to America arrived in 1619, and, though slavery was outlawed earlier in some states, it was not declared illegal in all states until 1865. Over the course of this period, millions of black people were enslaved (there were

almost four million enslaved black people in America in 1860 alone),* and they performed an estimated quarter billion hours of forced unpaid labor.†

- The era of slavery was quickly followed by the era of Jim Crow, a name given to a system of laws in various American states between the 1870s and 1960s that required racial segregation in public places and in organizations such as schools and the military. These laws thus effectively ensured that amenities and opportunities for black Americans were far inferior to those available to white Americans. Black-led protest movements led to the removal of many of these laws, but structural inequality and racism persist in the twenty-first century.

- The early 2010s saw the rise of Black Lives Matter, a protest movement combating contemporary black oppression, including the unjustified killing and brutal treatment of black people by police and the mass incarceration of black people (in America in the year Coates wrote *Between the World and Me*, a black man was six times more likely to be in jail than a white man).‡ *Between the World and Me* was published in the year following the 2014 death of Michael Brown, a black teenager who was killed, while unarmed, by a police officer who shot him six times. In Ferguson, Missouri, where the shooting occurred, weeks of protest followed his death, and protest resumed when the officer responsible was not indicted.

FROM *Between the World and Me*§

Son,

Last Sunday the host of a popular news show asked me what it meant to lose my body. The host was broadcasting from Washington, D.C., and I was seated in a remote studio on the far west side of Manhattan. A satellite closed the miles between us, but no machinery could close the gap between her world and the world for which I had been summoned to speak. When the host asked me about my body, her face faded from the screen, and was replaced by a scroll of words, written by me earlier that week.

The host read these words for the audience, and when she finished she turned to the subject of my body, although she did not mention it specifically. But by now I am accustomed to intelligent people asking about the condition of my body without realizing the nature of their request. Specifically, the host wished to know why I felt that white America's progress, or rather the progress of those Americans who believe that they are white,¶ was built on looting and violence. Hearing this, I felt an old and indistinct sadness well up in me. The answer to this question is the record of the believers themselves. The answer is American history.

There is nothing extreme in this statement. Americans deify democracy in a way that allows for a dim awareness that they have, from time to time, stood in defiance of their God. But democracy is a forgiving God and America's heresies—torture, theft, enslavement—are so common among individuals and nations that none can declare themselves immune. In fact, Americans, in a real sense, have never betrayed their God. When Abraham Lincoln declared, in 1863, that the battle of Gettysburg must ensure "that government of the people, by the people, for the people, shall not perish from the earth," he was not merely being aspirational; at the onset of the Civil War, the

---

* Ta-Nehisi Coates, "Slavery Made America," *The Atlantic*, June 24, 2014.
† Clarence J. Mumford, *Race and Reparations: A Black Perspective for the 21st Century* (Africa World Press, 1996), 428.
‡ "Fact Sheet: Trends in U.S. Corrections," The Sentencing Project, 2015.
§ Ta-Nehisi Coates, *Between the World and Me* (Spiegel & Grau, 2015).
¶ This phrasing echoes James Baldwin's 1987 essay "On Being 'White' ... and Other Lies": "[white Americans] have brought humanity to the edge of oblivion: because they think they are white. Because they think they are white, they do not dare confront the ravage and the lie of their history...."

United States of America had one of the highest rates of suffrage* in the world. The question is not whether Lincoln truly meant "government of the people" but what our country has, throughout its history, taken the political term "people" to actually mean. In 1863 it did not mean your mother or your grandmother, and it did not mean you and me. Thus America's problem is not its betrayal of "government of the people," but the means by which "the people" acquired their names.

This leads us to another equally important ideal, one that Americans implicitly accept but to which they make no conscious claim. Americans believe in the reality of "race" as a defined, indubitable feature of the natural world. Racism—the need to ascribe bone-deep features to people and then humiliate, reduce, and destroy them—inevitably follows from this inalterable condition. In this way, racism is rendered as the innocent daughter of Mother Nature, and one is left to deplore the Middle Passage or the Trail of Tears† the way one deplores an earthquake, a tornado, or any other phenomenon that can be cast as beyond the handiwork of men.

But race is the child of racism, not the father. And the process of naming "the people" has never been a matter of genealogy and physiognomy so much as one of hierarchy. Difference in hue and hair is old. But the belief in the pre-eminence of hue and hair, the notion that these factors can correctly organize a society and that they signify deeper attributes, which are indelible—this is the new idea at the heart of these new people who have been brought up hopelessly, tragically, deceitfully, to believe that they are white.

These new people are, like us, a modern invention. But unlike us, their new name has no real meaning divorced from the machinery of criminal power. The new people were something else before they were white—Catholic, Corsican, Welsh, Mennonite, Jewish—and if all our national hopes have any fulfillment, then they will have to be something else again. Perhaps they will truly become American and create a nobler basis for their myths. I cannot call it. As for now, it must be said that the process of washing the disparate tribes white, the elevation of the belief in being white, was not achieved through wine tastings and ice cream socials, but rather through the pillaging of life, liberty, labor, and land; through the flaying of backs; the chaining of limbs; the strangling of dissidents; the destruction of families; the rape of mothers; the sale of children; and various other acts meant, first and foremost, to deny you and me the right to secure and govern our own bodies.

The new people are not original in this. Perhaps there has been, at some point in history, some great power whose elevation was exempt from the violent exploitation of other human bodies. If there has been, I have yet to discover it. But this banality of violence can never excuse America, because America makes no claim to the banal. America believes itself exceptional, the greatest and noblest nation ever to exist, a lone champion standing between the white city of democracy and the terrorists, despots, barbarians, and other enemies of civilization. One cannot, at once, claim to be superhuman and then plead mortal error. I propose to take our countrymen's claims of American exceptionalism seriously, which is to say I propose subjecting our country to an exceptional moral standard. This is difficult because there exists, all around us, an apparatus urging us to accept American innocence at face value and not to inquire too much. And it is so easy to look away, to live with the fruits of our history and to ignore the great evil done in all of our names. But you and I have never truly had that luxury. I think you know.

I write you in your fifteenth year. I am writing you because this was the year you saw Eric Garner choked to death for selling cigarettes; because you know now that Renisha McBride was shot for seeking

---

* The right to vote.

† The Middle Passage refers to the forced sea transportation of enslaved people from Africa to the Americas. It was the second leg of a profitable eighteenth-century triangular trading route that went from Europe to West Africa (carrying manufactured trade goods), from Africa to America (carrying enslaved people), and then from the Americas back to Europe (carrying raw materials such as sugar, cotton, or tobacco). Travel conditions were deplorable and about 15 per cent of the enslaved people transported died before arrival. The Trail of Tears is the name given to the forced displacement of Cherokee people from their homes in Georgia to an area in what is now Oklahoma. The American government compelled the displaced people to march in large groups with inadequate provisions, and thousands died on the way, between 1830 and 1850.

help, that John Crawford was shot down for browsing in a department store. And you have seen men in uniform drive by and murder Tamir Rice, a twelve-year-old child whom they were oath-bound to protect.* And you have seen men in the same uniforms pummel Marlene Pinnock,† someone's grandmother, on the side of a road. And you know now, if you did not before, that the police departments of your country have been endowed with the authority to destroy your body. It does not matter if the destruction is the result of an unfortunate overreaction. It does not matter if it originates in a misunderstanding. It does not matter if the destruction springs from a foolish policy. Sell cigarettes without the proper authority and your body can be destroyed. Resent the people trying to entrap your body and it can be destroyed. Turn into a dark stairwell and your body can be destroyed. The destroyers will rarely be held accountable. Mostly they will receive pensions. And destruction is merely the superlative form of a dominion whose prerogatives include friskings, detainings, beatings, and humiliations. All of this is common to black people. And all of this is old for black people. No one is held responsible.

There is nothing uniquely evil in these destroyers or even in this moment. The destroyers are merely men enforcing the whims of our country, correctly interpreting its heritage and legacy. It is hard to face this. But all our phrasing—race relations, racial chasm, racial justice, racial profiling, white privilege, even white supremacy—serves to obscure that racism is a visceral experience, that it dislodges brains, blocks airways, rips muscle, extracts organs, cracks bones, breaks teeth. You must never look away from this. You must always remember that the sociology, the history, the economics, the graphs, the charts, the regressions all land, with great violence, upon the body.

That Sunday, with that host, on that news show, I tried to explain this as best I could within the time allotted. But at the end of the segment, the host flashed

a widely shared picture of an eleven-year-old black boy tearfully hugging a white police officer. Then she asked me about "hope." And I knew then that I had failed. And I remembered that I had expected to fail. And I wondered again at the indistinct sadness welling up in me. Why exactly was I sad? I came out of the studio and walked for a while. It was a calm December day. Families, believing themselves white, were out on the streets. Infants, raised to be white, were bundled in strollers. And I was sad for these people, much as I was sad for the host and sad for all the people out there watching and reveling in a specious hope. I realized then why I was sad. When the journalist asked me about my body, it was like she was asking me to awaken her from the most gorgeous dream. I have seen that dream all my life. It is perfect houses with nice lawns. It is Memorial Day cookouts, block associations, and driveways. The Dream is treehouses and the Cub Scouts. The Dream smells like peppermint but tastes like strawberry shortcake. And for so long I have wanted to escape into the Dream, to fold my country over my head like a blanket. But this has never been an option because the Dream rests on our backs, the bedding made from our bodies. And knowing this, knowing that the Dream persists by warring with the known world, I was sad for the host, I was sad for all those families, I was sad for my country, but above all, in that moment, I was sad for you.

That was the week you learned that the killers of Michael Brown would go free.‡ The men who had left his body in the street like some awesome declaration of their inviolable power would never be punished. It was not my expectation that anyone would ever be punished. But you were young and still believed. You stayed up till 11 P.M. that night, waiting for the announcement of an indictment, and when instead it was announced that there was none you said, "I've got to go," and you went into your room, and I heard you crying. I came in five minutes after, and I didn't

---

* This passage lists black people whose killing provoked public outcry: Eric Garner, killed by New York police in 2014 when he was arrested under suspicion of illegally selling individual cigarettes; Renisha McBride, a teenager who died in 2013 when, after having been in a traffic accident, she walked up to a house and was shot by its occupant; John Crawford III, who was shot by police in 2015 because he was carrying a BB gun that was for sale in the Walmart where he was shopping; and Tamir Rice, a child who was shot and killed by Cleveland police in 2014.

† A black woman who in 2014 was punched forcefully and repeatedly by a police officer, Pinnock has a mental health condition, and the officer claimed that he was attempting to prevent her from walking into traffic.

‡ See the Introduction section of this reading.

hug you, and I didn't comfort you, because I thought it would be wrong to comfort you. I did not tell you that it would be okay, because I have never believed it would be okay. What I told you is what your grandparents tried to tell me: that this is your country, that this is your world, that this is your body, and you must find some way to live within the all of it. I tell you now that the question of how one should live within a black body, within a country lost in the Dream, is the question of my life, and the pursuit of this question, I have found, ultimately answers itself.

This must seem strange to you. We live in a "goal-oriented" era. Our media vocabulary is full of hot takes, big ideas, and grand theories of everything. But some time ago I rejected magic in all its forms. This rejection was a gift from your grandparents, who never tried to console me with ideas of an afterlife and were skeptical of preordained American glory. In accepting both the chaos of history and the fact of my total end, I was freed to truly consider how I wished to live—specifically, how do I live free in this black body? It is a profound question because America understands itself as God's handiwork, but the black body is the clearest evidence that America is the work of men. I have asked the question through my reading and writings, through the music of my youth, through arguments with your grandfather, with your mother, your aunt Janai, your uncle Ben. I have searched for answers in nationalist myth, in classrooms, out on the streets, and on other continents. The question is unanswerable, which is not to say futile. The greatest reward of this constant interrogation, of confrontation with the brutality of my country, is that it has freed me from ghosts and girded me against the sheer terror of disembodiment....

[As a child] I could not retreat, as did so many, into the church and its mysteries. My parents rejected all dogmas. We spurned the holidays marketed by the people who wanted to be white. We would not stand for their anthems. We would not kneel before their God. And so I had no sense that any just God was on my side. "The meek shall inherit the earth" meant nothing to me. The meek were battered in West Baltimore, stomped out at Walbrook Junction, bashed up on Park Heights,* and raped in the showers of the city jail. My understanding of the universe was physical, and its moral arc bent toward chaos then concluded in a box....

Every February my classmates and I were herded into assemblies for a ritual review of the Civil Rights Movement. Our teachers urged us toward the example of freedom marchers, Freedom Riders, and Freedom Summers,† and it seemed that the month could not pass without a series of films dedicated to the glories of being beaten on camera. The black people in these films seemed to love the worst things in life—love the dogs that rent their children apart, the tear gas that clawed at their lungs, the fire-hoses that tore off their clothes and tumbled them into the streets. They seemed to love the men who raped them, the women who cursed them, love the children who spat on them, the terrorists that bombed them. *Why are they showing this to us?* Why were only our heroes nonviolent? I speak not of the morality of nonviolence, but of the sense that blacks are in especial need of this morality. Back then all I could do was measure these freedom-lovers by what I knew. Which is to say, I measured them against children pulling out in the 7-Eleven parking lot, against parents wielding extension cords, and "Yeah, nigger, what's up now?"‡ I judged them against the country I knew, which had acquired the land through murder and tamed it under slavery, against the country whose armies fanned out across the world to extend their dominion. The world, the real one, was civilization secured and ruled by savage means. How could the schools valorize men and women whose values society actively scorned? How could they send us out into the streets of Baltimore, knowing all that they were, and then speak of nonviolence?

---

* These areas of Baltimore have a predominantly black population and high rates of poverty and crime.
† The Freedom Rides of 1961 protested the segregation of public buses, while the Freedom Summer was an intensive campaign to register black voters in Mississippi in 1964. The nonviolent civil rights activists engaged in these projects, like those who participated in the freedom marches, often experienced brutal violence from both police and civilians.
‡ In a portion of this book not reprinted here, Coates discusses an incident in which, at the age of 11, he witnessed an older boy pull out a gun in a 7-Eleven parking lot. He also recounts that safety concerns forced him to belong to a "crew" that controlled a portion of the city; he mentions the phrase "Yeah, nigger, what's up now?" in the context of one crew returning aggression expressed by another.

I came to see the streets and the schools as arms of the same beast. One enjoyed the official power of the state while the other enjoyed its implicit sanction. But fear and violence were the weaponry of both. Fail in the streets and the crews would catch you slipping and take your body. Fail in the schools and you would be suspended and sent back to those same streets, where they would take your body. And I began to see these two arms in relation—those who failed in the schools justified their destruction in the streets. The society could say, "He should have stayed in school," and then wash its hands of him.

It does not matter that the "intentions" of individual educators were noble. Forget about intentions. What any institution, or its agents, "intend" for you is secondary. Our world is physical. Learn to play defense—ignore the head and keep your eyes on the body. Very few Americans will directly proclaim that they are in favor of black people being left to the streets. But a very large number of Americans will do all they can to preserve the Dream. No one directly proclaimed that schools were designed to sanctify failure and destruction. But a great number of educators spoke of "personal responsibility" in a country authored and sustained by a criminal irresponsibility. The point of this language of "intention" and "personal responsibility" is broad exoneration. Mistakes were made. Bodies were broken. People were enslaved. We meant well. We tried our best. "Good intention" is a hall pass through history, a sleeping pill that ensures the Dream....

I think now of the old rule that held that should a boy be set upon in someone else's chancy hood, his friends must stand with him, and they must all take their beating together. I now know that within this edict lay the key to all living. None of us were promised to end the fight on our feet, fists raised to the sky. We could not control our enemies' number, strength, nor weaponry. Sometimes you just caught a bad one. But whether you fought or ran, you did it together, because that is the part that was in our control. What we must never do is willingly hand over our own bodies or the bodies of our friends. That was the wisdom:

We knew we did not lay down the direction of the street, but despite that, we could—and must—fashion the way of our walk. And that is the deeper meaning of your name*—that the struggle, in and of itself, has meaning.

That wisdom is not unique to our people, but I think it has special meaning to those of us born out of mass rape, whose ancestors were carried off and divided up into policies and stocks. I have raised you to respect every human being as singular, and you must extend that same respect into the past. Slavery is not an indefinable mass of flesh. It is a particular, specific enslaved woman, whose mind is as active as your own, whose range of feeling is as vast as your own; who prefers the way the light falls in one particular spot in the woods, who enjoys fishing where the water eddies in a nearby stream, who loves her mother in her own complicated way, thinks her sister talks too loud, has a favorite cousin, a favorite season, who excels at dress-making and knows, inside herself, that she is as intelligent and capable as anyone. "Slavery" is this same woman born in a world that loudly proclaims its love of freedom and inscribes this love in its essential texts, a world in which these same professors† hold this woman a slave, hold her mother a slave, her father a slave, her daughter a slave, and when this woman peers back into the generations all she sees is the enslaved. She can hope for more. She can imagine some future for her grandchildren. But when she dies, the world—which is really the only world she can ever know—ends. For this woman, enslavement is not a parable. It is damnation. It is the never-ending night. And the length of that night is most of our history. Never forget that we were enslaved in this country longer than we have been free. Never forget that for 250 years black people were born into chains—whole generations followed by more generations who knew nothing but chains.

You must struggle to truly remember this past in all its nuance, error, and humanity. You must resist the common urge toward the comforting narrative of divine law, toward fairy tales that imply some irrepressible justice. The enslaved were not bricks in your road, and their lives were not chapters in your redemptive history.

---

* Coates's son is named after Samori Ture (c. 1830–1900), a West African emperor who achieved several victories against French colonial forces, although his resistance ultimately failed.
† Those who profess (love of freedom).

They were people turned to fuel for the American machine. Enslavement was not destined to end, and it is wrong to claim our present circumstance—no matter how improved—as the redemption for the lives of people who never asked for the posthumous, untouchable glory of dying for their children. Our triumphs can never compensate for this. Perhaps our triumphs are not even the point. Perhaps struggle is all we have because the god of history is an atheist, and nothing about his world is meant to be. So you must wake up every morning knowing that no promise is unbreakable, least of all the promise of waking up at all. This is not despair. These are the preferences of the universe itself: verbs over nouns, actions over states, struggle over hope.

The birth of a better world is not ultimately up to you, though I know, each day, there are grown men and women who tell you otherwise. The world needs saving precisely because of the actions of these same men and women. I am not a cynic. I love you, and I love the world, and I love it more with every new inch I discover. But you are a black boy, and you must be responsible for your body in a way that other boys cannot know. Indeed, you must be responsible for the worst actions of other black bodies, which, somehow, will always be assigned to you. And you must be responsible for the bodies of the powerful—the policeman who cracks you with a nightstick will quickly find his excuse in your furtive movements. And this is not reducible to just you—the women around you must be responsible for their bodies in a way that you never will know. You have to make your peace with the chaos, but you cannot lie. You cannot forget how much they took from us and how they transfigured our very bodies into sugar, tobacco, cotton, and gold. ◼

Suggestions for Critical Reflection

1. Coates asks himself this question: "How do I live free in this black body?" How does he respond to this question? Is his response satisfactory?
2. What, according to Coates, is race? In what way— if at all—should it be considered real? If you have read the article by Kwame Anthony Appiah in this chapter, you might want to consider how Coates's and Appiah's views on race fit together (if they do).
3. Coates's argument is focused on experiences of blackness in the United States. What portion (if any) of his key claims are applicable only to the United States, and what portion (if any) are applicable elsewhere? (If you live outside the United States, consider what claims are applicable to your own country; if you live within the United States, consider what claims are applicable globally.)
4. How does atheism shape the view of history put forward in *Between the World and Me*? How is this view of history reflected in the vision of personal ethics offered in the book?
5. What is "the Dream"? How is the Dream for people who are considered white different from the Dream for those who are considered black—and how is it similar?
6. What does Coates suggest about the relationship between the body and the self? How does this inform his interpretation of the harm done to individuals by racial injustice?
7. While *Between the World and Me* has been widely acclaimed, the book has also been criticized as advocating hopelessness in the face of black oppression rather than encouraging political resistance. Michelle Alexander, for example argues the following in her review of the book:

> [W]e must not ask whether it is possible for a human being or society to become just or moral; we must believe it is possible. Believing in this possibility—no matter how slim—and dedicating oneself to playing a meaningful role in the struggle to make it a reality focuses one's energy and attention in a useful way.*

Is this a legitimate objection to the ideas Coates puts forward? Why or why not?

---

* Michelle Alexander, "Ta-Nehisi Coates's 'Between the World and Me,'" *The New York Times*, 17 August 2015.

What Is the Meaning of Life?

What makes life meaningful? Does life have a purpose, and if so, what is it? Is this purpose—if there is one—something that comes from outside of ourselves, and that we need to discover, or are we responsible for creating our own purpose? In general, what is it to lead a good life? For example, if part of leading a good life is being happy, then how do we do that—how can we construct a happy life?

Many philosophers throughout history have sought to clarify and to answer these important questions, and if you have worked your way through the readings in the other chapters of this book—especially the chapter on Ethics—you will have already encountered some important efforts to address these issues. For example, Plato examined the connection between being good and being happy, and argued that true psychological health

comes from moral virtue; Aristotle influentially asserted that human beings have a *telos*—an intrinsic function or nature—and that human flourishing consists in living in accordance with this function; Kant argued carefully that the highest good for human beings is the good will; while Mill focused on sensations of pleasure and developed a nuanced view of the best way to cultivate and preserve human happiness.

What most pre-twentieth-century responses to the problem of the meaning of life have in common is that they depend upon some substantive metaphysical framework or other: a commitment to the position that the universe has meaning *built in to it*, either into human nature itself, or some super-natural organizing principle for the world (such as God's design, or pure rationality), or both. From this perspective, the task of the philosopher is to find out what the actual meaning of life really is, so that we can do a better job of living our lives in accordance with it; and this is a question that has a particular answer that we can either get right or get wrong. (Furthermore, since there is only one right answer and multiple competing theories, most people presumably get it at least partially wrong.)

Suppose, however, that the universe does not come with meaning baked in. Suppose that we, as human beings, are not responsible for finding and matching the predetermined pattern by which we (really, objectively) should live our lives—because there simply is no such pattern—but instead we have the awful responsibility of *creating* meaning—of bringing meaning into a universe that, prior to our decision, had no such meaning. What should we do then? Is this a counsel of despair, pure nihilism, or could there still be a satisfying story to be told about the meaning of life under such conditions? Could we still be happy? This, roughly, is the starting point for the readings in this chapter.

Epictetus represents the ancient Greek and Roman school of thought called stoicism. A guiding principle of stoicism is that the universe is driven by deterministic natural principles that are beyond our control, and the secret of happiness is to bring our will into line with what is going to happen anyway—to accept each moment as it presents itself, rather than struggling against it and wishing it were otherwise than it is.* Epictetus lays out some concrete advice for how to achieve this kind of serenity.

We then jump to the twentieth century and a selection from A.J. Ayer who argues briskly, as a logical positivist, that the question "What is the meaning of life?" makes no sense—is nonsensical—and therefore has no coherent answer. We should not regret being unable to answer this impossible question, therefore, but instead, Ayer advises, should decide as individuals how we want to live, based on our own personal interests and projects.

In "The Myth of Sisyphus" Albert Camus introduces the notion of the Absurd: the idea that the human condition is that we live in a world that offers neither meaning nor clear understanding and yet—absurdly—we yearn for both. Camus argues that our response to this fact of life should be heroic defiance.

Finally, Kathy Behrendt addresses the question of whether "any reason for living is a reason for not dying." She runs through a series of theories about what makes for a good life, and argues that it is less clear than it might first seem what our response to this question should be.

Want to know more about what philosophers have said about the meaning of life? Some good starting points are: Julian Baggini, *What's It All About?: Philosophy and the Meaning of Life* (Granta, 2004); Christopher Belshaw, *10 Good Questions about Life and Death* (Blackwell, 2005); David Benatar, ed., *Life, Death & Meaning* (Rowman & Littlefield, 2016); Jon Cottingham, *On the Meaning of Life* (Routledge, 2002); Terry Eagleton, *The Meaning of Life: A Very Short Introduction* (Oxford University Press, 2008); Dennis Ford, *The Search for Meaning: A Short History* (University of California Press, 2007); Daniel Klein, *Every Time I Find the Meaning of Life, They Change It: Wisdom of the Great Philosophers on How to Live* (Penguin, 2015); Klemke and Cahn, eds., *The Meaning of Life: A Reader* (Oxford University Press, 2017); Runzo and Martin, eds., 2000, *The Meaning of Life in the World Religions* (Oneworld Publications, 2000); Joshua W. Seachris, ed., *Exploring the Meaning of Life: An Anthology and Guide* (Wiley-Blackwell, 2012); and Julian Young, *The Death of God and the Meaning of Life* (Routledge, 2014).

---

* Stoicism is not a perfect fit with the rough classification described above, between metaphysical and nihilistic approaches to the meaning of life, since the stoics in fact did believe that the deterministic principles guiding the universe are rational principles that we might be able to understand and endorse, and so we might come to understand that what looks like misfortune is really nothing of the sort.

EPICTETUS

FROM *Enchiridion*

Who Was Epictetus?

Epictetus was born a slave in about 55 CE in Phrygia, a region of what is now south-western Turkey. The name his parents gave him is unknown: Epictetus is the Greek word (*epíktetos*) for a thing that is acquired as property. He was brought up in Rome as an enslaved person in the household of a wealthy master who was himself a former slave but had been freed and had risen to become a secretary to the notorious Roman emperor Nero. Because of this, Epictetus would have been familiar with life at the imperial court and would have had some exposure to the shifting world of Roman politics. He also seems to have been given unusual privileges by his master, Epaphroditus, and was given permission to attend lectures by one of the foremost Stoic philosophers of the time, Musonius Rufus.

At some point—we don't know exactly when—Epictetus was granted his freedom, and from that point until his old age he devoted his life entirely to the study and teaching of philosophy. In 95 CE Nero's successor Domitian expelled all the philosophers in Italy, suspecting them of stirring up republican sympathies, and Epictetus moved to Greece, where he founded a school at Nicopolis. His boarding school was successful and became a destination for the sons of upper-class Roman families who admired and wanted to learn from Greek culture and philosophy. Epictetus focused on teaching practical philosophical lessons, based on rational arguments, aimed at inspiring his students to make a break with received moral and social notions and to learn to live better lives. Over time his reputation grew, and his school may even have been visited by the emperor Hadrian.

Epictetus did not write down any of his lectures, but they were recorded by some of his students, in particular one named Arrian. The written lectures (only half of which survived) are now known as the *Discourses*, and Arrian also prepared a practical guide to Epictetus's thought called the *Manual* or, in Greek, *Enchiridion*. Although not written by Epictetus himself, these works were thought at the time and since to be essentially his words.

In accordance with his philosophy, Epictetus lived very simply and had few attachments or possessions. It was only late in his life that he retired from teaching and the responsibilities of being a philosopher and allowed himself to take on a family, adopting an abandoned child and taking in a female servant to act as a mother and domestic helper. Though Epictetus suffered from ill health and walked with a limp throughout his life,* he lived to the age of about 80 and died in 135 CE.

What Is the Structure of This Reading?

The *Enchiridion* is not intended to be a summary of Epictetus' overall thought but instead is a compilation of practical pieces of advice for daily life based on his philosophy. These are the kinds of things Epictetus would have taught his students, though presented here without the rhetorical flourish that can be found in his *Discourses*, and separated from much of the argumentation he would have used to support them.

Some Useful Background Information

1. Epictetus is known as a Stoic philosopher. Stoicism was a school of thought founded in the third century BCE by Zeno of Citium in Athens, and largely developed by his successor Chrysippus between about 230 and 210 BCE. It was the dominant philosophy

---

* There is an apocryphal story which goes that, while he was enslaved, he was tortured by his master who twisted his leg. Enduring the pain with apparent indifference, Epictetus warned Epaphroditus that his leg would break; when it did break, he said, "There, did I not tell you that it would break?" From then on Epictetus was lame.

of the Roman world until the rise of Christianity as a state religion in the fourth century CE. At its core Stoicism combines a belief in a deterministic natural world, governed by natural laws or *logos*, with an emphasis on the human capacity to make free choices and to use our reason to see the world as it really is rather than merely as it appears to be. It is thus up to us how to act, and wise persons will bring their actions into line with the natural course of things—which, according to Stoicism, is itself part of the larger rationality of the universe and not merely arbitrary—rather than try to change things that cannot be changed. For Epictetus, as for the other Stoics, philosophy is not merely an intellectual discipline but a way of life, involving constant training and practice. We should seek to free ourselves from the undue influence of our passions and instead follow the path of reason, in order to achieve peace of mind and clear judgment. Following Socrates, the Stoics believed that unhappiness and (apparent) misfortune are the results of human ignorance of the reason inherent in nature.

Some Common Misconceptions

1. Today the word "stoic" has come to mean unemotional and able to endure hardship without complaint. This meaning is not completely disconnected from its origins in this philosophical movement, but it can be misleading: the Stoics did not seek to eliminate or ignore emotion, but to train themselves to use careful, clear judgment to assess the appropriateness of these passions or sensations rather than passively reacting to them.

2. Epictetus advises, in part, that we can find peace of mind by adapting our will to how the world is, rather than by vainly seeking to impose our will on something that cannot be changed. This is more than the simple fatalism it might seem, however. According to Stoic philosophy the world of things that are beyond our power, understood properly, is a universe that contains an inherent rational order—in fact, is sometimes described as God becoming immanent—and so it is not just prudent but also right to make ourselves in tune with it.

How Important and Influential Is This Passage?

Epictetus' writings had enormous influence for hundreds of years after his death. Marcus Aurelius, Roman Emperor from 161 to 180 CE and the author of the very influential *Meditations*, describes reading Epictetus' *Discourses* as a crucial event in his intellectual development. Epictetus' work was one of only a handful of pagan writings that were respected and protected by the early Christian Church, and the *Enchiridion* was used almost verbatim as a rulebook for Eastern Orthodox monasteries. With the advent of the printing press, the *Discourses* and *Enchiridion* were some of the first works to be mechanically printed and they have remained continuously in print since 1535. Epictetus' views are often a touchstone of modern self-help psychology, especially in holding that our emotional responses to events are what create anxiety and depression, rather than the events themselves, and that with proper counseling these responses can be understood as irrational and unnecessary.

FROM *Enchiridion**

I

There are things which are within our power, and there are things which are beyond our power. Within our power are opinion, aim, desire, aversion—in a word, whatever affairs are our own. Beyond our power are body, property, reputation, status, and, in a word, anything we don't have the power to control.

Now the things within our power are by nature free, unrestricted, unhindered; but those beyond our power are weak, dependent, restricted, alien. Remember, then, that if you attribute freedom to things by nature dependent and take what belongs to others for your own, you will be hindered, you will lament, you will be disturbed, you will find fault both with gods and men. But if you take for your own only that which is your own and view what belongs to others just as it really is, then no one will ever compel you, no one will restrict you; you will find fault with no one, you will accuse no one, you will do nothing against your will; no one will hurt you, you will not have an enemy, nor will you suffer any harm.

Aiming, therefore, at such great things, remember that you must not allow yourself any inclination, however slight, toward the attainment of the others;[†] but that you must entirely give up on some of them, and for the present postpone the rest. But if you would have these, and possess power and wealth likewise, you may miss the latter in seeking the former; and you will certainly fail to get the only thing which can bring happiness and freedom.

Seek at once, therefore, to be able to say to every unpleasing appearance, "You are but an appearance and by no means the real thing." And then examine it by those rules which you have; and first and chiefly by this: whether it concerns the things which are within our own power or those which are not; and if it concerns anything beyond our power, be prepared to say that it is nothing to you.

II

Remember that desire demands the attainment of that of which you are desirous; and aversion demands the avoidance of that to which you are averse; that he who fails of the object of his desires is disappointed; and he who incurs the object of his aversion is wretched. If, then, you shun only those undesirable things which you can control, you will never incur anything which you shun; but if you shun sickness, or death, or poverty, you will run the risk of wretchedness. Remove the habit of aversion, then, from all things that are not within our power, and apply it to things undesirable which are within our power. But for now, suspend desire completely; for if you desire any of the things not within our own power, you must necessarily be disappointed; and you are not yet secure of those which are within our power, and so are legitimate objects of desire. Where it is practically necessary for you to pursue or avoid anything, do even this with discretion and gentleness and moderation.

III

With regard to whatever objects either delight the mind or are useful or are tenderly beloved, remind yourself of what nature they are, beginning with the merest trifles: if you have a favorite cup, that it is but a cup of which you are fond—for thus, if it is broken, you can bear it; if you embrace your child or your wife, that you embrace a mortal—and thus, if either of them dies, you can bear it.

...

V

Men are disturbed not by things, but by the views which they take of things. Thus death is nothing terrible, or otherwise it would have appeared so to Socrates. But the terror consists in our notion of death, that it is terrible. When, therefore, we are hindered or

---

*　Translated by Thomas Wentworth Higginson, with modifications by the editor.
†　Things you cannot control, such as riches or reputation.

disturbed, or grieved, let us never impute it to others, but to ourselves—that is, to our own views. It is the action of an uninstructed person to reproach others for his own misfortunes; of one entering upon instruction, to reproach himself; and one perfectly instructed, to reproach neither others nor himself.

VI

Be not elated at any excellence not your own. If a horse should be elated, and say, "I am handsome," it might be endurable. But when you are elated and say, "I have a handsome horse," know that you are elated only on the merit of the horse. What then is your own? The use of the phenomena of existence.* So that when you are in harmony with nature in this respect, you will be elated with some reason; for you will be elated at some good of your own.

...

VIII

Don't demand that events should happen as you wish; but wish them to happen as they do happen, and you will find peace.

IX

Sickness is an impediment to the body, but not to the mind unless the mind decides that it is. Lameness is an impediment to the leg, but not to the mind. Say this to yourself with regard to everything that happens. For you will find it to be an impediment to something else, but not truly to yourself.

...

XII

If you would improve, lay aside such reasonings as these: "If I neglect my affairs, I shall not have enough to live on; if I do not punish my servant, he will be good for nothing." For it is better to die of hunger, free from grief and fear, than to be wealthy but uneasy;

and it is better that your servant should be bad than you unhappy.

Begin therefore with little things. Is a little oil spilled or a little wine stolen? Say to yourself, "This is the price paid for peace and tranquillity; and nothing is to be had for nothing." And when you call your servant, consider that it is possible he may not come at your call; or, if he does, that he may not do what you wish. But it is not at all desirable for him, and very undesirable for you, that it should be in his power to disrupt your peace of mind.

XIII

If you would improve, be content to be thought foolish and dull with regard to externals.† Do not desire to be thought to know anything; and though you should appear to others to be somebody, distrust yourself. For be assured, it is not easy simultaneously to keep your will in harmony with nature and to secure externals; while you are absorbed in the one, you must necessarily neglect the other.

XIV

If you wish your children and your wife and your friends to live forever, you are foolish, for you wish things to be in your power which are not so, and what belongs to others to be your own. Similarly, if you wish your servant to be without fault, you are foolish, for you wish vice not to be vice but something else. But if you wish not to be disappointed in your desires, that is in your own power. Exercise, therefore, what is in your power. A man's master is he who is able to provide or remove whatever that man seeks or shuns. Whoever then would be free, let him wish nothing, let him decline nothing, which depends on others; otherwise he must necessarily be a slave.

XV

Remember that you must behave as at a banquet. Is anything brought round to you? Put out your hand and take a moderate share. Does it pass by you? Do

---

* "The phenomena of existence": the appearances of things, impressions.
† Merely external or conventional signs (e.g., status symbols), as opposed to the genuinely important things.

not stop it. Is it not yet come? Do not yearn in desire toward it, but wait till it reaches you. Behave like this with regard to children, wife, status, riches, and you will in time be worthy to feast with the gods. And if you do not so much as take the things which are set before you, but are able even to forego them, then you will not only be worthy to feast with the gods, but to rule with them also. For, by thus doing, Diogenes and Heraclitus,* and others like them, deservedly became divine, and were so recognized.

XVI

When you see anyone weeping for grief, either that his son has gone abroad or that he has lost some money or property, take care not to be overcome by the apparent evil, but discriminate and be ready to say, "What hurts this man is not this occurrence itself—for another man might not be hurt by it—but the view he chooses to take of it." As far as conversation goes, however, do not disdain to sympathize with him and, if need be, to groan with him. Take heed, however, not to groan inwardly, too.

...

XX

Remember that it is not he who gives abuse or blows, who affronts, but the view we take of these things as insulting. When, therefore, anyone provokes you, be assured that it is your own opinion which provokes you. Try, therefore, in the first place, not to be bewildered by appearances. For if you take some time before reacting, you will more easily command yourself.

...

XXII

If you have an earnest desire toward philosophy, prepare yourself from the very first to have the multitude laugh and sneer, and say, "Suddenly we have a philosopher among us"; and, "What makes him so pretentious now?" Now, for your part, don't be pretentious, but keep steadily to those things which appear best to you, as one appointed by God to the role of philosopher. For remember that, if you are persistent, those very people who at first ridiculed you will afterwards admire you. But if you let them persuade you not to be a philosopher, you will incur a double ridicule.

XXIII

If you ever happen to turn your attention to externals, for the pleasure of anyone, be assured that you have ruined your scheme of life. Be content, then, in everything, with being a philosopher; and if you wish to seem so likewise to anyone, appear so to yourself, and it will be enough for you.

...

XXV

Is anyone given preferential treatment over you at a formal party, or in being honoured, or in being asked to join a confidential conversation? If these things are good, you ought to rejoice that he has them; and if they are evil, do not be grieved that you have them not. And remember that you cannot be permitted to rival others in externals without using the same means to obtain them. For how can he who will not haunt the door of any man, will not attend him, will not praise him, have an equal share with him who does these things? You are unjust, then, and unreasonable if you are unwilling to pay the price for which these things are sold, and would have them for nothing. For how much are lettuces sold? An obol,† for instance. If another, then, paying an obol, takes the lettuces, and you, not paying it, go without them, do not imagine that he has gained any advantage over you. For as he has the lettuces, so you have the obol which you did not give. So, in the present case, you have not been invited to such a person's formal dinner because you have not paid him the price for which a supper is sold. It is sold for praise; it is sold for paying court. Give him, then, the value if it be for your advantage. But if you would at the same time not pay the one, and

---

* Diogenes of Apollonia (fifth century BCE) and Heraclitus of Ephesus (c. 535–c. 475 BCE) were Greek philosophers and precursors of Socrates.
† A small Greek coin.

yet receive the other, you are unreasonable and foolish. Have you nothing, then, in place of the dinner? Yes, indeed, you have—not to praise him whom you do not like to praise; not to bear the insolence of his lackeys.

XXVI

The will of nature may be learned from things upon which we are all agreed. As when our neighbor's boy has broken a cup, or the like, we are ready at once to say, "These are casualties that will happen"; be assured, then, that when your own cup is likewise broken, you ought to be affected just as when another's cup was broken. Now apply this to greater things. Is the child or wife of another dead? There is no one who would not say, "This is an accident of mortality." But if anyone's own child happens to die, it is immediately, "Alas! how wretched am I!" It should be always remembered how we are affected on hearing the same thing concerning others.

...

XXIX

In every affair consider what precedes and what follows, and then undertake it. Otherwise you will begin enthusiastically, indeed, careless of the consequences, and when these are developed, you will shamefully give up. "I would conquer at the Olympic Games." But consider what precedes and what follows, and then, if it be for your advantage, engage in the affair. You must conform to rules, submit to a diet, refrain from rich food; exercise your body, whether you choose it or not, at a stated hour, in heat and cold; you must drink no cold water, and sometimes no wine—in a word, you must give yourself up to your trainer as to a physician. Then, in the combat, you may be thrown into a ditch, dislocate your arm, turn your ankle, swallow an abundance of dust, be whipped, and, after all, lose the victory. When you have reckoned up all this, if your inclination still holds, set about the combat. Otherwise, take notice, you will behave like children who sometimes play at being wrestlers, sometimes gladiators, sometimes blow a trumpet, and sometimes act a tragedy, when they happen to have seen and admired these shows. Thus you too will be at one time a wrestler, and another a gladiator; now a philosopher, now an orator; but nothing in earnest. Like an ape you mimic all you see, and one thing after another is sure to please you, but is out of favor as soon as it becomes familiar. For you have never entered upon anything thoughtfully; nor after having surveyed and tested the whole matter, but carelessly, and with a halfway zeal. Thus some, when they have seen a philosopher and heard a man speaking like Euphrates*—though, indeed, who can speak like him?—have a mind to be philosophers, too. Consider first, friend, what the matter is, and what your own nature is able to bear. If you would be a wrestler, consider your shoulders, your back, your thighs; for different persons are made for different things. Do you think that you can act as you do and be a philosopher, that you can eat, drink, be angry, be discontented, as you are now? You must watch, you must labor, you must get the better of certain appetites, must break off with your friends and family, be despised by your servant, be laughed at by those you meet; come off worse than others in everything—in positions, in honors, before tribunals. When you have fully considered all these things, approach, if you please—that is, if, by parting with them, you have a mind to purchase serenity, freedom, and tranquillity. If not, do not come hither; do not, like children, be now a philosopher, then a tax collector, then an orator, and then one of Caesar's officers. These things are not consistent. You must be one man, either good or bad. You must cultivate either your own reason or else externals; apply yourself either to things within or without you—that is, be either a philosopher or one of the mob.†

XXX

Duties are universally defined by social relations. Is a certain man your father? In this are implied taking care of him, submitting to him in all things, patiently receiving his reproaches, his correction. But he is a bad

---

* Euphrates was a well-known Stoic philosopher from the generation before Epictetus, who lived in the southern area of what is today Syria between 35 and 118 CE. Several contemporaries praise his great talent as an orator.

† Common people, masses.

father. Is your natural tie, then, to a *good* father? No, but to a father. Is a brother unjust? Well, preserve your own just relation toward him. Consider not what *he* does, but what *you* are to do to keep your own mind in a state conforming to nature, for another cannot hurt you unless you allow it. You will then be hurt when you consent to be hurt. In this manner, therefore, if you accustom yourself to contemplate the relations of neighbor, citizen, commander, you can deduce from each the corresponding duties.

...

XXXIII

Begin by prescribing to yourself some character and demeanor, which you are able to stick to whether alone or in company.

Be mostly silent, or speak only what is necessary, and in few words. We may, however, enter sparingly into discourse sometimes, when occasion calls for it; but let it not run on any of the common subjects, as gladiators, or horse races, or athletic champions, or food, or drink—the vulgar* topics of conversation—and especially not on men, so as either to blame, or praise, or make comparisons. If you are able, then, by your own conversation, bring over that of your company to proper subjects; but if you happen to find yourself among strangers, be silent.

Let not your laughter be loud, frequent, or abundant.

Avoid taking oaths, if possible, altogether; at any rate, so far as you are able.

Avoid public and vulgar entertainments; but if ever an occasion calls you to them, pay attention not to imperceptibly slide into vulgarity. For be assured that if a person be ever so pure himself, yet, if his companion be corrupted, he who converses with him will be corrupted likewise.

Provide things relating to the body no further than absolute need requires, as meat, drink, clothing, house, servants. But cut off everything that looks toward show and luxury.

Before marriage guard yourself with all your ability from unlawful sexual intercourse with women; yet be not uncharitable or severe to those who are led into this, nor boast frequently that you yourself do otherwise.

If anyone tells you that a certain person speaks ill of you, do not make excuses about what is said of you, but answer: "He was ignorant of my other faults, otherwise he would have mentioned these as well."

It is not necessary for you to appear often at public spectacles;† but if ever there is a proper occasion for you to be there, do not appear more solicitous for any other than for yourself—that is, wish things to be only just as they are, and only the best man to win; for thus nothing will go against you. But abstain entirely from acclamations and derision and violent emotions. And when you come away, do not discourse a great deal on what has passed, or no more than is necessary to get it out of your system. For it would appear by such discourse that you were dazzled by the show.

Be not eager or ready to attend private recitations;‡ but if you do attend, preserve your gravity and dignity, and yet avoid making yourself disagreeable.

When you are going to confer with anyone, and especially with one who seems your superior, think about how Socrates or Zeno§ would behave in such a case, and you will not be at a loss to meet properly whatever may occur.

When you are going to meet someone powerful, imagine to yourself that you may not find him at home, that you may be shut out, that the doors may not be opened to you, that he may not notice you. If, with all this, it be your duty to go, bear what happens and never say to yourself, "It was not worth so much"; for this is vulgar, and like a man bewildered by externals.

In company, avoid a frequent and excessive mention of your own actions and adventures. For however agreeable it may be to yourself to allude to the risks you have run, it is not equally agreeable to others to hear about your exploits. Avoid likewise an endeavor to excite laughter, for this may readily slide you into

---

* Characteristic of ordinary, unsophisticated people (from the Latin *vulgaris* meaning "of the common people").
† Public games, such as sporting events.
‡ Private lectures or poetry recitals.
§ Socrates and Zeno were famous Greek philosophers. Zeno of Cyprus (335–263 BCE) was the founder of Stoicism.

vulgarity, and, besides, may be apt to lower you in the esteem of your acquaintance. Approaches to indecent conversation are likewise dangerous. Therefore, when anything of this sort happens, use the first fit opportunity to rebuke him who makes advances that way, or, at least, by silence and blushing and a serious look show yourself to be displeased by such talk.

...

XLI

It is a sign of lack of intellect to spend much time in things relating to the body, as to be immoderate in exercises, in eating and drinking, and in the discharge of other animal functions. These things should be done incidentally and our main strength be applied to our reason.

XLII

When any person does ill by you, or speaks ill of you, remember that he acts or speaks from an impression that it is right for him to do so. Now it is not possible that he should follow what appears right to you, but only what appears so to himself. Therefore, if he judges from false appearances, he is the person hurt, since he, too, is the person deceived. For if anyone takes a true proposition to be false, the proposition is not hurt, but only the man is deceived. Setting out, then, from these principles, you will meekly bear with a person who reviles you, for you will say upon every occasion, "It seemed so to him."

...

XLVIII

The condition and characteristic of a vulgar person is that he never looks for either help or harm from himself, but only from externals. The condition and characteristic of a philosopher is that he looks to himself for all help or harm. The marks of a proficient are that he censures no one, praises no one, blames no one, accuses no one; says nothing concerning himself as being anybody or knowing anything. When he is in any instance hindered or restrained, he accuses himself; and if he is praised, he smiles to himself at the person who praises him; and if he is censured, he makes no defense. But he goes about with the caution of a convalescent, careful of interference with anything that is doing well but not yet quite secure. He restrains desire; he transfers his aversion to only those things which thwart the proper use of our own will; he employs his energies moderately in all directions; if he appears stupid or ignorant, he does not care; and, in a word, he keeps watch over himself as if he were an enemy waiting in ambush. ■

Suggestions for Critical Reflection

1. Does Epictetus say that you can avoid being disappointed by disciplining yourself not to want the things that you can't—or might not—get? How practical, or healthy, is this advice?
2. "Sickness is an impediment to the body, but not to the mind unless the mind decides that it is." What do you make of this?
3. Why do you think Epictetus says that "it is not easy simultaneously to keep your will in harmony with nature and to secure externals"?
4. How attractive do you find Epictetus' stoicism? Is it a good guide for everyday life? Does it seem to you a good way to be happy?

A.J. AYER

The Claims of Philosophy

Who Was A.J. Ayer?

Sir Alfred Jules Ayer (1910–89), known to all his friends as Freddie, was born into a wealthy European-origin family in London. He attended the pre-eminent English private school Eton, then went on scholarship to Oxford. He served as an officer in a British espionage and sabotage unit during World War II, then taught at University College London and at Oxford.

When only 24, Ayer wrote *Language, Truth, and Logic*, the book that made his name. In it, he briefly, simply, and persuasively to many, argued for logical positivism, a form of radical empiricism that had been developed largely by the group of philosophers called the Vienna Circle, whose ideas Ayer had picked up while studying with them in Austria. Logical positivism dominated Anglophone philosophy for decades; while objections (especially to Ayer's rather simplified version) came thick and fast, everyone was at least aware of it as a philosophical force to be reckoned with.

While *Language, Truth, and Logic* was by far his best-seller, Ayer wrote a good deal of other important work, especially in epistemology. Though his work is not now generally included in lists of all-time philosophical landmarks, he was considered, in terms of influence if not of originality, second only to Bertrand Russell among the English philosophers of his day. He was also known for his advocacy of humanism and was the first executive director of the British Humanist Association, a charitable organization working towards "a tolerant world where rational thinking and kindness prevail."*

Ayer was extraordinarily well-known by the British public. He wrote and spoke on all sorts of popular issues, all over the media. In those days, TV networks programmed witty intellectual chatter, and Ayer was a master at this. He loved his celebrity, and hobnobbed with the famous and influential. He was knighted in 1970.

What Is the Structure of This Reading?

Ayer begins by distinguishing between two types of philosophy; he raises criticisms of both types, and argues that neither can help with the question "what is the meaning of life?" This is because, he argues, the question makes no sense and has no possible coherent answer. In Part III he argues that appealing to God's purpose for the universe will not provide an answer, and in Part IV he similarly argues that appeals to human nature or to evolution cannot tell us how we should behave. All we are left with are our own individual goals and values.

Some Useful Background Information

The background to this article is Ayer's philosophy of logical positivism. The core principle of logical positivism is a view of meaning called *verificationism*. On this view, what a statement means can be wholly captured by understanding what difference it makes whether it is true or not—by understanding its 'truth conditions.' For example, if I say that my dog has three legs then this is true just so long as, if you were to meet my dog and count its legs, there were three of them; if it had any other number of legs, my claim would be false. For logical positivists, the only way that we can make sense of a statement having truth conditions is by thinking about the possible ways in which our sensory experiences might differ depending on whether the statement is true or false—ultimately, we can verify that a dog has three legs only by looking at it (or perhaps feeling it in a dark room) and counting the appendages. In the end, even very complicated scientific propositions boil down to some set of claims about what we would experience under such and such conditions; they are true just in case we do (or would) have those experiences, and false if we do (or would) not.

---

* https://humanism.org.uk/about/

This may seem a fairly straightforward and sensible account of how language works, but it has quite far-reaching consequences. One of these is that certain pieces of language may masquerade as meaningful statements but, if the truth or falsity of those claims would make no difference to our possible sensory experiences, then they in fact are not meaningful at all. They are not false (which would have to be discovered by experience)—they are simply not the kind of thing that could be true *or* false. Despite surface grammatical appearances, they tell us nothing about how the world might be. Notorious examples include "There exists a transcendent God" or "Stealing is morally wrong."

If these sorts of non-empirical sentences—sentences about metaphysics or values, for example—have no literal meaning, then what is their function? According to some logical positivists, including Ayer, they are rather like exclamations or expressive actions. Saying "ouch" when you stub your toe, or giving someone a heart-felt hug, are not things that have literal meaning—they are not things that can be true or false—but they nevertheless are a kind of expression. In a similar way, perhaps, saying "stealing is deeply immoral" might have the function of expressing strong disapproval of stealing—metaphorically, punching stealing in the face—even if it is not a claim that could be either true or false.

The Claims of Philosophy*

I

Contemporary philosophers may be divided into two classes: the pontiffs and the journeymen.† As the names that I have chosen indicate, the basis of this division is not so much a difference of opinion as a difference of attitude. It is not merely that the journeyman denies certain propositions which the pontiff asserts, or that he asserts certain propositions which the pontiff denies. It is rather that he has a radically different conception of the method of philosophy and of the ends that it is fitted to achieve. Thus, it is characteristic of those whom I describe as pontiffs that they think it within the province of philosophy to compete with natural science. They may, indeed, be willing to admit that the scientist achieves valuable results in his own domain, but they insist that he does not, and cannot, attain to the complete and final truth about reality; and they think that it is open to the philosopher to make this deficiency good. In support of this view, they may, for example, argue that every scientific theory is based upon presuppositions which cannot themselves be scientifically proved; and from this they may infer, in the interests of their own 'philosophical' brand of irrationality, that science itself is fundamentally irrational; or else they may have recourse to metaphysics to supply the missing proof. Alternatively, they may hold that the scientist deals only with the appearances of things, whereas the philosopher by the use of his special methods penetrates to the reality beyond. In general, the ideal of the pontiff is to construct a metaphysical system. Such a system may actually include some scientific hypotheses, either as premises or, more frequently, as deductions from metaphysical first principles. It may, on the other hand, be uncompromisingly metaphysical. In either case, the aim is to give a complete and definitive account of 'ultimate' reality.

Unfortunately, as the journeymen on their side have been at pains to show, this 'ultimate' reality is a fiction, and the ideal of a metaphysical system that is anything other than a scientific encyclopaedia is devoid of any basis in reason. To some extent, indeed, this fact has been borne in upon the pontiffs, and the result is

---

*   Published in *Polemic* 7 (March 1947).

†   A pontiff is a high priest, and a journeyman is a skilled worker who has completed an apprenticeship in a particular trade.

that they now tend to desert reason and even to decry it. This separates them sharply from their philosophical ancestors, who at least professed to reason, even if they did not always reason well. Few men, indeed, can ever have reasoned worse than Hegel, the arch-pontiff of the nineteenth century,* but at least he claimed the support of reason for his fantasies. His ground for thinking that a mobile logic is needed to describe a mobile world may have been no better than the principle that 'who drives fat oxen must himself be fat'; but at least, if he rejected the 'static' Aristotelian logic, he did so in favour of what he, no doubt mistakenly, believed to be a superior logic of his own. Though he misused logic abominably, he did not affect to be above it. But now if we turn to Heidegger, the high priest of the modern school of existentialists, and the leading pontiff of our times,† we find ourselves in a country from which the ordinary processes of logic, or indeed reasoning of any kind, appear to have been banished. For what we learn from him is that it is only in the clear light of Nothing that Being has being, and consequently that it is the supreme privilege of the philosopher to concern himself with Nothing.[1] For this he requires no special intellectual discipline. It is sufficient that he experiences anguish, provided always that it is an anguish without any special object. For it is thus, according to Heidegger, that the Nothing reveals itself. This strange thesis is indeed backed by a pretence of argument, but since the argument depends upon the elementary fallacy of treating 'nothing' as a name, it is hardly to be taken seriously. Nor does Heidegger himself appear to attach very much weight to it. For it is not by logic that he seeks to convince: nor is his the Socratic method of following an argument wherever it may lead. Like the sermons of Dr. Dodd,[2] his work is addressed to the passions; and it is no doubt for this reason that it has succeeded in becoming fashionable.

Now just as William James thought that all prigs must sooner or later end by becoming Hegelians, so it seems to me that the fate of the contemporary pontiff must be to go the way of Heidegger. I do not mean by this that he will have to subscribe to Heidegger's doctrines. There are other types of 'deeply significant nonsense' available. But inasmuch as his quest for ultimate reality cannot be made to prosper by any rational means, he is likely, if he adheres to it, to seek some non-rational source of enlightenment. At this point he devolves into a mystic or a poet. As such he may express an attitude to life which is interesting in itself and even a source of inspiration to others; and perhaps it would be churlish to refuse him the title of philosopher. But it is to be remarked that when philosophy has been brought to this stage then, whatever its emotional value, it has ceased to be, in any ordinary sense, a vehicle of knowledge.

II

The history of philosophy, as it is taught in the textbooks, is largely a parade of pontiffs; and it might be thought that the only course open to the budding philosopher was either to enrol himself under one of their banners, or else to try to become a pontiff in his own right. But in this, as in so many other cases, the textbooks are behind the times. For, at least in England and America, the philosophical scene has been dominated for the last fifty years, not by the pontiffs, but by those whom I describe as journeymen. Unlike the pontiffs, the journeymen do not set out in quest of ultimate reality. Nor do they try to bring philosophy into competition with the natural sciences. Believing, as they do, that the only way to discover what the world is like is to form hypotheses and test them by observation, which is in fact the method of science, they are content to leave the scientist in full possession of the field of speculative knowledge. Consequently they do not try to build systems. The task of the philosopher, as they see it, is rather to deal piecemeal with a special set of problems. Some of these problems are historical, in the sense that they involve the criticism and interpretation of the work of previous philosophers; others are primarily mathematical, as belonging to the specialized

---

* Georg Wilhelm Friedrich Hegel (1770–1831) was a German philosopher who expounded a very influential form of "absolute idealism." He developed the dialectical method of logic, whereby a thesis and its antithesis are resolved into their synthesis.

† Martin Heidegger (1889–1976) is another German philosopher who made important and original contributions to phenomenology and existentialism.

field of formal logic; others again are set by the sciences: they involve the analysis of scientific method, the evaluation of scientific theories, the clarification of scientific terms. It is, for example, a philosophical problem to decide what is meant by 'probability': and the journeymen have already contributed much towards its solution. Finally, there are a number of problems, such as the problem of perception, the problem of our knowledge of other minds, the question of the significance of moral judgments, that arise out of the common usages and assumptions of everyday life. In a broad sense, all these problems are semantic: that is to say, they can all be represented as concerned with the use of language. But since the term 'semantics' is technically applied to a particular formal discipline which does not, even for the journeymen, comprehend the whole of philosophy, I think it better to resume their philosophical activities under the general heading of logical analysis.

Essentially, the journeymen are technicians; and from this point of view the comparison with the pontiffs is very much to their advantage. They suffer, however, from a certain thinness of material. Consider, for example, the so-called philosophers of common-sense, who follow the distinguished leadership of Professor G.E. Moore.* In the opinion of this school, it is not sensible for a philosopher to question the truth of such common-sense statements as that this is a sheet of paper or that I am wearing shoes on my feet. And if anyone were to question it, they would reply simply that, on the relevant occasions, they knew for certain that statements of this sort were true. Thus, Professor Moore himself has proved, to his own satisfaction, the existence of external objects, a question much canvassed by philosophers, by the simple method of holding up his hands and saying that he knows for certain that they exist;[3] and indeed there is no denying that in its way this is a valid proof. At the same time these philosophers confess to being very doubtful of the correct analysis of the common-sense propositions which they know to be true. The question whether or not this really

is a sheet of paper does not puzzle them at all; but the question of what precisely is implied by saying that it is puzzles them a great deal. In technical language, it is a matter of discovering the relationship between the sense-data† which are immediately experienced and the physical objects which it is their function to present; and this is a problem which, in the opinion of our common-sense philosophers, has not yet been satisfactorily solved. Now I do not wish to suggest that this is not a difficult problem, or to belittle the ingenuity with which the journeymen have tackled it. But I am afraid that a layman who was told that a question of this sort was of sufficient interest to a modern philosopher to occupy him for a lifetime would be inclined to think that modern philosophy was degenerating into scholasticism.‡ If he were told, as he might be by a pontiff, that there was serious doubt of the existence of this piece of paper he would be very properly incredulous, but he might also be impressed: he might even be brought to think that he himself had been excessively naïve in taking such a thing for granted. But once he had been assured that the truth of his common-sense assumption that the paper existed was not after all in doubt, I think it would be difficult to interest him in a meticulous analysis of its implications. He would remark that he understood very well what he meant by saying that this was a piece of paper, and that he did not see what was to be gained by a laborious attempt at further clarification. To this it could, indeed, be objected that he might think very differently if he had been properly educated in philosophy; and that in any case there is no reason why the layman's judgments of value should be binding upon the philosopher. But even so it is difficult not to feel some sympathy for our layman. It is difficult not to suspect that the philosopher of common-sense must sometimes be inclined to say to himself what the poet Clough said when he found himself exclusively engaged in doing up parcels for Florence Nightingale: 'This that I see is not all, and this that I do is but little. It is good but there is better than it.'§ ...

* G.E. Moore (1873–1958) was an English philosopher and one of the founders of twentieth-century analytic philosophy.
† The, presumably mental, sensations of which we are non-inferentially conscious, such as a red, round visual image of a tomato (as opposed to the tomato itself).
‡ The method of teaching and learning that dominated medieval universities in Europe. Ayer is using the term in a pejorative way to mean nit-picking attention to little details within a closed system of thought.
§ Arthur Hugh Clough (1819–61) was an English poet; in the 1850s he devoted himself to working as a secretarial assistant to his wife's cousin Florence Nightingale and wrote virtually no poetry for six years during this period. Florence

III

On the side of the pontiffs, imaginative literature. On the side of the journeymen, the reintegration of philosophy with science or the piece-meal solution of logical or linguistic puzzles. Surely, it will be said, this is not what the public expects of its philosophers. Surely, the business of the philosopher is to make clear the meaning of life, to show people how they ought to live. Call him a pontiff or a journeyman, according to his method of approach; the distinction is not of any great importance. What is important is the message that he has to give. It is wisdom that is needed, not merely scientific knowledge. Of what use to us is the understanding of nature if we do not know the purpose of our existence or how we ought to live? And who is to answer these supremely important questions if not the philosopher?

The reply to this is that there is no true answer to these questions; and since this is so it is no use expecting even the philosopher to provide one. What can be done, however, is to make clear why, and in what sense, these questions are unanswerable; and once this is achieved it will be seen that there is also a sense in which they can be answered. It will be found that the form of answer is not a proposition, which must be either true or false, but the adoption of a rule, which cannot properly be characterized as either true or false, but can nevertheless be judged as more or less acceptable. And with this the problem is solved, so far as reasoning can solve it. The rest is a matter of personal decision, and ultimately of action.

Let us begin then by considering the purpose of our existence. How is it possible for existence to have a purpose? We know very well what it is for a man to have a purpose. It is a matter of his intending, on the basis of a given situation, to bring about some further situation which for some reason or other he conceives to be desirable. And in that case it may be said that events have a meaning for him according as they conduce, or fail to conduce, towards the end* that he desires. But how can life in general be said to have

any meaning? A simple answer is that all events are tending towards a certain specifiable end: so that to understand the meaning of life it is necessary only to discover this end. But, in the first place, there is no good reason whatever for supposing this assumption to be true, and secondly, even if it were true, it would not do the work that is required of it. For what is being sought by those who demand to know the meaning of life is not an explanation of the facts of their existence, but a justification. Consequently a theory which informs them merely that the course of events is so arranged as to lead inevitably to a certain end does nothing to meet their need. For the end in question will not be one that they themselves have chosen. As far as they are concerned it will be entirely arbitrary; and it will be a no less arbitrary fact that their existence is such as necessarily to lead to its fulfilment. In short, from the point of view of justifying one's existence, there is no essential difference between a teleological explanation of events and a mechanical explanation.[†] In either case, it is a matter of brute fact that events succeed one another in the ways that they do and are explicable in the ways that they are. And indeed what is called an explanation is nothing other than a more general description. Thus, an attempt to answer the question why events are as they are must always resolve itself into saying only how they are. But what is required by those who seek the meaning of life is precisely an answer to their question 'Why?' that is something other than an answer to any question 'How?' And just because this is so they can never legitimately be satisfied.

But now, it may be objected, suppose that the world is designed by a superior being. In that case the purpose of our existence will be the purpose that it realizes for him; and the meaning of life will be found in our conscious adaptation to his purpose. But here again, the answer is, first, that there is no good reason whatsoever for believing that there is any such superior being; and, secondly, that even if there were, he could not accomplish what is here required of him. For let us

---

Nightingale (1820–1910) was a pioneer of modern nursing, coming to prominence as a manager and trainer of nurses during the Crimean War (1853–56); she was also a social reformer, and an innovator in the graphical presentation of statistical data.

* Goal, outcome.

† A teleological explanation explains in terms of purposes, while a mechanical explanation explains by appealing to causes.

assume, for the sake of argument, that everything happens as it does because a superior being has intended that it should. As far as we are concerned, the course of events still remains entirely arbitrary. True, it can now be said to fulfil a purpose; but the purpose is not ours. And just as, on the previous assumption, it merely happened to be the case that the course of events conduced to the end that it did, so, on this assumption, it merely happens to be the case that the deity has the purpose that he has, and not some other purpose, or no purpose at all. Nor does this unwarrantable assumption provide us even with a rule of life. For even those who believe most firmly that the world was designed by a superior being are not in a position to tell us what his purpose can have been. They may indeed claim that it has been mysteriously revealed to them, but how can it be proved that the revelation is genuine? And even if we waive this objection, even if we assume not only the world as we find it is working out the purpose of a superior being, but also that we are capable of discovering what this purpose is, we are still not provided with a rule of life. For either his purpose is sovereign or it is not. If it is sovereign, that is, if everything that happens is necessarily in accordance with it, then this is true also of our behaviour. Consequently, there is no point in our deciding to conform to it, for the simple reason that we cannot do otherwise. However we behave, we shall fulfil the purpose of this deity; and if we were to behave differently, we should still be fulfilling it; for if it were possible for us not to fulfil it it would not be sovereign in the requisite sense. But suppose that it is not sovereign, or, in other words, that not all events must necessarily bear it out. In that case, there is no reason why we should try to conform to it, unless we independently judge it to be good. But that means that the significance of our behaviour depends finally upon our own judgments of value; and the concurrence of a deity then becomes superfluous.

The point is, in short, that even the invocation of a deity does not enable us to answer the question why things are as they are. At the most it complicates the answer to the question how they are by pushing the level of explanation to a further stage. For even if the ways of the deity were clear to those who believed in him, which they apparently are not, it would still be, even to them, a matter of brute fact that he behaved as he did, just as to those who do not believe in him it is a matter of brute fact that the world is what it is. In either case the question 'Why?' remains unanswered, for the very good reason that it is unanswerable. That is to say, it may be answerable at any given level but the answer is always a matter of describing at a higher level not why things are as they are, but simply how they are. And so, to whatever level our explanations may be carried, the final statement is never an answer to the question 'Why?' but necessarily only an answer to the question 'How?'

It follows, if my argument is correct, that there is no sense in asking what is the ultimate purpose of our existence, or what is the real meaning of life. For to ask this is to assume that there can be a reason for our living as we do which is somehow more profound than any mere explanation of the facts; and we have seen that this assumption is untenable. Moreover it is untenable in logic and not merely in fact. The position is not that our existence unfortunately lacks a purpose which, if the fates had been kinder, it might conceivably have had. It is rather that those who inquire, in this way, after the meaning of life are raising a question to which it is not logically possible that there should be an answer. Consequently, the fact that they are disappointed is not, as some romanticists would make it, an occasion for cynicism or despair. It is not an occasion for any emotional attitude at all. And the reason why it is not is just that it could not conceivably have been otherwise. If it were logically possible for our existence to have a purpose, in the sense required, then it might be sensible to lament the fact that it had none. But it is not sensible to cry for what is logically impossible. If a question is so framed as to be unanswerable, then it is not a matter for regret that it remains unanswered. It is, therefore, misleading to say that life has no meaning; for that suggests that the statement that life has a meaning is factually significant, but false; whereas the truth is that, in the sense in which it is taken in this context, it is not factually significant.

There is, however, a sense in which it can be said that life does have a meaning. It has for each of us whatever meaning we severally choose to give it. The purpose of a man's existence is constituted by the ends to which he, consciously or unconsciously, devotes himself. Some men have a single overriding purpose to which all their activities are subordinated. If they are at all successful in achieving it, they are probably the happiest, but they are the exceptions. Most men pass from one object to another; and at any one time they may pursue a number of different ends, which may or may not be capable of being harmonized. Philosophers, with a preference for tidiness, have sometimes tried to show that all these apparently diverse objects can really be reduced to one: but the fact is that there is no end that is common to all men, not even happiness. For setting aside the question whether men ought always to pursue happiness, it is not true even that they always do pursue it, unless the word 'happiness' is used merely as a description of any end that is in fact pursued. Thus the question what is the meaning of life proves, when it is taken empirically, to be incomplete. For there is no single thing of which it can truly be said that this is the meaning of life. All that can be said is that life has at various times a different meaning for different people, according as they pursue their several ends.

That different people have different purposes is an empirical matter of fact. But what is required by those who seek to know the purpose of their existence is not a factual description of the way that people actually do conduct themselves, but rather a decision as to how they should conduct themselves. Having been taught to believe that not all purposes are of equal value, they require to be guided in their choice. And thus the inquiry into the purpose of our existence dissolves into the question 'How ought men to live?'

IV

The question how ought men to live is one that would seem to fall within the province of moral philosophy; but it cannot be said of every moral philosopher that he makes a serious attempt to answer it. Moreover, those who do make a serious attempt to answer it are mostly pontiffs, who approach it wrongly. For having decided, on metaphysical grounds, that reality is of such and such a character they try to deduce from this the superiority of a certain mode of life. But, quite apart from the merits or demerits of their metaphysics, it is a mistake on their part to suppose that a mere description of reality is sufficient to establish any rule of life at all. A familiar instance of this mistake is the claim that men ought to live in such and such a way because such and such is their real nature. But if what is meant by their having such and such a real nature is that they really are of the nature in question, then all that can possibly be established is that they really do

behave in the manner indicated. For if they behaved differently, they thereby show that they had a different nature. Thus in telling men that they ought to live in accordance with their real nature you are telling them to do what they do; and your pretended rule of life dissolves into nothing, since it is equally consistent with any course of conduct whatsoever. If, on the other hand, what is meant by a man's real nature is not the nature that he actually displays but the nature that he ought to display, then the moral rule that the argument is supposed to justify is assumed at the outset, and assumed without proof. As a moral rule, it may be acceptable in itself; but the supposed deduction of it from a non-moral premiss turns out inevitably to be a fraud.

It is not only metaphysicians who commit this fallacy. There is, for example, a brand of 'scientific ethics' according to which the right rule of life is that which harmonizes with the course of human evolution. But here again the same ambiguity arises. For if 'the course of human evolution' is understood as an actually existent process, then there is no sense in telling people that they ought to adapt themselves to it, for the very good reason that they cannot possibly do otherwise. However they may behave they will be acting rightly, since it is just their behaving as they do that makes the course of evolution what it is. In short, if progress is defined in terms of merely historical development, all conduct is progressive; for every human action necessarily furthers the course of evolution, in the straightforward sense of adding to its history. If on the other hand, it is only some among the many possible developments of human history that are considered to be progressive, then there is some sense in saying that we ought to strive to bring them about; but here again the moral rule which we are invited to adopt is not deduced but simply posited. It is neither itself a scientific statement of fact, nor a logical consequence of any such statement. By scientific methods we can indeed discover that certain events are more or less likely to occur; but the transition from this to deciding that some of these possible developments are more valuable than others carries us outside the domain of science altogether. In saying this, I do not wish to repudiate the humanistic values of those who put forward the claims of scientific ethics, or even to suggest that any other system of values is more securely founded. My objection to these moralists is simply that they fall into the logical error of confusing normative* judgments of value with scientific statements of fact. They may have the advantage of the metaphysicians, in that their factual premises are more deserving of belief, but the fundamental mistake of trying to extract normative rules from supposedly factual descriptions is common to them both.

In moral, as in natural, philosophy it is characteristic of the journeyman to have detected the flaw in the method of the pontiffs, but here also they have purchased their freedom from error at the price of a certain aridity. For not only do they not attempt to prove their judgments of value; for the most part they refrain from expressing them at all. What they do instead, apart from criticizing other moral philosophers, is to subject the terminology of ethics to logical analysis. Thus the questions that they discuss are whether the term 'good' or the term 'right' is to be taken as fundamental, and whether either is definable; whether it is a man's duty to do an action or merely to set himself to do it; whether his duty is to do what is objectively right or merely what he thinks to be right; whether the rightness of an action depends upon its actual consequences, or upon its probable consequences, or upon its consequences as foreseen by the agent, or not upon its consequences at all; whether it is possible to fulfil an obligation unintentionally; whether the moral goodness of an action depends upon its motive; and many other questions of a similar sort. Such questions can be interesting, though they are not always made so, and I do not wish to say that they are not important; but to the practical man they must appear somewhat academic. By taking a course in this kind of moral philosophy a man may learn how to make the expression of his moral judgments secure from formal criticism. What he will not learn is what, in any concrete situation, he actually ought to do.

I think, then, that it can fairly be made a reproach to the journeymen that they have overlooked the Aristotelian principle that the end of moral philosophy is 'not knowledge but action'.[4] But their excuse is that once the philosopher who wishes to be practical has said this, there is very little more that he can say. Like anyone else, he can make moral recommendations, but he cannot legitimately claim for them the sanction of philosophy. He cannot prove that his judgments of value are correct, for the sufficient reason that no judgment of value is capable of proof. Or rather, if it is capable of proof, it is only by reference to some other judgment of value, which must itself be left unproved. The moral philosopher can sometimes affect men's conduct by drawing their attention to certain matters of fact; he may show, for example, that certain sorts of action have unsuspected consequences, or that the motives for which they are done are different from what they appear to be; and he may then hope that when his audience is fully aware of the circumstances it will assess the situation in the same way as he does himself. Nevertheless there may be some who differ from him, not on any question of fact, but on a question of value, and in that case he has no way of demonstrating that his judgment is superior. He lays down one rule, and they lay down another; and the decision between them is a subject for persuasion and finally a matter of individual choice.

Since judgments of value are not reducible to statements of fact, they are strictly speaking neither true nor false; and it is tempting to infer from this that no course of conduct is better or worse than any other. But this would be a mistake. For the judgment that no course of conduct is better or worse than any other is itself a judgment of value and consequently neither true nor false. And while an attitude of moral indifference is legitimate in itself, it is not easily maintained. For since we are constantly faced with the practical necessity of action, it is natural for most of us to act in accordance with certain principles; and the choice of principles implies the adoption of a positive set of values. That these values should be consistent is a necessary condition of their being fully realized; for it is logically impossible to achieve the complete fulfilment of an inconsistent set of ends. But, once their consistency is established, they can be criticized only on practical grounds, and from the standpoint of the critic's own moral system, which his adversary may or may not accept. No doubt, in practice, many people are content to follow the model rules that are prescribed to them by others; but the decision to submit oneself to authority on such a point is itself a judgment of value. In the last resort, therefore, each individual has the responsibility of choice; and it is a responsibility that is not to be escaped.

---

*   Having to do with values.

V

... No more than the scientist is the philosopher specially privileged to lay down the rules of conduct, or to prescribe an ideal form of life. If he has strong opinions on these points, and wishes to convert others to them, his philosophical training may give him a certain advantage in putting them persuasively: but, whether or not the values that he recommends are found to be acceptable, it is not from his philosophy that they can derive their title to acceptance. His professional task is done when he has made the issues clear. For in morals and in politics, at the stage where politics become a matter of morals, there is no repository of truth to which only the learned few have access. The question how men ought to live is one to which there is no authoritative answer. It has to be decided by each man for himself. ■

Suggestions for Critical Reflection

1. Ayer distinguishes between two kinds of philosopher, the "pontiffs" and the "journeymen," but he is critical of both kinds. What do you make of this distinction? Is there a third option for philosophy? How fair are Ayer's complaints?

2. "Surely, the business of the philosopher is to make clear the meaning of life, to show people how they ought to live." Ayer denies that this is a coherent task—for philosophers or anyone else—but then admits that there is "a sense" in which philosophy can be useful here. How effectively do you think Ayer argues for his main claim: that the question "what is the meaning of life?" makes no sense because it has no possible answer? What is left over, on Ayer's account, for philosophers to say about the meaning of life?

3. Ayer raises the possibility (which he doubts) that there exists a God who has designed the universe to serve a certain purpose, and that we could come to understand this cosmic purpose and consciously choose to endorse it. *Even then*, Ayer, says this would not answer, for us, the question "what is the meaning of life?" How does Ayer argue for this conclusion? Is he right?

4. Ayer insists that it is misleading to say that life has no meaning. Why does he say this?

5. Ayer makes a sharp distinction between *describing* how things are and judging how they *ought* to be; his arguments in Part III often depend on this contrast—sometimes called the fact-value distinction—being clear. But is it really? Are all facts value-free and are all values completely independent of facts? If this distinction can be blurred, what does this do to Ayer's argument?

6. "In the last resort, therefore, each individual has the responsibility of choice; and it is a responsibility that is not to be escaped." In the end, is Ayer's stance on the meaning of life empowering or deflating?

Notes

1 *Vide* [see] *Was ist Metaphysik*. Published by Friedrich Cohen in Bonn, 1929.

2 *Vide* Boswell's *Life of Johnson*. 'A clergyman (whose name I do not recollect): "Were not Dodd's sermons addressed to the passions?" Johnson: "They were nothing, sir, be they addressed to what they may."'

3 *Vide* his 'Proof of an External World'. Proceedings of the British Academy, vol. XXV.

4 *Vide* 'Nicomachean Ethics' Book I, Section 3.

ALBERT CAMUS

FROM *The Myth of Sisyphus*

Who Was Albert Camus?

Albert Camus was born in 1913 to a poor family in Algeria, north Africa, at that time a French colony. He studied at the University of Algiers—studying part time and supporting himself through a succession of temporary jobs—and was also a serious soccer player, playing as goalkeeper for a high-profile university team until tuberculosis ended his career. After completing the equivalent of an MA degree (on the Greek philosopher Plotinus) he became a journalist. In 1935 he founded a theater company in Algeria called the Théâtre de l'Équipe, which aimed to bring excellent plays to working-class audiences. At the outbreak of World War II Camus was working in France for *Paris-Soir* magazine and was at first a pacifist. He became radicalized in his opposition to the German occupation after reading about executions of members of the French Resistance. He joined the Resistance cell *Combat*, which published an underground newspaper of the same name, and became editor of the newspaper in 1943. He was in Paris in 1944 when the Allies liberated the city, and reported on the fighting. After the war he founded the French Committee for the European Federation, one of several groups that joined together into the European Federalist Movement, a precursor of the European Union.

Camus was awarded the Nobel Prize for Literature in 1957, at 44 the second youngest person ever to receive that honor (after Rudyard Kipling, who received it at 42). Among his major works are the novels *The Stranger* (1942), *The Plague* (1947), and *The Fall* (1956), the plays *Caligula* (1944) and *The Misunderstanding* (1944), and the philosophical essays *The Myth of Sisyphus* (1942) and *The Rebel* (1951). The reading included here is the fourth and final part of *The Myth of Sisyphus*. Camus died in a car accident in France in 1960, at the age of only 46. In his coat pocket was an unused train ticket. He had planned to travel by train with his wife and children, but, fatefully, he accepted his publisher's last minute proposal to travel with him by car instead.

Camus was a political radical who rejected any form of authoritarianism and campaigned against capital punishment. Although broadly left-wing in his views, Camus became a strong critic of Communism. This caused him to split from Jean-Paul Sartre, the well-known French existentialist philosopher.

Some Useful Background Information

1. For Camus, the human condition is that we live in a world that offers neither meaning nor clear understanding and yet—absurdly—we yearn for both. Our lives will end with an inevitable, final, and meaningless death, and nothing outside of ourselves determines or constrains what we should or should not do. Camus argued that the best response, that of the Absurd Hero, is to embrace this condition of absurdity. The alternative is to commit "philosophical suicide": to falsely endorse non-existent external standards—such as those from religion—in order to give life the fake appearance of meaning. In reality, though, according to Camus there is no escape from the Absurd. One of the purposes of *The Myth of Sisyphus* is to examine what kinds of lives can be worth living despite their absolute meaninglessness. Futilely seeking to avoid death, Camus thought, prevents us from fully appreciating and experiencing life.

2. One of the consequences of this view of the human condition as being absurd is the importance of choice, and this is one of the main ways in which Camus's work is related to existentialism. If there are no external sources of meaning, there are no standards by which we can choose rightly or wrongly. We are absolutely free to make our lives any way we want. On the other hand, terrifyingly, we are absolutely responsible for those choices—we cannot evade the responsibility to choose by appealing to some unavoidable external standard, as there are no such standards unless we choose them.

3. The well-known first line of the first section of *The Myth of Sisyphus* (not reprinted here) is "There is but one truly serious philosophical problem, and that is suicide." It is striking that Camus focuses his philosophical investigation not on a quest for understanding or analysis, but on the choice of an action. For him, philosophy is not the hopeless attempt to formulate a rational theory of a meaningless universe, but instead is the practical question of how (and whether) to live in that universe.

FROM *The Myth of Sisyphus**

The gods had condemned Sisyphus† to ceaselessly rolling a rock to the top of a mountain, whence the stone would fall back of its own weight. They had thought with some reason that there is no more dreadful punishment than futile and hopeless labor.

If one believes Homer, Sisyphus was the wisest and most prudent of mortals. According to another tradition, however, he was disposed to practice the profession of highwayman. I see no contradiction in this. Opinions differ as to the reasons why he became the futile laborer of the underworld. To begin with, he is accused of a certain levity in regard to the gods. He stole their secrets. Ægina, the daughter of Æsopus, was carried off by Jupiter.‡ The father was shocked by that disappearance and complained to Sisyphus. He, who knew of the abduction, offered to tell about it on condition that Æsopus would give water to the citadel of Corinth. To the celestial thunderbolts he preferred the benediction of water. He was punished for this in the underworld. Homer tells us also that Sisyphus had put Death in chains. Pluto§ could not endure the sight of his deserted, silent empire. He dispatched the god of war, who liberated Death from the hands of her conqueror.

It is said that Sisyphus, being near to death, rashly wanted to test his wife's love. He ordered her to cast his unburied body into the middle of the public square. Sisyphus woke up in the underworld. And there, annoyed by an obedience so contrary to human love, he obtained from Pluto permission to return to earth in order to chastise his wife. But when he had seen again the face of this world, enjoyed water and sun, warm stones and the sea, he no longer wanted to go back to the infernal darkness. Recalls, signs of anger, warnings were of no avail. Many years more he lived facing the curve of the gulf, the sparkling sea, and the smiles of earth. A decree of the gods was necessary. Mercury¶ came and seized the impudent man by the collar and, snatching him from his joys, led him forcibly back to the underworld, where his rock was ready for him.

You have already grasped that Sisyphus is the absurd hero. He *is*, as much through his passions as through his torture. His scorn of the gods, his hatred of death, and his passion for life won him that unspeakable penalty in which the whole being is exerted toward accomplishing nothing. This is the price that must be paid for the passions of this earth. Nothing is told us about Sisyphus in the underworld. Myths are made for the imagination to breathe life into them. As for this myth, one sees merely the whole effort of a body straining to raise the huge stone, to roll it, and push it up a slope a hundred times over; one sees the face screwed up, the cheek tight against the stone, the shoulder bracing the claycovered mass, the foot wedging it, the fresh start with arms outstretched, the wholly human security of two earth-clotted hands. At the very end of his long effort measured by skyless space and time without depth, the purpose is achieved. Then Sisyphus watches the stone rush down in a few

---

* Albert Camus, *The Myth of Sisyphus*, trans. Justin O'Brien (Alfred A. Knopf).
† In Greek mythology, Sisyphus was the founding king of the Greek city-state of Corinth, from a time long before written history.
‡ Æsopus is a river god (and the name of a river in Corinthia), and Jupiter is the Roman name for Zeus, the king of the Greek gods.
§ The ruler of the underworld in classical mythology, also known as Hades.
¶ The Roman name for the Greek messenger god Hermes, who among other roles conducted souls into the afterlife.

moments toward that lower world whence he will have to push it up again toward the summit. He goes back down to the plain.

It is during that return, that pause, that Sisyphus interests me. A face that toils so close to stones is already stone itself! I see that man going back down with a heavy yet measured step toward the torment of which he will never know the end. That hour like a breathing-space which returns as surely as his suffering, that is the hour of consciousness. At each of those moments when he leaves the heights and gradually sinks toward the lairs of the gods, he is superior to his fate. He is stronger than his rock.

If this myth is tragic, that is because its hero is conscious. Where would his torture be, indeed, if at every step the hope of succeeding upheld him? The workman of today works every day in his life at the same tasks, and his fate is no less absurd. But it is tragic only at the rare moments when it becomes conscious. Sisyphus, proletarian of the gods,* powerless and rebellious, knows the whole extent of his wretched condition: it is what he thinks of during his descent. The lucidity that was to constitute his torture at the same time crowns his victory. There is no fate that cannot be surmounted by scorn.

If the descent is thus sometimes performed in sorrow, it can also take place in joy. This word is not too much. Again I fancy Sisyphus returning toward his rock, and the sorrow was in the beginning. When the images of earth cling too tightly to memory, when the call of happiness becomes too insistent, it happens that melancholy arises in man's heart: this is the rock's

victory, this is the rock itself. The boundless grief is too heavy to bear. These are our nights of Gethsemane.† But crushing truths perish from being acknowledged. Thus, Œdipus‡ at the outset obeys fate without knowing it. But from the moment he knows, his tragedy begins. Yet at the same moment, blind and desperate, he realizes that the only bond linking him to the world is the cool hand of a girl.§ Then a tremendous remark rings out: "Despite so many ordeals, my advanced age and the nobility of my soul make me conclude that all is well." Sophocles' Œdipus, like Dostoevsky's Kirilov,¶ thus gives the recipe for the absurd victory. Ancient wisdom confirms modern heroism.

One does not discover the absurd without being tempted to write a manual of happiness. "What! by such narrow ways—?"** There is but one world, however. Happiness and the absurd are two sons of the same earth. They are inseparable. It would be a mistake to say that happiness necessarily springs from the absurd discovery. It happens as well that the feeling of the absurd springs from happiness. "I conclude that all is well," says Œdipus, and that remark is sacred. It echoes in the wild and limited universe of man. It teaches that all is not, has not been, exhausted. It drives out of this world a god who had come into it with dissatisfaction and a preference for futile suffering. It makes of fate a human matter, which must be settled among men.

All Sisyphus' silent joy is contained therein. His fate belongs to him. His rock is his thing. Likewise, the absurd man, when he contemplates his torment, silences all the idols. In the universe suddenly restored

---

* Forced to work for the (higher) gods.

† The garden of Gethsemane was the place where Jesus spent the night before his crucifixion and, knowing that he was about to be betrayed and executed, agonized about his fate before coming to terms with it.

‡ A tragic hero in Greek mythology, Oedipus was fated to fulfill a prophecy that he would accidentally kill his father and marry his mother, and thereby bring disaster down upon his family and his city. When he realizes what he has done he blinds himself. This story is the subject of three plays by Sophocles (c. 497–406 BCE): *Oedipus Rex*, *Oedipus at Colonus*, and *Antigone*.

§ This refers to his daughters Antigone and Ismene, whom Oedipus asked to hold one last time before his exile.

¶ A character in Russian author Fyodor Dostoevsky's novel *Demons* (1872, sometimes called *The Possessed*), who commits suicide because he is convinced that for life to be worth living God must exist, and yet he is also convinced that God cannot exist. To Camus this suicide is not an act of despair but of revolt, and an expression of the unbounded freedom that we have if God does not exist.

** A reference to the biblical passage, "Enter by the narrow gate; for wide is the gate and broad is the way that leads to destruction, and there are many who go in by it. How narrow is the gate and confined is the way which leads to life, and there are few who find it" (Matthew 7:13–14).

to its silence, the myriad wondering little voices of the earth rise up. Unconscious, secret calls, invitations from all the faces, they are the necessary reverse and price of victory. There is no sun without shadow, and it is essential to know the night. The absurd man says yes and his efforts will henceforth be unceasing. If there is a personal fate, there is no higher destiny, or at least there is but one which he concludes is inevitable and despicable. For the rest, he knows himself to be the master of his days. At that subtle moment when man glances backward over his life, Sisyphus returning toward his rock, in that slight pivoting he contemplates that series of unrelated actions which becomes his fate, created by him, combined under his memory's eye and soon sealed by his death. Thus, convinced of the wholly human origin of all that is human, a blind man eager to see who knows that the night has no end, he is still on the go. The rock is still rolling.

I leave Sisyphus at the foot of the mountain! One always finds one's burden again. But Sisyphus teaches the higher fidelity that negates the gods and raises rocks. He too concludes that all is well. This universe henceforth without a master seems to him neither sterile nor futile. Each atom of that stone, each mineral flake of that night-filled mountain, in itself forms a world. The struggle itself toward the heights is enough to fill a man's heart. One must imagine Sisyphus happy. ▪

Suggestions for Critical Reflection

1. According to Camus, hope is a mistake. Why does he believe this? Is he right? What do you think might be the benefits of abandoning hope?

2. If the absurd hero abandons objective values and does not seek explanation or justification, then why did Camus write an essay apparently trying to explain and justify the absurd worldview? Does Camus write philosophy or does he reject philosophy?

3. "One must imagine Sisyphus happy." Must one? Why? What happens to Camus's position if Sisyphus is not happy?

4. "There is no fate that cannot be surmounted by scorn." What do you think Camus means by this?

KATHY BEHRENDT

Reasons to Live versus Reasons Not to Die

Who Is Kathy Behrendt?

Kathy Behrendt is a Canadian philosopher teaching at Wilfrid Laurier University in Waterloo, Ontario. She obtained a Doctorate in Philosophy at the University of Oxford in 2000, where she then taught for several years. Behrendt has published on issues of personal identity, memory, and the fear of death, among other topics. Her related published works include "Whole Lives and Good Deaths" (2014), which discusses narrative conceptions of the self in connection with the end of life, and "A Special Way of Being Afraid" (2010), which examines the fear of non-existence.

What Is the Structure of This Reading?

Behrendt frames this paper as a response to a line from philosopher Steven Luper-Foy: "any reason for living is an excellent reason for not dying." While this sentiment might seem at first sight to be obviously true, Behrendt shows that it is not only possible to disagree with it but that it might not even be an attractive position if it is true.

Her starting point is one well-known theory of the good life from ancient Greece: Epicureanism. For the Epicurean, a happy life is one which is peaceful, self-sufficient, filled with reliable pleasures (such as friendship), and free from anxiety or pain. Philosophy can help us to lead such a life, according to Epicurus, and one of the ways it does so is by freeing us from the fear of death—a natural but irrational fear which is the source of a great deal of unnecessary anxiety and (through the desire to cling to life) selfishness and immorality.

Behrendt points out that, according to Epicureanism, it is in fact not true that what makes life worth living is also a reason to prefer not dying. A modification of the Epicurean position produces a view, which Behrendt calls Acquisitionism, on which reasons to live are also reasons not to die—but this view is unattractive, she argues. A better view than either Epicureanism or Acquisitionism is another conception of the good life that

Behrendt labels Completionism—but with Completionism we are again back to a view that accepts that death need not always be undesirable to those leading a good life. Indeed, for the Completionist, "death has a positive and necessary role to perform in helping to articulate and shape the primary reasons to live."

The final position that Behrendt considers is one formulated by Thomas Nagel. One can think of this account as a blending of Completionism with Acquisitionism and, if we accept it, it makes it once again true that reasons for living are always reasons for not dying. Behrendt does not issue a final verdict on whether the Nagelian conception of the good life is adequate, but concludes by noting that what might have seemed at first like an obvious connection between reasons to live and reasons not to die has turned out to be more complex than it appeared, and we are left not quite sure what we should want to say about it.

Some Common Misconceptions

1. Much of Behrendt's paper is presented as a response to the Epicurean understanding of life and death. Epicurus is often regarded as a "hedonist" philosopher, in that he advocates the pursuit of pleasure and avoidance of pain. The term "hedonism" is now often used to mean the unrestricted pursuit of physical appetites such as sexual gratification and the gluttonous consumption of food. To Epicurus, however, the best life is a moderate one in which pain is avoided and desires are limited to those things that can be easily acquired.

2. Neither Behrendt nor any of the philosophers she discusses are advocating for death. Epicurus' position is that death is simply nothing to the one who dies, because one no longer exists once death has come. Though this means that a person should not fear their own death because they can't be harmed by it, this doesn't entail that death is in any way positive (or that it doesn't seriously harm other people who are still alive—such as friends and family).

Reasons to Live versus Reasons Not to Die*

"Any reason for living is an excellent reason for not dying"—Luper-Foy, "Annihilation," 278

Some claims seem so clearly right that we don't think to question them. Steven Luper-Foy's remark is like that. It borders on the 'trivially true' (i.e. so obviously true as to be uninteresting). If I have a reason to live, surely I likewise have a reason not to die. It may then be surprising to learn that so many philosophers disagree with this claim—either directly or by implication. I will look at some of the things people say that stand in opposition to Luper-Foy's claim. I will also consider what is needed in order to agree with it. The views canvassed cover broad issues concerning life and death, and what matters to us with respect to both.

Epicurus† (341–271 B.C.) made claims about death that are still debated today. Perhaps his most notorious was that death is 'nothing to us' (*Leading Doctrines*, 2). There is a sense in which, for Epicurus, the claim that death is nothing to us is quite literally true. We have nothing to do with death because so long as we are alive, it is not present for us. And if it were present for us we would be absent (*Letter to Menoeceus*, 125). At no point do 'I' and 'death' coincide. So it cannot have an impact upon me.

Sometimes when reinforcing this point Epicurus emphasises that I will not sense or perceive anything when I am dead. Sometimes he merely emphasises that I will not exist when I am dead. There are unspoken assumptions in either case: either I need to sense something in order for something to be bad for me, or I need to exist in order for it to be bad for me. Both assumptions have come in for considerable criticism, especially the first one. But we can set this aside for the time being. Instead, I want to investigate how Epicurus deals with the issue of reasons for living. Understanding Epicurus'

views on life, it turns out, can help shed light on his view of death.

If death is nothing to us, do we have any reason to live? An uncharitable reading of Epicurus might say we do not. Certainly Epicurus and his followers were known for having challenging views about what in life is valuable. Life is good in so far as it yields pleasurable experience. But pleasurable experience is characterised by Epicurus in terms of the absence of pain. This being so, according to Epicurus, the benefits of pleasure do not increase with duration—more is not better. This can be difficult for people to understand and accept. But consider an analogy with health, which is sometimes used to explain the Epicurean view of pleasure: if you are healthy your health does not get better the longer it goes on. Likewise with pleasure in the Epicurean sense—the absence of pain, like the condition of being in good health, is a stable quality. It does not increase with time.

Epicurus would be the first to admit that this view of pleasure goes against the norm; his goal in part was to reform the common view. Thus it is not surprising that his understanding of pleasure is a far cry from the types of things many people often think of as pleasurable, e.g. sensual, often short-lived activities, such as the pursuit of physical pleasure beyond what is needed to survive and stave off appetites. Lucretius‡ (c.94–c.50 B.C.), a later follower of Epicurus, compared the relentless accumulation of pleasures to the pouring of water into a sieve or cracked vessel (*On the Nature of Things* 3.1005–1008)—a time-involving, never-ending and ultimately frustrating procedure. People who engage in such pursuits enjoy the act of drinking more than they appreciate the sensation of quenched thirst. Therefore they are constantly compelled to seek further pleasures. There are various names for such people but I am going to call them '*Acquisitionists*'; their key trait is that, for anything they deem good, the pleasure lies

* Kathy Behrendt, "Reasons to Live versus Reasons Not to Die," *Think* 10, 28 (Summer 2011): 67–76.
† Epicurus was an Ancient Greek philosopher who argued for a materialistic conception of the universe and defended a conception of the good life focused on tranquility and the avoidance of pain. He wrote numerous works, only a few of which have survived to the present day. See the introduction for more details regarding Epicurean philosophy.
‡ Titus Lucretius Carus (c. 99 BCE–c. 55 BCE) was a Roman poet and philosopher, known primarily for the six-book poem *On the Nature of Things*, in which he describes and defends Epicurean philosophy.

in the experience of obtaining it, and they will always crave more of it. By contrast to the Acquisitionist, Epicurus' view of non-time-bound pleasure invites us to rest content with the state of well-being that ensues when appetites and wants have been fulfilled.

What has this got to do with the relation between reasons for living and reasons for not dying? The Acquisitionist's compulsion to pursue and enlarge on fleeting pleasures is an ongoing endeavour that can be cut off by death at any time. Someone afflicted with this compulsion always wants more of what she wants, and so death stands in the way of her achieving this. Her reasons for living are reasons for not dying; she abhors and fears death because it interferes with a project that in theory has no end. That is part of why the thought of her own death produces fear and anxiety. However, once we rid ourselves of such wants, 'we no longer need unlimited time', according to Epicurus (*Leading Doctrines*, 20). We therefore stop being afraid that life is not eternal. We don't need to live forever in order to live well, since a good life can happen in a finite amount of time and isn't increased with duration. This is why, for the Epicureans, reasons for living are not reasons for not dying. Whatever it is that makes life good for an Epicurean, it cannot be anything we insist on pursuing ad infinitum.* The thinking person, who follows the 'mind' and not the 'body' does not 'avoid pleasure', but nor does he regret 'departure from life' (*Leading Doctrines*, 20); his pleasures are time-bound and death does not infringe on them. In short, and in contrast to the Acquisitionist, the Epicurean has reasons to live but they are not reasons not to die.

Some people think that Epicurus' difficult view of death is tied to his having rather spectacularly missed the point of life. He paints a picture in which our choices are between life as frustrated and fearful persons of the flesh trying to fill the cracked vessel of our endless, fleeting desires, and life as the person of the mind who basks in a state of simple well-being in the form of the absence of pain, with no great need to prolong this state. But perhaps these are not the only options. There are many valuable things in life that do take considerable time but don't demand endless renewal. Consider having a child, pursuing a career, undertaking a project of scientific discovery, or athletic

excellence, or artistic creation. These are all potential reasons for living. For many people, such things constitute *the* reasons for living. They propel us into the future and make us want to go on—as opposed to the day-to-day mundane things we do in order merely to pass the time we have been allotted.

These reasons for living take time to see through to the end. However, time is needed not because, like the Acquisitionist with the insatiable appetite, we just want to do these sorts of things again and again, but because in order to accomplish these tasks we need to follow a certain complex path. We need to do certain things in a certain order over a considerable stretch of time. If I want to become a successful lawyer I need to reach adulthood, and undergo a long period of education, apprenticeship, and work before achieving my goal. If I want to have and raise a child, biology determines that this too takes time. Successfully completing a marathon is unthinkable unless one follows a lengthy and structured regimen of training. But crucially, unlike the ongoing, endless pursuit of additional pleasures, *completion* of these goals and activities is also possible. The partnership in a firm can be obtained. The child can grow and thrive and be sent off into the world. The race can be run to the finish line. And so on.

The people who hold some form of this view are a diverse lot and differ amongst themselves on many of the details. For the purposes of this discussion, I am going to group them together and call them 'Completionists'. The key feature which they share is that they believe in and value time-extended but completable goals. The completion of valued life projects requires time, and the time required can be interrupted by death. Such an interruption, far from being nothing to them, would be a disaster, coming as it does before the goals are fully realised. As far as Completionists are concerned, Epicurus' composure about death was gained at the expense of ignoring these time-extended but completable goals.

Notice that the Completionists' disagreement with Epicurus here is not total. Like the Epicureans, Completionists also reject Steven Luper-Foy's claim. The reasons they give for living are not reasons for not dying. Or not ultimately—there is a qualification in this case. Prior to the completion of one's goals, these

---

* Latin: to infinity.

goals provide reasons to avoid death. But it is understood that the goals can be completed. So they cannot stand as permanent, unqualified reasons for wanting to avoid death. In fact, many Completionists emphasise that a limited life-span is necessary for us to form, pursue, and appreciate certain activities. I would not be motivated to become a top lawyer or star athlete if my time on earth were unlimited. I might not even be able to imagine goals for my self in the future if that future had no limit. I also may not value my accomplishments if they are amongst countless that I will be able to go on to pursue. Reasons for living here go hand-in-hand with reasons for dying. The time-extended but completable goals discussed have the fact of our mortality built into them, because mortality is part of what helps us formulate them and makes them valuable. So Completionists cannot embrace Luper-Foy's edict that any reason for living is an excellent reason for not dying. They have many reasons for living but these do not ultimately stand in the way of accepting death—indeed, death has a positive and necessary role to perform in helping to articulate and shape the primary reasons to live.

Does anyone other than the Acquisitionist agree with Luper-Foy? Maybe we should be satisfied with the Acquisitionist's endorsement. But even apart from Epicurus' criticisms, Acquisitionists are usually portrayed as shallow and unthinking. They are motivated by the spirit of acquisitiveness; emphasis is placed on the pursuit of more and further pleasures for their own sake, rather than on any satisfaction they bring about. The Completionist tends to view the Acquisitionist with despair—she is unwilling to undergo hardship for the sake of a long-term goal. And nothing will ever be finished for her, so she cannot achieve closure and contentment. That this is no way to live is another point the Completionists and the Epicureans can agree on. Furthermore, Lucretius' cracked vessel metaphor strikes a chord; there is something perhaps empty and unsatisfying in the constant accumulation of more short-lived pleasurable experiences. If we want to do justice to Luper-Foy's point, it would be nice to have a better representative of it than the Acquisitionist. Let's consider what we might need here, in light of where we have got to so far.

Epicurus and his followers cannot accept that any reason for living is an excellent reason for not dying, because the pleasures of life are not increased with time. While there are things we can enjoy in life, death does not detract from that enjoyment, which would not increase if we did not die. Completionists hold, against Epicurus, that death *can* undermine what is good in life. In particular, death is bad when it comes before we have completed certain time-extended goals. But once those goals are completed death is not a threat, and in order to form and appreciate those goals, it is necessary that we are beings who can and will die. Therefore in so far as those goals are our reasons to live, they are still not always reasons not to die. If we want reasons for living that are also reasons for not dying, it seems we need the following: reasons for living that are time-extended (*contra** the Epicurean), but are also open-ended, in the sense of not limited by time (*contra* the Completionist). And ideally, we would like those reasons not to consist entirely in obtaining the maximal experience of pleasure for its own sake (*contra* the Acquisitionist).

One person who may point us in the right direction here is Thomas Nagel.[†] He is amongst the many who do not accept Epicurean detachment about death. Death is bad, according to Nagel, and it is bad because it deprives us of the goods in life. These goods consist in not just momentary, experienced pleasures, but hopes and possibilities that death may undermine. A person, for Nagel, is 'identified by his history and his possibilities' more so than by his experiential state at any particular moment (5). So far this does not necessarily differ from the Completionist view that we need a decent stretch of time in order to complete meaningful goals. Both Nagel and the Completionist seem to agree that many of the goods of life are time-extended and death is bad in so far as it can curtail them. But Nagel adds a key point that pushes him into a separate camp, namely that the possibilities apparently open to a person may be unlimited. This changes matters considerably. As Nagel puts it, 'if there is no limit to the amount of life that it would be good to have, then it may be that a bad end is in store for us all' (10). What he is suggesting here is that death may always come at the wrong time, depriving us of possible goods of life.

---

*   Latin: in opposition to, in contrast to.

†   See the introduction to Thomas Nagel earlier in this volume.

Nagel is perfectly well aware that we cannot in fact live forever. Nature dictates this. So his talk of the limitless possible goods death deprives us of cannot mean 'possible' only within the current bounds of nature. There is clearly a limit to what possibilities are in fact available to us, given that we are mortal and our lives are short. But there may be no limit to the possibilities that we can imagine or conceive of for ourselves. It is when we dwell on these that we enter Nagel's realm of limitless possibilities for the self. Our sense of our own experience, says Nagel, 'does not embody this idea of a natural limit' (9–10); we can and often do plan as though there were no tomorrow. And even when we know it is not true, we are capable of imagining another career, another race, another goal worthy of pursuit, which could bring us further happiness. The Completionist's apparent acceptance of death under certain circumstances rings hollow when we let our imagination take flight and think of all the good experiences we have yet to have, or want to have again.

In Nagel we find the time-extended but open-ended reasons for living that we were looking for. These reasons to live propel us beyond the present experience and into the (theoretically open-ended) future. This is in contrast to the Epicurean view, where good is associated with an experiential state defined by the absence of pain, and does not increase with time. But it is also in contrast to the Completionist, who views the goods in life to be time-extended but completable; for here is a view that claims, in theory anyway, these goods may have no limit. In so far as death poses a threat to the realisation of the possible goods we can conceive of, the threat, like the possibilities themselves, is unlimited. Hence reasons for living, on Nagel's view, are always reasons for not dying.

Has this view avoided association with the shallow Acquisitionist position? That depends on what about Nagel's view we choose to emphasise. There are some apparent similarities with the Acquisitionist, in that the view Nagel considers implies that more of what is good is better, so to speak. Hence death's permanent potential to deprive us of the goods in life: 'death, no matter how inevitable, is an abrupt cancellation of indefinitely extensive possible goods' (10).

But Nagel also says that some things can be good or bad independently of how they feel for a person at the time. For instance, he disparages the 'man who wastes his life in the cheerful pursuit of a method of communicating with asparagus plants' (5). Similarly, but more seriously, he views the adult who suffers a brain injury and is reduced to the state of a contented child to be the subject of a great misfortune. The asparagus-man and the brain-injured person are in a contented state. The Acquisitionist would have trouble saying that anything is wrong for them or that they suffer any harm, so long as they can go on experiencing the pleasures of being fed and well cared for. Nagel's view that they do suffer harm connects with his belief that persons are defined not just in terms of their present state, but their history and possibilities. These possibilities must, for Nagel, be richer and more complex than the potential to live in a state of physical comfort indefinitely (otherwise he would not view these people as unfortunate). He speaks of the importance of success and failure and aspects of our life that are like processes rather than individual moments of well-being. 'Processes' here can plausibly include the longer-term goals of the Completionist—achievements which require time and, often, some pain and sacrifice. If we include such things amongst the possible goods of life, we arrive at something quite different from the Acquisitionist's understanding of the goods that death can deprive us of.

Despite such differences between himself and the Acquisitionist, Nagel will also have to contend with criticism of his claim that the goods of life may be 'indefinitely extensive'. The Epicurean objects to the notion of time-extended goods, and will criticise Nagel for suggesting that someone in a good state might still be deprived, and that this deprivation might be alleviated by additional time. The Completionist objects to the notion of *indefinitely* extended goods, and will criticise Nagel for suggesting that anything could retain its value indefinitely, or that we can imagine an open-ended future of limitless possibilities for ourselves.

It may be possible to maintain that any reason for living is a reason for not dying. But the claim is hard-won, if we are to give it the seriousness it deserves and ensure that the reasons in question are ones that we are prepared to live for, for all time. The Acquisitionist's reasons for never dying could wear thin after a finite amount of time; simply revelling in the experience of pleasure may lose its appeal given enough time, and thereby cease to be a reason for living. The Completionists arguably offer us better reasons for living (or at least what many of us would recognise as good and enduring reasons to go on). However, they added that those reasons gained their strength and possibly their coherence from being placed in the context of a finite, mortal lifespan. Nagel disagreed, and he is not alone in holding that the complex, rich and varied possibilities that give us, now, reasons to go on, can in some form provide grounds for continuing on indefinitely.

We cannot here resolve the disagreements that remain between the various parties. But we can at least note that Luper-Foy's claim that any reason for living is an excellent reason for not dying, regardless of its truth, is certainly not trivial. There are a number of ways of disagreeing with it. What is more, there are arguable advantages to disagreeing with it. The fact that the Epicurean and the Completionist have reasons for living that are not always reasons for not dying helps them accept their mortality. Their reasons for living won't necessarily place them in the unhappy position of having to dread or regret their inevitable demise. On the other hand, we may, like Nagel, think our reasons for living are always reasons for not dying—and excellent reasons at that, going far beyond the Acquisitionists' superficial, perhaps unsustainable, values. But if that is what we think then it is hard to avoid the view that, in so far as our reasons for living are sustainable and unlimited, a bad end is indeed in store for us all. ∎

Suggestions for Critical Reflection

1. The Epicurean position is meant to provide relief from the fear of death. But shouldn't one fear death, to at least some degree? Is indifference toward death helpful in relieving us of anxiety, or might it lead to a lack of sensible caution or a lack of appreciation for life?

2. According to the Completionist, "a limited life-span is necessary for us to form, pursue, and appreciate certain activities. I would not be motivated to become a top lawyer or star athlete if my time on earth were unlimited." Do you agree with this claim? Some have speculated that future technology may allow humans to live for an indefinite length of time. Would the prospect of immortality undermine the motivation to form and pursue life goals?

3. Are there good reasons to prefer the "richer and more complex" goals advocated by the Completionist and Nagel, such as long-term career and relationship success, artistic excellence, and the raising of children, over the simple and deliberately unambitious desires of the Epicurean? If so, what are those reasons? Are they moral reasons, or reasons of some other sort?

4. Behrendt suggests that Luper-Foy's statement strikes many people as an obvious (or "trivial") truth. His claim could, however, be interpreted in at least two different ways: (1) *At any particular time*, any reason for living is an excellent reason for not dying *at that time*"; or (2) "Any reason for living is an excellent reason *to never die.*" Which of these two interpretations seems more plausible? Are both interpretations contrary to the Epicurean and Completionist positions? Does Behrendt's argument hold equally with regard to both interpretations?

5. In the end, do you think that what makes life worth living is also a reason to prefer not dying? What kind of a harm, if any, is death to the one who dies?

6. Is "a bad end in store for us all"? (And what exactly is this supposed to mean?)

References

Epicurus, *Leading Doctrines*, in *The Philosophy of Epicurus*, ed. and trans. George K. Strodach (Chicago: Northwestern University Press, 1963).

Epicurus, *Letter to Menoeceus*, in *The Philosophy of Epicurus*.

Lucretius, *On the Nature of Things*, ed. and trans. Anthony M. Esolen (Baltimore: Johns Hopkins Univ. Press, 1995).

Luper-Foy, S., 'Annihilation', in *The Metaphysics of Death*, ed. J.M. Fischer (Stanford: Stanford University Press, 1993).

Nagel, T., 'Death', in *Mortal Questions* (Cambridge: Cambridge University Press, 1979).

PERMISSIONS ACKNOWLEDGMENTS

Appiah, Kwame Anthony. "How to Decide If Races Exist," *Proceedings of the Aristotelian Society* 106 (2006): 365–82. Copyright © The Aristotelian Society, 2006. Reprinted by permission of Oxford University Press, conveyed by Copyright Clearance Center.

Aristotle. Excerpts from *The Nicomachean Ethics*, Books I, II, and X, translated by Terence Irwin. Hackett Publishing Company, 1999. Copyright © 1999 by Terence Irwin. Reprinted with the permission of Hackett Publishing Company, Inc. All rights reserved.

Ayer, A.J. "The Claims of Philosophy," *Polemic* 7 (March 1947). Reprinted with the permission of Ted Honderich, Literary Executor to A.J. Ayer.

Beauvoir, Simone de. "Introduction," from *The Second Sex*, translated by Constance Borde and Sheila Malovany-Chevallier. Translation copyright © 2009 by Constance Borde and Sheila Malovany-Chevallier. Used by permission of Alfred A. Knopf, an imprint of the Knopf Doubleday Publishing Group, a division of Penguin Random House LLC. All rights reserved.

Behrendt, Kathy. "Reasons to Live versus Reasons Not to Die," *Think* 10.28 (Summer 2011): 67–76. Copyright © The Royal Institute of Philosophy. Reproduced by permission of Cambridge University Press through PLSclear.

Bettcher, Talia Mae. "Trans Women and the Meaning of 'Woman,'" from *Philosophy of Sex: Contemporary Readings*, 6th ed., edited by A. Soble, N. Power, and R. Halwani. Rowman & Littlefield, 2013. Originally published as "Without a Net: Starting Points for Trans Stories," in the *American Philosophical Association Newsletter on Philosophy and LGBT Issues* 10.2 (Spring 2011): 2–5. Reprinted with the permission of the American Philosophical Association and Rowman & Littlefield.

Camus, Albert. Excerpt from *The Myth of Sisyphus*, translated by Justin O'Brien. *Le Mythe de Sisyphe*. Copyright © Editions Gallimard, Paris, 1942. All rights reserved. Reprinted by permission of the Estate of Albert Camus and Editions Gallimard, conveyed by The Wylie Agency. Translation copyright © 1955; copyright renewed 1983 by Penguin Random House LLC. Used by permission of Alfred A. Knopf, an imprint of the Knopf Doubleday Publishing Group, a division of Penguin Random House LLC. All rights reserved.

Chalmers, David. "The Puzzle of Conscious Experience," from *Scientific American*, December 1995. Reprinted with the permission of David Chalmers.

Coates, Ta-Nehisi. Excerpt from *Between the World and Me*. Copyright © 2015 by Ta-Nehisi Coates. Used by permission of Spiegel & Grau, an imprint of Random House, a division of Penguin Random House LLC. All rights reserved.

Dennett, Daniel C. "Where Am I?" pages 310–23 of *Brainstorms: Philosophical Essays on Mind and Psychology*. Copyright © 1981 Massachusetts Institute of Technology. Reprinted with the permission of The MIT Press.

Frankfurt, Harry. "Alternate Possibilities and Moral Responsibilities," Chapter 1 of *The Importance of What We Care About: Philosophical Essays*. Cambridge University Press, 1998. Originally published in *Journal of Philosophy* LXVI (66.23), December 1969. Reprinted with the permission of Joan Gilbert and The Journal of Philosophy.

Gettier, Edmund. "Is Justified True Belief Knowledge?" *Analysis* 23.6 (June 1963): 121–23. Copyright © 1963 Oxford University Press. Reprinted by permission of Oxford University Press, conveyed by Copyright Clearance Center.

Held, Virginia. "Feminist Transformations of Moral Theory," [abridged] *Philosophy and Phenomenological Research* 50, Supplement (Autumn 1990): 321–44. Copyright © 1990 International Phenomenological Society. Reprinted by permission of the publisher, conveyed by Copyright Clearance Center.

Kind, Amy. "How to Believe in Qualia," pages 285–98 of *The Case for Qualia*, edited by Edmond Wright. Copyright © 2008 Massachusetts Institute of Technology. Reprinted with the permission of The MIT Press.

Longino, Helen. "Can There Be a Feminist Science?" *Hypatia* 2.3 (1987): 51–64. Copyright © 1987 by Hypatia, Inc. Reprinted with the permission of Cambridge University Press, conveyed by Copyright Clearance Center.

Mackie, J.L. "Evil and Omnipotence," *Mind* (New Series) 64.254 (April 1955): 200–12. Copyright © 1955 Oxford University Press. Reprinted by permission of Oxford University Press, conveyed by Copyright Clearance Center.

Nagel, Thomas. "What Is It Like to Be a Bat?" *The Philosophical Review* 83.4 (October 1974): 435–50. Reprinted with the permission of Thomas Nagel and The Journal of Philosophy.

Nozick, Robert. Excerpt from Chapter 7, "Distributive Justice," in *Anarchy, State and Utopia*. Copyright © 1974, 2008, 2013. Reprinted by permission of Basic Books, an imprint of Hachette Book Group, Inc.

Okin, Susan Moller. Excerpt from "Justice and Gender," *Philosophy and Public Affairs* 16.1 (1987): 42–72. Philosophy & Public Affairs © 1987 Wiley. Reprinted with the permission of Blackwell Publishing, Inc., conveyed by Copyright Clearance Center.

Parfit, Derek. "Personal Identity," *The Philosophical Review* 80.1 (Jan. 1971): 3–27.

Plato. "The Allegory of the Cave," from *The Republic*, translated by Benjamin Jowett, 1892. Excerpts from Book II (357a–367e) of the *Republic*, translated by G.M.A. Grube; revised by C.D.C. Reeve. Copyright © 1992 by Hackett Publishing Company, Inc. Reprinted with the permission of Hackett Publishing Company, Inc. All rights reserved.

Rawls, John. Excerpts from *Justice as Fairness: A Restatement*. Cambridge, MA: The Belknap Press of Harvard University Press, Copyright © 2001 by the President and Fellows of Harvard College. Used by permission. All rights reserved.

Rée, Paul. "The Illusion of Free Will" ("Die Illusion der Willensfreiheit"), Chapters 1 and 2, from *Die Illusion der Willensfreiheit* (1885) translated by Stefan Bauer-Mengelberg, in *A Modern Introduction to Philosophy*, 3rd ed., edited by Paul Edwards and Arthur Pap. The Free Press, 1973.

Saul, Jennifer. "Scepticism and Implicit Bias," *Disputatio* 5.37 (2013): 243–63. Copyright © 2013 Jennifer Saul. Reprinted by permission of the author.

Thomson, Judith Jarvis. "The Trolley Problem," *The Yale Law Journal* 94.6 (May 1985): 1395–1415. Copyright © 1985 The Yale Law Journal Company, Inc. Reprinted with the permission of the publisher conveyed by Copyright Clearance Center.

Young, Iris Marion. "Five Faces of Oppression," Chapter 2 of *Justice and the Politics of Difference*. Princeton University Press, 1990. Copyright © 1990 by Princeton University Press. Republished with the permission of Princeton University Press, conveyed by Copyright Clearance Center.

Images

Introduction
"Top Hat," by Eli W. Buel, ca. 1870.
https://commons.wikimedia.org/wiki/File:Accession_
Number-_1969-0183-0156_(2720792408).jpg

Philosophy of Religion
"Sunlight Seeping through Heavy Tungnath Clouds," by
Sriramskumar, 2016. Licensed under the Creative Commons
Attribution-Share Alike 4.0 International license, https://
creativecommons.org/licenses/by-sa/4.0/deed.en

Epistemology
"Self Portrait," by Nadar (Gaspard-Félix Tournachon),
n.d. National Library of France, Prints and Photographs
Department, FOL-EO-15 (3), https://gallica.bnf.fr/ark:/12148/
btv1b105358981

Philosophy of Mind
"Faradisation du muscle frontal," by Guillaume-Benjamin-
Amand Duchennede Boulogne, ca. 1854–1856. The Horace
W. Goldsmith Foundation Fund, through Joyce and Robert
Menschel, 2013. Metropolitan Museum of Art (US), 2013.229

Free Will
"Silvan Omerzu's Interpretation of Pinocchio Ostržek," by
Miha Fras, 2015. Licensed under the Creative Commons
Attribution-No Derivatives 4.0 International license, https://
creativecommons.org/licenses/by-nd/4.0/

Personal Identity
[No title], Anonymous, n.d. Licensed under the CC0
1.0 Universal Public Domain Dedication license, https://
creativecommons.org/publicdomain/zero/1.0/

Ethical Theory
"Washington, D.C. Class in the Banneker Junior High
School," by Marjory Collins, March 1942. Farm Security
Administration–Office of War Information photograph
collection (Library of Congress).

Justice
"Shanty Homes near a Railway Station, Mumbai, India," by
Anonymous (MM), December 2010. Licensed under the
Creative Commons Attribution-Share Alike 2.0 Generic
License, https://creativecommons.org/licenses/by-sa/2.0/
deed.en

Equality and Fairness
"2017.01.21 Women's March Washington, DC USA 00095,"
by Ted Eytan, 21 January 2017. Licensed under the Creative
Commons Attribution-Share Alike 2.0 Generic License,
https://creativecommons.org/licenses/by-sa/2.0/deed.en

Life, Death, and Happiness
[No title], Anonymous, n.d. Licensed under the CC0 1.0
Universal Public Domain Dedication license, https://
creativecommons.org/publicdomain/zero/1.0/

From the Publisher

A name never says it all, but the word "Broadview" expresses a good deal of the philosophy behind our company. We are open to a broad range of academic approaches and political viewpoints. We pay attention to the broad impact book publishing and book printing has in the wider world; for some years now we have used 100% recycled paper for most titles. Our publishing program is internationally oriented and broad-ranging. Our individual titles often appeal to a broad readership too; many are of interest as much to general readers as to academics and students.

Founded in 1985, Broadview remains a fully independent company owned by its shareholders—not an imprint or subsidiary of a larger multinational.

To order our books or obtain up-to-date information, please visit broadviewpress.com.

broadview press
www.broadviewpress.com

MARQUIS

Québec, Canada